10 personality introduces the digital personality of Tank, a robot receptionist at Carnegie Mellon University.

13 treatment of psychological disorders focuses on Dr. Daniel Foster, a psychologist working on an Indian reservation, and Laura Lichti, a licensed therapist just beginning her career.

14 chapters,
26 ordinary people,
26 extraordinary stories

D0817190

11 stress and health examines stress from the perspectives of Eric Flansburg, a police officer, and Kehlen Kirby, an emergency medical services (EMS) provider.

14 social psychology explores the life of Olympic runner Julius Achon, who adopted 11 orphans from his homeland of Uganda. This chapter also features the story of Joe and Susanne Maggio, a married couple whose union was made possible by the Internet.

12 psychological disorders tells the story of Ross Szabo, a young man with bipolar disorder, and Melissa Hopely, a young woman with obsessive-compulsive disorder.

PRESENTING PSYCHOLOGY

· A PARTNERSHIP BETWEEN ·
WORTH PUBLISHERS & SCIENTIFIC AMERICAN

PRESENTING PSYCHOLOGY

DEBORAH M. LICHT   MISTY G. HULL   COCO BALLANTYNE

Pikes Peak Community College,
Colorado

Pikes Peak Community College,
Colorado

· A PARTNERSHIP BETWEEN ·

WORTH PUBLISHERS   &   SCIENTIFIC AMERICAN

worth publishers
Macmillan Learning

New York

Vice President, Editorial: Charles Linsmeier

Publisher for Psychology and Sociology: Rachel Losh

Executive Acquisitions Editor: Daniel McDonough

Developmental Editor: Moira Lerner

Marketing Manager: Lindsay Johnson

Market Development Manager: Shannon Howard

Executive Media Editor: Rachel Comerford

Associate Media Editor: Anthony Casciano

Director, Content Management Enhancement: Tracey Kuehn

Managing Editor: Lisa Kinne

Project Editor: Jeanine Furino

Editorial Assistant: Kimberly Morgan-Smith

Production Manager: Sarah Segal

Art Manager: Matthew McAdams

Photo Editor: Cecilia Varas

Photo Researchers: Jacqui Wong, Deborah Anderson

Media Producer: Joe Tomasso

Interior Designer: Barbara Reingold

Cover Designer: Blake Logan

Layout Designer: Lee McKevitt

Illustrations: Todd Buck, Northeastern Graphic

Composition: codeMantra

Printing and Binding: RR Donnelley

Cover Photo: PCN Photography

Library of Congress Control Number: 2015946015

Paperback:

ISBN-13: 978-1-319-01637-1

ISBN-10: 1-319-01637-5

Loose-leaf:

ISBN-13: 978-1-319-02837-4

ISBN-10: 1-319-02837-3

Worth Publishers

One New York Plaza

New York, NY 10004-1562

www.macmillanhighered.com

Chapter opening photo credits:

CO1a, p. xLii, Worn pickaxe, Image Source/Getty Images; CO1b, p. xLii, Metallic copper nugget, Karin Rollett-Vlcek/Getty Images; CO1c, p. xLii, Underground safety gear, Eduard Andras/Getty Images; CO1d, p. 1, Coal Miner, Joshua Ets-Hokin/Getty Images; CO2a, p. 46, Dogtags, Thinkstock; CO2b, p. 47, Female soldier, Thinkstock; CO2c, p. 46, Human brain (left and right hemisphere), Pasieka/Science Photo Library; CO3a, p. 87, Cute little ballerina, Bobbie Osborne/Getty Images; CO3b, p. 86, Hands showing Chinese way of counting, ICHIRO/Getty Images; CO3c, p. 86, Bath toys, Bernard Jaubert/age fotostock/SuperStock; CO4a, p. 129, African American male nurse, Curt Pickens/Getty Images; CO4b, p. 128, Silhouette of people in different poses, iStock Vectors/Getty Images; CO4c, p. 128, Pillow without pillowcase, © D. Hurst/Alamy; CO4d, p. 128, Pillow with white pillowcase, © D. Hurst/Alamy; CO4e, p. 128, Drip bag on stand, © mood-board/Alamy; CO4f, p. 128, Close-up of eye mask, Exactostock/SuperStock; CO5a, p. 172, Training shoe close-up, Zoonar/P Gudella/age fotostock; CO5b, p. 173, Woman runner, © Pixattitude/Dreamstime.com; CO5c, p. 172, Sport silhouettes basketball, Thinkstock CO6a, p. 214, Young woman's work life, ZoneCreative/Getty Images; CO6b, p. 215, Conductor, C Squared Studios/Getty Images; CO6c, p. 214 Lute © Bob Jacobson/Corbis; CO7a, p. 258, Studio shot of fencer, Tetra Images/Getty Images; CO7b, p. 258, Skull x-ray (side angle), Stockbyte/Getty Images; CO7c, p. 258, Accident in the city, Nancy Brammer/Getty Images; CO7d, p. 259 Professional businesswoman using a digital tablet, londoneye/Getty Images; CO8a, p. 305 Pregnant woman, Kais Tolmats/Getty Images; CO8b, p. 304, Blue socks, Tatyana Nikitina/Getty Images; CO8d, p. 304, Infant's filled milk bottle, Creative Crop/Getty Images; CO9a, p. 357, Boy holding globe over head, Jose Luis Pelaez Inc./Getty Images; CO9b, p. 356, Toy shark, Image Source/Getty Images; CO9c, p. 356, Reference books, notebooks, and pen, Christina Norwood/Getty Images; CO10a, p. 407, Black video conference camera, E+/Getty images; CO10b, p. 402, Computer keyboard, Kyoungil Jeon/Getty Images; CO10c, p. 403, Keys from a keyboard, spxChrome/Getty Images; CO10e, p. 402, Mask Jupiter, Images; CO11a, p. 440, CO11b, p. 440, Studio portrait of firefighter, Tetra Images/SuperStock; CO11c, p. 440, The rear of a parked New York City police car, © Paul Hakimata/Alamy; CO12a, p. 474, A car key and remote starter, Kathleen Wauters/Getty Images; CO12b, p. 475, Businessman at podium, Comstock/Getty Images; CO12c, p. 474, Light switch in the on position, Samuel Kessler/Getty Images; CO13a, p. 514, Young businessman sitting on swivel chair, allindiaimages/Super-Stock; CO13b, p. 515, Young woman standing and smiling, Glow Asia/SuperStock; CO13c, p. 514, Pipe stem, Plains People, © The Trustees of the British Museum/Art Resource, NY; CO14, p. 552, Four sides of cardboard box with jute and packaging tape, pixhook/Getty Images; CO14b, p. 553, Father and daughter, Edward Carlile Portraits/Getty Images; CO14c, p. 552, Two long-stemmed roses on a laptop computer, cpaquin/Getty Images

Video still images credit:

Chapter 3, Worldwide Features/Barcroft Media/Landov; Chapter 6, Jiri Rezac/-Polaris/Newscom; All other chapters, WHF/Worth archive Silhouettes on page i: Businessman on podium: Comstock/Getty Images; Officer: Exactostock/Superstock; Standing woman: Glow Asia/Superstock; Woman Pointing: Blue Jean Images/Superstock; Runner: Photodisc/Getty Images; Father/Daughter: Edward Carlie Portraits/Getty Images; Depressed Man: elkor/Getty Images; Man sitting: allindiaimages/Superstock; Firefighter: Tetra Images/Superstock; Baseball Player: Photodisc/Getty Images

For our students and children,
our greatest teachers.

about the authors

Deborah Licht is a professor of psychology at Pikes Peak Community College in Colorado Springs, Colorado. She has over two decades of teaching and research experience in a variety of settings, ranging from a small private university in the midwest to a large public university in Copenhagen, Denmark. She has taught introductory psychology, psychology of the workplace, abnormal psychology, the history of psychology, child development, and elementary statistics. She has experience in traditional, online, and hybrid courses, and is particularly inspired by first-generation college students who turn to community colleges to pursue their education. She received a BS in psychology from Wright State University, Dayton, Ohio; an MS in clinical psychology from the University of Dayton; and a PhD in psychology (experimental psychopathology) from Harvard University. She continues to be interested in research on causal beliefs and their influence on behavior, particularly in relation to how college students think about their successes and failures as they pursue their degrees.

Misty Hull is a professor of psychology at Pikes Peak Community College in Colorado Springs, Colorado. She has taught a range of psychology courses at Pikes Peak Community College, including introductory psychology, human sexuality, and social psychology in a variety of delivery formats (traditional, online, and hybrid). Her love of teaching comes through in her dedication to mentoring new and part-time faculty in the teaching of psychology. She received her BS in human development and family studies from Texas Tech University in Lubbock, Texas, and an MA in professional counseling at Colorado Christian University in Lakewood, Colorado. She has served in a variety of administrative roles at Pikes Peak Community College, including interim associate dean, and coordinator of the Student Crisis Counseling Office. From 2002-2010, Misty served as the psychology discipline chair for the Colorado Community College System, helping develop the state system's approach to teaching psychology. One of her many professional interests is research on the impact of student persistence in higher education.

Coco Ballantyne is a New York–based journalist and science writer with a special interest in psychology. Before collaborating with Deborah Licht and Misty Hull to write *Scientific American: Psychology* and *Scientific American: Presenting Psychology,* Coco worked as a reporter for *Scientific American* online, covering the health, medicine, and neuroscience beats. She has also written for *Discover* magazine and *Nature Medicine.* Coco earned an MS from Columbia University School of Journalism, where she received a Horgan Prize for Excellence in Critical Science Writing. Prior to her journalistic career, Coco worked as a teacher and tutor, helping high school and college students prepare for standardized tests such as the SAT, GRE, and MCAT. She also worked as a physics and math teacher at Eastside College Preparatory School in East Palo Alto, California, and as a Human Biology course associate at Stanford University, where she earned a BA in human biology.

brief contents

contents

CHAPTER 1 introduction to the science of psychology 1

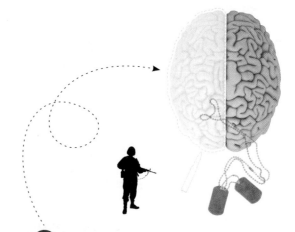

CHAPTER 2 biology and behavior 47

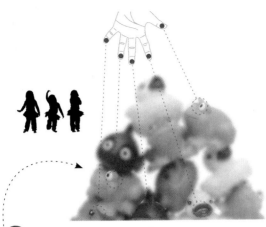

CHAPTER 3 sensation and perception 87

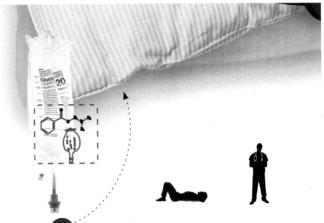

CHAPTER 4 consciousness 129

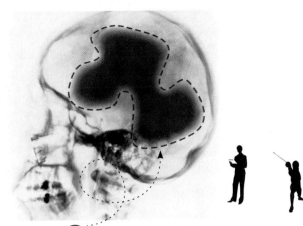

CHAPTER 7 cognition, language, and intelligence 259

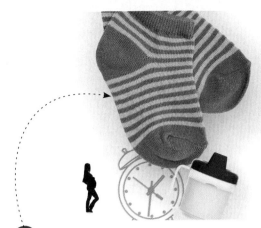

CHAPTER 8 human development 305

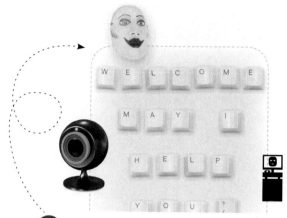

CHAPTER 9 motivation and emotion 357

CHAPTER 10 personality 403

CHAPTER 11 stress and health 441

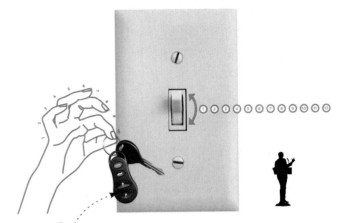

CHAPTER 12 psychological disorders 475

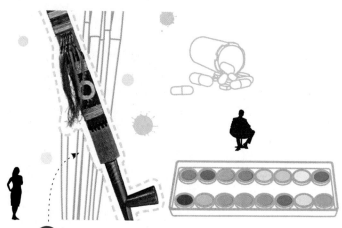

CHAPTER **13** treatment of psychological disorders 515

CHAPTER **14** social psychology 553

preface

In this new work, we have continued our partnership with *Scientific American* to produce an innovative textbook designed to engage and motivate introductory psychology students as they explore and learn the fundamental concepts of psychology. In planning and writing this book, we benefited significantly from extensive needs-based research conducted by Worth Publishers. By gathering feedback and insights from instructors across the country, Worth has identified the most common challenges of teaching introductory psychology, both in traditional classrooms and online.

Written in a stimulating, journalistic style and featuring distinct pedagogical and content characteristics, this text is meant to be a student-friendly introduction to psychology that readily applies compelling scientific information to everyday life. Many years of teaching introductory psychology have taught us the value and necessity of helping students connect with the material. They want to learn about concepts and issues that are practical and relevant to their lives. The research conducted by Worth Publishers clearly and consistently reinforced the importance of achieving a higher degree of student engagement. Thus, we set out to write a text with stimulating content that would offer students a model for thinking critically about a complex world filled with behaving, emoting, and thinking humans.

As instructors, we understand that students' time is limited. To help them get the most out of their reading experience, we have crafted this text, line-by-line, to ensure every piece of information is relayed in a clear and concise manner. We have organized the material to deliver content in the most logical and efficient way. The result of these painstaking efforts is a streamlined and user-friendly textbook. *Scientific American: Presenting Psychology* increases efficiency without compromising the integrity of content.

We recognize that a student's learning experience does not end with the printed text. Accordingly, we have created a text that marries the printed page with the online space, and uses multimedia to seamlessly reinforce concepts. The online experience of this text—and the digital authorship of its components—are not an afterthought. We have been intimately involved in curating the online lessons that accompany the book in LaunchPad (Worth's online course space, described in extensive detail below), and we have written questions for LearningCurve, its online adaptive quizzing system.

What's Different and Why

An emphasis on engagement and comprehension

The combination of our teaching experience, our partnership with *Scientific American*, and the knowledge we have gleaned from needs-based research has led to the creation of an innovative text with several distinctive characteristics. These characteristics, which combine to enhance student engagement and comprehension, are described here:

1. Stories of real people, which provide a relevant and meaningful context for the psychological concepts presented, are seamlessly

Infancy and Child Development

26 AND PREGNANT The circumstances surrounding the birth mine's second child were strikingly different from those of her first Eddie came into the world, Jasmine was a married, working woma 10 more years of life experience; and a decade can make a world o ence in development. As Jasmine can testify. "The mental capacity different between a 16- and a 26-year-old." By this time in life, Jasmine h become much more aware of how her decisions impacted others, especiall her children.

integrated throughout each chapter. These stories also offer real-world examples of strength and resilience.

2. There are free, easy-to-access *Online Video Profiles* of people featured in the chapters. These "In Their Own Words" and "You Asked, They Answered" segments engage students on a personal level. Assessable versions of the Online Video Profiles also exist in LaunchPad and incorporate thoughtful questions that tighten the link between the video and chapter content, creating a more relevant and memorable learning experience.

Christina, in Her Own Words:

http://qrs.ly/fd4qsy1

You Asked, Christina Answers

http://qrs.ly/dx4qsyd

Which medical professional had the biggest impact on your recovery?

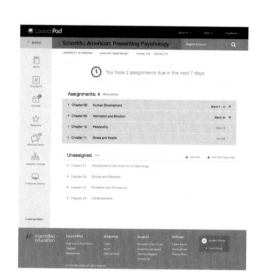

3. Our authorship extends beyond the printed book and into the digital space. As instructors with experience teaching traditional, online, and hybrid courses, we have helped curate LaunchPad, the online course space—ensuring that the online experience complements the printed text and supports assessment in accordance with learning outcomes.

4. The unique partnership with *Scientific American* has infused a journalistic style throughout the text, particularly through the involvement of coauthor Coco Ballantyne, a science writer who came to the project directly from *Scientific American*. In addition, enrichment material from the magazine is provided in a LaunchPad feature titled *From the Pages of Scientific American;* one or more of these pieces are linked to each chapter.

5. *Infographics,* 50+ full-page visual presentations, are integrated throughout the text, combining concepts and/or data into a single storyboard format (patterned after those featured in *Scientific American*). The majority illuminate concepts identified through research as the most challenging for instructors to teach and students to master. Examples include communication within neurons, and positive and negative reinforcement and punishment.

6. *Integrated thematic features* emphasizing conceptual relationships and everyday relevance are woven throughout the text. There are seven themes for the integrated features, and each of these themes relates to issues in contemporary psychology. For each chapter, we have chosen only those themes that logically and directly reinforce content. They are seamlessly integrated into the narrative, never relegated to a "box" or an aside.

CONNECTIONS

7. *Connections* appear liberally throughout, beginning in Chapter 2. These annotated cross-references to material covered in previous chapters explain the

relationships between topics, helping students understand the "big picture" issues in psychology.

8. All substantive content, including the stories and thematic features, flows within the narrative in an uninterrupted fashion. This absence of boxes places all coverage on an equal footing and allows examples to occur precisely where they are needed to illuminate and reinforce concepts.

Compelling Life Stories Woven Through Each Chapter

Stories stimulate interest and help students connect concepts with real life.

Stories are often the key to how we organize information and apprehend meaning in the world around us. Most textbook authors understand this, and many texts contain opening vignettes to introduce each chapter. Similarly, their pages are peppered with examples to help students apply and grasp material along the way.

This text is different. It integrates the compelling stories of real people with essential psychological content throughout the chapter. Students encounter both famous figures, such as NBA star Jeremy Lin (Chapter 5), and everyday people who find themselves in extraordinary circumstances, like shark attack victim Lucy Mangum (Chapter 9). The stories of these people are tightly interwoven into the body of the chapter, helping students comprehend and recall critical material. Readers do not have to guess how psychology relates to everyday life because our stories dovetail the content with the application. In other words, we return to the same human stories throughout the chapter, linking psychology content to the lives of real people.

We have intentionally chosen people from all walks of life, providing a diverse spread of gender, culture, race, age, nationality, and occupation. (See TABLES P.1 and P.2 on pages xx–xxi for a full list of gender and cultural coverage throughout the book.) Students will read about an Iraq War veteran, an immigrant from Somalia, a neuroanatomist, and a community college student who is balancing work, school, and parenting. Our goal is for every student to see aspects of him- or herself in the stories presented in this book, and to convey our strong sense of optimism and hope. Most chapters feature ordinary people who encounter difficult circumstances but persevere and grow nevertheless.

When we say this book has a journalistic element, we really mean it. The majority of the chapter stories are based on direct interviews with subjects—not simply background information gathered from secondary sources. Interview questions have been content driven, or designed to gather information that reinforces chapter concepts.

Online Video Profiles of Featured Stories

Videos allow students to know the people we have featured in a more personal way.

Videos of people featured in the book accompany most chapters and are strategically placed to complement written content. All videos are free and easily accessed via students' mobile devices (by scanning the QR code in the text) and computers (by using the URL that appears alongside the QR code).

Table P.1 CULTURE AND MULTICULTURAL COVERAGE

Culture and multicultural topics are covered on the following pages:

Aggression, pp. 26–27, 580

Alcohol, pp. 156–158

Attractiveness, pp. 588–590

Body ideal, pp. 374–375

Colors, meaning of, p. 101

Conformity, pp. 568–570

Cultural norms, p. 147

Daily hassles, pp. 450–451

Deaf culture, p. 106

Death, pp. 350–351

Depression, pp. 449–450, 494

Development

    adolescence, protracted, pp. 342–343

    attachment, pp. 330–331

    child rearing, p. 327

    cognitive development, p. 327

    moral development, pp. 337–339

Discrimination, p. 581

Eating disorders, pp. 373–375

Facebook and other social media, pp. 32, 546

Facial expression

    display rules, pp. 392–393

    universality, pp. 391–392

Fasting and hierarchy of needs, p. 367

Homosexuality

    genes, pp. 377–378

Hunger, p. 367

Hypnosis, pp. 166–168

Intelligence, p. 286

    cultural aspects, p. 287

    culture-fair intelligence tests, p. 294

    socioeconomic factors and, p. 294

    testing bias, p. 294

Intrinsic motivation, pp. 360–361

Language

    bilingualism, p. 282

    and environment, p. 321

    and personality, pp. 426–427

    syntax, p. 283

    and thought, pp. 284–285

Learning outcomes, in children, p. 327

Marriage, p. 343

Mate preferences, pp. 589–590

Memory, pp. 233–234

Media violence, pp. 205–206

Minorities in psychology, p. 10

Motivation, learning a new culture, pp. 357–359

Musical training and cognitive benefits, p. 72

Obesity, pp. 370, 370–373

Observational learning, pp. 175, 203–204, 206–207

Perceptual illusions, pp. 118–119

Personal control, p. 465

Prejudice and stereotyping, p. 582

Psychological disorders

    antisocial personality disorder, pp. 504–506

    dissociative identity disorder, p. 507

    eating disorders, pp. 373–375

    schizophrenia, pp. 515–517

    social anxiety, pp. 489–490

Psychotherapy, pp. 517–518

Racism

    stress, pp. 459–450

Safety needs, pp. 365–366

Sex, pp. 382, 589

Sleep, p. 147

Smoking, pp. 160–161

Social anxiety disorder, pp. 489–490

Social loafing, pp. 575–576

Social support, p. 469

Stereotype threat, p. 582

Stereotyping, pp. 428, 581, 582

Stress

    adjusting to a new culture, pp. 449–450

    poverty and inequality, p. 448

Suicide, p. 494

Therapy, pp. 541–542

The first video, "In Their Own Words," introduces the person and important themes of his or her story, answers questions, and provides thought-provoking, and often poignant, commentary. The shorter "You Asked, They Answered" clips are interspersed elsewhere in the chapter, showing the same individuals responding to questions posed by students who reviewed the manuscript. These student-generated questions are associated with chapter concepts and offer insight from the reader's perspective. Within LaunchPad, our curated online course space, students find the Online Video Profiles again, only this time as assessable capstone activities for each chapter. Instructors can assign the Online Video Profiles within LaunchPad and require students to answer questions linking the video to important chapter content. Students will never wonder how these stories relate to the course material: The quizzes highlight the connection and reinforce key concepts.

Table P.2 GENDER COVERAGE

Topics relating to gender are covered on the following pages:

Aggression and biology, p. 494

Alcohol
   binge drinking, pp. 156–157
   pregnancy, p. 158

Attraction, p. 96

Beauty, standards of, pp. 588–589

Biological sex/gender, pp. 312–313

Body image, pp. 373–374, 588–590

Cancer and stressors, p. 455

Cognition, pp. 268, 340

Couples therapy, pp. 533–534

Dating, pp. 553–554

Degrees awarded, p. 65

Development, motor skills, p. 328

Dieting, p. 465

Early maturation, p. 334

Eating disorders, pp. 370, 373–375

Emotions, pp. 397–398

Freud's views, pp. 407–414, 417–418

Gender roles, pp. 339–340

Hardiness, p. 464

Hormones, pp. 494, 496

Jealousy, p. 543

Life expectancy, p. 349

Marriage, pp. 343, 379

Mate preferences
   biological, p. 589
   cultural, p. 589

MDMA, p. 162

Menarche, pp. 333–334

Moral development, p. 339

Nature and nurture, p. 65

Personal control, p. 465

Personality, pp. 427–428

Physical development, pp. 333–334

Pregnancy
   teen, p. 311

Psychological disorders
   anxiety and obsessive-compulsive
     disorders, p. 486

bipolar disorder, p. 497

depression, pp. 492, 497

dissociative identity disorder, p. 507

panic disorder, pp. 487–488

schizophrenia, pp. 499–501

Psychodynamic therapy, p. 524

REM sleep behavior disorder, pp. 144–145

Sex
   gender differences, p. 380
   motivation for, pp. 375–376, 589
   and relationships, pp. 379–380

Sexual activity, p. 380

Sexual orientation, pp. 377–378

Sexually transmitted infections, p. 334

Stereotyping, pp. 64–65, 397–398

Stress, coping, pp. 465–466

Suicide, pp. 494–495

Tend and befriend, pp. 63–64

Women and work, pp. 64–65

Women in psychology, p. 10

Digital Authorship That Extends Beyond the Book

The online course space complements the printed text.

As professors who have taught traditional, online, and hybrid courses, we understand the importance of digital materials. Many texts divorce their media content from the written content, so that the online experience seems bolted onto the text. Our book is integrated with digital materials in LaunchPad, Worth's online course space. There, you'll find online materials that truly echo the features of the book—and use online tools to enhance them. Examples are the assessable versions of the Online Video Profiles and infographics. We've helped compose the LearningCurve adaptive quizzes in LaunchPad, to ensure that they match the text seamlessly. And we've curated the LaunchPad units so that they reflect the online lessons we use in our own classes. For instructors to teach effectively, the text and multimedia must be in conversation with each other. Our goal has been to create a text and online system that is in tune with the way contemporary students experience the text and multimedia together.

Engaging Visual Program with Unique Infographics

Our visuals help students understand processes and combine related concepts.

Students are bombarded with different forms of visual media, and they have come to expect visual representations of concepts.

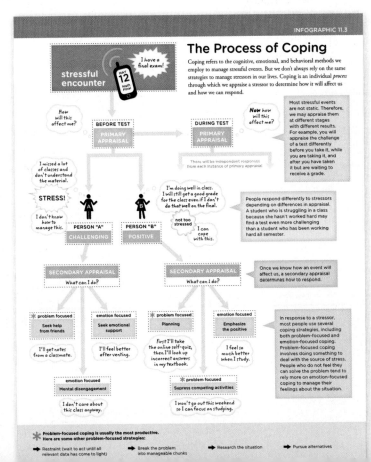

Textbooks have responded to this development with flashy magazine-style images and engaging photos. Again, based on extensive research with instructors and students, including those in our own classes, our text seeks to find a desirable middle ground between the visual clutter of contemporary texts and the traditional, less stimulating pages of those from the past. We have used visuals to reinforce students' understanding of critical and more challenging concepts—without stimulus overload.

Working closely with experienced science illustrators, we have developed infographics with introductory psychology students in mind. Our visuals are attractive and modern, but they have been conceived and developed for their pedagogical value, not their flash. Many of these infographics were inspired by the whiteboard illustrations we create to elucidate concepts in our own classes. Others have been suggested by our thoughtful and creative manuscript reviewers.

Clear and easy to navigate, these full-page infographics combine stimulating images with straightforward explanations in a format that is accessible to the novice psychology student. All chapters include at least two infographics, and many contain three or more. These learning tools are designed to accomplish one or more of the following:

- Describe a step-by-step process or tell a sequential story.

- Compare two concepts that are distinct but well suited to being presented together in a fresh context. For example, we've included four theories of emotion in one infographic to show how each explains the sequence of events leading to an emotion.

- Provide visual representations of data so students who are new to statistics can easily grasp complex analyses.

There is another reason our infographics differ from those found in other texts: They can stand alone. By reviewing and studying an infographic, students can examine concepts without necessarily referring to the main text, making them a great study and review tool. That being said, our infographics also provide an excellent way to reinforce material in the narrative. Finally, use of the infographics is not limited to the printed page. LaunchPad provides assessable versions of the infographics, which quiz students on their content and encourage them to make connections with everyday life.

Integrated Thematic Features

Our thematic features seamlessly enhance understanding of core material.

Most introductory textbooks contain a standard or uniform set of boxes that provide enrichment content. Unfortunately, many students see the outline of the box and skip right over it because they believe it lacks importance or is "unnecessary" content they don't need to master for tests. Instructors may not even assign these boxes if they seem superfluous—not only to their students, but also to them.

We strongly believe enrichment features should deepen and build on students' understanding of chapter concepts. This perspective, fully reinforced by the publisher's research, led us to eliminate boxes and embed this content within the narrative. Our thematic examples and applications always occur precisely where they provide maximal reinforcement of concepts, and seamlessly flow within the chapter narrative. The intent of this approach is to have students continue reading, that is, not stop because they see a box with information (sometimes set off to the side, at

INFOGRAPHIC 2.1

Communication Within Neurons

Neural communication involves different processes *within* and *between* neurons. In this infographic, we follow the electrical action that conveys messages *within* the neuron, from one end to the other.

1. THE NEURON AT REST
Before communication begins, the neuron is "at rest." Closed channels in the cell membrane prevent some positive ions from entering the cell, and the inside of the cell is slightly more negative than the charge outside. At -70 mV, the cell is at its resting potential.

2. THE ACTION POTENTIAL
This graph shows the characteristic electrical trace of the action potential. When the neuron is stimulated, positive ions enter the cell, making the axon less negative (A). When the charge reaches threshold (-55 mV), an action potential is triggered. Positive ions flood the cell, quickly reversing the charge from negative to positive (B). Afterward, the cell is restored to resting potential (C).

3. ACTION POTENTIAL TRAVELS LENGTH OF AXON
The action potential occurring in one axon segment causes a voltage change in the next, initiating an entirely new action potential there. This sequential action travels along the axon like a wave, carrying the message from axon hillock to terminal buds.

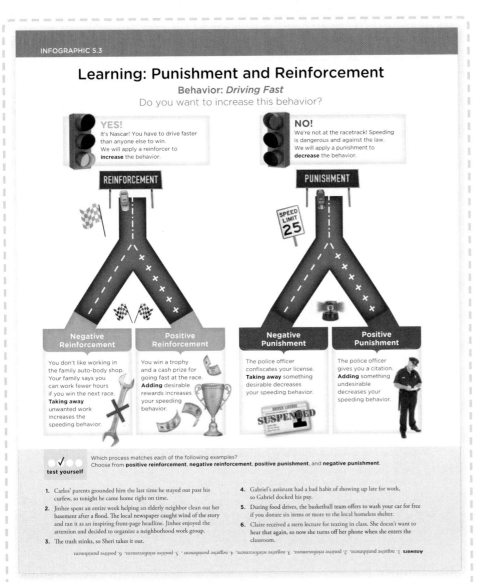

INFOGRAPHIC 5.3

Learning: Punishment and Reinforcement

Behavior: *Driving Fast*
Do you want to increase this behavior?

YES!
It's Nascar! You have to drive faster than anyone else to win.
We will apply a reinforcer to **increase** the behavior.

NO!
We're not at the racetrack! Speeding is dangerous and against the law.
We will apply a punishment to **decrease** the behavior.

REINFORCEMENT

PUNISHMENT

SPEED LIMIT 25

Negative Reinforcement	**Positive Reinforcement**	**Negative Punishment**	**Positive Punishment**
You don't like working in the family auto-body shop. Your family says you can work fewer hours if you win the next race. **Taking away** unwanted work increases the speeding behavior.	You win a trophy and a cash prize for going fast at the race. **Adding** desirable rewards increases your speeding behavior.	The police officer confiscates your license. **Taking away** something desirable decreases your speeding behavior.	The police officer gives you a citation. **Adding** something undesirable decreases your speeding behavior.

test yourself ✓ Which process matches each of the following examples?
Choose from **positive reinforcement**, **negative reinforcement**, **positive punishment**, and **negative punishment**.

1. Carlos' parents grounded him the last time he stayed out past his curfew, so tonight he came home right on time.

2. Jinhee spent an entire week helping an elderly neighbor clean out her basement after a flood. The local newspaper caught wind of the story and ran it as an inspiring front-page headline. Jinhee enjoyed the attention and decided to organize a neighborhood work group.

3. The trash stinks, so Sheri takes it out.

4. Gabriel's assistant had a bad habit of showing up late for work, so Gabriel docked his pay.

5. During food drives, the basketball team offers to wash your car for free if you donate six items or more to the local homeless shelter.

6. Claire received a stern lecture for texting in class. She doesn't want to hear that again, so now she turns off her phone when she enters the classroom.

Answers 1. negative punishment, 2. positive reinforcement, 3. negative reinforcement, 4. negative punishment, 5. positive reinforcement, 6. positive punishment.

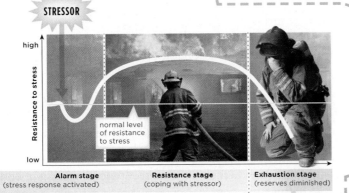

STRESSOR

Resistance to stress

high

low

normal level of resistance to stress

Alarm stage
(stress response activated)

Resistance stage
(coping with stressor)

Exhaustion stage
(reserves diminished)

INFOGRAPHIC 11.1

Physiological Responses to Stress

When faced with an emergency, our bodies go through a series of physiological responses that assist us in coping with a stressor. Activation of the *fight-or-flight* response and *hypothalamic-pituitary-adrenal (HPA)* system gives us the energy and resources we need to cope with a temporary stressor. Studying these physiological responses, Hans Selye (1956) suggested that the sequence follows the same path no matter the stressor. He found that when the stressor remains, our bodies can no longer adapt. Selye called this sequence the *general adaptation syndrome (GAS)*.

GENERAL ADAPTATION SYNDROME (GAS)
In the alarm stage, short-term responses are activated, giving us energy to combat a threat. In the resistance stage, resources remain mobilized, and we continue to cope with the stressor. But eventually we enter the exhaustion stage when we become weak and susceptible.

STRESSOR

high

normal level of resistance to stress

Alarm stage (stress response activated)   **Resistance stage** (coping with stressor)   **Exhaustion stage** (reserves diminished)

SHORT-TERM RESPONSES TO STRESS

Amygdala processes information about stressor. If threat is perceived, hypothalamus triggers short-term stress response.

STRESSOR

Hypothalamus

FIGHT-OR-FLIGHT RESPONSE   **HYPOTHALAMIC-PITUITARY-ADRENAL (HPA) SYSTEM**

Pituitary gland

Sympathetic Nervous System   Pituitary gland

Adrenal Medulla (core of adrenal glands)   Adrenal Cortex (outside layer of adrenal glands)

Catecholamines epinephrine, norepinephrine   Corticosteroids including cortisol

PROLONGED STRESS

Relative risk of a cold

no stress   less than 1   1–6   7–24   more than 24

Duration of stressor (in months)

Prolonged stress can cause the immune system to break down. As you can see, the risk of becoming sick is directly related to the duration of a stressor. This effect is seen even when the stressor is not traumatic. Data in this study were collected from people reporting on interpersonal conflicts and problems concerning work (Cohen et al., 1998).

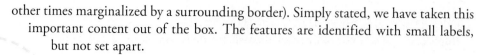

other times marginalized by a surrounding border). Simply stated, we have taken this important content out of the box. The features are identified with small labels, but not set apart.

The seven themes for the integrated features are described below. We chose these features because they are both *relevant* and *practical* in their content and placement. We've created them with the knowledge that the more students are able see how psychology is relevant to their lives, the easier it will be for them to learn and retain the information. In utilizing these thematic features, we follow one simple guideline: Features (typically, four or five per chapter) are *only* included in a chapter where there is a *clear and meaningful relationship to the main discussion.* In other texts, a fixed set of topics is selected for presentation in boxes and statically appears in each chapter, regardless of fit. Our thematic topics vary: Sometimes they are applications of a concept introduced in the chapter; other times they can be used to launch lectures or classroom discussion. As a result, these features are unlikely to be skipped. They offer high-interest content you and your students can use in and out of the classroom—not to mention information you can include on exams. Each theme is briefly described below. (For a full list of thematic pieces, see TABLE P.3.)

Social media provide an easy way for young people to create and cultivate relationships, but the quality of some of these associations is questionable. Experts worry that teenagers place excessive importance on the number of online interactions they have, rather than the depth of those interactions (Fox News, 2013, March 20). Another concern is that social media may serve as staging grounds for negative behaviors like bullying. According to one survey, approximately 8% of Internet-using teenagers say they have been bullied online in the past year; 88% have observed others being "mean or cruel" on a social media site; 25% say their interactions through social media have led to offline arguments; and 8% claim their online conversations have served as the impetus for physical fights (Lenhart et al., 2011).

But it's not all bad news. The majority of teens who use social media say that their interactions through these networks have made them feel better about themselves and more deeply connected to others (Lenhart et al., 2011). Online communities provide teens with a space to explore their identities and interact with people from diverse backgrounds. They serve as platforms for the exchange of ideas and art (sharing music, videos, and blogs), and places for students to study and collaborate on school projects (O'Keeffe, Clarke-Pearson, & Council on Communications and Media, 2011).

NETWORK BULLIES AND FRIENDS

 1. *Apply This* Illustrates how psychology concepts readily apply to our daily experiences and observations. Sections of the text, infographics, tables, and other items with special relevance to students' lives are labeled with the suggestion to Apply This. *Example:* "Protecting Your Senses" (Chapter 3).

 2. **SOCIAL MEDIA and psychology** Highlights contemporary research exploring how social media applications, such as Facebook and Twitter, impact behavior. *Example:* "Facebook in the Brain" (Chapter 2).

 3. **didn't SEE that coming** Raises student interest by detailing an unexpected, high-interest, and newsworthy development related to the chapter's focus. *Example:* "The Perks of Being Bilingual" (Chapter 7).

 4. **nature and nurture** Presents important findings related to twin studies, genetic research, and heritability studies. Students will get a sense of how difficult it is to gauge the relative degrees to which nature and nurture shape human behavior. *Example:* "The Case of Bruce Reimer" (Chapter 8).

 5. **across the WORLD** Focuses on cross-cultural studies, highlighting salient findings on behavior variation across cultures. *Example:* "Know Thy Client" (Chapter 13).

Table P.3 INTEGRATED THEMATIC FEATURES

Topics grouped under this book's themes can be found on the listed pages:

 APPLY THIS

Study Smart, p. 7
How to Read a Scientific Article, p. 19
Don't Believe Everything You Read, p. 40
Where's My Morning Antagonist?, p. 59
You Are in Control: Subliminal Influences, p. 92
Protecting Your Senses, p. 117
7 Sleep Myths, 149
How to Get a Good Night's Sleep, p. 150
Warning Signs of Problematic Drinking, p. 158
Think Positive Reinforcement, p. 201
Multitasking and Memory, p. 225
Study Smarter: Methods of Improving Your Memory, p. 231
Facts About Memory Loss, p. 253
Problem Solving, p. 270
Move It or Lose It, p. 346
Weight Loss: Making It Fit, p. 373
Protect Yourself, p. 383
Are You a Self-Actualizer?, p. 419
Everyday Stress Relievers, p. 467
Think Positive, p. 470
Try This, p. 528
I Think I Need Help: What Should I Do?, p. 545
Cut the Loafing, p. 576

 SOCIAL MEDIA and psychology

Facebook in the Brain, p. 78
Can't Get Enough, p. 163
Contagious Behaviors, p. 194
The Social Networking Teen Machine, p. 337
Network Needs, p. 368
It's Written All Over Your Facebook, p. 433
Therapist or Friend?, p. 546
Relationships Online, p. 588

 didn't SEE that coming

SpongeBob on the Brain, p. 38
Rescuing Animals with Classical Conditioning, p. 182
Google Brain, p. 242
The Perks of Being Bilingual, p. 282
Inside the Brain of a Rapper, p. 299
"On Being Sane in Insane Places," p. 482
Something Doesn't Feel Right, p. 562

 nature and nurture

What Kind of Sleeper Are You?, p. 142
Why Dyslexia?, p. 296
Destiny of the Difficult Baby, p. 329
The Case of Bruce Reimer, p. 341
The Funny Thing About Personality, p. 406
Four Sisters, p. 501
Why The Attitude?, p. 561

 across the WORLD

The Many Faces of Facebook, p. 32
Memory and Culture, p. 233
Death in Different Cultures, p. 350
A Cross-Cultural Look at Eating Disorders, p. 374
What They are Doing in Bed...or Elsewhere, p. 382
Can You Feel the Culture?, p. 392
Culture of Personality, p. 428
The Stress of Starting Anew, p. 449
The Many Faces of Social Anxiety, p. 490
Know Thy Client, p. 541
Slackers of the West, p. 576

 CONTROVERSIES

Conflicted Feelings About Cochlear Implants, p. 106
False Claims About Hypnosis, p. 166
Spotlight on Spanking, p. 200
The Debate over Repressed Childhood Memories, p. 245
Do Animals Use Language, Too?, p. 285
How Birth Order May—or May Not—Affect Your Personality, p. 416
Meditate on This, p. 468
The Stanford "Prison," p. 582
Are You My Natural Selection?, p. 589

 THINK again

What's in a Number?, p. 16
Male Brain, Female Brain, p. 64
Extrasensory Perception, p. 124
Chickens Can't Play Baseball, p. 189
Fearing the Friendly Skies, p. 276
Let Them Eat Cake, p. 278
Language Without Sound, p. 284
Genie the "Feral Child," p. 323
Sext You Later, p. 381
Think Positive, p. 470
The Insanity Plea, p. 478

6. **CONTROVERSIES** Examines debates over contemporary research and provocative issues in the psychological community. *Example:* "The Debate over Repressed Childhood Memories" (Chapter 6).

7. **THINK again** Helps students zero in on key concepts or deconstruct popular psychological myths, providing a fun and interesting way to hone their critical thinking skills. *Example:* "Chickens Can't Play Baseball" (Chapter 5).

Connections: Emphasizing the "Big Picture"

Frequently occurring short asides point out conceptual links across chapters.

As instructors, we have spent years consistently pointing out important conceptual relationships among psychology topics and subdisciplines. Research by Worth Publishers confirms that the vast majority of instructors (over 90%) believe it is important for students to grasp the "big picture" issues of psychology. Yet most texts fall short in this respect. Many present psychology's subdisciplines as "silos" or independent areas of study and then, in an attempt to counter this limitation, include brief cross-references (frequently limited to a page number), or boxed inserts that are nicely annotated, but used too infrequently.

With considerable help from our reviewers, we believe we've overcome this long-standing problem. Beyond the introductory chapter, students will encounter numerous **Connections**, clearly annotated to establish key conceptual relationships across chapters. In Chapter 6 on memory, for example, we connect our discussion of attention to the topic of consciousness (Chapter 4), pointing out that we can only attend to, and thus remember, a certain amount of information at any given time. In Chapter 8 on human development, we link our discussion of language development to the principles of learning (Chapter 5), noting that operant conditioning and observational learning play a role in language acquisition.

CONNECTIONS

In **Chapter 1** we presented the four major goals of psychology: describe, explain, predict, and control behavior. These four goals guide psychologists' investigation of how biology influences behavior. As you read through this chapter, try to keep these goals in mind.

From Administrator to Adjunct: Assessment That Helps

Our assessment components encourage students to become more proactive about learning.

In the interest of more student engagement, psychology instructors continue to request that authors provide more applications and exercises. In our own classrooms, we have noted that the use of these "learning by doing" tools has become increasingly popular and very effective. Accordingly, our chapters include Try This exercises that ask students to apply key concepts by performing simple activities. They are typically fast and easy-to-do, and reinforce chapter content. For example, in Chapter 7 on cognition, we provide students with a list of six words and ask them to create as many sentences as possible. The point of this activity is to show that language is a creative medium. In Chapter 9 on motivation and emotion, we ask students to hold a pen in their mouth in two different ways and then reflect on how they feel. This exercise demonstrates the facial feedback hypothesis.

try this

Take 15 seconds and try to memorize these seven words in the order they appear:
puppy stop sing sadness soccer kick panic.
Now close your eyes, and see how many you recall. How did you do?

Another key pedagogical tool is the Show What You Know at the end of each major section. Our questions are carefully tied to the chapter's learning objectives, and rather than limit their assessment purpose to recall and recognition, each set includes one or more questions that require application and conceptual synthesis. In turn, these questions serve to continuously remind students of the importance of achieving a deeper understanding of key principles. A typical example of such a question comes from Chapter 2 on biology and behavior: "When confronted with a potentially threatening situation, the sympathetic nervous system sometimes prepares for 'fight or flight' and/or 'tend and befriend.' How would you explain these two very different responses using the evolutionary perspective?"

As instructors, we understand the value of both formative and summative assessment. We've read the research and we have seen it play out in the classroom: Students learn better when they are tested on the material. But testing needn't be restricted to high-stakes exams and stressful pop quizzes. We can build assessment into the learning process using end-of-section and end-of-chapter questions that reward students for reading carefully and encourage them to think critically. This is the purpose of our Show What You Know and *Test Prep* features. We can also incorporate fun explorative activities where appropriate (the Try This feature), and give students the opportunity to challenge themselves further with online assessment. Worth's research-driven Learning-Curve adaptive quizzing system (available via LaunchPad) provides students with formative assessment and immediate and personalized feedback. We, the authors, have written and reviewed quiz questions for LearningCurve, so instructors and students can be confident that the online formative assessment is seamlessly aligned with the text.

FRANCKREPORTER/ GETTY IMAGES

Alignment with the American Psychological Association and Disciplines Beyond Psychology

APA Learning Guidelines 2.0

We aim to prepare students for successful careers in psychology and other fields. For this reason, we have aligned our content with the goals of psychology's principal professional organization, the American Psychological Association (APA). Even more granular alignment can be found in our Test Bank, which allows instructors to sort questions by APA learning goal.

ALIGNMENT WITH APA LEARNING GUIDELINES 2.0

GOAL 1: KNOWLEDGE BASE IN PSYCHOLOGY

APA LEARNING OBJECTIVES:

1.1 Describe key concepts, principles, and overarching themes in psychology

1.2 Develop a working knowledge of psychology's content domains

1.3 Describe applications of psychology

APA Learning Goal 1 aligns with the following *Scientific American: Presenting Psychology* content and *Scientific American: Presenting Psychology* objectives (numbered by chapter).

CHAPTER 1: 1.1–1.10

CHAPTER 2: 2.1–2.16

CHAPTER 3: 3.1–3.15

CHAPTER 4: 4.1–4.12

CHAPTER 5: 5.1–5.15

CHAPTER 6: 6.1–6.15

CHAPTER 7: 7.1–7.12

CHAPTER 8: 8.1–8.20

CHAPTER 9: 9.1–9.17

CHAPTER 10: 10.1–10.15

CHAPTER 11: 11.1–11.12

CHAPTER 12: 12.1–12.11

CHAPTER 13: 13.1–13.12

CHAPTER 14: 14.1–14.12

APPENDIX A: Introduction to Statistics

APPENDIX B: Careers in Psychology

INTEGRATED THEMATIC features in each chapter

ALL CONNECTIONS in Chapters 2–15 and Appendix A

ALIGNMENT WITH APA LEARNING GUIDELINES 2.0 (CONTINUED)

INFOGRAPHICS in each chapter

TRY THIS application activities in Chapters 1–7, 9, 11, 13, 14, and Appendix A: Introduction to Statistics

LAUNCHPAD RESOURCES

LEARNINGCURVE

INSTRUCTOR'S RESOURCE MANUAL

GOAL 2: SCIENTIFIC INQUIRY AND CRITICAL THINKING

APA LEARNING OBJECTIVES:

2.1 Use scientific reasoning to interpret psychological phenomena

2.2 Demonstrate psychology information literacy

2.3 Engage in innovative and integrative thinking and problem solving

2.4 Interpret, design, and conduct basic psychological research

2.5 Incorporate sociocultural factors in scientific inquiry

APA Learning Goal 2 aligns with the following *Scientific American: Presenting Psychology* content and *Scientific American: Presenting Psychology* objectives (numbered by chapter). (Objectives noted as "From the Pages of *Scientific American*" may be found on Launch Pad.)

CHAPTER 1: 1.6–1.10; Think Again: What's in a Number?; Didn't See That Coming: SpongeBob on the Brain; From the Pages of *Scientific American:* Murder She Wrote; Infographic 1.2: How to Read a Scientific Article; Infographic 1.3: The Scientific Method; Infographic 1.4: The Correlation Coefficient: What's in a Number?; Infographic 1.5: The Experimental Method: Are You in Control?

CHAPTER 2: 2.2; Think Again: Male Brain, Female Brain; Social Media and Psychology: Facebook in the Brain; Infographic 2.1: Ways to Study the Living Brain

CHAPTER 3: 3.11, 3.15; Controversies: Conflicted Feelings About Cochlear Implants; Didn't See That Coming: Think Again: Extrasensory Perception; From the Pages of *Scientific American:* Physically Out of Tune; From the Pages of *Scientific American:* Brain Freeze Explained; Infographic 3.4: Gestalt Organizing Principles: The Whole is Greater

CHAPTER 4: Nature and Nurture: What Kind of Sleeper Are You?; Apply This: 7 Sleep Myths; Controversies: False Claims About Hypnosis; From the Pages of *Scientific American:* More than Just a Bad Dream; Social Media and Psychology: Can't Get Enough

CHAPTER 5: Didn't See That Coming: Rescuing Animals with Classical Conditioning; Think Again: Chickens Can't Play Baseball; Controversies: Spotlight on Spanking; From the Pages of *Scientific American:* The Taste of Immune Suppression; Infographic 5.1: Learning Through Classical Conditioning; Infographic 5.2: Learning Through Operant Conditioning; Infographic 5.3: Learning: Punishment and Reinforcement

CHAPTER 6: Apply This: Multitasking and Memory; Didn't See That Coming: Google Brain; Controversies: The Debate Over Repressed Childhood Memories; From the Pages of *Scientific American:* Why Testing Boosts Learning; From the Pages of *Scientific American:* What Marijuana Reveals About Memory; Infographic 6.1: Sensory Memory; Infographic 6.2: Study Smarter: Methods of Improving Your Memory

CHAPTER 7: Think Again: Fearing the Friendly Skies; Think Again: Let Them Eat Cake; Didn't See That Coming: The Perks of Being Bilingual; Think Again: Language Without Sound; Controversies: Do Animals Use Language Too?; Nature and Nurture: Why Dyslexia?; Didn't See That Coming: Inside the Brain of a Rapper; From the Pages of *Scientific American:* Laughter Leads to Insight; Infographic 7.1: Concepts and Prototypes; Infographic 7.2: Problem Solving; Infographic 7.4: How Smart Are Intelligence Tests?

CHAPTER 8: 8.19; Think Again: Genie the "Feral Child"; Nature and Nurture: Destiny of the Difficult Baby; From the Pages of *Scientific American:* Changing Social Roles Can Reverse Aging; Infographic 8.1: Research Methods in Developmental Psychology; Infographic 8.3: Piaget's Theory of Cognitive Development

CHAPTER 9: From the Pages of *Scientific American:* Lunchtime Leniency; From the Pages of *Scientific American:* Happy in the Morning; Infographic 9.2: Mechanisms in Hunger Regulation; Infographic 9.4: The Anatomy of Fear

CHAPTER 10: Nature and Nurture: The Funny Thing About Personality; Controversies: How Birth Order May—or May Not—Affect Your Personality; From the Pages of *Scientific American:* Open Mind, Longer Life; Infographic 10.1: Ego Defense Mechanisms; Infographic 10.2: The Social-Cognitive Perspective on Personality; Infographic 10.3: Examining the Unconscious: Projective Personality Tests

CHAPTER 11: 11.2–11.3; Controversies: Meditate on This; Think Again: Think Positive; From the Pages of *Scientific American:* Meditate That Cold Away; Infographic 11.2: Physiological Responses to Stress; Infographic 11.3: The Process of Coping; Infographic 11.1: Stressed Out

CHAPTER 12: 12.9; Think Again: The Insanity Plea; Didn't See That Coming: "On Being Sane in Insane Places"; Nature and Nurture: Four Sisters; From the Pages of *Scientific American:* Inflammation Brings on the Blues

CHAPTER 13: 13.9; Infographic 13.2: Classical Conditioning in Behavior Therapies; From the Pages of *Scientific American:* A Brighter Tune

CHAPTER 14: 14.10; Nature and Nurture: Why the Attitude?; Didn't See That Coming: Something Doesn't Feel Right; Controversies: The Stanford "Prison"; Controversies: Are You My Natural Selection?; From the Pages of *Scientific American:* Following the Crowd; From the Pages of *Scientific American:* Rudeness on the Internet

APPENDIX A: Introduction to Statistics

DIVERSE CHARACTER profiles integrated throughout each chapter

INTEGRATIVE CONNECTIONS found in Chapters 2–14 and Appendix A

LAUNCHPAD

LEARNINGCURVE

INSTRUCTOR'S RESOURCE MANUAL

ALIGNMENT WITH APA LEARNING GUIDELINES 2.0 (CONTINUED)

GOAL 3: ETHICAL AND SOCIAL RESPONSIBILITY IN A DIVERSE WORLD

APA LEARNING OBJECTIVES:

3.1 Apply ethical standards to evaluate psychological science and practice

3.2 Build and enhance interpersonal relationships

3.3 Adopt values that build community at local, national, and global levels

APA Learning Goal 3 aligns with the following *Scientific American: Presenting Psychology* content and *Scientific American: Presenting Psychology* objectives (numbered by chapter). (Objectives noted as "From the Pages of *Scientific American*" may be found on Launch Pad.)

CHAPTER 1: 1.10; Across the World: The Many Faces of Facebook

CHAPTER 2:

CHAPTER 3: Controversies: Conflicted Feelings About Cochlear Implants

CHAPTER 5: Social Media and Psychology: Contagious Behaviors

CHAPTER 6: Across the World: Memory and Culture

CHAPTER 7:

CHAPTER 8: Across the World: Death in Different Cultures; Social Media and Psychology: The Social Networking Teen Machine

CHAPTER 9: Across the World: A Cross-Cultural Look at Eating Disorders; Across the World: Can You Feel the Culture?; Social Media and Psychology: Network Needs

CHAPTER 10: Across the World: Culture of Personality; Social Media and Psychology: It's Written All Over Your Facebook

CHAPTER 11: Across the World: The Stress of Starting Anew

CHAPTER 12: Across the World: The Many Faces of Social Anxiety

CHAPTER 13: 13.9; Across the Word: Know Thy Client; Social Media and Psychology: Therapist or Friend?

CHAPTER 14: 14.5–14.8, 14.11–14.12; Across the World: Slackers of the West; From the Pages of *Scientific American:* Rudeness on the Internet; Social Media and Psychology: Relationships Online; Infographic 14.3: Thinking About Other People: Stereotypes, Discrimination, and Prejudice

DIVERSE CHARACTER profiles integrated throughout each chapter.

GOAL 4: COMMUNICATION

APA LEARNING OBJECTIVES:

4.1 Demonstrate effective writing for different purposes

4.2 Exhibit effective presentation skills for different purposes

4.3 Interact effectively with others

APA Learning Goal 4 aligns with the following *Scientific American: Presenting Psychology* content and *Scientific American: Presenting Psychology* objectives (numbered by chapter).

CHAPTER 1: Infographic 1.2: How to Read a Scientific Article

CHAPTER 7: 7.8–7.9; Infographic 7.3: The Building Blocks of Language

CHAPTER 8: 8.8–8.9; Social Media and Psychology: The Social Networking Teen Machine

CHAPTER 9: 9.15; Social Media and Psychology: Network Needs; Across the World: Can You Feel the Culture?

CHAPTER 10: Nature and Nurture: The Funny Thing About Personality; Social Media and Psychology: It's Written All Over Your Facebook

CHAPTER 13: Across the World: Know Thy Client; Social Media and Psychology: Therapist or Friend?

CHAPTER 14: 14.3–14.6, 14.12; From the Pages of *Scientific American:* Rudeness on the Internet; Social Media and Psychology: Relationships Online

SHOW WHAT YOU KNOW AND TEST PREP: Are You Ready? Assessment questions in each chapter; "You Asked, They Answered" Online Video Profile questions

TEST BANK essay questions

LAUNCHPAD

LEARNINGCURVE

INSTRUCTOR'S RESOURCE MANUAL

GOAL 5: PROFESSIONAL DEVELOPMENT

APA LEARNING OBJECTIVES:

5.1 Apply psychological content and skills to career goals

5.2 Exhibit self-efficacy and self-regulation

5.3 Refine project-management skills

5.4 Enhance teamwork capacity

5.5 Develop meaningful professional direction for life after graduation

Learning Goal 5 aligns with the following *Scientific American: Presenting Psychology* content and *Scientific American: Presenting Psychology* objectives (numbered by chapter).

CHAPTER 1: 1.1

CHAPTER 2:

CHAPTER 3: From the Pages of *Scientific American:* Physically Out of Tune

CORRELATION WITH APA LEARNING GUIDELINES 2.0 (CONTINUED)

Learning Goal 5 aligns with the following *Scientific American: Presenting Psychology* content and *Scientific American: Presenting Psychology* objectives (numbered by chapter).

CHAPTER 4: Nature and Nurture: What Kind of Sleeper Are You?; From the Pages of *Scientific American:* More Than Just a Bad Dream; Apply This: 7 Sleep Myths

CHAPTER 5: Social Media and Psychology: Contagious Behaviors; Apply This: Think Positive Reinforcement

CHAPTER 6: 6.6; From the Pages of *Scientific American:* Psychology: Why Testing Boosts Learning; Apply This: Multitasking and Memory; Didn't See That Coming: Google Brain; Infographic 6.2: Study Smarter: Methods of Improving Your Memory

CHAPTER 7: 7.5–7.7; From the Pages of *Scientific American:* Laughter Leads to Insight; Think Again: Let Them Eat Cake; Didn't See That Coming: The Perks of Being Bilingual; Didn't See That Coming: Inside the Brain of a Rapper; Infographic 7.2: Problem Solving; Infographic 7.3: The Building Blocks of Language

CHAPTER 8: Nature and Nurture: Destiny of the Difficult Baby; Social Media and Psychology: The Social Networking Teen Machine; From the Pages of *Scientific American:* Changing Social Roles Can Reverse Aging

CHAPTER 9: 9.1–9.6, 9.8; Social Media and Psychology: Network Needs

CHAPTER 10: 10.6–10.7; Across the World: Culture of Personality; From the Pages of *Scientific American:* Open Mind, Longer Life; Social Media and Psychology: It's Written All Over Your Facebook; Infographic 10.1: Ego Defense Mechanisms

CHAPTER 11: 11.7, 11.10, 11.12; Across the World: The Stress of Starting Anew; Controversies: Meditate on This; From the Pages of *Scientific American:* Meditate That Cold Away; Think Again: Think Positive; Infographic 11.3: The Process of Coping; Infographic 11.1: Stressed Out

CHAPTER 12: Infographic 12.2: Suicide in the United States

CHAPTER 13: 13.11–13.12; From the Pages of *Scientific American:* A Brighter Tune; Across the World: Know Thy Client; Social Media and Psychology: Therapist or Friend?

CHAPTER 14: 14.2–14.6, 14.8, 14.10–14.12 Across the World: Slackers of the West; From the Pages of *Scientific American:* Following the Crowd

APPENDIX B: Careers in Psychology

LAUNCHPAD

LEARNINGCURVE

INSTRUCTOR'S RESOURCE MANUAL

Psychology Content on the MCAT

The Medical College Admission Test (MCAT) began including psychology on its exam in 2015. This new requirement stipulates that 25% of the test will include questions pertaining to the "Psychological, Social, and Biological Foundations of Behavior." Many of these topics are covered during the introductory psychology course, so we've made a useful chart that aligns the psychology topics to be covered on the MCAT with the location of that material in the book. A sample version appears below, and the entire chart is available for download from the *Scientific American: Presenting Psychology* page at worthpublishers.com.

PSYCHOLOGY CONTENT ON THE MCAT

MCAT 2015: Categories in Sensation and Perception

Content Category 6e: Sensing the environment	Scientific American: Presenting Psychology		Content Category 6e: Sensing the environment	Scientific American: Presenting Psychology	
	Section Topic	Page Number(s)		Section Topic	Page Number(s)
Sensation	Sensation and Perception (Ch 3)	86–127	Sensory receptors transduce stimulus energy and transmit signals to the central nervous system.	Transduction	89
	Studying Sensation	89–117			
Thresholds	Absolute Threshold	90			
	Difference Threshold	90–93	*Sensory pathways*	Light Is Sight	94–95
	Infographic 3.1: Studying Sensation	91		All Ears	104–107
				Smell: Nosing Around	109–110
Signal Detection Theory	Signal Detection Theory	93		Taste: Just Eat It	111–112
Sensory Adaptation	Sensory Adaption	90		Touch: Feel the Magic	112–113

PSYCHOLOGY CONTENT ON THE MCAT (CONTINUED)

Content Category 6e: Sensing the environment	Scientific American: Presenting Psychology	
	Section Topic	Page Number(s)
Types of sensory receptors	The Retina	98–99
	All Ears	104–107
	Smell: Nosing Around	109–110
	Taste: Just Eat It	111–112
	Touch: Feel the Magic	112–113
The cerebral cortex controls voluntary movement and cognitive functions.	The Cortex: A Peek Beneath the Skull	73–78
Information processing in the cerebral cortex	The Cortex: A Peek Beneath the Skull	73–78
Lateralization of cortical functions	Lateralization	70
	The Split-Brain Operation	68–70
	The Special Roles of the Left and the Right	70–71
Vision	Vision	93–102
Structure and Function of the Eye	You Won't Believe Your Eyes	96–100
Visual Processing	Is That Oprah Winfrey Over There?	99–100
Visual pathways in the brain	Infographic 3.2: Seeing	97
Feature detection	Is That Oprah Winfrey Over There?	99–100
Hearing	Hearing	102–108
Auditory processing	All Ears	104–107
Auditory pathways in the brain	From Sound Wave to Bone Movements	104
Perceiving loudness and pitch	Listen, Hear	102–104
Sensory reception by hair cells	From Bone Movement to Moving Fluid	106
Other senses	Extrasensory Perception	123–124
Sensory systems in the skin	Oh, the Pain	113–116
	The Reflex Arc	61–62

Content Category 6e: Sensing the environment	Scientific American: Presenting Psychology	
	Section Topic	Page Number(s)
Tactile pathways in the brain	Figure 3.6: Fast and Slow Pain Pathways	114
Types of pain	Oh, the Pain	113–116
Factors that influence pain	Gate Control	115–116
	Psychology of Pain	116
Taste	Taste: Just Eat it	111–112
Taste buds/ chemoreceptors that detect specific chemicals in the environment	Taste: Just Eat it	111–112
Gustatory pathways in the brain	Another Chemical Sense	111–112
	Figure 3.4: Tasting	111
Smell	Smell: Nosing Around	109–110
Olfactory cells/ chemoreceptors that detect specific chemicals in the environment	Figure 3.3: Olfaction	110
Olfactory pathways in the brain	Olfaction in the Brain	109–110
Role of smell in perception of taste	A Chemical Sense	109
Perception	Perception	118–124
Bottom-up/Top-down processing	Data-based and Knowledge-based Processing	89
Perceptual organization (i.e., depth, form, motion, constancy)	Perceptual Organization	119
	Depth Perception	119–122
	Perceptual Constancy and Perceptual Set	122–123
	Extrasensory Perception	123–124
Gestalt principles	Infographic 3.4: Gestalt Organizing Principles: The Whole is Greater	120

14 Chapters, 26 Extraordinary Stories

The scope and sequence of our text are consistent with the 14 chapters covered in most introductory psychology books. We've also included two instructional appendices. The first provides coverage of statistical concepts, allowing instructors to choose how deeply they want to explore statistics and experimental design. The second addresses careers in psychology. Both appendices supplement the related material in Chapter 1.

We have described the innovations that set this book apart, but how do they all connect? If we could identify the three unifying themes of this textbook, they would be the following: thinking critically, thinking positively, and connecting psychology to everyday life. Our experiences in academia and journalism have taught us to question what we see on television, encounter on the Internet, read in newspapers, and hear in conversation. Being a scientist means being a critical thinker, and we have made a conscious effort to impart a healthy dose of skepticism in our readers: highlighting areas where research is preliminary or inconclusive, where correlation does not imply causation, and where human bias may color research findings.

Being skeptical does not mean being negative, however. We believe that human beings are intrinsically good: capable of learning, evolving, and contributing to society in positive ways. The people featured in this book display the extraordinary sensibility and strength that all of us possess at some deep level. We have consciously chosen subjects who have faced daunting challenges with courage and optimism. Their stories, along with the other features woven through the text (Try This, Apply This, Think Again, etc.), demonstrate psychology's relevance to a broad spectrum of human experience. Psychology is not just for professors, researchers, and therapists; it's for all of us.

The chapters in this book can be taught in any order. However, we do recommend that students start with Chapter 1, which lays the groundwork for all the other chapters. Here is a brief overview of what lies ahead:

EDUARD ANDRAS/GETTY IMAGES

CHAPTER **1** **introduction to the science of psychology** demonstrates how psychology was intensely relevant to the 33 Chilean miners who spent over 2 months trapped underground. One of the key pedagogical tools in this chapter is an elegant infographic showing students how to read a research article.

CHAPTER **2** **biology and behavior** interweaves psychology concepts with the story of Iraq War veteran Brandon Burns, who experienced a miraculous recovery from a brain injury, and Christina Santhouse, a young woman who has thrived in school, work, and life in general—after having an operation to remove nearly half her brain. One of the highlights in this chapter is a Social Media and Psychology feature revealing a relationship between the number of Facebook friends and structural features of the brain.

© MOODBOARD / ALAMY

CHAPTER **3** **sensation and perception** tells the story of Liz Allen, a mother raising deaf and blind triplets. This chapter includes a detailed illustration of the eye, providing a close look at the retinal cells.

CHAPTER **4** **consciousness** offers a peek into the life of anesthesiologist Dr. Robert Julien, and explores the experiences of Matt Utesch, a young man with narcolepsy. Here, we feature a detailed infographic illustrating how different drugs combine to amplify or dampen neural activity.

CHAPTER **5** **learning** illustrates the principles of classical conditioning, operant conditioning, and observational learning using the examples of basketball pro Jeremy Lin and blind marathon runner/triathlete Ivonne Mosquera-Schmidt. Demonstrating the application aspect of psychological research, a Didn't See That Coming feature explores how conservationists are using conditioned taste aversion to protect endangered species.

CHAPTER **6** memory tells the poignant tale of the amnesiac Clive Wearing and follows Dorothea Seitz, a memory expert, to the World Memory Championships. A Think Again feature gets students to think critically about multitasking while doing schoolwork.

CHAPTER **7** cognition, language, and intelligence explores the cognitive breakdown of stroke survivor Dr. Jill Bolte Taylor and the reading difficulties of actor Orlando Bloom, who has dyslexia. An Apply This infographic illustrates various ways to handle real-world problems.

CHAPTER **8** human development details the lives of two community college students—Jasmine Mitchell, a single mother juggling education and career responsibilities with child rearing, and Chloe Ojeah, a young woman who cares for her aging grandparents between classes and homework. A useful infographic compares cross-sectional, longitudinal, and cross-sequential research designs.

CHAPTER **9** motivation and emotion relates the life experiences of Mohamed Dirie, a young man who immigrated to the United States from Somalia, and Lucy Mangum, a child who survived a shark attack. A Social Media and Psychology feature explores how people use Facebook to satisfy psychological needs (or not).

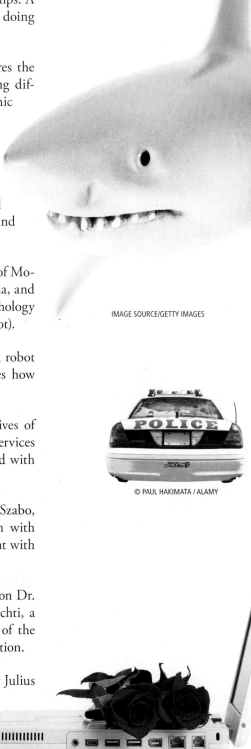

IMAGE SOURCE/GETTY IMAGES

CHAPTER **10** personality introduces the digital personality of Tank, a robot receptionist at Carnegie Mellon University. A Controversies feature explores how birth order may—or may not—influence personality.

CHAPTER **11** stress and health examines stress from the perspectives of Eric Flansburg, a police officer, and Kehlen Kirby, an emergency medical services (EMS) provider. An Across the World feature looks at the stressors associated with immigration.

© PAUL HAKIMATA / ALAMY

CHAPTER **12** psychological disorders tells the story of Ross Szabo, a young man with bipolar disorder, and Melissa Hopely, a young woman with obsessive-compulsive disorder. Here, we have carefully aligned chapter content with the changes outlined in the *DSM-5*.

CHAPTER **13** treatment of psychological disorders focuses on Dr. Dan Foster, a psychologist working on an Indian reservation, and Laura Lichti, a therapist beginning her career. An Across the World feature explores some of the cultural issues therapists should consider when serving a diverse client population.

CHAPTER **14** social psychology explores the life of Olympic runner Julius Achon, who adopted 11 orphans from his homeland of Uganda. In fact, his story is so inspirational that we chose to have him adorn our cover. This chapter also includes the story of Joe and Susanne Maggio, a married couple whose union was made possible by the Internet, and an Apply This feature offers strategies to minimize social loafing in workgroups.

CPAQUIN/GETTY IMAGES

FRAGILE

PIXHOOK/GETTY IMAGES

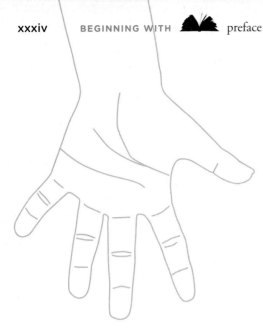

Multimedia to Support Teaching and Learning

☐ LaunchPad for *Scientific American: Presenting Psychology*

LaunchPad offers Worth's acclaimed online content curated by the authors and other experts, and organized for easy assignability. LaunchPad includes a full e-Book, LearningCurve quizzing, student self-assessment, simulations, videos, instructor resources, and an easy-to-use gradebook. It also includes Video Profile Assessments—versions of the text's Online Video Profiles that contain questions to help students connect the book's stories to core content. Infographic Assessments within the e-Book turn the printed infographics into mini-quizzes.

LearningCurve quizzing combines adaptive question selection, personalized study plans, and state-of-the-art question analysis reports. With questions for every chapter written by Deborah Licht and Misty Hull, LearningCurve provides a unique learning experience—a gamelike feel that keeps students engaged in the material while helping them learn the concepts.

LaunchPad is a breakthrough user interface distinguished by its powerful simplicity. Learn more and request access at worthpublishers.com/launchpad.

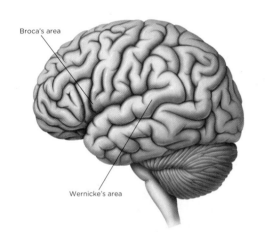

Broca's area

Wernicke's area

☐ E-Book for *Scientific American: Presenting Psychology*

With LaunchPad, the *Scientific American: Presenting Psychology* e-Book integrates the text with an assortment of media-powered learning tools, and a variety of customization options for both students and instructors. Worth's acclaimed e-Book platform was developed by a cognitive psychologist (PhD, Yale University) who taught undergraduate psychology at the University of Massachusetts. *Scientific American: Presenting Psychology* is also available as an online or downloadable e-Book at CourseSmart (www.coursesmart.com).

☐ Presentation and Video Resources

Worth Video Anthology for Introductory Psychology

Instead of having to search through all of Worth's vast video collection, users can now access a "best of" collection that showcases 250 videos from:

- Video Tool Kit for Introductory Psychology (including 30 additional videos co-produced by *Nature* and *Scientific American*)
  - Digital Media Archives, Volumes 1 and 2
  - *Scientific American Frontiers Teaching Modules,* Third Edition

Interactive Presentation Slides for Introductory Psychology

This series of "next generation" PowerPoint® lectures gives instructors a dynamic yet easy-to-use way to engage students during classroom presentations. Each lecture provides opportunities for discussion and interaction, and includes a wide array of embedded video clips and animations (including activities from Worth's ActivePsych).

ActivePsych: Classroom Activities, Projects, and Video Teaching Modules

ActivePsych is a series of interactive activities and video clips that will captivate your classroom and inspire student participation, with minimal instructor preparation necessary. ActivePsych includes more than 30 interactive activities, PowerPoint®-based demonstrations, 22 new short video clips, plus the new *Scientific American Frontiers Teaching Modules,* Third Edition.

Presentation Slides

- Illustration Slides feature all of the text art and illustrations (including infographics, tables, charts, and graphs) in PowerPoint® format.
- Lecture Slides focus on key concepts and themes from the text, and feature tables, graphs, and figures from both the text and selected videos from the Worth Anthology.
- Chapter Photos, Figures, and Tables give you access to all of the photographs from *Scientific American: Presenting Psychology,* organized by chapter.

☐ Assessment Tools

Diploma Computerized Test Bank

This comprehensive Test Bank, created specifically for *Presenting Psychology,* includes approximately 4,000 multiple-choice, true/false, and essay questions. Each question is keyed to a learning objective, page and section reference, and APA goal. Questions are also rated for level of difficulty and identified as either factual/definitional or conceptual/application. Diploma Test Banks allow you to add an unlimited number of questions, edit questions, format a test, scramble questions, and incorporate pictures, equations, or multimedia links. The computerized Test Bank also allows you to export into a variety of formats compatible with many Internet-based testing products.

iClicker Radio Frequency Classroom Response System

Offered by Worth Publishers, in partnership with iClicker.

☐ Instructor's Resources

Instructor's Resource Manual

Written and compiled by experienced instructors of introductory psychology, the *Instructor's Resource Manual* is the perfect tool for busy instructors who want to make the introductory psychology course more engaging for their students. This manual includes chapter objectives; chapter summaries; lecture, discussion, and classroom activity suggestions organized by section; multimedia suggestions from Worth's rich video and student media offerings; plus tips for embracing new classroom technologies and teaching online.

Faculty Lounge

Free to psychology instructors, Worth's Faculty Lounge is the place to find and share teaching ideas and materials that work best in the classroom. In no time, you'll be browsing through a wealth of publisher- and peer-provided resources—or uploading your own. All resources in the Lounge are faculty-reviewed for accuracy and quality, which means you can feel calm, cool, and collected in front of your class at a moment's notice!

- Videos, animations, and images
- News articles
- Lecture ideas and classroom activities
- Useful Web sites and images
  Explore at http://psych.facultylounge.worthpublishers.com.

TLC (Teaching, Learning, Community)

A breakthrough teaching service supervised by a team of faculty experts, Worth's TLC allows you to:

- Consult with leading psychology educators
- Participate in online symposia and events that may qualify for continuing education credit
- Share teaching tips and challenges
- Connect with your colleagues
  Explore at http://worthpublishers.com/tlc.

Student Study and Research Tools

Psychology and the Real World, FABBS Foundation
This reader provides a collection of brief, personal, original essays, ranging in length from 2,500 to 3,500 words, in which leading academic psychologists describe what their area of research has contributed to society. Free when packaged.

Pursuing Human Strengths: A Positive Psychology Guide, Martin Bolt, Calvin College
This workbook provides an overview of nine positive personality traits, such as hope, self-respect, and joy. It also offers self-assessment tools to help students gauge how much of the trait they have developed, and how they might work toward fostering these traits. Free when packaged.

Enhanced Course Management Solutions and Single Sign-On

Blackboard, Angel, Desire2Learn, Moodle, Sakai, and more
Course packs offer a completely integrated solution that you can easily customize and adapt to meet your teaching goals and objectives. Examples of instructor content now included in our enhanced solutions are the complete Test Bank, the complete Instructor's Resources, a variety of PowerPoint® slides, and much more. Course packs are available at www.bfwpub.com/lms. For information about arranging single sign-on/grade-sync between your department's course management system and Launch-Pad, inquire with your local sales representative.

Acknowledgments

Six years ago, we met in Manhattan to discuss the possibility of creating a bold new psychology textbook. Sipping coffee and watching taxis zoom past the window, we discussed our burgeoning partnership with Worth Publishers, and our excitement about creating an introductory text that would bring relevance and student engagement to a whole new level. We believe that dream has now materialized, but it would not have been possible without the hard work and talent of reviewers, focus group attendees, students, interview subjects, contributors, and editors.

Matt Ours, we joke with you about "getting us into this mess!" but it turns out we really do love this mess. Thank you for planting the seed for our involvement at Worth. We are forever grateful to Kevin Feyen and Erik Gilg for having the vision to go forward with this project, and believing in our ability to execute it. Catherine Woods, you have been with us from the beginning, and we are thankful for your ongoing support and oversight. Those early years were tough, but Jim Strandberg made sure we maintained our focus and sense of humor. Rachel Losh, you picked up this project and ran with it in all the right directions. It's hard to imagine a more enterprising and market-savvy leader to see this project through. Now that you are our publisher, we miss your hands-on involvement, but we know you continue to nurture this project from on high.

Acquisitions editor Daniel McDonough, you jumped into the mix with wonderful enthusiasm. Thank you, Dan, for appreciating our hard work, advocating on our behalf, and communicating with us in a refreshingly direct manner. Editorial assistant Kimberly Morgan-Smith, it was clear from the beginning that you were excited to join the team and invested in the project. We know you juggle many responsibilities, some quite difficult, but you always get the job done cheerfully.

Creating a textbook with streamlined content and precise language required extensive editing and revision. It's hard to imagine accomplishing this task without the bright ideas and gentle direction of Moira Lerner, our devoted developmental editor. Moira, thank you for grasping the big picture and keeping track of all the minute details—a daunting intellectual challenge, but one you handled beautifully.

Brad Rivenburgh, Glenn and Meg Turner of Burrston House, you came to this project just when we were in great need of your extensive publishing experience and vast fund of research knowledge. You knew what the market demanded, and you provided explicit directions for supplying it. Thank you for selecting an exceptional panel of reviewers, and distilling their feedback into practical suggestions for us to consider. The focus groups you organized have been an invaluable tool for fine-tuning our efforts.

Marna Miller, Anne DeMarinis, Dawn Albertson, Emily Stark, and Leah Georges, thank you for making the infographics come to life so elegantly. Photo editor Cecilia Varas and photo researchers Jacqui Wong and Deborah Anderson, your patience and persistence have paid off; thank you for working diligently to secure use of the desired photographs; we know it was challenging.

Producing a high-quality college textbook is a formidable task, but we had an expert to guide us through: project editor Jeanine Furino. Thank you, Jeanine, for working diligently to make the production process efficient, and for responding swiftly to our concerns and questions. Director of development Tracey Kuehn, you made the transition from development to production smooth and manageable—and perhaps more importantly, you kept us sane during that first production experience. We knew your heart was really in it when you spent part of your honeymoon with us! Copy editor Deborah Heimann, we are grateful for your help keeping track of all those citations, and answering innumerable questions about hyphens, semicolons, capital letters, and other copy issues. Cover and Interior Designer Blake Logan, you have done a remarkable job presenting densely packed information in a clear and stimulating visual format.

To all the managers, designers, illustrators, editors, and other team members with whom we did not have direct contact, please know that we are thoroughly impressed with your work; we feel lucky to have had you on our team. A huge thanks to production manager Sarah Segal, managing editor Lisa Kinne, layout designer Lee McKevitt, chapter opener designer Charles Yuen, art manager Matthew McAdams, illustrator Todd Buck, and supplements production manager Stacey Alexander.

Peter Levin, John Philp, and Barbara Parks of Splash Studios, your videos give us goose bumps, and some of them move us to tears. Thank you for conveying the chapter stories in a way that was real, yet respectful to the interview subjects. No one could have done it better. Jessica Bayne, your guidance on this project has been invaluable.

Rachel Comerford and Gayle Yamazaki, you have provided essential support to us in our development of online learning activities. Thanks to your expertise, our readers can take full advantage of Worth's online learning space, LaunchPad.

Marketing gurus Lindsay Johnson and Shannon Howard, thank you for helping us bond with the sales team and ensuring that real college students read this book! Without you, our work would be pointless. Market development manager Shannon Howard, thanks for giving this project the promotional attention it needed even before we had even finished our work on it! We also acknowledge the excellent work of Anthony Casciano, who has developed the supplements, and Debra Hollister, who assisted with

Appendix C—in addition to many other contributions.

We have benefited in countless ways from an exceptional group of academic reviewers. Some have been our greatest champions, and others our sharpest critics. We needed both. We are grateful for the hundreds of hours you spent examining this text, writing thoughtful critiques, and offering bright ideas—many of which we have incorporated into our text. This is your book, too.

Mary Beth Ahlum, *Nebraska Wesleyan University*

Winifred Armstead-Hannah, *City College of Chicago, Richard R. Daley College*

Sandra Arntz, *Carroll University*

Shaki Asgari, *Iona College*

Sherry Ash, *San Jacinto College Community College*

Diane Ashe, *Valencia College, West*

Nani Azman, *University of Hawaii, Maui College*

Rosenna Bakari, *Des Moines Area Community College*

Michael E. Barber, *Santa Fe College*

Nazira Barry, *Miami Dade College, Wolfson*

Holly Beard, *Midlands Technical College*

Patrick Bennett, *Indiana State University*

Garrett L. Berman, *Roger Williams University*

Leslie Berntsen, *University of Southern California*

John Bickford, *University of Massachusetts, Amherst*

David Biek, *Middle Georgia State College*

Andrew Blair, *Palm Beach State College*

Marilyn Bonem, *Eastern Michigan University*

Leanne Boucher, *Nova Southeastern University*

Saundra Boyd, *Houston Community College*

Amy A. Bradshaw, *Embry-Riddle Aeronautical University*

Karen Brakke, *Spelman College*

Lauren Brown, *Mott Community College*

Amy Buckingham, *Red Rocks Community College*

Michelle A. Butler, *U.S. Air Force Academy*

Judith Caprio, *Rhode Island College*

Jessica Carpenter, *Elgin Community College*

Gabriela Carrasco, *University of North Alabama*

Sharon Chacon, *Northeast Wisconsin Technical College*

Daniel Chadborn, *Southeastern Louisiana University*

Gabriela Chavira, *California State University–Northridge*

Regina Chopp, *University of Southern California*

Diana Ciesko, *Valencia College–East*

Shirley Clay, *Northeast Texas Community College*

Deborah Conway, *Community College of Allegheny County, South Campus*

Kristie Coredell-McNulty, *Angelo State University*

Cheryl Cotten, *Wor-Wic Community College*

Baine B. Craft, *Seattle Pacific University*

Margaret Davidson, *Rockwall-Heath High School*

Amber DeBono, *Winston-Salem State University*

David Devonis, *Graceland University*

Rebekah Phillips DeZalia, *Coastal Carolina Community College*

Amanda di Bartolomeo, *University of California, Los Angeles*

Matthew D. Diggs, *Collin College*

Evelyn Doody, *College of Southern Nevada*

Karen Trotty Douglas, *Alamo Colleges, San Antonio College*

Kimberly Duff, *Cerritos College*

Jeanne Edman, *Consumnes River College*

Mitchell Estaphan, *Bristol Community College*

Roel Evangelista, *Community College of Baltimore–Essex*

Frank Eyetsemitan, *Roger Williams University*

Kelvin Faison, *Pasco Hernando Community College*

Robert Fauber, *Temple University*

Dan Fawaz, *Georgia Perimeter College–Clarkston*

Christopher Ferguson, *Stetson University*

Frank M. Ferraro III, *Nebraska Wesleyan University*

Stephen Fox, *University of Hawaii–Maui College*

Lisa Fozio-Thielk, *Waubonsee Community College*

Susan Frantz, *Highline Community College*

Jeanette Gassaway, *Ohio University–Chillicothe*

Rachel Gentry, *Ball State University*

Sherry Ginn, *Rowan-Cabarrus Community College*

Gladys Green, *State College of Florida*

Jerry Green, *Tarrant County College, Northwest*

Bettye P. Griffin, *West Hills Community College District*

Donnell Griffin, *Davidson County Community College*

Lynn Haller, *Morehead State University*

Julie Hanauer, *Suffolk County Community College*

Keith Happaney, *Lehman College*

Christine Harrington, *Middlesex County College*

Carol Kozak Hawk, *Austin Community College*

Cathy Hawkins, *North Hennepin Community College*

Rickye Heffner, *University of Toledo*

Byron Heidenreich, *Illinois State University*

Bryan Hendricks, *University of Wisconsin, Madison*

Jennifer Higa-King, *Honolulu Community College*

Mia Holland, *Bridgewater State University*

Debra Hollister, *Valencia College–Lake Nona*

Amy Holmes, *Davidson County Community College*

Karen Y. Holmes, *Norfolk State University*

Nancy Honeycutt, *Alamance Community College*

Mary Susan Horton, *Mesa Community College*

Vivian Hsu, *Rutgers University*

Christopher Hubbell, *Rensselaer Polytechnic Institute*

Ken Hudson, *Florida Community College*

Mayte Insua-Auais, *Miami Dade College–North*

Judy Jankowski, *Grand Rapids Community College*

Joan Jensen, *Central Piedmont Community College*

Barry Johnson, *Davidson County Community College*

Jessica Jolly, *Gloucester County College*

Judith Josephs, *Salem State University*

Diana Joy, *Community College of Denver*

Nora Kametani, *Nunez Community College*

Carolyn Kaufman, *Columbus State Community College*

Zelida Keo-Trang, *Saddleback College*

Lynnel Kiely, *City Colleges of Chicago, Harold Washington College*

Yuthika Kim, *Oklahoma City Community College*

Cheri Kittrell, *State College of Florida*

Nicole Korzetz, *Lee College*

Michelle LaBrie, *College of the Canyons*

Cindy Lahar, *York County Community College*

Jennifer Lee, *Cabrillo College*

Juliet Lee, *Cape Fear Community College*

Kris Leppien-Christensen, *Saddleback College*

Christine Lofgren, *University of California–Irvine*

Pamela Joan Marek, *Kennesaw State University*

Alexander Marvin, *Seminole State College of Florida*

Kirsten Matthews, *Harper College*

Brent Mattingly, *Ashland University*

Cindy Matyi, *Ohio University, Chillicothe Campus*

Ashley Maynard, *University of Hawaii*

Dan McConnell, *University of Central Florida*

Cheryl McGill, *Florence-Darlington Technical College*

Lisa Moeller, *Devry University*

Thurla Moore, *Tallahassee Community College*

Kristie Morris, *SUNY Rockland Community College*

Julie Morrison, *Glendale Community College*

Paige Muellerleile, *Marshall University*

Robin Musselman, *Lehigh Carbon Community College*

Margaret Nauta, *Illinois State University*

Roderick Neal, *Patrick Henry Community College*

Ronn Newby, *Des Moines Area Community College*

John L. Oliver, *Florida Community College*

Jennifer Ounjian, *Contra Costa College*

Joanna Palmer, *Baker College of Flint*

Carol Pandey, *Los Angeles Pierce College*

Jan Pascal, *Johnson County Community College*

Melissa Patton, *Eastern Florida State College*

Linda Perrotti, *University of Texas at Arlington*

Kristin Price, *Owens Community College*

Judy Quon, *California State University–Long Beach*

Marianna Rader, *Rockingham Community College*

Barbara Radigan, *Community College of Allegheny County*

Elena Reigadas, *Los Angeles Harbor College*

Tanya Renner, *Kapiʻolani Community College*

Nan Rice, *Springfield Tech Community College*

Vicki Ritts, *St. Louis Community College, Meramec*

Michelle Robinson, *Saddleback College*

Fredric E. Rose, *Palomar College*

Karen Saenz, *Houston Community College*

Ronald Arthur Salazar, *San Juan College*

Carol Schachat, *Orange Coast College*

Rebecca E. Shepherd, *College of the Canyons*

Melinda Shoemaker, *Broward College–North*

Maria Shpurik, *Florida International University*

Joan Siebert, *Community College of Allegheny County*

Debra Silverman, *Keiser University*

Theresa Simantirakis, *Wright College*

Valerie A. Simon, *Wayne State University*

Karyn Skaar, *Northeast Texas Community College*

Don Smith, *Everett Community College*

Jerry Snead, *Coastal Carolina Community College*

Jonathan Sparks, *Vance-Granville Community College*

Jason Spiegelman, *Community College of Baltimore County–Catonsville*

Susan Nash Spooner, *McLennan Community College*

Chris Stanley, *Winston-Salem State University*

Betsy Stern, *Milwaukee Area Technical College*

Lara Tedrow, *Tidewater Community College*

Jennifer Thompson-Watson, *City Colleges of Chicago, Kennedy–King College*

Carole Toney, *Polk State College*

Elizabeth Tuckwiller, *George Washington University*

Mary Ann Valentino, *Fresno City College*

Jennifer M. Verive, *Western Nevada College*

Jeff Wachsmuth, *Napa Valley College*

Linda Walsh, *University of Northern Iowa*

Martha Weaver, *Eastfield College*

Melissa B. Weston, *El Centro College*

Tanya Whipple, *Missouri State University*

Ric Wynn, *County College of Morris*

Clare Zaborowshi, *San Jacinto College Community College*

Valerie Zurawski, *St. John's University*

Thank you to the following student reviewers who provided valuable feedback and contributed questions for our video interviews:

Nicole Adamcyzk, *Suffolk County Community College*

Hilary Allen, *Waubonsee Community College*

Wes Armstrong, *Georgia Perimeter College*

Michael Baker, *Suffolk County Community College*

Michael Blackburn, *Valencia College*

Rebecca Blackburn, *Valencia College*

Zandi Bosua, *Suffolk County Community College*

Michael Burt, *Valencia College*

Joseph Calabrese, *Waubonsee Community College*

Paul Calzada, *College of Southern Nevada*

Tracy Cleary, *Valencia College*

James Ferguson, *Suffolk County Community College*

Amanda Flood, *Suffolk County Community College*

Marie Forestal, *Valencia College*

Casey Frisque, *Northeast Wisconsin Technical College*

Jordana Gaines, *Suffolk County Community College*

Chris Henderson, *Georgia Perimeter College*

Daisy Hidalgo, *Valencia College*

Matthew Hirschland, *Georgia Perimeter College*

Eric Hollenback, *Waubonsee Community College*

Michael Hollenback, *Waubonsee Community College*

Meridith Hollister, *Valencia College*

Zane Howard, *Georgia Perimeter College*

Caitlyn Ingram, *Suffolk County Community College*

Carole Keef, *Valencia College*

Zoe Kiefer, *Waubonsee Community College*

Donya Kobari, *Georgia Perimeter College*

Emily Kolk, *Suffolk County Community College*

Deanna Krane, *Suffolk County Community College*

Kayla Krasnee, *Suffolk County Community College*

Amanda Landolt, *Northeast Wisconsin Technical College*

Joline Ledbetter, *College of Southern Nevada*

Adam R. Leicht, *Georgia Perimeter College*

Amanda Meyer, *Waubonsee Community College*

Justin Oge, *Tarrant County College–Northwest*

Melissa Ortiz, *Suffolk County Community College*

Kimberly Peterson, *Suffolk County Community College*

Jacob Rodgers, *Tarrant County College–Northwest*

Jared Rodgers, *Tarrant County College–Northwest*

Chloe Rodriguez, *Tarrant County College–Northwest*

Sarah Rogers, *Suffolk County Community College*

Carolina Rosales, *Waubonsee Community College*

Amber Roth, *Georgia Perimeter College*

Danika Sanders, *College of Southern Nevada*

Olivia Schlabra, *Georgia Perimeter College*

Whitney Schmidt, *Tarrant County College–Northwest*

Cheyenne Sharpe, *Tarrant County College–Northwest*

Monica Sheehan, *Tarrant County College–Northwest*

Lydia Simone, *College of Southern Nevada*

Analiese Smith, *Tarrant County College–Northwest*

Victoria Vallance, *Suffolk County Community College*

Katherine Weinmann, *Tarrant County College–Northwest*

Stephanie Willes, *College of Southern Nevada*

Courtney Williams, *Tarrant County College–Northwest*

Owen Wood, *Tarrant County College–Northwest*

Sarah Woolf, *Tarrant County College–Northwest*

The following instructors graciously attended our focus groups. Their feedback both informed and influenced many key aspects of the text, as well as the resources that accompany it.

Anora Ackerson, *Kalamazoo Valley Community College*

Winifred Armstead-Hannah, *City Colleges of Chicago, Richard R. Daley College*

Marina Baratian, *Brevard Community College*

Nazira Barry, *Miami College, Dade, Wolfson*

Sonia Bell, *Prince George's Community College*

Christopher Beverly, *St. Johns River State College*

Andrew Blair, *Palm Beach State College*

Marilyn Bonem, *Eastern Michigan University*

Leanne Boucher, *Nova Southeastern University*

Winfield Brown, *Florence-Darlington Technical College*

Alison Buchanan, *Henry Ford Community College*

Jessica Cail, *Pepperdine University*

Christie Cathey, *Missouri State University*

Shakiera Causey, *Guilford Technical Community College*

Ruby Christian-Brougham, *Los Angeles Valley College*

Julia Cohen, *Los Angeles Pierce College*

Bonnie Dennis, *Virginia Western Community College*

Dianne DeSousa, *Prairie State Community College*

Peggy Dombrowski, *Harrisburg Area Community College*

Susan Edwards, *Mott Community College*

Urminda Firlan, *Kalamazoo Valley Community College*

Amanda Frei, *University of Phoenix*

Sherry Ginn, *Rowan-Cabarrus Community College*

Marlene Groomes, *Miami Dade–Homestead*

Julie Hernandez, *Rock Valley College*

Sallie Herrin, *Rowan-Cabarrus Community College*

Debra Hollister, *Valencia College–Lake Nona*

Nancy Honeycutt, *Alamance Community College*

Kathleen Hughes-DeSousa, *Pasco Hernando Community College*

Susan Johnson, *Cypress College*

Paul Johnson, *Oakton Community College*

Lynda Karlis, *Macomb Community College–Center Campus*

Ken Kikuchi, *College of Lake County*

Andrew Kim, *Citrus College*

Cheri Kittrell, *State College of Florida*

Rachel Laimon, *Mott Community College*

Samuel Lamb, *Tidewater Community College, Virginia Beach*

Deborah Maher, *Orange Coast College*

Jeni Maijala, *University of Phoenix*

Richard Manley, *Antelope Valley College*

Randy Martinez, *Cypress College*

Myssie Mathis, *Cape Fear Community College*

Dan McConnell, *University of Central Florida*

Cheryl McGill, *Florence-Darlington Technical College*

David McGrevy, *Palomar Community College*

Russ McGuff, *Tallahassee Community College*

William Mellan, *Hillsborough Community College–Plant City*

Charles Miron, *Community College of Baltimore County–Catonsville*

Paulina Multhaupt, *Macomb Community College–Center Campus*

Sonia Nieves, *Broward Community College–South Campus*

James O'Brien, *Tidewater Community College, Virginia Beach*

Marco O'Brien, *Milwaukee Area Technical College*

Denise Orme, *Golden West College*

Jennifer Pemberton, *Community College of Baltimore County–Catonsville*

Kathleen Peters, *Brevard Community College*

Debbie Podwika, *Kankakee Community College*

James Previte, *Antelope Valley College*

Christopher Raye, *Santa Fe College*

Alan Richey, *Wilkes Community College*

Debra Rowe, *Oakland Community College-Royal Oak*

Carlos Sandoval, *Cypress College*

Spring Schaefer, *Delta College*

Alex Schwartz, *Santa Monica College*

Maria Shpurik, *Florida International University*

Morgan Slusher, *Community College of Baltimore County–Essex*

Steven Smith, *California State University, Fullerton*

Jason Spiegelman, *Community College of Baltimore County–Catonsville*

Eli Stav, *Broward Community College–North Campus*

Cari Stevenson, *Kankakee Community College*

Krishna Stilianos, *Oakland Community College–Highland Lakes*

Shawn Talbot, *Kellogg Community College*

Anne Taylor-Spitzer, *Antelope Valley College*

Chris Thomas, *Florence-Darlington Technical College*

Khia Thomas, *Broward Community College–North Campus*

Jennifer Thompson-Watson, *City Colleges of Chicago, Kennedy–King College*

Lora Vasiliauskas, *Virginia Western Community College*

Rebekah Wanic, *Grossmont College*

Linda Weldon, *Community College of Baltimore County–Essex*

Rhonda Whitten, *Tri-County Technical College*

Steve Withrow, *Guilford Technical Community College*

Dreama Witt, *Guilford Technical Community College*

Brandy Young, *Cypress College*

There is one "unofficial" reviewer whose contributions cannot be quantified. Working behind the scenes from start to finish, reading every line of this text alongside us, was Dr. Eve Van Rennes. Dr. Van Rennes, thank you for your intelligent critiques and unwavering support.

It goes without saying that this project would not have been the same without the hard work and dedication of our author team. Every sentence in this textbook has been a group effort: We have written and reviewed everything together. Our minds work differently and we have distinct skill sets, but we recognize and appreciate those in each other. Writing this book has been an arduous task (who knew three women could live on just a few hours of sleep every night?), but we have encouraged and supported each other along the way. We are more than a work team—we are lifelong friends. We should acknowledge that none of us would have written these words if it hadn't been for our parents and grandparents, who made our education their top priority.

Last, but certainly not least, we would like to thank the extraordinary people whose life stories are woven throughout these chapters. We selected you because your stories touched and inspired us. Learning about your lives has helped us become more thoughtful and compassionate people. We believe you will have the same effect on college students across the country.

A special thanks to Julius Achon and the late James Fee, who made it possible for us to use the beautiful photo gracing the cover of this text. We hope the inclusion of Julius's story raises awareness about the challenges facing people in Northern Uganda, and about the efforts of the Achon Uganda Children's Fund.

Deborah M. Licht
Misty G. Hull
Coco Ballantyne

1

Eduard Andras/Getty Images

Image Source/Getty Images

introduction to the science of psychology

Presenting Psychology

AND IT ALL CAME FALLING DOWN Thursday, August 5, 2010: It was a crisp morning in Chile's sand-swept Atacama Desert. The mouth of the San José copper mine was quiet and still, just a black hole in the side of a mountain. You would never know an avalanche was brewing inside. That morning, 33 men entered that dark hole thinking they would go home to their families at the end of their 12-hour shift. Unfortunately, this is not how the story unfolded (Franklin, 2011).

Darío Segovia started his workday reinforcing the mine's narrow passageways, a process that entailed covering the roof with metal nets. The nets were intended to catch falling rocks, like the one that had sheared off a fellow miner's leg just a month before, but Segovia knew the nets were nothing more than a stopgap solution. For over a century, miners had been chipping away at the mountain's rocky foundation, boring through its belly with drills and dynamite, and taking very few steps to ensure it remained stable (Franklin, 2011).

At about 11:30 A.M., the mountain issued its warning call. A loud splintering sound reverberated through the mine's dim caverns. Then about 2 hours later, the mountain hit its breaking point. A section of tunnel collapsed some 1,300 feet underground (a depth of 4 football fields), sending a thick whoosh of stones and dirt howling through the shaft (Associated Press, 2010, August 25; Franklin, 2011). The blast of air was so strong it knocked loose Victor Zamora's false teeth (Franklin, 2011). As miners scrambled up the dark passageways slipping on loose rocks and gravel, the mountain shook again, delivering a fresh downpour of debris. The final rumble ended with an enormous thunk—the sound of a massive 700,000-ton boulder plugging their only viable escape (Franklin, 2011).

Meanwhile above ground, workers stood by as a plume of dust collected at the entrance. They knew something was terribly wrong. Those thunderous noises from inside the mountain did not sound like routine dynamite detonations. Below the cave-in site, 33 men began making their way to *el refugio,* a safety shelter half a mile underground at the base of the mine. About the size of a studio apartment, the shelter contained two oxygen tanks, a few medical supplies, and enough food to sustain 10 miners for 2 days. Once all the men arrived, they closed the doors, turned off their lamps to save energy, and began to ponder what had just occurred. As journalists throughout the world would soon report, they had been buried alive (Franklin, 2011).

Beyond the Book: Watch the Video

http://qrs.ly/oe4qsgr

SCIENTIFIC AMERICAN ▶

PRESENTING PSYCHOLOGY

© 2016, Macmillan

Take a minute and put yourself in the place of the Chilean miners. Squeezed into a small, dark hole half a mile beneath the earth's surface, a place where it's approximately 90°F with 90% humidity (Cohen, 2011), you are crowded among 32 other sweaty men. The main supply of drinking water is tainted with oil and dirt, and your daily food ration amounts to one spoonful of canned tuna fish and a few sips of milk (Franklin, 2011). Sleep is dangerous because you never know when a slab of rock might break off the ceiling and crush you. Besides, there is no dry spot to lie on; water trickles through every vein and crevice of this miserable dungeon. Crouched on the wet rock floor, you wonder what your family is doing. Have they heard about the accident? Surely, they will worry when you don't show up for dinner tonight. Maybe a rescue team is on its way. Maybe there is no rescue team.

The story of the Chilean miners is largely based on Jonathan Franklin's *33 Men: Inside the Miraculous Survival and Dramatic Rescue of the Chilean Miners.* Publisher: G.P. Putnam's Sons.

Inside the Mine
A miner navigates through the dark caverns of a Chilean mineral mine. On August 5, 2010, a large section of the San José copper mine in Copiapo collapsed, sealing 33 miners deep inside the earth with barely any food or drinking water. © Marcelo Hernandez/ DPA/ZUMAPRESS.com

Hello from Below
A government video shows a handful of the trapped miners standing in *el refugio*, a safety shelter half a mile beneath the earth's surface. At the time this footage was captured, the men had been trapped for 23 days. They appear worn and weary, but if you look closely, you might notice a glimmer of hope in their eyes, for they know that rescue teams are working 24-7 to bring them home. AP Photo/ Chile's Government Video

In this type of situation, our first concern tends to be physical safety. The average healthy adult can only survive about 3 to 5 weeks without food (Lieberson, 2004, November 8); the humid, filthy mine shaft is an ideal breeding ground for dangerous skin infections; and the dust and noxious air particles are a perfect recipe for lung disease (Associated Press, 2010, September 7; Franklin, 2011). But was physical harm the only type of danger the miners faced? Think about what might happen to a man's mind when he is crowded into a sweltering rock pit for a prolonged period. How might it affect the way he thinks, feels, and acts? The miners' story can illustrate a great deal of what psychologists know about human thoughts, emotions, and behavior, and a variety of other topics covered in this textbook. For example, you can read about changes to sleep-wake cycles (Chapter 4), the relation between stress and health (Chapter 11), and the ways in which we perceive our environments (Chapter 3). As you progress through the chapters of this book, keep in mind that you are reading the stories of real people who feel and react (with one notable exception in Chapter 10). We can better understand these individuals through the field of psychology.

What Is Psychology?

LO 1 Define psychology and describe its scope.

Psychology is the scientific study of behavior and mental processes. Running, praying, and gasping were observable activities of the miners when the mountain collapsed above them, all potentially a focus of study in psychology. And although their thoughts and emotions were not observable, they are valid topics of study in psychology as well.

Psychologists are scientists who work in a variety of fields, all of which include the study of behavior and underlying mental processes. People often associate psychology with therapy, and many psychologists do provide therapy. These *counseling psychologists* and *clinical psychologists* might also conduct research on the causes and treatments of psychological disorders (**Table 1.1** on the next page; Chapters 12 and 13). Clinical practice is just one slice of the gigantic psychology pie. There are psychologists who spend their days observing rats in laboratories or assessing the capabilities of children in schools. Psychologists may also be found poring over

psychology The scientific study of behavior and mental processes.

psychologists Scientists who study behavior and mental processes.

TABLE 1.1   MENTAL HEALTH PROFESSIONALS

Degree	Occupation	Training	Focus	Prescribes Medications
Medical Doctor, MD	Psychiatrist	Medical school and residency training in psychiatry	Treatment of psychological disorders; may include research focus	Yes
Doctor of Philosophy, PhD	Clinical or Counseling Psychologist	Graduate school; includes dissertation and internship	Research-oriented and clinical practice	Varies by state
Doctor of Psychology, PsyD	Clinical or Counseling Psychologist	Graduate school; includes internship; may include dissertation	Focus on professional practice	Varies by state
Master's Degree, MA or MS	Mental Health Counselor	Graduate school; includes internship	Focus on professional practice	No

Mental health professionals come from a variety of backgrounds. Here, we present a handful of these, including general information on training, focus, and whether the training includes licensing to prescribe medication for psychological disorders.

brain scans in major medical centers, spying on monkeys in the Brazilian rainforest, and meeting with corporate executives in skyscrapers (**Figure 1.1**; see Appendix B for more on careers in psychology).

Psychology is a broad field that includes many perspectives and subfields. The American Psychological Association (APA), one of psychology's major professional organizations, has over 50 divisions representing various subdisciplines and areas of interest (APA, 2012a). The Association for Psychological Science (APS), another major professional organization in the field, offers a list on its Web site of over 100 different societies, organizations, and agencies that are considered to have some affiliation with the field of psychology (APS, 2012). In fact, each of the chapters in this textbook covers a broad subtopic that represents a subfield of psychology.

BASIC AND APPLIED RESEARCH   Psychologists conduct two major types of research. Basic research, which often occurs in university laboratories, focuses on collecting data to support (or refute) theories. The goal of basic research is not to find solutions to specific problems, but rather to gather knowledge for the sake of knowledge. General explorations of human sensory abilities, responses to trauma, and memory are examples of basic research. Applied research, on the other hand, focuses

FIGURE 1.1

Fields of Psychology

The pie charts on the right show the primary place of work for full-time doctorate-level psychologists working in 2009 and their areas of specialty. As you can see, psychologists work in diverse contexts and specialize in many subfields. The clinical psychologist above counsels displaced flood survivors in a Thai refugee camp. Research from: Michalski, Kohout, Wicherski, & Hart (2011); Photo: Boris Roessler/dpa/Landov

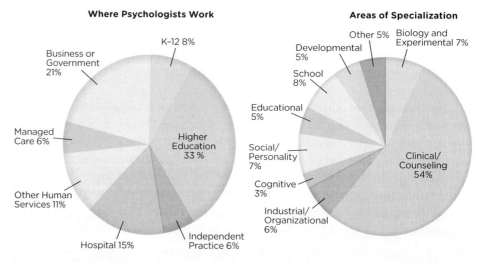

Where Psychologists Work

K-12 8%
Business or Government 21%
Managed Care 6%
Other Human Services 11%
Hospital 15%
Independent Practice 6%
Higher Education 33%

Areas of Specialization

Other 5%
Biology and Experimental 7%
Developmental 5%
School 8%
Educational 5%
Social/Personality 7%
Cognitive 3%
Industrial/Organizational 6%
Clinical/Counseling 54%

on changing behaviors and outcomes, and often leads to real-world applications, such as specific behavioral interventions for children with autism, or innovative keyboard layouts that improve typing performance. Applied research may incorporate findings from basic research, but it is often conducted in natural settings outside the laboratory and its goals are more practical.

MISCONCEPTIONS ABOUT PSYCHOLOGY Looking at Figure 1.1, you may have been surprised to learn about the variety of subjects that psychologists study. If so, you are not alone. Researchers report that students often have misconceptions about psychology (Hughes, Lyddy, & Lambe, 2013). Most of what the average person knows about psychology comes from the popular media, which fails to present an accurate portrayal of the field, its practitioners, and its findings. Frequently, guests who are introduced as "psychologists" or "therapists" by television talk show hosts really aren't psychologists as defined by the leading psychological organizations (Stanovich, 2013).

One common misconception is that psychology is simply common sense, meaning it is just a collection of knowledge that any reasonably smart person can pick up through everyday experiences. This sense of the obviousness of psychological findings might be related to the *hindsight bias,* or the feeling that "I knew it all along." When a student learns of a finding from psychology, she may believe she knew it all along because the finding seems obvious to her in retrospect, even though she wouldn't necessarily have predicted the outcome beforehand. We fall prey to the hindsight bias in part because we are constantly seeking to explain events; we come up with plausible explanations after we learn of a finding from psychological research (Lilienfeld, 2012). Or sometimes, students insist they know all there is to know about child development, for example, because they are parents. Just because a young man has experience as a father does not necessarily mean he can observe his family like a scientist. The problem is that common sense and "popular wisdom" are not always correct (Lilienfeld, 2012). Common sense is an important ability that helps us survive and adapt, but it should not take the place of scientific findings. As you learn more about the human mind, you will start to see that it is quite fallible and prone to errors (Chapter 6 and Chapter 7). **Table 1.2** identifies some common-sense myths that have been dispelled through research. Have you fallen for any of them?

▲ FIGURE 1.2
What Is This?
Throughout this book, you will find parenthetical notes like this one. These citations tell you the source of research or findings being discussed, in this case a book published by Stanovich in 2013. If you want to know more about a topic, you can look up the source and read the original article or book. Information provided in this brief citation allows you to locate the full reference in the alphabetized reference list at the back of the textbook: Look for **Stanovich, K. E. (2013)** on page R-41. There are many systems and formats for citing sources, but this textbook uses the APA style established by the American Psychological Association (APA, 2010c).

TABLE 1.2 DISPELLED: FIVE "COMMONSENSE" MYTHS	
Myth	**Reality**
"Blowing off steam" or expressing anger is good for you.	Unleashing anger actually may make you more aggressive (Lilienfeld, Lynn, Ruscio, & Beyerstein, 2010).
Most older people live sad and solitary lives.	People actually become happier with age (Lilienfeld et al., 2010).
Once you're married and have kids, your sex life goes down the tubes.	According to the Global Sex Survey (2005), people ages 35–44 are having more sex than any other age group.
After birth, your brain no longer generates new neurons.	Neurons in certain areas of the brain are replenished during adulthood (Eriksson et al., 1998).
Listening to Mozart and other classical music will make an infant smarter.	There is no solid evidence that infants who listen to Mozart are smarter than those who do not (Hirsh-Pasek, Golinkoff, & Eyer, 2003).

Here are a few examples of commonsense "wisdom" that have been debunked by psychological research.

Photo: Jessie Cowan/Getty Images

PSYCHOLOGY IS A SCIENCE   Unlike common sense, which is based on casual observations, psychology is a rigorous science based on meticulous and methodical observation, as well as data analysis. Psychology is a science in the same sense that chemistry and biology are sciences.

Science is a systematic approach to gathering knowledge through careful observation and experimentation. It requires sharing results and doing so in a manner that permits others to duplicate and therefore verify work. Using this scientific approach, psychologists have determined that many popular beliefs, such as *people only use 10% of their brains,* are not true. There is a great deal of this type of "psychomythology," which is "the collective body of misinformation about human nature" (Lilienfeld et al., 2010, p. 43). Reading this textbook, you might discover that some of your most cherished nuggets of commonsense "wisdom" do not stand up to scientific scrutiny.

The Goals of Psychology

LO 2   Summarize the goals of the discipline of psychology.

What exactly do those who study behavior and mental processes hope to accomplish? The answer to this question varies according to subfield, but there are four main goals: to describe, explain, predict, and control behavior. These goals lay the foundation for the scientific approach used in psychology. Let's take a closer look at each goal.

DESCRIBE   Goal 1 is simply to describe or report what is observed. Imagine a psychologist who wants to *describe* the aftereffects of being trapped in a mine for a prolonged period. What kind of study would she conduct? To start, she would need access to a group of people who have survived this type of ordeal, such as the 33 Chilean miners. Following the men's rescue, she might request permission to perform some assessments to evaluate their moods, social adjustment, and physical health. She might even monitor the miners over time, conducting more assessments at a later date. Eventually, she would present her observations in a scientific article published in a respected journal, and use her findings to help plan future research.

EXPLAIN   Goal 2 is to organize and make sense of what researchers have observed. If the psychologist noticed an interesting pattern in her assessments of the miners, she might develop an explanation for this finding. Let's say the miners' health after confinement seemed to be poor compared to their prior status; then the psychologist might look for factors that could influence immunological health. Searching the scientific literature for clues, she might come across studies of people with experiences in similar situations, for example, sailors living and working for long periods in submarines. If she determined that health-related changes were associated with the confinement experienced in a submarine, this could help *explain* the changes in the miners' medical status, although she still would have to conduct a controlled experiment to identify a causal relationship between confinement in a mine and health-related issues.

PREDICT   Goal 3 is to predict behaviors or outcomes on the basis of observed patterns. If the researcher determined that the miners' reduced immunological status resulted from sleep deprivation caused by confinement, then she could *predict* that prolonged confinement in another setting (such as a submarine) might lead to the same outcome: sleep deprivation, and therefore decreased immunity.

CONTROL   Goal 4 is to use research findings to shape, modify, and control behavior. When we say "control behavior," your mind might conjure up the image of an evil inventor who takes control of someone's mind and makes him carry out a malicious

Ready for the Plunge
A Chinese pilot in training boards a deep-sea submersible in the Indian Ocean. The cramped environment of an underwater vehicle provides an ideal setting for studying the psychological effects of confinement. Submarine crews may spend weeks at a time crowded into cramped quarters—a living arrangement that can affect mood, memory, and disease immunity (Thomas et al., 2003). XINHUA /LANDOV

Apply This

TABLE 1.3 STUDY SMART

Technique	What to Do
Survey	Skim the material to determine what may be useful to you: review questions, learning objectives, chapter summaries. Identify main ideas and concepts.
Question	Note any questions that arise after your survey. Create an outline to help organize your study based on the questions you generate.
Read	Read through your chapter and take notes on the content.
Recall	Go over the material you have read in your mind. Identify key points and crucial processes. Discuss how other material supports the key points and processes.
Review	Reread the material, and include additional material to enhance your notes. "Teach" the material to someone else.
Individualize the process	Break down the reading into small sections you can read, recall, and review effectively.
Space your study	Build in breaks and spread the study sessions over time.
Minimize distractions	Focus on the task at hand; multitasking while studying diverts attention, resulting in more time spent learning the material.
Test frequently	Test yourself frequently. Low-stakes feedback provides an opportunity to learn the material and retain it longer.
Sleep	Get enough rest. Good sleep helps us learn new material and retain it.

Listed above are some practical tips for remembering information you learn in your classes. This advice is largely based on research presented in Chapter 6.

INFORMATION FROM: AL FIRDAUS (2012); ROEDIGER, PUTNAM, & SMITH (2011); ROHRER & TAYLOR (2006).

plot. This is *not* the kind of control we are talking about. Instead, we are referring to how we can *apply* the findings of psychological research to change and direct (*control*) behaviors in a beneficial way. Perhaps the researcher could use her findings to help a mining company hire workers better suited to the confining characteristics of mining. Working in small spaces like mines and submarines is not for everyone.

Psychological research has important applications in your life, too. See **Table 1.3** for some useful tips on learning and remembering information for your classes. Much of this advice is based on studies presented in Chapter 6.

You have now learned the definition, scope, and goals of psychology. You will soon explore the ins and outs of psychological research: how psychologists use a scientific approach, the many types of studies they conduct, and the ethical standards for acceptable conduct that guide them through the process. But we will start with some history, meeting the people whose philosophies, insights, and research findings molded psychology into the vibrant science it is today.

show what you know

1. Psychology is the scientific study of _____ and _____ .

2. A researcher is asked to devise a plan to help improve behavior in the confined space of subway trains. Based on his research findings, he creates some placards that he believes will modify the behavior of subway riders. This attempt to change behaviors falls under which of the main goals of psychology?
   a. describe   b. explain
   c. predict   d. control

3. How is common sense different from the findings of psychology? If one of your friends says, "I could have told you that!" when you describe the findings of various studies on confinement, how would you respond?

✓ CHECK YOUR ANSWERS IN APPENDIX C.

Roots, Schools, and Perspectives of Psychology

The field of psychology is almost 140 years old, very young compared to other scientific disciplines, but its core questions are as old as humanity itself. Look at the works of the ancient Greeks, and you will see that they asked some of the same questions as modern psychologists—such as, *What is the connection between the body and mind? How do we obtain knowledge? Where does knowledge reside?* Making your way through this book, you will discover the answers to these questions take many forms.

Philosophy and Physiology

LO 3   Identify influential people in the formation of psychology as a discipline.

The roots of psychology lie in disciplines as diverse as philosophy and physiology. In ancient Greece, the great philosopher Plato (427–347 BCE) believed that truth and knowledge exist in the soul before birth; that is, humans are born with some degree of innate knowledge. Plato raised an important issue psychologists still contemplate: the contribution of *nature* in the human capacity for cognition.

One of Plato's most renowned students, Aristotle (384–322 BCE), eventually went on to challenge his mentor's basic teachings. Aristotle believed that we know reality through our perceptions, and we learn through our sensory experiences, an approach now commonly referred to as *empiricism.* Aristotle has been credited with laying the foundation for a scientific approach to answering questions, including those pertaining to psychological concepts such as emotion, sensation, and perception (Slife, 1990; Thorne & Henley, 2005). Ultimately, because he believed knowledge is the result of our experiences, Aristotle paved the way for scientists to study the world through their observations.

This notion that experience, or *nurture,* plays an all-important role in how we acquire knowledge contradicts Plato's belief that it is inborn. Aristotle thus provided the opposing position in the discussion of the relative contributions of nature and nurture, a central theme in the field of psychology. Today, psychologists agree that nature and nurture are both important, and current research explores the contribution of each through studies of heredity and environmental factors.

If Aristotle placed great confidence in human perception, French philosopher René Descartes (dā-'kärt; 1596–1650) practically discounted it. Famous for saying, "I think, therefore, I am," Descartes believed that most everything else was uncertain, including what he saw with his own eyes. He proposed that the body is like a tangible machine, whereas the mind has no physical substance. The body and mind interact as

Nature and Nurture
Would you believe that these trees belong to the same species? Both are Jeffrey pines (*Pinus jeffreyi*), but they have been exposed to dramatically different environmental pressures. Jeffrey pines typically reach 80 to 130 feet. The tree on the left appears to be growing in fertile soil in a thriving forest, whereas the one on the right has virtually sprung from a slab of rock on an 8,122-foot peak in Yosemite National Park (St. John, 2003, August 19). A testament to the power of nurture. left: Kent and Donna Dannen/Science Source; right: Bob Gibbons/Science Source

two separate entities, a view known as *dualism,* and Descartes (and many others) wondered how they were connected. Descartes' work allowed for a more scientific approach to examining thoughts, emotions, and other topics previously believed to be beyond the scope of study.

About 200 years later, another scientist experienced a "flash of insight" about the mind–body connection. It was October 22, 1850, when German physicist Gustav Theodor Fechner (1801–1887) suddenly realized that he could "solve" the mind–body conundrum, that is, figure out how they connect. Fechner reasoned that by studying the physical ability to sense stimuli, we are simultaneously conducting experiments on the mind. In other words, we can understand how the mind and body work together by studying sensation. Fechner is considered one of the founders of physiological psychology, and his efforts laid the groundwork for research on sensation and perception (Benjamin, 2007; Robinson, 2010).

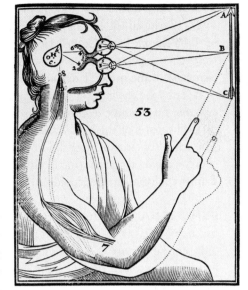

Descartes and Dualism
French philosopher René Descartes proposed that the eye and other body parts work like machines. The mind, he suggested, is separate and intangible. But as you will discover in this textbook, many activities of the mind have been traced back to physical interactions among nerve cells. National Library of Medicine

Psychology Is Born

Thus far, the only people in our presentation of psychology's history have been philosophers and a physicist. You might ask where all the psychologists were during the time of Descartes and Fechner. The answer is simple: There were no psychologists until 1879. That was the year Wilhelm Wundt (vǏl'hĕlm vŏont) (1832–1920) founded the first psychology laboratory, at the University of Leipzig in Germany, and for this he generally is considered the "father of psychology." Equipped with its own laboratory, research team, and meticulous accounts of experiments, psychology finally became a discipline in its own right.

The overall aim of Wundt's early experiments was to measure psychological processes through **introspection,** a method used to examine one's own conscious activities. For Wundt, introspection involved effortful reflection on the sensations, feelings, and images experienced in response to a stimulus, followed by reports that were *objective,* meaning free of opinions, beliefs, expectations, and values. In order to ensure reliable data, Wundt required all his participants to complete 10,000 "introspective observations" prior to starting data collection. His participants were asked to make quantitative judgments about physical stimuli—how strong they were, how long they lasted, and so on (Boring, 1953; Schultz & Schultz, 2012). The following Try This should give you a better sense of Wundt's method of introspection.

Wundt Measures the Mind
In 1861 Wilhelm Wundt conducted an experiment on reaction time, which was a turning point in the field of psychology. Using a pendulum that hit a bell upon reaching its outer limits, Wundt demonstrated a 10th of a second delay between hearing the bell and noting the position of the pendulum (and vice versa), and it was during that very brief period that a mental process occurred. Finally, activities of the mind could be measured (Thorne & Henley, 2005). Archives of the History of American Psychology, The Center for the History of Psychology, The University of Akron

The next time your cell phone vibrates, take the opportunity to engage in some introspection. Grab the cell phone and hold it in your hands (try to resist answering the call). Pay attention to what you experience as you wait for the vibrations to stop. Then put down the phone and consider your experience. Report on your sensations (the color, the shape, the texture, and so on) and feelings (anxiety, excitement, frustration), but make your observations *objective.*

try this

introspection The examination of one's own conscious activities.

STRUCTURALISM   A student of Wundt's, Edward Titchener (tĭch′ənər) (1867–1927) developed the school of psychology known as **structuralism.** In 1893 Titchener set up a laboratory at Cornell University in Ithaca, New York, where he conducted introspection experiments aimed at determining the structure and "atoms" (or most basic elements) of the mind. Titchener's participants, also extremely well trained, were asked to describe the elements of their current consciousness. In contrast to Wundt's focus on *objective,* quantitative reports of conscious experiences, Titchener's participants provided detailed reports of their *subjective* (unique or personal) experiences (Hothersall, 2004). The school of structuralism did not last past Titchener's lifetime, and even most of his contemporaries regarded structuralism as outdated. Nevertheless, Titchener demonstrated that psychological studies could be conducted through observation and measurement.

FUNCTIONALISM   In the late 1870s, William James (1842–1910) offered the first psychology classes in the United States, at Harvard University, where he was granted $300 for laboratory and classroom demonstration equipment (Croce, 2010). James had little interest in pursuing the experimental psychology practiced by Wundt and other Europeans; instead, he was inspired by the work of Charles Darwin (1809–1882). Studying the elements of introspection was not a worthwhile endeavor, James believed, because consciousness is an ever-changing "stream" of thoughts. Consciousness cannot be studied by looking for fixed or static elements, because they don't exist, or so he reasoned. But James believed consciousness does serve a function, and it is important to study the purpose of thought processes, feelings, and behaviors, and how they help us adapt to the environment. This focus on purpose and adaptation in psychological research is the overarching theme of the school of **functionalism.** Although it didn't endure as a separate field of psychology, functionalism has continued to influence the practice of psychology, as evidenced by educational psychology, studies of emotion, and comparative studies of animal behavior (Benjamin, 2007).

HERE COME THE WOMEN   Like most sciences, psychology began as a "boys' club," with men earning the degrees, teaching the classes, and running the labs. There were, however, a few women, as competent and inquiring as their male counterparts, who beat down the club doors long before women were formally invited. One of William James' students, Mary Whiton Calkins (1863–1930) completed all the requirements for a PhD at Harvard, but was not allowed to graduate from the then all-male college because she was a woman. Nonetheless, she persevered with her work and established her own laboratory at Wellesley College, eventually becoming the first female president of the APA. If you are wondering, the first woman to earn a PhD in psychology was Margaret Floy Washburn (1871–1939), a student of Titchener. Her degree, which was granted in 1894, came from Cornell University, which—unlike Harvard—allowed women to earn doctorates at the time.

Mamie Phipps Clark (1917–1983) was the first Black woman to be awarded a PhD in psychology from Columbia University. Her work, which she conducted with her husband Kenneth Bancroft Clark, examined the impact of prejudice and discrimination on child development. In particular, she explored how race recognition impacts a child's self-esteem (Pickren & Burchett, 2014). Her husband held a faculty position at City University of New York, but she was never allowed to teach there. Instead, she found a job analyzing research data and eventually became executive director of the Northside Center for Child Development in upper Manhattan (Pickren & Burchett, 2014).

Thanks to trailblazers such as Calkins, Washburn, and Clark, the field of psychology is no longer dominated by men. In fact, about three quarters of students earning master's degrees and PhDs in psychology are women, a statistic that now has some experts worrying about the need for more men in various subfields (Cynkar, 2007; Willyard, 2011).

Breaking Ground
Margaret Floy Washburn is perhaps most famous for becoming the first woman psychologist to earn a PhD, but her scholarly contributions must not be underestimated. Her book *The Animal Mind: A Textbook of Comparative Psychology* (1908), which drew on her extensive research with animals, had an enduring impact on the field (APA, 2013b; Washburn, 2010).

For the Children
The work of Mamie Phipps Clark raised awareness about the unique psychological issues affecting African American and other minority children. She and her husband founded Harlem's Northside Center for Child Development, an organization that continues to provide psychological and educational support to children in the community.

Psychology's Perspectives

LO 4   List and summarize the major perspectives in psychology.

Some of the early schools of psychology had a lasting impact and others seemed to fade. Nevertheless, they all contributed to the growth of the young science. Some of the early schools developed into perspectives that continue to help us understand the complex nature of human behavior. The descriptions below and **Infographic 1.1** on the next page show how the early roots of psychology and the perspectives fused and flow together.

PSYCHOANALYTIC   Toward the end of the 19th century, while many early psychologists were busy investigating the "normal" functioning of the mind (in experimental psychology), Sigmund Freud (1856–1939) focused much of his attention on the "abnormal" aspects. Freud believed that behavior and personality are influenced by conflicts between one's inner desires (such as sexual and aggressive impulses) and the expectations of society—clashes that occur for the most part unconsciously or outside of awareness (Gay, 1988; Chapter 10). The *psychoanalytic* perspective is used as an explanatory tool in many of psychology's subfields.

BEHAVIORAL   As Freud worked on his new theories of the unconscious mind, Ivan Pavlov (1849–1936), a Russian physiologist, was busy studying canine digestion. Pavlov got sidetracked by an intriguing phenomenon. The dogs in his study had learned to salivate in response to stimuli or events in the environment, a type of learning that eventually became known as *classical conditioning* (Chapter 5). Building on Pavlov's conditioning experiments, American psychologist John B. Watson (1878–1958) established **behaviorism,** which viewed psychology as the scientific study of behaviors that could be seen and/or measured. Consciousness, sensations, feelings, and the unconscious were not suitable topics of study, according to Watson.

Carrying on the behaviorist approach to psychology, B. F. Skinner (1904–1990) studied the relationship between behaviors and their consequences. Skinner's research focused on *operant conditioning,* a type of learning that occurs when behaviors are rewarded or punished (Chapter 5). Skinner acknowledged that mental processes such as memory and emotion might exist, but they are not topics to be studied in psychology. To ensure that psychology was a science, he insisted on studying behaviors that could be observed and documented.

HUMANISTIC   Psychologists such as Carl Rogers (1902–1987) and Abraham Maslow (1908–1970) took psychology in yet another direction. The founders of **humanistic psychology** were critical of the deterministic tilt of psychoanalysis and behaviorism, and the presumed lack of control people have over their lives. The humanistic perspective suggests that human nature is essentially positive, and that people are naturally inclined to grow and change for the better (Chapter 10) (Maslow, 1943; Rogers, 1961). Humanism challenged the thinking and practice of researchers and clinicians who had been "raised" on Watson and Skinner. Reflecting on the history of psychology, we cannot help but notice that new developments are often reactions to what came before. The rise of the humanistic perspective was, in some ways, a rebellion against the rigidity of psychoanalysis and behaviorism.

COGNITIVE   During the two-decade prime of *behaviorism* (1930–1950), many psychologists only studied observable behavior. Yet prior to behaviorism, psychologists had emphasized the study of thoughts and emotions. The situation eventually came full-circle in the 1950s, when a new force in psychology brought these unobservable elements back into focus. This renewed interest in the study of mental processes falls

Freud Takes Off
Psychology's most famous icon boards his first airplane in 1928, years after psychoanalysis had gotten off the ground in Europe and America. Freudian ideas are still alive and well, though people often overestimate their importance in psychology. About 90% of American Psychological Association members do not practice psychoanalysis, and most science-minded psychologists have distanced themselves from Freudian notions because they are not supported by solid experimental data (Stanovich, 2013; Hobson, 2006). AP Photo

structuralism An early school of psychology that used introspection to determine the structure and most basic elements of the mind.

functionalism An early school of psychology that focused on the function of thought processes, feelings, and behaviors and how they help us adapt to the environment.

behaviorism The scientific study of observable behavior.

humanistic psychology An approach suggesting that human nature is by and large positive, and the human direction is toward growth.

Psychology's Roots

The first laboratory dedicated to the new science of psychology was founded by Wilhelm Wundt at the University of Leipzig in Germany in 1879. But psychology's roots go back further than that. Philosophers and scientists have long been interested in understanding how the mind works. Early schools of thought like structuralism and functionalism developed into contemporary perspectives, each distinguished by different areas of emphasis, prompting different kinds of questions.

HUMANISTIC PERSPECTIVE

Maintain an optimistic focus on human behavior; believe that each person is a master of his own fate.

Carl Rogers
1902–1987

Abraham Maslow
1908–1970

Will tending to and nurturing this tree help me reach my fullest potential?

BIOPSYCHOSOCIAL PERSPECTIVE

Examine the biological, psychological, and sociocultural factors influencing behavior.

What biological, psychological, and social factors influence the way I manage my allergy to tree pollen?

PSYCHOANALYTIC PERSPECTIVE

Sigmund Freud
1856–1939

Interested in abnormal functioning and unconscious thought; personality is shaped by unconscious conflict.

How do your feelings about the size of this tree relate to your unconscious aggression toward your father?

SOCIOCULTURAL PERSPECTIVE

Mamie Phipps Clark
1917–1983

Lev Vygotsky
1896–1934

Understand behavior by examining influences of other people and the larger culture.

How do cultures differ in their attitudes toward nature?

EVOLUTIONARY PERSPECTIVE

Charles Darwin
1809–1882

Use knowledge about evolutionary forces to understand behavior.

Is my fear of heights inherited? Could it have contributed to my survival?

BEHAVIORAL PERSPECTIVE

B. F. Skinner
1904–1990

Ivan Pavlov
1849–1936

John Watson
1878–1958

Interested in studying only behavior that can be observed and measured.

Is spending time relaxing under this tree reinforced? If yes, I will come back again.

COGNITIVE PERSPECTIVE

George Miller
1920–2012

Renewed focus on mental processes, including physiological explanations.

How am I able to remember where this tree is in the forest?

STRUCTURALISM

Used reports of subjective experience (introspection) to describe the structure of the mind.

Edward Titchener
1867–1927

Wilhelm Wundt
1832–1920

Margaret Floy Washburn
1871–1939

Describe in detail each element of this tree, including color, shape, size, etc.

BIOLOGICAL PERSPECTIVE

Use knowledge about underlying physiology to explain behavior and mental processes.

How do my eyes and brain work together to sense and perceive this tree?

FUNCTIONALISM

Mary Whiton Calkins
1863–1930

William James
1842–1910

Interested in how the mind functions to help us adapt and survive.

How does resting under this tree promote my long-term survival?

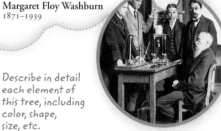

Wilhelm Wundt, "Father of Psychology," founded the first laboratory dedicated to psychology.

PHILOSOPHICAL AND SCIENTIFIC ROOTS

Plato
427–347 BCE

Aristotle
384–322 BCE

Descartes
1596–1650

Gustav Fechner
1801–1887

Ancient and modern philosophers and scientists explored the connection between mind and body.

 Does this tree exist in the physical world or only in my mind?

under the field of *cognitive psychology* (Wertheimer, 2012). And George Miller's (1920–2012) research on memory is considered an important catalyst for this cognitive revolution (Chapter 6). The cognitive perspective examines mental processes that direct behavior, focusing on concepts such as thinking, memory, and language. The *cognitive neuroscience* perspective, in particular, explores physiological explanations for mental processes, searching for connections between behavior and the human nervous system, especially the brain. With the development of brain-scanning technologies, cognitive neuroscience has flourished, interfacing with fields such as medicine, computer science, and psychology.

May the Biggest Beak Win
In a population of finches, some have little beaks that can only crack open small, soft seeds; others have big beaks that can open big seeds; and still others fall somewhere in between. During times of food scarcity (such as a drought), the big-beaked birds are more likely to survive and reproduce because they have a greater variety of seeds to choose from. Looking at the finch population during this period, you will see more birds being born with bigger beaks. It's natural selection right before your eyes (Grant, 1991). © A. & J. Binns/VIREO

EVOLUTIONARY   According to the evolutionary perspective, behaviors and mental processes are shaped by the forces of evolution. This perspective is based on Charles Darwin's theory of evolution and the principles of **natural selection.** As Darwin saw it, great variability exists in the characteristics of humans and other organisms. Natural selection is the process through which inherited traits in a given population either increase in frequency because they are adaptive or decrease in frequency because they are maladaptive. Humans have many adaptive traits and behaviors that appear to have evolved through natural selection.

BIOLOGICAL   The biological perspective uses knowledge about underlying physiology to explain behavior and mental processes. Psychologists who take this approach explore how biological factors, such as hormones, genes, and the brain, are involved in behavior and cognition. Chapter 2 provides a foundation for understanding this perspective.

Culture Matters
In a typical Middle Eastern market, the customer is expected to bargain with the seller. How does this compare to shopping in the United States, where prices are preestablished? When it comes to studying human thoughts and behavior, understanding cultural context is key. Craig Pershouse /Getty Images

SOCIOCULTURAL   The sociocultural perspective emphasizes the importance of social interactions and culture, including the roles we play. Lev Vygotsky (1896–1934) proposed that we must examine how social and cultural factors influence the cognitive development of children (Chapter 8). With this realization, researchers such as Mamie Phipps Clark have studied how prejudice, segregation, and discrimination impact the development of the self (Pickren & Burchett, 2014).

In the past, researchers often assumed that the findings of their studies were applicable to people of all ethnic and cultural backgrounds. Then in the 1980s, cross-cultural research began to uncover differences that called into question the presumed universal nature of these findings. New studies revealed that Western research participants are not always representative of people from other cultures. Even groups within a culture can influence behavior and mental processes; thus, we need to take into account these various settings and subcultures.

BIOPSYCHOSOCIAL   Many psychologists use the **biopsychosocial perspective** to explain behavior; in other words, they examine the biological, psychological, and sociocultural factors influencing behavior (Beauchamp & Anderson, 2010). The biopsychosocial perspective suggests that these factors are highly interactive: It's not just the convergence of factors that matters, but the way they interact.

COMBINING THE PERSPECTIVES   You can see that the field of psychology abounds with diversity. With so many perspectives (**Table 1.4** on the next page), how do we know which one is the most accurate and effective in achieving psychology's goals?

natural selection   The process through which inherited traits in a given population either increase in frequency because they are adaptive or decrease in frequency because they are maladaptive.

biopsychosocial perspective   Explains behavior through the interaction of biological, psychological, and sociocultural factors.

TABLE 1.4   CURRENT PERSPECTIVES IN PSYCHOLOGY

Perspective	Main Idea	Questions Psychologists Ask
Psychoanalytic	Proposes that underlying conflicts influence behavior.	How do our unconscious conflicts affect our decisions and behavior?
Behavioral	Explores human behavior as learned primarily through associations, reinforcers, and observation.	How does learning shape our behavior?
Humanistic	Focuses on the positive and growth aspects of human nature.	How do choice and self-determination influence behavior?
Cognitive	Examines the mental processes that direct behavior.	How do thinking, memory, and language direct behavior?
Evolutionary	Examines characteristics in terms of how they influence adaptation to the environment and survival.	How does natural selection advance our behavioral predispositions?
Biological	Uses knowledge about underlying physiology to explore and explain behavior and mental processes.	How do biological factors, such as hormones, genes, anatomy, and brain structures, influence behavior and mental processes?
Sociocultural	Examines the influences of other people as well as the larger culture to help explain behavior and mental processes.	How do culture and environment shape our attitudes?
Biopsychosocial	Investigates the biological, psychological, and sociocultural factors that influence behavior.	How do the interactions of biology, psychology, and culture influence behavior and mental processes?

Psychologists draw on a variety of theories in their research and practice. Listed above are the dominant theoretical perspectives, all of which reappear many times in this textbook. Human behaviors are often best understood when viewed through more than one lens.

Human behavior is complex and requires an integrated approach—using the findings of multiple perspectives—to explain its origins. In some cases, creating a theoretical *model* helps clarify a complex set of observations. Models often enable us to form mental pictures of what we seek to understand. Many psychologists pick and choose among the various approaches to explain and understand a given phenomenon. Remember this integrated approach as you learn more about the miners. What biological, psychological, social, and cultural factors were involved in their survival? How did these factors combine to form their overall experience?

THE FIRST 17 DAYS   Immediately following the mine collapse, the 33 trapped miners switched into survival mode. When faced with a life-or-death situation, the brain responds by unloading stress hormones. This stress response, which we will discuss in more detail in Chapter 11, leads to a boost of physical energy, alertness, and an overwhelming sense of urgency to deal with a threat. The miners found it difficult to stay calm and think rationally. Some lost their tempers and started to shout. They argued about what to do next: Should they stay in the safety shelter awaiting a rescue team or search the mine for exit routes? The shift foreman Luis Urzúa attempted to take command, but some of the miners refused to recognize his authority. That first night underground, all bets were off. There was no plan, no cooperation. It was every man for himself (Franklin, 2011).

After a sleepless night on the wet floor, the men arose in darkness (morning, noon, and midnight all look the same when you're half a mile beneath the earth's surface). But the day started off on a bright note when one of the older miners, José Henríquez, led the group in a prayer. With restored optimism, one group of men began to search the mine's winding tunnels for escape passages. Another team tried to alert rescue workers by blasting through rock with dynamite sticks, banging the roof with heavy machinery, and beeping the horns of trucks that had been sealed underground with them. Both missions failed, and the miners spent yet another night splayed on jagged slabs of rock (Franklin, 2011).

Several days passed without a sign from the world above, and the miners grew weak and weary. To stretch their food supply over several days, they had been forced to limit their intake to one spoonful of tuna fish, half a glass of milk, and one cracker every 24 hours—about 100 calories per day. Their only source of hydration was oil-tainted water so foul-tasting that one man opted to try his own urine as an alternative. For a toilet, they used an old oil drum, the smell of which was almost unbearable (Franklin, 2011).

By Day 16, each of the miners had lost what appeared to be about 20 pounds (Healy, 2010, August 23). Some had written goodbye letters to their wives and children. "Take care and protect your mother, your sister, you are now the man of the house," Mario Sepúlveda wrote his teenage son (Franklin, 2011, p. 111). For several days, the men had been hearing the hum of drills, a sure sign that a recovery effort was under way, but no rescue team had actually reached the part of the mine where they were trapped (Franklin, 2011). Then at 5:50 A.M. on the 17th day, a miracle came crashing through the roof of their dank dungeon: the tip of a drill bit. The rescue team had finally found them (Franklin, 2011).

Above ground, rescuers waited anxiously as the drill slowly emerged from underground. The tip of the bit surfaced with orange paint on the bottom and bags of letters— sure signs that at least one man had survived. But the real celebrations began with the discovery of a note scrawled in red marker: "Estamos bien en el refugio los 33" or "We are okay in the shelter, the 33 of us." It was a miracle: All 33 men were alive (Franklin, 2011, p. 124).

Now that the miners had a lifeline, a tiny borehole through which food, medicine, and other essentials could be delivered, attention in the media began to shift to their psychological status. Drilling a rescue tunnel wide enough to hoist them out of the mine could take up to 4 months: Were the miners emotionally prepared to wait that long? 📁

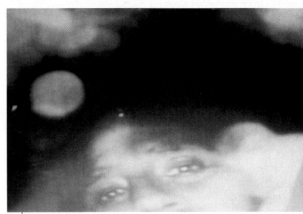

Are You There?

What do you see in the eyes of miner Florencio Ávalos? The image was captured on August 23, 2010, after the miners had endured over 2 weeks of starvation and isolation. © Ho New/Reuters

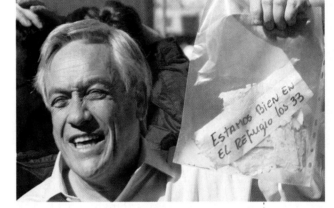

Estamos Bien

After 2 weeks of drilling the earth in search of the miners, rescuers finally pierced into a cavern located almost half a mile underground. When the drill bit resurfaced, it carried a bag full of notes, one of which read, "Estamos bien en el refugio los 33" or "We are okay in the shelter, the 33 of us." The rescuers— and eventually people all around the world—went wild in celebration. Now the challenge was drilling a hole wide enough to hoist the men to safety. © DPA/ZUMApress.com

---

✓○○○ show what you know

1. Wilhelm Wundt's research efforts all involved _____, which is the examination of one's own conscious activities.
   a. functionalism
   b. structuralism
   c. reaction time
   d. introspection

2. Your psychology instructor is adamant that psychologists should only study observable behaviors. She acknowledges consciousness exists, for example, but insists it cannot be observed or documented, so should not be a topic for psychological research. Which of the following perspectives is she using?
   a. psychoanalytic
   b. behavioral
   c. humanistic
   d. cognitive

3. The process through which inherited traits in a given population either increase in frequency because they are adaptive or decrease in frequency because they are maladaptive is called:
   a. natural selection.
   b. functionalism.
   c. structuralism.
   d. psychology.

4. We have presented eight perspectives in this section. Describe how two of them are similar. Pick two other perspectives and explain how they differ.

✓ CHECK YOUR ANSWERS IN APPENDIX C.

Science and Psychology

FRUSTRATED MINERS Extreme circumstances tend to awaken the darker elements of human nature, and the Chilean mining ordeal was no exception. During those first 17 days underground, the men split into three factions, each with its own designated leader and sleeping territory. They squabbled over pieces of cardboard that they used as mattresses, and a few arguments reportedly escalated into fistfights (CBS News/Associated Press, 2010, October 16; Franklin, 2011). But the same life-or-death situations that elicit what is most ugly about humankind can also summon what is most beautiful—our ability to feel compassion, to comfort and support one another, and to sacrifice personal needs for the benefit of the group. In the case of Los 33, the beautiful triumphed over the ugly.

The men were able to move beyond their personal disputes and see the big picture. They realized that banding together was the only sensible way to endure. Like players on a team, they began to assume special roles and responsibilities. The "pastor" José Henríquez led the group in regular prayers; the "electrician" Edison Peña cobbled together a bootleg lighting system; and the "doctor" Yonni Barrios drew from the knowledge of medicine he learned while caring for his sick mother. The miners selected two very different yet complementary leaders: the foreman Luis Urzúa and a second unofficial leader named Mario Sepúlveda. Formerly known as "El Loco" or the "Crazy One," Sepúlveda once pole-danced on the bus the miners daily rode, sending them into fits of laughter. Now they looked to him for strength and inspiration (Franklin, 2011).

To break the monotony of their subterranean existence, the miners coordinated their daily activities, starting their morning with a prayer, holding a midday "townhall" meeting where they voted democratically on all major decisions, and praying again in the afternoon. When it was time for their daily meal, they gathered like a family, politely waiting to eat until all 33 members had been served (Franklin, 2011).

The men experienced their share of psychological meltdowns during those first 17 days, but they found comfort in the bonds of brotherhood. "We were like a family," said Samuel Ávalos. "When someone falls, you pick them up" (Franklin, 2011, p. 103). And like very close family members, they could almost feel each other's pain. "I was more worried about my companions," said Ávalos, referring to the younger men who had just started families. "They had little babies, pregnant wives. That broke me. . . . To see my compañeros cry and cry" (p. 109).

Charismatic Leader
The miners looked to Mario Sepúlveda for support and guidance during their 10-week ordeal underground. Sepúlveda and the shift foreman Luis Urzúa had distinct, yet complimentary, leadership styles.
El Mercurio/Chile/GDA/El Mercurio de Chile/Newscom

The roles these men assumed, the ways in which they cooperated, and the emotional support they offered to each other are just the types of social dynamics that scientists would be interested in studying (Chapter 14). Equally interesting was the manner in which people throughout the world responded when they learned that rescuers had made contact with the miners.

THINK again

What's in a Number?

News of the trapped miners was headlined, broadcast, and tweeted across the globe. People found it difficult to believe that all 33 men had survived. Some said it was testament to the endurance of the human spirit. Others called it a miracle of God. Still others pointed to the mystical nature of numerology, which attempts to provide explanations for a variety of events and observations. The number 33, which numerologists consider a "master number" (Decoz, 2011, April 18), was thought to play an important role. Here is some of the "evidence" presented to support this claim (Agence France Presse, 2010, October 14; freedomflores, 2010, October 18; The Vigilant Citizen, 2010, October 14):

NUMEROLOGY TO THE
RESCUE?

- There were **33** miners.
- They sent up a note saying, "Estamos bien en el refugio los **33**." This statement contains **33** characters and spaces.
- The eventual rescue date was 10/13/10; the sum of these digits equals **33**.
- Drilling the rescue tunnel took **33** days, and the width of the rescue tunnel was said to be 66 centimeters, which is **33** times two.

Are you detecting a pattern? The fact is, anyone can draw a connection or find a pattern if they try hard enough, and these patterns do not necessarily represent a unifying theory or provide a scientific explanation. They are just coincidences. ●+

While the beliefs surrounding numerology may have provided a meaningful way for some people to interpret the miners' experiences, such beliefs have no scientific validity. In the following section, we'll examine "pseudosciences" like numerology and explain how we use *critical thinking* to evaluate how they compare to scientific research and thought.

LO 5 Evaluate pseudopsychology and its relationship to critical thinking.

As intriguing as this apparent 33 theme may be, it has no scientific meaning. Numerology is a prime example of **pseudopsychology,** an approach to explaining and predicting behavior and events that appears to be psychology but is not supported by objective evidence. Another familiar pseudopsychology is *astrology,* which uses a chart of the heavens called a *horoscope* to predict everything from the weather to romantic relationships. Surprisingly, many people have difficulty distinguishing between pseudosciences, like astrology, and true sciences, even after earning a college degree (Impey, Buxner, & Antonellis, 2012; Schmaltz & Lilienfeld, 2014).

Why does astrology often seem to be accurate in its descriptions and predictions? Consider this excerpt from a monthly Gemini horoscope: "You could meet a lot of fascinating people and make many new friends as autumn begins. You could also take up a creative new interest or hobby" (Horoscope.com, 2014). When you think about it, this statement could apply to just about any human being on the planet. We all are capable of starting new activities and meeting "fascinating people" (isn't every person "fascinating" in her own way?). How could you possibly prove such a statement wrong? You couldn't. That's why astrology is not science. A telltale feature of a pseudopsychology, like any pseudoscience, is its tendency to make assertions so broad and vague that they cannot be refuted (Stanovich, 2013).

"What's nice about working in this place is we don't have to finish any of our experiments."

S. Harris/Cartoonstock

Critical Thinking

Why can't we use pseudopsychology to help predict and explain behaviors? Because there is no solid evidence for its effectiveness, no scientific support for its findings. Critical thinking is absent from the "pseudotheories" used to explain the pseudosciences (Rasmussen, 2007; Stemwedel, 2011). What is critical thinking and when should we use it? **Critical thinking** is the process of weighing various pieces of evidence, synthesizing them (putting them together), and determining how each contributes to the bigger picture. Critical thinking requires one to consider the source of information and the

pseudopsychology An approach to explaining and predicting behavior and events that appears to be psychology, but has no empirical or objective evidence to support it.

critical thinking The process of weighing various pieces of evidence, synthesizing them, and evaluating and determining the contributions of each.

quality of evidence before making a decision on its validity. The process involves thinking beyond definitions, focusing on underlying concepts and applications, and being open-minded and skeptical at the same time. Psychology is driven by critical thinking.

Let's put our critical thinking skills to work by examining the numerological "evidence" pertaining to Los 33. First, can we trust the data? One source suggests the rescue hole was 66 centimeters, but another says it was 68 centimeters. Some miners were rescued on 10/13/10, but others emerged on 10/14/10 (the rescue took place over the course of 2 days). Hmm, some of the 33s appear to be fading into thin air. Lesson learned: We should use critical thinking to evaluate the evidence for a claim.

But critical thinking goes far beyond verifying the facts (Yanchar, Slife, & Warne, 2008). Even if every piece of numerological evidence was spot-on, you would still have to weigh the relative importance of each piece of information and combine them all in a logical way: What do all these 33s mean, and can your conclusion predict what happens next? Here, we run into trouble again. Numerology and other pseudosciences cannot effectively predict future events.

Critical thinking is an invaluable skill, whether you are a trapped miner struggling to survive, a psychologist planning an experiment, or a student trying to earn a good grade in psychology class. For example, has anyone ever told you that choosing "C" on a multiple-choice question is your best bet when you don't know the answer? There is little research showing this is the best strategy (Skinner, 2009). Next time you're offered a tempting niblet of folk wisdom, think before you bite: What kind of evidence exists to support this claim? Can it be used to predict future events?

The Scientific Method

LO 6   Describe how psychologists use the scientific method.

Critical thinking is an important component of the **scientific method,** the process scientists use to conduct research. The goal of the scientific method is to provide *empirical evidence,* or data from systematic observations or experiments. An **experiment** is a controlled procedure involving scientific observations and/or manipulations by the researcher to influence participants' thinking, emotions, or behaviors. In the scientific method, an observation must be objective, or outside the influence of personal opinion and preconceived notions. Humans are prone to errors in thinking (Chapter 7), but the scientific method helps to minimize their impact.

Suppose a researcher had tried to determine whether any of the Chilean miners was running a fever. He might have asked the crew's "doctor," Yonni Barrios, to place his hand on each man's forehead, but Barrios' measurement of "fever" could have been different from the researcher's. A more objective approach would have been to send down a thermometer to the mine. Observations that are truly objective do not differ from one person to the next based on beliefs or opinions. A thermometer will read the same whether it's being used by Yonni Barrios or a new parent. Now let's take a look at the 5 basic steps of the scientific method.

STEP 1: DEVELOP A QUESTION   The scientific method typically begins when a researcher observes something interesting in the environment and comes up with a research question. A great way to start this process is to read books and articles written by scientists. (See **Infographic 1.2** to get a sense of how best to find and read an article; learning these skills will help you in many classes you take, including psychology.) Imagine that a psychologist has decided to study the psychological health of the trapped miners. While reviewing the literature on this topic, he comes across several studies suggesting that disaster survivors face an elevated risk for depression (Bonanno, Brewin, Kaniasty, & La Greca, 2010). This makes the psychologist wonder: Will Los 33 experience rates of depression similar to those of other disaster victims, or do their unique circumstances place them in a category all their own?

scientific method The process scientists use to conduct research, which includes a continuing cycle of exploration, critical thinking, and systematic observation.

experiment A controlled procedure that involves careful examination through the use of scientific observation and/or manipulation of variables (measurable characteristics).

How to Read a Scientific Article

Psychologists publish their research findings in peer-reviewed, scientific journals. Scientific journal articles are different from news articles or blog posts that you might find through a typical Internet search. When you read news articles or blog posts about a research study, you can't assume these sources accurately interpret the study's findings or appropriately emphasize what the study's original authors think is important. For a full description of the background, methodology, results, and the application of a research study's findings, you must read a scientific article.

How Do I Find a Scientific Article?

You can find scientific journal articles through online journal databases such as PsycINFO, available through your school library, or Google Scholar, a search engine accessible on any computer. Search results can provide **references** that follow a standard format, like this:

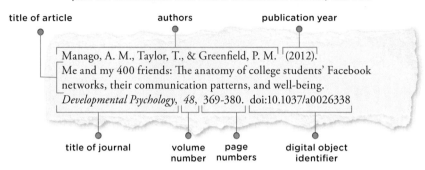

title of article   authors   publication year

Manago, A. M., Taylor, T., & Greenfield, P. M. (2012). Me and my 400 friends: The anatomy of college students' Facebook networks, their communication patterns, and well-being. *Developmental Psychology,* *48,* 369-380. doi:10.1037/a0026338

title of journal   volume number   page numbers   digital object identifier

What's in a Scientific Article?

At first glance, scientific articles can seem overwhelming. It helps to know what you will find in a typical article. Scientific articles follow a specific organizational style and include the following elements:

TITLE ○

Developmental Psychology
2012, Vol. 48, No. 2, 369–380

© 2012 American Psychological Association
0012-1649/12/$12.00 DOI: 10.1037/a0026338

Me and My 400 Friends: The Anatomy of College Students' Facebook Networks, Their Communication Patterns, and Well-Being

AUTHORS ○

Adriana M. Manago, Tamara Taylor, and Patricia M. Greenfield
University of California, Los Angeles

ABSTRACT ○

✔ Brief description of entire article.

✔ Helps you quickly decide if the article describes research you are interested in.

Is there a trade-off between having large networks of social connections on social networking sites such as Facebook and the development of intimacy and social support among today's generation of emerging adults? To understand the socialization context of Facebook during the transition to adulthood, an online survey was distributed to college students at a large urban university; participants answered questions about their relationships by systematically sampling their Facebook contacts while viewing their Facebook profiles online. Results confirmed that Facebook facilitates expansive social networks that grow disproportionately through distant kinds of relationship (acquaintances and activity connections), while also expanding the number of close relationships and stranger relationships, albeit at slower rates. Those with larger networks estimated that larger numbers of contacts in their networks were observing their status updates, a form of public communication to one's entire contact list. The major function of status updates was emotional disclosure, the key feature of intimacy. This finding indicates the transformation of the nature of intimacy in the environment of a social network site. In addition, larger networks and larger estimated audiences predicted higher levels of life satisfaction and perceived social support on Facebook. These findings emphasize the psychological importance of audience in the Facebook environment. Findings also suggest that social networking sites help youth to satisfy enduring human psychosocial needs for permanent relations in a geographically mobile world—college students with higher proportions of maintained contacts from the past (primarily high school friends) perceived Facebook as a more useful tool for procuring social support.

Keywords: social network site, peer relationships, emerging adulthood, intimacy development, wellbeing

KEYWORDS ○

✔ Identify themes or topics of article.
✔ Can be used to search for similar articles.

INTRODUCTION ○

✔ Explains topic of study, relevant previous research, and specific goals and hypotheses.

Psychological development during the transition from childhood to adulthood happens within the context of an expanding network of social relations, the details of which depend on cultural and historical context, socialization environments, and material affordances (Schlegel & Barry, 1991). One of the most striking aspects of the socialization environment in Western cultures in the early part of the 21st century is that adolescents and emerging adults have a variety of communication technologies at their disposal to manage quickly and efficiently very large webs of social connections. Nowhere is this expanse of social connections more clearly articulated than on social networking sites such as Facebook, the most popular social network in the United States and the fourth most visited website on the Internet (Comscore, 2010). From a sociocultural and historical perspective on human development (Co'te & Levine, 2002), it is not hard to imagine that the prominence of Facebook as a cultural phenomenon in the lives of college students in the United States would frame and shape developmental issues salient to them. Certainly, the current generation of college students has experienced an adolescence permeated by online peer interactions (Gross, 2004). Estimates are that 90% of un-

This article was published Online First January 30,

Other elements not shown here:

METHOD

✔ Describes how study was conducted.

✔ Provides details about participants, materials and procedures, allowing the study to be replicated.

RESULTS

✔ Describes data collected and outcome of study.

✔ Often includes tables, graphs or figures.

DISCUSSION

✔ Interprets results to determine support or lack of support for the research hypotheses.

✔ Often reports study's limitations, contributions, and implications for future research.

REFERENCES

✔ Listing of all articles cited.

✔ A *great* place to look for additional research articles!

It's in the Data
Sian Beilock, a psychologist from the University of Chicago, examines an fMRI scan. Using brain imaging and other types of objective data such as behavioral observations and cortisol levels in the saliva, Dr. Beilock studies the psychological mechanisms that underlie "choking under pressure," or faltering under stress (University of Chicago, 2013). AP Photo/M. Spencer Green

Variable	Record Number	Columns	Format
FAMILYID	1	3 - 7	Numeric
FROMWHO	1	9 - 12	Numeric
WHICHATT	1	14 - 17	Numeric
INT_T_	1	19 - 24	Numeric
INT_S_	1	26 - 31	Numeric
CON_T_	1	33 - 38	Numeric
CON_S_	1	40 - 46	Numeric
PERS	1	48 - 52	Numeric
GLOB	1	54 - 58	Numeric
STA_C_	1	60 - 64	Numeric
STA_O_	1	66 - 70	Numeric
BARR	1	72 - 76	Numeric
BREW	2	1 - 5	Numeric

165	1	1	0	1	0	0	1
165	1	2	1	0	1	0	0
165	1	3	1	0	9	0	

▲ **FIGURE 1.3**
Raw Data
The information in this figure comes from a data file. Until the researcher analyzes the data, these numbers will have little meaning.

hypothesis (hī-ˈpä-thə-səs) A statement that can be used to test a prediction.

theory Synthesizes observations in order to explain phenomena and guide predictions to be tested through research.

operational definition The precise manner in which a variable of interest is defined and measured.

STEP 2: DEVELOP A HYPOTHESIS   Once a research question has been developed, the next step in the scientific method is to formulate a **hypothesis** (hī-ˈpä-thə-səs), a statement that can be used to test a prediction. The psychologist might come up with a hypothesis that reads something like this: "If we treat half of the survivors from the San José mining disaster with therapy and put the other half on a waiting list for therapy, those on the waiting list will be more likely to receive a diagnosis of depression within 5 years of rescue." The data collected by the experimenter will either support or refute the hypothesis. Hypotheses are difficult to generate for studies on new and unexplored topics; in these situations, a general prediction may take the place of a formal hypothesis.

While developing research questions and hypotheses, researchers should always be on the lookout for information that could offer explanations for the phenomenon they are studying. For a study on depression, this might entail reviewing theories about the causes of depression. **Theories** synthesize observations in order to explain phenomena, and they can be used to make predictions that can then be tested through research. Many people believe scientific theories are nothing more than unverified guesses or hunches, but they are mistaken (Stanovich, 2013). A theory is a well-established body of principles that often rests on a sturdy foundation of scientific evidence. Evolution is a prime example of a theory that has been mistaken for an ongoing scientific controversy. Thanks to inaccurate portrayals in the media, many people have come to believe that evolution is an active area of "debate," when in reality it is a theory embraced by the overwhelming majority of scientists, including most psychologists.

STEP 3: DESIGN STUDY AND COLLECT DATA   Once a hypothesis has been developed, the researcher designs an experiment to test it. **Operational definitions** specify the precise manner in which the characteristics of interest are defined and measured. For example, the psychologist might have used a depression scale to measure the mood of the miners, and then defined depression based on a cutoff point (anyone with a score greater than 40, for example). According to the scientific method, a good operational definition helps others understand how to perform an observation or take a measurement.

The researcher then collects the data to test the hypothesis. Gathering data must be done in a very controlled fashion to ensure there are no errors, which could arise from recording problems or from unknown environmental factors. We will address the basics of data collection later in the chapter.

STEP 4: ANALYZE THE DATA   The researcher now has data that need to be analyzed, or organized in a meaningful way. As you can see from **Figure 1.3,** rows and columns of numbers are just that, numbers. In order to make sense of the "raw" data, one must use statistical methods. *Descriptive statistics* are used to organize and present data, often through tables, graphs, and charts. *Inferential statistics,* on the other hand, go beyond simply describing the data set, allowing researchers to make inferences and determine the probability of events occurring in the future (for a more in-depth look at statistics, see Appendix A).

Once the data have been analyzed, the researcher must ask several questions: Did the results support the hypothesis? Were the predictions met? He evaluates his hypothesis, rethinks his theories, and possibly designs a new study. This procedure is an important part of the scientific method because it enables us to think critically about our findings. In the hypothetical depression study of Los 33, what if the researcher found no differences between the therapy and nontherapy groups? Was the type of therapy used ineffective? Were the tools for measuring depression problematic? If these ideas are worth pursuing, the researcher could develop a new hypothesis and embark on a study to test it. Look at **Infographic 1.3** and notice the cyclical nature of the scientific method.

The Scientific Method

Psychologists use the scientific method to conduct research. The scientific method allows researchers to collect empirical (objective) evidence by following a sequence of carefully executed steps. In this infographic, you can trace the steps taken in an actual research project performed by two psychologists who were interested in the effect of "counting your blessings" (Emmons & McCullough, 2003). Notice that the process is cyclical in nature. Answering one research question often leads researchers to develop additional questions, and the process begins again.

The researchers see an article suggesting happiness is related to greater overall health. The researchers think about their own study and wonder:

ASK NEW QUESTIONS

Does counting your blessings also lead to better overall health?

To develop a question, a researcher will:
- observe the world around him;
- identify a personally interesting topic;
- review scientific literature on this topic.

To develop a hypothesis (a testable prediction), a researcher will:
- look for existing theories about the topic;
- establish operational definitions to specify variables being studied.

STEP 1: DEVELOP A QUESTION

Grandma always says, "Count your blessings." Why? What is the impact of a grateful outlook?

STEP 2: DEVELOP A HYPOTHESIS

HYPOTHESIS:
People who think about positive events in their lives will report greater psychological well-being than people who think about negative events.

STEP 5: PUBLISH THE FINDINGS

A researcher writes a description of the study and submits it to an academic journal, where it will be peer-reviewed and if approved, published for other researchers to read and use in their own research.

The researchers write an article titled, "Counting blessings versus burdens: An experimental investigation of gratitude and subjective well-being in daily life." It is published in the *Journal of Personality and Social Psychology*.

Group 1 participants reported significantly greater well-being than other groups. Researchers conclude that people who count their blessings feel better about their lives as a whole.

1 2 3 Researchers randomly assign participants to three groups. Every week, Group 1 participants list five things they are grateful for; Group 2 participants list five things that bother them; and Group 3 participants list any five things that happened. All three groups are surveyed weekly to determine their psychological well-being.

STEP 4: ANALYZE THE DATA

STEP 3: DESIGN STUDY & COLLECT DATA

A researcher organizes and analyzes the data and determines whether the hypothesis is supported.

A researcher plans a well-controlled study. Data are collected when the study is performed.
- A design can be experimental or descriptive.
- Data are collected using controlled measurement techniques.

STEP 5: PUBLISH THE FINDINGS Once the data have been analyzed and the hypothesis tested, it's time to share findings with other researchers who might be able to build on the work. This typically involves writing a scientific article and submitting it to a scholarly, peer-reviewed journal. Journal editors send these submitted manuscripts to subject-matter experts, or peer reviewers, who carefully read them and make recommendations for publishing, revising, or rejecting the articles altogether.

The peer-review process is notoriously meticulous, and it helps provide us with more certainty that findings from research can be trusted. This approach is not foolproof, of course. There have been cases of fabricated data slipping past the scrutiny of peer reviewers. In some cases, these oversights have had serious consequences for the general public. Case in point: the widespread confusion over the safety of routine childhood vaccines.

In the late 1990s, researchers published a study suggesting that vaccination against infectious diseases caused autism (Wakefield et al., 1998). The findings sparked panic among parents, including the actress Jenny McCarthy, who led a march in Washington, DC, calling for changes in vaccination policies. The study turned out to be fraudulent and the reported findings were deceptive, but it took 12 years for journal editors to retract the article (Editors of *The Lancet,* 2010). One reason for this long delay was that researchers had to investigate all the accusations of wrongdoing and data fabrication (Godlee, Smith, & Marcovitch, 2011). The investigation included interviews with the parents of the children discussed in the study, which ultimately led to the finding that the information in the published account was inaccurate (Deer, 2011).

Since the publication of that flawed study, several high-quality investigations have found no solid support for the autism-vaccine hypothesis (Honda, Shimizu, & Rutter, 2005; Madsen et al., 2002; Taylor et al., 2002). Still, the publicity given to the original article continues to cast a shadow: Approximately 18% of Americans believe that vaccines cause autism and 30% are "not sure" (Harris Interactive/HealthDay poll, 2011). Ultimately, even though the peer-review process is a safeguard against fraud and inaccuracies, sometimes the process is not successful, and problematic findings make their way into peer-reviewed journals.

Publishing an article is a crucial step in the scientific process because it allows other researchers to **replicate** an experiment, which might mean repeating it with other participants or altering some of the procedures. This repetition is necessary to ensure that the initial findings were not just a fluke or the result of a poorly designed experiment.

In the case of Wakefield's fraudulent autism study, other researchers tried to replicate the study for over 10 years, but could never establish a relationship between autism and vaccines (Godlee et al., 2011). This fact alone made the Wakefield findings suspect. The more a study is replicated and produces similar findings, the more confidence we can have in those findings.

ASK NEW QUESTIONS Most studies generate more questions than they answer, and here lies the beauty of the scientific process. The results of one scientific study raise a host of new questions, and those questions lead to new hypotheses, new studies, and yet another collection of questions. This continuing cycle of exploration uses critical thinking at every step in the process.

replicate To repeat an experiment, generally with a new sample and/or other changes to the procedures, the goal of which is to provide further support for the findings of the first study.

Research Basics

THE BIG WAIT   The miners' first 17 days underground were intense and grueling, but now they faced the ultimate test of psychological endurance: waiting up to 4 months for rescuers to bore an escape tunnel. Could they go the distance? The circumstances of their cave-home were not exactly conducive to mental stability: no personal space, zero privacy, stifling heat, nauseating odors, minimal contact with family and friends, and loads of time to kill.

Recognizing the extraordinary psychological battle the miners faced, a team of psychologists was assembled to oversee their mental health (Franklin, 2011). Physicians and the lead psychologist Alberto Iturra began holding daily conference calls with the miners using a makeshift telephone line running through one of the boreholes. (A total of three narrow bore holes were drilled in order to facilitate communication and the delivery of food, medicine, and other necessities [Associated Press, 2010, August 30].) The relationship between Iturra and the miners was congenial at first, but feelings turned sour when Iturra began to meddle with the men's communications. He recommended, for example, that the miners be allotted only 1 minute for their first conversation with family members. According to one miner, Iturra actually got on the line and said "cut" when a miner's time was up. The psychologists also began to read personal letters sent from the miners to their families, and vice versa, censoring every piece of mail flowing in and out of the mine. Apparently, they were concerned that certain types of news (such as family and financial troubles) might be too much for the already stressed miners to bear. But this censorship incited something of a rebellion among the group (Franklin, 2011).

Mental health experts across the globe weighed in on the matter. Psychiatrist Nick Kanas of the University of California deemed it unwise to censor communications between the miners and the outside world. "I would not screen anything. . . . Otherwise you are setting up a basis for mistrust," Kanas told journalist Jonathan Franklin (Franklin, 2011, p. 152). "Any attempt to be not entirely forthcoming [by rescuers] could be seen as a lack of trust," said psychologist Lawrence Palinkas of the University of Southern California in an interview with *Discovery News* (O'Hanlon, 2010, August 31).

No psychologist had ever studied human beings in a scenario quite like this. There were no "lessons learned" from past experience, no guidelines to follow, and certainly no research on the subject. The best Iturra and his colleagues could do was draw on studies of people in similar situations—such as miners who had been trapped for shorter periods of time, sailors confined in submarines, and astronauts on long-term space missions (Franklin, 2011).

Note from Above
The wife of trapped miner Mario Gomez writes him a letter. © Ronald Patrick/Action Press/ZUMApress.com

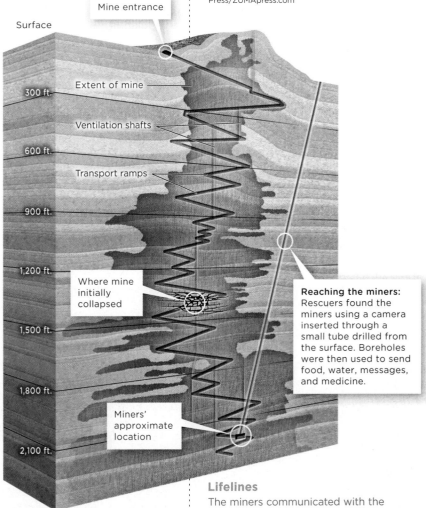

Mine entrance

Surface

300 ft.

Extent of mine

Ventilation shafts

600 ft.

Transport ramps

900 ft.

1,200 ft.

Where mine initially collapsed

1,500 ft.

Reaching the miners: Rescuers found the miners using a camera inserted through a small tube drilled from the surface. Boreholes were then used to send food, water, messages, and medicine.

1,800 ft.

Miners' approximate location

2,100 ft.

Lifelines
The miners communicated with the outside world through 6-inch-wide boreholes running from inside the mine to the ground above. Using one of these passageways, rescuers sent the men small containers known as *palomas,* or "doves," holding letters from family members (BBC News, 2010, October 14; Quilodran, 2010, August 24). Staff/MCT/Newsroom

Yum

On Chile's Independence Day, the miners received a special delivery from on high: *empanadas,* or delicious pastries filled with meat, olives, raisins, and egg (Penhaul, 2010, September 18). How might such comfort food have affected the men's moods?

Juanmonino/iStockphoto

Imagine you had the opportunity to conduct research on Los 33. Soon we will discuss two major categories of research design you could use—descriptive and experimental—but first, let's take a look at some of the concepts relevant to nearly all scientific studies.

VARIABLES   Virtually every psychology study includes **variables,** or measurable characteristics that vary, or change, over time or across people. In chemistry, a variable might be temperature, mass, or volume. In psychological experiments, researchers study a variety of characteristics pertaining to humans and other organisms. Examples of variables include personality characteristics (shyness or friendliness), cognitive characteristics (memory), number of siblings in a family, gender, socioeconomic status, and so forth. A psychologist studying the miners might be interested in variables related to mood, leadership qualities, competitiveness, or educational background. In many experiments, the goal is to see how changing one variable affects another. In the Chilean miner example, a researcher might be interested in knowing how the delivery of empanadas, delicious stuffed pastries, affected the miners' moods. Once the variables for a study are chosen, researchers must create operational definitions with precise descriptions and manners of measurement.

- -

LO 7   Summarize the importance of a random sample.

- -

POPULATION AND SAMPLE   How do researchers decide who should participate in their studies? It depends on the **population,** or overall group, the researcher wants to examine. If the population is large (all college students in the United States, for example), then the researcher selects a subset of that population called a **sample.**

There are many methods for choosing a sample. One way is to pick a **random sample,** that is, theoretically any member of the population has an equally likely chance of being selected to participate in the study. Think about the problems that may occur if the sample is not random. Suppose a researcher is trying to assess attitudes about banning supersized sugary sodas in the United States, but the only place she recruits participants is New York City, where such a ban was implemented for some time. How might this bias her findings? New York City residents do not constitute a **representative sample,** or group of people with characteristics similar to those of the population of interest.

It is important for the researcher to choose a representative sample, because this allows her to generalize her findings, meaning to apply information from a sample to the population at large. Let's say that 44% of the respondents in her study believe supersized sugary sodas should be banned. If her sample was similar enough to the overall U.S. population, then she may be able to infer that this finding from the sample is representative: "Approximately 44% of people in the United States believe that supersized sugary sodas should be banned."

Super Sample

If a researcher aimed to understand American attitudes about supersized soda bans, she would be foolish to limit her study to residents of New York City. Michael Bloomberg, the former mayor of the Big Apple, called for a ban on the sale of supersized sugary drinks in 2012. The controversial law probably affected attitudes about the issue, even though it was subsequently struck down. Thus, the people of New York City do not constitute a representative sample.

AP Photo/Kathy Willens

INFORMED CONSENT   The researcher has chosen the population of interest, and she has identified her sample, but she needs to make certain that these people are comfortable participating in her research. Before she can begin to collect data, she must obtain **informed consent,** or acknowledgment from the participants that they understand what their participation will entail, including any possible harm that could result. Informed consent is a participant's way of saying, "I understand my role in this study, and I am okay with it," and it's the researcher's way of ensuring that participants know what they are getting into.

DEBRIEFING   Following the study, there is another step of disclosure known as **debriefing.** In a debriefing session, researchers provide participants with useful information related to the study. In some cases, participants are informed of the deception or manipulation they were exposed to in the study, information that couldn't be shared with them beforehand. You will soon learn why a small dose of duplicity sometimes comes in handy for scientific research. And rest assured, all experiments on humans and animals must be approved by an **Institutional Review Board (IRB)** to ensure the highest degree of ethical standards.

The topics we have touched on thus far—variables, operational definitions, samples, informed consent, and debriefing—apply to psychology research in general. You will see how these concepts are relevant to studies when we explore descriptive and experimental research in the upcoming sections.

Synonyms
Institutional Review Board (IRB) reviewing committee, Animal Welfare Committee, Independent Ethics Committee, Ethical Review Board

THE MINERS GET THEIR WAY   After nearly a month of working with lead psychologist Alberto Iturra, the miners demanded that he be dismissed. They were tired of the psychologists reading and editing their letters, searching care packages, and punishing them for refusing to go along with Iturra's agenda. The miners issued an ultimatum: Either Iturra goes, or we stop eating. Their strategy worked, at least temporarily; Iturra agreed to take a 1-week break, while another psychologist, Claudio Ibañez, took charge (Franklin, 2011). Ibañez was much more relaxed in his approach. He put an end to the letter-editing and package-tampering and, in doing so, he placed more faith in the miners' ability to cope with whatever news might arrive from the world above.

Ibañez was trained in **positive psychology,** a relatively new approach that studies the positive aspects of human nature—happiness, creativity, love, and all that is best about people (Franklin, 2011; Seligman & Csikszentmihalyi, 2000). Historically, psychologists have tended to focus on the abnormal and maladaptive patterns of human behavior. Positive psychology does not deny the existence of these darker elements; it just directs the spotlight elsewhere. This has much in common with the humanistic perspective. In fact, positive psychologists often refer to the early work of the humanists as setting the stage for the current field of positive psychology (Robbins, 2008). There is a lot to be said for this approach. Evidence suggests that people who have a positive outlook tend to flourish and have better mental health than their less optimistic peers (Catalino & Fredrickson, 2011). You will read about such people in the many real-world stories woven into this textbook.

Ibañez's more laid-back style was a welcome relief to some of the miners, but soon it became clear that his method had its drawbacks as well. With much of the censorship stopped, families reportedly began to sneak forbidden items like marijuana, amphetamines, and chocolate into their care packages. Yes, chocolate. Sweets were a "no-no" because they could aggravate the miners' fragile dental health. Try living with an untreated toothache for days, weeks, or months. The arrival of prohibited items soon sparked envy and resentment among some of the men, disrupting the delicate social structure within the mine (Franklin, 2011). 📁

variables Measurable characteristics that can vary over time or across people.

population All members of an identified group about which a researcher is interested.

sample A subset of a population chosen for inclusion in an experiment.

random sample A subset of the population chosen through a procedure that ensures all members of the population have an equally likely chance of being selected to participate in the study.

representative sample A subgroup of a population selected so that its members have characteristics similar to those of the population of interest.

informed consent Acknowledgment from study participants that they understand what their participation will entail.

debriefing Sharing information with participants after their involvement in a study has ended, including the purpose of the study and of deception used in it.

Institutional Review Board (IRB) A committee that reviews research proposals to protect the rights and welfare of all participants.

positive psychology An approach that focuses on the positive aspects of human beings, seeking to understand their strengths and uncover the roots of happiness, creativity, humor, and so on.

show what you know

1. An instructor in the psychology department assigns a project requiring students to read several journal articles on a controversial topic. They are then required to weigh various pieces of evidence from the articles, synthesize the information, and determine how the various findings contribute to understanding the topic. This process is known as:
   a. pseudotheory.
   b. critical thinking.
   c. hindsight bias.
   d. applied research.

2. How would you explain to someone that astrology is a pseudopsychology?

3. A researcher identifies affection between partners by counting the number of times they gaze into each other's eyes while in the laboratory waiting room. The cutoff for those who would be considered very affectionate partners is gazing more than 10 times in 1 hour. The researcher has created a(n) _____ of affection.
   a. theory
   b. hypothesis
   c. replication
   d. operational definition

4. A researcher is interested in studying college students' attitudes about banning supersized sodas. She randomly selects a group of students from across the nation, trying to pick a _____ that will closely reflect the characteristics of college students in the United States.
   a. variable
   b. debriefing
   c. representative sample
   d. representative population

✓ CHECK YOUR ANSWERS IN APPENDIX C.

Descriptive Research

LO 8   Recognize the forms of descriptive research.

Suppose a researcher is interested in studying how the sudden arrival of drugs, sweets, and other prohibited goods affects the miners' social interactions. This is a great topic for **descriptive research,** the type of investigation psychologists conduct when they need to explore a subject of interest. Descriptive research is primarily concerned with describing, and is useful for studying new or unexplored topics when researchers might not have specific expectations about outcomes. But there are some things descriptive research cannot achieve. This method provides us with clues to the causes of behaviors, but it *cannot* unearth cause-and-effect relationships, a point that we will return to later in the chapter. But first, we will explore four descriptive research methods.

Naturalistic Observation

One form of descriptive research is **naturalistic observation,** which involves studying participants in their natural environments using systematic observation. And when we say "natural environments," we don't necessarily mean the "wild." It could be an office, a home, or even a preschool. In one naturalistic study, researchers explored the interactions that occurred when parents dropped off their children at preschool. One variable of interest was the length of time it took parents to leave the children at school. The researchers found that the longer parents or caregivers took to leave, the less time the children played with their peers and the more likely they were to stand by and watch other kids playing. The researchers also noted that women were somewhat more likely than men to hold the children and physically pick them up during drop-off. These drop-off interactions seemed to get in the way of children "settling into" the classroom (Grady, Ale, & Morris, 2012).

NATURALLY, IT'S A CHALLENGE   As with any type of research, naturalistic observation centers around variables, and those variables must be pinned down with operational definitions. Let's say a researcher is interested in studying aggressiveness in enclosed spaces and decides to examine aggression among Los 33: an intriguing topic given that research has linked stress and hot temperatures to more aggressive behaviors (Anderson, 2001; Fay & Maner, 2014; Kruk, Halász, Meelis, & Haller, 2004). At the beginning of the study, the researcher would need to operationally define aggression, including detailed descriptions of specific behaviors that illustrate it.

descriptive research   Research methods that describe and explore behaviors, but with findings that cannot definitively state cause-and-effect relationships.

naturalistic observation   A type of descriptive research that studies participants in their natural environment through systematic observation.

observer bias   Errors introduced into the recording of observations due to a researcher's value system, expectations, or attitudes.

case study   A type of descriptive research that closely examines one individual or small group.

Then she might create a checklist of aggressive behaviors like shouting and pushing, and a coding system to help keep track of them.

Naturalistic observation allows psychologists to observe participants going about their business in their normal environments, without the disruptions of artificial laboratory settings. Perhaps the most important requirement of naturalistic observation is that researchers must not disturb the participants or their environment, so participants won't change their normal behaviors (particularly those behaviors the researchers wish to observe). Some problems arise with this arrangement, however. Natural environments are cluttered with a variety of unwanted variables, and removing them can alter the natural state of affairs the researchers are striving to maintain. And because the variables in natural environments are so hard to control, researchers may have trouble replicating findings. Suppose the researcher opted to study the behavior of Los 33 during their heated dominoes matches. In this natural setting, she would not be able to control who played and when; whoever showed up at the dominoes table would become a participant in her study.

OBSERVER BIAS How can we be sure observers will do a good job recording behaviors? A researcher who detests dominoes might pay attention to very different aspects of domino-related behaviors than a researcher who relishes the game. One way to avoid such problems is to include multiple observers and then determine how similarly they record the behaviors. If the observers don't execute this task in the same way, there may be **observer bias,** which refers to errors introduced as a result of an observer's value system, expectations, attitudes, and so forth.

Case Study

Another type of descriptive research method is the **case study,** a detailed examination of an individual or small group. Case studies typically involve collecting a vast amount of data on one person or group, often using multiple avenues to gather information. The process might include in-depth interviews with the person being studied and her friends, family, and coworkers, and questionnaires about medical history, career, and mental health. The goal of a case study is to provide a wealth of information from a variety of resources. Case studies are invaluable for studying rare events, like 33 Chilean miners cooped up in a subterranean hole. Unlike naturalistic observation, where the researcher assumes the role of detached spectator, the case

Please Wash Your Hands
According to one study, male college students are less conscientious about hand-washing in the restroom than female college students. Even after a reminder was placed in the restroom, only 35% of men washed their hands, compared to 97% of women (Johnson, Sholcosky, Gabello, Ragni, & Ogonosky, 2003). Researchers in this study took great care to look as though they were regular people who just happened to be using the restroom themselves. Do you think more men would have washed their hands if they knew they were being observed? Jutta Klee/Getty Images

Rain Man
The subject of one of the most famous case studies in the history of psychology, Kim Peek was able to simultaneously read two pages of a book—one with each eye—and memorize nearly all the information it contained. Like the movie character he inspired ("Raymond Babbitt" in the movie *Rain Man*), Peek had extraordinary intellectual abilities but a low IQ (Brogaard & Marlow, 2012, December 11). Case studies are often used to explore rare psychological conditions relating to cognition, personality, and behavior.
Barton Glasser/Deseret News

TABLE 1.5 CLASSIC CASE STUDIES IN PSYCHOLOGY

Case Study	Description	Outcome
Phineas Gage	A railroad worker who survived after an iron rod blasted through his skull	Suggested the role that frontal lobes play in personality
H. M.	A man who suffered from profound memory loss following brain surgery	Showed how brain damage can be linked to memory loss
Little Albert	An 11-month-old who was conditioned to fear rats	Revealed the ability to classically condition fear in humans
The Genain Quadruplets	Identical quadruplet sisters who all developed schizophrenia	Demonstrated a genetic factor is involved in schizophrenia
"Rat Man"	A man with obsessive thoughts, including a punishment involving rats	Exemplified a case study on which Sigmund Freud based his theories
Lorenz's Geese	Goslings that became attached to Konrad Lorenz	Documented the imprinting phenomenon

Summarized here are some of the most colorful case studies in the history of psychology. These classic studies have provided psychologists with valuable insights into human behaviors, and you will read about many of them in the chapters to come.

study may require complete immersion in the participant's environment. How do you think this might impact the researcher's observations and the conclusions of the study? See **Table 1.5** for some examples of classic case studies, many of which we will examine in later chapters, helping us answer this question.

No matter how colorful or thought-provoking a case study may be, it cannot be used to support or refute a hypothesis (Stanovich, 2013). Like naturalistic observation, the case study method can help to further develop theories, but it can't provide answers to what is causing behaviors. This descriptive method can offer guidance for designing new studies on topics that may be relatively underexplored (Stanovich, 2013). But as knowledge advances and researchers are more concerned with testing hypotheses, the case study becomes increasingly irrelevant. Hypothesis testing involves drawing comparisons between different conditions (Stanovich, 2013). Case studies do not allow us to compare conditions to determine if there are other explanations for behaviors.

Suppose you are trying to examine how parent–child interactions at home might relate to preschoolers' transitions during morning drop-off. What would happen if you limited your research to a case study of a family with two working parents and 10 children? The dynamics of this family may not be representative of those in other families. We should not make sweeping generalizations based on our observations of a single person or group.

Survey Method

One of the fastest ways to collect descriptive data is the **survey method,** which relies on questionnaires or interviews. A survey is basically a series of questions that can be administered on paper, in face-to-face interviews, via telephone, or through a few mouse clicks. Your college might send out surveys to gauge student attitudes about new online classes and e-books (Some possible questions you may see on a college survey might be: How often do you encounter technical difficulties with your online courses? How would you rate your overall satisfaction with an assigned e-book?). The benefit of the survey method is that one can gather data from numerous people in a short period of time. Surveys can be used alone or in conjunction with other research methods.

survey method A type of descriptive research that uses questionnaires or interviews to gather data.

correlational method A type of descriptive research examining the relationships among variables.

correlation An association or relationship between two (or more) variables.

WORDING AND HONESTY Like any research design, the survey method has its limitations. The wording of surveys can lead to biases in responses. A question with a positive or negative spin may sway a participant's response one way or the other: Do you prefer a half-full glass of soda or a half-empty glass of soda? Take a look at **Figure 1.4** for an example of how the wording of a survey can influence participant responses.

More importantly, participants in studies using the survey method are not always forthright in their responses, particularly when they have to admit to things they are uncomfortable discussing face-to-face. In short, people lie. In one study, psychologists asked thousands of American women if they had ever cheated on their husbands. When a researcher questioned them in person, 1% of the wives admitted cheating; but when asked through a computer-based questionnaire, 6% confessed their infidelity (Whisman & Snyder, 2007). People often exhibit a desire not to reveal attitudes or behaviors that are embarrassing or deal with sensitive topics (Tourangeau & Yan, 2007). This may lead to an inaccurate representation of participants' attitudes and beliefs.

SKIMMING THE SURFACE Another disadvantage of the survey method is that it tends to skim the surface of people's beliefs or attitudes, failing to tap into the complex issues underlying responses. Ask 1,000 people if they *intend* to exercise regularly, and you might get more than a few affirmative responses. But *yes* might mean something quite different from one person to the next ("Yes, it crosses my mind, but I can never go through with it" versus "Yes, I have a specific plan, and I have been able to follow through"). To obtain more precise responses, researchers often ask people to respond to statements using a scale that indicates the degree to which they agree or disagree (for example, a 5-point scale ranging from *strongly agree* to *strongly disagree*), or the degree to which they have had an experience (for example, a 5-point scale ranging from *never* to *almost always*).

REPRESENTATIVE SAMPLES AND SURVEYS The representativeness of survey samples can also be called into question. Some surveys fail to achieve representative samples because their *response rates* fall short of ideal. If a researcher sends out 100 surveys to potential participants and only 20 people return them, how can we be sure that the answers of those 20 responders reflect those of the entire group? Without a representative sample, we cannot generalize the survey findings.

Correlational Method

The final form of descriptive research we will cover is the **correlational method,** which examines relationships among variables and assists researchers in making predictions. When researchers collect data on many variables, it can be useful to determine if these variables are related to each other in some way. A **correlation** represents a relationship or link between variables (**Infographic 1.4** on the next page). For example, there is probably a correlation between the years of working in a mine and yearly salary. The more time a miner has put in, the more cash he takes home.

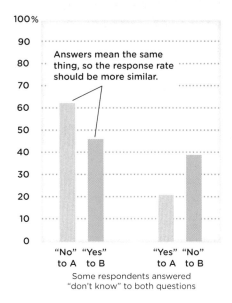

Answers mean the same thing, so the response rate should be more similar.

100%
90
80
70
60
50
40
30
20
10
0

"No" to A   "Yes" to B   "Yes" to A   "No" to B

Some respondents answered "don't know" to both questions

FIGURE 1.4
It Depends How You Ask
In a classic study, researchers asked two versions of the same question:

(A) Do you think the United States should allow public speeches against democracy?

(B) Do you think the United States should forbid public speeches against democracy?

Answering "no" to Question A (in other words, not allow speeches) *should* be the same as answering "yes" to Question B (in other words, forbid speeches). However, far more respondents answered "no" to Question A than answered "yes" to Question B. According to the researchers, "the 'forbid' phrasing makes the implied threat to civil liberties more apparent" than the "not allow" phrasing does (Rugg, 1941, p. 91). And that's something fewer people were willing to support.

"87% of the 56% who completed more than 23% of the survey thought it was a waste of time."

The Correlation Coefficient: What's in a Number?

A correlation indicates a relationship between two variables, such as the amount of time you spend studying and the grade you get on a test. This relationship is often indicated using a correlation coefficient, symbolized as *r*. To interpret the relationship using a correlation coefficient (*r*), ask yourself two questions:

(1) What is the *direction* of the relationship?

(2) What is the *strength* of the relationship?

A *scatterplot* helps us see what the relationship looks like.

And remember, a correlation between two variables does not necessarily mean that one variable caused the change in the other variable.

👁 What does the Correlation **look** like?

Using a scatterplot, we can express the relationship between two variables. One variable is labeled on the horizontal axis, and the second variable is labeled on the vertical axis. Each dot represents one participant's scores on the two variables. Notice how the shape of the graph changes depending on the direction and strength of the relationship between the variables.

$$r = + .73$$

↕ What Is the **Direction** of the Correlation?

- *positive* (+) correlation
  as one variable increases, the other also increases

- *negative* (−) correlation
  as one variable increases, the other decreases (an inverse relationship)

Example: +.73 is a positive number, showing a **positive correlation**. As hours spent studying increase, test grades also increase.

🏋 What Is the **Strength** of the Correlation?

strength ranges from +1.00 to −1.00

- a value close to +1.00 or −1.00 is a **strong** correlation

- a value close to 0.00 is a **weak** correlation

Example: +.73 is close to 1.00. This shows a **strong correlation** between hours spent studying and test grades.

⚠ BEWARE of the potential **Third Variable**

Correlation does not indicate that one variable *causes* a change in the other. A **third variable** may have influenced the results.

Example: Although time spent studying and exam grades are strongly and positively correlated, attendance is another variable. Students who attend classes regularly tend to spend more hours studying. Likewise, students who attend classes regularly know what to expect on the test and are therefore likely to get better grades.

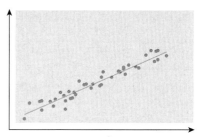

example:
+.73 (strong positive correlation)

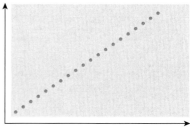

perfect positive correlation (+1.00)

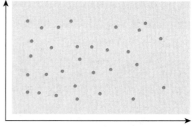

no relationship (.00)

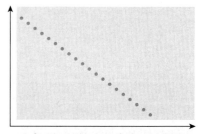

perfect negative correlation (−1.00)

This is an example of a positive correlation. As one variable increases, so does the other. A negative correlation, on the other hand, means as one variable goes up the other goes down (an inverse relationship). A good example would be the number of days trapped in the mine and body weight (at least before rescuers started delivering food). As the number of days increased, the miners' weight decreased. You have probably noticed correlations between variables in your own life. Increase the hours you devote to studying, and you will likely see your grades go up (a positive correlation). The more you hold a baby, the less she cries (a negative correlation).

CORRELATION COEFFICIENT   Some variables are not related to each other, whereas others have a link between them. Correlations indicate this type of information by representing the strength of the relationship between variables. Some relationships are strong and clear. Others are weak and barely noticeable. Lucky for researchers, there is one number that indicates the relationship's strength and direction (positive or negative): a statistical measure called the **correlation coefficient,** which is symbolized as r. Correlation coefficients range from +1.00 to –1.00, with positive numbers indicating a positive relationship between variables and negative numbers indicating an inverse relationship between variables. The closer r is to +1.00 or to –1.00, the stronger the relationship. The closer r is to .00, the weaker the relationship. When the correlation coefficient is very close to zero, there may be no relationship at all between the variables. For example, consider the variables of shoe size and intelligence. Are people with bigger (or smaller) feet more intelligent? Probably not; there would be no link between these two variables, so the correlation coefficient between them (the r value) is around zero. Take a look at Infographic 1.4 to see how correlation coefficients are portrayed on graphs called *scatterplots*.

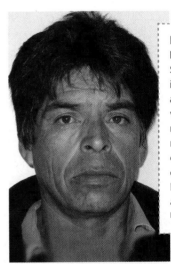

THIRD VARIABLE   Even if there is a very strong correlation between two variables, this does not indicate there is a causal link between them. No matter how high the r value is or how logical the relationship seems, it does not *prove* a cause-and-effect connection. If you discover a positive relationship between the years worked in the mine and salary, it's easy to jump to the conclusion that experience causes higher salary. But is it also possible that higher salary leads to greater experience (people keep jobs that pay well)? The direction of the relationship, or directionality, matters. It is also important to consider that some other variable or characteristic may be influencing both experience and salary. What additional variables might "cause" increased salary? One possibility is productivity, which could increase with the number of years on the job; more productive workers are rewarded with higher salaries. Here, we have a **third variable,** some unaccounted for characteristic of the participants or their environment that explains the changes in the two other variables. When you observe strong links between variables, consider other factors that could be related to both.

Remember, correlational and other descriptive methods can't identify the causes of behaviors. But this type of research *can* provide clues to what underlies behaviors, and thus it serves as a valuable tool when other types of experiments are unethical or impossible to conduct (in the previous example, researchers couldn't ethically manipulate real-world variables like salary or employment decisions). Moreover, descriptive research can produce interesting results. Just consider the following example.

Synonyms
third variable third factor

correlation coefficient The statistical measure (symbolized as r) that indicates the strength and direction of the relationship between two variables.

third variable An unaccounted for characteristic of participants or the environment that explains changes in the variables of interest.

The Many Faces of Facebook

You probably know that Facebook is the most widely used social networking site in the world, far more popular than Twitter and LinkedIn (eBizMBA, 2015). But you may be surprised to learn that 82% of Facebook's billion-plus users reside outside of North America (Facebook, 2015). Why do people in different parts of the world use this American invention? Do they use Facebook to rekindle an old friendship, create a new alliance, or spy on an ex?

WHAT'S THE NUMBER ONE REASON PEOPLE USE FACEBOOK?

Curious about patterns of Facebook use across time and culture, a team of European researchers set out to gather data from users in different countries (Vasalou, Joinson, & Courvoisier, 2010). With the help of Facebook walls and networks, they recruited 423 Facebook users from the United States, the United Kingdom, Italy, Greece, and France. Then they asked the participants to complete an online questionnaire and conducted a statistical analysis of the responses. Their findings were intriguing.

Across cultures, the primary motivation for using Facebook was "social searching," or connecting with people already known outside of Facebook (friends, family, colleagues, and so on). In second place was "social browsing," or looking for new acquaintances, which was particularly popular among French and Italian users. When it came to total time investment in Facebook, the British led the pack, averaging between 2 and 5 hours per week (compared to 2 hours or less for those in other countries). French and Greek users were not particularly interested in status updates, and the French did not place a high value on photographs (Vasalou et al., 2010). What do all these findings mean? The answer to this question is beyond the scope of the study. Surveys and other forms of descriptive research are information-gathering tools that illuminate behavioral tendencies, but they cannot explain the causes of those behaviors. This is the goal of experimental research, the focus of our next section.

show what you know

1. _____ is primarily useful for studying new or unexplored topics.
   a. An operational definition
   b. Observer bias
   c. Descriptive research
   d. A correlation

2. A researcher was interested in studying the behaviors of parents dropping off children at preschool. He trained several teachers to use a checklist and a stopwatch to record how long it took a caregiver to enter and leave the classroom, as well as the subsequent behaviors of the children. This approach to collecting data is referred to as:
   a. naturalistic observation.
   b. representative sampling.
   c. informed consent.
   d. applied research.

3. Describe the strengths and weaknesses of descriptive research.

✓ CHECK YOUR ANSWERS IN APPENDIX C.

Experimental Research

The nation of Chile went to heroic lengths to ensure that Los 33 made it out of the mountain alive. Most search-and-rescue missions are run by mine owners, but this was an extraordinary situation that demanded extraordinary measures. Lucky for the miners, Chilean President Sebastián Piñera decided that the government would lead the operation (Weiner, 2011, January 9). Engineers from the Chilean navy built the rescue capsule that ultimately lifted all 33 men back into the light of day, and the Health Ministry created a plan to care for the miners, which included voluntary psychological counseling for at least 6 months after the rescue (Kofman & Hopper, 2010, October 13; Kraul, 2010, October 11).

But the Chilean government was not in it alone. Governments, businesses, and individuals from all over the world flooded the Atacama Desert offering whatever help they could. Even a group from the National Aeronautics and Space Administration (NASA) showed up to lend a hand: two doctors, one engineer, and a psychologist named Albert Holland who had trained astronauts to cope with the stressful living conditions of outer space. The NASA crew was impressed with the efforts of the Chileans, but they also offered a few bits of advice, including a recommendation to increase the men's daily intake of vitamin D (Prengaman, 2010, September 3; Spotts, 2010, September 7).

Why would the miners need more vitamin D? Most people get a substantial amount of vitamin D through sun exposure. When the sun's UV rays strike the skin, its cells begin synthesizing vitamin D—an important process, as this "sunshine vitamin" is essential for maintaining healthy bones, a strong immune system, and perhaps even optimal cognitive performance (Lee, O'Keefe, Bell, Hensrud, & Holick, 2008; Medline Plus, 2014; Przybelski & Binkley, 2007; Wilkins, Sheline, Roe, Birge, & Morris, 2006). Deprived of sunlight for weeks on end, the miners were at risk of becoming vitamin D deficient.

Imagine you are a psychologist who has been following the Chilean miner saga. You've read the news reports about NASA recommending more vitamin D, which makes you wonder if giving vitamin D supplements will, in fact, improve the men's cognitive abilities. Here's the hypothesis you come up with: If one group of miners is given vitamin D supplements and the other group of miners a sugar pill, those receiving the vitamin D supplement will show improvements in cognitive functioning.

Eager to begin your study, you ask the Chilean government for permission to study the cognitive effects of vitamin D supplementation on Los 33. Sadly, your request is promptly denied. Not to worry. You have another option that may be even better: taking your study to a laboratory setting. Performing research in a controlled laboratory environment has huge benefits. You have greater control over who participates in the study, freedom to manipulate the variables, and the ability to draw comparisons between groups that differ only with respect to your target variables. In other words, you have the opportunity to use the *experimental method.*

Experimental Method

At last, we arrive at the type of research method we have been alluding to all along, a design that reveals cause and effect. Unlike the descriptive studies discussed earlier, the **experimental method** can tell us about cause and effect, because it aims to ensure that every variable except those being manipulated by the researcher is held constant, or controlled (**Infographic 1.5**). To identify a particular cause of an outcome, we assign research participants to two or more groups, and with the exception of some sort of manipulation or treatment done by the experimenter, these groups are equivalent. If following the manipulation or treatment the groups differ on a measure of interest, we can say with confidence that the experimental manipulation caused that change. This allows researchers to observe the variable of interest without interference from other variables.

If you are having trouble understanding what it means to control variables, consider this analogy: You are outside a football stadium, desperately trying to follow a friend lost in a swarm of people. Everyone is moving in different directions, making it exceedingly difficult to pinpoint your friend's location and direction of movement. But what if everyone in the crowd except your friend froze for a moment in time? Would it be easier to observe him now that he is the only one moving? This is similar to what researchers try to do with variables—hold everything steady except the variables they are examining.

Returning to the sun-deprived miners, let's examine how you might design a simple research study using the experimental method to investigate the cognitive effects of a vitamin D supplement. Your hypothesis is that participants housed in a laboratory setting without natural light who are given vitamin D supplements will perform better on a cognitive task than participants in the same laboratory setting who receive a sugar pill. Although we cannot study Los 33 per se, it's possible for us to put together a group of men who are very similar to the miners in age, educational background, physical health, and other variables that might affect their cognitive performance, and then subject them to a prolonged period of sun deprivation. Next you would divide the men into two groups—one receives vitamin D supplements and the other gets a sugar pill—and compare their performance on various mental tasks after a designated amount of time has passed. If the group receiving the vitamin D performs better, then you can attribute the difference to vitamin D. Although this may sound fairly straightforward, there are still a few more things you need to know.

RANDOM ASSIGNMENT Assigning participants to groups is a crucial step of the experimental method. Fail to divide participants in the correct way and your whole study is compromised. For this reason, researchers use **random assignment** to ensure that participants have an equal chance of being assigned to any of the groups. Randomly choosing which treatment the participants receive reduces the possibility of some participant characteristics influencing the findings. You may have noticed some similarities between random assignment and the "random sample" introduced earlier in the chapter. But here's the difference: Random sampling is used at the onset of a study to gather participants from a larger population. Random assignment comes into play later, when you are assigning participants to different groups. You can flip a coin, roll dice, or use a computer to generate numbers, but the goal of random assignment is always the same: to ensure that the groups are roughly equal on all characteristics. If the groups are lopsided with respect to some variable, the results may be affected. Getting back to your study on vitamin D and cognition, imagine that you assigned all the highly educated participants to one group and the less educated participants to the other. Might educational experience influence the results of a cognitive test? Perhaps. Random assignment helps reduce some of the interference resulting from these types of characteristics.

experimental method A type of research that manipulates a variable of interest (independent variable) to uncover cause-and-effect relationships.

random assignment The process of appointing participants in a research study to the experimental or control groups, ensuring that every person has an equal chance of being assigned to either.

The Experimental Method: Are You in Control?

The experimental method is the type of research that can tell us about causes and effects. It is different from descriptive studies in that key aspects of the experiment—participants, variables, and study implementation—are tightly controlled. The experiment typically includes at least two groups—an experimental group and a control group. This allows the researcher to isolate the effects of manipulating a single variable, called the independent variable.

Imagine you want to know if laws that ban texting while driving are worthwhile. Does texting really *cause* more accidents? Perhaps texting is merely correlated with higher accident rates in certain populations, such as college students, because college students are both more likely to text and more likely to have accidents. In order to find out, you have to perform an experiment.

VARIABLES

INDEPENDENT VARIABLE

The variable that researchers deliberately manipulate.

Example: The independent variable is texting while driving.

- **Experimental group** drives through obstacle course while texting.
- **Control group** drives through obstacle course without texting.

DEPENDENT VARIABLE

The variable measured as an outcome of manipulation of the independent variable.

Example: The dependent variable is the number of accidents (objects hit in obstacle course).

EXTRANEOUS VARIABLE

An unforeseen factor or characteristic that could unintentionally interfere with the outcome.

Example: Some participants have more driving experience than others. Without controlling the amount of driving experience, we can't be certain the independent variable caused more accidents.

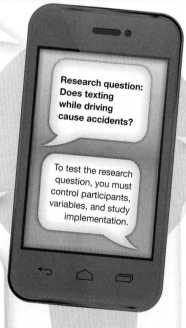

Research question: Does texting while driving cause accidents?

To test the research question, you must control participants, variables, and study implementation.

STUDY IMPLEMENTATION

PARTICIPANTS

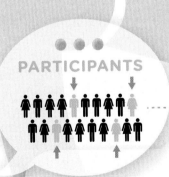

REPRESENTATIVE SAMPLE

Subset of the population chosen to reflect population of interest.

Example: Participants must be college students. Other groups might be affected differently by the independent variable.

RANDOM SAMPLE

Method used to ensure participants do not introduce unexpected bias.

Example: Researchers recruit participants by randomly selecting students from the college directory.

RANDOM ASSIGNMENT

Process by which researcher randomly assigns participants to experimental or control group.

Example: Experimenter flips coin to determine participant's group.

EXPERIMENTER BIAS

Researchers' expectations and unintentional behaviors can unwittingly change the outcome of a study.

Example: Without thinking, researcher says "good luck" to one group. This might unintentionally cause them to try harder.

Researchers control for these effects by using a **double-blind study** in which neither researcher nor participant knows what group participants are assigned to.

"Well, I guess we're the control group."

Cartoonstock

Synonyms
experimental group treatment group
independent variable explanatory variable
dependent variable response variable

experimental group The members of an experiment who are exposed to the treatment variable or manipulation by the researcher; represents the treatment group.

control group The participants in an experiment who are not exposed to the treatment variable; this is the comparison group.

independent variable (IV) In the experimental method, the variable manipulated by the researcher to determine its effect on the dependent variable.

dependent variable (DV) In the experimental method, the characteristic or response that is measured to determine the effect of the researcher's manipulation.

extraneous variable A variable in the environment or of the participants that could unintentionally influence the outcome of a study.

confounding variable A type of extraneous variable that changes in sync with the independent variable, making it difficult to discern which one is causing changes in the dependent variable.

double-blind study Type of study in which neither the researchers who are administering the independent variable nor the participants know what type of treatment is being given.

placebo (plə-ˈsē-ˌbō) An inert substance given to members of the control group; the fake treatment that has no benefit, but is administered as if it does.

LAB **EXPERIMENTAL AND CONTROL GROUPS** Let's assume you did use random assignment to divvy your participants into two groups. One will receive the treatment (a daily dose of vitamin D), and the other will receive no treatment at all (they will, however, be handed a sugar pill that looks identical to the vitamin D supplement). Those members of the group who get the treatment (the real vitamin D supplements) comprise the **experimental group,** and those participants who get the sugar pill are members of the **control group,** and they do not receive the treatment. (We explain the need for the fake treatment in a moment.)

INDEPENDENT AND DEPENDENT VARIABLES Let's restate a point we already made earlier in the section, this time using our new vocabulary terms: The only difference between the experimental and control groups should be the variable the researchers are manipulating—in this case, vitamin D intake. The different treatments the two groups receive is called the **independent variable (IV),** because it is the one variable the researchers are deliberately changing (in this case, some participants get vitamin D, others a sugar pill). In the experimental method, an independent variable is that which the researcher is manipulating, and due to the complex nature of human behavior, often more than one independent variable may be used. The **dependent variable (DV)** is the characteristic or response the researchers are trying to observe or measure. In the hypothetical study, the dependent variable is the participants' performance on cognitive tests. Just remember, the independent variable is what is manipulated and the dependent variable is what is being measured as a result of that manipulation. Stated slightly differently: The dependent variable, in this case, performance on the cognitive tests, "depends" on or is caused by the treatment (either vitamin D or the sugar pill).

EXTRANEOUS VARIABLES Another issue that must be considered by researchers as they plan their experiment is making sure that **extraneous variables** are not allowed to interfere with their measures. Extraneous variables are characteristics of the environment or participants that potentially interfere with the outcome of the research. While conducting your study of vitamin D supplements, you discover that three of the participants are reacting to the artificial light in the lab, making it very difficult for them to sleep. And this sleeplessness can definitely influence performance on cognitive tasks. Unfortunately, you failed to consider this very important variable in your research design, making it an extraneous variable. Researchers have to carefully contemplate the different kinds of variables that might influence the dependent variable.

There is a specific type of extraneous variable that can *confound* the results of an experiment. **Confounding variables** are a type of extraneous variable that changes in sync with the independent variable, making it very difficult to discern which variable—the independent variable or the confounding variable—is causing changes in the dependent variable. Imagine you house the participants in your study in a very nice lab setting, but because the lab can only hold half the participants at a time, you decide to wait and collect data from the control group later in the year. At that point, your lab assistant has gone on maternity leave, so you need to hire a new lab assistant, a young man who will administer the sugar pills to the control group. When the data are collected on cognitive performance, you can't be sure whether differences between groups on test scores result from the vitamin D pills, or some variables related to the gender of the lab assistants or even the time of year that the data were collected. These other variables could be confounding variables.

The good news is that there are numerous ways of eliminating the influence of an extraneous variable. This is called *controlling* a variable. As we mentioned earlier, random assignment to the treatment and control groups can help to lessen the impact of such variables. In this example, that means ensuring both groups have approximately the same number of participants who are having trouble sleeping in the lab. Or, if you wanted to control how sleep impacts the outcome of your study, you could just remove the poor sleepers from your sample and not include their information in your statistical analyses.

If you succeed in holding all variables constant except the independent variable, then you can make a statement about cause and effect. Let's say your study does uncover cognitive differences between the experimental and control groups. It is relatively safe to attribute that disparity to the independent variable. In other words, you can presume that the vitamin D caused the superior performance of the experimental group.

DOUBLE-BLIND STUDY   Earlier in the chapter, we mentioned that deception can sometimes be useful in scientific research. You are about to learn why. One way researchers use deception is by conducting a *single-blind study* in which participants do not know what treatment they are receiving. An even stronger experimental design is a **double-blind study,** an experiment in which neither the participants nor the researchers working directly with those participants know who is getting the real treatment and who is getting the pretend treatment. In our example, neither the person administering the pills nor the participants would know who was receiving the vitamin D supplement and who was receiving the sugar pill. Keeping participants in the dark is relatively easy; just make sure the treatment and sugar pill look the same from the outside (here, the vitamin D and sugar pill look identical). Blinding the researchers is a little trickier but can be accomplished with the help of clever assistants who make it appear that all participants are getting the same treatment.

THINKING IS BELIEVING   There are some very compelling reasons for making a study double-blind. Prior research tells us that the expectations of participants can influence results. If someone hands you a sugar pill but tells you it is real medicine, you might end up feeling better simply because this is what you expect will happen when you believe you are being treated. Apparently, thinking is believing. When people are given a fake pill or other inactive "treatment," known as a **placebo** (plə-'sē-,bō), they often get better even though the contents of the pill are inert. The *placebo effect* has been shown to ease pain, anxiety, depression, and the symptoms of Parkinson's disease. There are even some reports that, on occasion, the use of placebos has been linked to a reduction in the size of tumors (Niemi, 2009). Researchers believe that the placebo effect arises through both conscious expectations and unconscious associations between treatment cues and healing. One's expectation influences the placebo's actual effect.

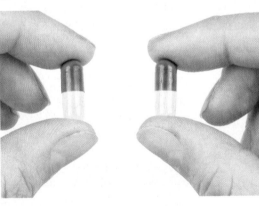

Looks Real
One of these pills contains an active ingredient; the other is a placebo. In placebo-controlled drug trials, researchers give some participants drugs and others placebos. People taking the placebos often experience effects that are similar to those reported by the participants taking the actual drug. Cordelia Molloy/Science Source

EXPERIMENTER BIAS   We've discussed the rationale for keeping participants in the dark, but why is it necessary to keep the researchers clueless as well? Researchers' expectations can influence the outcome of a study, a phenomenon known as **experimenter bias.** A researcher may unwittingly color a study's outcome through subtle verbal and/or nonverbal communication with the participants, conveying hopes or beliefs about

Synonyms
experimenter bias experimenter effect, researcher expectancy effect

experimenter bias Researchers' expectations that influence the outcome of a study.

TABLE 1.6 RESEARCH METHODS: ADVANTAGES AND DRAWBACKS

Research Method	Advantages	Disadvantages
Descriptive	Good for new research questions; can study phenomena in their naturally occurring environment.	Very little control; increased experimenter/participant bias; cannot determine cause and effect.
Correlational	Shows whether two variables are related; useful when an experiment is not possible.	Directionality and third-variable problems; cannot determine cause and effect.
Experimental	Can determine cause and effect; increased control over variables.	Results may not generalize beyond lab setting; potential for extraneous variables.

How does a researcher choose which method to use? It depends on the research question. Each research method has advantages and disadvantages.

Cartoonstock

"Good Morning, Here's your placebo—I mean medicine. . . well, I'm fired."

the experiment's results. A statement by the researcher like "I really have high hopes for this medicine" might influence participants' reactions to the treatment. The researcher's value system may also impact the results in barely noticeable but very important ways. Beliefs and attitudes can shape the way a researcher frames questions, tests hypotheses, or interprets findings (Rosenthal, 2002b).

Congratulations! You have now learned the nuts and bolts of the experimental method, one of psychology's greatest myth-debunking, knowledge-gathering tools. This method gives us more control over variables than any other type of study we have discussed; it also stands out in its ability to establish cause and effect. However, like any scientific approach, the experimental method is not without its flaws. Laboratory settings are inherently unnatural and therefore cannot always paint an accurate picture of behaviors that would occur in a natural setting. Remember, when people know they are being observed, their behavior changes. Other weaknesses of the experimental method include cost (it's expensive to maintain a laboratory) and time (collecting data in a laboratory setting can be much slower than, say, sending out a survey). **Table 1.6** gives an overview of some of the advantages and disadvantages of the research methods we have described.

Now it's time to test our understanding of the experimental method with the help of a sprightly yellow square named SpongeBob.

didn't SEE that coming

SpongeBob on the Brain

A little television won't hurt a child, will it? Kids' programs are interspersed with lessons on colors, words, and numbers, and only run for periods of 20 to 30 minutes. It seems reasonable to assume that little snippets of TV can't possibly have any measurable effect.

When it comes to the rapidly developing juvenile brain, however, it's probably not safe to assume anything. Consider the following controlled experiment examining the cognitive changes observed in preschool children after just 9 minutes of exposure to a talking yellow sponge zipping across a television screen.

TURNING YOUNG BRAINS TO "SPONGE"?

The research participants were 60 four-year-olds, most of whom came from White, upper-middle-class households. Researchers randomly assigned the children to one of three conditions: watching the extremely fast-paced cartoon *SpongeBob SquarePants,* viewing an educational program, or drawing with crayons and markers. Following 9 minutes of the assigned activities, the children took a series of four commonly used tests to assess their executive function—the collection of brain processes involved in self-control, decision making, problem solving, and other higher-level functions. The results were shocking: Children in the SpongeBob group performed considerably worse than those in the other groups (Lillard & Peterson, 2011). Just 9 minutes of SpongeBob produced a temporary lapse in cognitive function.

How do we know that this was not the result of a different variable, such as some children's preexisting attentional issues or television-watching habits at home? Those factors were accounted for in the study. In the experimental method, researchers hold nearly all variables constant except the one they want to manipulate—the 9-minute activity, in this case. This is the independent variable (IV). That way, the researchers can be somewhat confident that changes in the IV are driving changes in the dependent variable (DV)—performance on the cognitive tests.

What aspect of the cartoon caused these effects is not yet known, but the researchers suspect that it has something to do with the show's "fantastical events and fast pacing" (Lillard & Peterson, 2011, p. 648). Further studies are in the works, so stay tuned. ◉!

Sponge Brain
No one expects cartoons to make kids smarter, but can they hurt them? One study suggests that preschool children watching just 9 minutes of the high-energy, ultra-stimulating kids' show *SpongeBob SquarePants* experience a temporary dip in cognitive function.
PRNewsFoto/Nickelodeon

Research Ethics

LO 10 Demonstrate an understanding of research ethics.

Throughout this chapter, we have used the Chilean mining disaster as a subject for many hypothetical research endeavors, including studies on depression, aggression, and cognition. What we haven't yet addressed is the enormous ethical responsibility psychologists take on when they decide to conduct these types of studies. Psychologists do not examine dinosaur fossils or atomic particles. They study humans and other living creatures who experience pain, fear, and other complex feelings, and it is their professional duty to treat them with dignity and respect.

Like most other professionals, psychologists have established specific guidelines to help ensure ethical behavior in their field. Professional organizations such as the American Psychological Association (APA), the Association for Psychological Science (APS), and the British Psychological Society (BPS) provide written guidelines their members agree to follow. These guidelines ensure the ethical treatment of research participants (human and animal). They encourage psychologists to do no harm; safeguard the welfare of humans and animals in their research; know their responsibilities to society and community; maintain accuracy in research, teaching, and practice; and respect human dignity, to name a few examples (APA, 2010a).

CONFIDENTIALITY Confidentiality is a primary issue in psychology. Researchers must take steps to protect research data from misuse or theft. Psychologists who offer therapy services are obligated to keep client and therapy session information confidential; in fact, they are required to keep this information safeguarded in their offices. Confidentiality enables clients to speak freely about deeply personal issues. It ensures that research participants feel confident when they share sensitive information (sexual or controversial matters, for example), because they may rest assured researchers will protect it.

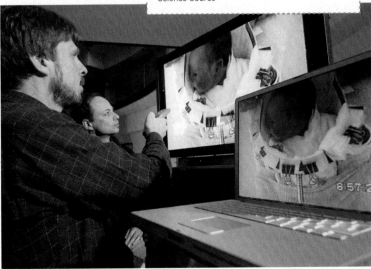

A Lofty Responsibility
Researchers study a newborn baby responding to smells such as curry and garlic. Certain flavors are familiar to babies because they were exposed to them in utero (through their mothers' diets). Conducting research on infants and other minors involves additional ethical considerations, and informed consent must be obtained from parents or legal guardians.
Thierry Berrod, Mona Lisa Production / Science Source

DECEPTION   Other important ethical topics are informed consent and debriefing, both of which we discussed earlier. Informed consent is the process by which research participants acknowledge their understanding of their role in the study and sign off on it. Debriefing refers to the process in which researchers disclose important information to their participants after wrapping up a study. This includes informing participants about any deception. Throughout this textbook, you will read about experiments in which the participants did not know ahead of time what was being studied. In addition, they were often purposely lied to as a part of the manipulation, or to conceal what was being studied until the debriefing phase. It is important to note that no one is ever forced to become a participant in a research study. Participation is completely voluntary, and participants can drop out at any time.

Apply This

Don't Believe Everything You Read

SCIENCE, SPIN, OR
SOUND BITES?

As you venture deeper into the study of psychology, you may find yourself becoming increasingly skeptical of media reports on psychological research. We encourage a healthy dose of skepticism. Although many news stories on scientific findings are accurate and balanced, others are flawed and overhyped. Look at these headlines about a 2012 study on the psychological impact of pacifier, or "binkie," use:

"Pacifier Use Can Lead to Emotional Problems in Boys, Study Finds"
(Fox News, 2012, September 19).

"UW Study Says Boys' Pacifier Use Limits Social Development"
(Seely, 2012, September 19).

It sounds as if pacifiers are *causing* emotional problems in males. We must have a cause-and-effect relationship, right? Wrong. The following is a rough description of the research, which is actually a combination of three studies described in one article. In a study of elementary school children, researchers found that boys (but not girls) who had used pacifiers during infancy were more likely to have trouble mimicking the facial expressions of others. (Mirroring facial expressions is believed to promote *empathy,* or the ability to put oneself in someone else's shoes, and pacifiers could potentially interrupt the development of this skill by blocking muscles around the mouth.) Additional studies of college students linked pacifier

Binkie Brouhaha
In 2012 researchers published a study showing a correlation between pacifier use in boys and lower levels of emotional intelligence later in life. The findings of this study could easily be interpreted as "pacifier use stunts emotional development," but this is a reckless conclusion. Think of all the other variables that might affect emotional development: parenting style, exposure to television, nutrition, interactions with siblings. Need we go on?
leungchopan/Shutterstock

use during infancy to lower levels of empathy and emotional intelligence, but only in males (Niedenthal et al., 2012).

Provocative as these findings may be, they do not allow us to conclude that pacifiers cause emotional impairments. Isn't it possible that the reverse is true? Infants with emotional problems are more likely to be given pacifiers (thus the emotional problems are leading to the pacifier use)? The authors explicitly highlight this problem: "The studies do not allow us to draw causal conclusions, as the children were not randomly assigned to pacifier use" (Niedenthal et al., 2012, p. 392). And while the researchers did control for some variables such as the mother's education and the child's anxiety level, it is impossible to control for every third variable that might influence emotional health. Can you think of any other factors that could impact the results?

The take-home message: If a news report claims that *X causes Y,* don't automatically assume that the media has it right. The only way to really understand the results and limitations of a psychological study is to read it for yourself. ➤

show what you know

1. The experimental method can provide findings on the _____ among variables.
   a. experimenter bias
   b. confounding
   c. random assignment
   d. cause-and-effect relationship

2. A researcher studying the impact of vitamin D on cognitive functioning gave supplements to the experimental group and a placebo to the control group. After 2 months, she tested the participants' cognitive functioning, which is a measure of the _____ variable.
   a. dependent
   b. independent
   c. extraneous
   d. confounding

3. Describe what a double-blind study is and explain why deception is necessary in this case.

4. Following a study involving a double-blind procedure with a treatment and a placebo, a researcher met with each participant individually to discuss important information about the study. This is known as:
   a. informed consent.
   b. debriefing.
   c. deception.
   d. naturalistic observation.

✓ CHECK YOUR ANSWERS IN APPENDIX C.

THE RESCUE Tuesday, October 12, 2010: The miners had been dreaming of this day for the last 10 weeks. Rescuers had finally blasted an escape tunnel down to the workshop area, a small cavern located above the safety shelter (Franklin, 2011). They would soon be lowering an elevator-like contraption known as the "Phoenix" down the tunnel to retrieve the miners. One by one, each man would travel back to the surface of the earth and into the arms of his family and friends. There would be a few onlookers, including President Piñera, a thousand journalists, and one billion people watching the rescue live on television (Craze & Crooks, 2010, October 13).

The first to ascend would be those believed to be most mentally stable. If something went wrong during the initial ascent, the rescuers wanted someone who could keep his cool onboard (Kraul, 2010, October 11). Florencio Ávalos, the soft-spoken 31-year-old father of two young boys, would go first, followed by the charismatic Mario Sepúlveda, 39; Juan Illanes, 51; and a 23-year-old Bolivian named Carlos Mamani. Next to go would be the men with medical problems, followed by those in good physical shape. The very last man to surface would be the determined and devoted leader, 54-year-old Luis Urzúa (CBS News/AP, 2010, October 12; Craze & Crooks, 2010, October 13; Kraul, 2010, October 11).

The rescue effort spanned 2 days. When all was said and done, all 33 men had been brought to safety. Now everyone wondered how the miners would cope with their new celebrity status. These 33 men had gone from

13 Down, 20 to Go
Carlos Barrios emerges from the Phoenix rescue capsule. He was the 13th miner to be hoisted to safety. AP Photo/Jorge Saenz

being ordinary working people to the most sought after interview subjects in the world. Reporters, publishing companies, and Hollywood all wanted a piece of Los 33. The group met with movie stars, attended galas, and led parades through Disneyland. One of the miners, Edison Peña, ran the New York City Marathon just weeks after emerging from the mine. He also appeared on *The Late Show with David Letterman* doing an Elvis impression (Pearson & Siemaszko, 2010, November 6).

But the same Peña who was seen gyrating on the *The Late Show* was later hospitalized for depression and anxiety. Other miners have also suffered from psychological troubles, including nightmares and difficulty readjusting to family life. Some are taking medications, and nearly a third have suffered from *post-traumatic stress disorder* (Chapter 11) (Barrionuevo, 2011, October 12; CBS News, 2011, February 10; Tobar, 2014, July 7). Despite these stark aftereffects, the rescue of these 33 men gives us many reasons to be hopeful. Just think about the teamwork, selflessness, and love the miners showed for each other. Remember the rescue workers who toiled around the clock to save the men from their underground nightmare; the wives, mothers, fathers, siblings, cousins, and friends who dropped everything and moved to the Atacama Desert to await the return of their loved ones; and the strangers all over the world who sat around their televisions, crying as they watched the miners emerge from the darkness. It is tragic that many of the miners have suffered psychological wounds, but as you will learn in this book, humans have an amazing way of overcoming adversity. Do not underestimate the positive potential of humanity.

At Last
Darío Segovia's family members erupted in celebration as they witnessed him emerge from the mine on October 13, 2010. They had waited 10 weeks for him to come home. AP Photo/Natacha Pisarenko, File

TABLE 1.7 RECURRING THEMES

Theme	Definition	What to look for
Nature and Nurture	The relative weight of heredity and environment in relation to behaviors, personality characteristics, and so on	Adaptation, heredity, environment, genes, instincts, reflexes, upbringing, peers, parents
Culture	The relative importance of cultural influences on behaviors, personality characteristics, and so on	Diversity, ethnicity, ethnic groups, cultural context, cross-cultural factors, ethnocentrism
Gender	The relative importance of one's gender as it relates to behaviors, personality characteristics, and so on	Gender bias, gender differences, social roles, masculinity, femininity, gender roles
Positive Psychology	The focus on positive aspects of human beings, as opposed to the more traditional focus on abnormality and maladaptive behavior	Strengths, optimal behavior, happiness, well-being, achievement, self-confidence, human potential

Throughout this textbook, you will come across four important themes: nature and nurture, culture, gender, and positive psychology.

Image Source/Getty Images

summary of concepts   1

LO 1 Define psychology and describe its scope. (p. 3)

Psychology is the scientific study of behavior and mental processes. Psychologists are scientists who work in a variety of fields, studying behavior and mental processes. They conduct two major types of research: basic and applied. Basic research focuses on collecting data to support or refute theories, gathering knowledge for the sake of knowledge. Applied research focuses on changing behaviors and outcomes, often leading to real-world applications.

LO 2 Summarize the goals of the discipline of psychology. (p. 6)

The goals of psychology are to describe, predict, explain, and control behavior. These goals lay the foundation for the scientific approach and the research designs used to carry out experiments.

LO 3 Identify influential people in the formation of psychology as a discipline. (p. 8)

The roots of psychology lie in disciplines such as philosophy and physiology. The early philosophers established the foundation for some of the longstanding discussions in psychology (nature and nurture). In 1879 psychology was officially founded when Wilhelm Wundt created the first psychology laboratory, located in Leipzig, Germany.

Edward Titchener established structuralism to study the elements of the mind. In the late 1870s, William James offered the first psychology class in the United States, at Harvard, and developed the early school of psychology known as functionalism.

LO 4 List and summarize the major perspectives in psychology. (p. 11)

Psychologists use different perspectives to understand and study issues and topics in the field. Each perspective provides a different vantage point for uncovering the complex nature of human behavior. The psychoanalytic perspective looks at the unconscious conflicts at the root of personality development. The behavioral perspective examines human behavior as learned primarily through associations, reinforcers, and observation. The humanistic perspective focuses on the positive and growth aspects of human nature. The cognitive perspective considers the mental processes that direct behavior. The evolutionary perspective examines heritable traits that increase or decrease in frequency across generations. The biological perspective identifies the physiological basis of behavior. The sociocultural perspective looks at the social and cultural influences that impact behavior. The biopsychosocial perspective explains human behavior in terms of biological, psychological, and sociocultural factors.

LO 5   Evaluate pseudopsychology and its relationship to critical thinking. (p. 17)

Pseudopsychology is any approach to explaining and predicting behavior and events that appears to be psychology but is not supported by empirical, objective evidence. Critical thinking, on the other hand, is the process of weighing various pieces of evidence, synthesizing them, and determining how each contributes to the bigger picture. Critical thinking is absent from the "pseudotheories" used to explain the pseudopsychologies.

LO 6   Describe how psychologists use the scientific method. (p. 18)

Psychologists use the scientific method to provide empirical evidence based on systematic observation or experiments. The scientific method includes five basic steps: develop a question, formulate a hypothesis, collect data, analyze the data, and publish the findings. The scientific method is a continuing cycle of exploration, which uses critical thinking at each step in the process, and asks new questions along the way.

LO 7   Summarize the importance of a random sample. (p. 24)

A population includes all members of an identified group a researcher is interested in exploring. If it is a large population, then the researcher will select a subset, called a sample. A random sample ensures that all members of a population have an equal chance of being selected to participate in a study, thus increasing the likelihood of a representative sample being used.

LO 8   Recognize the forms of descriptive research. (p. 26)

Descriptive research is a type of investigation used to describe and explore a phenomenon. It is especially useful for studying new or unexplored topics, when researchers might not have specific expectations about outcomes. Descriptive research methods include naturalistic observation, case studies, the survey method, and the correlational method.

LO 9   Explain how the experimental method relates to cause and effect. (p. 34)

The experimental method is a type of research that incorporates independent and dependent variables to uncover cause-and-effect relationships. A well-designed experiment holds everything constant, except for the variables being manipulated by the researcher. If following the manipulation the groups of participants differ on the measure of interest, we can say with confidence that the experimental manipulation caused that change.

LO 10   Demonstrate an understanding of research ethics. (p. 39)

Researchers must abide by guidelines to ensure the ethical treatment of research participants. These guidelines encourage psychologists to do no harm; safeguard the welfare of humans and animals in their research; know their responsibilities to society and community; maintain accuracy in research, teaching, and practice; and respect human dignity.

key terms

behaviorism, p. 11
biopsychosocial perspective, p. 13
case study, p. 27
confounding variable, p. 36
control group, p. 36
correlation, p. 29
correlation coefficient, p. 31
correlational method, p. 29
critical thinking, p. 17
debriefing, p. 25
dependent variable (DV), p. 36

descriptive research, p. 26
double-blind study, p. 37
experiment, p. 18
experimental group, p. 36
experimental method, p. 34
experimenter bias, p. 37
extraneous variable, p. 36
functionalism, p. 10
humanistic psychology, p. 11
hypothesis, p. 20
independent variable (IV), p. 36

informed consent, p. 25
Institutional Review Board (IRB), p. 25
introspection, p. 9
natural selection, p. 13
naturalistic observation, p. 26
observer bias, p. 27
operational definition, p. 20
placebo, p. 37
population, p. 24
positive psychology, p. 25
pseudopsychology, p. 17

psychologists, p. 3
psychology, p. 3
random assignment, p. 34
random sample, p. 24
replicate, p. 22
representative sample, p. 24
sample, p. 24
scientific method, p. 18
structuralism, p. 10
survey method, p. 28
theory, p. 20
third variable, p. 31
variables, p. 24

TEST PREP are you ready?

1. Researchers at a large university were asked to devise a stop-smoking campaign and assess its effectiveness. Using findings from prior research, they created a program to help students, faculty, and staff quit smoking. This is an example of:
   a. basic research.
   b. applied research.
   c. naturalistic observation.
   d. case studies.

2. _____ is a collection of knowledge that any reasonably smart person can pick up through casual observations of everyday experiences.
   a. Common sense
   b. Hindsight bias
   c. Psychology
   d. Psychomythology

3. The Greek philosopher Plato believed that truth and knowledge exist in the soul before birth and that humans have innate knowledge. This positions supports:
   a. empiricism.
   b. the nurture side of the nature–nurture issue.
   c. the nature side of the nature–nurture issue.
   d. dualism.

4. Inspired by the work of Charles Darwin, William James proposed that the purpose of thought processes, feelings, and behaviors is to adapt to the environment, which is an important concept of:
   a. introspection.
   b. behaviorism.
   c. structuralism.
   d. functionalism.

5. _____ suggests that human nature is by and large positive.
   a. Natural selection
   b. Psychoanalysis
   c. Structuralism
   d. Humanistic psychology

6. Psychology is driven by _____, but pseudopsychology is not.
   a. unverified guesses
   b. critical thinking
   c. lessons learned
   d. folk wisdom

7. The goal of _____ is to provide empirical evidence or data based on systematic observation or experimentation.
   a. operational definitions
   b. critical thinking
   c. the scientific method
   d. a hypothesis

8. _____ allow us to make inferences and determine the probability of certain events occurring.
   a. Inferential statistics
   b. Descriptive statistics
   c. Operational definitions
   d. Theories

9. A psychologist studying the Chilean miners was interested in their leadership qualities and educational backgrounds. These characteristics are generally referred to as:
   a. operational definitions.
   b. hypotheses.
   c. variables.
   d. empiricism.

10. One way to pick a random sample is to make sure every member of the population has:
    a. no extraneous variables.
    b. no confounding variables.
    c. an equally likely chance of having a characteristic in common.
    d. an equally likely chance of being picked to participate.

11. Descriptive research is invaluable to psychologists at the beginning stages of a study. Some forms of descriptive research can provide information on:
    a. cause-and-effect relationships.
    b. random assignment.
    c. relationships among variables.
    d. experimenter bias.

12. A researcher interested in learning more about the effect of isolation might choose the Chilean miners as a(n) _____, which is a type of descriptive research invaluable for studying rare events.
    a. experiment
    b. case study
    c. naturalistic observation
    d. correlational study

13. The _____ variable is what the researcher manipulates, and the _____ variable is the response the researcher measures.
    a. confounding; extraneous
    b. extraneous; confounding
    c. dependent; independent
    d. independent; dependent

14. With a(n) _____ study, neither the researchers nor the participants know who is getting the treatment or who is getting the placebo.
    a. double-blind
    b. experimental
    c. correlational
    d. blind

15. The members of the _____ include those participants who receive the real treatment as opposed to a placebo.
    a. control group
    b. experimental group
    c. population
    d. sample

16. Explain how a thorough review of the literature plays a part in the scientific method.

17. A researcher has suggested that handwriting analysis may reveal dishonesty through stroke size and pressure used. If you were to use the experimental method to further study this topic, what would your treatment and control groups be?

18. Which survey is potentially more accurate: a face-to-face interview or written questions to be answered in private? Explain your answer.

19. Find an article in the popular media that presents variables as having cause-and-effect relationships, but that is really a correlational study.

20. Reread the feature on the Sponge Bob study. If you were to replicate the study, what would you do to change or improve it?

✓ CHECK YOUR ANSWERS IN APPENDIX C.

Get personalized practice by logging into LaunchPad at **www.macmillanhighered.com/launchpad/ sciampresenting1e** to take the LearningCurve adaptive quizzes for Chapter 1.

2

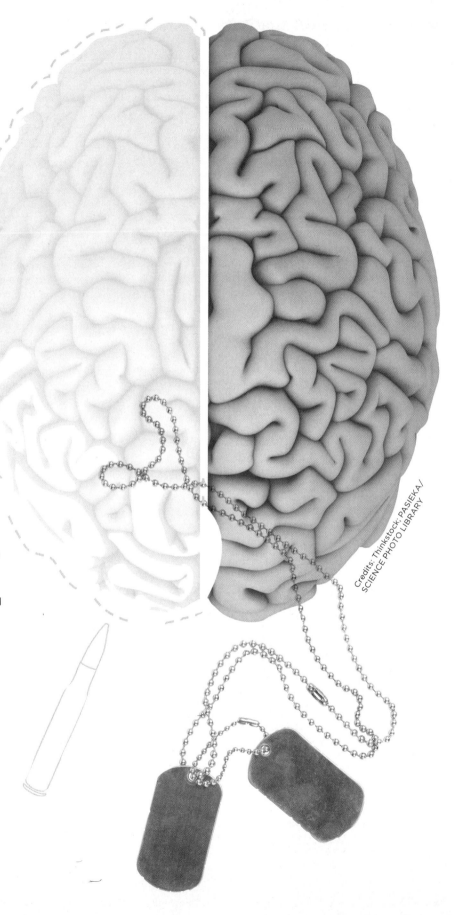

Credits: Thinkstock: PASIEKA/
SCIENCE PHOTO LIBRARY

biology and
behavior

Thinkstock

Introducing the Brain

IN THE LINE OF FIRE   It was November 9th, 2004, and U.S. Marine Brandon Burns was surrounded on all sides by gunfire. The enemy was everywhere, in the buildings, streets, and alleyways of Fallujah. "I was in the deepest part of the city [and] there was chaos," remembers Brandon. At age 19, Brandon was on the front lines in the Iraq War, fighting in the battle of Fallujah.

"I was on top of the Humvee automatic grenade launcher shooting round after round," Brandon recalls. Suddenly, there was darkness. A bullet from an enemy sniper had pierced Brandon's helmet and skull, and ricocheted through the back left side of his brain. Bleeding and unconscious, Brandon was rushed from Fallujah to Baghdad. Medics had to resuscitate him on five separate occasions during that ambulance ride. Brandon explains, "Five times I died."

From Baghdad, Brandon was transferred to a hospital in Germany. Doctors concluded that some parts of his brain were no longer viable. "They removed part of my skull and dug out the injured part of my brain," and now, Brandon says, "one third of my brain is gone." 📁

Ready for Duty
Brandon Burns poses for a photo at the Marine Corps Recruit Depot in Parris Island, South Carolina, in the fall of 2003. The following year, he was shot by an enemy sniper in the battle of Fallujah. Laura Burns

Front Lines
At the age of 17, Brandon signed up to join the Marines. Two years later, he found himself engaged in some of the most rigorous urban combat of the Iraq War (Filkins, 2004, November 21). ©Sa'ad Mohammed/epa/Corbis

Note: Quotations attributed to Brandon Burns, Laura Burns, and Christina Santhouse are personal communications.

A Complex Communication Network

Imagine that you lost a sizable chunk of your brain. How would it impact your life? Would you be the same person as before? Your brain houses your thoughts, emotions, and personality, and orchestrates your behavior. It files away all your memories and dark secrets, and is involved in your every move, from the beat of your heart to the blink of your eye.

However, the human brain is only one part of the most complex living entity known. The human *nervous system* is a communication network that conveys messages throughout your body, using electrical and chemical processes. The nervous system contains the brain, spinal cord, and other nerves and fibers, and includes some 100 billion (10^{11}) nerve cells. For a sense of what that number represents, consider that the population of the United States was approximately 320 million people in 2015; the number of nerve cells is approximately 313 times the number of people living in the United States. These cells are interlinked through some 100 quadrillion (10^{15}) connections (Tang, Nyengaard, De Groot, & Gundersen, 2001). This intricate, ever-adapting web of connections gives us the power to think and feel in ways that are different from—and vastly more complex than—the thinking and feeling capacities of most other organisms.

Consider the many tasks your brain is juggling at this very moment. As you scan the words on this page, your brain helps control the tiny muscles moving your eyes back and forth as well as the larger muscles in your neck and torso that keep you sitting upright. Light-sensitive cells in the back of your eyes relay signals, using electricity and chemicals, to various brain regions that transform the black marks on this page into words, sentences, and ideas for you to remember. And all the while, your brain is processing nonvisual sensory input such as sounds and smells, and working with other nerve cells in your body to make sure your heart keeps pumping, your lungs keep breathing, and your glands and organs keep releasing hormones properly.

The Last Frontier: From Bumps to Brain Scans

LO 1 Define neuroscience and biological psychology and explain their contributions to our understanding of behavior.

Brandon's injury resulted in a significant loss of his brain tissue. Remarkably, not only did he survive, but he can still talk about what occurred, think about the events, and feel emotions regarding what happened to him. How exactly does his

neuroscience The study of the brain and nervous system.

biological psychology The branch of psychology that focuses on how the brain and other biological systems influence human behavior.

phrenology An early approach to explaining the functions of the brain by trying to link the physical structure of the skull with a variety of characteristics.

brain orchestrate all these complex functions, especially after severe trauma? And how does a noninjured brain carry out these complicated processes? Scientists have developed a decent understanding of how individual brain cells communicate with each other, but they have yet to provide definitive answers to "big questions" involving the brain and other parts of the nervous system such as: How do we think? What is consciousness? Why must we sleep? This is why the brain may be regarded as the last frontier of medicine. **Neuroscience,** the study of the brain and nervous system, actually extends far beyond the borders of medicine and into disciplines as diverse as engineering, computer science, and our personal favorite—psychology. The subfield of psychology concerned with understanding how the brain and other biological systems influence human behavior is called **biological psychology,** which brings us to the goal of this chapter: to examine how biology influences our behavior.

Synonyms
biological psychology biopsychology, psychobiology, neuropsychology, physiological psychology, behavioral neuroscience

---

LO 2   Compare and contrast tools scientists use to study the brain.

Brandon underwent many brain scans before and after his surgeries, which allowed doctors to get a detailed look inside his head without lifting a scalpel. But had Brandon lived in a different era, brain scans would not have been an option.

Before there were technologies to study the brain, people could only speculate about what was going on beneath the skull of a living person. One theory was that bumps on a person's skull could reveal characteristics about him. Judging the topography of a person's head was a core part of **phrenology,** the now discredited brain "science" that achieved enormous popularity at the beginning of the 19th century through its founder Franz Joseph Gall (1757–1828). Another early (but more scientific) way of studying the brain was through *ablation,* a technique used by physiologist Pierre Flourens (1794–1867) to determine the functions of different brain regions (Pearce, 2009). This technique involved destroying parts of a living animal's brain and then determining whether some functioning was lost following this surgery. In spite of the limitations of their methodologies, Gall and Flourens advanced the idea that there might be areas of the brain with particular functions. In other words, there are locations in the brain that are responsible for specific brain activities: there is a *localization* of function.

Brain research has come a long way since the days of Gall and Flourens. The last century, and particularly the last few decades, has witnessed an explosion of technologies for studying the nervous system (see **Infographic 2.1** on the next page). Such advances

CONNECTIONS

In **Chapter 1,** we presented the four major goals of psychology, which are to describe, explain, predict, and control behavior. These four goals guide psychologists' investigations of how biology influences behavior. As you read through this chapter, try to keep these goals in mind.

CONNECTIONS

If phrenology were practiced today, we would consider it a *pseudoscience,* or an activity that resembles science but is not supported by objective evidence. (See **Chapter 1** to read more on pseudoscience.)

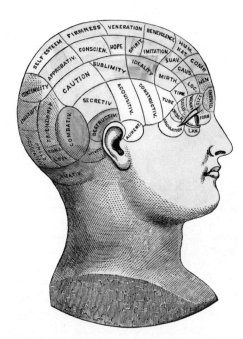

All in Your Head
Are you a secretive person? How high is your self-esteem? The answers to these questions lie on the surface of the skull, or so claimed 19th-century phrenologists, such as the one depicted in this 1886 illustration (right). The phrenological map (left) shows the locations of brain "organs" thought to be responsible for various psychological traits. left: © North Wind Picture Archives/The Image Works, right: Image Asset Management Ltd./SuperStock

Ways to Study the Living Brain

For hundreds of years, scientists interested in studying the brain were limited to surgical techniques, often on cadavers. Imaging and recording technologies now allow us to investigate the living brain by assessing structure, function, or both. CAT and MRI techniques provide static pictures of brain structures, while functional imaging and recording techniques allow us to see the relationship between brain activity and specific mental functions. Functional techniques can also be used to diagnose injuries and diseases earlier than techniques that look at structure.

New technologies are continually being developed, allowing us to study the brain in ways we couldn't imagine just a few years ago.

Looking at Brain STRUCTURE

COMPUTERIZED AXIAL TOMOGRAPHY CAT

Using X-rays, a scanner creates multiple cross-sectional images of the brain. Here, we see the brain from the top at the level of the ventricles, which form the butterfly-shaped dark spaces in the center.

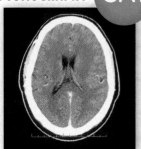

MAGNETIC RESONANCE IMAGING MRI

An MRI machine's powerful magnets create a magnetic field that passes through the brain. A computer analyzes the electromagnetic response, creating cross-sectional images similar to those produced by CAT, but with superior detail.

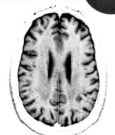

What's Next?
Making Connections

The intricate pathways of myelinated axons in the brain can't be seen in the imaging techniques above. But new technologies like diffusion spectrum imaging (DSI), which tracks the diffusion of water molecules through brain tissue, are being used to map neural connections. The resulting images show a complex information superhighway, with different colors indicating directions of travel.

Watching Brain FUNCTION

EEG ELECTROENCEPHALOGRAM

Electrodes placed on the scalp record electrical activity from the cortical area directly below. When the recorded traces are lined up, as in the computer readout seen here, we can see the scope of functional responses across the lobes.

PET POSITRON EMISSION TOMOGRAPHY

A radioactively labeled substance called a tracer is injected into the bloodstream and tracked while the subject performs a task. A computer then creates 3-D images showing degrees of brain activity. Areas with the most activity appear in red.

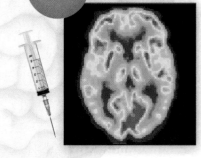

fMRI FUNCTIONAL MAGNETIC RESONANCE IMAGING

The flow of oxygen-rich blood increases to areas of the brain that are active during a task. fMRI uses powerful magnets to track changes in blood-oxygen levels. Like PET, this produces measurements of activity throughout the brain.

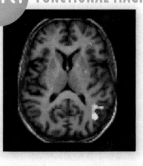

TABLE 2.1 IMAGING AND RECORDING TECHNOLOGIES

Technology	Limitations
Electroencephalogram (EEG)	Only records brain-wave activity happening on the surface of the brain.
Computerized Axial Tomography (CAT scan or CT scan)	Exposes people to radiation, potentially increasing cancer risk (National Cancer Institute, 2010).
Positron Emission Tomography (PET)	From injection to scan, PET scans are time-consuming. This procedure can be expensive, and it exposes people to radiation.
Magnetic Resonance Imaging (MRI)	MRIs produce more detailed images than CTs but are more time-consuming and expensive.
Functional Magnetic Resonance Imaging (fMRI)	Indirectly measures neural activity via blood flow, not necessarily identifying the precise location of cognitive processes.

In the past, most of what scientists learned about the brain came from probing the skulls of cadavers and observing the behavior of people suffering from brain damage. Today, researchers use a variety of technologies to study the brains of living people; however they are not without their limitations.

SOURCE: YASMIN ET AL., 2012.

have made it possible to observe the brain as it makes decisions, sleeps, and even tells lies (Dang-Vu et al., 2008; Hampton & O'Doherty, 2007; Kozel et al., 2009). See **Table 2.1** for information on the scope and limitations of these technologies.

With that overview, we are now ready to begin our chapter-long "learning tour" of the nervous system. Our journey begins in the microscopic world of nerve cells, or **neurons**. Neurons are specialized cells that communicate with each other through both electrical and chemical signals. They are the building blocks of the brain, spinal cord, and nerves. When large numbers of these building blocks are lost or damaged, as occurred in Brandon's injury, the consequences can be severe.

THE AWAKENING Two weeks after the shooting, Brandon finally awoke from his coma. He could not move or feel the right side of his body, and he had lost the ability to use language. There were so many things he wanted to say to his family, but when he opened his mouth, the only sound that came out was "ugh." Weeks went by before Brandon uttered his first word: "no." That was all he could say for months, even when he was dying to say "yes."

Apart from the paralysis to his right side and his difficulty with language, Brandon's other abilities appeared to be intact. He could remember people, places, and objects, and he reported no trouble hearing, smelling, or tasting. Although Brandon was not as outgoing and self-assured as before, he hadn't changed much overall.

Why did the trauma to Brandon's brain cause deficits in language, but not memory? Why was the right side of his body paralyzed, while the left side worked fine? Our discussion of the brain's organization later in this chapter will clear up these mysteries for you. But first, let's find out how neurons in the brain and body communicate, for this biological process underlies your every behavior, thought, and emotion.

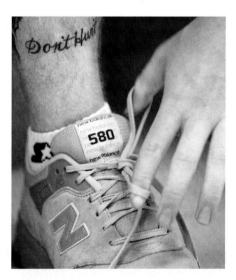

One-Handed
Brandon ties his shoelaces with his left hand. His traumatic brain injury occurred on the left side of his brain, causing paralysis and loss of sensation on the right side of his body. A. J. Wolfe/The Commercial Appeal

 show what you know

1. Made up of the brain, spinal cord, and other nerves, _____ is a communication network that conveys messages throughout the body, using electrical and chemical processes.
   a. consciousness
   b. the human nervous system
   c. a neuron
   d. the skull

2. A researcher studying the impact of Brandon's brain injury might work in the field of _____ , which includes the study of the brain and nervous system.

3. In the next section, you will learn much more about neurons, which are often referred to as the "building blocks" of the nervous system. What building blocks are you familiar with in other fields of study?

✓ CHECK YOUR ANSWERS IN APPENDIX C.

neurons The building blocks of the nervous system that transmit electrical and chemical signals in the body.

Neurons and Neural Communication

Just the Basics

LO 3   Label the parts of a neuron and describe an action potential.

Synonyms
cell body soma
terminal buds axon buds, synaptic knobs, terminal buttons
synapse synaptic cleft, synaptic gap

THE STRUCTURE OF A TYPICAL NEURON   A typical neuron has three basic parts: a cell body, dendrites, and an axon (**Figure 2.1**). The **cell body** of a neuron contains the standard components found in most human cells: protein-producing mechanisms, structures that nourish the cell, and a nucleus containing DNA. Extending from the cell body are many **dendrites** (den-drīts), which are tiny, branchlike fibers. Generally projecting in the opposite direction from the dendrites is a single **axon**, which is a long, skinny, tubelike extension of the cell body, with branches ending in *terminal buds.* Many axons are surrounded by a **myelin sheath** (mī-ə-lən shēth), a fatty substance that provides insulation. In such cases the axon is not entirely enclosed, but rather, covered in segments of myelin. The breaks between the myelin segments are called *nodes of Ranvier.*

The **synapse** (si-naps) is the tiny gap between a terminal bud of one axon and a neighboring dendrite of the next neuron (see image on page 58). Just for perspective, the synaptic gap is only about 0.000127 millimeters (1.27×10^4) wide, whereas a single sheet of printer paper is 0.1 millimeter thick.

HOLDING IT TOGETHER: GLIAL CELLS   The function of neurons is to transmit information up and down the body all day and night, and neurons need a little support and nurturing to get this

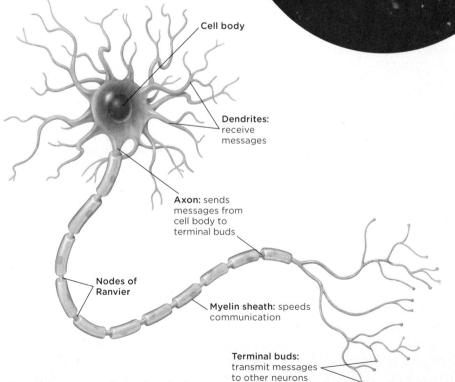

(see image on page 58)

FIGURE 2.1

The Neuron
The neuron, the basic building block of the nervous system, has three main components: (1) the *cell body,* which contains vital cellular structures; (2) bushy *dendrites* that receive messages from neighboring neurons; and (3) a long, thin *axon* that sends messages to other neurons through its branchlike *terminal buds.* James Cavallini/Photo Researchers, Inc.

Cell body

Dendrites: receive messages

Axon: sends messages from cell body to terminal buds

Nodes of Ranvier

Myelin sheath: speeds communication

Terminal buds: transmit messages to other neurons

tough job done. This is where the **glial cells** (glē-əl) come into play. In the human brain, glial cells outnumber neurons by approximately 50 to 1 (Yuhas & Jabr, 2012), holding neurons together and maintaining the structure of the nervous system. (*Glia* means "glue" in Greek.)

For many years, scientists believed that glial cells simply kept things together, but we now know they do much more (Ndubaku & de Bellard, 2008). For example, glial cells come to the rescue if the brain is injured. When Brandon was shot in the head, glial cells called *microglia* worked to defend his brain from infection and inflammation (d'Avila et al., 2012; Streit, 2000). Another class of glial cells called *astrocytes* began to restore the barrier between his brain and blood (Gruber, 2009). Astrocytes have been found to support communication between neurons as well (Araque & Navarrete, 2010). Another type of glial cells, *Schwann cells,* produce the myelin that envelops axons.

Glia to the Rescue
A scanning electron micrograph shows neurons (green) and glia (orange). Glial cells serve as the "glue" of the nervous system, providing cohesion and support for the neurons. Thomas Deerinck, NCMIR/Science Source

Processes Inside the Neuron

Neurons have properties that allow them to communicate with other cells. But what information do they convey? In essence, the message is simple: "I have been activated." Neurons are activated in response to sensations, thoughts, and other neurons, and this forms the basis for all that we think, feel, and do.

A neuron is surrounded by and contains electrically charged solutions (**Infographic 2.2** on the next page). If the total charge in each of these solutions is different, a voltage will be generated between the outside and the inside of the cell. This voltage is determined by the electrical characteristics of particles called *ions*. Some ions are negatively charged; others are positively charged. The difference in the charges inside and outside of the neuron determines its *polarity*, the degree to which it is positive or negative overall. Two processes direct the flow of positive and negative ions into or out of the cell. *Diffusion* is the natural tendency of the ions to spread out or disperse, and *electrostatic pressure* causes similarly charged ions to spread apart and oppositely charged ions to move toward each other (like the behavior of magnets). The concentrations, inside and outside of the cell, of positively charged ions (sodium and potassium) and negatively charged ions (protein molecules) determine the activity in most neurons.

A neuron is encased in a membrane that is selectively permeable, allowing only some of the ions to pass in and out of its channels. The membrane is impermeable to positive sodium ions and negative protein ions (it does not allow these ions to enter or exit). Positive sodium ions move toward the membrane from the outside, and negative protein ions move toward the membrane from the inside; each moves closer to its side of the membrane wall (because the opposite charges are attracted to each other).

Inside the neuron, the concentration of potassium ions is greater than that outside the membrane. Also inside the cell are negatively charged protein ions, which do not exist outside the cell. These protein ions are attracted to the excess positive charge outside and move toward the membrane, but they are too big to go through.

cell body The region of the neuron that includes protein-producing mechanisms, structures that nourish the cell, and a nucleus containing DNA.

dendrites (den-drīts) Tiny, branchlike fibers extending from the cell body that receive messages from other neurons and send information in the direction of the cell body.

axon Skinny tubelike structure of a neuron that extends from the cell body, and which sends messages to other neurons.

myelin sheath (mī-ə-lən shēth) Fatty substance that insulates the axon and speeds the transmission of neural messages.

synapse (si-naps) The tiny gap between a terminal bud of one axon and a neighboring dendrite of the next neuron; junction between neurons where communication occurs.

glial cells (glē-əl) Cells that support, nourish, and protect neurons; produce myelin that covers axons.

Communication Within Neurons

Neural communication involves different processes *within* and *between* neurons. In this infographic, we follow the electrical action that conveys messages *within* the neuron, from one end to the other.

Dendrites

Neuron cell body

Axon hillock

Axon

Myelin sheath

Node of Ranvier

+ + + + +
− −
+
+
− −
+ + + + +

Terminal buds

1. THE NEURON AT REST

Before communication begins, the neuron is "at rest." Closed channels in the cell membrane prevent some positive ions from entering the cell, and the solution inside of the cell is slightly more negative than the charge of the solution outside. At –70 mV, the cell is at its resting potential.

2. THE ACTION POTENTIAL

+30
0
−55
−70

A   + B   C

This graph above shows the characteristic electrical trace of the action potential. When the neuron is stimulated, positive ions enter the cell, making the axon less negative (A). When the charge reaches threshold (–55 mV), an action potential is triggered. Positive ions flood the cell, quickly reversing the charge from negative to positive (B). Afterward, the cell is restored to resting potential (C).

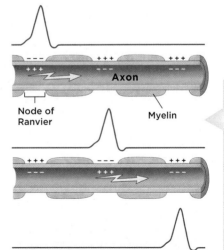

Axon

Node of Ranvier

Myelin

3. ACTION POTENTIAL TRAVELS LENGTH OF AXON

The action potential occurring in one axon segment causes a voltage change in the next, initiating an entirely new action potential there. This sequential activity travels along the axon like a wave, carrying the message from axon hillock to terminal buds.

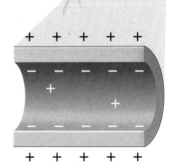

Because the protein ions can't get out, the inside of the neuron is negatively charged when the neuron is not active. The concentration of sodium ions inside the cell is much less than its concentration on the outside of the cell. As a result, the sodium ions on the outside are attracted to the cell wall (because of diffusion and electrostatic pressure). An electrical potential is created by the differences in charge between the outside and the inside of the neuron, which is its *resting potential*.

RESTING POTENTIAL   The **resting potential** represents the electrical potential of a cell "at rest," the condition of a cell when it is not activated. The solutions on either side of the membrane wall come into equilibrium with a slightly more negative charge inside. In the resting state, the voltage inside the cell is about –70 millivolts (mV) compared to the voltage on the outside. (Think of a resting neuron like a battery, which holds a charge. For comparison, one double A battery has a 1,500-mV charge.) This resting potential is only one part of the story. Let's look at what happens when a neuron stops "resting" and goes into "action."

ACTION POTENTIAL   Although the positive sodium ions are being pulled toward the inside of the cell, they cannot move into the cell until the neuron is stimulated by neighboring cells. When this happens, a signal instructs the channels, or gates, in the cell membrane to open up. The channels in the dendrites open, freeing the positive sodium ions to enter the cell through the dendrites, move into the cell body, and to finally reach the beginning of the axon, known as the *axon hillock*.

The influx of the positive sodium ions at the axon hillock raises the internal cell voltage of the first segment of the axon from the resting voltage of –70 mV to the *threshold potential* of –55 mV relative to the outside. This change in voltage causes the sodium gates to open, and the positive sodium ions flood the cell. The voltage inside that section of the axon rises rapidly, increasing from –55 mV to +30 mV, after which the sodium gates immediately close. This produces a spike in the value of the voltage within the cell, as the charge inside the cell becomes more positive than that outside of the cell. This is the **action potential,** or the spike in electrical energy that passes through the axon of a neuron.

The potassium gates open, and the positive potassium ions, now repelled by the much more positively charged cell interior, flow out of the cell. However, because the proportion of sodium and potassium ions inside and outside the cell is not the same as before (the ions are no longer at equilibrium), a sodium/potassium pump within the cell membrane brings them back to their original values by pumping the excess positive sodium ions back outside the cell and the positive potassium ions back in. In this way, the solutions inside and outside this segment of the axon return to equilibrium. In other words, it returns to resting potential.

MOVING DOWN THE AXON   The firing of the first segment of the axon produces excess sodium ions on the inside of the cell, and these positive sodium ions diffuse to the next segment within the axon. This causes the voltage of the second segment of the axon to reach the threshold potential (–55 mV), opening its sodium gates and causing a spike of voltage there (+30 mV). Meanwhile, the first segment of the axon returns to its resting potential, so that the electrical spike cannot travel back in that direction. This process repeats through each segment of the axon, like a row of dominos tumbling down. Every time a segment of the axon fires, the positive sodium ions flood in from the outside of the cell, while the prior segment returns to its resting potential, all along the length of the axon to its end. Each action potential takes about 1 millisecond to complete, and a typical neuron can fire several hundred times per second.

Synonyms
threshold potential stimulus threshold
action potential spike potential

resting potential The electrical potential of a cell "at rest"; the state of a cell when it is not activated.

action potential The spike in electrical energy that passes through the axon of a neuron, the purpose of which is to convey information.

EXCITATORY AND INHIBITORY SIGNALS   How do neighboring cells initially signal for the channels to open up to let the positive sodium ions move into the dendrites of a neuron? The message to fire begins at the dendrites. Chemical messages from surrounding neurons are sent to the cell body. If enough sending neurons signal the receiving neuron to pass along the message, their combined signal becomes *excitatory* and the neuron will fire. However, not all neighboring neurons send an excitatory signal. Some will send an *inhibitory* signal, instructing the neuron not to fire. For an excitatory signal to occur, there have to be more excitatory than inhibitory signals, and the difference between the two has to meet the threshold potential of –55 mV. If "enough" positively charged ions enter the cell, the potential of the neuron increases and reaches the threshold, or trigger point, and the cell "fires."

ALL-OR-NONE   Action potentials are **all-or-none:** They either happen or they don't. Their strength remains the same no matter what occurs. A neuron conveys the strength of a stimulus by firing more often and delivering its message to more neurons. This is how we sense the difference between a quiet sound and a loud bang, for example. When we hear a loud bang: (1) The number of sensory neurons fired is greater than the number fired for a quiet sound, and (2) each individual neuron fires more often than it would for a quiet sound. Thus, there is no such thing as a partial action potential, or a strong or weak action potential.

So Fast

Action potentials may travel as fast as 268 miles per hour through a myelinated axon (Susuki, 2010). Myelin is a protein that envelops and insulates the axon, facilitating faster transmission of the impulse. The action potential "skips" over the segments of myelin, hopping from one node of Ranvier to the next (see small space in the center), instead of traversing the entire length of the axon. JEAN-CLAUDE REVY, ISM/Phototake

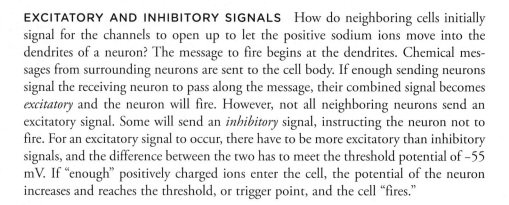

ROLE OF MYELIN SHEATH   The firing of a neuron is facilitated by the myelin sheath, which insulates and protects the tiny spikes in electricity happening inside the axon. Because myelin is such a good insulator, it does not allow the exchange of ion fluid between the inside and the outside of the cell membrane. However, the axon is not covered with myelin at the nodes of Ranvier (you can see this in the photograph to the left). The exchange of ion fluid can only happen at these nodes. The action potential thus appears to "jump" from node to node, as opposed to traversing the entire axon in one continuous movement, speeding the transmission of the signal. The speed of the action potential in an unmyelinated axon is approximately 1.1 to 4.5 miles per hour (mph), and a myelinated axon has transmission speeds of approximately 157 to 268 mph (Susuki, 2010). Unmyelinated axons, or those damaged from multiple sclerosis or other diseases, have slower transmission speeds, because the signal must make its way down the entire length of the axon. The damaged myelination caused by multiple sclerosis can lead to many symptoms, including fatigue, trouble with vision, and cognitive disabilities (Su, Banker, Bourdette, & Forte, 2009).

Communication Between Neurons

LO 4   Illustrate how neurons communicate with each other.

Neurons communicate with each other via chemicals called **neurotransmitters**. (**Infographic 2.3** illustrates communication between neurons in detail.) An action potential moves down the axon, eventually reaching the terminal buds. The signal to release neurotransmitters is the voltage change from the action potential, which results in *vesicles* (small fluid-filled sacs) that contain neurotransmitters attaching to the membrane on the terminal buds. This allows the neurotransmitters to be released into the synaptic gap. The majority of these neurotransmitters drift across the synaptic gap and come into contact with **receptor sites** of the receiving neuron's dendrites. Just as it takes the right key to unlock a door, the neurotransmitter must fit a corresponding receptor site to convey its message. Because there are a variety of neurotransmitters, a variety of receptor sites also exist.

all-or-none A neuron either fires or does not fire; action potentials are always the same strength.

neurotransmitters Chemical messengers that neurons use to communicate at the synapse.

receptor sites The location where neurotransmitters attach on the receiving side of the synaptic gap.

Communication Between Neurons

Messages travel within a neuron using electrical currents. But communication *between* neurons depends on the movement of chemicals—neurotransmitters. Though they all work in the same way, there are many different types of neurotransmitters, each linked to unique effects on behavior. However, drugs and other substances, known as *agonists* and *antagonists,* can alter this process of communication between neurons by boosting or blocking normal neurotransmitter activity.

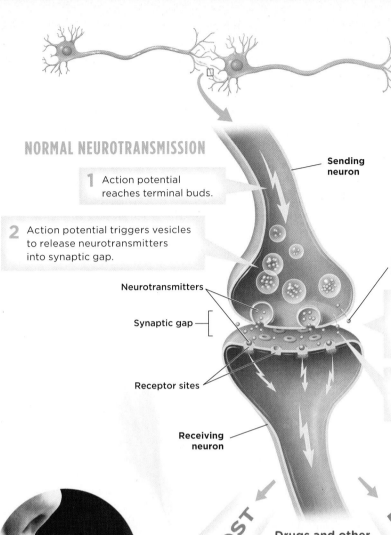

NORMAL NEUROTRANSMISSION

1 Action potential reaches terminal buds.

2 Action potential triggers vesicles to release neurotransmitters into synaptic gap.

Sending neuron

Neurotransmitters

Synaptic gap

Receptor sites

Receiving neuron

Excess neurotransmitter being reabsorbed by the sending neuron

3 Neurotransmitters bind to their matching receptor sites on receiving neuron's dendrite, causing positively charged particles to enter cell. Action potential is created.

4 After binding, neurotransmitters are reabsorbed or diffuse out of synaptic gap.

BOOST

BLOCK

Drugs and other substances can alter normal neurotransmission.

AGONIST

Agonists boost normal neurotransmitter activity. Nicotine mimics acetylcholine and causes this same activation. More receptors are activated, and more messages are sent.

Agonists

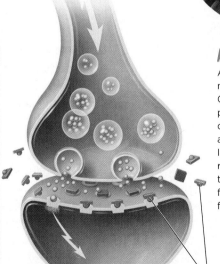

ANTAGONIST

Antagonists block normal neurotransmitter activity. Curare, the paralyzing poison used on blowgun darts, acts as an acetylcholine antagonist. It blocks acetylcholine receptors, preventing the neurotransmitter from activating them, so fewer messages are sent.

Antagonists

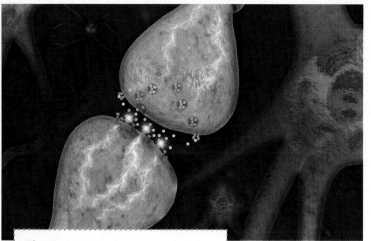

The Synapse
The terminal bud of a sending neuron (top) interacts with a dendrite of a receiving neuron by releasing chemical messengers (neurotransmitters) into the synapse. Once the neurotransmitters migrate across the gap and latch onto the dendrite's receptor sites, the message has been conveyed. Carol and Mike Werner/Science Source

When the neurotransmitters latch onto the receptors of the dendrites of the receiving neuron, the gates in the receiving cell's membrane fly open, ushering positively charged particles into the cell and thus restarting the cycle of the action potential (if the threshold is met). Keep in mind that the firing of one neuron contributes to the possibility for neighboring neurons to fire as a result of its chemical message.

When neurotransmitters are released into the synapse, many of them bind to receptors. Ultimately, they may be reabsorbed by the sending terminal bud in a process known as **reuptake.** Those that are not reabsorbed drift out of the synaptic gap, through diffusion. This is how the synaptic gap is cleared of neurotransmitters, in preparation for the next release of chemical messengers.

Neurotransmitters and Behavior

LO 5   List various neurotransmitters and summarize their involvement in human behavior.

As mentioned, there are different types of neurotransmitters. Researchers have identified approximately 100 of them, with many more yet to be discovered. We already know that neurotransmitters secreted by one neuron under certain conditions can cause neighboring neurons to fire, which can affect the regulation of mood, appetite, muscles, organs, arousal, and a variety of other functions. Here we will describe only a handful of neurotransmitters, starting with the first neurotransmitter discovered, *acetylcholine.*

ACETYLCHOLINE   Acetylcholine is a neurotransmitter that relays messages from neurons to muscles, thus enabling movement. Any time you move some part of your body, whether dancing your fingers across a keypad or bouncing your head to one of your favorite songs, you have, in part, acetylcholine to thank. Too much acetylcholine leads to muscle spasms; too little causes paralysis. Acetylcholine is also involved in memory. In particular, low levels in the brain have been linked to Alzheimer's disease (Kihara & Shimohama, 2004), which can lead to problems of memory, language, and thinking.

GLUTAMATE AND GABA   Much of the communication within the nervous system involves two neurotransmitters: *glutamate* and *GABA* (short for gamma-aminobutyric acid). Glutamate is an excitatory neurotransmitter, so its main job is to kick neurons into action (make them fire), whereas GABA is inhibitory (it puts the brakes on firing). Glutamate plays a central role in learning and memory (Riedel, Platt, & Micheau, 2003); its overactivity may be associated with strokes (Castellanos et al., 2008); and its underactivity is theorized to be involved in some of the symptoms of schizophrenia (Gordon, 2010).

Synonyms
norepinephrine noradrenaline

reuptake Process by which neurotransmitters are reabsorbed by the sending terminal bud.

NOREPINEPHRINE   *Norepinephrine* has a variety of effects in the nervous system, but one of its most important functions is to help prepare the body for stressful situations. Think about how Brandon was surrounded by gunfire during the battle of Fallujah. Norepinephrine was working to enable Brandon's nervous system to initiate action. In the brain, norepinephrine is involved in regulating arousal and sleep (Jones, 2003).

SEROTONIN   Serotonin plays a key role in controlling appetite, aggression, and mood, and also regulates sleep and breathing. Abnormally low serotonin activity is thought to drive depression. Antidepressants called serotonin reuptake inhibitors (SSRIs), including Prozac and Zoloft, boost the effects of this "feel good" neurotransmitter (Chapter 13). Normally, neurotransmitters that do not connect with receptor sites can be reabsorbed by the sending terminal bud in the reuptake process. SSRIs work to prevent this reabsorption. The longer the serotonin is available in the gap, the more time it has to attach to a receptor.

DOPAMINE   The neurotransmitter *dopamine* is known to play a role in problems with drug use. Repeated use of drugs overstimulates and damages the functioning of the neurons in the brain's reward circuit, theoretically making it more difficult to enjoy non-drug-related activities. Dopamine also plays a key role in attention, learning through reinforcement, and regulating body movements. Deterioration of neurons that produce dopamine is linked to Parkinson's disease, an incurable disorder that causes trembling of the hands, arms, legs, and face, and difficulty with movement, coordination, and balance.

ENDORPHINS   *Endorphins* are a group of naturally produced opioids (Chapter 4) that regulate the secretion of other neurotransmitters. The term endorphin is derived from the words "endogenous," meaning it is created within, and "morphine." Released in response to pain, endorphins block pain receptor sites. Brisk exercise increases their production, reducing the experience of pain and elevating mood.

Agonists and Antagonists

Drugs and other substances influence behavior by interfering at the level of the synapse (Chapters 4 and 13). Certain substances can be used to act like neurotransmitters and others can be used to block normal neurotransmitter activity. *Agonists* are substances that increase the normal activity of the neurotransmitter (whether it normally sends an excitatory or inhibitory signal) and *antagonists* reduce the activity or block the release of the neurotransmitter (Infographic 2.3). For example, some substances, such as nicotine and muscarine (found in poisonous mushrooms), increase the secretion of acetylcholine, causing sweating, pupil constriction, nausea, and respiratory distress. These substances increase the normal activity of acetylcholine; thus, they are agonists. On the other hand, the popular anti-wrinkle treatment Botox is an antagonist because it blocks acetylcholine release, paralyzing the facial muscles so they can no longer wrinkle the overlying skin (Kim, Oh, & Paik, 2006).

Apply This

Where's My Morning Antagonist?

Did you jump-start your day with a cup of coffee? Or perhaps you sipped a caffe latte, tea, or soda? Caffeine works its magic, perking you up at the crack of dawn or jolting you from that midafternoon daze, by manipulating the nervous system. One way caffeine works is by blocking the receptors for a neurotransmitter called *adenosine*. Thus, caffeine's primary role is as an antagonist. When adenosine latches onto receptors, it slows down their activity (making them less likely to fire), and this tends to make you feel drowsy. Caffeine resembles adenosine enough that it can dock onto the same receptors ("posing" as adenosine). With caffeine occupying its receptors, adenosine can no longer exert its calming effect (Julien, Advokat, & Comaty, 2011). The result: More neurons fire and you feel full of energy. The effects of caffeine do

istockphoto/thinkstock

not stop at the brain. As anyone who has enjoyed a double latte can testify, caffeine kicks the body into high gear by increasing activity in the branch of the nervous system serving the body (Corti et al., 2002).

What are the health consequences of regular caffeine consumption? When used in moderation, caffeine may boost your ability to form long-term memories (Borota et al., 2014). Drinking coffee, in particular, has been associated with a lower risk of type 2 diabetes, Parkinson's disease, and stroke among women, but these effects may be attributed to other compounds found in coffee—not necessarily the caffeine (Lopez-Garcia, 2009; Sääksjärvi et al., 2008; van Dam & Hu, 2005). Also note that continued use of caffeine can lead to anxiety, restlessness, and headaches if you reduce your consumption (Ozsungur, Brenner, & El-Sohemy, 2009; Chapter 4). And for some (pregnant women, children, and people with certain health conditions), caffeine use should be limited (Nawrot et al., 2003).

Now sit back, relax, and sip on a beverage, caffeinated or not. It's time to examine the nervous system running through your arms, legs, fingers, toes—and everywhere else.

show what you know

1. Many axons are surrounded by a _____, which is a fatty substance that insulates the axon.

2. When Brandon was injured, _____ played an important role in his recovery by defending against infection and inflammation of the brain, as well as holding neurons together and maintaining the structure of the nervous system.
   a. glial cells   b. dendrites
   c. action potentials   d. sodium ions

3. _____ are released into the _____ when an action potential reaches the branches of the terminal buds.
   a. Sodium ions; synaptic gap
   b. Neurotransmitters; synaptic gap
   c. Potassium ions; cell membrane
   d. Neurotransmitters; sodium gates

4. Neural communication is very complicated. Draw a diagram depicting the process of neural communication, then explain it to yourself while looking at what you have drawn.

✓ CHECK YOUR ANSWERS IN APPENDIX C.

The Supporting Systems

Like any complex system, the brain needs a supporting infrastructure to carry out its directives and relay essential information from the outside world. Running up and down your spine and branching throughout your body are neurons that provide connections between your brain and the rest of you. The **central nervous system (CNS)** is made up of the brain and spinal cord. The **peripheral nervous system (PNS)** includes all the neurons that are not in the central nervous system and is divided into two branches: the *somatic nervous system* and the *autonomic nervous system*. The peripheral nervous system provides the communication pathway between the central nervous system and the rest of the body. **Figure 2.2** gives an overview of the entire nervous system.

The Spinal Cord and Simple Reflexes

Brandon suffered a devastating brain injury that temporarily immobilized half of his body. The paralysis could have affected his entire body if the bullet had pierced his **spinal cord.** This bundle of neurons allows communication between the brain and the peripheral nervous system, which connects with the body's muscles, glands, and organs. The spinal cord has two major responsibilities: (1) receiving information from the body and sending it to the brain; and (2) taking information from the brain and sending it throughout the body. If this pathway is blocked, commands from the brain cannot reach the muscles responsible for making you walk, dance, and wash dishes. Likewise, the skin and other parts of the body have no pathway for communicating sensory information to the brain, like "Ooh, that burner is hot," or "Oh, this massage feels good."

central nervous system (CNS)
A major component of the human nervous system that includes the brain and spinal cord.

peripheral nervous system (PNS)
The part of the nervous system that connects the central nervous system to the rest of the body.

spinal cord The bundle of neurons that allows communication between the brain and the peripheral nervous system, connecting with the body's muscles, glands, and organs.

sensory neurons Neurons specialized for receiving information about the environment from the sensory systems and transmitting this information to the brain for further processing.

motor neurons Neurons specialized for transmitting information from the central nervous system to other parts of the body, such as muscles and glands.

interneurons Neurons that reside exclusively in the brain and spinal cord; act as a bridge connecting sensory and motor neurons.

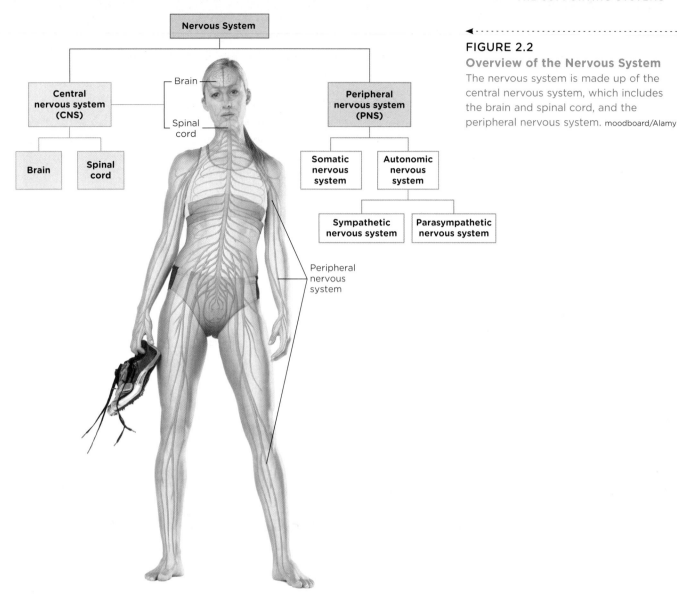

FIGURE 2.2
Overview of the Nervous System
The nervous system is made up of the central nervous system, which includes the brain and spinal cord, and the peripheral nervous system. moodboard/Alamy

LO 6   Explain how the central and peripheral nervous systems connect.

How do the brain and spinal cord, which make up the *central nervous system,* communicate with the rest of the body through the *peripheral nervous system?* In essence, there are three types of neurons participating in this back-and-forth communication. **Sensory neurons** receive information about the environment from the sensory systems and convey this information to the brain for processing. **Motor neurons** carry information from the central nervous system to produce movement in various parts of the body, such as muscles and glands. **Interneurons,** which reside exclusively in the brain and spinal cord, act as bridges connecting sensory and motor neurons. By assembling and processing sensory input from multiple neurons, interneurons facilitate the nervous system's most complex operations, from solving tough problems to forming lifelong memories. They are also involved in a relatively simple operation, the reflex.

THE REFLEX ARC   Some activities don't involve the interneurons in the brain (at least at the start). Consider the withdrawal reaction to painful stimuli (**Figure 2.3** on the next page). If you accidentally touch a hot pan, you activate a pathway of communication that goes from your sensory neurons through interneurons in your spinal cord and right back out through motor neurons, without initially involving the brain.

Synonyms
sensory neurons afferent neurons
motor neurons efferent neurons
interneurons association neurons, relay neurons

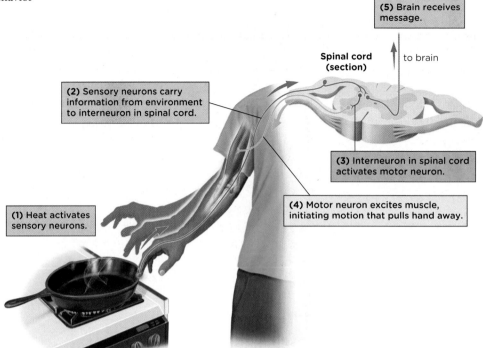

(5) Brain receives message.

Spinal cord (section)   to brain

(2) Sensory neurons carry information from environment to interneuron in spinal cord.

(3) Interneuron in spinal cord activates motor neuron.

(4) Motor neuron excites muscle, initiating motion that pulls hand away.

(1) Heat activates sensory neurons.

FIGURE 2.3
The Spinal Cord and Reflex Arc
Without any input from the brain, the spinal cord neurons are capable of creating some simple reflexive behavior. While this reflex is occurring, sensory neurons also send messages to the brain, letting it know what has happened.

This type of pain reflex includes a number of steps: (1) Your hand touches the hot pan, activating sensory receptors, which cause the sensory neurons to carry a signal from your hand to the spinal cord. (2) In the spinal cord, the signal from the sensory neurons is received by interneurons. (3) The interneurons quickly activate motor neurons and instruct them to respond. (4) The motor neurons then instruct your muscles to contract, causing your hand to withdraw quickly. A sensory neuron has a rendezvous with an interneuron, which then commands a motor neuron in the spinal cord to react—no brain required. We refer to this process, in which a stimulus causes an involuntary response, as a **reflex arc.**

Eventually, your brain does process the event; otherwise, you would have no clue it ever happened. You become consciously aware of your reaction *after* it has occurred (*My hand just pulled back; that pan was hot!*). Although many sensory and motor neurons are involved in this reaction, it happens very quickly, hopefully in time to reduce injury in cases when the reflex arc involves pain. Think about touching a flame or something sharp. You want to be able to respond, without waiting for information to get to the brain or for the brain to send a message to the motor neurons instructing the muscles to react.

try this

Check your answer in Appendix C.

Test your knowledge of the reflex arc using Brandon as an example. As you recall, Brandon's brain injury led to paralysis on the right side of his body. What do you think would happen if a doctor tapped on his right knee—would he experience a reflex?

What Lies Beyond: The Peripheral Nervous System

LO 7   Describe the organization and function of the peripheral nervous system.

The peripheral nervous system (PNS) includes all the neurons that are not in the central nervous system. These neurons are bundled together in collections called **nerves,** which act like electrical cables carrying signals from place to place. Nerves are the primary mechanism for communication by the peripheral nervous system, informing the central nervous system about the body's environment—both the exterior (for example, sights, sounds, and tastes) and the interior (for example, heart rate, blood pressure, and temperature). The central nervous system, in turn, makes sense of all this information and then responds by dispatching orders to the muscles, glands, and other tissues through the nerves of the peripheral nervous system. The PNS has two functional branches: the *somatic nervous system* and the *autonomic nervous system*.

THE SOMATIC NERVOUS SYSTEM　The **somatic nervous system** includes sensory nerves and motor nerves. (*Somatic* means "related to the body.") The sensory nerves gather information from sensory receptors and send it to the central nervous system. The motor nerves receive information from the central nervous system and send this information to the muscles, instructing them to initiate *voluntary* muscle activity (which results in movement). The somatic nervous system controls the skeletal muscles that give rise to voluntary movements, like using your arms and legs. It also receives sensory information from the skin and other tissues, providing the brain with constant feedback about temperature, pressure, pain, and other stimuli.

THE AUTONOMIC NERVOUS SYSTEM　Meanwhile, the **autonomic nervous system** (ȯ-tə-'nä-mik) is working behind the scenes, regulating *involuntary* activity, such as the pumping of the heart, the expansion and contraction of blood vessels, and digestion. Most of the activities supervised by the somatic nervous system are voluntary (within your conscious control and awareness), whereas processes directed by the autonomic nervous system tend to be involuntary (automatic) and outside of your awareness. Just remember: Autonomic controls the automatic. But this is not a hard-and-fast rule. The knee-jerk reflex, for instance, is managed by the somatic, or "voluntary," system even though it is an involuntary response.

The autonomic nervous system has two divisions involved in our physiological responses to stressful or crisis situations (**Figure 2.4** on the next page). The **sympathetic nervous system** initiates what is often referred to as the "fight-or-flight" response, which is how the body prepares to deal with a crisis. When faced with a stressful situation, the sympathetic nervous system preps the body for action by increasing heart rate and respiration, and by slowing digestion and other bodily functions. Earlier, we mentioned that caffeine makes you feel physically energized. This is because it activates the fight-or-flight response (Corti et al., 2002).

The **parasympathetic nervous system,** on the other hand, oversees the "rest-and-digest" process, which basically works to bring the body back to a noncrisis mode. The parasympathetic nervous system takes over when the crisis has ended by reversing the activity initiated by the sympathetic system (for example, lowering heart rate and respiration, increasing digestion and other maintenance activities). The two systems work together, balancing the activities of these primarily involuntary processes. Sometimes they even have a common goal. For example, parasympathetic stimulation increases blood flow to the penis to create an erection, but it is the sympathetic system that causes ejaculation (Goldstein, 2000). Working together, these two systems allow us to fight if we need to, flee when necessary, and calm down when danger has passed.

The fight-or-flight response would certainly come in handy if fleeing predators was part of your day-to-day life (as it may have been for our primitive ancestors), but you probably are not chased by wild animals very often. You may, however, notice your heart racing and your breathing rate increase during other types of anxiety-producing situations—going on a first date, taking a test, or speaking in front of an audience. You have your sympathetic nervous system to thank for these effects (Chapter 11).

TEND AND BEFRIEND　Fighting and running like mad are not the only ways we respond to stress. Many women have an inclination to "tend and befriend" in response to a threat—that is, they direct energy toward nurturing offspring and forging social bonds (Taylor et al., 2000). Men, too, exhibit this response, especially in high-pressure scenarios. In one small study, men placed in a stressful situation were

reflex arc An automatic response to a sensory stimulus, such as the "knee-jerk" reaction; a simple pathway of communication from sensory neurons through interneurons in the spinal cord back out through motor neurons.

nerves Bundles of neurons that carry information to and from the central nervous system; provide communication between the central nervous system and the muscles, glands, and sensory receptors.

somatic nervous system The branch of the peripheral nervous system that includes sensory nerves and motor nerves; gathers information from sensory receptors and controls the skeletal muscles responsible for voluntary movement.

autonomic nervous system (ȯ-tə-'nä-mik) The branch of the peripheral nervous system that controls involuntary processes within the body, such as contractions in the digestive tract and activity of glands.

sympathetic nervous system The division of the autonomic nervous system that mobilizes the "fight-or-flight" response to stressful or crisis situations.

parasympathetic nervous system The division of the autonomic nervous system that orchestrates the "rest-and-digest" response to bring the body back to a noncrisis mode.

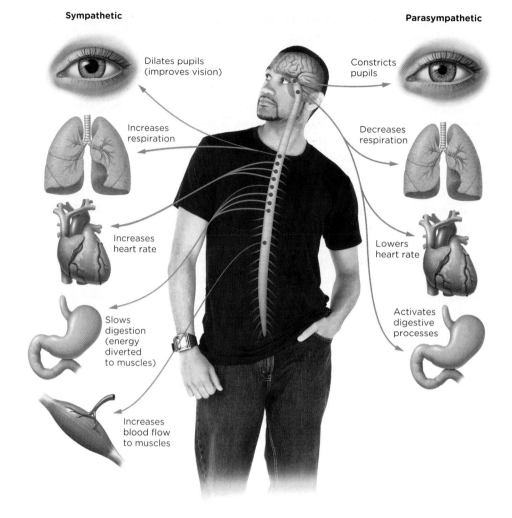

more likely to show increased trust of others; those others, in turn, were more likely to feel that these men were trustworthy. The trusting men were also more willing to share resources than were those who were not subjected to stress (von Dawans, Fischbacher, Kirschbaum, Fehr, & Heinrichs, 2012). While serving in Iraq, Brandon likely experienced this increase of trust with his fellow soldiers.

Women are generally more likely to "tend and befriend," but are there other gender disparities related to the nervous system? Some people believe males and females are "hardwired" differently; others believe they are socially conditioned to develop certain skills and tendencies. Let's take a look at some of the evidence.

THINK again

Male Brain, Female Brain

It is a well-known fact that the numbers of women employed in certain fields, particularly science, technology, engineering, and mathematics (STEM) continue to be low (Blickenstaff, 2005; **Figure 2.5**). Does society encourage boys to pursue science and technology interests while pushing girls into the social sciences and humanities? There is no denying that social and cultural factors influence female achievement in math and science. Studies suggest that gender stereotypes, which are commonly held beliefs about the nature of men and women, can influence performance in these fields. For example, when exposed to statements such as "women possess poor math ability" just before taking a test, some women will actually perform at a lower level (Josephs, Newman, Brown, & Beer, 2003; Chapter 14).

SCIENCE AND
THE SEXES

But there might also be something biological at play. Research shows that male and female brains are far more alike than they are different, but some intriguing disparities exist, both in terms of anatomy and function. For example, the cerebral hemispheres are not completely symmetric, and males and females differ somewhat in these asymmetries (Tian, Wang, Yan, & He, 2011). One fMRI study found that certain regions of the limbic cortex and the frontal lobes were larger in women, while areas of the parietal cortex, the amygdala, and hypothalamus were larger in men (Goldstein et al., 2001; the lobes and other regions of the brain are discussed in the second half of this chapter). MRI analyses point to sex differences in the brain networks involved in social cognition and visual-spatial abilities (Feis et al., 2013). The implications for behavior are not totally clear, but some of these gender disparities (for example, in regions involved in spatial reasoning, memory, and emotion) may be present very early in development, perhaps at the time of birth (Cahill, 2012). Some distinctions between male and female brains are believed to be influenced by hormones secreted prenatally, suggesting they have a biological basis (Sanders, Sjodin, & de Chastelaine, 2002).

It appears that both nature and nurture are responsible for the gender imbalance in math and the sciences. While women are statistically underrepresented in these fields, their participation has grown dramatically over the past 50 years, a clear sign of positive change. Researchers propose that "Having more women in STEM careers would decrease the gender wage gap in society, as STEM jobs for women pay about 33% more, on average, than non-STEM jobs for women" (Saucerman & Vasquez, 2014, p. 61). ●+

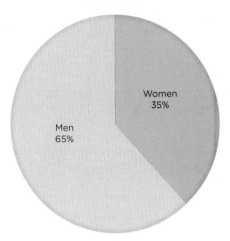

▲ **FIGURE 2.5**

Bachelor's Degrees Awarded in the United States
Women earn the majority (57.3%) of all bachelor's degrees awarded in the United States. But when it comes to degrees awarded in science, math, and engineering, the numbers look very different (National Science Foundation, 2015). Why do so many fewer women receive degrees in STEM fields?

CONNECTIONS

In **Chapter 1,** we presented the nature–nurture issue and its importance in the field of psychology. Here, we can see this issue in relation to the gender imbalance in math and science. Researchers continue to evaluate the relative influence of nature and nurture in the development of academic and career goals.

The Endocrine System and Its Slowpoke Messengers

Imagine that you are 19-year-old Brandon Burns fighting in the battle of Fallujah, one of the bloodiest battles of the Iraq War. The sound of gunfire rings through the air. Bullets zip past your helmet. People are dying around you. Your life could end at any moment. Unless you have been in a similar situation, it would be difficult to fathom how you would feel. But one thing seems certain: You would feel extremely stressed.

When faced with imminent danger, the sympathetic nervous system responds almost instantaneously. Activity in the brain triggers the release of neurotransmitters that cause increases in heart rate, breathing rate, and metabolism—changes that will come in handy if you need to flee or defend yourself. But the nervous system does not act alone. The endocrine system is also hard at work, releasing stress hormones, such as cortisol, which prompt similar physiological changes.

LO 8   Summarize the role of the endocrine system and how it influences behavior.

The **endocrine system** (en-də-krən) is a communication system that uses glands, rather than neurons, to send messages (**Figure 2.6** on the next page). These messages are delivered by **hormones,** chemicals released into the bloodstream that can cause aggression and mood swings, as well as influence growth, alertness, cognition, and appetite.

endocrine system (en-də-krən) The communication system that uses glands to convey messages by releasing hormones into the bloodstream.

hormones Chemical messengers released into the bloodstream that influence mood, cognition, appetite, and many other processes and behaviors.

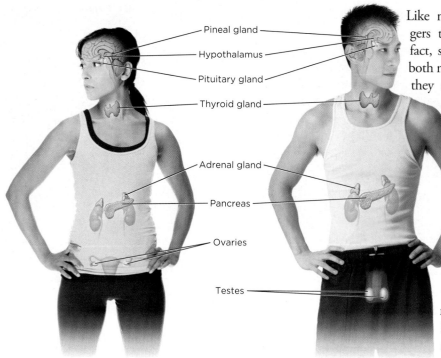

Pineal gland

Hypothalamus

Pituitary gland

Thyroid gland

Adrenal gland

Pancreas

Ovaries

Testes

▲ FIGURE 2.6

The Endocrine System
This system of glands communicates within the body by secreting hormones directly into the bloodstream.
left: (face) Hemera/Thinkstock, (body) Yuri Arcurs; right: Asiaselects/Getty Images

Like neurotransmitters, hormones are chemical messengers that can affect many processes and behaviors. In fact, some chemicals, such as norepinephrine, can act as both neurotransmitters and hormones depending on where they are released. Neurotransmitters are unloaded into the synapse, whereas hormones are secreted into the bloodstream by glands stationed around the body. These glands collectively belong to the endocrine system.

When neurotransmitters are released into a synaptic gap, their effects can be almost instantaneous. Hormones usually make long voyages to far-away targets by way of the bloodstream, creating a relatively delayed but usually longer-lasting impact. A neural impulse can travel over 250 mph, much faster than messages sent via hormones, which take minutes (if not longer) to arrive where they are going. However, the messages sent via hormones are more widely spread because they are disseminated through the bloodstream.

If the endocrine system had a chief executive officer, it would be the **pituitary gland,** a gland about the size of a pencil eraser located in the center of the brain, just under the *hypothalamus* (a structure of the brain we will explore later). Controlled by the hypothalamus, the pituitary gland influences all the other glands, as well as promoting growth through the secretion of hormones.

The **thyroid gland** regulates the rate of metabolism by secreting thyroxin, and the **adrenal glands** (ə-drē-nəl) are involved in responses to stress and regulation of salt balance. Other endocrine glands and organs directed by the pituitary include the pineal gland, which secretes melatonin (controls sleep–wake cycles); the pancreas, which secretes insulin (regulates blood sugar); and the ovaries and testes, whose secretion of sex hormones is one reason that men and women are different. Together, these glands and organs can impact: (1) growth and sex characteristics, (2) regulation of some of the basic body processes, and (3) responses to emergencies. Just as our behaviors are influenced by neurotransmitters we can't see and action potentials we can't feel, the hormones secreted by the endocrine system are also hard at work behind the scenes.

Now that we have discovered how information moves through the body via electrical and chemical signals, let's turn our attention toward the part of the nervous system that integrates this activity, creating a unified and meaningful experience. Let's explore the brain.

✔○○○ show what you know

1. _____ carry information from the central nervous system to activate various parts of the body, such as muscles and glands.
   - **a.** Interneurons
   - **b.** Dendrites
   - **c.** Sensory neurons
   - **d.** Motor neurons

2. When a stimulus causes an involuntary response, we refer to it as a reflex arc; the simple communication pathway goes from a sensory neurons through interneurons in the _____ and back out through motor neurons.
   - **a.** brain
   - **b.** spinal cord
   - **c.** axon hillock
   - **d.** nodes of Ranvier

3. The _____ gland, located in the center of the brain, just under the hypothalamus, is in charge of the endocrine system.

4. When confronted with a potentially threatening situation, the sympathetic nervous system sometimes prepares for "fight or flight" and/or "tend and befriend." How would you explain these two very different responses using the evolutionary perspective?

✔ CHECK YOUR ANSWERS IN APPENDIX C.

The Amazing Brain

THE GIRL WITH HALF A BRAIN   As Brandon Burns began his long journey to recovery, a 17-year-old girl in Bristol, Pennsylvania, was enjoying a particularly successful senior year of high school. Christina Santhouse was an honor roll student for the fourth year in a row, and she had been named captain of the varsity bowling team. But these accomplishments did not come so easily. It took Christina twice as much time as classmates to do homework assignments because her brain needed extra time to process information. She had to invent a new bowling technique because the left side of her body was partially paralyzed, and she was constantly aware of being "different" from the other kids at school. Christina wasn't simply *different* from her classmates, however. She was *extraordinary* because she managed to do everything they did (and more) with nearly half of her brain missing.

Christina's remarkable story began when she was 7 years old. She was a vibrant, healthy child who loved soccer and playing outside with her friends. Barring an occasional ear infection, she basically never got sick—that is, until the day she suffered her first seizure. It was the summer of 1995 and Christina's family was vacationing on the Jersey Shore. While playing in a swimming pool with her cousins, Christina hopped onto the deck to chase a ball and noticed that something wasn't quite right. She looked down and saw her left ankle twitching uncontrollably. Her life was about to change dramatically.

As the days and weeks wore on, the tremors in Christina's ankle moved up her left side and eventually spread throughout her body. In time, she was having seizures every 3 to 5 minutes. Doctors suspected she had Rasmussen's encephalitis, a rare disease that causes severe swelling in one side of the brain, impairing movement and thinking and causing seizures that come as often as every few minutes (National Institute of Neurological Disorders and Stroke, 2011b).

Christina and her mother decided to seek treatment at The Johns Hopkins Hospital in Baltimore, the premiere center for treating children with seizure disorders. They met with Dr. John Freeman, a pediatric neurologist and an expert in *hemispherectomy,* a surgery to remove nearly half of the brain. A rare and last-resort operation, the hemispherectomy is only performed on patients suffering from severe seizures that can't be controlled in other ways. After examining Christina, Dr. Freeman made the same diagnosis of her condition—Rasmussen's encephalitis—and indicated that the seizures would get worse, and they would get worse fast. He recommended a hemispherectomy and told Christina (and her mother) to let him know when she had reached her limit with the seizures. Then they would go ahead with the operation.

Why did Dr. Freeman recommend this drastic surgery to remove nearly half of Christina's brain? And what side of the brain did he suggest removing? Before addressing these important questions, we need to develop a general sense of the brain's geography. 📁

Right Brain, Left Brain: The Two Hemispheres

LO 9   Describe the functions of the two brain hemispheres and how they communicate.

If you look at a photo or an illustration of the brain, you will see a walnut-shaped wrinkled structure—this is the **cerebrum** (Latin for "brain"), the largest and most conspicuous part of the brain. The cerebrum includes virtually all parts of the brain

Staying Strong
Christina Santhouse relaxes with her mother at Johns Hopkins, where she had a dramatic brain surgery known as a hemispherectomy. Prior to the operation, Christina experienced hundreds of seizures a day. William Johnson

Christina, in Her Own Words:

http://qrs.ly/fd4qsy1

© 2016, Macmillan

pituitary gland   The pea-sized gland located in the center of the brain just under the hypothalamus; known as the master gland.

thyroid gland   Gland of the endocrine system that regulates the rate of metabolism by secreting thyroxin.

adrenal glands   (ə-drē-nəl) Part of the endocrine system involved in responses to stress as well as the regulation of salt balance.

cerebrum   The largest part of the brain, includes virtually all parts of the brain except primitive structures; has two distinct hemispheres.

Two Hemispheres

The cerebrum looks like a walnut with its two wrinkled halves. Regions of the left and right hemispheres specialize in different activities, but the two sides of the brain are constantly communicating and collaborating. Science Source/Photo Researchers, Inc. Colorization by: Eric Cohen

except the brainstem structures, which you will learn about later. Like a walnut, the cerebrum has two distinct halves, or *hemispheres*. Looking at the brain from above, you can see a deep groove running from the front of the head to the back, dividing it into the right cerebral hemisphere and the left cerebral hemisphere. Although the hemispheres look like mirror images of one another, with similar structures on the left and right, they do not have identical jobs nor are they perfectly symmetrical. Generally speaking, the right hemisphere controls the left side of the body, and the left hemisphere controls the right. This explains why Brandon, who was shot on the left side of his head, suffered paralysis and loss of sensation on the *right* half of his body. Christina's situation is roughly the opposite. Rasmussen's encephalitis struck the *right* side of her brain, which explains why her *left* ankle started twitching at the pool and why all of her subsequent seizures affected the left side of her body. This is why Dr. Freeman recommended the removal of her right hemisphere.

CHRISTINA MAKES THE DECISION   Within 2 months, Christina's seizures were occurring every 3 minutes, hundreds of times a day. She was unable to play soccer or go outside during school recess, and she sat on a beanbag chair in class so she wouldn't hurt herself when overcome with a seizure. "I couldn't do anything anymore," Christina says. "I wasn't enjoying my life."

In February 1996 the doctors at Johns Hopkins removed the right hemisphere of Christina's brain. The operation lasted some 14 hours. When Christina emerged from the marathon surgery, her head was pounding with pain. "I remember screaming and asking for medicine," she recalls. The migraines persisted for months but eventually tapered off, and ultimately the surgery served its purpose: Christina no longer experienced debilitating seizures. ▾

The Split-Brain Operation

LO 10 Explain lateralization and how split-brain operations affect it.

Removing nearly half of a brain may sound barbaric, but hemispherectomies have proven to be effective for eliminating and reducing seizures. In a study of the 111 children who had hemispherectomies at Johns Hopkins between 1975 and 2001, 65% no longer suffered seizures at all, and 21% experienced infrequent, "nonhandicapping" seizures. The remaining 14% still had seizures described as "troublesome" (Kossoff et al., 2003).

Hemispherectomies are exceptionally rare, used only when seizures occur many times a day, cannot be tempered with drugs, and stem from problems in one hemisphere (Choi, 2007, May 24). A less extreme, last-resort surgery for drug-resistant seizures is the **split-brain operation,** which essentially disconnects the right and left hemispheres. Normally, the two hemispheres are linked by a bundle of nerve fibers known as the **corpus callosum** (kòr-pəs ka-lō-səm). Through the corpus callosum, the left and right sides of the brain communicate and work together to process information. But this same band of nerve fibers can also serve as a passageway for the electrical storms responsible for seizures. With the split-brain operation, the corpus callosum is severed so that these storms can no longer pass freely between the hemispheres (Wolman, 2012, March 15).

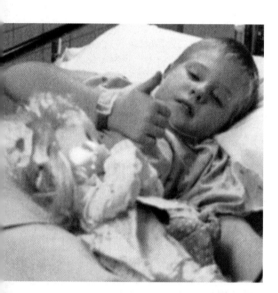

Pre-Op

Christina is wheeled into the operating room for her 14-hour hemispherectomy. She had a seizure in the elevator on the way to the surgery. William Johnson

Synonyms
split-brain operation callosotomy

split-brain operation A rare procedure used to disconnect the right and left hemispheres by cutting the corpus callosum.

corpus callosum (kòr-pəs ka-lō-səm) The thick band of nerve fibers connecting the right and left cerebral hemispheres; principal structure for information shared between the two hemispheres.

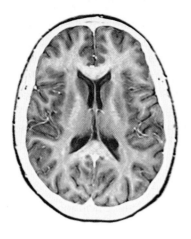
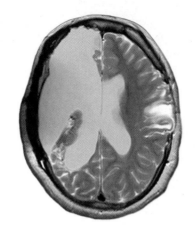

Hemispherectomy
On the left is an MRI scan of a brain with both hemispheres intact. The scan on the right shows the brain of a person who has undergone a hemispherectomy. The green area, once occupied by the removed hemisphere, is now filled with cerebrospinal fluid. left: Medical Body Scans/ Science Source. Colorization by Matthew Bologna; right: Medical Body Scans/Science Source

STUDYING THE SPLIT BRAIN In addition to helping many patients with severe, drug-resistant epilepsy (Abou-Khalil, 2010), the consequences of split-brain operations have provided researchers with an excellent opportunity to explore the specialization of the hemispheres. Before we start to look at this research, you need to understand how visual information is processed. Each eye receives visual sensations, but that information is sent to the opposite hemisphere, and shared between the hemispheres via the corpus callosum. Specifically, information presented in the right visual field is processed in the left hemisphere, and information presented in the left visual field is processed in the right hemisphere.

Equipped with this knowledge, American neuropsychologist Roger Sperry (1913–1994) and his student Michael Gazzaniga (1939–) conducted groundbreaking research on epilepsy patients who had undergone split-brain operations to alleviate their seizures. Not only did Sperry and Gazzaniga's "split-brain" participants experience fewer seizures, they had surprisingly normal cognitive abilities and showed no obvious changes in "temperament, personality, or general intelligence" as a result of their surgeries (Gazzaniga, 1967, p. 24). But under certain circumstances, the researchers observed, they behaved as though they had two separate brains (Gazzaniga, 1967, 1998; **Figure 2.7**).

FIGURE 2.7
The Split-Brain Experiment
The image to the left shows a top view of the corpus callosum, the bundle of neurons linking the right and left hemispheres. When the corpus callosum is severed, we can see clear functional differences between the two sides of the brain. Studies of people who have undergone this procedure are known as "split-brain" experiments. An example of this type of experiment is shown below. Terence H. Williams, Nedzad Gluhbegovic/Wolters Kluwer

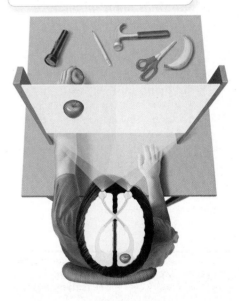

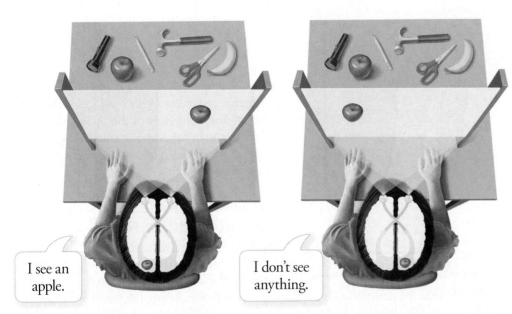

Touch the object matching the image on the screen.

I see an apple.

I don't see anything.

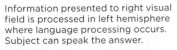

Information presented to right visual field is processed in left hemisphere where language processing occurs. Subject can speak the answer.

Information presented to left visual field is processed in right hemisphere. Subject can't use language to say what he was shown.

The subject can touch the correct object even if he can't say what has been projected in his left visual field. The subject uses his left hand, which is controlled by the right hemisphere, where the visual information has been processed.

You Asked, Christina Answers

http://qrs.ly/py4qsy7

How does your condition affect your confidence and social life?

Because the hemispheres are disconnected through the surgery, researchers can study each hemisphere separately to explore its own unique capabilities (or specializations). Imagine that researchers flashed an image (let's say an apple) on the right side of a screen, ensuring that it would be processed by the brain's *left* hemisphere. The split-brain participant could articulate what she had seen (*I saw an apple*). If, however, the apple appeared on the left side of the screen (processed by the *right* hemisphere), she would claim she saw nothing. But when asked to identify the image in a nonverbal way (pointing or touching with her left hand), she could do this without a problem (Gazzaniga, 1967, 1998).

LATERALIZATION   The split-brain experiments offered an elegant demonstration of **lateralization,** the tendency for the left and right hemispheres to excel in certain activities. When images are flashed in the right visual field, the information is sent to the left side of the brain, which excels in language processing. This explains why the split-brain participants were able to articulate the image they had seen on the right side of the screen. Images appearing in the left visual field are sent to the right side of the brain, which excels at visual-spatial tasks but is generally not responsible for processing language. Thus, the participants were tongue-tied when asked to report what they had seen on the left side of the screen. They could, however, reach out and point to it using their left hand, which is controlled by the right hemisphere (Gazzaniga, 1998; Gazzaniga, Bogen, & Sperry, 1965).

The split-brain studies revealed that the left hemisphere plays a crucial role in language processing and the right hemisphere in managing visual-spatial tasks. These are only generalizations, however. While there are clear differences in the way the hemispheres process information (and the speed at which they do it), they can also process the same types of information. In a split-brain individual, communication between the hemispheres is limited. This is *not* the case for someone with an intact corpus callosum. The hemispheres are constantly integrating and sharing all types of information (Lilienfeld, Lynn, Ruscio, & Beyerstein, 2011). Next time you hear someone claim that some people are more "left-brained" and others are more "right-brained," ask him to identify the research that backs up such a claim. Similarly, beware of catchy sales pitches for products designed to increase your "logical and analytical" left-brain thinking or to help you tap into the "creative" right brain. This way of thinking is oversimplified. Keep this in mind while reading the upcoming sections on specialization in the left and right sides of the brain. The two hemispheres may have certain areas of expertise, but they work as a team to create your experience of the world.

The Special Roles of the Left and the Right

Armed with this new knowledge of the split-brain experiments, let's return our focus to Brandon. Brandon's injury occurred on the left side of his brain, devastating his ability to use language. Before the battle of Fallujah, he had breezed through Western novels at breakneck speeds. After his injury, even the simplest sentence baffled him. Words on a page looked like nothing more than black lines and curls. Brandon remembers, "It was like a puzzle that I couldn't figure out."

HANDEDNESS AND LANGUAGE DOMINANCE   Brandon's difficulties with language are fairly typical for someone with a brain injury to the left hemisphere, because regions on the left side of the brain tend to predominate in language. This is not true for everyone, however. In a study examining handedness and language dominance, researchers measured participants' degree of handedness (righty or lefty) and used brain scan technology to determine their predominant side for language processing. They found that around 27% of strongly left-handed participants and 4% of strongly right-handed participants had language dominance in the *right* hemisphere (Knecht et al., 2000). What does this suggest? The left hemisphere controls language in most but not all people, though it doesn't always correspond to right- or left-handedness.

LO 11   Identify areas in the brain responsible for language production and comprehension.

BROCA'S AREA   Evidence for the "language on the left" notion appeared as early as 1861, when a French surgeon by the name of Pierre Paul Broca (1824–1880) encountered two patients who had, for all practical purposes, lost the ability to talk. One of the patients could only say the word "tan," and the other had an oral vocabulary of five words. When Broca later performed autopsies on the men, he found that both had sustained damage to the same area on the side of the left frontal lobe (right around the temple; **Figure 2.8**). Over the years, Broca identified several other speech-impaired patients with damage to the same area, a region now called **Broca's area** (brō-kəz) (Greenblatt, Dagi, & Epstein, 1997), which is involved in speech production. However, some researchers propose that other parts of the brain may also be involved in generating speech (Tate, Herbet, Moritz-Gasser, Tate, & Duffau, 2014).

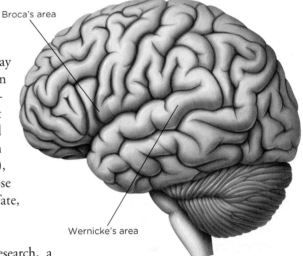

Broca's area

Wernicke's area

▲ **FIGURE 2.8**

Language Areas of the Brain
For most people, the left hemisphere controls language. Broca's area plays a critical role in language production, and Wernicke's area in language comprehension.

WERNICKE'S AREA   Around the same time Broca was doing his research, a German doctor named Karl Wernicke (1848–1905) pinpointed a different place in the left hemisphere that seemed to control speech comprehension. Wernicke noticed that patients suffering damage to a small tract of tissue in the left temporal lobe, now called **Wernicke's area** (ver-nə-kəz), struggled to make sense of what others were saying. Wernicke's area is the brain's headquarters for language comprehension.

Broca's and Wernicke's work, along with other early findings, highlighted the left hemisphere's critical role in language. Scientists initially suspected that Broca's area was responsible for speech creation and Wernicke's area for comprehension, but it is now clear the use of language is far more complicated. These areas may perform additional functions, such as processing music and interpreting hand gestures (Koelsch et al., 2002; Xu, Gannon, Emmorey, Smith, & Braun, 2009), and they cooperate with multiple brain regions to allow us to produce and understand language (Tate et al., 2014). Furthermore, some speech processing appears to occur in the right hemisphere.

THE ROLE OF THE RIGHT   Research involving two split-brain individuals suggests the right hemisphere is more proficient than the left in some visual tasks (Corballis, 2003), such as determining whether two objects are identical as opposed to mirror images of one another (Funnell, Corballis, & Gazzaniga, 1999), or judging if lines are oriented in the same direction (Corballis, Funnell, & Gazzaniga, 2002). Other findings suggest the right hemisphere is crucial for understanding abstract and humorous use of language (Coulson & Van Petten, 2007); somewhat better than the left for following conversations that change topic (Dapretto, Lee, & Caplan, 2005); and important for our ability to recognize faces (Kanwisher, McDermott, & Chun, 1997; Rossion, 2014).

lateralization   The idea that each cerebral hemisphere processes certain types of information and excels in certain activities.

Broca's area   (brō-kəz) A region of the cortex that is critical for speech production.

Wernicke's area   (ver-nə-kəz) A region of the cortex that plays a pivotal role in language comprehension.

Brain Games
Christina's dramatic recovery
was facilitated by physical,
occupational, vision, and speech
therapy. "The more therapy," says
Christina, "the better chance of
recovery." William Johnson

You Asked, Christina Answers

http://qrs.ly/jx4qsyb

**What kind of therapy
did you have and for
how long?**

CONNECTIONS

In **Chapter 1,** we described the guidelines
psychologists use to ensure the ethical
treatment of humans and animals. In order
to conduct the experiment described
here, the researchers had to get pre-
approval from an ethics board. The
board determined the proposed research
necessitated the surgery on the newborn
opossums and that they would be treated
humanely.

Baby Beethoven
For millions of Chinese children, learning to play
an instrument like the violin or piano begins early.
Children with musical training outperform their
untrained peers on tests of IQ and language skills
(Schellenberg, 2011; Schellenberg & Winner, 2011). Is
this because music lessons make children smarter,
perhaps by stimulating positive changes in the
brain? Or is it because smart children are more likely
to take lessons? Researchers are still trying to get to
the bottom of this conundrum. Lou Linwei/Sinopix

Neuroplasticity

When Christina was wheeled out of surgery, her mother approached,
grabbed hold of her right hand, and asked her to squeeze. Christina
squeezed, demonstrating that she could understand and respond to language. Remember, she still had her left hemisphere.

Losing the right side of her brain did come at a cost, however. We
know that Christina suffers partial paralysis on the left side of her body; this
makes sense, because the right hemisphere controls movement and sensation on the left. We also know that it took Christina extra time to do her
schoolwork. But if you ask Christina whether she has significant difficulty
with any of the "right-brain" tasks described earlier, her answer will be no.

In addition to making the honor roll and leading the bowling team,
Christina managed to get her driver's license (even though some of her
doctors said she never would), graduate from high school, and go to
college. These accomplishments are the result of Christina's steadfast
determination, but also a testament to the brain's amazing ability to heal
and regenerate.

LO 12 Define neuroplasticity and recognize when it is evident in the brain.

The brain undergoes constant alteration in response to experiences and is
capable of some degree of physical adaptation and repair. Its ability to heal, grow
new connections, and make do with what is available is a characteristic we refer to
as **neuroplasticity.** New connections are constantly forming between neurons, and
unused ones are fading away. Vast networks of neurons have the ability to reorganize
in order to adapt to the environment and an organism's ever-changing needs, a quality
particularly evident in the young. After brain injuries, younger children have better
outcomes than do adults; their brains show more plasticity (Johnston, 2009).

In one study, researchers removed the eyes of newborn opossums and found
that brain tissues normally destined to become visual processing centers took a developmental turn. Instead, they became areas that specialized in processing other types
of sensory stimuli, such as sounds and touch (Karlen, Kahn, & Krubitzer, 2006). The
same appears to happen in humans. Brain scans reveal that when visually impaired
individuals learn to read Braille early in life, a region of the brain that normally specializes in handling visual information becomes activated, suggesting it is used instead
for processing touch sensations (Burton, 2003; Liu et al., 2007).

Remarkably, this plasticity is evident even with the loss of an entire hemisphere.
Researchers report that the younger the patient is when she has a hemispherectomy,

the better her chances are for recovery. In fact, even with the loss of an entire left hemisphere (the primary location for language processing), speech is less severely impacted (though some impact is inevitable) in young patients. The younger the person undergoing the procedure, the less disability is evident in speech (Choi, 2008).

STEM CELLS   Scientists once thought that people were born with all the neurons they would ever have. Brain cells might die, but no new ones would crop up to replace them. Thanks to research beginning in the 1990s, that dismal notion has been turned on its head. In the last few decades, studies with animals and humans have shown that some areas of the brain are constantly generating new neurons, a process known as **neurogenesis,** which might be tied to learning and creating new memories (Eriksson et al., 1998; Gould, Beylin, Tanapat, Reeves, & Shors, 1999; Jessberger & Gage, 2014; Reynolds & Weiss, 1992).

The cells responsible for churning out these new neurons are known as **stem cells,** and they are quite a hot topic in biomedical research. Scientists hope to harness these little cell factories to repair tissue that has been damaged or destroyed. Imagine that you could use stem cells to bring back all the neurons that Brandon lost from his injury or replace those that Christina lost to surgery. Cultivating new brain tissue is just one potential application of stem cell science. These cellular cure-alls might also be used to alleviate the symptoms of Parkinson's disease, or replenish neurons of the spine, enabling people with spinal cord injuries to regain movement. Both have already been accomplished in mice (Keirstead et al., 2005; Wernig et al., 2008). Although embryonic stem cells can be used for such purposes, some stem cells can be found in tissues of the adult body, such as the brain and bone marrow.

Cure All?
Because stem cells can differentiate into any type of cell in the body, they have great therapeutic potential. The cells pictured here are derived from a human embryo, but stem cells also reside in various adult tissues such as the brain and bone marrow. Professor Miodrag Stojkovic/ Science Source

The Cortex: A Peek Beneath the Skull

Imagine you were one of the surgeons performing Christina's hemispherectomy. What exactly would you see when you peeled away the scalp and cut an opening into the skull? Before seeing the brain, you would come upon a layer of three thin membranes, the *meninges,* which envelop and protect the brain and spinal cord (**Infographic 2.4** on the next page). Perhaps you have heard of meningitis, a potentially life-threatening condition in which the meninges become inflamed as a result of an infection. The meninges are bathed in a clear watery substance called cerebrospinal fluid, which offers additional cushioning and helps in the transport of nutrients and waste in and out of the brain and the spinal cord. Once you peeled back the meninges, you would behold the pink cerebrum.

As Christina's surgeon, your main task would be to remove part of the cerebrum's outermost layer, the **cerebral cortex** (sə-rē-brəl). The cerebral cortex processes information and is the layer of cells surrounding nearly all the other brain structures. You'll remember our earlier comment that the cerebrum looks like a wrinkled walnut. This is because the cortex is scrunched up and folded onto itself to fit inside a small space (the skull). This outermost section of the brain is also the part that is "newest," or most recently evolved compared to the "older" structures closer to its core. We know this because researchers have compared the brains of humans with other primates. The structures we share with our primate relatives are considered more primitive, or less evolved, than the structures that are unique to humans.

LO 13 Identify the lobes of the cortex and explain their functions.

The cortex overlying each hemisphere is separated into different sections, or lobes. The major function of the **frontal lobes** is to organize information among the other lobes of the brain. The frontal lobes are also responsible for higher-level cognitive functions, such as thinking, perception, and impulse control. The **parietal lobes** (pə-rī-ə-təl) receive and process sensory information like touch, pressure, temperature, and spatial orientation.

neuroplasticity The brain's ability to heal, grow new connections, and reorganize in order to adapt to the environment.

neurogenesis The generation of new neurons in the brain.

stem cells Cells responsible for producing new neurons.

cerebral cortex (sə-rē-brəl) The wrinkled outermost layer of the cerebrum, responsible for higher mental functions, such as decision making, planning, and processing visual information.

frontal lobes The area of the cortex that organizes information among the other lobes of the brain and is responsible for higher-level cognitive functions and behavior.

parietal lobes (pə-rī-ə-təl) The area of the cortex that receives and processes sensory information such as touch, pressure, temperature, and spatial orientation.

Getting into the Brain

Finding Personality in the Brain

In 1848 an accidental blast drove a 3-foot iron bar through the head of railroad worker Phineas Gage. He survived, but his personality was markedly changed. Previously described as having a "well-balanced" mind, post-injury Gage was prone to angry outbursts and profanity (Harlow, 1968, 1969, as cited in Macmillan, 2000).

Phineas Gage holding the iron bar that injured him.

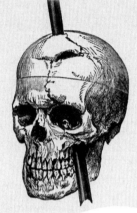

Using measurements from his fractured skull, scientists have been able to estimate where the damage occurred (Ratiu, Talos, Haker, Lieberman, & Everett, 2004; Van Horn et al., 2012). Cases like this have helped psychologists understand the role of different structures in the brain.

Getting TO the Brain

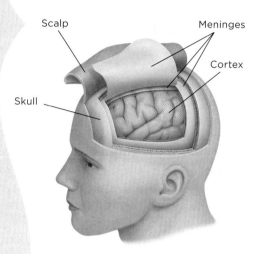

Scalp · Meninges · Cortex · Skull

In order to study the brain, we must get to it first. Peel away the scalp and cut away the bony skull, and you will find still more layers of protection. Three thin membranes—the meninges—provide a barrier to both physical injury and infection. Bypass them, and the outermost layer of the brain, the cortex, is revealed.

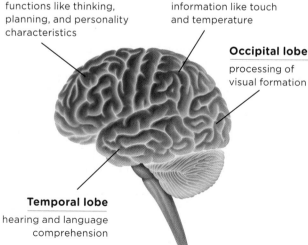

Frontal lobe
higher-level cognitive functions like thinking, planning, and personality characteristics

Parietal lobe
integration of sensory information like touch and temperature

Occipital lobe
processing of visual formation

Temporal lobe
hearing and language comprehension

Motor cortex
commands the body's movements

Somatosensory cortex
receives sensory information from the body

Wernicke's area
language comprehension

Broca's area
language production

Lobes of the Brain
This drawing shows the left hemisphere of the brain. Each hemisphere is divided into lobes, which are known for the major functions found there.

Specialized Areas of the Brain
Unlike the lobes, which are associated with many functions, some areas of the brain have one specialized function.

Visual information goes to the **occipital lobes** (äk-si-pə-təl) for processing, and hearing and language comprehension are largely handled by the **temporal lobes.** We'll have more to say about the lobes as we discuss them each in turn below.

The Lobes: Up Close and Personal

Prior to her hemispherectomy, Christina was extroverted, easygoing, and full of energy. "I had absolutely no worries," she says, recalling her pre-Rasmussen's days. After her operation, Christina became more introverted and passive. She felt more emotionally unsettled. "You go into surgery one person," she says, "and you come out another."

The transformation of Christina's personality may be a result of many factors, including the stress of dealing with a serious disease, undergoing a major surgery, and readjusting to life with disabilities. But it could also have something to do with the fact that she lost a considerable amount of brain tissue, including her right frontal lobe. Networks of neurons in the frontal lobes are involved in processing emotions, making plans, controlling impulses, and carrying out a vast array of mental tasks that each person does in a unique way (Williams, Suchy, & Kraybill, 2010). The frontal lobes play a key role in the development of personality (Stuss & Alexander, 2000). A striking illustration of this phenomenon involves an unlucky railroad foreman, Phineas Gage.

PHINEAS GAGE AND THE FRONTAL LOBES   The year was 1848, and Phineas Gage was working on the railroad. An accidental explosion sent a 3-foot iron tamping rod clear through his frontal lobes (Infographic 2.4). The rod, about as thick as a broom handle, drove straight into Gage's left cheek, through his brain, and out the top of his skull (Macmillan, 2000). What's peculiar about Gage's accident (besides the fact that he was walking and talking just hours later) is the extreme transformation it caused. Before the accident, Gage was a well-balanced, diligent worker whom his supervisors referred to as their "most efficient and capable foreman" (Harlow, 1848, as cited in Neylan, 1999, p. 280). After the accident, he was unreliable, unpleasant, and downright vulgar. His character was so altered that people acquainted with him before and after the accident claimed he was "no longer Gage" (Harlow, 1848, as cited in Neylan, 1999, p. 280). However, there is evidence that Gage recovered to some degree. He spent almost 8 years working as a horse caretaker and stagecoach driver (Harlow, 1968, 1969, as cited in Macmillan, 2000).

Modern scientists have revisited Gage's case, using measurements from his fractured skull and brain-imaging data to estimate exactly where the damage occurred. Their studies suggest that the metal rod caused destruction in both the left and right frontal lobes (Damasio, Grabowski, Frank, Galaburda, & Damasio, 1994), although, researchers now believe the rod did not pierce the right hemisphere (Ratiu et al., 2004; Van Horn et al., 2012). The only good thing about Gage's horrible accident, it seems, is that it illuminated the importance of the frontal lobes in defining personality characteristics.

DOGS, CARTOONS, AND THE MOTOR CORTEX   Toward the rear of the frontal lobes is a strip of the brain known as the **motor cortex,** which works with other areas to plan and execute voluntary movements (Infographic 2.4). Evidence for this region's involvement in muscle movement first came from a study of dogs by Gustav Fritsch (1838–1927) and Edvard Hitzig (1838–1907). Working from a makeshift lab, the two doctors discovered they could make the animals move by electrically stimulating their brains (Gross, 2007). A mild shock to the right side of the cortex might cause a twitch in the left forepaw or the left side of the face, whereas stimulating the left would spur movement on the right (Finger, 2001).

North American neurosurgeon Wilder Penfield (1891–1976) used a method similar to Fritsch and Hitzig with humans to create a map showing which points along the motor cortex corresponded to the various parts of the body (Penfield & Boldrey, 1937).

occipital lobes (äk-si-pə-təl) The area of the cortex in the back of the head that processes visual information.

temporal lobes The area of the cortex that processes auditory stimuli and language.

motor cortex A band of tissue toward the rear of the frontal lobes that works with other brain regions to plan and execute voluntary movements.

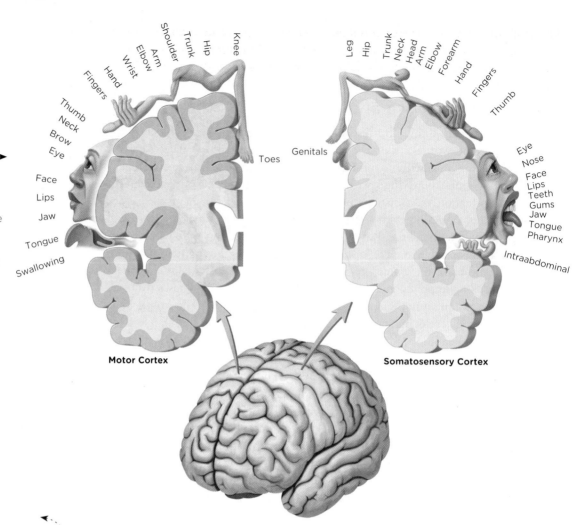

FIGURE 2.9

The Motor and Somatosensory Cortex
This drawing shows how the motor and somatosensory cortex correspond to the various regions of the body. Parts of the body that are shown larger, such as the face and hands, indicate areas of greater motor control or sensitivity. The size of each body part reflects the amount of cortex allocated to it.

Motor Cortex

Somatosensory Cortex

CONNECTIONS

This research compared one man's brain to a control group of 35 men. In **Chapter 1,** we discussed the importance of having a large enough sample size to give us reliable findings, which might be a consideration here. Also, we discussed the potential problems with using case studies for making generalizations to the population, and here, the use of Einstein as a single participant to compare to the control group could be considered a type of case study.

Superbrain

A photo of Einstein's brain shows what researchers have referred to as his "extraordinary prefrontal cortex" (Falk, Lepore, & Noe, 2012, p. 1). The irregularities in Einstein's parietal lobes may explain some of his spectacular mathematical and visual-spatial abilities (Witelson et al., 1999; Falk et al., 2012). Could it be that Einstein's mathematical activities caused changes to his parietal lobes? Harvey Collection. Otis Historical Archives, National Museum of Health and Medicine

Penfield's map is often represented by the "homunculus" (hō-mən-kyə-ləs; Latin for "little man") cartoon, a distorted image of a human being with huge lips and hands and a tiny torso (**Figure 2.9**). The size of each body part in the figure roughly reflects the amount of cortex devoted to it, which explains why parts requiring extremely fine-tuned motor control (the mouth and hands) are gigantic in comparison to other body parts.

ALBERT EINSTEIN AND THE PARIETAL LOBES   Directly behind the frontal lobes on the crown of your head are the parietal lobes (Infographic 2.4). The parietal lobes help orient the body in space, are involved in tactile processing (for example, interpreting sensations related to touch, such as pain and pressure), and may play a role in mathematical reasoning associated with spatial cognition (Desco et al., 2011; Grabner et al., 2007; Wolpert, Goodbody, & Husain, 1998). A study published in 1999 compared the brain of Albert Einstein to a control group of 35 brain specimens from men who had donated their bodies for use in research. Prior to their deaths, these men had normal cognitive functioning, average intelligence, and no mental health issues. The researchers reported that Einstein's brain did not weigh more than the average brain of the control group, but a region of his parietal lobe believed to be important for visual–spatial processing was 15% larger than those of the control group.

They proposed that the differences in that specific region of the parietal lobe in Einstein's brain may have been linked to his "exceptional intellect" in areas of visual-spatial cognition and mathematical thinking (Witelson, Kigar, & Harvey, 1999). Of course, the link between the size of Einstein's parietal region and his "exceptional intellect" is correlational in nature, so we should be cautious in our interpretations.

PENFIELD AND THE SOMATOSENSORY CORTEX The parietal lobes are home to the **somatosensory cortex,** a strip of brain running parallel to the motor cortex, which receives and integrates sensory information from all over the body (pain and temperature, for example). Penfield, the neurosurgeon who created the homunculus for the motor cortex, mapped the somatosensory cortex in the same way (Penfield & Boldrey, 1937; Figure 2.9). As you might expect, the most sensitive areas of the body like the face and tongue are oversized on the homunculus, whereas areas less sensitive to stimulation, such as the forearm and the calf, are smaller.

THE TEMPORAL LOBES AND THE AUDITORY CORTEX Below the parietal lobes, on the sides of your head, are the temporal lobes, which process auditory stimuli, recognize visual objects, especially faces, and play a key role in language comprehension and memory (Hickok & Poeppel, 2000; Infographic 2.4 on page 74). The temporal lobes are home to the *auditory cortex,* which receives information from the ears and allows us to "hear" sounds. In particular, researchers have supported the notion, based on studies of primate vocalizations, that the ability to recognize language has evolved over time and is processed within the temporal lobes (Scott, Blank, Rosen, & Wise, 2000; Squire, Stark, & Clark, 2004).

THE OCCIPITAL LOBES AND THE PRIMARY VISUAL CORTEX Visual information is initially processed in the occipital lobes, in the lower back of the head (Infographic 2.4). If you have ever suffered a severe blow to the rear of your head, you may remember "seeing stars," probably because activity in the occipital lobes was disrupted (hopefully only for a few seconds). It is here, where the optic nerve connects to the *primary visual cortex,* that visual information is received and interpreted, and where we process that information (for example, about color, shape, and motion). (See Chapter 3 for more on the visual process.) Even for a person with healthy eyes, if this area were damaged, severe visual impairment could occur. At the same time, the individual would still be able to "see" vivid *mental* images (Bridge, Harrold, Holmes, Stokes, & Kennard, 2012).

> **Seeing Stars**
> If you have ever been struck or fallen on the back of the head, you may recall perceiving bright blobs or dots floating by. The occipital lobes at the rear of the brain are home to the visual processing centers. TOSHIFUMI KITAMURA/ AFP/Getty Images

LO 14 Describe the association areas and identify their functions.

THE ASSOCIATION AREAS In addition to the specialized functions of the different lobes described above, the cortex contains **association areas** whose role is to integrate information from all over the brain. The association areas are located in all four lobes; however, they are much harder to pinpoint than are the motor and sensory areas. The association areas allow us to learn (just as you're doing now), to have abstract thoughts (for example, 2 + 2 = 4), and to carry out complex behaviors like texting and tweeting. The language-processing hubs we learned about earlier, *Broca's area* and *Wernicke's area,* are association areas that play a role in the production and comprehension of speech. In humans, the vast majority of the cortical surface is dedicated to the association areas.

Synonyms
association areas intrinsic processing areas

somatosensory cortex A band of tissue running parallel to the motor cortex that receives and integrates sensory information from all over the body.

association areas Regions of the cortex that integrate information from all over the brain, allowing us to learn, think in abstract terms, and carry out other intellectual tasks.

SOCIAL MEDIA and psychology

Facebook in the Brain

A major theme of this chapter is localization of function, the idea that certain areas of the brain tend to specialize in performing certain tasks. When we say "tasks," we mean just about any activity you can imagine, from riding a bicycle to managing friend networks on Facebook.

The average number of Facebook "friends" is 338, but the friend tally varies significantly from one person to the next, ranging from zero to 5,000, the maximum allowed by Facebook (Facebook Help Center, 2015; Pew Research Center, 2014, February 3). What does a Facebook friend number reveal about a person—job networking skills, offline popularity, time wasted at work? According to one preliminary study, friend volume may reflect something about the brain of the user.

FACEBOOK FRIENDS: A GRAY MATTER.

Using MRI technology, researchers studied the brain structures of a sample of Facebook users. They discovered a correlation between the number of Facebook friends and the density of gray matter (the primary tissue of the cerebral cortex) in areas of the brain important for social interaction. One of those regions, the *superior temporal sulcus,* is thought to be important for detecting socially meaningful movements such as hand gestures and eye shifts. Another, known as the *entorhinal cortex,* appears to play a key role in matching faces to names, a critical skill for Facebookers (Kanai, Bahrami, Roylance, & Rees, 2012). As anyone with a few hundred friends can testify, keeping track of all those names and faces can be challenging.

We should point out that this study is correlational. So it cannot reveal whether the number of friends causes changes in brain structure, or whether the characteristics of the brain structures determine the number of friends. Perhaps some other variable is responsible for both. This single study needs replication, but it has generated intriguing questions for researchers to tackle in the future.

✓ show what you know

1. The left hemisphere excels in language and the right hemisphere excels in visual-spatial tasks. This specialization of the two hemispheres is known as:
   a. split-brain.
   b. callosotomy.
   c. hemispherectomy.
   d. lateralization.

2. A man involved in a car accident suffered severe brain trauma. As he recovered, it became clear he was having difficulty producing speech, even though he could understand what people were saying. It is very likely he had suffered damage to the left frontal lobe in a part of the brain referred to as:
   a. Wernicke's area.
   b. Broca's area.
   c. the visual field.
   d. the corpus callosum.

3. The corpus callosum enables information sharing between the two hemispheres. In some cases, surgeons sever the corpus callosum to prevent seizures from spreading between the two hemispheres. How would you explain to a middle school student why this surgical procedure is used and how it is helpful?

4. The brain is constantly undergoing alterations in response to experiences and is capable of a certain degree of physical adaptation and repair. This ability is known as:
   a. neuroplasticity.
   b. phrenology.
   c. ablation.
   d. lateralization.

5. The major function of the _____ is to organize information among the other lobes of the brain.
   a. parietal lobes
   b. frontal lobes
   c. corpus callosum
   d. temporal lobes

6. The _____ integrate information from all over the brain, allowing us to learn, have abstract thoughts, and carry out complex behaviors.

✓ CHECK YOUR ANSWERS IN APPENDIX C.

Digging Below the Cortex

Now that we have surveyed the brain's outer terrain, identifying some of the hotspots for language and other higher cognitive functions, let's dig deeper and examine some of its older structures.

Drama Central: The Limbic System

LO 15 Distinguish the structures and functions of the limbic system.

Buried beneath the cortex is the **limbic system,** a group of interconnected structures that play an important role in our experiences of emotion, motivation, and memory. It also fuels our most basic drives, such as hunger, sex, and aggression. The limbic system includes the *hippocampus, amygdala, thalamus,* and *hypothalamus* (**Figure 2.10**).

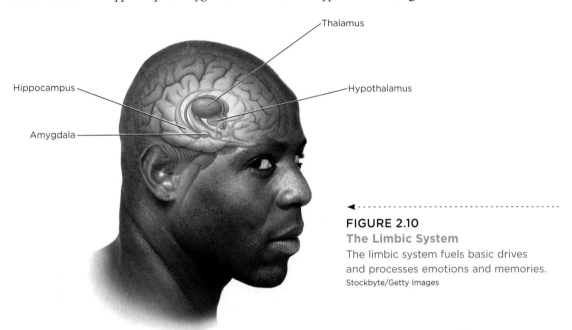

Thalamus

Hippocampus

Hypothalamus

Amygdala

◄ ⋯⋯⋯⋯⋯⋯⋯⋯⋯⋯⋯⋯⋯⋯⋯⋯

FIGURE 2.10
The Limbic System
The limbic system fuels basic drives and processes emotions and memories.
Stockbyte/Getty Images

HIPPOCAMPUS   The largest structure in the limbic system is the hippocampus, a pair of curved structures. The **hippocampus** is primarily responsible for processing and forming new memories from experiences, but it is not where memories are permanently stored (Eichenbaum, 2004). Given its key role in memory, it may come as no surprise that the hippocampus is one of the brain areas affected by Alzheimer's disease (Henneman et al., 2009; Wang et al., 2003). On the brighter side of things, the hippocampus is also one of the few places in the brain known to generate new neurons throughout life (Eriksson et al., 1998; Tate, Herbet, Moritz-Gasser, Tate, & Duffau, 2014).

AMYGDALA   Another structure of the limbic system is the **amygdala** (ə-mig-də-lə), which processes basic emotions like fear and aggression and the memories associated with them (Kalin, Shelton, & Davidson, 2004; Kluver & Bucy, 1939; LeDoux, 2000). Having spent many months in a war zone, Brandon encountered more than his fair share of fear-provoking near-death experiences. On one occasion, he was riding at nearly 60 mph in a Humvee that spun out of control and almost flipped over. "My heart was beating faster than ever before," Brandon recalls. In dangerous situations like this, the amygdala is activated and the nervous system orchestrates a whole-body response (racing heart, sweaty palms, and the like), as well as an emotional reaction (fear).

limbic system A collection of structures that regulates emotions and basic drives like hunger, and aids in the creation of memories.

hippocampus A pair of structures located in the limbic system; primarily responsible for creating new memories.

amygdala (ə-mig-də-lə) A pair of almond-shaped structures in the limbic system that processes basic emotions, such as fear and aggression, as well as associated memories.

THALAMUS   Seated at the center of the limbic system is the **thalamus** (tha-lə-məs), whose job is to process and relay sensory information to the appropriate parts of the cortex (visual information to the visual cortex, and so on). The great majority of the data picked up by all the sensory systems, except olfaction (sense of smell), pass through the thalamus before moving on to the cortex for processing (Kay & Sherman, 2007). You might think of the thalamus as an air traffic control tower guiding incoming aircraft; when pilots communicate with the tower, the controllers direct the route to take or the runway to use.

HYPOTHALAMUS   Just below the thalamus is the **hypothalamus** (hī-pō-tha-lə-məs; *hypo* means "under" in Greek), which keeps the body's systems in a steady state, making sure variables like blood pressure, body temperature, and fluid/electrolyte balance remain within a healthy range. The hypothalamus is also involved in regulating sleep–wake cycles (Saper, Scammell, & Lu, 2005), sexual arousal (Laan & Janssen, 2007), and appetite (Ahima & Antwi, 2008). For example, neurons from the digestive system send signals to the hypothalamus (such as "stomach is empty"), which then sends signals to higher regions of the brain (such as "it's time to eat"). But deciding what and when to eat does not always come down to being hungry or full. Other brain areas are involved in eating decisions and can override the hypothalamus, driving you to polish off the French fries or scarf down that chocolate bar even when you are not that hungry.

Deeper Yet: The Brainstem and Cerebellum

The brain is made up of structures responsible for processes as complex as rebuilding a car's engine or selecting the right classes for a degree program. Yet delving deeper in the brain, we find structures that control more primitive functions.

LO 16 Distinguish the structures and functions of the brainstem and cerebellum.

COMPONENTS OF THE BRAINSTEM   The brain's ancient core consists of a stalklike trio of structures called the *brainstem* (**Figure 2.11**). The brainstem, which includes the midbrain, pons, and medulla, extends from the spinal cord to the **forebrain,** which is the largest part of the brain and includes the cerebral cortex and the limbic system.

The top portion of the brainstem is known as the **midbrain,** and although there is some disagreement about which brain structures belong to the midbrain, most agree it plays a role in levels of arousal. The midbrain is also home to neurons that help generate movement patterns in response to sensory input (Stein, Stanford, & Rowland, 2009). For example, if someone shouted "Look out!" neurons in your midbrain would play a role when you flinch. Also located in the midbrain is part of the **reticular formation,** an intricate web of neurons that is responsible for levels of arousal—whether you are awake, dozing off, or somewhere in between. The reticular formation is also involved in your ability to attend selectively to important incoming information by sifting through sensory data on its way to the cortex, picking out what's relevant and ignoring the rest. Imagine how overwhelmed you would feel by all the sights, sounds, tastes, smells, and physical sensations in your environment if you didn't have a reticular formation to help you discriminate between information that is important (the sound of a honking car horn) and that which is trivial (the sound of a dog barking in the distance).

The **hindbrain** includes areas of the brain responsible for fundamental life-sustaining processes. The **pons,** which helps regulate sleep–wake cycles and coordinates movement between the right and left sides of the body, is an important structure of the hindbrain.

Synonyms
reticular formation reticular activating system

---

thalamus (tha-lə-məs) A structure in the limbic system that processes and relays sensory information to the appropriate areas of the cortex.

hypothalamus (hī-pō-tha-lə-məs) A small structure located below the thalamus that maintains a constant internal environment within a healthy range; helps regulate sleep–wake cycles, sexual behavior, and appetite.

forebrain Largest part of the brain; includes the cerebral cortex and the limbic system.

midbrain The part of the brainstem involved in levels of arousal; responsible for generating movement patterns in response to sensory input.

reticular formation A network of neurons running through the midbrain that controls levels of arousal and quickly analyzes sensory information on its way to the cortex.

hindbrain Includes areas of the brain responsible for fundamental life-sustaining processes.

pons A hindbrain structure that helps regulate sleep–wake cycles and coordinate movement between the right and left sides of the body.

medulla (mə-ˈdúl-ə) A structure that oversees vital functions, including breathing, digestion, and heart rate.

cerebellum (ser-ə-be-ləm) Structure located behind the brainstem that is responsible for muscle coordination and balance; Latin for "little brain."

The pons sits atop the **medulla** (mə-ˈdŭl-ə), a structure that oversees some of the body's most vital functions, including breathing and heart rate maintenance (Broadbelt, Paterson, Rivera, Trachtenberg, & Kinney, 2010).

CEREBELLUM Behind the brainstem, just above the nape of the neck, sits the orange-sized **cerebellum** (ser-ə-be-ləm). (Latin for "little brain," the cerebellum looks like a mini-version of the whole brain.) Centuries ago, scientists found that removing parts of the cerebellum from animals caused them to stagger, fall, and act clumsy. Although the cerebellum is best known for its importance in muscle coordination and balance, researchers are exploring how this "little brain" influences higher cognitive processes in the "big brain," such as abstract reasoning and language production (Fine, Ionita, & Lohr, 2002). People with damaged cerebellums struggle with certain fine distinctions, such as telling the difference between words that sound somewhat alike (for example, "pause" versus "paws") or producing emotional reactions that are appropriate to a given situation (Bower & Parsons, 2003).

Hooray! We have finally completed our tour of the nervous system. We started on the micro level, exploring electrical and chemical signaling between neurons, and then worked our way through the macro structures of the brain, spinal cord, and peripheral nervous system. As you delve into topics covered in other chapters, remember that communication between neurons underlies every psychological phenomenon. Do not hesitate to revisit this chapter throughout the course; this is your biological foundation.

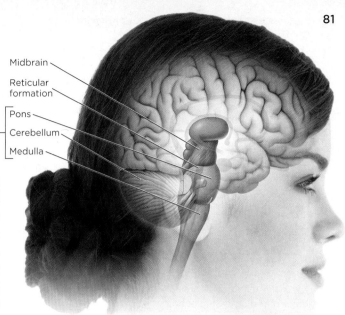

▲ FIGURE 2.11

The Brainstem and Cerebellum
Located beneath the structures of the limbic system, the brainstem includes the midbrain, pons, and medulla. These structures are involved in arousal, movement, and life-sustaining processes. The cerebellum is important for muscle coordination and balance and, when paired with the pons and medulla, makes up the hindbrain. © Fabrice Lerouge/Onoky/Corbis

---

✓○○○ show what you know

1. The _____ is a group of interconnected structures that process emotions, memories, and basic drives.
   a. left hemisphere
   b. limbic system
   c. corpus callosum
   d. superior temporal sulcus

2. The specific brain structure that processes basic emotions, such as fear and aggression and the memories associated with them, is the _____.

3. The primary role of the thalamus is to:
   a. relay sensory information.
   b. keep the body's systems in a steady state.
   c. generate movement patterns in response to sensory input.
   d. regulate sleep–wake cycles.

✓ CHECK YOUR ANSWERS IN APPENDIX C.

WHERE ARE THEY NOW? You may be wondering what became of Brandon Burns and Christina Santhouse. Three years after returning from Iraq, Brandon married a young woman named Laura who has witnessed his dramatic recovery. When Laura first met Brandon, he had a lot of trouble communicating his thoughts. His sentences were choppy; he often omitted words and spoke in a flat and emotionless tone. "His speech was very delayed, very slow," Laura recalls. Now he is able to use more humor and emotion, articulate his thoughts in lengthy, complex sentences; read a book; and write for his Web site. Much of Brandon's time is spent caring for his sons, 6-year-old Porter and 4-year-old Morgan, and his 2-year-old daughter MacCrea Iona. He also works in a church ministry and in that capacity has traveled to numerous countries, including Haiti, Kenya, and Honduras.

As for Christina, she continues to reach for the stars—and grab them. After studying speech-language pathology at Misericordia University in Dallas,

Life Is Good
Three years after his traumatic brain injury, Brandon celebrated his marriage to Laura. The couple now has three children. Laura Burns

Hard at Work
With her master's degree in speech–language pathology, Christina now works full time in Pennsylvania's public school system. Courtesy, Bucks County Courier Times/ William Johnson

Pennsylvania, for 5 years (and making the dean's list nearly every semester), Christina graduated with both a bachelor's and master's degree. But those years were not smooth sailing. Christina remembers the department chairman telling her that she wouldn't be able to handle the rigors of the program. According to Christina, on graduation day, that same chairman presented her with the department's Outstanding Achievement Award. "People often don't expect too much from people with disabilities," she says.

Today, Christina works as a full-time speech–language pathologist in Pennsylvania's public school system, helping elementary schoolchildren overcome their difficulties with stuttering, articulation, and other speech problems. She is also a member of the local school district's Brain STEPS team, which supports students who are transitioning back into school following brain injuries. "Hopefully, I have opened some doors for other people with disabilities," Christina offers. "There were never doors open for me; I've had to bang them down."

You Asked, Christina Answers

http://qrs.ly/dx4qsyd
Which medical professional had the biggest impact on your recovery?

Brandon and Christina provide breathtaking illustrations of neuroplasticity—the brain's ability to heal, grow new connections, and make do with what is available—and also of the skills of the neuropsychologists, physical therapists, occupational therapists, speech pathologists, and other professionals who assisted in their rehabilitation. The recoveries of Brandon and Christina bear testimony to the awesome tenacity of the human spirit. 📁

② summary of concepts

LO 1 Define neuroscience and biological psychology and explain their contributions to our understanding of behavior. (p. 48)

Neuroscience is the study of the nervous system and the brain, and it overlaps with a variety of disciplines and research areas. Biological psychology is a subfield of psychology focusing on how the brain and other biological systems influence behavior. These disciplines help us discover connections between behavior and the nervous system (particularly the brain) as well as physiological explanations for mental processes.

LO 2 Compare and contrast tools scientists use to study the brain. (p. 49)

Researchers use a variety of technologies to study the brain. An electroencephalogram (EEG) detects electrical impulses in the brain. Computerized axial tomography (CAT or CT) uses X-rays to create many cross-sectional images of the brain. Magnetic resonance imaging (MRI) uses magnets and pulses of radio waves to produce more detailed cross-sectional images; both MRI and CT scans only reveal the structure of the brain. Positron emission tomography (PET) uses radioactivity to track glucose consumption to construct a map of the brain. Functional magnetic resonance imaging (fMRI) captures changes in brain activity by tracking patterns of blood flow.

LO 3 Label the parts of a neuron and describe an action potential. (p. 52)

A typical neuron has three basic parts: a cell body, dendrites, and an axon. The dendrites receive messages from other neurons, and branches at the end of the axon send messages to neighboring neurons. These messages are electrical and chemical in nature. An action potential is the electrical signal that moves down the axon, causing a neuron to send chemical messages across the synapse. Action potentials are all-or-none, meaning they either fire or do not fire.

LO 4 Illustrate how neurons communicate with each other. (p. 56)

Neurons communicate with each other via chemicals called neurotransmitters. An action potential moves down the axon to the terminal buds, where the command to release neurotransmitters is conveyed. Most of the neurotransmitters released into the synapse drift across the gap and come into contact with receptor sites of the receiving neuron's dendrites.

Thinkstock

LO 5 List various neurotransmitters and summarize their involvement in human behavior. (p. 58)

Neurotransmitters are chemical messengers that neurons use to communicate. There are many types of neurotransmitters, including acetylcholine, glutamate, GABA, norepinephrine, serotonin, dopamine, and endorphins, and each has its own type of receptor site. Neurotransmitters can influence mood, cognition, behavior, and many other processes.

LO 6 Explain how the central and peripheral nervous systems connect. (p. 61)

The brain and spinal cord make up the central nervous system (CNS), which communicates with the rest of the body through the peripheral nervous system (PNS). There are three types of neurons participating in this back-and-forth communication: Motor neurons carry information from the CNS to various parts of the body such as muscles and glands; sensory neurons relay data from the sensory systems (for example, eyes and ears) to the CNS for processing; and interneurons, which reside exclusively in the CNS, act as bridges connecting sensory and motor neurons. Interneurons mediate the nervous system's most complex operations, including sensory processing, memory, thoughts, and emotions.

LO 7 Describe the organization and function of the peripheral nervous system. (p. 62)

The peripheral nervous system is divided into two branches: the somatic nervous system and the autonomic nervous system. The somatic nervous system controls the skeletal muscles that enable voluntary movement. The autonomic nervous system regulates the body's involuntary processes and has two divisions: the sympathetic nervous system, which initiates the fight-or-flight response, and the parasympathetic nervous system, which oversees the rest-and-digest processes.

LO 8 Summarize the role of the endocrine system and how it influences behavior. (p. 65)

Closely connected with the nervous system, the endocrine system uses glands to send messages around the body. These messages are conveyed by hormones—chemicals released into the bloodstream that can cause aggression and mood swings, and influence growth and alertness, among other things.

LO 9 Describe the two brain hemispheres and how they communicate. (p. 67)

The cerebrum includes virtually all parts of the brain except for the primitive brainstem structures. It is divided into two hemispheres: the right cerebral hemisphere and the left cerebral hemisphere. The left hemisphere controls most of the movement and sensation on the right side of the body. The right hemisphere controls most of the movement and sensation on the left side of the body. Connecting the two hemispheres is the corpus callosum, a band of fibers that enables them to communicate.

LO 10 Explain lateralization and how split-brain operations affect it. (p. 68)

Each hemisphere excels in certain activities, a phenomenon known as lateralization. The left hemisphere excels in language and the right hemisphere excels in visual-spatial tasks. Under certain experimental conditions, people who have had the split-brain operation act as if they have two separate brains.

LO 11 Identify areas in the brain responsible for language production and comprehension. (p. 71)

Several areas in the brain are responsible for language processing. Broca's area is primarily responsible for speech production, and Wernicke's area is primarily responsible for language comprehension.

LO 12 Define neuroplasticity and recognize when it is evident in the brain. (p. 72)

Neuroplasticity is the ability of the brain to form new connections between neurons and adapt to changing circumstances. Networks of neurons, particularly in the young, can reorganize to adapt to the environment and an organism's ever-changing needs.

LO 13 Identify the lobes of the cortex and explain their functions. (p. 73)

The outermost layer of the cerebrum is the cerebral cortex. The cortex is separated into different sections called lobes. The major function of the frontal lobes is to organize information among the other lobes of the brain. The frontal lobes are also responsible for higher-level cognitive functions, such as thinking and personality characteristics. The parietal lobes receive and process sensory information such as touch, pressure, temperature, and spatial orientation. Visual information goes to the occipital lobes for processing. The temporal lobes are primarily responsible for hearing and language comprehension.

LO 14 Describe the association areas and identify their functions. (p. 77)

The association areas in the lobes integrate information from all over the brain, allowing us to learn, have abstract thoughts, and carry out complex behaviors.

LO 15 Distinguish the structures and functions of the limbic system. (p. 79)

The limbic system is a group of interconnected structures that play an important role in our emotions and memories.

The limbic system includes the hippocampus, amygdala, thalamus, and hypothalamus. In addition to processing emotions and memories, the limbic system fuels the most basic drives, such as hunger, sex, and aggression.

LO 16 Distinguish the structures and functions of the brainstem and cerebellum. (p. 80)

The brain's ancient core consists of a stalklike trio of structures called the brainstem, which includes the midbrain, pons, and medulla. The brainstem extends from the spinal cord to the forebrain, which is the largest part of the brain that includes the cerebral cortex and the limbic system. Located at the top of the brainstem is the midbrain, which most agree plays a role in levels of arousal. The hindbrain includes areas responsible for fundamental life-sustaining processes. Behind the brainstem is the cerebellum, which is responsible for muscle coordination and balance.

key terms

action potential, p. 55
adrenal glands, p. 66
all-or-none, p. 56
amygdala, p. 79
association areas, p. 77
autonomic nervous system,
  p. 63
axon, p. 52
biological psychology, p. 49
Broca's area, p. 71
cell body, p. 52
central nervous system
  (CNS), p. 60
cerebellum, p. 81
cerebral cortex, p. 73
cerebrum, p. 67
corpus callosum, p. 68

dendrites, p. 52
endocrine system, p. 65
forebrain, p. 80
frontal lobes, p. 73
glial cells, p. 53
hindbrain, p. 80
hippocampus, p. 79
hormones, p. 65
hypothalamus, p. 80
interneurons, p. 61
lateralization, p. 70
limbic system, p. 79
medulla, p. 81
midbrain, p. 80
motor cortex, p. 75
motor neurons, p. 61
myelin sheath, p. 52

nerves, p. 62
neurogenesis, p. 73
neurons, p. 51
neuroplasticity, p. 72
neuroscience, p. 49
neurotransmitters, p. 56
occipital lobes, p. 75
parasympathetic nervous
  system, p. 63
parietal lobes, p. 73
peripheral nervous system
  (PNS), p. 60
phrenology, p. 49
pituitary gland, p. 66
pons, p. 80
receptor sites, p. 56
reflex arc, p. 62

resting potential, p. 55
reticular formation, p. 80
reuptake, p. 58
sensory neurons, p. 61
somatic nervous system, p. 63
somatosensory cortex, p. 77
spinal cord, p. 60
split-brain operation, p. 68
stem cells, p. 73
sympathetic nervous system,
  p. 63
synapse, p. 52
temporal lobes, p. 75
thalamus, p. 80
thyroid gland, p. 66
Wernicke's area, p. 71

TEST PREP are you ready?

1. _____ are the specialized cells that are the building blocks of the central and the peripheral nervous systems.
   a. Neurotransmitters
   b. The hemispheres
   c. Neurons
   d. Hormones

2. When positive ions at the axon hillock raise the internal cell voltage of the first segment of an axon from its resting voltage to its threshold potential, the neuron becomes activated. This spike in electrical energy causes _____ to occur.
   a. an action potential
   b. reuptake
   c. a reflex arc
   d. lateralization

3. A colleague of yours tells you that she has been diagnosed with multiple sclerosis. Luckily, the disease was diagnosed early and she is getting state-of-the-art treatment. So far, it does not appear that she has experienced problems with the _____ covering the axons in her nervous system.
   a. myelin sheath
   b. reticular formation
   c. glutamate
   d. neurotransmitters

4. Match the neurotransmitter with its primary role(s).
   ____ 1. acetylcholine
   ____ 2. glutamate
   ____ 3. endorphins
   ____ 4. serotonin
   a. reduction of pain
   b. learning, memory
   c. movement
   d. mood, aggression, appetite

5. A neuroscientist studying the brain and the spinal cord would describe her general area of interest as the:

a. central nervous system.

b. peripheral nervous system.

c. autonomic nervous system.

d. neurons.

6. A serious diving accident can result in damage to the _____, which is responsible for receiving information from the body and sending it to the brain, and for sending information from the brain throughout the body.

a. corpus callosum
b. spinal cord

c. reflex arc
d. somatic nervous system

7. While sitting at your desk, you hear the tone signaling an incoming e-mail. That sound is received by your auditory system and information is sent via sensory neurons to your brain. Here, we can see how the _____ provides a communication link between the central nervous system and the rest of the body.

a. endocrine system
b. cerebrum

c. corpus callosum
d. peripheral nervous system

8. After facing a frightening situation in a war zone, Brandon's parasympathetic nervous system reacts with a:

a. "fight-and-rest" response.

b. "fight-or-flight" response.

c. "tend-and-befriend" process.

d. "rest-and-digest" process.

9. Lately, your friend has been prone to mood swings and aggressive behavior. The doctor has pinpointed a problem in his _____, which is a communication system that uses _____ to convey messages via hormones.

a. endocrine system; action potentials

b. endocrine system; glands

c. central nervous system; glands

d. central nervous system; peripheral nervous system

10. Which of the following statements is correct regarding the function of the right hemisphere in comparison to the left hemisphere?

a. The right hemisphere is less competent handling visual tasks.

b. The right hemisphere is more competent handling visual tasks.

c. The left hemisphere is more competent judging if lines are oriented similarly.

d. The right hemisphere is more competent with speech production.

11. Although Gall's phrenology has been discredited as a true brain "science," Gall's major contribution to the field of psychology is the idea that:

a. locations in the brain are responsible for certain activities.

b. the left hemisphere is responsible for activity on the right side of the body.

c. the left hemisphere is responsible for language production.

d. stem cells can be used to repair tissue that has been damaged.

12. Broca's area is involved in speech production, and _____ is critical for language comprehension.

a. the corpus callosum
b. the right hemisphere

c. the parietal lobe
d. Wernicke's area

13. Match the structures with their principal functions:

_____ 1. association areas

_____ 2. temporal lobes

_____ 3. meninges

_____ 4. occipital lobes

_____ 5. parietal lobes

a. three thin membranes protect brain

b. integration of information from all over brain

c. hearing and language comprehension

d. receives sensory information, such as touch

e. processes visual information

14. The limbic system is a group of interconnected structures in the brain. Match the structures below with their principle functions:

_____ 1. amygdala

_____ 2. hippocampus

_____ 3. hypothalamus

_____ 4. thalamus

a. responsible for making new memories

b. processes basic emotions

c. relays sensory information

d. keeps body systems in steady state

15. The _____ is located in the midbrain and is responsible for levels of arousal and your ability to selectively attend to important stimuli.

a. cerebellum
b. thalamus

c. hippocampus
d. reticular formation

16. Describe how agonists and antagonists differ and develop an analogy to help you remember these differences.

17. The "knee-jerk" reaction that occurs when a doctor taps your knee with a rubber hammer provides a good example of a reflex arc. Describe this involuntary reaction and then draw your own diagram to show the reflex arc associated with it.

18. Describe two major differences between neurotransmitters and hormones and how they influence behavior.

19. The research conducted by Sperry and Gazzaniga examined the effects of surgeries that severed the corpus callosum. Describe what these split-brain experiments tell us about the lateralization of the hemispheres of the brain and how they communicate.

20. We described a handful of tools scientists use to study the brain. Compare their functions and limitations.

✓ CHECK YOUR ANSWERS IN APPENDIX C

Get personalized practice by logging into LaunchPad at **www.macmillanhighered.com/launchpad/ sciampresenting1e** to take the LearningCurve adaptive quizzes for Chapter 2.

3

sensation and perception

An Introduction to Sensation and Perception

GOOD MORNING, TRIPLETS Long before the sun rises, Liz Allen is awake, making sure that her 13-year-old triplets Emma, Zoe, and Sophie make it to school on time. First she walks into the bedroom of Emma and Zoe.

The floor may be sprinkled with toys if Emma has been awake in the night. She likes to climb inside her toy box and toss out everything. Zoe is a better sleeper, but she too might be up for several hours at a time. "They're pretty active at night," explains Liz. When sleeping, Emma and Zoe are almost certain to be found cuddled lengthwise, feet-to-head.

Gently shaking the girls, Liz says, "Wake up. Let's get ready," but she needn't utter a word. She

The Triplets
The Dunn sisters, Sophie (left), Zoe, and Emma (front), are the world's only deaf and blind triplets. Emma and Zoe can see nothing, while Sophie has very limited vision even when wearing corrective lenses. All three girls wear devices known as cochlear implants, which simulate the sensation of hearing.
Worldwide Features/Barcroft Media/Landov

"speaks" to Emma and Zoe by moving her hands, and they "listen" by feeling her fingers dance through the motions of sign language. Emma and Zoe are completely blind and deaf. During the day, the triplets use *cochlear implants,* electronic devices that provide them with some degree of hearing. But these implants only provide a hearinglike experience; they do not "fix" deafness (UCSF Medical Center, 2015). The third triplet, Sophie, is easier to rouse, as she possesses some limited vision. Flipping the light switch is enough to get her started on her morning routine.

Welcome to the world of Emma, Zoe, and Sophie. They are, as far as we know, the world's only deaf and blind triplets.

Liz, in Her Own Words:

http://qrs.ly/yp4qsef

Worldwide Features/
Barcroft Media/Landov

The Basics

LO 1 Define sensation and perception and explain how they are different.

Have you ever wondered what it is like to be blind and deaf? Most people depend on sights and sounds for virtually every daily activity, from buttering toast to answering the phone. Thanks to our eyes and ears, we can tell the difference between 12:00 noon and 12:00 midnight, soft jazz and a screaming ambulance. Sights and sounds are a source for thoughts and memories. When we think about people, we "see" their faces and "hear" their voices in our minds.

How does a deaf-blind person function in the world? We humans are adaptive creatures; when faced with disabilities, we make the best of what we have. Emma, Zoe, and Sophie have come to rely on their other senses—touch, smell, and taste—to compensate for what they cannot see or hear. Instead of rising to an alarm clock or the sunlight streaming through their window, Emma and Zoe feel their mother nudging them and signing "Wake up" and "Let's get ready" into their hands. They recognize Mom by touch and smell, and they find their way around new places by running their fingers along the edges and contours of objects and walls. "You would think . . . that they are missing out on a lot," Liz says, "but they don't miss much."

Sensory Blending
Painter David Hockney stands before his massive *Bigger Trees Near Warter* at an exhibition in London. Hockney reportedly has *synesthesia*, a rare condition whereby a person experiences a combination of perceptions in response to a "single sensory modality" (Rich & Mattingley, 2002). A synesthete may, for instance, describe the color green as having a scent, or the word "Tuesday" as being maroon with black stripes. Hockney created the stage sets for various operas by painting what he saw in the music (Ward, 2006, June 10). AP Photo/ Sang Tan

SENSATION VERSUS PERCEPTION The subject of this chapter is sensation and perception, the absorbing and deciphering of information from the environment. **Sensation** is the process by which receptors in our sensory organs (located in the eyes, ears, nose, mouth, skin, and other tissues) receive and detect stimuli. **Perception** is the process through which information about these stimuli is organized, interpreted, and transformed into something meaningful. Sensation is seeing a red burner on the stove; perception is thinking *hot*. Sensation is hearing a loud, shrill tone; perception is recognizing it as the warning sound of a fire alarm.

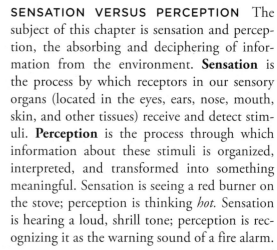

Note: Quotations attributed to Liz Allen are personal communications.

Sensation and perception work together to provide a coherent experience of the world around and inside you. But how does this happen without your effort or awareness? How does the vast amount of stimuli outside and inside your body get transformed into experiences that seem so personal—how are beams of light turned into an image of a beautifully colored sunrise, and chemical sensations into your experience of a sweet strawberry?

LO 2   Define transduction and explain how it relates to sensation.

TRANSDUCTION   Sensation begins when your sensory systems receive input from the environment. Each of your sensory systems is designed to respond to stimuli of a certain kind. Light waves and sound waves accost your eyes and ears, heat waves bathe your skin, molecules of different chemical compositions float into your nostrils and descend upon your taste buds, and physical objects press against your body. But none of these stimuli can have an impact on your brain unless they are translated into a language it understands: electrical and chemical signals. This is the job of the specialized sensory cells located in the back of your eyes, the caverns of your ears and nose, the spongy surface of your tongue and within your skin, muscle, and other tissues. The process of transforming stimuli into the electrical and chemical signals of neurons is called **transduction,** and it is the first step of sensation. The neural signals are then processed by the central nervous system, resulting in what we consciously experience as *sensations* (*seeing* a person's face or *smelling* smoke).

For sensations to be useful, we must assign meaning to them (*that face belongs to my girlfriend* or *the scent of smoke signals fire*). And even though we describe and explain sensation and perception as two distinct events, there is no physical boundary in the brain marking the end of sensation and the beginning of perception. The processing of stimuli into sensations and perceptions is quick and automatic.

DATA-BASED AND KNOWLEDGE-BASED PROCESSING   Psychologists often distinguish between two ways that we process sensory and perceptual information. **Data-based processing** describes how the brain takes basic sensory information and processes the incoming stimuli. **Knowledge-based processing** generally involves the next step, utilizing our past experiences and knowledge to understand sensory information. Data-based processing is the equivalent to what cameras and video recorders do best—collect data without any preconceived notions or expectations. Knowledge-based processing is the arena where humans excel. The brain constructs a representation of the world based on what we have learned and experienced in the past.

How do these concepts figure into *psychology,* the scientific study of behavior and mental processes? Sensation and perception are the starting points for every psychological process you can imagine, from writing an e-mail to building relationships. Psychologists continue to discover the many ways that sensation and perception affect such processes. How? Through careful and systematic observation of behavior.

Studying Sensation

Liz began to suspect that her triplets had vision and hearing impairments when she noticed irregularities in their behavior. When Zoe lost her hearing, for example, she became frustrated with one of her favorite toys—a cube that made music when she pushed its buttons. Liz's careful observation of her daughter's activities prompted her to consult a specialist. Eventually, it became clear that there was a problem with the *sensory* receptors in Zoe's ears, but Liz initially noticed a *behavioral* change.

CONNECTIONS

In **Chapter 2,** we described how neurons work together to shape our experiences. The electrical signals are active within the axon, and the chemical signals are at work in the synapse.

CONNECTIONS

As discussed in **Chapter 2,** the brain and the spinal cord make up the central nervous system. The peripheral nervous system includes the somatic and autonomic branches of the nervous system.

Synonyms
data-based processing bottom-up processing
knowledge-based processing top-down processing

sensation   The process by which sensory organs in the eyes, ears, nose, mouth, skin, and other tissues receive and detect stimuli.

perception   The organization and interpretation of sensory stimuli by the brain.

transduction   The process of transforming stimuli into neural signals.

data-based processing   Taking basic sensory information about incoming stimuli and processing it for further interpretation.

knowledge-based processing   Drawing on past experiences and knowledge to understand and interpret sensory information.

HUMAN SENSATION   Studying sensation means studying human beings, who are complex and variable. Not everyone is born with the same collection of stimulus-detecting equipment. Some people have eyes that see 20/20; others have been wearing glasses since they were toddlers. There is even variation within a given individual. The ability to detect faint stimuli, for instance, depends on your state of mind and body (such as how preoccupied or bored you happen to be, how stressed you feel, or whether you've had your morning cup of coffee).

This variability in one's ability to sense can have profound consequences. If you get in your car immediately following a heated argument, you may be less likely to notice (that is, sense) a bicyclist in your rearview mirror—who on any other day would catch your eye. This is because your attention is divided, just as it is when you are multitasking. Research has found that approximately 2% of people might be able to multitask flawlessly; however, the great majority of us are limited in our ability to attend to the environment, especially when focusing on more than one demanding task (Watson & Strayer, 2010). In particular, researchers have demonstrated that distracting social activities, such as Facebook and text messaging, are linked with poorer grades in college students (Junco & Cotten, 2012). Unfortunately, human beings do not have sensory organs that are equivalent to light meters, sound meters, motion detectors, and thermometers. Our sensory systems are prone to interferences from outside and within, which challenge psychologists as they search for ways to accurately measure sensory abilities.

LO 3   Describe and differentiate between absolute thresholds and difference thresholds.

ABSOLUTE THRESHOLDS   Researchers can determine various types of sensory *thresholds,* which are the smallest levels of stimulation people can detect. Of particular interest to psychologists are **absolute thresholds,** defined as the weakest stimuli that can be detected 50% of the time. The absolute threshold commonly cited for vision, for instance, is described as the equivalent of being able to see the flame of one candle, in the dark of night, 30 miles away 50% of the time (Galanter, 1962). But, remember, the state of a person's body and mind can influence his ability to sense a faint stimulus: Although absolute thresholds have been established for the general population (**Infographic 3.1;** Galanter, 1962), these thresholds are not necessarily *absolute* for a particular person over time. Absolute thresholds are important, but there is more to sensation than noting the presence of a stimulus. Many everyday sensory experiences involve detecting *changes* in environmental stimuli.

SENSORY ADAPTATION   Have you ever put on cologne or perfume and wondered if it was too strong, but within a matter of minutes you don't even notice it? Or perhaps you have jumped into an ice-cold swimming pool, and within 30 minutes you are oblivious to the frigid temperature. Our sensory receptors become less sensitive to constant stimuli through a process called **sensory adaptation,** a natural lessening of awareness of unchanging conditions. This allows us to focus instead on changes in our environment—a skill that has proven invaluable for survival.

DIFFERENCE THRESHOLDS   Intrigued by this keen sensitivity to change, early psychologists decided to figure out *how different* stimuli need to be in order for someone to notice their difference. Through careful experimentation, they established various **difference thresholds,** or the minimum differences between two stimuli noticed 50% of the time.

Let's say you are blindfolded, holding a 100-gram stick of butter, and somebody places a thinly sliced pat of butter weighing only 0.5 grams on top of the stick (adding 0.5% of the weight of the stick of butter). Do you think you'd notice the added weight

Getting Accustomed
Most people are painfully aware of their new braces, but after a while they begin to notice them less. If a stimulus is ongoing and steady, we tend to become less aware of it. This process of *sensory adaptation* helps keep us on alert for changes in the environment. © Caroline Schiff/ Blend Images/Corbis

CONNECTIONS

In **Chapter 1,** we presented the evolutionary perspective. Here, it is used to explain how sensory adaptation has evolved. By ignoring unchanging stimuli, we are better prepared to detect changes in the environment. For our ancestors, picking up new information often meant the difference between life and death.

Synonyms
difference thresholds just noticeable differences

absolute threshold   The weakest stimuli that can be detected 50% of the time.

sensory adaptation   Sensory receptors tend to become less sensitive to constant stimuli.

difference threshold   The minimum difference between two stimuli that can be noticed 50% of the time.

Studying Sensation

An airplane manufacturer designs a control panel covered with dials and lights. In addition to checking the panel in a factory setting, the manufacturer must also be sure the panel works for the people who will be using it. For example, will pilots notice when a warning light is on?

Human factors engineers study how sensation and perception interact with machines and equipment. A pilot might be tested to see how dim a light she can detect 50% of the time (absolute threshold). A pilot might also be tested to determine how different the intensity of two lights would have to be for her to detect a change 50% of the time (difference threshold). Using information gathered by a human factors engineer, the manufacturer could accurately set the brightness of lights on the panel.

Absolute thresholds

are the weakest stimuli that can be detected 50% of the time. Absolute thresholds for each of the five senses (GALANTER, 1962):

Touch
a bee's wing falling on your cheek

Hearing
the tick of a clock at 20 feet

Smell
one drop of perfume throughout a six-room apartment

Vision
candle flame seen from 30 miles away on a clear dark night

Taste
1 teaspoon of sugar in 2 gallons of water

In order to be detected, a light must be bright enough to be seen. Lights weaker than the absolute threshold would be considered subliminal stimuli— stimuli so weak you don't sense them consciously and reliably.

50%

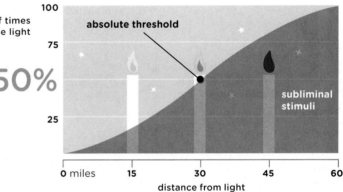

percent of times you can see the light

absolute threshold

subliminal stimuli

distance from light

Signal detection theory

Our ability to detect a stimulus depends on sensory factors (such as the intensity of the stimulus or the presence of interfering stimuli) and our psychological state (such as how alert we are). After determining minimum brightness for airplane control panel lights, a human factors engineer would also use signal detection theory to assess real-life situations. Lights that are noticeable in a controlled test situation might not be detected when other stimuli interfere.

During a real flight, natural light might be coming in through the cockpit windows.

The pilot might be busy communicating with air traffic control.

✳ How much more intense does a stimulus need to be for it to be detected in real-life situations?

Ever So Subtle
Participants from China and the Netherlands were asked to choose the less colorful image. Can you tell there's a difference in brightness? The *difference threshold,* or just noticeable difference, is the minimum difference between two stimuli noticed 50% of the time. Qin, S., Ge, S., Yin, H., Xia, J., & Heynderickx, I. (2010). *Displays, 31,* 25-34.

CONNECTIONS

In **Chapter 1,** we presented the sociocultural perspective, which helps us understand how some behaviors differ across cultures, and others are universal. Here, we see how difference thresholds are the same across cultures.

CONNECTIONS

In **Chapter 1,** we discussed critical thinking and psychomythology. The claim that subliminal advertising can make us buy things we don't want is an example of this type of "misinformation" about human behavior. An important component of critical thinking is determining if there is scientific evidence to support or refute claims, including those conveyed in urban myths.

of the pat of butter? Probably not. But if someone added a much larger pat of butter on top, say, a pat weighing 5 grams (5% of the stick's weight), then you would almost definitely notice the change, right? Somewhere in between that tiny pat and the larger pat of butter is the difference threshold.

According to Ernst Heinrich Weber (1795–1878), difference thresholds are determined by ratios, not absolute numbers. In fact, the *just noticeable difference* for weight is 2%; that is, the proportion of added weight needed for you to feel the difference 50% of the time. Getting back to our stick of butter (which is getting a little soft now), we only need to add a slice of butter weighing 2 grams (2% of the weight of the stick) for you to notice someone has added to your burden. What if you were holding 500 grams (or 5 sticks) of butter? How much would need to be added for you to detect the difference in weight*? **Weber's law** states that *ratios,* not raw number values, determine these difference thresholds. The five senses each have their own constant Weber ratios.

Difference thresholds vary slightly from person to person because each of us has a unique sensory toolkit. But is there variation across people from different cultures? In one study, researchers compared participants' ability to detect changes to pictures (for example, their brightness and color) of flowers, balloons, rabbits, and other objects (see photo above). The just noticeable difference was the same for the Chinese and Dutch participants "for most images" (Qin et al., 2010, p. 25). The implication is that this aspect of sensation and perception might not be influenced by cultural factors.

Apply This ➤

You Are in Control: Subliminal Influences

The absolute thresholds and difference thresholds discussed above pertain to stimuli that we can detect at least 50% of the time. What about stimuli below these thresholds? Do *subliminal* stimuli, which are well below our absolute thresholds (such as light that is too dim to see and sounds that are too faint to hear), have an impact on us? Perhaps you have heard of "subliminal advertising," or stealthy attempts by marketers to woo you into buying their products. Here's an example: You're in a theater and suddenly the words "Buy Popcorn!" flash across the screen, but only for a few milliseconds. Your sensory receptors may detect this fleeting stimulus, but so briefly that you don't notice. According to urban myth, subliminal marketing can make you run out and buy popcorn, soft drinks, or whatever products happen to be advertised. But these messages cannot affect behavior in this way. They cannot manipulate you to purchase something you had not planned on purchasing, or to quit smoking, for example (Karremans, Stroebe, & Claus, 2006). Remember, you have conscious authority over the purchases and life choices you make. ➤

That being said, the brain does register information presented at an unconscious or nonconscious level. Neuroimaging studies suggest that neural activity is evident in response to the "subliminal presentation" of stimuli (Axelrod, Bar, Rees, & Yovel, 2014; Kouider & Dehaene, 2007). These subliminal messages may be able to

*Answer: 2% of 500 grams is 10 grams.

influence fleeting moods through *priming* (stimulating memories beneath awareness through previous exposure; Chapter 6). One study found that if you expose people to ugly scenes (for example, pictures of dead bodies or buckets of snakes) for several milliseconds (thus "priming" them), they then will rate a neutral picture of a woman's face as less likable than when exposed to feel-good subliminal images (such as pictures of kittens and bridal couples) (Krosnick, Betz, Jussim, & Lynn, 1992).

Thus far, we have focused on the stimulus itself. But what about other environmental factors, such as background stimuli competing for the observer's attention, or internal factors like the observer's state of mind—do these variables enter the equation as well?

SIGNAL DETECTION THEORY   As previously noted, our ability to detect weak stimuli in the environment is based on many factors, and the theory that draws them all together is called **signal detection theory** (Infographic 3.1). It is based on the idea that "noise" from our internal and external environments can interfere with our ability to detect weak signals. Imagine you are participating in an experiment studying the detection of weak stimuli, and you are told to push a button when you see a light flash. The strength of the flashes will range from clearly noticeable to undetectable. You sometimes press the button, but it turns out no light flash occurred: a false alarm. Other times you will press the button and be correct: a hit. How many hits and false alarms you have depends on many internal factors, including how tired you are, when you last ate, your expectations about the importance of success, your motivation, and so on. It also depends on external variables, such as the light level in the room and the dust in the air.

Signal detection theory is useful in a variety of real-world situations. In one study, researchers applied the theory to explain how nurses respond and make decisions about patient safety—how background noises influence their ability to hear patient alarm monitors, for example. One of the specific issues raised by this study was the impact of "missed signals," that is, medical errors resulting from interference with the nurses' ability to detect and interpret patient signs and symptoms (Despins, Scott-Cawiezell, & Rouder, 2010).

In situations like this, the ability to sense and perceive may have life or death implications. But how exactly does each of the five senses collect and process information? Let's start by exploring the sense that is generally considered most dominant: vision.

✓ ○ ○ ○ **show what you know**

1. _____ makes the information received by the sensory receptors more meaningful by drawing from experience to organize and interpret sensory data.
   a. Perception
   b. Transduction
   c. Sensation
   d. Signal detection

2. Transduction is the process of transforming stimuli into neural signals. Identify some stimuli in your current surroundings that are being transformed into neural signals you experience as sensations.

3. A woman standing next to you at the supermarket has some very strong-smelling cheese in her basket. You notice the odor immediately, but within a matter of minutes you can barely detect it. This reduced sensitivity to a constant smell results from the process of:
   a. sensation.
   b. transduction.
   c. perception.
   d. sensory adaptation.

✓ CHECK YOUR ANSWERS IN APPENDIX C.

Vision

THE EYES OF THE TRIPLETS   When Liz became pregnant with triplets, she was busy caring for her firstborn child, 3-year-old Sarah. Her marriage wasn't working. In fact, she and her husband had already begun to contemplate divorce. It could not have been a worse time for Liz to discover she was going to have not one, not two, but three babies.

Many triplets are fraternal, meaning they come from three distinct egg–sperm combinations, each with its own genetic makeup. Liz was pregnant with

Weber's law The law stating that each of the five senses has its own constant ratio determining difference thresholds.

signal detection theory A theory explaining how various factors influence our ability to detect weak signals in the environment.

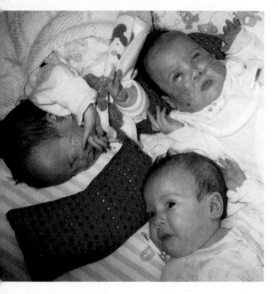

Extreme Preemies
Emma, Zoe, and Sophie were born over 3 months early, long before fetal development had run its course. Premature infants are at risk for serious complications, including respiratory distress, heart irregularities, and vision problems (March of Dimes, 2013).
Worldwide Features/Barcroft Media/Landov

identical triplets, which results when one fertilized egg splits three ways. The babies were born more than 3 months early by emergency cesarean delivery due to grave concerns about Zoe's fetal heartbeat. Each baby weighed less than 2 pounds. Liz was well aware of the health dangers associated with prematurity (breathing problems, brain bleeds, visual impairment, and so on), but she could only hope for the best.

After spending their first months of life in the hospital, hooked to feeding tubes, breathing tubes, and IVs, the triplets finally came home—Sophie first, Emma second, and finally Zoe. But 2 days after Emma arrived home, Liz realized that something was wrong. Emma's eyes weren't "tracking," or following moving objects. Liz took Emma to a specialist, who said she was blind. Soon it became clear that Zoe and Sophie also had vision problems.

What happened to the triplets' eyes? To understand how the girls lost their vision, we must first learn how the eye turns light into electrical and chemical impulses for the brain to interpret. 📁

Light Is Sight

LO 4   Explain how electromagnetic energy is transduced into a sensation of vision.

When you look at a stop sign, would you believe you are sensing light waves bouncing off the stop sign and into your eyes? The eyes do not sense faces, objects, or scenery. They detect light. Remember, if you don't have light, you don't have sight. But what exactly *is* light? Light is an electromagnetic energy wave, composed of fluctuating electric and magnetic fields zooming from place to place at a very fast rate. And when we say "fast," we mean from Atlanta to Los Angeles in a tenth of a second. Electromagnetic energy waves are everywhere all the time, zipping past your head, and bouncing off your nose. As you can see in **Figure 3.1,** light that is visible to humans falls along a spectrum, or range, of electromagnetic energy.

WAVELENGTH   The various types of electromagnetic energy can be distinguished by their **wavelength,** which is the distance from one wave hump to the next (like the distance between the crests of waves rolling in the ocean; Figure 3.1). Gamma waves

FIGURE 3.1
Visible Light and the Electromagnetic Spectrum
Only a small part of the electromagnetic spectrum can be detected by the human visual system. Visible light wavelengths range from approximately 400 to 700 nanometers. We use electromagnetic energy for a variety of purposes, from warming our dinners to carrying on digital conversations. Radioactive symbol, Thinkstock; X-Ray hand, AJ Photo/Science Source; Marines, Lance Cpl. Tucker S. Wolf. U.S. Marine Corps; Hand holding phone, © Rob Bartee/Alamy; Radio tower, TERADAT SANTIVIVUT/Getty Images

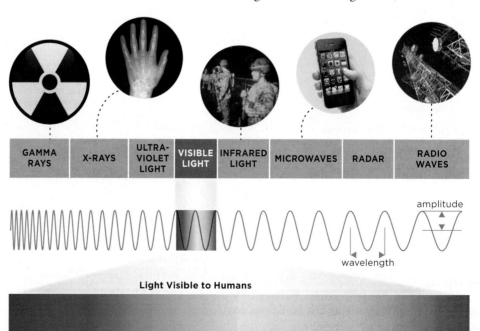

have short wavelengths and are located on the far left of the spectrum. At the opposite extreme (far right of the spectrum) are the long radio waves. The light humans can see falls in the middle of the spectrum, measuring between 400 and 700 nanometers (nm) or billionths of a meter (Brown & Wald, 1964). Wavelength also plays an important role in determining the colors humans and animals can detect.

The Colors We See

Although dogs can only see the world in blues, yellows, and grays (Coren, 2008, October 20), primates, including humans, can detect a wider spectrum of colors, including reds and oranges. This ability to see reds and oranges may be an adaptation to spot ripe fruits against the green backdrop of tree leaves (Rowe, 2002). Other creatures can see "colors" that we can't. Snakes can detect infrared waves radiating off the bodies of their prey, and birds size up potential mates using the ultraviolet waves reflected by feathers (Bennett, Cuthill, Partridge, & Maier, 1996; Gracheva et al., 2010).

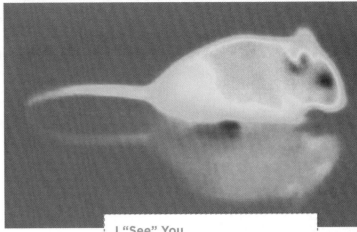

I "See" You
This is what you might perceive if you were a snake searching for dinner in the dark. The western diamondback rattlesnake has facial sensors that detect infrared radiation from warm-blooded prey. Scientists have yet to determine exactly how the heat waves are transduced into neural signals, but the process depends on specialized channels in nerve fibers of the face (Gracheva et al., 2010). Julius Lab at UCSF

FEATURES OF COLOR   The colors you see result from light reflecting off of objects and reaching your eyes. Every color can be described according to three factors: hue, brightness, and saturation. The first factor, **hue,** is what we commonly refer to as "color" (blue jeans have a blue hue). Hue is determined by the wavelength reflecting off of an object: Violet has the shortest wavelength in the visible spectrum (400 nm), and red has the longest (700 nm). The *brightness* of a color represents a continuum from bright to dim, or the intensity of the color. Brightness depends on wave height, or **amplitude,** the distance from midpoint to peak (or from midpoint to trough; Figure 3.1). Just remember, the taller the height, the brighter the light. **Saturation,** or color purity, is determined by uniformity of wavelength. Saturated colors are made up of same-size wavelengths. Objects we see as pure violet, for instance, are reflecting only 400-nm light waves. We can "pollute" the violet light by mixing it with other wavelengths and the result will be a less saturated, pale lavender. Most colors in the environment are not pure. The red pigments in Kerry Washington's red lipstick probably reflect a mixture of waves in the 600–700 nm range, rather than pure 700-nm red. Combinations of these three basic features—hue, brightness, and saturation—can produce an infinite number of colors; our eyes are just not sensitive enough to tell them all apart. Amazingly, though, the average person sees some 2.3 million colors (Linhares, Pinto, & Nascimento, 2008).

Really Red
Kerry Washington sported intensely red lipstick at the Daily Front Row's 2015 Annual Fashion Los Angeles Awards. Her lipstick may appear to be a pure red, but the color is most likely a blend of various red wavelengths. Most colors we encounter in the real world are a mix of different wavelengths. John Kopaloff/FilmMagic/Getty Images

PERCEPTION OF COLORS   And now, the 2.3 million-dollar question: Most of us agree that stop signs are red and taxicabs are yellow, but can we be sure that one person's *perception* of color is identical to another's? Is it possible that your "red" may be someone else's "yellow"? Without getting inside the mind of another person and perceiving the world as he does, this question is very difficult to answer. The colors we perceive do not actually exist in the world around us; they are the product of what is in our environment, including properties of the object and the wavelength of the light it reflects, and the brain's interpretation of that light. When these factors change, so too do the colors we see.

wavelength   The distance between wave peaks (or troughs).

hue   The color of an object, determined by the wavelength of light it reflects.

amplitude   The height of a wave; the distance from midpoint to peak, or from midpoint to the trough of a wave.

saturation   Color purity.

try this

Go find the brightest, most saturated object you possess that has a yellow hue, and grab a strong flashlight while you are at it. Wait until it is dark outside. Now put the object on a table right in front of you and look at it with a dim light shining overhead. Next, shine the flashlight directly onto the yellow object and notice how your perception of the color changes. Finally, turn off all the lights in the room and notice again how your perception of the color changes.

Your three perceptions of this same yellow object will be very different—not because the object itself has changed, but rather because the light shining upon it (and thus, the light it reflects) has changed. Color perception results from the interaction between light and brain activity. The eyes take light energy and transform it into neural code for the brain to interpret. The exquisite specificity of this code allows us to distinguish between electric blue and cobalt, lime green and chartreuse. All this is made possible by the eye's remarkable biology.

You Won't Believe Your Eyes

The human eye is nothing short of an engineering marvel (**Infographic 3.2**). When you look in the mirror, you see only a fraction of each ping-pong-sized eyeball; the rest is hidden inside your head. Let's explore this biological wonder, starting from the outside and working our way toward the brain.

THE CORNEA   The surface of the eye looks wet and glassy. This clear outer layer over the colored portion of the eye is called the **cornea,** and it has two important jobs: (1) shielding the eye from damage by dust, bacteria, or even a poke, and (2) focusing incoming light waves. About 65–75% of the focusing ability of the eye comes from the cornea, which is why imperfections in its shape can lead to blurred vision (National Eye Institute, 2012). Corneal flaws are primarily to blame for so many people (about a third of the American population) needing glasses or contact lenses. LASIK eye surgery, a popular alternative to corrective lenses, uses a laser to reshape the cornea so that it can focus light properly.

THE IRIS AND THE PUPIL   Directly behind the cornea is the donut-shaped **iris.** When you say someone has velvety brown eyes, you are really talking about the color of her irises. The black hole in the center of the iris is called the pupil. In dim lighting, the muscles of the iris relax, widening the pupil to allow more light inside the eye. In bright sunlight, the iris muscles squeeze, constricting the pupil to limit the amount of light. Studies show that men are more enticed by women with enlarged pupils (Hess, 1975; Tombs & Silverman, 2004). When looking at someone she finds attractive, a woman's pupils dilate—especially during the most fertile time of her monthly cycle (Laeng & Falkenberg, 2007).

THE LENS AND ACCOMMODATION   Behind the pupil is the lens, a tough, transparent structure that is similar in size and shape to an "M&M's candy" (Mayo Clinic, 2014). Like the cornea, the lens specializes in focusing incoming light, but it can also change shape in order to adjust to images near and far, a process called **accommodation.** If you take your eyes off this page and look across the room, faraway objects immediately come into focus because your lens changes shape. As we age, the lens begins to stiffen, impairing our ability to focus on up-close images like the words you are reading right now. You can tell if a person has this condition, called *presbyopia,* when she strains to read a book or restaurant menu at arm's length. Most people develop some degree of presbyopia between 40 and 65 years of age (Mayo Clinic, 2014).

cornea The clear, outer layer of the eye that shields it from damage and focuses incoming light waves.

iris The muscle responsible for changing the size of the pupil.

accommodation The process by which the lens changes shape in order to focus on images near and far.

Seeing

"Seeing" involves more than simply looking at an object. Vision is a complex process in which light waves entering the eye are directed toward the retina where they are transduced into messages the brain can understand. The triplets all experienced vision loss from retinopathy of prematurity (ROP), a condition in which blood vessels in the retina grow incorrectly. Damage to this crucial structure has a severe impact on vision.

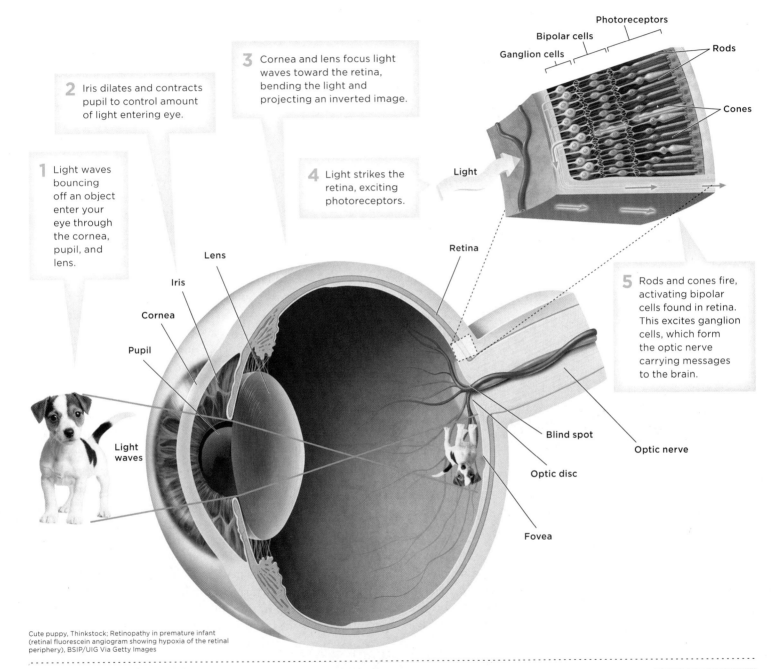

Photoreceptors

Bipolar cells

Ganglion cells

Rods

Cones

2 Iris dilates and contracts pupil to control amount of light entering eye.

3 Cornea and lens focus light waves toward the retina, bending the light and projecting an inverted image.

1 Light waves bouncing off an object enter your eye through the cornea, pupil, and lens.

4 Light strikes the retina, exciting photoreceptors.

Light

Retina

5 Rods and cones fire, activating bipolar cells found in retina. This excites ganglion cells, which form the optic nerve carrying messages to the brain.

Lens

Iris

Cornea

Pupil

Light waves

Blind spot

Optic disc

Optic nerve

Fovea

Cute puppy, Thinkstock; Retinopathy in premature infant (retinal fluorescein angiogram showing hypoxia of the retinal periphery), BSIP/UIG Via Getty Images

RETINOPATHY OF PREMATURITY (ROP)

is a condition characterized by irregular blood vessel growth in the eye. If a baby is born too early (before 31 weeks), blood vessels serving the retina may fail to develop properly, leaving part of the retina without blood vessels. Scar tissue may also pull the retina away from its normal position in the back of the eye (National Eye Institute, 2009). Even when light waves are received by the eye, vision is impossible without a healthy retina to transduce light into messages the brain can understand.

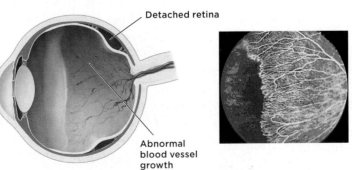

Detached retina

Abnormal blood vessel growth

Here we see the incomplete blood vessel growth characteristic of ROP. The vessels, shown here in yellow, stop before they reach the front of the eye.

The Retina

After passing through the cornea, pupil, and lens, light waves travel through the eyeball's jellylike filling and land on the **retina,** a carpet of neurons covering the back wall of the eye. This area was the source of the triplets' visual impairments. Emma, Zoe, and Sophie all suffered from retinopathy of prematurity (ROP), a condition in which blood vessels in the retina grow incorrectly (Chawla et al., 2012). The last 3 months of pregnancy are critical for fetal eye development, when webs of blood vessels rapidly branch from the center of the retina outward, delivering crucial oxygen and nutrients to the developing tissue. After the triplets' very early birth, these vessels began to branch abnormally, eventually pulling the retina from the back of the eye.

The retina is responsible for the *transduction* of light energy into neural activity; that is, sensing light and relaying a message to the brain. Without the retina, vision is impossible.

LO 5   Describe the function of rods and cones.

PHOTORECEPTORS AND OTHER NEURONS   The retina is home to millions of specialized neurons called **photoreceptors,** which absorb light energy and turn it into chemical and electrical signals for the brain to process. Two types of photoreceptors are located along the back of the retina, *rods* and *cones,* which get their names from their characteristic shapes. **Rods** are extremely sensitive, firing in response to even a single *photon,* the smallest possible packet of light (Rieke & Baylor, 1998). If rods were all we had, the world would look something like an old black-and-white movie. **Cones** enable us to enjoy a visual experience more akin to HDTV (except for those of us with *color deficiencies,* which we will discuss later). In addition to providing color vision, cones allow us to see fine details, such as the small print on the back of a shampoo bottle.

The rods and cones are just the first step in a complex neural signaling cascade that ultimately leads to a visual experience in the brain (see Infographic 3.2 on page 97). Near the rods and cones are *bipolar cells,* another specialized type of neuron, located approximately in the middle of the retina. When a rod or cone is stimulated by light energy, it conveys its signal to nearby bipolar cells. These in turn convey their signal to *ganglion cells,* yet another type of neuron, located toward the front of the retina. Axons of the ganglion cells bundle together in the **optic nerve,** which is like an electrical cable (one extending from each eye) hooking the retina to the brain. The optic nerve exits the retina at the *optic disc,* causing a **blind spot,** since this area lacks rods and cones. You can find your blind spot by following the instructions in the Try This.

CONNECTIONS

In **Chapter 2,** we noted that neurons are activated in response to sensations. In the case of vision, the sensation is light and the neurons being stimulated start with the photoreceptors in the retina. When a photoreceptor fires, its message is sent on its way to the brain.

Rods and Cones
You can see why the light-sensing neurons in the back of the eye are called rods (tan) and cones (green). Rods outnumber cones by a factor of 20 and are found everywhere in the retina except the centrally located fovea. The color-sensing cones are mostly in the fovea. Steve Gschmeissner/Science Photo Library

try this

Holding your book at arm's length, close your right eye and stare at the orange with your left eye. Slowly bring the book closer to your face. The apple on the left will disappear when light from that picture falls on your blind spot.

THE FOVEA   The retina in each eye is home to some 120 million rods and 6 million cones (Amesbury & Schallhorn, 2003). Rods are found everywhere in the retina, except in the optic disc (mentioned earlier) and a tiny central spot called the *fovea.* Cones are packed most densely in the fovea, but are also sprinkled through the rest of the retina. When you need to study something in precise detail (like the tiny serial number on the back of a computer), hold it under a bright light and stare at it straight-on. The cones in the fovea excel at sensing detail and operate best in ample light. If, however, you want to get a look at something in dim light, focus your gaze slightly to its side, stimulating the super-light-sensitive rods outside the fovea.

Dark and Light Adaptation

The eye has an amazing ability to adjust to drastic fluctuations in light levels. This process starts with the pupil, which rapidly shrinks and expands in response to light changes, and then continues with the rods and cones, which need more time to adjust to changes in lighting. When you walk into a dark movie theater after being outside in the bright sun, you can barely see an inch in front of your face. After a few minutes, your eyes start to adjust to the dark in a process called **dark adaptation,** which takes about 8 minutes for cones and 30 minutes for rods (Hecht & Mandelbaum, 1938; Klaver, Wolfs, Vingerling, Hoffman, & de Jong, 1998). Cones respond more quickly, so they are more useful in the first few minutes of dark adaptation. Then the rods kick into action, allowing you to make out silhouettes of objects and people. Why are these photoreceptors so sluggish in their responses to darkness? To restore their sensitivity to light, rods and cones must undergo a chemical change associated with protein molecules, and this takes time (Caruso, 2007, August 13; Ludel, 1978). Also keep in mind that, for most of human evolution, dark adaptation meant adjusting to the gradual setting of the sun (Caruso, 2007, August 13).

When you *leave* the dark theater and return to the blinding light of day, the eyes also adjust. With **light adaptation,** the pupil constricts to reduce the amount of light flooding the retina, and the rods and cones become less sensitive to light. Light adaptation occurs relatively quickly, lasting at most 10 minutes (Ludel, 1978).

Is That Oprah Winfrey Over There?

Let's stop for a moment and examine how information flows through the visual pathway (Infographic 3.2 on page 97). Suppose you are looking at Oprah Winfrey's face. Remember, you're actually seeing the light that her face reflects. Normally, light rays bouncing off Oprah would continue moving along a straight-line path, but they encounter the bulging curvature of the cornea covering your pupil, which bends them. (The light is further bent by the lens, but to a lesser extent.) Rays entering the top of the cornea bend downward and those striking the base bend upward. The result is an inverted, or flip-flopped, projection on your retina. It's like your eye is a movie theater, the retina is its screen, and the feature film being played is *Your World, Turned Upside Down* (Kornheiser, 1976; Stratton, 1896). The neurons of the retina respond to the stimulus; signals are sent from the photoreceptor cells to the bipolar cells, which then signal the ganglion cells that bundle into the optic nerves.

The optic nerves (one from each eye) intersect at a place in the brain called the *optic chiasm.* From there, information coming from each eye gets split, with about half traveling to the same-side thalamus and half going to the opposite-side thalamus. Interneurons then shuttle the data to the *visual cortex,* located in the occipital lobes in the back of your head. Neurons in the visual cortex called **feature detectors** specialize in detecting specific features of your visual experience, such as angles, lines, and movements. How these features are pieced together into a unified visual experience (*I see Oprah!*) is complex.

> CONNECTIONS
>
> Interneurons are found in the central nervous system (the brain and the spinal cord). As described in **Chapter 2**, the interneurons receive and help process signals from sensory neurons.

retina The layer of the eye that contains photoreceptor cells and the location for the transduction of light energy into neural activity.

photoreceptors Cells that absorb light energy and turn it into chemical and electrical signals for the brain to process.

rods Specialized light receptors in the retina that are responsible for sight when the light level is low; not sensitive to color, but useful for night vision.

cones Specialized light receptors responsible for our sensation of color and our ability to sense details.

optic nerve The bundle of axons from ganglion cells leading to the visual cortex.

blind spot The location where the optic nerve exits the retina.

dark adaptation Ability of the eyes to adjust to dark after exposure to brightness.

light adaptation Ability of the eyes to adjust to light after being in the dark.

feature detectors Neurons in the visual cortex specialized in detecting specific features of the visual experience, such as angles, lines, and movements.

Hubel and Wiesel (1979) proposed that visual processing begins in the visual cortex, where teams of cells respond to specifically oriented lines (as opposed to just pixel-like spots of light), and then continues in other parts of the cortex, where information from both eyes is integrated. Scientists have now identified at least 30 different areas in the brains of humans and other primates that play a role in visual processing (Ramachandran & Rogers-Ramachandran, 2009).

In Living Color

Although we have discussed various features of color, we have not yet explained *how* waves of electromagnetic energy result in our perception of colors. How does the brain know red from maroon, green from turquoise, yellow from amber? Two main theories explain human color vision—the *trichromatic theory* and the *opponent-process theory*—and you need to understand both because they address different aspects of the phenomenon.

LO 6   Compare and contrast the theories of color vision.

Light Mixing
The color of a light is the result of a mixture of wavelengths from the visible spectrum. When red, blue, and green light wavelengths are combined in equal proportions, they produce white light. This may seem counterintuitive, because most of us have learned that mixing different-colored paints yields brown (not white). The rules of light mixing differ from those of paints and other pigmented substances. © 2009 Richard Megna - Fundamental Photographs

THE TRICHROMATIC THEORY   Proposed in the 1800s by an English physician–scientist, Thomas Young (1773–1829), and expanded upon decades later by Hermann von Helmholtz (1821–1894), a Prussian physicist, the **trichromatic theory** (trī-krō-ˈma-tik) suggests that we have three types of cones. Red cones are excited by electromagnetic energy with wavelengths in the red range (about 620–700 nm); green cones fire in response to electromagnetic energy with wavelengths in the green realm (500–575 nm); and blue cones are activated by electromagnetic energy with wavelengths corresponding to blues (about 450–490 nm; Mollon, 1982).

So how is it that we can detect millions of colors when our cones are only sensitive to red, green, and blue? The primary colors of light are also red, green, and blue, and when mixed together in equal proportions, they appear as white light (see the photograph to the left). According to the trichromatic theory, the brain identifies a precise hue by calculating patterns of excitement among the three cone populations. When you look at a yellow banana, for example, both the red and green cones fire, but not the blue ones. The brain interprets this pattern of red and green activation as "yellow." And because white light is actually a mixture of all the wavelengths in the visible spectrum, it excites all three cone types, creating a sensation of "white" in the mind's eye. Thus, it is the relative activity of the three types of cones that the brain uses to make its color calculations.

COLOR DEFICIENCY AND COLOR BLINDNESS   Loss or damage to one or more of the cone types leads to *color deficiency*, more commonly known as "color blindness." These terms are often used interchangeably, but true color blindness is extremely rare. Sometimes color blindness is accompanied by extreme sensitivity to light and poor vision for detail, both resulting from deficient or missing cones (Tränkner et al., 2004). The condition associated with red–green color defects occurs in about 8% of men and less than 1% of women with European ancestors (Deeb, 2005). Most

---

trichromatic theory (trī-krō-ˈma-tik) The perception of color is the result of three types of cones, each sensitive to particular wavelengths in the red, green, and blue spectrums.

afterimage An image that appears to linger in the visual field after its stimulus, or source, is removed.

opponent-process theory Perception of color derives from a special group of neurons that respond to opponent colors (red-green, blue-yellow).

people with color deficiencies have trouble distinguishing between red and green because they are missing or deficient in the red or green receptors, but they can see other colors very well. If you can't see the number shown in the Ishihara color plate to the right, then you may have a red–green deficiency (Wong, 2011).

Ample research backs up the trichromatic theory, but there are some color-related phenomena it cannot explain. A prime example is the *afterimage effect*. An **afterimage** is an *image* that appears to linger in your visual field *after* its stimulus, or source, is gone.

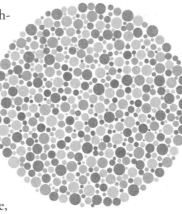

See It?
If you cannot make out the number 45 in this Ishihara color plate, then you might have a red–green color deficiency, the most common variation of "color blindness." Red–green deficiency results from a problem with the red or green cones. SSPL/Getty Images.

try this
Fix your eyes on the black cross in the center of the image to the left. After 30 seconds, shift your gaze to the blank white area. What colors do you see now?
Jacquelyn S. Wong/ViewFinder Exis, LLC

OPPONENT-PROCESS THEORY German physiologist Ewald Hering (1834–1918) realized that the trichromatic theory could not explain the visual phenomenon of the afterimage effect and thus developed the **opponent-process theory** of color vision. Hering proposed that in addition to the color-sensitive cones, a special group of neurons responds to opponent colors—pairs of colors such as red–green and blue–yellow that cannot be perceived simultaneously (there is no such thing as reddish-green or bluish-yellow light). One neuron in an opponent pair fires when you look at red, but is inactive when you see green. The other neuron gets excited by green but turned off by red. If you spend enough time staring at the red and blue picture in the Try This above, the neurons excited by these colors become exhausted and stop responding. When you shift your gaze to the white surface, the opponent neurons fire in response to the green and yellow wavelengths. Meanwhile, the red and blue neurons are too fatigued to fire. You end up seeing a green and yellow afterimage. Research has provided strong support for the opponent-process theory, identifying particular types of neurons in a region of the thalamus (DeValois & DeValois, 1975; Jameson & Hurvich, 1989).

As it turns out, we need both the trichromatic and opponent-process theories to clarify different aspects of color vision. Color perception occurs both in the light-sensing cones in the retina and in the opponent cells serving the brain. The ability to perceive color is not based on processing at a single point along the visual pathway, or even one area of the brain (Gegenfurtner, 2003; Solomon & Lennie, 2007).

Vision is a highly complex—and fragile—sensory system. The same could be said of hearing, the subject of our next section. Let's find out how the auditory system takes sound waves from the environment, and turns them into perceptions of clapping thunder, buzzing mosquitos, and joyful giggles.

Wed in Red
A couple in China poses for a wedding photo. The bridal gown and roses are red, a color that connotes luck in Chinese culture. Many brides also wear red in India, where this color is associated with purity (Akcay, Dalgin, & Bhatnagar, 2011). © Hou Jiansen/Xinhua/ZUMAPRESS.com

✓ show what you know

1. The hue of a color is determined by the _____ of the light reflecting off an object.

2. Cells in the retina that absorb light energy and turn it into chemical and electrical signals are called _____.

   a. opponent-processing   **b.** photoreceptors

   c. fovea   **d.** feature detectors

3. Explain the two major theories of color vision.

4. It's dark in your house, and you are struggling to see what time it is without turning on the light. You notice that if you turn your gaze slightly to the side of your watch, you can make out the large numbers. The ability to see these large details in the dark is due to your:

   a. presbyopia.   **b.** optic disc.

   c. cones.   **d.** rods.

✓ CHECK YOUR ANSWERS IN APPENDIX C.

Hearing

Toddling Triplets
Liz sits with her firstborn Sarah (left back), and the triplets (left to right) Sophie, Emma, and Zoe. The triplets were about 12 months when this photo was taken. Worldwide Features/Barcroft Media/Landov

 **THE EARS OF THE TRIPLETS**   Taking care of three blind infants and a preschooler was no easy task, but Liz was strong, stubborn, and determined to see her girls thrive. They were beginning to reach the major developmental milestones of babyhood—walking and talking—when, at 20 months, everything fell apart.

It started with Zoe, who out of the blue stopped playing with her favorite toy, the cube that made different sounds when she pushed on its sides. Zoe would push the buttons over and over, then burst into tears. Eventually, Zoe and her sisters stopped responding to Liz's voice. It was also during this period that the triplets began to act as if they had some kind of stomach illness—refusing to eat, vomiting during car rides, curling up in the fetal position, and banging their heads against the floor. These behaviors did not stem from a simple stomachache, but something much more troubling: vertigo, a dizzying sensation of spinning or whirling.

Both conditions—the deafness and the vertigo—arose from deterioration of the inner ear, home to the delicate structures responsible for hearing and balance. The damage traced to the triplets' first few months in the hospital when doctors had given them antibiotics. The drugs may have saved the girls' lives, but they had a devastating side effect: ototoxicity, or "ear poisoning." 📁

Listen, Hear

LO 7   Summarize how sound waves are transduced into the sensation of hearing.

The wind howling. A baby crying. Raindrops pelting the roof of a car. These sounds are perceived so differently, yet they all begin with the same type of stimulus: a sound wave moving through the environment. When we use our sense of hearing, or **audition,** we are detecting sound waves that enter our ears. Sound waves are rhythmic vibrations of molecules traveling through air or other materials, like water, metal, or wood.

SOUND WAVES   Every sound wave begins with a vibration. That could mean a pulsating loudspeaker, a quivering guitar string, or vocal chords fluttering in your throat. When an object vibrates, it sends a pressure disturbance through the molecules of the surrounding medium (usually air). Imagine a very quiet environment, such as the inside of a parked car, where the air molecules are evenly distributed for the most part. Now turn on the radio, and the membrane of the amplified speaker immediately bulges outward, pushing air molecules out of its way. This creates a zone where the particles are tightly packed and the pressure is high; the particles directly in front of the speaker will hit the particles right in front of them, and so

audition The sense of hearing.

on throughout the interior of your car. As the speaker retracts, or pulls back, it gives the air particles ample room to move, creating a zone where particles are spread out and pressure is low. As the speaker rhythmically pushes back and forth, it sends *cycles* of high pressure waves (with particles "bunched up") and low pressure waves (with particles "spread out") rippling through the air (Ludel, 1978). It's important to note that molecules are not being transmitted when you speak to a friend across the room; air particles from your mouth do not travel to his ears, only the sound wave does.

Now that we have established what sound waves are—alternating zones of high and low pressure moving through the environment—let's address the immense variation in sound quality. Why are some noises loud and others soft, some shrill like a siren and others deep like a bullfrog? Sounds can be differentiated by three main qualities: *loudness, pitch,* and *timbre.*

Synonyms
loudness volume

LOUDNESS Let's begin by exploring loudness. We sense the loudness of a sound based on the amplitude, or height, of the wave it generates. A kitten purring generates low-amplitude sound waves; a NASCAR engine generates high-amplitude sound waves. Just remember: The taller the mound, the louder the sound. Loudness is measured in decibels (dB), with 0 dB being the absolute threshold for human hearing; normal conversation is around 60 dB. Noises at 140 dB can be instantly detrimental to hearing (Yost, 2007). But you needn't stand next to a 140-dB jet engine to sustain hearing loss, as **Figure 3.2** illustrates. Prolonged exposure to moderately loud sounds such as traffic and loud music can also cause damage.

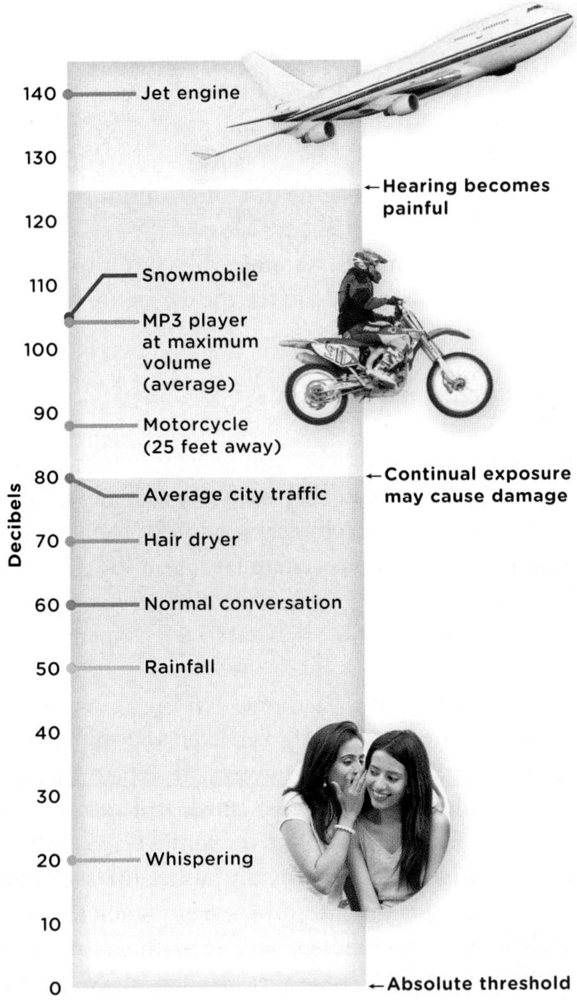
Decibels
140
130
120
110
100
90
80
70
60
50
40
30
20
10
0
Jet engine
Snowmobile
MP3 player at maximum volume (average)
Motorcycle (25 feet away)
Average city traffic
Hair dryer
Normal conversation
Rainfall
Whispering
Hearing becomes painful
Continual exposure may cause damage
Absolute threshold

FIGURE 3.2
Decibels and Damage
Loudness is measured in decibels (dB). The absolute threshold for human hearing—the softest sound a human can hear—is described as 0 dB. Loud noises, such as the 140 dB produced by a jet engine, cause immediate nerve damage leading to hearing loss. Chronic exposure to moderately loud noise, such as traffic or an MP3 player near maximum volume, can also cause damage (Keith, Michaud, & Chiu, 2008). Airplane, istockphoto/Thinkstock; Motorcycle: Vasiliy Vishnevskiy/Alamy; Whispering women, Photosindia/Getty Images

Table 3.1 RANGE OF FREQUENCIES THAT CAN BE DETECTED BY SPECIES	
Species	**Approximate Frequency Range (Hz)**
Elephant	16–12,000
Rabbit	360–42,000
Dog	67–45,000
Cat	45–64,000
Mouse	1,000–91,000
Bat	2,000–110,000
Beluga whale	100–123,000

Bats cannot see very well, but they have an exquisite sense of hearing. Like many animal species, bats can detect sound frequencies well beyond the range of human hearing.

SOURCE: ADAPTED FROM STRAIN (2003).

PITCH   The **pitch** of a sound describes how high or low it is. An example of a high-pitched sound is a flute at its highest notes; a low-pitched sound is a tuba at its lowest notes. Pitch is based on wave **frequency.** We measure frequency with a unit called the *hertz* (Hz), which indicates the number of wave peaks passing a given point in 1 second. If you are hearing a 200-Hz sound wave, then theoretically 200 waves enter your ear per second. A higher-pitched sound will have a higher frequency of waves; the time between the "bunched up" particles and the "spread out" particles will be less than that for a lower-pitched sound. Humans can detect frequencies ranging from about 20 Hz to 20,000 Hz, but we tend to lose the higher frequencies as we get older. **Table 3.1** shows the range of frequencies that can be detected by various species. And just remember, faster peaks mean higher squeaks; waves moving slow make pitch sound low.

When Emma, Zoe, and Sophie began to go deaf, they lost their ability to hear high frequencies first, which means they stopped hearing high-pitched sounds, like female voices. It pains Liz to reminisce about this period because she wonders how her babies felt when it seemed like their mom had stopped talking to them.

TIMBRE   We know that sounds can have different levels of loudness and pitch, but how is it possible that two sounds with similar loudness and pitch (Beyoncé and Ariana Grande belting the same note at the same volume) can sound so different? The answer to this question lies in their timbre. The texture of a sound, or *timbre* ('tam-bər), describes its unique combination of frequencies. Most of the "racket" you hear on a regular basis—people's voices, traffic noises, humming air conditioners—is made up of many frequencies. Timbre is the reason we can tell the difference between two sounds with exactly the same pitch and loudness.

All Ears

We have outlined the basic properties of sound. Now let's learn how the ears transform sound waves into the language of the brain. As you will see, your ears are extraordinarily efficient at what they do—transducing the physical motion of sound waves into the electrical and chemical signals of the nervous system (**Infographic 3.3**).

FROM SOUND WAVE TO BONE MOVEMENTS   What exactly happens when a sound wave reaches your ear? First it is ushered inside by the ear's funnel-like structure. Then it sweeps down the auditory canal, a tunnel leading to a delicate membrane called the eardrum, which separates the outer ear from the middle ear. The impact of the sound wave bouncing against the eardrum sets off a chain reaction through the three tiny bones in the middle ear: the hammer, anvil, and stirrup. The chain reaction of the tiny bones moving each other amplifies the sound wave, turning it into a physical motion that has great strength. The hammer pushes the anvil; the anvil moves the stirrup; and the stirrup presses on a drumlike membrane called the *oval window* leading to the ear's deepest cavern, the inner ear. It is in this cavern that transduction occurs.

pitch The degree to which a sound is high or low determined by the frequency of its sound wave.

frequency The number of sound waves passing a given point per second; higher frequency is perceived as higher pitch, and lower frequency is perceived as lower pitch.

Can You Hear Me Now?

Side effects of lifesaving drugs given to the triplets as newborns eventually led to deterioration of the inner ear, home of the delicate structures where vibrations are converted to electrical and chemical signals that the brain understands as sound. Without this conversion, sound waves may enter the ear, but we do not "hear." Hearing is a process in which stimuli (sound waves) are mechanically converted to vibrations that are transduced to neural messages. If one part of this complicated system is compromised, hearing loss results. In the triplets' case, cochlear implants provide a sense of sound.

1 The pinna funnels sound waves into the auditory canal, focusing them toward the eardrum.

2 Vibrations in the eardrum cause hammer to push anvil, which moves stirrup, which presses on oval window, amplifying waves.

3 Pressure on oval window causes fluid in cochlea to vibrate.

4 Vibrating fluid in cochlea bends hair cells on basilar membrane, triggering action potentials in the auditory nerve.

5 Auditory nerve carries signals to auditory cortex in brain, where sounds are given meaning.

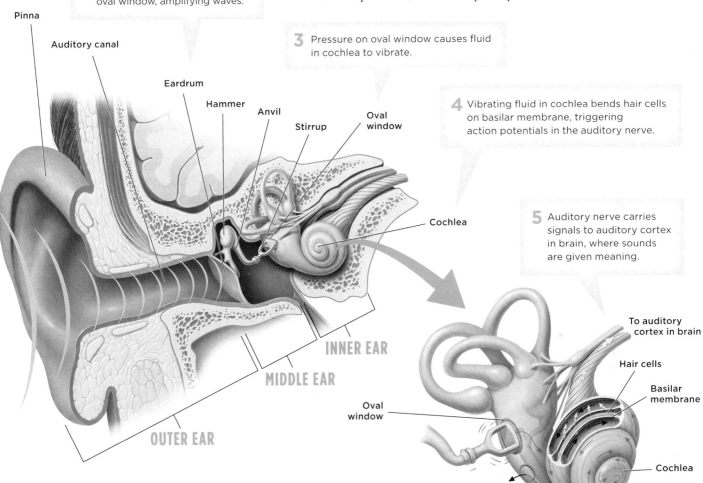

Pinna
Auditory canal
Eardrum
Hammer
Anvil
Stirrup
Oval window
Cochlea

INNER EAR
MIDDLE EAR
OUTER EAR

To auditory cortex in brain
Hair cells
Basilar membrane
Oval window
Cochlea

COCHLEAR IMPLANTS enable hearing by circumventing damaged parts of the inner ear. An external microphone gathers sound, which is organized by a speech processor. Internally, an implanted receiver converts this signal into electrical impulses that directly stimulate the auditory nerve.

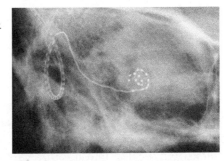

This X-ray shows the cochlear implant's electrode array coiling into the cochlea, directly reaching nerve fibers leading to the auditory nerve.

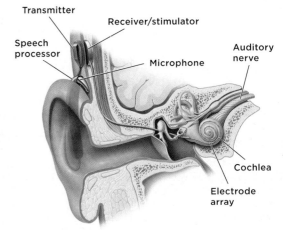

Transmitter
Receiver/stimulator
Speech processor
Microphone
Auditory nerve
Cochlea
Electrode array

FROM BONE MOVEMENT TO MOVING FLUID   The primary component of the inner ear is the **cochlea** (kō-klē-ə), a snail-shaped structure filled with liquid. The entire length of the cochlea is lined with the *basilar membrane,* which contains about 16,000 hair cells. These hair cells are the receptor cells for sound waves, which are transformed into liquid waves inside the cochlea. When the stirrup pushes on the oval window (a result of sound waves entering the ear), fluid in the cochlea vibrates and the hair cells bend in response. Below the base of the hair cells are dendrites of neurons whose axons form the *auditory nerve* (Ludel, 1978). If a vibration is strong enough in the cochlear fluid, the bending of the hair cells causes the nearby nerve cells to fire. Signals from the auditory nerve pass through various processing hubs in the brain, including the thalamus, and eventually wind up in the auditory cortex, where sounds are given meaning. Let's summarize this process: (1) Sound waves hit the eardrum, (2) the tiny bones in the middle ear begin to vibrate, (3) this causes the fluid in the cochlea to vibrate, (4) the hair cells bend in response, initiating a neural cascade that eventually leads to the sensation of sound.

COCHLEAR IMPLANTS   The cochlea is an extremely delicate structure. If the hair cells are damaged or destroyed, they will not regrow like blades of grass (at least in humans and other mammals). So when Emma, Zoe, and Sophie lost their hearing around age 2, there was no magical drug or surgical procedure that could restore their hearing. Hope arrived about a year later, when the triplets were outfitted with cochlear implants, electronic devices that help those who are deaf or hard-of-hearing. These "bionic ears," as they are sometimes called, pick up sound waves from the environment with a microphone and turn them into electrical impulses that stimulate the auditory nerve, much as the cochlea would do were it functioning properly. From there, the auditory nerve transmits electrical signals to the brain, where they are "heard," or interpreted as human voices, hip-hop beats, and dog barks.

Cochlear implants have enabled many people to understand language and appreciate music, but "hearing" with a cochlear implant is not exactly the same as hearing with two ears. Voices may sound computerized or Mickey Mouse-like (Oakley, 2012, May 30). Liz had no idea how the girls would respond to their first experience hearing with the implants. They reacted the same way they do to most everything in life—each in her own way. Zoe broke into a huge grin; Emma sat still, just listening; and Sophie started crying (Hudson & Paul, 2007).

CONTROVERSIES

Conflicted Feelings About Cochlear Implants

➡️ ⬅️   Cochlear implants are a marvel of modern technology. To take a brain full of silence and fill it with sound—now, that is an accomplishment worth celebrating, right? Not everyone in the deaf community thinks so. Cochlear implants may sound like a "miracle cure" for people with hearing difficulties, but they are not without controversy (Papsin & Gordon, 2007). The deaf community is divided on the issue, with many saying that deafness is not a medical problem that needs to be fixed, but instead is a culture with its own language, literature, art, and educational system (Swanson, 1997). Some individuals view their deafness as a gift and would choose to remain deaf even if given the opportunity to acquire normal hearing (Sparrow, 2005). Sign language bonds the deaf community, and cochlear implants threaten to weaken that bond by assimilating deaf people into the hearing world. The issue becomes particularly prominent in cases involving young children, whose parents are making decisions for them. When it comes to cochlear implants, there is no right or wrong—only choices appropriate for the unique needs of each individual. ➡️ ⬅️

SOME DEAF INDIVIDUALS VIEW THEIR DEAFNESS AS A GIFT. . . .

You might be wondering why the triplets were provided with cochlear implants, not *hearing aids.* Hearing aids work by increasing the amplitude of incoming sound waves (making them louder) so the hair cells in the inner ear can better detect them. If hair cells are damaged beyond repair, as was the case for Emma, Zoe, and Sophie, then the inner ear cannot pass along messages to the brain. There will be no sensation of hearing, no matter how much you turn up the volume.

How the Brain Perceives Pitch

We know how sound waves are transformed into auditory sensations, but there are many types of sounds. How does the brain know the difference between the yap of a Chihuahua and the deep bark of a Rottweiler, the sweet song of a flute and the bellow of a tuba? In other words, how do we distinguish between sound waves of high and low frequencies? There are two complementary theories that explain how the brain processes pitch.

LO 8   Illustrate how we sense different pitches of sound.

PLACE THEORY   According to **place theory,** the location of neural activity along the cochlea allows us to sense the different pitches of high-frequency sounds. Hair cells toward the oval-window end of the basilar membrane vibrate more to higher-frequency sounds. Hair cells toward the opposite end of the basilar membrane vibrate more in response to lower-frequency sounds. The brain determines the pitch of high-frequency sounds by judging where along the basilar membrane neural signals originate.

Place theory works well for explaining higher-pitch sounds, but not so well for lower-pitch sounds. This is because lower-frequency sounds produce vibrations that are more dispersed along the basilar membrane, with less precise locations of movement.

FREQUENCY THEORY   To understand how humans perceive lower pitches, we can use the **frequency theory,** which suggests it is not where along the cochlea hair cells are vibrating, but how frequently they are firing (the number of neural impulses per second). The entire basilar membrane vibrates at the same frequency as a sound wave, causing the hair cells to be activated at that frequency, too. The nearby neurons fire at the same rate as the vibrations, sending signals through the auditory nerve at this rate. If the sound wave has a frequency of 200 Hz, then the basilar membrane vibrates at 200 Hz, and the neurons in the auditory nerve fire at this rate as well.

Neurons, however, can only fire so fast, the maximum rate being about 1,000 times per second. How does the frequency theory explain how we hear sounds higher than 1,000 Hz? According to the **volley principle,** neurons can "work" together so that their combined firing can exceed 1,000 times per second. Imagine a hockey team practicing for a tournament. The coach challenges the players to fire shots on goal at a faster rate than one individual. The team members get together and decide to work in small groups and alternate shots on the goal. The first group skates and shoots, and as they are skating away from the goal to return to the back of the line, the next group takes their shots. Each time a group is finished shooting, the next group is ready to shoot. Neurons grouped together in the same way will fire in *volleys;* as one group of neurons finishes firing and is "recovering," the next group will fire. The frequency of the combined firing of all groups results in one's perception of the pitch of the sound.

ALL TOGETHER NOW   Let's draw this all together. Human beings can hear sounds ranging in frequency from 20 to 20,000 Hz. The frequency theory explains how we perceive sounds from 20 to 400 Hz; the volley principle covers the 400- to

CONNECTIONS

In **Chapter 2,** we described how neurons must recover after they fire, so that each neuron can return to its resting potential. It is during this period that they cannot fire, that is, they are "recovering."

---

cochlea (kō-klē-ə) Fluid-filled, snail-shaped organ of the inner ear lined with the basilar membrane.

place theory States that pitch corresponds to the location of the vibrating hair cells along the cochlea.

frequency theory States that pitch is determined by the vibrating frequency of the sound wave, basilar membrane, and associated neural impulses.

volley principle States that the perception of pitches between 400 and 4,000 Hz is made possible by neurons working together to fire in volleys.

4,000-Hz range; and the place theory accounts for frequencies from 4,000 to 20,000 Hz. At times, both place theory and the volley principle can be used to explain perceptions of sounds between 1,000 and 4,000 Hz.

We have now examined what occurs in a hearing system working at an optimal level. But many of us have auditory functioning that is far from perfect.

I Can't Hear You

At least one third of people over age 65 and half of those over 80 have difficulty hearing (Desai, Pratt, Lentzner, & Robinson, 2001; Gordon-Salant & Callahan, 2009). At the onset of hearing loss, high frequencies become hard to hear, making it difficult to understand certain consonant sounds such as the "th" in thumb (American Speech-Language-Hearing Association, 2012). Everyone experiences some degree of hearing loss as they age, primarily resulting from normal wear and tear of the delicate hair cells. Damage to the hair cells or the auditory nerve leads to *sensorineural deafness. Conduction hearing impairment* results from damage to the eardrum or the middle-ear bones that transmit sound waves to the cochlea.

But it's not just older adults who ought to be concerned. One large study found that about 20%, or 1 in 5, of American teenagers suffer from some degree of hearing loss, and the problem appears to be on the rise (Shargorodsky, Curhan, Curhan, & Eavey, 2010). Exposure to loud sounds, such as listening to music at high volume through earbuds, may play a role. A study of Australian children determined that using personal stereo devices increased the risk of hearing loss by 70% (Cone, Wake, Tobin, Poulakis, & Rickards, 2010).

As you know from the triplets' story, certain medications can also harm the fragile structures of the ear, as can ear infections, tumors, and trauma. Some babies (between 1 and 6 of every 1,000) are born with severe to profound hearing loss (Cunningham & Cox, 2003). How do you think those babies adjust to their hearing deficit? How does anyone with a sensory weakness cope? They find ways to compensate, and often that means fine-tuning other sensory systems. Case in point: Zoe and her exquisite sense of smell.

Not Too Loud
Next time you use your earbuds, remember that long-term exposure to loud music can cause hearing damage. A sound needn't be earsplitting to harm your delicate auditory system. Granger Wootz/Blend Images

✓○○○ show what you know

1. The pitch of a sound is based on the _____ of its waves.
   - **a.** frequency
   - **b.** timbre
   - **c.** amplitude
   - **d.** purity

2. When a sound wave hits the eardrum, it causes vibrations in the bones of the middle ear, making the fluid in the cochlea vibrate. Hair cells on the basilar membrane bend in response to the motion, causing nerve cells to fire. This process is known as:
   - **a.** the volley principle.
   - **b.** transduction.
   - **c.** the frequency theory.
   - **d.** audition.

3. A researcher studying the location of neural activity in the cochlea finds that hair cells nearest the oval window vibrate more to high-frequency sounds. This supports the _____ theory of pitch perception.

4. The mechanisms underlying how we sense the pitch of a sound are complicated. We have included two theories and one principle to explain pitch sensation. Try to solidify your understanding of how we hear pitch by creating a sketch of the process.

✓ CHECK YOUR ANSWERS IN APPENDIX C.

Smell, Taste, Touch: The Chemical and Skin Senses

THE SCENT OF A MOTHER One day when Zoe was walking in the park with a friend, Liz decided to pay her an unexpected visit. As soon as her mom came within 15 feet, Zoe turned off the trail and made a beeline toward her with outstretched arms. She knew her mother had arrived because she could smell her, and she could do it while strolling through the breezy outdoors and eating a potent-smelling orange. Zoe was so confident in her sense of smell, explains Liz, "[that] she was willing to walk off the path into the grass to unknown territory, positive that's where I was." Either Zoe's sense of smell is extraordinarily sharp, or she has learned to use it more effectively than the average person. Do you think your nose could accomplish the same? 📁

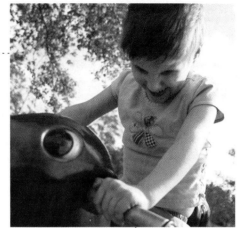

At Play
Zoe rocks on a spring rider at the playground. The triplets spend much of their time outdoors—at the playground, the park, and the swimming pool. Worldwide Features/Barcroft Media/Landov

Smell: Nosing Around

LO 9   Describe the process of olfaction.

Many people take **olfaction** (ōl-'fak-shən)—the sense of smell—for granted. But such individuals might think twice if they actually understood how losing olfaction would affect their lives. People with the rare condition of *anosmia* are unable to perceive odors. They cannot smell smoke in a burning building or a gas leak from a stove. They cannot tell whether the fish they are about to eat is spoiled. Nor can they savor the complex palates of pesto, curry, chocolate, coffee, or prime rib. Because, without smell, food doesn't taste as good.

A CHEMICAL SENSE   Olfaction and taste are called chemical senses because they involve sensing chemicals in the environment. For olfaction, those chemicals are odor molecules riding currents of air. For taste, they are flavor molecules surfing on waves of saliva. Odor molecules, which are emitted by a variety of sources (for example, spices, fruits, flowers, bacteria, and skin), make their way into the nose by hitchhiking on currents of air flowing into the nostrils or through the mouth. About 3 inches into the nostrils is a patch of tissue called the *olfactory epithelium*. Around the size of a typical postage stamp, the olfactory epithelium is home to millions of olfactory receptor neurons that provide tiny docking sites, or receptors, for odor molecules (much as a lock acts as a docking site for a key; **Figure 3.3** on the next page). When enough odor molecules attach to an olfactory receptor neuron, it fires, causing an action potential, illustrating how *transduction* occurs in the chemical sense of olfaction.

OLFACTION IN THE BRAIN   Olfactory receptor neurons stimulate a part of the brain called the *olfactory bulb,* where they converge in clusters called *glomeruli* (Figure 3.3). Then the signal is passed along to higher brain centers, including the hippocampus, amygdala, and olfactory cortex (Firestein, 2001). The other sensory systems relay data through the thalamus before going to higher brain centers. But the wiring of the olfactory system is unique; olfaction is on a fast track to the limbic system, where emotions like fear and anger are processed.

Humans have about 350 different *types* of odor receptors, yet we can distinguish over 1 trillion smells (Bushdid, Magnasco, Vosshall, & Keller, 2014). Each receptor

CONNECTIONS

In **Chapter 2,** we introduced the concept of *neuroplasticity,* which refers to the ability of the brain to heal, grow new connections, and make do with what's available. Here, we suggest that Zoe's heavy reliance on other senses is made possible by the plasticity of her nervous system.

CONNECTIONS

In **Chapter 2,** we discussed the properties that allow neurons to communicate with other cells. When sending neurons signal a receiving neuron to pass along its message, their combined signal becomes *excitatory* and the neuron will fire. Here we are discussing olfactory receptor neurons stimulated by odor molecules. If enough odor molecules are present, an *action potential* occurs, causing a spike in electrical energy to pass through the axon.

olfaction (ōl-'fak-shən) The sense of smell.

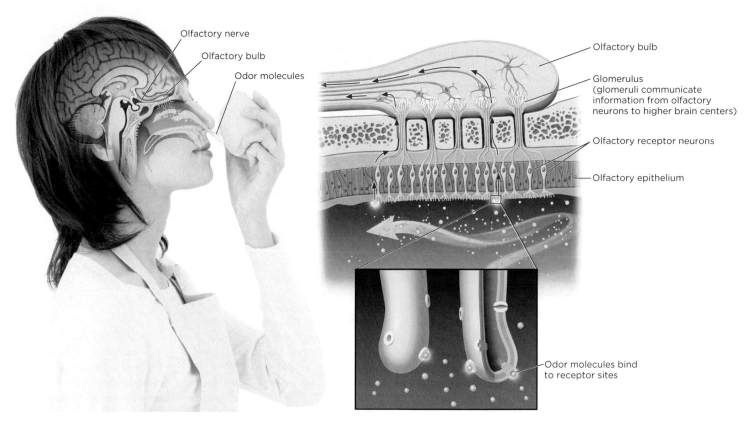

▲ **FIGURE 3.3**

Olfaction

When enough odor molecules attach to an olfactory receptor neuron, it fires, sending a message to the olfactory bulb in the brain. Glomeruli then communicate the signal to higher brain centers.

Collage Photography/Veer

type recognizes several odors, and each odor activates several receptors; a given scent creates a telltale pattern of electrical activity that the brain recognizes as lemon, garlic, or smelly feet. The types of receptors and the degree to which they are activated identify the odor (Firestein, 2001).

Scents have a powerful influence on human behavior and thought. Minutes after birth, babies use the scent of their mother's breast to guide them toward the nipple, and they quickly learn to discriminate Mom's milk from someone else's (Makin & Porter, 1989; Porter & Winberg, 1999). Research suggests that odor-induced memories are not necessarily more accurate than those evoked by touching, hearing, or seeing (Herz, 1998), but they are more emotional and "associated with stronger feelings of being brought back in time" (Larsson & Willander, 2009, p. 318). Why are memories triggered by smell drenched in emotion? Remember that olfactory information is communicated directly to the limbic system. Evidence suggests that smells activate this emotion-processing hub more than other sensations. Brain-imaging research indicates that smelling a perfume remembered from one's past activates the amygdala more than looking at its bottle (Herz, 2007; Herz, Eliassen, Beland, & Souza, 2004).

RECEPTOR REPLENISHMENT   There is another reason smell is special. Olfactory receptor neurons are one of the few types of neurons that regenerate. Once an olfactory receptor neuron is born, it does its job for a minimum of 30 days, then dies and is replaced (Schiffman, 1997). This process slows with age, impairing odor sensitivity (Larsson, Finkel, & Pedersen, 2000). If it weren't for this continual replenishment of olfactory neurons, we wouldn't smell much of anything. Olfactory neurons are in direct contact with the environment, so they are constantly under assault by bacteria, dirt, and noxious chemicals. Some toxins—like the fumes and dust at New York City's World Trade Center site after the terrorist attacks in 2001—can even cause long-term damage to the olfactory system. Many workers involved in the clean-up effort following 9/11 may be permanently impaired in their ability to smell (Dalton et al., 2010).

gustation (gəs-ˈtā-shən) The sensation of taste.

Taste: Just Eat It

Eating is as much an olfactory experience as it is a taste experience. Just think back to the last time your nose was clogged from a really bad cold. How did your meals taste? When you chew, odors from food float up into your nose, creating a flavor that you perceive as "taste," when it's actually smell. If this mouth–nose connection is blocked, there is no difference between apples and onions, Sprite and Coke, or wine and cooled coffee (Herz, 2007). Don't believe us? Then do the Try This experiment below.

Tie on a blindfold, squeeze your nostrils, and ask a friend to hand you a wedge of apple and a wedge of onion, both on toothpicks so that you can't feel their texture. Now bite into both. Without your nose, you probably can't tell the difference (Rosenblum, 2010).

try this

LO 10 Discuss the structures involved in taste and describe how they work.

ANOTHER CHEMICAL SENSE If the nose is so crucial for flavor appreciation, then what role does the mouth play? Receptors in the mouth are sensitive to five basic but very important tastes: sweet, salty, sour, bitter, and umami. You are likely familiar with all these tastes, except perhaps umami, which is a savory taste found in seaweed, aged cheeses, protein-rich foods, mushrooms, and monosodium glutamate (MSG; Chandrashekar, Hoon, Ryba, & Zuker, 2006). We call the ability to detect these stimuli our sense of taste, or **gustation** (gəs-ˈtā-shən; **Figure 3.4**).

Receptor cells for taste are found in the taste buds on the tongue, the roof of the mouth, and lining the cheeks. Somewhere between 5,000 to 10,000 taste buds are embedded in the *papillae*, those bumps you can see on a person's tongue (Society for Neuroscience, 2012). Jutting from each of these buds are 50 to 100 taste receptor cells, and it is onto these cells that food molecules bind (similar to the lock-and-key mechanism of an odor molecule binding to a receptor in the nose).

FIGURE 3.4

Tasting

Taste buds located in the papillae are made up of receptor cells that communicate signals to the brain when stimulated by chemicals from food and other substances. Omikron/Science Source

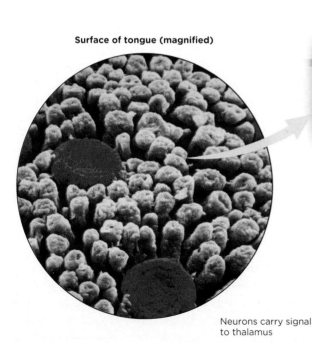

Surface of tongue (magnified)

Cross-section of papilla

Taste bud

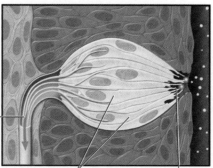

Taste bud

Neurons carry signal to thalamus

Taste receptor cells   Receptor sites

As you bite into a juicy orange and begin to chew, chemicals from the orange (sour acid and sweet sugar) are released into your saliva, where they dissolve and bathe the taste buds throughout your mouth. The chemicals find their way to matching receptors and latch on, sparking action potentials in sensory neurons, another example of *transduction.* Signals are then sent through sensory neurons to the thalamus, and then on to higher brain centers for processing.

Receptors for taste are constantly being replenished, but their life span is only about 10 days (Schiffman, 1997). If they didn't regenerate, you would be in trouble every time you burned your tongue sipping hot coffee or soup. Even so, by age 20, you have already lost half of the taste receptors you had at birth. And as the years go by, their turnover rate gets slower and slower, making it harder to appreciate the basic taste sensations (Kaneda et al., 2000). Drinking alcohol and smoking worsen the problem by impairing the ability of receptors to receive taste molecules. Losing taste is unfortunate, and it may take away from life's simple pleasures, but it's probably not going to kill you—at least not if you are a modern human. We can't be so sure about our primitive ancestors.

CONNECTIONS

In **Chapter 2,** we learned that sensory neurons receive information from the sensory system and send it to the brain for processing. With gustation, the sensory neurons are sending information about taste. Once processed in the brain, information can be sent back through motor neurons signaling you to take another bite!

Supertaster

A graduate student performs a taste test at Rutgers University's Sensory Evaluation Laboratory. Researchers have found that some people are more sensitive than others to bitter-tasting foods. These "supertasters" tend to eat fewer vegetables because of their texture and slightly bitter taste (Marris, 2006). AP Photo/Brian Branch-Price

EVOLUTION AND TASTE   The ability to taste has been essential to the survival of our species. Tastes push us toward foods we need and away from those that could harm us. We gravitate toward sweet, calorie-rich foods for their life-sustaining energy—an adaptive trait if you are a primitive human foraging in trees and bushes, not so adaptive if you are a modern human looking for something to eat at the food court in your local shopping mall. We are also drawn to salty foods, which tend to contain valuable minerals, and to umami, which signals the presence of proteins essential for cellular health and growth. Bitter and sour tastes we tend to avoid, on the other hand. This also gives us an evolutionary edge because poisonous plants or rancid foods are often bitter or sour. It is interesting to note that our *absolute threshold* for bitter is lower than the threshold for sweet. Can you see how this is advantageous?

Every person experiences taste in a unique way. You like cilantro; your friend thinks it tastes like bath soap. Taste preferences may begin developing before birth, as flavors consumed by a pregnant woman pass into amniotic fluid and are swallowed by the fetus. In one study, infants who had been exposed to the flavor of carrots before birth (through their mothers' consumption of carrot juice in the last trimester) showed fewer disapproving facial expressions when fed carrot-flavored cereal compared to plain cereal. This suggests exposure to the carrot flavor before birth led to greater enjoyment of this taste compared to that of plain cereal. This preference was not evident in infants who had not been exposed to the flavor of carrots in utero (Mennella, Coren, Jagnow, & Beauchamp, 2001).

We have made some major headway in this chapter, examining four of the major sensory systems: vision, hearing, smell, and taste. Now it is time to get a feel for a fifth sense. Are you ready for tingling, tickling, and titillating touch?

Touch: Feel the Magic

If you were introduced to Zoe, she would probably explore your face for about 20 seconds, and then return to whatever she was doing. Emma would likely spend more time getting to know you. She might give you a hug, put her cheek against yours, and carefully examine your head with her fingers. At the dinner table, Emma is neat and tidy, and does not like to get food on her hands and face. Zoe loves to dig in and make a mess. These two girls, who are genetically identical, experience the world of touch in dramatically different ways. But both rely on touch receptors within the body's main touch organ—the skin.

Take a moment to appreciate your vast *epidermis,* the outer layer of your skin. Weighing around 6 pounds on the average adult, the skin is the body's biggest organ and the barrier that protects our insides from cruel elements of the environment (bacteria, viruses, and physical objects) and distinguishes us from others (fingerprints, birthmarks). It also shields us from the cold, sweats to cool us down, and makes vitamin D (Bikle, 2004). And perhaps most importantly, skin is a data collector. Every moment of the day, receptors in our skin gather information about the environment. Among them are *thermoreceptors* that sense hot or cold, *Pacinian corpuscles* that detect vibrations, and *Meissner's corpuscles* sensitive to the slightest touch, like a snowflake landing on your nose (Bandell, Macpherson, & Patapoutian, 2007; **Figure 3.5**).

Feeling Around
Zoe approaches eating in a very tactile way, digging in and feeling the food on her skin. While Zoe cannot see or hear, her senses of smell, taste, and touch are extremely fine-tuned. Worldwide Features/ Barcroft Media/Landov

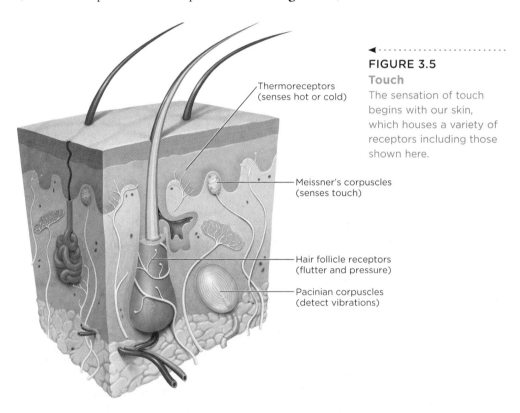

Thermoreceptors (senses hot or cold)

Meissner's corpuscles (senses touch)

Hair follicle receptors (flutter and pressure)

Pacinian corpuscles (detect vibrations)

FIGURE 3.5
Touch
The sensation of touch begins with our skin, which houses a variety of receptors including those shown here.

Oh, the Pain

Not all touch sensations are as pleasant as the tickle of a snowflake. Touch receptors can also communicate signals that are interpreted as pain. *Nociceptive pain* is caused by heat, cold, chemicals, and pressure. *Nociceptors* that respond to these stimuli are primarily housed in the skin, but they also are found in muscles and internal organs.

In very rare cases, a baby is born without the ability to feel pain. Children with this type of genetic disorder may face a greater risk of serious injury (Romero, Simón, Garcia-Recuero, & Romance, 2008). When scrapes and cuts are not felt, they may not receive the necessary protection and treatment. Pain can protect us from minor bangs and bruises as well as serious bodily harm. The "ouch" that results from the stub of a toe or the prick of a needle tells us to stop what we are doing and tend to our wounds. Let's find out how this protective mechanism works.

TWO PATHWAYS FOR PAIN   Thanks to the elaborate system of nerves running up and down our bodies, we are able to experience unpleasant, yet very necessary, sensations of pain. *Fast nerve fibers,* made up of large, myelinated neurons, are responsible for conveying information about pain occurring in the skin and muscles, generally experienced as a stinging feeling in a specific location. If you stub your toe, your first perception is a painful sting where the impact occurred. *Slow nerve fibers,* made up of smaller, unmyelinated neurons, are responsible for conveying information about pain throughout the body. Pain conveyed by the slow nerve fibers is more like a dull ache, not necessarily concentrated in a specific region. The diffuse aching sensation that follows the initial sting of the stubbed toe results from activity in the slow nerve fibers. As the names suggest, fast nerve fibers convey information quickly (at a speed of 30–110 meters/sec) and slow nerve fibers convey information more slowly (8–40 meters/sec; Somatosensory Function, 2004). But where are they sending this information?

The axons of these fast and slow sensory nerve fibers band together as nerves on their way to the spinal cord and up to the brain (**Figure 3.6**). The bundled fast nerve fibers make their way to the reticular formation of the brain, alerting it that something important has happened. The information then goes to the thalamus and on to the somatosensory cortex, where sensory information from the skin is processed further (for example, indicating where it hurts most). The bundled slow nerve fibers start out in the same direction, toward the brain, with processing occurring in the brainstem, hypothalamus, thalamus, and limbic system. In the midbrain and amygdala, for example, emotional reactions to the pain are processed (Gatchel,

CONNECTIONS

In **Chapter 2,** we explained how a myelin sheath insulates the axon and speeds up the conduction of electrical impulses. The myelin covering the fast nerve fibers allows them to convey their information about pain more quickly than the slow nerve fibers that are unmyelinated.

FIGURE 3.6
Fast and Slow Pain Pathways
When you stub your toe, two kinds of pain messages can be communicated to your brain. Your first perception of pain may be a sharp, clear feeling where the impact occurred. The message quickly travels through your spinal cord to your brain, signaling arousal and alerting you to react. Slow nerve fibers also travel through your spinal cord to carry messages about the pain that lingers after the initial injury, often generating an emotional response.

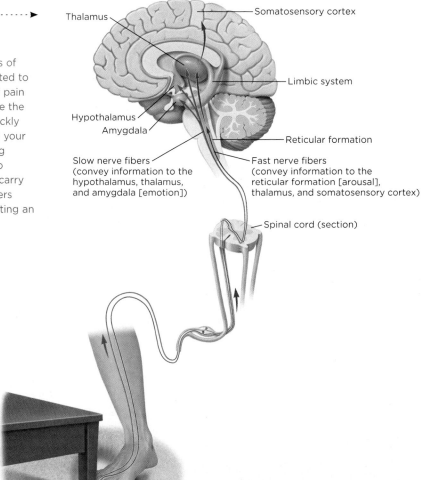

Thalamus — Somatosensory cortex

Limbic system

Hypothalamus
Amygdala

Reticular formation

Slow nerve fibers
(convey information to the hypothalamus, thalamus, and amygdala [emotion])

Fast nerve fibers
(convey information to the reticular formation [arousal], thalamus, and somatosensory cortex)

Spinal cord (section)

gate-control theory Suggests that the perception of pain will either increase or decrease through the interaction of biopsychosocial factors; signals are sent to open or close "gates" that control the neurological pathways for pain.

Peng, Peters, Fuchs, & Turk, 2007). As with other neurons, the transmission of information, in this case about pain, occurs through electrical and chemical activities. *Substance P* and glutamate are two important neurotransmitters that work together to increase the firing of the pain fibers at the injury location.

Understanding the mechanisms of pain at the neural level is important, but biology alone cannot explain how we perceive pain and why people experience it so differently. How can the same flu shot cause great pain in one person but mere discomfort in another? And why does our sensitivity to pain seem to fluctuate from one day to the next?

LO 11   Describe how the biopsychosocial perspective is used to understand pain.

As with most complex topics in psychology, pain is best understood using a multilevel method, such as the biopsychosocial perspective. Chronic pain, for example, can be explained by biological factors (the neurological pathways involved), psychological factors (distress, cognition), and social factors (immediate environment, relationships; Gatchel et al., 2007). Prior experiences, environmental factors, and cultural expectations influence how the pain is processed (Gatchell & Maddrey, 2004).

Researchers studying pain once searched for a direct path from pain receptors to specific locations in the brain, but this simple relationship does not exist (Melzack, 2008). Instead, there is a complex interaction between neurological pathways and psychological and social factors, and *gates* involved in the shuttling of information back and forth between the brain and the rest of the body.

GATE CONTROL   The most influential theory of pain perception is the **gate-control theory.** It states that a person's perception of pain is either increased or decreased by how the brain interprets pain through an interaction of biopsychosocial factors (Melzack & Wall, 1965). Once pain messages are received in the brain (through the mechanisms outlined above), the brain interprets the incoming information, and then sends signals back down through the spinal cord to either open or close the "gates" that control the neurological pathways for pain. Depending on the situation and psychological and social factors, the gates may open to increase the experience of pain, or close to decrease it. In situations where it's important to keep going in spite of an injury (athletes in competitions, soldiers in danger), the gates might be instructed to close. In situations where feeling intense pain has value (when you are ill, and your body needs to rest, for instance), the gates may be instructed to remain open.

Escape the Pain
The last thing you want to look at while undergoing an unpleasant or painful medical procedure is the ceiling tiles in your hospital room. Being immersed in a virtual winter scene, complete with snowmen and penguins, can help take one's mind off the pain (Li, Montaño, Chen, & Gold, 2011). Army Sergeant Oscar Liberato (left) gets lost in the virtual reality video game SnowWorld (right) as he undergoes a painful procedure. left: Steve Elliot, U.S. Army Photo; right: Image by Ari Hollander and Howard Rose, Seattle, copyright Hunter Hoffman, UW, www.vrpain.com.

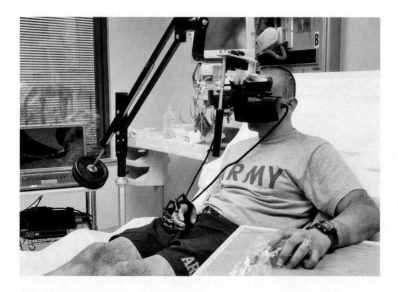

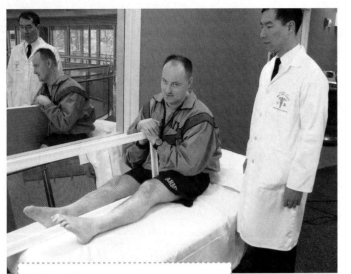

Mirror Therapy
Neurologist Jack Tsao uses mirror therapy to help Army Sergeant Nicholas Paupore at the Walter Reed Army Medical Center. The reflection of a leg in the mirror seems to take on the identity of the one that is missing, which may help the patient resolve his phantom limb pain. Mirror therapy is a promising development, but further studies are needed to evaluate its efficacy (Moseley, Gallace, & Spence, 2008). Donna Miles/ American Forces Press Service

CONNECTIONS

In **Chapter 2,** we reported that endorphins are naturally produced opioids that regulate the secretion of other neurotransmitters.

kinesthesia (ki-nəs-'thē-zhē-ə) Sensory system that conveys information about body position and movement.

proprioceptors (proh-prē-uh-sep-tərs) Specialized nerve endings primarily located in the muscles and joints that provide information about body location and orientation.

vestibular sense (ve-'sti-byə-lər) The sense of balance and equilibrium.

Signals to shut the gate do not always come from the brain (Melzack, 1993, 2008). Information sent from the pain receptors in the body can also open and close the neurological gates from the bottom up, depending on which type of fiber is active. If the small unmyelinated fibers are active, the gates are more likely to open, sending the pain message up the spinal cord to the brain. If the large myelinated fibers are active, the gates are more likely to close, inhibiting pain messages from being sent on. Suppose you stub your toe. One way to ease the pain is by rubbing the injured area, stimulating the pressure receptors of the large fibers. This activity closes the gates, interfering with the pain message that would otherwise be sent to the brain.

It is clear that everyone experiences pain in a unique way. But are there factors that predispose a person to be more or less sensitive to pain?

THE PSYCHOLOGY OF PAIN Pain sensitivity can ebb and flow for an individual, with psychological factors exerting a powerful effect (Gatchel et al., 2007; Raichle, Hanley, Jensen, & Cardenas, 2007). Negative feelings such as fear and anxiety can amplify pain, whereas laughter and distraction can soften it, interfering with the ability to attend to pain. Certain types of stressors (for example, running in a marathon, or giving birth) trigger the release of endorphins. Endorphins reduce pain by blocking the transmission of pain signals to the brain and spinal cord, possibly through the inhibition of substance P, a neurotransmitter in the spinal cord and brain (Rosenkranz, 2007).

PHANTOM LIMB PAIN Perhaps the most striking illustration of pain's complexity is phantom limb pain. Some 50–80% of people who have lost an arm or leg through amputation can experience burning, tingling, intense pain, cramping, and other sensations that they feel originate in their missing limb (Ramachandran & Brang, 2009; Ramchandran & Hauser, 2010; Rosenblum, 2010). Researchers are still trying to determine what causes phantom limb pain, but they have proposed a variety of plausible mechanisms, ranging from changes in the structure of neurons to reorganization of the brain in relation to sensations felt in different locations in the body (Flor, Nikolajsen, & Jensen, 2006). When the brain doesn't receive normal signals from the limb, conflicting messages are sent to the brain from nerve cells and seem to be interpreted as pain.

Kinesthesia: Body Position and Movement

LO 12 Illustrate how we sense the position and movement of our bodies.

You may have thought "touch" was the fifth and final sense, but there is more to sensation and perception than the traditional five categories. Closely related to touch is the sense of **kinesthesia** (ki-nəs-'thē-zhē-ə), which provides feedback about body position and movement. Kinesthesia endows us with the coordination we need to walk gracefully, dance the salsa, and put on our clothes without looking in the mirror. This knowledge of body location and orientation is made possible by specialized nerve endings called **proprioceptors** (proh-prē-uh-sep-tərs), which are primarily located in the muscles and joints. Proprioceptors monitor changes in the position of body parts and the tension in muscles. When proprioception is impaired, our ability to perform physical tasks like holding a book or driving a car is compromised.

You may recall from earlier in the chapter that Emma, Zoe, and Sophie began to curl up in the fetal position and vomit while riding in the car during the same period that they lost their hearing. This was because they were losing their **vestibular sense** (ve-'sti-byə-lər), which helps the body maintain balance as it deals with the effects

 *Apply This*

TABLE 3.2	PROTECTING YOUR SENSES
Sense	**Simple Steps to Guard Against Damage**
Vision	Don't smoke. Wear sunglasses and a hat in the sun. Both smoking and sun exposure heighten your risk of developing cataracts and other eye diseases. Put on protective eye gear when doing work or playing sports that could endanger your eyes (mowing the lawn or playing baseball, for example); 90% of eye injuries can be avoided by wearing the right eye gear (American Academy of Ophthalmology, 2014a, b, & c).
Hearing	Listen to iPods and other media players at or below half volume. Wear earplugs or earmuffs when using leaf-blowers, power tools, and other loud devices (American Speech-Language-Hearing Association, 2014). If the sound level seems too high at your workplace, talk to your employer; you are legally entitled to a working environment that is safe for your ears (Occupational Safety & Health Administration, 2014).
Smell	Two of the leading causes of olfactory loss are head trauma and upper respiratory infections like the common cold and sinus infections (Keller & Malaspina, 2013; Temmel et al., 2002). Avoid head injuries by buckling your seatbelt, wearing a bike helmet, and using protective headgear for contact sports. Minimize your exposure to respiratory viruses with regular hand washing.
Taste	Don't smoke. Nicotine may change the structure and function of the tongue's papillae, which could explain why most smokers have decreased sensitivity to taste (Pavlos et al., 2009). Smoking also impairs olfaction (Katotomichelakis et al., 2007), and therefore dampens the appreciation of flavors.
Touch	Touch receptors are located in the skin and throughout the body, so protecting your sense of touch means taking good care of your body in general. Spinal cord or brain injuries can lead to widespread loss of sensation, so take commonsense precautions like buckling your seatbelt and wearing protective headgear for biking, football, construction work, and so on.

Here are just a few tips for protecting your precious senses. These measures should be considered in addition to regular medical checkups, such as annual eye exams.

of gravity, movement, and position. Astronauts often become nauseated during their first days in space because their vestibular systems are confused. The vestibular system comprises fluid-filled organs in the inner ear: the *semicircular canals* and the nearby *vestibular sacs*. When the head tilts, fluid moves the hairlike receptors in these structures, causing neurons to fire, initiating a signal that travels to the cerebellum (transduction once again). Motion sickness, which many people experience on boats and roller coasters, is caused by conflicting information coming from the eyes and vestibular system. This is known as *sensory conflict theory* (Johnson, 2005).

Before we move on to the next section on perception, let's take a moment to appreciate the sensory systems that allow us to know and adapt to the surrounding world. How would you function without vision, hearing, smell, taste, and touch, and what steps can you take to preserve them (**Table 3.2**)?

Walk the Wire
Without his sense of kinesthesia, stuntman Nik Wallenda never would have crossed the Niagara Falls on an 1,800-foot tightrope. Kinesthesia enables us to know our body position and movement. AP Photo/The Canadian Press, Frank Gunn

✓ **show what you know**

1. The chemical sense called _____ provides the sensation of smell.

2. Chemicals from food are released in saliva, where they dissolve and bathe the taste buds. The chemicals find matching receptors and latch on, sparking action potentials. This is an example of:
   a. olfaction.
   b. transduction.
   c. sensory adaptation.
   d. thermoreceptors.

3. List five things you are currently doing that involve the use of kinesthesia.

4. Maya consulted her physician about severe back pain. In order to help her understand pain perception, the doctor recommended she consider _____, which suggests that a variety of biopsychosocial factors can interact to amplify or diminish pain perception.
   a. the theory of evolution
   b. an absolute threshold
   c. the gate-control theory
   d. gustation

 **✓** CHECK YOUR ANSWERS IN APPENDIX C.

Perception

We have learned how the sensory systems absorb information and transform it into the electrical and chemical language of neurons. Now let's look more closely at the next step: *perception,* which draws from experience to organize and interpret sensory information, turning sensory data into something meaningful. Perhaps the most important lesson you will learn in this section is that *perception is far from foolproof.* We don't see, hear, smell, taste, or feel the world exactly as it is, but as our brains judge it to be.

Illusions: The Mind's Imperfect Eye

What you see is not always what you get. Consider this experiment: Researchers asked a group of undergraduates studying *oenology* (the study of wine) to sample two beverages. One was a white wine, and the other was the exact same white wine—colored red with flavorless dye. When it came time to evaluate the aromas, the students used the standard white-wine adjectives (for example, honey and apple) to describe the white wine, and this came as no surprise. When asked to describe the "red wine," which was really the same white wine, the tasters used the standard red-wine adjectives (for example, raspberry and peppery; Morrot, Brochet, & Dubourdieu, 2001). It appeared they were tricked by their eyes! What they *saw* was red wine, so what they *perceived* were red wine aromas, even though they were not actually smelling red wine aromas. *Perception* is essential to our functioning, but as the wine-tasting example illustrates, it is sometimes misleading.

A great way to detect distortions in perceptual processes is to study illusions. An **illusion** is a perception that is incongruent with real sensory data, conveying an inaccurate representation of reality. Looking at perception when it is working "incorrectly" allows us to examine knowledge-based processing, which draws upon past experience to make sense of incoming information. If a clock stops ticking, you can open it up to see what's wrong and better understand how it works. Illusions serve a similar purpose. Let's examine one.

Look at the Müller-Lyer illusion in **Figure 3.7.** It appears lines (b) and (d) are longer, but in fact all four lines (a–d) are equal in length. Why does this illusion occur? Our experiences looking at buildings tell us that the corner presented in line (c) is nearer because it is jutting toward us. The corner presented in line (d) seems to be farther away because it is jutting away. Two objects that are the same size will project different images on the retina if one is farther away; the farther object will project a smaller image on the retina. People living in "carpentered worlds" (that is, surrounded by structures constructed with corners, angles, and straight lines, as opposed to living in more "traditional" settings) are more likely to be tricked by this illusion because of their experience seeing manufactured structures. People in more traditional settings, without all the hard edges and straight lines, are less likely to fall prey to such an illusion (Segall, Campbell, & Herskovits, 1968).

LOL :-)
When your friend texts you a smiley face, data-based processing enables you to see two dots, a hyphen, and a parenthesis. But how does your brain understand the collective meaning of these symbols? Through knowledge-based processing, you draw on past experience to make sense of the new information you encounter.
Mathias Wilson/Getty Images

FIGURE 3.7
The Müller-Lyer Illusion
Which line looks longer? They are actually the same length. Visual depth cues cause you to perceive that (b) and (d) are longer because they appear farther away.

(a)   (b)   (c)   (d)

Another visual illusion is *stroboscopic motion,* the appearance of motion produced when a sequence of still images are shown in rapid succession. (Think of drawing stick figures on the edges of book pages and then flipping the pages to see your figure "move.") The brain interprets this as movement. Even infants appear to perceive this kind of motion (Valenza, Leo, Gava, & Simion, 2006). Although illusions provide clues about how perception works, they cannot explain everything. Let's take a look at principles of perceptual organization, which provide universal guidelines on how we perceive our surroundings.

Stroboscopic
The golf club and golf ball seem to be moving because their images appear in rapid succession. Stroboscopic motion is an example of a visual illusion.
Vandystadt/Michael Hans/Science Source

Perceptual Organization

LO 13 Identify the principles of perceptual organization.

Many psychologists turn to the Gestalt (gə-'stält) psychologists to understand how perception works. Gestalt psychologists, who were active in Germany in the late 1800s and early 1900s, became interested in perception after observing illusions of motion. They wondered how stationary objects could be perceived as moving and thus attempted to explain how the human mind organizes stimuli in the environment. Noting the tendency for perception to be organized and complete, they realized that the whole is greater than the sum of its parts; the brain naturally organizes stimuli in their entirety rather than perceiving the parts and pieces. **Gestalt** means "whole" or "form" in German. The Gestalt psychologists, and others who followed, studied the principles that explain how the brain perceives objects in the environment as wholes or groups (**Infographic 3.4** on the next page).

One central idea illuminated by the Gestalt psychologists is the **figure-ground** principle (Fowlkes, Martin, & Malik, 2007). As you focus your attention on a figure (for example, the vase at right and in Infographic 3.4), all other features drop into the background. If, however, you direct your gaze onto the faces, the vase falls into the background with everything else. The figure and ground continually change as you shift your focus. Other gestalt organizational principles include the following:

- *Proximity*—Objects close to each other are perceived as a group.
- *Similarity*—Objects similar in shape or color are perceived as a group.
- *Connectedness*—Objects that are connected are perceived as a group.
- *Closure*—Gaps tend to be filled in if something isn't complete.
- *Continuity*—Parts tend to be perceived as members of a group if they head in the same direction.

Although these organizational principles have been demonstrated for vision, it is important to note that they apply to the other senses as well. Imagine a mother who can discern her child's voice amid the clamor of a busy playground: Her child's voice is the figure and the other noises are the ground.

Depth Perception

LO 14 Identify concepts involved in depth perception.

That same mother can tell that the slide extends from the front of the jungle gym, thanks to her brain's ability to pick up on cues about depth. How can a two-dimensional image projected on the retina be perceived in three dimensions? There appear to be inborn abilities and learned cues for perceiving depth and distance. Let's start by examining one inborn ability to recognize depth and its potential for danger. Watch out, baby.

illusion A perception incongruent with sensory data.

gestalt (gə-'stält) The natural tendency for the brain to organize stimuli into a whole, rather than perceiving the parts and pieces.

figure-ground A central principle of Gestalt psychology, involving the shifting of focus; as attention is focused on one object, all other features drop or recede into the background.

Gestalt Organizing Principles: The Whole is Greater

The Gestalt psychologists identified principles that explain how the brain naturally organizes sensory information into meaningful wholes rather than distinct parts and pieces. These principles help you navigate the world by allowing you to see, for example, that the path you are walking on continues on the other side of an intersection. Gestalt principles also help you make sense of the information presented in your textbooks. Let's look at how this works.

figure-ground

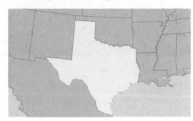

We tend to perceive visual stimuli as figures existing on a background. On this map, one area becomes the focus, while the rest functions as background context.

Some stimuli, such as this classic figure-ground vase, are *reversible figures*. You see something different depending on whether you focus on the yellow or the black portion.

LAW OF proximity

We tend to perceive objects that are near each other as a unit. This set of dots is perceived as three groups rather than six separate columns or 36 individual dots.

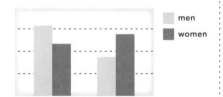

men
women

Proximity helps us read graphs like this one. We understand that bars close together should be compared.

LAW OF similarity

We see objects as a group if they share features such as color or shape. In this example, we perceive eight vertical columns rather than four rows of alternating squares and dots.

Canada
U.S.
Mexico

0   5   10   15   20   25

Similarity helps us read color-coded charts and graphs. We understand the graph above as having horizontal bars because we naturally group the similarly colored icons.

LAW OF connectedness

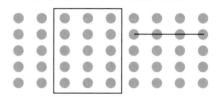

We tend to see objects as a group if there is something that connects them. In this group of dots, the ones enclosed in or connected by lines appear related even though all dots are the same.

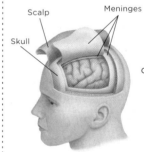

Scalp
Meninges
Skull

In a textbook figure, connectedness helps us understand what is being labeled.

LAW OF closure

We tend to fill in incomplete parts of a line or figure. In this example, we perceive a circle even when the line is broken.

Closure allows us to read letters and images that are interrupted. We can read this letter even though it is made up of unconnected lines.

LAW OF continuity

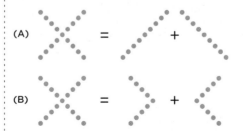

(A)
(B)

We perceive groups where objects appear to be going in the same direction. In this example, we perceive the figure as made up of two continuous lines that intersect (A) rather than two angles that are brought together (B).

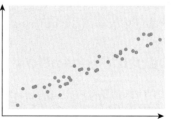

Continuity helps us read graphs like this scatterplot, where we perceive the overall pattern.

VISUAL CLIFF In order to determine whether **depth perception** is innate or learned, researchers studied the behavior of babies approaching a "visual cliff," a flat, clear glass surface with a checkered tablecloth-like pattern directly underneath that gives the illusion of a drop-off (Gibson & Walk,1960). The researchers placed infants ages 6 to 14 months at the edge of the glass. At the other end of the glass were the babies' mothers, coaxing them to crawl over. For the most part, the children refused to move toward what they perceived to be a drop-off, suggesting that the perception of depth was innate. Without ever having explored the edge of an actual abyss, these infants seemed instinctively to know it should be avoided.

BINOCULAR CUES Some cues for perceiving depth are the result of information gathered by both eyes. **Binocular cues** provide information from the right and left eyes to help judge depth and distance. For example, **convergence** is the brain's interpretation of the tension (or lack thereof) in the eye muscles that direct where both eyes focus. If an object is close, there is more muscular tension (as the muscles turn our eyes inward toward our nose), and the object is perceived as near. This perception of distance is based on experience; throughout life, we have learned that the more muscular tension, the closer an object. Let's take a moment and feel that tension.

Point your finger up to the ceiling at arm's length with both eyes open. Now slowly bring your finger close to your nose. Can you feel tension and strain in your eye muscles? Your brain uses this type of convergence cue to determine distance.

> **try this**

Another binocular cue is **retinal disparity,** which is the difference between the images seen by the right and left eyes. The greater the difference, the closer the object. The more similar the two images, the farther the object. With experience, our brains begin using these image disparities to judge distance. The following Try This provides an example of retinal disparity.

Hold your index finger about 4 inches in front of your face pointing up to the ceiling. Quickly open your right eye as you are closing your left eye, alternating this activity for a few seconds; it should appear as if your finger is jumping back and forth. Now do the same thing, but this time with your finger out at arm's length. The image does not seem to be jumping as much.

> **try this**

depth perception The ability to perceive three-dimensional objects and judge distances.

binocular cues Information gathered from both eyes to help judge depth and distance.

convergence A binocular cue used to judge distance and depth based on the tension of the muscles that direct where the eyes are focusing.

retinal disparity A binocular cue that uses the difference between the images the two eyes see to determine the distance of objects.

Monocular Cues
You can gauge the distance and depth in this photo with at least four types of monocular cues: (1) People that are farther away look smaller (relative size). (2) The two sides of the street start out parallel but converge as distance increases (linear perspective). (3) The trees in the front block those that are behind (interposition). (4) Textures are more apparent for closer objects (texture gradient). Yoan Valat/epa/Corbis

MONOCULAR CUES Judgments about depth and distance can also be informed by **monocular cues,** which do not necessitate the use of both eyes. An artist who paints pictures can transform a white canvas into a three-dimensional perceptual experience by using techniques that take advantage of monocular cues. The monocular cues include (but are not limited to) the following:

- *Relative Size*—If two objects are similar in actual size, but one is farther away, it appears to be smaller. We interpret the larger object as being closer.
- *Linear Perspective*—When two lines start off parallel, then come together, where they converge appears farther away than where they are parallel.
- *Interposition*—When one object is in front of another, it partially blocks the view of the other object, and this partially blocked object appears more distant.
- *Texture Gradient*—When objects are closer, it is easier to see their texture. As they get farther away, the texture becomes less visible. The more apparent the texture, the closer the object appears.

Perceptual Constancy and Perceptual Set

All these perceptual skills are great—if you are standing still—but the world around us is constantly moving. How do our perceptual systems adapt to changes? We possess the ability to perceive objects as having constant properties, although our environments are constantly changing. **Perceptual constancy** refers to the tendency to perceive objects as maintaining their shape, size, and color even when the angle, lighting, and distance change. A door is shaped like a rectangle, but when it opens, the image projected on our retina is not a rectangle. Yet, we still perceive the door as having a rectangular shape. This is called **shape constancy.** As you gaze on cars and trucks from the window of an airplane, they may look like bugs scurrying around, but you know some are as big as elephants because your perceptual toolkit includes **size constancy.** Through experience, we get to know the size of everyday objects and perceive them accordingly, regardless of whether they are far or near. Similarly, **color constancy** allows us to see the world in stable colors, even when the sensory data arriving at our photoreceptors change. A bright red backpack appears bright red outside in the sunshine or inside a house. The light waves bouncing off of the backpack have changed, but your understanding of the color has not been altered.

Although examples of these organizational tendencies occur with robust regularity, some of these perceptual skills are not necessarily universal, as the Müller-Lyer illusion

Once a Rectangle, Always a Rectangle
How do you know that all these doors are the same size and shape? The images projected onto your retina suggest that the opened doors are narrower, nonrectangular shapes. Your brain, however, knows from experience that all the opened doors are identical rectangles. This phenomenon is known as shape constancy. Getty Images/Image Source

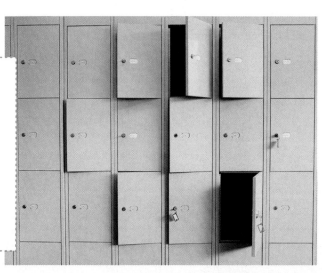

demonstrates. Some studies suggest that children *learn* to perceive size constancy (Granrud, 2009), and this skill may not develop properly when children are deprived of certain types of stimuli.

Learning also plays a role in the phenomenon of **perceptual set**—the tendency to perceive stimuli in a specific manner based on past experiences and expectations. If someone handed you a picture of two women and said, "This is a mother with her daughter," you would be more likely to rate them as looking alike than if you had been given the exact same picture and told, "These women are unrelated." Indeed, research shows that people who believe they are looking at parent–child pairs are more likely to rate the pairs as similar than those who believe the members of the pairs are not related (even though they are looking at the same adult–child pairs; Oda, Matsumoto-Oda, & Kurashima, 2005). In short, we tend to see what we are looking for.

Perceptual sets are molded by the context of the moment. If you hear the word "sects" in a TV news report about feuding religious groups, you are unlikely to think the reporter is saying "sex" even though "sects" and "sex" sound the same. Similarly, if you see a baby swaddled in a blue blanket, you are probably more likely to assume it's a boy than a girl. Studies show that expectancies about male or female infants influence viewers' perceptions of gender (Stern & Karraker, 1989). Simply labeling infants as *premature* or *full-term* will shape people's attitudes about them (Porter, Stern, & Zak-Place, 2009).

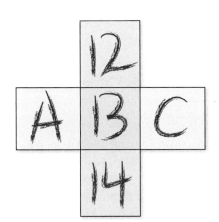

Letters or Numbers?
Look in the green square. What do you see? That depends on whether you viewed the symbol as belonging to a row of letters (A B C) or a column of numbers (12 13 14). Perceptions are shaped by the context in which a stimulus occurs, and our expectations about that stimulus.

Although our perceptual sets may not always lead to the right conclusions, they do help us organize the vast amount of information flooding our senses. But can perception exist in the absence of sensation? In other words, is it possible to perceive something without seeing, hearing, smelling, tasting, or feeling it?

Extrasensory Perception: Where's the Evidence?

LO 15 Define extrasensory perception and explain why psychologists dismiss claims of its legitimacy.

Have you ever had a dream that actually came to pass? Perhaps you have heard of psychics who claim that they can read people's "auras" and decipher their thoughts. **Extrasensory perception (ESP)** is this purported ability to obtain information about the world without any sensory stimuli. And when we say "no sensory input," we are not referring to sights, sounds, smells, tastes, and feelings occurring subliminally, or below absolute thresholds. We mean absolutely no measurable sensory data. The study of these kinds of phenomena is called **parapsychology.**

monocular cues Depth and distance cues that require the use of only one eye.

perceptual constancy The tendency to perceive objects in our environment as stable in terms of shape, size, and color, regardless of changes in the sensory data received.

shape constancy An object is perceived as maintaining its shape, regardless of the image projected on the retina.

size constancy An object is perceived as maintaining its size, regardless of the image projected on the retina.

color constancy Objects are perceived as maintaining their color, even with changing sensory data.

perceptual set The tendency to perceive stimuli in a specific manner based on past experiences and expectations.

extrasensory perception (ESP) The purported ability to obtain information about the world without any sensory stimuli.

parapsychology The study of extrasensory perception.

CONNECTIONS

The importance of replicating experiments was discussed in **Chapter 1.** The more a study is replicated and produces similar findings, the more confident we can be in them; replication is a key step in the scientific method. If similar results cannot be reproduced using the same methods, then the original findings may have resulted from chance or experimenter bias.

... THERE IS NO SCIENTIFIC EVIDENCE TO SUPPORT ITS EXISTENCE.

Mother and Daughters
Liz and her eldest daughter Sarah (back left) relax with the triplets: Zoe (front left), Emma (front right), and Sophie (back right). Zoe and Emma currently attend the Texas School for the Blind and Visually Impaired, while Sophie goes to school in the local district.
Worldwide Features/Barcroft Media/Landov

THINK again

Extrasensory Perception

 ESP, psychic powers, the sixth sense—call it what you will, there is no scientific evidence to support its existence (Farha, 2007; Wiseman & Watt, 2006). Nevertheless, a handful of respected researchers have published research suggesting it exists. In 2011, Cornell University's Daryl Bem set off a firestorm of controversy with a journal article offering evidence for ESP. The article, which reported nine experiments involving some 1,000 participants, suggested that human beings have the ability to predict the future (Bem, 2011). Other psychologists pointed out flaws in Bem's statistical analysis (Wagenmakers, Wetzels, Borsboom, & van der Maas, 2011), which Bem then defended (Bem, Utts, & Johnson, 2011). The research was further called into question in 2012, when a team of scientists tried to replicate Bem's results using his same methodology and failed (Ritchie, Wiseman, & French, 2012).

Despite ESP's lack of scientific credibility, many people remain firm believers. Most often, their "evidence" comes in the form of personal anecdotes. Aunt Tilly predicted she was going to win the lottery based on a dream she had one night, and when she did win, it was "proof" of her ESP abilities. This is an example of what psychologists might call an *illusory correlation,* an apparent link between variables that are not closely related at all. Aunt Tilly dreamed she won the lottery, but so did 1,000 other people around the country, and they didn't win—what about that evidence? Although some may find the idea of ESP compelling, you should be *very* skeptical about it, because there is no reliable data to back it up (Farha, 2007; Wiseman & Watt, 2006). 💬+

More interesting than ESP, we would argue, are the remarkable (and real) stories of people who thrive despite difficulties with sensation and perception. Are you wondering what became of Emma, Zoe, and Sophie?

MOVING FORWARD   When the triplets were about 5 years old, Liz and her husband got a divorce, and Liz faced the daunting task of caring for four young children. Today, Sarah is a high school graduate, Emma and Zoe study at the prestigious Texas School for the Blind and Visually Impaired, and Sophie is holding her own in the public school system. Liz operates her own business and recently wed her true love from two decades past.

With the love and support of family, Emma and Zoe have made significant strides in their social and linguistic skills. Both can communicate with about 50 signs, but they understand many more and are building their vocabulary all the time. As for Sophie, having limited vision has enabled her to take classes alongside sighted children. 📁

  show what you know

1. _____ means the "whole" or "form" in German.

2. One binocular cue called _____ is based on the brain's interpretation of the tension in muscles of the eyes.
   a. convergence
   b. retinal disparity
   c. interposition
   d. relative size

3. Using what you have learned so far in the textbook, how would you try to convince a friend that extrasensory perception does not exist?

4. Have you ever noticed how the shape of a door seems to change as it opens and closes, yet you know its actual shape remains the same? The term _____ refers to the fact that even though sensory stimuli may change, we know that objects do not change their shape, size, or color.
   a. perceptual set
   b. perceptual constancy
   c. convergence
   d. texture-gradient

✓ CHECK YOUR ANSWERS IN APPENDIX C.

summary of concepts ③

LO 1 Define sensation and perception and explain how they are different. (p. 88)

Sensation is the manner in which physical stimuli are received and detected. Perception gives meaning to the information the sensory receptors receive. Data-based processing describes how the brain takes basic sensory information and processes the incoming stimuli. Knowledge-based processing utilizes our past experiences and knowledge in order to understand sensory information.

LO 2 Define transduction and explain how it relates to sensation. (p. 89)

Sensory organs receive stimuli from the environment (for example, sound waves, light energy). The transformation of these stimuli into neural signals is known as transduction. The neural signals are then processed by the central nervous system, resulting in what we consciously experience as sensations.

LO 3 Describe and differentiate between absolute thresholds and difference thresholds. (p. 90)

One of the important goals of studying sensation and perception is to determine absolute thresholds, the weakest stimuli that can be detected 50% of the time. Difference thresholds indicate the minimum difference between two stimuli noticed 50% of the time. Weber's law states the ratios that determine these difference thresholds. The ability to detect weak signals in the environment is based on many factors.

LO 4 Explain how electromagnetic energy is transduced into a sensation of vision. (p. 94)

For vision, light is transduced into neural activity. The neural signals are processed by the central nervous system, resulting in visual experiences. The wavelength of the light shining on objects and reflecting back at our eyes determines the color. Our experience or perception of color results from the interaction between the light in our environment and the activities in our brains.

LO 5 Describe the function of rods and cones. (p. 98)

Rods are photoreceptors in the retina that are extremely sensitive to light. Rods do not provide the sensation of color. Cones, also in the retina, are responsible for our sensation of color and our ability to see the details of objects. Cones are not used when ambient light is low. Cones are concentrated in the fovea.

LO 6 Compare and contrast the theories of color vision. (p. 100)

The trichromatic theory of color vision suggests there are three types of cones, each sensitive to particular wavelengths in the red, green, and blue spectrums. The three types of cones fire in response to different electromagnetic wavelengths. The opponent-process theory of color vision suggests that in addition to the color-sensitive cones, we also have neurons that respond differently to opponent colors (for example, red–green, blue–yellow).

LO 7 Summarize how sound waves are transduced into the sensation of hearing. (p. 102)

Audition is the term used for the sense of hearing. When we hear, we are sensing sound waves, which are rhythmic vibrations of molecules traveling through a variety of forms of matter (including air). The cochlea is a fluid-filled, snail-shaped organ of the inner ear. When the oval window vibrates, it causes the fluid in the cochlea to move. The cochlea is lined with the basilar membrane, which contains hair cells. When the fluid moves, the hairs lining the basilar membrane bend in response. The hair cells cause the nerve cells nearby to fire, sending neural messages through the auditory nerve to the auditory cortex via the thalamus.

LO 8 Illustrate how we sense different pitches of sound. (p. 107)

Place theory suggests that the location of neural activity along the cochlea allows us to sense different pitches of high-frequency sounds. With a high-frequency sound, vibrations occur closer to the end of the basilar membrane near the oval window. Frequency theory suggests that the frequency of the neural impulses determines the experience of pitch. The entire basilar membrane vibrates at the same rate as the sound wave; the neural impulses occur at this same rate. The frequency theory explains how we perceive the pitch of sounds from 20 to 400 Hz. The volley principle explains our perception of the different pitches between 400 and 4,000 Hz. And, the place theory explains our perception of pitches from 4,000 to 20,000 Hz.

LO 9 Describe the process of olfaction. (p. 109)

The chemical sense referred to as olfaction provides the sensation of smell. Molecules from odor-emitting objects in our environments make their way into our nostrils up through the nose or mouth. The olfactory epithelium is home to millions of olfactory receptor neurons, which provide receptors for odor molecules.

LO 10 Discuss the structures involved in taste and describe how they work. (p. 111)

Gustation is the sense of taste. The receptor cells for taste are located in the taste buds, which are located on the tongue, the roof of the mouth, and inside the mouth on the cheeks. Taste buds are embedded in the papillae on the tongue. Jutting from each of these buds are 50 to 100 taste receptor cells. Taste is essential to the survival of species. Tastes push organisms toward needed foods and away from harmful ones.

LO 11 Describe how the biopsychosocial perspective is used to understand pain. (p. 115)

The biopsychosocial perspective explains the perception of pain by exploring biological, psychological, and social factors. This multilevel method examines how these factors play a role in the experience of pain. According to the gate-control theory, how the brain interprets pain will either increase or decrease the perception of pain. Neural activity makes its way to the brain, where it is processed. The brain is capable of blocking pain by sending a message through the interneurons to "close the gate" so the pain won't be felt.

LO 12 Illustrate how we sense the position and movement of our bodies. (p. 116)

Kinesthesia is the sense of position and movement of the body, including body parts. We are aware of where the parts of our bodies are in space because of specialized nerve endings called proprioceptors, which are primarily located in the muscles and joints. Our proprioceptors monitor changes in the position of body parts and the tension in our muscles. The vestibular sense helps us deal with the effects of gravity, movement, and body position to keep us balanced.

LO 13 Identify the principles of perceptual organization. (p. 119)

Gestalt psychologists sought to explain how the human mind organizes stimuli from the environment. They realized the whole is greater than the sum of its parts, meaning the brain naturally organizes stimuli as a whole rather than parts and pieces. Gestalt indicates a tendency for human perception to be organized and complete. The organizational principles include: proximity, similarity, connectedness, closure, and continuity.

LO 14 Identify concepts involved in depth perception. (p. 119)

Depth perception appears partially to be an innate ability. Children in the visual cliff experiment, for example, refuse to move toward what they perceive to be a drop-off. Binocular cues use information gathered from both eyes to help judge depth and distance. Monocular cues can be used by either eye alone and also help judge depth and distance.

LO 15 Define extrasensory perception and explain why psychologists dismiss claims of its legitimacy. (p. 123)

Extrasensory perception (ESP) is the purported ability to obtain information about the world without any sensory stimuli. The study of these kinds of phenomena is called parapsychology. There is no scientific evidence to back up claims of ESP and other parapsychology phenomena.

key terms

TEST PREP are you ready?

1. Stimuli are detected through the process called:
   a. perception.
   b. data-based processing.
   c. sensation.
   d. knowledge-based processing.

2. You're listening to music on your iPod. The sound waves transmitted through the earbuds lead to vibrations in the fluid in your cochlea. This activity causes the hair cells to bend, which causes nearby nerve cells to fire. This process of transforming stimuli into electrical and chemical signals of neurons is:
   a. transduction.
   b. perception.
   c. knowledge-based processing.
   d. convergence.

3. According to signal detection theory, our ability to detect weak stimuli in the environment is based on many factors, including which of the following?
   a. characteristics of the experimenter
   b. fatigue and motivation
   c. false alarms
   d. hits

4. While rollerblading outside, you get something in your eye. As the day goes on, your eye still feels irritated. It is possible you've scratched your _____, which is the transparent outer layer, the function of which is to protect the eye and bend light to help focus light waves.
   a. lens   b. retina
   c. iris   d. cornea

5. The blind spot of the retina lacks _____ because it is the location where the optic nerve exits the retina.
   a. binocular cues   b. rods and cones
   c. interposition   d. feature detectors

6. In color vision, the opponent-process theory was developed to explain the _____, which could not be explained by the _____ theory.
   a. afterimage effect; trichromatic
   b. blind spot; place
   c. feature detectors; trichromatic
   d. color deficiencies; frequency

7. A developmental psychologist is interested in studying children's _____, which is the term we use for the sense of hearing.
   a. wavelength   b. amplitude
   c. pitch   d. audition

8. Frequency theory of pitch perception suggests it is the number of _____ that allows us to perceive differences in pitch.
   a. sound waves greater than 1,000 Hz
   b. the timbre
   c. neural impulses firing
   d. the amplitude

9. One large study conducted in the United States by Shargorodsky and colleagues (2012) found hearing loss in what percentage of teenagers?
   a. 5%   b. 20%
   c. 50%   d. 65%

10. The wiring of the olfactory system is unique, because other sensory systems relay data through the _____ before information is passed along to higher brain centers, but this is not the case for olfactory information.
    a. thalamus   b. corpus callosum
    c. reticular formation d. basilar membrane

11. _____ specialize in recognizing specific characteristics of your visual experience, such as angles, lines, and movements.
    a. Feature detectors   b. Rods
    c. Cones   d. Photoreceptors

12. We are aware of where the parts of our bodies are in space because of specialized nerve endings called _____, which are primarily located in the joints and muscles.
    a. proprioceptors   b. Meissner's corpuscles
    c. Pacinian corpuscles d. nociceptors

13. Hector is staring at the small print on the back of a credit card. Which of the following would be a binocular cue to indicate how close the credit card is to his face?
    a. tension of the muscles focusing the eyes
    b. relative size of two similar objects
    c. two lines initially some distance apart coming together
    d. interposition

14. One of the gestalt organizational principles suggests that objects close to each other are perceived as a group. This is known as:
    a. continuity.   b. closure.
    c. similarity.   d. proximity.

15. When two objects are similar in actual size and one of these objects is farther away than the other, the object at a distance appears to be smaller than the closer object. This is a monocular cue called:
    a. linear perspective.   b. interposition.
    c. relative size.   d. texture gradient.

16. Use the evolutionary perspective of psychology to explain the importance of any two aspects of human taste.

17. How is extrasensory perception different from the perception of subliminal stimuli?

18. The transformation of a sound wave into the experience of something heard follows a complicated path. To better understand the process, draw a diagram starting with a sound in the environment and ending with the sound heard by an individual.

19. Why does placing ice on a sore shoulder stop the pain?

20. Describe the difference between absolute threshold and difference threshold.

✓ CHECK YOUR ANSWERS IN APPENDIX C.

4

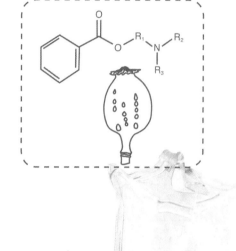

iStock Vectors/Getty Images

consciousness

An Introduction to Consciousness

MIND-ALTERING MEDICINE   Robert Julien, M.D., did not choose a typical 9-to-5 job. His profession involves paralyzing people, interfering with their memory formation, and numbing their senses—but only temporarily. Dr. Julien is an *anesthesiologist,* a medical doctor whose primary responsibility is to monitor a patient's vital functions (for example, respiration and pulse) and manage pain before, during, and after surgery. With the help of powerful drugs that manipulate the nervous system, Dr. Julien has eased the pain and anxiety of over 30,000 patients undergoing procedures that otherwise could have been very unpleasant.

In ancient times, people may have sought pain relief by dipping their wounds in cold rivers and streams. They concocted mixtures of crushed roots, barks, herbs, fruits, and flowers to ease pain and induce sleep in surgical patients (Keys, 1945). Many of the plant chemicals discovered by these early peoples are still given to patients today, although in slightly different forms. Opium was used by the ancient Egyptians (El Ansary, Steigerwald, & Esser, 2003), and its chemical relatives are used by modern-day physicians and hospitals all over the world (for example, *morphine* for pain relief and *codeine* for cough suppression).

Seasoned Anesthesiologist
Dr. Robert Julien is an anesthesiologist, a physician who keeps patients comfortable and monitors their vital signs during surgery. Anesthesiologists administer drugs that interfere with pain, paralyze the muscles, and induce a sleeplike state. How these substances alter consciousness is still somewhat mysterious (Geddes, 2011, November 29). Judith Julien

Nevertheless, it took many centuries for anesthesia to become a regular part of surgery. Before the mid-1800s, surgery was so painful that patients writhed and screamed on operating tables, sometimes held down by four or five people (Bynum, 2007). During the Mexican-American War, a band would play when Mexican soldiers had their limbs amputated so the men's cries would not be heard by others (Aldrete, Marron, & Wright, 1984). The only anesthetic available may have been whiskey, wine, or a firm blow to the head that literally knocked the patient out. Fortunately, the science of anesthesia has come a long way. It is now possible to have a tooth extracted or a mole removed without a twinge of discomfort. A patient undergoing open heart surgery can lie peacefully as surgeons pry open his chest and poke around with their instruments, then leave the hospital with no memory of the actual operation. But anesthesia is a curious thing. Drugs used to ease pain and anxiety also influence sensations, perceptions, and one's awareness of self and the environment: They can dramatically alter "conscious" experiences. 🗂

Ancient Opium
Wall art from the Tomb of Horemheb in Egypt's Valley of the Kings depicts a person holding two round vessels representing poppy flowers. The ancient Egyptians used the poppy opiate morphine for pain relief, but its therapeutic role was controversial (El Ansary et al., 2003).
© Gianni Dagli Orti/Corbis

Note: Unless otherwise specified, quotations attributed to Dr. Robert Julien and Matt Utesch are personal communications.

LO 1   Define consciousness.

Consciousness is a concept that can be difficult to pinpoint. Psychologist G. William Farthing offers a good starting point: **Consciousness** is "the subjective state of being currently aware of something either within oneself or outside of oneself" (1992, p. 6). Consciousness is best defined as the state of being aware of oneself, one's thoughts, and/or the environment. According to this definition of subjective awareness, one can be asleep and still be aware (Farthing, 1992). Consider this example: You are dreaming about a siren blaring and you wake up to discover it is your alarm clock; you were clearly asleep but aware at the same time, as the sound registered in your brain. This ability to remain aware while asleep was especially useful for our primitive ancestors, who needed to be vigilant about dangers day and night.

Consciousness and Memory

Several years ago, Dr. Julien had a patient who didn't want to have general anesthesia during her hysterectomy, an operation to remove the uterus. Anesthesiologists typically put patients "to sleep" for hysterectomies, but Dr. Julien agreed to honor the patient's unusual request. He gave her a drug called Versed (midazolam) to help her relax, but not enough to knock her out. (Versed belongs to a class of calming drugs called *depressants*, which you will learn about later.) The woman seemed to be wide awake throughout the $2^1/_2$-hour procedure, chatting with doctors and nurses and even requesting that certain music be played in the operating room (much to the dismay of the surgical team).

CONNECTIONS

In **Chapter 1,** we introduced the evolutionary perspective. The adaptive trait to remain aware even while asleep has evolved through natural selection, allowing our ancestors to defend against predators and other dangerous situations.

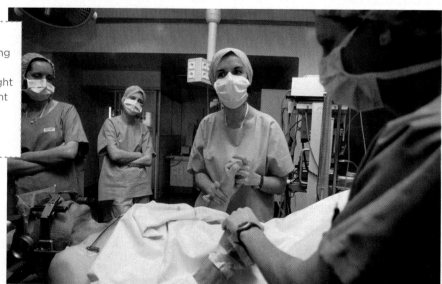

Comfortably Numb
A patient lies awake on the operating table as doctors stimulate his brain with electrical currents. With the right combination of anesthetics, a patient can be wide awake yet feel no pain and form no lasting memory of the procedure. © ASTIER

consciousness The state of being aware of oneself, one's thoughts, and/or the environment; includes various levels of conscious awareness.

At 11:00 P.M. that night, a nurse called Dr. Julien saying the patient was furious that he had used general anesthesia during the operation (which he had not done). The drug Dr. Julien had used to help the patient relax can also cause memory loss for events experienced while under its influence. Unable to remember the surgery, the patient logically assumed she had been given general anesthesia. "I went to the hospital at midnight to explain to the patient that I had honored her request and that she had been wide awake during the procedure but was unable to form memory proteins because the Versed had blocked their formation," Dr. Julien explained. In other words, the Versed had interfered with the production of a protein needed for memory creation. "To this day, I'm not sure she ever accepted my explanation or forgave me for taking away any memory of the procedure" (Julien & DiCecco, 2010, p. 11).

Would you say Dr. Julien's patient was conscious during the operation? If consciousness is a "subjective state of being currently aware" (Farthing, 1992, p. 6), then it would appear she was conscious during the surgery. She was alert and talking, yet her awareness of the event vanished within hours. Was this a problem with her consciousness or her memory? Although memory plays an important role in conscious processes, it is not equivalent to consciousness. The patient appeared to be "aware" during the procedure, but later had no memory of the event. As Dr. Julien explained to her, a failure occurred in the process involved in memory formation, perhaps in the *encoding* or *storage* of the event (Chapter 6).

Millions of Americans suffer from memory problems similar to that experienced by Dr. Julien's patient. They are aware, alert, and able to have meaningful conversations, yet they cannot form new memories because they suffer from Alzheimer's (Chapter 6) or another form of dementia. There are also people who cannot form memories because they are taking consciousness-altering drugs. In very rare cases, people taking certain types of prescription sleeping pills have been known to "sleep drive," or get behind the wheel in a trancelike state (Dolder & Nelson, 2008; Southworth, Kortepeter, & Hughes, 2008; Zammit, 2009).

Studying Consciousness

The field of psychology began with the study of consciousness. Wilhelm Wundt and his disciple Edward Titchener founded psychology as a science based on exploring consciousness and its contents. Another early psychologist, William James, regarded consciousness as a "stream" that provides a sense of day-to-day continuity (James, 1890/1983). Think about how this "river" of thoughts is constantly rushing through your head. An e-mail from an old friend appears in your inbox, jogging your memory of the birthday party she threw last month, and that reminds you that tomorrow is your *mother's* birthday (better not forget that one), and you need to swing by the store to pick up a gift. You notice your shoe is untied, think about school starting tomorrow, and remember the utility bill sitting on the counter, all within a matter of seconds. Thoughts interweave and overtake each other like currents of flowing water; sometimes they are connected by topic, emotion, events, but other times they don't seem to be connected by anything other than your stream of consciousness.

Although psychology started with the introspective study of consciousness, American psychologists John Watson, B. F. Skinner, and other behaviorists insisted that the science of psychology should restrict itself to the study of observable behaviors. This attitude persisted until the 1950s and 1960s, when psychology underwent a revolution of sorts. Researchers began to direct their focus back on the unseen mechanisms of the mind. *Cognitive psychology*, the scientific study of conscious processes such as thinking, problem solving, and language, emerged as a major subfield.

◢ **CONNECTIONS**

In **Chapter 1,** we discussed the contributions of these early psychologists. Wundt founded the first psychology laboratory, edited the first psychological journal, and used experimentation to measure psychological processes. Titchener was particularly interested in examining consciousness and the "atoms" of the mind.

Behavior, Behavior, Behavior
B. F. Skinner works with a pigeon in the laboratory. A die-hard behaviorist, Skinner believed that psychology should restrict itself to the study of observable behaviors. Consciousness and other unseen mental activities were beyond the realm of psychological research.
Sam Falk/Science Source

Today, understanding consciousness is an important goal of psychology, and many believe science can be used to investigate its mysteries.

Advanced technology for examining brain processes and functions has added to our growing knowledge of consciousness, but barriers to studying it remain. One is that consciousness is subjective, pertaining only to the individual who experiences it. Thus, it is impossible to *objectively* study another's conscious experience (Blackmore, 2005; Farthing, 1992). To make matters more complicated, one's consciousness changes from moment to moment. Right now you are concentrating on these words, but in a few seconds you might be thinking of something else or slip into light sleep. In spite of these challenges, researchers around the world are inching closer to understanding consciousness by studying it from many perspectives. Welcome to the world of consciousness and its many shades of gray.

The Nature of Consciousness

There are many elements of conscious experience, including desire, thought, language, sensation, perception, knowledge of self, and of course memory, as conscious experiences usually involve the retrieval of memories. Simply stated, any cognitive process is potentially a part of your conscious experience. Let's look at what this means, for example, when you go shopping on the Internet. Your ability to navigate from page to page hinges on your recognition of visual images (*Is that the PayPal home page or my e-mail log-in?*), language aptitude (for reading), and motor skills (for typing and clicking). While browsing products, you access various memories (which link you just clicked, the shoes you saw last week, and so on)—all of this is part of your consciousness, your stream of thought.

CONNECTIONS

In **Chapter 1,** we presented the concept of objective reports, which are free of opinions, beliefs, expectations, and values. Here, we note that descriptions of consciousness are more subjective in nature, and do not lend themselves to objective reporting.

try this

Stop reading and listen. Do you hear background sounds you didn't notice before—a soft breeze rustling through the curtains or a car passing by? *You* may not have picked up on these sounds, but your brain was keeping tabs. You are constantly monitoring all this activity whether you are aware of it or not. It happens *automatically*.

LO 2   Explain how automatic processing relates to consciousness.

AUTOMATIC PROCESSING   In describing consciousness, psychologists often distinguish between cognitive processes that occur *automatically* (without effort, awareness, or control) and cognitive activity that requires us to focus our attention on specific sensory input (with effort and awareness, we choose what to attend to and where to direct our focus). Our sensory systems absorb an enormous amount of information, and the brain must sift through this data and determine what is important and needs immediate attention, what can be ignored, and what can be processed and stored for later use. This **automatic processing** allows information to be collected and saved (at least temporarily) with little or no conscious effort (McCarthy & Skowronski, 2011; Schmidt-Daffy, 2011). Without automatic processing, we would be overwhelmed with data. Just imagine having to manage your brain's behind-the-scenes responsibilities (for example, keeping track of your heart rate or filtering unimportant noises) while taking a psychology midterm exam.

Automatic processing can also refer to the involuntary cognitive activity guiding some behaviors. We are seemingly able to behave and act without focusing our attention. Behaviors seem to occur without intentional awareness, and without getting in the way of our other activities (Hassin, Bargh, & Zimerman, 2009). Do you remember the last time you drove your car on a familiar route, daydreaming the entire time? Somehow you arrived at your destination without noticing much about your driving, the traffic, and

CONNECTIONS

In **Chapter 3,** we introduced the concept of *sensory adaptation,* which is the tendency to become less sensitive to and less aware of constant stimuli after a period of time. This better prepares us to detect changes in the environment, which can signal important activities that require our attention. Here, we see how this can occur through automatic processing.

Automatic Processing
Do you recall dropping your keys in your bag this morning? Many routine activities, such as putting away keys and locking the door, occur without our awareness. We might not remember these events because we never gave them our attention in the first place. Ariel Skelley/Blend/Getty Images

so forth. Or have you ever been listening to music while cleaning the kitchen, and then realized you were almost finished without once being aware that you had scrubbed the countertop or mopped the floor? You were conscious enough to complete complex tasks, but not enough to realize that you were doing so.

Although unconscious processes direct various behaviors, we can also make conscious decisions about where to focus our attention. While walking to class you might focus intently on a conversation you just had with your friend or an exam you will take in an hour. With this type of conscious activity, we deliberately channel or direct our attention.

LO 3   Describe how we narrow our focus through selective attention.

SELECTIVE ATTENTION   Although we have access to a vast amount of information in our internal and external environments, we can only focus our attention on a small portion at one time. This narrow focus on specific stimuli is known as **selective attention.** Talking to someone in a crowded room, you are able to block out the chatter and noise around you and immerse yourself in the conversation. This efficient use of selective attention is known as the *cocktail-party effect* (Koch, Lawo, Fels, & Vorländer, 2011). Studies suggest selective attention can be influenced by emotions. Anger, for example, increases our ability to selectively attend to something or someone (Finucane, 2011). So too does repeated exposure to important stimuli (Brascamp, Blake, & Kristjánsson, 2011). We also get better at ignoring distractions as we age (Couperus, 2011).

This doesn't mean other information goes undetected (remember we are constantly gathering data through automatic processing). Our tendency is to adapt to continuous input, and ignore the unimportant sensory stimuli that bombard us every moment. We are designed to pay attention to abrupt, unexpected changes in the environment, and to stimuli that are unfamiliar or especially strong (Bahrick & Newell, 2008; Daffner et al., 2007; Parmentier & Andrés, 2010). Imagine you are studying in a busy courtyard. You are aware the environment is bustling with activity, but you fail to pay attention to every person—until something changes (someone yells, for example). Then your attention might be directed to that novelty.

automatic processing Detection, encoding, and sometimes storage of information without conscious effort or awareness.

selective attention The ability to focus awareness on a small segment of information that is available through our sensory systems.

What Umbrella?
In an elegant demonstration of *inattentional blindness,* researchers asked a group of participants to watch a video of men passing around a basketball. As the participants kept careful tabs on the players' passes, a semi-transparent image of a woman with an umbrella appeared among them. Only 21% of the participants (1 out of 5) even noticed; the others had been focusing their attention elsewhere (Most et al., 2001).

INATTENTIONAL BLINDNESS   Selective attention is great if you need to study for a psychology test while others are watching a movie, but it can also be dangerous. Suppose a friend sends you a hilarious text message while you are walking toward a busy intersection. Thinking about the text can momentarily steal your attention away from signs of danger, like a car turning right on red without stopping. While distracted by the text message, you might step into the intersection—without seeing the car turning in your path. This "looking without seeing" is referred to as inattentional blindness, and it can have serious consequences (Mack, 2003).

Ulric Neisser illustrated just how blind we can be to objects directly in our line of vision. In one of his studies, participants were instructed to watch a video of men passing a basketball from one person to another (Neisser, 1979; Neisser & Becklen, 1975). As the participants diligently followed the basketball with their eyes, counting each pass, a partially transparent woman holding an umbrella was superimposed walking across the basketball court. Only 21% of the participants even noticed the woman (Most et al., 2001; Simons, 2010); the others had been too fixated on counting the basketball passes to see her (Mack, 2003).

LEVELS OF CONSCIOUSNESS   People often equate consciousness with being awake and alert, and unconsciousness with being passed out or comatose. But the distinction is not so clear, because there are different *levels of conscious awareness* including wakefulness, sleepiness, drug-induced states, dreaming, hypnotic states, and meditative states, to name but a few. One way to define these levels of consciousness is to determine how much control you have over your awareness. A high level of awareness might occur when you focus intensely on a task (using a sharp knife); a lower level might occur as you daydream, although you are able to snap out of it as needed. Sometimes we can identify an agent that causes a change in the level or state of consciousness. Psychologists typically delineate between *waking consciousness* and *altered states of consciousness* that may result from drugs, alcohol, or hypnosis—all topics covered in this chapter.

Wherever your attention is focused at this moment, that is your conscious experience—but there are times when attention essentially shuts down. What's going on when we lie in bed motionless, lost in a peaceful slumber? Sleep, fascinating sleep, is the subject of our next section.

 show what you know

1. One barrier to studying consciousness is the fact that it is _____, pertaining only to the person who experiences it.

2. While studying for an exam, your sensory systems absorb an inordinate amount of information from your surroundings, most of which escapes your awareness. Because of _____, you generally do not get overwhelmed with incoming sensory data.

   a. consciousness   **b.** automatic processing
   c. depressants   **d.** encoding

3. Inattentional blindness is the tendency to "look without seeing." Given what you know about selective attention, how would you advise someone to avoid inattentional blindness?

✔ CHECK YOUR ANSWERS IN APPENDIX C.

Sleep

When Matt Utesch reminisces about childhood, he remembers having a lot of energy. "I was the kid that would wake up at 6:00 A.M. and watch cartoons," Matt recalls. As a teenager, Matt channeled his energy through sports—playing basketball, running cross-country, and competing in one of the nation's top-ranking private soccer leagues. But everything changed during Matt's sophomore year of high school. That was the year the sleepiness hit.

At first it seemed like nothing serious. Matt just dozed off in class from time to time. But his mini-naps gradually became more frequent. Eventually, the sleepiness would take hold of him in every class except physical education. "Matt, you just fell asleep," his friends would say. "No I didn't," he would shoot back, unaware he had nodded off. Most of Matt's teachers assumed he was just another teenager exhausted from late-night partying. Nobody, not even Matt's doctor, suspected he had a serious medical condition—until the accident happened.

Matt, In His Own Words
http://qrs.ly/nd4qsyj

© 2016, Macmillan

It was the summer before junior year, and Matt was driving his truck home from work at his father's appliance repair shop. One moment he was rolling along the street at a safe distance from other cars, and the next he was ramming into a brown Saturn that had slowed to make a left turn. What had transpired in the interim? Matt had fallen asleep. He slammed on the brake pedal, but it was too late; the two vehicles collided. Unharmed, Matt leaped out of his truck and ran to check on the other driver—a woman who, as he remembers, "was totally out of it." Her backrest had broken, and her back had nearly broken along with it. A few weeks after the accident, Matt went to the woman's home to bring her flowers. She invited him inside, and they sat down and began to chat. Then, right in the midst of their conversation, Matt fell asleep. 📁

Sleep Troubles
Matt Utesch was active and full of energy as a child, but come sophomore year in high school, he periodically fell asleep throughout the day. Matt was beginning to experience the symptoms of a serious sleep disorder. Courtesy Matthew Utesch

An Introduction to Sleep

All animals sleep or engage in some rest activity that resembles sleep (Horne, 2006). Dolphins snooze while swimming, keeping one eye cracked open at all times; horses usually sleep standing up; and some birds appear to doze mid-flight (Siegel, 2005; U.S. Fish & Wildlife Service, 2006). There are animals that require loads of sleep—bats and opossums sleep 18 to 20 hours a day—and those that need barely any—elephants and giraffes get by on 3 or 4 hours (Siegel, 2005). Sleep needs vary greatly among people, ranging from as little as 4 hours a night to as long as 11 or more (Horne, 2006). But most of us require between 7 and 8 hours to stay mentally and physically healthy (Banks & Dinges, 2007). Do the math and that translates to about a third of the day, and therefore a third of your *life*. Clearly, sleep serves some important function, but what is it? And how does it relate to consciousness? How can sleep go so wrong, as happened for Matt? Before tackling these questions, let's get a handle on the basics.

LO 4   Identify how circadian rhythm relates to sleep.

CIRCADIAN RHYTHM   Have you ever noticed that you often get sleepy in the middle of the afternoon? Even if you had a good sleep the night before, you inevitably begin feeling tired around 2:00 or 3:00 P.M.; it's like clockwork. That's because it is clockwork. Many things your body does, including sleep, are regulated by a biological clock. Body temperature rises during the day, reaching its maximum in the early evening. Hormones are secreted in a cyclical fashion. Growth hormone is released at night, and the stress hormone cortisol soars in the morning, reaching levels 10 to 20 times higher than at night (Wright, 2002). These are just a few of the body functions that follow predictable daily patterns, affecting our behaviors, alertness, and activity levels. Such patterns in our physiological functioning roughly follow the 24-hour cycle of daylight and darkness; they follow a **circadian rhythm** (sər-ˈkā-dē-ən).

In the circadian rhythm for sleep and wakefulness, there are two times when the desire for sleep hits hardest. The first is between 2:00 and 6:00 A.M., the same window of time when most car accidents caused by sleepiness occur (Horne, 2006). The second, less intense desire for sleep strikes midafternoon, around 2:30 P.M., when many college students have trouble keeping their eyes open in class (Mitler & Miller, 1996).

Not all biological rhythms are circadian. Some occur over longer time intervals (monthly menstruation), and others cycle much faster (90-minute sleep cycles, to be discussed shortly). Many animals migrate or hibernate during certain seasons and mate according to a yearly pattern. Even when deprived of cues like changing levels of sunlight, some animals continue to follow these cycles. Birds caged indoors, for example, exhibit mood and behavioral changes at the times of year when they would normally be migrating. Biological clocks are everywhere in nature, acting as day planners for organisms as basic as bacteria and slime mold (Wright, 2002).

SUPRACHIASMATIC NUCLEUS   Where in the human body do these inner clocks and calendars dwell? Miniclocks are found in cells all over your body, but a master clock is nestled deep within the hypothalamus, a brain structure whose activities revolve around maintaining homeostasis, or balance, in the body's systems. This master of clocks, known as the *suprachiasmatic nucleus (SCN)*, actually consists of two clusters, each no bigger than an ant, totaling around 20,000 neurons (Forger & Peskin, 2003; Wright, 2002). The SCN plays a role in our circadian rhythm by communicating with other areas of the hypothalamus, which regulates daily patterns of hunger and temperature, and the reticular formation, which regulates alertness and sleepiness (**Infographic 4.1**).

Although tucked away in the recesses of the brain, the SCN knows the difference between day and night. That's because it receives signals from a special type of light-sensing cells in the eye, called *retinal ganglion cells*. With the help of these informants, the clock adjusts to the light and dark cycling of the planet. When light beams upon the earth, your clock tells you to rise and shine, and when darkness hits, it urges you to bed. One way the SCN keeps you on schedule is by indirectly communicating with the pineal gland, a part of the endocrine system, to regulate the release of *melatonin,* a hormone that promotes sleep. In dark conditions, the clock commands the pineal gland to produce melatonin, making it easier to sleep. When light hits the eye, melatonin secretion slows down. So if you want to sleep, turn down the lights, and let your brain turn up the melatonin.

What would happen if you lived in a dark cave with no cell phones or computers to help you keep track of time? Would your body stay on a 24-hour cycle or get confused? Studies of people living in conditions with no indication of the time of day show that the internal clock continues to hum along at a slightly slower pace, eventually settling on a cycle that runs a little over 24 hours (Carskadon, Labayak, Acebo, & Seifer, 1999; Czeisler et al., 1999). But depriving the clock of its external light cues is generally not a good idea. Sleep–wake cycles can be disrupted, leading to exhaustion, irritability, impairment of memory, and other negative outcomes.

CONNECTIONS

In **Chapter 2,** we explained the functions of the hypothalamus. For example, it maintains blood pressure, temperature, and electrolyte balance. It also is involved in regulating sleep–wake cycles, sexual arousal, and appetite.

In **Chapter 3,** we described how light enters the eye and is directed to the retina. The rods and cones in the retina are photoreceptors, which absorb light energy and turn it into electrical and chemical signals. Here, we see how light-sensing cells relay information to the SCN.

In **Chapter 1,** we presented the experiences of the 33 Chilean miners who spent 2 months trapped in the dark caverns of a collapsed mine. When they were rescued, actions were taken to protect their eyes because they had not been exposed to natural light for more than 2 months.

circadian rhythm (sər-ˈkā-dē-ən) The daily patterns roughly following the 24-hour cycle of daylight and darkness; and 24-hour cycle of physiological and behavioral functioning.

The Suprachiasmatic Nucleus

The suprachiasmatic nucleus (SCN) of the hypothalamus is the body's internal master clock, playing a role in regulating our circadian rhythms. These rhythms roughly follow the 24-hour cycle of daylight and darkness. But one doesn't have to consciously perceive light for the SCN to function properly; there is a dedicated, *nonvisual* pathway that carries light information from the eyes to the SCN.

Pineal gland
produces melatonin

Hypothalamus
regulates patterns of hunger and temperature

Reticular formation
regulates alertness and sleepiness

Suprachiasmatic nucleus (SCN)

The SCN is actually two tiny bundles of neurons within the hypothalamus. The SCN sends messages about light to the rest of the hypothalamus and the reticular formation, and regulates the pineal gland's production of melatonin, a sleep-inducing hormone.

The SCN is located deep in the brain, far away from visual processing areas. So how does it get information about light? Our eyes contain a separate nonvisual pathway made of retinal ganglion cells. This pathway goes directly to the SCN.

SCN

Pathway for visual information

Optic chiasm

Visual processing area

Nonvisual pathway for signals about light

Supra is Latin for "above."
Suprachiasmatic means "above the chiasm."
The SCN's long name helps you find it in the brain!

For the 20% of the U.S. workforce doing shift work, normal sleep schedules are disrupted. This leads to health problems and increased accidents (Harrington, 2001). Using what we know about how the SCN works, researchers are helping industries ease these effects. Bright lights, such as those installed in this power station control room, contain a high proportion of the blue light found in morning sun, fooling the SCN into thinking it is daytime. That makes it easier for workers to synchronize sleep patterns with work activities.

Credits: Head, Citizen Stock/Alamy; Control room, © Hank Morgan/Science Source

LARKS AND OWLS   Everyone has her own unique clock, which helps explain why some of us are "morning people" or so-called "larks," and others are "night owls." If you are a lark, you roll out of bed feeling energized and alert, get more accomplished early in the day, yet grow weary as the day drags on. One study characterized larks as preferring to go to bed before 11:00 P.M. and rising before 8:00 A.M. (Gale & Martyn, 1998). Owls, on the other hand, get up late and hit the sack late. If you slam the "snooze" button on your alarm clock five times every morning, shower with your eyes closed, and act like a grouch at breakfast, you're probably an owl. But being an owl often means your energy level builds throughout the day, making it easy to stay up late posting to Instagram or reading your textbook. About 20% of us are true owls, 20% are genuine larks, and the rest fall somewhere in between (Horne, 2006).

try this

Check your answers in Appendix C.

College students are often portrayed as owls, but is this just a stereotype? Does something in the college environment influence sleep–wake cycles, or is there a biological explanation? If you were to explore this question, what kind of experiment would you design? What would your independent and dependent variables be?

JET LAG AND SHIFT WORK   Whether you are a lark or an owl, your biological clock is likely to become confused when you travel across time zones. Your clock does not automatically reset to match the new time. The physical and mental consequences of this delayed adjustment, known as "jet lag," may include difficulty concentrating, headaches, and gastrointestinal distress. Fortunately, the biological clock can readjust by about 1 or 2 hours each day, eventually falling into step with the new environmental schedule (Cunha & Stöppler, 2011). Jet lag is frustrating, but at least it's only temporary.

Now imagine plodding through life with a case of jet lag you just can't shake. This is the tough reality for some of the world's shift workers—firefighters, nurses, miners, power plant operators, and other professionals who work while the rest of the world is snuggled under the covers. Shift workers represent about 20% of the workforce in the United States and other developed countries, or 1 in 5 people who are employed (Di Lorenzo et al., 2003). Some work rotating shifts, which means they are constantly going to bed and waking up at different times; others consistently work the overnight shift, so their sleep-wake cycles are permanently out-of-step with the light and dark cycles of the earth. Constantly fighting the clock takes a heavy toll on the mind and body. An irregular sleep schedule may lead to symptoms of *insomnia,* or difficulty falling asleep and sleeping soundly. Picture yourself coming off the night shift and arriving home at 7:00 A.M.: The sun is shining brightly, the birds are chirping, and the rest of the family is chatting over their cornflakes. This is not an ideal environment for sleep. Insomnia resulting from shift work can lead to decreased job productivity, depression, anxiety, diabetes, and other chronic diseases (Morin et al., 2006; Vgontzas et al., 2009). Shift workers also face an elevated risk of becoming overweight, and of developing stomach ulcers and heart disease (Di Lorenzo et al., 2003; Knutsson, 2003). In addition, an estimated 5% to 10% of

Jet Lag
Rapidly traveling through time zones puts a strain on the body and brain. Most of us can adjust by 1 or 2 hours per day. So if you travel across 3 time zones (Los Angeles to New York), it could take as long as 3 days to adapt (Cunha & Stöppler, 2011). © Beard & Howell/Getty Images

shift workers have been diagnosed with *circadian rhythm sleep–wake disorders,* characterized by excessive sleepiness at work and insomnia at home (American Psychiatric Association, 2013).

Dr. Lawrence J. Epstein of Harvard Medical School suggests ways in which night workers can minimize circadian disturbances and increase their productivity. Remember that light is the master clock's most important external cue. Dr. Epstein suggests maximizing light exposure during work time and steering clear of it close to bedtime. Some night shifters don sunglasses on their way home, to block the morning sun, and head straight to bed in a quiet, dark room (Epstein & Mardon, 2007). Taking 20- to 30-minute power naps in the middle of a night shift can also help shift workers stay awake and alert (Harvard Medical School, 2007).

Night Shift
Factory workers are among the many professionals who clock in and out at all hours of the day. Working alternating or night shifts can disrupt circadian rhythms, leading to fatigue, irritability, and diminished mental sharpness. Physical activity and good sleep habits will help counteract the negative effects (Costa, 2003). Michael Reynolds/EPA/Newscom

The Stages of Sleep

LO 5   Summarize the stages of sleep.

Have you ever watched someone sleeping? The person looks blissfully tranquil: body still, face relaxed, chest rising and falling like a lazy ocean wave. Don't be fooled. Underneath the body's quiet front is a very active brain, as revealed by an electroencephalogram (EEG), a device that picks up electrical signals from the brain and displays this information on a screen. If you could look at an EEG trace of your brain right this moment, you would probably see a series of tiny, short spikes in rapid-fire succession. These high-frequency brain waves are called **beta waves,** and they appear when you are solving a math problem, reading a book, or any time you are alert. Now let's say you climb into bed, close your eyes, and relax. As you become more and more drowsy, the EEG would likely begin showing **alpha waves,** which are lower in frequency than beta waves (Cantero, Atienza, Salas, & Gómez, 1999). At some point, you drift into a different level of consciousness known as sleep.

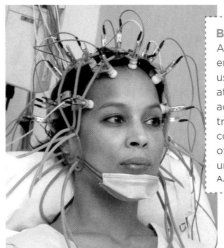

Brain Waves
A woman receives an electroencephalogram (EEG), a test commonly used in sleep studies. The electrodes attached to her head pick up electrical activity from her brain, which is transformed into a series of spikes on a computer screen. Through careful study of EEG data, researchers have come to understand the various stages of sleep. AJPhoto/Science Source

NON-REM SLEEP   A normal sleeper begins the night in **non-rapid eye movement (non-REM),** or nondreaming, sleep, which has four stages (**Infographic 4.2** on the next page). The first and lightest is Stage 1 sleep, also known as "light sleep." During Stage 1, muscles go limp and body temperature starts to fall. The eyeballs may move gently beneath the lids. If you looked at an EEG of a person in Stage 1, you would likely see **theta waves,** which are lower in frequency than both alpha and beta waves. This is the type of sleep many people deny having. Example: Your friend begins to snooze while watching TV, so you poke her in the ribs and say, "Wake up!" but she swears she wasn't asleep. It is also during this initial phase of sleep that

beta waves Brain waves that indicate an alert, awake state.

alpha waves Brain waves that indicate a relaxed, drowsy state.

non-rapid eye movement (non-REM) The nondreaming sleep that occurs during sleep Stages 1 to 4.

theta waves Brain waves that indicate light sleep.

Sleep

Looking in on a sleep study, you'll see that the brain is actually very active during sleep, cycling through non-REM stages and ending in REM sleep approximately five times during the night. Transitions between stages are clearly visible as shifts in EEG patterns.

Graphs illustrating the human sleep cycle typically present an 8-hour time span, as shown below. But this doesn't tell the whole story of sleep. The amount of time spent sleeping and the content of our sleep changes across the life span. And while a *normal* night's sleep lasts approximately 7 hours for a healthy young adult, 30% of working adults get 6 hours or fewer of sleep per night (Centers for Disease Control and Prevention, 2012f).

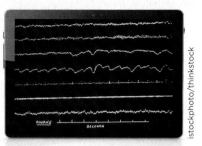

This sleep study participant wears electrodes that will measure her brain waves and body movements during sleep.

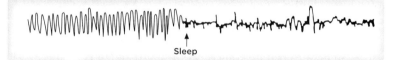

Sleep

Looking at brain waves allows us to trace a person's stage of sleep. Here we can see a clear shift from waking to sleeping patterns.
(FROM DEMENT & VAUGHAN, 1999.)

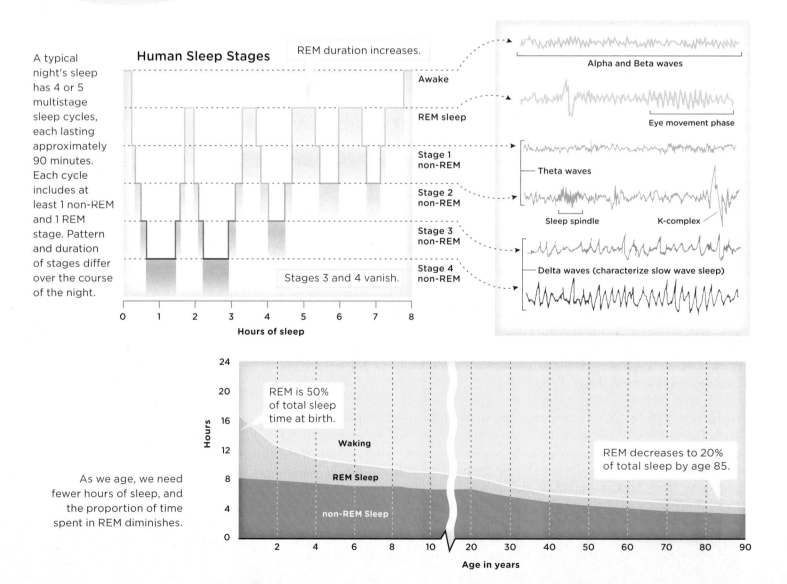

A typical night's sleep has 4 or 5 multistage sleep cycles, each lasting approximately 90 minutes. Each cycle includes at least 1 non-REM and 1 REM stage. Pattern and duration of stages differ over the course of the night.

Human Sleep Stages

REM duration increases.
Awake
REM sleep
Stage 1 non-REM
Stage 2 non-REM
Stage 3 non-REM
Stage 4 non-REM
Stages 3 and 4 vanish.

Alpha and Beta waves
Eye movement phase
Theta waves
Sleep spindle   K-complex
Delta waves (characterize slow wave sleep)

Hours of sleep

As we age, we need fewer hours of sleep, and the proportion of time spent in REM diminishes.

REM is 50% of total sleep time at birth.
Waking
REM Sleep
non-REM Sleep
REM decreases to 20% of total sleep by age 85.

Age in years

hallucinations, or imaginary sensations, can occur. Do you ever see blotches of color or bizarre floating images as you drift off to sleep? Or perhaps you have felt a sensation of falling or swinging and then jerked your arms or legs in response? False perceptions that occur during the limbo between wakefulness and sleep are called *hypnagogic* (ˌhip-nə-ˈgäj-ik) *hallucinations,* and they are no cause for concern—in most cases. More on this when we return to Matt's story.

After a few minutes in Stage 1, you move on to the next phase of non-REM sleep, called Stage 2 sleep, which is slightly deeper than Stage 1, so you are harder to awaken. Theta waves continue showing up on the EEG, along with little bursts of electrical activity called *sleep spindles* and large waves called *K-complexes* appearing every 2 minutes or so. Researchers suspect sleep spindles are associated with memory consolidation and intelligence (Fogel & Smith, 2011). The exact function of K-complexes is up for debate: Some suggest they are the brain's way of being ready to awaken when the need arises, while others believe they are the mechanism for remaining asleep in spite of disturbing stimuli (Colrain, 2005).

After passing through Stages 1 and 2, the sleeper descends into Stage 3, and then into an even deeper Stage 4, when it is most difficult to awaken. Both Stages 3 and 4 are known as slow-wave sleep, because they are characterized by tall, low-frequency **delta waves.** Stages 3 and 4 are really very similar, but Stage 4 contains a higher proportion of delta waves (delta waves are evident more than 50% of the time). Waking a person from slow-wave sleep is not easy. Most of us feel groggy, disoriented, and downright irritated when jarred from a slow-wave slumber. This is also the peak time for the secretion of growth hormone, which helps children to grow taller and stronger, and to build tissue (Awikunprasert & Sittiprapaporn, 2012).

REM SLEEP   You don't stay in deep sleep for the remainder of the night, however. After about 40 minutes of Stage 4 sleep, you work your way back through the lighter stages of sleep, from Stage 4, to Stage 3, to Stage 2, and finally to Stage 1. Then, instead of waking up, you enter a fifth stage known as **rapid eye movement (REM)** sleep. During REM, the eyes often dart around, even though they are closed (hence the name "rapid eye movement" sleep). The brain is very active, with EEG recordings showing faster and shorter waves similar to that of someone who is wide awake. Pulse and breathing rate fluctuate, and blood flow to the genitals increases, which explains why people frequently wake up in a state of sexual arousal. Another name for REM sleep is *paradoxical sleep,* because the sleeper appears to be quiet and resting, but the brain is full of electrical activity. People roused from REM sleep often report having vivid, illogical dreams. Thankfully, the brain has a way of preventing us from acting out our dreams. During REM sleep, certain neurons in the brainstem control the voluntary muscles, keeping most of the body still.

What would happen if the neurons responsible for disabling the muscles during REM sleep were destroyed or damaged? Researchers led by Michel Jouvet in France and Adrian Morrison in the United States found the answer to that question in the 1960s and 1970s. Both teams showed that severing these neurons in the brains of cats caused them to act out their kitty dreams. Not only did the sleeping felines stand up; they arched their backs in fury, groomed and licked themselves, and hunted imaginary mice (Jouvet, 1979; Sastre & Jouvet, 1979).

You Asked, Matt Answers

http://qrs.ly/dm4qsyu

In hindsight, did you notice any changes that may have foreshadowed the onset of narcolepsy?

Kitty Dreams
This cat may be dreaming of chasing mice and birds, but its body is essentially paralyzed during REM sleep. Disable the neurons responsible for this paralysis and you will see some very interesting behavior— the cat will act out its dream. Thinkstock

delta waves Brain waves that indicate a deep sleep.

rapid eye movement (REM) The stage of sleep associated with dreaming; sleep characterized by bursts of eye movements, with brain activity similar to that of a waking state, but with a lack of muscle tone.

SLEEP ARCHITECTURE Congratulations. You have just completed one sleep cycle, working your way through Stages 1, 2, 3, and 4 of non-REM sleep and ending with a dream-packed episode of REM. Each of these cycles lasts about 90 minutes, and the average adult sleeper loops through five of them per night. The composition of these 90-minute sleep cycles changes during the night. During the first two cycles, a considerable amount of time is devoted to the deep sleep Stages 3 and 4. Halfway through the night, however, Stages 3 and 4 vanish. Meanwhile, the REM periods become progressively longer, with the first REM episode lasting only 5 to 10 minutes, and the final one lasting nearly a half-hour (Siegel, 2005). Therefore, we pack in most of our restorative sleep early in the night and most of the dreaming toward the end; and the sleep stage we spend the most time in—nearly half the night—is Stage 2 (Epstein & Mardon, 2007).

As we age, the makeup of our sleep cycles, or *sleep architecture,* changes. Older people spend less time in REM sleep and the deeply refreshing stages of non-REM sleep (3 and 4). Instead, they experience longer periods of light sleep (Stages 1 and 2), which can be interrupted easily by noises and movements (Ohayon, Carskadon, Guilleminault, & Vitiello, 2004). Could this be the reason many older people complain of sleeping poorly, waking up often, and feeling drowsy during the day? Not all elderly people have trouble sleeping, of course. Like most everything in life, sleep patterns vary considerably from one individual to the next.

Wake Up!
Some of us feel refreshed after sleeping 6 or 7 hours. Others can barely grasp a glass of orange juice without a solid 8. Sleep habits appear to be a blend of biological and environmental forces—both nature and nurture. © Ariel Skelley/Blend Images/Corbis

Nature and Nurture

What Kind of Sleeper Are You?

On a typical weeknight, the average American sleeps 6 hours and 40 minutes, but there is significant deviation from this "average." A large number of people—about 20% of the population—get fewer than 6 hours, and another 28% snooze longer than 8 hours (National Sleep Foundation, 2009). What explains this variation in the duration of sleep?

When it comes to understanding sleep patterns, we cannot ignore what is in our *nature,* or genetics. Some studies suggest sleep needs are inherited from parents, and there are probably many genes involved (He et al., 2009; Hor & Tafti, 2009). Evidence also suggests that "short sleepers" (people who average fewer than 6 hours per night) and "long sleepers" (those who sleep more than 9 hours) are running on different circadian rhythms. Nighttime increases of the "sleep hormone" melatonin, for example, tend to be reduced for those who get fewer zzz's (Aeschbach et al., 2003; Rivkees, 2003).

But it is also possible that some short sleepers are really just average sleepers getting by on less than an optimal amount of sleep. Given the opportunity to catch up for a few days, would they sleep for hours upon hours? This is just what happened in a small study of healthy young adults. On Day 1 of sleep catch-up, all the participants slept more than usual. But by Day 3, the longer sleepers were engaged in less catch-up than the shorter sleepers, who seemed to be chipping away at a "sleep debt" they had accumulated (Klerman & Dijk, 2004). We do not have access to the genetic codes of these participants, so it is impossible to know what heritable factors might have influenced the results. But the findings do suggest sleep patterns are, to some degree, shaped by the circumstances of our lives. If the short sleepers in the study were getting sufficient sleep, then we wouldn't expect them to show signs of sleep debt. Sleep patterns, like virtually every psychological phenomenon, appear to be dictated by both nature and nurture. ◊🏠

ARE "SHORT SLEEPERS" ALWAYS IN SLEEP DEBT?

Sleep Disturbances

LO 6 Recognize various sleep disorders and their symptoms.

 **PROBLEM IDENTIFIED: NARCOLEPSY** Shortly after the car accident, Matt was diagnosed with **narcolepsy,** a neurological disorder characterized by excessive daytime sleepiness and other sleep-related disturbances. The most striking symptoms of narcolepsy include the "irrepressible need to sleep, lapsing into sleep, or napping occurring within the same day" (American Psychological Association [APA], 2013a, p. 372). With narcolepsy, sleepiness can strike anytime, anywhere—during a job interview, while riding a bicycle, or in the midst of a passionate kiss. One time Matt fell asleep while making a sandwich. When he awoke, he was still holding a slice of meat in his hand. Some people with narcolepsy report a waking alert level and then falling asleep, while others report an overwhelming feeling of sleepiness all the time. "Sleep attacks" can occur several times a day. Most are measured in seconds or minutes, but episodes of an hour or longer have been reported (National Institute of Neurological Disorders and Stroke, 2011a). By the time Matt was a junior in high school, his uncontrollable naps were striking upward of 20 to 30 times a day. 🗀

CATAPLEXY And that wasn't all. Matt developed another debilitating symptom of narcolepsy: *cataplexy,* an abrupt loss of strength or muscle tone that occurs when a person is awake. During a severe cataplectic attack, some muscles go limp, and the body may collapse slowly to the floor like a rag doll. One moment Matt would be standing in the hallway laughing with friends; the next he was splayed on the floor unable to move a muscle. "It was like a tree being cut down [and] tipping over," he recalls. Cataplexy attacks come on suddenly, usually during periods of emotional excitement (American Psychiatric Association, 2013). The effects usually wear off after several seconds, but severe attacks can render a person immobilized for minutes.

Cataplexy may completely disable the body, but it produces no loss in consciousness. Even during the worst attack, Matt remained completely aware of himself and his surroundings. He could hear people talking about him; sometimes they snickered in amusement. "Kids can be cruel," Matt says. By junior year, Matt was having 60 to 100 attacks a day.

SLEEP PARALYSIS AND HYPNAGOGIC HALLUCINATIONS Matt also developed two other common narcolepsy symptoms: sleep paralysis and hypnagogic hallucinations. *Sleep paralysis* is a temporary paralysis that strikes just before falling asleep or upon waking (American Psychiatric Association, 2013). Recall that the body becomes paralyzed during REM sleep, but sometimes this paralysis sets in prematurely or fails to turn off on time. Picture yourself lying in bed, awake and fully aware yet unable to roll over, climb out of bed, or even wiggle a toe. You want to scream for help, but your lips won't budge. Sleep paralysis is a common symptom of narcolepsy, but it can also strike ordinary sleepers. One study found that nearly a third of college students had experienced sleep paralysis at least once in their lives (Cheyne, Newby-Clark, & Rueffer, 1999). Episodes usually last a few seconds, but some go on for several minutes—a terrifying experience for most people.

Sleep paralysis may seem scary, but now imagine seeing bloodthirsty vampires standing at the foot of your bed just as you are about to fall asleep. Earlier we discussed

Tired Teen
Matt's battle with narcolepsy climaxed during his junior year of high school. In addition to falling asleep 20 to 30 times a day, he was experiencing frequent bouts of cataplexy, an abrupt loss of muscle tone that occurs while one is awake. Cataplexy struck Matt anytime, anywhere—up to 100 times a day.
Courtesy Matthew Utesch

Sleep Attack
Eight-year-old Lucas Carlton of Liverpool, England, suffers from narcolepsy, a neurological disorder characterized by frequent bouts of uncontrollable sleepiness and other symptoms. Lucas sleeps as many as 20 hours per day. Mercury Press/ZUMAPRESS.com

narcolepsy A neurological disorder characterized by excessive daytime sleepiness, which includes lapses into sleep and napping.

the *hypnagogic hallucinations* people can experience during Stage 1 sleep (seeing strange images, for example). But not all hypnagogic hallucinations involve harmless blobs. They can also be realistic visions of axe murderers or space aliens trying to abduct you (McNally & Clancy, 2005). Matt had a recurring hallucination of a man with a butcher knife racing through his doorway, jumping onto his bed, and stabbing him in the chest. Upon awakening, Matt would often quiz his mother with questions like, "When is my birthday?" or "What is your license plate number?" He wanted to verify she was real, not just another character in his dream. Like sleep paralysis, vivid hypnagogic hallucinations can occur in people without narcolepsy, too. Shift work, insomnia, and sleeping faceup are all factors that appear to heighten one's risk (Cheyne, 2002; McNally & Clancy, 2005).

BATTLING NARCOLEPSY   Throughout junior year, Matt took various medications to control his narcolepsy, but his symptoms persisted. Narcolepsy was beginning to interfere with virtually every aspect of his life. At the beginning of high school, Matt had a 4.0 grade point average; now he was working twice as hard and earning lower grades. Playing sports had become a major health hazard because his cataplexy struck wherever and whenever, without notice. If he collapsed while sprinting down the soccer field or diving for a basketball, he might twist an ankle, break an arm, or worse. It was during this time that Matt realized who his true friends were. "The people that stuck with me [then] are still my close friends now," he says. Matt's loyal buddies learned to recognize the warning signs of his cataplexy (for example, when he suddenly stands still and closes his eyes) and did everything possible to keep him safe, grabbing hold of his body and slowly lowering him to the ground. His buddies had his back—literally.

Approximately 1 in 2,500 people suffers from narcolepsy (Ohayon, 2011). It is believed to result from a failure of the brain to properly regulate sleep patterns. Normally, the boundaries separating sleep and wakefulness are relatively clear—you are awake, in REM sleep, or in non-REM sleep. With narcolepsy, the lines separating these different realms of consciousness fade, allowing sleep to spill into periods of wakefulness. The loss of muscle tone during cataplexy, sleep paralysis, and dreamlike hypnagogic hallucinations may be explained by occurrences of REM sleep in the midst of wakefulness (Attarian, Schenck, & Mahowald, 2000). In other words, REM sleep occurs in the wrong place, at the wrong time (see a summary of this and other sleep disturbances in **Table 4.1**).

REM SLEEP BEHAVIOR DISORDER   Problems with REM regulation can also lead to other sleep disturbances, including **REM sleep behavior disorder.** The defining characteristics of this disorder include "repeated episodes of arousal often associated with vocalizations and/or complex motor behaviors arising from REM sleep" (American Psychiatric Association, 2013, p. 408). People with REM sleep behavior disorder are much like the cats in Morrison's and Jouvet's experiments; something has gone awry with the brainstem mechanism responsible for paralyzing their bodies during REM sleep, so they are able to move around and act out their dreams (Schenck & Mahowald, 2002). This is not a good thing, since the dreams of people with REM sleep behavior disorder tend to be unusually violent and action-packed, involving fights with wild animals and other attackers (Fantini, Corona, Clerici, & Ferini-Strambi, 2005). According to some research, up to 65% of REM sleep behavior disorder sufferers have injured either themselves or their bedmates at one point or another. Scrapes, cuts, and bruises are common, and traumatic brain injuries have also been reported (American Psychiatric Association, 2013; Aurora et al., 2010). REM sleep behavior disorder primarily affects older men (age 50 and up) and frequently foreshadows the development of serious neurodegenerative disorders— conditions such as Parkinson's disease and dementia that are associated with the

You Asked, Matt Answers

http://qrs.ly/tr4qsyv

What kind of physician did you visit in order to be diagnosed with narcolepsy?

REM sleep behavior disorder
A sleep disturbance in which the mechanism responsible for paralyzing the body during REM sleep is not functioning, resulting in the acting out of dreams.

obstructive sleep apnea hypopnea (hī-pop-ˈnē-ə) A serious disturbance of non-REM sleep characterized by complete absence of air flow (apnea) or reduced air flow (hypopnea).

insomnia Sleep disorder characterized by an inability to fall asleep or stay asleep, impacting both the quality and the quantity of sleep.

TABLE 4.1   SLEEP DISTURBANCES

Sleep Disturbance	Definition	Defining Characteristics
Narcolepsy	Neurological disorder characterized by excessive daytime sleepiness, which includes lapses into sleep and napping.	Irrepressible need to sleep; daytime napping; cataplexy; sleep paralysis; hypnagogic hallucinations.
REM Sleep Behavior Disorder	The mechanism responsible for paralysis during REM not functioning, resulting in the acting out of dreams.	Dreamers vocalize and act out dreams; violent and active dreams are common; upon awakening the dream is remembered; risk of injury to self and sleeping partners.
Obstructive Sleep Apnea Hypopnea	Serious disturbance characterized by a complete absence of air flow (apnea) or reduced air flow (hypopnea).	Upper throat muscles go limp; airway closes; breathing stops for 10 seconds or longer; sleeper awakens, gasping for air.
Insomnia	Inability to fall asleep or stay asleep.	Poor sleep quantity or quality; tendency to wake up too early; cannot fall back asleep; not feeling refreshed after a night's sleep.
Sleepwalking	Disturbance of non-REM sleep characterized by complex motor behavior during sleep.	Expressionless face; open eyes; may sit up in bed, walk around, or speak gibberish; upon awakening has limited recall.
Sleep Terrors	Disturbance of non-REM sleep generally occurring in children.	Screaming, inconsolable child; usually no memory of the episode the next day.

Problems can arise during both REM and non-REM sleep. This table outlines some of the most common sleep disturbances and their defining characteristics.

gradual decline and death of neurons (Boeve et al., 2007; Fantini et al., 2005; Postuma et al., 2009; Schenck & Mahowald, 2002). But, women and younger people are diagnosed with this disorder as well (American Psychiatric Association, 2013).

BREATHING-RELATED SLEEP DISORDERS   There are several breathing-related sleep disorders, but the most common is **obstructive sleep apnea hypopnea** (hī-pop-'nē-ə), characterized by a complete absence of air flow (apnea) or reduced air flow (hypopnea). During normal sleep, the airway remains open, allowing air to flow in and out of the lungs. With obstructive sleep apnea hypopnea, the upper throat muscles go limp, allowing the upper airway to close shut (American Psychiatric Association, 2013). Breathing stops for 10 seconds or more, causing blood oxygen levels to drop (Chung & Elsaid, 2009). The brain responds by commanding the body to *wake up and breathe!* The sleeper awakes and gasps for air, sometimes with a noisy nasal sound, and then drifts back to sleep. This process can repeat itself several hundred times per night, preventing a person from experiencing the deep stages of sleep so crucial for feeling reenergized in the morning. Most people have no memory of the repeated awakenings and wonder why they feel so exhausted during the day; they are completely unaware that they suffer from this serious sleep disturbance. Obstructive sleep apnea hypopnea is more common among men than women and is more prevalent in the obese, and in women after menopause. This condition is linked to increased risk of death in the elderly, traffic accidents, and reduced quality of life, as well as elevated blood pressure, which increases the risk of cardiovascular disease (American Psychiatric Association, 2013).

INSOMNIA   The most prevalent sleep disorder is **insomnia,** which is characterized by an inability to fall asleep or stay asleep. People with insomnia often report that the quantity or quality of their sleep is not good. They may complain of waking up in the middle of the night or arising too early, and not being able to fall back asleep.

Does Rosie Snore?
Actor and TV personality Rosie O'Donnell is among the millions of Americans who suffer from obstructive sleep apnea (Schocker, 2012, September 25). Research suggests this sleep disorder affects between 3% and 7% of the adult population (Punjabi, 2008). Steve Mack/ FilmMagic/Getty Images

Restless Gaga
Pop diva Lady Gaga glows at the Vanity Fair Oscar Party in 2014. Gaga appears to get plenty of beauty sleep, but she reportedly suffers from insomnia. "Fame is like rocket fuel," she said in a 2010 interview with *OK!* magazine. "The more my fans like what I'm doing, the more I want to give back to them. And my passion is so strong I can't sleep. I haven't slept for three days" (Simpson, 2010, April 5, para. 3). Jon Kopaloff/FilmMagic/Getty Images

Synonyms
sleep terrors night terrors
sleepwalking somnambulism
(säm-ˈnam-byə-ˌli-zəm)

Sleepiness during the day and difficulties with cognitive tasks are also reported (American Psychiatric Association, 2013). About a third of adults experience some symptoms of insomnia, and 6% to 10% suffer from *insomnia disorder* (American Psychiatric Association, 2013; Mai & Buysse, 2008; Roth, 2007). Insomnia symptoms can be related to many factors, including the stress of a new job, college studies, depression, anxiety, jet lag, aging, and drug use.

OTHER SLEEP DISTURBANCES A common sleep disturbance that can occur during non-REM sleep (typically Stages 3 and 4) is *sleepwalking*. A quarter of all children will experience at least one sleepwalking incident, and it seems to run in families (Licis, Desruisseau, Yamada, Duntley, & Gurnett, 2011). Here are some ways to spot a sleepwalker: Her face is expressionless; her eyes are open; and she may sit up in bed, walk around in confusion, or speak gibberish. (The garbled speech of sleepwalking is different from sleep *talking,* which can occur in either REM or non-REM sleep, but is not considered a sleep disturbance.) Sleepwalkers may have "limited recall" of the event upon awakening (American Psychiatric Association, 2013). They are capable of accomplishing a variety of tasks such as opening doors, going to the bathroom, and getting dressed, all of which they are likely to forget by morning. Most sleepwalking episodes are not related to dreaming, and contrary to urban myth, awakening a sleepwalker will not cause sudden death or injury. What's dangerous is leaving the front door unlocked and the car keys in the ignition, as sleepwalkers have been known to wander into the streets and even attempt driving (American Psychiatric Association, 2013).

Sleep terrors are non-REM sleep disturbances primarily affecting children. A child experiencing a night terror may sit up in bed, stare fearfully at nothing, and scream. Parents may find the child crying hysterically, breathing rapidly, and sweating. No matter what the parents say or do, the child remains inconsolable. Fortunately, sleep terrors only last a few minutes, and most children outgrow them. Sleep terrors are often worse for parents than they are for the child, who generally won't remember the episode the next day (American Psychiatric Association, 2013).

Nightmares are frightening dreams that occur in REM sleep. They affect people of all ages. And unlike night terrors, nightmares can often be recalled in vivid detail. Because nightmares usually occur during REM sleep, they are generally not acted out (American Psychiatric Association, 2013).

Who Needs Sleep?

Matt's worst struggle with narcolepsy stretched through the last two years of high school. During this time, he was averaging 20 to 30 naps a day. You might think that someone who falls asleep so often would at least feel well rested while awake. This was not the case. Matt had trouble sleeping at night, and it was taking a heavy toll on his ability to think clearly. He remembers nodding off at the wheel a few times but continuing to drive, reassuring himself that everything was fine. He forgot about homework assignments and simple things people told him. Matt was experiencing two of the most common symptoms of sleep deprivation: impaired judgment and lapses in memory (Goel, Rao, Durmer, & Dinges, 2009).

Let's face it. No one can function optimally without a good night's sleep. But the expression "good night's sleep" means something quite different from one person to the next. Newborns sleep anywhere from 10.5 to 18 hours per day, toddlers 11 to 14 hours, school-aged children 9 to 11 hours, and teens 8 to 10 hours (National Sleep Foundation, 2015a, 2015c). The average adult needs between 7 and 8 hours to feel restored, though some (including Madonna and Jay Leno) claim they get by on just 4 (Breus, 2009, May 6). People who average less than 4 or more than 11 hours, otherwise known as "extreme sleepers," are very rare (Horne, 2006).

"Wake up, Tom. You're having the American dream again."

Peter Steiner/The New Yorker Collection/www.cartoonbank.com.

SLEEP DEPRIVATION What happens to animals when they don't sleep at all? Laboratory studies show that sleep deprivation kills rats faster than starvation (Rechtschaffen & Bergmann, 1995; Siegel, 2005). Curtailing sleep in humans leads to rapid deterioration of mental and physical well-being. Stay up all night for 48 hours and you can expect your memory, attention, reaction time, and decision making to suffer noticeably (Goel et al., 2009; Lim & Dinges, 2010). Sleepy people find it especially challenging to accomplish tasks that are monotonous and boring; those deprived of sleep have trouble focusing on a single activity, like keeping their eyes on the road while driving (Lim & Dinges, 2010). Using driving simulators and tests to measure alertness, hand-eye coordination, and other factors, researchers report that getting behind the wheel while sleepy is similar to driving drunk. Staying awake for just 17 to 19 consecutive hours (which many of us with demanding jobs, children, and social lives do regularly) produces the same effect as having a blood alcohol content (BAC) of 0.05%, the legal limit in many countries (Williamson & Feyer, 2000). Sleep loss also makes you more prone to *microsleeps*, or uncontrollable mini-naps lasting several seconds—enough time to miss a traffic light turning red. Staying awake for several days at a time (11 days is the current world record, based on experimental data; Gillin, 2002, March 25) produces a host of disabling effects, including fragmented speech, cognitive deficits, mood swings, and hallucinations (Gulevich, Dement, & Johnson, 1966).

A more chronic form of sleep deprivation results from insufficient sleep night-upon-night for weeks, months, or years. People in this category are less likely than their well-rested peers to exercise, eat healthy foods, have sex, and attend family events (National Sleep Foundation, 2009). They also face a greater risk for heart disease, diabetes, and weight gain (Sigurdson & Ayas, 2007), and have decreased immune system responses and slower reaction times (Besedovsky, Lange, & Born, 2012; Orzeł-Gryglewska, 2010). Many researchers suspect the obesity epidemic currently plaguing Western countries is linked to chronic sleep deprivation. Skimping on sleep appears to disrupt appetite-regulating hormones, which may lead to excessive hunger and overeating (Willyard, 2008).

REM DEPRIVATION So far we have only covered sleep loss in general, but remember there are two types of sleep: REM and non-REM. What happens if only one of these is compromised? Studies show that depriving people of Stages 3 and 4 sleep leads to physical symptoms such as fatigue and increased sensitivity to pain (Roehrs,

sleep terrors A disturbance of non-REM sleep, generally occurring in children; characterized by screaming, staring fearfully, and usually no memory of the episode the following morning.

nightmares Frightening dreams that occur during REM sleep.

TABLE 4.2 THEORIES OF SLEEP

Theory	Description	Reflection
Restorative	Sleep allows for growth and repair of the body and brain.	Growth hormone secreted during non-REM sleep; protein production increases during REM; replenishment of neurotransmitters.
Evolutionary	Sleep serves adaptive function; evolved as it helped survival.	Dark environments were unsafe; humans have poor night vision compared to animals hunting at night.
Consolidation	Sleep aids in the consolidation of memories and learning.	Assists in creation of memories, learning difficult concepts; similar patterns of brain activity when learning and sleeping afterwards.

We spend approximately a third of our lives sleeping, yet the precise purpose of sleep is still to be established. Above are three of the dominant theories.

Hyde, Blaisdell, Greenwald, & Roth, 2006). Preliminary research suggests depriving people of REM sleep in particular can cause emotional overreactions to threatening situations (Rosales-Lagarde et al., 2012). REM deprivation can also lead to **REM rebound,** an increased amount of time spent in REM sleep when one finally gets an opportunity to sleep in peace.

WHY DO WE SLEEP?   The exact purpose of sleep has yet to be identified. Drawing from sleep deprivation studies and other types of experiments, researchers have constructed various theories to explain *why* we spend so much time sleeping (**Table 4.2**). Here are three of the major ones:

- The *restorative theory* says we sleep because it allows for growth and repair of the body and brain. Growth hormone is secreted during non-REM sleep and protein production ramps up in the brain during REM. Some have suggested that sleep is a time for rest and replenishment of neurotransmitters, especially those important for attention and memory (Hobson, 1989).

- An *evolutionary theory* says sleep serves an adaptive function; it evolved because it helped us survive. For much of human history, nighttime was very dark—and very unsafe. Humans have poor night vision compared to animals hunting for prey, so it was adaptive for us to avoid moving around our environments in the dark of night. The development of our circadian rhythms driving us to sleep at night has served an important evolutionary purpose.

- Another compelling theory suggests that sleep helps with the *consolidation* of memories and learning. Researchers disagree about which stage of sleep might facilitate such a process, but one thing seems clear: Without sleep, our ability to lay down complex memories, and thus learn difficult concepts, is hampered (Farthing, 1992). Studies show that areas of the brain excited during learning tasks are reawakened during non-REM sleep. When researchers monitored the neuronal activity of rats exploring a new environment, they noticed certain neurons firing. These same neurons became active again when the rats fell into non-REM sleep, suggesting that the neurons were involved in remembering the experience (Diekelmann & Born, 2010). Similarly, in humans, PET scans have shown common patterns of brain activity when research participants were awake and learning and later while asleep (Maquet, 2000).

REM rebound An increased amount of time spent in REM during the first sleep session after sleep deprivation.

Whatever the purpose of sleep, there is no denying its importance. After a couple of sleepless nights, we are grumpy, clumsy, and unable to think straight. Although we may appreciate the value of sleep, we don't always practice the best sleep habits—or know what they are. Read on to discover some behaviors and assumptions you should avoid.

Apply This

7 Sleep Myths

Everyone seems to have their own bits of "expert knowledge" about sleep. Read on to learn about claims (in **bold**) that are false.

- **Drinking alcohol before bed helps you sleep better:** Alcohol helps you fall asleep, but it undermines sleep quality and may cause you to awaken in the night (Ebrahim, Shapiro, Williams, & Fenwick, 2013). So, too, can one or two cups of coffee. Although moderate caffeine consumption heightens alertness (Epstein & Mardon, 2007), be careful not to drink too much or too close to bedtime; either action may lead to further sleep disruption (Drake, Roehrs, Shambroom, & Roth, 2013).

- **Exercising right before bed sets you up for a good night's sleep:** Generally speaking, exercise promotes slow-wave sleep, the type that makes you feel bright-eyed and bushy-tailed in the morning (Driver & Taylor, 2000; Youngstedt & Kline, 2006). However, working out too close to bedtime (2 to 3 hours beforehand) may prevent good sleep (National Institutes of Health [NIH], 2012).

- **Everyone needs 8 hours of sleep each night:** Most people require between 7 and 8 hours (Banks & Dinges, 2007), but sleep needs can range greatly from person to person. Some people do fine with 6 hours; others genuinely need 9 or 10.

- **Watching TV or using your computer just before bed helps get you into the sleep zone:** Screen time is not advised as a transition into sleep time. The stimulation of TV and computers can inhibit sleep (National Sleep Foundation, 2015b).

- **You can catch up on accumulated sleep loss with one night of "super-sleep":** Settling any sleep debt is not easy. You may feel refreshed upon waking from 10 hours of "recovery" sleep, but the effects of sleep debt will likely creep up later on (Cohen et al., 2010).

- **Insomnia is no big deal. Everyone has trouble sleeping from time to time:** Insomnia is a mentally and physically debilitating condition that can result in mood changes, memory problems, difficulty with concentration and coordination, and other life-altering impairments (Pavlovich-Danis & Patterson, 2006).

- **Sleep aids are totally safe:** When taken according to prescription, sleep aids are relatively safe and effective, although they do not guarantee a normal night of sleep. That being said, research has linked some of these medications to an increased risk of death (Kripke, Langer, & Kline, 2012), as well as an increased risk of sleep eating, sleep sex, and "driving while not fully awake" (U.S. Food and Drug Administration, 2013, para. 5).

NO IPADS ALLOWED
IN THE BED!

Before moving on to the next section, look at **Table 4.3** on the next page for some ideas on how to get better sleep. ➡

Apply This

TABLE 4.3 HOW TO GET A GOOD NIGHT'S SLEEP

To Get Good Sleep	Reasoning
Get on a schedule.	The body operates according to daily cycles, or circadian rhythms. Putting your body and brain on a regular schedule—going to bed and waking up at roughly the same time every day—is critical.
Set the stage for sleep.	Turn down the lights, turn off your phone, and slip into soft pajamas. Do everything possible to create a quiet, dark, and comfortable sleeping environment.
Watch eating, drinking, and smoking.	Beware of foods that create heartburn, and avoid excessive use of alcohol, caffeine, and nicotine (known enemies of sleep) especially late in the day.
Move it or lose it.	Exercise is associated with better sleep, but not right before bed. Exercising 2 to 3 hours before bed can actually prevent good sleep.

If you frequently wake up feeling groggy and unrestored, above are several simple measures you can take to improve the quality of your sleep.

SOURCE: NIH, 2012.

✓ **show what you know**

1. The suprachiasmatic nucleus obtains its information about day and night from:
   a. circadian rhythms.
   b. beta waves.
   c. K-complexes.
   d. retinal ganglion cells.

2. In which of the following stages of sleep do adults spend the most time at night?
   a. Stage 1
   b. Stage 2
   c. Stage 3
   d. Stage 4

3. Narcolepsy is a neurological disorder characterized by excessive daytime sleepiness and other sleep-related disturbances such as _____, which refers to an abrupt loss of muscle tone that occurs when a person is awake.

4. Make a drawing of the 90-minute sleep cycle. Label each stage with its associated brain wave(s).

✓ CHECK YOUR ANSWERS IN APPENDIX C.

Dreams

Sleep is an exciting time for the brain. As we lie in the darkness, eyes closed and bodies limp, our neurons keep firing. REM is a particularly active sleep stage, characterized by brain waves that are fast and irregular. During REM, anything is possible. We can soar through the clouds, kiss superheroes, and ride roller coasters with frogs. Time to explore the weird world of dreaming.

 SLEEP, SLEEP, GO AWAY Just 2 months before graduating from high school, Matt began taking a new medication that vastly improved the quality of his nighttime sleep. He also began strategic power napping, setting aside time in his schedule to go somewhere peaceful and fall asleep for 15 to 30 minutes. "Power naps are probably the greatest thing a person with narcolepsy can do," Matt insists. The naps helped eliminate the daytime sleepiness, effectively preempting all those unplanned naps that had fragmented his days. Matt also worked diligently to create structure in his life, setting a predictable rhythm of going to bed, taking medication, going to bed again, waking up in the morning, attending class, taking a nap, and so on.

Now a college graduate and working professional, Matt manages his narcolepsy quite successfully. All of his major symptoms—the spontaneous naps, cataplexy, sleep paralysis, and hypnagogic hallucinations—have faded. "Now if I fall asleep, it's because I choose to," Matt says. "Most people don't even know I have narcolepsy."

You Asked, Matt Answers

http://qrs.ly/nu4qsyx

What sorts of medications help to control narcolepsy?

Not everyone with narcolepsy is so fortunate. The disorder is often mistaken for another ailment, such as depression or insomnia. Most people with narcolepsy don't even know they have it, and by the time an expert offers them a diagnosis (sometimes years after the symptoms began), they have already suffered major social and professional consequences (Stanford School of Medicine, 2015). While several medications are available to help control symptoms, there is no known cure for narcolepsy. Scheduling "therapeutic naps," avoiding monotonous activities, and controlling emotional highs are all behavioral treatments for narcolepsy.

Now when Matt goes to sleep at night, he no longer imagines people coming to murder him. In dreams, he soars through the skies like Superman, barreling into outer space to visit the planets. "All my dreams are now pleasant," says Matt, "[and] it's a lot nicer being able to fly than being stabbed by a butcher knife." If you wonder what Matt is doing these days, he works at a credit union (one of the top producers in his company) and is pursuing his master's of business administration (MBA). Onward and upward, like Superman. 🗂

In Your Dreams

LO 7   Summarize the theories of why we dream.

What are dreams, and why do we have them? People have contemplated the significance of dreams for millennia, and scholars have developed many intriguing theories to explain them.

PSYCHOANALYSIS AND DREAMS   The first comprehensive theory of dreaming was developed by the father of psychoanalysis, Sigmund Freud (Chapters 10 and 13). In 1900 Freud laid out his theory in the now-classic *The Interpretation of Dreams,* proposing that dreams were a form of "wish fulfillment," or a playing out of unconscious desires. As Freud saw it, many of the desires expressed in dreams are forbidden and would produce great anxiety in a dreamer if she were aware of them. In dreams, these desires are disguised so they can be experienced without danger of discovery. Freud believed dreams have two levels of content: *manifest* and *latent*. **Manifest content,** the apparent meaning of a dream, is the actual story line of the dream itself—what you remember when you wake up. **Latent content** is the hidden meaning of a dream, and represents unconscious conflicts and desires. During therapy sessions, psychoanalysts look deeper than the actual story line of a dream, using its latent content to uncover what's occurring unconsciously. (Critics of Freud's approach to dream analysis would note there are an infinite number of ways to interpret any dream, all of which are impossible to prove wrong.)

ACTIVATION-SYNTHESIS MODEL   In contrast to Freud's theory, the **activation-synthesis model** suggests that dreams have no meaning whatsoever (Hobson & McCarley, 1977). During REM sleep, the motor areas of the brain are inhibited (remember, the body is paralyzed), but sensory areas of the brain hum with a great deal of neural activity. According to the activation-synthesis model, we respond to this activity as if it has meaning, even though this sensory excitement is only random chatter among neurons. Our creative minds make up stories to match this activity, and these stories are our dreams. During REM sleep the brain is also trying to make sense of neural activity in the vestibular system. If the vestibular system is active while we are lying still, then the brain may interpret this as floating or flying—both common experiences reported by dreamers.

Under Control
After a few very challenging years, Matt developed effective strategies for managing his narcolepsy. In addition to using a medication that helps him sleep more soundly at night, Matt takes strategic power naps and sticks to a regular bedtime and wake-up schedule.
Courtesy Matthew Utesch

⟋ CONNECTIONS

In **Chapter 3** we noted that the vestibular system is responsible for our balance. Accordingly, if its associated area in the nervous system is active while we are asleep, the sensations normally associated with this system when we are awake will be interpreted in a congruent manner.

manifest content The apparent meaning of a dream; the remembered story line of a dream.

latent content The hidden meaning of a dream, often concealed by the manifest content of the dream.

activation–synthesis model This theory proposes that humans respond to random neural activity while in REM sleep as if it has meaning.

NEUROCOGNITIVE THEORY OF DREAMS The neurocognitive theory of dreams proposes that a network of neurons exists in the brain, including some areas in the limbic system and the forebrain, that is necessary for dreaming to occur (Domhoff, 2001). People with damage to these brain areas either do not have dreams, or their dreams are not normal. Additional support for this theory comes from studies of children; it turns out that the dreams of children differ from those of adults. Before about 13 to 15 years of age, children report dreams that are less vivid and seem to have less of a story line. Apparently, an underlying neural network must develop or mature before a child can dream like an adult. And as noted earlier, memory consolidation seems to be facilitated by sleep, with some theorists emphasizing the important role REM sleep plays in this process. The neurocognitive theory of dreams does not suggest, however, that dreams serve a purpose. Instead, they seem to be the result of how sleep and consciousness have evolved in humans (Domhoff, 2001).

Dream a Little Dream

Most dreams feature ordinary, everyday scenarios like driving a car or sitting in class. The content of dreams is repetitive and in line with what we think about when we are awake, and includes similar ideas about relationships, bad luck, people, and negative feelings. In fact, the content of dreams is relatively consistent across cultures. Dreams are more likely to include sad events than happy ones and, contrary to popular assumption, less than 12% of dream time is devoted to sexual activity (Yu & Fu, 2011). If you're one of those people who believe they don't dream, you are probably wrong. Most individuals who insist they don't dream simply fail to remember their dreams. If awakened during a dream, one is more likely to recall it at that moment than if asked to remember it at lunchtime. The ability to remember dreams is dependent on the length of time since the dream.

Most dreaming takes place during REM sleep and is jam-packed with rich sensory details and narrative. Dreams also occur during non-REM sleep, but they lack the vivid imagery and storylike quality of REM dreams. The average person starts dreaming about 90 minutes into sleep, then goes on to have about four to six dreams during the night. Add up the time and you get a total of about 1 to 2 hours of dreaming per night. An interesting feature of dreams is that they happen in real time. In one early study investigating this phenomenon, researchers roused sleepers after they had been in a 5-minute REM cycle and again after a 15-minute REM cycle, asking them how long they had been dreaming (5 or 15 minutes). The majority of the participants—four out of five—gave the right answer (Dement & Kleitman, 1957).

Have you ever realized that you are in the middle of a dream? A *lucid dream* is one that you are aware of having, and research suggests that about half of us have had one (Gackenbach & LaBerge, 1988). There are two parts to a lucid dream: the dream itself and the awareness that you are dreaming. Some suggest lucid dreaming is actually a way to direct the content of dreams (Gavie & Revonsuo, 2010), but this is a controversial claim because there is no way to confirm people's subjective reports; dreams cannot be experienced by an outsider.

Dreaming Brain
PET scans reveal the high levels of brain activity during REM sleep (left) and wakefulness (right). During REM, the brain is abuzz with excitement. (This is especially true of the sensory areas.) According to the activation-synthesis model, dreams may result when the brain tries to make sense of all this neural activity. Hank Morgan/Science Source

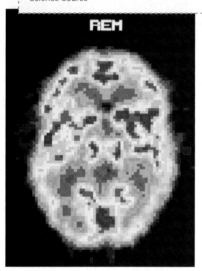
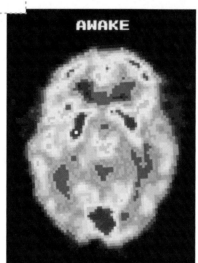

Jack Ziegler/The New Yorker Collection/www.cartoonbank.com

"Uh-oh. I think I'm having one of those dreams again."

Fantastical, funny, or frightening, dreams represent a distinct state of consciousness, and consciousness is a fluid, ever-changing entity. Now it's time to explore how consciousness transforms when chemicals are introduced into our bodies.

✓ show what you know

1. Freud believed dreams have two levels. The _____ refers to the apparent meaning of the dream, whereas the _____ refers to its hidden meaning.

2. According to the _____, dreams have no meaning whatsoever. Instead, the brain is responding to random neural activity as if it has meaning.
   a. psychoanalytic perspective   b. neurocognitive theory
   c. activation–synthesis model   d. evolutionary perspective

3. What occurs in the brain when you dream?

4. Your 6-year-old cousin does not have dreams with a true story line; her dreams seem to be fleeting images. This supports the neurocognitive theory of dreams, as does the fact that:
   a. until children are around 13 to 15 years old, their reported dreams are less vivid.
   b. dream content is not the same across cultures.
   c. children younger than 13 can report very complicated story lines from their dreams.
   d. dream content is the same for people, regardless of age.

✓ CHECK YOUR ANSWERS IN APPENDIX C.

Altered States of Consciousness

We have now explored many levels of consciousness, from wide-awake to sound asleep, but we have yet to address states of consciousness that result from the influence of agents such as drugs and alcohol, or hypnosis. Let's take a look at these altered states.

 **EMERGENCY IN THE NIGHT** You wake in the middle of the night with a dull pain around your belly button. By morning, the pain is sharp and stabbing and has migrated to your lower right abdomen, so you head to the local emergency room where doctors diagnose you with appendicitis, an inflammation of the appendix often caused by infection. You need an emergency operation to remove your appendix, and a strong anesthetic is in order: a combination of drugs to paralyze the abdominal muscles, dull the pain, and wipe out your memory of the procedure. Dr. Julien, introduced at the start of the chapter, is your anesthesiologist.

For paralysis, Dr. Julien would probably give you a drug similar to *curare,* an arrowhead poison used by South American natives. Curare works by blocking the activity of the neurotransmitter acetylcholine, which stimulates muscle contractions in the body. But curare does not cross into the brain, and therefore it does not have the power to transport you to another level of consciousness (Czarnowski, Bailey, & Bal, 2007). If curare were the only drug Dr. Julien administered, you would be lying on the operating table paralyzed yet completely awake and aware of your pain—not a pleasant scenario. 📁

Psychoactive Drugs

LO 8   Define psychoactive drugs.

To dull the perception of pain, Dr. Julien might administer fentanyl, which belongs to a class of drugs called opioids that we will soon discuss. And to stamp out your memory of the surgery, he would lull you into a sleeplike stupor with a drug such as propofol and then maintain that state of sleep with other drugs. One moment you are awake, sensing, perceiving, thinking, and talking. The next moment you see nothing, hear nothing, feel nothing. It's like you are gone. Fentanyl and propofol are considered **psychoactive drugs** because the chemicals they contain cause changes in

CONNECTIONS

In **Chapter 2,** we described neurotransmitters and the role they play in the nervous system. Acetylcholine is a neurotransmitter that relays messages from motor neurons to muscles, which enables movement. Too little acetylcholine causes paralysis. Here, we see how drugs can block the normal activity of acetylcholine, causing the paralysis useful during surgery.

psychoactive drugs Substances that can cause changes in psychological activities such as sensation, perception, attention, judgment, memory, self-control, emotion, thinking, and behavior; substances that cause changes in conscious experiences.

Vulnerable Youth
Young smokers are more inclined than their nonsmoking peers to use illegal drugs, display aggression, and develop mental health problems. They also have a harder time quitting than those who start smoking in adulthood (American Cancer Society, 2012).
Aaron Huey/National Geographic/Getty Images

Synonyms
depressants downers
barbiturate yellow jackets, pink ladies, goof balls, reds, rainbows

---

depressants A class of psychoactive drugs that *depress* or slow down activity in the central nervous system.

barbiturate (bär-ˈbi-chə-rət) Depressant drug that decreases neural activity and reduces anxiety; a type of sedative.

---

psychological activities such as sensation, perception, attention, judgment, memory, self-control, emotion, thinking, and behavior—all of which are associated with our conscious experiences.

You don't need to visit a hospital to have a psychoactive drug experience. Mind-altering drugs are everywhere—in the coffee shop around the corner, at the liquor store down the street, and probably in your own kitchen. About 90% of people in the United States regularly use *caffeine*, a psychoactive drug found in coffee, soda, tea, and medicines (Alpert, 2012; Gurpegui, Aguilar, Martínez-Ortega, Diaz, & de Leon, 2004). Trailing close behind caffeine are *alcohol* (found in beer, wine, and liquor) and *nicotine* (in cigarettes and other tobacco products), two substances that present serious health risks. Another huge category of psychoactive drugs is prescription medications—drugs for pain relief, depression, insomnia, and just about any ailment you can imagine. Don't forget the illicit, or illegal, drugs like LSD and Ecstasy. An estimated 9.4% of Americans aged 12 and older say they used illegal drugs in the past month (Substance Abuse and Mental Health Services Administration [SAMHSA], 2014).

Psychoactive drugs alter consciousness in an untold number of ways. They can rev you up, slow you down, let down your inhibitions, and convince you that the universe is on the verge of collapse. We will discuss the three major categories of psychoactive drugs—depressants, stimulants, and hallucinogens—but keep in mind that some drugs fall into more than one group.

Depressants

LO 9   Identify several depressants and stimulants and know their effects.

In his 25 years as an anesthesiologist, Dr. Julien has primarily relied on a group of psychoactive drugs that *depress* activity in the central nervous system, or slow things down. For this reason, they are called **depressants**. Dr. Julien sometimes *premedicates* patients, administering drugs to calm them while they wait to be wheeled into the operating room. He might use a benzodiazepine, which would act as a *tranquilizer*—a type of depressant that has a calming, sleep-inducing effect. Other examples of tranquilizers are Valium (diazepam) and Xanax (alprazolam), which are used to treat anxiety disorders. A more recent addition to the tranquilizer family is Rohypnol (flunitrazepam), also known as the "date rape drug" or "roofies," which is legally manufactured and approved as a treatment for insomnia in other countries, but banned in the United States (Drug Enforcement Administration [DEA], 2012). Sex predators have been known to slip roofies into their victims' drinks, especially darker-colored cocktails where the blue pills dissolve unseen. Rohypnol can cause confusion, amnesia, lowered inhibitions, and sometimes loss of consciousness, preventing victims from defending themselves or remembering the details of a sexual assault.

BARBITURATES   Once a patient is in the operating room and ready for surgery, Dr. Julien puts him to sleep. This process is called "induction," and it is sometimes accomplished using another type of depressant termed a **barbiturate** (bär-ˈbi-chə-rət), which is a sedative (calming or sleep-inducing) drug that decreases neural activity. In low doses, barbiturates cause many of the same effects as alcohol (discussed below)—relaxation, lowering of spirits, or alternatively, aggression (Julien, Advokat, & Comaty, 2011)—which may explain why they have become so popular among recreational users. But these substances are addictive and extremely dangerous when taken in excess or mixed with other drugs. If barbiturates are taken alongside alcohol, for example, the muscles of the diaphragm may relax to the point of suffocation (**Infographic 4.3**).

The Dangers of Drugs in Combination

Taking multiple drugs simultaneously can lead to unintended and potentially fatal consequences because of how they work in the brain. Drugs can modify neural communication by increasing or decreasing the chemical activity. When two drugs work on the same system, their effects can be additive, greatly increasing the risk of overdose. For example, alcohol and barbiturates both bind to GABA receptors. GABA's inhibitory action has a sedating effect, which is a good thing when you need to relax. But too much GABA will relax physiological processes to the point where unconscious, life-sustaining activities shut down, causing you to stop breathing and die.

Hundreds of deaths are caused annually in the U.S. when drugs like alcohol and barbiturates are taken in combination (Kochanek et al., 2012). In 2009 alone, 519,650 emergency room visits were attributed to use of alcohol in combination with other drugs (SAMHSA, 2010).

NORMAL GABA ACTIVITY

- ○ GABA
- ◼ Alcohol
- ▲ Barbiturate

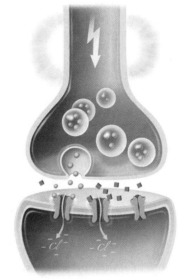

Action potential

Sending neuron

GABA receptor

Receiving neuron

GABA message communicated

GABA activation, which calms nervous system activity, is essential for proper functioning of the central nervous system. Without GABA, nerve cells fire too frequently.

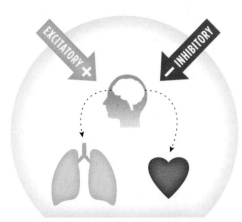

When systems are functioning normally, GABA's inhibitory signals perfectly balance excitatory signals in the central nervous system (CNS). This results in regular breathing and heart rate.

ALCOHOL

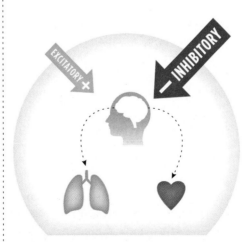

Alcohol activates the same receptors, increasing GABA's activity.

When alcohol increases GABA's inhibitory signals, excitatory and inhibitory signals in the CNS are out of balance. Along with increased relaxation, heart and breathing rates decrease. Increasing levels of alcohol could eventually lead to stupor and coma.

ALCOHOL + BARBITURATE

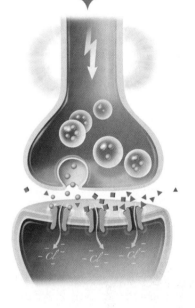

Barbiturates bind to and activate GABA receptors too, creating even more GABA-related inhibition.

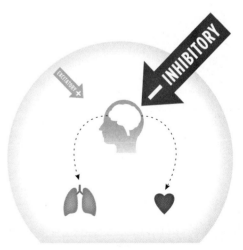

Together, alcohol and barbiturates further unbalance excitatory and inhibitory signals, suppressing heart rate and the impulse to breathe.

Opium Poppy

Naturally occurring opioids, or *opiates,* are found in the opium poppy, the same plant that produces those little black seeds on your breakfast bagel. Doctors have been using the poppy opiate *morphine* to alleviate pain since the early 1800s (Julien et al., 2011). Getty Images/Vetta

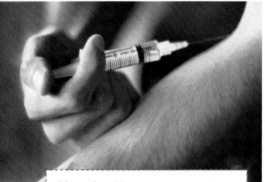

Shooting Up

Heroin is one of the most pleasure-inducing—and dangerous—drugs in the world. About 23% of heroin users get hooked, and the consequences of chronic use are serious: boils on the skin, HIV and hepatitis (from contaminated needles), liver disease, spontaneous abortion, and many others (National Institute on Drug Abuse, 2013b). © PhotoAlto/Alamy

opioids A class of psychoactive drugs that minimizes perceptions of pain.

opiates A class of psychoactive drugs that cause a sense of euphoria; a drug that imitates the endorphins naturally produced in the brain.

OPIOIDS   Putting a patient to sleep is not enough to prepare him for a major surgery; he also needs drugs that combat pain. Even when a patient is out cold on the operating table, his brain receives pain impulses that without proper painkilling drugs can give rise to what Dr. Julien calls "autonomic instability," a disruption of heart rate, blood pressure, and other activities regulated by the autonomic nervous system. One way to maintain autonomic stability is to give the patient an **opioid,** a drug that minimizes the brain's perception of pain. "Opioid" is an umbrella term for a large group of similarly acting drugs, some found in nature and others concocted in laboratories (synthesized replacements such as methadone). Opioids block pain, induce drowsiness and euphoria, and slow down breathing (Julien et al., 2011). There are two types of naturally occurring opioids: the endorphins produced by your body, and the **opiates** found in the opium poppy. Morphine, which is derived from the opium poppy, is used to alleviate pain in medical settings; it also serves as the raw material for making the street drug heroin, which enters the brain more quickly and has 3 times the strength (Julien et al., 2011).

PRESCRIPTION DRUG ABUSE   Few people in the United States actually use heroin (less than 1%; SAMHSA, 2014), and some studies suggest that number is decreasing. But another class of opioids appears to be taking its place—synthetic painkillers such as Vicodin (hydrocodone) and OxyContin (oxycodone; Fischer & Rehm, 2007; SAMHSA, 2010). Unlike heroin, these medications are legally manufactured by drug companies and legitimately prescribed by physicians. Intentionally using a medication without a doctor's approval or in a way not prescribed by a doctor (for example, taking too much of a medication) can lead to *prescription drug abuse,* and this behavior is shockingly common among teenagers, who are more vulnerable to becoming hooked or addicted (Zhang et al., 2009). Where are teens getting prescription meds? The majority obtain these drugs from friends and family members (National Institute on Drug Abuse, 2014a). Opioid abuse is an epidemic among high school students, and many don't understand how easy it is to become hooked on these drugs. Sadly, drug overdose deaths have surpassed the number of deaths resulting from car accidents in the United States (Moisse, 2011, September 20).

Alcohol

We end our coverage of depressants with alcohol, which, like other drugs in its class, has played a central role in the history of anesthesia. The ancient Greek doctor Dioscorides gave his surgical patients a special concoction of wine and mandrake plant (Keys, 1945), and 19th-century Europeans used an alcohol-opium mixture called *laudanum* for anesthetic purposes (Barash, Cullen, Stoelting, & Cahalan, 2009). These days, you won't find anesthesiologists knocking out patients with alcohol, but you will encounter plenty of people intoxicating themselves.

BINGE DRINKING   Alcohol is the most commonly used depressant in the United States. Around 15% of adults and 25% of teenagers report that they *binge drink* (consuming four or more drinks for women and five or more for men, on one occasion or within a short time span) at least once a month (Naimi et al., 2003; Wen et al., 2012). Many people think binge drinking is fun, but they might change their minds if they reviewed the research. Studies have linked binge drinking to poor grades, aggressive behavior, sexual promiscuity, and accidental death. In 2005 almost 2,000 college students in the United States died in alcohol-related accidents (Hingson, Zha, & Weitzman, 2009). Think getting wasted is sexy? Consider this: Alcohol impairs sexual performance, particularly for men, who may have trouble obtaining and sustaining an erection.

You don't have to binge drink in order to have an alcohol problem (**Figure 4.1**). Some people cannot get through the day without a midday drink; others need alcohol to unwind or fall asleep. The point is there are many forms of alcohol misuse. About 8.5% of the adult population in the United States (nearly 1 in 10 people) struggle with alcohol dependence or some other type of drinking problem (Grant et al., 2004). Drinking can destroy families, careers, and human lives.

ALCOHOL AND THE BODY   Let's stop for a minute and examine how alcohol influences consciousness (Figure 4.1). People sometimes say they feel "high" when they drink. How can such a statement be true when alcohol is a *depressant,* a drug that slows down activity in the central nervous system? Alcohol boosts the activity of GABA, a neurotransmitter that dampens activity in certain neural networks, including those that regulate social inhibition—a type of self-restraint that keeps you from doing things you will regret the next morning. This release of social inhibition can lead to feelings of euphoria. Drinking affects other conscious processes, such as reaction time, balance, attention span, memory, speech, and involuntary life-sustaining activities like breathing (Howland et al., 2010; McKinney & Coyle, 2006). Drink enough, and these vital functions will shut down entirely, leading to coma and even death (Infographic 4.3).

The female body is less efficient at breaking down (metabolizing) alcohol. Even when we control for body size and muscle-to-fat ratio, we see that women achieve higher blood alcohol levels (and thus a significantly stronger "buzz") than men who have consumed equal amounts. Why? Because men have more of an alcohol-metabolizing enzyme in their stomachs, which means they start to break down alcohol almost immediately after ingestion. In a woman, most of the alcohol clears the stomach and enters the bloodstream and brain before the liver finally breaks it down (Toufexis, 2001).

Binge Drinking
Binge drinking has been associated with reduced mental and physical health. This effect appears to intensify with increasing levels of alcohol ingestion (Wen et al., 2012).
© Pascal Deloche/GODONG/Godong/Corbis

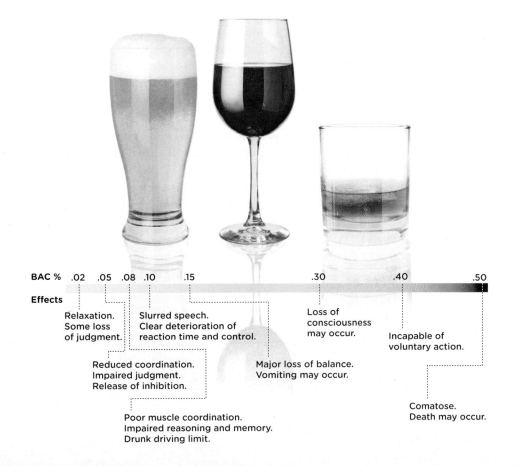

| BAC % | .02 | .05 | .08 | .10 | .15 | .30 | .40 | .50 |

Effects

Relaxation. Some loss of judgment.

Slurred speech. Clear deterioration of reaction time and control.

Loss of consciousness may occur.

Incapable of voluntary action.

Reduced coordination. Impaired judgment. Release of inhibition.

Major loss of balance. Vomiting may occur.

Poor muscle coordination. Impaired reasoning and memory. Drunk driving limit.

Comatose. Death may occur.

FIGURE 4.1
Blood Alcohol Concentration (BAC) and Effects on Behavior
The effects of one drink—a 12-oz bottle of beer, 4-oz glass of wine, or 1-oz shot of hard liquor—vary depending on weight, ethnicity, gender, and other factors. Across most of the United States, a BAC of .08 is the legal limit for driving. But even at lower levels, our coordination and focus may be impaired. Source: Centers for Disease Control and Prevention, 2011, February 11; (Photos: left & center) Danny Smythe/Shutterstock; (right) Thinkstock

THE CONSEQUENCES OF DRINKING   Light alcohol consumption by adults—one to two drinks of wine, beer, or liquor a day—may have some cardiovascular and cognitive benefits (Cervilla, Prince, Joels, Lovestone, & Mann, 2000; Mukamal, Maclure, Muller, Sherwood, & Mittleman, 2001). Excessive drinking, on the other hand, is associated with a host of health problems. Overuse of alcohol can lead to malnourishment, cirrhosis of the liver, and *Wernicke–Korsakoff syndrome,* whose symptoms include confusion and memory problems. Excessive drinking has also been linked to heart disease, various types of cancer, tens of thousands of yearly traffic deaths, and fetal-alcohol syndrome in children whose mothers drank during pregnancy. Deaths due to overuse of alcohol, numbering about 75,000 annually, have been reported as the third most common type of preventable death in the United States (Centers for Disease Control and Prevention [CDC], 2004; Mokdad, Marks, Stroup, & Gerberding, 2004). If you suspect that you or someone you care about is overusing alcohol, take a look at the warning signs of problematic drinking presented in **Figure 4.2.**

Apply This

FIGURE 4.2
Warning Signs of Problematic Drinking
The presence of one or more of these warning signs could indicate a developing problem with alcohol. *Sources:* APA, 2012, March; NIH, National Institute on Alcohol Abuse and Alcoholism, 2013.

- Having your friends or relatives express concern.
- Becoming annoyed when people criticize your drinking behavior.
- Feeling guilty about your drinking behavior.
- Thinking you should drink less but being unable to do so.
- Needing a morning drink as an "eye-opener" or to relieve a hangover.
- Not fulfilling responsibilities at work, home, or school because of your drinking.
- Engaging in dangerous behavior (like driving under the influence).
- Having legal or social problems due to your drinking.

Stimulants

Not all drugs used in anesthesia are depressants. Did you know that some doctors use cocaine as a local anesthetic for nose and throat surgeries (MedicineNet, 2014)? Cocaine is a **stimulant**—a drug that increases neural activity in the central nervous system, producing heightened alertness, energy, elevated mood, and other effects (Julien et al., 2011). When applied topically, cocaine blocks sensation in the peripheral nerves and thereby numbs the area.

COCAINE   The first to tap into cocaine's pain-zapping potential were the ancient Peruvians, who chewed the leaves of the coca plant (which contain about 1% cocaine) and then applied their saliva to surgical incisions. The coca plant, they believed, was a divine gift; chewing the leaves quenched their hunger, lifted their sadness, and restored their energy. Thousands of years later, in 1860, a German chemist named Albert Niemann extracted the active ingredient in the coca leaf and dubbed it "cocaine" (Julien et al., 2011; Keys, 1945). Within a few decades, doctors were using cocaine for anesthesia, Sigmund Freud was giving it to patients (and himself), and Coca-Cola was putting it in soda (Keys, 1945; Musto, 1991).

While cocaine is illegal in the United States and most other countries, it is among the most widely used illicit drugs. Depending on the form in which it is prepared (powder, rocks, and so on), it can be snorted, injected, or smoked. The sense of energy, euphoria, and other alterations of consciousness that cocaine induces after entering the bloodstream and infiltrating the brain last anywhere from 5 to 30 minutes (National Institute on Drug Abuse, 2013a). Cocaine produces a rush of pleasure and excitement by amplifying the effects of dopamine and norepinephrine. But the coke high comes at a steep price. Any time you take cocaine, you put yourself at risk

Cocaine in Cola
The original recipe for Coca-Cola included cocaine, but the company removed the drug from its cola in 1900, one year before the city of Atlanta banned its nonprescription use (Musto, 1991). © Bettmann/CORBIS

for suffering a stroke or heart attack, even if you are young and healthy. Cocaine is implicated in more emergency room visits than any other illegal drug (Drug Abuse Warning Network, 2011). It is also extremely addictive. Many users find they can never quite duplicate the high they experienced the first time, so they take increasingly higher doses, developing a physical need for the drug, increasing their risk of effects such as anxiety, insomnia, and schizophrenia-like psychosis when they stop using it (Julien et al., 2011).

Cocaine use grew rampant in the 1980s. That was the decade *crack*—an ultra-potent (and ultra-cheap) crystalline form of cocaine—began poisoning America's inner cities. Although cocaine is still a major problem, another stimulant—methamphetamine—has come to rival it in popularity.

Synonyms
methamphetamine meth, crystal meth, crank
amphetamines speed, uppers, bennies

AMPHETAMINES *Methamphetamine* belongs to a family of stimulants called the **amphetamines** (am-ˈfe-tə-ˌmēnz). Doctors used amphetamines to treat medical conditions as diverse as head injury and excessive hiccups in the 1930s and 1940s (Julien et al., 2011). During World War II, soldiers and factory workers used methamphetamine to increase energy and boost performance (Lineberry & Bostwick, 2006). Nonprescription use of methamphetamine is illegal, but people have learned how to brew this drug in their own laboratories, using ingredients from ordinary household products such as drain cleaner, battery acid, and over-the-counter cough medicines. "Cooking meth" is a dangerous enterprise. The flammable ingredients, combined with the reckless mentality of "tweaking" cookers, make for toxic fumes and thousands of accidental explosions every year (Lineberry & Bostwick, 2006). Despite the enormous risk, many people continue to cook meth at home, endangering and sometimes killing their own children.

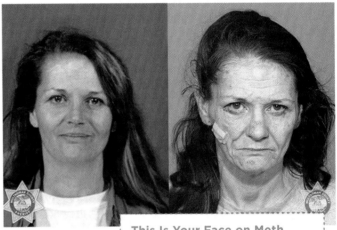

This Is Your Face on Meth
This woman appears to have aged 15 or 20 years, but the time elapsed between these two photos is just 2 ½ years. Methamphetamine ravages the body, the brain, and one's overall appearance. Some meth users have lingering symptoms: Imagine experiencing horrific tactile hallucinations that cause you to believe bugs have invaded your skin and are crawling underneath it, and that in response you tear your skin to the bone in order to kill them. Newscom

Ridiculously cheap, easy to make, and capable of producing a euphoric high lasting many hours, methamphetamine stimulates the release of the brain's pleasure-producing neurotransmitter dopamine, causing a surge in energy and alertness similar to a cocaine high. It also tends to increase sex drive and suppress appetite for food. But unlike cocaine, which the body eliminates quickly, meth lingers in the body (National Institute on Drug Abuse, 2013c). Brain-imaging studies show that chronic meth use causes serious brain damage in the frontal lobes and other areas, still visible even among those who have been clean for 11 months. This may explain why so many meth users suffer from lasting memory and movement problems (Krasnova & Cadet, 2009; Volkow et al., 2001). Other severe consequences of meth use include extreme weight loss; tooth decay ("meth mouth"); and psychosis with hallucinations that can come and go for months, if not years, after quitting (National Institute on Drug Abuse, 2013c).

CAFFEINE Most people have not experimented with illegal stimulants like cocaine and meth, but many are regular users of caffeine. We usually associate caffeine with beverages like coffee, but this pick-me-up drug also lurks in places you wouldn't expect, such as in over-the-counter cough medicines, chocolate, and energy bars. Caffeine works by blocking the action of adenosine, a neurotransmitter that normally muffles the activity of excitatory neurons in the brain (Julien et al., 2011). By interfering with adenosine's calming effect, caffeine makes you feel physically and mentally wired. A cup of coffee might help you stay up later, exercise longer and harder, and get through more pages in your textbooks.

Moderate caffeine use (up to four cups of coffee per day) has been associated with increased alertness, enhanced recall ability, elevated mood, and greater endurance

stimulants A class of drugs that increase neural activity in the central nervous system.

amphetamines (am-ˈfe-tə-ˌmēnz) Stimulant drugs; methamphetamine falls in this class of drugs.

during physical exercise (Ruxton, 2008). Some studies have also linked moderate long-term consumption with lower rates of depression and suicide, and reduced cognitive decline with aging (Lara, 2010; Rosso, Mossey & Lippa, 2008). But just because researchers find a link between caffeine and positive health outcomes, we should not necessarily conclude that caffeine is responsible for it. We need to remember that correlation does not prove causation. What's more, too much caffeine can make your heart race, your hands tremble, and your mood turn irritable. It takes several hours for your body to metabolize caffeine, so a late afternoon mocha latte may still be present in your system as you lie in bed at midnight counting sheep—with no luck.

TOBACCO   What do you think is the number one cause of premature death worldwide—AIDS, illegal drugs, road accidents, murder . . . suicide? None of the above (**Figure 4.3**). Tobacco causes more deaths than any of these other factors combined (BBC News, 2010, November 20; World Health Organization [WHO], 2008b). The use of cigarettes and other tobacco products claims 5 million lives every year, and half a million in the United States alone (Kasisomayajula et al., 2010). Smoking can lead to lung cancer, emphysema, heart disease, and stroke (American Lung Association, 2014). The average smoker loses approximately 10 to 15 years of her life.

Despite these harrowing statistics, about 1 in 5 adults in the United States continues to light up (CDC, 2010). They say it makes them feel relaxed yet more alert, less hungry, and more tolerant of pain. And those who try to kick the habit find it exceedingly difficult. Cigarettes and other tobacco products contain a highly addictive stimulant called *nicotine,* which sparks the release of epinephrine and norepinephrine. Nicotine use appears to be associated with activity in the same brain area activated by cocaine, another drug that is extremely difficult to give up (Pich et al., 1997; Zhang, Dong, Doyon, & Dani, 2012). The few who succeed face a steep uphill battle. Around 90% of quitters relapse within 6 months (Nonnemaker et al., 2011), suggesting that relapse is a normal experience when quitting, not a sign of failure.

CONNECTIONS

In **Chapter 1,** we discussed the problem with possible third factors and correlations. Here, we need to be cautious about making too strong a statement about coffee causing positive health outcomes, because third factors could be involved in increased caffeine consumption and better health.

FIGURE 4.3

Leading Causes of Death in the United States

The leading killers in this country—heart disease, cancer, and chronic lower respiratory diseases—are largely driven by smoking. Tobacco exposure is behind nearly half a million deaths every year.

Source: Kochanek et al., 2011; photo: © David J. Green—Lifestyle/Alamy

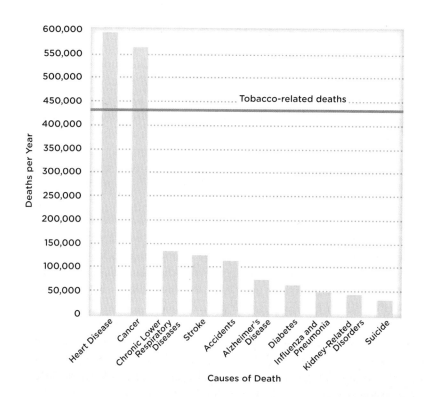

Smoking is not just a problem for the smoker. It is a problem for spouses, children, friends, and anyone who is exposed to the _secondhand smoke_. Secondhand smoke is particularly dangerous for children, whose developing tissues are highly vulnerable (Chapter 8). By smoking, parents increase their children's risk for sudden infant death syndrome (SIDS), respiratory infections, asthma, and bronchitis (CDC, 2014). Secondhand smoke contributes to 21,400 lung cancer deaths and 379,000 heart disease deaths worldwide (Öberg, Jaakkola, Woodward, Peruga, & Prüss-Ustün, 2011), and according to the Centers for Disease Control and Prevention (2014), "there is no risk-free level of exposure" (para. 3). Researchers have also become concerned about the health implications of thirdhand smoke, the combination of cigarette toxins (including lead, which is a known neurotoxin) that lingers in rooms, elevators, and other small spaces long after a smoker has left the scene. Thirdhand smoke is what you smell when you walk into a hotel room and think, _Hmm, someone's been smoking in here_ (Winickoff et al., 2009).

Hallucinogens

LO 10 Discuss some of the hallucinogens.

We have learned how various depressants and stimulants are used in anesthesia. Believe it or not, there is also a place for **hallucinogens** (hə-'lü-sə-nə-jənz)—drugs that produce hallucinations (sights, sounds, odors, or other sensations of things that are not actually present), altered moods, and distorted perception and thought. Phencyclidine (PCP or _angel dust_) and ketamine (_Special K_) are sometimes referred to as _psychedelic anesthetics_ because they were developed to block pain and memory in surgical patients during the 1950s and 1960s (Julien et al., 2011). PCP is highly addictive and extremely dangerous. Because users cannot feel normal pain signals, they run the risk of unintentionally harming or killing themselves. Long-term use can lead to depression and memory impairment. The milder of the two, ketamine, continues to be used in hospitals, but PCP was abandoned long ago. Its effect was just too erratic.

LSD Sheets
Lysergic acid diethylamide, or LSD, is usually taken by mouth, administered through candy, sugar cubes, or blotter sheets like the one pictured here. A popular drug during the "hippie" era of the 1960s and 1970s, LSD has now fallen out of favor.
Science Source

LSD The most well-known hallucinogen is probably **lysergic acid diethylamide (LSD**; lə-'sər-jik; dī-,e-thə-'la-,mīd)—the odorless, tasteless, and colorless substance that produces extreme changes in sensation and perception. People using LSD may report seeing "far out" colors and visions of spirals and other geometric forms. Some experience a crossover of sensations, such as "tasting sound" or "hearing colors." Emotions run wild and bleed into one another; the person "tripping" can quickly flip between depression and joy, excitement and terror (Julien et al., 2011). Trapped on this sensory and emotional roller coaster, some people panic and injure themselves. Others believe that LSD opens their minds, offers new insights, and expands their consciousness. The outcome of a "trip" depends a great deal on the environment and people who are there. LSD is not often overused, and its reported use has remained at an all-time low (Johnston, O'Malley, Bachman, & Schulenberg, 2012).

Synonyms
secondhand smoke passive smoke
hallucinogens psychedelic drugs

hallucinogens (hə-'lü-sə-nə-jənz) A group of psychoactive drugs that can produce hallucinations (auditory, visual, or kinesthetic), distorted sensory experiences, alterations of mood, and distorted thinking.
lysergic acid diethylamide (LSD) (lə-'sər-jik; dī-,e-thə-'la-,mīd) A synthetically produced, odorless, tasteless, and colorless hallucinogen that is very potent; produces extreme changes in sensations and perceptions.

Long-term use may be associated with depression and other psychological problems, including flashbacks that can occur weeks, months, or years after taking the drug. LSD flashbacks may be triggered by fatigue, stress, and illness (Thurlow & Girvin, 1971).

MDMA   In addition to the traditional hallucinogens, there are quite a few "club drugs," or synthetic "designer drugs," used at parties, raves, and dance venues. The most popular among them is **methylenedioxymethamphetamine** (**MDMA**; meth'ĭ-lēn-dī-ok'sē-meth'am-fet'ă-mēn), commonly known as *Ecstasy* or *Molly*. Ecstasy is chemically similar to the stimulant methamphetamine and the hallucinogen mescaline, and thus produces a combination of stimulant and hallucinogenic effects (Barnes et al., 2009; National Institute on Drug Abuse, 2013d).

An Ecstasy trip might bring on feelings of euphoria, love, openness, heightened energy, and floating sensations, as well as intense anxiety and depersonalization, with the user feeling like a detached spectator, watching himself from the outside without having any control. Ecstasy can also cause a host of changes to the body, including decreased appetite, lockjaw, blurred vision, dizziness, rapid heart rate, and dehydration (Gordon, 2001, July 5; Noller, 2009). Dancing in hot, crowded conditions while on Ecstasy can lead to severe heat stroke, seizures, even cardiac arrest and death (Parrott, 2004). Every year, thousands of Ecstasy users leave raves and all-night parties in ambulances. Despite its dangers, Ecstasy is still a popular illicit drug (SAMHSA, 2012).

Ecstasy triggers a sudden general unloading of serotonin in the brain, after which serotonin activity is temporarily depleted until its levels are restored (Klugman & Gruzelier, 2003). Studies of animals have shown that even short-term exposure to MDMA can cause long-term, perhaps even permanent, damage to the brain's serotonin pathways, and there is mounting evidence that a similar type of damage affecting reuptake from the synapse and storage of serotonin occurs in humans as well (Campbell & Rosner, 2008; Reneman et al., 2001; Ricaurte & McCann, 2001). One study found that women's brains are more susceptible to Ecstasy damage than men's, but larger studies are needed to confirm this finding (Reneman et al., 2001). The growing consensus is that even light-to-moderate Ecstasy use can handicap the brain's memory system, and heavy use may impair higher-level cortical functions, such as planning for the future and shifting attention (Klugman & Gruzelier, 2003). Studies also suggest that Ecstasy users are more likely to experience symptoms of depression (Guillot, 2007).

MARIJUANA   The most widely used illegal (in most states) drug, and one of the most popular in all the Western world, is *marijuana* (Compton, Grant, Colliver, Glantz, & Stinson, 2004; Degenhardt & Hall, 2012; SAMHSA, 2014). Forty-four percent of high school seniors in the United States have tried this drug (National Institute on Drug Abuse, 2014b). "It's no big deal," a user might say, "you can't get addicted." But these kinds of assumptions are misleading. Studies suggest that marijuana use can lead to dependence, memory impairment, and deficits in attention and learning (Harvey, Sellman, Porter, & Frampton, 2007; Kleber & DuPont, 2012). Others identify it as a cause of some chronic psychological disorders (Reece, 2009). Long-term use has been associated with reduced motivation (Reece, 2009), as well as respiratory problems, impaired lung functioning, and suppression of the immune system (Iversen, 2003; Pletcher et al., 2012). In addition, the smoke from marijuana contains 50% to 70% more cancer-causing hydrocarbons

CONNECTIONS

In **Chapter 2,** we reported that serotonin is critical for the regulation of mood, appetite, aggression, and automatic behaviors like sleep. Here, we see how the use of Ecstasy can alter levels of this neurotransmitter.

Synonyms
marijuana Mary Jane, M.J., grass, reefer, weed, pot, ganja, hemp
methylenedioxymethamphetamine E, X

Cannabis
Marijuana is the most commonly used illicit drug in the world, consumed by 2.6% to 5% of the adult population. It is also the primary reason people seek drug treatment in many regions of the world, including North America (United Nations, 2012). Thinkstock

than tobacco (Kothadia et al., 2012). Smoking marijuana also causes a temporary dip in sperm production and a greater proportion of abnormal sperm (Brown & Dobs, 2002).

Marijuana comes from the hemp plant, *Cannabis sativa,* which has long been used as—surprise—an anesthetic (Keys, 1945). These days, doctors prescribe marijuana to stimulate patients' appetites and suppress nausea, but its medicinal use is not without debate. Studies suggest that marijuana does effectively reduce the nausea and vomiting linked to chemotherapy (Grotenhermen & Müller-Vahl, 2012; Iversen, 2003), but there is conflicting evidence about its long-term effects on the brain (Schreiner & Dunn, 2012).

Marijuana's active ingredient is **tetrahydrocannabinol (THC;** te-trə-hī-drə-kə-ˈna-bə-ˌnȯl), which toys with consciousness in a variety of ways, making it hard to classify the drug into a single category (for example, stimulant, depressant, or hallucinogen). In addition to altering pain perception, THC can induce mild euphoria, and create intense sensory experiences and distortions of time. At higher doses, THC may cause hallucinations and delusions (Murray, Morrison, Henquet, & Di Forti, 2007).

Some of marijuana's effects linger long after the initial high is over. Impairments in learning and memory may persist for days in adults (weeks for adolescents), and long-term use may lead to *addiction* (National Institute on Drug Abuse, 2015; Schweinsburg, Brown, & Tapert, 2008).

Overuse and Addiction

We often joke about being "addicted" to our coffee or soda, but do we understand what this really means? In spite of frequent references to *addiction* in everyday conversations, the term has been omitted from the American Psychiatric Association's diagnostic manual due to its "uncertain definition and potentially negative connotation" (American Psychiatric Association, 2013, p. 485). Historically, the term *addiction* has been used (both by laypeople and professionals) to refer to the urges people experience for using a drug or engaging in an activity to such an extent that it interferes with their functioning or is dangerous. This could mean a gambling habit that depletes your bank account, a sexual appetite that destroys your marriage, or perhaps even a social media fixation that prevents you from holding down a job.

SOCIAL MEDIA and psychology

Can't Get Enough

Is it difficult for you to sit through a movie without checking your Twitter "Mentions"? Are you constantly looking at your Facebook News Feed in between work e-mails? Do you sleep with your iPhone? If you answered "yes" to any of the above, you are not alone. People around the world, from Indonesia to the United Kingdom, are getting hooked on social media—so hooked in some cases that they are receiving treatment for social media *addiction* (Maulia, 2013, February 15; NBC Universal, 2013, February 12).

Facebook and Twitter may be habit forming, but you would think these sites would be easier to resist than, say, coffee or cigarettes. Such is not the case, according to one recent study. With the help of smartphones, researchers kept tabs on the daily desires of 205 young adults and found the urge to use media was harder to resist than sex, spending money, alcohol, coffee, or cigarettes (Hofmann, Vohs, & Baumeister, 2012). These findings are thought provoking, and this line of research is one to follow, but don't allow one study to minimize the serious and long-standing issue of drug addiction. The American Psychiatric Association (2013) does not consider

". . .THE URGE TO USE MEDIA WAS HARDER TO RESIST THAN SEX, SPENDING MONEY, ALCOHOL. . . ."

methylenedioxymethamphetamine (MDMA) (meth′ī-lēn-dī-ok′sē-meth′am-fet′ă-mēn) A synthetic drug chemically similar to the stimulant methamphetamine and the hallucinogen mescaline; produces a combination of stimulant and hallucinogenic effects.

tetrahydrocannabinol (THC) (te-trə-hī-drə-kə-ˈna-bə-ˌnȯl) The active ingredient of marijuana.

behavioral addictions to be mental disorders. Further, the National Institute on Drug Abuse (2014c) defines addiction to drugs, in particular, as "a chronic, relapsing brain disease that is characterized by compulsive drug seeking and use, despite harmful consequences" (para. 1). You read it right: Addiction changes your brain.

FIGURE 4.4
Rates of Drug Dependence in the United States

This graph depicts the rates of drug dependence/abuse in the United States. As you can see, alcohol tops the list, followed by marijuana, and then pain relievers such as Vicodin and Oxycontin. The sedatives category includes barbiturates, which are powerful nervous system depressants. *Source:* National Institute on Drug Abuse, 2012; (photo) © Alec Macdonald/Alamy

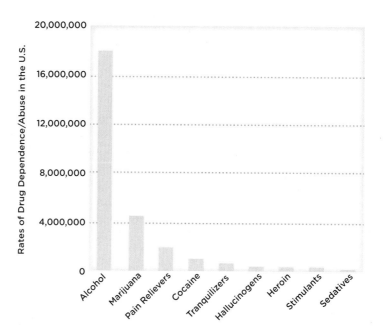

LO 11 Explain how physiological and psychological dependence differ.

PHYSIOLOGICAL AND PSYCHOLOGICAL DEPENDENCE Substance use can be fueled by both *physiological* and *psychological* dependence. **Physiological dependence** means the body no longer functions normally without the drug (see **Figure 4.4** on drug dependence in the United States). Want to know if you are physiologically dependent on your morning cup of Joe? Try removing it from your routine for a few days and see if you get a headache or feel fatigued. If your answers are yes and yes, odds are that you have experienced *withdrawal*, a sign of physiological dependence. **Withdrawal** is the constellation of symptoms that surface when a drug is removed or withheld from the body, and it's not always as mild as a headache and fatigue. An alcoholic who suddenly stops drinking (or significantly cuts down) may suffer from **delirium tremens (DTs),** withdrawal symptoms that include sweating, restlessness, hallucinations, severe tremors, and seizures. Withdrawal symptoms disappear when you take the drug again, and this of course makes you more likely to continue using it. (The removal of the unpleasant symptoms acts as negative reinforcement for taking the drug, a process you can learn about in Chapter 5.) In this way, withdrawal powers the addiction cycle.

Another sign of physiological dependence is **tolerance.** Persistent use of alcohol and other drugs alters the chemistry of the brain and body. Over time, your system adapts to the drug and therefore needs more and more to re-create its original effect. If it once took you 2 beers to unwind, but now it takes you 4, then tolerance has probably set in. Tolerance increases the risk for accidental overdose, because more drug is needed to obtain the desired effect.

Psychological dependence is indicated by a host of problematic symptoms distinct from tolerance and withdrawal. Individuals with psychological dependence believe, for example, they need the drug because it will increase their emotional or mental well-being. The "pleasant" effects of a drug can act as positive reinforcement for taking the drug (Chapter 5). Let's say a smoker has a cigarette, fulfilling her

physiological dependence With constant use of some psychoactive drugs, the body no longer functions normally without the drug.

withdrawal With constant use of some psychoactive drugs, a condition in which the body becomes dependent and then reacts when the drug is withheld; a sign of physiological dependence.

delirium tremens (DTs) Withdrawal symptoms that can occur when a heavy drinker suddenly stops or significantly cuts down alcohol consumption; can include sweating, restlessness, hallucinations, severe tremors, and seizures.

tolerance With constant use of some psychoactive drugs, a condition in which the body requires more and more of the drug to create the original effect; a sign of physiological dependence.

psychological dependence With constant use of some psychoactive drugs, a strong desire or need to continue using the substance occurs without the evidence of tolerance or withdrawal symptoms.

TABLE 4.4   PSYCHOACTIVE DRUGS

Drug	Classification	Effects	Potential Harm
Alcohol	Depressant	disinhibition, feeling "high"	coma, death
Barbiturates	Depressant	decreased neural activity, relaxation, possible aggression	loss of consciousness, coma, death
Caffeine	Stimulant	alertness, enhanced recall, elevated mood, endurance	heart racing, trembling, insomnia
Cocaine	Stimulant	energy, euphoria, rush of pleasure	heart attack, stroke, anxiety, psychosis
Heroin	Depressant	pleasure-inducing, reduces pain, rush of euphoria and relaxation	boils on the skin, hepatitis, liver disease, spontaneous abortion
LSD	Hallucinogen	extreme changes in sensation and perception, emotional roller coaster	depression, long-term flashbacks, other psychological problems
Marijuana	Hallucinogen	stimulates appetite, suppresses nausea, relaxation, mild euphoria, distortion of time, intense sensory experiences	respiratory problems, immune system suppression, cancer, memory impairment, deficits in attention and learning
MDMA	Stimulant; hallucinogen	euphoria, heightened energy, anxiety, and depersonalization	blurred vision, dizziness, rapid heart rate, dehydration, heat stroke, seizures, cardiac arrest, and death
Methamphetamine	Stimulant	energy, alertness, increases sex drive, suppresses appetite	lasting memory and movement problems, severe weight loss, tooth decay, psychosis, sudden death
Opioids	Depressant	blocks pain, induces drowsiness, euphoria, slows down breathing	respiratory problems during sleep, falls, constipation, sexual problems, overdose
Tobacco	Stimulant	relaxed, alert, more tolerant of pain	cancer, emphysema, heart disease, stroke, reduction in life span

Most drugs can be classified under one of the major categories listed above, but there are substances, such as MDMA, that fall into more than one class. Psychoactive drugs carry serious risks.

physical need for nicotine. If the phone rings, she might answer it and light up a cigarette, because she has become accustomed to smoking and talking on the phone at the same time. Psychological dependence is an urge or craving, not a physical need. The cues associated with using the telephone facilitate the smoker's urge to light up (Bold, Yoon, Chapman, & McCarthy, 2013).

Psychologists and psychiatrists use specific criteria for drawing the line between use and overuse of drugs. Overuse is maladaptive and causes significant impairment or distress to the user and/or his family: problems at work or school, neglect of children or household duties, physically dangerous behaviors, and so forth. In addition, the behavior has to be sustained for a certain period of time (that is, over a 12-month period). The American Psychiatric Association (2013) has established these criteria to help professionals distinguish between drug use and substance use disorder.

Depressants, stimulants, hallucinogens, marijuana—every drug we have discussed, and every drug imaginable—must gain entrance to the body in order to access the brain. Some are inhaled, others snorted or injected directly into the veins, all altering the state of consciousness of the user (**Table 4.4**). But is it possible to enter an altered state of consciousness without using a substance? It is time to explore hypnosis.

Hypnosis

The term *hypnosis* was taken from the Greek root word for "sleep," but hypnosis is by no means the equivalent of sleep. Most would agree **hypnosis** is an altered state of consciousness in which changes in perceptions and behaviors result from suggestions made by a hypnotist. "Changes in perceptions and behaviors" can mean a lot of things, of course, and there is some debate about what hypnosis is. Before going any further, let's be clear about what hypnosis *isn't*.

CONTROVERSIES

False Claims About Hypnosis

➡️⬅️ Popular conceptions of hypnosis often clash with scientists' understanding of the phenomenon. Let's take a look at some examples:

- **People can be hypnotized without consent:** You cannot force someone to be hypnotized; they must be willing.
- **Hypnotized people will act against their own will:** Stage hypnotists seem to make people walk like chickens or miscount their fingers, but these are things they would likely be willing to do when not hypnotized.
- **Hypnotized people can exhibit "superhuman" strength:** Hypnotized or not, people have the same capabilities (Druckman & Bjork, 1994). Stage hypnotists often choose feats that their hypnotized performers could achieve under normal circumstances.
- **Hypnosis helps people retrieve lost memories:** Studies find that hypnosis may actually promote the formation of false memories and one's confidence in those memories (Kihlstrom, 1985).
- **Hypnotized people experience age regression. In other words, they act childlike:** Hypnotized people may indeed act immaturely, but the underlying cognitive activity is that of an adult (Nash, 2001).
- **Hypnosis induces long-term amnesia:** Hypnosis cannot make you forget your first day of kindergarten or your wedding. Short-term amnesia is possible if the hypnotist specifically suggests that something will be forgotten after the hypnosis wears off. ➡️⬅️

NO ONE CAN FORCE YOU TO BECOME HYPNOTIZED

Now that some misconceptions about hypnosis have been cleared up, let's focus on what we know. Researchers propose the following characteristics are evident in a hypnotized person: (1) ability to focus intently, ignoring all extraneous stimuli; (2) heightened imagination; (3) an unresisting and receptive attitude; (4) decreased pain awareness; and (5) high responsivity to suggestions (Kosslyn, Thompson, Costantini-Ferrando, Alpert, & Spiegel, 2000; Silva & Kirsch, 1992).

Does this process have any application to real life? With some limited success, hypnosis has been used therapeutically to treat phobias and commercially to help people change lifestyle habits (Green, 1999;

Mesmerizing
A 19th-century doctor attempts to heal a patient using the hypnotic techniques created by Franz Mesmer in the 1770s. Mesmer believed that every person was surrounded by a magnetic field, or "animal magnetism," that could be summoned for therapeutic purposes (Wobst, 2007). The word "mesmerize" derives from Mesmer's name. Jean-Loup Charmet/Science Source

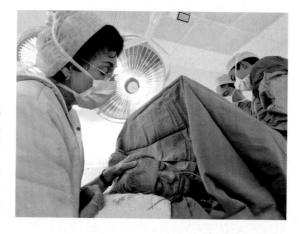

Hypnosis for Pain
A doctor in Belgium performs hypnosis on a patient undergoing a painful procedure. For those who are susceptible to hypnosis, this approach may diminish the need for anesthesia.
BSIP/UIG Via Getty Images

Kraft, 2012). Hypnosis can also be used to reduce headaches and other pains associated with stress (Patterson & Jensen, 2003). Research also suggests that hypnosis does ease the pain associated with childbirth and surgery, reducing the need for painkillers (Cyna, McAuliffe, & Andrew, 2004; Wobst, 2007).

A SESSION WITH A HYPNOTIST   Imagine you are using hypnosis for one of these purposes—headaches, for example. How would a session with a hypnotist proceed? Probably something like this: The hypnotist talks to you in a calm, quiet voice, running through a list of suggestions on how to relax. She might suggest that you sit back in your chair and choose a place to focus your eyes. Then she quietly suggests that your eyelids are starting to droop, and you feel like you need to yawn. You grow tired and more relaxed. Your breathing slows. Your arms feel so heavy that you can barely lift them off the chair. Alternatively, the hypnotist might suggest that you are going down steps, and ask you to focus attention on her voice. Hypnotists who are very good at this procedure can perform an induction in less than a minute, especially if they know the individual being hypnotized.

Once in this altered state of consciousness, you may be open to suggestion. If, say, the hypnotist suggested you could not lift your feet off the ground, then you might actually feel this way. Or if she suggested that you will not remember your own middle name after coming out of hypnosis, this *posthypnotic suggestion* may very well play out.

People in hypnotic states sometimes report having sensory experiences that deviate from reality; they may, for example, see or hear things that are not there. In a classic experiment, participants were hypnotized to believe they wouldn't experience pain when asked to place one hand in a container filled with ice-cold water. With their other hand, they were asked to press a button if they experienced pain. Amazingly, the participants gave *spoken reports* of feeling no pain. However, they actually did press the button indicating pain during their hypnotic session (Hilgard, Morgan, & Macdonald, 1975). This suggests a "divided consciousness," that is, part of our consciousness is always aware, even when hypnotized and instructed to feel no pain. People under hypnotic states can also experience temporary blindness and deafness.

With the help of PET scans, some researchers have found evidence that hypnosis induces changes in the brain that might explain this diminished pain perception (Faymonville et al., 2000; Rainville, Duncan, Price, Carrier, & Bushnell, 1997). Dr. Julien agrees that hypnosis, meditation, and other relaxation techniques may indeed reduce anxiety and pain, but only to a certain extent. So if you plan to go under the knife with hypnosis as your sole form of pain management, don't be surprised if you feel the piercing sensation of the scalpel.

THEORIES OF HYPNOSIS   There are many theories to explain hypnosis. One hypothesis, referred to briefly above, is that hypnotized people experience a "split" in awareness or consciousness (Hilgard, 1977, 1994). According to this perspective, there is an ever-present hidden observer that oversees the events of our daily lives. You are listening to a boring lecture, picking up a little content here and there, but also thinking about that juicy gossip you heard before class. Your mind is working on different levels, and the hidden observer is keeping track of everything. In a hypnotic state, the hidden observer is still aware of what is transpiring in the environment, while another stream of mental activity focuses on the hypnotic suggestions.

Others have suggested that hypnosis is not a distinct state of consciousness, but more of a role-playing exercise. Have you ever watched a little boy pretend he was a firefighter? He becomes so enthralled in his play that he really believes he is a firefighter. His tricycle is now his fire engine; his baseball cap his firefighter's hat.

hypnosis An altered state of consciousness allowing for changes in perceptions and behaviors, which result from suggestions made by a hypnotist.

He *is* the firefighter. Something similar happens when we are hypnotized. We have an expectation of how a hypnotized person should act or behave; therefore, our hypnotized response is nothing more than the role we think we should take on. And this is particularly true when there is a good rapport between the hypnotist and the person being hypnotized.

FADE TO BLACK   It is time to conclude our discussion of consciousness, but first let's run through some of the big picture concepts you should take away from this chapter. Consciousness refers to a state of awareness—awareness of self and things outside of self—that has many gradations and dimensions. During sleep, awareness decreases, but it does not fade entirely (remember that alarm clock that becomes part of your dream about a wailing siren). Sleep has many stages, but the two main forms are non-REM and REM. Dreams may serve a purpose, but they may also be nothing more than your brain's interpretation of neurons signaling in the night. You learned from Dr. Julien that anesthetic drugs can profoundly alter consciousness. The same is true of drugs used outside of medical supervision, the use of which can lead to dependence, health problems, and death. Lastly, although somewhat controversial and misunderstood, hypnosis appears to induce an altered state of consciousness and may have useful therapeutic applications.

✓ ○ ○ ○ show what you know

1. Match the agent in the left column with the most appropriate outcome in the right column:

   _____ 1. depressant   a. blocks pain
   _____ 2. opioid   b. slows down activity in the CNS
   _____ 3. alcohol   c. increases neural activity in the CNS
   _____ 4. cocaine   d. cirrhosis of the liver

2. An acquaintance described an odorless, tasteless, and colorless substance he took many years ago. He discussed a variety of changes to his sensations and perceptions, including seeing colors and spirals. It is likely he had taken which of the following hallucinogens:

   a. alcohol
   b. nicotine
   c. LSD
   d. cocaine

3. Dr. Julien uses a range of _____ to dull the perception of pain, to inhibit memories of surgery, and to change a variety of psychological activities.

4. People often describe dangerous or risky behaviors as being addictive. You might hear a character in a movie say that he is addicted to driving fast, for example. Given what you have learned about physiological and psychological dependence, how would you determine if behaviors are problematic?

✓ CHECK YOUR ANSWERS IN APPENDIX C.

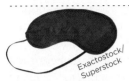

Exactostock/Superstock

LO 1 Define consciousness. (p. 130)

Consciousness is the state of being aware of oneself, one's thoughts, and/or the environment. There are various levels of conscious awareness, including wakefulness, sleepiness, drug-induced states, dreaming, hypnotic states, and meditative states.

LO 2 Explain how automatic processing relates to consciousness. (p. 132)

Because our sensory systems absorb large amounts of information, being consciously aware of all of it is not possible. Without our awareness, the brain determines what is important, what requires immediate attention, and what can be processed and stored for later use if necessary.

LO 3 Describe how we narrow our focus through selective attention. (p. 133)

We can only direct our attention toward a small portion of the information that is available to us. This narrow focus on specific stimuli is referred to as selective attention. In particular, we are designed to pay attention to changes in environmental stimuli, to unfamiliar stimuli, and to especially strong stimuli.

LO 4 Identify how circadian rhythm relates to sleep. (p. 136)

Predictable daily patterns influence our behaviors, alertness, and activity levels in a cyclical fashion. These circadian rhythms in our physiological functioning roughly follow the 24-hour cycle of daylight and darkness. In the circadian rhythm for sleep and wakefulness, there are two times when the desire for sleep hits hardest. The first occurs in the early hours of the morning, between about 2:00 to 6:00 A.M., and the second, less intense desire for sleep strikes midafternoon, around 2:00 or 3:00 P.M.

LO 5 Summarize the stages of sleep. (p. 139)

Sleep begins in non-rapid eye movement (non-REM), or nondreaming sleep, which has four stages. The lightest is Stage 1; this is the time during which imaginary sensations can occur. Stage 1 lasts only a few minutes before Stage 2 begins. At this point, it is more difficult to rouse the sleeper before she drifts even further into Stage 3 and then Stage 4, also known as slow-wave sleep. The sleeper then works her way back up to Stage 1. And instead of waking up, she enters a 5th stage known as rapid eye movement (REM) sleep. During this stage, closed eyes dart around, and brain activity changes. People awakened from REM sleep often report having vivid dreams. Each cycle, from Stage 1 through REM, lasts about 90 minutes, and the average adult loops through five complete cycles per night. The composition of these cycles changes as the night progresses.

LO 6 Recognize various sleep disorders and their symptoms. (p. 143)

Narcolepsy is a neurological disorder characterized by excessive daytime sleepiness and other sleep-related disturbances. REM sleep behavior disorder occurs when the mechanism responsible for paralyzing the body during REM sleep does not function properly. As a result, the individual is able to move around and act out dreams. Obstructive sleep apnea hypopnea is a serious disturbance of non-REM sleep characterized by periodic blockage of breathing. The upper throat muscles go limp, allowing the airway to close. The sleeper awakens and gasps for air, then drifts back to sleep. Insomnia is the inability to fall asleep or stay asleep. People with insomnia report poor quantity or quality of sleep, and some may complain about waking up too early and being unable to fall back to sleep.

LO 7 Summarize the theories of why we dream. (p. 151)

Freud believed dreams have two levels of content. Manifest content, the apparent meaning of the dream, is the actual story line of the dream itself. Latent content contains the hidden meaning of the dream, consisting of unconscious conflicts and desires. The activation–synthesis model suggests that dreams have no meaning whatsoever: we respond to random neural activity of the sleeping brain as if it has meaning. Neurocognitive theory suggests there is a network of neurons in the brain necessary for dreaming to occur. According to this theory, dreams are the result of how sleep and consciousness have evolved in humans.

LO 8 Define psychoactive drugs. (p. 153)

Psychoactive drugs can cause changes in psychological activities such as sensation, perception, attention, judgment, memory, self-control, emotion, thinking, and behavior. These drugs alter consciousness in an untold number of ways. They can, for example, depress activity in the central nervous system, produce hallucinations, or cause a sense of euphoria.

LO 9 Identify several depressants and stimulants and know their effects. (p. 154)

Depressants decrease activity in the central nervous system. These include barbiturates, opioids, and alcohol. Stimulants increase activity in the central nervous system, producing effects such as heightened alertness, energy, and mood. These include cocaine, amphetamines, methamphetamine, caffeine, and nicotine.

LO 10   Discuss some of the hallucinogens. (p. 161)

Hallucinogens produce hallucinations, altered moods, and distorted perception and thought. The most well-known is lysergic acid diethylamide (LSD). This odorless, tasteless, and colorless substance often produces extreme changes in sensation and perception. Others are the "club drugs," or synthetic "designer drugs," used at parties, raves, and dance venues. Of these the most popular is methylenedioxymeth-amphetamine (MDMA), which is chemically similar to the stimulant methamphetamine, producing a combination of stimulant and hallucinogenic effects. The most widely used illegal (in most states) drug is marijuana. At high doses, its tetrahydrocannabinol (THC) can induce mild euphoria and create intense sensory experiences.

LO 11   Explain how physiological and psychological dependence differ. (p. 164)

With constant use of some psychoactive drugs, a condition can develop in which the body becomes dependent on the drug. Signs of this physiological dependence include tolerance and withdrawal. Psychological dependence occurs without the evidence of tolerance or withdrawal symptoms, but is indicated by many other problematic symptoms. People with psychological dependence believe they need the drug because it increases their emotional or mental well-being. Physiological dependence is physical and has serious health consequences.

LO 12   Describe hypnosis and explain how it works. (p. 166)

Hypnosis is an altered state of consciousness that can create changes in perceptions and behaviors, usually resulting from suggestions made by a hypnotist. It is known to ease pain associated with childbirth and surgery, and can reduce the need for painkillers. One theory suggests that hypnotized people experience a "split" in awareness or consciousness. Others suggest hypnosis is a role-playing exercise.

key terms

activation–synthesis model, p. 151
alpha waves, p. 139
amphetamines, p. 159
automatic processing, p. 132
barbiturate, p. 154
beta waves, p. 139
circadian rhythm, p. 136
consciousness, p. 130
delirium tremens (DTs), p. 164
delta waves, p. 141
depressants, p. 154

hallucinogens, p. 161
hypnosis, p. 166
insomnia, p. 145
latent content, p. 151
lysergic acid diethylamide (LSD), p. 161
manifest content, p. 151
methylenedioxymethamphet-amine (MDMA), p. 162
narcolepsy, p. 143
nightmares, p. 146
non-rapid eye movement (non-REM), p. 139

obstructive sleep apnea hypopnea, p. 145
opiates, p. 156
opioid, p. 156
physiological dependence, p. 164
psychoactive drugs, p. 153
psychological dependence, p. 164
rapid eye movement (REM), p. 141
REM rebound, p. 148

REM sleep behavior disorder, p. 144
selective attention, p. 133
sleep terrors, p. 146
stimulant, p. 158
tetrahydrocannabinol (THC), p. 163
theta waves, p. 139
tolerance, p. 164
withdrawal, p. 164

TEST PREP are you ready?

1. William James was interested in studying _____, which he described as a "stream" that provides day-to-day continuity.
   a. dreams
   b. automatic processing
   c. selective attention
   d. consciousness

2. A great deal of information is available in our internal and external environments, but we can only focus on a small portion of it. This narrow focus on specific stimuli is known as:
   a. stream of consciousness.
   b. selective attention.
   c. waking consciousness.
   d. encoding of memories.

3. _____ refers to the ability to block out the chatter and noise in a busy environment so that you can pay attention to your ongoing conversation with someone.
   a. The cocktail-party effect
   b. Inattentional blindness
   c. Automatic processing
   d. The circadian rhythm

4. The daily patterns of our physiological functioning, such as our temperature, roughly follow the 24-hour cycle of daylight and darkness. This pattern is driven by our:
   a. blood pressure.
   b. need for sleep.
   c. levels of consciousness.
   d. circadian rhythm.

5. The suprachiasmatic nucleus (SCN) can be thought of as a master clock for our daily rhythm. The SCN sends messages to the _____, which regulates patterns of hunger and temperature, and the _____, which regulates alertness and sleepiness.
   a. reticular formation; retinal ganglion cells
   b. retinal ganglion cells; hypothalamus
   c. hypothalamus; reticular formation
   d. thalamus; hypothalamus

6. Shift workers can have problems with their sleep–wake cycles, sometimes resulting in _____, which refers to difficulty falling asleep and sleeping soundly.
   a. insomnia
   b. cataplexy
   c. narcolepsy
   d. hypnagogic hallucinations

7. If we hook you up to an electroencephalogram (EEG) as you become drowsy, the EEG would begin to show _____ waves.
   a. fast
   b. alpha
   c. beta
   d. theta

8. The fifth stage of sleep is known as _____, when brain activity looks similar to that of someone who is wide awake.
   a. sleep paralysis
   b. cataplexy
   c. non-REM sleep
   d. REM sleep

9. Depriving people of REM sleep can result in:
   a. REM rebound.
   b. insomnia.
   c. more beta waves while they sleep.
   d. increased energy levels.

10. According to Sigmund Freud's theory, dreams are a form of:
    a. REM rebound.
    b. wish fulfillment.
    c. microsleep.
    d. sleep terror.

11. People with damage to specific areas of the limbic system and forebrain do not have dreams or experience abnormal dreams. Which of the following explains this finding?
    a. the theory of evolution
    b. the activation–synthesis model
    c. the psychoanalytic theory
    d. the neurocognitive theory

12. _____ such as caffeine, alcohol, and hallucinogens can cause changes in psychological activities, for example, sensation, perception, attention, and judgment.
    a. Tranquilizers
    b. Depressants
    c. Psychoactive drugs
    d. Stimulants

13. Methamphetamine stimulates the release of the brain's pleasure-producing neurotransmitter _____, causing a surge in energy and alertness.
    a. dopamine
    b. serotonin
    c. acetylcholine
    d. adenosine

14. Which is the number one cause of premature death worldwide?
    a. AIDS
    b. tobacco
    c. road accidents
    d. illegal drugs

15. Drug use can be fueled by dependence. _____ dependence means the body no longer functions normally without the drug, and one sign of this type of dependence is _____, as indicated by the symptoms that occur when the drug is withheld.
    a. Psychological; tolerance
    b. Physiological; substance abuse
    c. Physiological; withdrawal
    d. Psychological; withdrawal

16. Give an example showing that you are still conscious when asleep.

17. Describe automatic processing, and give two reasons why it is important.

18. Interns and residents in hospitals sometimes work 48-hour shifts. Why would you not want a doctor keeping such a schedule to care for you at the end of her shift?

19. Name and describe four different sleep disturbances. Differentiate them by describing their characteristics.

20. Give four examples of drugs that people use legally on a daily basis.

✓ CHECK YOUR ANSWERS IN APPENDIX C.

Get personalized practice by logging into LaunchPad at **www.macmillanhighered.com/launchpad/ sciampresenting1e** to take the LearningCurve adaptive quizzes for Chapter 4.

5

a t h l e t e

Zoonar/P Gudella/Agefotostock; Thinkstock

learning

© Pixattitude | Dreamstime.com

An Introduction to Learning

Palo Alto, California: It was the spring of 1999, and Ivonne Mosquera was about to graduate from Stanford University with a bachelor's degree in mathematics. Math majors typically spend a lot of time manipulating numbers on paper, graphing functions, and trying to understand spatial relationships—all activities that draw on their sense of vision. But Ivonne had no memory of seeing an equation, a number, or even a piece of paper. She had been blind since the age of 2, when doctors removed both of her eyes to arrest the spread of an aggressive cancer.

Blindness never stopped Ivonne from doing much of anything. Growing up in New York City, she used to ride her bicycle across the George Washington Bridge as her father ran alongside. She went to school with sighted kids, climbed trees in the park, and studied ballet, tap, and jazz dance (Boccella, 2012, May 6; iminmotion.net, n.d., para. 3). She tried downhill skiing, hiking, and rock climbing. Now Ivonne was graduating from college with a degree in one of the most rigorous academic disciplines, a great accomplishment indeed. Yet there were bigger things to come for Ivonne. In the next decade, she would become a world-class runner and triathlete.

Meanwhile, just a few miles from the Stanford campus, a 10-year-old boy named Jeremy Lin was finishing fifth grade and working on his basketball game. In the evenings, Jeremy and his brothers would go with their father to the nearby YMCA to run drills and shoot hoops late into the night (Dalrymple, 2012). It was during this period that Jeremy's future high school coach, Peter Diepenbrock, first caught a glimpse of the scrappy young player. "He was very small," Coach Diepenbrock recalls, "but [had] just an incredible, incredible amount of confidence." Jeremy knew exactly how to play and was determined to do so, regardless of his size. Even so, no one could have predicted the "Linsanity" he would be capable of inspiring across the globe.

At first glance, Ivonne Mosquera (now Ivonne Mosquera-Schmidt) and Jeremy Lin don't seem to have much in common. But as you read their stories, you will see how their relentless determination, work ethic, and optimism led to their athletic achievements—Ivonne as a runner and triathlete and Jeremy as a basketball player. You will also see how *learning* changed their lives and paved the way for their success. 📁

World Champion
Ivonne Mosquera-Schmidt runs in the Capital of Texas Triathlon on May 28, 2012. Blind since the age of 2, Ivonne has always been extremely active. She has danced across the stage of New York City's Lincoln Center, climbed Tanzania's Mount Kilimanjaro, and competed in over 25 triathlons. Brightroom.com

He's Got Game
Playing for the Los Angeles Lakers in the 2014/2015 NBA season, Jeremy Lin races past Ryan Hollins of the Sacramento Kings. Jeremy's basketball accomplishments are the result of talent, motivation, and extensive *learning*. © Michael Goulding/The Orange County Register/ZUMA Wire

Note: Quotations attributed to Ivonne Mosquera-Schmidt and Peter Diepenbrock are personal communications.

Ivonne, In Her Own Words

http://qrs.ly/kt4qq64

@ 2016, Macmillan

CONNECTIONS

In **Chapter 2,** we described circumstances in which learning influences the brain and vice versa. For example, dopamine plays an important role in learning through reinforcement, attention, and regulating body movements. *Neurogenesis* (the generation of new neurons) is also thought to be associated with learning.

In **Chapter 3,** we discussed *sensory adaptation,* which is the tendency to become less aware of constant stimuli. Becoming habituated to sensory input keeps us alert to *changes* in the environment.

learning A relatively enduring change in behavior or thinking that results from experiences.

habituation (hah-bi-chü-ā-shən) A basic form of learning evident when an organism does not respond as strongly or as often to an event following multiple exposures to it.

stimulus An event or occurrence that generally leads to a response.

What Is Learning?

LO 1 Define learning.

Psychologists define **learning** as a relatively enduring change in behavior or thinking that results from our experiences. Studies suggest that learning can begin before we are even born—prior to birth, a baby has already begun to single out the sound of his mother's voice (Kisilevsky et al., 2008). And learning may continue until our dying day. But even though learning leads to changes in the brain, including alterations to individual neurons as well as their networks, these modifications of behavior and thinking are not always permanent.

The ability to learn is not unique to humans. Trout can learn to press a pendulum to get food (Yue, Duncan, & Moccia, 2008); orangutans can pick up whistling (Wich et al., 2009); and even honeybees can be trained to differentiate among photos of human faces (Dyer, Neumeyer, & Chittka, 2005). One of the most basic forms of learning occurs during the process of **habituation** (hah-bi-chü-ā-shən), which is evident when an organism does not respond as strongly or as often to an event following multiple exposures to its occurrence. This type of learning is apparent in a wide range of living beings, from humans to sea slugs (Chapter 6). An animal might initially *respond* to a **stimulus,** which is an event that generally leads to a response, but with repeated exposures, the stimulus is increasingly ignored and habituation occurs. Essentially, an organism *learns* about a *stimulus* but begins to ignore it as it is repeated.

Animals Learn to Help
Army Specialist Antonio Ingram gets a kiss from Emma, one of the therapy dogs that works with soldiers at Fort Hood, Texas (Flaherty, 2011, October 29). Therapy animals like Emma help ease the stress of wounded veterans, abused children, cancer patients, and others suffering from psychological distress (American Humane Association, 2013). The dogs are trained using the principles of learning. AP Photo/ The Killeen Daily Herald, Marianne Lijewski

Researchers have studied learning using a variety of animals. The history of psychology is full of stories about scientists who began studying animal *biology* but then switched their focus to animal *behavior* as unexpected events unfolded in the laboratory. These scientists were often excited to find the connections between biology and experience that became evident as they explored the principles of learning.

Animals are often excellent models for studying and understanding human behavior. Conducting animal research sidesteps many of the ethical dilemmas that arise with human research. It's generally considered okay to keep rats, cats, and birds in cages to ensure control over experimental variables (as long as they are otherwise treated humanely), but locking up people in laboratories would obviously be unacceptable.

This chapter focuses on three major types of learning: classical conditioning, operant conditioning, and observational learning. As you make your way through these pages, you will begin to realize that learning is very much about creating associations. Through *classical conditioning,* we associate two different stimuli: for example, the sound of a bell and the arrival of food. In *operant conditioning,* we make connections between our behaviors and their consequences: for example, through rewards and punishments. With *observational learning,* we learn by watching and imitating other people, establishing a closer link between our behavior and the behavior of others.

Learning can occur in predictable or unexpected ways. It allows us to grow and change, and it is a key to achieving goals. Now let's see how learning has shaped the lives of Ivonne Mosquera-Schmidt and Jeremy Lin.

CONNECTIONS

In **Chapter 1,** we described the theme of nature and nurture, which examines the relative weight of heredity and environment. Some scientists who initially studied the biological and innate aspects (nature) of animals shifted their focus and began to study how experiences and learning (nurture) influenced these animals.

In **Chapter 1,** we discussed Institutional Review Boards, which must approve all research with human participants *and* animal subjects to ensure safe and humane procedures.

Suited Up to Swim
Ivonne and her guide prepare for the 2012 Paratriathlon World Championships in Auckland, New Zealand. Ivonne is about to begin the swim portion of the triathlon, which takes place in the frigid ocean waters along Queens Wharf. She wears a wetsuit to keep her warm. The red string just below her knee is the tether that keeps her connected to the guide. G. John Schmidt/Courtesy Ivonne Mosquera-Schmidt

AN OMINOUS SMELL Ivonne is on her way to swim practice. As she walks through the locker room and approaches the pool entrance, she catches a whiff of chlorine. Immediately, her shoulders tense and her heart rate jumps. The smell of chlorine gives Ivonne the jitters, not because there is something inherent about the chemical that causes a physical reaction, but because it is associated with something she dreads: swimming.

"I've never been a strong swimmer," Ivonne says. "I just survive in water." Submerging her ears in water, which is necessary when she swims the freestyle stroke in triathlons, makes Ivonne feel disoriented. "I can't hear what's around me," she explains. "There aren't sounds or echoes for me to follow."

Imagine navigating a mile in the frigid ocean bordering Canada in the Vancouver Triathlon, or plowing through choppy waves (not to mention dodging pieces of trash) in the Hudson River in New York City's triathlon. Now imagine doing all of that swimming in the darkness. It's no surprise that Ivonne feels a little apprehensive about being in the water.

To understand why the smell of chlorine seems to evoke such a strong physiological response for Ivonne, we need to travel back in time and into the lab of a young Russian scientist: Ivan Pavlov.

✔✔◯◯ **show what you know**

1. Learning is a relatively enduring change in _____ that results from our _____.

2. Learning is often described as the creation of _____, for example, between two stimuli or between a behavior and its consequences.
   a. habituation
   b. ethical dilemmas
   c. associations
   d. unexpected events

✔ CHECK YOUR ANSWERS IN APPENDIX C.

Classical Conditioning

LO 2   Explain what Pavlov's studies teach us about classical conditioning.

The son of a village priest, Ivan Pavlov (1849–1936) had planned to devote his life to the church. He changed his mind at a young age, however, when he discovered his love for science. Although he won a Nobel Prize in 1904 for his research on the physiology of digestion, Pavlov's most enduring legacy was his trailblazing research on learning (Fancher & Rutherford, 2012).

Pavlov spent the 1890s studying the digestive system of dogs at Russia's Institute of Experimental Medicine (Watson, 1968). One of his early experiments involved measuring how much dogs salivate in response to food. Initially, the dogs salivated as expected, but as the experiment progressed, they began salivating to other stimuli as well. After repeated trials with an assistant giving a dog its food and then measuring the dog's saliva output, Pavlov noticed that instead of *salivating* the moment it received food, the dog began to salivate at the mere sight or sound of the lab assistant arriving to feed it. The assistant's footsteps, for example, seemed to act like a trigger (the *stimulus*) for the dog to start salivating (the *response*). Pavlov had discovered how associations develop through the process of learning, which he referred to as *conditioning*. The dog was associating the sound of footsteps with the arrival of food; it had been *conditioned* to associate certain sights and sounds with eating. Intrigued by his discovery, Pavlov decided to shift the focus of his research to investigate the dogs' salivation (which he termed "psychic secretions") in these types of scenarios (Fancher & Rutherford, 2012, p. 248; Watson, 1968).

CONNECTIONS

A dog naturally begins to salivate when exposed to the smell of food, even before tasting it. This is an involuntary response of the autonomic nervous system, which we explored in **Chapter 2.** Dogs do not normally salivate at the sound of footsteps. Here, we see this response is a *learned* behavior, as the dog salivates without tasting or smelling food.

Pavlov's Basic Research Plan

Pavlov followed up on his initial observations with numerous studies in the early 1900s, examining the link between stimulus (for example, the sound of human footsteps) and response (the dog's salivation). The type of *behavior* Pavlov was studying (salivating) is not voluntary, but involuntary or reflexive (Pavlov, 1906). The connection between food and salivating is innate and universal, whereas the link between the sound of footsteps and salivating is learned. Learning has occurred whenever a new, nonuniversal link between stimulus (footsteps) and response (salivation) is established.

Many of Pavlov's studies had the same basic format (**Infographic 5.1**). Prior to the experiment, the dog had a tube surgically inserted into its cheek to allow for the precise collection of saliva. When the dog salivated, instead of the secretions being swallowed, they were emptied from that tube into a measuring device so Pavlov could determine exactly how much the dog was producing.

Tick Tick

Pavlov conditioned his dogs to salivate in response to auditory stimuli, such as bells and ticking metronomes. A metronome is a device that musicians often use to maintain tempo. This "old-fashioned" metronome has a wind-up knob and a pendulum that ticks at various speed settings. Modern metronomes are digital and often come with additional features such as adjustable volume. Perhaps Pavlov could have used these features to test different aspects of classical conditioning. Galina Ermolaeva/Dreamstime.com

Learning Through Classical Conditioning

During his experiments with dogs, **Ivan Pavlov** noticed them salivating before food was even presented. Somehow the dogs had learned to associate the lab assistant's approaching footsteps with eating. This observation led to Pavlov's discovery of the process of classical conditioning, in which we learn to associate a neutral stimulus with an unconditioned stimulus that produces an automatic, natural response. The crucial stage of this process involves repeated pairings of the two stimuli.

PAVLOV'S EXPERIMENT

Before conditioning

Dog salivates automatically when food is presented.

Unconditioned stimulus → Unconditioned response (salivates)

Bell means nothing to dog, so there is no response.

Neutral stimulus (ringing bell) No response

During conditioning

In the process of conditioning, bell is repeatedly played right before dog receives food. Over time, dog learns that bell signals arrival of food.

Neutral stimulus (ringing bell) + Unconditioned stimulus = Unconditioned response (salivates)

repeated over time

After conditioning

Dog has now learned to associate bell with food and will begin salivating when bell rings.

Conditioned stimulus (ringing bell) → Conditioned response (salivates)

HAVE YOU BEEN CONDITIONED?

Before conditioning

Neutral stimulus   No response

Unconditioned stimulus → Unconditioned response (stomach growls)

During conditioning

Neutral stimulus + Unconditioned stimulus

Unconditioned response (stomach growls)   repeated over time

After conditioning

Conditioned stimulus → Conditioned response (stomach growls)

Classical conditioning prompts learning that occurs naturally, without studying or other voluntary effort. And it happens every day. Do you feel hungry when you see a pizza box or McDonald's "golden arches"? Just like Pavlov's dogs, we learn through repeated pairings to associate these neutral stimuli with food, and the sight of a cardboard box or a yellow "M" can be enough to get our stomachs rumbling.

CONNECTIONS

In **Chapter 1,** we discussed the importance of control in the *experimental method.* In this case, if the sound of footsteps was the stimulus, then Pavlov would need to *control* the number of steps taken, the type of shoes worn, and so on, to ensure the stimulus was identical for each trial. Otherwise, he would be introducing extraneous variables, which are characteristics that interfere with the outcome of research, making it difficult to determine what exactly was causing the dog to salivate.

CONNECTIONS

In **Chapter 1,** we discussed operational definitions, which are the precise ways in which characteristics of interest are defined and measured. Although earlier we described the research in everyday language, here we provide operational definitions for the procedures of the study.

Synonyms
classical conditioning Pavlovian conditioning

neutral stimulus (NS) A stimulus that does not cause a relevant automatic or reflexive response.

classical conditioning Learning process in which two stimuli become associated with each other; when an originally neutral stimulus is conditioned to elicit an involuntary response.

unconditioned stimulus (US) A stimulus that automatically triggers an involuntary response without any learning needed.

unconditioned response (UR) A reflexive, involuntary response to an unconditioned stimulus.

conditioned stimulus (CS) A previously neutral stimulus that an organism learns to associate with an unconditioned stimulus.

conditioned response (CR) A learned response to a conditioned stimulus.

acquisition The initial learning phase in both classical and operant conditioning.

Because Pavlov was interested in exploring the link between a stimulus and the dog's response, he had to pick a stimulus that was more controlled than the sound of someone walking into a room. Pavlov used a variety of stimuli, such as sounds produced by metronomes, buzzers, and bells, which under normal circumstances have nothing to do with food. In other words, they are *neutral* stimuli in relation to feeding and responses to food.

On numerous occasions during an experimental trial, Pavlov and his assistants presented a dog with a chosen sound—the tone of a bell, for instance—and then moments later gave the dog some meat powder. Each time the tone was sounded, the assistant would wait a couple of seconds and then offer the dog the meat powder. All the while, its saliva was being measured. After repeated pairings, the dog learned to link the tone with the meat powder. We know this procedure resulted in learning, because after several pairings the dog would salivate in response to the tone alone, with no meat powder present. The dog had been conditioned to associate the tone with food.

Time for Some Terms

LO 3   Identify the differences between the US, UR, CS, and CR.

Now that you know Pavlov's basic research procedure, it is important to learn the specific terminology psychologists use to describe what is happening (Infographic 5.1). Before the experiment began, the tone was a **neutral stimulus (NS)**—something in the environment that *does not* normally cause a relevant *automatic* or reflexive response. In the current example, salivation is the automatic response associated with food; dogs do not normally respond to the tone of a bell by salivating. But through experience, the dogs learned to link this neutral stimulus (the tone) with another stimulus (food) that prompts an automatic, unlearned response (salivation). This type of learning is **classical conditioning,** and it occurs when an originally neutral stimulus is conditioned to elicit or induce an involuntary response, such as salivation, eye blinks, and other types of *reflex* reactions.

US, UR, CS, AND CR   At the start of a trial, before the dogs were conditioned or had learned anything about the neutral stimulus, they salivated when they smelled or were given food. The food is called an **unconditioned stimulus (US)** because it triggers an automatic response without any learning needed. Salivation by the dogs when exposed to food is an **unconditioned response (UR)** because it doesn't require any conditioning (learning); the dog just does it involuntarily. The salivation (the UR) is an automatic response elicited by the smell or taste of food (the US). After conditioning has occurred, the dog responds to the tone of the bell almost as if it were food. The tone, previously a *neutral stimulus,* has now become a **conditioned stimulus (CS)** because it triggers the dog's salivation. When the salivation occurs in response to the tone, it is called a **conditioned response (CR);** the salivation is a learned response.

THE ACQUISITION PHASE   The pairings of the neutral stimulus (the tone) with the US (the meat powder) occur during the **acquisition** or initial learning phase. Some points to remember:

- The meat powder is always a US (the dog never has to learn how to respond to it).
- The dog's salivating is initially a UR to the meat powder, but eventually becomes a CR as it occurs in response to the tone (without the sight or smell of meat powder).
- The US is always different from the CS; the US automatically triggers the response, but with the CS, the response has been *learned* by the organism.

Pavlov's work paved the way for a new generation of psychologists who considered behavior to be a topic of objective, scientific study. Like many who would follow, he believed that scientists should focus only on observable behaviors; his work transformed our understanding of learning and our approach to psychological research.

Nuts and Bolts of Classical Conditioning

We have learned about Pavlov's dogs and their demonstration of classical conditioning. We have defined the terminology associated with that process. Now it's time to take our learning (about learning) to the next level and examine some of the principles that guide the process.

LO 4   Recognize and give examples of stimulus generalization and stimulus discrimination.

STIMULUS GENERALIZATION   What would happen if a dog in one of Pavlov's experiments heard a slightly higher-frequency tone? Would the dog still salivate? Pavlov (1927/1960) asked this same question and found that a stimulus similar to the CS caused the dogs to salivate as well. This is an example of **stimulus generalization.** Once an association is forged between a CS and a CR, the learner often responds to similar stimuli as if they are the original CS. When Pavlov's dogs learned to salivate in response to a metronome ticking at 90 beats per minute, they also salivated when the metronome ticked a little more quickly (100 beats per minute) or slowly (80 beats per minute; Hothersall, 2004). Their response was *generalized* to metronome speeds ranging from 80 to 100 beats per minute. Perhaps you have been classically conditioned to salivate at the sight of a tall glass of lemonade. Stimulus generalization predicts you would now salivate when seeing a shorter glass of lemonade, or even a mug, if you knew it contained your favorite drink.

STIMULUS DISCRIMINATION   Next let's see what would happen if you presented Pavlov's dogs with two stimuli that differed significantly. Believe it or not, the dogs would be able to tell them apart. If you presented the meat powder with a high-pitched sound, they would associate that pitch with the meat powder and salivate. However, they would not salivate in response to low-pitched sounds. The dogs would display **stimulus discrimination,** the ability to differentiate between a particular CS and other stimuli sufficiently different from it. With enough training, Pavlov's dogs could differentiate among high and low tones (Watson, 1968). Similarly, someone who's been stung by a bee might only become afraid at the sight of bees (and not flies, for example) because he has learned to discriminate among various flying insects. He has only been conditioned to experience fear in response to bees.

EXTINCTION   Once the dogs in a classical conditioning experiment associate the tone of a bell with meat powder, can they ever listen to the sound without salivating? The answer is yes—if they are repeatedly exposed to the sound of the tone *without* the meat powder. If the CS is presented time and again without the US, the association may fade. The CR decreases and eventually disappears in a process called **extinction.** In general, if dogs are repeatedly exposed to a CS (for example, a metronome or bell) without any tasty treats to follow, they produce progressively less saliva in response to the stimulus and, eventually, none at all (Watson, 1968).

SPONTANEOUS RECOVERY   But take note: Even with extinction, the connection is not necessarily gone forever. For example, Pavlov (1927/1960) used classical conditioning with a dog to form an association between the tone of a bell and meat

CONNECTIONS

In **Chapter 1,** we described the scientific method and how it depends on *objective* observations. An objective approach requires scientists to make their observations without the influence of personal opinion or preconceived notions. We are all prone to biases, but the scientific method helps minimize their effects. Pavlov was among the first to insist that behavior must be studied objectively.

Layland Masuda/Shutterstock

CONNECTIONS

In **Chapter 3,** we introduced the concept of a *difference threshold,* which is the minimum difference between two stimuli that is noticed 50% of the time. Here, we see that difference thresholds can play a role in stimulus discrimination tasks. The conditioned stimulus and the comparison stimuli must be sufficiently different to be distinguished; that is, their difference is greater than the difference threshold.

stimulus generalization The tendency for stimuli similar to the conditioned stimulus to elicit the conditioned response.

stimulus discrimination The ability to differentiate between a conditioned stimulus and other stimuli sufficiently different from it.

extinction In classical conditioning, the process by which the CR decreases after repeated exposure to the CS in the absence of the US; in operant conditioning, the disappearance of a learned behavior through the removal of its reinforcer.

powder. Once the tone was associated with the salivation, he stopped presenting the meat powder, and the association was extinguished (the dog didn't salivate in response to the tone). Two hours following this extinction, Pavlov presented the tone again and the dog salivated. This reappearance of the conditioned response following its extinction is called **spontaneous recovery.** With the presentation of a CS after a period of rest, the CR reappears. The dog had not "forgotten" the association when the pairing was extinguished. Rather, the CR was "suppressed" when the dog was not being exposed to the US. Two hours later when the bell (the CS) sounded in the absence of food (the US), the association reemerged; the link between the tone and the food had been simmering beneath the surface. Let's return to that refreshing glass of lemonade—a summer drink you may not consume for 9 months out of the year. It is possible that your CR (salivating) will be suppressed because of the process of extinction from September to the end of May, but when June rolls around, spontaneous recovery may occur, and once again you are salivating at the sight of that lemonade glass (the CS).

HIGHER ORDER CONDITIONING After the acquisition phase, it is possible to add another layer to the conditioning process. Suppose the tone of the bell has become a CS for the dog, such that every time it sounds, the dog has learned to salivate. Once this conditioning is established, the researcher can add a new neutral stimulus, such as a light flashing, every time the dog hears the sound of the tone. After pairing the sound and the light together (without the meat powder anywhere in sight or smell), the light will become associated with the sound and the dog will begin to salivate in response to seeing the light alone. This is called **higher order conditioning** (**Figure 5.1**). With repeated pairings of the CS (the tone) and a new neutral stimulus (the light), the second neutral stimulus becomes a CS as well. When all is said and done, both stimuli (the sound and the light) have gone from being neutral stimuli to conditioned stimuli, and either of them can elicit the CR (salivation). But in higher order conditioning, the second neutral stimulus is paired with a CS instead of being paired with the original US (Pavlov, 1927/1960). In our example, the light is associated with the sound, not with the food directly.

Humans also learn to salivate when presented with stimuli that signal the delivery of food. Perhaps your nightly routine includes making dinner during television commercial breaks, and your mouth begins to water as you prepare your food. Initially,

FIGURE 5.1
Higher Order Conditioning
Once an association has been made through classical conditioning, the conditioned stimulus can be used to acquire new learned associations. Here, when a conditioned stimulus (such as a bell that now triggers salivation) is repeatedly paired with a neutral stimulus (NS) such as a flashing light, the dog will learn to salivate in response to the light—without food ever being present! These multiple layers of learning help us understand how humans form associations between many different stimuli. Jack Russell terrier: Thinkstock; Bell: Thinkstock; Dog bowl: Thinkstock; Bulb: Shutterstock

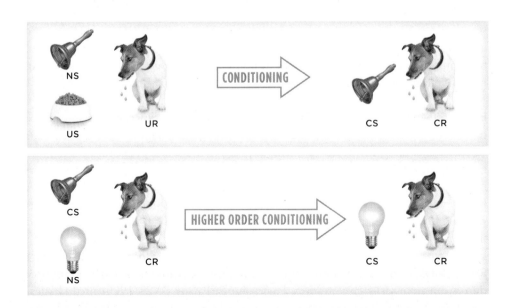

the commercials are neutral stimuli, but maybe you have gotten into the habit of preparing food only during those breaks. Making your food (CS) causes you to salivate (CR), and because dinner preparation always happens during commercials, those commercials will eventually have the power to make you salivate (CR) as well, even in the absence of food. Here we have an example of higher order conditioning, wherein additional stimuli elicit the CR.

Classical conditioning is not limited to examples of salivation. It affects you in ways you may not even realize. Think of what happens to your heart rate, for example, when you walk into a room where you have had a bad experience. See Table 5.1 on page 184 for some additional real-life examples of classical conditioning. Now let's observe how classical conditioning might apply to Ivonne's experiences.

From Dogs to Triathletes: Extending Pavlov

Getting in the water has always made Ivonne uneasy, making her muscles tighten and her heart pump faster. She experiences this physiological fear response (the UR) because she feels disoriented when her ears, which she uses for navigation, are submerged. Her disorientation would be considered an *unconditioned stimulus* (US). During the acquisition phase, Ivonne began to associate the smell of chlorine (a neutral stimulus) with the disorientation she feels (US) while swimming. Every time she went to the pool, the odor of chlorine was in the air. With repeated pairings of the chlorine smell and the disoriented feeling, the neutral stimulus became linked with the US. Now, simply smelling chlorine evokes the same physiological response she has when she feels disoriented in the water. The chlorine odor went from being a *neutral stimulus* to a *conditioned stimulus* that elicits the now *conditioned response* of her fear reaction.

Now let's explore a more hypothetical situation. If Ivonne were to smell dishes rinsed in a bleach solution or chlorine-smelling household cleaners, she might have a *CR,* suggesting *stimulus generalization* has occurred. This explains how we can react in ways that make no sense to us; Ivonne may wonder to herself why she is reacting so strongly to those dishes.

Stimulus discrimination also applies to Ivonne's example. A gym locker room is filled with all sorts of odors: hair spray, shampoo, and sweaty socks, just to mention a few. Of all the scents in the locker room, chlorine is the only one that gets her heart racing. The fact that Ivonne can single out this odor even when bombarded with other smells and sounds demonstrates her ability to differentiate the CS from other stimuli.

It would be nice for Ivonne if the smell of chlorine no longer made her heart race. There are two ways that she could get rid of this classically conditioned response. First, she could stop swimming for a very long time, and the association might fade away through *extinction.* But quite often avoidance does not extinguish a classically conditioned response, as the possibility of spontaneous recovery always exists. (Recovery in this sense means recovering the conditioned response of fear, not the more familiar sense of "getting better.") And clearly, this approach is not practical for Ivonne.

The second option is to pair a new response with the US or the CS. For example, Ivonne could practice relaxation skills and positive race visualization that includes a successful completion of the swim, until swimming itself no longer triggers the anxiety. With this accomplished, the chlorine would cease to stir up anxiety as well. Or Ivonne could gradually expose herself to the smell of chlorine while maintaining a state of relaxation, thus preventing the learned anxiety and fear response. In Chapter 13, we present some techniques therapists use to help individuals struggling with anxiety and fear.

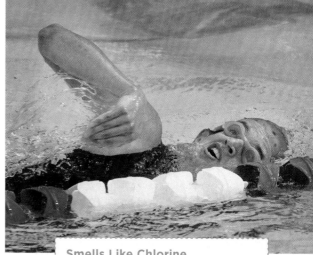

Smells Like Chlorine
Although Ivonne has now completed over 25 triathlons, she is not particularly comfortable with the swimming portion of the event. Just smelling chlorinated pool water makes her heart beat faster and her muscles tense—physiological responses resulting from classical conditioning. How might this reaction be eliminated? If Ivonne were to stay away from the pool for some period of time, the association between the chlorine smell and the disorientation she feels in the water may fade through the process of extinction.

spontaneous recovery The reappearance of a conditioned response following its extinction.

higher order conditioning With repeated pairings of a conditioned stimulus and a neutral stimulus, the second neutral stimulus becomes a conditioned stimulus as well.

Yuck: Conditioned Taste Aversion

LO 5   Summarize how classical conditioning is dependent on the biology of the organism.

Have you ever experienced food poisoning? After falling ill from something you ate, whether it was sushi, uncooked chicken, or tainted peanut butter, you probably steered clear of that particular food for a while. This is an example of **conditioned taste aversion,** a *powerful* form of classical conditioning that occurs when an organism learns to associate the taste of a particular food or drink with illness. Imagine a grizzly bear that avoids poisonous berries after vomiting all day from eating them. Often it only takes a single pairing between a food and a bad feeling—that is, one-trial learning—for an organism to learn its lesson. In the case of the bear, the US is the poison in the berries; the UR is the vomiting. After acquisition, the CS would be the sight of the berries, and the CR would be a nauseous feeling, as well as avoiding the berries in the future.

Avoiding foods that induce sickness has **adaptive value**, meaning it helps organisms survive, upping the odds they will reproduce and pass their genes along to the next generation. According to the evolutionary perspective, humans and other animals have a powerful drive to ensure that they and their offspring reach reproductive age, so it's critical to steer clear of tastes that have been associated with illness.

How might conditioned taste aversion play out in your life? Suppose you eat a hot dog a few hours before coming down with a stomach virus that's coincidentally spreading throughout your college. The hot dog isn't responsible for your illness—and you might even be aware of this—but the thought of eating one can make you feel sick even after you have recovered. Physical experiences like this can sometimes be so strong that they override our knowledge of the facts.

RATS WITH BELLYACHES   American psychologist John Garcia and his colleagues provided a demonstration of taste aversion in their well-known studies with laboratory rats (Garcia, Ervin, & Koelling, 1966). They designed a series of experiments to explore how rats respond to eating and drinking foods associated with sickness. In one study, Garcia and his colleagues provided the animals with flavored water followed by injections of a drug that upset their stomachs. The animals rejected that flavored drink thereafter.

The rats in Garcia's studies seemed naturally inclined to link their "internal malaise" (sick feeling) to tastes and smells and less likely to associate the nausea with other types of stimuli related to their hearing or vision, such as noises or things they saw (Garcia et al., 1966). This is clearly an adaptive trait, because nausea often results from ingesting food that is poisonous or spoiled. In order to survive, an animal must be able to recognize and shun the tastes of dangerous substances. Garcia's research highlights the importance of **biological preparedness,** the predisposition or inclination of animals (and people) to form certain kinds of associations through classical conditioning. Conditioned taste aversion is a powerful form of learning; would you believe it can be used to save endangered species?

didn't SEE that coming

Rescuing Animals with Classical Conditioning

 Using your newfound knowledge of conditioned taste aversion, imagine how you might solve the following problem: An animal is in trouble in Australia. The northern quoll, a meat-eating marsupial that might be described as a cute version of an opossum, is critically endangered because a non-native "cane toad" is invading its territory. Cane toads may look delicious (at least to the quolls, who eat them right up), but they pack a lethal dose of poison—often enough to kill a quoll

CONNECTIONS

In **Chapter 1,** we introduced the *evolutionary perspective,* which suggests that adaptive behaviors and traits are shaped by *natural selection.* Here, the evolutionary perspective helps clarify why some types of learning are so powerful. In the case of conditioned taste aversion, species gain an evolutionary advantage through quick and efficient learning about poisonous foods.

conditioned taste aversion   A form of classical conditioning that occurs when an organism learns to associate the taste of a particular food or drink with illness.

adaptive value   The degree to which a trait or behavior helps an organism survive.

biological preparedness   The tendency for animals to be predisposed or inclined to form associations.

conditioned emotional response   An emotional reaction acquired through classical conditioning; process by which an emotional reaction becomes associated with a previously neutral stimulus.

in just one eating. Wherever the toads have settled, quoll populations have diminished or disappeared (O'Donnell, Webb, & Shine, 2010). The quolls are now in danger of becoming extinct. How could you use conditioned taste aversion to save them?

EATING A POISONOUS TOAD CAN TAKE A QUOLL!

Remember that conditioned taste aversion occurs when an organism rejects a food or drink after consuming it and becoming very sick. To condition the quolls to stop eating the toxic toads, you must teach them to associate the little amphibians with nausea. You could do this by feeding them non-poisonous cane toads containing a drug that causes nausea. A group of researchers from the University of Sydney recently used this approach with the quolls, and the strategy turned out to be quite successful. Quolls that were submitted to conditioned taste aversion were less likely than their unconditioned comrades to eat the poisonous toads and die (O'Donnell et al., 2010).

Learning to the Rescue
Australia's northern quoll (left) is threatened by the introduction of an invasive species known as the cane toad (right). The quolls eat the toads, which carry a lethal dose of poison, but they can learn to avoid this toxic prey through conditioned taste aversion (O'Donnell et al., 2010).
left: Eric and David Hosking/CORBIS;
right: Chris Mattison/FLPA/Science Source

Similar approaches are being tried across the world. For example, the U.S. Fish and Wildlife Service is using taste aversion to discourage endangered Mexican wolves from feasting on livestock in New Mexico and Arizona (Bryan, 2012, January 28). As you see, lessons learned by psychologists working in a lab can have far-reaching consequences. 👁!

Little Albert and Conditioned Emotional Response

LO 6   Describe the Little Albert study and explain how fear can be learned.

So far, we have focused chiefly on the classical conditioning of physical responses—salivation, nausea, and increased heart rate. Now let's take a closer look at some of the emotional reactions classical conditioning can produce, through the pairing of a stimulus with an emotional response. We call this a **conditioned emotional response:** an emotional reaction acquired via classical conditioning.

The classic case study of "Little Albert," conducted by John B. Watson and Rosalie Rayner, provides a famous illustration of a conditioned emotional response (Watson & Rayner, 1920). Little Albert was an 11-month-old baby who initially had no fear of rats. When he saw the white rats scurrying about Watson and Rayner's lab, he didn't seem the least bit scared. In fact, he was rather intrigued and sometimes reached out to touch them. But all this changed when the researchers began banging a hammer against a steel bar (a US for a fear response in younger children) every time he reached for the rat (Harris, 1979). After seven pairings of the loud noise and the appearance of the rat, Little Albert began to fear rats and generalized this fear to other furry objects, including a sealskin coat and a rabbit (Harris, 1979). The sight of the rat went from being a neutral stimulus to a conditioned stimulus (CS), and Little Albert's fear of the rat became a conditioned response (CR).

CONNECTIONS
In **Chapter 1,** we introduced two types of research. *Basic research* is focused on gathering knowledge for the sake of knowledge. *Applied research* focuses on changing behaviors and outcomes, often leading to real-world applications. Here, we see how classical conditioning principles are *applied* to help save wildlife.

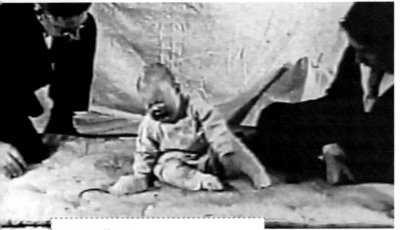

Poor Albert
"Little Albert" was an 11-month-old baby who developed a fear of rats through his participation in an ethically questionable experiment by John B. Watson and Rosalie Rayner (Watson & Rayner, 1920). Watson and Rayner repeatedly showed the child a rat while terrifying him with a loud banging sound. Albert quickly learned to associate the sight of the rat with the scary noise, and his resulting fear of rats is known as a conditioned emotional response.
Archives of the History of American Psychology, The Center for the History of Psychology, The University of Akron

Nobody knows exactly what happened to Little Albert after he participated in Watson and Rayner's research. Some psychologists believe Little Albert's true identity is still unknown (Powell, 2010; Reese, 2010). Others have proposed Little Albert was Douglas Merritte, who at age 6 died of hydrocephalus (Beck & Irons, 2011; Beck, Levinson, & Irons, 2009). More recently, researchers have proposed that Little Albert was William Albert Barger (later known as William Albert Martin), who lived until 2007 and reportedly did not like animals (Powell, Digdon, Harris, & Smithson, 2014). Did Barger's distaste for animals stem from his participation in Watson and Rayner's experiment, or was it the result of seeing a childhood pet killed in an accident? Researchers cannot be sure, and we may never know the true identity of Little Albert or the long-term effects of his exposure to this type of unethical conditioning.

The Little Albert study would never happen today; at least, we hope it wouldn't. Contemporary psychologists conduct research according to stringent ethical guidelines, and instilling terror in a baby would not be considered acceptable (and would not be allowed at research institutions). However, it is not too far out to imagine a similar scenario playing out in real life. Picture a toddler who is about to reach for a rat on the kitchen floor. A parent sees this happening and shouts "NO!" It would not take many pairings of the toddler reaching for the rat and the parent shouting "NO!" for the child to develop a fear of the rat. In this real-world scenario, you would be hard-pressed to find someone who would say the parent's behavior was unethical.

Classical Conditioning: Do You Buy It?

Classical conditioning has applications in marketing and sales (**Table 5.1**). Some research suggests that advertisements can instill emotions and attitudes toward product brands through classical conditioning, and that these responses may linger as long as 3 weeks (Grossman & Till, 1998). In one study, some participants were shown pictures

TABLE 5.1 REAL-LIFE EXAMPLES OF CLASSICAL CONDITIONING

Type	Pairing of Neutral Stimulus and US	Expected Response
Advertising	Repeated pairing of products such as cars (neutral stimulus) with celebrities (US)	Automatic response to celebrity (UR), such as sexual arousal, heart racing, desire; pairing leads to similar response, such as sexual arousal, heart racing, desire (CR) to the product (CS).
Fears	Pairing of a dog lunging (US) at you on the street (neutral stimulus) where you take your morning run	Automatic response to the dog lunging at you is fear (UR); pairing leads to similar response of fear (CR) to the street (CS) where the dog lives.
	One pairing of seeing a car in the rearview mirror (neutral stimulus) and being rear-ended by that car (US)	Automatic response to the impact of the collision is fear (UR); with one pairing, the sight of a car approaching in the rearview mirror (CS) elicits a fearful reaction (CR).
Fetishes	Repeated pairings of originally nonsexual objects like shoes (neutral stimuli) and sexual activity (US)	Automatic response to sexual activity is sexual arousal (UR), leading to an association of sexual pleasure (CR) with the objects (CS).
Romance	Repeated pairings of a cologne (neutral stimulus) with your romantic partner (US)	Automatic response to your feelings for your partner is sexual arousal (UR); paired with the cologne (CS), leads to sexual arousal (CR).

The implications of classical conditioning extend far beyond salivating dogs. These are just a few examples of how this form of learning impacts daily life.

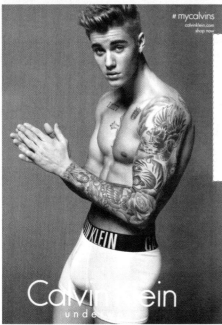

Does Sexy Sell?
Justin Bieber models underwear for Calvin Klein's Spring 2015 ad campaign. Research suggests that advertisements may instill attitudes toward brands through classical conditioning (Grossman & Till, 1998), but how do these attitudes affect sales? Now that is a question worth researching.
The Advertising Archives

of pleasant scenes (such as a tropical location or a panda in a natural setting) paired with a fictitious mouthwash brand. Participants who were exposed to the mouthwash (originally a neutral stimulus) and the favorable pictures (the US) were more likely to retain a positive enduring attitude (now the CR) toward the mouthwash (which became a CS) than participants who were exposed to the entire same set of pictures paired in random order. In other words, the researchers were able to create "favorable attitudes" toward the fictitious brand of mouthwash by pairing pictures of the mouthwash with scenery that evoked positive emotions (Grossman & Till, 1998). The study did not address whether this favorable attitude leads to a purchase, however.

Do you think you are susceptible to this kind of conditioning? We would venture to say that we all are. Complete the following Try This to see if classical conditioning affects your attitudes and feelings toward everyday products.

Marketers use classical conditioning to instill positive emotions and attitudes toward product brands. List examples of recent advertisements you have seen on television or the Internet that use this approach to get people to buy products. Which of your recent purchases may have been influenced by such ads?

try this

Remember that classical conditioning is a type of learning associated with automatic (or involuntary) behaviors. You don't "learn" to go out and buy a particular brand of mouthwash through classical conditioning. Classical conditioning can influence our attitudes toward products, but it can't teach us voluntary behaviors. Well then, how do we learn these types of deliberate behaviors? Read on.

 show what you know

1. _____ is the learning process in which two stimuli become associated.

2. Because of _____, animals and people are predisposed or inclined to form associations that increase their chances of survival.

3. Hamburgers were once your favorite food, but ever since you ate a burger tainted with salmonella (which causes food poisoning), you cannot smell or taste one without feeling nauseous. Which of the following is the unconditioned stimulus?
   a. salmonella
   b. nausea
   c. hamburgers
   d. the hamburger vendor

4. Watson and Rayner used classical conditioning to instill fear in Little Albert. Create a diagram of the neutral stimulus, US, UR, CS, and CR used in their experiment. In what way does Little Albert show stimulus generalization?

✓ CHECK YOUR ANSWERS IN APPENDIX C.

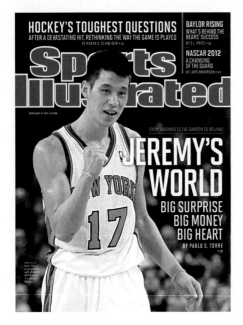

Rising Star
Jeremy Lin appears on a 2012 cover of *Sports Illustrated*. This rookie player amazed the world on February 4 of that same year when he came off the bench and led the New York Knicks to victory against the New Jersey Nets. It was the first game of a Lin-led winning streak—the beginning of "Linsanity."
Sports Illustrated/Getty Images

Operant Conditioning

THE JEREMY LIN SHOW Madison Square Garden, February 4, 2012: The New York Knicks are playing their third game in three nights, hoping to end a losing streak. But they are already trailing far behind the New Jersey Nets in the first quarter. That's when Jeremy Lin, a third-string point guard who is dangerously close to being cut from his third NBA team, bounds off the bench and leads the Knicks to a stunning victory. By the end of the game, the crowd is going crazy, the Knicks players are laughing like giddy schoolboys, and the Pearl Jam song "Jeremy" reverberates through the stadium (Beck, 2012, February 4; Dalrymple, 2012). One commentator perfectly sums up the state of affairs: "It's the Jeremy Lin Show here at Madison Square Garden" (Dalrymple, 2012, p. 24).

Jeremy Lin was an overnight sensation. People around the world were fascinated by him for many reasons. He was the fourth Asian American player in NBA history, the first Harvard graduate to play in the league since the 1950s, and previously a bench-warmer, not even drafted out of college (Beck, 2011, December 28). Everyone was asking the same question: Would Jeremy be a one-game wonder or something bigger?

Jeremy ended up leading the Knicks through a seven-game victory spree, the highlights of which included scoring 38 points against the Los Angeles Lakers—more points in that game than the Lakers' mighty Kobe Bryant (ESPN.com, 2012, February 10). Suddenly, Jeremy's face was everywhere—on the covers of *TIME Magazine* and *Sports Illustrated* (twice) and all over the Internet (Dalrymple, 2012, p. xv). Where did this guy come from?

Like any of us, Jeremy is a unique blend of nature and nurture. He was blessed with a hearty helping of physical capabilities (nature), such as speed, agility, and coordination. But he was also shaped by the circumstances of his life (nurture). This second category is where learning comes in. Let's find out how.

The Shaping of Behavior

When Jeremy began his freshman year at Palo Alto High School, he was about 5′3″ and 125 pounds—not exactly NBA material. During his sophomore year, he learned to dunk, and by senior year, he was over 6 feet tall and leading his team to victory in the Division II state championship (Dalrymple, 2012; Tennis, 2012, February 20).

We Did It, Coach!
Jeremy and his teammates from Palo Alto High School celebrate a victory that led them to the 2006 state finals. Pictured in the center is Coach Peter Diepenbrock, who has maintained a friendship with Jeremy since he graduated. Prior to Jeremy's sensational season with the Knicks, Diepenbrock helped him with his track workouts. Keith Peters/Palo Alto Weekly

Jeremy was a big fish in a small pond—so big that he didn't need to work very hard to maintain his level of success. However, college recruiters did not observe anything exceptional in his strength or overall athleticism (Viera, 2012, February 12). This may be the reason Jeremy did not receive any athletic scholarship offers from Division I colleges, despite his basketball prowess and 4.2 grade point average (McGregor, 2012, February 15; Spears, 2012, February 18).

Things changed when Jeremy found himself in a bigger pond, playing basketball at Harvard University. That's when Coach Diepenbrock says the young player began working harder on aspects of practice he didn't particularly enjoy, such as weight lifting, ball handling, and conditioning. When Jeremy was picked up by the NBA, his diligence soared to a new level. While playing with the Golden State Warriors, he would eat breakfast at the team's training facility by 8:30 A.M., three and a half hours before practice. "Then, all of sudden, you'd hear a ball bouncing on the floor," Keith Smart, a former coach told *The New York Times* (Beck, 2012, February 24, para. 14). Between NBA seasons, Jeremy returned to his alma mater Palo Alto High School to run track workouts with Coach Diepenbrock. He also trained with a shooting coach and spent "an inordinate amount of time" honing his shot, according to Diepenbrock.

Jeremy's persistence paid off. The once-scrawny scrapper, now 6′3″ and 200 pounds (ESPN.com, 2015), is exploding with power and agility. According to Diepenbrock, "He has gotten to the point where now, as far as the strength and the athleticism, he is on par—or good enough—with veteran NBA athletes."

OPERANT CONDITIONING DEFINED   What has kept Jeremy working so hard all these years? Psychologists might attribute Jeremy's ongoing efforts to **operant conditioning,** a type of learning in which people or animals come to associate their voluntary actions with their consequences. Whether pleasant or unpleasant, the effects of a behavior influence future actions. Think about some of the consequences of Jeremy's training—short-term results like seeing his free throw shot improve, and long-term rewards like victory, fame, and fortune. How do you think these outcomes might have influenced (and continue to influence) Jeremy's behavior? Before addressing this question, we need to take a closer look at operant conditioning.

LO 7   Describe Thorndike's law of effect.

THORNDIKE AND HIS CATS   One of the first scientists to objectively study the effect of consequences on behavior was American psychologist Edward Thorndike (1874–1949). Thorndike's early research focused on chicks and other animals, many of which he kept in his apartment. But after an incubator almost caught fire, his landlady insisted he get rid of the chicks (Hothersall, 2004). It was in the lab that Thorndike conducted his research on cats. His most famous experimental setup involved putting a cat in a latched cage called a "puzzle box" and planting enticing pieces of fish outside the door. When first placed in the box, the cat would scratch and paw around randomly, but after a while, just by chance, it would pop the latch, causing the door to release. The cat would then escape the cage to devour the fish (**Figure 5.2**). The next time the cat was put in the box, it would repeat this random

FIGURE 5.2
Puzzle Box
Early psychologist Edward Thorndike conducted his well-known cat experiments using "puzzle boxes" like the one shown below. At the start of the experiment, Thorndike's cats pawed around haphazardly until they managed to unlatch the cage and then eat the fish treats outside the door. As the trials wore on, the felines learned to free themselves more quickly. After several trials, the amount of time needed to escape the box dropped significantly (see graph below). Thorndike attributed this phenomenon to the *law of effect,* which states that behaviors are more likely to reoccur if they are followed by pleasurable outcomes. Data from Thorndike, 1898

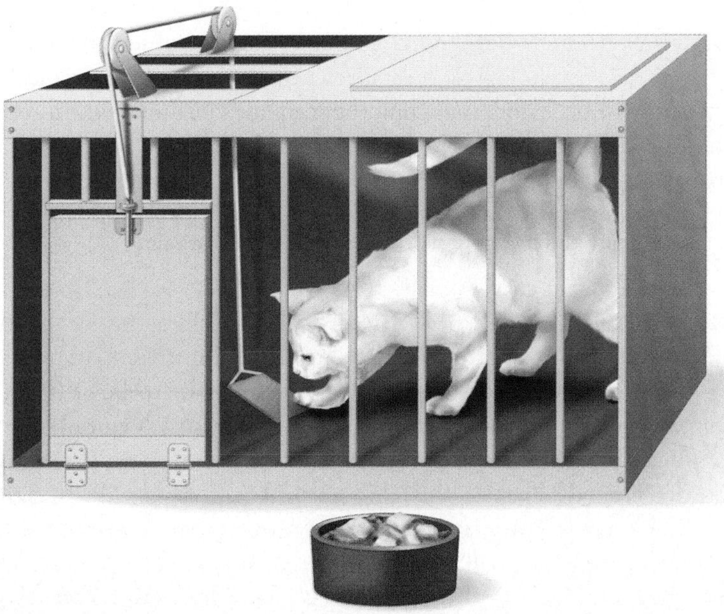

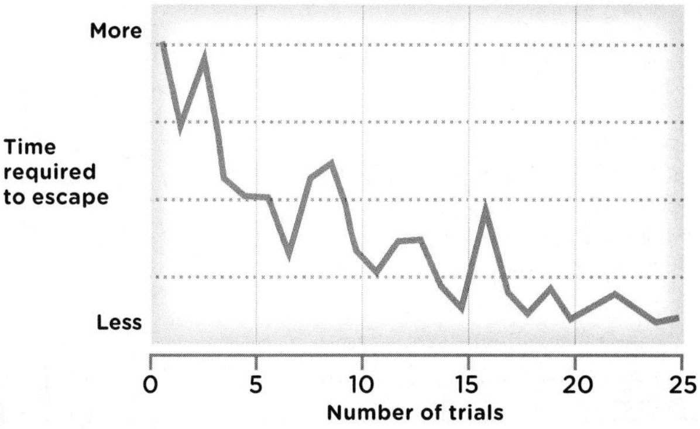

operant conditioning Learning that occurs when voluntary actions become associated with their consequences.

activity, scratching and pawing with no particular direction. And again, just by chance, the cat would pop the latch that released the door and freed it to eat the fish. Each time the cat was returned to the box, the number of random activities decreased until eventually it was able to break free almost immediately (Thorndike, 1898).

We should highlight a few important issues relating to this early research. First, these cats discovered the solution to the puzzle box accidentally, while exhibiting their naturally occurring behaviors (scratching and exploring). So, they initially obtained the fish treat by accident. The other important point is that the measure of learning was not an exam grade or basketball score, but the amount of time it took the cats to break free.

The cats' behavior, Thorndike reasoned, could be explained by the **law of effect,** which says that a behavior (opening the latch) is more likely to happen again when followed by a pleasurable outcome (delicious fish). Behaviors that lead to pleasurable outcomes will be repeated, while behaviors that don't lead to pleasurable outcomes (or are followed by something unpleasant) will not be repeated. The law of effect is not limited to cats. When was the last time your behavior changed as a result of a pleasurable outcome?

Most contemporary psychologists would call the fish in Thorndike's experiments **reinforcers,** because the fish increased the likelihood that the preceding behavior (escaping the cage) would occur again. Reinforcers are consequences that follow behaviors, and they are a key component of operant conditioning. Our daily lives abound with examples of reinforcers. Praise, hugs, good grades, enjoyable food, and attention are all reinforcers that increase the probability the behaviors they follow will be repeated. Through the process of **reinforcement,** targeted behaviors become more frequent. A child praised for sharing a toy is more likely to share in the future. A student who studies hard and earns an A on an exam is more likely to prepare well for upcoming exams.

SKINNER AND BEHAVIORISM Some of the earliest and most influential research on operant conditioning came out of the lab of B. F. Skinner (1904–1990), an American psychologist. Like Pavlov, Skinner had not planned to study learning. Upon graduating from college, Skinner decided to become a writer and a poet, but after a year of trying his hand at writing, he decided he "had nothing to say" (Skinner, 1976). Around this time, he began to read the work of Watson and Pavlov, which inspired him to pursue a graduate degree in psychology. He enrolled at Harvard, took some psychology classes that he found "dull," and eventually joined a lab in the Department of Biology, where he could study the subject he found most intriguing: animal behavior.

Skinner was devoted to **behaviorism,** the scientific study of observable behavior. Behaviorists believed that psychology could only be considered a "true science" if it was based on the study of behaviors that could be seen and documented. In relation to learning, Skinner and other behaviorists proposed that *all* behaviors, thoughts, and emotions are shaped by factors in the external environment.

LO 8 Explain shaping and the method of successive approximations.

SHAPING AND SUCCESSIVE APPROXIMATIONS Building on Thorndike's law of effect and Watson's approach to research, Skinner demonstrated, among other things, that rats can learn to push levers and pigeons can learn to bowl (Peterson, 2004). Since animals can't be expected to immediately perform such complex behaviors, Skinner employed **shaping,** the use of reinforcers to change behaviors through small steps toward a desired behavior (see **Infographic 5.2** on page 190). Skinner used shaping to teach a rat to "play basketball" (dropping a marble through a hole) and pigeons to "bowl" (nudging a ball down a miniature alley). As you can see in the

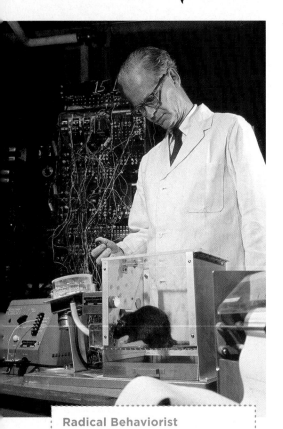

Radical Behaviorist
American psychologist Burrhus Frederic Skinner, or simply B. F. Skinner, is one of the most influential psychologists of all time. Skinner believed that every thought, emotion, and behavior (basically anything psychological) is shaped by factors in the environment. Using animal chambers known as "Skinner Boxes," he conducted carefully controlled experiments on animal behavior. Nina Leen/Time & Life Pictures/ Getty Images

law of effect Thorndike's principle stating that behaviors are more likely to be repeated when followed by pleasurable outcomes, and those followed by something unpleasant are less likely to be repeated.

reinforcers Consequences, such as events or objects, that increase the likelihood of a behavior reoccurring.

reinforcement Process by which an organism learns to associate a voluntary behavior with its consequences.

behaviorism The scientific study of observable behavior.

shaping The use of reinforcers to guide behavior to the acquisition of a desired, complex behavior.

photo on page 188. Skinner placed animals in chambers, or <u>Skinner boxes</u>, which were outfitted with food dispensers the animals could activate (by pecking a target or pushing on a lever, for instance) and recording equipment to monitor these behaviors. These boxes allowed Skinner to conduct carefully controlled experiments, measuring activity precisely and advancing the scientific and systematic study of behavior.

How in the world did Skinner get pigeons to bowl? The first task was to break the bowling lessons into small steps that pigeons could accomplish. Next, he introduced reinforcers as consequences for behaviors that came closer and closer to achieving the desired goal—bowling a strike! Choosing the right increments for the behaviors was crucial. If his expectations started too high, the pigeons would never be given any reinforcers. If his expectations were too low, the pigeons would get reinforcers for everything they did. Either way, they would be unable to make the critical connection between desired behavior and reward. So Skinner devised a plan such that every time the animals did something that brought them a step closer to completing the desired behavior, they would get a reinforcer (usually food). The first reward might be given for simply looking at the ball; the second for bending down and touching it; and the third, for nudging the ball with their beaks. Since each incremental change in behavior brings the birds closer to accomplishing the larger goal of bowling, this method is called shaping by **successive approximations.** By the end of the experiment, the pigeons were repeatedly driving balls down miniature alleys, knocking down pins with a swipe of the beak (Peterson, 2004).

Successive approximations can also be used with humans, who are sometimes unwilling or unable to change problematic behaviors overnight. For example, psychologists have used successive approximation to change truancy behavior in adolescents (Enea & Dafinoiu, 2009). The truant teens were provided reinforcers for consistent attendance, but with small steps requiring increasingly more days in school.

It is amazing that the principles used for training animals can also be harnessed to keep teenagers in school. Is there anything operant conditioning *can't* accomplish?

Synonyms
Skinner boxes operant chambers

Musical Bunny
Keller and Marian Breland observe one of their animal performers at the IQ Zoo in Hot Springs, Arkansas, circa 1960. Using the operant conditioning concepts they learned from B. F. Skinner, the Brelands trained ducks to play guitars, raccoons to shoot basketballs, and chickens to tell fortunes. But their animal "students" did not always cooperate; sometimes their instincts interfered with the conditioning process (Bihm, Gillaspy, Lammers, & Huffman, 2010). The Central Arkansas Library System/Courtesy of Bob Bailey

THINK again

Chickens Can't Play Baseball

Rats can be conditioned to press levers; pigeons can be trained to bowl; and—believe it or not—chickens can learn to dance and play the piano (Breland & Breland, 1951). Keller and Marian Breland, a pair of Skinner's students, managed to train 6,000 animals not only to boogie but also to vacuum, dine at a table, and play sports and musical instruments (Breland & Breland, 1961). But as hard as they tried, the Brelands could not coax a chicken to play baseball.

Here's a rundown of what happened: The Brelands placed a chicken in a cage adjacent to a scaled down "baseball field," where it had access to a loop attached to a baseball bat. If the chicken managed to swing the bat hard enough to send the ball into the outfield, a food reward was delivered at the other end of the cage. Off the bird would go, running toward its meal dispenser like a baseball player sprinting to first base—or so the routine was supposed to go. But as soon as the Brelands took away the cage, the chicken behaved nothing like a baseball player; instead, it madly chased and pecked at the ball (Breland & Breland, 1961).

BASEBALL? NO. PIANO? YES.

How did the Brelands explain the chickens' behavior? They believed that the birds were demonstrating **instinctive drift,** the tendency for instinct to undermine conditioned behaviors. A chicken's pecking, for example, is an instinctive food-getting behavior. Pecking is useful for opening seeds or killing insects (Breland & Breland, 1961), but it won't help the bird get to first base. Animal behavior can be conditioned, but instinct may interfere with the process.

successive approximations A method of shaping that uses reinforcers to condition a series of small steps that gradually approach the target behavior.

instinctive drift The tendency for animals to revert to instinctual behaviors after a behavior pattern has been learned.

Learning Through Operant Conditioning

Operant conditioning is a type of learning in which we associate our voluntary actions with the consequences of those actions. For example, a pigeon naturally pecks things. But if every time the pigeon pecks a ball, he is given a *reinforcer,* the pigeon will soon learn to peck the ball more frequently.

B. F. Skinner showed that operant conditioning could do more than elicit simple, isolated actions. Through the process of *shaping,* in which reinforcers are used to change behaviors toward a more complex behavior, Skinner taught his pigeons to perform behaviors involving a series of actions, like bowling and tennis. Today, shaping is used routinely by parents, teachers, coaches, and employers to train all kinds of complex behaviors.

SKINNER'S EXPERIMENT: TRAIN A PIGEON TO PLAY TENNIS

Pigeon is rewarded with seeds for pecking the ball.

peck   **REINFORCEMENT**

reinforcement with seeds

Ball-pecking behavior increases.

peck   **REINFORCEMENT**   peck   **REINFORCEMENT**   peck

REINFORCEMENT

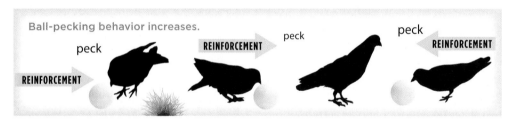

Now only the next step toward "tennis" is rewarded.

peck   peck   pushing the ball   **REINFORCEMENT**

reinforcement with seeds

Ball-pushing behavior increases.

pushing the ball   pushing the ball   pushing the ball

REINFORCEMENT   **REINFORCEMENT**   **REINFORCEMENT**

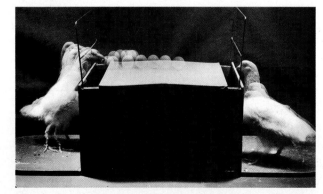

After behavior has been shaped through reinforcement, the pigeon has learned to play tennis.

HAVE YOU BEEN TRAINED?

Not every child is born loving the healthy foods his parent offers. But shaping can help a child learn to eat his vegetables. Over a period of time, reinforcement is given for behaviors that are closer and closer to this goal. Can you think of anything that would be a reward for eating vegetables? Praise or the excitement of a contest may work in this way.

1 Child refuses to eat vegetables.

2 YES! Reinforced for touching fork

3 GOOD JOB! Now, reinforced for touching vegetables

4 After behavior has been shaped through reinforcement, the child has learned to eat his vegetables.

Term	Classical Conditioning	Operant Conditioning
The Association	Links different stimuli, often through repeated pairings	Links behavior to its consequence, often through repeated pairings
Response	Involuntary behavior	Voluntary behavior
Acquisition	The initial learning phase	The initial learning phase
Extinction	The process by which the conditioned response decreases after repeated exposure to the conditioned stimulus in the absence of the unconditioned stimulus	The disappearance of a learned behavior through the removal of its reinforcer
Spontaneous Recovery	The reappearance of the conditioned response following its extinction.	Following extinction due to the absence of reinforcers, the behavior reemerges in a similar setting

These fundamental learning concepts apply to both classical and operant conditioning.

These examples involve researchers deliberately shaping behaviors with reinforcers in a laboratory setting. Many behaviorists believe behaviors are being shaped all of the time, both in and out of the laboratory. What factors in the environment might be shaping your behavior?

Common Features of Operant and Classical Conditioning

Both operant and classical conditioning are forms of learning, and they share many common principles (**Table 5.2**). As with classical conditioning, behaviors learned through operant conditioning go through an *acquisition* phase. Jeremy Lin learned to dunk a basketball when he was a sophomore in high school. The cats in Thorndike's experiments learned how to escape their puzzle boxes after a certain number of trials. In both cases, the acquisition stage occurred through the gradual process of shaping. Behaviors learned through operant conditioning are also subject to *extinction*—that is, they may fade in the absence of reinforcers. A rat in a Skinner box eventually gives up pushing on a lever if there is no longer a reinforcer awaiting. But that same lever-pushing behavior can make a sudden comeback through *spontaneous recovery*. After a rest period, the rat returns to his box and reverts to his old lever-pushing ways.

With operant conditioning, stimulus generalization is seen when a previously learned response to one stimulus occurs in the presence of a similar stimulus. A rat is conditioned to push a particular type of lever, but it may push a variety of other lever types similar in shape, size, and color. Horses also show stimulus generalization. With successive approximations using a tasty oat-molasses grain reinforcer, a small sample of horses learned to push on a "rat lever" with their lips in response to the appearance of a solid black circle with a 2.5-inch diameter. After conditioning, the horses were presented with a variety of black circles of different diameters; demonstrating stimulus generalization, they pressed the lever most often when shown circles close in size to the original (Dougherty & Lewis, 1991).

Stimulus discrimination is also at work in operant conditioning, as organisms can learn to discriminate between behaviors that do and do not result in reinforcement. With the use of reinforcers, turtles can learn to discriminate among black, white, and gray paddles. In one study, researchers rewarded a turtle with morsels of meat when it chose a black paddle over a white one; subsequently, the turtle chose the black paddle over other-colored paddles (Leighty et al., 2013).

Stimulus discrimination even applies to basketball players. Jeremy Lin certainly has learned to discriminate between teammates and opponents. It's unlikely he would get reinforcement from the crowd if he mistook an opponent for a teammate and passed the ball to the other team. Making a perfect pass to a teammate, on the other hand, would likely earn approval. This brings us to the next topic, *positive reinforcement,* where we start to see how classical and operant conditioning differ.

Types of Reinforcement

LO 9   Identify the differences between positive and negative reinforcement.

POSITIVE REINFORCEMENT   With operant conditioning, an organism learns to associate voluntary behaviors with their consequences. *Any* stimulus that increases a behavior is a reinforcer. What we haven't addressed is that a reinforcer can be something added or something taken away. In the process of **positive reinforcement,** reinforcers are presented (added) following the targeted behavior, and reinforcers in this case are generally pleasant (see Infographic 5.3 on page 199). By presenting positive reinforcers following a target behavior, we are increasing the chances that the target behavior will occur again. If the behavior doesn't increase after the stimulus is presented, that particular stimulus should not be considered a reinforcer. The fish treats that Thorndike's cats received immediately after escaping the puzzle box and the morsels of bird feed that Skinner's pigeons got for bowling are examples of positive reinforcement. In both cases, the reinforcers were *added* following the desired behavior and were pleasurable.

There were also many potential positive reinforcers driving Jeremy Lin. The praise that his coaches gave him for passing a ball to a teammate would be an example of positive reinforcement. Back in high school, Coach Diepenbrock rewarded players with stickers to provide feedback on their performance ("kind of middle schoolish," he admits, but effective nonetheless). Jeremy averaged the highest sticker score of any player ever. Did the sticker system have an effect on Jeremy's behavior? Coach Diepenbrock cannot be certain, but if it did, seeing his sticker-filled poster would have served as a positive reinforcer for him to practice.

You may be wondering if this approach could be used in a college classroom. The answer would inevitably depend on the people involved. Remember, the definition of a positive reinforcer depends on the organism's response to its presence (Skinner, 1953). You may love getting stickers, but your classmate may be offended by them.

Keep in mind, too, that not all positive reinforcers are pleasant; when we refer to *positive* reinforcement, we mean that something has been *added*. For example, if a child is starved for attention, then any kind of attention (including a reprimand) would be experienced as a positive reinforcer. Every time the child misbehaves, she gets reprimanded, and reprimanding is a form of attention, which the child craves. The scolding reinforces the misbehavior.

NEGATIVE REINFORCEMENT   We have established that behaviors can be increased or strengthened by the addition of a stimulus. But it is also possible to increase a behavior by taking something away. Behaviors can increase in response to **negative reinforcement,** through the process of *taking away* (or subtracting) something unpleasant. Skinner used negative reinforcement to shape the behavior of his rats. The rats were placed in Skinner boxes with floors that delivered a continuous mild electric shock—except when they pushed on a lever. The animals would begin

Good Work
Georgia preschool teacher Inyite (Shell) Adie-Ikor with a bouquet of roses. She is the recipient of the Early Childhood Educator Award and a $10,000 check from the international education organization Knowledge Universe. Awards and money often reinforce the behaviors they reward, but every individual responds differently to reinforcement. Craig Bromley/Getty Images for Knowledge Universe

the experiment scampering around the floors to escape the electric current, but every once in a while they would accidentally hit the lever and turn off the current. Eventually, they learned to associate pushing the lever with the removal of the unpleasant stimulus (the mild electric shock). After several trials, the rats would push the lever immediately, reducing their shock time.

Think about some examples of negative reinforcement in your own life. If you try to drive your car without your seat belt, does your car make an annoying beeping sound? If so, the automakers have employed negative reinforcement to *increase* your use of seat belts. The beeping provides an annoyance (an unpleasant stimulus) that prompts most people to put on their seat belts (the desired behavior increases) to make the beeping stop, and thus remove the unpleasant stimulus. The next time you get in the car, you will be faster to put on your seat belt, because you have learned that buckling up immediately makes the annoying sound go away. For another example of negative reinforcement, picture a dog that constantly begs for treats. The begging (an unpleasant stimulus) stops the moment the dog is given a treat, a pattern that increases *your* treat-giving behavior. The problem is that the dog's begging behavior is being strengthened through positive reinforcement; the dog has learned that the more it begs, the more treats it receives.

Notice that with negative reinforcement, the target behaviors increase in order to remove an unwanted condition. Returning to our example of Jeremy Lin, how might a basketball coach use negative reinforcement to increase a behavior? Of course, the coach can't build an electric grid in the flooring (as Skinner did with his rats) to get his players moving faster. He might, however, start each practice session by whining and complaining (a very annoying stimulus) about how slow the players are moving. But as soon as their level of activity increases, he stops his annoying behavior. The players then learn to avoid the coach's whining and complaining simply by running faster and working harder at every practice. Thus, the removal of the annoying stimulus (whining and complaining) increases the desired behavior (running faster). Keep in mind that the goal of negative reinforcement is to *increase* a desired behavior. Try to remember this when you read the section on punishment.

LO 10 Distinguish between primary and secondary reinforcers.

PRIMARY AND SECONDARY REINFORCERS   There are two major categories of reinforcers: primary and secondary. The food with which Skinner rewarded his pigeons and rats is considered a **primary reinforcer** (innate reinforcer), because it satisfies a biological need. Food, water, and physical contact are considered primary reinforcers (for both animals and people) because they meet essential requirements. Many of the reinforcers shaping human behavior are **secondary reinforcers,** which means they do not satisfy biological needs but often derive their power from their connection with primary reinforcers. Although money is not a primary reinforcer, we know from experience that it gives us access to primary reinforcers, such as food, a safe place to live, and perhaps even the ability to attract desirable mates. Thus, money is a secondary reinforcer. The list of secondary reinforcers is long and varied, because different people find different things and activities to be reinforcing. Listening to music, washing dishes, taking a ride in your car—these would all be considered secondary reinforcers for people who enjoy doing them. Ready for a tongue twister? A reinforcer is only a reinforcer if the person receiving it finds it reinforcing. In other words, the designation of a reinforcer depends on its ability to increase a target behavior.

Secondary reinforcers are evident in everyday social interactions. Think about how your behaviors might change in response to praise from a boss, a pat on the back from a coworker, or even a nod of approval from a friend on Facebook or Instagram. Yes, reinforcers can even exert their effects through the digital channels of social media.

Synonyms
negative reinforcement omission training
secondary reinforcers conditioned reinforcers

positive reinforcement The process by which reinforcers are added or presented following a targeted behavior, increasing the likelihood of it occurring again.

negative reinforcement The removal of an unpleasant stimulus following a target behavior, which increases the likelihood of it occurring again.

primary reinforcer A reinforcer that satisfies a biological need, such as food, water, physical contact; innate reinforcer.

secondary reinforcer Reinforcers that do not satisfy biological needs but often gain their power through their association with primary reinforcers.

Infectious Goodness
Standing before a giant red mailbox, London postal worker Imtiyaz Chawan holds a Guinness World Records certificate. Through the Royal Mail Group's Payroll Giving Scheme, British postal workers donated money to 975 charitable groups, setting a record for the number of charities supported by a payroll giving scheme (Guinness Book of World Records News, 2012, February 6). Charitable giving is the type of positive behavior that can spread through social networks. Many charities are now using social media for fundraising purposes.
David Parry/PA Wire

SOCIAL MEDIA and psychology

Contagious Behaviors

Why do you keep glancing at your Facebook page, and what compels you to check your phone 10 times an hour? All those little tweets and updates you receive are reinforcing. It feels good to be retweeted, and it's nice to see people "like" your Instagram posts.

With its never-ending supply of mini-rewards, social media often sucks away time that would otherwise be devoted to offline relationships and work—a clear drawback. But the reinforcing power of social media can also be harnessed to promote positive behaviors. A study by MIT researcher Damon Centola found that people are more likely to explore healthy behaviors when alerted that others in their social media networks are doing the same. This is especially true for those in "clustered" networks, where people share many of the same contacts. As Centola observed: "People usually require contact with multiple sources of 'infection' before being convinced to adopt a behavior" (Centola, 2010, p. 1194). Each of these sources of infection, it seems, provides social reinforcement for the positive behavior. Thus, if you want to develop a healthier lifestyle, it can't hurt to surround yourself with online friends who exercise, eat well, and don't smoke.

WHY DO YOU CHECK YOUR PHONE 10 TIMES AN HOUR?

Now that we have a basic understanding of operant conditioning, let's take things to the next level and examine its guiding principles.

The Power of Partial Reinforcement

LO 11   Describe continuous reinforcement and partial reinforcement.

A year after graduating from Stanford, Ivonne returned to New York City and began looking for a new activity to get her outside and moving. She found the New York Road Runners Club, which connected her with an organization that supports and trains runners with all types of disabilities, including paraplegia, amputation, and cerebral palsy. Having no running experience (apart from jogging on a treadmill), Ivonne showed up at a practice one Saturday morning in Central Park and ran 2 miles with one of the running club's guides. The next week she came back for more, and then the next, and the next.

CONTINUOUS REINFORCEMENT When Ivonne first started attending practices, her teammates promised to buy her hot chocolate whenever she increased her distance. "Every time they would try to get me to run further, they'd say, 'We'll have hot chocolate afterwards!'" Ivonne remembers. "They actually would follow through with their promise!" The hot chocolate was given in a schedule of **continuous reinforcement,** because the reinforcer was presented *every* time Ivonne ran a little farther. Continuous reinforcement can be used in a variety of settings: a child getting praise *every* time he does the dishes; a dog getting a treat *every* time it comes when called. You get the commonality: reinforcement *every* time the behavior is produced.

For the Love of Running
Ivonne runs tethered to her husband, G. John Schmidt. She sets the pace, while he warns her of any changes in terrain, elevation, and direction. When Ivonne started running in 2001, her friends reinforced her with hot chocolate. These days, she doesn't need sweet treats to keep her coming back. The pleasure she derives from running is reinforcement enough. MICHAEL S. WIRTZ/The Inquirer/Daily News/Philly.com

PARTIAL REINFORCEMENT Continuous reinforcement comes in handy for a variety of purposes and is ideal for establishing new behaviors during the acquisition phase. But delivering reinforcers intermittently, or every once in a while, works better for maintaining behaviors. We call this approach **partial reinforcement.** Returning to the examples listed for continuous reinforcement, we can also imagine partial reinforcement being used: The child gets praise *almost* every time he does the dishes; a dog gets a treat every third time it comes when called. The reinforcer is not given every time the behavior is observed, only *some* of the time.

Early on, Ivonne received a reinforcer from her training buddies for *every* workout she increased her mileage. But how might partial reinforcement be used to help a runner increase her mileage? Perhaps instead of hot chocolate on every occasion, the treat could come after every other successful run. Or, a coach might praise the runner's hard work only some of the time. The amazing thing about partial reinforcement is that it happens to all of us, in an infinite number of settings, and we might never know how many times we have been partially reinforced for any particular behavior. Common to all of these partial reinforcement situations is that the target behavior is exhibited, but the reinforcer is *not* supplied each time this occurs.

The hard work and reinforcement paid off for Ivonne. In 2003 she ran her first marathon—New York City—and has since competed in more than a dozen others.

Hope Springs Eternal
Why are slot machines so enticing? The fact that they deliver rewards occasionally and unpredictably makes them irresistible to many gamblers. Slot machines take advantage of the partial reinforcement effect, which states that behaviors are more persistent when reinforced intermittently, rather than continuously.
David Sacks/Getty Images

PARTIAL REINFORCEMENT EFFECT When Skinner put the pigeons in his experiments on partial reinforcement schedules, they would peck at a target up to 10,000 times without getting food before giving up (Skinner, 1953). According to Skinner, "Nothing of this sort is ever obtained after continuous reinforcement" (p. 99). The same seems to be true with humans. In one study from the mid-1950s, researchers observed college students playing slot machines. Some of the slot machines provided continuous reinforcement, delivering pretend coins every time students pulled their levers. Others followed partial reinforcement schedules, dispensing coins only some of the time. After the students played eight rounds, all of the machines stopped giving coins. Without any coins to reinforce them, the students stopped pulling the levers—but not at the same time. Those who had received coins with every lever pull gave up more quickly than did those rewarded intermittently. In other words, lever-pulling behavior was less likely to be extinguished when established through partial reinforcement (Lewis & Duncan, 1956). Psychologists call this phenomenon the **partial reinforcement effect:** Behaviors take longer to disappear (through the process of *extinction*) when they have been acquired or maintained through partial, rather than continuous, reinforcement.

Remember, partial reinforcement works very well for maintaining behaviors, but not necessarily for establishing behaviors. Imagine how long it would take Skinner's pigeons to learn the first step in the shaping process (looking at the ball) if they were rewarded for doing so only 1 in 5 times. The birds learn fastest when reinforced every time, but their behavior will persist longer if they are given partial reinforcement thereafter. Here's another example: Suppose you are housetraining your puppy. The best plan is to start the process with continuous reinforcement (praise the dog every time it "goes" outside), but then shift to partial reinforcement once the desired behavior is established.

Synonyms
partial reinforcement intermittent reinforcement

continuous reinforcement A schedule of reinforcement in which every target behavior is reinforced.

partial reinforcement A schedule of reinforcement in which target behaviors are reinforced intermittently, not continuously.

partial reinforcement effect The tendency for behaviors acquired through intermittent reinforcement to be more resistant to extinction than those acquired through continuous reinforcement.

Timing Is Everything: Reinforcement Schedules

LO 12 Name the schedules of reinforcement and give examples of each.

Skinner identified various ways to administer partial reinforcement, or *partial reinforcement schedules*. As often occurs in scientific research, he stumbled on the idea by chance. Late one Friday afternoon, Skinner realized he was running low on the food pellets he used as reinforcers for his laboratory animals. If he continued rewarding the animals on a continuous basis, the pellets would run out before the end of the weekend. With this in mind, he decided only to reinforce some of the desired behaviors (Skinner, 1956, 1976). The new strategy worked like a charm. The animals kept performing the target behaviors, even though they weren't given reinforcers every time.

Clearly partial reinforcement is effective, but how exactly should it be delivered? Four different reinforcement schedules can be used: fixed-ratio, variable-ratio, fixed-interval, and variable-interval (**Figure 5.3**).

nilovsergey/shutterstock

FIGURE 5.3

Schedules of Reinforcement
Continuous reinforcement is ideal for establishing new behaviors. But once learned, a behavior is best maintained with *partial* reinforcement. Partial reinforcement can be delivered according to four different schedules of reinforcement, as shown here.

Fixed-Ratio: *Reinforcer is given after a predetermined number of desired responses.*

Variable-Ratio: *Reinforcer is given after a certain number of desired responses—and this number changes from trial to trial.*

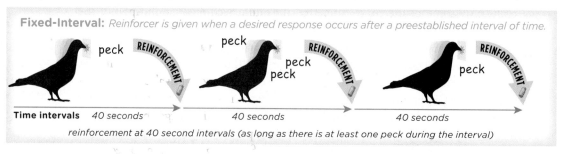

Fixed-Interval: *Reinforcer is given when a desired response occurs after a preestablished interval of time.*

reinforcement at 40 second intervals (as long as there is at least one peck during the interval)

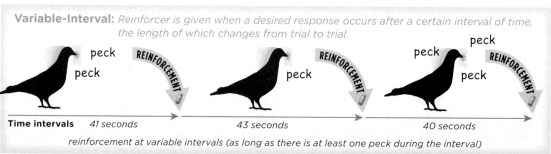

Variable-Interval: *Reinforcer is given when a desired response occurs after a certain interval of time, the length of which changes from trial to trial.*

reinforcement at variable intervals (as long as there is at least one peck during the interval)

FIXED-RATIO SCHEDULE   In some situations, the best approach to reinforcement is a **fixed-ratio schedule.** With this arrangement, the subject must exhibit a predetermined number of desired responses or behaviors before a reinforcer is given. A pigeon in a Skinner box may have to peck a spot five times in order to score a delicious pellet (5:1). A third-grade teacher might give students prizes when they pass three multiplication tests (3:1). Generally, the fixed-ratio schedule produces a high response rate, but with a characteristic dip immediately following the reinforcement. Pigeons rest briefly before pecking away at the target again, and students take a short break before studying for another multiplication test.

VARIABLE-RATIO SCHEDULE   Other times, it is best to use reinforcement that is unpredictable. In a **variable-ratio schedule,** the number of desired responses or behaviors that must occur before a reinforcer is given changes across trials. (This number is based on an average number of responses to be reinforced.) If the goal is to train a pigeon to peck a spot on a target, a variable-ratio schedule can be used as follows: Trial 1, the pigeon gets a pellet after pecking the spot twice; Trial 2, the pigeon gets a pellet after pecking the spot once; Trial 3, the pigeon gets a pellet after pecking the spot three times; and so on. In the third-grade classroom, the teacher might not tell the students how many tests they will need to pass to get a prize. She may give a prize after two tests, then the next time after seven tests. This variable-ratio schedule tends to produce a high response rate (pecking and studying in our examples) and behaviors that are difficult to extinguish because of the unpredictability of the reinforcement schedule.

FIXED-INTERVAL SCHEDULE   In some cases, it might be important to focus on the interval of time between reinforcers, as opposed to the number of desired responses. In a **fixed-interval schedule,** the reinforcer comes after a preestablished interval of time; a reinforcer is given for the first target behavior *after* that period has elapsed. If a pigeon is on a fixed-interval schedule of 30 seconds, it can peck at the target as often as possible once the interval starts, but it will only get a reinforcer following its first response after the 30 seconds has ended. If the third graders are on a fixed-interval schedule of 1 week, the teacher gives prizes only on Fridays for children who do well on their math quiz that day; it doesn't matter how they performed on other math quizzes earlier that week. With this schedule, the target behavior tends to increase as each time interval comes to an end. The pigeon pecks the spot more often when the time nears 30 seconds, and the students study harder as Friday approaches.

VARIABLE-INTERVAL SCHEDULE   In a **variable-interval schedule,** the length of time between reinforcements is unpredictable. In this schedule, the reinforcer comes after an interval of time goes by, but the length of the interval changes from trial to trial (within a predetermined range based on an average interval length). As with the fixed-interval schedule, reinforcement follows the first target behavior that occurs after the time interval has elapsed. Training a pigeon to peck a spot on a target using a variable-interval schedule might include the following: Trial 1, the pigeon gets a pellet after 41 seconds; Trial 2, the pigeon gets a pellet after 43 seconds; Trial 3, the pigeon gets a pellet after 40 seconds; and so on. In each trial, the pigeon is rewarded for the first response it makes after the interval of time has passed (which varies from trial to trial). The third-grade teacher might think that an average of 4 days should go by between quizzes. So, instead of giving reinforcers every 7 days (that is, always on Friday), she gives quizzes separated by a variable interval. The first quiz might be after a 2-day interval, the next after a 3-day interval, and the students do not know when to expect them. The variable-interval schedule tends to encourage steady patterns of behavior. The pigeon tries its luck pecking a target once every 40 seconds or

fixed-ratio schedule A schedule in which the subject must exhibit a predetermined number of desired behaviors before a reinforcer is given.

variable-ratio schedule A schedule in which the number of desired behaviors that must occur before a reinforcer is given changes across trials and is based on an average number of behaviors to be reinforced.

fixed-interval schedule A schedule in which the reinforcer comes after a preestablished interval of time goes by; the behavior is only reinforced after the given interval is over.

variable-interval schedule A schedule in which the reinforcer comes after an interval of time goes by, but the length of the interval changes from trial to trial.

so, and the students come to school prepared to take a quiz every day (their amount of study holding steady).

So far, we have learned about *increasing* desired behaviors through reinforcement, but not all behaviors are desirable. Let's turn our attention to techniques used to suppress undesirable behaviors.

The Trouble with Punishment

In contrast to reinforcement, which makes a behavior more likely to recur, the goal of **punishment** is to *decrease* or stop a behavior (**Infographic 5.3**). Punishment is used to reduce unwanted behaviors by instilling an association between a behavior and some unwanted consequence (for example, between stealing and going to jail, or between misbehaving and a spanking). Punishment isn't always effective, however; people are often willing to accept unpleasant consequences to get something they really want.

POSITIVE AND NEGATIVE PUNISHMENT   There are two major categories of punishment: *positive* and *negative*. With **positive punishment,** something aversive or disagreeable is applied following an unwanted behavior. For example, getting a ticket for speeding is a positive punishment, the aim of which is to decrease driving over the speed limit. Paying a late fine for overdue library books is a positive punishment, the goal of which is to decrease returning library books past their due date. In basketball, a personal foul (for example, inappropriate physical contact) might result in positive punishment, such as a free throw for the opposing team. Here, the *addition* of something aversive (the other team getting a wide open shot) is used with the intention of decreasing a behavior (pushing, shoving, and the like).

The goal of **negative punishment** is also to reduce an unwanted behavior, but in this case, it is done by *taking away* something desirable. A person who drives while inebriated runs the risk of negative punishment, as his driver's license may be taken away. This loss of driving privileges is a punishment designed to *reduce* drunken driving. If you never return your library books, you might suffer the negative punishment of losing your borrowing privileges. The goal is to *decrease* behaviors that lead to lost or stolen library books. What kind of negative punishment might be used to rein in illegal conduct in basketball? Just ask one of Jeremy Lin's former teammates, superstar Carmelo Anthony, one of many players suspended for participating in a 2006 brawl between the Knicks and the Denver Nuggets. Anthony, a Nuggets player at the time (how ironic that he was later traded to the Knicks), was dealt a 15-game suspension (and no salary for those games not played) for slugging a Knicks player in the face (Lee, 2006, December 19). Anthony's suspension is an example of negative punishment, because it involves subtracting something desirable (the privilege to compete and his salary for those games) to decrease a behavior (throwing punches on the court).

Punishment may be useful for the purposes of basketball, but how does it figure into everyday life? Think about the last time you tried using punishment to reduce unwanted behavior. Perhaps you scolded your puppy for having an accident, or snapped at your housemate for leaving dirty dishes in the sink. If you are a parent or caregiver of a young child, perhaps you have tried to reign in misbehavior with various types of punishment, such as spanking.

Time-Out
Sending a child to a corner for a "time-out" is an example of negative punishment because it involves removing something (the privilege to play) in order to decrease an unwanted behavior. Spanking is a positive punishment because it involves the addition of something (a slap on the bottom) to discourage an undesirable behavior.
Design Pics/Ron Nickel/ Getty Images

punishment The application of a consequence that decreases the likelihood of a behavior recurring.

positive punishment The addition of something unpleasant following an unwanted behavior, with the intention of decreasing that behavior.

negative punishment The removal of something desirable following an unwanted behavior, with the intention of decreasing that behavior.

Learning: Punishment and Reinforcement
Behavior: *Driving Fast*
Do you want to increase this behavior?

Red sports cars, © lenka - Fotolia.com; Police officer writing a ticket, © Lisa F. Young - Fotolia.com; Flags, © FreeSoulProduction - Fotolia.com; Green Traffic Light, Thinkstock; Red Traffic Light, Thinkstock; Wrench, Thinkstock; Green highway sign isolated, Thinkstock; Speed limit road sign with post and different numbers, © Thomaspajot/ Dreamstime.com; Red flashing light on a white background, © Fotovika/Dreamstime.com; Trophy, Comstock/Thinkstock; Falling money, istockphoto/Thinkstock; Vector design set of racing flags, freesoulproduction/Shutterstock.

YES!
It's Nascar! You have to drive faster than anyone else to win.
We will apply a reinforcer to **increase** the behavior.

NO!
We're not at the racetrack! Speeding is dangerous and against the law.
We will apply a punishment to **decrease** the behavior.

REINFORCEMENT

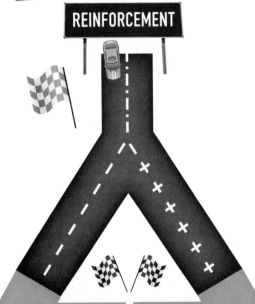

PUNISHMENT

Negative Reinforcement

You don't like working in the family auto-body shop. Your family says you can work fewer hours if you win the next race. **Taking away** unwanted work increases the speeding behavior.

Positive Reinforcement

You win a trophy and a cash prize for going fast at the race. **Adding** desirable rewards increases your speeding behavior.

Negative Punishment

The police officer confiscates your license. **Taking away** something desirable decreases your speeding behavior.

Positive Punishment

The police officer gives you a citation. **Adding** something undesirable decreases your speeding behavior.

---

test yourself

Which process matches each of the following examples?
Choose from **positive reinforcement, negative reinforcement, positive punishment,** and **negative punishment**.

1. Carlos' parents grounded him the last time he stayed out past his curfew, so tonight he came home right on time.

2. Jinhee spent an entire week helping an elderly neighbor clean out her basement after a flood. The local newspaper caught wind of the story and ran it as an inspiring front-page headline. Jinhee enjoyed the attention and decided to organize a neighborhood work group.

3. The trash stinks, so Sheri takes it out.

4. Gabriel's assistant had a bad habit of showing up late for work, so Gabriel docked his pay.

5. During food drives, the basketball team offers to wash your car for free if you donate six items or more to the local homeless shelter.

6. Claire received a stern lecture for texting in class. She doesn't want to hear that again, so now she turns off her phone when she enters the classroom.

Answers 1. negative punishment, 2. positive reinforcement, 3. negative reinforcement, 4. negative punishment, 5. positive reinforcement, 6. positive punishment

Spotlight on Spanking

➡️⬅️ Were you spanked as a child? Would you or do you spank your own children? Statistically speaking, there is a good chance your answer will be *yes* to both questions. Studies suggest that about two thirds of American parents use corporal (physical) punishment to discipline their young children (Gershoff, 2008; Regalado, Sareen, Inkelas, Wissow, & Halfon, 2004; Zolotor, Theodore, Runyan, Chang, & Laskey, 2011). But is spanking an effective and acceptable means of discipline?

There is little doubt that spanking can provide a fast-acting fix: If a child is beating up his brother, a swift slap on his bottom will probably make him stop

TO SPANK OR NOT TO SPANK . . .

pronto. But think about the larger lesson the boy learns in the process. His parents are trying to teach him not to be aggressive toward his brother, but in doing so, they demonstrate an aggressive behavior (hitting). Children are experts at mimicking adults' behaviors (see the next section on observational learning), and several studies suggest that spanking is linked to future aggression and other antisocial behaviors (Gershoff, 2010; Taylor, Manganello, Lee, & Rice, 2010).

Apart from sending children the message that aggression is okay, corporal punishment may promote serious long-term mental health problems. Harsh physical punishment, which includes spanking, grabbing, and pushing, has been linked to an elevated risk for developing mood, anxiety, and personality disorders (Afifi, Mota, Dasiewicz, MacMillan, & Sareen, 2012). It may also interfere with cognitive development, retarding growth in various parts of the frontal lobes (Tomoda et al., 2009), a region of the brain that processes complex thoughts. One study even found that spanked children score lower on intelligence tests than their nonspanked peers (Straus & Paschall, 2009).

Critics argue that studies casting a negative light on spanking are primarily *correlational*, meaning they show only a link—not necessarily a cause-and-effect relationship—between physical punishment and negative outcomes (Larzelere & Baumrind, 2010). They point to other factors that might explain some of the problems spanked children seem to develop. Perhaps these children are aggressive and antisocial to begin with (that would explain why they were spanked in the first place), or maybe their parents are more likely to be abusive, and the abuse (not the spanking) is to blame (Baumrind, Larzelere, & Cowan, 2002). Spanking, or "striking a child with an open hand on the buttocks or extremities with the intention of modifying behavior without causing physical injury" (American Academy of Pediatrics, 1998, pp. 725–726), may be an effective way to modify young children's behavior, according to some experts (Baumrind, Larzelere, & Cowan, 2002; Larzelere & Baumrind, 2010). But it must be delivered by a parent whose approach is "warm, responsive, rational, and temperate" (Baumrind, 1996, p. 857).

Scholars on both sides make valid points, but the debate is somewhat lopsided, as an increasing number of studies suggest that spanking is ineffective and emotionally damaging (Gershoff & Bitensky, 2008; Smith, 2012; Straus, 2005). ➡️⬅️

CONNECTIONS

In **Chapter 2,** we noted the primary roles of the *frontal lobes:* to organize information processed in other areas of the brain, orchestrate higher-level cognitive functions, and direct behaviors associated with personality. Here, we note that harsh physical punishment interferes with normal development of the frontal lobes—a good example of the ongoing interaction between nature (physical development of the brain) and nurture (physical punishment).

LO 13 Explain how punishment differs from negative reinforcement.

PUNISHMENT VERSUS NEGATIVE REINFORCEMENT   Punishment and negative reinforcement are two concepts that students often find difficult to distinguish (**Table 5.3**; also see Infographic 5.3 on p. 199). Remember that punishment (positive or negative) is designed to *decrease* the behavior that it follows, whereas

TABLE 5.3 REINFORCEMENT VERSUS PUNISHMENT

Term	Defined	Goal	Example
Positive Reinforcement	Addition of a pleasant stimulus following a target behavior	Increase desired behavior	Students who complete an online course 15 days before the end of semester receive 10 points of extra credit.
Negative Reinforcement	Removal of an unpleasant stimulus following a target behavior	Increase desired behavior	Students who have perfect attendance for the semester do not have to take the final exam.
Positive Punishment	Addition of something unpleasant following an unwanted behavior	Decrease undesired behavior	Students who are late to class more than two times have to write an extra paper.
Negative Punishment	Removal of something pleasant following an unwanted behavior	Decrease undesired behavior	Students late to class on exam day are not allowed to use their notes when taking the exam.

The positive and negative forms of reinforcement and punishment are easy to confuse. Above are some concrete definitions, goals, and examples to help you sort them out.

reinforcement (positive or negative) aims to *increase* the behavior. Operant conditioning uses reinforcers (both positive and negative) to *increase* target behaviors, and punishment to *decrease* unwanted behaviors.

If all the positives and negatives are confusing you, just think in terms of math: Positive always means adding something, and negative means taking it away. Punishment can be *positive,* which means the addition of something viewed as unpleasant ("Because you made a mess of your room, you have to wash all the dishes!"), or *negative,* which involves the removal of something viewed as pleasant or valuable ("Because you made a mess of your room, no ice cream for you!"). For basketball players, a positive punishment might be *adding* more wind sprints to *decrease* errors on the free throw line. An example of negative punishment might be benching the players for brawling on the court; *taking away* the players' court time to *decrease* their fighting behavior.

 *Apply This*

Think Positive Reinforcement

With all this talk of chickens, basketball players, and triathletes, you may be wondering how operant conditioning applies to you. Just think about the last time you earned a good grade on a test after studying really hard. How did this grade affect your preparation for the next test? If it made you study more, then it served as a positive reinforcer. A little dose of positive reinforcement goes a long way when it comes to increasing productivity. Let's examine three everyday dilemmas and brainstorm ways we could use positive reinforcers to achieve better outcomes.

Problem 1: Your housemate frequently goes to sleep without washing his dinner dishes. Almost every morning, you walk into the kitchen and find a tower of dirty pans and plates sitting in the sink. No matter how much you nag and complain, he simply will not change his ways. *Solution:* Nagging and complaining are getting you nowhere. Try positive reinforcers instead. Wait until a day your housemate takes care of his dishes and then pour on the praise. You might be pleasantly surprised the next morning.

REINFORCEMENT
STRATEGIES YOU
CAN PUT TO GOOD USE

Problem 2: Your child is annoying you with her incessant whining. She whines for milk, so you give it to her. She whines for someone to play with, so you play with her. Why does your child continue to whine although you are responding to all her needs? *Solution:* Here, we have a case in which positive reinforcers are driving the problem. When you react to your child's gripes and moans, you are reinforcing them. Turn off your ears to the whining. You might even want to say something like, "I can't hear you when you're whining. If you ask me in a normal voice, I'll be more than happy to help." Then reinforce her more mature behavior by responding attentively.

Problem 3: You just trained your puppy to sit. She was cooperating wonderfully until about a week after you stopped rewarding her with dog biscuits. You want her to sit on command, but you can't keep doling out doggie treats forever. *Solution:* Once the dog has adopted the desired behavior, begin reinforcing unpredictably. Remember, continuous reinforcement is most effective for establishing behaviors, but a variable schedule (that is, giving treats intermittently) is a good bet if you want to make the behavior stick (Pryor, 2002). ➤

Classical and Operant Conditioning: What's the Difference?

Students sometimes have trouble differentiating classical and operant conditioning (**Figure 5.4**). After all, both forms of conditioning—classical and operant—involve forming associations. In classical conditioning, the learner links different *stimuli;* in operant conditioning, the learner connects her behavior to its *consequences* (reinforcement and punishment). Another key similarity is that the principles of acquisition, stimulus discrimination, stimulus generalization, extinction, and spontaneous recovery apply to both types of conditioning.

But there are also key differences between classical and operant conditioning. In classical conditioning, the learned behaviors are involuntary, or reflexive. Ivonne cannot directly control her heart rate any more than Pavlov's dogs can decide when to salivate. Operant conditioning, on the other hand, concerns voluntary behavior. Jeremy Lin had power over his decision to practice his shot, just as Skinner's pigeons had control over swatting bowling balls with their beaks. In short, classical conditioning is an involuntary form of learning, whereas operant conditioning requires active effort.

Another important distinction is the way in which behaviors are strengthened. In classical conditioning, behaviors become more frequent with repeated pairings of stimuli. The more often Ivonne smells chlorine before swim practice, the tighter the association she makes between chlorine and swimming. Operant conditioning is also strengthened by repeated pairings, but in this case, the connection is between a behavior and its consequences. Reinforcers strengthen the behavior; punishment weakens it. The more benefits (reinforcers) Jeremy gains from succeeding in basketball, the more likely he will keep practicing.

Often classical conditioning and operant conditioning occur simultaneously. A baby learns that he gets fed when he cries; getting milk reinforces the crying behavior (operant conditioning). At the same time, the baby learns to associate

FIGURE 5.4
Differences Between Classical and Operant Conditioning

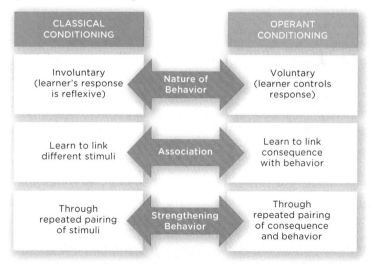

milk with the appearance of the bottle. As soon as he sees his mom or dad take the bottle from the refrigerator, he begins salivating in anticipation of gulping it down (classical conditioning).

Classical and operant conditioning are not the only ways we learn. There is one major category of learning we have yet to cover. Use this hint to guess what it might be: How did you learn to peel a banana, open an umbrella, and throw a Frisbee? Somebody must have shown you.

☑○○○ show what you know

1. According to Thorndike and the _____, behaviors are more likely to be repeated when they are followed by pleasurable outcomes.

2. A third-grade teacher gives her students prizes for passing math tests. Not only do the students improve their math scores, they also begin studying harder for their spelling tests as a result of this reinforcement schedule. Their increased studying of spelling is an example of:
   a. classical conditioning.
   b. an unconditioned response.
   c. an unconditioned stimulus.
   d. stimulus generalization.

3. A child disrupts class and the teacher writes her name on the board. For the rest of the week, the child does not act up. The teacher used _____ to decrease the child's disruptive behaviors.
   a. positive punishment
   b. negative punishment
   c. positive reinforcement
   d. negative reinforcement

4. Think about a behavior you would like to change (either yours or someone else's). Devise a schedule of reinforcement using positive and negative reinforcement to change that behavior. Also contemplate how you might use successive approximations. What primary and secondary reinforcers would you use?

5. How do continuous and partial reinforcement differ?

✓ CHECK YOUR ANSWERS IN APPENDIX C.

Observational Learning and Cognition

BASKETBALL IQ   Jeremy Lin is not the fastest runner or highest jumper on the planet, and he is certainly not the biggest guy in professional hoops. In the world of the NBA, where the players' average height is about 6′7″ and the average weight is 220 pounds, Jeremy is actually somewhat small (NBA.com, 2007, November 20; NBA.com, 2007, November 27). So what is it about this benchwarmer-turned-big-shot that makes him so special? Jeremy's success, we suspect, is largely a result of qualities that are extremely hard to measure, like unstoppable confidence, dogged determination, and a penetrating *basketball IQ*, or mental mastery of the sport. "There are very few people that have the same basketball IQ," Coach Diepenbrock explains. "That's what separates him from other players."

The roots of Jeremy's hoop smarts reach back to his father's native country. Growing up in Taiwan, Gie-Ming Lin didn't have much exposure to basketball, but he was fascinated by what he saw of the sport. When Gie-Ming arrived in America, he fell head over heels in love with basketball, taping NBA games and watching them any chance he got.

Lincredible
Playing for the Los Angeles Lakers, Jeremy Lin charges past Jerryd Bayless of the Milwaukee Bucks. Jeremy may not be the tallest player in the NBA, but he more than makes up for that in confidence and game smarts. Tannen Maury/EPA/Landov

Basketball Family
Baby Jeremy poses with his father Gie-Ming, a basketball aficionado who learned the game by studying NBA greats like Kareem Abdul-Jabbar and Larry Bird (O'Neil, 2009, December 10).
HANDOUT/Reuters/Landov

Synonyms
observational learning social learning

This 5′6″ engineering student had never picked up a basketball, but he managed to learn the techniques of the game by closely watching the moves of NBA legends like Kareem Abdul-Jabbar, Larry Bird, and Magic Johnson (O'Neil, 2009, December 10). Eventually, he tried those moves on the court, and passed them along to Jeremy and his other two sons. ▼ 🗀

The NBA greats that Gie-Ming studied served as **models,** demonstrating behaviors that could be observed and imitated. We call this process **observational learning,** as it results from watching the behavior of others. According to Bandura (1986), this type of learning is more likely to occur when the learner: (1) is *paying attention* to the model; (2) *remembers* what she observed (Bahrick, Gogate, & Ruiz, 2002); (3) is *capable of performing* the behavior she has observed; and (4) is *motivated* to demonstrate the behavior.

The Power of Observational Learning

Think about how observational learning impacts your own life. Speaking English, eating with utensils, and driving a car are all skills you probably picked up in part by watching and mimicking others. Do you ever use slang? Phrases like "gnarley" (cool) from the 1980s, "Wassup" (What is going on?) from the 1990s, and "peeps" (my people, or friends) from the 2000s caught on because people copy what they observe others saying and writing. Consider some of the phrases trending today that 20 years from now people won't recognize.

Observational learning doesn't necessarily require sight. Let's return to Ivonne, who competes in triathlons, consisting of 1 mile of swimming, 25 miles of biking, and 6 miles of running. Ivonne performs the swimming and running sections of the triathlon attached to a guide with a tether, and the bike section on a tandem bike with the guide. To fine-tune her swimming technique, she *feels* her swim coach demonstrate the freestyle stroke. Standing in the water behind him, Ivonne places one hand on his back and the other on his arm while he goes through the motions of a stroke. She feels the angle of his arms as they break the water's surface, the distance between his fingers as he plows through the water, and the position of his wrist throughout the motion. Then she imitates the movement she *observed* through her sense of touch.

Tandem Triathletes
Ivonne (rear) and her guide, Marit Ogin, ride together in the Nickel City Buffalo Triathlon. The guide is responsible for steering, breaking, and communicating to Ivonne when it is time to shift gears or adjust body position for a turn. G. John Schmidt/Courtesy Ivonne Mosquera-Schmidt

----
LO 14 Summarize what Bandura's classic Bobo doll study teaches us about learning.

PLEASE PLAY NICELY WITH YOUR DOLL Just as observational learning can lead to positive outcomes like sharper basketball and swimming skills, it can also breed undesirable behaviors. The classic Bobo doll experiment conducted by psychologist Albert Bandura and his colleagues revealed just how fast children can adopt aggressive ways they see modeled by adults, as well as exhibit their own novel aggressive responses (Bandura, Ross, & Ross, 1961). In one of Bandura's studies, 76 preschool children were placed in a room alone with an adult and allowed to play with stickers and prints for making pictures. During their playtime, some of the children were paired with adults who acted aggressively toward a 5-foot-tall inflatable Bobo doll—punching it in the nose, hitting its head with a mallet, kicking it around the room, and yelling phrases such as, "Sock him in the nose" and "Pow!" The other children in the study were paired with adults who played with toys peacefully (Bandura et al., 1961).

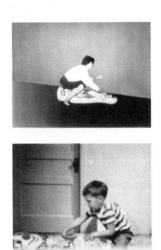

Bobo Doll
Preschool children in Albert Bandura's famous Bobo doll experiment performed shocking displays of aggression after seeing violent behaviors modeled by adults. The children were more likely to copy models who were rewarded for their aggressive behavior and less likely to mimic those who were punished (Bandura, 1986).
Courtesy Dr. Albert Bandura

At the end of the experiment, all the children were allowed to play with a Bobo doll themselves. Those who had observed adults attacking and shouting were much more likely to do the same. Boys were more likely than girls to mimic physical aggression, especially if they had observed it modeled by men. Boys and girls were about equally likely to imitate verbal aggression (Bandura et al., 1961).

Identify the independent variable and dependent variable in the experiment by Bandura and colleagues. What might you change if you were to replicate this experiment?

try this

Check your answers in Appendix C.

VIOLENCE IN THE MEDIA Psychologists have followed up Bandura's research with studies investigating how children are influenced by violence they see on television, the Internet, and in movies and video games. The American Academy of Pediatrics sums it up nicely: "Extensive research evidence indicates that media violence can contribute to aggressive behavior, desensitization to violence, nightmares, and fear of being harmed" (American Academy of Pediatrics, 2009, p. 1495). One large study found that children who watched TV programs with violent role models, such as *Starsky and Hutch* (a detective series from the 1970s that included violence and suspense), were at increased risk when they became adults of physically abusing their spouses and getting into trouble with the law (Huesmann, Moise-Titus, Podolski, & Eron, 2003). A more recent study conducted in New Zealand followed over 1,000 children from as early as birth until they were around 26 years old. The researchers found that the more television the children watched, the more likely they were to show antisocial behaviors as young adults. Interestingly, this association was between antisocial behaviors and excessive television viewing, regardless of the content (Robertson, McAnally, & Hancox, 2013).

model The individual or character whose behavior is being imitated.
observational learning Learning that occurs as a result of watching the behavior of others.

Critics caution, however, that an *association* between media portrayals and violent behaviors doesn't mean there is a cause-and-effect relationship (establishing an association is not the same as pinning down a cause). There are other factors related to parenting that could influence *both* television viewing and aggression (Huesmann et al., 2003). If a parent is emotionally neglectful and places a child in front of the television all day, the child may eventually imitate some of the aggression she sees on TV. At the same time, the child may resent the parent for ignoring her, and this resentment could lead to aggression. But how do you know which of these factors—television exposure or parenting approach—is more important in the development of aggressive tendencies? This is an active area of psychological research, but experts agree that television and other forms of media may influence aggressive tendencies in children (Clemente, Espinosa, & Vidal, 2008; Office of the Surgeon General, National Center for Injury Prevention and Control, National Institute of Mental Health, & Center for Mental Health Services, 2001). The American Academy of Pediatrics has recommended that children should be limited to less than 1–2 hours of total screen time per day (American Academy of Pediatrics, 2001, 2013). Unfortunately, children and their parents have not followed this recommendation. In fact, the average screen time for preschool-age children in the United States has been reported to be as much as 4 hours a day (Tandon, Zhou, Lozano, & Christakis, 2011). Instead of focusing on the number of hours children watch television, some have suggested that we should focus on program content, encouraging families and caregivers to reduce exposure to programs that contain violence and aggression, and to increase the amount of content with prosocial behavior (Christakis et al., 2013; McCarthy, 2013).

PROSOCIAL BEHAVIOR AND OBSERVATIONAL LEARNING   Here's the flip side to this issue: Children also have a gift for mimicking positive behaviors. When children watch shows similar to *Sesame Street,* they receive messages that encourage **prosocial behaviors,** meaning these programs foster kindness, generosity, and forms of behavior that benefit others.

Let's look more closely at research on the impact of prosocial models. Using scales to measure children's stereotypes and cultural knowledge before and after they watch TV shows, a group of researchers found evidence that shows like *Sesame Street* can have a positive influence (Cole, Labin, & del Rocio Galarza, 2008). Based on their review of multiple studies, these researchers made recommendations to increase prosocial behaviors. Children's shows should have intended messages, include prosocial information about people of other cultures and religions, be relevant to children in terms of culture and environment, and be age-appropriate and contain intentional and direct (unhidden) messages aimed at educating children about people from different backgrounds.

Adults can also pick up prosocial messages from media. In a multipart study, researchers exposed adults to prosocial song lyrics (as opposed to neutral lyrics). The first experiment found that listening to prosocial lyrics increased the frequency of prosocial thoughts. Findings from the second experiment indicated that listening to a song with prosocial lyrics increased empathy, or the ability to understand what another person is going through. The third experiment found that listening to a song with prosocial lyrics increased helping behavior. These researchers only looked at the short-term effects, but exposing people continuously to prosocial lyrics may have a lasting impact (Greitemeyer, 2009).

Sunny Days
The prosocial behaviors demonstrated by Big Bird and *Sesame Street* friends appear to have a meaningful impact on child viewers. Children have a knack for imitating positive behaviors such as sharing and caring (Cole et al., 2008).
AP Photo/Mark Lennihan

Whistling Ape
Bonnie the orangutan seems to have learned whistling by copying workers at the Smithsonian National Zoological Park in Washington, DC. Her musical skill is the result of observational learning (Stone, 2009; Wich et al., 2009). Courtesy of Smithsonian National Zoological Park

When learning occurs through observation, often it is visible. Children watching aggression toward a Bobo doll imitate the behaviors they see, which researchers can witness and document. Not all forms of learning are so obvious.

Latent Learning

LO 15 Describe latent learning and explain how cognition is involved in learning.

Ivonne's feet pound the streets of Boston. She is among some 20,000 runners competing in the city's oldest annual 26.2-mile running race, the Boston Marathon. (Ivonne has nabbed first place in the Women's Visually Impaired Division three times.) She runs with teammates who make sure the path is clear, allowing her to focus on her performance instead of worrying about obstacles.

A MAP THAT CANNOT BE SEEN Before a race, Ivonne checks online to see if there is a description of the course or studies a map with her husband or a friend in order to learn the location of important landmarks such as hills, major turns, bridges, railroad tracks, and so on. "Doing this helps me feel that I have an idea of what to expect, and when to expect it," Ivonne says. The mental layout she creates contributes to her **cognitive map,** a mental representation of the physical surroundings, and it continues to come together in the race. As Ivonne runs, she hears sounds from all directions—the breathing of other runners, their feet hitting the ground, chatter from the sidelines—and uses these auditory cues to produce a mental map of her surroundings. In fact, we all create these cognitive maps, which provide a spatial representation to help us navigate our environment. These maps are developed through **latent learning,** a type of learning that occurs without awareness and regardless of reinforcement, and that remains hidden until there is a need to use it.

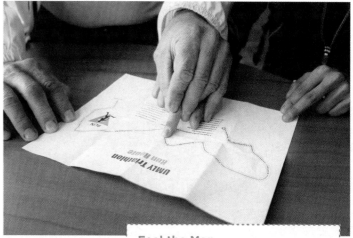

Feel the Map
Ivonne's husband guides her hand over the map of a racecourse. She is beginning to form a cognitive map of the route, one that will continue to crystallize as she races. While running, Ivonne's ears collect clues about the relative positions of objects and the direction of motion—information that goes into creating a cognitive map. MICHAEL S. WIRTZ/The Inquirer/Daily News/Philly.com

RATS THAT KNOW WHERE TO GO Edward Tolman and his colleague C. H. Honzik demonstrated latent learning in rats in their classic 1930 maze experiment (**Figure 5.5** on the next page). The researchers took three groups of rats and let them run free in mazes for several days. One group received food for reaching the goal boxes in their mazes; a second group received no reinforcement; and a third received nothing until the 11th day of the experiment, when they, too, received food for finding the goal box. As you might expect, rats getting the treats from the onset solved the mazes more quickly as the days wore on. Meanwhile, their unrewarded compatriots wandered through the twists and turns, showing only minor improvements from one day to the next. But on Day 11 when the researchers started to give treats to the third group of rats, their behavior changed markedly. After just one round of treats, the rats were scurrying through the mazes and scooping up the food as if they had been rewarded throughout the experiment (Tolman & Honzik, 1930). They had apparently been learning, even when there was no reinforcement for doing so—or in simpler terms, learning just for the sake of learning.

We all do this as we acquire cognitive maps of our environments. Without realizing it, we remember locations, objects, and details of our surroundings, and bring this information together in a mental layout (Lynch, 2002). Research suggests that visually impaired people forge cognitive maps without the use of visual information. Instead, they use "compensatory sensorial channels" (hearing and sense of touch, for example) to gather information about their environments (Lahav & Mioduser, 2008).

prosocial behaviors Actions that are kind, generous, and beneficial to others.
cognitive map The mental representation of the layout of a physical space.
latent learning Learning that occurs without awareness and regardless of reinforcement, and is not evident until needed.

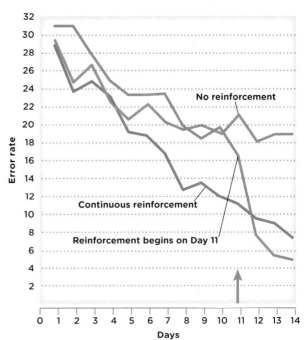

FIGURE 5.5
Latent Learning
In a classic experiment, groups of rats learned how to navigate a maze at remarkably different rates. Rats in a group receiving reinforcement from Day 1 (the green line on the graph) initially had the lowest rate of errors and were able to work their way through the maze more quickly than the other groups. But when a group began to receive reinforcement for the first time on Day 11, their error rate dropped immediately. This shows that the rats were learning the basic structure of the maze even when they weren't being reinforced.
Data from Tolman, 1948

This line of research highlights the importance of cognitive processes underlying behavior and suggests that learning can occur in the absence of reinforcement. Because of the focus on cognition, this research approach conflicts with the views of Skinner and some other 20th-century psychologists who adhered to a strict form of behaviorism.

Many other studies have challenged Skinner's views. Wolfgang Köhler's (1925) research on chimpanzees suggests that animals are capable of thinking through a problem before taking action. He designed an experiment in which chimps were presented with out-of-reach bananas, and showed that the animals were able to plan a variety of banana-fetching strategies, including stacking crates to climb on. Here, the chimps displayed *insight,* a sudden coming together of awareness of a situation, leading to the solution of a problem (Chapter 7).

Today, most psychologists agree that both observable, measurable behaviors and internal cognitive processes such as insight are necessary and complementary elements of learning. Environmental factors have a powerful influence on behavior, as Pavlov, Skinner, and others discovered, but every action can be traced to activity in the brain. Understanding how cognitive processes translate to behaviors remains one of the great challenges facing psychologists.

IT KEEPS GETTING BETTER   Wondering what became of Jeremy Lin following "Linsanity?" After suffering a knee injury in the spring of 2012, Jeremy was out of commission for the remainder of the season with the Knicks. He then signed a deal with the Houston Rockets, had a good run with that team for two seasons, and was traded to the Los Angeles Lakers in the summer of 2014. As of the printing of this book, Jeremy is playing for the Charlotte Hornets. He has proven he can hold his own as a point guard in the NBA, and we suspect he will continue stirring up "Linsanity" in the future.

Ivonne Mosquera-Schmidt continues to be an unstoppable force. Between 2012 and 2014, she set three American records, running faster than any totally blind woman in the 1,500-meter, the 3,000-meter, and the 5,000-meter distances. She won a gold medal at the 2013 Paratriathlon World Championships, her second gold medal in this competition. In the summer of 2014, Ivonne was diagnosed with a rare type of bladder cancer, a challenge she faced with incredible courage and optimism. She underwent

Shoot for the Stars
Jeremy works with an aspiri[ng]
player in Taipei, Taiwan. His [work with]
children continues through t[he]
Lin Foundation, a nonprofit [organization]
devoted to serving young people and
their communities. AP Photo/Chiang Ying-ying

chemotherapy and surgery, and was back on the track within weeks of leaving the hospital. Ivonne is currently preparing for the 2016 Paralympics, which are scheduled to be held in Rio de Janeiro, Brazil. What keeps this amazing woman going? Apart from the obvious reasons, such as love of sport, Ivonne derives great satisfaction from bridging the gap between the able-bodied and disabled communities. Blind and sighted athletes have a common appreciation for exercise, and training and racing unite them in a very human way. "We can have the same dreams, the same goals, the same ambitions," Ivonne says, "and [exercise] gets us working together."

Peace of Mind
Ivonne does the triangle pose during a visit to Queenstown, New Zealand. Yoga helps develop the strength and flexibility she needs for racing, and keeps her grounded. G. John Schmidt/Courtesy Ivonne Mosquera-Schmidt

✓◯◯◯ show what you know

1. You want to learn how to play basketball, so you watch videos of Jeremy Lin executing plays. If your game improves as a result, this would be considered an example of:
   a. observational learning.
   b. association.
   c. prosocial behavior.
   d. your cognitive map.

2. Bandura's Bobo doll study shows us that observationall learning results in a wide variety of learned behaviors. Describe several types of behaviors you have learned by observing a model.

3. Although Skinner believed that reinforcement is the cause of learning, there is robust evidence that reinforcement is not always necessary. This comes from experiments studying:
   a. positive reinforcement.
   b. negative reinforcement.
   c. latent learning.
   d. stimulus generalization.

✓ CHECK YOUR ANSWERS IN APPENDIX C.

5 summary of concepts

LO 1   Define learning. (p. 174)

Learning is a relatively enduring change in behavior or thinking that results from experiences. Organisms as simple as fish and as complex as humans have the ability to learn. Learning is about creating associations. Sometimes we associate two different stimuli (*classical conditioning*). Other times we make connections between our behaviors and their consequences (*operant conditioning*). We can also learn by watching and imitating others (*observational learning*), creating a link between our behavior and the behavior of others.

LO 2   Explain what Pavlov's studies teach us about classical conditioning. (p. 176)

The dogs in Pavlov's studies learned to associate various stimuli with the anticipation of food, which resulted in them salivating when the stimuli were introduced. He discovered how such associations are learned, and referred to this process as *conditioning*. Classical conditioning is the process in which two stimuli become associated; once this association has been established, an originally neutral stimulus is conditioned to elicit an involuntary response.

LO 3   Identify the differences between the US, UR, CS, and CR. (p. 178)

In classical conditioning, a neutral stimulus is something in the environment that does not normally cause a relevant automatic or reflexive response. This neutral stimulus is repeatedly paired with an unconditioned stimulus (US) that triggers an unconditioned response (UR). The neutral stimulus thus becomes a conditioned stimulus (CS) that the organism has learned to associate with the US. This CS elicits a conditioned response (CR). The initial pairing of a neutral stimulus with a US is called acquisition.

LO 4   Recognize and give examples of stimulus generalization and stimulus discrimination. (p. 179)

Once an association is forged between a CS and a CR, the learner often responds to similar stimuli as if they are the original CS. This is called stimulus generalization. For example, someone who has been bitten by a small dog and reacts with fear to all dogs, big and small, demonstrates stimulus generalization. Stimulus discrimination is the ability to differentiate between a CS and other stimuli sufficiently different from it. Someone who was bitten by a small dog may be afraid of small dogs, but not large dogs, thus demonstrating stimulus discrimination.

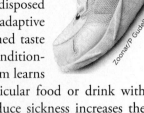

Zoonar/P Gudella/Agefotostock

LO 5   Summarize how classical conditioning is dependent on the biology of the organism. (p. 182)

Animals and people show biological preparedness, meaning they are predisposed to learn associations that have adaptive value. For example, a conditioned taste aversion is a form of classical conditioning that occurs when an organism learns to associate the taste of a particular food or drink with illness. Avoiding foods that induce sickness increases the odds the organism will survive and reproduce, passing its genes along to the next generation.

LO 6   Describe the Little Albert study and explain how fear can be learned. (p. 183)

The case study of Little Albert illustrates the conditioned emotional response, an emotional reaction (fear in Little Albert's case) acquired via classical conditioning. When Little Albert heard a loud bang, this was a US that elicited a fear response (the UR). Through conditioning, the sight of a rat became paired with the loud noise and went from being a *neutral stimulus* to a CS. Little Albert's fear of the rat became a CR.

LO 7   Describe Thorndike's law of effect. (p. 187)

Thorndike's law of effect was important in the development of operant conditioning, a type of learning in which people or animals come to associate their voluntary actions with consequences. The law of effect states that if a behavior is followed by a pleasurable outcome, that behavior is more likely to reoccur.

LO 8   Explain shaping and the method of successive approximations. (p. 188)

Building on Thorndike's law of effect and Watson's behaviorism, Skinner used reinforcers to guide behavior to the acquisition of a desired complex behavior, a process called shaping. Successive approximations is a method of shaping that uses reinforcers to condition a series of small steps that gradually approach a target behavior. Animal behavior can be shaped using successive approximations, but instinct can interfere with the process. This instinctive drift is the tendency for animals to revert to instinctual behaviors after a behavior pattern has been learned.

LO 9 Identify the differences between positive and negative reinforcement. (p. 192)

Positive reinforcement refers to the process of applying reinforcers that increase future occurrences of a targeted behavior. The fish treats that Thorndike gave his cats are examples of positive reinforcers (they increased the likelihood of the cats opening the latch). Behaviors can also increase in response to negative reinforcement through the process of taking away (or removing) something unpleasant. Putting on a seat belt in a car to stop an annoying beep is an example of negative reinforcement (it increases the likelihood of wearing a seat belt). Both positive and negative reinforcement increase desired behaviors.

LO 10 Distinguish between primary and secondary reinforcers. (p. 193)

There are two major categories of reinforcers. Primary reinforcers satisfy biological needs. Food, water, and physical contact are considered primary reinforcers. Secondary reinforcers do not satisfy biological needs, but often derive their power from their connection with primary reinforcers. Money is an example of a secondary reinforcer; we know from experience that it gives us access to primary reinforcers, such as food, a safe place to live, and perhaps even the ability to attract desirable mates.

LO 11 Describe continuous reinforcement and partial reinforcement. (p. 194)

Reinforcers can be delivered on a constant basis (continuous reinforcement) or intermittently (partial reinforcement). Continuous reinforcement is generally more effective for establishing a behavior, whereas learning through partial reinforcement is more resistant to extinction (the partial reinforcement effect) and useful for maintaining behavior.

LO 12 Name the schedules of reinforcement and give examples of each. (p. 196)

In a fixed-ratio schedule, reinforcement follows a predetermined number of desired responses or behaviors. In a variable-ratio schedule, the number of desired responses or behaviors that must occur before a reinforcer is given changes across trials and is based on an average number of responses to be reinforced. In a fixed-interval schedule, the reinforcer comes after a preestablished interval of time goes by; the response or behavior is only reinforced after the given interval passes. In a variable-interval schedule, the reinforcement comes after an interval of time passes, but the length of the interval changes from trial to trial. The lengths of these intervals are within a predetermined range based on a desired average interval length.

LO 13 Explain how punishment differs from negative reinforcement. (p. 200)

In contrast to reinforcement, which makes a behavior more likely to recur, the goal of punishment is to *decrease* a behavior. Negative reinforcement differs from punishment because it strengthens a behavior that it follows by removing something aversive or disagreeable. Punishment decreases a behavior by instilling an association between a behavior and some unwanted consequence (for example, between stealing and going to jail, or between misbehaving and a spanking).

LO 14 Summarize what Bandura's classic Bobo doll study teaches us about learning. (p. 204)

Observational learning can occur when we watch a model demonstrate a behavior. Albert Bandura's classic Bobo doll experiment showed that children readily imitate aggression when they see it modeled by adults. Studies suggest that children and adults may be inclined to mimic aggressive behaviors seen in TV shows, movies, video games, and on the Internet. Observation of prosocial behaviors, on the other hand, can encourage kindness, generosity, and forms of behavior that benefit others.

LO 15 Describe latent learning and explain how cognition is involved in learning. (p. 207)

Learning can occur without reinforcement. Edward Tolman showed that rats could learn to navigate mazes even when given no rewards. Their learning only became apparent when it was needed (latent learning). The rats were learning without reinforcement, just for the sake of learning. This cognitive approach reminds us that measurable behaviors and cognitive processes are necessary and complementary elements in the study of learning.

key terms

TEST PREP are you ready?

1. One basic form of learning occurs during the process of _____, which is evident when an organism does not respond as strongly or as often to an event following multiple exposures to it.
   a. insight
   b. habituation
   c. classical conditioning
   d. operant conditioning

2. Even trout can learn through operant conditioning, as evidenced by their
   a. innate urge to get food.
   b. reaction to an unconditioned stimulus.
   c. ability to press a pendulum to get food.
   d. reactions to predators.

3. The behaviors learned with classical conditioning are _____, whereas those learned with operant conditioning are _____.
   a. involuntary; voluntary
   b. voluntary; involuntary
   c. voluntary; innate
   d. involuntary; innate

4. Every time you open the pantry where dog food is stored, your dog starts to salivate. His reaction is a(n)
   a. unconditioned response.
   b. conditioned response.
   c. stimulus discrimination.
   d. reaction based on observational learning.

5. Your first love wore a musky-scented perfume, and your heart raced every time he or she appeared. Even now when you smell that scent, your heart speeds up, suggesting the scent is a(n)
   a. unconditioned stimulus.
   b. conditioned stimulus.
   c. conditioned response.
   d. unconditioned response.

6. Avoiding foods that induce sickness has _____. This taste aversion helps organisms survive.
   a. adaptive value
   b. stimulus generalization
   c. stimulus discrimination
   d. higher order conditioning

7. Little Albert was an 11-month-old baby who originally had no fear of rats. In an experiment conducted by Watson and Rayner, he was classically conditioned to fear white rats through the pairing of a loud noise with exposure to a rat. His resulting fear is an example of a(n)
   a. unconditioned stimulus.
   b. operant conditioning.
   c. conditioned emotional response.
   d. biological preparedness.

8. _____ indicates that if a behavior is followed by a pleasurable outcome, it likely will be repeated.
   a. Latent learning
   b. Classical conditioning
   c. Biological preparedness
   d. The law of effect

9. Which of the following is an example of negative reinforcement?
   a. working hard to get an A on a paper
   b. a child getting more computer time when he finishes his homework
   c. a dog whining in the morning, leading an owner to wake up and take it outside
   d. getting a speeding ticket and then not exceeding the speed limit afterward

10. All your friends tell you that you look fabulous in your new jeans, so you start wearing them all the time. This is an example of
    a. positive reinforcement.
    b. negative reinforcement.
    c. positive punishment.
    d. negative punishment.

11. A child is reprimanded for misbehaving, but then she seems to misbehave even more! This indicates that reprimanding her was
    a. negative punishment.
    b. positive reinforcement.
    c. positive punishment.
    d. an unconditioned response.

12. In Bandura's Bobo doll study, children who saw an adult attacking and shouting at the doll:
    a. were more likely to display aggressive behavior.
    b. were less likely to display aggressive behavior.
    c. did not play with the Bobo doll at all.
    d. began to cry when they saw the adult acting aggressively.

13. According to research, children who watch TV programs with violent role models are:
    a. more likely to have parents with legal troubles.
    b. less likely to get in trouble with the law as adults.
    c. at decreased risk of abusing their spouses when they become adults.
    d. at increased risk of abusing their spouses when they become adults.

14. Rats allowed to explore a maze, without getting reinforcers until the 11th day of the experiment, subsequently behaved in the maze as if they had been given reinforcers throughout the entire experiment. Their behavior is evidence of
    a. latent learning.
    b. observational learning.
    c. classical conditioning.
    d. operant conditioning.

15. Wolfgang Köhler's research on chimpanzees suggests that animals are capable of thinking through a problem before taking action, and having a sudden coming together of awareness of a situation, leading to the solution of a problem. This is called:
    a. observational learning.
    b. insight.
    c. modeling.
    d. higher order conditioning.

16. What is the difference between stimulus generalization and stimulus discrimination?

17. Describe an example of how you have used shaping and partial reinforcement to change your behavior. Which schedule of reinforcement do you think you were using?

18. What is the difference between primary reinforcers and secondary reinforcers? Give an example of each and explain how they might be used to change a behavior.

19. How are punishment and negative reinforcement different? Give examples of negative reinforcement, positive punishment, and negative punishment and explain how they aim to change behavior.

20. Some studies show that watching violent films is associated with violent behaviors. Why are such studies unable to show a cause-and-effect relationship between a film's content and viewers' behavior?

CHECK YOUR ANSWERS IN APPENDIX C.

Get personalized practice by logging into LaunchPad at **www.macmillanhighered.com/launchpad/ sciampresenting1e** to take the LearningCurve adaptive quizzes for Chapter 5.

6

An Introduction to Memory

Flow with It: The Stages of Memory

Retrieval and Forgetting

The Biology of Memory

153   209   17

189   192

ZoneCreative/GettyImages

©Bob Jacobson/Corbis

memory

An Introduction to Memory

MEMORY BREAKDOWN: THE CASE OF CLIVE WEARING   Monday, March 25, 1985:
Deborah Wearing awoke in a sweat-soaked bed. Her husband Clive had been up all night perspiring, vomiting, and with a high fever. He said that he had a "constant, terrible" headache, like a "band" of pain tightening around his head (Wearing, 2005, p. 27). The symptoms worsened over the next few days, but the two doctors caring for Clive reassured Deborah that it was just a bad case of the flu. By Wednesday, Clive had spent three nights awake with the pain. Confused and disoriented, he turned to Deborah and said, "Er, er, darling. . . . I can't . . . think of your name" (p. 31).

The doctor arrived a couple of hours later, reassured Deborah that her husband's confusion was merely the result of sleep deprivation, and prescribed sleeping pills. Deborah came home later that day, expecting to find her husband in bed. But no Clive. She shouted out his name. No answer, just a heap of pajamas. After the police had conducted an extensive search, Clive was found when a taxi driver dropped him off at a local police station; he had gotten into the cab and couldn't remember his address (Wearing, 2005). Clive returned to his flat (which he did not recognize as home), rested, and took in fluids. His fever dropped, and it appeared that he was improving. But when he awoke Friday morning, his confusion was so severe he could not identify the toilet among the various pieces of furniture in his bathroom. As Deborah placed urgent calls to the doctor, Clive began to drift away. He lost consciousness and was rushed to the hospital in an ambulance (Wearing, 2005; Wilson & Wearing, 1995).

Prior to this illness, Clive Wearing had enjoyed a fabulous career in music. As the Director of the London Lassus Ensemble, he spent his days leading singers and instrumentalists through the emotionally complex music of his favorite composer, Orlande de Lassus. A renowned expert on Renaissance music, Clive produced music for the prestigious British Broadcasting Corporation (BBC), including that which aired on the wedding day of Prince Charles and Lady Diana Spencer (Sacks, 2007, September 24; Wilson, Baddeley, & Kapur, 1995; Wilson, Kopelman, & Kapur, 2008). But Clive's work—and his whole life—tumbled into chaos when a virus that normally causes blisters on the mouth invaded his brain.

Millions of people carry herpes simplex virus type 1 (HSV-1). Usually, it causes unsightly cold sores on the mouth and face. (There is also HSV-2, more commonly associated with genital herpes.) But for a small minority of the adult population—as few as 1 in 500,000 annually—the virus invades the central nervous system and causes a life-threatening infection called *encephalitis*. Left untreated, herpes encephalitis causes death in over 70% of its victims. Most who survive have lasting neurological deficits (Sabah, Mulcahy, & Zeman, 2012; Whitley & Gnann, 2002).

The Conductor
In 1985 conductor Clive Wearing (pictured here with his wife Deborah) developed a brain infection—viral encephalitis—that nearly took his life. Clive recovered physically, but his memory was never the same.
© Ros Drinkwater/Alamy

Although Deborah saw to it that Clive received early medical attention, having two doctors visit the house day and night for nearly a week, these physicians mistook his condition for the flu with meningitis-like symptoms (Wilson & Wearing, 1995). Misdiagnosis is common with herpes encephalitis (even to this day), as its symptoms resemble those of other conditions, including the flu, meningitis, a stroke, and epilepsy (Sabah et al., 2012). When Clive and Deborah arrived at the hospital on the sixth day of his illness, they waited another 11 hours just to get a proper diagnosis (Wearing, 2005; Wilson & Wearing, 1995).

Clive and Deborah, in Their Own Words

http://qrs.ly/gz4qq6y

Jiri Rezac/Polaris/Newscom

LEARNING OBJECTIVES After reading and studying this chapter, you should be able to:

LO 1	Define memory.		**LO 8**	Describe long-term memory.
LO 2	Identify the processes of encoding, storage, and retrieval in memory.		**LO 9**	Illustrate how encoding specificity relates to retrieval cues.
LO 3	Explain the stages of memory described by the information-processing model.		**LO 10**	Identify some of the reasons why we forget.
LO 4	Describe sensory memory.		**LO 11**	Explain how the malleability of memory influences the recall of events.
LO 5	Summarize short-term memory.		**LO 12**	Define rich false memory.
LO 6	Give examples of how we can use chunking to improve our memory span.		**LO 13**	Compare and contrast anterograde and retrograde amnesia.
LO 7	Explain working memory and how it compares with short-term memory.		**LO 14**	Identify the brain structures involved in memory.
			LO 15	Describe long-term potentiation.

The Diary
Looking at a page from Clive's diary, you can see the fragmented nature of his thought process. He writes an entry, forgets it within seconds, and then returns to the page to start over, often writing the same thing. Encephalitis destroyed areas of Clive's brain that are crucial for learning and memory, so he can no longer recall what is happening from moment to moment.
Jiri Rezac / Polaris/Newscom

Clive survived, but the damage to his brain was extensive and profound; the virus had destroyed a substantial amount of neural tissue. And though Clive could still sing and play the keyboard (and spent much of the day doing so), he was unable to continue working as a conductor and music producer (D. Wearing, personal communication, June 18, 2013; Wilson & Wearing, 1995). In fact, he could barely get through day-to-day life. In the early stages of recovery, simple activities like eating baffled him. He ate the menu and attempted to spread cottage cheese on his bread, apparently mistaking it for butter. He confused basic concepts such as "scarf" and "umbrella," and shaved his eyebrows and nose (Wearing, 2005; Wilson & Wearing, 1995).

In the months following his illness, Clive was overcome with the feeling of just awakening. His senses were functioning properly, but every sight, sound, odor, taste, and feeling registered for just a moment, and then vanished. As Deborah described it, Clive saw the world anew with every blink of his eye (Wearing, 2005). The world must have seemed like a whirlwind of sensations, always changing, never stable. Desperate to make sense of everything, Clive would pose the same questions time and again: "How long have I been ill?" he would ask Deborah and the hospital staff members looking after him. "How long's it been?" (Wearing, p. 181). For much of the first decade following his illness, Clive repeated the same few phrases almost continuously in his conversations with people. "I haven't heard anything, seen anything, touched anything, smelled anything," he would say. "It's just like being dead" (Wearing, p. 160).

The depth of Clive's impairment is revealed in his diary, where he wrote essentially the same entries all day long. On August 25, 1985, he wrote, "I woke at 8:50 A.M. and baught [sic] a copy of *The Observer*," which is then crossed out and followed by "I woke at 9:00 A.M. I had already bought a copy of *The Observer*." The next line reads, "This (officially) confirms that I awoke at 9:05 A.M. this morning" (Wearing, 2005, p. 182). Having forgotten all previous entries, Clive reported throughout the day that he had just become conscious. His recollection of writing in his journal—along with every experience in his life—came and went in a flash. The herpes virus had ravaged his memory system.

The story of Clive Wearing launches our journey through *memory*. This chapter will take us to the opposite ends of a continuum: from memory loss to exceptional feats of remembering. We will travel to the World Memory Championships, an annual event where competitors from around the globe gather to see how many numbers, words, and images they can squeeze into their brains in 3 days. You will learn some tricks that might help you remember material for exams and everyday life: terms, concepts, passwords, pin numbers, people's names, and where you left your keys. You, too, can develop superior memorization skills; you just have to practice using memory aids. But beware: No matter how well you exercise your memory "muscle," it does not always perform perfectly. Like anything human, memory is prone to error.

Three Processes of Memory: Encoding, Storage, and Retrieval

LO 1   Define memory.

Memory refers to information the brain collects, stores, and may retrieve for later use. Much of this process has gone haywire for Clive. You may be wondering why we chose to start this chapter with the story of a person whose memory system failed. When it comes to understanding complex cognitive processes like those of memory, sometimes it helps to examine what happens when elements of the system are not working.

What is your earliest memory and how was it created? Do you know if it is accurate? And how can you recall it after so many years? Psychologists have been asking questions like these since the 1800s. Exactly how the brain absorbs information from the outside world and files it for later use is still not completely clear, but scientists have proposed many theories and models to explain how the brain processes, or works on, data on their way to becoming memories. As you learn about various theories and models, keep in mind that none of them are perfect. Rather than labeling one as *right* and another as *wrong,* most psychologists embrace a combination of approaches, taking into consideration their various strengths and weaknesses.

One often-used model likens the brain's memory system to a computer. Think about how a computer operates: It receives data from external sources, like your fingers typing on the keyboard, and converts that data into a code it can manipulate. Once this is accomplished, the information can be saved on the hard drive so you can open up the documents, MP3s, and other data files you need. The brain's memory system accomplishes similar tasks, but it is very different from a computer. Communication among neurons in the brain is more complicated than signals running between electrical components in a circuit. And unlike a computer, which maintains your files exactly how you last saved them, memories are subject to modifications over time, and this means they may be somewhat different each time you access them. Finally, the brain has seemingly unlimited storage capabilities, and the ability to process many types of information simultaneously, both consciously and unconsciously. We don't completely understand how a functioning memory system works, but there is basic agreement on its general processes, particularly *encoding, storage,* and *retrieval.*

LO 2   Identify the processes of encoding, storage, and retrieval in memory.

ENCODING   During the course of a day, we are bombarded with information coming from all of our senses and internal data from thoughts and emotions. Some of this information we will remember, but the majority of it will not be retained for very long. What is the difference between what is kept and what is not? Most psychologists agree that it all starts with **encoding,** the process through which information enters our memory system. Think about what happens when you pay attention to an event

CONNECTIONS

In **Chapter 2,** we described the electrical and chemical processes involved in the communication between neurons. We also reported that the human nervous system, which includes the brain, contains 100 billion cells interlinked by about 100 quadrillion (10^{15}) connections.

memory Information collected and stored in the brain that is generally retrievable for later use.

encoding The process through which information enters our memory system.

unfolding before you; stimuli associated with that event (sights, sounds, smells) are taken in by your senses and then converted to neural activity that travels to the brain. Here, the neural activity continues, at which point the information takes one of two paths: Either it enters our memory system (it is encoded to be stored for a longer period of time) or it slips away. For Clive Wearing, much of this information slips away.

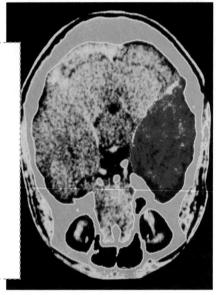

CONNECTIONS

In **Chapters 2** and **3,** we described how sensory information is taken in by sensory receptors and transduced; that is, transformed into neural activity. Here, we explore what happens after *transduction,* when information is processed in the memory system.

Encephalitis

The red area in this computerized axial tomography (CAT or CT) scan reveals inflammation in the temporal lobe. The cause of this swelling is herpes simplex virus, the same virus responsible for Clive's illness. Many people carry this virus (it causes cold sores), but herpes encephalitis is extremely rare, affecting as few as 1 in 500,000 people annually (Sabah et al., 2012). Even with early treatment, this brain infection frequently leaves its victims with cognitive damage (Kennedy & Chaudhuri, 2002). Airelle-Joubert/Science Source

STORAGE   For information that is successfully encoded, the next step is **storage.** Storage is exactly what it sounds like: preserving information for possible recollection in the future. Before Clive Wearing fell ill, his memory was excellent. His brain was able to encode and store a variety of events and learned abilities. Following his bout with encephalitis, however, his ability for long-term storage of new memories was destroyed—he could no longer retain new information for more than seconds at a time.

RETRIEVAL   After information is stored, how do we access it? Perhaps you still have a memory of your first-grade teacher's face, but can you remember his or her name? This process of coming up with the name is called **retrieval.** Sometimes information is encoded and stored in memory but cannot be accessed, or retrieved. Have you ever felt that a person's name or a certain vocabulary word was just sitting "on the tip of your tongue"? Chances are you were struggling from a retrieval failure, which we will discuss later in this chapter.

Before taking a closer look at the three processes of memory—encoding, storage, and retrieval—let's see what the memory system can do when it's functioning at an optimal level. Welcome to the world of memory sport.

MEET THE MEMORY ATHLETES   The 18th Annual World Memory Championships had officially kicked off. Dorothea Seitz felt her heart pound as she flipped over her memorization sheet. The page was filled with row upon row of black-and-gray "abstract images" that any ordinary person would see as meaningless blobs, distinguishable only by subtle differences in shape, shade, and texture. But to Dorothea, these blobs were rabbits leaping off the page, fish splashing in water, or bizarre human faces—anything her mind could conjure up. Because one of the keys to memorization, most any memory champion will tell you, is a lively imagination. She had 15 minutes to memorize as many images as possible, a maximum of 330, in the order given.

Dorothea was the reigning junior champion, and she had come to defend her title. Sitting in that same London conference room were 73 other contestants from all over the world, including

Memory Jocks

Competitors at the 2013 World Memory Championships study stacks of playing cards. Many wear earmuffs and other devices to block out background noises that might interfere with their concentration. Matthew Lloyd/The Times/Newscom

most of the hotshots in memory sport. Many wore large ear plugs or earmuffs to cancel out any noises that might derail their train of thought. Others donned dark glasses with tiny holes cut out of the centers, or side blinders like the kind race-horses wear—anything to keep their eyes from wandering from the task at hand.

When the 15 minutes were up, contest supervisors circulated the room collecting memorization sheets and distributing "recall sheets"—pieces of paper with the same images arranged in a different order. The contestants had only 30 minutes to unscramble them. Speeding through the recall phase of the event, Dorothea managed to remember 214 images. That put her in fourth place overall—not bad for a 17-year-old high school student competing against adults.

Dorothea had started the competition strong, but there were still nine events to go. The competitors would spend the next 3 days memorizing meaningless strings of numbers, random lists of words, imaginary historic dates, and other pieces of contrived "information." 📁

MEMORY COMPETITORS AND THE REST OF US The brains of memory champions are not wired in a special way; these are regular people who have trained themselves to excel in memory. Just ask eight-time World Memory Champion Dominic O'Brien if he thinks anyone can acquire an exceptional memory, and he will tell you there's no doubt about it. When O'Brien first began to train his memory at age 30, he could remember no more than 6 or 7 playing cards in a row. Eventually, he was able to memorize 2,808 cards (54 decks) after looking at each card only once. "I transformed my memory power very quickly as a result of applying simple techniques and practicing regularly," Dominic says. "If I can become a memory champion then anybody can" (D. O'Brien, personal communication, January 10, 2010). Just like a gymnast or a wrestler, a memory athlete prepares, trains, and practices. A powerful memory takes work!

One small study actually compared memory competitors to "normal" people and found nothing extraordinary about their intelligence or brain structure. What they did find was heightened activity in specific brain areas (particularly in regions used for spatial memory). This activity seemed to be associated with the use of a method for remembering items by associating them with an imagined "journey" (Maguire, Valentine, Wilding, & Kapur, 2003). As it turns out, memory champions like Dorothea and Dominic rely heavily on this type of imagined journey, which is rich with visual images. We will learn about this memory aid later in the chapter, when we discuss memory improvement, but first we must get a grasp of how the entire system works.

The Information-Processing Model of Memory

LO 3   Explain the stages of memory described by the information-processing model.

Psychologists employ several models to explain how the memory system is organized. Among the most influential is the *information-processing model* first developed by Atkinson and Shiffrin. This model suggests that memory operates in a series of stages (**Figure 6.1** on the next page), and these stages represent a *flow of information* (Anderson, 1971; Atkinson & Shiffrin, 1968; Wood & Pennington, 1973).

According to the information-processing model, the brain has three types of memory storage, each associated with a stage of memory: **Sensory memory** can hold vast amounts of sensory stimuli for a sliver of time, **short-term memory** can temporarily maintain and process limited information for a longer stretch, and **long-term memory** has essentially unlimited capacity and stores enduring information.

Note: Quotations attributed to Dorothea Seitz are personal communications.

2,808 Cards
Memory master Dominic O'Brien took 54 decks of playing cards and memorized their correct order after flipping through them just once. By practicing memory techniques, Dominic went from being a person with an average memory to an eight-time World Memory Champion.
musk/Alamy

CONNECTIONS

In **Chapter 1,** we described the importance of using theories and models to organize and conceptualize observations. In this chapter, we present several of these to explain the human memory system.

Synonyms
sensory memory sensory register

storage The process of preserving information for possible recollection in the future.
retrieval The process of accessing information encoded and stored in memory.
sensory memory A stage of memory that captures near-exact copies of vast amounts of sensory stimuli for a very brief period of time.
short-term memory A stage of memory that temporarily maintains and processes a limited amount of information.
long-term memory A stage of memory with essentially unlimited capacity that stores enduring information about facts and experiences.

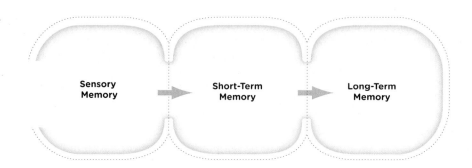

FIGURE 6.1
The Information-Processing Model of Memory

Sensory Memory → Short-Term Memory → Long-Term Memory

↗ CONNECTIONS

In **Chapter 3,** we defined *sensation* as the process by which receptors receive and detect stimuli. *Perception* is the process by which sensory data are organized to provide meaningful information. Some critics of the information-processing model suggest that sensory memory is an important component of perception, not a stage of memory.

FIGURE 6.2
The Levels of Processing Framework of Memory
Information can be processed along a continuum from shallow to deep, affecting the probability of recall. Shallow processing, in which only certain details like the physical appearance of a word might be noticed, results in brief memories that may not be recalled later. We are better able to recall information we process at a deep level, thinking about meaning and tying it to memories we already have. Gunnar Pippel/Shutterstock

Shallow: notice some physical features

Intermediate: notice patterns and a little more detail

Deep: think about meaning

PROCESSING

FISH fish *fish*

fish/dish

In the upcoming pages, you will read much more about these stages of memory and how they relate to Clive Wearing, whose short- and long-term memory are severely impaired.

The information-processing model is a valuable tool for learning about and researching memory, but like any scientific model, it has flaws. Some critics contend that *sensory memory* is really a primary component of perception. Others doubt that a clear boundary exists between *short-term* and *long-term memories* (Baddeley, 1995). And still others argue that this "pipeline" model is a simplistic representation because information does not necessarily flow through the memory system in a straight-line path (Cowan, 1988). Despite its weaknesses, the information-processing model remains an essential tool for explaining how memory works.

Levels of Processing

Another way to conceptualize memory is from a processing standpoint. To what degree does information entering the memory system get worked on? According to the *levels of processing* framework, there is a "hierarchy of processing stages" that corresponds to different depths of information processing (Craik & Lockhart, 1972). Thus, processing can occur along a continuum from shallow to deep (**Figure 6.2**). Shallow-level processing is primarily concerned with physical features, such as the brightness or shape of an object, or the number of letters in a word. Deeper-level processing relies on characteristics related to patterns and meaning, and generally results in longer-lasting and easier-to-retrieve memories. So when you pay only a little attention to data entering your sensory system, shallow processing occurs, resulting in more transient memories. If you really contemplate incoming information and relate it to memories you already have, deeper processing occurs, and the new memories are more likely to persist (Craik & Tulving, 1975; Francis & Gutiérrez, 2012; Newell & Andrews, 2004).

Fergus Craik and Endel Tulving explored levels of processing in their classic 1975 study. After presenting college students with various words, the researchers asked them yes or no questions, prompting them to think about and encode the words at three different levels: shallow, intermediate, and deep. The shallow questions required the students to study the appearance of the word: "Is the word in capital letters?" The intermediate-level questions related to the sound of the word: "Does the word rhyme with 'weight'?" And finally, the deep questions challenged the students to consider the word's meaning: "Is the word a type of fish?" When the researchers surprised the students with a test to see which words they remembered without any cues or clues, the students were best able to recall words whose meaning they had thought about (Craik & Tulving, 1975). The take-home message: Deep thinking helps create strong memories (Foos & Goolkasian, 2008).

Ask several people to try to remember the name "Clive Wearing." (1) Tell some of them to picture it written out in uppercase letters (CLIVE WEARING). (2) Tell others to imagine what it sounds like *(Clive Wearing rhymes with dive daring)*. (3) Ask a third group to contemplate its underlying significance *(Clive Wearing is the musician who suffers from an extreme case of memory loss)*. Later, test each person's memory for the name and see if a *deeper* level of processing leads to better encoding and a stronger memory.

> try this

Most people have the greatest success with (3) deep processing, but it depends somewhat on how they are prompted to retrieve information. For example, if someone asks you to remember any words that rhyme with "dive daring," the name "Clive Wearing" will probably pop into your head regardless of whether you used deep processing.

The levels of processing model helps us understand why testing, which often requires you to connect new and old information, can improve memory and help you succeed in school. Research strongly supports the idea that "testing improves learning," as long as the stakes are low (Dunlosky, Rawson, Marsh, Nathan, & Willingham, 2013). The Show What You Know and Test Prep resources in this textbook are designed with this in mind. Repeated testing, or the *testing effect,* results in a variety of benefits: better information retention; identification of areas needing more study; and increased self-motivated studying (Roediger, Putnam, & Smith, 2011). Speaking of testing, why not take a moment and show what you know?

 show what you know

1. _____ refers to the information that your brain collects, stores, and may use at a later time.

2. _____ is the process whereby information enters the memory system.
   - **a.** Retrieval
   - **b.** Encoding
   - **c.** Communication
   - **d.** Spatial memory

3. After suffering from a devastating illness, Clive Wearing essentially lost the ability to use which of the following stages of the information-processing model?
   - **a.** long-term memory
   - **b.** sensory memory
   - **c.** memory for keywords
   - **d.** sensory register

4. How might you illustrate shallow processing versus deep processing as it relates to studying?

✓ CHECK YOUR ANSWERS IN APPENDIX C.

Flow with It: The Stages of Memory

Think of all the information streaming through your sensory channels at this very moment. Your eyes may be focused on this sentence, but you are also collecting data through your peripheral vision. You may be hearing noises (the hum of a fan), smelling odors (dinner cooking in the kitchen), tasting foods (if you are snacking), and even feeling things (your back pressed against a chair). Many of these sensory stimuli never catch your attention, but some are being registered in your *sensory memory,* the first stage of the information-processing model (**Infographic 6.1** on the next page).

Sensory Memory: The Here and Now

LO 4   Describe sensory memory.

The bulk of information entering sensory memory comes and goes like the images on a movie screen. A few things catch your attention—the beautiful eyes of Mila Kunis, the sound of her voice, and perhaps the color of her shirt—but not much more before the frame switches and you're looking at another image. Information floods our sensory memory through multiple channels—what we see enters through one channel, what we taste through another, and so on.

Sensory Memory

On your way to class, you notice a dog barking at a passing car. You see the car, smell its exhaust, hear the dog. All this information coming through your sensory systems registers in your *sensory memory*, the first in a series of stages, according to the information-processing model of memory.

But what happens to information once it enters your sensory memory? Sensory memory is difficult to study. Research such as George Sperling's classic experiment involving iconic memory helps us understand how sensory memories are registered and processed.

Sensory information is constantly taken in, creating different types of sensory memory.

woof!

Most information registers in sensory memory.

Echoic Memory

"I hear the dog barking."
- auditory impressions/ sounds
- duration 1–10 seconds
- very accurate

Iconic Memory

"I see the dog."
- visual impressions/ images
- duration less than 1 second
- very accurate

SENSORY MEMORY

woof!

→ **SHORT-TERM MEMORY***

→ **LONG-TERM MEMORY**

*Not all information processed in sensory memory ends up in short-term memory.

"I smell the car's exhaust."
- smell, pain, touch, taste, etc.
- duration and accuracy vary

How do we know how long iconic memory lasts?

George Sperling (1960) developed a creative way to measure how quickly iconic memories fade from awareness. Participants were shown an array of letters and were asked to recall one row. Participants performed well when recalling that one row, but couldn't recall other letters: Their sensory memory for them had faded. This technique is still used today to study fleeting sensory memories.

| K Z R A |
| Q B T P |
| S G N Y |

Letters flash on screen, then disappear.

High Tone
MediumTone
Low Tone

A tone sounds. Participants report only the row associated with that tone.

Q B T P

Participants can report row associated with tone, but no other row. All letters initially registered in their sensory memory, but the iconic memory dissolves before more letters can be reported.

ICONIC MEMORY: "MORE IS SEEN THAN CAN BE REMEMBERED"   Interested in how the brain processes data entering the visual channel, Harvard graduate student George Sperling (1960) designed an experiment to determine how much information can be detected in a brief exposure to visual stimuli. Sperling set up a screen that flashed multiple rows of letters for one-twentieth of a second, and then asked participants to report what they saw. His first goal was to determine how many letters the participants could remember when an *array* of letters (for example, three rows of four letters) was flashed briefly; he found that, on average, the participants only reported four letters. But Sperling wasn't sure if this meant they were only able to store one row at a time in their memory, or if they stored all the rows at once, but just not long enough to recite them before they were forgotten.

Sperling was convinced that "more is seen than can be remembered" (1960, p. 1), so he devised a clever method called *partial report* to provide evidence. As with the original experiment, he briefly flashed an array of letters (for example, three rows of four letters), with all rows visible. But instead of having the participants report what they remembered from all the rows, he asked them to report what they remembered from just one row at a time (Infographic 6.1). Here's how the study went: The array of letters was flashed, and once it disappeared, a tone was sounded. When participants heard a high-pitched tone, they were to report the letters in the top row; with a medium-pitched tone, the letters in the middle row; and with a low-pitched tone, the letters in the bottom row. The participants were only asked to give a partial report, that is, to report on just one of the rows, but they did not know which row ahead of time. In this version of the study, the participants doubled their performance, recalling approximately 76% of the letters (Sperling, 1960). Sperling's research suggests that the *visual impressions* in our sensory memory, also known as **iconic memory**, are photograph-like in their accuracy but dissolve in less than a second. Given the short duration of iconic memory, can you predict what would happen to the participants' performance if there were a delay before they reported what they saw?

Anthony Asael/Art in All of Us/Corbis

try this

Stare at the photo of the child laughing and then shut your eyes. Does an image of the child linger in your mind's eye for just a moment? How long do you think this iconic memory lasts?

EIDETIC IMAGERY   Perhaps you have heard friends talk about someone who claims to have a "photographic memory" that can record and store images with the accuracy of a camera: "My cousin Dexter can look at a textbook page, remember exactly what it says in a few seconds, and then recall the information days later, seeing the pages exactly as they were." That may be what Dexter claims, but is there scientific evidence to back up such an assertion? We doubt it.

According to some reports, though, researchers have documented a phenomenon that comes fairly close to photographic memory. It's called *eidetic imagery* (ī-'de-tik),

iconic memory   Visual impressions that are photograph-like in their accuracy but dissolve in less than a second; a form of sensory memory.

and those who have this ability can "see" an image or object for as long as several minutes after it has been removed from sight, describing its parts with amazing specificity. However, the details they "see" are not always accurate, and thus their memories are not quite "photographic." Eidetic imagery is rare and usually only occurs in young children (Searleman, 2007, March 12).

ECHOIC MEMORY   Exact copies of the sounds we hear linger longer than visual impressions; **echoic memory** (ə-kō-ik) can last from about 1 to 10 seconds (Lu, Williamson, & Kaufman, 1992; Peterson, Meagher, & Ellsbury, 1970), and it can capture very subtle changes in sound. Research has shown that the introduction of a single tone played for 300 milliseconds initiates changes in cortical activity (Inui et al., 2010). Even if you are not aware of it, your auditory system is picking up slight changes in stimuli and storing them in echoic memory for a brief moment, so you don't have to pay attention to every incoming sound. Perhaps you have had the following experience: During class, your instructor notices a classmate daydreaming and tries to bring her back to reality: "Olivia, could you please restate the question for us?" Her mind was indeed wandering, but amazingly she can recall the instructor's last sentence, responding, "You asked us if brain scans should be allowed as evidence in courtrooms." For this, Olivia can thank her echoic memory.

Although brief, sensory memory is critical to the creation of memories. Without it, how would information enter the memory system in the first place? We have discussed iconic and echoic memory, which register sights and sounds, but memories can also be rich in smells, tastes, and touch. Remember, data received from all the senses are held momentarily in sensory memory. The bulk of research has focused on iconic and echoic memories, but psychologists propose that we also have similar sensory stores for the other senses.

Short-Term Memory

LO 5   Summarize short-term memory.

When information enters your sensory memory, it does not linger. So where does it go next? If not lost in the overwhelming array of sensory stimuli, the data proceed to *short-term memory,* the second stage in the information-processing model proposed by Atkinson and Shiffrin (1968). The amount of time information is maintained and processed in short-term memory depends on how much you are distracted by other cognitive activities, but the duration can be about 30 seconds (Atkinson & Shiffrin, 1968). You can stretch short-term memory further with **maintenance rehearsal,** a technique of repeating what you want to remember over and over in your mind. With maintenance rehearsal, it is theoretically possible to hold information there as long as desired. It comes in handy when you need to remember a series of numbers or letters (for example, phone numbers or zip codes). Imagine this: While strolling down the street, you witness a hit-and-run accident: a truck runs a red light, smashes into a car, and then speeds away. As the truck zooms off, you manage to catch a glimpse of the license plate number, "PRZ-7659," but how will you remember it long enough before reaching the 911 operator? If you're like most people, you will say the plate number to yourself over and over, either aloud or in your mind, using maintenance rehearsal.

But maintenance rehearsal does not work so well if you are distracted. In a classic study examining the duration of short-term memory, most participants were unable to recall three-letter combinations beyond 18 seconds while performing another task (Peterson & Peterson, 1959; **Figure 6.3**). The task (counting backward by 3s)

CONNECTIONS

In **Chapter 3,** we described *sensory adaptation,* the process by which we become less aware of constant stimuli. This allows us to focus on changes in our environment, an ability invaluable to survival. Humans are exquisitely sensitive to even the slightest changes in auditory stimuli, and our echoic memory allows us to store and follow changes in sounds.

Synonyms
maintenance rehearsal rote rehearsal

FIGURE 6.3
Duration of Short-Term Memory
Distraction can reduce the amount of time information remains in short-term memory. When performing a distracting cognitive task, most people were unable to recall a letter combination beyond 18 seconds. *Source:* From Peterson and Peterson (1959), Figure 3, p. 195

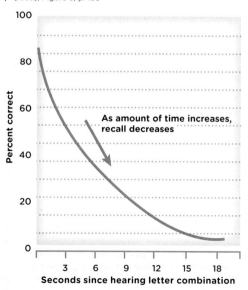

As amount of time increases, recall decreases

interfered with their natural inclination to mentally repeat the letter combinations; in other words, they were limited in their ability to use maintenance rehearsal. What this study reveals is that short-term memory has a limited capacity.

At any given moment, you can only concentrate on a tiny percentage of the data flooding your sensory memory. Items that capture your attention can move into your short-term memory, but most everything else disappears faster than you can say the word "memory." Please remember this when you are texting during class or watching TV while studying; if your goal is to remember what you *should be* concentrating on, you need to give it your full attention.

Apply This ➤

Multitasking and Memory

It's Sunday evening, and you need to catch up on the reading for your psychology class. You sit down in a quiet place and open your textbook. But just as you are getting into the psychology groove, a little "bloop bloop" jolts you out of the mental flow. A text bubble appears in the corner of your computer screen: OMG . . . blah blah blah . . . LOL! You begin an instant messaging (IM) conversation that continues on-and-off throughout your study session, periodically taking away your attention from psychology. By the evening's end, you do manage to finish a chapter, but how do you think your digital chitchat affected your memory of its material?

Psychologists from Central Connecticut State University wondered the same thing, so they did what any good researchers would do: They designed an experiment to find answers. The participants in their study were people very much like you— college students ranging from ages 17 to 46 who had enrolled in a general psychology course. All 89 students were asked to read a passage from a psychology textbook; some were allowed to read undisturbed, while others had to carry on IM conversations at the same time. Once the students had completed the assignment, the researchers quizzed them on their knowledge of the material (Bowman, Levine, Waite, & Gendron, 2010).

Here's what they found: The students who IMed during the reading task performed at roughly the same level as their non-IMing peers, but they needed much more time to read the passage: about 22–59% longer, and that's not including the time they spent reading and writing instant messages (Bowman et al., 2010). Thus, in order to achieve the same level of understanding, the IMers had to spend a lot more time making their way through the text. What does this mean for you? IMing might be seriously slowing the rate at which you learn. Spend enough time bouncing text bubbles back-and-forth, and you might even see your grades head south; there is some evidence that college students who spend a lot of time IMing or who frequently text and use Facebook while studying may have lower grade point averages than those who do not (Fox, Rosen, & Crawford, 2009; Junco & Cotten, 2012). ➤

HOW TO LOWER YOUR GPA USING FACEBOOK

Multitasking, whether it involves texting, using Facebook, or IMing, inevitably requires a shift in attention, and this is hard work for the brain, which has to engage and disengage different networks (Clapp, Rubens, Sabharwal, & Gazzaley, 2011). Keep this in mind the next time you consider using your smart phone behind the wheel. Texting while driving increases the likelihood of crashing or coming close to crashing by 23 times (Olson, Hanowski, Hickman, & Bocanegra, 2009), and studies show that using a cell phone impairs driving to the same degree as drunkenness (Strayer & Watson, 2012, March).

CONNECTIONS

Here, we see how memory is related to attention. In **Chapter 4,** we talked about the limited capacity of human attention. At any given point in time, there are only so many items you can attend to and thus move into your memory system.

CONNECTIONS

In **Chapter 1,** we discussed *correlations,* or relationships between two variables. Here, we note a negative correlation: As time spent using communication technologies goes up, GPA goes down. But correlation does not prove causation; perhaps people with lower GPAs have less interest in studying, and thus more time to socialize. Or, maybe there is a *third factor,* such as the ability to manage time effectively, influencing both variables.

echoic memory (ə-ˈkō-ik) Exact copies of the sounds we hear; a form of sensory memory.
maintenance rehearsal Technique of repeating information to be remembered, increasing the length of time it can be held in short-term memory.

2390
45791
340982
0128957
93781256
501298347

▲ FIGURE 6.4
Digit Span Test
The Digit Span test is a simple way to assess memory. Participants are asked to listen to a string of numbers and then repeat them. The string of numbers grows longer as the test progresses. Ask a friend to give you this test and see how many numbers you can remember. For a real challenge, you can even try to recite the list backward!

LO 6   Give examples of how we can use chunking to improve our memory span.

Now that we have established how important attention is for your success and safety, let's return to the memory stage to which it is so intimately tied: short-term memory. We mentioned that people frequently try to remember numbers and letters by repeating them over and over in their minds. This maintenance rehearsal is useful, but how many items can we realistically hold in our short-term memory at one time? Using a task called the Digit Span test (**Figure 6.4**), cognitive psychologist George Miller (1956) determined that most people can retain only five to nine digits: He called this the "magical number seven, plus or minus two." Indeed, most people can only attend to about five to nine items at one time (Cowan, Chen, & Rouder, 2004; Cowan, Nugent, & Elliott, 2000). But what exactly constitutes an "item?" Must it be a single-digit number? Not necessarily; we can expand short-term memory by packing more information into the items we need to remember.

Consider this example: Your friend has just gotten a new phone number, which she tells you as the elevator door is closing between you. How are you going to remember her number long enough to create a new entry in your cell phone? You could try memorizing all 10 digits in a row (8935550172), but a better strategy is to break the number into more manageable pieces (893-555-0172). Here, you are using **chunking,** Miller's name for grouping numbers, letters, or other types of information into meaningful subsets, or "chunks." Can you think of situations in which you might chunk information to help you remember it more easily?

Short-term memory can only hold so much, but we can increase its storage potential by chunking. The fact that short-term memory is actively processing information and is flexible in this regard suggests that it may be more than just a stage in which information is briefly stored. Indeed, many psychologists believe that short-term memory is more than an inactive storage facility.

Working Memory: Where the Action Is

LO 7   Explain working memory and how it compares with short-term memory.

Subsequent conceptualizations of the information-processing model include a concept known as **working memory** (Baddeley & Hitch, 1974), which refers to what is *going on* in short-term memory. Working memory is the active processing through which we maintain and manipulate information in the memory system. Let's use an analogy of a "bakery" and what goes on inside it. Think of short-term memory as the bakery, that is, the place that hosts your current thoughts and whatever your brain is working on at this very moment. According to this conceptualization, working memory is analogous to the making of bread, cakes, and pastries inside the bakery.

But not everyone agrees on the distinctions between short-term and working memory (Cowan, 2008; Rose, Myerson, Roediger, & Hale, 2010). Some psychologists do not differentiate between short-term and working memory, and use the terms interchangeably. For our purposes, we will identify "short-term memory" as a stage in the original information-processing model as well as the "location" where information is temporarily held, and "working memory" as the activities and processing occurring within.

Now let's take a closer look at the model of working memory originally proposed by psychologists Alan Baddeley and Graham Hitch (1974), which has been updated and revised over the years (Baddeley, 2002). According to this model, the purpose of working memory is to actively maintain information, aiding the mind as it performs complex cognitive tasks. To accomplish this, working memory has four components with specific functions: the phonological loop, the visuospatial sketchpad, the central executive, and the episodic buffer (Baddeley, 2002; **Figure 6.5**).

chunking Grouping numbers, letters, or other items into meaningful subsets as a strategy for increasing the quantity of information that can be maintained in short-term memory.

working memory The active processing of information in short-term memory; the maintenance and manipulation of information in the memory system.

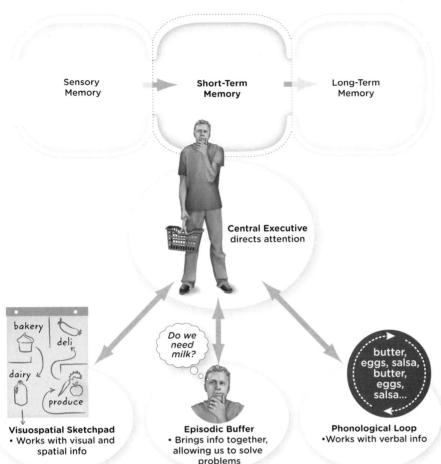

Sensory Memory

Short-Term Memory

Long-Term Memory

Central Executive
directs attention

bakery
deli
dairy
produce

Visuospatial Sketchpad
• Works with visual and spatial info

Do we need milk?

Episodic Buffer
• Brings info together, allowing us to solve problems

butter, eggs, salsa, butter, eggs, salsa...

Phonological Loop
•Works with verbal info

FIGURE 6.5
Model of Working Memory
Working memory represents the active processing occurring in short-term memory. Overseeing the big picture is the central executive, which directs attention and integrates processing among three subsystems: the phonological loop, the visuospatial sketchpad, and the episodic buffer. To see how this model works, imagine you have stopped by the supermarket to pick up groceries. You rehearse the shopping list with your phonological loop, produce a mental layout of the store with your visuospatial sketchpad, and use the episodic buffer to access long-term memories and determine whether you need any additional items. Tying together all these activities is the central executive.
Source: Baddeley (2002)

PHONOLOGICAL LOOP   The *phonological loop* is responsible for working with verbal information for brief periods of time; when exposed to verbal stimuli, we "hear" an immediate corollary in our mind. This component of working memory is what we use, for example, when we are reading, trying to solve problems, or learning new vocabulary. Most of us can only manipulate about 2 seconds' worth of verbal material in this loop without actively trying to repeat it (Baddeley, 2000; Baddeley & Hitch, 1994). Imagine you are trying to remember the passcode for your debit card. You know it is somehow related to your first zip code, so you retrieve your zip code from long-term memory. You then "hear" the five numbers played in your phonological loop as you desperately try to remember your passcode (*I remember it was 02138*). Once you figure out your passcode, the numbers of your zip code are no longer needed, and they slip quietly back into your long-term memory.

VISUOSPATIAL SKETCHPAD   The *visuospatial sketchpad* is where visual and spatial data are briefly stored and manipulated, including information about your surroundings and where things are in relation to each other and you. This working memory component allows you to close your eyes and reach for the coffee mug you just set down. We can also use information from long-term memory in our visuospatial sketchpad. Imagine you are standing at the entrance to the mall, determined to make your shopping excursion short and sweet. Thinking back to the last time you were there, you bring forth a mental image of how the stores are laid out. Excellent! You now have a map of the mall in your visuospatial sketchpad, which allows you to make more strategic decisions (*Victoria's Secret? No, JCPenney is closer*). But as you start considering the items you need to buy, the memory of the mall layout begins to slide back into your long-term memory. Studies by Baddeley and colleagues show that we have difficulty trying to perform even two visuospatial tasks at the same time (Baddeley, 1999, 2006).

CENTRAL EXECUTIVE   The *central executive* has responsibilities similar to those of the chief executive in any organization—it directs attention, makes plans, and coordinates activities (Baddeley, 2002). Part of its role is to determine what information is important, and to help organize and manipulate consciousness. Why is it that we cannot actually text, eat, and safely drive all at once? Like a juggler, the central executive can only catch and toss one ball at a time. We may think we are doing all three tasks at once, but we are really just swapping the alternatives in and out at a fast pace.

EPISODIC BUFFER   The *episodic buffer* is the part of working memory where information from the phonological loop, visuospatial sketchpad, and long-term memory can be brought together temporarily, under the direction of the central executive (Baddeley, 2000). The episodic buffer forms the bridge between memory and conscious awareness. It enables us to assign meaning to past events, solve problems, and make plans for the future.

As you know, working memory is limited in its capacity and duration. So how do we maintain so much information over the years? What aspect of memory makes it possible to memorize thousands of vocabulary words, scores of names and facts, and lyrics to your favorite songs? Enter long-term memory.

Long-Term Memory: Save It for Later

Items that enter short-term memory have two possible fates: Either they fade away or they move into *long-term memory* (**Figure 6.6**). Think of how much information is stored in your long-term memory: funny jokes, important conversations, images of faces, multiplication tables, and so many vocabulary words—between 30,000 (Lessmoellmann, 2006, October/November) and 60,000 words (Pinker, 1994) for the average English speaker. Could it be that long-term memory has an endless holding capacity? It may be impossible to answer this question, but for all practical purposes our long-term memory has no limits. And the memories stored there, such as street names from your childhood, may even last a lifetime (Schmidt, Peeck, Paas, & van Breukelen, 2000).

FIGURE 6.6
Long-Term Memory

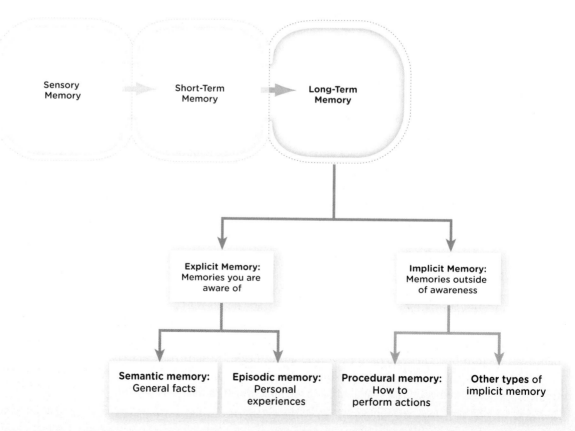

LO 8   Describe long-term memory.

EXPLICIT MEMORY   Long-term memory can be described in a variety of ways, but psychologists often distinguish between two categories: explicit and implicit. <u>**Explicit**</u> <u>**memory**</u> is the type of memory you are aware of having and can consciously express in words or declare: *Roses are red, guacamole is made with avocados; I wore bootcut jeans yesterday.* Tulving (1972) proposes two forms of explicit memory: semantic and episodic. **Semantic memory** pertains to general facts about the world (*the sky is blue; the United States holds presidential elections every four years*). But there is also a type of memory you can call your own. This personal form is called **episodic memory** (e-pə-sä-dik). It is your record of the memorable experiences, or "episodes," in your life, including when and where they occurred (Tulving, 1985).

FLASHBULB MEMORIES   Often our most vivid episodic memories are associated with intense emotion. Think about an emotionally charged experience from your past: receiving news that a loved one has died, getting engaged, or being the victim of an assault. If recollecting these events feels like watching a 4-D movie, you might be experiencing what psychologists call a **flashbulb memory,** a detailed account of circumstances surrounding an emotionally significant or shocking, sometimes historic, event (Brown & Kulik, 1977). Some people remember what they were doing when they heard about the terrorist attacks of September 11, 2001, or the horrific events that unfolded at Sandy Hook Elementary School in Newtown, Connecticut, on December 14, 2012. They recall where they were, who or what source relayed the news, how it made them feel, what they did next, and other random details about their experience (Brown & Kulik, 1977).

Because flashbulb memories seem so strong, vivid, and rich in detail, we often place great confidence in them, but research suggests that we should be cautious about doing this. Flashbulb memories sometimes include inaccuracies or lack some specific details (Neisser, 1991; Talarico & Rubin, 2003).

IMPLICIT MEMORY   Unlike explicit memory, which can easily flow into conscious thought, <u>**implicit memory**</u> is difficult to bring into awareness and express. It is a memory for something you know or know how to do, but which might be automatic or unconscious. Many of the physical activities we take for granted, such as playing an instrument, driving a car, and dribbling a basketball, use a special type of implicit

Effortless
Following his bout with encephalitis in 1985, Clive could still read music and play the piano, demonstrating that his procedural memory was not destroyed. Researchers documented a similar phenomenon in a professional cello player who battled herpes encephalitis in 2005 (Vennard, 2011, November 21). Jiri Rezac/ Polaris/Newscom

Synonyms
explicit memory declarative memory
implicit memory nondeclarative memory

explicit memory A type of memory you are aware of having and can consciously express in words or declare, including memories of facts and experiences.

semantic memory The memory of information theoretically available to anyone, which pertains to general facts about the world; a type of explicit memory.

episodic memory (e-pə-sä-dik) The record of memorable experiences or "episodes" including when and where an experience occurred; a type of explicit memory.

flashbulb memory A detailed account of circumstances surrounding an emotionally significant or shocking, sometimes historic, event.

implicit memory A memory of something you know or know how to do, but that might be automatic or unconscious; this type of memory is often difficult to bring to awareness and express.

memory called **procedural memory,** that is, the memory of how to carry out an activity without conscious control or attention. After his illness, Clive Wearing could still pick up a piece of music and play it on the piano. He had no recollection of learning to sight-read or play, yet he could execute these skills like the professional he had always been (Vennard, 2011, November 21). Therefore, Clive's procedural memory was still working.

Memories acquired through classical conditioning are also implicit. Let's say you enjoy eating food at McDonald's and the very sight of the golden arches makes you salivate like one of Pavlov's dogs. Somewhere along the line, you formed an association, a memory linking the appearance of that restaurant to juicy hamburgers and creamy shakes, but the association does not require your conscious awareness (Cowan, 1988). It is implicit.

CONNECTIONS

In **Chapter 5,** we introduced the concept of classical conditioning, which occurs when an originally neutral stimulus is conditioned to *elicit* or induce an involuntary response, such as salivation, eyeblinks, and other types of *reflex* reactions. Here we can see how closely linked learning and memory are.

Improving Memory

How does the process of moving data into the memory system create long-term memories? Some activities work well for keeping information in short-term memory (maintenance rehearsal, for example). Others involve moving information from short-term memory to long-term memory. Let's take a look at some of these processes, kicking off our discussion with a little test.

try this

Take 15 seconds and try to memorize these seven words in the order they appear.

puppy stop sing sadness soccer kick panic

Now close your eyes, and see how many you recall. How did you do?

You just completed a miniversion of "Random Words," Dorothea's favorite event in the World Memory Championships. Dorothea won a gold medal in this category, committing 244 words to memory in 15 minutes. What's her secret? She uses **mnemonic** (nih-ˈmän-ik) devices—techniques for improving memory. You have probably used several mnemonic devices in your own life. For example, have you ever relied on the *first-letter technique,* such as *Every Good Boy Deserves Fudge,* to learn the line notes of the treble clef scale? Or perhaps you have used an *acronym,* such as ROY G BIV, to remember the colors of the rainbow (**Figure 6.7**)? Chunking, which we discussed earlier, is also a mnemonic technique. As you can see in **Infographic 6.2,** mnemonic devices and other memory strategies can enhance retention of material as you study.

METHOD OF LOCI   One of the mnemonics Dorothea relies on most is the *method of loci* (lō-ˌsī, meaning "places"). Here's how it works: When presented with a series of words to remember, Dorothea takes them on a mental journey through the place she knows best: her bedroom and bathroom. Walking through her room, she puts the items-to-be-remembered at predetermined spots along the way. Let's say she is trying to remember the seven words from above. Dorothea visualizes herself entering her bedroom.

procedural memory The unconscious memory of how to carry out a variety of skills and activities; a type of implicit memory.

mnemonic (nih-ˈmän-ik) Technique to improve memory.

FIGURE 6.7

Mnemonics

Mnemonics enable us to translate information into a form that is easier to remember. For example, the common acronym ROY G BIV helps us remember the order of the seven colors in the rainbow. And when music students have trouble remembering the notes on the lines of the treble clef (EGBDF), they often rely on the first-letter technique, creating a sentence out of words beginning with these ▼ letters: *Every Good Boy Deserves Fudge.*

Red
Orange
Yellow
Green
Blue
Indigo
Violet

Study Smarter: Methods of Improving Your Memory

You may never need to memorize the order of 2,808 playing cards as memory champion Dominic O'Brien did. But you do need to be able to understand and recall hundreds of details when your teacher hands you an exam. Luckily, research shows that certain strategies and memory techniques will help you retain information when you study.

start studying

Recall details
Mnemonics translate information into a more easily remembered form.

Acronyms and first-letter technique
It's easier to remember a short phrase than a string of information.

ROYGBIV

Chunking
It's easier to remember a few chunks than a long string.

8935550172
893-555-0172

Method of loci
It's easier to remember information when you deliberately link it to locations along a familiar route.

Organize information
Hierarchical structures organize information into a meaningful system. The process of organizing aids encoding and, once encoded, the information is easier to recall.

furniture

fruit

flowers

Make connections
Elaborative rehearsal is deep processing that boosts transfer to long-term memory by connecting new information to older memories.

Give yourself time
Distributed practice creates better memory than study crammed into a single session.

NOVEMBER **13**
NOVEMBER **15**
NOVEMBER **18**
NOVEMBER **21**
↶ *study* ↷
NOVEMBER **23**   ↖ *test*

Get some rest
Sleep, or even wakeful resting after study, allows newly learned material to be encoded better.

ZZZ

A *test*

Credits: Single lotus flower, Shutterstock; Pine chest of drawers, Shutterstock; Pansy, Shutterstock; Green sofa, Shutterstock; Marigold, Shutterstock; City map with labels, Shutterstock; Vintage wooden rocking chair, Shutterstock; Red grape, Shutterstock; Peach, Shutterstock; November calendar icon, Shutterstock; Banana, Shutterstock; Portrait of teenage girl with hand on chin, BLOOMimage/Getty Images; High education (student with chemical models and chemical formula on the blackboard), zorani/ Getty Images

The first thing she comes upon is the bed, so she might imagine a cute *puppy* playing with the pillow. Then she encounters a bedside table, which suddenly becomes a bus *stop* with a bus parked in front. She walks over to the sofa, climbs onto it, and begins to *sing*. The next object on her path is a box, but not an ordinary box, because it's weeping tears of *sadness*. Next in her path is a mirror that she shatters to pieces with a *soccer* ball. When she gets to the sink, she *kicks* it with her foot. Finally, she imagines aliens climbing out of the toilet, causing her to *panic*. If she needs to remember the items, she retraces the journey, stopping at each point to observe the image she left there.

You can use the method of loci, too. Just pick a familiar route—through your favorite restaurant, college campus, even your own body—and mentally place things you need to remember at points along the way. For remembering short lists, memory champion Dominic O'Brien suggests tagging items to preestablished points along the body (O'Brien, 2005). Suppose you need to pick up five items at the grocery: *milk, eggs, olive oil, bananas,* and *cherries.* Choose some body parts and then visually connect them to the items you need. For example, your hair is slicked back in *olive oil;* your nose is a big long *banana;* you can't see because someone threw *eggs* in your eyes; *cherries* dangle from your ears like earrings; and you have a *milk* mustache.

HIERARCHICAL STRUCTURES   Another way to boost your memory is to arrange the material you are trying to memorize into a hierarchy, or a system of meaningful categories and subcategories. In a classic study, researchers found that if participants were given a list of words that followed a hierarchical structure, they were better able to recall the words than participants learning the same words not organized in any meaningful way. In fact, the participants who had learned the words using the hierarchy were able to recall three times as many words as the other group (Bower, Clark, Lesgold, & Winzenz, 1969).

try this

Try to remember the various divisions of the nervous system. Sketch a diagram like the one here (this is from Figure 2.2 from Chapter 2) showing the relationships among the concepts, starting with the most general and ending with the most specific.

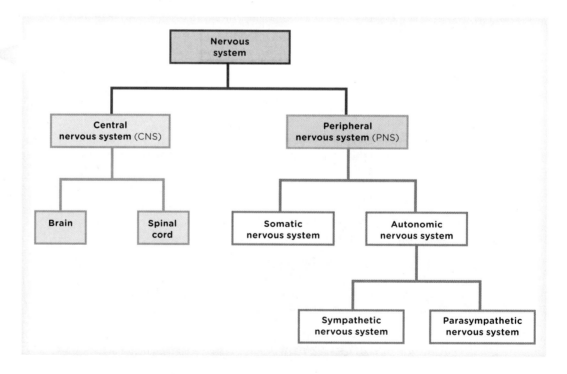

AUTOMATIC AND EFFORTFUL PROCESSING   As you recall from earlier in the chapter, the levels of processing framework suggests that stronger memories result when you think about information on a deep level. Dorothea and her rivals came to the championships expecting to use **effortful processing.** As the name implies, effortful processing is not only intentional but also requires work (Hartlage et al., 1993; Hasher & Zacks, 1979). Some types of effortful processing, such as maintenance rehearsal, are useful for extending the amount of time you can hold onto information in short-term memory. Others employ patterns and meaning to encode information for longer storage. For example, Dorothea links hundreds of elaborate images (like the puppy playing on the pillow, or aliens rising out of the toilet) on a mental journey—not an easy task to perform in 15 minutes. Her effortful processing occurs at a deep level, and as the levels of processing framework suggests, results in more successful learning and retention of information.

We should note that some encoding occurs through automatic processing— that is, with little or no conscious effort or awareness (Hartlage, Alloy, Vázquez, & Dykman, 1993; Hasher & Zacks, 1979). For example, when Dorothea walked into the conference room at the World Memory Championships, she processed all sorts of information without even trying—like the fact that most of the people milling around the room were men and that the team from China was wearing matching orange-and-white tracksuits. She did not make an effort to pick up on these details, but she remembers them nevertheless. Her memory system absorbed the data automatically.

ELABORATIVE REHEARSAL AND VISUALIZATION   Effortful processing is evident in **elaborative rehearsal,** the method of connecting incoming information to knowledge in long-term memory. Here, we can see that the *level of processing* occurs at a deep level, which suggests the encoding of information will be more successful. Dorothea's mental walks involve this type of deeper processing (elaborative rehearsal) because she takes new information and puts it in the familiar framework of her home. By picturing the journey and the objects-to-be-remembered in her mind's eye, Dorothea is taking advantage of *visualization,* another effective encoding strategy. People tend to remember verbal information better when it's accompanied by vivid imagery. Some research suggests, for example, that children recall news stories better when they see them presented on television, as opposed to reading about them in a printed article (Walma van der Molen & van der Voort, 2000).

DISTRIBUTED PRACTICE   What other strategies might improve encoding and help you move information into long-term memory? You've probably heard this before, but you should avoid cramming for long periods of time without breaks (also referred to as **massed practice**). Research dating back to the 1800s shows that **distributed practice**—spreading out study sessions, with breaks in between—is much more effective than packing information into your brain all at once (Ebbinghaus, 1885/1913; Rohrer & Taylor, 2006). When researchers asked students to learn a new mathematical skill, they found that participants who practiced the new skill in two sessions (separated by a week) did better on a practice test (4 weeks later) than those who spent the same amount of time practicing in one session (Pashler, Rohrer, Cepeda, & Carpenter, 2007). Surprisingly, how students apply distributed practice to studying may be associated with their culture and beliefs (Schommer-Aikins & Easter, 2008). But when it comes to studying groups, there are no hard-and-fast rules that apply to every member. Each individual should be viewed as such—an individual. Keep this in mind as you read on.

across the WORLD

Memory and Culture

Ask a person from the United States and a person from China to recount some life memories, and you may detect some interesting cultural themes in their reports. Research suggests that Chinese people are more likely than Americans to remember social and historical occurrences and focus their memories on other

---

> **CONNECTIONS**
>
> In **Chapter 4,** we described *automatic processing,* the collection and retention (sometimes temporary) of information with little or no conscious effort. Automatic processing can also refer to the automatic cognitive activity that guides some behaviors, enabling us to act without focusing attention on what we are doing. Without our awareness, the brain determines what needs attention and what can be processed for later use.

Synonyms
distributed practice spacing effect

> **CONNECTIONS**
>
> In **Chapter 1,** we presented the sociocultural perspective of psychology, which suggests that we should examine the influences of social interactions and culture to understand behavior. Here, we see how culture can influence decisions about the way to study.

effortful processing The encoding and storage of information with conscious effort, or awareness.

elaborative rehearsal The method of connecting incoming information to knowledge in long-term memory; a deep level of encoding.

massed practice Studying for long periods of time without breaks.

distributed practice Spreading out study sessions over time with breaks in between.

people. Americans, on the other hand, tend to recall events as they relate to their individual actions and emotions (Wang & Conway, 2004). Why is this so?

MEMORIES OF WE, OR MEMORIES OF ME?

It may have something to do with the fact that China—like many countries in East Asia, Africa, and Latin America—has a *collectivist* culture, whereas the United States is more *individualistic*. People in collectivist societies tend to prioritize the needs of family and community over those of the individual. Individualistic cultures are more "me" oriented, or focused on autonomy and independence. Thus, it would make sense that participants from China, a collectivist culture, would have more community-oriented memories than their American counterparts.

Memories East and West
A group of Chinese boys enjoy each other's company. China has a community-oriented, or collectivist, culture, which is reflected in the memories of its people. Compared to their U.S. counterparts, the Chinese are more inclined to recollect events in the context of society and history, emphasizing the roles played by other people (Wang & Conway, 2004).
Xinhua/ZUMApress/Newscom

SLEEP AND MEMORY   We have touched on many strategies for boosting memory, from chunking to visualization to distributed practice. If we could leave you with one final piece of advice, it would be the following: SLEEP. Exactly how sleep promotes memory is still not completely understood, but there is no question that good sleep makes for better processing of memories (Born, Rasch, & Gais, 2006; Diekelmann & Born, 2010; Marshall & Born, 2007). Even periods of "wakeful resting" can be of benefit. Participants who experienced a 15-minute period of wakeful resting (sitting in a darkened quiet room) displayed better retention of newly learned material than did participants who played a game for 15 minutes. Wakeful resting seems to allow newly learned material to be encoded better, and thus retained in memory longer (Dewar, Alber, Butler, Cowan, & Della Sala, 2012). What might this mean for you? Make sure you allow yourself some quiet time following the learning of new material. Don't end your study sessions with an activity that might interfere with your encoding. Of course, it takes more than good rest to succeed in college; you need to be able to analyze, apply, and synthesize material, not just remember it.

"Wow, that's a lot to remember," you may be saying. Hopefully, you can retain it with the help of some of the mnemonic devices we have presented. You might also take a wakeful resting break in preparation for the next section, which focuses on the topic of memory retrieval.

CONNECTIONS

In **Chapter 4,** we discussed how sleep and dreams relate to memory. For example, researchers suspect that *sleep spindles* are associated with memory consolidation, and some theorists emphasize the importance of *REM* sleep in this process.

show what you know

1. According to the information-processing model, our short-term memory can hold onto information for up to about _____ if we are not distracted by something else.
   a. 10 seconds
   b. 30 seconds
   c. 45 seconds
   d. 60 seconds

2. As you enter the airport, you try to remember the location of the baggage claim area. You remember the last time you picked up your friend at this airport, and using your visuospatial sketchpad, realize the area is to your left. This ability demonstrates the use of your:
   a. sensory memory.
   b. working memory.
   c. phonological loop.
   d. flashbulb memory.

3. _____ memory is the type of memory you are aware of having and can consciously declare, whereas _____ memory is for something you know or know how to do, but that might be automatic or unconscious.

4. On 9/11 Tanya was watching television when a news bulletin announced the terrorist attacks. She has vivid memories of that moment, including what she was doing, the friends she was with, and many details of her surroundings. This type of memory is known as a(n):
   a. phonological loop.
   b. sensory memory.
   c. implicit memory.
   d. flashbulb memory.

5. Develop a mnemonic device to help you memorize the following terms from this section: explicit memory, semantic memory, episodic memory, flashbulb memory, implicit memory, and procedural memory.

✓ CHECK YOUR ANSWERS IN APPENDIX C.

Retrieval and Forgetting

Have you ever heard the saying "an elephant never forgets?" Granted, this might be somewhat of an overstatement, but as far as animals go, elephants do have remarkable memories. Consider the story of two elephants that briefly worked together in the circus and then were separated for 23 years. When they reencountered one another at an elephant sanctuary in Tennessee, the two animals started to inspect each other's trunk scars and "bellowed" in excitement: The long-lost friends had recognized one another (Ritchie, 2009, January 12)! An elephant's memory—and yours, too—is only as good as its ability to retrieve stored memories. Let's return to the World Memory Championships and examine the critical process of retrieval.

What Can You Retrieve?

LO 9 Illustrate how encoding specificity relates to retrieval cues.

Every event in the World Memory Championships begins with *encoding* data into the memory system and *storing* that information for later use. Contestants are presented with information—numbers, words, historic dates, and the like—and provided a certain amount of time to file it away in long-term memory. But no matter how much information they absorb, the contestants' efforts are meaningless if they can't *retrieve* it in the recall phase of the event.

RETRIEVAL CUES AND PRIMING One of the most grueling events in the World Memory Championships is "One Hour Numbers," a race to see who can memorize the greatest number of random digits in an hour. Contestants are given four sheets of paper, each containing 1,000 random digits, and 1 hour to cram as many as possible into their long-term memories. During the recall phase that follows, they get 2 hours to scrawl the correctly ordered numbers on blank sheets of paper. This is a backbreaker because there are no reminders, or *retrieval cues,* to help contestants locate the information in their long-term memory. **Retrieval cues** are stimuli that help you retrieve stored information that is difficult to access (Tulving & Osler, 1968). For example, let's say you were trying to remember the name of the researcher who created the working memory model introduced earlier in the chapter. If we gave you the first letter of his last name, *B,* would that help you retrieve the information? If your mind jumped to "Baddeley" (the correct answer), then *B* served as your retrieval cue.

Friends Forever
Elephants Jenny and Shirley remembered one another after being separated for 23 years. Reunited at the Elephant Sanctuary in Hohenwald, Tennessee, they examined one another's trunks and hollered with joy (Ritchie, 2009, January 12). Courtesy of Carolyn Buckley, http://www.carolbuckley.com

retrieval cues Stimuli that help in the retrieval of stored information that is difficult to access.

One Hour Numbers Discipline
Memorisation Sheet

World MEMORY Championships

```
9 9 8 4 4 5 7 1 8 7 3 4 3 2 8 8 5 8 0 5 1 4 5 1 1 6 6 0 4 1 5 4 9 0 9 4 3 1 7 8    Row 1
2 2 5 3 0 9 9 7 5 6 7 8 2 9 7 8 2 2 4 6 7 9 0 5 4 2 6 7 8 0 1 2 8 0 1 6 4 5 3 6    Row 2
6 6 9 3 4 7 9 7 2 1 8 6 5 4 2 3 8 7 5 5 6 5 5 6 9 3 2 8 8 2 1 1 2 4 3 1 9 8 9 4    Row 3
7 2 0 6 1 3 9 9 2 0 5 0 4 8 1 4 5 4 3 1 3 8 9 4 8 3 2 2 0 8 9 1 9 8 4 2 7 9 7 6    Row 4
1 4 6 2 7 7 1 9 7 5 0 2 2 2 9 5 6 3 0 5 8 2 6 5 3 9 1 6 2 8 9 9 9 2 7 6 8 5 9 4    Row 5
5 5 7 7 3 1 0 1 0 7 7 7 1 8 7 8 4 5 6 6 1 0 6 7 8 3 1 8 1 2 3 1 9 7 2 9 8 6 5 7    Row 6
8 9 7 7 8 7 4 9 5 7 7 4 5 4 3 5 0 0 8 3 7 8 1 5 2 3 2 9 9 1 5 1 7 4 3 8 3 0 5 5    Row 7
9 9 5 4 1 3 7 3 9 8 9 4 4 4 9 8 8 3 0 2 6 3 9 8 7 8 8 2 9 8 9 5 4 8 6 4 2 8 2 3    Row 8
8 0 4 0 8 3 7 1 1 7 2 1 6 4 2 4 0 8 4 0 8 2 1 7 9 2 1 8 9 3 5 0 5 5 0 3 6 5 0 5    Row 9
8 7 8 3 0 0 7 2 3 5 1 3 1 3 4 9 7 6 7 5 0 4 1 6 6 7 0 4 5 9 3 1 4 7 3 1 8 3 0 4    Row 10
9 2 5 7 9 1 3 3 9 7 9 2 5 2 1 4 5 7 0 9 7 1 4 0 0 0 9 8 5 9 6 6 1 8 2 8 2 9 2    Row 11
4 9 6 6 8 9 3 5 1 2 6 2 2 7 2 6 1 1 0 4 8 4 9 8 7 7 9 8 0 5 4 8 4 3 4 3 8 9 8 9    Row 12
9 4 4 1 2 8 8 2 0 7 3 4 7 9 9 6 5 5 6 5 1 6 0 5 6 8 7 6 5 6 8 7 9 5 4 0 6 6 9 9    Row 13
9 2 7 7 3 2 0 6 5 1 5 3 2 0 0 8 8 8 5 8 2 0 4 1 0 9 2 0 3 4 7 2 7 3 0 2 4 3 6 7    Row 14
7 9 8 9 8 3 4 6 2 6 9 8 8 3 1 8 0 3 8 9 1 7 0 7 3 1 5 0 9 6 0 1 8 6 1 0 0 9 5 8    Row 15
2 4 8 2 7 2 8 9 7 4 5 3 0 5 0 9 1 6 9 8 7 4 0 8 8 2 5 1 7 2 3 6 3 7 5 2 7 7 0 3    Row 16
5 4 1 2 1 2 5 4 5 4 7 8 3 2 2 5 7 9 5 2 5 9 1 2 8 0 0 2 8 6 0 7 7 9 6 6 2 5 0 1    Row 17
3 4 2 2 5 6 0 2 0 4 4 8 1 0 3 1 7 6 6 2 1 6 4 7 3 0 8 0 6 1 8 2 9 3 9 0 3 9 6 0    Row 18
0 8 2 9 8 3 0 4 4 8 2 3 1 2 2 7 4 4 8 3 2 4 3 9 1 5 1 7 0 9 3 1 0 9 9 0 0 5 9 1    Row 19
9 7 7 8 0 3 5 7 5 0 8 4 0 5 2 5 6 2 6 8 7 5 2 1 9 9 2 0 8 0 5 7 7 0 6 7 3 5 5 7    Row 20
9 3 1 8 4 6 7 6 3 7 8 5 4 4 4 9 7 9 1 4 6 2 7 8 3 6 6 9 2 2 1 7 0 0 6 1 9 0 0 9    Row 21
1 4 0 7 9 9 0 3 2 5 9 8 7 6 7 3 7 7 2 7 7 7 4 9 0 6 9 2 5 7 1 3 1 9 8 4 7 1 7 6    Row 22
4 5 8 8 0 6 0 6 8 1 0 8 8 8 7 7 7 0 5 8 3 3 7 4 5 4 1 1 3 8 0 3 4 0 0 7 8 6 5 9    Row 23
9 7 9 8 3 4 0 5 2 0 7 3 9 9 9 8 4 8 9 6 6 0 3 6 7 2 1 6 5 6 7 1 6 0 4 4 3 4 9 4    Row 24
                                                                                  Row 25
```

The Ultimate Test
"One Hour Numbers" is one of the most demanding events in the World Memory Championships. Contestants are given 1 hour to memorize as many numbers as possible, and then 2 hours to write them in order on paper. The world record, currently held by Wang Feng of China, is 2,660 digits (World Memory Statistics, 2015). World Memory Championships

priming The stimulation of memories as a result of retrieval cues in the environment.

recall The process of retrieving information held in long-term memory without the help of explicit retrieval cues.

recognition The process of matching incoming data to information stored in long-term memory.

serial position effect The ability to recall items in a list depends on where they are in the series.

primacy effect The tendency to remember items at the beginning of a list.

recency effect The tendency to remember items at the end of a list.

encoding specificity principle Memories are more easily recalled when the context and cues at the time of encoding are similar to those at the time of retrieval.

Even Clive Wearing, who could not remember what was happening from one moment to the next, showed evidence of using retrieval cues. For instance, Clive spent 7 years of his life at St. Mary's Hospital in Paddington, England, yet had no conscious memory of living there. And, according to his wife Deborah, Clive was "completely devoid" of knowledge of his own location; the hospital name was not at all connected with his sense of location (D. Wearing, personal communication, June 25, 2013). But if Deborah prompted him with the words "St. Mary's," he would chime back, "Paddington," oblivious to its connection (Wearing, 2005, p. 188). In this instance, the *retrieval cue* in Clive's environment (the sound of the word "St. Mary's") was **priming** his memory of the hospital name. Priming is the process of awakening memories with the help of retrieval cues.

At this point, you may be wondering how priming can occur in a person with severe amnesia. Clive's conscious, *explicit* memory is diminished, but his unconscious, *implicit* memory still functions. Just because he could not articulate, or "declare," the name of the hospital does not mean that the previously known word combination had entirely vanished from his memory system.

RECALL AND RECOGNITION Now let's return to the "One Hour Numbers" event of the World Memory Championships. This type of challenge relies on pure **recall,** the process of retrieving information held in long-term memory without the help of explicit retrieval cues. Recall is what you depend on when you answer fill-in-the-blank or short-answer essay questions on exams. Say you are given the following prompt: "Using a computer metaphor, what are the three processes involved in memory?" In this situation, you must come up with the answer from scratch: "The three processes are *encoding, storage,* and *retrieval.*"

Now let's say you are faced with a multiple-choice question: "One proven way of retaining information is: (a) distributed practice, (b) massed practice, or (c) eidetic imagery." Answering this question relies on **recognition,** the process of matching incoming data to information stored in long-term memory. Recognition is generally a lot easier than recall because the information is right before your eyes; you just have to identify it (*Hey, I've seen that before*). Recall, on the other hand, requires you to come up with information on your own. Most of us find it easier to *recognize* the correct answer from a list of possible answers in a multiple-choice question than to *recall* the same correct answer for a fill-in-the-blank question.

SERIAL POSITION EFFECT Recall and recognition come into play outside of school as well. Just think about the last time someone asked you to pick up some items at the store. In order to find the requested goods, you had to recognize them (*There's the ketchup*), but even before that you had to recall them—a much harder task. The ability to recall items from a list depends on where they fall in the list, a phenomenon psychologists call the **serial position effect** (**Figure 6.8**). When given a list of words to memorize, research participants are better able to remember items at the beginning of the list, which is known as the **primacy effect,** as well as items at the end, which is called the **recency effect** (Deese & Kaufman, 1957; Murdock, 1962).

Imagine you are on your way to the store to buy supplies for a dinner party, but your cell phone battery is about to die. Your phone rings; it's your housemate asking you to pick up the following items: napkins, paper towels, dish soap, butter, laundry soap, paper plates, sparkling water, ice cream, plastic spoons, bread, pickles, and flowers. Without any way to write down this list, you are at the mercy of the serial position effect. In all likelihood (and if you don't use mnemonics), you will return home with napkins, paper towels, and a bottle of dish soap (due to the primacy effect), as well as bread, pickles, and flowers (due to the recency effect); the items in the middle will more likely be forgotten.

The Encoding Specificity Principle

When it comes to retrieving memories, context matters. Where were you when you encoded the information, and what was occurring around you? Researchers have found that environmental factors play a key role in determining how easily memories are retrieved.

CONTEXT IS EVERYTHING   In a classic study by Godden and Baddeley (1975), participants learned lists of words under two conditions: while underwater (using scuba gear) and on dry land. They were then tested for recall in both conditions: If they learned the list underwater, they were tested underwater and on dry ground; if they learned the list on dry ground, they were tested on dry ground and underwater. The participants were better able to retrieve words when the learning and recall occurred in the same location (**Figure 6.9**). If they learned the words underwater, they had an easier time recalling them underwater. Words learned on land were easier to recall on land. Here we have an example of *context-dependent memory;* memories are easier to access when the encoding and retrieval occur in similar contexts.

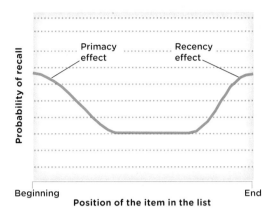

▲ FIGURE 6.8
The Serial Position Effect
Items at the beginning and the end of a list are more likely to be recalled.

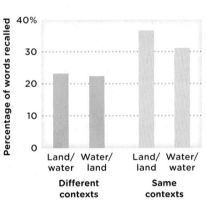

◀ FIGURE 6.9
Does Context Influence Memory Retrieval?
Researchers asked participants to learn a list of words in two contexts: underwater and on dry land. The participants had an easier time recalling words when learning and recall happened in the same setting (learning underwater and recalling underwater or learning on dry land and recalling on dry land). *Source:* Godden and Baddeley, 1975 Photo: Sergey Dubrov/Shutterstock

Context-dependent memory is part of a broader phenomenon conveyed by the **encoding specificity principle,** which states that memories are more easily recalled when the context and cues at the time of encoding are similar to those at the time of retrieval (Smith, Glenberg, & Bjork, 1978; Tulving & Thompson, 1973). There is even evidence that summoning a memory for an event reactivates the same brain areas that became excited during the event itself (Danker & Anderson, 2010). This suggests that the activity in your brain at the time of encoding is similar to that at retrieval, and researchers using fMRIs have found support for this (Gottfried, Smith, Rugg, & Dolan, 2004).

CONNECTIONS

In **Chapter 2,** we presented a variety of technologies used to explore the brain. fMRI captures changes in brain activity by revealing patterns of blood flow in a particular area. This is a good indicator of how much oxygen is being used as a result of activity there.

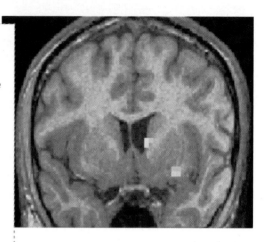

Context Matters
Using fMRI scans, researchers observed the brain activity of people trying to remember images they had first viewed in the presence of a specific scent (Gottfried et al., 2004). When recalling images they had linked to smells, odor-processing areas of the brain became noticeably excited, even in the absence of any odors. The scan shows the activity in the brain (see yellow on scan) of a person recalling an odor-linked image. (Gottfried, J. A., Smith, A. P. R., Rugg, M. D., & Dolan, R. J. (2004). Remembrance of odors past: Human olfactory cortex in cross-modal recognition memory. *Neuron, 42,* 687-895.)

Cues . . . Retrieval Cues
While watching your favorite James Bond movie, you pick up on all sorts of background stimuli from the environment. These sights, sounds, smells, tastes, and feelings have become entwined with your memory of the movie, so they can serve as retrieval cues for scenes in the film. Next time you smell buttery popcorn, don't be surprised if the ice blue eyes of Daniel Craig pop into your head. Apc/ZUMAPRESS/Newscom

IT ALL COMES FLOODING BACK   In your own life, you may have noticed that old memories tend to emerge from the woodwork when you return to the places where they were created. Dining at a restaurant you once frequented with an ex-boyfriend or girlfriend probably sparks memories of romantic moments (or perhaps a bitter argument) you had there. Going to a high school reunion might bring back memories of football games, dances, and classrooms not recalled in years. How does returning to the birthplace of a memory help bring it to mind? Places where memories are created often abound with retrieval cues—sights, sounds, tastes, smells, and feelings present at the time of encoding. These retrieval cues help awaken stored memories.

Suppose you go to a friend's house to watch the James Bond movie *Skyfall*. While encoding a memory of the movie, you are exposed to all sorts of stimuli in the environment, such as the hum of an air conditioner, the taste of the chips and salsa you are munching on, the tabby cat purring next to you on the sofa. All these feelings have nothing to do with *Skyfall,* but they are strongly linked to your experience of watching the film. So the next time you are at your friend's house and you see that tabby cat purring on a sofa, thoughts of 007 might come back to you.

MOODS, INTERNAL STATES, AND MEMORY   The encoding specificity principle does not merely apply to the context of the surroundings. Remembering things is also easier when physiological and psychological conditions, including moods and emotions, are similar at the time of encoding and retrieval. Sometimes memories can be best retrieved under such circumstances; we call this *state-dependent memory*. One morning upon awakening, you spot a red cardinal on your window ledge. You forget about the cardinal for the rest of the day—even when you pass the very same window. But come tomorrow morning when you are once again half-awake and groggy, memories of the red bird return. Here, your ability to recall the cardinal is dependent on your internal or physiological state being the same as it was at the time of encoding. Retrieval is also easier when the content of a memory corresponds to our present emotional state, a phenomenon known as mood congruence (Bower, Gilligan, & Menteiro, 1981; Drace, Ric, & Desrichard, 2010). If you are in a happy mood, you are more likely to recollect a happy-go-lucky character from a book, but if you are in a sour mood, you are more inclined to remember the character whose bad mood matches yours.

How Easily We Remember: Memory Savings

Retrieval is clearly at work in recall and recognition, the two processes we compared above. But there is another, less obvious form of retrieval that occurs in the process of **relearning.** Perhaps you've noticed that you learn material much more quickly a second time around. Math equations, vocabulary, and grammar rules seem to make more sense when you've seen them before. Some information seems to stick better when we learn it twice (Storm, Bjork, & Bjork, 2008).

HERMANN EBBINGHAUS   The first person to quantify the effect of relearning was Hermann Ebbinghaus (1850–1909), a German psychologist and pioneering researcher of human memory. Ebbinghaus was the sole participant in his experiments, so his research actually shed light on *his* memory, although the trends he uncovered in himself seem to apply to human memory in general.

Thorough scientist that he was, Ebbinghaus spent hour upon hour, day after day memorizing lists of "nonsense syllables"—meaningless combinations of vowels and consonants such as DAZ and MIB. Once Ebbinghaus had successfully remembered a list, meaning he could recite it smoothly and confidently, he would put it aside. Later, he would memorize it all over again and calculate how much time he had saved in Round 2, a measure called the "savings score" (Ebbinghaus, 1885/1913). In a study that supports Ebbinghaus' theory of savings in relearning, participants who were asked to memorize number–word pairs (for example, 17-snake, 23-crown) showed significant savings in the amount of time needed to relearn the number–word pairs 6 weeks later (Marmurek & Grant, 1990).

Since no one spends all day memorizing nonsense syllables, you may wonder how Ebbinghaus' research and the "savings score" apply to real life. At some point in school, you probably had to memorize a famous speech like Dr. Martin Luther King's "I Have a Dream." Let's say it took you 100 practice sessions to recite the speech flawlessly. Then, a month later, you tried memorizing it again and it only took 50 attempts. Because you cut your learning time in half (from 100 practice sessions to 50), your savings score would be 50%.

A FOREIGN LANGUAGE?   Learning is a lot like blazing a trail through freshly fallen snow. Your first attempt plowing through the powder is hard work and slow going, but the second time (relearning) is easier and faster because the snow is packed and the tracks already laid down. This also seems to be true for relearning a forgotten childhood language. One small study focused on native English speakers who as children had been exposed to either Hindi or Zulu to varying degrees. Although none of the adults in the study had any *explicit* memories of those languages, those who were under 40 were still able to distinguish sounds from their childhood languages better than members of a control group with no exposure to these languages (Bowers, Mattys, & Gage, 2009). The implication is that people who have some knowledge of a language (even if they don't realize it) benefit from this memory, by showing a "memory savings" if they try to learn the language again. They are a step ahead of other adults learning that language for the first time.

How Easily We Forget: Memory Slips Explained

LO 10 Identify some of the reasons why we forget.

Once Dorothea has memorized numbers, images, and other bits of information for the World Memory Championships, how long do they stick in her mind—an hour, a day, a week? Dorothea reports that images and words can last for several days, but meaningless strings of numbers, like the hundreds of digits memorized for the "One Hour Numbers" event, tend to fade within a day.

CONNECTIONS

As we noted in **Chapter 1,** case studies generally have only one participant. Here we see that Ebbinghaus, the researcher, was the sole participant. It is important to consider this when interpreting the findings, especially as we try to generalize to the population.

relearning Material learned previously is acquired more quickly in subsequent exposures.

FIGURE 6.10
Ebbinghaus' Curve of Forgetting
Ebbinghaus discovered that most forgetting occurs within 1 hour of learning and then levels off.

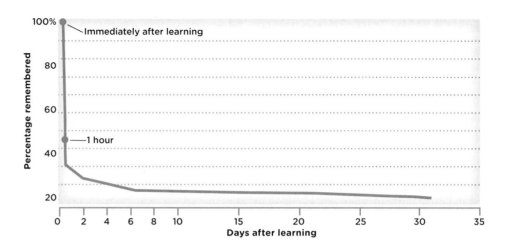

This would probably come as no surprise to Hermann Ebbinghaus, who, in addition to demonstrating the effects of relearning, was the first to illustrate just how rapidly memories vanish. Through his experiments with nonsense syllables, Ebbinghaus (1885/1913) found that the bulk of forgetting occurs immediately after learning. If you look at his *curve of forgetting* (**Figure 6.10**), you will see his memory of word lists plunging downward the hour following learning, then leveling off thereafter. Think about how the curve of forgetting applies to you. Some of what you hear in a psychology lecture will disappear from memory as soon as you walk out the door, but what you remember a week later will probably not differ much from what you recall in a month.

ENCODING FAILURE   What exactly causes us to forget? That may depend on the stage of memory processing—encoding, storage, or retrieval—at which a given instance of memory failure occurs. Sometimes details and events we think we have forgotten were actually never encoded in the first place. Take this example: After a long and stressful day, you stop at the supermarket to pick up a frozen dinner. While fumbling through your bag in search of your wallet, you take out your gloves and place them on the cashier's counter, but because your attention is focused on finding your wallet, you don't even notice where you've placed the gloves. Then you pay and walk out the door, only to wake up the next morning wondering where you left your gloves! This is an example of *encoding failure* because the data never entered your memory system. You never registered putting your gloves on the counter in the first place, so how can you expect to remember where you left them? For a classic demonstration of encoding failure, take a look at the 10 pennies appearing in the Try This. You've looked at a penny hundreds of times in your life, so identifying the real penny should be no problem, right?

try this

Look at the 10 pennies to the right. Which one is correct? Check your answer in Appendix C.

proactive interference   The tendency for information learned in the past to interfere with the retrieval of new material.

If you're like most people, chances are you picked the wrong coin because you have never taken the time to study a penny and *encode* its visual details (Nickerson & Adams, 1979).

STORAGE FAILURE AND MEMORY DECAY   Memory lapses can also result from *storage* failure. Take a moment and try to remember your high school locker combination. At one point you knew these numbers by heart, but they have slipped your mind because you no longer use them. Many memories decay over time, but there is plenty of evidence that we can store a vast fund of information, sometimes for very long periods. Such memories might include the name of the street where you grew up (Schmidt et al., 2000), grades in college (Bahrick, Hall, & Da Costa, 2008), and factual knowledge from college courses (Conway, Cohen, & Stanhope, 1991). However, these types of memories are subject to a variety of inaccuracies and distortions, and tapping into them is not always easy.

TIP-OF-THE-TONGUE PHENOMENON   Sometimes we know that we have knowledge of something but just can't pull it out of storage, or retrieve it. The name of that college classmate or that new blockbuster movie, it's just sitting on the tip of your tongue but it won't slide off! This simple *retrieval* failure is called the *tip-of-the-tongue phenomenon*. Most of us have this feeling about once a week, but luckily we are able to retrieve the elusive phrase approximately 50% of the time (James & Burke, 2000; Schwartz, 2012). Often we can correctly guess the first letter of the word or how many syllables it has (Hanley & Chapman, 2008). Studies suggest that the tip-of-the-tongue phenomenon becomes more common with age (Brown & Nix, 1996).

HYPERTHYMESTIC SYNDROME   What would happen if you had the opposite problem—that is, instead of forgetting all the time, you remembered everything? Imagine how overwhelming it would be to remember all the experiences you have had, all the people you have met, all the meals that you have eaten over the years, and so on. The ability to forget seems to have great adaptive value, because forgetting allows you to attend to what's going on in the here and now. Some people, however, cannot forget. This type of memory ability is known as *hyperthymestic syndrome* (Parker, Cahill, & McGaugh, 2006). The irony is that having this type of "super" memory has drawbacks, including problems with abstract thinking and the ability to make generalizations, although it doesn't necessarily impair day-to-day functioning.

PROACTIVE INTERFERENCE   You now know that forgetting can stem from problems in encoding and storage. And the tip-of-the-tongue phenomenon tells us that it can also result from glitches in *retrieval*. Studies also show that retrieval is influenced, or in some cases blocked, by information we learn before and after a memory is made, which we refer to as *interference* (Waugh & Norman, 1965). If you have studied more than one foreign language, you have probably experienced interference. Suppose you take Spanish in middle school, and then begin studying Italian in college. As you try to learn Italian, you may find Spanish words creeping into your mind and confusing you; this is an example of **proactive interference,** the tendency for information learned in the past to interfere with the retrieval of new material. People who learn to play a second musical instrument experience the same problem; the fingering of the old instrument interferes with the retrieval of new fingering.

Who Are They?
Sometimes a name we are trying to remember feels so close, yet we cannot quite pull it out of storage. This feeling of near-retrieval is known as the *tip-of-the-tongue phenomenon*, and it happens frequently when we try to recall the names of celebrities. top: © Bettmann/ CORBIS; middle: AP Photo; bottom: Charley Gallay/WireImage/Getty Images

RETROACTIVE INTERFERENCE   Now let's say you are going on a trip to Mexico and need to use the Spanish you learned back in middle school. As you approach a vendor in an outdoor market in Costa Maya, you may become frustrated when the only words that come to mind are *ciao bello* and *buongiorno* (Italian for "hello

FIGURE 6.11
Proactive and Retroactive
Interference

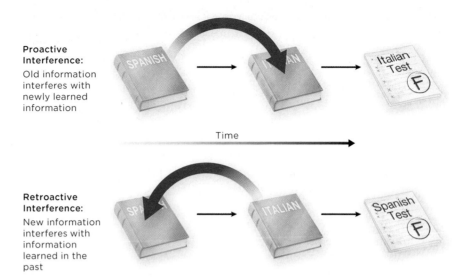

Proactive Interference:
Old information interferes with newly learned information

Time

Retroactive Interference:
New information interferes with information learned in the past

handsome" and "good day"), when you really are searching for phrases with the same meaning in Español. Here, recently learned information interferes with the retrieval of things learned in the past. We call this **retroactive interference.** This type of interference can also impact the musician; when she switches back to her original instrument, the fingering techniques she uses to play the new instrument interfere with her old techniques. Thus, proactive interference results from knowledge acquired in the past and retroactive interference is caused by information learned recently (**Figure 6.11**).

Although our memories fail us all the time, we manage to get by with a little help from our friends, who remind us to set our alarm clocks, study for tests, and say "happy birthday" to so and so. We have cell phones to store phone numbers and e-mail accounts to maintain addresses. The news media remind us what day it is. And then of course, there is Google.

didn't SEE that coming

Google Brain

Google. What would life be like without it? Every day, we use Google to find the answers to questions we are too embarrassed to ask out loud. It enables us stay abreast of the latest news, provides us with immediate access to the voices and faces of friends, and helps us schedule our lives. Google is, without doubt, one of the modern brain's greatest helpers. But here's the question: Is all of Google's hard work making us lazy?

Maybe "resourceful" is a better word. One study found that people essentially use computers as storage places for information they would otherwise have to remember (Sparrow, Liu, & Wegner, 2011). The researchers asked participants to read and type 40 statements referring to trivia-like information (for example, "An ostrich's eye is bigger than its brain"). Those who were told they would need the information later *and* that it would be available on the computer were less likely to try memorizing it than those denied computer access. Even those who were *not* asked to remember the information showed better recall if they had no expectations of searching for it on the computer. It seems we as a culture have adapted to being constantly "plugged in" and having information at our fingertips. Remember the last time you lost Internet service? "The experience of losing our Internet connection becomes more and more like losing a friend" (Sparrow et al., 2011, p. 4).

IS GOOGLE MAKING US LAZY?

retroactive interference The tendency for recently learned information to interfere with the retrieval of things learned in the past.

Misinformation: Can Memories Be Trusted?

Why do we need computers to help us keep track of the loads of information flooding our brains throughout the day? The answer is simple. We can't remember everything. We forget, and we forget often. Sometimes it's obvious an error has occurred (*I can't remember where I left my cell phone*), but other times it's less apparent. Have you noticed that when you recall a shared event, your version is not always consistent with those of other people? As you will soon discover, memories are not reliable records of reality. They are malleable (that is, capable of being changed or reshaped by various influences) and constantly updated and revised, like a wiki. Let's see how this occurs.

LO 11 Explain how the malleability of memory influences the recall of events.

Elizabeth Loftus, a renowned psychologist and law professor, has been studying memory and its reliability for the last 4 decades. During the course of her career, she has been an expert witness in over 200 trials. The main focus of her work is the very problem we just touched upon: If two people have different memories of an event, whom do we believe?

MEMORY RECONSTRUCTED   Loftus suggests that we should not expect our accounts of the past to be identical to those of other people or even of our own previous renditions of events. According to Loftus, episodic memories are not exact duplicates of past events (recent or distant). Instead, she and others propose a *reconstructionist* model of memory "in which memories are understood as creative blendings of fact and fiction" (Loftus & Ketcham, 1994, p. 5). Over the course of time, memories can fade, and because they are permeable, they become more vulnerable to the invasion of new information. In other words, your memory of some event might include revisions to what really happened, based on knowledge, opinions, and information you have acquired since the event occurred.

Suppose you watch a debate between two presidential candidates on live television. A few days later, you see that same debate parodied on *Saturday Night Live*. Then a few weeks later, you try to remember the details of the actual debate—the topics discussed, the phrases used by the candidates, the clothes they wore. In your effort to recall the real event, you may very well incorporate some elements of the *Saturday Night Live* skit (for example, words or expressions used by the candidates). The memories we make are not precise depictions of reality, but representations of the world as we perceive it. With the passage of time, we lose bits and pieces of a memory, and unknowingly we replace them with new information.

THE MISINFORMATION EFFECT   If you witnessed a car accident, how accurately would you remember it? Elizabeth Loftus and John Palmer (1974) tested the reliability of people's memories for such an event in a classic experiment. After showing participants a short film clip of a multiple-car accident, Loftus and Palmer quizzed them about what they had seen. They asked some participants, "About how fast were the cars going when they smashed into each other?" Replacing the word "smashed" with "hit," they asked others, "About how fast were the cars going when they hit each other?" Can you guess which version resulted in the highest estimates of speed? If you guessed "smashed," you are correct.

One week later, the researchers asked the participants to recall the details of the accident, including whether they had seen any broken glass in the film. Although no broken glass appears in the film, the researchers nevertheless predicted there would be some "yes" answers from participants who had initially been asked about the speed of

CONNECTIONS

In **Chapter 1,** we introduced the concepts of expectations and bias, noting that these can produce inaccuracies in thinking and research. Here, we describe the ways in which our memories can fail. As accurate as our thoughts and memories may seem, we must be aware that they are vulnerable to error.

Comedy or Reality
Did former vice presidential candidate Sarah Palin (right) really say, "I can see Russia from my house!" during a one-on-one interview, or was that just Tina Fey (left) doing a Palin impersonation on *Saturday Night Live*? Sometimes, we unknowingly edit our memories, incorporating bits and pieces of information learned after the fact. left: Photo by Dana Edelson/NBC/NBCU Photo Bank Getty Images; right: WHITNEY CURTIS/EPA/Newscom

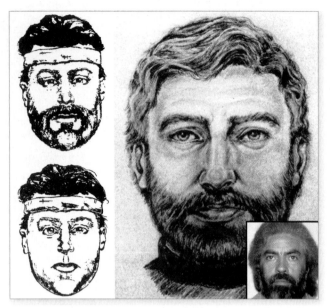

Memory Sketches
Comparing the two police sketches (left) and the more accurate drawing by sketch artist Jeanne Boylan (right), you see how renderings of the same individual can be dramatically different, even though all three were based on eyewitness information. Police sketches are based on the memories of eyewitnesses, each of whom has a unique—and potentially erroneous—memory of the suspect.
Composite by Nate Caplin KRT/Newscom

the cars that "smashed" into each other. Their predictions were correct. Participants who had heard the word "smashed" apparently incorporated a faster speed in their memories, and were more likely to report having seen broken glass. Participants who had not heard the word "smashed" seemed to have a more accurate memory of the filmed car collision. The researchers concluded that memories can change in response to new information, and specifically that the participants' recollections were altered by the wording of a questionnaire (Loftus & Palmer, 1974). This research suggests that eyewitness accounts of accidents, crimes, and other important events might be altered by factors that come into play *after* the event occurs. Because memories are malleable, the wording of questions can change the way events are recalled, and care must be taken when questioning people about the past, whether it's in a therapist's office, a social service agency, or a police station.

Researchers have since conducted numerous studies on the **misinformation effect,** or the tendency for new and misleading information to distort one's memory of an incident. Studies with a variety of participants have resulted in their "remembering" a stop sign that was really a yield sign, a screwdriver that was really a hammer, and a barn that did not actually exist (Loftus, 2005).

Prosecutors often tell people who have witnessed crimes not to speak to each other, and with good reason. Suppose two people witnessed an elderly woman being robbed. One eyewitness remembers seeing a bearded man wearing a blue jacket swiping the woman's purse. The other noticed the blue jacket but *not* the beard. If, however, the two eyewitnesses exchange stories of what they saw, the second eyewitness may unknowingly incorporate the beard into his "memory." Information learned after the event (that is, the "fact" that the thief had a beard) can unknowingly get mixed in with memories of that event (Loftus, 2005; Loftus, Miller, & Burns, 1978). If we can instill this type of "false" information into a "true" memory, do you suppose it is possible to give people memories for events that never happened? Indeed, it is.

False Memories

LO 12 Define rich false memory.

Elizabeth Loftus knows firsthand what it is like to have a memory implanted. Tragically, her mother drowned when she was 14 years old. For 30 years, she believed that someone else had found her mother's body in a swimming pool. But then her uncle, in the middle of his 90th birthday party, told her that she, Elizabeth, had found her mother's body. Loftus initially denied any memory of this horrifying experience, but as the days passed, she began to "recall" the event, including images of the pool, her mother's body, and numerous police cars arriving at the scene. These images continued to build for several days, until she received a phone call from her brother informing her that her uncle had been wrong, and that all her other relatives agreed Elizabeth was not the one who found her mother. According to Loftus, "All it took was a suggestion, casually planted" (Loftus & Ketcham, 1994, p. 40), and she was able to create a memory of an event she never witnessed. Following this experience, Loftus began to study **rich false memories,** that is, "wholly false memories" characterized by "the subjective feeling that one is experiencing a genuine recollection, replete with sensory details, and even expressed with confidence and emotion, even though the event never happened" (Loftus & Bernstein, 2005, p. 101).

Would you believe that about 25% of participants in rich false memory studies are able to "remember" an event that never happened? Using the "lost in the mall"

misinformation effect The tendency for new and misleading information obtained after an incident to distort one's memory of it.

rich false memories Recollections of an event that never occurred, which are expressed with emotions and confidence and include details.

technique, Loftus and Pickrell (1995) showed just how these imaginary memories take form. The researchers recruited a pair of family members (for example, parent–child or sibling–sibling) and then told them they would be participating in a study on memory. With the help of one of the members of the pair (the "relative"), the researchers recorded three true events from the pair's shared past and created a plausible story of a trip to a shopping mall that never happened. Then they asked the true "participant" to recall as many details as possible about each of the four events (remember, only three of the events were real), which were presented in a book provided by the researchers. If the participant could not remember any details from an event, he was instructed to write, "I do not remember this." In the "lost in the mall" story, the participant was told that he had been separated from the family in a shopping mall around the age of 5. According to the story, the participant began to cry, but was eventually helped by an elderly woman and was reunited with his family. Mind you, the "lost in the mall" episode was pure fiction, but it was made to seem real through the help of the participant's relative (who was working with the researchers). Following a series of interviews, the researchers concluded that 29% of the participants were able to "recall" either part or all of the fabricated "lost in the mall" experience (Loftus & Pickrell, 1995). These findings may seem shocking (they certainly caused a great uproar in the field), but keep in mind that a large majority of the participants did not "remember" the fabricated event (Hyman, Husband, & Billings, 1995; Loftus & Pickrell, 1995).

False Memories
Would you believe that looking at photoshopped pictures can lead to the creation of false memories? In one study, researchers discovered that participants could "remember" hot air balloon rides they never took after looking at doctored photos of themselves as children on balloon rides. The researchers speculate that a photo "helps subjects to imagine details about the event that they later confuse with reality" (Garry & Gerrie, 2005, p. 321). Mike Sonnenberg/E+/Getty Images

CONTROVERSIES

The Debate over Repressed Childhood Memories

➡️ ⬅️ Given what you learned from the "lost in the mall" study, do you think it's possible that false memories can be planted by psychotherapy? Imagine a clinical psychologist or psychiatrist who firmly believes that her client was sexually abused as a child. The client has no memory of abuse, but the therapist is convinced that the abuse occurred and that the traumatic memory for it has been *repressed*, or unconsciously pushed below the threshold of awareness. Using methods such as hypnosis and dream analysis, the therapist helps the client resurrect a "memory" of the abuse (that presumably never occurred). Angry and hurt, the client then confronts the "abuser," who happens to be a close relative, and forever damages the relationship. Believe it or not, this scenario is very plausible. Consider these true stories picked from a long list:

- With the help of a psychiatrist, Nadean Cool came to believe that she was a victim of sexual abuse, a former member of a satanic cult, and a baby killer. She later claimed these to be false memories brought about in therapy (Loftus, 1997).
- Under the influence of prescription drugs and persuasive therapists, Lynn Price Gondolf became convinced that her parents molested her during childhood. Three years after accusing her parents of such abuse, she concluded the accusation was a mistake (Loftus & Ketcham, 1994).
- Laura Pasley "walked into her Texas therapist's office with one problem, bulimia, and walked out with another, incest" (Loftus, 1994, p. 44).

In the history of psychology, few topics have stirred up as much controversy as repressed memories. Some psychologists believe that painful memories can indeed be repressed and recovered years or decades later (Knapp & VandeCreek, 2000). The majority, however, would agree that the studies supporting the existence of repressed

CONNECTIONS

In **Chapter 4,** we described an altered state of consciousness called *hypnosis* that allows for changes in perceptions and behavior, resulting from suggestions made by the hypnotist. Here, we discuss the use of hypnosis in a therapeutic setting; the hypnotist is a therapist trying to help a client "remember" an abuse that the therapist believes has been repressed.

memories have many shortcomings (Piper, Lillevik, & Kritzer, 2008). Although childhood sexual abuse is shockingly common, affecting some 30–40% of girls (about 1 in 3) and 13% of boys (about 1 in 8) in the United States (Bolen & Scannapieco, 1999), there is *not* good evidence that these traumas are repressed. Even if they were, retrieved memories of them would likely be inaccurate (Roediger & Bergman, 1998). Many trauma survivors face quite a different challenge—letting go of painful memories that continue to haunt them. (See the discussion of posttraumatic stress disorder in Chapter 11.)

REAL OR IMAGINED?

The American Psychological Association (APA) and other authoritative mental health organizations have investigated the repressed memory issue at length. In 1998 the APA issued a statement offering its main conclusions, summarized below:

- Sexual abuse of children is very common and often unrecognized, and the repressed memory debate should not detract attention from this important issue.
- Most victims of sexual abuse have at least some memory of the abuse.
- Memories of past abuses can be forgotten and remembered at a later time.
- People sometimes do create false memories of experiences they never had.
- We still do not completely understand how accurate and flawed memories of childhood abuse are formed (APA, 1998a). ➜ ◄

The main message of this section is that memory is malleable, or changeable. What are the implications for eyewitness accounts, especially those provided by children? If we are aware of how questions are structured and understand rewards and punishments from the perspective of a child, then the interview will produce fewer inaccuracies (Sparling, Wilder, Kondash, Boyle, & Compton, 2011). Researchers have found that having children close their eyes increases the accuracy of the testimony (Vredeveldt, Baddeley, & Hitch, 2013, February), but relying solely on their accounts has contributed to many cases of mistaken identity. In addition, the presence of someone in a uniform appears to put added pressure on child eyewitnesses, resulting in more guessing and inaccurate recall (Lowenstein, Blank, & Sauer, 2010).

Before you read on, take a minute and allow the words of Elizabeth Loftus to sink in: "Think of your mind as a bowl filled with clear water. Now imagine each memory as a teaspoon of milk stirred into the water. Every adult mind holds thousands of these murky memories. . . . Who among us would dare to disentangle the water from the milk?" (Loftus & Ketcham, 1994, pp. 3–4). What is the basis for all this murkiness? Time to explore the biological roots of memory.

✓ show what you know

1. _____ suggests that retrieving memories is easier in the context in which they were made.
   a. The encoding specificity principle
   b. Retroactive interference
   c. Proactive interference
   d. The curve of forgetting

2. Ebbinghaus reported that his memory of word lists plunged the first hour after he learned them; he displayed this in his:
   a. encoding specificity principle.   b. curve of forgetting.
   c. recency effect.   d. serial position effect.

3. Your uncle claims he attended a school play in which you played the "Cowardly Lion." He has described the costume you wore, the lines you mixed up, and even the flowers he gave you. At first you can't remember the play, but eventually you seem to. Your mother insists you were never in that school play, and your uncle wasn't in the country that year, so he couldn't have attended the performance at all. Instead, you have experienced a:
   a. curve of forgetting.   b. state-dependent memory.
   c. savings score.   d. rich false memory.

4. Loftus and Palmer (1974) conducted an experiment in which the wording of a question (using "smash" versus "hit") significantly influenced participants' recall of the event. What does this suggest about the malleability, or changeability, of memory?

✓ CHECK YOUR ANSWERS IN APPENDIX C.

The Biology of Memory

What did you do today? Did you have breakfast, brush your teeth, put your clothes on, drive your car, read an assignment, text a friend? Whatever you did, we are sure of one thing: It required a whole lot of memory. You could not send a text message without knowing how to spell, read, and use a cell phone—all things you had to learn and remember. Likewise, you could not drive without remembering how to unlock your car, start the engine, use the pedals. Memory is involved in virtually everything you do.

If memory is behind all your daily activities, important processes must be occurring in the brain to make this happen: both on the macro (large) and micro (small) scale. But as we learned from Clive's example, these processes are fragile and can be profoundly disrupted. Exploring the causes of memory failure can help us understand the biological basis of memory.

Amnesia

LO 13 Compare and contrast anterograde and retrograde amnesia.

In the months and years following Clive's illness, researchers administered many tests to assess his cognitive functioning. They found his IQ to be within an average range but his ability to remember past events deeply impaired. When prompted to name as many musical composers as possible in 1 minute, Clive— a man who had devoted his career to the study of music—could only produce four: Mozart, Beethoven, Bach, and Haydn. He denied that dragonflies have wings and claimed he had never heard of John F. Kennedy (Wilson et al., 1995).

Clive was even more disabled when it came to developing new memories. Initially, he could not hold onto incoming information for more than a blink of an eye. If his wife Deborah left the room, even for a short trip to the restroom, he would welcome her back as if she had been away for years—embracing, celebrating, sometimes weeping. "How long have I been ill?" he would ask, forgetting the answer and repeating himself within seconds (Wearing, 2005, p. 181). 📁

Love Triumphs
Clive forgot many things, but not the love he has for his wife. Every time Deborah came to visit, he recognized her but could not recall their last meeting, even if it happened just minutes before. Hugging, kissing, and sometimes twirling Deborah in the air, he would ask how much time had passed (Wearing, 2005). Jiri Rezac/Polaris/Newscom

Amnesia, or memory loss, can result from either a physical or psychological condition. There are different types and degrees of amnesia, ranging from extreme (losing decades of autobiographical memories) to mild (temporarily forgetting people's names after a concussion).

ANTEROGRADE AMNESIA According to researchers, Clive suffers from "a more severe anterograde amnesia than any other patient previously reported" (Wilson et al., 1995, p. 680). **Anterograde amnesia** (an-tə-,rō-,grād) is the inability to "lay down" or create new long-term memories (**Figure 6.12** on the next page), and it is generally caused by damage or injury to the brain, resulting from surgery, alcohol, head trauma, or illness. Someone with anterograde amnesia cannot form memories of events and experiences that occur following the brain damage, regardless of its cause. People affected by anterograde amnesia may be incapable of holding down a job, as their inability to lay down new

anterograde amnesia (an-tə-,rō-,grād)
A type of memory loss; an inability to create new memories following damage or injury to the brain.

FIGURE 6.12
Retrograde and Anterograde Amnesia
Retro means "before," so retrograde amnesia is the inability to retrieve memories for events that occurred *before* an amnesia-causing injury. *Antero* means "after," so anterograde amnesia is the inability to form memories for events that occur *after* an injury.
Chris McGrath/Getty Image

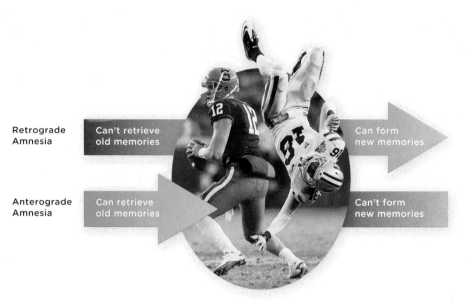

Retrograde Amnesia — Can't retrieve old memories — Can form new memories

Anterograde Amnesia — Can retrieve old memories — Can't form new memories

memories affects their capacity to remember daily tasks. For Clive, his short-term memory still functioned to a certain extent, but he could only absorb and process information for several seconds before it was lost. From his perspective, every experience was fresh, and every person (with the exception of some he knew well from the past) a total stranger.

RETROGRADE AMNESIA A second type of memory loss is **retrograde amnesia,** an inability to access memories created before a brain injury or surgery (Brandt & Benedict, 1993; Figure 6.12). With retrograde amnesia, a person has difficulty retrieving old memories, though how "old" depends on the extent of trauma to the brain. People with retrograde amnesia generally remember who they are and the most important events of their earlier lives (Manns, Hopkins, & Squire, 2003; Squire & Wixted, 2011). Remember that *retrograde* refers to the inability to access old memories, and *anterograde* refers to the inability to create new memories.

Clive suffered from retrograde amnesia in addition to his anterograde amnesia. While he appeared to retain a vague outline of his past (hazy information about his childhood, the fact that he had been a choral scholar at Clare College, Cambridge, and so on), he could not retrieve the names of his children unless prompted. And although Clive's children were all adults when he developed encephalitis, he came out of the illness thinking they were young children. The retrograde amnesia has improved, but only minimally. In 2005, for example, Clive asked his 40-something son what subjects he was studying in grammar school (equivalent to American high school). Nowadays when inquiring about his children, Clive simply asks, "What are they doing?" (D. Wearing, personal communication, June 18 and 25, July 11, 2013).

In spite of the severe retrograde and anterograde amnesia, some of Clive's memory functions continued to operate quite well. At one point, Deborah arranged for Clive to be reunited with the singers from the London Lassus Ensemble, a group he had conducted for more than a decade before his illness. At first Clive paused and looked at the musicians with uncertainty, but then he raised his hands and began conducting, leading them through the music with precision and grace. Remembering the piece (which he had edited himself), Clive mouthed its words in Latin and employed the same tempo and conducting style he had used in the past (D. Wearing, personal communication, July 11, 2013). After the performance, the musicians left and Clive sat in the empty chapel wondering what had gone on there earlier (Wearing, 2005). When shown a video of himself leading the chorus, he remarked, "I wasn't conscious then" (Wilson et al., 2008). Clive's explicit memory of the event vanished in seconds, but his implicit memory—knowing how to conduct—was intact.

retrograde amnesia A type of memory loss; an inability to access memories formed prior to damage or injury to the brain, or difficulty retrieving them.

memory trace The location where memories are etched in the brain via physiological changes.

How is it possible that some of Clive's long-term memories were blotted out, while others, such as how to conduct music, remained fairly clear? The evidence suggests that different types of long-term memories have distinct processing routes in the brain. Thus, damage to one area of the brain may impair some types of memory but not others. Let's take a closer look at where memories seem to be stored in the brain.

Where Memories Live in the Brain: A Macro Perspective

LO 14 Identify the brain structures involved in memory.

A few years after the onset of Clive's illness, doctors evaluated his brain using an MRI scan. A troubling picture emerged; the virus had destroyed many parts of his brain, notably the hippocampus, which plays a vital role in the creation of new memories (Wilson et al., 2008).

Only in the last 50 years have scientists come to appreciate the role of the hippocampus in memory (**Infographic 6.3** on the next page). Back in the 1920s, psychologist Karl Lashley set out to find a **memory trace:** the physical spot where memories are etched in the brain, also called an *engram*. Lashley selected a group of rats that had learned the layout of specific mazes, and then made large cuts at different places in their cortices to see how this affected their memory of the mazes. No matter where Lashley sliced, the rats still managed to maneuver their way through the mazes (Costandi, 2009, February 10; Lashley, 1950). These findings led Lashley and other scientists to believe that memory is spread throughout the brain rather than localized in a particular region (Costandi, 2009, February 10; Kandel & Pittenger, 1999). *Connectionism* is a model that suggests our memories are distributed throughout the brain in a network of interlinked neurons.

THE CASE OF H.M.   Henry Molaison (better known as "H.M.") forced scientists to completely reevaluate their understanding of the brain's memory system. From the onset of his amnesia in 1953 until his death in 2008, H.M. served as a research participant for some 100 scientists (Corkin, 2002), making him the most extensively studied amnesic patient.

H.M.'s brain troubles began at the age of 10, a year or so after being knocked unconscious in a bicycle accident. He began to experience seizures, which worsened with age and eventually became so debilitating that he could no longer hold a steady job. Antiseizure medications were unsuccessful in controlling his seizures, so at the age of 27, H.M. opted for an experimental surgery to remove parts of his brain: the temporal lobes (just beneath the temples), including the hippocampus (Scoville & Milner, 1957).

H.M.'s surgery succeeded in reining in his epilepsy but left his memory in shambles. Upon waking from the operation, he could no longer find his way to the bathroom or recognize the hospital workers caring for him. He played with the same jigsaw puzzles and read the same magazines day after day as if he were seeing them for the first time (Scoville & Milner, 1957). Like Clive, H.M. suffered from profound *anterograde amnesia,* the inability to encode new long-term memories, and a

CONNECTIONS

In **Chapter 2,** we described the hippocampus as a pair of curved structures buried deep within the temporal lobes. The hippocampus is primarily responsible for processing and making new memories, but is not where memories are permanently stored. It is also one of the brain areas where *neurogenesis* occurs, that is, where new neurons are generated.

Synonyms
connectionism parallel distributed processing (PDP)

Project H.M.
Dr. Jacopo Annese, director of the Brain Observatory at the University of San Diego, stands in front of a massive digital image rendered from a slice of brain tissue preserved on a slide. Dr. Annese and his team have carved the brain of amnesiac Henry Molaison, or "H.M.," into 2,401 slices to be digitized and studied (Brain Observatory, 2013). John Gibbins/U-T San Diego/Zuma Press/Newscom

Tracking Memory in the Brain

Whether with lab rats or case studies, psychologists have spent decades tracking the location of memory in the brain. What they've found so far should be no surprise: Memory is a complex system involving multiple structures and regions of the brain. Memory is formed, processed, and stored throughout the brain, and different types of memory have different paths. So to find memory in the brain, it helps to know your way around the brain's structures. Remembering the amygdala's role in processing basic emotion, for instance, can help you understand its role in processing the emotional content of memories.

Forming New Memories

In an attempt to control the disabling seizures of a man named Henry Molaison (H.M.), doctors surgically removed portions of his brain, including the hippocampus. The surgery affected H.M.'s memory. He had profound anterograde amnesia: He could tap into old memories, but he could no longer make new explicit memories. However, he could still create implicit memories. Using information gathered about H.M.'s brain, scientists have been able to directly connect the hippocampus to the creation of new explicit memories.

After his death, H.M.'s brain was cut into over 2,000 slices that were preserved and digitized for research.

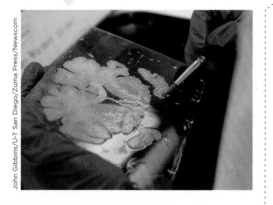

John Gibbins/U-T San Diego/Zuma Press/Newscom

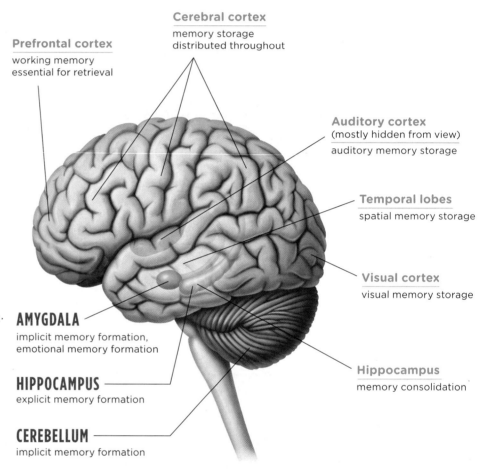

Prefrontal cortex
working memory
essential for retrieval

Cerebral cortex
memory storage
distributed throughout

Auditory cortex
(mostly hidden from view)
auditory memory storage

Temporal lobes
spatial memory storage

Visual cortex
visual memory storage

Hippocampus
memory consolidation

AMYGDALA
implicit memory formation,
emotional memory formation

HIPPOCAMPUS
explicit memory formation

CEREBELLUM
implicit memory formation

Storing Memories

Through his experiments slicing the cortices of rats that had learned to navigate mazes, Karl Lashley concluded that complex memories are not localized to a particular region in the cortex, but are instead widely distributed. Later research has established the interrelated roles of specific structures in the process of encoding, storing, and retrieving memories.

In a process called *memory consolidation,* which begins in the hippocampus, memories are moved to other parts of the cerebral cortex for long-term storage. Research on this topic is ongoing. For instance, scientists have been able to link explicit memory storage to areas of the brain where the original sensation was processed (see Harris, Petersen, & Diamond, 2001).

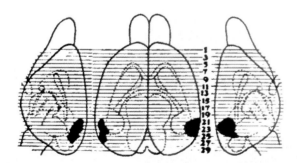

Lashley kept a careful record of the sizes and locations of lesions made in each rat as part of his experiments.

Credit: Lashley's sketches showing where he made incisions in rat brains, *Journal of Comparative Neurology,* K. S. Lashley, L. E. Wiley. Copyright © 1933 The Wistar Institute of Anatomy and Biology

milder form of *retrograde amnesia*, trouble retrieving existing memories from storage. Although H.M. had difficulty recalling what occurred during the few years leading up to his surgery (Scoville & Milner, 1957), he did remember events from the more distant past, for example, the 1929 stock market crash and the events of World War II (Carey, 2008).

H.M. maintained a working implicit memory, which he demonstrated in an experiment involving the complex task of tracing a pattern reflected in a mirror. With repeated practice sessions (none of which he remembered), H.M. improved his performance on the drawing task, learning it as well as someone without amnesia (Gabrieli, Corkin, Mickel, & Growdon, 1993). Clive can also acquire new implicit memories, but his ability is very limited. According to Deborah, it took years for Clive to learn how to get to his bedroom in the small community residence where he moved after leaving the hospital (Wearing, 2005).

THE ROLE OF THE HIPPOCAMPUS   Imagine you are a scientist trying to figure out exactly what role the hippocampus plays in memory. Consider the facts you know about H.M.: (1) He has virtually no hippocampus; (2) he has lost the ability to make new *explicit* memories, yet can create *implicit* memories; and (3) he can still tap into memories of the distant past. So what do you think the hippocampus does? Evidence suggests that the hippocampus is essential for creating new explicit memories but *not* implicit memories. Researchers have also shown that explicit memories are processed and stored in other parts of the brain, including the temporal lobes and areas of the frontal cortex (García-Lázaro, Ramirez-Carmona, Lara-Romero, & Roldan-Valadez, 2012).

As in H.M.'s case, Clive's ability to form explicit memories is profoundly compromised, largely a result of the destruction of his hippocampus. Yet Clive also struggles with the creation of implicit memories—not surprising given the extensive damage to other regions of his brain, such as the amygdala and temporal lobes (Wilson et al., 2008). Studies have zeroed in on other brain areas, such as the cerebellum and amygdala, as processing hubs for implicit memory (Thompson & Kim, 1996; Thompson & Steinmetz, 2009). The amygdala plays a central role in the processing of emotional memories (García-Lázaro et al., 2012). See Infographic 6.3 for more information about memory processing in the brain.

So although the hippocampus plays a central role in laying down new memories, it does not appear to serve as their ultimate destination. This process of memory formation, which moves a memory from the hippocampus to other areas of the brain, is called *memory consolidation* (Squire & Bayley, 2007). The consolidation that begins in the hippocampus allows for the long-term storage of memories. According to Kandel and Pittenger (1999): "The final locus of storage of memory is widely assumed to be the cerebral cortex, though this is a difficult assertion to prove" (p. 2041). As for retrieval, the hippocampus appears to be in charge of accessing young memories, but then passes on that responsibility to other brain regions as memories grow older (Smith & Squire, 2009).

This idea that the hippocampus is essential for creating explicit memories (as opposed to implicit memories) is supported by what we know about *infantile amnesia*, that is, the inability to remember events from our earliest years. Most adults cannot remember events before the age of 3, though it is not clear why. Some researchers suggest that it is because the hippocampus and frontal cortex, both important for the creation of long-term explicit memories, are not fully developed in children (Bauer, 2006; Willoughby, Desrocher, Levine, & Rovet, 2012).

This macrolevel perspective allows us to see the "big picture" of memory, but what's going on microscopically? The next section focuses on the important changes occurring in and between neurons.

Where Memories Live in the Brain: A Micro Perspective

LO 15 Describe long-term potentiation.

How does your brain change when you learn a new driving route to school? If we could peer into your skull, we might see a change in your hippocampus. As one study found, London taxicab drivers with greater time spent on the job had structural changes in some regions of the hippocampus, particularly to an area that processes "spatial knowledge" (Maguire, Woollett, & Spiers, 2006). Zooming in for a closer look, we might actually see changes at the level of the neuron. If you are looking for a memory imprint, the best place to look is the synapse.

LONG-TERM POTENTIATION As it turns out, the more neurons communicate with each other, the better the connections between them. **Long-term potentiation** occurs when sending neurons release neurotransmitters more effectively, and receiving neurons become more sensitive, boosting synaptic strength for days or even weeks (Lynch, 2002; Malenka & Nicoll, 1999; Whitlock, Heynen, Shuler, & Bear, 2006). In other words, long-term potentiation refers to the increased efficiency of neural communication over time, resulting in learning and the formation of memories. Researchers suggest long-term potentiation may be the biological basis of many kinds of learning. As you learn a new skill, for example, the neurons involved in performing that skill increase their communication with each other. It might start with a somewhat random firing of neurons, but eventually the neurons responsible for the new skill develop pathways through which they communicate more efficiently. Having trouble visualizing the process? Imagine this scenario: Your college has opened a new campus with an array of brand-new buildings, but it has yet to construct the sidewalks connecting them. In order to go from one class to the next, students have to wade through tall grass and weeds. All the trampling eventually gives way to a system of paths linking the buildings, including a multitude of efficient paths that develop among them. Long-term potentiation of neural connections occurs in a similar fashion: over time, the communication among neurons improves and strengthens, allowing for the skill to develop and become more natural (Whitlock et al., 2006). These paths represent how a skill, whether tying your shoes or driving a stick shift, is learned and thus becomes a memory.

APLYSIA Amazingly, we have learned much about long-term potentiation from the sea slug *Aplysia*. Why the sea slug? One reason is that *Aplysia* has only about 20,000 neurons (Kandel, 2009)—a little easier to work with than the 100 billion neurons of a human brain. The sea slug's neural simplicity, that is, the fact that the synapses are relatively easy to examine individually, also allows for the intensive study of habituation and other processes involved in classical conditioning. Studies using sea slugs as their subjects indicate that long-term potentiation, or increases in synaptic "strength," is associated with learning and memory. What can a sea slug learn? They can be classically conditioned to retract their gills in response to being squirted with water. Researchers report that when the sea slugs are conditioned in this way, there are structural changes in both presynaptic and postsynaptic cells, including changes to connections between neurons (Kandel, 2009)—evidence of long-term potentiation. So never, ever complain to your instructor that you cannot learn: If a sea slug can do it, so can you!

ALZHEIMER'S DISEASE On a less positive note, disruptions in long-term potentiation appear to be at work in *Alzheimer's disease,* a progressive, devastating brain illness that causes cognitive decline, including memory, language, and thinking problems. Alzheimer's affects as many as 5.1 million Americans (National Institute on Aging, 2013). The disease was first discovered by Alois Alzheimer, a German

CONNECTIONS

In **Chapter 2,** we introduced the synapse: the tiny gap between two neurons. Neurons communicate with each other via chemicals called neurotransmitters, which are released into the synapse. Here, we see how the activities at the neural level are related to the formation and maintenance of memories.

Smart Slug

Studying the neurons of sea slugs, researchers have observed the synaptic changes that underlie memory. Long-term potentiation enables a sea slug to retract its gills in anticipation of being squirted with water. NaturePL/SuperStock

CONNECTIONS

In **Chapter 5,** we discussed classical conditioning and how a neutral stimulus can be paired with an unconditioned stimulus, ultimately leading to a conditioned stimulus resulting in a conditioned response. In the case of the sea slug, the squirt of water is the conditioned stimulus and its involuntary response of retracting its gills is the conditioned response.

neuropathologist, in the early 1900s. He had a patient with severe memory problems whose autopsy revealed that neurons in her brain were tangled like the wires of your earbud headphones. These *neurofibrillary tangles,* as they came to be called, were eventually shown to result from twisted protein fibers accumulating inside brain cells. In addition to the tangles, the other distinctive sign of Alzheimer's is the presence of *amyloid plaques,* protein clumps that build up between neurons, blocking their lines of communication (Vingtdeux, Davies, Dickson, & Marambaud, 2011).

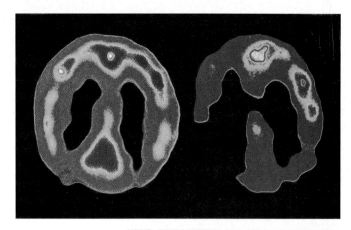

There is no cure for Alzheimer's disease, and current treatments focus only on reducing the severity of symptoms rather than correcting the brain damage responsible. But there is also reason to be hopeful. Promising new drugs are coming down the pipeline, and there is some preliminary evidence suggesting that simple lifestyle changes, like becoming more physically active and pursuing intellectually and socially stimulating activities, may actually decrease the speed and severity of cognitive decline (Hertzog, Kramer, Wilson, & Lindenberger, 2009, July/August; Wilson & Bennett, 2003). Additional good news comes from research suggesting that we should not think of cognitive decline as inevitable in aging. We have more control of aging than previously thought, especially when we focus on the lifelong possibilities of learning and autonomy (Hertzog et al., 2009). Furthermore, it's not only the strengthening of synapses that makes for enduring memories, but also the activation of new ones (Yu, Ponomarev, & Davis, 2004), and this process could offset cognitive decline (**Table 6.1**).

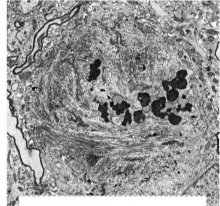

Inside Alzheimer's
The PET scan (top left) depicts the brain of a normal person, while the scan to its right shows that of a person with Alzheimer's. Studies using PET suggest a slowing of brain activity in certain regions of the Alzheimer's brain (Alzheimer's Association, 2013). The neurofibrillary tangles (bottom image, with tangles in pink) result from twisted protein fibers accumulating inside brain cells. top: Jessica Wilson/Science Source; bottom: Thomas Deerinck, NCMIR/Science Source

Apply This

TABLE 6.1 FACTS ABOUT MEMORY LOSS

There is no definitive way to know whether you or a family member will suffer from a neurocognitive disorder; most cases result from a complex combination of genetic, environmental, and lifestyle factors.

Studies of both animals and people have linked physical exercise to a variety of positive changes in the brain, including enhanced blood flow, increased thickness of the cortex, and less age-related deterioration of the hippocampus (Polidori, Nelles, & Pientka, 2010).

Some research suggests that people who begin exercising in their thirties (and stick with it) experience less cognitive decline than their sedentary peers by the time they reach their forties and fifties (Hertzog et al., 2009), although consistent exercise at any age has lasting cognitive benefits (Cotman & Berchtold, 2002; Kramer, Erickson, & Colcombe, 2006).

Intellectually engaging activities such as reading books and newspapers, writing, drawing, and solving crossword puzzles have been associated with a lower risk of memory loss (Hertzog et al., 2009; Wang, Karp, Winblad, & Fratiglioni, 2002).

Being socially active and hooked into social networks may reduce the risk of developing dementia (Fratiglioni, Paillard-Borg, & Winblad, 2004).

Memory loss needn't be an inevitable part of aging. Above are some facts you should know about memory.

Like many topics psychologists study, the biological mechanisms that give rise to memory remain somewhat mysterious. We know we have memories; we know they are formed in the brain; and we know the brain is a physical entity, yet we still don't know exactly how we go from a bunch of firing neurons to a vivid recollection of your 21st birthday bash, your high school prom, or the image of Bruno Mars banging on

long-term potentiation The increased efficiency of neural communication over time, resulting in learning and the formation of memories.

his drums at the Super Bowl halftime show. Studies attempting to test the various theories of memory formation are inconclusive, often generating more questions than answers. But one thing seems certain: Memory researchers have plenty of exciting work ahead.

✓○○ show what you know

1. _____ refers to the inability to lay down new long-term memories, generally resulting from damage to the brain.
   a. Anterograde amnesia
   b. Retrograde amnesia
   c. Infantile amnesia
   d. Long-term potentiation

2. The _____ is a pair of curved structures in the brain that play a central role in memory.
   a. engram   b. temporal lobe
   c. hippocampus   d. aplysia

3. _____ is the process of memory formation, which moves a memory from the hippocampus to other areas of the brain.
   a. Long-term potentiation   b. Memory consolidation
   c. Priming   d. The memory trace

4. Infantile amnesia makes it difficult for people to remember events that occurred before the age of 3. What is your earliest memory and how old were you when that event occurred?

✓ CHECK YOUR ANSWERS IN APPENDIX C.

FINAL THOUGHTS   At this point, you may be wondering what became of the two people featured in this chapter, Clive Wearing and Dorothea Seitz. After living in the hospital for 7 years, Clive moved to a country residence specially designed for people suffering from brain injuries. As he left the hospital, some of the staff members offered him a farewell and said they would miss him. Addressing them with a polite bow, Clive exclaimed, "You're the first people I've seen!" When Deborah would visit Clive in his new home, she found him happy and relaxed, spending much of his time on walks through gardens and the local village (Wearing, 2005, p. 293). In 2002 Clive and Deborah renewed their marriage vows. Clive participated fully in the service, reciting scripture he had memorized during his career as a professional singer decades before (D. Wearing, personal communication, June 10, 2013). After the ceremony, he had no recollection of what had taken place but nevertheless was very happy, laughing and devouring sponge cake (Wearing, 2005).

As for Dorothea, she succeeded in defending her title of Junior World Memory Champion in 2009 and finished the competition in 11th place overall. After completing high school, Dorothea spent a year doing volunteer work in Peru. She is currently studying political science and sociology in Freiburg, Germany.

Onward
(left) Nearly two decades after falling ill, Clive renewed his wedding vows with Deborah. Now in his seventies, Clive lives in a country residence for people suffering from brain injuries (Vennard, 2011, November 21). (right) Dorothea became the Junior World Memory Champion for the second time in 2009. Although she no longer competes in memory sport, she continues to exercise her intellect as a student of political science and sociology. left: Jiri Rezac/Polaris/ Newscom; right: © Ilona Huege

summary of conc

LO 1 Define memory. (p. 217)

Memory refers to the information collected and stored in the brain that is generally available for later use. Exactly how the brain absorbs information from the outside world and files it for later use is still not completely understood. However, scientists have proposed many theories and constructed various models to help explain how the brain processes, or works on, data on their way to becoming memories.

© Bob Jacobson/Corbis

LO 2 Identify the processes of encoding, storage, and retrieval in memory. (p. 217)

Encoding is the process through which new information enters our memory system. Information is taken in by our senses and converted into neural activity that travels to the brain, and if successfully encoded, it is stored. Storage preserves the information for possible recollection in the future. Retrieval is the process of accessing information stored in memory.

LO 3 Explain the stages of memory described by the information-processing model. (p. 219)

According to the information-processing model, the brain has three types of memory storage associated with the stages of memory: sensory memory, short-term memory, and long-term memory. The levels of processing framework suggests there is a hierarchy of stages that corresponds to different depths of information processing.

LO 4 Describe sensory memory. (p. 221)

Data picked up by the senses enter sensory memory, where sensations are registered. Here, almost exact copies of our sensations are processed for a very brief moment. Information from the outside world floods our sensory memory through multiple channels. Although this stage of memory is fleeting, it is critical to the creation of memories.

LO 5 Summarize short-term memory. (p. 224)

Short-term memory is the second stage of the original information-processing model. This is where information is temporarily maintained and processed before moving on to long-term memory or leaving the memory system. Short-term memory has a limited capacity; how long and how much it can hold depends on how much you are distracted by other cognitive activities. Through maintenance rehearsal, we can prolong short-term memory.

LO 6 Give examples of how we can use chunking our memory span. (p. 226)

Grouping numbers, letters, or other items into meaningful subsets, or "chunks," is an effective strategy for juggling and increasing the amount of information in short-term memory. In addition, chunking can help nudge the same information into long-term memory.

LO 7 Explain working memory and how it compares with short-term memory. (p. 226)

The active processing component of short-term memory, working memory, has four important parts. The phonological loop is responsible for working with verbal information for brief periods of time. The visuospatial sketchpad is where visual and spatial data are briefly stored and manipulated. The central executive directs attention, makes plans, coordinates activities, and determines what information should be ignored. The episodic buffer is where information from the phonological loop, visuospatial sketchpad, and long-term memory can all be brought together temporarily, as directed by the central executive.

LO 8 Describe long-term memory. (p. 229)

Long-term memory is a stage of memory with essentially unlimited capacity. Long-term memories may be explicit or implicit. Explicit memory is the type of memory you are aware of having and can consciously express, and can be further divided into semantic and episodic memory. Semantic memory pertains to general facts about the world, while episodic memory is your record of the memorable experiences in your life. Implicit memory is for something you know or you know how to do, but that might be automatic or unconscious, and therefore difficult to articulate.

LO 9 Illustrate how encoding specificity relates to retrieval cues. (p. 235)

Retrieval cues are stimuli that help you retrieve stored information that is difficult to access. The encoding specificity principle states that memories are more easily recalled when the context and cues at the time of encoding are similar to those at the time of retrieval. Thus, the context (external or internal) at the time of encoding and retrieval provides retrieval cues. Priming, recall, and recognition also play a role in the retrieval of stored information.

LO 10 Identify some of the reasons why we forget. (p. 239)

Memory failure may occur during any of the three stages of memory processing: encoding, storage, and retrieval. One example of memory failure is the tip-of-the-tongue phenomenon, which occurs when we cannot retrieve a stored memory.

LO 11 Explain how the malleability of memory influences the recall of events. (p. 243)

Eyewitness accounts are not always reliable because people's memories are far from perfect. Memories can change over time, which means we should be careful when questioning people about crimes and other events they have witnessed. Studies on the misinformation effect suggest that information obtained after an incident can distort one's memory of it.

LO 12 Define rich false memory. (p. 244)

Rich false memories are experienced as true recollections of an event, including details, emotions, and confidence that the event occurred, although it never did. Some researchers have implanted memories of events that never occurred.

LO 13 Compare and contrast anterograde and retrograde amnesia. (p. 247)

There are varying degrees of amnesia, or memory loss, due to medical or psychological conditions. Anterograde amnesia is the inability to "lay down" or create new long-term memories, and is generally caused by damage to the brain

resulting from surgery, alcohol, head trauma, or illness. Retrograde amnesia is an inability to access memories created before a brain injury or surgery.

LO 14 Identify the brain structures involved in memory. (p. 249)

Researchers have identified many brain structures involved in the processing and storage of memory. The hippocampus is essential for creating new explicit memories, as are the temporal lobes and frontal cortex. Other areas, such as the cerebellum and amygdala, are integral in the processing of implicit memories.

LO 15 Describe long-term potentiation. (p. 252)

Long-term potentiation refers to the increased efficiency of neural communication over time, resulting in learning and the formation of memories. The communication among neurons improves and strengthens, allowing for new skills to develop and become more natural. These new pathways explain how a skill, for example, is learned and thus becomes an implicit memory.

key terms

TEST PREP are you ready?

1. You try to remember the name of a movie you watched last year, but you are struggling. When you do finally remember it was *Lincoln*, which memory process were you using?
   a. short-term memory
   b. sensory memory
   c. encoding
   d. retrieval

2. According to the levels of processing framework, there is a _____ that corresponds to the depth at which information is processed, as well as reflecting how durable and retrievable a memory may be.
   a. hierarchy of processing
   b. computer metaphor
   c. method of loci
   d. phonological loop

3. Using the partial report method, Sperling (1960) showed that participants could recall 76% of the letters briefly flashed on a screen. The findings from this study indicate the capabilities of:
   a. eidetic imagery.
   b. depth of processing.
   c. iconic memory.
   d. the phonological loop.

4. Miller (1956) reviewed findings on the Digit Span test and found that short-term memory capacity is limited to between 5 and 9 numbers, that is, the "magical number seven, plus or minus two." However, through the use of _____, we can improve the span of our short-term memory.
   a. echoic memory
   b. iconic memory
   c. multitasking
   d. chunking

5. Baddeley and colleagues proposed that the purpose of _____ is to actively maintain information while the mind is performing complex tasks. The phonological loop, visuospatial sketchpad, central executive, and episodic buffer all play a role in this process.
   a. eidetic imagery
   b. working memory
   c. short-term memory
   d. semantic memory

6. In a classic study, Godden and Baddeley (1975) asked participants to learn lists of words under two conditions: while underwater and on dry land. Participants were better able to recall the information in the same context in which it was encoded. This finding supports:
   a. the encoding specificity principle.
   b. Baddeley's working memory model.
   c. the serial position effect.
   d. the information-processing model of memory.

7. Your friend tells you she prefers multiple-choice tests because she is able to identify an answer when she sees it listed as one of the choices for a question. She is describing her _____, which is the process of matching incoming data to information stored in long-term memory.
   a. relearning
   b. recall
   c. recognition
   d. retrieval

8. _____ causes problems with the retrieval of memories because of information you learned in the past and _____ causes problems with retrieval due to recently learned information.
   a. The recency effect; the primacy effect
   b. The primacy effect; the recency effect
   c. Proactive interference; retroactive interference
   d. Retroactive interference; proactive interference

9. According to _____, memories can fade over time, becoming more vulnerable to new information. Thus, your memory of an event might include revisions of what really happened.
   a. the information-processing model of memory
   b. the levels of processing framework
   c. Baddeley's model of working memory
   d. a reconstructionist model of memory

10. In studies by Loftus and colleagues, around 25% of participants are able to "remember" an event that never happened. This type of _____ shows us how the malleability of memory can influence recall.
    a. hyperthymestic syndrome
    b. rich false memory
    c. proactive interference
    d. serial position effect

11. In one study, Loftus and Palmer (1974) found that when they told participants two cars had "smashed" into each other, these same participants were more likely to report they had seen broken glass in a previously viewed film than participants who were told the cars had "hit" each other. This tendency for new and possibly deceptive information to distort one's memory of a past incident is known as:
    a. the misinformation effect.
    b. retroactive interference.
    c. proactive interference.
    d. the serial position effect.

12. Traumatic experiences that are thought to be pushed out of consciousness are often referred to as _____ memories.
    a. long-term
    b. short-term
    c. repressed
    d. sensory

13. Retrograde amnesia is generally caused by some sort of trauma to the brain. People with retrograde amnesia generally cannot:
    a. form memories of events that occur following the trauma.
    b. access memories of events created before the trauma.
    c. form semantic memories following the trauma.
    d. use procedural memories.

14. _____ refers to the increased efficiency of neural communication over time, resulting in learning and the formation of memories.
    a. Memory consolidation
    b. Long-term potentiation
    c. Memory trace
    d. Priming

15. The _____ is essential for creating new explicit memories, but not implicit memories.
    a. parietal lobe
    b. amygdala
    c. cerebellum
    d. hippocampus

16. A friend says, "My grandmother has terrible short-term memory. She can't remember anything from a couple of hours ago." This statement represents a very common mistake people make when discussing memory. How would you explain this confusion about short-term memory versus long-term memory?

17. How are iconic memory and echoic memory different from each other?

18. How does working memory differ from short-term memory?

19. Provide two examples of mnemonics you've used.

20. Imagine you are a teacher creating a list of classroom rules in case of an emergency. If you were expecting your students to remember these rules after only reading through them once, where in the list would you position the most important rules? Why?

✓ CHECK YOUR ANSWERS IN APPENDIX C.

Get personalized practice by logging into LaunchPad at www.macmillanhighered.com/launchpad/sciampresenting1e to take the LearningCurve adaptive quizzes for Chapter 6.

7

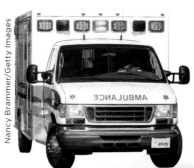

Nancy Brammer/Getty Images

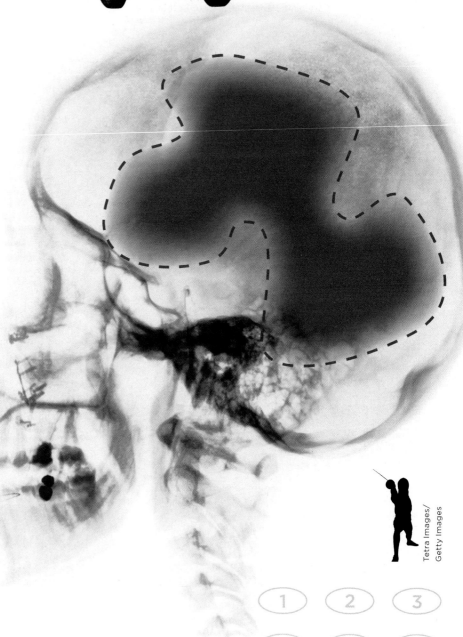

Stockbyte/Getty Images

Tetra Images/
Getty Images

cognition, language, and intelligence

londoneye/Getty Images

An Introduction to Cognition

BLEEDING BRAIN   December 10, 1996, was the day a blood vessel in Dr. Jill Bolte Taylor's brain began to bleed. At approximately 7:00 A.M., Dr. Jill awoke to a pain behind her left eye, a stabbing sensation she found similar to the "brain freeze" felt after a hasty gulp of ice cream. It seemed strange for a healthy 37-year-old woman to experience such a terrible headache, but Dr. Jill was not the type to lounge in bed all day. Pushing through the pain, she got up and climbed onto her exercise machine. But as soon as she began moving her limbs back and forth, a weird out-of-body sensation took hold. "I felt as though I was observing myself in motion, as in the playback of a memory," Dr. Jill writes in her book, *My Stroke of Insight.* "My fingers, as they grasped on to the handrail, looked like primitive claws" (Taylor, 2006, p. 37).

The Brain Scientist
An accomplished neuroanatomist, Dr. Jill Bolte Taylor had devoted her career to studying the brains of others. But one winter morning in 1996, she was given the frightening opportunity to observe her own brain in the midst of a meltdown. AJ Mast/ The New York Times/Redux

The pain, meanwhile, kept hammering away at the left side of her head. She stepped off the workout machine and headed toward the bathroom, but her steps seemed plodding, and maintaining balance demanded intense concentration. Finally reaching the shower, Dr. Jill propped herself against the wall and turned on the faucet, but the sound of the water splashing against the tub was not the soothing *whoosh* she had expected to hear. It was more like an earsplitting roar. Dr. Jill's brain was no longer processing sound in a normal way. For the first time that morning, she began to wonder if her brain was in serious trouble (Taylor, 2006).

"What is going on?" she thought. "What is happening in my brain?" (Taylor, 2006, p. 41). If anyone was poised to answer these questions, it was Dr. Jill herself. A devoted neuroanatomist, she spent her days studying neurons at a prestigious laboratory affiliated with Harvard Medical School. She now imagined herself rummaging through her mental library for any memories that might help diagnose her condition. This method of **recall** was something

CONNECTIONS

In **Chapter 6,** we presented the process of retrieval in memory. Dr. Taylor was having difficulty retrieving her memories. We assume that the information she was trying to access had been successfully encoded and stored prior to the stroke.

Story and quotations from *My Stroke of Insight,* by Jill Bolte Taylor, © 2006 by Jill Bolte Taylor. Used by permission of Viking Penguin, a division of Penguin Group (USA) Inc.

LEARNING OBJECTIVES After reading and studying this chapter, you should be able to:

LO 1 Define cognition and explain how it is related to thinking.

LO 2 Define concepts and identify how they are organized.

LO 3 Differentiate between formal concepts and natural concepts.

LO 4 Describe the biological processes associated with cognition.

LO 5 Explain how trial and error and algorithms can be used to solve problems.

LO 6 Identify different types of heuristics used to solve problems.

LO 7 Define decision making and explain how heuristics can lead us astray.

LO 8 Define language and give examples of its basic elements.

LO 9 Explain the linguistic relativity hypothesis and its relation to language and thought.

LO 10 Examine and distinguish among various theories of intelligence.

LO 11 Describe how intelligence is measured and identify important characteristics of assessment.

LO 12 Define creativity and its associated characteristics.

she habitually used, but all the files seemed to be locked. The knowledge was there, but she could not tap into it (Taylor, 2006).

Dr. Jill sensed that something was terribly wrong, but she could not help feeling mesmerized by the "tranquil euphoria" of her new state of consciousness. She no longer felt separate from the outside world. Like a fluid running fast and free, her body drifted in and out of surrounding space. Memories of the past floated into the distance, everyday worries evaporated, and the little voices in her mind that normally narrated her train of thought fell silent (Taylor, 2006).

Wading in a dreamlike fog, Dr. Jill managed to shower and put on clothes. Then, just as she began visualizing the journey to work, her right arm fell limp like a dead fish. It was paralyzed. At that moment she knew: "Oh my gosh, I'm having a stroke! I'm having a stroke!" (Taylor, 2006, p. 44). Her next thought was: "Wow this is so cool! . . . How many scientists have the opportunity to study their own brain function and mental deterioration from the inside out?" (p. 44).

Dr. Jill was indeed having a rare form of stroke caused by a defective linkage between blood vessels in the brain. This faulty connection in the central nervous system, known as an arteriovenous malformation (AVM), is present in a substantial number of people—about 300,000 in the United States alone (around 0.1% of the population). Most individuals born with AVMs are symptomless and unaware of their condition, but about 12% (36,000 people) experience effects ranging from annoying headaches to life-threatening brain bleeds like the kind Dr. Jill was experiencing (National Institute of Neurological Disorders and Stroke, 2015).

Dr. Jill, in Her Own Words:
http://qrs.ly/o74qslk

© 2016, Macmillan

Tangled
The tangled intersection of arteries (red) and veins (blue) is an arteriovenous malformation (AVM), the anatomical abnormality that led to Dr. Taylor's stroke. An AVM is essentially a clump of blood vessels that results when there are no capillaries linking arteries to veins. Sometimes the vessels of an AVM burst under pressure, allowing blood to pool in the brain; this is called a *hemorrhagic stroke* (American Stroke Association, 2012; National Institute of Neurological Disorders and Stroke, 2015).
Medical Body Scans/Science Source

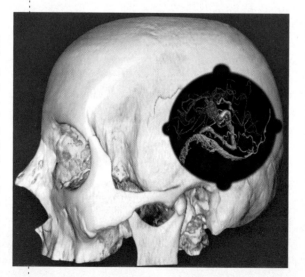

Having a backstage pass to her own stroke was a once-in-a-lifetime learning opportunity for a neuroanatomist, but it was also a serious condition requiring an immediate response. Aware of this urgency, Dr. Jill walked into her home office and took a seat by the phone, racking her brain for ideas of how to get help. The usual strategies like calling 911 or knocking on a neighbor's door simply did not cross her mind. As she gazed at the phone keypad, a string of digits materialized in her brain. It was the phone number of her mother in Indiana.

Calling her mom was certainly an option, but what would she say? Dr. Jill didn't want to worry her mother, so she sat and waited, hoping that another set of digits would appear (Taylor, 2006).

Finally, another number flickered by in two separate chunks—it was her work number. She scrawled the digits as fast as she could, but looking at what she had written, she only saw cryptic lines and curves. Fortunately, those lines and curves matched the figures she saw on the phone keypad. Dr. Jill picked up the receiver and dialed her coworker and friend, Dr. Stephen Vincent (Taylor, 2006). Steve answered the phone immediately, but his words were incomprehensible to Dr. Jill. "Oh my gosh, he sounds like a golden retriever!" she thought. Mustering all her mental might, she opened her mouth and said, "This is Jill, I need help!" Well, that's what she hoped she had said. Her own voice sounded like a golden retriever as well (Taylor, 2006, p. 56; TED.com, 2008). Luckily, Steve recognized that the murmurs and cries belonged to his friend Jill, and before long he was driving her to the hospital (Taylor, 2006).

As blood hemorrhaged into Dr. Jill's brain, she became increasingly unable to process sensory information, tap into memories, and use language. As she later reflected: "In the course of four hours, I watched my brain completely deteriorate in its ability to process all information" (TED.com, 2008). The bleeding was beginning to limit her capacity for cognition.

Cognition. You've probably heard the word tossed around in conversation, and perhaps you know that it has something to do with thinking. But what exactly do we mean by cognition, and where does it figure in the vast landscape of psychology? 📁

Cognition and Thinking

The study of cognition is deeply rooted in the history of psychology. Early psychologists were intensely focused on understanding the mysterious workings of the mind, often using introspection (examination of one's own conscious activities) in their studies. With the rise of behaviorism in the 1930s, the emphasis shifted away from internal processes and on to behavior. Researchers shunned the study of thoughts, emotions, and anything they could not observe or measure objectively. In the 1950s, psychologists once again began to probe the private affairs of the mind. Psychology experienced a *cognitive revolution,* and research on cognition and thinking has flourished ever since.

LO 1   Define cognition and explain how it is related to thinking.

Cognition is the mental activity associated with obtaining, converting, and using knowledge. But how is this different from *thinking?* Thinking is a specific type of cognition that requires us to "go beyond" information or to manipulate information to reach a goal. **Thinking** involves coming to a decision, reaching a solution, or forming a belief (Matlin, 2013). Cognition is a broad term that describes mental activity, and thinking is a subset of cognition. These definitions are not universally accepted, however; some psychologists consider cognition and thinking to be one and the same activity. Regardless of how the terms are defined, Dr. Jill was clearly experiencing significant impairments in both cognition and thinking on the morning of her stroke.

HOSPITAL HUBBUB   Upon arriving at Mount Auburn Hospital, Dr. Jill got a **computerized axial tomography** (CT or CAT) brain scan. The cross-sectional slices provided by the scan merged into a troubling picture: a giant hemorrhage in the left side of her brain. According to Dr. Jill, "My left hemisphere was swimming in a pool of blood and my entire brain was swollen in response to the trauma" (Taylor, 2006, p. 68).

CONNECTIONS

In **Chapter 1,** we introduced early psychologists who used *introspection* as a research method. Wundt used it to examine psychological processes experienced in response to stimuli. Titchener used introspection to determine the structure of the mind. Their work set the stage for the field of cognitive psychology, the study of mental processes, and *cognitive neuroscience,* which explores the physiological basis of mental processes.

CONNECTIONS

In **Chapter 2,** we described CAT scans. This technology uses X-rays to create cross-sectional "slices" of the brain that come together to form a three-dimensional image. CAT scans can detect tumors and brain damage and display the brain's structural features.

cognition The mental activity associated with obtaining, converting, and using knowledge.

thinking Mental activity associated with coming to a decision, reaching a solution, or forming a belief.

Bleeding Brain
The red zone on the right of the CT scan shows a hemorrhage on the left side of the brain. (Note that the patient's left is your right.) In Dr. Jill's case, the bleeding interfered with activity in Broca's and Wernicke's areas, impairing her ability to produce and understand language. Her frontal lobe function also deteriorated the morning of the stroke, as illustrated by the difficulty she had in devising a coherent strategy to get medical help.
Scott Camazine/Science Source

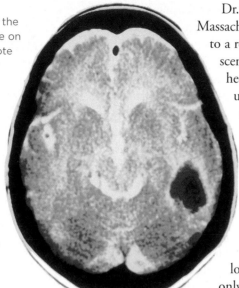

Dr. Jill was rushed by ambulance to the emergency room at Massachusetts General Hospital, where she was eventually assigned to a room in the neurological intensive care unit. The hospital scene, with its blinding lights and loud noises, was far too hectic for Dr. Jill's fragile sensory systems, which had become ultra-sensitive to stimulation. Light assaulted her eyes and scorched her brain "like fire" (Taylor, 2006, p. 67). Hospital workers grilled her with questions that seemed nothing more than a bewildering racket. "Sound streaming in through my ears blasted my brain senseless so that when people spoke, I could not distinguish their voices from the underlying clatter of the environment," she remembers (p. 75). Some of the hospital personnel, who didn't understand Dr. Jill's condition and were insensitive to her vulnerability, tried to communicate by speaking louder and louder, as if she were hearing impaired, but this only upset and confused her more. What she needed was for those addressing her to speak slowly, pronounce clearly, and show a bit of compassion (Taylor, 2006). Fortunately, the neurologist overseeing her case was one of the few people who saw what Dr. Jill needed. Dr. Anne Young looked into Dr. Jill's eyes, spoke quietly, and touched her body with respect. "Although I could not completely understand her words, I completely understood her intention," Dr. Jill recalls. "This woman understood that I was not stupid but that I was wounded" (p. 86). 📁

You Asked, Dr. Jill Answers

http://qrs.ly/6v4qsxf

How did you communicate thoughts and ideas to others when you weren't able to effectively express yourself?

Concepts

On Day 2 in the hospital, Steve told Dr. Jill that her mother, who went by the name of "G.G.," would be coming to visit. Dr. Jill found the news perplexing (Taylor, 2006). What on Earth was a *mother,* and who or what was a *G.G.?* "Initially, I didn't understand the significance of G.G.—as I had lost the *concept* of what a mother was," she writes (p. 88). The following day, G.G. appeared at the doorway, walked over to her daughter's bed, and climbed in alongside her. As Dr. Jill recalls, "She immediately wrapped me up in her arms and I melted into the familiarity of her snuggle" (p. 90).

LO 2   Define concepts and identify how they are organized.

Although the touch of G.G. felt familiar, the *concept* of her had slipped away, at least temporarily. *Concepts* are a central ingredient of cognitive activity, and are used in important processes such as memory, reasoning, and language (Slaney & Racine, 2011). **Concepts** are mental representations of *categories* of objects, situations, and ideas that belong together based on their central features or characteristics. The concept of *superhero,* for example, includes a variety of recognizable characteristics, such as: has supernatural powers, battles villains, protects innocent people, and wears unbecoming tights. Abstract concepts (such as love, belonging, and honesty) are far harder to pinpoint than concrete concepts (like animals, furniture, and telephones). Personal experiences and culture shape the construction of abstract concepts, and we don't always agree on their most important characteristics.

Without concepts, it would be quite difficult to understand the tidal wave of data flooding our brains every day. For example, we all know what *dessert* is. But if the concept *dessert* did not exist, we would have to describe all the characteristics that we expect of a dessert whenever one comes up in conversation: "Yesterday I ate the most delicious food—you know, those sweet-tasting, mouth-watering, high-calorie items

concepts Mental representations of categories of objects, situations, and ideas that belong together based on their central features or characteristics.
formal concepts The mental representations of categories that are created through rigid and logical rules or features.

typically consumed after lunch or dinner?" Thanks to our dessert concept, however, we can simply use the word "dessert" as shorthand for all of them. ("Yesterday I ate the most delicious dessert.") And even if someone offers you an unfamiliar dessert (for example, a chocolate tartelette), you still know that you are being offered a sweet food typically eaten after a meal. Concepts allow us to organize and synthesize information, and to draw conclusions about specific objects, situations, and ideas that we have never encountered before. Imagine how exhausting thinking and talking would be if we did not have concepts to fall back on.

HIERARCHIES OF CONCEPTS   One way to understand concepts is to consider how they can be organized in *hierarchies.* Generally, psychologists use a three-level concept hierarchy to categorize information.

At the top of the hierarchy are *superordinate* concepts. This is the broadest category, encompassing all the objects belonging to a concept. The superordinate concept of furniture is depicted at the top of the hierarchy in **Infographic 7.1** on the next page. This is a very broad group, including everything from couches to nightstands.

Narrowing our focus to include only couches, we are considering the *midlevel* or basic level of our hierarchy. This is still a fairly general grouping, but not as broad as a superordinate concept such as furniture.

Subordinate-level concepts are even narrower, in this case referring to specific types or instances of couches, such as a loveseat, a La-Z-Boy, or my own couch with crumbs between the cushions.

The midlevel category is what we use most often to identify objects in everyday experience. Most children learn the midlevel concepts first, followed by the superordinate and subordinate concepts (Mandler, 2008; Rosch, Mervis, Gray, Johnson, & Boyes-Braem, 1976). Although a child might grasp the meaning of *couch,* she may not understand *furniture* (the superordinate level) or *chaise lounge* (the subordinate level).

Reconstructing concept hierarchies was a formidable task for Dr. Jill, because so many of their layers had been washed away by the hemorrhage. But with hard work, relentless optimism, and the help of G.G., she slowly reconstructed concepts as diverse as *alphabet letters* and *tuna salad.* Using children's books like *The Puppy Who Wanted a Boy,* G.G. helped her daughter retrain her brain to read, and by putting together puzzles, Dr. Jill was able to recreate concepts such as *right side up* and *edge* (Taylor, 2006). A trip to the laundromat became a lesson in first-grade math concepts—and in the challenges of learning concepts all over again. Putting a few coins in her daughter's hand, G.G. posed the following question: "What's one plus one?" Perplexed, Dr. Jill came back with a more basic question: "What's a one?" (p. 108).

- -
LO 3   Differentiate between formal concepts and natural concepts.
- -

FORMAL CONCEPTS   Now let's take a look at the way concepts develop. **Formal concepts** are based on rigid and logical rules (or "features" of a concept). When a child learns that 1 is an odd number because, like all other odd numbers, it cannot be divided evenly by 2 without a remainder, she is developing a simple formal concept. An object, idea, or situation must explicitly adhere to strict criteria in order to meet the definition of a particular formal concept. Science uses formal concepts to develop laws, theorems, and rules. Formal concepts introduced in this textbook include the pitch of a sound (defined by the frequency of the sound wave) and iconic memory (with a span of less than 1 second).

Mouthwatering Concepts
Which dessert do you prefer: the American sundae (middle), the Turkish baklava (left), or the French tart (right)? You may not have tasted every one of these desserts, but you know they are sweet foods eaten after meals because you have developed a "dessert" concept.
left: Shutterstock; middle: M. Unal Ozmen/Shutterstock. com; right: Kheng Guan Toh/shutterstock.com

Synonyms
formal concepts artificial concepts

CONNECTIONS

In **Chapter 1,** we introduced *operational definitions,* which specify the precise manner in which a variable is defined and measured. Creating operational definitions for formal concepts is relatively straightforward, because they are already defined by rigid and logical rules. Natural concepts are more challenging, as experts do not always agree on how to define or measure them.

Concepts and Prototypes

Concepts are used to organize information in a manner that helps us understand things even when we are encountering them for the first time. *Formal concepts*, like "circle," allow us to categorize objects and ideas in a very precise way— something either meets the criteria to be included in that category, or it doesn't. *Natural concepts* develop as a result of our everyday encounters, and vary according to our culture and individual experiences. We tend to use *prototypes*, ideal representations with features we associate most with a category, to identify members of natural concepts.

formal
CONCEPT
Defined by rigid, precise rules

A circle is a two-dimensional shape in which all points are the same distance from its center.

natural
CONCEPT
Defined by general characteristics established through everyday encounters

A couch is a large piece of furniture used for sitting.

Concepts can be organized into **HIERARCHIES**

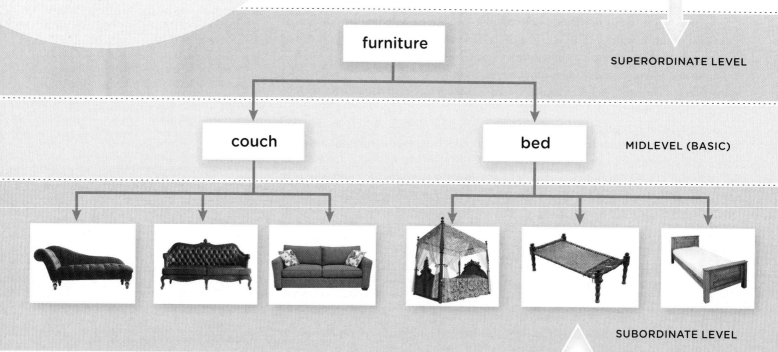

furniture — **SUPERORDINATE LEVEL**

couch   bed — **MIDLEVEL (BASIC)**

SUBORDINATE LEVEL

Did you think of this? Maybe not. But if you're from India, the traditional charpai may be your prototype—the first image that comes to mind when someone says "bed." What comes to mind when you think of the concept "fruit?" Researchers studying the development of categories organized a group of items from the most prototypical to the least prototypical (Rosch & Mervis, 1975). How long would it take you to think of an olive?

most prototypical

least prototypical

orange   apple   banana   strawberry   pineapple   lemon   date   coconut   tomato   olive

Credits: Vintage bed, Shutterstock; Two green olives, Shutterstock; Ripe pineapple, Shutterstock; Ripe orange, Shutterstock; Ripe banana, Shutterstock; Red apple, Shutterstock; Lemon, Shutterstock; Fresh tomato, Shutterstock; Fresh red strawberry, Shutterstock; Dried dates, Shutterstock; Coconut, Shutterstock; Black sofa, Shutterstock; Charpoy bedstead cot furniture, © Dinodia/age fotostock; 3D rendering of the canopy bed of Louis XV, Shutterstock; Red daybed, Thinkstoc Upholstered Sofa, Thinkstock

NATURAL CONCEPTS In contrast to formal concepts, **natural concepts** are defined by general characteristics and are acquired during the course of our daily lives (Rosch, 1973). Identifying objects that fall into such categories is more difficult because their boundaries are imprecise and harder to define; natural concepts don't have the same types of rigid rules for identification that formal concepts do (Hampton, 1998). This makes them more difficult to outline and therefore less useful in science.

Consider the natural concept of *mother.* Your concept of *mother* may be quite different from that of the person sitting next to you. What criteria do you use to determine if someone is a mother? Is it necessary for a person to get pregnant and have a baby? If so, the large group of women who adopt children are not included. What about someone who gives birth but then immediately puts the baby up for adoption—is she a mother?

PROTOTYPES In our daily use of natural concepts, we rely on **prototypes,** which are the ideal or most representative examples of natural concepts (Mervis & Rosch, 1981). Prototypes help us categorize or identify specific members of a concept. If you were asked to identify the ideal example of a mother, you might very well begin describing the characteristics of your *own* mother, because she is probably the mother with whom you are most familiar. If we asked you to name an example of a fruit, you would most likely say apple or orange—and *not* olive, unless, of course, you happen to be from Greece where olives are practically a staple. Infographic 7.1 presents a list of fruit organized from the most frequently suggested prototype—orange—to the least frequently suggested prototype—olive (Rosch & Mervis, 1975).

Items are easier to identify when they closely resemble prototypes. If shown an image of a papaya, many people in the United States would take longer to identify it as belonging to the fruit category than if they were shown an image of a peach (which is more similar to the common prototypes of apples and oranges). We suspect it would take them even longer to identify a durian or rambutan. Because natural concepts develop through daily experiences, prototypes vary from one person to the next. One study comparing adults in the United States and China found cross-cultural differences in the prototypical examples for mythological figures and tropical fish (Yoon et al., 2004).

We now know how the brain organizes information into meaningful categories, or concepts. But how is that information represented inside our heads, even for concepts related to people, places, and things that aren't present? With the help of *mental imagery,* another key ingredient of cognition, we see them in our mind's eye and imagine how they look, sound, smell, taste, and feel.

Mental Imagery

Dr. Taylor's stroke devastated certain aspects of her cognitive activity, such as language and memory. But some functions, like her ability to think visually, continued humming along quite smoothly (Taylor, 2006). If asked a question, she would search for answers in her arsenal of mental images. As Dr. Jill describes it, "Language with linear processing was out. But thinking in pictures was in" (p. 78).

When people try to describe cognitive activity, they often provide descriptions of images from the "mind's eye," or *mental images.* Try to imagine, for instance, where your cell phone is right now. Did a picture of your beloved mobile device suddenly materialize in your head? If so, you have just created a mental image. Whether contemplating the whereabouts of cell phones or daydreaming about celebrities walking the red carpet, our brains are constantly whipping up vivid pictures. These mental images are not two-dimensional scenes frozen in time. Our brains have an amazing knack for manipulating them in three dimensions.

natural concepts The mental representations of categories resulting from experiences in daily life.

prototype The ideal or most representative example of a natural concept; helps us categorize or identify specific members of a concept.

Let's consider what we do when we examine a *new* object for the first time. We typically hold it in our hands (if it's not too heavy) and rotate it to get a better sense of what we are looking at. If the object is too large to hold, we often walk around it to see how it looks from various angles. Researchers are particularly interested in finding out if we *mentally* behave this way as well, and they have spent a great deal of time studying mental imagery and the rotation of objects.

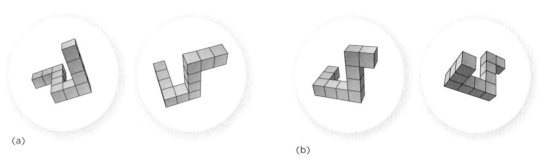

FIGURE 7.1

Manipulating Mental Images
Can you tell which object pair is congruent? In order to figure this out, you must hold images of these figures in your mind and mentally manipulate them. (Answer at the bottom of page.)
Source: Shepard and Metzler (1971)

(a)

(b)

IMAGINING OBJECTS AND MAPS In one of the earliest studies on this topic, Roger Shepard and Jacqueline Metzler (1971) had eight participants look at 1,600 pairs of object drawings like those displayed in **Figure 7.1** and then asked them to mentally rotate one of the objects in the pair to determine if they were identical. In calculating the reaction times, the researchers discovered that the amount of time it took participants to rotate the object depended on the degree of difference between the orientations of the two objects. The greater the rotation, the longer it took participants to decide if the objects were identical.

The ability to mentally rotate objects is extremely useful in everyday life. Remember the last time you tried to fit a large piece of furniture through a doorway, squeeze rolling luggage into the overhead bin of an airplane, or cram just one more container of leftovers into an overflowing refrigerator. In each case, you probably relied on some type of mental rotation to plan how to get each of these objects into or through a small space.

Perhaps you have heard the stereotype that men outperform women when it comes to packing a car or trunk. Research does suggest that men are better than women in tasks requiring the mental rotation of objects (Collins & Kimura, 1997), but this disparity is not absolute. With practice, women may catch up. In one study, women who practiced mentally rotating objects while playing computer games showed greater improvement on measures of mental rotation than did the men (Cherney, 2008).

FIGURE 7.2

Scanning Mental Images
Researchers asked participants to imagine this fictional map and "find" objects there. As with a real object, it took longer to find objects that were farther apart. Source: Kosslyn, Ball, & Reiser (1978)

In another fascinating study on mental imagery, participants were instructed to study a map of a small fictional island (**Figure 7.2**). The researchers then asked them to close their eyes and imagine the map, first picturing one object (the hut) and then scanning across their mental image of the map until they "arrived" at a second object (the rock). The researchers found that it took longer for participants to "find" objects on the mental map when the objects were farther apart. As with the scanning of real objects, the amount of time it takes to scan a mental image is relative to the distances between the objects in the image (Kosslyn, Ball, & Reiser, 1978). In addition, Kosslyn (1978) suggests that the size of the image is connected to how much detail people can see in their mind's eye. Fewer details can be detected on smaller images.

AUDITORY IMAGERY Stop for a moment and imagine the smell of chocolate chip cookies baking in the oven, the tang of lemon on your tongue, or the sound of a cat meowing. It is important to remember that not all imagery is visual; other sensory experiences can be used to construct imagery in our minds. A review of research on auditory imagery indicated that auditory images are similar to true auditory stimuli (such as music and language) in their properties (for example, pitch and loudness), and that auditory images involve the brain regions used in auditory perception, such as Broca's area (Hubbard, 2010). Interestingly, auditory imagery is associated with a person's musical background and ability. When asked to think about two known song lyrics, study participants with musical training were better than other participants at identifying which of the songs would be sung at a higher pitch (Janata & Paroo, 2006).

We use mental images all the time—so often it's hard to conceive of thinking without them. Imagine reading this chapter without being able to visualize Dr. Jill staggering around her house the morning of her stroke. How would your brain interpret the description of Steve's voice sounding like a golden retriever if you could not "hear" the sound in your mind? Mental images, like concepts, lie at the heart of cognition.

Every cognitive activity we have discussed thus far, from establishing prototypes of fruit to mentally rotating leftovers in the refrigerator, is made possible by the electric and chemical bustle of billions of neurons. Let's dive into that bustle and get acquainted with the biology of cognition.

Biology of Cognition

LO 4   Describe the biological processes associated with cognition.

Dr. Jill's story provides a stark illustration of the following principle: If the brain's biological integrity is compromised, cognition is likely to suffer. The bleeding in her brain began in a small region on the left side of her cerebral cortex but soon spread across large areas of her brain (Taylor, 2006). Among those affected was her left frontal lobe, a part of the brain critical for a broad array of higher cognitive functions such as processing emotions, controlling impulses, and making plans. Remember that Dr. Jill experienced enormous difficulty devising a simple plan to save her own life (for example, she was unable to think of calling 911).

The stroke also ravaged brain regions critical for another major element of cognition: language processing. "As the blood interrupted the flow of information transmission between my two language centers (Broca's anteriorly and Wernicke's posteriorly). . . . I could neither create/express language nor understand it," Dr. Jill recalls in her book (Taylor, 2006, p. 62). Broca's and Wernicke's areas work with other parts of the brain to generate and understand language.

COGNITION AND NEURONS   The biology of cognition can also be observed on a micro scale. Normally, changes at the level of neurons make it possible to store and retrieve information—like how to call 911 in a dire emergency. Apparently, the stroke had interfered with neurons involved in the retrieval of memories. It is also at the neuronal level where we see the amazing plasticity of the brain at work. Following a stroke, healing and regeneration begin with changes to neurons. These changes include greater excitability of the neurons, rewiring to take advantage of both hemispheres, increases in dendritic connections, and increased efficiency of connections at the synapses (Dobkin, 2005).

MEASURING COGNITION IN THE BRAIN   Reading Dr. Jill's CT scans, the doctors were able to see the cause of all these cognitive malfunctions—an enormous hemorrhage on the left side of her brain: "It didn't take someone with a Ph.D. in neuroanatomy to figure out that the huge white hole in the middle of the brain scan didn't belong there!" (Taylor, 2006, p. 68).

CONNECTIONS

In **Chapter 1,** we emphatically noted that a correlation does not prove a cause-and-effect link between variables. Here, we need to determine if musical training made participants better at identifying the pitch, or whether some other *third factor* was involved. Perhaps the musicians had better auditory abilities to begin with and decided to study music because of that.

CONNECTIONS

In **Chapter 2,** we described the *association areas,* which integrate information from all over the brain. Dr. Taylor's stroke impacted her ability to use language, presumably by disrupting the normal activities of two association areas: Broca's area, pivotal for speech production, and Wernicke's area, for language comprehension.

CONNECTIONS

In **Chapter 6,** we described how learning and memory are evident at the neural level. Through the process of *long-term potentiation,* communication between sending and receiving neurons is enhanced. This increased synaptic strength facilitates learning and memory formation, and is apparent in the aftermath of a stroke.

Technologies such as CT are extremely useful for detecting abnormalities like strokes and tumors, but they also tell us a lot about normal cognitive functioning. Many interesting studies on cognition have investigated the biological basis of mental imagery. As it turns out, the brain often displays similar patterns of activity, whether we are imagining something or seeing it in real life.

In one study, researchers implanted electrodes in the brains of participants with severe epilepsy. This allowed the researchers to monitor individual neurons as participants looked at houses, animals, famous people, and other images. They found that some neurons responded to certain objects but not to others. A neuron would fire when the participant was looking at a picture of a baseball but not at an image of a face, for example. The researchers could identify the image the person was viewing simply by observing his brain activity. They also observed that *the same* neurons that became excited when the person was looking at an actual object also were active when the person was merely imagining that object (Kreiman, Koch, & Fried, 2000).

Using technologies such as PET and fMRI, researchers have found that the visual cortex can be activated by mental imagery as well as by external stimuli (Ganis, Thompson, & Kosslyn, 2004). Information (from either an external stimulus or a mental image) is processed by the visual cortex, which works with other areas of the brain to identify images based on knowledge stored in memory. Researchers have noted that similar areas of the frontal and parietal regions of the brain are activated when study participants look at, for example, an image of a tree *and* when they imagine a tree. Once again, it appears that perception and imagery use many of the same neural mechanisms (Ganis et al., 2004).

Gender and Cognition

Clearly, there are substantial biological differences between men and women, but how do the sexes compare in their cognitive abilities? In childhood, girls tend to perform better on tests of verbal ability, but the discrepancies are so small that they don't provide useful information for making educational decisions (Hyde & Linn, 1988; Wallentin, 2009). Meanwhile, boys are able to mentally rotate objects earlier in infancy than girls (Moore & Johnson, 2008). But differences in cognitive development between boys and girls are "minimal," and are only responsible for a small proportion of the variability in children's scores on cognitive tasks (Ardila, Rosselli, Matute, & Inozemtseva, 2011).

Research suggests that some cognitive gender disparities carry over into adulthood, with women outperforming men in verbal tasks and men showing greater spatial and mathematical abilities. These gender differences have declined over the past several decades, suggesting changes in sociocultural factors are at work, such as greater availability of advanced math courses and more support for both men and women to pursue careers that interest them (Deary, Penke, & Johnson, 2010; Wai, Cacchio, Putallaz, & Makel, 2010). When it comes to mathematics performance in children, gender is not the best future indicator; environmental factors such as mother's education, the learning environment of the home, and effectiveness of the elementary school are "far stronger predictors" (Lindberg, Hyde, Petersen, & Linn, 2010).

CONNECTIONS

In **Chapter 2,** we reported that the visual cortex is the part of the brain where visual information is received, interpreted, and processed. Here, we see that the information processed by the visual cortex does not always arise from visual stimuli.

CONNECTIONS

In **Chapter 2,** we learned there are many similarities between male and female brains, but some disparities do exist. The differences in brain function, although biological, can also be explained in terms of experience and its effect on the brain's structure and function.

 show what you know

1. _____ is the mental activity associated with obtaining, converting, and using knowledge.

2. If you were to define the _____ of *superhero,* you might suggest that characters in this category have supernatural powers, battle villains, and protect people.
   a. cognition
   b. concept
   c. hierarchy
   d. mental imagery

3. Your instructor explains that the pitch of a sound is defined by the frequency of the sound wave. She is describing a _____, which is created through rigid rules or features.
   a. prototype
   b. natural concept
   c. formal concept
   d. cognition

4. Give two examples of how biology is associated with cognition.

✓ CHECK YOUR ANSWERS IN APPENDIX C.

Problem Solving and Decision Making

THE BIG DILEMMA   On Day 3 at the hospital, a team of doctors arrived at Dr. Jill's bedside to discuss the possibility of performing surgery. One of the doctors, an expert in AVMs (the blood vessel abnormality responsible for her stroke), informed Dr. Jill that there was a blood clot as big as a "golf ball" on the left side of her brain. Both the clot and the remainder of the AVM needed to be extracted; otherwise, she risked suffering another stroke (Taylor, 2006).

Dr. Jill did not understand much of what she heard from the doctors because her language-processing neurons were, as she puts it, "swimming in a pool of blood" (Taylor, 2006, p. 91). But she did catch the part about slicing open her skull, a prospect that she found quite unappealing. "Any self-respecting neuroanatomist would *never* allow anyone to cut their head open!" she writes (p. 91). Dr. Jill had good reason to worry, for brain surgery is not without risks. When surgeons go into the brain to fix one problem, there is always the possibility that they will unintentionally create a new one. No one could be certain of the operation's outcome.

Dr. Jill had a very big problem on her hands and a very important decision to make. This section of the chapter is devoted to problem solving and decision making, two distinct yet tightly interwoven topics. Read carefully: The knowledge we are about to share may be very useful to you. Understanding problems and how they are solved can make life's difficulties a lot more manageable. ▶

What's the Problem?

Have you ever considered the multitude of problems you encounter and solve every day? Problems crop up when something gets in the way of a goal, like a computer crashing when you are racing to finish a project or a tricky scheduling situation at work. Problems range from the mundane (*my profile picture on Facebook is old*) to the potentially overwhelming (*I have a life-threatening brain bleed*). In psychology, **problem solving** refers to the variety of approaches we can use to achieve a goal.

COMPONENTS OF PROBLEM SOLVING Problem solving has intrigued psychologists for generations. Newell, Shaw, and Simon (1958) developed an information-processing model, suggesting that problem solving proceeds from an initial state (the situation at the start of a problem) to a goal state (the situation when the problem is solved; Matlin, 2013). Think about how this model applies to Dr. Jill. Her *initial state* included two very big problems: a massive blood clot and a troublesome clump of blood vessels in the left hemisphere of her brain. The *goal state* was maximizing her health, both physically and cognitively.

Another crucial component of problem solving is recognizing obstacles that block the path to a solution (Matlin, 2013). Think about a problem you want to solve and try to identify the initial state, the goal state, and the obstacles in your way. If your initial state is unfinished homework and your goal state is the completion of your homework in a timely manner, the obstacles might include the competing duties of household chores or something more internal, like sleepiness or lack of motivation.

STEPS TO SOLVING PROBLEMS The first step in problem solving is understanding the problem (see **Infographic 7.2** on the next page). If you can't identify or label a problem, then solving it is going to be difficult. Once you grasp the problem, you must choose one of many available approaches or strategies to tackle it. Which one you settle on—and the speed, accuracy, and success of your solution—will depend on many factors, including your fund of knowledge, your organization of knowledge, and the amount of time you spend assessing the problem (Ericsson, 2003; Goldstein, 2011).

"As soon as we solve one problem, another one appears. So let's keep this problem going for as long as we can!"

problem solving The variety of approaches that can be used to achieve a goal.

Problem Solving

Problem solving involves figuring out how to achieve a goal. Once you understand a problem, you can identify an approach to solving it. A successful approach will help you manage obstacles that come from the problem itself, such as a rigid deadline for an essay you're struggling to write. But sometimes the way we think about a problem can itself be a barrier, preventing us from identifying available approaches.

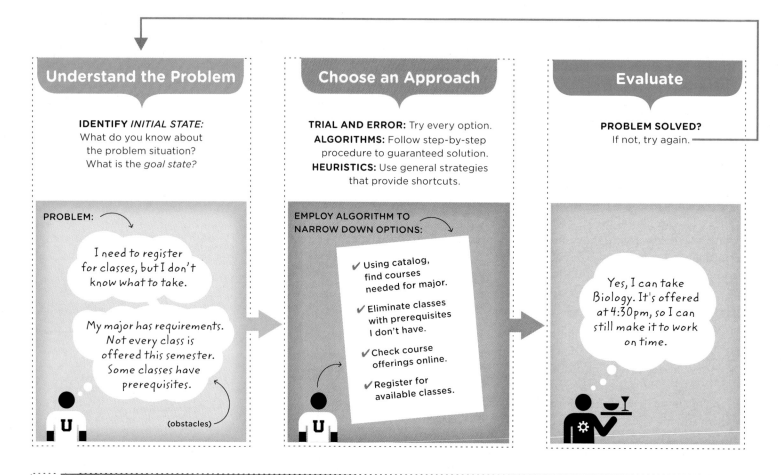

Understand the Problem

IDENTIFY *INITIAL STATE:*
What do you know about the problem situation?
What is the *goal state?*

PROBLEM:

I need to register for classes, but I don't know what to take.

My major has requirements. Not every class is offered this semester. Some classes have prerequisites.

(obstacles)

Choose an Approach

TRIAL AND ERROR: Try every option.
ALGORITHMS: Follow step-by-step procedure to guaranteed solution.
HEURISTICS: Use general strategies that provide shortcuts.

EMPLOY ALGORITHM TO NARROW DOWN OPTIONS:

✔ Using catalog, find courses needed for major.

✔ Eliminate classes with prerequisites I don't have.

✔ Check course offerings online.

✔ Register for available classes.

Evaluate

PROBLEM SOLVED?
If not, try again.

Yes, I can take Biology. It's offered at 4:30pm, so I can still make it to work on time.

Barriers to Problem Solving

Being stuck in a certain way of thinking about a problem can limit what we see as available approaches. For example, our student registering for classes may assume that "classes" must be in-person meetings with an instructor on campus. This assumption prevents the student from investigating more flexible online classes, hybrid classes, or classes that could be transferred from another college.

Sticking with our usual solution strategies is called a **mental set**. To see if you can overcome your mental set, try solving this problem:

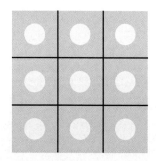

Without lifting your pencil, can you connect all nine dots using only 4 straight lines and without crossing any dot more than once? *(Solution on page 272.)*

Functional fixedness is another barrier in which we can only imagine using familiar objects in their usual way. Say you need to tie two ropes together, but you can't reach them both at the same time. Will functional fixedness keep you from solving this problem? *(Solution on page 274.)*

Problems are a constant part of life, but they are much easier to manage if we understand the strategies available to solve them. The aim of the upcoming discussion is to provide you with several approaches for solving problems, while also examining the various factors that come into play during the process.

Approaches to Problem Solving

LO 5   Explain how trial and error and algorithms can be used to solve problems.

TRIAL AND ERROR   One common approach to problem solving is **trial and error,** the process of finding a solution through a series of attempts. Mistakes will likely be made along the way, but attempts that don't work are simply eliminated. Let's say you have a HUGE set of keys and you have to unlock a door you don't use very often. With the trial-and-error approach, you would insert keys, one by one, hoping the correct key is on the ring. If one key doesn't work, then you move on to another, and if that key doesn't work, you try yet another key, and so on.

Trial and error is only useful in certain circumstances. It should not be used if the stakes are extremely high, particularly in situations where a wrong selection could be harmful or life-threatening. Imagine, for example, if Dr. Jill's physicians had used trial and error to figure out what procedure she needed. *Let's try this surgery first: If it doesn't work, we'll try a different one next week, and then another the following week.* When people's health and well-being are on the line, trial and error is clearly not the way to go.

Nor is this approach recommended for problems with too many possible solutions. If your keychain has 1,000 keys, you probably would not want to spend your time randomly selecting keys until one fits (potentially trying the same key more than once). Trial and error is somewhat of a gamble because there is no guarantee it will lead to a solution. By the way, computer hackers may use this approach to get your password and gain uninvited access to your digital world. More about this to come.

64,000 Combos
Forgot your lock combination? Trying to figure it out by trial and error is not an effective strategy, as there are 64,000 possible solutions. Better buy a new lock. Pixel Embargo/shutterstock.com

ALGORITHMS   If you're looking for a problem-solving approach that is more of a sure thing, an *algorithm* is probably your best bet. **Algorithms** (al-gə-ri-thəmz) use formulas or sets of rules that provide solutions to problems. Unlike trial and error, algorithms ensure a solution, as long as you follow all the steps. Suppose you are trying to figure out a 20% tip for a server at a restaurant. Here's an easy algorithm to calculate your tip—take the total amount of your bill, move the decimal to the left one space, and multiply by 2. This will result in 20% of your bill. This simple algorithm provides a guaranteed "correct" solution to the problem.

As reliable as algorithms may be, they are not always practical. If you don't know the algorithm's formula, you obviously cannot use it, and sometimes the steps may require too much time. Let's return to our example of computer hacking. After losing patience with trial and error, the hacker designs an algorithm that generates a series of possible passwords made up of letters, numbers, and symbols. Because algorithms guarantee solutions, the hacker eventually will generate your password. But the question is: Will it happen in this century? If you have chosen your password wisely, the algorithm may not work within a time frame that the hacker is willing—or able—to wait. For example, simply changing your eight-letter password by one character (lowercase to uppercase) and adding an * can increase a hacker's processing time from 2.4 days to 2.1 centuries (Mahmood, 2010, March 31). Ha ha, hacker!

trial and error An approach to problem solving that involves finding a solution through a series of attempts and eliminating those that do not work.

algorithm (al-gə-ri-thəm) An approach to problem solving using a formula or set of rules that, if followed, ensures a solution.

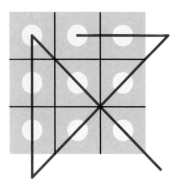

▲ **FIGURE 7.3**
Solution to the Dot Problem in Infographic 7.2
Did your mental set cause you to assume the square implied boundaries? If so, it may not have occurred to you that you could draw lines extending outside the square.

LO 6   Identify different types of heuristics used to solve problems.

HEURISTICS   If using an algorithm is not an option, which is often the case with everyday problems, we can turn to **heuristics** (hyü-ris-tiks). A heuristic is a problem-solving approach that employs a "rule of thumb" or broad application of a strategy. Although heuristics are not always reliable in their results, they do help us identify and evaluate possible solutions to our problems. Let's say you are cooking rice, but the instructions are unavailable. One good rule of thumb, is to use 2 cups of water for every cup of rice. Another heuristic is to put the rice in the pot and add water until it is one thumb-knuckle above the rice. But unlike algorithms, which use formulas and sets of rules, there is no guarantee a heuristic will yield a correct solution. The advantage of heuristics is that they allow you to shrink the pool of possible solutions to a size that is manageable.

Heuristics provide shortcuts, allowing you to ignore the many approaches you know will not work and move on to solutions more likely to be successful. But you might need to use trial and error to choose the best solution from that smaller pool of possibilities. A hacker might use a heuristic that combines a commonly used password (123456, password, football) and then add something from the domain itself. For example, if the hacker is trying to break into a Sony PlayStation account, her heuristic might be to try a variety of commonly used passwords and add "PS" at the end (123456PS, passwordPS, footballPS). She would then use trial and error until she breaks into the account. Most problems in life do not come with ready-made algorithms for reaching a correct solution, so we tend to fall back on heuristics.

Heuristics come in a variety of forms. One commonly used heuristic involves *creating subgoals* or *subproblems.* In the days following her stroke, Dr. Jill had a great deal of trouble moving her body. One of her main challenges was sitting up, but she was able to solve this problem "by breaking the effort of sitting up into the smaller steps of rocking and then rolling upward" (Taylor, 2006, p. 93). When writing your last term paper, did you break it into shorter, more achievable parts? If so, you were using this type of heuristic, which instructors often recommend to students.

Another frequently used heuristic is **means–ends analysis.** Here, you try to figure out how to decrease the distance between your goal and your current point in the process. You determine *how* to reach your goal (the means), which allows you to *solve the problem* (the end). Using means–ends analysis may also involve breaking your problem into subproblems that can be solved independently, incorporating the heuristic described in the last paragraph. The challenge is to decide which subproblem to address first. If you are struggling with your term paper, you must first identify the problem (finding appropriate support for your thesis) and then divide the problem into two subproblems: (1) identifying an appropriate database to search for articles in the field; and (2) finding a library where you can obtain and read the articles.

INSIGHT   Another manner of reaching a solution is through **insight,** an understanding that occurs in a sudden stroke of clarity (that oh-so-satisfying "aha!" moment). It can stem from experience solving previous problems, or it can be totally new. Insight often comes as a pleasant surprise because we are not aware of the mental "work" we did to achieve it.

Insight happens so suddenly that we sometimes say to ourselves: *Why did it take me so long to figure that out? The answer seems so obvious now.* Theories suggest that, without our conscious awareness, our minds are busy reorganizing the way the problem is represented, and this allows us suddenly and inexplicably to see things in a new light. Sometimes stepping away from a problem for a short time allows the solution to "suddenly appear" (Sio & Ormerod, 2009). There is evidence that activity in the frontal and temporal lobes immediately precedes the "aha!" moment (Kounios & Beeman, 2009).

heuristics (hyü-ris-tiks) Problem-solving approaches that incorporate a rule of thumb or broad application of a strategy.

means–ends analysis Heuristic used to determine how to decrease the distance between a goal (the means) and the current status, leading to the solution of a problem (the end).

insight An understanding or solution that occurs in a sudden stroke of clarity (the feeling of "aha!").

functional fixedness A barrier to problem solving that occurs when familiar objects can only be imagined to function in their normal or usual way.

Wolfgang Köhler, a Gestalt psychologist, made some remarkable discoveries on insight in chimpanzees. As early as 1913, he created various problems for chimps to solve. For example, Köhler put bananas just out of the chimps' reach, supplied them with various "tools" (crates, sticks, and so forth), and watched how they went about getting the bananas. The chimps were very clever; they stacked crates, used sticks, and managed to retrieve the bananas using what Köhler hypothesized was intelligence and insight (Köhler, 1925).

The Gestalt psychologists believed that humans and animals solve problems through perception and cognition—by creating mental representations of objects and their relationships (Whitman, 2011). To solve the banana problem, the chimp's mind reorganizes the relative positions of the banana-getting objects. We humans manipulate pictures in our minds in a similar fashion, and it requires no conscious effort. Ah, the beauty of insight.

I Want Bananas
In a classic study, Wolfgang Köhler provided chimpanzees with some out-of-reach bananas and materials that could potentially be used to fetch them. Resourceful chimps they were, building towers of crates and poking at the fruit with sticks. Rather than using trial and error to solve the problem, they seemed to rely on intelligence and insight. Wolfgang Köhler Papers/American Philosophical Society

Barriers to Problem Solving

With the capacity for insight, we can be masterful problem solvers. But as you probably know from personal experience, great ideas do not always materialize when we need them; there are many barriers to problem solving (Infographic 7.2). One such barrier is **functional fixedness,** which occurs when we can only imagine using familiar objects in their usual way. This *fixation* can hinder problem solving, because it stops us from being able to find other, creative uses for objects. Suppose the hem of your pants gets caught on something and the thread starts unraveling. A roll of tape and a stapler are on your desk, and both could be used to "fix" your wardrobe malfunction. But because of functional fixedness, you only view these items in their "usual" capacities. Children have less trouble with functional fixedness than adults because they have not become accustomed to using familiar objects in a fixed way (German & Defeyter, 2000).

Mental sets represent another barrier to problem solving. When faced with a problem, we tend to fall back on solution strategies we have always used—even if they don't work so well. For example, when your hem comes out of your pants, you grab a needle and thread because that is the solution you have always used. With mental sets, an approach that has worked in the past will often come immediately to mind and be reused, preventing us from seeing other solutions.

Emotional barriers can also get in the way of problem solving. If you are trying to figure out how to fix the dripping faucet and someone is peering over your shoulder saying, "Hurry up! What's taking you so long?" you may feel rushed, anxious, and annoyed. These negative emotions affect your ability to think clearly and creatively. Positive emotions, on the other hand, may set the stage for innovative thinking. Good feelings are thought to promote a "flexible" way of thinking, one that enables quick attention shifting and the ability to develop new strategies in response to a changing environment (Isen, 2008). Keep this in mind when you are trying to help someone solve a problem.

Think Outside the Box
Who knew that a paint roller could be used for holding toilet paper and that car tires doubled as planters? Sometimes it's hard to imagine using objects for unconventional purposes. Our resistance toward using familiar objects in new ways is known as *functional fixedness,* and it can get in the way of problem solving. left: Andrea Jones/Garden World Images/age fotostock; right: Andreas Schlegel/age fotostock

FIGURE 7.4
Solution to the Two-Rope Problem in Infographic 7.2
Using a shovel to create a pendulum will allow you to swing the second rope. When it swings near you, you can grab it and hold both ropes at the same time.
Shutterstock

Decisions, Decisions

UNDER THE KNIFE With the help of her mother's gentle coaxing, Dr. Jill made the decision to go through with surgery. On the afternoon of December 27, 1996, she awoke in the recovery room with the left side of her head shaved clean and a 9-inch wound in the shape of a horseshoe (Taylor, 2006). Dr. Jill had survived the operation, and she didn't feel drained and confused, as you might expect: "Upon awakening, I realized that I felt different now. There was brightness in my spirit again and I felt happy" (p. 112).

"Say something!" demanded G.G., as she approached her daughter's bedside (Taylor, 2006, p. 113). G.G. needed to know that her daughter could still use language. Surgeons had just spent hours poking around her left hemisphere, home to the language processing regions of Broca's and Wernicke's areas. The surgeons might have inadvertently short-circuited one of these key regions, compromising her ability to understand or produce words. Dr. Jill opened her mouth and responded, and she and G.G. both became teary-eyed. The operation appeared to have gone well; Dr. Jill, it seemed, had made the right decision (Taylor, 2006). 🗀

Post-Op
Dr. Jill poses with her mother, G.G., who played an instrumental role in the recovery process. When Dr. Jill emerged from surgery, G.G. was anxious to know whether her daughter's language-processing abilities were still intact. When Dr. Jill opened her mouth and spoke, it seemed clear that everything was going to be okay.
© My Stroke of Insight, Inc. Photo by Kip May

LO 7   Define decision making and explain how heuristics can lead us astray.

You may be wondering how decision making differs from problem solving. As you now know, problem solving refers to the variety of approaches we can use to achieve a goal. **Decision making** is the cognitive process of choosing from those alternative approaches. Thus, problem solving and decision making can occur at the same time.

PREDICTING THE FUTURE Decision making often involves predicting the future: What is the likelihood that Event A will occur under these circumstances? How about Event B? In cases like these, we can make an educated guess, but some situations lend themselves to more accurate guesses than others. If the weather channel predicts there is a 99% chance of thunderstorms today, it's fairly safe to assume it's going to rain. Better bring your umbrella.

decision making The cognitive process of choosing from alternatives that might be used to reach a goal.

availability heuristic A decision-making strategy that predicts the likelihood of something happening based on how easily a similar type of event from the past can be recalled.

But there are many times when predicting the future is like rolling dice—you have almost no way of knowing the outcome. Suppose you are searching for a used car on craigslist. How do you choose a "gently used" car from among the hundreds listed in your locality? With no prior knowledge of the cars or their owners (apart from whatever information they decide to post on craigslist), all you can do is hope the car you choose is not a lemon. But who knows if your gamble is going to work? Choices that hinge on predictions can be very risky, and we sometimes make the wrong decision.

SINGLE FEATURE   There are many ways to go about making decisions. One way is to focus on a single aspect, or feature, of the situation. Let's say you are trying to decide where to stop for gas. If your only criterion is cost, you will seek out the gas station with the cheapest gasoline, paying no attention to what kind of donuts they sell inside or how clean their bathroom may be. The *single feature* on which you are basing your decision (where to stop for gas) is the price of the fuel (not tasty donuts or a clean bathroom).

ADDITIVE MODEL   The single-feature approach may not be effective for making complex decisions, in which there are *many* features to consider. With a more complex decision, such as which car to purchase, you might create a list of the primary features you consider important (gas mileage, safety ratings, sound system, and so on). Using this list, you could rate each of the possible choices (for example, Ford Focus versus Toyota Prius) according to their features, and then tally these ratings to see which car comes out on top. This method of calculating the highest rating is often referred to as an *additive model* of decision making.

The Trouble with Heuristics and the Confirmation Bias

At the start of the section, we mentioned that decision making often involves making predictions, and different scenarios afford different levels of certainty about the future. Heuristics, which involve a rule of thumb or a broad application of a strategy, can help predict the probability of an event occurring. Unfortunately, heuristics can also lead us astray in our assessment of situations and prediction of outcomes. Daniel Kahneman and Amos Tversky (1973) were among the first to systematically research the ways in which heuristics can be ineffective. They found that people are prone to ignore important information while using heuristics (Kahneman & Tversky, 1996). This is particularly true for the *availability heuristic* and the *representativeness heuristic.*

THE AVAILABILITY HEURISTIC   Using the **availability heuristic,** we predict the probability of something happening in the future based on how easily we can recall a similar type of event from the past. The availability heuristic is essentially a decision-making strategy that relies on memory. If we can easily recall a certain event, then we tend to base our decisions on the assumption that it can happen again. Many factors make an event more available, including its recency, frequency, familiarity, and vividness. Let's look at each of these categories.

Imagine the year is 2010 and you have just learned about the mine collapse that left 33 Chilean workers trapped underground. If asked to predict the likelihood of a similar mining collapse occurring in the near future, your estimation would likely be higher than normal because you just heard about the Chilean incident. Our predictions using the availability heuristic are based on how easily we can recall similar events from the past, and the *more* recently a similar situation has occurred, the more easily it will be recalled. With an event still fresh in our minds, we are more likely to overestimate the odds of a similar event occurring in the future.

"Would you be interested in adding a few options?"

➤ **CONNECTIONS**

In **Chapter 6,** we described the *recency effect,* which is the tendency to remember items more accurately when they appear at the end of a list or series. Here, we discuss the tendency to remember *similar* events better if they have occurred recently.

Now imagine that you were asked to decide the following: Do more students at your college use Macs or PCs? Before deciding how to answer, you would probably think about the number of students you have seen using these types of computers and make an estimation based on that tally. In this case, the *frequency* of occurrence influences your decision. You rely on your recall of seeing students using computers in the halls, classrooms, and library. If you are in the graphic design department, for example, chances are you'll see more Macs than PCs. Based strictly on your observations from a single department, your sample would not be representative of the entire college, and the availability heuristic would lead you to the wrong answer. The availability heuristic can be accurate, but only when based on appropriate information.

The *familiarity* of an event might also lead to inaccurate estimates. If you and your friends are all avid PC users, you may overestimate the extent to which others are using PCs. The more familiar you are with a situation, the more likely you are to predict a similar occurrence in the future.

Finally, the *vividness* of an event can influence our recall. Try to conjure up an image of someone winning the "big one" at a casino. There are lights, sounds, and a lot of hubbub. The prizewinner jumps joyfully in the air, hollering and crying at the top of his lungs, with onlookers clapping and shouting in approval. This type of dramatic display never occurs when some poor guy loses his last $100; the details of a losing bet would consequently be far more difficult to recall. Because the winning image is more vivid, we are more likely to recall it and thus to overestimate the likelihood it will occur in our own lives. Memorable imagery leads us to believe that these types of wins happen all the time, when in fact they are very rare. If an event has made a striking impression on you, even a rare occurrence such as an airplane crash, you will be more likely to overestimate the probability of it happening again (Tversky & Kahneman, 1982).

CONNECTIONS

In **Chapter 1**, we discussed the importance of using a *representative sample* for making generalizations from a sample to the population. With the use of the availability heuristic, we must be careful that the sample used is representative; sometimes the memories in our "sample" are not randomly selected. Instead, they are chosen because of their recency, frequency, familiarity, and vividness.

THINK again

Fearing the Friendly Skies

Are people generally more afraid of flying in an airplane or riding in a car? Airplanes seem frightening to many people, yet the statistics suggest we should be more concerned about driving. The odds of getting into a fatal traffic accident are 1 in 98, compared to about 1 in 7,000 for a plane crash (National Safety Council, 2012).

Now consider the weeks and months following the terrorist attacks of September 11, 2001. How did people feel about flying after seeing what happened to the hijacked planes on the news? Countless people stayed away from airports and airplanes. So many would-be air travelers took to the roads after 9/11 that there was a temporary surge in traffic fatalities. In the 3 months following September 11, more people died in car accidents (apparently trying to avoid air travel) than did in the four hijacked airplanes (Gigerenzer, 2004). In this unfortunate case, people were increasing their risk of death by trying to reduce it.

Risk perception is complex. A number of factors contribute to an overblown fear of flying. The fact that airplane crashes and terrorist attacks are beyond one's control and represent the potential for enormous disaster tends to increase many people's perceptions of risk (Slovic & Weber, 2002, April). And, as we've learned from our earlier discussion of the availability heuristic, people tend to deem events more probable when similar scenarios are easy to recall. 💭+

SIT BACK, RELAX AND ENJOY THE FLIGHT

Safer Than Your Car
The odds of dying in a plane crash are extremely low—lower than perishing in a fall, a drowning incident, or a car accident (National Safety Council, 2012). Still, many people are petrified of flying. This is partly a result of the availability heuristic; we tend to overestimate the likelihood of events that easily spring to mind. ssuaphotos/shutterstock.com

THE REPRESENTATIVENESS HEURISTIC   Sometimes we have to make decisions based on our judgment of a situation or person. The **representativeness heuristic** evaluates the degree to which their primary characteristics are similar to our prototypes. With the representativeness heuristic, we make quick, effortless judgments about how closely a person or situation fits our preconceived prototype (Shah & Oppenheimer, 2008). In contrast, the availability heuristic requires us to access information from long-term memory and use it to make predictions about events.

Let's examine how the representativeness heuristic works in practice. Peter is a middle-aged man. He is conservative, a lovely speaker, thoughtful, and well read. He lives alone in an apartment in the city. Is Peter a truck driver or a poet? Forced to choose between these two occupations and using the representativeness heuristic, the majority of people would likely guess that Peter is a poet because his description better matches their prototype of a poet than their prototype of a truck driver. But this approach fails to consider the *base rate* (the prevalence of features or events in the population) of these occupations. There are far more truck drivers than poets, suggesting the better guess would be that Peter is a truck driver. The representativeness heuristic can be useful, but the accuracy of our information must also be taken into account; our conclusions should be drawn from base rates, not stereotypes. The other limitation of the representativeness heuristic is that prototypes are based on exposure to limited samples, which may not provide a good representation of the population.

THE CONFIRMATION BIAS   We can also miss important information through the **confirmation bias,** when we unintentionally look for evidence that upholds our beliefs. People tend to overlook or discount evidence that runs counter to their original beliefs or positions. For example, you decide to go on a date with someone you are *really* interested in, even though you don't know him very well. You Google stalk him and look on his Facebook page, and immediately connect with one of the "likes" he has. With this information in hand, you stop your search, convinced you now have evidence to support your decision to go out with him. We tend to focus on information that supports favorable outcomes (Krizan & Windschitl, 2007; Scherer, Windschitl, O'Rourke, & Smith, 2012), but what other sources of information could you use to avoid the confirmation bias in this case? The danger of the confirmation bias is that we miss or ignore relevant (and possibly contradictory) information without conscious intent; we don't deliberately set out looking for information to support what we already think.

"Give it to me straight, Doc. How long do I have to ignore your advice?"

You've Been Framed!

We have spent a great deal of time discussing factors that impede the decision maker. But in many situations, the characteristics of the problem itself, or the presentation of the problem, are to blame.

WHAT'S IN A FRAME?   The **framing effect** demonstrates how the presentation or context of a problem can influence the outcome of a decision. To look at this effect, researchers conducted a study in which they instructed participants to imagine that they had purchased a $10 ticket to attend a show, but lost their ticket on the way to the theater. Each participant was then asked whether he or she would be willing to pay $10 for another ticket. Only 46% of participants indicated that they would spend another $10 for a new ticket. Participants were next instructed to imagine another situation: In it, they planned to buy a $10 ticket to attend a show, but once they got in the ticket line, they suddenly realized that they had lost one of their $10 bills. Faced with this second scenario, 88% of the participants were willing to fork over the $10. In each case, the participants were faced with the proposition of spending an additional and unexpected $10, but they tended to make different decisions in

representativeness heuristic
A decision-making strategy used to evaluate the degree to which the primary characteristics of a person or situation are similar to our prototype of that type of person or situation.

confirmation bias   The tendency to look for evidence that upholds our beliefs and overlook evidence that runs counter to them.

framing effect   Occurs when the wording of questions or the context of a problem influences the outcome of a decision.

response to the different circumstances. The background information framing these hypothetical scenarios influenced the decisions made, even though the outcomes would have been identical—a net loss of $10 (Kahneman & Tversky, 1984; Tversky & Kahneman, 1981).

WHAT'S IN A QUESTION?   The specific wording of questions should also be considered. One study found that people are more likely to prefer ground beef if it is described as "80% lean," as opposed to "20% fat." Although 80% lean and 20% fat describe exactly the same product, these phrases evoke very different responses (Johnson, 1987). Another study investigated the effects of question framing on women using a telephone-based counseling service to inquire about the side effects of drugs taken during pregnancy (Jasper, Goel, Einarson, Gallo, & Koren, 2001). The women calling in were assigned to one of two groups. Members of the first group were told that "in every pregnancy there is a 1% to 3% chance that a woman will give birth to a child who has a major birth defect. This drug has not been shown to change that" (p. 1237). Women in the second group were told that "in every pregnancy, there is a 97–99% chance that a woman will give birth to a child who does not have a major birth defect. This drug has not been shown to change that" (p. 1237). The researchers then followed up with a series of questions. Participants in the first group believed that they faced a greater risk of bearing a child with a birth defect if they had taken the drug than those in the second group. Decision making is often influenced by whether a question is worded in a positive way (the glass is half full) or in a negative way (the glass is half empty) (Huber, Neale, & Northcraft, 1987).

THINK again

Let Them Eat Cake

Decisions can also be influenced by how much we have "on our plate" at a given time. Imagine making a decision when you are trying to cook dinner, watch the nightly news, and discipline your dog all at the same time. External demands can have a powerful impact on how we make decisions. In one study, researchers asked a group of participants to memorize two numbers and another group to keep a string of seven numbers in their minds. Meanwhile, both groups were offered the choice of fruit or chocolate cake. Surprisingly, the people who only had to memorize the two numbers selected the fruit every time, whereas those trying to remember the string of seven numbers tended to choose the cake (Shiv & Fedorikhin, 1999)! What this suggests is that our stress level impacts our decisions—and not in a way that benefits our waistlines.

HOW MUCH DO YOU HAVE ON YOUR PLATE?

show what you know

1. Imagine it is the first day of classes, but you forgot to write down the number of the room where your psychology class is meeting. You decide you will try to find your classroom by sticking your head in a random number of rooms until you see the assigned psychology textbook on someone's desk. This approach to finding your classroom uses:

   a. means–ends analysis.   b. an algorithm.
   c. trial and error.   d. heuristics.

2. One assignment in your psychology class is to design an experiment. Describe how you would use means–ends analysis to choose a topic for your experiment and write a review of the literature.

3. _____ refers to the cognitive process of choosing from a variety of alternatives you might use to reach your goal.

4. We often predict the probability of an event happening in the future based on how easily we can recall a similar type of event from the past. This is known as the:

   a. framing effect.
   b. confirmation bias.
   c. representativeness heuristic.
   d. availability heuristic.

5. A good friend is terrified of flying. How would you use your knowledge of heuristics to make him feel less afraid?

✓ CHECK YOUR ANSWERS IN APPENDIX C.

Language

ELVES, PIRATES, AND READING TROUBLES   Right around the time that Dr. Jill Bolte Taylor's life was uprooted by a massive brain hemorrhage, an aspiring actor by the name of Orlando Bloom was launching his career on the big screen. In 1997 the 19-year-old native of Canterbury, Kent, England, made his first appearance in a major film, playing a small part in *Wilde,* a movie about the life of playwright and poet Oscar Wilde (Braun, 2015). A couple of years later, the young Orlando was riding horseback through the rolling hills of New Zealand and shooting arrows at goblinlike *orcs,* playing the role of a pointy-eared elf named Legolas Greenleaf in a film trilogy that would make him a superstar: *The Lord of the Rings.* Not long after battling evil alongside hobbits and wizards, Orlando dueled with villainous pirates in another blockbuster film series: *Pirates of the Caribbean.* Now, with many major motion pictures under his belt, Orlando is one of the top actors in Hollywood (Braun, 2015; Sella, 2005).

Starring in adventure films requires extensive training in sword fighting, archery, and martial arts, but according to those who have seen Orlando in action, the athletic demands of the job are not an issue. "Orlando is all physical grace," says fellow actor Liam Neeson (Sella, 2005, para. 39). Acting also presents a major *cognitive* challenge, as it requires reading and memorizing thousands of lines. This part of the job may not come so easily for Orlando, however, because he has dyslexia.

Dyslexia, or specific reading disability, is characterized by difficulty reading, writing, spelling, and/or pronouncing (International Dyslexia Association, 2015). Although people with dyslexia struggle with reading, all the presumed prerequisites for good reading (adequate intelligence and eyesight, desire to learn, access to good instruction, for example) appear to be in place. Yet, the person still has trouble mastering fundamental skills (Shaywitz, 1996; Shaywitz & Shaywitz, 2005).

School was an endless struggle for Orlando. "Homework was always hard for me. Writing essays . . . getting my thoughts on the page, it was so difficult," he acknowledged in a 2010 interview with the Child Mind Institute (Freedom of Speech Ltd, 2014, March 10). Whenever it was time to read aloud in class, young Orlando would say that his throat was hurting, or that he felt ill—anything to avoid the embarrassment of reading before his peers (Child Mind Institute, 2010, October 18). Teachers didn't understand why Orlando was so distracted in class. As a progress report once said (according to Orlando): "If he would only stop looking out the window or into the hamster cage, we think he's probably a bright boy" (Child Mind Institute, 2010, October 18, para. 3). 📁

A-Lister
A close-up shot of Orlando Bloom during the Los Angeles premiere of *The Lord of The Rings: The Two Towers.* His performance as the elven character Legolas in *The Rings* trilogy established him as a major force in Hollywood. Gregg DeGuire/ WireImage/Getty Images

Synonyms
dyslexia developmental reading disorder

The impact of dyslexia can be far-reaching. In order to write an essay on a novel in English class, you have to read the book. To answer word problems in math, you must understand the written part of the question. Every standardized test requires fast and fluid reading. So many aspects of modern life reflect a general assumption that every adult knows how to read.

When dyslexia was first recognized over a century ago, many people assumed children fell behind in reading because they were ignorant or lazy, or had bad teachers (Shaywitz, 2003; Wolf, 2007; Zimmerman, 2014, June 19). Scientists have since discovered that dyslexia is rooted in the brain. With scanning technologies such as fMRI, scientists can examine the brain of someone with dyslexia as she reads, writes, or speaks. "We now know exactly where and how dyslexia manifests itself in the brain," writes dyslexia researcher Sally Shaywitz (2003, p. 4). Dyslexia, the evidence suggests, is caused by defects in the brain's ability to retrieve and manipulate certain components of language (Démonet, Taylor, & Chaix, 2004).

The Power of Language

Language is an amazing ability. Try to imagine human relationships in its absence. There would be no saying "What's wrong?" or "I love you." Language gives us the power to explicitly convey complex thoughts and feelings to others, and that is a remarkable feat.

LO 8   Define language and give examples of its basic elements.

Language can be defined as a system for using symbols to think and communicate. These symbols are words, gestures, or sounds put together according to specific rules. While a small number of words are onomatopoetic—or formed by sounds that resemble the realities they represent ("plop" to signify something dropping into the water)—the majority of the words we use are just arbitrary symbols that don't match their content (Pinker, 1994). Within a language, speakers generally agree on the meaning of these symbols, and use them to think, solve problems, make decisions, and daydream. Language is the ultimate medium for creativity. We can use words, gestures, and sounds to create an infinite number of statements.

> **try this**   Construct as many sentences as you can that include the following words: "giraffe," "kitten," "blue," "pretty," "rough," "run."

The average English speaker is familiar with some 30,000 (Lessmoellmann, 2006, October 4) to 60,000 words (Pinker, 1994). What's more, humans are always finding new meanings for old words or inventing new ones. If we say "apple product," for example, we could be referring to a crunchy red fruit or to a fancy new computer. Just think of how many new words have come from the use of digital technologies like text messaging and social media. Do you know what "friend farming" is? (We didn't, btw.) It is the "practice of adding many contacts (on Facebook or other social media) by using a list of another person's friends" (*Merriam-Webster's Open Dictionary,* n.d.). Another example, "phonecrastinate," means "to put off answering the phone until caller ID displays the name and number" (*Merriam-Webster's Open Dictionary,* n.d.).

The Basic Elements of Language

Language can be written, spoken, and signed. Speaking comes naturally to us because we are born with brains evolved for that purpose (Shaywitz, 1996). Young Orlando did not need speaking and listening lessons; neither did you. Children learn to speak by hearing others talk. (In Chapter 8, we will describe the consistent pathways through which language develops for children.)

Dyslexia usually begins to manifest itself as soon as a child starts learning to read, often in kindergarten. Think back to your first reading lesson. Your teacher probably introduced you to written language by teaching you to break words into their basic sound units (for example, the combination of *kuh, aah,* and *tuh* to form the word "cat"; Shaywitz, 1996). She was introducing you to phonemes.

PHONEMES   **Phonemes** (fō-nēmz) are units of sound that serve as the basic building blocks of all spoken languages. The symbols we call words are made up of phonemes. Examples of English phonemes include the sounds made by the letter *t* in the word "tail" and the letter *s* in the word "sail." Every phoneme has its own individual characteristic(s) (**Infographic 7.3**). For example, the letter *i* can represent two clearly different phonemes, as in the words "bit" and "bite."

---

language   A system for using symbols to think and communicate.

phonemes   (fō-nēmz)   The basic building blocks of spoken language.

The Building Blocks of Language

Language is made up of a collection of units and rules. These build upon each other to help us think and communicate. At the base are phonemes, which combine to make up morphemes, the smallest unit of language that carries meaning. At the top is displacement, which is the human ability to refer to things that are abstract or hypothetical.

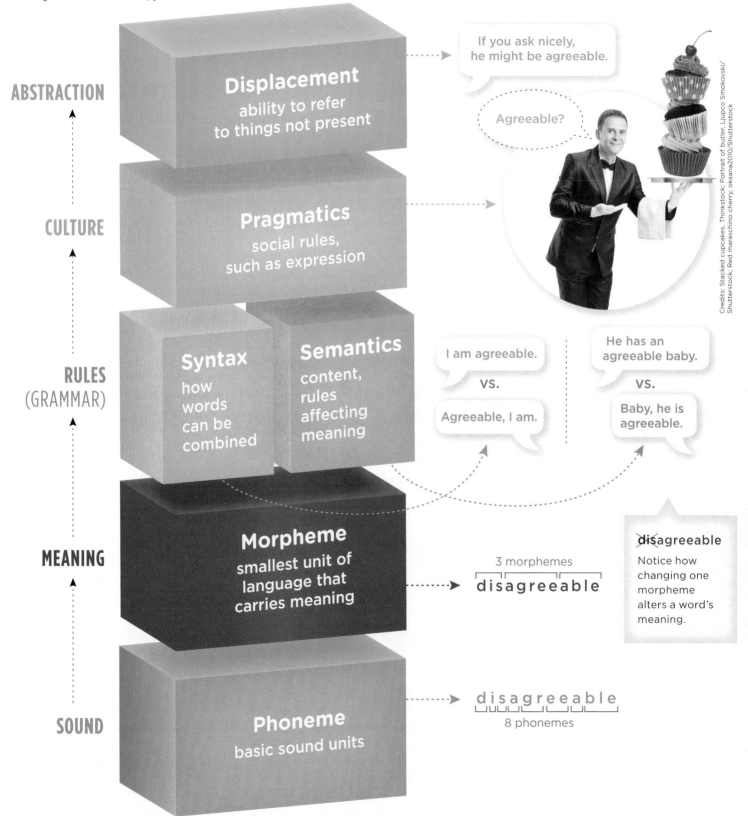

ABSTRACTION

Displacement
ability to refer
to things not present

If you ask nicely,
he might be agreeable.

Agreeable?

CULTURE

Pragmatics
social rules,
such as expression

RULES
(GRAMMAR)

Syntax
how
words
can be
combined

Semantics
content,
rules
affecting
meaning

I am agreeable.

vs.

Agreeable, I am.

He has an
agreeable baby.

vs.

Baby, he is
agreeable.

MEANING

Morpheme
smallest unit of
language that
carries meaning

3 morphemes
disagreeable

di̶s̶agreeable
Notice how
changing one
morpheme
alters a word's
meaning.

SOUND

Phoneme
basic sound units

disagreeable
8 phonemes

Credits: Stacked cupcakes, Thinkstock; Portrait of butler, Ljupco Smokovski/
Shutterstock; Red maraschino cherry, oksana2010/Shutterstock

Infants can recognize all phonemes from all languages until about 9 months of age. After that, they can no longer distinguish between phonemes that are not in the language(s) they regularly hear spoken (de Boysson-Bardies, Halle, Sagart, & Durand, 1989; Werker & Tees, 1984). This is what makes it so difficult for older children and adults to learn to speak a foreign language without an accent.

If you have children (or plan to have them), it wouldn't hurt for them to learn more than one language very early in life. Not only will their pronunciation sound natural; they may enjoy some cognitive perks, too.

didn't SEE that coming

The Perks of Being Bilingual

Psychologists once thought that the brain was best suited for learning a single language, and that exposing children to more than one language frustrated their intellectual development (Klass, 2011, October 10). Researchers are now uncovering evidence that learning two languages does not lead to word mix-ups and other cognitive troubles; in fact, it may actually improve a child's performance on various cognitive tasks (Westly, 2011, July/August).

DOES BEING BILINGUAL CLUTTER YOUR BRAIN?

Bilingualism has been associated with enhanced creativity, abstract thought, and working memory. Among the most striking qualities associated with bilingualism are strong executive control and more efficient *executive functioning* (Bialystok, 2011; Engel de Abreu, Cruz-Santos, Tourinho, Martin, & Bialystok, 2012; Westly, 2011, July/August). As the name implies, executive control is concerned with managing the brain's precious resources, deciding what's important and where to focus attention. Executive functioning refers to abilities related to planning ahead and solving problems.

A study of 7-month-old babies found that those growing up in bilingual homes already had an executive control advantage over their peers from monolingual environments. They could, for example, adjust their responses in order to get a reward (the appearance of a puppet) in ways that the monolingual babies could not (Kovács & Mehler, 2009). Research further demonstrates that bilingual children carry this executive control advantage into adulthood (Bialystok, 2011).

Why is this so? The bilingual brain is constantly exercising its executive control system. A person who speaks two languages cannot just turn on one language and turn off the other; the knowledge of both is always present and awake. The speaker is eternally torn between the two competing languages. Resolving this ongoing conflict seems to keep the executive control system very busy and always practicing (Bialystok, 2011).

Pays to Be Bilingual
A sign conveys a message in English and Spanish, suggesting that both languages are spoken in this area. Speaking two languages may boost the brain's ability to manage many different activities (Bialystok, 2011). glenda/Shutterstock

HOW WE READ Understanding phonemes is the first and most essential step in reading. In order to digest writing on a page, your brain must chop words into these fundamental sound bites (Shaywitz, 1996, 2003). This is where young Orlando probably encountered his first and most disabling roadblocks. A growing body of evidence suggests that the roots of dyslexia frequently lie in a person's problems with phonological processing (Shaywitz, Mody, & Shaywitz, 2006), the ability to distinguish and manipulate phonemes. Like most children with dyslexia, Orlando probably had trouble naming letters in the alphabet and knowing what sounds they make, identifying words that rhyme (for example, "hat," "mat," "rat"), and understanding how a word changes when one letter is swapped for another (for example, the transformation of "cat" to "cut" when the middle vowel is changed; L. Hecker, personal communication, July 22, 2011). If a child with dyslexia does not receive the special instruction he needs to overcome difficulties with phonemes, mastering the more complex layers of written language will be very challenging.

MORPHEMES   **Morphemes** (mòr-fēmz) represent the next level of language. They consist of one or more phonemes. It is the morpheme that brings meaning to a language. For example, the word "unimaginable" has three morphemes, *un, imagine,* and *able.* Each morpheme has a meaning and communicates something. Remove just one, and the word takes on a whole new significance. Clipping off *un,* for example, produces the word "imaginable," which means the exact opposite of the word you started with.

SYNTAX   The **syntax** of a language is the collection of rules dictating where words and phrases should be placed. Syntax guides both word choice and word order, providing consistency in sentence organization (Brandone, Salkind, Golinkoff, & Hirsh-Pasek, 2006). We say, "I love you," not "Love you I," because English syntax demands that the words appear in this order. Different languages have different syntaxes. In German, helping verbs often come toward the end of sentences, a variation in syntax that is striking to English speakers learning to speak German.

GRAMMAR AND SEMANTICS   **Grammar** refers to the rules associated with both word and sentence structure (Evans & Green, 2006). It tells us how words are made from sounds, how sentences are formed with words, where to place punctuation, and which word tenses to use. It combines syntax (the rules governing word choice and word order) and semantics. **Semantics** represents the rules used to bring meaning to words and sentences. Here are two sentences with different syntax, but the same semantics: *Jill kicked the ball. The ball was kicked by Jill.*

Wiley Miller/Cartoonstock.com

Semantics also refers to the context in which words appear. Let's consider the word "chip":

- I would like to eat a *chip.*
- You have a *chip* on your shoulder.
- I lost my last *chip* in that hand.
- You need to make a *chip* shot.
- The new policy will finally start to *chip* away at the retirement benefits.
- The store just installed a new computer *chip.*

In each instance, we determine the meaning of the word "chip" based on the context in which it is used in the sentence.

PRAGMATICS   Language is used in social interactions, which are governed by certain norms and expectations. **Pragmatics** are the social rules that help organize language. We have to learn how to take turns in a conversation, what gestures to use and when, and how to address people according to social standing (speaking with someone who occupies a higher status, an equal status, and so on) (Steiner, 2012, September 4; Yule, 1996). When addressing the Queen of Denmark, you would say, "Good day, Your Majesty," but when addressing your friend, you might say, "Hey, there."

How do we "know" these rules for language? Learning theorists propose that children learn language just like they learn other behaviors, through processes such as reinforcement and modeling (Bandura, 1977a; Skinner, 1957). In contrast, linguist Noam Chomsky (1928–) suggests that humans are born with innate language abilities.

morphemes (mòr-fēmz) The fundamental units that bring meaning to language.

syntax The collection of rules concerning where to place words or phrases.

grammar The rules associated with word and sentence structure.

semantics The rules used to bring meaning to words and sentences.

pragmatics The social rules that help to organize language.

Children needn't be taught the basics of language, according to Chomsky (2000); language develops like other organs in the body. Chomsky's position is based on the observation that children possess a much deeper knowledge of language than that which could have been acquired through experience. Their knowledge of language is not simply the result of hearing and imitating; it is hardwired within the brain. A built-in *language acquisition device* (LAD) accounts for the universality of language development. In fact, researchers have observed this innate capacity for language across cultures, and in nonhearing children (Chomsky, 2000; Petitto & Marentette, 1991).

THINK again

Language Without Sound

If Chomsky is right, then children would learn all languages, including signed languages, in basically the same way. Evidence suggests this is exactly what happens.

DEAF BABIES BABBLE WITH THEIR HANDS

No one sat down with you and "taught" you language. You just picked it up because people around you were using it. The same is true for all native speakers, whether they converse in Russian, Mandarin, or American Sign Language (ASL). ASL is a language with symbols, syntax, and a grammatical structure that parallels spoken language (Petitto, 1994). When people speak sign, some of the same regions of the brain are activated as when spoken language is used (Horwitz et al., 2003; Levänen, Uutela, Salenius, & Hari, 2001).

Spoken and signed languages also share the same critical period for acquisition. Between birth and 5 years old, the brain is highly plastic and ready to incorporate any language, but after that critical period, fluency is difficult to develop (Humphries et al., 2012).

Even the stages of language acquisition appear to proceed along the same path. Research suggests, for example, that deaf babies pass through a babbling stage around the same time as hearing babies. If you are unfamiliar with babbling, we are referring to the *ba-ba-ba* or *dah-dah-dah* sounds babies like to make while cruising on all fours. Babbling is accompanied by activation of the left hemisphere, a clue that it represents a step in language acquisition, not simply a new motor skill (Holowka & Petitto, 2002). Deaf babies who are exposed to ASL engage in "manual babbling," using their hands to repeat the fundamental units of sign language (Petitto & Marentette, 1991).

Babble
Deaf babies who are exposed to sign language develop their own version of babbling. Instead of rattling off spoken syllables (*da-da-da* or *ma-ma-ma*) as hearing infants typically do, they babble with their hands, repeating the basic units of sign language (Petitto & Marentette, 1991).
© Boaz Rottem/Alamy

DISPLACEMENT   Many scientists argue that language, more than any other human ability, truly sets us apart from other species. Animals have evolved complex systems of communication, but some features of human language appear to be unique. One of these unique features is *displacement*—the ability to talk and think about things that are not present at the moment. "I wonder if it's going to rain today," you might say to a friend. This statement demonstrates displacement, because it refers to an abstract concept and a hypothetical event. Displacement allows us to communicate about the future and the past, and fantasize about things that may or may not exist.

Thinking What We Say or Saying What We Think?

LO 9   Explain the linguistic relativity hypothesis and its relation to language and thought.

Psychologists are not in total agreement about the relationship between language and thought. The major controversy concerns the potential effect language can have on thinking. According to the *linguistic relativity hypothesis* (earlier known as the

Sapir–Whorf hypothesis) developed by Benjamin Lee Whorf (1956), languages have different effects on thinking and perception. For example, the Inuit and other Alaska Natives have many terms that refer to "snow" (in contrast to the single word used in English). This may cause them to perceive and think about snow differently than English speakers.

Whorf's hypothesis is not universally accepted, however. Critics suggest that he exaggerated the number of words the Inuit and other Alaska Natives had for "snow" and underestimated the number of words in English (Pullum, 1991). For example, although English doesn't have different words for "snow," this does not mean that we don't understand or cannot express understanding using word combinations (such as "light snow," "wet snow," and the like).

Whorf also observed different color-naming systems across languages. For example, there are 11 generally recognized words referring to color in English (black, white, red, green, yellow, blue, brown, purple, pink, orange, and grey). The Dani of New Guinea have far fewer names for color. The linguistic relativity hypothesis would predict that the Dani's experience of color is different from an English-speaking person's (Rosch, 1973). However, most research has not found this to be the case; color discrimination across cultures does not consistently indicate differences of color perception.

Although language might not determine thinking and perception, it certainly has an influence. Consider the role of gender in language. The English language tends to use "he" and "his" when gender is unspecified. Research indicates that the use of masculine pronouns often results in people ignoring females and focusing on males when forming mental images (Gastil, 1990; Hegarty & Buechel, 2006). "He" and "his" in these situations theoretically refer to either males or females, but the majority of English-speaking Americans think of males. Perhaps you can predict the potential downside of this tendency. Narrowing the focus to male images inevitably promotes gender bias and stereotyping.

The capacity for language is one of the defining characteristics of humanity. But it is not certain whether this capacity is unique to human beings. Animals communicate with a variety of instinctual (unlearned) behaviors (for example, chirping, whistling, tail slapping, and dancing). Is it possible they use language as well? Read on and draw your own conclusions.

CONTROVERSIES

Do Animals Use Language Too?

➡️⬅️ Rico was a border collie in Germany who knew 200 vocabulary words, including the name of a bunny toy, "Kaninchen," and a little Santa Claus named "Weihnachtsmann" (*Newsweek,* 2004, June 20). When Rico's owners instructed him to fetch a certain toy, he would run into the next room and race back with **HOT DOG!** that exact toy in his mouth. So impressive was the dog's verbal comprehension that a team of researchers decided to make him the focus of a case study. They concluded that Rico was capable of "fast-mapping," the ability to deduce the meaning of a word by hearing someone use it just once (Kaminski, Call, & Fischer, 2004).

Rico is not alone in possessing exceptional communication skills. The green-rumped parrotlet of Venezuela learns its early contact calls, or socially meaningful songs, from its parents. In other words, it learns to communicate through social interaction as opposed to instinct (Berg,

Bright Dog
Rico the border collie demonstrated his linguistic prowess by learning to recognize 200 words. More recently, researchers trained another border collie by the name of Chaser to recognize the names of 1,022 objects (Pilley & Reid, 2011). Rolf Haid Deutsch Presse Agentur/Newscom

Delgado, Cortopassi, Beissinger, & Bradbury, 2012). Kanzi the bonobo can create simple sentences with the help of pictograms, or images that represent words (Lessmoellmann, 2006, October 4). And Sarah the chimpanzee reportedly learned to read 130 word symbols and connect them into meaningful combinations such as, "Mary give raisin Sarah" (Premack & Premack, 1972, p. 6).

There is no question that animals are capable of sophisticated communication. But does that communication qualify as *language?* Keep in mind that animals need extensive training to learn and use vocabulary (you don't think Rico learned 200 words on his own, do you?), while human children pick up language through exposure. To our knowledge, only people have the ability to convey a vast number of ideas through complex grammatical constructs, and apply those constructs to critical thinking. Even if animals do possess rudimentary language abilities, humans appear to be the only species capable of grasping and using intricate sentence structures (Lessmoellmann, 2006, October 4; Pinker, 2003). ➡◀

 show what you know

1. _____ are the basic building blocks of spoken language.

2. According to the linguistic relativity hypothesis, language differences lead to differences in:
   a. phonemes.
   b. thinking and perception.
   c. the language acquisition device.
   d. displacement.

3. The Dutch word *gezelligheid* does not really have a one-word counterpart in English. It refers to a primary component of Dutch culture: a cozy type of setting that can be quaint, fun, and intimate. Most languages have these types of untranslatable words. How might this be an advantage for people who know more than one language?

✓ CHECK YOUR ANSWERS IN APPENDIX C.

Intelligence

Orlando Bloom was first diagnosed with dyslexia at the age of 7. Fortunately, he had a mother who believed in him and a school that allowed him to leave campus and attend special classes to address the issue (Child Mind Institute, 2010, October 18; Ryon, 2011, October 3). But many children are not identified as having dyslexia until they have lost considerable academic ground. Even those who receive an early diagnosis may not get into effective reading programs. Despite such challenges, people with dyslexia can be very successful.

Many great intellectuals have battled dyslexia, among them Nobel Prize winners Pierre Curie, Archer Martin, and Carol Greider (Allen, 2009, October 30); financier Charles Schwab; acclaimed writer John Irving; and the president of the esteemed Cleveland Clinic, Dr. Delos Cosgrove (Shaywitz, 2003). Dyslexia, it turns out, is not a gauge of intelligence (Ferrer, Shaywitz, Holahan, Marchione, & Shawyitz, 2010).

Nothing Can Stop Us Now
Nobel Prize winner Carol Greider (left) and financier Charles Schwab (right) are just two examples of successful people with dyslexia. There are many others, including Jay Leno, Tom Cruise, Anderson Cooper, and Ingvar Kamprad, the creator of IKEA (Allen, 2009, October 30; Turgeon, 2011, July 14). left: UPI/Landov; right: Erin Lubin/Landov

What Is Intelligence?

LO 10 Examine and distinguish among various theories of intelligence.

Generally speaking, **intelligence** is one's innate ability to solve problems, adapt to the environment, and learn from experiences. Intelligence relates to a broad array of psychological processes, including memory, learning, perception, and language, and how it is defined may sometimes depend on the variable being measured.

In the United States, intelligence is often associated with "book smarts." We think of "intelligent" people as those who score high on tests measuring academic abilities. But intelligence is more complicated than that—so complicated, in fact, that psychologists have yet to agree on precisely what it encompasses. It is not even clear whether intelligence is a single unified entity, or a collection of capabilities.

We do know that intelligence is, to a certain degree, a cultural construct. So although people in the United States tend to equate intelligence with school smarts, this is not the case everywhere in the world. Children living in a village in Kenya, for example, grow up using herbal medicine to treat parasitic diseases in themselves and others. Identifying illness and developing treatment strategies is a regular part of life. These children would score much higher on tests of intelligence relating to practical knowledge than on tests assessing vocabulary (Sternberg, 2004). Even within a single culture, the meaning of intelligence changes across time. "Intelligence" for modern Kenyans may differ from that of their 14th-century ancestors.

As we explore the theories of intelligence below, please keep in mind that intelligence does not always go hand in hand with *intelligent behavior*. People can score high on intelligence measures but exhibit a low level of judgment.

THE *g* FACTOR   Very early in the history of intelligence measurement, Charles Spearman (1863–1945) speculated that humans have a **general intelligence** (or ***g* factor**), by which he meant a singular underlying aptitude or intellectual ability. This *g* factor, Spearman asserted, drives capabilities in many areas, including verbal, spatial, and reasoning competencies. The *g* factor is the common link.

MULTIPLE INTELLIGENCES   Howard Gardner (1999, 2011) suggested that intelligence can be divided into *multiple intelligences* (**Figure 7.5**). According to Gardner, there are eight types of intelligences or "frames of mind": linguistic (verbal), logical-mathematical, spatial, bodily-kinesthetic, musical, intrapersonal, interpersonal, and naturalist. He has proposed that there also may be an existential intelligence, but the evidence is, for now, only suggestive (Gardner, 2011; Visser, Ashton, & Vernon, 2006). Take a look at **Table 7.1** on the next page and consider how different occupations might be well suited for individuals who excel in Gardner's original seven intelligences.

According to Gardner (2011), partial evidence for multiple intelligences comes from studying people with brain damage. Some mental capabilities are lost, whereas others remain intact, suggesting that they are really distinct categories. Further evidence for multiple intelligences (as opposed to just a *g* factor) comes from observing people with savant syndrome. Individuals with *savant syndrome* generally score low on intelligence tests but have some area of extreme singular ability (calendar calculations, art, mental arithmetic, and so on). Interestingly, the majority of individuals with savant syndrome are male (Treffert, 2009).

Some psychologists question whether these abilities qualify as intelligence, as opposed to skills. Critics contend that there is little empirical support for the existence of multiple intelligences (Geake, 2008; Waterhouse, 2006).

Survival Smarts
Maasai children in Kenya go through the motions of starting a fire. Definitions of intelligence vary according to culture. In the United States, intelligence is typically associated with high grades and test scores. Elsewhere in the world, being "smart" may have more to do with knowing how to survive and stay healthy.
Harald WENZEL-ORF/age fotostock

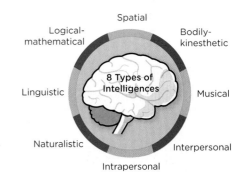

▲ **FIGURE 7.5**
Gardner's Theory of Multiple Intelligences

intelligence Innate ability to solve problems, adapt to the environment, and learn from experiences.

general intelligence (*g* factor) A singular underlying aptitude or intellectual competence that drives abilities in many areas, including verbal, spatial, and reasoning abilities.

TABLE 7.1   GARDNER'S ORIGINAL MULTIPLE INTELLIGENCES

Logical-mathematical	Scientist Mathematician	Sensitivity to, and capacity to discern logical or numerical patterns; ability to handle long chains of reasoning.
Linguistic	Poet Journalist	Sensitivity to the sounds, rhythms, and meanings of words; sensitivity to the different functions of language.
Musical	Composer Violinist	Abilities to produce and appreciate rhythm, pitch, and timbre; appreciation of the forms of musical expressiveness.
Spatial	Navigator Sculptor	Capacities to perceive the visual-spatial world accurately and to perform transformations on one's initial perceptions.
Bodily-kinesthetic	Dancer Athlete	Abilities to control one's body movements and to handle objects skillfully.
Interpersonal	Therapist Salesman	Capacities to discern and respond appropriately to the moods, temperaments, motivations, and desires of other people.
Intrapersonal	Person with detailed, accurate self-knowledge	Access to one's own feelings and the ability to discriminate among them and draw upon them to guide behavior; knowledge of one's own strengths, weaknesses, desires, and intelligences.

This table reprinted with permission from Gardner and Hatch (1989) presents Gardner's original 7 intelligences. Each intelligence has associated strengths and capabilities.

SOURCE: GARDNER AND HATCH (1989).

THE TRIARCHIC THEORY OF INTELLIGENCE   Robert Sternberg (1988) proposed three kinds of intelligence. Sternberg's **triarchic theory of intelligence** (trī-är-kik) suggests that humans have varying degrees of analytical, creative, and practical competencies (**Figure 7.6**). *Analytic intelligence* refers to our capacity to solve problems. *Creative intelligence* represents the knowledge and skills we use to handle new situations. *Practical intelligence* includes our ability to adjust to different environments.

Let's take a moment and see how the triarchic theory of intelligence relates to Dr. Jill Bolte Taylor. Following the stroke, Dr. Jill struggled with what Sternberg referred to as *analytic intelligence,* or the ability to solve problems. She did, however, demonstrate evidence of *creative intelligence,* using knowledge and skills to handle new situations. While recovering at the hospital, Dr. Jill had routine meetings with a doctor who regularly assigned her three items to remember. On his way out, he would ask her to recall these three items. Since the stroke had dismantled much of Dr. Jill's memory system, she found this assignment nearly impossible. But on one particular day, she was dead set on remembering the assigned items: *firefighter, apple,* and *33 Whippoorwill Drive.* Using all her available brain power, she recited the words over and over in her mind, but when the doctor finally quizzed her, she could not remember the "33" part of *33 Whippoorwill Drive.* She did, however, come up with a creative theoretical solution: She told the doctor that she would walk down Whippoorwill Drive and knock on every door until she identified the house (Taylor, 2006).

Dr. Jill also maintained some degree of *practical intelligence,* the ability to adjust to her surroundings. Her world was thrown into turmoil by the stroke, but she developed pragmatic coping mechanisms to deal with the novelty of it all. Quickly realizing that talking to people and watching television caused

FIGURE 7.6
Sternberg's Triarchic Theory of Intelligence

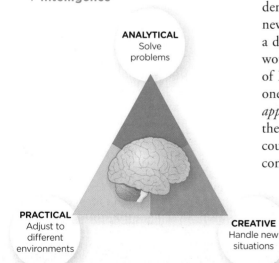

ANALYTICAL
Solve problems

PRACTICAL
Adjust to different environments

CREATIVE
Handle new situations

mental exhaustion, she and G.G. decided to limit these overstimulating activities so that her brain could heal in tranquility. This practical strategy turned out to be a key component of her recovery (Taylor, 2006).

TABLE 7.2   THEORIES OF INTELLIGENCE

Theory	Advantages	Further Thoughts
Spearman's general intelligence (*g*) There is a general intelligence driving abilities in many areas.	There is a connection among different abilities such as verbal, spatial, and reasoning competencies.	Given the complexity of the mind, can intelligence really be explained by a single general factor?
Gardner's multiple intelligences There are eight types of intelligences, which go beyond academic smarts and scholarship.	Linguistic, logical-mathematical, spatial, bodily-kinesthetic, musical, intrapersonal, interpersonal, and naturalist are "frames of mind" that allow humans to succeed.	What differentiates intelligence from skills?
Sternberg's triarchic theory Humans have varying degrees of analytical, creative, and practical competencies.	Analytic intelligence allows us to solve problems, creative intelligence represents knowledge and skills used to handle new situations, and practical intelligence includes the ability to adjust to different environments, all of which can be assessed.	Are each of these areas separate, or do they share something in common (like a *g* factor)?

A summary of the main theories of intelligence, each with its own set of strengths and other considerations.

Needless to say, there are different ways to conceptualize intelligence (**Table 7.2**), none of which appear to be categorically "right" or "wrong." Given these varied approaches, you might expect there are also many tools to measure intelligence. Let's explore several ways psychologists assess intellectual ability.

Measuring Brainpower

LO 11   Describe how intelligence is measured and identify important characteristics of assessment.

Recall that Orlando was 7 years old when he was diagnosed with dyslexia. Around the same time, he took an intelligence test and scored very high (Child Mind Institute, 2010, October 18). Tests of intelligence generally aim to measure **aptitude,** or a person's potential for learning. On the other hand, measures of **achievement** are designed to assess acquired knowledge (what a person has learned). Many brilliant people with dyslexia have performed poorly on achievement tests but very well on aptitude tests, demonstrating normal to high intelligence. The writer John Irving, for example, got a low score on the verbal portion of the SAT, and the renowned physician Delos Cosgrove performed poorly on the Medical College Admission Test (Shaywitz, 2003). Fortunately, they did not allow a single test to deter them. The line between aptitude and achievement tests is somewhat hazy, however; most tests are not purely one or the other.

A BRIEF HISTORY OF INTELLIGENCE TESTING   Intelligence testing is more than a century old. In 1904 psychologist Alfred Binet (1857–1911) joined a commission of the French government that sought to create a way to identify students who might have trouble learning in regular classroom settings. A new French law had recently required school attendance by all children. The Minister

You Asked, Dr. Jill Answers

http://qrs.ly/zs4qsxn

Did you undergo any psychological treatment during your recuperation?

---

triarchic theory of intelligence (trī-är-kik) Sternberg's theory suggesting that humans have varying degrees of analytical, creative, and practical abilities.

aptitude   An individual's potential for learning.

achievement   Acquired knowledge, or what has been learned.

of Public Instruction recognized that this transition would be difficult because some French children had never attended school. For the law to be implemented successfully, it was necessary to identify children who had potential to succeed. A measure was needed to predict the performance of these schoolchildren (Fancher & Rutherford, 2012; Watson, 1968).

Binet worked with one of his students, Théodore Simon (1872–1961), to construct an assessment of intelligence. They studied Binet's daughters and Parisian schoolchildren, coming up with the 30 items in the original assessment. These items were designed to be of increasing difficulty, starting with a simple test to see if a child could follow a lit match that the tester moved in front of her. The items became more difficult as testing progressed—explaining how paper and cardboard are different, and making rhymes with words, for instance (Fancher & Rutherford, 2012).

Binet and Simon assumed that children generally follow the same path of intellectual development. Their primary goal was to compare a child's mental ability with the mental abilities of other children of the same age. They would determine the **mental age (MA)** of a child by comparing his performance to that of other children in the same age category. For example, a 10-year-old boy with average intellectual abilities would score similarly to other 10-year-old children and thus would have a *mental age* of 10. An intelligent 10-year-old boy would score better than other 10-year-old children and thus have a higher mental age (for example, a mental age of 12) compared to his chronological age. Similarly, a child who was intellectually slower would have a mental age lower than his chronological age. Although Binet and Simon's measure of intelligence was groundbreaking at the time, it had many shortcomings that were eventually addressed by others.

One of the problems with relying on mental age as an index is that it cannot be used to compare intelligence levels across age groups. For example, you can't use mental age to compare the intelligence levels of an 8-year-old girl and a 12-year-old girl. In 1912, William Stern solved this problem by devising the **intelligence quotient (IQ)**. To calculate IQ, a child's mental age is divided by her chronological age and multiplied by 100. A 10-year-old girl with a mental age of 8 would have an IQ score of $(8 \div 10) \times 100 = 80$. If her mental age and chronological age were the same, her IQ would be 100. The IQ score can be used to compare the level of intelligence of this 10-year-old girl with children of other ages.

This method does not apply to adults, however. It wouldn't make sense to give a 60-year-old man who scores the same as a 30-year-old man an IQ score of 50 (that is, $30 \div 60 \times 100 = 50$). Modern intelligence tests still assign a numerical score (which we continue to refer to as "IQ"), although they no longer use the actual quotient score.

What's Your IQ?
French psychologist Alfred Binet collaborated with one of his students, Théodore Simon, to create a systematic assessment of intelligence. The materials pictured here come from Lewis Terman and Maude Merrill's 1937 version of Binet and Simon's test. Using these materials, the test administrator prompts the test taker with statements such as "Point to the doll's foot," or "What advantages does an airplane have over a car?" (Sattler, 1990). right: Albert Harlingue/Roger-Viollet/The Image Works; far right: SSPL/Getty Images

THE STANFORD-BINET TEST American psychologist Lewis Terman (1916) revised Stern's work so that Binet's test could be used in the United States, where it came to be known as the Stanford–Binet. Terman changed some items, added items, developed standards based on American children, and extended the test to include teens and adults. *The Stanford–Binet Intelligence Scales,* as it is now known in its fifth edition (Roid, 2003), includes the assessment of verbal and nonverbal abilities (for instance, defining words, tracing paths in a maze). The Stanford–Binet yields an overall score for general intelligence, as well as scores relating to more specific abilities, such as knowledge, reasoning, visual processing, and working memory (Becker, 2003).

THE WECHSLER TESTS In the late 1930s, David Wechsler began creating intelligence tests for adults (Anastasi & Urbina, 1997). Although many had been using the Stanford–Binet with adults, it was not an ideal measure, given that adults might not react positively to the questions geared to the daily experiences of school-age children. The Wechsler Adult Intelligence Scale (WAIS) was published in 1955 and has since been revised numerous times (1981, 1997), with the most recent revision in 2008 (WAIS–IV). In addition to creating assessments for adults, Wechsler also developed scales for older children (Wechsler Intelligence Scale for Children, WISC–IV) and younger children (Wechsler Preschool and Primary Scale of Intelligence, WPPSI–III).

The Wechsler assessments of intelligence consist of a variety of subtests designed to measure different aspects of intellectual ability. The 10 subtests on the WAIS–IV target four domains of intellectual performance: verbal abilities, perceptual reasoning, working memory, and processing speed. Results from the WAIS–IV include an overall IQ score, as well as scores on the four domains. Psychologists look for consistency among the domain scores and subtest scores. Substantial inconsistency may suggest an issue that should be further explored, such as a reading or language disability. In the United States, Wechsler tests are now used more frequently than the Stanford–Binet.

Let's Test the Intelligence Tests

As you read about the history of intelligence assessment, did you wonder how effective those early tests were? We hope so, because this would indicate you are thinking critically. Psychologists make great efforts to ensure the accurate assessment of intelligence, paying close attention to three important characteristics: validity, reliability, and standardization.

VALIDITY **Validity** is the degree to which an assessment measures what it intends to measure. We can assess the validity of a measure by comparing its results to those of other assessments that have been found to measure the factor of interest. In addition, we determine the validity of an assessment by seeing if it can predict what it is designed to measure, or its *predictive validity.* Thus, to determine if an intelligence test is valid, we would check to see if the scores it produces are consistent with those of other intelligence tests. A valid intelligence test should also be able to predict future performance on tasks related to intellectual ability.

RELIABILITY Another important characteristic of assessment is **reliability,** the ability of a test to provide consistent, reproducible results. If given repeatedly, a reliable test will continue producing the same types of scores. If we administer an intelligence test to an individual, we would expect (if it is reliable) that the person's scores will remain consistent across time. We can also determine the reliability of an assessment by splitting the test in half and then determining whether the findings of

mental age (MA) A score representing the mental abilities of an individual in relation to others of a similar chronological age.

intelligence quotient (IQ) A score from an intelligence assessment; originally based on mental age divided by chronological age, multiplied by 100.

validity The degree to which an assessment measures what it intends to measure.

reliability The ability of an assessment to provide consistent, reproducible results.

Measuring Achievement
Tests such as the SAT and ACT are called achievement tests because they are geared toward measuring learned knowledge, as opposed to innate ability. These tests are also standardized, making it possible to compare scores of people who are demographically similar.
Rui Vieira/PA Wire/AP Photos

Synonyms
normal curve normal distribution

standardization Occurs when test developers administer a test to a large sample and then publish the average scores for specified groups.

normal curve Depicts the frequency of values of a variable along a continuum; bell-shaped symmetrical distribution, with the highest point reflecting the average score.

the first and second halves of the test agree with each other. It is important to note that it is possible to have a reliable test that is not valid. For this reason, we always have to determine *both* reliability and validity.

STANDARDIZATION   In addition to being valid and reliable, a good intelligence test provides standardization. Perhaps you have taken a test that measured your achievement in a particular area (for example, an ACT or SAT), or an aptitude test to measure your innate abilities (for example, an IQ test). Upon receiving your scores, you may have wondered how you performed in comparison to other people in your class, college, or state. Most aptitude and achievement tests allow you to make these judgments through the use of **standardization.** Standardization occurs when test developers administer a test to a large sample of people and then publish the average scores, or *norms,* for specified groups. The sample must be representative of the population of interest; that is, it must include a variety of individuals who are similar to the population using the test. This allows you to compare your own score with people of the same age, gender, socioeconomic status, or region. Test norms permit evaluation of the relative performance (often provided as percentiles) of an individual compared to others with similar characteristics.

It is also critical that assessments are given and scored using standard procedures. This ensures that no one is given an unfair advantage or disadvantage. Intelligence tests are subject to tight control. The public does not have access to the questions or answers, and all testing must be administered by a professional. What about those IQ tests found on the Internet? They simply are not valid due to lack of standardization.

THE NORMAL CURVE   Have you ever wondered how many people in the population are really smart? Or perhaps how many people have average intelligence? With aptitude tests like the Wechsler assessments and the Stanford–Binet, we can predict what percentage of the population will have scores between two intervals by using a **normal curve,** which depicts the frequency of values along a continuum (**Infographic 7.4**). The normal curve is symmetrical and shaped like a bell. The highest point on the graph reflects the average score.

The normal curve shown in Infographic 7.4 portrays the distribution of scores for the Wechsler tests. As you can see, the *mean* or average score is 100. As you follow the horizontal axis, notice that the higher and lower scores occur less and less frequently in the population. A score of 145 or 70 is far less common than a score of 100, for example.

One final note about the normal curve is that it applies to a variety of traits, including IQ, height, weight, and personality characteristics, and that we use it to make predictions about these traits. Consult Appendix A for more information on the normal curve and a variety of other topics associated with statistics.

BUT ARE THEY FAIR?   A major concern with intelligence tests is that IQ scores consistently differ across certain groups of people. For example, researchers have reported that Black Americans in general score lower on intelligence tests than do White Americans. The difference in the average of these two groups is around 10 to 15 IQ points (Ceci & Williams, 2009; Dickens & Flynn, 2006). Group differences are also apparent for East Asians, who score around 6 points higher than average White Americans, and for Hispanics, who score around 10 points lower than average White Americans (Rushton & Jensen, 2010). Although researchers disagree about what causes these gaps in IQ scores, they are in general agreement that there is *no* evidence to support a "genetic hypothesis" (Nisbett et al., 2012). Instead, researchers generally attribute these group differences to environmental factors.

How Smart Are Intelligence Tests?

Tests that claim to measure intelligence are everywhere—online, in your favorite magazine, at job interviews, and in many elementary and secondary schools. But can all of these tests be trusted? The results of an intelligence test aren't meaningful unless the test is *valid, reliable,* and *fair*. But what do those concepts mean, and how can we be sure whether a test is valid, reliable, or fair—let alone all three? Let's take a look.

validity DOES THE TEST MEASURE WHAT IT INTENDS TO MEASURE?

Is a bathroom scale valid for measuring length?

How about a ruler missing its first inch?

A shortened ruler would not be a valid measure because it would provide different results than other rulers.

A valid intelligence test will provide results that:
- ✔ agree with the results of other valid intelligence tests
- ✔ predict performance in an area related to intelligence, such as academic achievement

reliability WILL YOUR SCORE BE CONSISTENT EVERY TIME YOU TAKE THE TEST?

A shortened ruler isn't valid, but it is *reliable* because it will give the same result every time it's used.

A reliable intelligence test will provide results that:
- ✔ are reproducible (produce a similar score if taken a second time)
- ✔ show the first and second halves of the test are consistent with each other

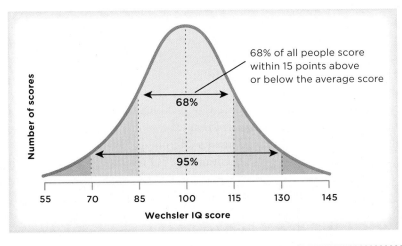

68% of all people score within 15 points above or below the average score

Number of scores (y-axis)

68%

95%

55   70   85   100   115   130   145

Wechsler IQ score

Because most intelligence tests are *standardized*, you can determine how well you have performed in comparison to others. Test scores tend to form a bell-shaped curve—called the normal curve—around the average score of 100. Most people (68%) score within 15 points above or below the average. If the test is reliable, each person's score should stay around the same place on the curve across multiple testings.

fairness IS THE TEST VALID FOR THE GROUP?

An animal weighing 2 stone is likely to be a:
(a) sparrow   (b) small dog
(c) mature lion   (d) blue whale

Unless you live in the United Kingdom, where the imperial system of weights is used, you probably wouldn't know that a stone is approximately 14 pounds, and therefore the correct answer is (b). Does this mean that you are less intelligent, or that the test is biased against people without a specific background? A test that is culture-fair is designed to minimize the bias of cultural background.

3 inches

2.286 Chinese Imperial cùn

.1667 cubits

The evidence for environmental influence is strong and points to a variety of factors that contribute to this gap in IQ scores. One adoption study, for example, found that Black and mixed-race children adopted by White families had significantly higher IQ scores than did Black and mixed-race children adopted by Black families (Moore, 1986). This indicates strongly that differences in household environments accounted for disparities in IQ scores. Another likely environmental explanation for the IQ gap is stress (Nisbett et al., 2012). Research suggests that Black families often live in more stressful environments than White families. Chronic stress can have a negative impact on the function of the brain, particularly those areas responsible for attention and memory (short-term, long-term, and working memory), which are vulnerable to sustained high levels of stress (McEwen, 2000).

Socioeconomic status (SES) is yet another important variable to consider. The disproportionate percentage of minorities in the lower strata may, in fact, mask the critical issue of environmental factors and their relationship with IQ. For example, children raised in homes with lower SES tend to watch more TV, have less access to books and technology, and are not read to as often. In addition, individuals with lower SES frequently live in disadvantaged neighborhoods and have limited access to quality schools (Hanscombe et al., 2012).

CULTURE-FAIR INTELLIGENCE TESTS   It has not yet been determined whether group differences in IQ scores also reflect biases of the tests themselves. Can an assessment tool be valid for some groups but not others? For example, are these IQ tests solely aptitude tests, or do they incorporate some level of achievement (learned content)? If that is the case, then people with limited exposure to certain types of test content may be at a disadvantage. Early versions of the IQ tests exhibited some bias against individuals from rural areas, people of lower socioeconomic status, and African Americans. Bias may result from language, dialect, or the culture of those who have created the tests (Sattler, 1990; Sternberg, 2004).

To address these problems, psychologists have tried to create **culture-fair intelligence tests,** designed to measure intelligence without putting people at a disadvantage because of their cultural backgrounds. One way to avoid bias is to use questions that would be familiar to people from a variety of backgrounds. Another method is to use nonverbal questions. (The Raven's Progressive Matrices uses this approach; see **Figure 7.7.**) Since intelligence is defined within a culture and tests are created within a culture, some have suggested that we can only create culture-relevant tests, not culture-fair or culture-free assessments (Sternberg, 2004).

Ultimately, IQ tests are good at predicting academic success. They are highly correlated with SATs, ACTs, and GREs, for example, and the correlations are stronger for the higher and lower ranges of IQ scores. Strong correlations help us make predictions about future behavior. Researchers have found, however, that self-discipline may be a better predictor of success than IQ tests (Duckworth & Seligman, 2005).

The study of intelligence is far from straightforward. Assessing a concept with no universally accepted definition is not an easy task, but these tests do serve useful purposes. The key is to be mindful of their limitations, while appreciating their ability to measure an array of cognitive abilities.

CONNECTIONS

In **Chapter 6,** we discussed the biology of memory, exploring areas of the brain responsible for memory formation and storage (hippocampus, cerebellum, and amygdala) as well as changes at the level of the neuron (long-term potentiation). Here, we note that stressful environments can impact the functioning of the memory system.

FIGURE 7.7

Nonverbal Intelligence

The Raven's Progressive Matrices test is used to assess components of nonverbal intelligence. For the sample question pictured here, the test taker is required to choose the item that completes the matrix pattern. The correct answer is choice 2. This type of test is generally considered culturally fair, meaning it does not favor certain cultural groups over others.

Sample items similar to those found in the Raven's® Progressive Matrices. Copyright © 1998 NCS Pearson, Inc. Reproduced with permission. All rights reserved. "Raven's" is a trademark, in the US and/or other countries, of Pearson Education, Inc. or its affiliate(s)

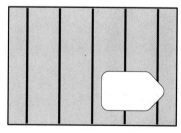

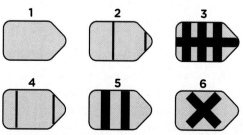

The Diversity of Human Intelligence

Once called mental retardation, *intellectual disability* consists of a delay in thinking, intelligence, and social and practical skills that is evident before age 18. Psychologists can assess intellectual functioning with IQ scores; for example, disability is identified as an IQ below approximately 70 on the Wechsler tests. It can also be assessed in terms of one's ability to adapt; for example, being able to live independently, and understanding number concepts, money, and hygiene. Although intellectual disability is the preferred term, the phrase "mental retardation" is still used in most laws and policies relating to intellectual disability (for example, Individuals with Disabilities Education Act, 2004; Social Security Disability Insurance; and Medicaid Home and Community Based Waiver) (Schalock et al., 2010).

There are many causes of intellectual disability, but we cannot always pinpoint them. According to the American Association on Intellectual and Developmental Disabilities (AAIDD), nearly half of intellectual disability cases have unidentifiable causes (Schalock et al., 2010). We do know the causes for Down syndrome (an extra chromosome in what would normally be the 21st pair), fetal alcohol syndrome (exposure to alcohol while in utero), and fragile X syndrome (a defect in a gene on the X chromosome leading to reductions in protein needed for development of the brain). There are also known environmental factors, such as lead and mercury poisoning, lack of oxygen at birth, various diseases, and exposure to drugs during fetal development.

At the other end of the intelligence spectrum are the intellectually **gifted,** those who have IQ scores of 130 or above. Above 140, one is considered a "genius." As you might imagine, very few people—about 2% of the population—are classified as gifted. An even smaller proportion falls in the genius range: only the top 1% of the population (Simonton, 2012, November/December). What roles do you think these gifted people take on in our society?

TERMAN'S STUDY OF THE GIFTED American psychologist Lewis Terman was interested in discovering if gifted children could function successfully in adulthood. His work led to the longest-running longitudinal study on genius and giftedness, begun in the early 1900s. This study, formerly called the Genetic Studies of Genius, is now called the Terman Study of the Gifted. Terman (1925) monitored 857 boys and 671 girls with IQs ranging from 130 to 200. These children (known as "Termites") were well adjusted socially, showed leadership skills, and were physically healthy and attractive (Terman & Oden, 1947). Following the participants into adulthood, the study found that they earned more academic degrees and achieved more financial success than their nongifted peers (Fancher & Rutherford, 2012; Holahan & Sears, 1995). Compelling as these findings may be, they do not necessarily indicate that high IQ scores guarantee success in all areas of life.

LIFE SMARTS The ability to function in everyday life also is influenced by *emotional intelligence* (Goleman, 1995). **Emotional intelligence** is the capacity to perceive, understand, regulate, and use emotions to adapt to social situations. People with emotional intelligence use information about their emotions to direct their behavior in an efficient and creative way (Salovey, Mayer, & Caruso, 2002). They are self-aware and can properly judge how to behave in social situations. A high level of emotional intelligence is indicated by self-control—the ability to manage anger, impulsiveness, and anxiety. Other attributes include empathy, awareness of emotions, and persistent self-motivation. Research suggests that emotional intelligence is related to performance on the job and at school (MacCann, Fogarty, Zeidner, & Roberts, 2011).

Feel the Music
Chinese conductor Hu Yizhou rehearses for an upcoming concert in Korea. Yizhou, who has Down syndrome, is part of the China Disabled Peoples Performing Art Troupe. REUTERS/You Sung-Ho

culture-fair intelligence test Assessments designed to minimize cultural bias.

gifted Highly intelligent; defined as having an IQ score of 130 or above.

emotional intelligence The capacity to perceive, understand, regulate, and use emotions to adapt to social situations.

As you may have observed in your own life, people display varying degrees of emotional intelligence. Where does this diversity in emotional intelligence—or any characteristic of intelligence—arise? Like many topics in psychology, it comes down to nature and nurture. Let's see how this principle applies to dyslexia.

Nature and Nurture

Why Dyslexia?

We don't have access to Orlando Bloom's genetic code, and we certainly are not in a position to speculate on what caused his dyslexia. In some cases, however, it appears that reading difficulties are written into the genes. Dyslexia is, to a certain extent, inherited. Some of the earliest dyslexia researchers noticed that the condition runs in families, and many studies have confirmed this observation (Fisher & DeFries, 2002). If you have dyslexia and you have children, there is a good chance one of your kids will develop it as well.

But genes aren't the whole story. Your genetic code provides a blueprint for the development of a human brain and body—not the finished product. Just as nutrition can affect the growth of a child's bones and muscles, early learning experiences can shape cognitive development. Strong reading, for example, is fostered by a variety of factors, including providing children with access to books, activities that help them understand phonemes (rhyming and other word games), and good schooling (Shaywitz, 2003).

DYSLEXIA CAN BE TRACED TO ATYPICAL CONNECTIONS IN THE BRAIN. . . .

The nurture side of the coin even has value for adults, whose brains are still receptive to training. Dyslexia can be traced to atypical connections in the brain, and, specifically, decreased activity in various areas, including the left parietotemporal region. fMRI research suggests this region can be awakened when a person with dyslexia receives intensive phonological training and learns to read more efficiently (Eden et al., 2004). The takeaway: Nature isn't everything. With proper intervention (nurture), the brain of someone with dyslexia can begin to behave more like the brain of an average reader (Shaywitz, 2003).

Origins of Intelligence

Now let's examine how nature and nurture impact intelligence in general. Twin studies (research involving identical and fraternal twins) are an excellent way to evaluate the relative weights of nature and nurture for virtually any psychological trait. The Minnesota twin studies (Johnson & Bouchard, 2011; McGue, Bouchard, Iacono, & Lykken, 1993) indicate there are strong correlations between the IQ scores of identical twins—stronger than the correlations between the IQ scores of fraternal twins or other siblings. In other words, the closer the genetic relationship (identical twins have identical genes), the more similar their IQ scores are. This suggests that genes play a major role in determining intellectual abilities. According to the Minnesota twin studies, identical twins' IQ scores have correlations as high as .86 (remembering that ±1.00 is a perfect correlation) (**Figure 7.8**).

Heritability refers to the degree to which heredity is responsible for a particular characteristic or trait. As psychologists study the individual differences associated with a variety of traits, they try to determine the heritability of each one. Many traits have a high degree of heritability (for example, eye color, height, and other physical characteristics), but others are determined by the environments in which we are raised (for example, manners; Dickens & Flynn, 2001). Results from twin and adoption studies suggest that heritability for "general cognitive abilities" is about 50%

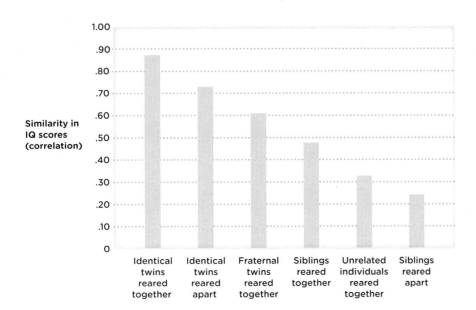

FIGURE 7.8
The Impact of Nature and Nurture on Intelligence
The most genetically similar people, identical twins, have the strongest correlation between their scores on IQ tests. This suggests that genes play a major role in determining intelligence. But if identical twins are raised in different environments, the correlation is slightly lower, showing some environmental effect (McGue et al., 1993).

(Plomin & DeFries, 1998; Plomin, DeFries, Knopik, & Niederhiser, 2013). In other words, about half of the variation in intellectual or cognitive ability can be attributed to genetic make-up, and the other half to environment.

It is important to emphasize that heritability applies to groups of people, not individuals. We cannot say, for example, that an individual's intelligence level is 40% due to genes and 60% the result of environment. We can only make general predictions about groups and how they are influenced by genetic factors (Dickens & Flynn, 2001).

So where does gender figure into the intelligence equation? Despite differences in brain size and structure, males and females do *not* differ significantly in terms of general intelligence (Burgaleta et al., 2012; Halpern et al., 2007). Many researchers find this pairing remarkable: "Apparently, males and females can achieve similar levels of overall intellectual performance by using differently structured brains in different ways" (Deary, Penke, & Johnson, 2010, p. 209). Although researchers do find different patterns of neurological activity in males and females, these differences are not necessarily due to nature. The brain can change in response to experience (nurture), and sex differences may be due to changes in synaptic connections and neural networks that result from experiences of being male or female (Hyde, 2007).

We have now explored the various approaches to assessing and conceptualizing intelligence. Let's shift our focus to a quality that is associated with intelligence but far more difficult to measure: *creativity*.

Creativity

LO 12 Define creativity and its associated characteristics.

Do you remember the last time you encountered a situation or problem that required you to "put on your thinking cap?" Sometimes it takes a little creativity to solve a problem. In a problem-solving scenario, **creativity** is the ability to construct valuable results in innovative ways. Creativity and intelligence are not equivalent, but they are correlated, and a basic level of intelligence is necessary for creativity to flow. For example, you need to have a certain level of intelligence to generate original ideas, as opposed to just more ideas (Benedek, Franz, Heene, & Neubauer, 2012; Nusbaum & Silvia, 2011).

heritability The degree to which hereditary factors (genes) are responsible for a particular characteristic observed within a population; the proportion of variation in a characteristic attributed to genetic factors.

creativity In problem solving, the ability to construct valuable results in innovative ways; the ability to generate original ideas.

CHARACTERISTICS OF CREATIVITY Because creativity doesn't present itself in a singular or uniform manner, it is difficult to measure. Most psychologists agree that there are several basic characteristics associated with creativity (Baer, 1993; Sternberg, 2006a, 2006b):

- Originality: the ability to come up with unique solutions when trying to solve a problem
- Fluency: the ability to create many potential solutions
- Flexibility: the ability to use a variety of problem-solving tactics to arrive at solutions
- Knowledge: a sufficient base of ideas and information
- Thinking: the ability to see things in new ways, make connections, see patterns
- Personality: characteristics of a risk taker, someone who perseveres and tolerates ambiguity
- Intrinsic motivation: influenced by internal rewards, motivated by the pleasure and challenge of work

DIVERGENT AND CONVERGENT THINKING **Divergent thinking** is an important component of creativity. It refers to the ability to devise many solutions to a problem (Baer, 1993). A classic measure of divergent thinking is the *unusual uses test* (Guilford, 1967; Guilford, Christensen, Merrifield, & Wilson, 1960; **Figure 7.9**). A typical prompt would ask the test taker to come up with as many uses for a brick as she can imagine. (What ideas do you have? Paperweight? Shot put? Stepstool?) Remember that we often have difficulty thinking about how to use familiar objects in atypical ways because of functional fixedness.

In contrast to divergent thinking, **convergent thinking** focuses on finding a single best solution by converging on the correct answer. Here, we fall back on previous experience and knowledge. This conventional approach to problem solving leads to one solution, but, as we have noted, many problems have multiple solutions.

FIGURE 7.9
Instructions for Guilford's Alternate Uses Task
The sample question at right is from Guilford's Alternate Uses Task, a revised version of the *unusual uses test,* which is designed to gauge creativity.
Reproduced by special permission of the Publisher, MIND GARDEN, Inc., www.mindgarden.com from the Alternate Uses by J.P. Guilford, Paul R. Christensen, Philip R. Merrifield, & Robert C. Wilson. Copyright 1960 by SheridanSupply Co. Further reproduction is prohibited without the publisher's written consent.

In this test, you will be asked to consider some common objects. Each object has a common use, which will be stated. You are to list as many as six other uses for which the object or parts of the object could serve.

Example:
Given: A NEWSPAPER (used for reading). You might think of the following other uses for a newspaper.

a. Start a fire
b. Wrap garbage
c. Swat flies
d. Stuffing to pack boxes
e. Line drawers or shelves
f. Make a kidnap note

Notice that all of the uses listed are different from each other and different from the primary use of a newspaper. Each acceptable use must be different from others and from the common use.

Creativity comes with many benefits. People with this ability tend to have a broader range of knowledge and interests. They are open to new experiences and often are less inhibited in their thoughts and behaviors (Feist, 2004; Simonton, 2000). The good news is that we can become more creative by practicing divergent thinking, taking risks, and looking for unusual connections between ideas (Baer, 1993).

Sometimes finding those new connections takes a little relaxing on the part of the brain. Let's see how this phenomenon might come into play by peering into the brain of a rapper.

didn't SEE that coming

Inside the Brain of a Rapper

👁️❗ How long would it take you to come up with a rhyme that looks something like this?

I shine and glow, even in the dark,
Stay smart, stay sharp, as a harp,
Played by a musician in this position,
Feel blessed to make the whole world listen,
And just glisten without even trying
Even when I die, I won't stay dead,
And it's straight off the head,
And it's straight out the lungs,
Looking fly, fresh, old man, so young
(Mos Def, 2011, February 28)

Hip-hop artist Mos Def came up with these rhymes off the top of his head one night at a club in New York City. He was freestyle rapping alongside fellow performer Kanye West ("freestyle" means to invent lyrics in the moment—no cheat sheets involved, no memorizing the night before). In a true freestyle session, rappers essentially create poetry as it flows from their mouths. An amazing cognitive feat, don't you think? Something special must be going on in the brain of a rapper in order for freestyle to occur.

Researchers have studied the brains of freestyle rappers as they "flow," or "spit rhymes," and they have discovered an interesting pattern of excitement and calmness in different areas of the brain. Using fMRI, Siyuan Liu and colleagues (2012) compared the brain activity of rappers as they freestyled and performed lyrics they had rehearsed. Freestyle sessions were correlated with greater activity in language-processing hot spots on the left side of the brain—not surprising, given the extraordinary language demands of improvisational rhyming. There was also heightened activity in an area of the frontal lobes known as the medial prefrontal cortex (MPFC) and a quieting down of another area known as the dorsolateral prefrontal cortex (DLPFC). This calming down of the DLPFC, which receives and filters input from the MPFC about internal intentions, may effectively relax the rules about which intentions are turned into action, setting the stage for creativity. "Letting go," it seems, is an essential part of the creative process. 👁️❗

MOS DEFINITELY CREATIVE!

Let It Flow
Generating rap lyrics on the spot appears to involve a slowdown of activity in the dorsolateral prefrontal cortex (DLPFC), a part of the brain thought to play a role in deciding which intentions are transformed into actions (Liu et al., 2012). This loosening of inhibition may facilitate creative expression. AP Photo/Joe Giblin

DR. JILL'S NEWFOUND INTELLIGENCE   It took Dr. Jill 8 years to recuperate from what she now calls her "stroke of insight," and it was not smooth sailing. Regaining her physical and cognitive strength required steadfast determination and painstaking effort. "Recovery was a decision I had to make a million times a day," she writes (Taylor, 2006, p. 115). She also had many people cheering her on—family and friends who had faith in her brain's plasticity, or ability to repair and rewire (Taylor, 2006).

If stroke victims fail to regain all faculties by 6 months, they never will. At least that is what Dr. Jill remembers hearing her doctors say. But she proved all the naysayers wrong. Within 2 years, Dr. Jill was living back in her home

divergent thinking The ability to devise many solutions to a problem; a component of creativity.

convergent thinking A conventional approach to problem solving that focuses on finding a single best solution to a problem by using previous experience and knowledge.

New Beginnings
Dr. Jill currently serves as the national spokesperson for the Harvard Brain Tissue Resource Center, where scientists conduct research on brain tissue from cadavers. It took 8 years for Dr. Jill to recover from her stroke. Her bestselling book *My Stroke of Insight* is being adapted for the big screen by Sony Pictures and Imagine Entertainment (drjilltaylor. com, 2010; IMDB, 2015).
© My Stroke of Insight, Inc.
Photo by Kip May

state of Indiana and teaching college courses in anatomy/physiology and neuro-science. Four years after the operation, she had retrained her body to walk gracefully and her brain to multitask. By Year 5, she could solve math problems, and by Year 7, she had accepted another teaching position, this time at Indiana University (Taylor, 2006).

Today, Dr. Jill is working on various projects to increase awareness and understanding of the brain, overseeing her nonprofit organization Jill Bolte Taylor BRAINS, and collaborating with the HAWN Foundation to create a high school curriculum, among other things (drjilltaylor.com, 2010). Dr. Jill finds she has become more open to new experiences and ways of thinking (a prerequisite for creativity), and that she has emerged from her ordeal more empathetic and emo-
▼ tionally aware. ☐

 show what you know

1. Sternberg believed that intelligence is made up of three types of competencies, including:
   a. linguistic, spatial, musical.
   b. intrapersonal, interpersonal, existential.
   c. analytic, creative, practical.
   d. achievement, triarchic, prototype.

2. Some tests of intelligence measure _____, or a person's potential for learning, and other tests measure _____, or acquired knowledge.

3. Define IQ. How is it derived?

4. An artist friend of yours easily comes up with unique solutions when trying to solve problems. This _____ is one of the defining characteristics of creativity.

✓ CHECK YOUR ANSWERS IN APPENDIX C.

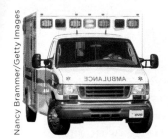

summary of concep

LO 1 Define cognition and explain how it is related to thinking. (p. 261)

Cognition is the mental activity associated with obtaining, converting, and using knowledge. Thinking is a specific type of cognition, which involves coming to a decision, reaching a solution, forming a belief, or developing an attitude. Cognition is a broad term that describes mental activity, and thinking is a subset of cognition.

LO 2 Define concepts and identify how they are organized. (p. 262)

Concepts are mental representations of *categories* of objects, situations, and ideas that belong together based on their central features or characteristics. Psychologists often use a three-level hierarchy to categorize objects. At the top of the hierarchy are superordinate concepts, the broadest category encompassing all the objects belonging to it. Below is the more specific midlevel of the hierarchy, the category used most often to identify objects. At the bottom of the hierarchy is the subordinate-level, the most specific category.

LO 3 Differentiate between formal concepts and natural concepts. (p. 263)

Formal concepts are created through rigid and logical rules or features of a concept. Natural concepts, on the other hand, are acquired through everyday experience. Natural concepts don't have the same types of rigid rules for identification that formal concepts do, and this makes them harder to outline. We organize our worlds with the help of prototypes, which are the ideal or most representative examples of particular natural concepts.

LO 4 Describe the biological processes associated with cognition. (p. 267)

The biology of cognition is evident in the brain, both on a micro and macro level. Changes at the level of the neuron, whether through rewiring, heightened excitability, or increased efficiency of synaptic transmission, make it possible to store, retrieve, and manipulate information. The plasticity of the brain enables dramatic recoveries from trauma.

LO 5 Explain how trial and error and algorithms can be used to solve problems. (p. 271)

Problem solving refers to the variety of approaches used to achieve goals. One approach to problem solving is trial and error, which involves finding a solution through a s attempts. Algorithms provide a virtually guaranteed solution to a problem by using formulas or sets of rules. Unlike trial and error, algorithms ensure that you will reach a solution if you follow all the steps.

LO 6 Identify different types of heuristics used to solve problems. (p. 272)

Heuristics are problem-solving approaches that incorporate a rule of thumb or broad application of a strategy. One commonly used heuristic involves creating subgoals or subproblems. Another commonly used heuristic is means–ends analysis, which involves figuring out how to decrease the distance between a goal and the current status. Using means–ends analysis, you can break a problem into subproblems and solve them independently.

LO 7 Define decision making and explain how heuristics can lead us astray. (p. 274)

Decision making generally refers to the cognitive process of choosing among various ways to reach a goal. Sometimes a decision is based on a single feature. With more complex decisions, we tend to consider a variety of features. Using the availability heuristic, we predict the probability of something happening in the future based on how easily we can recall a similar type of event from the past. If we can easily recall a similar type of event, then we judge that event as being more likely to occur. With the representativeness heuristic, we evaluate the degree to which the primary characteristics of an event, person, or situation are similar to our prototype.

LO 8 Define language and give examples of its basic elements. (p. 280)

Language is a system for using symbols to think and communicate. These symbols are words, gestures, or sounds, and there are specific rules for putting them together. Phonemes are the basic building blocks of spoken language. Morphemes consist of one or more phonemes and represent the fundamental units of meaning. The syntax of a language refers to the collection of rules guiding word choice and word order. Grammar refers to the rules associated with word and sentence structures and how these are formed from their components. Semantics refers to rules that are used to bring meaning to words and sentences. Pragmatics refers to the social rules for using language.

LO 9 Explain the linguistic relativity hypothesis and its relation to language and thought. (p. 284)

The linguistic relativity hypothesis proposes that language differences lead to disparities in thinking and perception. Most psychologists agree that although language might not determine thinking and perception, it certainly can influence it.

LO 10 Examine and distinguish among various theories of intelligence. (p. 287)

Charles Spearman speculated that intelligence consists of a general intelligence (or *g* factor), which refers to a singular underlying aptitude or intellectual ability. Howard Gardner suggested we have multiple intelligences, proposing eight different types of intelligences or "frames of mind": linguistic (verbal), logical-mathematical, spatial, bodily-kinesthetic, musical, intrapersonal, interpersonal, and naturalist. Robert Sternberg proposed three kinds of intelligences. His triarchic theory of intelligence suggests that humans have varying degrees of analytical, creative, and practical abilities.

LO 11 Describe how intelligence is measured and identify important characteristics of assessment. (p. 289)

Some tests of intelligence aim to measure aptitude, or a person's potential for learning. Measures of achievement are designed to assess acquired knowledge (what a person has learned). Psychologists must ensure the accurate assessment of intelligence by determining validity, that is, the degree to which the test measures what it intends to measure. Another important characteristic is reliability, the ability of a test to provide consistent, reproducible results. A reliable test, given repeatedly, will result in similar scores.

LO 12 Define creativity and its associated characteristics. (p. 297)

Creativity is the ability to construct valuable results in innovative ways. Most psychologists agree on the basic characteristics of creativity, including originality, fluency, and flexibility. Because creativity is not evident in a singular or uniform manner, it is difficult to measure.

key terms

achievement, p. 289

algorithm, p. 271

aptitude, p. 289

availability heuristic, p. 275

cognition, p. 261

concepts, p. 262

confirmation bias, p. 277

convergent thinking, p. 298

creativity, p. 297

culture-fair intelligence test, p. 294

decision making, p. 274

divergent thinking, p. 298

emotional intelligence, p.295

formal concepts, p. 263

framing effect, p. 277

functional fixedness, p. 273

general intelligence (*g* factor), p. 287

gifted, p. 295

grammar, p. 283

heritability, p. 296

heuristics, p. 272

insight, p. 272

intelligence, p. 287

intelligence quotient (IQ), p. 290

language, p. 280

means–ends analysis, p. 272

mental age (MA), p. 290

morphemes, p. 283

natural concepts, p. 265

normal curve, p. 292

phonemes, p. 280

pragmatics, p. 283

problem solving, p. 269

prototypes, p. 265

reliability, p. 291

representativeness heuristic, p. 277

semantics, p. 283

standardization, p. 292

syntax, p. 283

thinking, p. 261

trial and error, p. 271

triarchic theory of intelligence, p. 288

validity, p. 291

TEST PREP are you ready?

1. _____ is a mental activity associated with obtaining, converting, and using knowledge, and _____ refers to coming to a decision, reaching a solution, or forming a belief.
   a. Thinking; formal concept
   b. Cognition; superordinate concept
   c. Thinking; cognition
   d. Cognition; thinking

2. _____ are the mental representations of categories of objects, situations, and ideas that belong together based on their central features or characteristics.
   a. Concepts   b. Prototypes
   c. Algorithms   d. Heuristics

3. The boundaries of _____ are imprecise and hard to define, because they do not have rigid rules for identification. For example, not everyone agrees with what qualities make a *mother*.
   a. algorithms   b. heuristics
   c. natural concepts   d. formal concepts

4. Following a stroke, the neurons in the brain exhibit greater excitability, rewiring occurs, and there is increased efficiency of synaptic connections, all indicating _____ of the brain.
   a. algorithms   b. the plasticity
   c. means–ends analysis   d. the functional fixedness

5. You are at dinner with a friend and you are struggling to determine the tip you should leave. Your friend suggests you do what she does to calculate a 20% tip: Move the decimal to the left one space and multiply by 2. This is an example of using _____ to solve the problem.
   a. prototypes   b. a heuristic
   c. trial and error   d. an algorithm

6. _____ is thought of as an understanding or solution that occurs in a sudden stroke of clarity. Research suggests activity occurs in the frontal and temporal lobes immediately preceding an "aha!" moment, implying that a reorganization occurs without our awareness.
   a. Insight   b. Functional fixedness
   c. A superordinate concept   d. A mental set

7. Factors such as the frequency and vividness of an event make us more likely to predict such an event will occur in the future. This is known as using the:
   a. representativeness heuristic.
   b. availability heuristic.
   c. additive model.
   d. confirmation bias.

8. Sometimes we do not gather important information when making decisions because we are only looking for evidence that upholds our beliefs. This is known as the:
   a. availability heuristic.
   b. framing effect.
   c. single-feature approach to decision making.
   d. confirmation bias.

9. The wording of a question can influence the outcome of a decision. People are more likely to prefer ground beef if it is described as 80% lean as opposed to 20% fat. This is an example of:
   a. insight.
   b. the confirmation bias.
   c. the framing effect.
   d. the vividness of an event.

10. Infants can recognize and distinguish among all _____ from all languages until about 9 months of age. This is why it is so much more difficult for older children and adults to learn to speak a foreign language without an accent.
    a. morphemes   b. phonemes
    c. words   d. semantics

11. One important component of creativity is _____, which refers to the ability to devise many solutions to a problem.
    a. divergent thinking   b. convergent thinking
    c. emotional intelligence   d. the normal curve

12. The word "unexcitable" can be broken into three parts (*un, excite, able*). Remove one of these and the meaning of the word changes. These three parts represent _____, the fundamental units that bring meaning to a language.
    a. grammar   b. phonemes
    c. morphemes   d. semantics

13. _____ is one's innate ability to solve problems, adapt to the environment, and learn from experience.
    a. Heritability   b. Giftedness
    c. Insight   d. Intelligence

14. To determine the _____ of an intelligence test, you could give the assessment to a sample of participants and then compare the results with another assessment of intelligence to make sure the test is measuring what it intends to measure.
    a. reliability   b. validity
    c. standardization   d. norms

15. Although there is a consistent gap between how Black Americans and White Americans score on IQ tests, research suggests this is the result of:
    a. environmental factors such as chronic stress.
    b. heritability.
    c. genetic differences.
    d. emotional intelligence.

16. How are formal and natural concepts different? Give examples of each.

17. Explain how the theories of intelligence differ.

18. Many people on the Jersey Shore had to leave their homes when Hurricane Irene hit in 2011. On returning home, they found that no significant damage had occurred. When told to evacuate for Superstorm Sandy in 2012, many of these same residents did not leave. What heuristic do you think they used?

19. Why are reliability and validity important in test construction? What is at risk if you have developed an unreliable IQ test? What might happen if your IQ test is not valid?

20. Using divergent thinking, how many uses can you think of for a hammer?

✓ CHECK YOUR ANSWERS IN APPENDIX C.

Get personalized practice by logging into LaunchPad at **www.macmillanhighered.com/launchpad/ sciampresenting1e** to take the LearningCurve adaptive quizzes for Chapter 7.

8

Baby socks: Tatyana Nikitina/Getty Images, Sippy Cup: Creative Crop/ Getty Images

human
development

Kais Tolmats/Getty Images

The Study of Human Development

A DAY IN THE LIFE   Montgomery, Illinois: Mondays are especially hectic for working mom and college student Jasmine Mitchell. The 31-year-old starts the day at 5:00 A.M. with a morning workout of hip-swaying, shoulder-shimmying Zumba® dance. Then, in between catching her breath and folding laundry, she wakes up her 14-year-old daughter Jocelyn and her 5-year-old son Eddie. At 7:00 A.M., two more children appear at Jasmine's doorstep, a 14-year-old nephew and a 9-year-old niece. Jasmine takes care of the kids in the morning to help out her mother, who is their legal guardian. It is now 7:15 A.M., and Jasmine is fixing eggs and sausage for a house full of children.

Meanwhile, in Austin, Texas, 22-year-old Chloe Ojeah is dropping an array of multicolored pills into her grandparents' pill dividers. This painstaking task is something she needs to do carefully because it's critical that both her grandmother and grandfather take the correct medication in the morning and again at night. Her 79-year-old grandmother is struggling with Alzheimer's disease and her 85-year-old grandfather is recovering from a stroke. After skipping breakfast herself, Chloe heads out the door and drives to Austin Community College, where she is working toward a degree in communications and, down the road, a career in teaching.

Back in Illinois, it is now 8:30 A.M., and Jasmine has already dropped the four children off at three different schools. She returns home, cleans up the mess from breakfast, showers, and starts her homework. Jasmine is a student at Waubonsee Community College, where she is studying to be a social worker. There's not much time for homework, though, because Jasmine needs to be at her job by 11:00 A.M. (She works 40 hours a week as a receptionist at the college.)

Right around the time Jasmine walks into the office, Chloe is returning home from her morning class. She checks in with her grandparents' caregiver (*How did the morning go? Do we need anything from the store?*), chats with her grandfather, grabs lunch, and hits the books. Within a few hours, she is cooking dinner—enchiladas, a cheeseburger pie, or something else warm and comforting—and dispensing her grandparents' evening pills. They chat over supper, but Chloe's grandmother sometimes loses track of the conversation and stares blankly out the window.

Supermom
Jasmine Mitchell is coping with the complex issues of childhood, adolescence, and young adulthood. She juggles motherhood with college and a full-time job. Jasmine Mitchell

For the Love of Family
Chloe Ojeah is balancing her college education with the responsibility of caring for two elderly grandparents. Her grandmother, 79, struggles with Alzheimer's disease, and her grandfather, 85, continues to recover from a stroke. Courtesy Chloe Ojeah

Note: Quotations attributed to Jasmine Mitchell, Chloe Ojeah, and J. M. Richard are personal communications.

Other Voices: Allie Fuentes

http://qrs.ly/ll4qsdp

© 2016, Macmillan

Back in Illinois, Jasmine is just about to leave work. Around 8:30 P.M., she arrives at the home of her mother, who has picked up the kids at the end of their school day and cooked dinner for them. Once home, Eddie heads straight to bed and Jocelyn stays up late, working on homework. After finishing her own homework and tying up some odds and ends around the house, Jasmine finally goes to bed at 11:00 P.M.

It's nighttime in Texas, and Chloe is sitting footsteps away from her grandparents' bedroom. They've long since retired. She likes to stay close by, though, until 11:00 P.M., in case they need her. Finally, in the silence of the night, Chloe climbs the stairs and crawls into bed. 📁

Jasmine Mitchell and Chloe Ojeah are actual college students with real-world responsibilities. They are pursuing challenging degree programs, launching careers, and finding their place in the world. Both women are making their way through a busy, often tumultuous, period of life called *young adulthood*. At the same time, they are up to their necks in issues pertinent to other stages of life: *childhood* and *adolescence* for Jasmine, the young mother, and *late adulthood* for Chloe, the caretaker of two elderly family members.

These young women are people whose lives, in many respects, may resemble your own. Psychologists often focus their research on "normal" or "average" individuals, as it helps them uncover common themes and variations across the life span.

Developmental Psychology

LO 1 Define human development.

What do psychologists mean when they say "development?" Obviously, humans do not stay the same from conception to death. Development refers to the changes that occur in our bodies, minds, and social functioning. The goal of **developmental psychology** is to examine these changes. The study of development is, in many ways, an attempt to understand the struggles and triumphs of everyday people at different stages of their lives. Many of the topics presented in this chapter, such as personality, learning, and emotion, are covered elsewhere in this book. Here, we focus on how these evolve over the course of a lifetime, homing in on three major categories of developmental change: physical, cognitive, and socioemotional.

THREE CATEGORIES OF DEVELOPMENT *Physical development* begins the moment a sperm unites with an egg, and it continues until we take our final breath. The physical growth beginning with conception and ending when the body stops growing is referred to as **maturation.** For the most part, maturation follows a progression that is universal in nature and biologically driven, as these changes are common across all cultures and ethnicities, and generally follow a predictable pattern. After maturation, physical changes continue, but not necessarily in a positive or growth direction (Stuen & Faye, 2003). Changes in memory, problem-solving abilities, decision making, language, and intelligence all fall under the umbrella of *cognitive development.* Like physical development, cognitive development tends to follow a universal course early in life, but there is enormous variation in the way cognitive abilities change, particularly as people get older (Skirbekk, Loichinger, & Weber, 2012; Small, Dixon, & McArdle, 2011; von Stumm & Deary, 2012). *Socioemotional development* refers to social behaviors, emotions, and the changes people experience with respect to their relationships, feelings, and overall disposition.

I Can Sit!
Most babies become physically capable of sitting up alone at approximately 5½ months, though it ranges from 4 to 9 months (WHO Multicentre Growth Reference Study Group, 2006). Sitting upright is one of the milestones of physical development. Maturation tends to follow a predictable pattern, regardless of ethnicity or culture. Getty Images/Blend Images

BIOPSYCHOSOCIAL PERSPECTIVE In this chapter, we draw on the biopsychosocial perspective, which recognizes the contributions of biological, psychological, and social forces shaping human development. We consider the intricate interplay of heredity, chemical activity, and hormones (biological factors); learning and personality traits (psychological factors); and family, culture, and media (social factors). When examining complex psychological phenomena, it is important to incorporate a variety of approaches.

Three Debates

LO 2 Describe three longstanding discussions in developmental psychology.

Science is, at its core, a work in progress, full of unresolved questions and areas of disagreement. In developmental psychology, longstanding debates and discussions tend to cluster around three major themes: stages and continuity, nature and nurture, and stability and change. Each of these themes relates to a basic question: (1) Does development occur in separate or discrete stages, or is it a steady, continuous process? (2) What are the relative roles of heredity and environment in development? (3) How stable is one's personality over a lifetime and across situations?

STAGES OR CONTINUITY Some aspects of development occur in discrete stages; others in a steady, continuous process. Abrupt changes are often related to environmental circumstances. High school graduation, for example, marks the time when many young people feel free to move out of the family home. This response is not universal, however. Chloe graduated from high school years ago, but she is living with her grandparents so she can care for them. Physical changes may also occur in stages, such as learning to walk and talk, or developing the physical characteristics of a sexually mature adult.

One line of evidence supporting developmental stages with definitive beginnings and endings comes to us indirectly through the animal kingdom. Konrad Lorenz (1937) documented the *imprinting* phenomenon, showing, for example, that when baby geese hatch, they become attached to the first "moving and sound-emitting object" they see, whether it's their mother or a nearby human (p. 269). Lorenz made sure he was the first moving creature several goslings saw, and he found that they followed him as soon as they could stand up and walk, becoming permanently attached to him because he was that first "object." But there appeared to be a limited time frame within

You Asked, Allie Answers

http://qrs.ly/yd4qsdu
How does being a parent affect your work and school?

developmental psychology A field of psychology that examines physical, cognitive, and socioemotional changes across the life span.

maturation Physical growth beginning with conception and ending when the body stops growing.

He Must Be My Mother
A brood of baby geese follows scientist Konrad Lorenz. The goslings treated Lorenz like a mother because he was the first "moving and sound-emitting" object with whom they had contact (Lorenz, 1937, p. 269). As Lorenz discovered, there appears to be a critical period during which imprinting occurs. Time & Life Pictures/ Getty Images

which this imprinting occurred. Experiences during a **critical period** for this type of automatic response result in permanent and "irreversible changes" in brain function (Knudsen, 2004). Critical periods are a type of *sensitive period* of development, during which "certain capacities are readily shaped or altered by experience" (p. 1412). Young barn owls, for example, learn how to navigate their environment during a sensitive period in which auditory information is used to create a type of mental map, but this period is not considered critical because it is not characterized by irreversible brain changes (Knudsen, 2004).

How does all this talk of geese and owls relate to people? Some psychologists suggest there is a critical period for language acquisition. Until a certain age, children are highly receptive to learning language, but after that critical period ends, it is difficult for *them* to acquire a first language that is age-appropriate and "normal" (Kuhl, Conboy, Padden, Nelson, & Pruitt, 2005). Others suggest that language acquisition is not subject to a critical period, but rather to sensitive periods that all children experience (Knudsen, 2004). (For more on this topic, read about Genie the "feral child" later in this chapter.)

Although some aspects of development occur in stages, others occur gradually, without a clear distinction between them (McAdams & Olson, 2010). Observing a toddler making her transition into early childhood, you probably won't be able to pinpoint her shift from the "terrible twos" to the more emotionally self-controlled young child.

HEREDITARY AND ENVIRONMENTAL INFLUENCES Psychologists also debate the degree to which heredity (nature) and environment (nurture) influence behavior and development, but few would dispute the important contributions of both (Mysterud, 2003). Researchers can study a trait like impulsivity, which is the tendency to act before thinking, to determine the extent to which it results from hereditary factors and from the environment. In this particular case, nature and nurture appear to have equal weight (Bezdjian, Baker, & Tuvblad, 2011). Later in this chapter, we will examine the balance of nature and nurture in relation to brain and intellectual development, a longstanding, sometimes controversial debate in psychology and beyond.

STABILITY AND CHANGE How much does a person change from childhood to old age? Some researchers suggest that personality traits identified early in life can be used to predict behaviors across the life span (McAdams & Olson, 2010). Others report that personality characteristics change as a result of the relationships and experiences we have throughout life (Specht, Egloff, & Schmukle, 2011). Psychologists often discuss how experiences in infancy can set the stage for stable cognitive characteristics, particularly when it comes to early enrichment and its long-term impact on intellectual abilities (more on this topic later).

Three Methods

LO 3   Identify the types of research psychologists use to study developmental processes.

critical period Specific time frame in which an organism is sensitive to environmental factors, and certain behaviors and abilities are readily shaped or altered by events or experiences.

cross-sectional method A research design that examines people of different ages at a single point in time.

Developmental psychologists use a variety of methods to study differences across ages and time (**Infographic 8.1**).

THE CROSS-SECTIONAL METHOD The **cross-sectional method** enables researchers to examine people of different ages at a given point in time. In one study, for example, researchers used the cross-sectional method to investigate developmental

Research Methods in Developmental Psychology

Developmental psychologists use several research methods to study changes that occur with age. Imagine you want to know whether using social media helps protect against feelings of loneliness over time. How would you design a study to measure that? Let's compare methods.

Longitudinal

Measure a **single group** at **different points in time**

Example: Researchers follow a sample of participants, interviewing them every decade for a total of three measurements. As they age, participants report lower levels of loneliness than expected. But because the study is longitudinal, we can't eliminate the possibility that this particular group of participants is less lonely because of some historically specific effect.

GROUP 1

 20 YEARS OLD   30 YEARS OLD   40 YEARS OLD

2005　　　**2015**　　　**2025**

BENEFITS
+ Can track age-related changes.

PROBLEMS
- Measured changes could be specific to the particular group of participants.
- Takes a long time, leading some participants to drop out before study is complete.

Cross-sectional

Measure groups of people of **different ages** (for example, 20-, 40-, and 60-year-olds) at a **single point in time**

Example: Researchers interview participants in three different age groups: 20-, 40-, and 60-year-olds. The oldest group reports higher levels of loneliness. But because the study is cross-sectional, we can't be sure if this finding reflects a *cohort effect,* in which differences may be due to age or to common experiences within the group, as opposed to developmental changes in physical, cognitive, or socioemotional functioning.

GROUP 3　60 YEARS OLD

GROUP 2　40 YEARS OLD

GROUP 1　20 YEARS OLD

2005　　　**2015**　　　2025

BENEFITS
+ Allows comparison between age groups.
+ Can be completed relatively quickly.

PROBLEMS
- Susceptible to cohort effect.

Cross-sequential

Measure groups of people of **different ages**, following them across **different points in time**

Example: Researchers interview participants from three age groups every decade for a total of three measurements. This results in data showing how social media use and loneliness change within each group as they age.

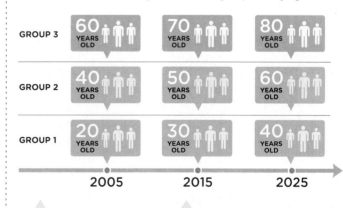

GROUP 3　60 YEARS OLD　70 YEARS OLD　80 YEARS OLD

GROUP 2　40 YEARS OLD　50 YEARS OLD　60 YEARS OLD

GROUP 1　20 YEARS OLD　30 YEARS OLD　40 YEARS OLD

2005　　　**2015**　　　**2025**

BENEFITS
+ Shows changes within individuals and between groups.
+ Better addresses cohort effect.

PROBLEMS
- Requires substantial resources and many participants.
- Takes a long time, leading some participants to drop out before study is complete.

CONNECTIONS

In **Chapter 6,** we described recall as the process of retrieving information held in long-term memory without the help of explicit retrieval cues. Here, we will see how these memory processes change as a function of development.

CONNECTIONS

In **Chapter 1,** we described confounding variables as unaccounted factors that change in sync with the independent variable, making it very hard to discern which one is causing changes in the dependent variable. Here, we consider how a cohort can act as a confounding variable.

changes in the efficiency of memory recall (Castel et al., 2011). They divided their 320 participants into groups according to age (children, adolescents, younger adults, middle-aged adults, young-old adults, and old-old adults) and compared the scores of the different groups to see if changes occur across the life span. One advantage of the cross-sectional method is that it can provide a great deal of information quickly; by studying differences across age groups, we don't have to wait for people to get older.

But a major problem with the cross-sectional method is that it doesn't tell us whether differences across age groups result from actual developmental changes or from common experiences within groups, a phenomenon known as the cohort effect. Members of each age group have lived through similar historical and cultural eras, and these common experiences may be responsible for some differences across groups. For example, the "old-old adults" in the memory recall study described above were not raised on cell phones, iPads, Google, or Facebook, so they probably have different perspectives than those in the younger adult group. The authors of the study were quick to point out this pitfall: "The present design was cross-sectional, whereas (in some ways) a longitudinal design would allow for stronger conclusions regarding . . . *changes* with age" (Castel et al., 2011, p. 1562).

THE LONGITUDINAL METHOD   Researchers can avoid the cohort effect by using the **longitudinal method,** which follows one group of individuals over a period of time. Curious to find out what "lifestyle activities" are associated with age-related cognitive decline, one team of researchers studied 952 individuals over a 12-year period (Small, Dixon, McArdle, & Grimm, March 2012). Every 3 to 4 years, they administered tests to all participants, assessing, for example, cognitive abilities and health status. The more engaged and socially active the participants were, the better their long-term cognitive performance. Using the longitudinal method, we can compare the same individuals over time, identifying similarities and differences in the way they age. But these studies are difficult to conduct because they require a great deal of money, time, and participant investment. Common challenges include attrition (people dropping out of the study) and practice effects (people performing better on measures as they get more "practice").

THE CROSS-SEQUENTIAL METHOD   The **cross-sequential method,** also used by developmental psychologists, is a mixture of the longitudinal and cross-sectional methods. You might call it the best of both worlds. Participants are divided into age groups and followed over time, so researchers can examine developmental changes within individuals and across different age groups. One team of researchers used this approach to identify the age at which cognitive decline becomes evident (Singh-Manoux et al., 2012). They recruited 10,308 participants, assigning each to a 5-year age group (45–49, 50–54, 55–59, 60–64, and 65–70), and then followed them for 10 years. Using this approach, they could observe changes in individuals as they aged *and* identify differences across age groups.

Human development is very complex. Some processes are universal; others are specific to an individual, and it is this combination that makes the field so fascinating. As you learn about the development of Chloe, Jasmine, and their families, you may be struck by the degree of similarity (or differences) in your own family.

✓◯◯◯   show what you know

1. A 3-year-old decides he doesn't need diapers, and much to his parents' surprise, he starts using the toilet. This physiological change likely results from his maturation, which follows a progression that is universal and biologically driven. This is an example of human _____, which includes changes in physical, cognitive, and socioemotional characteristics.

2. Explain the three longstanding discussions of developmental psychology.

3. A researcher is interested in studying developmental changes in memory recall. She asks 300 participants to take a memory test and then compares the results across five different age groups. This researcher is using which of the following methods?
   a. cross-sequential
   b. longitudinal
   c. cross-sectional
   d. biopsychosocial

✓ CHECK YOUR ANSWERS IN APPENDIX C.

Genetics, Conception, and Prenatal Development

16 AND PREGNANT   Jasmine has always had a mind of her own. As a teenager, she pretty much did as she pleased. If her mother forbade her to leave the house, she would go out and party extra-hard, her basic philosophy being, *If I'm going to get in trouble anyway, I might as well have a really good time.* Jasmine did not like high school, so on her 16th birthday, she walked into the principal's office and announced she was dropping out.

A few months later, she began dating an older guy who was, as she describes, "the definition of a bad boy." He was 19 years old, ran with the wrong crowd, and would soon become the father of her firstborn child. Getting pregnant was not exactly planned, nor was it something she couldn't have predicted; at 16, Jasmine was well aware of the consequences of sexual intercourse. But like many adolescents, she was living in the moment, not giving a whole lot of thought to the long-term consequences of her decisions.

Being pregnant with Jocelyn was a breeze. Apart from having strange cravings (bologna sandwiches and Doritos), Jasmine did not experience typical symptoms such as morning sickness and fatigue. "I didn't feel like I was pregnant." And like any normal 16-year-old, Jasmine wanted to hang out with friends and have fun. She continued to hit the party scene throughout the 9 months of her pregnancy (she was actually at a party when her water broke), but refrained from using alcohol and other drugs—a very wise decision, and you will soon discover why.

After a grueling labor lasting 36 hours, Jasmine was somewhat surprised by her newborn's appearance. "I was grossed out, honestly," Jasmine says. "She was covered with slime and ooze." But as soon as the nurses cleaned baby Jocelyn, she looked much more like a sweet little cherub. Okay, thought Jasmine, *She is kind of cute . . . and she came out of me!* It was mind-boggling to think that her body had produced this 7-pound, 9-ounce infant from the ground up—in less than a year. How did this living, breathing baby with 10 little fingers and toes emerge from a single cell roughly the size of the dot at the bottom of this question mark? We thought you'd never ask.

Chromosomes and Genes

LO 4   Examine the role genes play in our development and identify the biological factors that determine sex.

In order to understand human development, you must have a basic understanding of *chromosomes* and *genes*. With the exception of red blood cells, every cell in the human body has a nucleus at its center. Within this nucleus is material containing the blueprint or plan for the building of a complete person. This material is coiled tightly into 46 **chromosomes,** the threadlike structures we inherit from our biological parents (23 from our father and 23 from our mother). A chromosome contains one molecule of **deoxyribonucleic acid (DNA).** Looking at the DNA molecule in **Figure 8.1** on the next page, you can see a specific section along its length has been identified. This section corresponds to a **gene,** and genes provide the instructions for making proteins. The proteins encoded by genes determine the texture of your hair, the color of your eyes, and some aspects of your personality. Genes influence nearly every dimension of the complex living system known as YOU.

Your chromosomes, and all the genes they contain, come from your biological parents. In the moment of conception, your father's sperm united with your mother's

longitudinal method A research design that examines one sample of people over a period of time to determine age-related changes.

cross-sequential method A research design that examines groups of people of different ages, following them across time.

chromosomes Inherited threadlike structures composed of deoxyribonucleic acid (DNA).

deoxyribonucleic acid (DNA) A molecule that provides the instructions for the development and production of cells.

gene Specified segment of a DNA molecule.

FIGURE 8.1

Chromosomes, DNA, and Genes

Every cell in your body, except red blood cells and sex cells (sperm or egg), contains a full set of 23 chromosome pairs like those shown in the photo on the far right. These 23 chromosome pairs contain the full blueprint for you as a complete, unique person. The primary component of each chromosome is a single, tightly wound molecule of DNA. Within that DNA are around 21,000 genes, each determining specific traits such as hair texture. Note the sex chromosomes (X and Y) on the lower right, indicating the sex is male. CNRI/Science Source

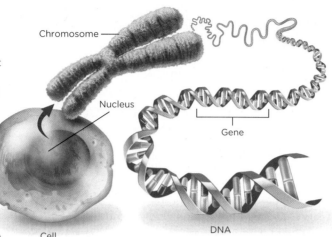
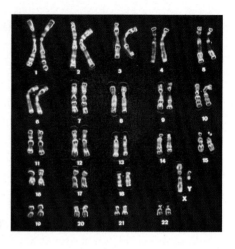

Chromosome

Nucleus

Gene

Cell

DNA

egg to form a **zygote,** a single cell that eventually gave rise to the trillions of cells that now make up your body (Sherwood, 2010). Typically, both sperm and egg contain 23 chromosomes, so the resulting zygote has 23 *pairs* of chromosomes, or 46 total. The 23rd pair of chromosomes, also referred to as the *sex chromosomes,* includes specific instructions for the zygote to develop into a male or female. Let's learn how this happens.

SEX DETERMINATION   The egg from the mother contributes an *X chromosome* to the 23rd pair, and the sperm from the father contributes either an *X chromosome* or a *Y chromosome.* If the sperm carries an *X,* the genetic sex is *XX,* and the zygote generally develops into a female. If the sperm carries a *Y,* the genetic sex is *XY,* and the zygote typically develops into a male. This designation of genetic sex is called *sex determination,* and it guides the activity of hormones that direct the development of reproductive organs and structures (Ngun, Ghahramani, Sánchez, Bocklandt, & Vilain, 2011). About 50% of sperm carry the X chromosome, and 50% carry the Y chromosome, which explains why about half the population is male (XY) and the other half is female (XX).

Genetic sex is established at the moment of conception and remains constant throughout life, but what happens next? In other words, how does the developing person acquire male or female reproductive anatomy? In a genetic male, the presence of the Y chromosome causes the fetal sex glands (also known as *gonads*) to become testes. If the Y chromosome is not present, as in the case of a genetic female, then the gonads develop into ovaries (Hines, 2011a). Both the testes and ovaries secrete sex hormones that influence the development of reproductive organs: **androgens** in the case of the testes and **estrogen** in the case of the ovaries. **Testosterone,** for example, is an androgen that influences whether male or female genitals develop. Beginning about 7 weeks after conception, the sex of the developing person can be determined through blood tests (Devaney, Palomaki, Scott, & Bianchi, 2011). By the end of the first trimester, genital anatomy can be determined by ultrasound (Scheffer et al., 2010).

DIFFERENCES OF SEXUAL DEVELOPMENT   In some cases, hormonal imbalances and genetic abnormalities lead to differences of sex development (Topp, 2013). Such disparities result from "congenital conditions in which development of chromosomal, gonadal, or anatomic sex is atypical" (Lee, Houk, Ahmed, & Hughes, 2006, p. e488). According to the American Psychiatric Association, **intersexual** refers to having "conflicting or ambiguous biological indicators" of male or female in sexual structures and organs (2013, p. 451). Around 1% of infants are found to have differences

zygote A single cell formed by the union of a sperm cell and egg.

androgens The male hormones secreted by the testes in males.

estrogen The female hormone secreted primarily by the ovaries in females.

testosterone An androgen produced by the testes.

intersexual Ambiguous or inconsistent biological indicators of male or female in the sexual structures and organs.

genotype An individual's complete collection of genes.

phenotype The observable expression or characteristics of one's genetic inheritance.

TABLE 8.1 DIFFERENCES OF SEXUAL DEVELOPMENT

Condition	Frequency
Intersex (atypical genitalia)	1 in 1,500 births
Klinefelter's syndrome	1 in 1,000 births
Turner's syndrome	1 in 2,500 female births
Androgen-insensitivity syndrome	1 in 13,000 births
5-alpha reductase deficiency	Very rare—incidence unknown

People with ambiguous sexual characteristics are considered to have differences of sexual development. Listed above are the frequency estimates for some common causes of intersexuality.

INFORMATION FROM: GENETICS HOME REFERENCE (2008); INTERSEX SOCIETY OF NORTH AMERICA (2008); NATIONAL INSTITUTES OF HEALTH, EUNICE KENNEDY SHRIVER NATIONAL INSTITUTE OF CHILD HEALTH AND HUMAN DEVELOPMENT (N.D.).

of sex development at birth. They once might have been called "hermaphrodites," but such terminology is outdated, derogatory, and misleading because it refers to the impossible condition of being both fully male and fully female (Vilain, 2008). There are various types of intersexual development (**Table 8.1**), but one example might be a genetic female (XX) or male (XY) who has sexual structures and organs that are ambiguous or inconsistent with genetic sex. In this case, we see that genes do not tell the whole story of human development. Let's explore the relationship between *genotype* and *phenotype*.

LO 5   Discuss how genotype and phenotype relate to development.

GENOTYPE AND PHENOTYPE   Recall that most of the cells in your body have 23 chromosome pairs (46 chromosomes total). These chromosomes are unique to you and are known as your **genotype.** Genotypes do not change in response to the environment, but they do interact with the environment. Because so much variability exists in the surrounding world, the outcome of this interaction is not predetermined. The color and appearance of your skin, for example, result from an interplay between your genotype and a variety of environmental factors including sun and wind exposure, age, nutrition, and smoking—all of which can impact how your genes are expressed (Kolb & Whishaw, 2011; Rees, 2003). The results of this interaction are the observable expression or characteristics of an individual, or **phenotype.** A person's phenotype is apparent in her unique physical, psychological, and behavioral characteristics (Scarr & McCartney, 1983).

You might be wondering what all this talk of genotype and phenotype has to do with psychology. Our genetic makeup influences our behavior, and psychologists are interested in learning how this process occurs. Consider schizophrenia, a psychological disorder (Chapter 12) with symptoms ranging from hallucinations to emotional problems. A large body of evidence now suggests that a person's genotype may predispose him to developing schizophrenia. Researchers report heritability rates as high as 80% to 85% (Craddock, O'Donovan, & Owen, 2005; Tandon, Keshavan, & Nasrallah, 2008b). But the expression or manifestation of the disorder results from a combination of genotype and experience, including diet, stress, toxins, and early parenting (Champagne & Mashoodh, 2009; Zhang & Meaney, 2010). Identical twins, who have the same genotype, may display different

CONNECTIONS

In **Chapter 7,** we described heritability as the degree to which heredity is responsible for a particular characteristic. Here, we see that around 80–85% of the population-wide variation in schizophrenia can be attributed to genetic makeup and 20% to the environment.

Seas of DNA
The colored lights are an artistic representation of the human genome, the complete set of DNA found in most cells in the body. Researchers with the Human Genome Project have decoded the entire human genome, which contains about 21,000 DNA segments known as genes (Pennisi, 2012, September 5). Genes are the blueprints for proteins that endow you with a unique set of traits, including eye color, hair texture, and—to a certain extent—psychological characteristics. Mario Tama/Getty Images

Can You Roll?
Urban myth tells us that tongue-rolling ability is determined by the presence of a single, dominant gene (Starr, 2005, June 10). It's probably more complicated than that, though. Many people who cannot roll their tongues as young children eventually learn to do so, suggesting that environmental factors also play a role in the development of this skill (Komai, 1951). © Graham Dunn/Alamy

phenotypes, including distinct expressions of schizophrenia if they both have this disorder. This is because schizophrenia, or any psychological phenomenon, results from complex relationships between genes and environment. Understanding these relationships is the main thrust of **epigenetics,** a field that examines the processes involved in the development of phenotypes.

DOMINANT AND RECESSIVE GENES Genes are behind just about every human trait you can imagine—from height, to shoe size, to behavior. But remember, you possess two copies of each chromosome (one from mom, one from dad), and therefore two of each gene. Sometimes the genes in a pair are identical (both of them encode dimples, for instance). In other cases, the two genes differ, providing dissimilar instructions about the outcome (one encodes dimples, while the other encodes no dimples). Often one gene variant has more power than the other. This **dominant gene** governs the expression of the inherited characteristic, overpowering the recessive, or subordinate, gene in the pair. A **recessive gene** cannot overcome the influence of a dominant gene. For example, "dimples" are dominant, and "no dimples" are recessive. If one gene encodes for dimples and the other no dimples, then dimples will be expressed. If both genes encode for no dimples, no dimples will be expressed. This all sounds relatively straightforward, but it's not. Psychological traits—and the genetics behind them—are exceedingly complex. Characteristics such as intelligence and aggressive tendencies are influenced by multiple genes, most of which have yet to be identified.

Now that we have a basic handle on genetics, let's shift our attention toward the developmental changes that occur within the womb.

From Zygote to Embryo to Fetus

LO 6   Describe the progression of prenatal development.

As you may recall, Jasmine's pregnancy with Jocelyn was not particularly difficult. She "didn't feel" pregnant. But the changes occurring within her body were extraordinary. The making of a human being, from a single cell to a sensing, perceiving, aware individual, is nothing short of awesome. Let's take a look at *prenatal development,* the 38–40 weeks between conception and birth.

epigenetics A field of study that examines the processes involved in the development of phenotypes.

dominant gene One of a pair of genes that has power over the expression of an inherited characteristic.

recessive gene One of a pair of genes that is dominated by the other gene in the pair.

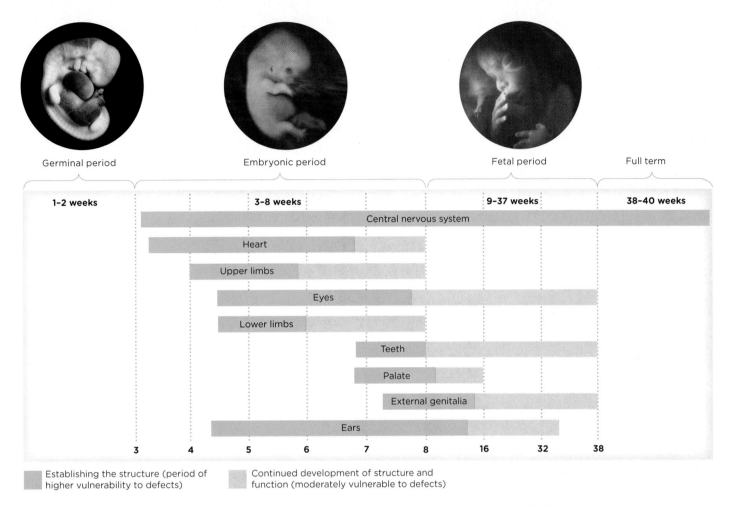

| Germinal period | Embryonic period | Fetal period | Full term |

Central nervous system
Heart
Upper limbs
Eyes
Lower limbs
Teeth
Palate
External genitalia
Ears

■ Establishing the structure (period of higher vulnerability to defects)

■ Continued development of structure and function (moderately vulnerable to defects)

THE ZYGOTE   In the beginning, before you became you, an egg (also known as an *ovum*) from your biological mother and a sperm cell from your biological father came together at the moment of *conception.* Together, the egg and sperm formed a single cell called a *zygote,* which is smaller than the tip of a needle. Under normal circumstances, a zygote immediately begins to divide into two cells, then each of those cells divides, and so on.

Conception sometimes results in twins or multiples. Identical or **monozygotic twins** develop from one egg inseminated at conception. This egg is fertilized by one sperm and then it splits, forming separate zygotes. Monozygotic twins have identical sets of 46 chromosomes, as they originate from the same zygote; the resulting infants are the same sex and have almost identical features. Fraternal or **dizygotic twins**, on the other hand, occur when two eggs are inseminated by two different sperm, leading to the development of two distinct zygotes. This can occur naturally, but assisted reproductive technology may increase the odds of a woman releasing more than one egg (Manninen, 2011). Twins and multiples resulting from these distinct sperm–egg combinations are like other biological siblings; they share around 50% of their genes.

GERMINAL AND EMBRYONIC PERIODS   From conception to the end of the 2nd week is the *germinal period,* during which the rapidly dividing zygote implants in the uterine wall. Between the 3rd and 8th weeks of development, the growing mass of cells is called an **embryo.** The embryo is protected in the amniotic sac and eventually receives nourishment, hydration, and oxygen through the umbilical cord, which is attached to the placenta. For the most part, the placenta ensures that the blood of the mother and the baby do not mix and disposes of carbon dioxide and waste. During the germinal period, all the cells were identical. In the *embryonic period,* the cells differentiate and the major organs and systems begin to form (**Figure 8.2**).

▲ **FIGURE 8.2**

Prenatal Development and Periods of Critical Growth

During prenatal development, individual structures form and are fine-tuned at different times. As each structure is being established, it is particularly vulnerable to interference. Once their critical periods are complete, the structures are fully established. left: Omikron/Science Source; center: Anatomical Travelogue/Science Source; right: Neil Bromhall/Science Source

monozygotic twins Identical twins who develop from one egg inseminated at conception, which then splits into two separate cells.

dizygotic twins Fraternal twins who develop from two eggs inseminated by two sperm, and are as genetically similar as any sibling pair.

embryo The unborn human from the beginning of the 3rd week of pregnancy, lasting through the 8th week of prenatal development.

This differentiation allows for the heart to begin to beat, the arms and legs to grow, and the spinal cord and intestinal system to develop. But less than half of all zygotes actually implant in the uterine wall (Gold, 2005). Of reported pregnancies, around 21% end in a miscarriage (Buss et al., 2006), many of which result from genetic abnormalities of the embryo (Velagaleti & Moore, 2011).

TERATOGENS   The embryo may be safely nestled in the amniotic sac, but it is not protected from all environmental dangers. **Teratogens** (tə-'ra-tə-jən) are agents that can damage a zygote, embryo, or fetus (**Table 8.2**). Radiation, viruses, bacteria, chemicals, and drugs are all considered teratogens. The damage depends on the agent, as well as the timing and duration of exposure, and can result in miscarriage, decreased birth weight, heart defects, and other adverse outcomes. One well-known teratogen is alcohol, which can lead to *fetal alcohol spectrum disorders (FASD)*. In particular, **fetal alcohol syndrome** (FAS) is the result of moderate to heavy alcohol use during pregnancy, which can cause delays in normal development, a small head, lower intelligence, and distinct facial characteristics (for example, wide-spaced eyes, flattened nose). Researchers continue to debate what constitutes an acceptable amount of alcohol use during pregnancy, but they do agree that even a small amount poses risks (Nathanson, Jayesinghe, & Roycroft, 2007; O'Brien, 2007).

Dad and Daughter
A father enjoys time with his 25-year-old adopted daughter. The young woman has fetal alcohol syndrome, a condition that results from exposure to alcohol during fetal development. The symptoms of fetal alcohol syndrome—which can be avoided by abstaining from alcohol during pregnancy—include delays in physical growth, learning disabilities, and problems with anxiety, attention, and impulse regulation (Mayo Clinic, 2014, June 2). Stuart Wong KRT/Newscom

TABLE 8.2	THE DANGERS OF TERATOGENS
Teratogens	**Potential Effects**
Alcohol	Fetal alcohol syndrome: developmental delay, poor growth, heart problems, growth delay
Caffeine	High exposure associated with miscarriage
Cocaine	Birth defects, miscarriage
Lead	High exposure linked with miscarriage
Lithium	Heart defects, malformations
LSD	Arm and leg defects, central nervous system problems
Mercury	Cerebral palsy, developmental delay, blindness
Nicotine	Malformations, low birth weight, cleft lip or palate, heart defects
Radiation exposure	Small skull, blindness, spina bifida, cleft palate

From conception until birth, the developing human is nestled deep inside a woman's body, but it remains vulnerable to threats from the outside. Listed here are some common teratogens and their effects.

SOURCE: BRENT (2004) AND LANGWITH (2010).

CONNECTIONS

In **Chapter 4,** we noted that the daily patterns in some of our physiological functioning roughly follow the 24-hour cycle of daylight and darkness, driven by our *circadian rhythm*. Here, we can see that even before birth, sleep–wake cycles are becoming evident.

THE FETAL PERIOD   Between 2 months and birth, the growing human is called a **fetus** (Figure 8.2). During the *fetal period*, the developing person grows from the size of a pumpkin seed to a small watermelon, the average birth weight being approximately 7 pounds (by North American standards). The fetus rapidly gains weight and begins to prepare for birth, and it already has clear sleep–wake cycles (Suwanrath & Suntharasaj, 2010). Under normal circumstances, all organs, systems, and structures are fully developed at birth, and the brain is approximately one-quarter the weight of an adult brain (Sherwood, Subiaul, & Zawidzki, 2008).

If you step back and contemplate the baby-making phenomenon, it's really quite amazing. But many more exciting developments are in store. Are you ready for some shrieking, babbling, and a little game of peekaboo? Let's move on to infancy and childhood.

✓ show what you know

1. _____ are threadlike structures humans inherit from their biological mothers and fathers.
   a. Teratogens
   b. Zygotes
   c. Genes
   d. Chromosomes

2. _____ represents a complete collection of genes, and _____ represents the observed expression of inherited characteristics.

3. A coworker tells you that she is in her 6th week of pregnancy. She is excited because she has learned that during this _____, her baby is developing a spinal cord, its heart is beginning to beat, and its intestinal system is forming.
   a. embryonic period
   b. phenotype
   c. germinal period
   d. genotype

4. How would you describe the difference between dominant and recessive genes to someone who has never taken an introductory psychology course?

✓ CHECK YOUR ANSWERS IN APPENDIX C.

Infancy and Child Development

26 AND PREGNANT The circumstances surrounding the birth of Jasmine's second child were strikingly different from those of her first. When Eddie came into the world, Jasmine was a married, working woman with 10 more years of life experience; and a decade can make a world of difference in development. As Jasmine can testify, "The mental capacity is way different between a 16- and a 26-year-old." By this time in life, Jasmine had become much more aware of how her decisions impacted others, especially her children.

Being pregnant with Eddie was nothing like the carefree experience of carrying Jocelyn. Jasmine noticed every ache and pain, and her nausea was so severe that she lost 20 pounds during the first few months. About midway into the pregnancy, doctors put her on strict bed rest in an effort to prevent a premature delivery, but Eddie still arrived 9 weeks early. In developed countries like the United States, the *age of viability,* or the earliest point at which a baby can survive outside of the mother's womb, has dropped to 22 weeks gestational age (Lawn et al., 2011).

During the fetal period, the digestive, respiratory, and other organ systems become fully developed. For babies born early, those systems may not be fully prepared to function. Eddie needed a breathing tube, a feeding tube, and an incubator because he could not yet control his body temperature. For a week following his delivery, Jasmine could only make contact by sticking her hands through a hole in his incubator. When she finally did get to hold Eddie, his response was breathtaking. Not only did he stop fussing and whining, he reacted with measurable physiological changes. "His vital signs went up," Jasmine says. "He breathed better on his own." 📁 ▼

Kangarooing
Jasmine "kangaroos" with her son Eddie in the neonatal intensive care unit. Kangarooing, or holding a premature baby to facilitate skin-to-skin contact, benefits both babies and parents. Premature babies who receive this type of attention have shorter stays in the hospital and an easier time learning how to nurse (Gregson & Blacker, 2011). Some researchers have found that preemies who were kangarooed performed better later on in tests of cognitive and motor skills than those kept in incubators (Feldman, Eidelman, Sirota, & Weller, 2002). Jasmine Mitchell

Newborn Growth and Development

LO 7 Summarize the physical changes that occur in infancy.

Newborn babies exhibit several *reflexes,* or unlearned patterns of behavior. Some are necessary for survival; others do not serve any obvious purpose. A few fade away in the first weeks and months of life, but many will resurface as voluntary movements as the infant grows and develops motor control (Thelen & Fisher, 1982). Let's take a look at two of these reflexes.

teratogens (tə-ˈra-tə-jən) Environmental agents that can damage the growing zygote, embryo, or fetus.

fetal alcohol syndrome (FAS) Delays in development that result from moderate to heavy alcohol use during pregnancy.

fetus The unborn human from 2 months following conception to birth.

ROOTING AND SUCKING REFLEXES What does a newborn do when you stroke her cheek? She opens her mouth and turns her head in the direction of your finger, apparently in search of a nipple. This *rooting reflex* typically disappears at 4 months, never to be seen again. The *sucking reflex,* evident when you touch her lips, also appears to be a feeding reflex. Sucking and swallowing abilities don't fully mature until the gestational age of 33 to 36 weeks, so babies who are born before that time—like Jasmine's son Eddie—may struggle with feeding (Lee et al., 2011). But that doesn't mean they cannot enjoy the benefits of breast milk, which is thought to have important effects on growth and cognitive development (Chaimay, 2011; de Lauzon-Guillain et al., 2012; Horwood & Fergusson, 1998). Jasmine pumped her breast milk, making it possible for Eddie to get its nutritional benefits through his feeding tube.

A newborn spends most of his time eating, sleeping, and crying. Sounds like a simple routine, but waking every 2 to 3 hours to feed a wailing baby can be very exhausting. Nevertheless, this stage soon gives way to a period of change that is far more interactive, and includes waving, clapping, walking, and dangerous furniture climbing. **Infographic 8.2** details some of the sensory and motor milestones of infancy. Keep in mind that the listed ages are averages; significant variation does exist across infants. The general sequence and timing, however, are fairly universal.

THE NEWBORN SENSES Babies come into the world equipped with keen sensory capabilities that seem to be designed for facilitating relationships. For example, infants prefer to look at human faces as opposed to geometric shapes (Salva, Farroni, Regolin, Vallortigara, & Johnson, 2011). Within hours of birth, they can discriminate their mother's voice from those of other women, and they show a preference for her voice (DeCasper & Fifer, 1980). Research suggests babies come to recognize their mother's voice while in the womb (Kisilevsky et al., 2003; Sai, 2005). Jocelyn came into the world crying but calmed down instantly when placed in Jasmine's arms, as if she already knew the sound of her mother speaking and singing. Hearing is developed and functioning before a baby is born, but sounds are initially distorted. It takes some time for amniotic fluid to dry up completely before a baby can hear clearly (Hall, Smith, & Popelka, 2004).

Smell and taste are also well developed in newborn infants. These tiny babies can distinguish the smell of their own mothers' breast milk from that of other women within days of birth (Nishitani et al., 2009). Babies prefer sweet tastes, react strongly to sour tastes, and notice certain changes to their mothers' diets because those tastes are present in breast milk. If a mother eats something very sweet, for instance, the infant tends to breastfeed longer.

The sense of touch is evident before birth; as early as 2 months after conception, for example, a fetus will show the rooting reflex. It was once believed that newborns were incapable of experiencing pain. But research suggests otherwise. Newborns respond to pain with reactions similar to those of older infants, children, and adults (Gradin & Eriksson, 2011; Urso, 2007).

Sight is the weakest sense in newborns, who have difficulty seeing things that are not in their immediate vicinity. The optimal distance for a newborn to see an object is approximately 8–14 inches away from his face (Cavallini et al., 2002), which happens to be the approximate distance between the face of a nursing baby and his mother. Eye contact is thought to strengthen the relationship between mother and baby. A newborn's vision can be blurry for several months, one reason being that the light-sensitive cones in the back of the eye are still developing (Banks & Salapatek, 1978).

CONNECTIONS

In **Chapter 3,** we reported that cones are specialized neurons called *photoreceptors,* which absorb light energy and turn it into chemical and electrical signals for the brain to process. Cones enable us to see colors and details. Newborns have blurry eyesight in part because their cones have not fully developed.

Infant Brain and Sensorimotor Development

As newborns grow, they progress at an astounding rate in seen and unseen ways. When witnessing babies' new skills, whether it be reaching for a rattle or pulling themselves into a standing position, it's easy to marvel at how far they have come. But what you can't see is the real action. These sensorimotor advancements are only possible because of the incredible brain development happening in the background.

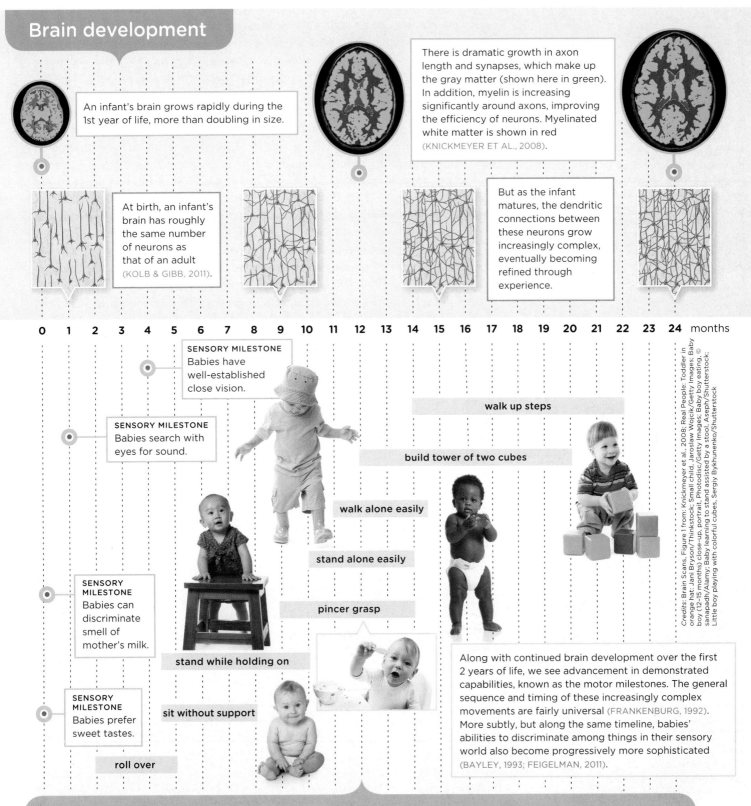

Brain development

An infant's brain grows rapidly during the 1st year of life, more than doubling in size.

At birth, an infant's brain has roughly the same number of neurons as that of an adult (KOLB & GIBB, 2011).

There is dramatic growth in axon length and synapses, which make up the gray matter (shown here in green). In addition, myelin is increasing significantly around axons, improving the efficiency of neurons. Myelinated white matter is shown in red (KNICKMEYER ET AL., 2008).

But as the infant matures, the dendritic connections between these neurons grow increasingly complex, eventually becoming refined through experience.

0 1 2 3 4 5 6 7 8 9 10 11 12 13 14 15 16 17 18 19 20 21 22 23 24 months

SENSORY MILESTONE Babies have well-established close vision.

SENSORY MILESTONE Babies search with eyes for sound.

SENSORY MILESTONE Babies can discriminate smell of mother's milk.

SENSORY MILESTONE Babies prefer sweet tastes.

walk up steps

build tower of two cubes

walk alone easily

stand alone easily

pincer grasp

stand while holding on

sit without support

roll over

Along with continued brain development over the first 2 years of life, we see advancement in demonstrated capabilities, known as the motor milestones. The general sequence and timing of these increasingly complex movements are fairly universal (FRANKENBURG, 1992). More subtly, but along the same timeline, babies' abilities to discriminate among things in their sensory world also become progressively more sophisticated (BAYLEY, 1993; FEIGELMAN, 2011).

Credits: Brain Scans, Figure 1 from: Knickmeyer et al., 2008; Real People: Toddler in orange hat: Jani Bryson/Thinkstock; Small child, Jaroslaw Wojcik/Getty Images; Baby boy (12–15 months) close-up, portrait, Photodisc/Getty Images; Baby boy eating, © sanapadh/Alamy; Baby learning to stand assisted by a stool, Aseph/Shutterstock; Little boy playing with colorful cubes, Sergiy Bykhunenko/Shutterstock

Motor and Sensory Development

THE GROWING BRAIN   The speed of brain development in the womb and immediately after birth is astounding. There are times in fetal development when the brain is producing some 250,000 new neurons per minute! The creation of *new* neurons is mostly complete by the end of the 5th month of fetal development (Kolb & Gibb, 2011). At the time of birth, a baby's brain has approximately 100 billion neurons (Toga, Thompson, & Sowell, 2006)—roughly the same number as that of an adult. Meanwhile, axons are growing longer, and more neurons—particularly those involved in motor control—are developing a myelin sheath around their axons. The myelin sheath increases the efficiency of neural communication, which leads to better motor control, enabling a baby to reach the milestones described earlier (waving, walking, and so forth).

SYNAPTIC PRUNING   Neurons rapidly sprout new connections to each other, a dramatic phase of synaptic growth that is influenced by the infant's experiences and stimulation from the environment. The increase in connections is not uniform throughout the brain. Between the ages of 3 and 6, for example, the greatest increase in neural connections occurs in the frontal lobes, the area of the brain involved in planning and attention (Thompson et al., 2000; Toga et al., 2006). As more links are established, more associations can be made between different stimuli, and between behavior and consequences. A young person needs to learn quickly, and this process makes it possible.

However, the extraordinary growth in synaptic connections does not last forever, as their number decreases by 40% to 50% by the time a child reaches puberty (Thompson et al., 2000; Webb, Monk, & Nelson, 2001). In a process known as *synaptic pruning,* unused synaptic connections are downsized or eliminated (Chechik, Meilijson, & Ruppin, 1998).

Synaptic pruning and other aspects of brain development are strongly influenced by experiences and input from the outside world. In the 1960s and 1970s, Mark Rosenzweig and his colleagues at the University of California, Berkeley, demonstrated how much environment can influence the development of nonhuman animal brains (Kolb & Whishaw, 1998). They found that rats placed in stimulating environments (furnished with opportunities for exploration and social interaction) experience greater increases in brain weight and synaptic connections than those put in nonstimulating environments (Barredo & Deeg, 2009, February 24; Kolb & Whishaw, 1998; Rosenzweig, 1984). Environmental stimulation (or lack thereof) also appears to influence the brain development of infants and children. Some research suggests that orphanage-raised babies who receive minimal care and human interaction experience delays in cognitive, social, and physical development. There is, however, a great deal of variability in later development when the children are placed in adoptive homes (Rutter & O'Connor, 2004).

CONNECTIONS

In **Chapter 2,** we described the structure of a typical neuron, which includes an axon projecting from the cell body. Many axons are surrounded by a myelin sheath, which is a fatty substance that insulates the axon. This insulation allows for faster communication within and between neurons. Here we see how this impacts motor development.

Stimulate the Brain
A kindergarten teacher leads students through dance movements (left) in what appears to be an enriched environment. Opportunities for physical exercise, social interaction, and other types of stimulating activity characterize enriched environments, which promote positive changes in the brain (van Praag, Kempermann, & Gage, 2000). Fewer signs of enrichment appear in the photo on the right, which shows another teacher with her class of preschoolers in a sparse room without books or even furniture. left: *Goh Chai Hin/Afp/Getty Images;* right: © *Robert Van Der Hilst/Corbis*

The Language Explosion

The brain development that occurs during childhood and the cognitive changes associated with it are remarkable. Consider the fact that babies come into the world incapable of using language, yet by the age of 6, most have amassed a vocabulary of about 13,000 words (Pinker, 1994). Let's take a look at some of the theories that attempt to explain the language explosion.

LO 8 Describe the theories explaining language acquisition.

BEHAVIORISM AND LANGUAGE Behaviorists propose that all behavior—including the use of language—is learned through associations, reinforcers, and observation. Infants and children learn language in the same way they learn everything else, through positive attention to correct behavior (for example, praising correct speech), unpleasant attention to incorrect behavior (for example, criticizing incorrect speech), and the observation of others.

LANGUAGE ACQUISITION DEVICE But the behaviorist theory may not explain all the complexities of language acquisition. If a young child tries to imitate a particular sentence structure, such as "I am going to the kitchen," he might instead say something grammatically incorrect, "I go kitchen." Children are not directly taught the structure of grammar, because its rules are too difficult for their developing brains to understand. Linguist Noam Chomsky (1959) suggested humans have a language acquisition device (LAD) that provides an innate mechanism for learning language. With the LAD, children compare the language they hear in their environment to a framework already hardwired in their brains. The fact that children all over the world seem to learn language in a fixed sequence, and during approximately the same sensitive period, is evidence that this innate language capacity exists.

INFANT-DIRECTED SPEECH (IDS) More recent theories of language acquisition focus on parents' and other caregivers' use of *infant-directed speech* (IDS). High-pitched and repetitive, IDS is observed throughout the world (Singh, Nestor, Parikh, & Yull, 2009). Can't you just hear Jasmine saying to baby Jocelyn in a high-pitched, sing-song voice, "Who's my little girl?" Researchers report that infants as young as 5 months old pay more attention to people who use IDS, which allows them to choose "appropriate social partners," or adults who are more likely to provide them with chances to learn and interact (Schachner & Hannon, 2011).

LANGUAGE IN THE ENVIRONMENT It's not only the type of voice that matters but also the amount of talking. Infants may not be the best conversation partners, but they benefit from a lot of chatter. It turns out that the amount of language spoken in the home correlates with socioeconomic status. Children from high-income families are more likely to have parents who engage them in conversation. Just look at these numbers for parents of toddlers: 35 words a minute spoken by high-income parents; 20 words a minute spoken by middle-income parents; 10 words a minute spoken by low-income parents (Hoff, 2003). The consequences of such interactions are apparent, with toddlers from high-income households having an average vocabulary of 766 words, and those from low-income homes only 357 (Hart & Risley, 1995). How might this disparity impact these same children when they start school? Research suggests that children from lower socioeconomic households begin school already lagging behind in reading, math, and academic achievement in general (Lee & Burkan, 2002), all of which could potentially be linked to decreased verbal interactions.

CONNECTIONS

In **Chapter 7,** we introduced the basic elements of language, such as phonemes, morphemes, and semantics, and explored how language relates to thought. In this chapter, we discuss how language develops.

CONNECTIONS

Chapter 5 presented the principles of learning. Here, we see how *operant conditioning*, through reinforcement and punishment, and *observational learning*, through modeling, can be used to understand how language is acquired.

Synonyms
infant-directed speech motherese

THE SEQUENCE OF ACQUISITION   Coo. Babble. Talk. No matter what language infants speak, or who raises them, you can almost be certain they will follow the universal sequence of language development (Chomsky, 2000). At the age of 2 to 3 months, infants typically start to produce vowel-like sounds known as **cooing.** These "oooo" and "ahhh" sounds are often repeated in a joyful manner.

When infants reach the age of 4 to 6 months, they begin to combine consonants and vowels in the **babbling** stage. These sounds are meaningless, but babbling can resemble real language ("ma, ma, ma, ma, ma" *Did you say . . . mama?*). Jasmine distinctly remembers Jocelyn as a tiny infant repeating "da, da, da, da," as if she were saying "Dadda" over and over. Amused by the irony of the situation (Jasmine was a single mother), she would put her face close to Jocelyn's and repeatedly say, "ma, ma, ma, ma." Nonhearing infants also go through this babbling stage, but they move their hands instead of babbling aloud (Petitto & Marentette, 1991). For both hearing and deaf infants, the babbling stage becomes an important foundation for speech production; when infants babble, they are on their way to their first words.

When do real words begin? At around 12 months, infants typically begin to utter their magical first words. Often, these are nouns used to convey an entire message, or *holophrase.* Perhaps you have heard an infant say something emphatically, such as "JUICE!" or "UP!" What she might be trying to say is "I am thirsty, could I please have some juice?" or "I want you to pick me up."

At about 18 months, infants start to use two-word phrases in their **telegraphic speech.** These brief statements might include only the most important words of a sentence, such as nouns, verbs, and adjectives, but no prepositions or articles. "Baby crying" might be a telegraphic sentence meaning the baby at the next table is crying loudly. As children mature, they start to use more complete sentences. Their grammar becomes more complex and they pack more words into statements. A "vocabulary explosion" tends to occur around 2 to 3 years of age (McMurray, 2007; **Figure 8.3**). By 5 to 6, most children are fluent in their native language, although their vocabulary does not match that of an adult.

There are two important components of normal language acquisition: (1) physical development, particularly in the language-processing areas of the brain (Chapter 2); and (2) exposure to language. If a child does not observe people using language during the first several years of life, normal language skills will not develop. Evidence for this phenomenon comes from case studies of people

Benefits of Sign
A baby and a caregiver communicate with sign language. Introducing sign to children as young as 6 months may help them communicate before they use verbal speech (Doherty-Sneddon, 2008). Early use of sign may also provide a verbal advantage down the road when they enter elementary school (Barnes, 2010). © Pop! Studio Photography/www.alamy.com/Corbis

cooing Production of vowel-like sounds by infants, often repeated in a joyful manner.
babbling The combining of consonants with vowels typically displayed at the age of 4 to 6 months.
telegraphic speech Two-word phrases typically used by infants around the age of 18 months.
schema A collection of ideas that represents a basic unit of understanding.

FIGURE 8.3
The Vocabulary Explosion
During the second year of life, a child's vocabulary increases dramatically.
Data from Mitchell and McMurray (2008).

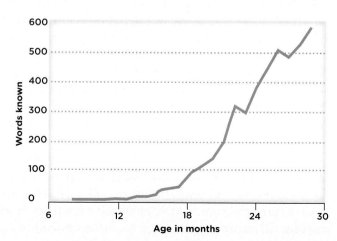

who were deprived of language in childhood (Goldin-Meadow, 1978). One of the most well-documented—and deeply troubling—cases of childhood deprivation centers on a young girl known as Genie.

Genie the "Feral Child"

In 1970 a social worker in Arcadia, California, discovered a most horrifying case of child neglect and abuse. "Genie," as researchers came to call her, was 13 at the time her situation came to the attention of the authorities, though she barely looked 7. Feeble and emaciated, the child could not even stand up straight. Genie was not capable of chewing food or using a toilet. She could not articulate a single word (Curtiss, Fromkin, Krashen, Rigler, & Rigler, 1974; PBS, 1997, March 4).

Between the ages of 20 months and 13 years, Genie had been locked away in a dark room, strapped to a potty chair or confined in a cagelike crib. Her father beat her when she made any type of noise. There, Genie stayed for 12 years, alone in silence, deprived of physical activity, sensory stimulation, and affection (Curtiss et al., 1974).

When discovered and brought to a hospital at age 13, Genie would not utter a sound (Curtiss et al., 1974). She did seem to understand simple words, but that was about it for her language comprehension. Researchers tried to build Genie's vocabulary, teaching her basic principles of syntax, and she made considerable gains, eventually speaking meaningful sentences. But some aspects of language, such as the ability to use the passive tense ("The carrot was given to the rabbit") or words such as "what" and "which" continued to mystify her (Goldin-Meadow, 1978). Why couldn't Genie master certain linguistic skills? Was it because she missed a critical period for language development? This is a real possibility.

AT AGE 13, GENIE COULD NOT EVEN SPEAK

We should note that Genie's story does end with a glimmer of hope. Genie is reported to be "happy," living in a group home for adults with intellectual disabilities (James, 2008, May 7). 💬➕

Piaget and Cognitive Development

LO 10 Summarize the key elements of Piaget's and Vygotsky's theories of cognitive development.

Language is just one domain of cognitive development. How do other processes like memory and problem solving evolve through childhood? As noted earlier, psychologists do not always agree on whether development is continuous or occurs in steps. Swiss biologist and developmental psychologist Jean Piaget (pyä-'zhā; 1896–1980) was among the first to suggest that infants have cognitive abilities, a notion that was not widely embraced at the time. Children do not think like adults, suggested Piaget, and their cognitive development takes place in stages.

One of the basic units of cognition, according to Piaget (1936/1952), is the **schema,** a collection of ideas or notions representing a basic unit of understanding. Young children form schemas based on functional relationships. The schema "toy," for example, might include any object that can be played with (such as dolls, trucks, and balls). As children mature, so do their schemas, which begin to organize and structure their thinking around more abstract categories, such as "love" (romantic love, love for one's country, and so on). As they grow, children expand their schemas in response to interactions with the environment and other life experiences.

At Play with Piaget
Developmental psychologist Jean Piaget (center) works with students in a New York City classroom. Piaget's research focused on school-age children, including his own three, who became participants in some of his studies. Children think differently from adults, Piaget proposed, and they experience cognitive development in distinct stages.
Bill Anderson/Science Source

Piaget (1936/1952) believed humans are biologically driven to advance intellectually, partly as a result of an innate need to maintain *cognitive equilibrium,* or a feeling of cognitive balance. Suppose a kindergartener's schema of airplane pilots includes only men, but then he sees a female pilot on television. This experience shakes up his notion of who can be a pilot, causing an uncomfortable sense of *disequilibrium* that motivates him to restore cognitive balance. There are two ways he might accomplish this. He could use **assimilation,** an attempt to understand new information using his already existing knowledge base, or schema. For example, the young boy might think about the female bus drivers he has seen and connect that to the female pilot idea (*Women drive buses, so maybe they can fly planes too*). However, if the new information is so disconcerting that it cannot be assimilated, he might use **accommodation,** a restructuring of old notions to make a place for new information. With accommodation, we remodel old schemas or create new ones. If the child had never seen a female driving anything other than a car, he might become confused at the sight of a female pilot. To eliminate that confusion, he could create a new schema (*Women drive all sorts of vehicles*). This is how we make great strides in cognitive growth. We assimilate information to fit new experiences into our old ways of thinking, and we accommodate our old way of thinking to understand new information.

Piaget (1936/1952) also proposed that cognitive development occurs in four periods or stages, and these stages have distinct beginnings and endings (**Infographic 8.3**).

SENSORIMOTOR STAGE From birth to about 2 years old is the **sensorimotor stage.** Infants use their sensory abilities and motor activities (such as reaching, crawling, and handling things) to learn about the surrounding world, exploring objects with their mouths, fingers, and toes. It's a nerve-racking process for parents ("Please do *not* put that shoe in your mouth!"), but an important part of cognitive development.

One significant milestone of the sensorimotor stage is **object permanence,** or an infant's realization that objects and people still exist when they are out of sight or touch. Have you ever watched a young infant play peekaboo? Her surprise when your face reappears suggests that she forgot you were there when your face was hidden. Jasmine tried to play peekaboo with Eddie when he was a baby, but he had a mixed reaction to the game, crying when she hid her face behind a blanket and laughing as soon as she pulled it away. Eddie's fear of his mother's disappearance and surprise at her reappearance didn't last; he learned about object permanence.

PREOPERATIONAL STAGE The next stage in cognitive development is the **preoperational stage,** which applies to children from 2 to 7 years old. During this time, children start using language to explore and understand their worlds (rather than relying primarily on sensory and motor activities). In this stage, children ask questions and use symbolic thinking. They may use words and images to refer to concepts. This is a time for pretending and magical thinking. Eddie, for example, likes to pretend he is Harry Potter. He drives Jasmine and Jocelyn crazy, racing around the house with a wand. Children in this stage are somewhat limited by their **egocentrism.** They can only imagine the world around them from their own perspective (see the Three Mountains task in Infographic 8.3).

According to Piaget (1936/1952), children in this stage have not yet mastered *operations* (hence, the name *preoperational* stage), which are the logical reasoning processes that older children and adults use to understand the world. For example, these children have a difficult time understanding the *reversibility* of some actions or events.

Does That Taste Good?
Babies are notorious for putting just about everything, including toys, shoes, and sand, in their mouths. Mouthing is one of the main ways babies experience their worlds, and it is an important aspect of cognitive development. It also provides exposure to viruses and other environmental pathogens, which helps prepare the developing immune system to fight infections (Fessler & Abrams, 2004). Elie Bernager/Getty Images

assimilation Using existing information and ideas to understand new knowledge and experiences.

accommodation A restructuring of old ideas to make a place for new information.

sensorimotor stage Piaget's stage of cognitive development during which infants use their sensory capabilities and motor skills to learn about the surrounding world.

object permanence A milestone of the sensorimotor stage of cognitive development; an infant's realization that objects and people still exist even when out of sight or touch.

preoperational stage Piaget's stage of cognitive development during which children can start to use language to explore and understand their worlds.

egocentrism Only able to imagine the world from one's own perspective.

Piaget's Theory of Cognitive Development

Jean Piaget proposed that children's cognitive development occurs in stages characterized by particular cognitive abilities. These stages have distinct beginnings and endings.

Formal Operational

Child is now able to think logically and systematically and is capable of hypothetical thinking.

Concrete Operational

Child understands operations and thinks more logically in reference to concrete objects and circumstances.

Preoperational

Child uses symbolic thinking to explore and understand the world. Children at this stage are known for magical thinking and egocentrism.

Sensorimotor

Child uses sensory capabilities and motor activities to learn about the world; develops object permanence.

Piaget's four stages of cognitive development

Sensorimotor
birth–2 yrs

Preoperational
2–7 yrs

Concrete Operational
7–11 yrs

Formal Operational
11 yrs and up

Child playing peekaboo, © Peter Polak/Fotolia.com; Child playing vet with Teddy bear, © Gina Sanders/Fotolia.com; Object permanence test, Doug Goodman/Science Source; Blocks silo, Thinkstock; Teenage girl writing on chalkboard, Creatas/Thinkstock; Young Asian boy pouring cooking oil into cake batter, iStockphoto/Thinkstock: Hands open, iStockphoto/Thinkstock; Piaget Conservation-Girl with milk glasses, Bianca Moscatelli/Worth Publishers ; Eye featured in the hand: © Flashon Studio/Dreamstime.com

How do we assess a child's stage of cognitive development?
Piaget developed techniques to test characteristic capabilities associated with each stage.

Object permanence test determines whether a child realizes that hidden objects still exist. Infants who have developed object permanence will search for an object.

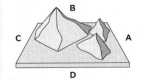

Three Mountains task tests egocentrism. Can the child imagine a perspective different than her own? "What would you see if you were standing at Point B?"

Conservation of Volume test assesses understanding of operations. Does a child understand that the amount of liquid remains constant when it is poured into a container with a different shape?

Third Eye task tests formal operational thought. "If you had a third eye, where would you put it?" Children at this stage come up with logical, innovative answers.

FIGURE 8.4

FIGURE 8.4
Conservation Tasks
Children in the preoperational stage don't realize that properties like volume and mass stay constant when items are only rearranged or reshaped. Tasks like those outlined here are used to test children's understanding of the concept of conservation.

Type of Conservation Task	Original Presentation	Alteration	Question	Preoperational Child's Answer
Volume	Two equal beakers of liquid 	Pour one into a taller, narrower beaker. 	Does one beaker have more liquid?	The taller beaker has more liquid.
Mass	Two equal lumps of clay 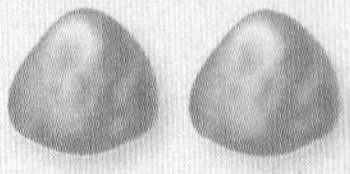	Roll one lump into a long, hotdog shape. 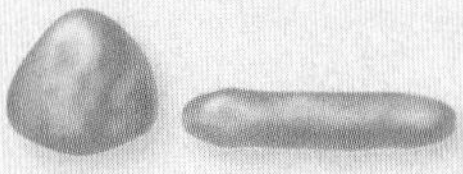	Does one lump weigh more?	The original lump weighs more.
Length	Two equal lengths of rope 	Move one rope. 	Is one rope longer?	The top rope is longer.
Number	Two equal lines of buttons 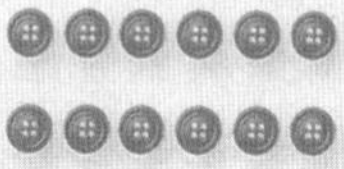	Increase amount of space between buttons in one line. 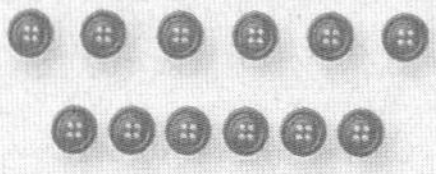	Does one line have more buttons?	The longer line has more buttons.

They may have trouble comprehending that vanilla ice cream can be refrozen after it melts, but not turned back into sugar, milk, and vanilla. This difficulty with operations is also apparent in errors involving **conservation,** which refers to the unchanging properties of volume, mass, or amount in relation to appearance (**Figure 8.4**). For example, if you take two masses of clay of the same shape and size, and then roll only one of them out into a hotdog shape, a child in this stage may think that the longer-shaped clay is now made up of more clay than the undisturbed clump of clay. Or, the child may see that the newly formed clump of clay is skinnier and therefore assume it is smaller. Why is this so? Children at this age generally focus on only one characteristic of an object. They do not understand how the object stays fundamentally the same, even if it is manipulated or takes on a different appearance.

CONCRETE OPERATIONAL STAGE   Around age 7, children enter what Piaget called the **concrete operational stage.** They begin to think more logically, but mainly in reference to concrete objects and circumstances: things that can be seen or touched, or are well defined by strict rules. Children in this stage tend to be less egocentric and can understand the concept of conservation. However, they still have trouble with abstract concepts. Around age 8 or 9, Jocelyn tended to take everything literally. Once she asked to go outside when it was pouring rain, and Jasmine replied, "Are you crazy? It's raining cats and dogs!" Jocelyn became distressed and cried, "The poor little kitties are gonna get hurt when they fall from the sky!" Children in this stage also have trouble thinking hypothetically. A 7-year-old may respond with a blank stare if you ask her a "what if?" type of question. (*If you were able to travel to the future, what kind of animals would your great-grandchildren see in the wild?*)

FORMAL OPERATIONAL STAGE   Children enter the **formal operational stage** at age 11; they begin to think more logically and systematically. They can solve problems such as those in the Third Eye task in Infographic 8.3. This activity asks a

conservation Refers to the unchanging properties of volume, mass, or amount in relation to appearance.

concrete operational stage Piaget's stage of cognitive development during which children begin to think more logically, but mainly in reference to concrete objects and circumstances.

formal operational stage Piaget's stage of cognitive development during which children begin to think more logically and systematically.

scaffolding Pushing children to go just beyond what they are competent and comfortable doing, while providing help in a decreasing manner.

child where she would put a third eye, and why. (*I'd put it in the back of my head so that I could see what is going on behind my back.*) These types of capabilities do not necessarily develop overnight, and logical abilities are likely to advance in relation to interests and to skills developed in a work setting. Piaget suggested that not everyone reaches this stage of formal operations. But to succeed in most colleges, this type of logical thinking is essential; students need to think critically and use abstract concepts to solve problems.

THE CRITICS Critics of Piaget suggest that although cognitive development might occur in stages with distinct characteristics, the transitions from one stage to the next are likely to be gradual, and do not necessarily represent a complete leap from one type of thinking to the next. Some believe Piaget's theory underestimates children's cognitive abilities. For example, some researchers have found that object permanence occurs sooner than suggested by Piaget (Baillargeon, Spelke, & Wasserman, 1985). Others question Piaget's assertion that the formal operational stage is reached by 11 to 12 years of age, and that no further delineations can be made between the cognitive abilities of adolescents and adults of various ages. One solution is to account for cognitive changes occurring in adulthood by considering stages beyond Piaget's original formulation.

Vygotsky and Cognitive Development

One other major criticism of Piaget's work is that it does not take into consideration the social interactions that influence the developing child. Russian psychologist Lev Vygotsky (vī-'gät-skē; 1896–1934) was particularly interested in how social and cultural factors affect a child's cognitive development (Vygotsky, 1934/1962).

How might social interactions impact a child's cognitive development? Children are like apprentices in relation to others who are more capable and experienced (Zaretskii, 2009). Those children who receive help from older children and adults progress more quickly in their cognitive abilities. For example, when parents help their children solve puzzles by providing support for them to succeed on their own, the children show advancement in goal-directed behavior and the ability to plan ahead (Bernier, Carlson, & Whipple, 2010; Hammond, Müller, Carpendale, Bibok, & Liebermann-Finestone, 2012).

One way we can support children's cognitive development is through **scaffolding:** pushing them to go just beyond what they are competent and comfortable doing, but also providing help in a decreasing manner. A parent or caregiver provides support when necessary, but allows a child to solve problems independently: "Successful scaffolding is like a wave, rising to offer help when needed and receding as the child regains control of the task" (Hammond et al., 2012, p. 275).

Vygotsky also emphasized that learning always occurs within the context of a child's culture. Children across the world have different sets of expected learning outcomes, from raising sheep to weaving blankets to playing basketball. We need to keep these cross-cultural differences in mind when exploring cognitive development in children.

Culture and Cognition
A man and a boy work together threshing rice in the fields of Madagascar. What this child learns and how his cognitive development unfolds are shaped by the circumstances of his environment. Children reared in agricultural societies may acquire different cognitive skill sets than those raised in urban, industrialized settings.
© Yvan Travert/Photononstop/Corbis

SOME THINGS NEVER CHANGE Jocelyn and Eddie have very different personalities, and their unique characteristics began to surface early in their development. Jocelyn has always been easygoing and mild-mannered. As an infant, she would cry and fuss as infants do, but her discontent could usually be traced to a clear cause (for example, she was hungry or tired). Eddie was more apt to cry for no obvious reason; he was more difficult to please; and Jasmine describes him as having had a "hot" temper.

Jocelyn was a social butterfly from the start. As an infant, she would perk up on hearing a voice or spotting a person's face, and she began to talk at an early age. Baby Eddie was not such a "people person." He was more entranced by the bright colors and shapes he saw on TV programs for infants and toddlers. He also began to talk and walk considerably later than Jocelyn. But as his pediatrician said, these developmental discrepancies probably had a lot to do with gender (boys tend to lag behind girls in language and motor skills) and the fact that Eddie was born 2½ months early.

Many of Jocelyn's and Eddie's personality traits remained stable through toddlerhood. Both children started day care around the age of 2, but their adjustments to this change in routine were starkly different. Jocelyn, always very social, never cried after being dropped off. Eddie, the more introverted sibling, cried every day for 3 or 4 months. Why he had such a hard time saying goodbye is unclear, but there are probably many reasons. Perhaps he preferred the quiet solitude of home to the bustling environment of the childcare center, or maybe it had something to do with his parents' marital problems at the time. Eddie was experiencing *separation anxiety,* and we usually see this peak at approximately 13 months (Hertenstein & McCullough, 2005). Now that Eddie has spent years in daycare and school, he has no problem being away from home. Any delays in language or motor development he experienced as a result of prematurity have long since vanished. "Now," says Jasmine, "he is 5 going on 15, mentally and physically." 📁

Temperament and Attachment

Until now, we have mostly discussed physical and cognitive development, but recall we are also interested in *socioemotional* development. When thinking about Jocelyn and Eddie, it is important to consider their relationships, emotional processes, and *temperaments.*

TEMPERAMENT From birth, infants display characteristic differences in their behavioral patterns and emotional reactions, that is, their **temperament.** Some babies and toddlers can be categorized as having an exuberant temperament, showing an overall positive attitude and sociability (Degnan et al., 2011). "High-reactive" infants exhibit a great deal of distress when exposed to unfamiliar stimuli, such as new sights, sounds, and smells. "Low-reactive" infants do not respond to new stimuli with great distress (Kagan, 2003). Classification as high- and low-reactive is based on measures of behavior, emotional response, and physiology (such as heart rate and blood pressure; Kagan, 1985, 2003).

These different characteristics seem to be innate, as they are evident from birth and consistent in the infants' daily lives. There is also evidence that some of these characteristics remain fairly stable throughout life (Kagan & Snidman, 1991). However, the environment can influence temperament (Caspi, Roberts, & Shiner, 2005). Factors such as maternal education, neighborhood, and paternal occupation through adolescence can predict characteristics of adult temperament, such as persistence, shyness, and impulsiveness (Congdon et al., 2012).

temperament Characteristic differences in behavioral patterns and emotional reactions that are evident from birth.

EASY, DIFFICULT, OR SLOW TO WARM UP   Researchers have found that the majority of infants can be classified as having one of three fundamental temperaments (Thomas & Chess, 1986). Around 40% are considered "easy" babies; they are easy to care for because they follow regular eating and sleeping schedules. These happy babies can be soothed when upset and don't appear to get rattled by transitions or changes in their environments. Jasmine would put Jocelyn in this category. Baby Jocelyn's crying was usually for an obvious reason, and she settled down when the problem was resolved.

"Difficult" babies (around 10%) are more challenging because they don't seem to have a set schedule for eating and sleeping. And they don't deal well with transitions or changes in the environment. Difficult babies are often irritable and unhappy, and compared to easy babies, they are far less responsive to the soothing attempts of caregivers. They also tend to be very active, kicking their legs on the changing table and wiggling like mad when you try to put on their clothes.

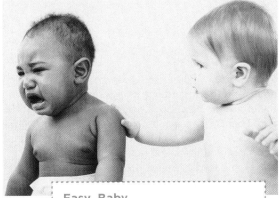

Easy, Baby
Most babies can be classified according to one of three fundamental temperaments: about 40% are "easy," meaning they are generally content and follow predictable schedules; approximately 10% are "difficult," or hard to please and irregular in their schedules; and another 15% are "slow to warm up," meaning they struggle with change but eventually adjust. The remaining 35% do not fall into any one category. JGI/Jamie Grill/Getty Images

"Slow to warm up" babies (around 15%) are not as irritable (or active) as difficult babies, but they are not fond of change. Give them enough time, however, and they will adapt. Jasmine would place Eddie in this category. Eddie was not keen on the new day-care environment, but he eventually adjusted. He was just slow to warm up to the unfamiliar place and people.

These categories of baby temperaments are useful, but we should remember that 35% of babies are considered hard to classify because they share the characteristics of more than one type.

Nature and Nurture

Destiny of the Difficult Baby

Perhaps you are wondering about the long-term implications of baby temperaments. What becomes of infants—particularly the difficult bunch—when they get older? Do they grow up to be difficult children, stirring up trouble in school and alienating other kids with their grumpy behavior? If the answer were unequivocally yes, then we would chalk it up to nature: Difficult is written into the genes and no amount of excellent parenting is going to change such babies. Fortunately, this does *not* appear to be the case. Research suggests that difficult babies are unusually sensitive to input from their parents, a characteristic that—depending on environmental circumstances—can be either a blessing or a curse (Stright, Gallagher, & Kelley, 2008).

Stright and colleagues (2008) studied over a thousand mothers and babies during the first 6 years of life. Baby temperament was assessed at 6 months, and the mothers and their children were observed interacting on six separate occasions, from 6 months old until the time they were first graders. The children's first-grade teachers also participated, filling out questionnaires about their pupils' academic and social skills.

DO DIFFICULT BABIES BECOME OBNOXIOUS CHILDREN?

The researchers found that children with mothers demonstrating "higher-quality parenting styles" (being emotionally responsive and respectful of their children's need for independence) fared better than those with moms exhibiting lower-quality parenting (emotional distance and disregard for autonomy). Come first grade, children exposed to higher-quality parenting were more likely to succeed academically and maintain positive relationships with peers and teachers. Meanwhile, first graders raised by more detached and controlling mothers had the most trouble adjusting to school. The effects—both good and bad—were magnified for the difficult babies, suggesting these children are more receptive to parenting in general (Stright et al., 2008). Nature may have endowed them with a "difficult" temperament, but with some encouragement and respect from loving parents, their energy could be channeled in a very constructive way.

CONNECTIONS

In **Chapter 1,** we discussed *research ethics* and the importance of ensuring the ethical treatment of research participants (human and nonhuman animal). Psychologists must do no harm and safeguard the welfare of participants. This would not have been possible if the Harlows had taken human newborns from their parents to study the importance of physical contact. Many even question the ethics of their use of newborn monkeys in this manner.

Soft Like Mommy

A baby monkey in a laboratory experiment clings to a furry mother surrogate. Research by Harry and Margaret Harlow and colleagues at the University of Wisconsin showed that physical comfort is important for the socioemotional development of these animals. When given the choice between a wire mesh "mother" that provided milk and a cloth-covered "mother" without milk, most of the monkeys opted to snuggle with the cuddly cloth-covered one. Photo Researchers

As you can see, parents have the power to steer the development of their children in positive and negative directions. But what exactly makes a good parent? The adjectives or phrases that come to our minds are "patience," "sensitivity," "acceptance," "strength," and "unconditional love." It also helps to be soft, warm, and snuggly—especially if you happen to be a monkey.

THE HARLOWS AND THEIR MONKEYS   Research suggests that physical touch is a very important part of infant development. Among the first to explore this topic in an experimental situation were Harry Harlow, Margaret Harlow, and their colleagues at the University of Wisconsin (Harlow, Harlow, & Suomi, 1971). The researchers were initially interested in learning how physical contact affects the development of loving relationships between infants and mothers. But they realized this would be difficult to study with human infants; instead, they turned to newborn macaque monkeys (Harlow, 1958).

Here's how the experiment worked: Infant monkeys were put in cages alone, each with two artificial "surrogate" mothers. One surrogate was outfitted with a soft cloth and heated with a bulb. The other surrogate mother was designed to be lacking in "contact comfort," as she was made of wire mesh and not covered in cloth. Both of these surrogates could be set up to feed the infants. In one study, half the infant monkeys received their milk from the cloth surrogates and the other half got their milk from the wire surrogates. The great majority of the infant monkeys spent most of their time clinging to or in contact with the cloth mother, even if she was not the mother providing the milk. The baby monkeys spent 15 to 18 hours a day physically close to the cloth mother, and only 1 to 2 hours touching the wire mother.

Harlow and colleagues also created situations in which they purposefully scared the infants with a moving toy bear, and found that the great majority of the infant monkeys (around 80%) ran to the cloth mother, regardless of whether she was a source of milk. In times of fear and uncertainty, these infant monkeys found more comfort in the soft and furry mothers. Through their experiments, Harlow and his colleagues showed how important physical contact is for these living creatures (Harlow, 1958; Harlow & Zimmerman, 1959).

ATTACHMENT Physical contact plays an important role in **attachment,** or the degree to which an infant feels an emotional connection with primary caregivers. Using a design called the *Strange Situation,* Mary Ainsworth (1913–1999) studied the attachment styles of infants between 12 and 18 months (Ainsworth, 1979, 1985; Ainsworth & Bell, 1970; Ainsworth, Blehar, Waters, & Wall, 1978). The Strange Situation goes roughly like this: A mother and child are led into a room. A stranger enters, and the mother then exits the room, leaving the child in the unfamiliar environment with the stranger, who tries to interact with the child. The mother returns to the room but leaves again, and then returns once more. At this point, the stranger departs. During this observation, the researchers note the amount of anxiety displayed by the child before and after the stranger arrives, the child's willingness to explore the unfamiliar environment, and the child's reaction to the mother's return. The following response patterns were observed:

- **Secure attachment:** Around 65% of the children were upset when their mothers left the room, but were easily soothed upon her return, quickly returning to play. These children seemed confident that their needs would be met and felt safe exploring their environment, using the caregiver as a "secure base."

attachment The degree to which an infant feels an emotional connection with primary caregivers.

- **Avoidant attachment:** Approximately 20% of the children displayed no distress when their mothers left, and they did not show any signs of wanting to interact with their mothers when they returned, seemingly happy to play in the room without looking at their mothers or the stranger. They didn't seem to mind when their mothers left, or fuss when they returned.

- **Ambivalent:** Children in this group (around 10%) were quite upset and very focused on their mothers, showing signs of wanting to be held, but unable to be soothed by their mothers. These children were angry (often pushing away their mothers) and not interested in returning to play.

Ideally, parents and caregivers provide a *secure base* for infants, and are ready to help regulate emotions (soothe or calm) or meet other needs. This makes infants feel comfortable exploring their environments. Ainsworth and colleagues (1978) suggested that development, both physical and psychological, is greatly influenced by the quality of an infant's attachment to caregivers. But much of the early research in this area focused on infants' attachment to their mothers. Subsequent research suggests that we should examine infants' attachment to multiple individuals (mother, father, caregivers at day care, and close relatives), as well as cross-cultural differences in attachment (Field, 1996; Rothbaum, Weisz, Pott, Miyake, & Morelli, 2000).

Critics of the Strange Situation method suggest it creates an artificial environment and does not provide good measures of how infant-mother pairs act in their natural settings. Some suggest that the temperament of infants predisposes them to react the way they do in this setting. Infants prone to anxiety and uncertainty are more likely to respond negatively to such a scenario (Kagan, 1985). More generally, attachment theories are criticized for not considering cross-cultural differences in relationships (Rothbaum et al., 2000).

Feeling Secure
A childcare worker plays with toddlers at Moore Community Center's Early Head Start program in Biloxi, Mississippi. Children are more willing to explore their environments when they have caregivers who consistently meet their needs and provide a secure base. Jim West/Photo Edit

Attachments are formed early in childhood, but they have implications for a lifetime: "Experiences in early close relationships create internal working models that then influence cognition, affect, and behavior in relationships that involve later attachment figures" (Simpson & Rholes, 2010, p. 174). People who experienced ambivalent attachment as infants have been described as exhibiting an "insatiability for closeness" in their adult relationships. Those who had secure attachments are more likely to expect that they are lovable and that others are capable of love. They are aware that nobody is perfect, and this attitude allows for intimacy in relationships (Cassidy, 2001). Infant attachment may even have long-term health consequences. One 32-year longitudinal study found that adults who had been insecurely attached as infants were more likely to report inflammation-based illnesses (for example, asthma, cardiovascular disease, and diabetes) than those with secure attachments (Puig, Englund, Simpson, & Collins, 2013).

Erikson's Psychosocial Stages

LO 11 Describe how Erikson's theory explains psychosocial development through puberty.

One useful way to understand socioemotional development is to consider its progression through stages. According to Erik Erikson (1902–1994), human development is marked by eight psychosocial stages, spanning infancy to old age (Erikson & Erikson, 1997). Each of these stages is marked by a developmental task or an emotional crisis that must be handled successfully to allow for healthy psychological growth.

TABLE 8.3   ERIKSON'S EIGHT STAGES

Stage	Age	Positive Resolution	Negative Resolution
Trust versus mistrust	Birth to 1 year	Trusts others, has faith in others.	Mistrusts others, expects the worst of people.
Autonomy versus shame and doubt	1 to 3 years	Learns to be autonomous and independent.	Learns to feel shame and doubt when freedom to explore is restricted.
Initiative versus guilt	3 to 6 years	Becomes more responsible, shows the ability to follow through.	Develops guilt and anxiety when unable to handle responsibilities.
Industry versus inferiority	6 years to puberty	Feels a sense of accomplishment and increased self-esteem.	Feels inferiority or incompetence, which can later lead to unstable work habits.
Ego identity versus role confusion	Puberty to twenties	Tries out roles and emerges with a strong sense of values, beliefs, and goals.	Lacks a solid identity, experiences withdrawal, isolation, or continued role confusion.
Intimacy versus isolation	Young adulthood (twenties to forties)	Creates meaningful, deep relationships.	Lives in isolation.
Generativity versus stagnation	Middle adulthood (forties to mid-sixties)	Makes a positive impact on the next generation through parenting, community involvement, or work that is valuable and significant.	Experiences boredom, conceit, and selfishness.
Integrity versus despair	Late adulthood (mid-sixties and older)	Feels a sense of accomplishment and satisfaction.	Feels regret and dissatisfaction.

These are the eight stages of psychosocial development proposed by Erik Erikson. Each stage is marked by a developmental task or an emotional crisis that must be handled successfully to allow for healthy psychological growth.

SOURCE: ERIKSON AND ERIKSON (1997).

The crises, according to Erikson, stem from conflicts between the needs of the individual and the expectations of society (Erikson, 1993). Successful resolution of a stage enables an individual to approach the following stage with more tools. Unsuccessful resolution leads to more difficulties during the next stage. Take a look at **Table 8.3** to see the stages associated with infancy, childhood, and beyond.

show what you know

1. The _____ reflex occurs when you stroke a baby's cheek; she opens her mouth and turns her head toward your hand. The _____ reflex occurs when you touch the baby's lips; this reflex helps with feeding.

2. Your instructor describes how he is teaching his infant to learn new words by showing her flashcards with images. Every time the infant uses the right word to identify the image, he gives her a big smile. When she uses an incorrect word, he frowns. Your instructor is using which of the following to guide his approach:
   a. theories of behaviorism
   b. Chomsky's language acquisition device
   c. infant-directed speech
   d. telegraphic speech

3. Piaget suggested that when we try to understand new information and experiences by incorporating them into our existing knowledge and ideas, we are using:
   a. the rooting reflex.   b. schemas.
   c. accommodation.   d. assimilation.

4. Vygotsky recommended supporting children's cognitive development by _____, pushing them a little harder than normal while gradually reducing the amount of help you give them.

5. Erikson proposed that socioemotional development comprises eight psychosocial stages, and these stages include:
   a. scaffolding.
   b. physical maturation.
   c. developmental tasks or emotional crises.
   d. conservation.

6. What can new parents expect regarding the sequence of their child's language development, and how might they help encourage it?

✔ CHECK YOUR ANSWERS IN APPENDIX C.

Adolescence

THE WALKING, TALKING HORMONE   Jocelyn is no longer a cute little bundle of girlhood; nowadays, she is a "walking, talking hormone," says Jasmine. "Boys, make-up, and friends are the center of her world now." At age 14, Jocelyn can also be mouthy; she cares a lot about what other people think of her; and she is mortified by her 31-year-old mother whom she thinks of as "so old." There are times when Jocelyn blatantly disregards her mother's instructions. She might, for example, go to a friend's house even after Jasmine has explicitly denied her permission to do so.

Jocelyn's behaviors are stereotypical of teenagers, or *adolescents*. **Adolescence** refers to the transition period between late childhood and early adulthood, and it can be challenging for both parents and kids. As you may recall from earlier in the chapter, Jasmine proved to be quite a challenge for her own mom when she was a teen, skipping school and carousing until late at night with friends. "At 14, I had already started the crazy life," says Jasmine, who considers herself blessed to have a daughter like Jocelyn, who gets As and Bs in her classes, doesn't use drugs or alcohol, and participates in her school's volleyball, basketball, and dance teams.

In the United States, adult responsibilities often are distant concepts for adolescents. But this is not universal. For example, in underdeveloped countries, children take on adult responsibilities as soon as they are able. In some parts of the world, girls younger than 18 are already married and dealing with grown-up responsibilities. In Bolivia, girls can legally marry at 14 years old (Nour, 2009). However, adolescence generally allows for a much slower transition to adult duties in America. Although adolescents might develop adult bodies, including the ability to become parents, the more extensive schooling and training they must complete in order to perform at an adult level keep them dependent on parents and caregivers ▼ for a longer time.

Physical and Cognitive Development in Adolescence

LO 12 Give examples of significant physical changes that occur during adolescence.

PHYSICAL DEVELOPMENT   Adolescence is a time of dramatic physical growth, comparable to that which occurs during fetal development. The "growth spurt" includes rapid changes in height, weight, and bone growth, and usually begins between ages 9 and 10 for girls and ages 12 and 16 for boys. Sex hormones, which influence this growth and development, are at high levels.

Puberty is the period during which the body changes and becomes sexually mature and able to reproduce (**Figure 8.5** on the next page). During puberty, the **primary sex characteristics** (reproductive organs) mature; these include the ovaries, uterus, vagina, penis, scrotum, and testes. At the same time, the **secondary sex characteristics** (physical features not associated with reproduction) become more distinct; these include pubic, underarm, and body hair. Breast changes also occur in boys and girls (with the areola increasing in size), and fat increases in girls' breasts. Adolescents experience changes to their skin and overall body hair. Girls' pelvises begin to broaden, while boys experience a deepening of their voices and broadening of their shoulders.

It is during this time that girls experience **menarche** ('me-ˌnär-kē), the point at which menstruation begins. Menarche can occur as early as age 9 or after age 14,

Growing Up Fast
Members of the St. Thomas Boys Choir in Leipzig, Germany, practice a chant in rehearsal. Choir directors are struggling with the fact that young boys' voices are deepening earlier as the years go by. In the mid-1700s, voice changes reportedly occurred in singers aged 17 or 18; today, the average age is closer to 10 (Mendle & Ferrero, 2012). No one is certain why boys are hitting puberty sooner, but some researchers point to a correlation with increasing body mass index (Sørensen, Aksglaede, Petersen, & Juul, 2010). Wolfgang Kluge/picturealliance/dpa/AP Images

adolescence The transition period between late childhood and early adulthood.
puberty The period of development during which the body changes and becomes sexually mature and capable of reproduction.
primary sex characteristics Organs associated with reproduction, including the ovaries, uterus, vagina, penis, scrotum, and testes.
secondary sex characteristics Body characteristics, such as pubic hair, underarm hair, and enlarged breasts, that develop in puberty but are not associated with reproduction.
menarche ('me-ˌnär-kē) The point at which menstruation begins.

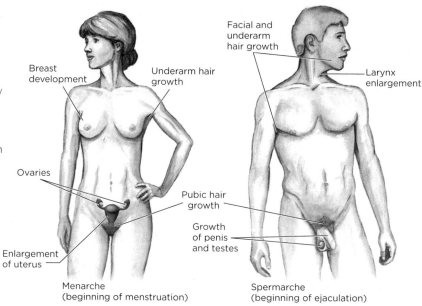

········· ▶

FIGURE 8.5
Physical Changes at Puberty
During puberty, the body changes and becomes sexually mature and able to reproduce. The primary sex characteristics mature, and the secondary sex characteristics become more distinct. Primary sex characteristics are related to reproductive organs. The reproductive organs, present at birth, begin to function differently at puberty. For instance, the testes and ovaries are involved in stimulating more visible changes, such as breast development and growth of the penis.

Michelle was the first in her class to pupate.

Synonyms
sexually transmitted infections sexually transmitted diseases

but typical onset is around 12 or 13. Boys experience **spermarche** (ˈspər-ˌmär-kē), their first ejaculation, during this time period as well (Ladouceur, 2012). But when it occurs is more difficult to specify, as boys may be reluctant to talk about the event (Mendle, Harden, Brooks-Gunn, & Graber, 2010).

Not everyone goes through puberty at the same time. Some evidence suggests that early maturing adolescents face a greater risk of engaging in unsafe behaviors, such as drug and alcohol use (Shelton & van den Bree, 2010). Compared to their peers, girls who mature early seem to experience more negative outcomes than those who mature later, including increased anxiety, particularly social anxiety; they also appear to face a higher risk of emotional problems and delinquent behaviors (Blumenthal et al., 2011; Harden & Mendle, 2012). Early maturing girls are more likely to smoke, drink alcohol, have lower self-confidence, and later take on jobs that are "less prestigious." There are certain factors that can reduce such risks, though, including parents who show warmth and support (Shelton & van den Bree, 2010).

Boys who mature early generally have a more positive experience and do not show evidence of increased anxiety (Blumenthal et al., 2011). But, when researchers examine the "tempo," or speed, with which boys reach full sexual maturity, they find that rapid development can be associated with a range of problems, including aggressive behavior, cheating, and temper tantrums (Marceau, Ram, Houts, Grimm, & Susman, 2011).

Adolescence is a time when sexual interest peaks, yet teenagers don't always make the best choices when it comes to sexual activity. A study by the Centers for Disease Control and Prevention (CDC, 2008a) found that over 25% of girls (approximately 1 in 4) between ages 14 and 19 are infected with "at least one of the most common sexually transmitted diseases" (para. 1). Over half of new *sexually transmitted infections* affect young people ages 15–24; keep in mind that this group represents only 25% of the sexually active population (CDC, 2013). Sexually transmitted infections are especially risky for adolescents because they often go untreated and can lead to a host of problems, including long-term sterility.

LO 13 Explain how Piaget described cognitive changes that take place during adolescence.

COGNITIVE DEVELOPMENT Alongside the remarkable physical changes of adolescence are equally remarkable cognitive developments. As noted earlier, children in this age range are better able to distinguish between abstract and hypothetical situations.

This ability is an indication that a teenager has entered Piaget's formal operational stage, which begins in adolescence and continues into adulthood. During this period, the adolescent begins to use deductive reasoning to draw conclusions and critical thinking to approach arguments. She can reason abstractly, classify ideas, and use symbols. The adolescent can think beyond the current moment, pondering the future and considering many possibilities. She may begin to contemplate what will happen beyond high school, including career choices and education.

A specific type of egocentrism emerges in adolescence. Before this age, children can only imagine the world from their own perspective, but during adolescence they begin to be aware of others' perspectives. Egocentrism is still apparent, however, as they believe others share their preoccupations. For example, a teenager who focuses on his appearance will think that others are focusing on his appearance as well (Elkind, 1967). Adolescents also tend to believe that everyone thinks the same way they do.

This intense focus on the self may lead to a feeling of immortality, which can result in risk-taking behaviors (Elkind, 1967). Because they have not had many life experiences, adolescents may fail to consider the long-term consequences of their behaviors. They may fail to consider the repercussions of unprotected sex or drug use, for instance. Their focus on the present (for example, having fun in the moment) outweighs their ability to assess the potential harm in the future (pregnancy or addiction). So to help adolescents stop engaging in risky behaviors such as smoking, we might focus on short-term consequences, like bad breath when kissing a partner, rather than long-term dangers such as lung cancer (Robbins & Bryan, 2004).

THE ADOLESCENT BRAIN Risk taking in adolescence is thought to result from characteristics of the adolescent brain. The limbic system, which is responsible for processing emotions and perceiving rewards and punishments, undergoes significant development during adolescence. Another important change is the increased myelination of axons in the prefrontal cortex, which improves the connections within the brain involved in planning, weighing consequences, and multitasking (Steinberg, 2012). But the relatively quicker development of the limbic system in comparison to the prefrontal cortex can lead to risk-taking behavior. Because the prefrontal cortex has not yet fully developed, the adolescent may not foresee the possible consequences of reward-seeking activities that are supported by the reward center of the limbic system. Changes to the structure of the brain continue through adolescence, resulting in a fully adult brain between the ages of 22 and 25, and a decline in risk-taking behaviors (Giedd et al., 2009; Steinberg, 2010, 2012). But the studies on brain structure provide results for groups, which may not apply to every person. We cannot use such findings to draw definitive conclusions about individual teenagers (Bonnie & Scott, 2013).

Socioemotional Development in Adolescence

Adolescence is also a time of great socioemotional development. During this period, children become more independent from their parents. Conflicts may result as an adolescent searches for his **identity,** or sense of who he is based on his values, beliefs, and goals. Until this point in development, the child's identity was based primarily on the parents' or caregivers' values and beliefs. Adolescents explore who they are by trying out different ideas in a variety of categories, including politics and religion.

http://qrs.ly/mb4qsdy

How has your relationship with your son changed as he's entered adolescence?

Too Young
A teen inmate sits in her room at a maximum-security juvenile facility in Illinois. As a result of the 2005 *Roper v. Simmons* decision (Borra, 2005), defendants being tried for crimes committed before age 18 are no longer candidates for the death penalty. The U.S. Supreme Court arrived at this decision after carefully weighing evidence submitted by the American Psychological Association (APA) and others, which suggests that the juvenile mind is still developing and vulnerable to impulsivity and poor decision making (APA, 2013c). Heather Stone/Chicago Tribune/MCT via Getty Images

spermarche (ˈspər-ˌmär-kē) A boy's first ejaculation.

identity A sense of self based on values, beliefs, and goals.

Once these areas have been explored, they begin to commit to a particular set of beliefs and attitudes, making decisions to engage in activities related to their evolving identity. However, their commitment may shift back and forth, sometimes on a day-to-day basis (Klimstra et al., 2010).

LO 14 Describe how Erikson explained changes in identity during adolescence.

ERIKSON AND ADOLESCENCE Erikson's theory of development addresses this important issue of identity formation (Erikson & Erikson, 1997). The time from puberty to the twenties is the stage of *ego identity versus role confusion,* which is marked by the creation of an adult identity. The adolescent strives to define himself. If the tasks and crises of Erikson's first four psychosocial stages have not been successfully resolved, the adolescent may enter this stage with distrust toward others, and feelings of shame, guilt, and inadequacy (see Table 8.3 on p. 332). In order to be accepted, he may try to be all things to all people.

It is during this period that one wrestles with some important life questions: *What career do I want to pursue? What kind of relationship should I have with my parents? What religion (if any) is compatible with my views, beliefs, and goals?* This stage often involves "trying out" different roles. A person who resolves this stage successfully emerges with a stronger sense of her values, beliefs, and goals. One who fails to resolve *role confusion* will not have a solid sense of identity and may experience withdrawal, isolation, or continued role confusion. However, just because we reach adulthood doesn't mean our identity stops evolving. As we will soon see, there is still plenty of growth throughout life.

PARENTS AND ADOLESCENTS What role does a parent play during this difficult period? Generally speaking, parent–adolescent relationships are positive (Paikoff & Brooks-Gunn, 1991), but conflict does increase during early adolescence (Van Doorn, Branje, & Meeus, 2011), and it frequently relates to issues of control and parental authority. Often these parent–teen struggles revolve around everyday issues such as curfews, chores, schoolwork, and personal hygiene. Fortunately, conflict tends to decline as both parties become more comfortable with the adolescent's growing sense of autonomy and self-reliance (Lichtwarck-Aschoff, Kunnen, & van Geert, 2009; Montemayor, 1983).

FRIENDS Friends become increasingly influential during adolescence. Some parents express concern about the negative influence of peers; however, it is typical for adolescents to form relationships with others of the same age and with whom they might share beliefs and interests. These friendships tend to support the types of behaviors and beliefs parents encouraged during childhood (McPherson, Smith-Lovin, & Cook, 2001). Adolescents tend to behave more impulsively in front of their peers than do adults. It appears that social pressure may inhibit their ability to "put the brakes on" impulsivity in decision making (Albert, Chein, & Steinberg, 2013). But peers can also have a positive influence, supporting prosocial behaviors—getting good grades or helping others, for example (Roseth, Johnson, & Johnson, 2008; Wentzel, McNamara Barry, & Caldwell, 2004). With the use of smartphones and tablets, these negative and positive influences are often transmitted through digital space.

It's My Life!
Relationships between teens and parents are generally positive, but most involve some degree of conflict. Many disputes center on everyday issues, like clothing and chores, but the seemingly endless bickering does have a deeper meaning. The adolescent is breaking away from his parents, establishing himself as an autonomous person. SW Productions/ Getty Images

SOCIAL MEDIA and psychology

The Social Networking Teen Machine

Social media provide an easy way for young people to create and cultivate relationships, but the quality of some of these associations is questionable. Experts worry that teenagers place excessive importance on the number of online interactions they have, rather than the depth of those interactions (Fox News, 2013, March 20). Another concern is that social media may serve as staging grounds for negative behaviors like bullying. According to one survey, approximately 8% of Internet-using teenagers say they have been bullied online in the past year; 88% have observed others being "mean or cruel" on a social media site; 25% say their interactions through social media have led to offline arguments; and 8% claim their online conversations have served as the impetus for physical fights (Lenhart et al., 2011).

But it's not all bad news. The majority of teens who use social media say that their interactions through these networks have made them feel better about themselves and more deeply connected to others (Lenhart et al., 2011). Online communities provide teens with a space to explore their identities and interact with people from diverse backgrounds. They serve as platforms for the exchange of ideas and art (sharing music, videos, and blogs), and places for students to study and collaborate on school projects (O'Keeffe, Clarke-Pearson, & Council on Communications and Media, 2011).

Social media are here to stay, and will continue to impact the socioemotional development of adolescents. The challenge for parents is to find ways to direct this online activity while still recognizing their child's need for space and autonomy (Yardi & Bruckman, 2011). What steps do you think parents should take to ensure that teenagers are using social media in a positive way?

NETWORK BULLIES AND FRIENDS

Kohlberg's Stages of Moral Development

LO 15 Summarize Kohlberg's levels of moral development.

Moral development is another important aspect of socioemotional growth. Lawrence Kohlberg (1927–1987), influenced by the work of Piaget, proposed three levels of moral development that occur in sequence over the life span. These levels, which are further divided into two stages, focus on specific changes in beliefs about right and wrong (**Figure 8.6** on the next page).

Kohlberg used a variety of fictional stories about moral dilemmas to determine the stage of moral reasoning of participants in his studies. The *Heinz dilemma* is a story about a man named Heinz who was trying to save his critically ill wife. Heinz did not have enough money to buy a drug that could save her, so after trying unsuccessfully to borrow money, he finally decided to steal the drug. The two questions asked of individuals in Kohlberg's studies were these: "Should the husband have done that? Was it right or wrong?" (Kohlberg, 1981, p. 12). Kohlberg was not really interested in whether his participants thought Heinz should steal the drug or not; instead, the goal was to determine the moral reasoning behind their answers.

Although Kohlberg described moral development as sequential and universal in its progression, he noted that environmental influences and interactions with others (particularly those at a higher level of moral reasoning) support its continued development. Additionally, not everyone progresses through all three levels; an individual may get stuck at an early stage and remain at that level of morality throughout life. Let's look at these three levels.

Kohlberg at Work
American psychologist Lawrence Kohlberg proposed that moral reasoning progresses through three major levels: preconventional, conventional, and postconventional. The rate at which we move through these developmental levels partly depends on environmental factors, such as interactions with parents and siblings. Critics contend that Kohlberg's research focused too heavily on men in Western cultures (Endicott, Bock, & Narvaez, 2003; Gilligan, 1982). Lee Lockwood/Time & Life Pictures/Getty Images

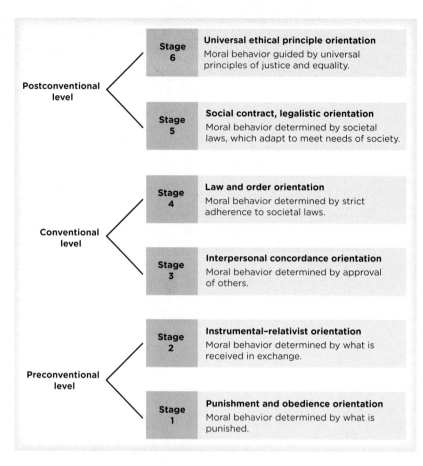

FIGURE 8.6
Kohlberg's Stages of Moral Development

PRECONVENTIONAL MORAL REASONING From the time a toddler or pre-schooler begins to understand the connection between behavior and its consequences, she can begin to think about moral issues and make decisions about what is right and wrong. **Preconventional moral reasoning** usually applies to young children, and it focuses on the consequences of behaviors, both good and bad. For children in Stage 1 (*punishment and obedience orientation*), "goodness" and "badness" are determined by whether a behavior is punished. For example, a child decides not to cheat on a test because she is worried about getting caught and then punished. Thus, consequences drive the belief about what is right and wrong. Regarding the Heinz dilemma, a child at this level may say the husband should not steal the drug because he may go to jail if caught. Children in Stage 2 (*instrumental–relativist orientation*) behave in accordance with a "marketplace" mentality, looking out for their own needs most of the time. The world is seen as an exchange of goods and services, so giving to others does not occur out of loyalty or fairness, but for the hope of reciprocity—"You scratch my back and I'll scratch yours" (Kohlberg & Hersh, 1977, p. 55).

CONVENTIONAL MORAL REASONING At puberty, **conventional moral reasoning** is used, and determining right and wrong is informed by expectations from society and important others, not simply personal consequences. The emphasis is on conforming to society's rules and regulations. In Stage 3 (*interpersonal concordance orientation*), actions that are helpful or please others are considered "good." Gaining approval (being a "good boy" or "nice girl") is an important motivator. Faced with the Heinz dilemma, the adolescent might suggest that because society says a husband must take care of his wife, Heinz should steal the drugs so that others won't think poorly of him. In Stage 4 (*law and order orientation*), the focus is on rules and social order. Duty and obedience to authorities define what is right. Heinz should not steal because stealing is against the law. Cheating on exams is not right because one is obligated to uphold a student code of conduct (Kohlberg & Hersh, 1977).

preconventional moral reasoning Kohlberg's stage of moral development in which a person, usually a child, focuses on the consequences of behaviors, good or bad, and is concerned with avoiding punishment.

conventional moral reasoning Kohlberg's stage of moral development that determines right and wrong from the expectations of society and important others.

postconventional moral reasoning Kohlberg's stage of moral development in which right and wrong are determined by the individual's beliefs about morality, which sometimes do not coincide with society's rules and regulations.

gender The dimension of masculinity and femininity based on social, cultural, and psychological characteristics.

gender identity The feeling or sense of being either male or female, and compatibility, contentment, and conformity with one's gender.

gender roles The collection of actions, beliefs, and characteristics that a culture associates with masculinity and femininity.

POSTCONVENTIONAL MORAL REASONING The third level of Kohlberg's theory is **postconventional moral reasoning.** Right and wrong are determined by the individual's beliefs about morality, which may be inconsistent with society's rules and regulations. Stage 5 (*social contract, legalistic orientation*) reasoning suggests that laws should be followed when they are upheld by society as a whole; but, if a law does not exhibit "social utility," it should be changed to meet the needs of society. In other words, a law-and-order approach isn't always morally right. Someone using this type of reasoning might suggest that Heinz should steal the drug because the laws of society fail to consider his unique situation. In Stage 6 (*universal ethical principle orientation*), moral behavior is determined by universal principles of justice, equality, and respect for human life. An understanding of the "right" thing to do is guided not only by what is universally regarded as right, but also by one's conscience and personal ethical perspective. With regard to the Heinz dilemma, someone using post-conventional moral reasoning would thoughtfully consider all possible options, but ultimately decide that human life overrides societal laws.

CRITICISMS Kohlberg's theory of moral development has not been without criticism. Carol Gilligan (1982) leveled a number of serious critiques, suggesting that the theory did not represent women's moral reasoning. She noted that Kohlberg's initial studies included only male participants, introducing bias into his research findings. Gilligan suggested that Kohlberg had discounted the importance of caring and responsibility and that his choice of an all-male sample was partially to blame. Another issue with Kohlberg's theory is that it focuses on the moral reasoning of individuals, and thus is primarily applicable to Western cultures; in more collectivist cultures, the focus is on the group (Endicott, Bock, & Narvaez, 2003). One last concern about Kohlberg's theory is that we can define and measure moral reasoning, but predicting moral behavior is not always easy. Research that examines moral reasoning and moral behavior indicates that the ability to predict moral behavior is weak at best (Blasi, 1980; Krebs & Denton, 2005).

Gender Development

LO 16 Define gender and explain how culture plays a role in its development.

One important developmental process, which can unfold at any point in life but often occurs during childhood and adolescence, is the establishment of gender identity. **Gender** refers to the dimension of masculinity and femininity based on social, cultural, and psychological characteristics. Men are typically perceived as masculine, and women are assumed to be feminine. But concepts of masculine and feminine vary according to culture, social context, and the individual. According to the American Psychiatric Association (2013), "gender" also indicates the public and often legally recognized role a person has as a man or woman, boy or girl. **Gender identity** is the feeling or sense of being either male or female, and compatibility, contentment, and conformity with one's gender (Egan & Perry, 2001; Tobin et al., 2010).

LEARNING GENDER ROLES We learn how to *behave* in gender-appropriate ways through the **gender roles** designated by our culture. This understanding of expected male and female behavior is generally demonstrated by around age 2 or 3. So too is the ability to differentiate between boys and girls, and men and women (Zosuls, Miller, Ruble, Martin, & Fabes, 2011). Let's explore how these gender roles are learned.

The social-cognitive theory suggests that gender roles can be acquired through observational learning (Bussey & Bandura, 1999; Else-Quest, Higgins, Allison, & Morton, 2012; Tenenbaum & Leaper, 2002). We learn from our observations of others in our environment, particularly those of the same gender. Children also learn and model the behaviors represented in electronic media and books (Kingsbury & Coplan, 2012).

CONNECTIONS

In **Chapter 1,** we discussed the importance of collecting data from a *representative sample,* whose members' characteristics closely reflect the population of interest. Kohlberg's early research included only male participants, but he and others *generalized* his findings to females. Generalizing from an all-male sample to females in the population may not be justifiable.

CONNECTIONS

In **Chapter 5,** we described how learning can occur by observing and imitating a model. Here we see how this type of learning can shape the formation of gender roles.

CONNECTIONS

In **Chapter 5,** we discussed operant conditioning, which is learning that results from consequences. Here, the positive reinforcer is encouragement, which leads to an increase in a desired behavior. The punishment is discouragement, which reduces the unwanted behavior.

Gender Free

Toronto parents Kathy Witterick and David Stocker decided to raise their third child gender free. When baby Storm was born, Witterick and Stocker informed family and friends that the sex of the child would remain a secret for some time; they wanted Storm to make his or her own decision about gender identity (Poisson, 2011, December 26). Pictured here is Storm with big brother Jazz. STEVE RUSSELL/TORONTO STAR, Kathy Witterick

Monkey Play

A male vervet monkey rolls a toy car on the ground (left), and a female examines a doll (right). When provided with a variety of toys, male vervet monkeys spend more time playing with cars and balls, whereas females are drawn to dolls and pots (Alexander & Hines, 2002). Similar behaviors have been observed in rhesus monkeys (Hassett, Siebert, & Wallen, 2008). These studies suggest a biological basis for the gender-specific toy preferences often observed in human children. MCT/MCT via Getty Images

Gender roles are also established through *operant conditioning.* Children often receive reinforcement for behaviors considered gender-appropriate and punishment (or lack of attention) for those viewed as inappropriate. Parents, caregivers, relatives, and peers reinforce gender-appropriate behavior by smiling, laughing, or encouraging. But when children exhibit gender-inappropriate behavior (a boy playing with a doll, for example), the people in their lives might frown, get worried, or even put a stop to it. Through this combination of encouragement and discouragement a child learns to conform to society's expectations.

Keep in mind that not all parents and caregivers are passionate about preserving traditional gender roles. Researchers have found that children develop more fluid ideas about gender-appropriate behavior in environments that do not specify strict gender roles (Hupp, Smith, Coleman, & Brunell, 2010).

COGNITION AND GENDER SCHEMAS Children also seem to develop gender roles by actively processing information (Bem, 1981). In other words, kids think about the behaviors they observe, including the differences between males and females. They watch their parents' behavior, often following suit (Tenenbaum & Leaper, 2002). Using the information they have gathered, they develop a variety of gender-specific rules they believe should be followed—for example, girls help around the house, boys play with model cars (Yee & Brown, 1994). These rules provide the framework for **gender schemas,** which are the psychological or mental guidelines that dictate how to be masculine or feminine.

BIOLOGY AND GENDER Clearly, culture and learning influence the development of gender-specific behaviors and interests, but could biology play a role too? Research on nonhuman primates suggests this is the case (Hines, 2011a). A growing body of literature points to a link between testosterone exposure *in utero* and specific play behaviors (Swan et al., 2010). For example, male and female infants as young as 3 to 8 months demonstrate gender-specific toy preferences that cannot be explained by mere socialization or learning (Hines, 2011b). Research using eye-tracking technology reveals that baby girls spend more time looking at dolls, while boys tend to focus on toy trucks (Alexander, Wilcox, & Woods, 2009). And thus it seems, not all gender-specific behaviors can be attributed to culture and upbringing; this principle is well illustrated by the heartbreaking story of Bruce Reimer.

Nature and Nurture

The Case of Bruce Reimer

Bruce Reimer and his twin brother were born in 1965. During a circumcision operation at 8 months, Bruce's penis was almost entirely burnt away by electrical equipment used in the procedure. When he was about 2 years old, his parents took the advice of Johns Hopkins psychologist John Money and decided to raise Bruce as a girl (British Broadcasting Corporation [BBC], 2014, September 17). The thinking at the time was that what made a person a male or female was not necessarily the original structure of the genitals, but rather how he or she was raised (Diamond, 2004).

Just before Bruce's second birthday, doctors removed his testicles and used the tissues to create the beginnings of female genitalia. His parents began calling him Brenda, dressing him like a girl and encouraging him to engage in stereotypically "girl" activities such as baking and playing with dolls (BBC, 2014, September 17). But Brenda did not adjust so well to her new gender assignment. An outcast at school, she was called cruel names like "caveman" and "gorilla." She brawled with both boys and girls alike, and eventually got kicked out of school (Diamond & Sigmundson, 1997).

When Brenda hit puberty, the problem became even worse. Despite ongoing psychiatric therapy and estrogen replacement, she could not deny what was in her *nature*—she refused to consider herself female (Diamond & Sigmundson, 1997). Brenda became suicidal, prompting her parents to tell her the truth about the past (BBC, 2014, September 17).

At age 14, Brenda decided to "reassign himself" to be a male. He then changed his name to David, began taking male hormones, and underwent a series of penis construction surgeries (Colapinto, 2000; Diamond & Sigmundson, 1997). At 25, David married and adopted his wife's children, and for some time it appeared he was doing quite well (Diamond & Sigmundson, 1997). But sadly, at the age of 38, he took his own life.

We are in no position to explain the tragic death of David Reimer, but we cannot help but wonder what role his traumatic gender reassignment might have played. Keep in mind that this is just an isolated *case*. As discussed in Chapter 1, we should be extremely cautious about making generalizations from case studies, which may or may not be representative of the larger population. Many people who undergo sex reassignment go on to live happy and fulfilling lives.

HIS PARENTS. . . . DECIDED TO RAISE BRUCE AS A GIRL.

GENDER-ROLE STEREOTYPES The case of Bruce Reimer touches on another important topic: gender-role stereotypes. Growing up, David (who was called "Brenda" at the time) did not enjoy wearing dresses and playing "girl" games. He didn't adhere to the *gender-role stereotypes* assigned to little girls. Gender-role stereotypes, which begin to take hold around age 3, are strong ideas about the nature of males and females—how they should dress, what kinds of games they should like, and so on. Decisions about children's toys, in particular, follow strict gender-role stereotypes (boys play with trucks, girls play with dolls), and any crossing over risks ridicule from peers, sometimes even adults. Gender-role stereotypes are apparent in toy commercials (Kahlenberg & Hein, 2010) and pictures in coloring books (Fitzpatrick & McPherson, 2010). They also manifest themselves in academic settings. For example, many girls have negative attitudes about math, which seem to be associated with parents' and teachers' expectations about gender differences in math competencies (Gunderson, Ramirez, Levine, & Beilock, 2012).

Children, especially boys, tend to cling to gender-role stereotypes very tightly. You are much more likely to see a girl playing with a "boy" toy than a boy playing

gender schemas The psychological or mental guidelines that dictate how to be masculine and feminine.

Androgynous Idol
American Idol sensation Adam Lambert reportedly embraces androgyny, the mixing of stereotypically male and female qualities. "I'm trying to make it current again," Lambert told the *Daily Xtra*. "I've always been attracted to that" (Thomas, December 30, 2009). Steve Jennings/WireImage

with a "girl" toy. Society, in turn, is more tolerant of girls who cross gender stereotypes. In many cultures, the actions of a tomboy (a girl who behaves in ways society considers masculine) are more acceptable than those of a "sissy"—a derogatory term for a boy who acts in a stereotypically feminine way (Martin & Ruble, 2010; Thorne, 1993). Despite such judgments, some children do not conform to societal pressure (Tobin et al., 2010).

ANDROGYNY   Those who cross gender-role boundaries and engage in behaviors associated with both genders are said to exhibit **androgyny.** An androgynous person might be nurturing (generally considered a feminine quality) and assertive (generally considered a masculine quality), thus demonstrating characteristics associated with both genders (Johnson et al., 2006). But concepts of masculine and feminine—and therefore what constitutes androgyny—are not consistent across cultures. In North America, notions about gender are revealed in clothing colors; parents frequently dress boy babies in blue and girl babies in pink. In the African nation of Swaziland, on the other hand, children are dressed androgynously, wearing any color of the rainbow (Bradley, 2011).

TRANSGENDER AND TRANSSEXUAL   At birth, most people are identified as male or female; this is referred to as an infant's *natal gender,* or gender assignment. When natal gender does not feel right, an individual may have *transgender* experiences. According to the American Psychological Association, **transgender** refers to people "whose *gender identity, gender expression,* or behavior does not conform to that typically associated with the sex to which they were assigned at birth" (APA, 2011a, p. 1). Remember that gender identity is the feeling or sense of being either male or female. For a person who is transgender, a mismatch occurs between that sense of identity and the gender assignment at birth. This disparity can be temporary or persistent (American Psychiatric Association, 2013). Approximately 700,000 individuals in the United States (around 0.2% of the population) consider themselves to be transgender (Gates, 2011).

From Man to Woman
In April 2015, former Olympian and reality TV personality Bruce Jenner announced he would be making a transition from male to female (Steel, 2015, April 25). There is a lot of inconsistency in the terminology and labels associated with trans, that is, those who are transgender, transsexual, or nonconforming to traditional gender identities. Thus, we should be sensitive about labeling and, when possible, ask trans people how they would like to be identified (Hendricks & Testa, 2012, October). Ethan Miller/Getty Images for Michael Jordan Celebrity Invitational

When the discrepancy between natal gender and gender identity leads to significant experiences and/or expression of distress, an individual might meet the criteria for a *gender dysphoria* diagnosis (American Psychiatric Association, 2013). Some transgender individuals try to resolve this discontent through medical intervention. According to the American Psychiatric Association, a person is considered **transsexual** if he or she seeks or undergoes "a social transition from male to female or female to male, which in many, but not all, cases also involve[s] a somatic transition by cross-sex hormone treatment and genital surgery (*sex reassignment surgery*)" (p. 451, italics in original).

androgyny The tendency to cross gender-role boundaries, exhibiting behaviors associated with both genders.

transgender Refers to people whose gender identity and expression do not typically match the gender assigned to them at birth.

Emerging Adulthood

Childhood and adolescence pave the way for the stage of life known as *adulthood.* In the United States, the legal age of adulthood is 18 for some activities (voting, military enlistment) and 21 for others (drinking, financial responsibilities). These ages are not consistent across cultures and countries (the legal drinking age in some nations is as young as 16). Many cultures and religions mark the transition into adulthood by

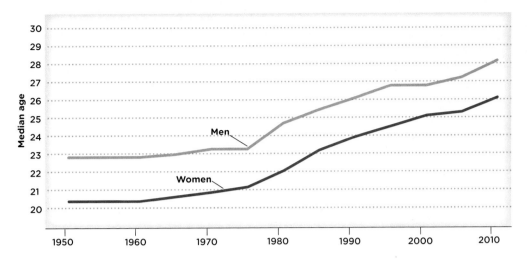

FIGURE 8.7

Age of First Marriage
Many developmental psychologists consider marriage a marker of adulthood because it can represent the first time a person leaves the family home to set out on his or her own. Since the 1950s and 1960s, the median age at which men and women marry for the first time has increased, a trend that appears likely to continue.
Data from U.S. Census Bureau (2011).

ceremonies and rituals (for example, Jewish *bar/bat mitzvahs,* Australian walkabouts, Christian confirmations, Latin American *quinceañeras*), starting as early as age 12.

Complicating the demarcation between adolescence and adulthood is the fact that young people in today's Western societies are marrying much later (Arnett, 2000; Elliott, Krivickas, Brault, & Kreider, 2012), and remaining dependent on their families for longer periods of time (**Figure 8.7**). Psychologists now propose a phase known as **emerging adulthood,** which is the time of life between 18 and 25 years of age. Emerging adulthood is neither adolescence nor early adulthood, and it is a period of exploration and opportunity. The emerging adult has neither the permanent responsibilities of adulthood nor the dependency of adolescence. By this time, most adolescent egocentrism has disappeared, which is apparent in intimate relationships and empathy (Elkind, 1967). During this stage, one can seek out loving relationships, education, and new views of the world before settling into the relative permanency of family and career (Arnett, 2000).

✓ ○○○ show what you know

1. The physical features not associated with reproduction, but that become more distinct during adolescence, are known as
   a. primary sex characteristics.
   b. secondary sex characteristics.
   c. menarche.
   d. puberty.

2. Your cousin is almost 14, and she has begun to use deductive reasoning to draw conclusions and critical thinking to support her arguments. Her cognitive development is occurring in Piaget's
   a. formal operational stage.
   b. concrete operational stage.
   c. ego identity versus role confusion stage.
   d. instrumental–relativist orientation.

3. _____ moral reasoning usually is seen in young children, and it focuses on the consequences of behaviors, both good and bad.

4. "Helicopter" parents pave the way for their children, troubleshooting problems for them, and making sure they are successful in every endeavor. How might this type of parenting impact an adolescent in terms of Erikson's stage of ego identity versus role confusion?

✓ CHECK YOUR ANSWERS IN APPENDIX C.

Adulthood

A WORK IN PROGRESS   At the very beginning of this chapter, we introduced Chloe Ojeah, a 22-year-old community college student caring for two aging grandparents, a 79-year-old grandmother with Alzheimer's disease and an 85-year-old grandfather recovering from a stroke. Like Jasmine, Chloe is immersed in young adulthood, a time when many people are continuing to forge their identities and lay the groundwork for enduring lifelong relationships. Many of the "Who am I?" type of questions that pop up

transsexual An individual who seeks or undergoes a social transition to the other gender, and who may make changes to his or her body through surgery and medical treatment.

emerging adulthood A phase of life between 18 and 25 years that includes exploration and opportunity.

A Good Life
Chloe's grandfather, J. M. Richard, enjoys breakfast with his wife of six decades. Mr. Richard says that his greatest accomplishment was marrying Mrs. Richard, whom he still loves deeply. Mrs. Richard struggles with Alzheimer's disease, but her impaired memory does not stop her from enjoying many daily activities. Chloe Ojeah

in adolescence may spill over into this stage of life. Chloe, for example, still hasn't decided where she stands politically, even though her family clearly leans in a certain direction. Nor has she settled on a religious faith, despite her exposure to at least two different churches. "It's not a decision I can make with my family," says Chloe, who wants to find answers on her own terms. "I'm still questioning everything."

Like many young adults, Chloe is also beginning to explore her capacity to form deep and loving relationships. Her first serious romantic relationship evolved out of a close friendship she had established while living in Houston. Chloe trusted this boyfriend; she was committed to him; she even loved him, though she wouldn't say she was "in love" with him. "More than anything," Chloe insists, "we just enjoyed being around each other." But spending time together was not much of an option when Chloe relocated to Austin to care for her grandparents. Since they parted ways, Chloe has remained on good terms with her ex-boyfriend and his relatives.

As Chloe is just beginning to experience her first meaningful relationships, her grandfather, J. M. Richard, is enjoying his 61st year of married life. When you ask Mr. Richard what he considers his most important achievements, the first thing he says is "marrying my wife." The last few years have been trying, given her battle with Alzheimer's disease, but Mr. Richard continues to be deeply committed to her. As he himself offers, "We still love each other."

Looking back on nearly nine decades of life, Mr. Richard says he feels satisfied: "I am happy with my life, and I am happy with my accomplishments." His fulfillment does not just stem from marriage and fatherhood. "I am also deep into the Baptist church," Mr. Richard notes. "The other thing I have been blessed with up until a year ago was good health." Before the stroke, Mr. Richard was able to drive his car, which allowed him the freedom to take care of business at his funeral home, maintain the various buildings he rents out to tenants, and oversee building projects on his properties. Now he has nerve damage on the left side of his body, which causes persistent pain. He walks with a cane, is visually impaired, and can no longer drive.

But Mr. Richard hasn't thrown in the towel. With the help of an occupational therapist, he hopes to get behind the wheel again one day. And unlike many people, even those who are half his age, he spends 30 to 40 minutes pedaling on his exercise bike each day. Mr. Richard also maintains a vibrant intellectual life, and he continues to talk on the phone with his employees at the funeral home several times a day. 🗁

Whatever you want from life, you are most likely to pursue and attain it during the developmental stage known as adulthood. Developmental psychologists have identified various stages of this long period, each corresponding to an approximate age group: *early adulthood* spans the twenties and thirties, *middle adulthood* the forties to mid-sixties, and *late adulthood* everything beyond.

Physical Development

LO 17 Name some of the physical changes that occur across adulthood.

The most obvious signs of aging tend to be physical in nature. Often you can estimate a person's age just by looking at his hands or facial lines. Let's get a sense of some of the basic body changes that occur through adulthood.

EARLY ADULTHOOD   During early adulthood, our sensory systems are sharp, and we are at the height of our muscular and cardiovascular ability. But some systems have already begun their downhill journey. Hearing, for instance, often starts to decline as a result of noise-induced hearing impairment that commences in early adolescence (Niskar et al., 2001). The body is fairly resilient at this stage, but lifestyle choices can have profound health consequences. Heavy drinking, drug use, poor eating habits, and sleep deprivation can make a person look, feel, and function like someone much older.

As we head toward our late thirties, fertility-related changes occur for both men and women. Women experience a 6% reduction in fertility in their late twenties, 14% in their early thirties, and 31% in their late thirties (Menken, Trussell, & Larsen, 1986; Nelson, Telfer, & Anderson, 2013). Men also experience a fertility dip, but it appears to be gradual and results from fewer and poorer quality sperm (Sloter et al., 2006). It is not until age 50 that male fertility declines substantially (Kidd, Eskenazi, & Wyrobek, 2001).

MIDDLE ADULTHOOD   In middle adulthood, the skin wrinkles and sags due to loss of collagen and elastin, and skin spots may appear (Bulpitt, Markowe, & Shipley, 2001). Hair starts to turn gray and may fall out. Hearing loss continues and may be exacerbated by exposure to loud noises (Kujawa & Liberman, 2006). Eyesight may decline. The bones weaken. Oh, and did we mention you might shrink? But do not despair. There are measures you can take to slow the aging process. For example, genes influence height and bone mass, but research suggests we can limit the shrinking process through continued exercise. In one study, researchers followed over 2,000 people for three decades. Everyone in the study got shorter (the average height loss being 4 centimeters, or about 1.6 inches), but those who had engaged in "moderate vigorous aerobic" exercise lost significantly less (Sagiv, Vogelaere, Soudry, & Ehrsam, 2000). To maintain your stature and overall physique, you would be wise to participate in lifelong moderate endurance activities such as jogging, walking, and swimming.

For women, middle adulthood is a time of major physical change. Estrogen production decreases, the uterus shrinks, and menstruation no longer follows a regular pattern. This marks the transition toward **menopause,** the time when ovulation and menstruation cease, and reproduction is no longer possible. Menopausal women can experience hot flashes, sweating, vaginal dryness, and breast tenderness (Newton et al., 2006). These symptoms may sound unpleasant, but many women consider menopause to be a temporary inconvenience, reporting a sense of relief following the cessation of their menstrual periods, as well as increased interest in sexual activity (Etaugh, 2008).

Men experience their own constellation of midlife physical changes, sometimes referred to as male menopause or *andropause*. Some suggest calling it *androgen decline,* as there is a reduction in testosterone production, not an end to it (Morales, Heaton, & Carson, 2000). Men in middle adulthood may complain of depression, fatigue, and cognitive difficulties, which might be associated with lower testosterone. But research suggests this link between hormones and behavior is evident in only a tiny proportion of aging men (Pines, 2011).

LATE ADULTHOOD   Late adulthood, which begins around 65, is also characterized by the decline of many physical and psychological functions. Eye problems, such as cataracts and impaired night vision, are common. Hearing continues on a downhill course, and reaction time increases (Fozard, 1990). The brain processes information more slowly, and brain regions responsible for memory deteriorate (Eckert, Keren, Roberts, Calhoun, & Harris, 2010).

CONNECTIONS

In **Chapter 3,** we described causes for hearing impairment. Damage to the hair cells or the auditory nerve is called sensorineural deafness. Conduction hearing impairment results from damage to the eardrum or the middle-ear bones that transmit sound waves. Exposure to loud sounds, such as listening to music through earbuds, may play a role in hearing impairment starting in adolescence.

Get a Move On!
Exercise is one of the best ways to fight the aging process. Working out on a regular basis improves cardiovascular health, bone and muscle strength, and mood. A study of more than 400,000 people in Taiwan found that those who exercised just 15 minutes a day lived an average of 3 years longer than their sedentary peers (Wen et al., 2011). © yellowdog/cultura/Corbis

menopause   The time when a woman no longer ovulates, her menstrual cycle stops, and she is no longer capable of reproduction.

Apply This

Move It or Lose It

Some physical decline is inevitable with age, but it is possible to grow old gracefully. One of the best ways to fight aging is to get your body moving. Aerobic exercise improves bone density and muscle strength, and lowers the risk for cardiovascular disease and obesity. It's good for your brain too. "A single bout of moderate [aerobic] exercise" seems to provide a short-term boost in working memory for adults of various ages (Hogan, Mata, & Carstensen, 2013, para. 1). Maintaining a certain level of day-to-day aerobic activity also seems to make a difference, as older people who are physically active tend to perform better on working memory tasks (Guiney & Machado, 2013). We cannot offer a surefire biological explanation for these findings, but it is interesting to note that exercise might foster the development of neural networks, helping with the production of new hippocampus nerve cells, which are important in memory (Deslandes et al., 2009; Erickson et al., 2011; **Figure 8.8**). Would you believe that working out may even reduce the risk of Alzheimer's disease and other disorders of the nervous system (Radak et al., 2010)? When you take good care of your body, you're also taking good care of your mind. ➔

CONNECTIONS

In **Chapter 2,** we reported that studies with nonhuman animals and humans have shown that some areas of the brain are constantly generating new neurons, in a process known as *neurogenesis*. As we age, this production of new neurons seems to be supported by physical exercise.

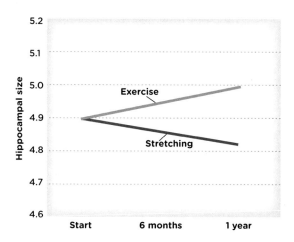

FIGURE 8.8

Exercise to Build Bigger . . . Brains?
Researchers interested in the effects of exercise on the aging brain randomly assigned participants to two groups: One group engaged in a program of gentle stretching exercises, and the other began doing more aerobic activity. During the course of the yearlong study, the researchers found typical levels of age-related shrinkage in the hippocampi of the stretching group. However, in the group that exercised more vigorously, not only was age-related deterioration prevented, hippocampal volume actually increased, with corresponding improvements in memory.
Source: Adapted from Erickson et al. (2011).

Cognitive Development

What's going on in the brain as we pass through the various stages of adulthood, and how do these changes affect our ability to function? Let's explore cognitive development in adulthood.

LO 18 Identify some of the cognitive changes that occur across adulthood.

EARLY ADULTHOOD Measures of aptitude, such as intelligence tests, indicate that cognitive ability remains stable from early to middle adulthood (Larsen, Hartmann, & Nyborg, 2008), though processing speed begins to decline (Schaie, 1993). Young adults are theoretically in Piaget's formal operational stage, which means they can think logically and systematically, but some researchers estimate that only 50% of adults ever exhibit formal operational thinking (Arlin, 1975).

MIDDLE AND LATE ADULTHOOD Much of the discussion of middle adulthood has focused on decline: declining skin elasticity, testosterone, cardiovascular health, and so on. Yet cognitive function does not necessarily decrease during middle adulthood. Longitudinal studies by Schaie and colleagues indicate that decreases in cognitive abilities cannot be reliably measured before 60 (Gerstorf, Ram, Hoppmann,

Golden Years
Old age can be a time of great artistic, intellectual, and humanitarian achievement. Frank Lloyd Wright (left) was 89 when he completed the design for New York's Guggenheim Museum; Nelson Mandela (middle) was 76 when he became the first Black president of South Africa; and Mother Teresa (right) was 69 when she received the Nobel Peace Prize.
left: Ben Schnall/Time & Life Pictures/Getty Images; center: Per-Anders Pettersson/Getty Images; right: Jean-Claude FRANCOLON/Gamma-Rapho via Getty Images

Willis, & Schaie, 2011; Schaie, 1993, 2008). There are some exceptions, however. Midlife is a time when information processing and memory can decline, particularly the ability to remember past events (Ren, Wu, Chan, & Yan, 2013).

After the age of 70, cognitive decline is more apparent. The Seattle Longitudinal Study has shown that the cognitive performance of today's 70-year-old participants is similar to the performance of 65-year-olds tested 30 years ago (Gerstorf et al., 2011; Schaie, 1993, 2008). So from a cognitive abilities perspective, turning 65 does not mean it is time to retire. Processing speed may slow with old age, but older adults are still capable of amazing accomplishments. Frank Lloyd Wright finished designing New York's Guggenheim Museum when he was 89 years old and Nelson Mandela became president of South Africa when he was 76. Age does not limit us unless we allow it to.

Some types of cognitive skills diminish in old age and others become more refined. Older people may not remember all of their academic knowledge, but their practical abilities seem to grow. Life experiences allow people to develop a more balanced understanding of the world around them, one that only comes with age (Sternberg & Grigorenko, 2005).

When studying cognitive changes across the life span, psychologists frequently describe two types of intelligence: **crystallized intelligence,** the knowledge we gain through learning and experience, and **fluid intelligence,** the ability to think in the abstract and create associations among concepts. As we age, the speed with which we acquire new material and create associations decreases (von Stumm & Deary, 2012). In one study, researchers examined performance on fluid and crystallized intelligence tasks in adults between the ages of 20 and 78. Crystallized abilities increased with age, whereas fluid abilities increased from 20 to 30 years of age and remained stable until age 50 (Cornelius & Caspi, 1987). Working memory, the active processing component of short-term memory that maintains and manipulates information, also becomes less efficient with age (Nagel et al., 2008; Reuter-Lorenz, 2013).

Earlier we mentioned that physical exercise provides a cognitive boost. The same appears to be true of mental exercises, such as those required for playing a musical instrument (Hanna-Pladdy & MacKay, 2011). That said, there does appear to be a lot of hype surrounding the "use it or lose it" mantra of aging. The declaration that exercising the brain will stop cognitive decline might be a slight overstatement (Salthouse, 2006). Although there are clear benefits of doing crossword puzzles and reading the newspaper, the evidence is not conclusive that this activity has the same effect it would have on a child, for example. When older adults exercise their brains in a particular domain (for example, playing a musical instrument or using

crystallized intelligence Knowledge gained through learning and experience.
fluid intelligence The ability to think in the abstract and create associations among concepts.

Wii *Big Brain Academy* software), the results do not necessarily transfer to other general abilities, such as cognitive and perceptual information processing (Ackerman, Kanfer, & Calderwood, 2010). However, tasks that specifically focus on training working memory may improve fluid intelligence, even into older age (Nisbett et al., 2012). But research suggests that people who continue to work, both physically and mentally, and remain in good physical shape are less likely to experience significant cognitive decline (Rohwedder & Willis, 2010). Thus, if your goal is to maintain a sharp mind as you age, don't just increase your Sudoku playing or reading time. You need to maintain a balanced approach incorporating a broad range of activities and interests.

Socioemotional Development

Socioemotional development does not always occur in a neat, stepwise fashion. Some of us become parents as teenagers, others not until our forties. This next section describes a host of social and emotional transformations that typically occur during adulthood.

LO 19 Explain some of the socioemotional changes that occur across adulthood.

ERIKSON AND ADULTHOOD   Earlier we described Erikson's approach to explaining socioemotional development from infancy through adolescence, noting that unsuccessful resolution of prior stages has implications for the stages that follow (see Table 8.3 on page 332). During young adulthood (twenties to forties), people are challenged by *intimacy versus isolation.* Young adults tend to focus on creating meaningful, deep relationships, and failing at this endeavor may lead to a life of isolation. Erikson also believed that we are unable to form these relationships if identity has not been clearly established in the identity versus role confusion of adolescence.

Moving into middle adulthood (forties to mid-sixties), we face the crisis of *generativity versus stagnation.* Positive resolution of this stage includes feeling like you have made a real impact on the next generation, through parenting, community involvement, or work that is valuable and significant. Those who do not have a positive resolution of this stage face stagnation, characterized by boredom, conceit, and selfishness.

In late adulthood, we look back on life and evaluate how we have done, a crisis of *integrity versus despair* (mid-sixties and older). If previous stages have resulted in positive resolutions, we feel a sense of accomplishment and satisfaction. A negative resolution of this stage indicates that we have regrets and dissatisfaction.

Before we further explore socioemotional development in adulthood, we must note that Erikson's theory, though very important in the field of developmental psychology, has provided more framework than substantive research findings. His theory was based on case studies, with limited supporting research. In addition, the developmental tasks of Erikson's stages might not be limited to the particular time frame proposed. For example, creating an adult identity is not limited to adolescence, as this stage may resurface at any point in adulthood (Schwartz, 2001).

ROMANCE AND RELATIONSHIPS   Young adulthood is a time when romantic relationships move in a new direction. The focus shifts away from fun-filled first experiences with sex and love to deeper connections. For many people, the twenties are a transition period between the "here and now" type of relationships of adolescence to the serious, long-term partnerships of adulthood (Arnett, 2000). Some of these relationships lead to what many people consider the most challenging, yet rewarding, role in life: parenthood.

PARENTING   Do you ever find yourself watching parent-child interactions at the store? You likely have noticed a vast spectrum of child-rearing approaches. Diana Baumrind (1966, 1971) has been studying parenting for over four decades, and her

---

CONNECTIONS

Here, we are reminded of an issue presented in **Chapter 1:** We must be careful not to equate correlation with causation. In this case, if you experience a decline in cognitive ability, you are less likely to work. Thus, it is the cognitive decline that would lead to the lack of work.

work has led to the identification of four parenting behavioral styles. These styles seem to be stable across situations, and are distinguished by levels of warmth, responsiveness, and control (Maccoby & Martin, 1983).

Parents who insist on rigid boundaries, show little warmth, and expect high control exhibit **authoritarian parenting.** They want things done in a certain way, no questions asked. "Because I said so" is a common justification used by such parents. Authoritarian parents are extremely strict and demonstrate poor communication skills with their children. Their kids, in turn, tend to have lower self-assurance and autonomy, and experience more problems in social settings (Baumrind, 1991).

Authoritative parenting may sound similar to authoritarian parenting, but it is very different. Parents who practice authoritative parenting set high expectations, demonstrate a warm attitude, and are responsive to their children's needs. Being supported and respected, children of authoritative parents are quite responsive to their parents' expectations. They also tend to be self-assured, independent, responsible, and friendly (Baumrind, 1991).

With **permissive parenting,** the parent demands little of the child and imposes few limitations. These parents are very warm but often make next to no effort to control their children. Ultimately, their children tend to lack self-control, act impulsively, and show no respect for boundaries.

Uninvolved parenting describes parents who seem indifferent to their children. Emotionally detached, these parents exhibit minimal warmth and devote little time to their children, although they do provide for their children's basic needs. Children raised by uninvolved parents tend to exhibit behavioral problems, poor academic performance, and immaturity (Baumrind, 1991).

Keep in mind that the great majority of research on these parenting styles has been conducted in the United States, which should make us wonder how applicable these categories are in other countries and cultures (Grusec, Goodnow, & Kuczynski, 2000). Additional factors to consider include the home environment, the child's personality and development, and the unique parent–child relationship. A child who is irritable will react to an authoritarian parent's restrictions in a different way than one who is easygoing, for example (Grusec & Goodnow, 1994).

GROWING OLD WITH GRACE   When many people think of growing older, they imagine a frail old woman (or man) sitting in a bathrobe and staring out the window, unable to care for herself. This stereotype is not accurate. As of 2000, fewer than 5% of Americans older than 65 lived in a nursing home (Hetzel & Smith, 2001). Most older adults in the United States enjoy active, healthy, independent lives. They are involved in their communities, faiths, and social lives, and contrary to popular belief—a large number have active sex lives (Lindau et al., 2007). Researchers have discovered that happiness generally increases with age (Jeste et al., 2013). Positive emotions become more frequent than negative ones, and emotional stability increases, meaning that we experience fewer extreme emotional swings (Carstensen et al., 2011). Stress and anger begin to diminish in early adulthood, and worry becomes less apparent after age 50 (Stone, Schwartz, Broderick, & Deaton, 2010).

Older people might feel happy because they no longer care about proving themselves in the world, they are pleased with the outcome of their lives, or they have developed a strong sense of emotional equilibrium (Jeste et al., 2012). Research suggests that older adults who are healthy, independent, and engaged in social activities also report being happy, and there is some evidence that this increased happiness may result in a longer life (Oerlemans, Bakker, & Veenhoven, 2011). Americans are now living longer than ever, with the average life expectancy of women being 81.1 years and men 76.3 years (Hoyert & Xu, 2012). Could happiness be one of the factors driving this increase in life span?

authoritarian parenting A rigid parenting style characterized by strict rules and poor communication skills.

authoritative parenting A parenting style characterized by high expectations, strong support, and respect for children.

permissive parenting A parenting style characterized by low demands of children and few limitations.

uninvolved parenting A parenting style characterized by a parent's indifference to a child, including a lack of emotional involvement.

Death and Dying

We have spent this entire chapter discussing life. Many of the stages and changes described occur at different times for different people, sometimes overlapping, other times skipped altogether. When it comes to life, nothing is certain—except, of course, the arrival of death.

LO 20 Describe Kübler-Ross' theory regarding reactions to imminent death.

Apart from sex, few topics are as difficult to address as death and dying. Psychiatrist Elisabeth Kübler-Ross (2009) opened the discussion in the early 1960s, while working with people facing the end of life. She found they experienced similar reactions when confronted with the news that their deaths were imminent: stages of denial, anger, bargaining, depression, and acceptance. These stages, Kübler-Ross suggested, are coping mechanisms for dealing with what is to come.

- **Denial:** In the denial stage, a person may react to the news with shock and disbelief, perhaps even suggesting the doctors are wrong. Unable to accept the diagnosis, he may seek other medical advice.
- **Anger:** A dying person may feel anger toward others who are healthy, or toward the doctor who does not have the cure. *Why me?* she may wonder, projecting her anger and irritability in a seemingly random fashion.
- **Bargaining:** This stage may involve negotiating with God, doctors, or other powerful figures for a way out. Usually, this involves some sort of time frame: *Let me live to see my firstborn get married,* or *Just give me one more month to get my finances in order.*
- **Depression:** There comes a point when a dying person can no longer ignore the inevitable. Depression may be due to the symptoms of the patient's actual illness, but it can also result from the overwhelming sense of loss—the loss of the future.
- **Acceptance:** Eventually, a dying person accepts the finality of his predicament; death is inevitable, and it is coming soon. This stage can deeply impact family and close friends, who, in some respects, may need more support than the person who is dying. According to one oncologist, the timing of acceptance is quite variable. For some people, it occurs in the final moments before death; for others, soon after they learn there is no chance of recovery from their illness (Lyckholm, 2004).

Kübler-Ross was instrumental in bringing attention to the importance of attending to the dying person (Charlton & Verghese, 2010; Kastenbaum & Costa, 1977). The stages she proposed provide a valuable framework for understanding death, but keep in mind that every person responds to death in a unique way. For some people, the stages are overlapping; others don't experience the stages at all (Schneidman, 1973). We should also note that there is little research supporting the validity of stages of death, and that the theory arose in a Western cultural context. Evidence suggests that people from other backgrounds may view death and dying from very different perspectives.

across the WORLD

Death in Different Cultures

What does death mean to you? Some of us believe death marks the beginning of a peaceful afterlife. Others see it as a crossing over from one life to another. Still others believe death is like turning off the lights; once you're gone, it's all over.

Views of death are very much related to religion and culture. A common belief among Indian Hindus, for example, is that one should spend a lifetime preparing for a "good death" (*su-mrtyu*). Often this means dying in old age, after conflicts have been put to rest, family matters settled, and farewells said. To prepare a loved one for a good death, relatives place the person on the floor at home (or on the banks of the Ganges River, if possible) and give her water from the hallowed Ganges. If these and other rituals are not carried out, the dead person's soul may be trapped and the family suffers the consequences: nightmares, infertility, and other forms of misfortune (Firth, 2005). Imagine a psychologist trying to assist grieving relatives without any knowledge of these beliefs and traditions.

EVERY CULTURE HAS ITS OWN IDEAS ABOUT DEATH.

In Japan and other parts of East Asia, families often make medical decisions for the dying person (Matsumura et al., 2002). They may avoid using words like "cancer" to shield them from the bad news, believing this knowledge may cause them to lose hope and deteriorate further (Koenig & Gates-Williams, 1995; Searight & Gafford, 2005). Yet, healthy East Asians are more likely than European Americans to engage in and enjoy life when reminded of the imminence of death (Ma-Kellams & Blascovich, 2012).

Interesting as these findings may be, remember they are only cultural trends. Like any developmental step, the experience of death is shaped by countless social, psychological, and biological factors. 🌐

Celebrating the Dead
A mariachi band plays at a cemetery in Mexico's Michoacan state on Dia de los Muertos, "Day of the Dead." During this holiday, people in Mexico and other parts of Latin America celebrate the lives of the deceased. Music is played, feasts are prepared, and graves are adorned with flowers to welcome back the spirits of relatives who have passed. In this cultural context, death is not something to be feared or dreaded, but rather a part of life that is embraced (National Geographic, 2015).
© Christian Kober/Robert Harding World Imagery/Corbis

LATEST DEVELOPMENTS   Do you wonder what became of Jasmine Mitchell and Chloe Ojeah? Both women continue to stay busy, pursuing careers and looking after their families. Chloe is still studying hard and caring for her grandparents. Jasmine graduated from Waubonsee Community College, went on to study social work at Aurora University, and is now earning her Master's degree in social work at Aurora. Eddie is busy practicing baseball and mixed martial arts, while Jocelyn juggles her honors classes with college preparation and church youth group activities. 📁

✓◯◯◯   show what you know

1. Physical changes during middle adulthood include declines in hearing, eyesight, and height. Research suggests which of the following can help limit the shrinking process?
   a. physical exercise
   b. elastin
   c. andropause
   d. collagen

2. As we age, our _____ intelligence, or ability to think abstractly, decreases, but our knowledge gained through experience, our _____ intelligence, increases.

3. When faced with death, a person can go through five stages. The final stage is _____, and sometimes family members need more support during this stage than the dying person.
   a. denial
   b. anger
   c. bargaining
   d. acceptance

4. An aging relative in his mid-seventies is looking back on his life and evaluating what he has accomplished. He feels satisfied with his work, family, and friends. Erikson would say that he has succeeded in solving the crisis of _____ versus _____.

✓ CHECK YOUR ANSWERS IN APPENDIX C.

8 summary of concepts

LO 1   Define human development. (p. 306)

Development refers to the changes that occur in physical, cognitive, and socioemotional functioning over the course of the life span. These changes begin at conception and end at death. The goal of developmental psychology is to examine these changes.

LO 2   Describe three longstanding discussions in developmental psychology. (p. 307)

Developmental psychologists' longstanding debates and discussions have centered on three major themes: stages and continuity; nature and nurture; and stability and change. Each of these themes relates to a basic question: (1) Does development occur in separate or discrete stages, or is it a steady, continuous process? (2) What are the relative roles of heredity and environment in human development? (3) How stable is one's personality over a lifetime and across situations?

LO 3   Identify the types of research psychologists use to study developmental processes. (p. 308)

Developmental psychologists use several methods to explore changes across the life span. The cross-sectional method examines people of different ages at one point in time, and the longitudinal method follows one sample of individuals over a period of time. In the cross-sequential method, participants are divided into age groups as well as followed over time, so researchers can examine developmental changes within individuals and across different age groups.

LO 4   Examine the role genes play in our development and identify the biological factors that determine sex. (p. 311)

All the cells in the human body (except for red blood cells) include a nucleus at their center. Inside this nucleus are our chromosomes, which contain genes made of deoxyribonucleic acid (DNA). Genes provide the blueprint for our physiological development and structure, the inherited framework for how we will develop. The 23rd pair of chromosomes, also referred to as the sex chromosomes, provides specific instructions for the individual to develop into a female or male. The egg from the mother contributes an X chromosome to the 23rd pair, and the sperm from the father contributes either an X chromosome or a Y chromosome. When both members of the 23rd pair are X chromosomes (XX), the zygote generally develops into a female. When the 23rd pair contains an X chromosome and a Y chromosome (XY), the zygote generally develops into a male.

LO 5   Discuss how genotype and phenotype relate to development. (p. 313)

Genotype refers to the 23 chromosome pairs that are unique to each individual and do not change in response to the environment. The genotype interacts with the environment, which results in a phenotype. This phenotype consists of a person's unique physical, psychological, and behavioral characteristics resulting from his or her particular combination of genotype and experiences.

LO 6   Describe the progression of prenatal development. (p. 314)

At conception, when the sperm and egg merge, they form a single cell called a zygote. During the germinal period, the zygote grows through cell division and eventually becomes implanted in the uterine wall. Between the 3rd and 8th weeks of development, the mass of cells is called an embryo. From 2 months following conception to birth, the growing human is identified as a fetus. The amniotic sac serves as a protective barrier; however, harmful environmental agents called teratogens can damage the growing embryo or fetus.

LO 7   Summarize the physical changes that occur in infancy. (p. 317)

As newborns grow, they experience astounding changes both seen and unseen. We see advancement in demonstrated capabilities, known as the motor milestones, and an increasingly sophisticated ability to discriminate among sensory stimuli. These sensorimotor advancements are made possible by the incredible brain development that is occurring. Neurons rapidly sprout new connections, and this dramatic synaptic growth is influenced by experiences and stimulation from the environment.

LO 8   Describe the theories explaining language acquisition. (p. 321)

The behaviorist's view of language development proposes that infants and children learn language in the same way they learn everything else—through positive attention from others for correct behavior, unpleasant attention for incorrect behavior, and by their own observations. Chomsky suggested that humans have a language acquisition device (LAD), an innate mechanism that provides a framework for children to learn language. Infant-directed speech (IDS) also plays a role in language acquisition. Infants pay more attention to adults who use IDS and are more likely to provide them with chances to learn and interact, thus allowing more exposure to language.

LO 9   Outline the universal sequence of language development. (p. 322)

At age 2–3 months, infants typically start to produce vowel-like sounds known as cooing. At 4–6 months, in the babbling stage, infants combine consonants with vowels. This progresses to the one-word stage around 12 months, followed by two-word telegraphic speech at approximately

Creative Crop/Getty Images

18 months. As children mature, they start to use more complete sentences.

LO 10 Summarize the key elements of Piaget's and Vygotsky's theories of cognitive development. (p. 323)

Piaget proposed that one of the basic units of cognition is the schema, which is a collection of ideas or notions that represent a basic unit of understanding. Humans have a need to maintain cognitive equilibrium, and use assimilation and accommodation for that purpose. When we assimilate, we attempt to understand new information using an already existing knowledge base or schema, and when we accommodate, we restructure old notions to make a place for new information. Piaget proposed that cognitive development occurs in four stages: the sensorimotor stage, preoperational stage, concrete operational stage, and formal operational stage. Vygotsky was particularly interested in how social and cultural factors affect cognitive development. He proposed that one way to help children's cognitive development is through scaffolding—pushing them to go just beyond what they are competent and comfortable doing, but also providing help, when needed, in a decreasing manner.

LO 11 Describe how Erikson's theory explains psychosocial development through puberty. (p. 331)

According to Erikson, human development is marked by eight psychosocial stages, spanning infancy through old age. Each stage is marked by a developmental task or an emotional crisis that must be handled successfully to allow for healthy psychological growth: trust versus mistrust, autonomy versus shame and doubt, initiative versus guilt, and industry versus inferiority.

LO 12 Give examples of significant physical changes that occur during adolescence. (p. 333)

Adolescence is characterized by many physical changes: a growth spurt in height, weight, and bones; sex hormones, which influence this growth and development, are also at high levels. In addition, primary sex characteristics (features associated with reproductive organs) and secondary sex characteristics (features not associated with reproductive organs) mature in both boys and girls.

LO 13 Explain how Piaget described cognitive changes that take place during adolescence. (p. 334)

During the formal operational stage of cognitive development, adolescents begin to use deductive reasoning and logic to draw conclusions. A specific type of egocentrism also emerges in adolescence. Adolescents may believe everyone thinks the same way they do. Because they have not had a lot of life experiences, they may fail to consider long-term consequences associated with their behaviors.

LO 14 Describe how Erikson explained changes in identity during adolescence. (p. 336)

The stage of ego identity versus role confusion occurs during adolescence and is marked by the creation of an adult identity. During this stage, the adolescent seeks to define himself through his values, beliefs, and goals. Erikson believed that the period of role confusion is important for the adolescent to navigate, as it provides a chance to "try out" different roles. Successful resolution of this stage results in stronger fundamental values, beliefs, and goals with a firmer sense of identity.

LO 15 Summarize Kohlberg's levels of moral development. (p. 337)

Kohlberg proposed three levels of moral reasoning that occur in sequence. Preconventional moral reasoning usually applies to young children and focuses on the personal consequences of behaviors, both good and bad. At puberty, conventional moral reasoning is used, with the determination of right and wrong based on the expectations of society and important others. In postconventional moral reasoning, right and wrong are determined by the individual's beliefs about morality, which may not coincide with society's rules and regulations.

LO 16 Define gender and explain how culture plays a role in its development. (p. 339)

Gender refers to the dimension of masculinity and femininity based on social, cultural, and psychological characteristics. It is often used in reference to the cultural roles that distinguish males and females. We generally learn these roles by observing other people's behavior and by adopting cultural beliefs about what is appropriate for men and women.

LO 17 Name some of the physical changes that occur across adulthood. (p. 344)

Adulthood brings about many physical changes. We are physically at our peak in early adulthood, but that typically declines as we reach late adulthood. Gradual physical changes occur, including hearing and vision loss, wrinkles, graying hair, reduced stamina, and for women menopause. Lifestyle choices can have significant influences on health. Heavy drinking, drug use, poor eating habits, and sleep deprivation can make one look, feel, and function like someone much older.

LO 18 Identify some of the cognitive changes that occur across adulthood. (p. 346)

Cognitive ability remains stable from early to middle adulthood, but midlife is a time when information processing and memory can decline, particularly the ability to remember past events. Processing speed may slow with old age.

Crystallized intelligence refers to the knowledge we gain through experience, and fluid intelligence refers to the ability to think in the abstract and create associations among concepts. As we age, the speed with which we learn new material and create associations decreases, but crystallized intelligence increases.

LO 19 Explain some of the socioemotional changes that occur across adulthood. (p. 348)

According to Erikson, during young adulthood, people face the crisis of intimacy versus isolation, and failure to create meaningful, deep relationships may lead to a life of isolation. In middle adulthood, we face the crisis of generativity versus stagnation. Positive resolution of this stage includes feeling like one has made a valuable impact on the next generation.

In late adulthood, in the crisis of integrity versus despair, we look back on life and evaluate how we have done.

LO 20 Describe Kübler-Ross' theory regarding reactions to imminent death. (p. 350)

Kübler-Ross documented similar reactions among people faced with the news of their imminent death: denial (reacting with shock and disbelief), anger (toward others who are healthy, or about the lack of a cure), bargaining (negotiating for more time), depression (due to illness or the overwhelming sense of loss), and acceptance (accepting death is inevitable). Yet people vary greatly in how they deal with and experience dying. Many of these reactions or coping mechanisms may occur simultaneously or in stages, or the dying individual might not experience any of these stages.

key terms

accommodation, p. 324
adolescence, p. 333
androgens, p. 312
androgyny, p. 342
assimilation, p. 324
attachment, p. 330
authoritarian parenting p. 349
authoritative parenting, p. 349
babbling, p. 322
chromosomes, p. 311
concrete operational stage, p. 326
conservation, p. 326
conventional moral reasoning, p. 338
cooing, p. 322
critical period, p. 308
cross-sectional method, p. 308

cross-sequential method, p. 310
crystallized intelligence, p. 347
deoxyribonucleic acid (DNA), p. 311
developmental psychology, p. 306
dizygotic twins, p. 315
dominant gene, p. 314
egocentrism, p. 324
embryo, p. 315
emerging adulthood, p. 343
epigenetics, p. 314
estrogen, p. 312
fetal alcohol syndrome (FAS), p. 316
fetus, p. 316
fluid intelligence, p. 347
formal operational stage, p. 326

gender, p. 339
gender identity, p. 339
gender roles, p. 339
gender schemas, p. 340
gene, p. 311
genotype, p. 313
identity, p. 335
intersexual, p. 312
longitudinal method, p. 310
maturation, p. 307
menarche, p. 333
menopause, p. 345
monozygotic twins, p. 315
object permanence, p. 324
permissive parenting, p. 349
phenotype, p. 313
postconventional moral reasoning, p. 339
preconventional moral reasoning, p. 338

preoperational stage, p. 324
primary sex characteristics, p. 333
puberty, p. 333
recessive gene, p. 314
scaffolding, p. 327
schema, p. 323
secondary sex characteristics, p. 333
sensorimotor stage, p. 324
spermarche, p. 334
telegraphic speech, p. 322
temperament, p. 328
teratogens, p. 316
testosterone, p. 312
transgender, p. 342
transsexual, p. 342
uninvolved parenting, p. 349
zygote, p. 312

TEST PREP are you ready?

1. A researcher is interested in studying changes across the life span with regard to memory, problem solving, and language. She chooses a large sample of college seniors and decides to follow them for the next 30 years. This is an example of:
   a. socioemotional development.
   b. longitudinal research.
   c. cross-sectional research.
   d. epigenetics.

2. Chloe's grandmother suffers from Alzheimer's disease. Chloe wonders if she will experience a similar future because of her biological relationship to her grandmother. What Chloe is contemplating is similar to which of the following debates in developmental psychology?
   a. stability and change
   b. stages or continuity
   c. critical or sensitive period
   d. nature and nurture

3. DNA molecules include sections corresponding to _____ , which encode proteins that determine the texture of hair, color of eyes, and some aspects of personality.

    a. phenotypes   b. epigenetics

    c. zygotes   d. genes

4. Your psychology instructor often discusses the factors in the environment that can influence how genes are expressed. This topic is a part of the field studying:

    a. epigenetics.   b. maturation.

    c. the cohort effect.   d. prenatal development.

5. Human development is influenced by the interaction of many factors. Brain development, for example, is influenced by biological maturation and experiences in the environment. This is evident in _____, which occurs when unused synaptic connections are eliminated.

    a. myelin

    b. socioemotional development

    c. synaptic pruning

    d. the rooting reflex

6. _____ are agents that can damage a growing embryo or fetus.

    a. Phenotypes   b. Genotypes

    c. Zygotes   d. Teratogens

7. Your friend's daughter starts to say "ma, ma, ma" over and over when you walk in the room. This _____ is a stage that starts at around 4 to 6 months, and it is generally characterized by meaningless combinations of consonants and vowels.

    a. cooing   b. babbling

    c. telegraphic speech   d. infant-directed speech

8. Erikson proposed that human development is characterized by eight psychosocial stages, each marked by a developmental task or emotional crisis. In the first stage, the infant must resolve the _____ conflict. Caregivers who are not responsive might lead the infant always to expect the worst in people.

    a. autonomy versus shame and doubt

    b. industry versus inferiority

    c. trust versus mistrust

    d. ego identity versus role confusion

9. According to Vygotsky, _____ is an approach that helps children learn, providing support when necessary but allowing them to problem solve as much as possible on their own.

    a. assimilation   b. scaffolding

    c. phenotype   d. schema

10. _____ further develop during adolescence. These changes are associated with reproductive organs, such as the maturation of ovaries, uterus, penis, and testes.

    a. Gender schemas

    b. Temperaments

    c. Primary sex characteristics

    d. Secondary sex characteristics

11. Adolescents begin thinking more logically and systematically, and start to use deductive reasoning to draw conclusions. They have entered what Piaget would refer to as the:

    a. formal operational stage.

    b. postconventional moral reasoning stage.

    c. industry versus inferiority stage.

    d. concrete operational stage.

12. One of the important tasks of adolescence is to _____, that is, to find a sense of self based on values, beliefs, and goals.

    a. use preconventional moral reasoning

    b. search for identity

    c. establish secure attachment

    d. use scaffolding

13. During middle adulthood, one major physical change for women is _____, which is often preceded by a decrease in estrogen production and a reduction in the size of the uterus.

    a. andropause   b. menarche

    c. shrinking in height   d. menopause

14. A research team has followed a large sample of men from their college graduation in 1955 through their retirement, trying to understand better how their cognitive abilities change over time. They interview and test these men once every 5 years. This would be considered a:

    a. cohort effect.   b. longitudinal method.

    c. cross-sectional method.   d. phenotype.

15. A woman learns that her death is imminent. According to Kübler-Ross, her initial reaction to this news will likely be shock and disbelief, which are common to the _____ stage.

    a. denial

    b. conventional moral reasoning

    c. late adulthood

    d. preoperational

16. Developmental psychologists explain changes across the life span using the biopsychosocial perspective. Categorize the following as biological, psychological, or social influences: family, learning, media, heredity, hormones, traits, culture.

17. Describe the stages in the development of a fertilized egg, from conception to birth.

18. Infants as young as 5 months old pay more attention to people who use infant-directed speech. Using the evolutionary perspective, explain why this might be the case.

19. Create a tool to help you remember the names of the four parenting styles observed by Baumrind.

20. We have described how cognitive abilities tend to decline with age. What kinds of cognitive activities might actually improve with age?

✓ CHECK YOUR ANSWERS IN APPENDIX C.

Get personalized practice by logging into LaunchPad at www.macmillanhighered.com/launchpad/ sciampresenting1e to take the LearningCurve adaptive quizzes for Chapter 8.

9

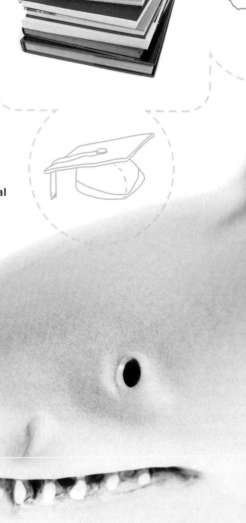

Shark: Image Source/Getty Images. Reference books, notebooks, and pen: Christina Norwood/Getty Images

motivation and emotion

Motivation

FIRST DAY OF SCHOOL   When Mohamed Dirie started first grade, he did not know his ABCs or 123s. He had no idea what the words "teacher," "cubby," or "recess" meant. In fact, he spoke virtually no English. As for his classmates, they were beginning first grade with basic reading and writing skills from preschool and kindergarten. Mohamed's early education had taken place in an Islamic school, where he spent most of his time learning to read and recite Arabic verses of the Qur'an (kə-'rän). But Arabic wasn't going to be much help to a 6-year-old trying to get through first grade in St. Paul, Minnesota.

Months earlier, Mohamed and his mother, father, and older sister had arrived in St. Paul from the East African nation of Kenya, some 8,000 miles across the globe. Kenya was not their native country, just a stopping point between their homeland, Somalia, and a new life in America.

Perhaps you have heard about Somalia. Many of the news stories coming out of this nation in the past two decades have told of bloody clashes between rival factions, kidnappings by pirates, suicide bombings, and starving children. Somalia's serious troubles began in 1991, when rebel forces overthrew the government of President Siad Barre. With gunshots ringing through the streets of their home city of Mogadishu, Mohamed's family, like thousands of others, fled the country, narrowly escaping death.

Mohamed, In His Own Words

http://qrs.ly/b14qshc

© 2016, Macmillan

War-Torn Somalia
Mohamed's family comes from the East African nation of Somalia (shaded red on the map). They fled their homeland in 1991 during a violent government overthrow that led to more than 20,000 civilian deaths (Gassmann, 1991, December 21). The image here shows a group of Somali rebels in the capital city of Mogadishu about a month after the regime was toppled. left: Globe Turner, LLC/Getty; right: AP Photo

Note: Quotations attributed to Mohamed Dirie are personal communications.

The Scholar
Four-year-old Mohamed (below) dressed in special attire to celebrate his completion of a *surah,* or chapter in the Qur'an. When this photograph was taken, the Dirie family had left Somalia and was living in a temporary home in Kenya. Some 14 years later, Mohamed graduated from high school in St. Paul, Minnesota (right). Courtesy of Mohamed Dirie

The first day of school in St. Paul, little Mohamed strapped on his backpack and walked with his mother to the bus stop. When the yellow bus pulled up to the curb, Mohamed's mother followed him inside and insisted on accompanying him to school. But Mohamed was ready to make the journey alone. "No, Mom, I got this," he remembers saying in his native Somali.

When Mohamed arrived at his new school, he found his way to the first-grade classroom and discovered a swarm of children chattering and making friends. Mohamed wanted to mingle, too, so he endeared himself to the other kids the best way he could—by smiling. Flashing a grin was Mohamed's way of communicating, *Hey, I am a good person and you should get to know me.* His strategy worked. "I really felt like other people approached me better," he says. Mohamed's warm and welcoming demeanor may have been one reason his teacher took a special interest in him, providing the individual attention he needed to catch up to his peers. And Mohamed caught up quickly.

By the end of third grade, he had graduated from an English as a Second Language (ESL) program and could converse fluently with classmates. He sailed through the rest of elementary school with As and Bs in all subjects. Middle school presented new challenges, as Mohamed attended one of the poorest schools in the district and occasionally got picked on, but he continued to excel academically, taking the most challenging classes offered. In high school, he took primarily international baccalaureate (IB) or pre-IB classes, which prepped him for his undergraduate work at the University of Minnesota. Now, with his bachelor's degree in scientific and technical communication, Mohamed is contemplating his next step. Will it be law school? A master's degree? Maybe a PhD?

If you think about where Mohamed began and where he is today, it's hard not to be awed. He entered the United States' school system 2 years behind his peers, unable to speak a word of English, an outsider in a culture radically different from his own. Without any tutoring from his parents (who couldn't read the class assignments, let alone help him with schoolwork), he managed to propel himself to the upper levels of the nation's educational system in just 12 years.

How do you explain Mohamed's success? This young man definitely is intelligent. You can tell he is bright after 5 minutes of conversation. But intelligence is not the only ingredient in the recipe for outstanding achievement. Other factors are important as well, including something psychologists consider essential for success in school: *motivation* (Conley, 2012; Hodis, Meyer, McClure, Weir, & Walkey, 2011; Linnenbrink & Pintrich, 2002). 📁

What Is Motivation?

There are people who get kicks from bungee jumping out of helicopters, and those who feel completely invigorated by a rousing match of chess. Human behaviors can be logical: We eat when hungry, sleep when tired, and go to work to pay the rent. Our behaviors can also be senseless and destructive: A beautiful fashion model starves herself, or an aspiring politician throws away an entire career for a fleeting sexual adventure. Why do people spend their hard-earned money on lottery tickets when the chances of winning may be 1 in 175 million (Wasserstein, 2013, May 16)? And what in the world drives teenagers to wrap houses in toilet paper on Halloween night?

One way to explain human behavior is through learning. We know that people (not to mention dogs, chickens, and slugs) can *learn* to behave in certain ways through classical conditioning, operant conditioning, and observational learning (Chapter 5). But learning isn't everything. Another way to explain behavior is to consider what might be motivating it. In the first half of this chapter, you will learn about different forms of motivation and the theories explaining them. Keep in mind that human behavior is complex and should be studied in the context of culture, biology, and the environment. Every behavior is likely to have a multitude of causes (Maslow, 1943).

LO 1   Define motivation.

Psychologists propose that **motivation** is a stimulus or force that can direct the way we behave, think, and feel. A motivated behavior tends to be guided (that is, it has a direction), energized, and persistent. Mohamed's academic behavior has all three features: *guided* because he sets specific goals like getting into graduate school, *energized* because he goes after those goals with zeal, and *persistent* because he sticks with his goals even when challenges arise.

INCENTIVE   Let's take a look at how operant conditioning, particularly the use of *reinforcers,* can help us understand the relationship between learning and motivation. When a behavior is reinforced (with positive or negative reinforcers), an association is established between the behavior and its consequence. If we consider motivated behavior, this association becomes the **incentive,** or reason to repeat the behavior. Imagine there is a term paper you have been avoiding. You decide you will treat yourself to an hour of Web surfing for every three pages you write. *Adding* a reinforcer (surf time) increases your writing behavior; thus, we call it a *positive reinforcer.* The association between the behavior (writing) and the consequence (Web surfing) is the incentive. Before you know it, you begin to expect this break from work, which motivates you to write.

CONNECTIONS

In **Chapter 7,** we described intellectually *gifted* people as those with very high IQ scores. We also presented the concept of *emotional intelligence.* Here, we see that in addition to intelligence, *motivation* plays a role in success.

You Asked, Mohamed Answers

http://qrs.ly/5k4qshh
What motivated you to go to college and better your education?

CONNECTIONS

In **Chapter 5,** we introduced *positive* and *negative reinforcers,* which are stimuli that increase future occurrences of target behaviors. In both cases, the behavior becomes associated with the reinforcer. Here, we see how these associations become incentives.

motivation A stimulus that can direct behavior, thinking, and feeling.

incentive An association established between a behavior and its consequences, which then motivates that behavior.

Adrenaline Junkie

Why are some people drawn to thrill-seeking activities like bungee jumping? Their behaviors are best explained by intrinsic motivation—the stimulation from these experiences is highly rewarding. "Sensation seeking" appears to be an inherited trait associated with certain patterns of dopamine activity in the brain (Derringer et al., 2010). VisualCommunications/Getty Images

LO 2   Explain how extrinsic and intrinsic motivation impact behavior.

EXTRINSIC MOTIVATION   When a learned behavior is motivated by the incentive of external reinforcers in the environment, we would say there is an **extrinsic motivation** to continue that behavior (Deci, Koestner, & Ryan, 1999; **Table 9.1**). In other words, the motivation comes from consequences that are found in the environment or situation. Bagels and coffee might provide extrinsic motivation for people to attend a boring meeting. Sales commissions provide extrinsic motivation for sales people to sell more goods. For most of us, money serves as a powerful form of extrinsic motivation.

INTRINSIC MOTIVATION   But learned behaviors can also be motivated by personal satisfaction, interest in a subject matter, and other variables that exist within a person. When the urge to continue a behavior comes from within, we call it **intrinsic motivation** (Deci et al., 1999). Reading a textbook because it is inherently interesting exemplifies intrinsic motivation. The reinforcers originate inside of you (learning feels good and brings you satisfaction), and not from the external environment.

What compels you to offer your seat to an older adult on a bus: Is it because you've been praised for helping others before (extrinsic motivation), or because it simply feels good to help someone (intrinsic motivation)? Perhaps your response is a combination of both.

EXTRINSIC VERSUS INTRINSIC   Many behaviors are inspired by a blend of extrinsic and intrinsic motivation, but there do appear to be potential disadvantages to extrinsic motivation (Deci et al., 1999). Researchers have found that using rewards, such as money and marshmallows, to reinforce already interesting activities (like doing puzzles, playing word games, and so on) can lead to a decrease in what was initially intrinsically motivating. Perhaps the use of external reinforcers causes people to feel less responsible for initiating their own behaviors.

TABLE 9.1   EXAMPLES OF INTRINSIC, EXTRINSIC, AND NEUTRAL PHRASES USED IN A MOTIVATION STUDY

Intrinsic Motivation Phrases	Extrinsic Motivation Phrases	Neutral Phrases
Writing an enjoyable paper	Writing an extra-credit paper	Writing an assigned paper
Working on the computer out of curiosity	Working on the computer for bonus points	Working on the computer to meet a deadline
Participating in a fun project	Participating in a money-making project	Participating in a required project
Pursuing my personal interests in class	Pursuing an attractive reward in class	Pursuing a routine task in class
Working with freedom	Working for incentives	Working with pressure
Having options and choices	Having prizes and awards	Having pressures and obligations
Working because it's fun	Working because I want money	Working because I have to
Feeling interested	Anticipating a prize	Feeling frustrated

Listed here are descriptions of activities that typically arouse intrinsic motivation, extrinsic motivation, or no motivation.

In general, behavior resulting from intrinsic motivation is likely to include "high-quality learning," but only when the activities are novel, challenging, or have aesthetically pleasing characteristics. Extrinsic motivation may be less effective, resulting in resentment or disinterest (Ryan & Deci, 2000). Unfortunately, researchers have found that "tangible rewards—both material rewards, such as pizza parties for reading books, and symbolic rewards, such as good student awards—are widely advocated by many educators and are used in many classrooms, yet the evidence suggests that these rewards tend to undermine intrinsic motivation for the rewarded activity" (Deci, Koestner, & Ryan, 2001, p. 15).

For Mohamed, the most powerful source of extrinsic motivation was the approval of his mother. He recalls how proud she was after returning from a parent–teacher conference in which his first-grade teacher said, "Your child is as bright as the sun." Mohamed doesn't remember his mom rewarding him with material things like toys and candy; apparently, making her proud was gratifying enough. But there were also forces driving Mohamed from within (intrinsic motivation). He enjoyed the process of learning. It was rewarding to master a second language and nail down his multiplication tables. Outside of class, Mohamed read books for fun. He still enjoys reading science fiction, so much that he hopes to write his own novel one day. Says Mohamed, "I want to be the first Somali to write a science fiction [book] in Somali."

Instinct Theory

GOODBYE, SOMALIA Somalia was not a safe place in 1991. The groups that orchestrated the revolution began warring among themselves, and the country plunged into bloody chaos. Over 20,000 innocent people were killed in the crossfire (Gassmann, 1991, December 21). A famine and food crisis ensued, which, in addition to the ongoing fighting, led to 240,000 to 280,000 deaths within the next 2 years (Gundel, 2003). It is easy to understand why Mohamed's parents, or anyone, would want to remove their family from Somalia during this period. Faced with a life-or-death situation, they were motivated by what you might call a "survival" instinct.

LO 3   Summarize instinct theory.

What are instincts, do humans really have them, and how do they relate to motivation? First observed by scientists studying animals, **instincts** are complex behaviors that are fixed, unlearned, and consistent within a species. Instincts motivate South American ovenbirds to construct elaborate cavelike nests, and sea turtles to swim back hundreds of miles to feeding grounds they visited years earlier (Broderick, Coyne, Fuller, Glen, & Godley, 2007). No one teaches the birds to build their nests or the turtles to retrace migratory routes; through evolution, these behaviors appear to be etched into their genetic make-up.

Instincts form the basis of one of the earliest theories of motivation. Inspired in part by Charles Darwin's theory of evolution, early scholars proposed that humans have a variety of instincts (McDougall, 1912). American psychologist William James (1890/1983) suggested we could explain some human behavior through instincts such as attachment and cleanliness. At the height of instinct theory's popularity, several thousand human "instincts" had been named, among them curiosity, flight, and aggressiveness (Bernard, 1926; Kuo, 1921). Yet there was little evidence they were true instincts—that is, complex behaviors that are fixed, unlearned, and consistent within a species. Only a handful of human behaviors might be considered instincts, such as rooting behavior in newborn infants (Chapter 8). But even these are more related to reflexes than is a complex activity like nest building.

Hungry and Waiting
A group of starving Somalis hope to receive food from an aid center in the city of Bardera. The situation in Somalia turned to chaos and desperation after rebels toppled the government in 1991. Over 240,000 people died in the ensuing war and famine (Gundel, 2003). Les Stone/Zuma

extrinsic motivation The drive or urge to continue a behavior because of external reinforcers.

intrinsic motivation The drive or urge to continue a behavior because of internal reinforcers.

instincts Complex behaviors that are fixed, unlearned, and consistent within a species.

Nesting Instinct
South American ovenbirds build cozy cavelike nests using mud, grass, and bark. Elaborate home-building behaviors, which are seen in all 240 ovenbird species, appear to be innate, or unlearned (Wuethrich, 1999, November 29). Their architectural aptitude seems to be the result of instinct. Fritz Poelking/ Age Fotostock

Although instinct theory faded into the background, some of its themes are apparent in the evolutionary perspective. A substantial body of research suggests that evolutionary forces influence human behavior. For example, emotional responses, such as fear of snakes, heights, and spiders, may have evolved to protect us from danger (Plomin, DeFries, Knopik, & Neiderhiser, 2013). But these fears are not instincts, because they are not universal. Not everyone is afraid of snakes and spiders; some of us have learned to fear (or not fear) them through experience. When trying to pin down the motivation for behavior, it is difficult to determine the relative contributions of learning (nurture) and innate factors (nature) such as instinct (Deckers, 2005).

CONNECTIONS

In **Chapter 1,** we presented the *evolutionary perspective,* which suggests humans have evolved adaptive traits through natural selection. Behaviors that improve the chances of survival and reproduction are most likely to be passed along to offspring, whereas less adaptive behaviors decrease in frequency. Humans do appear to have innate responses that have been shaped by our ancestors' behaviors.

FOUR YEARS IN KENYA After fleeing the bullet-riddled city of Mogadishu, Mohamed and his family made their way across the border into the neighboring country of Kenya, where they lived for about 4 years. Mohamed considers himself one of the "more fortunate ones." Many Somalis had no choice but to settle in squalid, overcrowded refugee camps, while Mohamed's family had the means to rent a small apartment in the capital city of Nairobi.

Being an outsider in Kenya was not easy, however. Back in Somalia, Mohamed's father had earned a solid living constructing buildings, and his mother had been a successful entrepreneur selling homemade food from their house. In Kenya, neither parent could find employment. They had no choice but to live off "remittances," or money sent from family members outside of Africa, and relying on other people was not their style. "You're waiting on other people to feed you," Mohamed says, "and [my father] didn't like that."

Daily life presented its fair share of challenges, too. Mohamed's diet was painfully monotonous, with most meals centering around *ugali,* a dense gruel made of corn or millet flour—similar to oatmeal, but harder in consistency. At times,

Surviving in Somalia
Habiba Ibrahim hauls wood to build a new home near Baidoa, Somalia, in December 1993. The 30-year-old mother was pushed off her land by fighting between ethnic groups. In the years following the government overthrow, 1–2 million Somalis fled their homes. Some resettled in the Western world, but most became refugees within their own country or in the neighboring nations of Kenya and Ethiopia (Gundel, 2003).
AP Photo/Ricardo Mazalan

the apartment building lost electricity for weeks, or water stopped flowing from faucets. During water shortages, the whole family would carry empty buckets and tubs to a nearby army base and ask for water. Despite these difficulties, Mohamed never went hungry or thirsty. His basic *physiological needs* were met.

Drive-Reduction Theory

Humans and nonhuman animals have basic physiological **needs** or requirements that must be maintained at some baseline or constant state to ensure continued existence. **Homeostasis** refers to the way in which our bodies maintain these constant states through internal controls. In order to survive, there is a continuous monitoring of oxygen, fluids, nutrients, and other physiological variables. If these fall below desired or necessary levels, an urge to restore equilibrium surfaces. And this urge motivates us to act.

LO 4   Describe drive-reduction theory and explain how it relates to motivation.

The **drive-reduction theory** of motivation proposes that this biological balancing act is the basis for motivation (Hull, 1952). According to this theory, behaviors are driven by the need to maintain homeostasis—that is, to fulfill basic biological needs for nutrients, fluids, oxygen, and so on (see **Infographic 9.1** on the next page). If a need is not fulfilled, this creates a **drive,** or state of tension, that pushes us or motivates behaviors to meet the need. The urges to eat, drink, sleep, seek comfort, or have sex are associated with physiological needs. Once a need is satisfied, the drive is reduced, at least temporarily, because this is an ongoing process, as the need inevitably returns. For example, when the behavior (let's say eating) stops, the deprivation of something (such as food) causes the need to increase again.

Let's look at another concrete example of drive reduction. Imagine you visit a mountainous area 6,500 feet above sea level, which puts a strain on breathing. While jogging, you find yourself gasping for air because your oxygen levels have dropped. Motivated by the need to maintain homeostasis, you stop what you are doing until your oxygen levels return to normal. Having an unfulfilled *need* (not enough oxygen) creates a *drive* (state of tension) that pushes you to modify your behavior in order to restore homeostasis (you stop and breathe deeply, allowing your blood oxygen levels to return to a normal level). The drive-reduction theory helps us understand how physiological needs can be motivators, but it is less useful for explaining why we climb mountains, go to college, or drive cars too fast.

Arousal Theory

Mohamed arrived in America when he was 6 years old. Stepping off the plane in the Twin Cities (Minneapolis/St. Paul) was quite a shock for a young boy who had lived most of his childhood in the crowded, pavement-covered city of Nairobi. "It was really strange to me," Mohamed says. "At that time, I hadn't really seen a place that had space." How odd it was to see patches of green grass in front of every house. "Everything looked like it sparkled."

New places, people, and experiences can be frightening. They can also be delightfully exhilarating. Humans are fascinated by novelty, and you see evidence of this innate curiosity in the earliest stages of life. Babies grab, suck, and climb on just about everything they can get their hands on, including (much to the horror of their parents) dangerous electrical devices. Ignoring the most forceful parental warnings (*Do NOT touch that hot plate!*), many toddlers still reach out and touch extremely hot cookware or recklessly leap between pieces of furniture. But mind you, children are not the only ones seeking new experiences. Grown men and women will pay hundreds of dollars to parachute out of airplanes or float over jagged mountains in hot-air balloons.

needs Physiological or psychological requirements that must be maintained at some baseline or constant state.

homeostasis The tendency for bodies to maintain constant states through internal controls.

drive-reduction theory Suggests that homeostasis motivates us to meet biological needs.

drive A state of tension that pushes us or motivates behaviors to meet a need.

Theories of Motivation

Motivational forces drive our behaviors, thoughts, and feelings. Psychologists have proposed different theories addressing the needs that create these drives within us. Let's look at the three most prominent theories of motivation. Some theories, like drive-reduction theory, best explain motivation related to physiological needs. Other theories focus on psy-chological needs, such as the need for an optimum level of stimulation, as described in arousal theory. In his hierarchy of needs, Abraham Maslow organizes various drives and proposes that we are motivated to meet some needs before others.

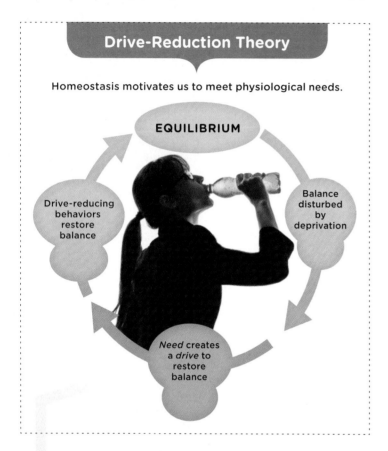

Drive-Reduction Theory

Homeostasis motivates us to meet physiological needs.

EQUILIBRIUM

Drive-reducing behaviors restore balance

Balance disturbed by deprivation

Need creates a *drive* to restore balance

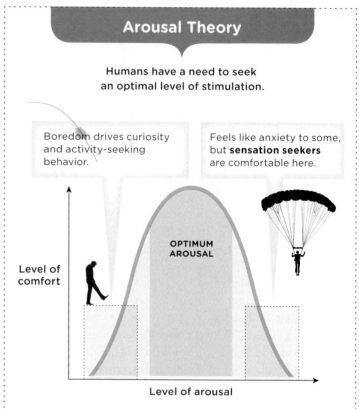

Arousal Theory

Humans have a need to seek an optimal level of stimulation.

Boredom drives curiosity and activity-seeking behavior.

Feels like anxiety to some, but **sensation seekers** are comfortable here.

OPTIMUM AROUSAL

Level of comfort

Level of arousal

Credits: Woman with water bottle, iStockphoto/Thinkstock; Sad business-man silhouette, shutterstock; Skydiver silhouette, shutterstock

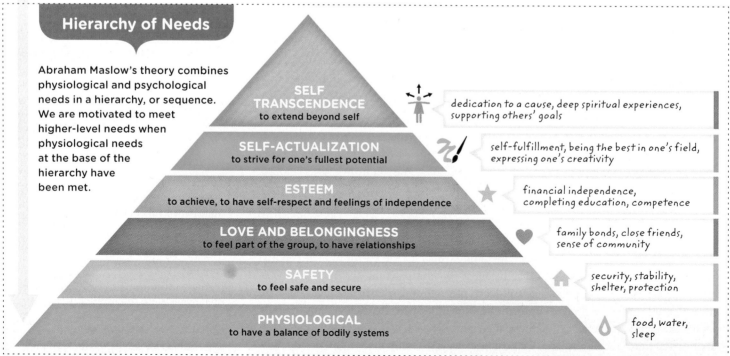

Hierarchy of Needs

Abraham Maslow's theory combines physiological and psychological needs in a hierarchy, or sequence. We are motivated to meet higher-level needs when physiological needs at the base of the hierarchy have been met.

SELF TRANSCENDENCE
to extend beyond self

dedication to a cause, deep spiritual experiences, supporting others' goals

SELF-ACTUALIZATION
to strive for one's fullest potential

self-fulfillment, being the best in one's field, expressing one's creativity

ESTEEM
to achieve, to have self-respect and feelings of independence

financial independence, completing education, competence

LOVE AND BELONGINGNESS
to feel part of the group, to have relationships

family bonds, close friends, sense of community

SAFETY
to feel safe and secure

security, stability, shelter, protection

PHYSIOLOGICAL
to have a balance of bodily systems

food, water, sleep

They also spend hours tooling around Web sites like Wikipedia and YouTube—just to learn about new things. Why engage in activities that have little, if anything, to do with satisfying basic biological needs? Humans are driven by other types of urges, including the apparent need for stimulation.

Our primate cousins are also inquisitive, which suggests that they too have an innate need for enrichment and sensory stimulation. Researchers have found that monkeys will attempt to open latches without extrinsic motivation; apparently, their curiosity motivates their behavior (Butler, 1960; Harlow, Harlow, & Meyer, 1950).

LO 5 Explain how arousal theory relates to motivation.

According to **arousal theory,** humans (and perhaps other primates) seek an optimal level of arousal, as not all motivation stems from physical needs. Arousal, or engagement in the world, can be a product of anxiety, surprise, excitement, interest, fear, and many other emotions. Have you ever had an unexplained urge to make simple changes to your daily routines, like taking a new route to work, preparing your morning eggs differently, or adding new clothes to your wardrobe? These behaviors may stem from your need to increase arousal, as *optimal* arousal is a personal or subjective matter that is not the same for everyone (Infographic 9.1). Evidence suggests that some people are *sensation seekers;* that is, they appear to seek activities that increase arousal (Zuckerman, 1979, 1994). Popularly known as "adrenaline junkies," these individuals relish activities like cliff diving, racing motorcycles, and watching horror movies. High sensation seeking is not necessarily a bad thing, as it may be associated with a higher tolerance for stressful events (Roberti, 2004).

Needs and More Needs: Maslow's Hierarchy

LO 6 Outline Maslow's hierarchy of needs.

Have you ever been in a car accident, lived through a hurricane, or witnessed a violent crime? At the time, you probably were *not* thinking about what show you were going to watch on HBO that night. When physical safety is threatened, everything else tends to take a backseat. This is one of the themes underlying the **hierarchy of needs** theory of motivation proposed by Abraham Maslow (1908–1970), a leading figure in the humanistic movement. Maslow organized human needs into a hierarchy of biological and psychological needs, often depicted as a pyramid (Infographic 9.1). The needs in the hierarchy are considered universal and are ordered according to the strength of their associated drives, with the most critical needs at the bottom. Food and water, for example, are situated at the base of the hierarchy, and generally take precedence over higher-level needs.

PHYSIOLOGICAL NEEDS *Physiological needs,* as stated earlier, include the requirements for food, water, sleep, and an overall balance of bodily systems. If a life-sustaining need such as fluid intake goes unsatisfied, other needs are placed on hold and the person is motivated to find ways to satisfy it. For example, the Chilean miners introduced in Chapter 1 spent weeks trapped underground with no clean drinking water. To quench their thirst, they were willing to drink oil-contaminated water (and urine, in the case of one man).

SAFETY NEEDS For most North Americans, basic physiological needs are "relatively well gratified" (Maslow, 1943), and thus Maslow would suggest their behavior is motivated by the next higher level in the hierarchy: *safety needs.* But how you define safety depends on the circumstances of your life. If you were living in Mogadishu during the 1991 revolution (and many times subsequent to that period), staying safe

Dangerous Fun
Babies and toddlers are notorious for climbing on furniture, mouthing nonfood items, and reaching for hazardous objects (this is why many parents "baby proof" their homes). Like adults looking for exciting places to travel and new electronic gadgets to own, these babies may be searching for novel forms of stimulation. BSIP/Phototake

CONNECTIONS

In **Chapter 1,** we discussed Maslow and his involvement in *humanistic psychology.* The humanists suggest that people are inclined to grow and change for the better, and this perspective is apparent in the hierarchy of needs. Humans are motivated by the universal tendency to move up the hierarchy and meet needs toward the top.

arousal theory Suggests that humans are motivated to seek an optimal level of arousal, or alertness and engagement in the world.

hierarchy of needs A continuum of needs that are universal and ordered in terms of the strength of their associated drives.

might have involved dodging bullets and artillery fire. For those currently living in Somalia, safety includes having access to safe drinking water and disease-preventing vaccines. Most people living in America do not have to worry about access to clean water or routine vaccinations. Here, safety is more likely equated with the need for predictability and order: having a steady job, a home in a safe neighborhood, health insurance, and living in a country with a stable economy. What does safety mean for you?

LOVE AND BELONGINGNESS NEEDS If safety needs are being met, then people will be motivated by *love and belongingness needs.* Maslow suggested this includes the need to avoid loneliness, to feel like part of a group, and to maintain affectionate relationships. Except for a rare run-in with neighborhood bullies, Mohamed enjoyed a fairly secure existence in Minnesota. His need for safety was met, so he was motivated at this next level of the hierarchy. In addition to cultivating deep family bonds, Mohamed befriended two boys he met in middle school, one who had emigrated from Bangladesh and the other a first-generation Mexican American. The three pals all ended up going to the University of Minnesota, and they remain very close.

We all want to belong, and failing to meet this need has significant consequences. People who feel disconnected or excluded may demonstrate less prosocial behavior (Twenge, Baumeister, DeWall, Ciarocco, & Bartels, 2007) and behave more aggressively and less cooperatively, which only tends to intensify their struggle for social acceptance (DeWall, Baumeister, & Vohs, 2008).

ESTEEM NEEDS If the first three levels of needs are being met, then the individual might be motivated by *esteem needs,* including the need to be respected by others, to achieve, and to have self-respect, self-confidence, and feelings of independence. Cultivating and fulfilling these needs foster a sense of confidence and self-worth, both qualities that Mohamed seems to possess. It was early in life that Mohamed began doing things for himself. His parents may have been there to encourage him, but they could not hold his hand when it came to tasks demanding proficiency in English— like filling out employment applications. But Mohamed did just fine on his own, landing his first job at a nonprofit student loan company just after ninth grade, and performing so well that the company employed him throughout college. Mohamed, it appears, began meeting esteem needs very early on.

SELF-ACTUALIZATION Even with the above-mentioned needs actively being met, Maslow suggested that the need for **self-actualization** would provide motivation "to become more and more what one is, to become everything that one is capable of becoming" (Maslow, 1943, p. 382). Self-actualization is the need to reach one's fullest potential. Some will meet this need by being the best possible parent, while others will strive to be the best artist or musician. Self-actualization is at the heart of the humanistic movement: It represents the human tendency toward growth and self-discovery (Chapter 10). For Mohamed, self-actualization means being an exceptional scholar, employee, and father.

SELF-TRANSCENDENCE Toward the end of his life, Maslow proposed an additional need: that for *self-transcendence.* This need motivates us to go beyond our own needs and feel outward connections through "peak experiences" of ecstasy and awe. Fulfilling this need might mean devoting oneself to a humanitarian cause, pursuing a lofty ideal, or achieving spiritual enlightenment. If you walked into Mohamed's room, you would see a huge poster that says, "Live a simple life so others can simply live." What this means, explains Mohamed, is that you should do the best you can in life, but also strive to allow others to do the same. "It's balancing your life so that

Love, Affection, and Belongingness
Relationships with friends help fulfill what Maslow called love and belongingness needs. TobKatrina/ Shutterstock

self-actualization The need to be one's best and strive for one's fullest potential.

self-determination theory (SDT) Suggests that humans are born with the needs for competence, relatedness, and autonomy, which are always driving us in the direction of growth and optimal functioning.

need for achievement (n-Ach) A drive to reach attainable and challenging goals, especially in the face of competition.

need for power (n-Pow) A drive to control and influence others.

you're always doing the most positive good," he says. As president of the University of Minnesota's Somali Student Association, Mohamed put this slogan to work, organizing activities to support Somali students, and arranging cultural awareness events at the university and in the greater Twin Cities communities.

EXCEPTIONS TO THE RULE   Maslow's hierarchy provides suggestions for the order of needs, but this sequence is not set in stone. In some cases, people abandon physiological needs in order to meet a self-actualization need—going on a hunger strike or giving up material possessions, for example. During the Islamic holy month of Ramadan, Mohamed refrains from drinking or eating from dawn to dusk—not an easy task during August in Minnesota, where the sun rises at about 6:00 A.M. and sets well after 8:00 P.M. The practice of fasting, which also occurs in Christianity, Hinduism, and Judaism, illustrates how basic physiological needs (food and water) can temporarily be placed on hold for a greater purpose (religion).

Safety is another basic need often relegated in the pursuit of something more transcendent. Just think of all the soldiers who have given their lives fighting for causes like freedom and social justice. Somali parents living in a war zone and battling hunger may neglect their own basic needs to ensure their children's well-being, thus fulfilling higher needs such as love and esteem.

SELF-DETERMINATION THEORY   Building on the ideas of both Maslow and Erik Erikson, Edward Deci and Richard Ryan (2008) proposed the **self-determination theory (SDT),** which suggests that humans are born with three universal, fundamental needs that are always driving us in the direction of optimal functioning: competence, relatedness, and autonomy (**Figure 9.1;** Stone, Deci, & Ryan, 2009). Competence represents the need to reach our goals through successful mastery of day-to-day responsibilities. Relatedness is the need to create meaningful and lasting relationships. And autonomy means managing one's behavior to reach personal goals. Self-determination theory does not focus on overcoming one's shortcomings, but on moving in a positive direction.

NEED FOR ACHIEVEMENT   In the early 1930s, Henry Murray proposed that humans are motivated by 20 fundamental human needs. One of these has been the subject of a great deal of research: the **need for achievement (n-Ach),** or a drive to reach attainable and challenging goals especially in the face of competition. McClelland, Atkinson, Clark, and Lowell (1976) suggested that people tend to seek out situations that provide opportunities for satisfying this need. A child who aspires to become a professional basketball player might start training at a very young age, read books about the sport, and apply for basketball camp scholarships. A high school student dead set on going to college may set up meetings with the college counselor, take practice SATs, and read books about how to write an exceptional application essay.

NEED FOR POWER   According to McClelland and colleagues (1976), some people are motivated by a **need for power (n-Pow),** or a drive to control and influence others. People with this need may project their importance through outward appearances. They may drive around in luxury cars, wear flashy designer clothing, and buy expensive houses. Some even flex their influence muscles on the pages of Facebook, building massive numbers of contacts just to show how important and popular they are.

Breaking Fast
Iraqi families gather for Iftar, the evening meal eaten after the daytime fast. During the holy month of Ramadan, Muslims foreswear food and water from dawn to dusk. They also step up charity work and other efforts to help those less fortunate (Huffington Post, 2012, July 16). Here, basic needs (food and water) are put on hold for something more transcendent. Johan Spanner/Polaris

CONNECTIONS

In **Chapter 8,** we introduced Erikson's theory of psychosocial development, which suggests that stages of development are marked by a task or emotional crisis. These crises often touch on issues of competence, relatedness, and autonomy.

FIGURE 9.1
Self-Determination Theory
Deci and Ryan's theory proposes that we are born with fundamental needs for competence, relatedness, and autonomy.
© 2005 by the American Psychological Association. Adapted with permission from Lyubormirsky, Sheldon, and Schkade (2005); photo: Justin Horrocks/Getty Images

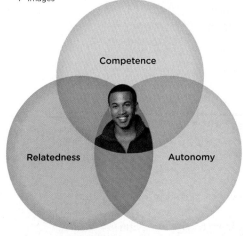

SOCIAL MEDIA and psychology

Network Needs

Some of the most enthusiastic users of Facebook—those who tend to have large numbers of contacts, status updates, and wall posts—score high on assessments of a personality trait called *narcissism* (Buffardi & Campbell, 2008; Mehdizadeh, 2010). Narcissistic people are vain and self-absorbed; they seek prestige and power, and they may feel a sense of superiority over others. These characteristics shine through online, and presumably have a negative impact on the Facebook social climate (Buffardi & Campbell, 2008; Carpenter, 2012).

Social media users are driven by the desire for love and belonging (the third level from the bottom on Maslow's hierarchy). Facebook seems to appeal to people who struggle to get those needs met in real life (Song et al., 2014), but it may not be the answer to their problems. One study of college students, for example, found no evidence that using Facebook eliminated loneliness. Those who were socially isolated offline were also socially isolated online (Freberg, Adams, McGaughey, & Freberg, 2010). In some cases, using social media actually intensified feelings of loneliness (DiSalvo, 2010, January/February). Perhaps this is because interactions with network "friends" tend to be more superficial than those in real life. Can anyone really maintain deep and meaningful relationships with 300 Facebook friends?

FACEBOOK: A CURE FOR LONELINESS?

But there is a bright side. Facebook does appear to be a useful tool for strengthening established relationships (DiSalvo, 2010). A century ago, families were not as geographically scattered as they are today. Grandparents, siblings, and cousins might have lived in the same town or county, and this would have created more opportunities for love, affection, and belonging. These days, families are dispersed all over the globe, and staying connected through social media may be a lot easier (and cheaper) than buying airplane tickets.

In the next section, we return our focus to the base of Maslow's pyramid, where basic drives such as hunger and thirst are represented. Sadly, many people in the world do not get those needs fulfilled.

  show what you know

1. _____ is a stimulus that directs the way we behave, think, and feel.

2. Imagine you are a teacher trying to motivate your students. Explain why you would want them to be influenced by intrinsic motivation as opposed to extrinsic motivation.

3. Your instructor suggests that gender differences in dating behavior are ultimately motivated by evolutionary forces. She is using which of the following to support her explanation?
   a. operant conditioning
   b. arousal theory
   c. instinct theory
   d. homeostasis

4. The _____ theory of motivation suggests that the need to maintain homeostasis motivates us to meet our biological needs.
   a. arousal
   b. instinct
   c. incentive
   d. drive-reduction

5. According to Maslow, the biological and psychological needs that motivate us to behave are arranged in a _____.

6. How does drive-reduction motivation differ from arousal motivation?

✓ CHECK YOUR ANSWERS IN APPENDIX C.

Back to Basics: Hunger

STARVING IN SOMALIA Like many Somali Americans, Mohamed regularly sends money back home to relatives in need. Without assistance from family members living in more prosperous countries like the United States, many Somalis would not be able to afford food, medicine, and other necessities. As Mohamed says, "You can't just leave your family back home to starve."

In the spring of 2011, the Horn of Africa was hit by a drought that plunged Somalia into one of the greatest humanitarian crises of our time—a famine responsible for the starvation deaths of 250 children every day, or 1 child every 6 minutes (British

Broadcasting Corporation [BBC], 2011, July 22). Refugees poured out of Somalia by the thousands. Desperate for food, they walked for weeks to reach refugee camps in neighboring countries. Aid workers said they encountered wounded children, dehydrated and emaciated, arriving at the camps with no shoes (BBC, 2011, June 28). According to a 2011 report, nearly half of Somalia's population was in need of "lifesaving assistance" (United Nations Office for the Coordination of Humanitarian Affairs, 2011, September 5). The situation has since improved, but food shortages continue (Agence France-Presse, 2014, July 26).

In the coming pages, we will explore hunger, one of the most powerful motivators of human behavior. You will learn what happens in the brain and body when a person is in dire need of food, either because of external circumstances (a famine) or deep-seated psychological factors (an eating disorder). We will also investigate the causes of overeating. So fasten your waist belt and get ready for a journey into the psychological realm of hunger. 📁

Hungry Brain, Hungry Body

It's midnight; you are struggling to get through the final pages of your psychology chapter. Suddenly, your stomach lets out a desperate gurgling cry. "Feed me!" *Time to heat up that frozen burrito,* you say to yourself as you head into the kitchen. But wait! Are you really hungry?

LO 7 Discuss how the stomach and the hypothalamus make us feel hunger.

THE STOMACH AND HUNGER In a classic study, Walter Cannon and A. L. Washburn (1912) sought to answer this question (well, not this *exact* question, but they did want to learn what causes stomach contractions). Here's a brief synopsis of the experiment: To help monitor and record his stomach contractions, Washburn swallowed a balloon that the researchers could inflate. The researchers also kept track of Washburn's hunger levels, having him push a button anytime he felt "hunger pangs" (**Figure 9.2**). What did the experiment reveal? Anytime he felt hunger, his stomach contracted.

BLOOD CHEMISTRY AND HUNGER Cannon and Washburn's experiment demonstrates that the stomach plays an important role in hunger, but it's just one piece of the puzzle. One reason we know this is that cancer patients who have had their stomachs surgically removed do not differ from people with their stomachs intact in regard to feelings of satiety (that is, feeling full) or the amount of food eaten during a meal (Bergh, Sjöstedt, Hellers, Zandian, & Södersten, 2003). We also must consider the chemicals in the blood, such as glucose, or blood sugar. When glucose levels dip, the stomach and liver send signals to the brain that something must be done about this reduced energy situation. The brain, in turn, will initiate a sense of hunger.

THE HYPOTHALAMUS AND HUNGER One part of the brain that helps regulate hungry feelings is the hypothalamus, which can be divided into functionally distinct areas. When the *lateral hypothalamus* is activated, appetite increases. This occurs even in well-fed animals if this region is stimulated electrically. Destroy this area of the brain, and animals lose interest in food, even to the point of starvation. The lateral hypothalamus is also involved in motivating behavior, ultimately helping to preserve the balance between energy supply and demand (Leinninger, 2011).

Food Aid
A Somali woman hauls a bag of food aid through the massive Dadaab refugee settlement in Kenya. When famine struck the Horn of Africa in 2011, tens of thousands of Somalis fled their homeland and resettled in overcrowded refugee camps like Dadaab (Gettleman, 2011, July 15).
Oli Scarff/Getty Images

FIGURE 9.2
Cannon and Washburn's Classic Hunger Study
Washburn swallowed a special balloon attached to a device designed to monitor stomach contractions. While the balloon was in place, he pressed a key every time he felt hungry. Comparing the record of key presses against the balloon measurements, Washburn was able to show that stomach contractions accompany feelings of hunger.

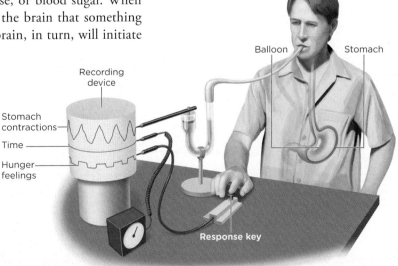

Recording device

Stomach contractions

Time

Hunger feelings

Balloon

Stomach

Response key

If the *ventromedial hypothalamus* becomes activated, appetite declines, causing an animal to stop eating. Disable this region of the brain, and the animal will overeat to the point of obesity. The ventromedial hypothalamus receives information about levels of blood glucose and other feeding-related stimuli, as it too works to maintain the body's energy balance (King, 2006).

The hypothalamus has a variety of sensors that react to information about appetite and food intake. Once this input is processed, appropriate responses are communicated via hormones in the bloodstream (**Infographic 9.2**). One such hormone is *leptin,* a protein emitted by fat cells that plays a role in suppressing hunger. Another is *insulin,* a pancreatic hormone involved in controlling levels of glucose in the bloodstream. With input from these and other hormones, the brain can monitor energy levels and respond accordingly. This complex system enables us to know when we are hungry, full, or somewhere in between.

Let's Have a Meal: Cultural and Social Context

Biology is not the only factor influencing eating habits. We must also consider the culture and social context in which we eat. In the United States, most of our social activities, holidays, and work events revolve around food. We may not even be hungry, but when presented with a spread of food, we find ourselves eating. All too often we eat too fast, rushing to our next event, class, or meeting, not taking the time to experience the sensation of taste. We tend to match our food intake to those around us, although we may not be aware of their influence (Herman, Roth, & Polivy, 2003; Howland, Hunger, & Mann, 2012). Gender plays a role in eating habits as well. Using naturalistic observation, researchers found that women choose lower-calorie meals when eating with a man than when eating with another woman (Young, Mizzau, Mai, Sirisegaram, & Wilson, 2009).

PORTION DISTORTION   A variety of factors drive our decisions to begin or stop eating, including hunger, satiety, and food taste (Vartanian, Herman, & Wansink, 2008). But more subtle variables, such as portion size, come into play too. In one study, participants at a movie theater were given free popcorn, some in medium-sized buckets and others in large buckets. Some of the buckets contained popcorn that was fresh, and others were filled with popcorn that was 14 days old. Participants given large buckets consistently ate 33% more than those given medium-size buckets, regardless of whether the popcorn was fresh or stale. The stale popcorn was described as "soggy" or "terrible," yet the participants still ate more of it when given larger portions (Wansink & Kim, 2005). Remember this the next time you sit down in front of the TV with an entire bag of snack food.

Portion size is just one factor influencing food intake. Visual cues are also important, especially when they provide feedback about how much you have eaten. To study this, researchers gave college students tubes of potato chips to eat while watching a movie. In some of the tubes, every 7th chip was dyed red. Participants given tubes with the occasional red chips consumed 50% less than those given tubes with no red chips. Thus we see, interrupting mindless eating (*Wait a second, that's a red chip*) can decrease the amount of food consumed in one sitting (Geier, Wansink, & Rozin, 2012).

Obesity

In today's world, a growing number of people are struggling with obesity, fueling popular interest in strategies for cutting down food intake. Two-thirds of adults in the United States are overweight, and one-third meet the criteria for *obesity,* defined as having a body mass index (BMI) of 30 or higher (Flegal, Carroll, Ogden, & Curtin,

CONNECTIONS

In **Chapter 2,** we described *hormones* as chemical messengers released in the bloodstream. Hormones do not act as quickly as neurotransmitters, but their messages are more widely spread throughout the body. Here, we see how hormones are involved in communicating information about hunger and feeding behaviors.

CONNECTIONS

In **Chapter 1,** we discussed *naturalistic observation,* a form of descriptive research that studies participants in their natural environments. One important feature of this type of study is that researchers do not disturb participants or their environment. Here, we assume the researchers were able to measure and record the meals chosen without interfering in the participants' natural behaviors.

Mechanisms in Hunger Regulation

We are all aware—sometimes uncomfortably so—when our stomachs are grumbling. But most hunger signals are communicated in an imperceptible cycle throughout our bodies. Feelings of hunger and satisfaction are the result of many independent signals. Different organs are involved in monitoring blood chemistry, prompting the communication of hunger or satiety signals to the brain. These messages are received by the hypothalamus, which regulates basic physiological needs. Separate areas of the hypothalamus then send signals to other parts of the brain, motivating us to increase or decrease eating.

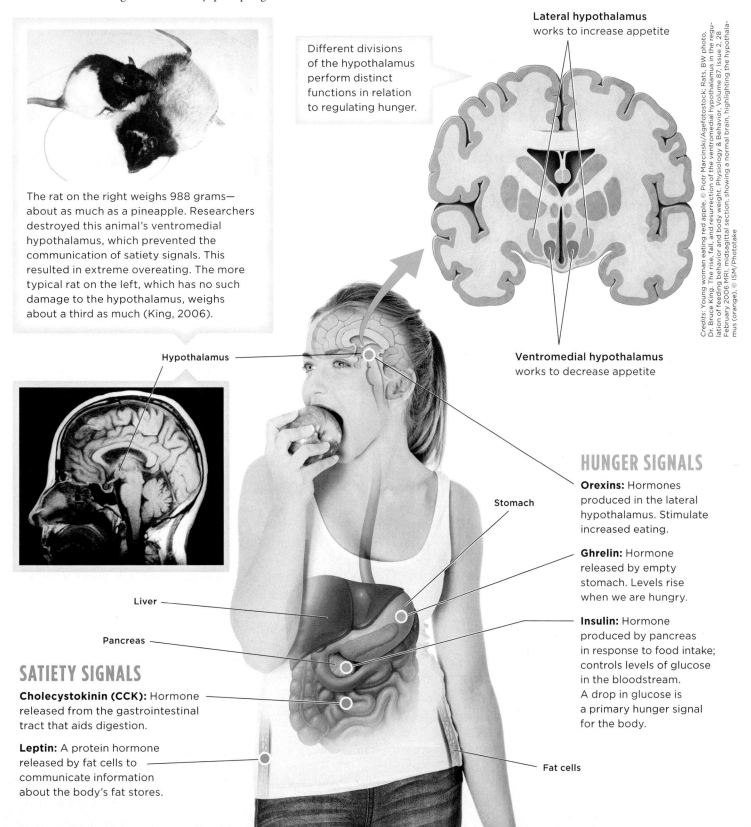

The rat on the right weighs 988 grams—about as much as a pineapple. Researchers destroyed this animal's ventromedial hypothalamus, which prevented the communication of satiety signals. This resulted in extreme overeating. The more typical rat on the left, which has no such damage to the hypothalamus, weighs about a third as much (King, 2006).

Different divisions of the hypothalamus perform distinct functions in relation to regulating hunger.

Lateral hypothalamus works to increase appetite

Ventromedial hypothalamus works to decrease appetite

Hypothalamus

Liver

Pancreas

Stomach

Fat cells

SATIETY SIGNALS

Cholecystokinin (CCK): Hormone released from the gastrointestinal tract that aids digestion.

Leptin: A protein hormone released by fat cells to communicate information about the body's fat stores.

HUNGER SIGNALS

Orexins: Hormones produced in the lateral hypothalamus. Stimulate increased eating.

Ghrelin: Hormone released by empty stomach. Levels rise when we are hungry.

Insulin: Hormone produced by pancreas in response to food intake; controls levels of glucose in the bloodstream. A drop in glucose is a primary hunger signal for the body.

Obesity Epidemic
More than a third of U.S. adults are obese, meaning they have a body mass index (BMI) greater than or equal to 30 (Ogden et al., 2014). Obesity has become a worldwide phenomenon, affecting countries as far-flung as Canada and Iran. Some researchers suspect the problem is related to the growing availability of cheap, processed, and well-marketed food (Swinburn et al., 2011). Digital Vision/Thinkstock

CONNECTIONS

In **Chapter 7,** we presented *heritability,* the degree to which heredity is responsible for a particular characteristic in a population. The heritability for BMI is 65%, indicating that around 65% of the variation in BMI can be attributed to genes, and 35% to environmental influences.

2010; Ogden, Carroll, Kit, & Flegal, 2014). Adults aren't the only ones battling the bulge; one-third of America's children and teens are overweight (American Heart Association, 2014).

SET POINT, SETTLING POINT, AND HEREDITY   Surprisingly, there is relatively little fluctuation in adult weight over time. The communication between the brain and the appetite hormones help regulate the body's **set point,** or stable weight that we tend to maintain despite variability in day-to-day exercise and intake of food. If you don't consume enough calories and your weight falls below this set point, metabolism decreases, causing you to gain weight and return to your set point. Exceed the set point, and metabolism increases, once again moving you back toward your stable weight (Keesey & Hirvonen, 1997). The set point acts like a thermostat, helping to maintain a consistent weight in part through changes in metabolism.

Some critics of the *set point* model suggest that it fails to appreciate the importance of social and environmental influences (Stroebe, van Koningsbruggen, Papies, & Aarts, 2013). These theorists suggest we should consider a *settling point,* which is less rigid and can explain how the "set" point can actually change based on the relative amounts of food consumed and energy used. A settling point can help us understand how body weight may shift to a newly maintained weight, and why so many people are overweight as a result of environmental factors, such as bigger meal portions, calorie-dense foods, increased dining at restaurants, and eating while engaged in another activity like watching television. Nevertheless, there does seem to be a genetic component of body weight. Studies suggest that the heritability of BMI is around 65% (Speakman et al., 2011). More research is needed, but it seems we may be genetically predisposed to stay within a certain weight range.

OVEREATING, SLEEP, AND SCREEN TIME   As you well know, deciding what and when to eat does not always come down to being hungry or full. We must consider how motivation plays a role in our eating patterns. Some people eat not because they are hungry, but because they are bored, sad, or anxious. Others eat simply because the clock indicates that it is mealtime. Higher brain regions involved in eating decisions can override the hypothalamus, driving you to devour that cheesy burrito even when you don't need the calories.

If our set point helps us maintain a certain weight, how does this impact people who struggle with *obesity?* Obesity is both a physiological and psychological issue. There is some evidence that genes play a role, and we also know some illnesses can lead to obesity (Anis et al., 2010; Plomin et al., 2013). But one often overlooked lifestyle factor related to obesity is sleep. Preliminary research suggests that inadequate sleep is linked to weight problems (a negative correlation between sleep and weight gain). In contrast, individuals who sleep between 6 and 8 hours are more likely to lose weight. Additionally, a positive correlation exists between screen time and weight gain: the more screen time, the more weight gain. When screen time interferes with making healthy eating choices and getting regular physical exercise, weight loss is not as successful (Elder et al., 2012).

To lose weight, one must eat less and move more (**Table 9.2**); in other words, use more calories than you are taking in. Our ancestors didn't have to worry about this. They *had* to choose foods rich in calories to give them energy to sustain themselves. Although this was a very efficient means of survival for them, it doesn't work out so well for us. When experiencing a "famine" (decrease in the caloric intake our bodies are accustomed to), our metabolism naturally slows down, requiring fewer calories and making it harder to lose weight.

In response to the obesity problem in the United States, policies have been implemented to raise awareness and discourage overeating. One such intervention is

Apply This ❱

TABLE 9.2 WEIGHT LOSS: MAKING IT FIT

Strategies	Description
Set realistic goals.	Set goals and expectations that are specific, realistic, and flexible.
Get regular exercise.	Exercising just 30 minutes a day 5 times a week can help with weight loss. Add a variety of physical activity to your daily routines.
Eat regularly and track intake.	Eat on a set schedule to minimize mindless eating. Eat only when hungry, and write down what and how much you consume by using a food diary.
Control portions.	Watch your portions. This is the amount you decide to eat. Read labels to determine the recommended serving size.
Drink water.	Eliminate sweetened beverages.
Join a weight loss support group.	Social support helps promote healthier coping strategies and accountability.

Losing weight is not an easy task, but it doesn't have to be painful. Making basic lifestyle changes in your daily routines can have significant benefits.

SOURCE: KRUGER, BLANCK, AND GILLESPIE (2006).

requiring information about calories to be clearly labeled, which can serve as a visual cue or reminder. Providing this information can impact healthy food choices. However, accessibility to comparably priced healthy alternatives must be increased (in vending machines, for example)—but this too may require changes in policy (Stroebe et al., 2013).

Eating Disorders

LO 8   Outline the characteristics of the major eating disorders.

Although many people deal with obesity, others struggle with food in a different way. Eating disorders are serious dysfunctions in eating behavior that can involve restricting food consumption, obsessing over weight or body shape, eating too much, and purging (American Psychiatric Association, 2013). Eating disorders usually begin in the early teens and typically affect girls. That doesn't mean boys do not struggle with eating disorders; 1 in 4 children ages 5–13 with an eating disorder is male (Madden, Morris, Zurynski, Kohn, & Elliot, 2009). However, the causes of body image distortions often differ according to gender. Females desire to be smaller and thinner, whereas males seek an "idealized masculine shape" (Darcy et al., 2012). Let's take a look at three of the most recognized eating disorders.

ANOREXIA NERVOSA   One of the most commonly known eating disorders is **anorexia nervosa,** which is characterized by self-imposed restrictions on calories needed to maintain a healthy weight. These restrictions lead to extremely low body weight in relation to age, sex, development, and physical health. Someone with this disorder has an extreme fear of gaining weight and getting fat, even though her body weight is extremely low. Often there is an altered and distorted sense of body weight and figure, and no realization of the "seriousness" of her low body weight (American Psychiatric Association, 2013). In some cases, women experience an absence of menstrual periods, a condition called *amenorrhea* (Attia & Roberto, 2009). Other severe symptoms may

set point The stable weight that is maintained despite variability in exercise and food intake.

anorexia nervosa An eating disorder identified by significant weight loss, an intense fear of being overweight, a false sense of body image, and a refusal to eat the proper amount of calories to achieve a healthy weight.

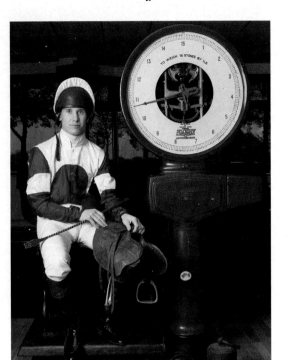

Must Be Thin

A British jockey weighs in at a horse racetrack near Manchester, England. Jockeys must satisfy strict weight requirements in order to ride in races. For many competitions, this means weighing 110 pounds or less. In an effort to stay thin, jockeys have been known to restrict their intake of food and liquid, sweat off water weight in saunas, and force themselves to vomit (Associated Press, 2008, April 25; McKenzie, 2012, October 23).
Lichfield/Getty Images

include brain damage, multiorgan failure, infertility, and thinning of the bones (National Institute of Mental Health [NIMH], n.d.). Anorexia is associated with the highest death rates of all psychological disorders (Darcy et al., 2012; Harris & Barraclough, 1998; Smink, van Hoeken, & Hoek, 2012). Approximately 20% of those deaths are due to suicide (Smink et al., 2012). Although anorexia nervosa affects mostly women and adolescent girls, males can also be affected (particularly those involved in wrestling, running, or dancing, who are required to maintain a certain weight).

BULIMIA NERVOSA Another eating disorder is **bulimia nervosa,** which involves recurrent episodes of binge eating, or consuming a large amount of food in a short period of time (with that amount being greater than most people would eat in the same time frame). While bingeing, the person feels a lack of control and thus engages in purging behaviors to prevent weight gain—for example, self-induced vomiting, misuse of laxatives, fasting, or excessive exercise (American Psychiatric Association, 2013). Like anorexia, bulimia more often affects women and girls (Stice, Marti, Shaw, & Jaconis, 2009). Bulimia also has serious health risks, such as high blood pressure, heart disease, and Type 2 diabetes (Haedt-Matt & Keel, 2011). Other symptoms include decaying teeth, damage to the throat, gastrointestinal disorders, and electrolyte imbalance from vomiting, which can lead to heart attack (NIMH, n.d.). Research has found that 23% of deaths associated with bulimia nervosa result from suicide (Smink et al., 2012).

BINGE-EATING DISORDER   You may have also heard of **binge-eating disorder** (American Psychiatric Association, 2013), characterized by episodes of excessive food consumption (eating more than most people would eat in the same amount of time and in similar situations). As in bulimia, the individual feels unable to control her eating during that period of time, but the difference is that she does not engage in excessive weight control or purging behaviors. Some psychological effects could include feelings of embarrassment about how much food has been consumed, depression, and guilt after overeating.

We know that eating disorders are apparent in America—we see evidence of them on television, in magazines, and in everyday life. But are these disorders also observed in India, South Africa, Egypt, and other parts of the world?

across the WORLD

A Cross-Cultural Look at Eating Disorders

Close your eyes and imagine the stereotypical beauty queen. Is she curvy like a Coke bottle or long and lean like a Barbie doll? We suspect the image that popped into your mind's eye looked more like the famed plastic doll. Let's face it: Western concepts of beauty, particularly female beauty, often go hand-in-hand with *thinness*.

With all this pressure to be slender, it's no wonder eating disorders like anorexia and bulimia are most commonly diagnosed and treated in Western societies such as the United States (Keel & Klump, 2003; Littlewood, 2004). Psychologists once believed eating disorders *only* occurred in regions of the world influenced by Western culture. Anorexia and bulimia were thought to be psychological disorders unique to certain societies. But evidence suggests it is not that simple.

Keel and Klump (2003) conducted a large review of studies and concluded that anorexia occurs throughout the

THEY . . . FOUND EVIDENCE OF PEOPLE, PARTICULARLY YOUNG WOMEN, STARVING THEMSELVES SINCE MEDIEVAL TIMES. . . .

non-Western world, from Hong Kong to Malaysia to Iran. They also found evidence of people, particularly young women, starving themselves since medieval times—long before Barbie dolls and runway models began making "normal" people feel "fat." Fear of fat may be an important factor driving self-starvation, but it is not necessarily the only one. There are other reasons people forgo food—a desire for some type of control, for instance (Simpson, 2002).

However, Keel and Klump (2003) found no evidence of bulimia (based on strict criteria) existing in regions isolated from Western culture. They also determined that the prevalence of the disorder dramatically increased during the second half of the 1900s, just as the fixation with thin was beginning to take hold. This pattern might not be as strong outside of Western culture, but such a focus on body image is becoming more prevalent across the world.

Skinny Around the World Admiration for thin body types is becoming more prevalent across cultures. Anorexia nervosa has been documented in both the Western and non-Western world (Keel & Klump, 2003). Camera Press/Redux

show what you know

1. Washburn swallowed a special balloon to record his stomach contractions. He also pressed a button to record his feelings of hunger. The findings indicated that whenever he felt hunger, his
   a. stomach was contracting.
   b. stomach was still.
   c. blood sugar went up.
   d. ventromedial hypothalamus was active.

2. Bulimia nervosa is an eating disorder characterized by
   a. restrictions of energy intake.
   b. extreme fear of gaining weight, although one's body weight is extremely low.
   c. a distorted sense of body weight and figure.
   d. extreme overeating followed by purging.

3. Describe how the hypothalamus triggers hunger and influences eating behaviors.

✓ CHECK YOUR ANSWERS IN APPENDIX C.

Sexual Motivation

It's obvious we need food, water, and sleep to survive. But where does sex fit into the needs hierarchy? "Sex may be studied as a purely physiological need," according to Maslow, "[but] ordinarily sexual behavior is multi-determined" (Maslow, 1943, p. 381). In other words, there are many forces motivating us to engage in sexual activity. These include the need for affection and love, and that means "both giving and receiving love" (p. 381). Every person is different, of course. There is tremendous variability in human **sexuality**—that is, our sexual activities, attitudes, and behaviors.

The Birds and the Bees

To grasp the complexity of human sexuality, we must understand the basic physiology of the sexual response. Enter William Masters and Virginia Johnson and their pioneering laboratory research, which included the study of approximately 10,000 distinct sexual responses of 312 male and 382 female participants (Masters & Johnson, 1966).

LO 9 Describe the human sexual response as identified by Masters and Johnson.

HUMAN SEXUAL RESPONSE CYCLE Masters and Johnson began their research in 1954, not exactly a time when sex was thought to be an acceptable subject for dinner conversation. Nevertheless, almost 700 people volunteered to participate in their study, which lasted a little more than a decade (Masters & Johnson, 1966). Using a variety of instruments to measure blood flow, body temperature, muscular changes,

bulimia nervosa An eating disorder characterized by extreme overeating followed by purging, with serious health risks.

binge-eating disorder An eating disorder characterized by episodes of extreme overeating, during which a larger amount of food is consumed than most people would eat in a similar amount of time under similar circumstances.

sexuality Sexual activities, attitudes, and behaviors.

Sexy Science
In the mid-1950s, William Masters teamed with Virginia Johnson to study the bodily changes occurring during masturbation and sex. Their research was groundbreaking, and it upended many long-held misconceptions about sex. For example, Masters and Johnson found that the length of a man's penis does not determine his ability to give pleasure (Fox, 2013, July 25).
© Bettmann/CORBIS

and heart rate, they discovered that most people experience a similar physiological sexual response, which can result from oral stimulation, manual stimulation, vaginal intercourse, or masturbation. Men and women tend to follow a similar pattern or cycle: *excitement, plateau, orgasm,* and *resolution* (**Figure 9.3**). These phases vary in duration for different people.

Sexual arousal begins during the *excitement phase.* This is when physical changes start to become evident. Muscles tense, the heartbeat quickens, breathing accelerates, the nipples become firm, and blood pressure rises a bit. In men, the penis becomes erect, the scrotum constricts, and the testes pull up toward the body. In women, the vagina lubricates and the clitoris swells (Levin, 2008).

Next is the *plateau phase.* There are no clear physiological signs to mark the beginning of the plateau, but it is the natural progression from the excitement phase. During the plateau phase, the muscles continue to tense, breathing and heart rate increase, and the genitals begin to change color as blood fills the area. This phase is usually quite short-lived, lasting only a few seconds to minutes.

The shortest phase of the sexual response cycle is the *orgasm phase.* As the peak of sexual response is reached, an **orgasm** occurs, which is a powerful combination of extremely gratifying sensations and a series of rhythmic muscular contractions. When men and women are asked to describe their orgasmic experiences, it is very difficult to differentiate between them. Brain activity observed via PET scans is also quite similar (Georgiadis, Reinders, Paans, Renken, & Kortekaas, 2009; Mah & Binik, 2001).

The final phase of the sexual response cycle, according to Masters and Johnson, is the *resolution phase.* This is when bodies return to a relaxed state. Without further sexual arousal, the blood flows out of the genitals, and blood pressure, heart rate, and breathing return to normal. Men lose their erection, the testes move down, and the skin of the scrotum loosens. Men will also experience a **refractory period,** an interval during which they cannot attain another orgasm. This can last from minutes to hours, and typically the older a man is, the longer the refractory period lasts. For women, the resolution phase is characterized by a decrease in clitoral swelling and a return to the normal labia color. Women do not experience a refractory period, and if sexual stimulation continues, some are capable of having multiple orgasms.

Masters and Johnson's landmark research has led to further studies of the physiological aspects of the sexual response cycle, and although their basic model is viewed as valid, research suggests there may be the need for "correction or modification, or additional explanation" (Levin, 2008, p. 2). As mentioned, sex is different for every person, and not everyone fits neatly into the same model. This idea applies not only to the physical experience of sex, but to all aspects of sexuality, including *sexual orientation.*

FIGURE 9.3

Masters and Johnson's Human Sexual Response Cycle

In the male sexual response (left), excitement is typically followed by a brief plateau, orgasm, and then a refractory period during which another orgasm is not possible. In the female sexual response (right), there is no refractory period. Orgasm is typically followed by resolution (a) or, if sexual stimulation continues, additional orgasms (b).

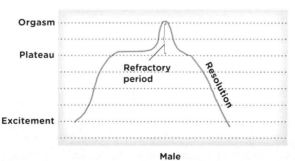

Male

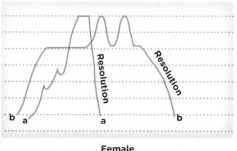

Female

Sexual Orientation

LO 10 Define sexual orientation and summarize how it develops.

Sexual orientation is the "enduring pattern" of sexual, romantic, and emotional attraction that individuals exhibit toward the same sex, opposite sex, or both sexes (APA, 2008). When attracted to members of the opposite sex, sexual orientation is **heterosexual.** When attracted to members of the same sex, sexual orientation is **homosexual,** commonly referred to as "lesbian" for women and "gay" for men (APA, 2008). When attracted to members of the same sex *and* members of the opposite sex, sexual orientation is **bisexual,** although most people tend to prefer one sex or the other. Those who do not feel sexually attracted to others are *asexual.* Lack of interest in sex does not necessarily prevent a person from maintaining relationships with spouses, partners, or friends, but little is known about the impact of asexuality because research on the topic is scarce.

WHAT'S IN A NUMBER? What percentage of the population is heterosexual? How about homosexual and bisexual? These questions may seem straightforward, but they are not easy to answer, partly because there are no clear-cut criteria for classifying people this way. Sexual orientation represents a vast spectrum; at one end are people who are "exclusively heterosexual" and at the other end are those considered "exclusively homosexual." Between these two poles is considerable variation (Kinsey, Pomeroy, & Martin, 1948; **Figure 9.4**). Some people might be exploring their sexuality, but not necessarily exhibiting a particular orientation, and this adds to the variability of rates. Estimates are available, but definitions of sexual orientation vary across cultures, and findings can be inconsistent as a result of differing survey designs: data collection in different years, the use of different age groups, different wording of questions, and so forth (Mosher, Chandra, & Jones, 2005, September 15). According to one estimate, 8 million people in the United States, or 3.5% of the adult population, are homosexual or bisexual (Gates, 2011).

How Sexual Orientation Develops

We are not sure how sexual orientation develops, although most research supports biological factors. Among professionals in the field, there is near agreement that human sexual orientation is not a matter of choice. Research has focused on everything from genetics to culture, but there is no strong evidence that sexual orientation is determined by one particular factor (or set of factors). Instead, it appears to result from an interaction between nature and nurture, but this is still under investigation, and may never be fully determined or understood (APA, 2008).

GENETICS AND SEXUAL ORIENTATION To determine the influence of biology in sexual orientation, we turn to twin studies, which are commonly used to examine the degree to which nature and nurture contribute to psychological traits. Since monozygotic twins share 100% of their genetic make-up, we expect them to share more genetically influenced characteristics than dizygotic twins, who only share about 50% of their genes. In a large study of Swedish twins, researchers explored the impact of genes and environment on "same-sex sexual behavior" (2,320 monozygotic twin pairs, 1,506 dizygotic twin pairs). In their sample, the monozygotic twins were moderately more likely than the dizygotic twins to have the same sexual orientation.

FIGURE 9.4
The Kinsey Sexuality Rating Scale
When interviewing people for a study on human sexuality, Alfred Kinsey and his colleagues (1948) discovered that people were not always exclusively heterosexual or homosexual. Instead, some described thoughts and behaviors that put them somewhere in between. This finding led the Kinsey team to develop the scale below, which shows that sexual orientation lies on a continuum.
Reprinted by permission of the Kinsey Institute for Research in Sex, Gender, and Reproduction, Inc.

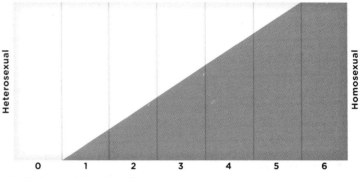

0 Exclusively heterosexual
1 Predominantly heterosexual, only incidentally homosexual
2 Predominantly heterosexual, but more than incidentally homosexual
3 Equally heterosexual and homosexual
4 Predominantly homosexual, but more than incidentally heterosexual
5 Predominantly homosexual, only incidentally heterosexual
6 Exclusively homosexual

orgasm A powerful combination of extremely gratifying sensations and a series of rhythmic muscular contractions.

refractory period An interval of time during which a man cannot attain another orgasm.

sexual orientation A person's enduring sexual interest in individuals of the same sex, opposite sex, or both sexes.

heterosexual Attraction to members of the opposite sex.

homosexual Attraction to members of the same sex.

bisexual Attraction to members of both the same and opposite sex.

They also found that same-sex sexual behavior for monozygotic twins had heritability estimates around 34–39% for men, and 18–19% for women (Långström, Rahman, Carlström, & Lichtenstein, 2010). These findings highlight two important factors: Men and women differ in terms of the heritability of same-sex sexual behavior, and the influence of the environment is substantial.

Researchers have searched for specific genes that might influence sexual orientation. Some have suggested that genes associated with male homosexuality might be transmitted by the mother. In one key study, around 64% of male siblings who were both homosexual had a set of several hundred genes in common, and these genes were located on the X chromosome (Hamer, Hu, Magnuson, Hu, & Pattatucci, 1993). But critics suggest this research was flawed, and no replications of this "gay gene" finding have been published since the original study (O'Riordan, 2012). Despite numerous attempts to identify genetic markers for homosexuality, researchers have had very little success (Dar-Nimrod & Heine, 2011). Some suggest that the search for genes underlying homosexuality is misguided. Why do we spend so much time and money seeking biological explanations for a "valid alternative lifestyle" (Jacobs, 2012)?

THE BRAIN AND SEXUAL ORIENTATION   Researchers have also studied the brains of people across sexual orientations, and their findings are interesting. Neuroscientist Simon LeVay (1991) discovered that a "small group of neurons" in the hypothalamus of homosexual men was almost twice as big as that found in heterosexual men. He did not suggest this size difference was indicative of homosexuality, but he did find it intriguing. LeVay also noted that these differences could have been the result of factors unrelated to sexual orientation. More recently, researchers using MRI technology found the corpus callosum to be thicker in homosexual men (Witelson et al., 2008).

HORMONES AND SEXUAL ORIENTATION   How do such differences arise in the brain? They may emerge before birth; hormones (estrogen and androgens) secreted by the fetal gonads play a role in the development of reproductive anatomy. One hypothesis is that the presence of androgens (the hormones secreted primarily by the male gonads) influences the development of a sexual orientation toward women. This would lead to heterosexual orientation in men, but homosexual orientation in women (Mustanski, Chivers, & Bailey, 2002). Because it would be unethical to manipulate hormone levels in pregnant women, researchers rely on cases in which hormones are elevated because of a genetic abnormality or medication taken by a mother. For example, high levels of androgens early in a pregnancy may cause girls to be more "male-typed," and promote the development of a homosexual orientation (Berenbaum, Blakemore, & Beltz, 2011; Jordan-Young, 2012).

Interestingly, having older brothers in the family seems to be associated with homosexuality in men (Blanchard, 2008). Why is this so? Evolutionary theory would suggest that the more males there are in a family, the more potential for "unproductive competition" among the male siblings. A homosexual younger brother would present less competition for older brothers in terms of securing mates and resources to support offspring.

BIAS   Although differences in sexual orientation are universal and have been evident throughout recorded history, individuals identified as members of the nonheterosexual minority have been subjected to stereotyping, prejudice, and discrimination. Nonheterosexual people in the United States, for example, have been, and continue to be, subjected to harassment, violence, and unfair practices related to housing and employment.

EVOLUTIONARY PSYCHOLOGY AND SEX   What is the purpose of sex? Evolutionary psychology would suggest that humans have sex to make babies and ensure the survival of the species (Buss, 1995). But if this were the only reason, then why would so many people choose same-sex partners? Some researchers believe it has

Love and Marriage
Comedian Wanda Sykes (left) and her wife, Alex Sykes, were married in 2008, when same-sex marriage was banned throughout most of the country (Jordan, 2009, May 13). In 2015, the Supreme Court legalized same-sex marriage across the nation, a legal shift that seems to parallel the changing attitudes of Americans. Between 2004 and 2015, support for same-sex marriage grew from 30% to 59% (Hook, 2015, March 9). Jason LaVeris/FilmMagic

something to do with "kin altruism," which suggests that homosexual men and women support reproduction in the family by helping relatives care for their children. Homosexual individuals may not "spend their time reproducing," but they can nurture the reproductive efforts of their "kin" (Erickson-Schroth, 2010).

There are other reasons to believe that there is more to human sex than making babies. If sex were purely for reproduction, we would expect to see sexual activity occurring only during the fertile period of the female cycle. Obviously, this is not the case. People have sex throughout a woman's monthly cycle and long after she goes through menopause. Sex is for feeling pleasure, expressing affection, and forming social bonds.

The Sex We Have

It is only natural for us to wonder if what we are doing between the sheets (or elsewhere) is typical or healthy. Is it normal to masturbate? Is it normal to fantasize about sex with strangers? The answers to these types of questions depend somewhat on cultural context. Most of us unknowingly learn *sexual scripts,* or cultural rules that tell us what types of activities are "appropriate" and don't interfere with healthy sexual intimacy. In some cultures, the sexual script suggests that women should have minimal, if any, sexual experience before marriage, but men are expected to explore their sexuality, or "sow their wild oats." Of course, not everyone follows the sexual scripts they are assigned.

KINSEY BREAKS GROUND When did researchers begin exploring sexuality in a systematic way? Alfred Kinsey and colleagues were among the first to try to scientifically and objectively examine human sexuality in America (Kinsey, Pomeroy, & Martin, 1948; Kinsey, Pomeroy, Martin, & Gebhard, 1953). Using the survey method, Kinsey and his team collected data on the sexual behaviors of 5,300 White males and 5,940 White females. Their findings were surprising; both men and women masturbated, and participants had experiences with premarital sex, adultery, and sexual activity with someone of the same sex. Perhaps more shocking was the fact that so many people were willing to talk about their personal sexual behavior in post–World War II America. At that time, people generally did not talk openly about sexual topics.

The Kinsey study was groundbreaking in terms of its data content and methodology, which included accuracy checks and assurances of confidentiality. The data have served as a valuable reference for researchers studying how sexual behaviors have evolved over time. However, Kinsey's work was not without limitations. For example, Kinsey and colleagues (1948, 1953) utilized a biased sampling technique that resulted in a group of participants that was not representative of the population. It was a completely White sample, with an overrepresentation of well-educated Protestants (Potter, 2006; Wallin, 1949). Another criticism of the Kinsey study is that it failed to determine the context in which orgasms occurred. Was a partner involved? Was the orgasm achieved through masturbation (Potter, 2006)?

SEXUAL ACTIVITY IN RELATIONSHIPS Subsequent research has been better designed, using samples that are more representative of the population (Herbenick et al., 2010; Michael, Laumann, Kolata, & Gagnon, 1994). Some of the findings may surprise you, others probably not. Around 77% of adults in the United States report they engaged in intercourse by age 20, regardless of cultural background or ethnicity. By the age of 44, 95% of adults have had intercourse. And the overwhelming majority did not wait for marriage (Finer, 2007). However, married people do have more sex than those who are unmarried (Laumann, Gagnon, Micheal, & Michaels, 1994). According to a large study of Swedish adults, the frequency of penile–vaginal intercourse is associated with sexual satisfaction, as well as satisfaction with relationships, mental

Radical Research
Alfred Kinsey meets with an interview subject in his office at the Institute for Sex Research, now The Kinsey Institute. Kinsey began investigating human sexuality in the 1930s, when talking about sex was taboo. He started gathering data with surveys, but then switched to personal interviews, which he believed to be more effective. These interviews often went on for hours and included hundreds of questions (Public Broadcasting Service [PBS], 2005, January 27). Wallace Kirkland/Time Life Pictures/Getty Images

CONNECTIONS

In **Chapter 1,** we emphasized that representative samples enable us to generalize findings to populations. Here we see that inferences about sexual behaviors for groups *other* than White, well-educated Protestants could be problematic, as few members of these groups participated in the Kinsey study.

TABLE 9.3 WHAT'S GOING ON?		
Sexual Activity	Average Frequency in Prior Month for Men	Average Frequency in Prior Month for Women
Penile–vaginal intercourse	5.2	4.8
Oral sex	2.3	1.9
Anal sex	0.10	0.08
Masturbation	4.5	1.5

How often do people engage in different types of sexual activity? Here are the monthly averages for adult men and women (the average age being 41). Keep in mind that significant variation exists around these numbers.

SOURCE: BRODY AND COSTA (2009), TABLE 1, P. 1950.

health, and life in general. Other sexual activities, such as masturbation, were found to have an inverse relationship with a variety of measures of satisfaction (Brody & Costa, 2009). Many studies indicate not only psychological benefits, but also physiological benefits of penile–vaginal intercourse. Correlations are apparent between the frequency of penile–vaginal intercourse and greater life expectancy, lower blood pressure, slimmer waistline, and lower prostate and breast cancer risk (Brody, 2010).

SEXUAL ACTIVITY AND GENDER DIFFERENCES As stereotypes might suggest, men think about sex more often than women (Laumann et al., 1994), and they consistently report a higher frequency of masturbation (Peplau, 2003; see **Table 9.3** for reported gender differences in frequency of sexual activity). Men in the United States tend to be more tolerant than women when it comes to casual sex before marriage, as well as more permissive in their attitudes about extramarital sex (Laumann et al., 1994). But these attitude differences are not apparent in heterosexual teenagers and young adults (Garcia, Reiber, Massey, & Merriwether, 2012). For these young people, attitudes about casual sex are apparent in their "hookup" behavior (**Table 9.4**).

TABLE 9.4 HOOKING UP	
Hookup Behavior	Undergraduates Reporting Behavior (%)
Kissing	98
Sexual touching above waist	58
Sexual touching below the waist	53
Performed oral sex	36
Received oral sex	35
Sexual intercourse	34

What exactly do college students mean when they say they "hooked up" with someone? As you can see from the data presented here, hooking up can signify anything from a brief kiss to sexual intercourse.

SOURCE: GARCIA ET AL. (2012).

Sext You Later

What kinds of factors do you think encourage casual attitudes about sex among teens? Most adolescents have cell phones these days (78%, according to one survey; Madden, Lenhart, Duggan, Cortesi, & Gasser, 2013), and a large number of those young people are using their phones to exchange text messages with sexually explicit words or images. In other words, today's teenagers are doing a lot of *sexting.* One study found that 20% of high school students have used their cell phones to share sexual pictures of themselves, and twice as many have received such images from others (Strassberg, McKinnon, Sustaíta, & Rullo, 2013). Teens who sext are more likely to have sex and take sexual risks, such as having unprotected sex (Rice et al., 2012).

ARE TEENS WHO SEXT MORE LIKELY TO HAVE SEX?

Sexting carries another set of risks for those who are married or in committed relationships. As many people see it, sexting outside a relationship is a genuine form of cheating. And because text messages can be saved and forwarded, it becomes an easy and effective way to damage the reputations of people, sometimes famous ones. Perhaps you have read about the sexting scandals associated with golfer Tiger Woods, ex-footballer Brett Favre, and former U.S. Congressman Anthony Weiner?

Now that's a lot of bad news about sexting. But can it also occur in the absence of negative behaviors and outcomes? When sexting is between two consenting, or shall we say "consexting," adults, it may be completely harmless (provided no infidelity is involved). According to one survey of young adults, sexting was not linked to unsafe sex or psychological problems such as depression and low self-esteem (Gordon-Messer, Bauermeister, Grodzinski, & Zimmerman, 2013). For some, sexting is just a new variation on flirting; for others, it may fulfill a deeper need, like helping them feel more secure in their romantic attachments (Weisskirch & Delevi, 2011). 💬+

SEX EDUCATION One way to learn about this relatively new phenomenon of sexting—or any sexual topic, for that matter—is through sex education in the classroom. School is the primary place where American children get information about sex (Byers, 2011), yet it is somewhat controversial. Many parents are afraid that some types of sex education essentially condone sexual activity among young people. Until 2010, Title V federal funding was limited to states that taught abstinence only (Chin et al., 2012). Yet, research suggests that programs promoting abstinence are associated with more teenage pregnancies: States with a greater emphasis on abstinence (as reflected in state laws and policies) have higher teenage pregnancy and birth rates (Stanger-Hall & Hall, 2011).

Teenagers who are provided a thorough education on sexual activity, including information on how to prevent pregnancy, are less likely to become pregnant (or get someone pregnant). Research shows that formal sex education increases safe-sex practices, reducing the likelihood of disease transmission (Kohler, Manhart, & Lafferty, 2008; Stanger-Hall & Hall, 2011). Sex education clearly impacts the behaviors of teenagers and young adults.

SEXUAL ACTIVITY AND AGE Now let's look at some data comparing the sexual behaviors of people at various stages of life. Would you expect to see major differences among people young, old, and in-between? According to a large cross-sectional survey of Americans ages 14 to 94, masturbation is more common than partnered sexual activities among adolescents and people over the age of 70. The same study found that more than half of those aged 18 to 49 had engaged in oral sex in the past

Sext Offender
Sending sexually explicit text messages, or "sexting," has become increasingly popular among young people. Although it may seem casual and fun, sexting can have serious repercussions. When 18-year-old Phillip Alpert texted a naked photo of his 16-year-old girlfriend, police arrested him for distributing child pornography. He was then assigned 5 years of probation and required to register as a sex offender (Feyerick & Steffen, 2009, April 8). Ricardo Ramirez Buxeda/Orlando Sentinel/MCT/Getty Images

year, with a lower proportion of the younger and older age groups engaging in this activity. Penetrative sex (vaginal and anal) was most common among adults ages 20 to 49 (Herbenick et al., 2010). In another large study (57- to 85-year-olds), researchers reported that aging did not seem to adversely affect interest in sexual activity. In fact, through the age of 74, the frequency of sexual activity remained steady, even with a high proportion of "bothersome sexual problems."

What They Are Doing in Bed . . . or Elsewhere

How often do people in New Zealand have sex? How many lovers has the average Israeli had? And are Chileans happy with the amount of lovemaking they do? These are just a few of the questions answered by the Global Sex Survey (2005), which, we dare to say, is one of the sexiest scientific studies out there (and which was sponsored by Durex, a condom manufacturer). We cannot report all the survey results, but here is a roundup of those we found most interesting:

PEOPLE IN GREECE ARE HAVING THE MOST SEX.

- People in Greece have the most sex—an average of 138 times per year, or 2 to 3 times per week.
- People in Japan have the least amount of sex—an average of 45 times per year, or a little less than once per week.
- The average age for losing one's virginity is lowest among Icelanders (between 15 and 16) and highest for those from India (between 19 and 20).
- Across nations, the average number of sexual partners is 9. If gender is taken into account, that number is a little higher for men (11) and lower for women (7).
- Of respondents, 50% reported having sex in cars, 39% in bathrooms, and 2% in airplanes.
- Nearly half the people around the world are happy with their sex lives.

As you reflect on these results, remember that surveys have limitations. People are not always honest when it comes to answering questions about personal issues (like sex), and the wording of questions can influence responses. Even if responses are accurate, we can only speculate about the beliefs and attitudes underlying them.

Happy Between the Sheets
Nearly half (44%) of adults participating in the Global Sex Survey said they were happy with their sex lives. Men were more likely than women to say they wanted to have sex more often (Global Sex Survey, 2005).
East/Shutterstock

Sexual Dysfunction

When there is a "significant disturbance" in the ability to respond sexually or to gain pleasure from sex, we call this **sexual dysfunction** (American Psychiatric Association, 2013). In the National Health and Social Life Survey, researchers found 43% of women and 31% of men suffered from some sort of sexual dysfunction (Laumann, Paik, & Rosen, 1999). Temporary sexual difficulties may be caused by everyday stressors or situational issues but can be resolved once the stress or the situation has passed. Longer-term sexual difficulties stem from a variety of issues, including beliefs about sex, ignorance about sexual practices, and even performance expectations. Health conditions can also give rise to sexual difficulties. The *biopsychosocial* perspective is invaluable for helping to untangle the roots of sexual problems. Sexual dysfunction may result from problems with desire, arousal, orgasm, and pain, but these are not mutually exclusive categories.

DESIRE Situational issues such as illness, fatigue, or frustration with one's partner can lead to temporary problems with desire. In some cases, however, lack of desire is persistent and distressing. Although either sex can be affected, women tend to report desire problems more frequently than men (Brotto, 2010; Heiman, 2002).

CONNECTIONS

In **Chapter 1,** we discussed limitations of using self-report surveys. People often resist revealing attitudes or behaviors related to sensitive topics, such as sexual activity. The risk is gathering data that do not accurately represent participants' attitudes and beliefs, particularly with face-to-face interviews.

AROUSAL   Problems with arousal occur when the psychological desire to engage in sexual behavior is there, but the body does not cooperate. Men may have trouble getting or maintaining an erection, or they may experience a decrease in rigidity, which is called *erectile disorder* (American Psychiatric Association, 2013). More than half of all men report they have occasionally experienced problems with erections (Hock, 2012). Women can also struggle with arousal. *Female sexual interest/arousal disorder* is apparent in reduced interest in sex, lack of initiation of sexual activities, reduced excitement, or decreased genital sensations during sexual activity (American Psychiatric Association, 2013).

ORGASM   *Female orgasmic disorder* is diagnosed when a woman is consistently unable to reach orgasm, has reduced orgasmic intensity, or does not reach orgasm quickly enough during sexual activity (American Psychiatric Association, 2013). Men who experience frequent delay or inability to ejaculate might have a condition known as *delayed ejaculation* (American Psychiatric Association, 2013; Segraves, 2010). With this disorder, the ability to achieve orgasm and ejaculate is inhibited or delayed during partnered sexual activity. Men who have trouble controlling when they ejaculate (particularly during vaginal sex) may suffer from *premature (early) ejaculation* (American Psychiatric Association, 2013).

PAIN   Women typically report more problems with intercourse-related pain than men. *Genito-pelvic pain/penetration disorder* refers to four types of co-occurring symptoms specific to women: difficulty having intercourse, pain in the genitals or pelvis, fear of pain or vaginal penetration, and tension of the pelvic floor muscles (American Psychiatric Association, 2013). Up to 15% of women in North America report frequent pain during intercourse, and issues related to pain are associated with reduced desire and arousal.

"I really think you should see a specialist about your lack of libido Sharon."

Sexually Transmitted Infections

LO 11   Identify the most common sexually transmitted infections.

Although sex is pleasurable and exciting for most, it is not without risks. Many people carry **sexually transmitted infections (STIs)**—diseases or illnesses passed on through sexual activity (Centers for Disease Control and Prevention [CDC], 2012f). There are many causes of STIs, but most are *bacterial* or *viral* (see **Table 9.5** on the next page for data on their prevalence). Bacterial infections such as *syphilis, gonorrhea,* and *chlamydia* often clear up with antibiotics. Viral infections like *genital herpes* and *human papillomavirus (HPV)* have no cure, only treatments to reduce symptoms.

Protect Yourself

The more sexual partners you have, the greater your risk of acquiring an STI. But you can lower your risk by communicating with your partner. People who know that their partners have had (or are having) sex with others face a lower risk of acquiring an STI than those who do not know. Why is this so? If you are aware of your partner's activities, you may be more likely to take preventative measures, such as using condoms. Of course, there is always the possibility that your sexual partner (or you) has a disease but doesn't know it. Some people with STIs are asymptomatic, meaning they have no symptoms. Others know they are infected but lie because they are ashamed, in denial, afraid of rejection, or for any number of reasons. ▼ Given all these unknowns, your best bet is to play it safe and use protection. ➤

sexual dysfunction   A significant disturbance in the ability to respond sexually or to gain pleasure from sex.

sexually transmitted infections (STIs)   Diseases or illnesses transmitted through sexual activity.

TABLE 9.5 SEXUALLY TRANSMITTED INFECTIONS

STI	Symptoms	Estimated Annual Prevalence of New Infections in the U.S.
Chlamydia	Women often have no symptoms; men can experience discharge from penis, burning when urinating, and pain/swelling of the testicles. Women may develop *pelvic inflammatory disease*, which can result in lower back pain, menstrual difficulties, and headaches.	2.86 million
Gonorrhea	No symptoms may be present in men or women. Men can experience burning when urinating, or white, yellow, or green discharge. Women can experience pain/burning when urinating, or vaginal discharge. Untreated gonorrhea can lead to sterility in both sexes.	820,000
Herpes	Blisters on the genitals, rectum, or mouth; painful sores after blisters break; fever, body aches, and swollen glands.	776,000
Human papillomavirus (HPV)	Warts growing in the genitals or the throat. Over 100 types of HPV have been identified, and research shows that untreated HPV can lead to the development of cervical, vaginal, urethral, penile, and anal cancers. Many HPV carriers have no symptoms and unknowingly spread the disease to others.	14.1 million
Syphilis	Firm, round sores that first appear where the infection enters the body and can then spread to other parts of the body. If the infection proceeds untreated over the course of years, it can lead to heart failure, blindness, liver damage, severe mental disturbance, or death.	55,400

Sexually transmitted infections (STIs) are extremely common. HPV, for example, is so widespread that nearly all sexually active people are infected at one time or another.

SOURCES: CDC (2012F, 2013, 2014A, 2014B, 2014C, 2015).

We have now explored many facets of motivation, from basic physiological drives to transcendent needs for achievement. As you may have guessed from the title of this chapter, motivations are intimately tied to emotions. In the sections to come, we will explore the complex world of human emotion, with a focus on fear and happiness.

✓○○○ **show what you know**

1. Masters and Johnson studied the physiological changes that accompany sexual activity. They determined that men and women experience a similar sexual response cycle, including the following ordered phases:
   a. excitement, plateau, orgasm, and resolution.
   b. plateau, excitement, orgasm, and relaxation.
   c. excitement, plateau, and orgasm.
   d. excitement, orgasm, and resolution.

2. Explain how twin studies have been used to explore the development of sexual orientation.

3. _____ and _____ are both bacterial infections that are spread through unprotected sexual activity.
   a. Syphilis; gonorrhea
   b. Pelvic inflammatory disease; herpes
   c. Human papillomavirus; herpes
   d. Syphilis; acquired immune deficiency syndrome

✓ CHECK YOUR ANSWERS IN APPENDIX C.

Emotion

RubberBall / SuperStock

SHARK ATTACK For those longing for a quiet beach escape, Ocracoke Island on the North Carolina coast is hard to beat. Wrapped in 16 miles of pristine beach, Ocracoke is a perfect place for building sandcastles, collecting seashells, and riding waves. Circumstances are ideal for young children, except for the occasional rip current. Oh, and there's one more thing: Beware of sharks.

One summer night in 2011, 6-year-old Lucy Mangum was splashing around on her boogie board at her family's favorite Ocracoke beach. She was close to shore in water no deeper than 2 feet. Suddenly, Lucy let out a spine-chilling scream. Her mother Jordan, just feet away, spotted the fin of a shark cutting through the water. Running to swoop up her daughter, Jordan did not realize what had occurred—until she saw the blood streaming from her daughter's right leg, which was "completely open" from heel to calf (Allegood, 2011, July 27). The shark had attacked Lucy.

Jordan did the right thing. She applied pressure to the gushing wound and called for help. Lucy's father Craig, who happens to be an emergency room doctor, rushed over and looked at the wound. Right away, he knew it was severe and needed immediate medical attention (Stump, 2011, July 26). In the moments following the attack, Lucy was remarkably calm. "Am I going to die?" she asked her mom. "Absolutely not," Jordan replied. "Am I going to walk?" Lucy asked. "Am I going to have a wheelchair?" It was too early to know (CBS News, 2011, July 26, para. 16). 📁 ▾

Lucy the Brave
Lucy Mangum was just 6 years old when she was attacked by a shark in the shallow waters of Ocracoke Island in North Carolina. Mangum Family Archives

What Is Emotion?

Unprovoked shark attacks are extremely uncommon, occurring less than 100 times per year worldwide. And most attacks are not fatal. To put things in perspective, you are 75 times more likely to be killed by a bolt of lightning and 33 times more likely to be killed by a dog (Florida Museum of Natural History, 2014). Despite their rarity, shark attacks seem to be particularly fear provoking. Maybe the thought of becoming the prey of a wild creature reminds us that we are still, at some level, animals: vulnerable players in the game of natural selection.

Fear is an emotion you experience throughout your life. When you were a baby, you might have been afraid of the vacuum cleaner or the hair dryer. As you matured, your fears may have shifted to the dog next door or the monster in the closet. These days you might be scared of growing older, being diagnosed with a serious disease, or losing someone you love.

LO 12 Define emotions and explain how they are different from moods.

But what exactly is fear? That's an easy question: Fear is an emotion. Now here's the hard question: What is an *emotion?* An **emotion** is a psychological state that includes a subjective or inner experience. In other words, emotion is intensely personal; we cannot actually feel each other's emotions firsthand. Emotion also has a physiological component; it is not only "in our heads." For example, anger can make you feel hot, anxiety might cause sweaty palms, and sadness may sap your physical energy. Finally, emotion entails a behavioral expression. We scream and run when frightened, gag in disgust, and shed tears of sadness. Think about the last time you felt joyous. What was your inner experience of that joy, how did your body react, and what would someone have noticed about your behavior?

Thus, emotion is a subjective psychological state that includes both physiological and behavioral components. But are these three elements—psychology, physiology, and behavior—equally important, and in what order do they occur? The answers to these questions are still under debate, as is the very definition of emotion (Davidson, Scherer, & Goldsmith, 2002). Given the complexity of emotion, it comes as no surprise that academics and scientists from many fields and perspectives are studying it (Coan, 2010).

MOODS VERSUS EMOTIONS Most psychologists agree that emotions are different from moods. Emotions are quite strong, but they don't generally last as long as moods, and they are more likely to have an identifiable cause. An emotion is initiated by a stimulus, and it is more likely than a mood to motivate someone to action. Moods are longer-term emotional states that are less intense than emotions and do not appear to have distinct beginnings or ends (Kemeny & Shestyuk, 2008; Matlin, 2009; Oatley,

emotion A psychological state that includes a subjective or inner experience, a physiological component, and a behavioral expression.

Keltner, & Jenkins, 2006). An example might help clarify: Imagine your mood is happy, but a car cuts you off on the highway, creating a negative emotional response like anger.

Now let's see how the three distinguishing characteristics of emotion (as opposed to moods) might apply to Lucy's situation. When Lucy's mother saw the wound from the shark bite, she remembers feeling "afraid" (CBS News, 2011, July 26). Her emotion (1) had a clear cause (the shark attacking her daughter), (2) likely produced a physiological reaction (heart racing, for example), and (3) motivated her to action (applying pressure to the wound and calling for help).

LANGUAGE AND EMOTION   If you were Lucy's mom, what words might you use to describe your fear—frightened, terrified, horrified, scared, petrified, spooked, aghast? Having a variety of labels at your disposal certainly helps when it comes to communicating your emotions. "I feel *angry* at you" conveys a slightly different meaning than "I feel *resentful* of you," or "I feel *annoyed* by you." The English language includes about 200 words to describe emotions. But does that mean we are capable of feeling only 200 emotions? Probably not. Words and emotions are not one and the same, but they are closely linked. In fact, their relationship has captivated the interest of linguists from fields as different as anthropology, psychology, and evolutionary biology (Majid, 2012).

Rather than focusing on words or labels, scholars typically characterize emotions along different dimensions. Izard (2007) suggests that we can describe emotions according to valence and arousal (**Figure 9.5**). The *valence* of an emotion refers to how pleasant or unpleasant it is. Happiness, joy, and satisfaction are on the pleasant end of the valence dimension; anger and disgust lie on the unpleasant end. The *arousal level* of an emotion describes how active, excited, and involved a person is while experiencing the emotion, as opposed to how calm, uninvolved, or passive she may be. With valence and arousal level, we can compare and contrast emotions. The emotion of ecstasy, for example, has a high arousal level and a positive valence. Feeling relaxed has a low arousal level and a positive valence. When Lucy looked down and saw the shark, she likely experienced an intense fear—high arousal, but negative valence. Fortunately, for Lucy and her family, fear eventually gave way to more positive emotions. Let's find out what happened.

FIGURE 9.5
Dimensions of Emotion
Emotions can be compared and contrasted according to their valence (how pleasant or unpleasant they are) and their arousal level. © 1980 by the American Psychological Association. Adapted with permission from Russell (1980)

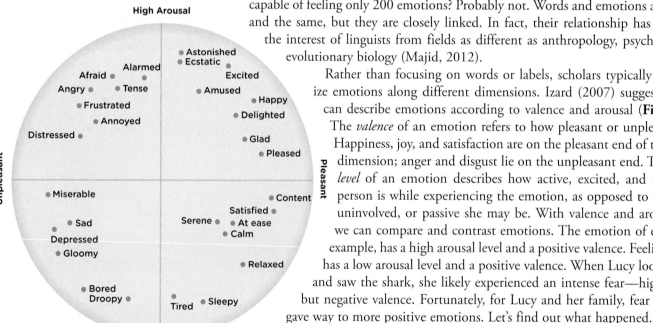

Emotion and Physiology

FIGHT BACK   Within 35 minutes of the attack, Lucy was lifted off Ocracoke Island by helicopter and was on her way to a trauma center in Greenville, North Carolina. The damage to her leg was extensive, with large tears to the muscle and tendons. She would need two surgeries, extensive physical therapy, and a wheelchair for some time after leaving the hospital (WRAL.com, 2011, July 26).

How did Lucy hold up during this period of extreme stress? According to lead surgeon Dr. Richard Zeri, the 6-year-old was "remarkably calm" (Allegood, 2011, July 27). She even forgave the shark: "I don't care that the shark bit me," she told reporters, "I forgive him" (Stump, 2011, July 26, para. 4). But Lucy also seemed to harbor some negative feelings, at least initially. "I hate sharks," she told her parents (Stump, 2011, July 26, para. 2). "I should have kicked him in the nose," she reportedly said (Allegood, 2011, July 27, para. 3). Fighting back is not an unusual response; some victims have prevented sharks from attacking by grabbing their tails, punching them in the gills, and gouging their eyes (Cabanatuan & Sebastian, 2005, October 19; Caldicott, Mahajani, & Kuhn, 2001).

Such acts of self-defense are mediated by the sympathetic nervous system's fight-or-flight response (Chapter 11). When faced with a crisis situation like a shark attack, stress hormones are released into the blood; breathing rate increases; the heart pumps faster and harder; blood pressure rises; the liver releases extra glucose into the bloodstream; and blood surges into the large muscles. All these physical changes prepare the body for confronting or fleeing the threat; hence the expression "fight or flight." But fear is not the only emotion that involves dramatic physical changes. Tears pour from the eyes during intense sadness and joy. Anger is associated with sweating, elevated heart rate, and heightened blood flow to the hands, apparently in anticipation of a physical confrontation (Ekman, 2003).

LO 13 List the major theories of emotion and describe how they differ.

Most psychologists agree that emotions and physiology are deeply intertwined, but they have not always agreed on the precise order of events. What happens first: the body changes associated with emotion or the emotions themselves? That's a no-brainer, you may be thinking. Emotions occur first, and then the body responds. American psychologist William James would have disagreed.

JAMES–LANGE THEORY In the late 1800s, James and Danish physiologist Carl Lange independently derived similar explanations for emotion (James, 1890/1983; Lange & James, 1922). What is now known as the **James–Lange theory of emotion** suggests that a stimulus initiates a physiological reaction (for example, the heart pounding, muscles contracting, a change in breathing) and/or a behavioral reaction (such as crying or striking out), which leads to an emotion (**Infographic 9.3** on the next page). Emotions *do not* cause physiological or behavioral reactions to occur, as common sense might suggest. Instead, "we feel sorry because we cry, angry because we strike, afraid because we tremble" (James, 1890/1983, p. 1066). In other words, changes in the body and behavior pave the way for emotions. Our bodies automatically react to stimuli, and awareness of this physiological response leads to the subjective experience of an emotion.

How might the James–Lange theory apply to our shark attack victim Lucy? It all begins with a stimulus, in this case the appearance of the shark and the pain of the bite. Next occur the physiological reactions (increased heart rate, faster breathing, and so on) and the behavioral responses (screaming, trying to swim away). Finally, the emotion registers. Lucy feels fear. Imagine that Lucy, for some reason, had no physiological reaction to the shark—no rapid heartbeat, and so forth. Would she still experience the same degree of terror? According to the James–Lange theory, no. Lucy might see the shark and decide to flee, but she wouldn't *feel* afraid.

The implication of the James–Lange theory is that each emotion has its own distinct physiological fingerprint. If this were the case, it would be possible to identify an emotion based on a person's physiological/behavioral responses. A person who is sad would display a different physiological/behavioral profile compared to when feeling angry, for example. PET scans have confirmed that different emotions such as happiness, anger, and fear do indeed have distinct activation patterns in the brain, lending evidence in support of the James–Lange theory (Berthoz, Blair, Le Clec'h, & Martinot, 2002; Carlsson et al., 2004; Damasio et al., 2000; Salimpoor, Benovoy, Larcher, Dagher, & Zatorre, 2011).

However, critics of the James–Lange theory of emotion suggest it cannot fully explain emotional phenomena because (1) people who are incapable of feeling physiological reactions of internal organs (as a result of surgery or spinal cord injuries, for example) can still experience emotions; (2) the speed of an emotion is much faster than physiological changes occurring in internal organs; and (3) when physiological changes are made to the functions of internal organs (through a hormone injection,

CONNECTIONS

In **Chapter 2,** we explained how the sympathetic nervous system prepares the body to respond to an emergency, whereas the parasympathetic nervous system brings the body back to a noncrisis mode through the "rest-and-digest" process. Here, we see how the autonomic nervous system is involved in physical experiences of emotion.

Ha Ha Ha!
Does laughing make you happy? According to the James–Lange theory of emotion, yes. It suggests that a behavioral response such as laughing paves the way for an emotion (happiness). Some clinicians actually incorporate "laugh therapy" into their treatment, and encouraging results have been seen in cancer patients and elderly people (Joshua, Cotroneo, & Clarke, 2005; Ko & Youn, 2011). Jason Stitt/Shutterstock

James–Lange theory of emotion
Suggests that a stimulus initiates the experience of a physiological and/or behavioral reaction, and this reaction leads to the feeling of an emotion.

Theories of Emotion

Imagine you are swimming and you think you see a shark. Fear pierces your gut, sending your heart racing as you swim frantically to shore. Or is it actually your churning stomach and racing heart that cause you to feel so terrified? And what part, if any, do your thoughts play in this process?

Psychologists have long debated the order in which events lead to emotion. Let's compare four major theories, each proposing a different sequence of events.

Credit: Sharks, Shutterstock

Body changes lead to emotions.	Body changes and emotions happen together.	Our thoughts about our body changes lead to emotions.	Our thoughts about our situation lead to emotions.
James–Lange	**Cannon–Bard**	**Schachter–Singer**	**Cognitive Appraisal**

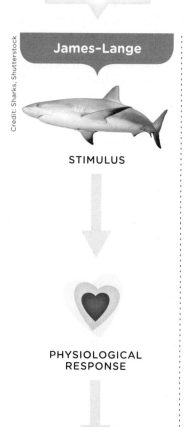

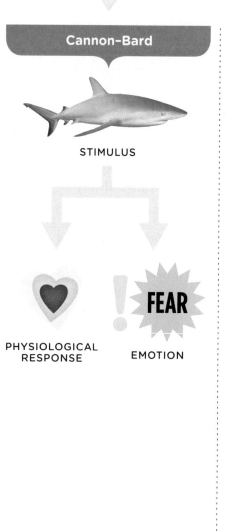

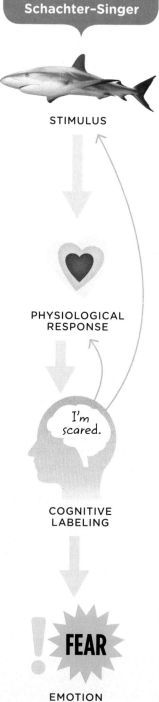

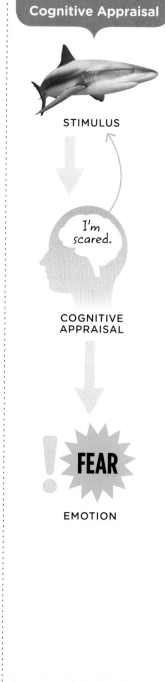

James–Lange

STIMULUS → PHYSIOLOGICAL RESPONSE → **FEAR** EMOTION

Cannon–Bard

STIMULUS → PHYSIOLOGICAL RESPONSE / **FEAR** EMOTION

Schachter–Singer

STIMULUS → PHYSIOLOGICAL RESPONSE → COGNITIVE LABELING (*I'm scared.*) → **FEAR** EMOTION

Cognitive Appraisal

STIMULUS → COGNITIVE APPRAISAL (*I'm scared.*) → **FEAR** EMOTION

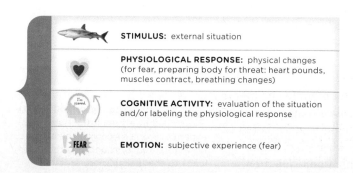

STIMULUS: external situation

PHYSIOLOGICAL RESPONSE: physical changes (for fear, preparing body for threat: heart pounds, muscles contract, breathing changes)

COGNITIVE ACTIVITY: evaluation of the situation and/or labeling the physiological response

EMOTION: subjective experience (fear)

for instance), emotions do not necessarily change (Bard, 1934; Cannon, 1927; Hilgard, 1987). In one experiment, researchers used surgery to stop animals from becoming physiologically aroused, yet the animals continued to exhibit behaviors associated with emotions, such as growling and posturing (Cannon, 1927).

CANNON–BARD THEORY   Walter Cannon (1927) and his student Philip Bard (1934) were among those who believed the James–Lange theory could not explain all emotions. The **Cannon–Bard theory of emotion** suggests that we do *not* feel emotion as a result of physiological and behavioral reactions; instead, the emotions and the body responses occur simultaneously (Infographic 9.3). The starting point of this response is a stimulus in the environment.

Let's use the Cannon–Bard theory to see how the appearance of a snake might lead to an emotional reaction. Imagine you are about to crawl into bed for the night. You pull back the sheets, and there, in YOUR BED, is a snake! According to the Cannon–Bard theory, the image of the snake will stimulate sensory neurons to relay signals in the direction of your cortex. But rather than rushing to the cortex, these signals pass through the thalamus, splitting in two directions—one toward the cortex and the other toward the hypothalamus.

When the neural information reaches the cortex and hypothalamus, several things could happen. First, the "thalamic–hypothalamic complex will be thrown into a *state of readiness*" (Krech & Crutchfield, 1958, p. 343), in a sense, waiting for the determination of whether the message will continue to the skeletal muscles and internal organs, instructing them to react. The neural information from the thalamus will arrive in the cortex at the same time, enabling you to "perceive" the snake on your bed. If it is just a rubber snake, this news will be sent from the cortex to the thalamic–hypothalamic complex, preventing the emergency signal from being sent to the skeletal muscles and internal organs. However, if the object in your bed is a real snake, then the emergency message will be forwarded to your skeletal muscles and internal organs, prompting a physiological and/or behavioral response (heart racing, jumping backward). It is at this point, along with the perception of the snake, that an emotion is experienced. The emotion and physiological reaction occur simultaneously.

Critics of the Cannon–Bard theory suggest that the thalamus might not be capable of carrying out this complex processing on its own and that other brain areas may contribute (Beebe-Center, 1951; Hunt, 1939). Research suggests that the limbic system, hypothalamus, and prefrontal cortex are also substantially involved in processing emotions (Kolb & Whishaw, 2009; Northoff et al., 2009).

Eek, a Snake!
Most people would be terrified to see a snake slithering across their bedsheets. Does the feeling of fear come before or after the heart starts racing and the body flinches? According to the Cannon-Bard theory of emotion, everything happens simultaneously: the emotional reaction, physiological changes, and a behavioral response. fivespots/shutterstock

Do Polygraphs Work?
The polygraph, or so-called "lie detector" test, operates on the premise that emotions are accompanied by measurable physiological changes. When some people lie, they feel anxious, which causes changes in blood pressure, heart rate, breathing, and production of sweat. By monitoring these variables, the polygraph can theoretically detect when a person feels stressed from lying (APA, 2004). However, the polygraph is not as effective as Hollywood may lead you to believe. Research suggests that error rates may be anywhere from 25% to 75% (Saxe, 1994). Guy Bell/Alamy

Cannon–Bard theory of emotion Suggests that environmental stimuli are the starting point for emotions, and physiological or behavioral responses occur at the same time emotions are felt.

Cognition and Emotion

SCHACHTER–SINGER THEORY　Stanley Schachter and Jerome E. Singer (1962) also took issue with the James–Lange theory, primarily because different emotions do not have distinct and recognizable physiological responses. They suggested there is a *general* pattern of physiological arousal caused by the sympathetic nervous system, and this pattern is common to a variety of emotions. The **Schachter–Singer theory of emotion** proposes that the experience of emotion is the result of two factors: (1) physiological arousal, and (2) a cognitive label for this physiological state (the arousal). According to this theory, if someone experiences physiological arousal, but doesn't know why it has occurred, she will label the arousal and explain her feelings based on her "knowledge" of the environment (that is, in recognition of the context of the situation). Depending on the "cognitive aspects of the situation," the physiological arousal might be labeled as joy, fear, anxiety, fury, or jealousy (Infographic 9.3).

To test their theory, Schachter and Singer injected participants (male college students) with either epinephrine to mimic physiological reactions of the sympathetic nervous system (such as increased blood pressure, respiration, and heart rate) or a placebo. The researchers also divided the participants into the following groups: those who were informed correctly about possible side effects (for example, tremors, palpitations, flushing, or accelerated breathing), those who were misinformed about side effects, and others who were told nothing about side effects.

The participants were left in a room with a "stooge," a confederate secretly working for the researcher, who was either euphoric or angry. When the confederate behaved euphorically, the participants who had been given no explanation for their physiological arousal were more likely to report feeling happy or appeared happier. When the confederate behaved angrily, participants given no explanation for their arousal were more likely to appear or report feeling angry. Through observation and self-report, it was clear the participants who did not receive an explanation for their physiological arousal could be manipulated to feel either euphoria or anger, depending on the confederate they were paired with. The participants who were accurately informed about side effects did not show signs or report feelings of euphoria or anger. Instead, they accurately attributed their physiological arousal to the side effects clearly explained to them at the beginning of the study (Schachter & Singer, 1962).

Some have criticized the Schachter–Singer theory, suggesting it overstates the link between physiological arousal and the experience of emotion (Reisenzein, 1983). Studies have shown that people can experience an emotion without labeling it, especially if neural activity sidesteps the cortex, heading straight to the limbic system (Dimberg, Thumberg, & Elmehed, 2000; Lazarus, 1991a). We will discuss this process in the upcoming section on fear.

COGNITIVE APPRAISAL AND EMOTION　Rejecting the notion that emotions result from cognitive labels of physiological arousal, Richard Lazarus (1984, 1991a) suggested that emotion is the result of the way people appraise or interpret interactions they have in their surroundings. It doesn't matter if someone can label an emotion or not; he will experience the emotion nonetheless. We've all felt emotions such as happiness, anxiety, and shame, and we don't need an agreed upon label or word to experience them. Babies, for example, can feel emotions long before they are able to label them with words.

Lazarus also suggested that emotions are adaptive, because they help us cope with the surrounding world. In a continuous feedback loop, as an individual's appraisal or interpretation of his environment changes, so do his emotions (Folkman & Lazarus, 1985; Lazarus, 1991b). Emotion is a very personal reaction to the environment. This notion became the foundation of the **cognitive appraisal approach** to emotion (Infographic 9.3), which suggests that the appraisal causes an emotional reaction. In contrast, Schachter–Singer theory asserts the arousal comes first and then has to be labeled.

Schachter–Singer theory of emotion
Suggests that the experience of emotion is the result of physiological arousal and a cognitive label for this physiological state.

cognitive appraisal approach
Suggests that the appraisal or interpretation of interactions with surroundings causes an emotional reaction.

Responding to the cognitive-appraisal approach, Robert Zajonc (ZI-yənce; 1984) suggested that thinking does not always have to be involved when we experience an emotion. As Zajonc (1980) saw it, emotions can precede thoughts and may even cause them. He also suggested we can experience emotions without interpreting what is occurring in the environment. Emotion can influence cognition, and cognition can influence emotion.

One of the main areas of disagreement among the theories just described concerns the role of cognition. Forgas (2008) proposed that the association between emotion and cognitive activity is complex and bidirectional: "Cognitive processes determine emotional reactions, and, in turn, affective states influence how people remember, perceive, and interpret social situations and execute interpersonal behaviors" (p. 99).

It's Written All over Your Face

We now know that emotions are complex and closely related to cognition, physiology, and perception. But how do these internal changes affect a person's appearance? Think about the clues you rely on when trying to "read" another person's emotions. Where do you look for signs of anger, sadness, or surprise? It's written all over his face, of course.

FACE VALUE   Lucy was lucky. With a 90% tear to the muscle and tendon and a severed artery, she could have easily lost her leg. But the surgeries went well. Just a week after the horrific incident, she was flashing a bashful grin on national television. Seated between mom and dad, Lucy played with her mother's fingers, squirmed, and then nestled her head under her father's arm. She looked as bright-eyed and vibrant as any child her age (MSNBC.com, 2011, July 26).

"The prognosis is great," Lucy's father Craig told *TODAY*'s Ann Curry. "It's going to take some time and some physical therapy, but she's going to be, you know, back and running and playing like she should" (MSNBC.com, 2011, July 26). The look on Craig's face was calm, happy. Jordan also appeared relieved. Their little girl was going to be okay.

Suppose you knew nothing about Lucy's shark attack, and someone showed you an image of Lucy's parents during that television interview. Would you be able to detect the relief in their facial expressions? How about someone from Nepal, Trinidad, or Bolivia: Would a cultural outsider also be able to "read" the emotions written across Craig and Jordan's faces? 📁

Road to Recovery
Despite the large cast on her leg, Lucy looks happy and healthy. Her shark-bite injuries were severe, but she received prompt, high-quality medical care.
Mangum Family Archives

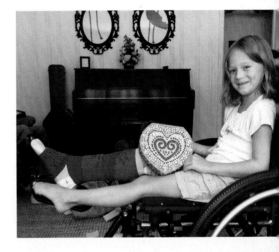

LO 14 Discuss evidence to support the idea that emotions are universal.

Writing in *The Expression of the Emotions in Man and Animals* (1872/2002), Charles Darwin suggested that interpreting facial expressions is not something we learn but rather is an innate ability that evolved because it promotes survival. Sharing the same facial expressions allows for communication. Being able to identify the emotions of others—like the fear in a friend who has just spotted a snake on the trail—would seem to come in handy. If facial expressions are truly unlearned and universal, then people from all different cultures ought to interpret them in the same way. A "happy face" should look much the same wherever you go, from the United States to the Pacific island of New Guinea.

EKMAN'S FACES   Some four decades ago, psychologist Paul Ekman traveled to a remote mountain region of New Guinea to study an isolated group of indigenous peoples. Ekman and his colleagues were very careful in selecting their participants, choosing only those who were unfamiliar with *Western facial behaviors*—people who were unlikely to know the signature facial expressions we equate with basic emotions

Universal Smile
A smile in India (right) means the same thing as a smile in Lithuania (middle) or Kenya (left). Facial expressions associated with basic emotions like happiness, disgust, and anger are strikingly similar across cultures (Ekman & Friesen, 1971). left: M Lohmann/ agefotostock; middle: Wojtek Buss/ age fotostock/Robert Harding; right: © Design Pics Inc/Alamy

like disgust and sadness. The participants didn't speak English, nor had they watched Western movies, worked for anyone with a Caucasian background, or lived among Westerners. The study went something like this: The researchers told the participants stories conveying various emotions such as fear, happiness, and anger. In the story conveying fear, for example, a man is sitting alone in his house with no knife, axe, bow, or any weapon to defend himself. Suddenly, a wild pig appears in his doorway, and he becomes frightened that the pig will bite him. Next, the researchers asked the participants to match the emotion described in the story to a picture of a person's face (choosing from 6–12 sets of photographs). The results indicated that the same facial expressions represent the same basic emotions across cultures (Ekman & Friesen, 1971). And so it seems, a "happy face" really does look the same to people in the United States and New Guinea.

Further evidence for the universal nature of these facial expressions is apparent in children born blind; although they have never seen a human face demonstrating an emotion, their smiles and frowns are similar to those of sighted children (Galati, Scherer, & Ricci-Bitti, 1997; Matsumoto & Willingham, 2009).

LO 15 Indicate how display rules influence the expression of emotion.

across the WORLD

Can You Feel the Culture?

Although the expression of some basic emotions appears to be universal, culture acts like a filter, determining the appropriate contexts in which to exhibit them. According to Mohamed (the Somali American we introduced earlier in the chapter), people from Somalia tend to be much less expressive than those born in the United States. "I have cousins who have just come to America, and even [now] when they have been here for about five years, they still like to keep to themselves about personal feelings," says Mohamed. This is especially true when it comes to interacting with people outside the immediate family.

WHEN TO REVEAL, WHEN TO CONCEAL

These differences Mohamed observes are probably reflections of display rules. A culture's **display rules** provide the framework or guidelines for when, how, and where an emotion is expressed. Think about some of the display rules in American culture. Negative emotions such as anger are often hidden in social situations. Suppose you are furious at a friend for forgetting to return a textbook she borrowed last night. You probably won't reveal your anger as you sit among other students. Other times display rules compel you to express an emotion you are *not* feeling. Your friend gives you a birthday gift that *really* isn't you. Do you say, "This is not my style. I think I'll exchange it for a store credit," or "Thank you so much" and smile graciously?

display rules Framework or guidelines for when, how, and where an emotion is expressed.

facial feedback hypothesis The facial expression of an emotion can affect the experience of that emotion.

Generally speaking, Americans tend to be fairly expressive. Showing emotion, particularly positive emotions, is socially acceptable. This is less the case in Japan, where people rarely reveal their feelings in public. One group of researchers secretly videotaped Japanese and American students while they were watching film clips that included surgeries, amputations, and other events commonly viewed as repulsive. Japanese and American participants showed no differences in their responses to the clips when they didn't think researchers were watching. The great majority demonstrated similar facial expressions of disgust and emotional reactions in response to the stress-inducing clips. But when a researcher was present, the Japanese were more likely than the Americans to conceal their negative expressions with smiles (Ekman et al., 1987). This tendency to hide feelings from the researcher is the result of cultural display rules. 🌐➔

FACIAL FEEDBACK HYPOTHESIS   While we are on the topic of facial expressions, let's take a brief detour back to the very beginning of the chapter when Mohamed arrived in his first-grade classroom speaking no English. Without a common language to communicate, Mohamed turned to a more universal form of communication: smiling. It is probably safe to assume that most of Mohamed's classmates took this to mean he was enjoying himself, as smiling is viewed as a sign of happiness in virtually every corner of the world. It also seems plausible that Mohamed's smiling had a positive effect on his classmates, making them more likely to approach and befriend him. But how do you think the act of smiling affected Mohamed?

Believe it or not, the simple act of smiling can make a person *feel* happier. Although facial expressions are caused by the emotions themselves, they sometimes affect the experience of those emotions. This is known as the **facial feedback hypothesis** (Buck, 1980), and if it is correct, we should be able to manipulate our emotions through our facial activities. Try this for yourself.

> **try this**

Take a pen and put it between your teeth, with your mouth open for about half a minute. Now, consider how you are feeling. Next, hold the pen with your lips, making sure not to let it touch your teeth, for half a minute. Again, consider how you are feeling.

If you are like the participants in a study conducted by Strack, Martin, and Stepper (1988), holding the pen in your teeth should result in your seeing the objects and events in your environment as funnier than if you hold the pen with your lips. Why would that be? Take a look at the photo to the right and note how the person holding the pen in his teeth seems to be smiling—the feedback of those smiling muscles leads to a happier mood.

We are now nearing the end of this chapter—and what an emotional one it has been! Before wrapping things up, let's examine various kinds of emotions humans can experience, narrowing our gaze onto fear and happiness.

✓◯◯◯ show what you know

1. _____ is a psychological state that includes a subjective or inner experience, physiological component, and behavioral expression.
   a. Valence
   b. Instinct
   c. Mood
   d. Emotion

2. On the way to a wedding, you get mud on your clothing. Describe how your emotion and mood would differ.

3. The _____ theory of emotion suggests that changes in the body and behavior lead to the experience of emotion.

4. _____ of a culture provide a framework for when, how, and where an emotion is expressed.
   a. Beliefs
   b. Display rules
   c. Feedback loops
   d. Appraisals

5. Name two ways in which the Cannon–Bard and Schachter–Singer theories of emotion are different.

6. What evidence exists that emotions are universal?

✓ CHECK YOUR ANSWERS IN APPENDIX C.

Types of Emotions

Imagine the whirlwind of emotions you would feel if you witnessed a loved one being attacked by a shark. Fear is probably the most obvious, but there are others, including *anger* toward the shark, *disgust* at the sight of blood, *anxiety* about the outcome, *gratitude* toward those who came to the rescue, and *guilt* (*it should have been me*).

Are such feelings common to all people? Some researchers have proposed that there is a set of "biologically given" emotions, which includes anger, fear, disgust, sadness, and happiness (Coan, 2010). These types of feelings are considered *basic emotions* because people all over the world experience and express them in similar ways; they appear to be innate and have an underlying neural basis (Izard, 1992). The fact that children born deaf and blind have the same types of expressions of emotion (happiness, anger, and so on) suggests the universal nature of such displays (Hess & Thibault, 2009).

It is also noteworthy that unpleasant emotions (fear, anger, disgust, and sadness) have survived throughout our evolutionary history, and are more prevalent than positive emotions such as happiness, surprise, and interest (Ekman, 1992; Forgas, 2008; Izard, 2007). This suggests that negative emotions have "adaptive value"; in other words, they may be useful in dangerous situations, like those that demand a fight-or-flight response (Forgas, 2008).

The Biology of Fear

LO 16 Describe the role the amygdala plays in the experience of fear.

Have you ever wondered what takes place in your brain when you feel afraid? Researchers certainly have. With the help of brain-scanning technologies, they have zeroed in on an almond-shaped structure in the limbic system (Cheng, Knight, Smith, & Helmstetter, 2006; Pape & Pare, 2010). This structure, known as the amygdala, is central to our experience of fear (Davis & Whalen, 2001; Hariri, Tessitore, Mattay, Fera, & Weinberger, 2002). If a person views threatening images, or even looks at an image of a frightened face, the amygdala is activated (Chiao et al., 2008; Laeng et al., 2010).

PATHWAYS TO FEAR What exactly does the amygdala do? When confronted with a fear-provoking situation, the amygdala enables an ultrafast and unconscious response. Sensory information (sights, sounds) entering the thalamus can either go to the cortex for processing, or head straight for the amygdala without stopping at the cortex (LeDoux, 1996, 2000, 2012). The direct path that goes from the thalamus to the amygdala conveys raw information about the threat, enabling your brain and body to respond to danger without your awareness. Like a panic button, the amygdala issues an alert, summoning other parts of the brain that play a role in the experience of fear (for example, the hypothalamus and medulla), which then alert the sympathetic nervous system. A pathway also goes to the pituitary gland, resulting in the secretion of stress hormones (LeDoux, 2012).

The snake-in-the-bed example from earlier in the chapter provides a clear example of an immediate fear response. Visual information about the snake goes directly to the thalamus, and from there to the amygdala, which triggers an alarm reaction. Your heart rate increases and breathing becomes rapid, preparing you to flee the slithery reptile. Meanwhile, information that was sent to the sensory processing centers of the visual cortex results in a visual representation of the snake. Let's suppose the "snake" is merely a rubber toy planted by a mischievous child. In this case, your cortex sends a message to the amygdala: "False alarm. The snake in the bed is a rubber toy." The key thing to note is that it takes longer for neural information to go from the thalamus to the cortex than from the thalamus to the amygdala. This explains why one generally needs a moment to calm down: The physiological reaction starts before the false alarm message from the cortex reaches the amygdala (**Infographic 9.4**).

Jaws the Terrible
The 1975 movie *Jaws* was America's first "summer blockbuster." *Jaws* told the tale of a great white shark that stalked beachgoers in a summer vacation spot. So frightening were the film's story and imagery that many Americans stopped going to the beach that summer (BBC, 2001, November 16). Universal/The Kobal Collection

The Anatomy of Fear

You instantly recoil when you spot a snake—then sigh with relief just a moment later when it registers that the snake is a rubber toy. Have you ever wondered why you react with fear when a "threat" turns out to be nothing? Why does it take longer for you to process a threat than react to it? Sensory information (sights, sounds) entering the brain travels to the thalamus and is then routed to the cortex for processing. Sensory information can also go directly to the amygdala. In the case of a threat, the amygdala alerts other areas of the brain and the endocrine system instantly without waiting for a conscious command. This enables a response to a threat before you are even fully aware of what you are reacting to.

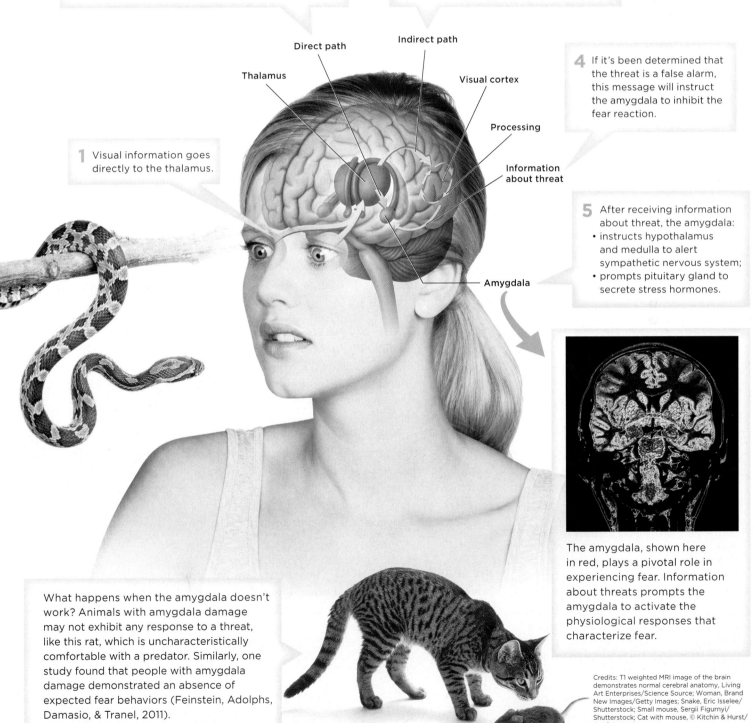

2 Basic information about threat is conveyed directly to the amygdala, enabling rapid response.

3 It takes longer for neural information to go to the visual cortex for processing.

Direct path

Indirect path

Thalamus

Visual cortex

4 If it's been determined that the threat is a false alarm, this message will instruct the amygdala to inhibit the fear reaction.

1 Visual information goes directly to the thalamus.

Processing

Information about threat

5 After receiving information about threat, the amygdala:
• instructs hypothalamus and medulla to alert sympathetic nervous system;
• prompts pituitary gland to secrete stress hormones.

Amygdala

The amygdala, shown here in red, plays a pivotal role in experiencing fear. Information about threats prompts the amygdala to activate the physiological responses that characterize fear.

What happens when the amygdala doesn't work? Animals with amygdala damage may not exhibit any response to a threat, like this rat, which is uncharacteristically comfortable with a predator. Similarly, one study found that people with amygdala damage demonstrated an absence of expected fear behaviors (Feinstein, Adolphs, Damasio, & Tranel, 2011).

Credits: T1 weighted MRI image of the brain demonstrates normal cerebral anatomy, Living Art Enterprises/Science Source; Woman, Brand New Images/Getty Images; Snake, Eric Isselee/ Shutterstock; Small mouse, Sergii Figurnyi/ Shutterstock; Cat with mouse, © Kitchin & Hurst/ Agefotostock

EVOLUTION AND FEAR   LeDoux (2012) suggested an evolutionary advantage to having direct and indirect routes for processing information about potential threats. The direct route (thalamus to amygdala, causing an emotional reaction) enables us to react quickly to threats for which we are biologically prepared (snakes, spiders, aggressive faces). The other pathway allows us to evaluate more complex threats (such as nuclear weapons, job layoffs) with our cortex, overriding the fast-response pathway when necessary.

The amygdala also plays an important role in the creation of "emotional memories," which are fairly robust and detailed (Johnson, LeDoux, & Doyère, 2009; LeDoux, 2002). This is useful because we are more likely to survive if we remember threats in our environments. For some people, however, emotional memories cause troublesome fear and anxiety (Chapter 11).

What other evidence points to the evolutionary benefit of fear and other emotions? Research suggests that the biological response patterns accompanying emotions are both innate and universal (they appear to be preprogrammed and shared by all). These patterns are the same irrespective of gender or age, although responses in older adults tend to be less extreme (Levenson, Carstensen, Friesen, & Ekman, 1991).

Happiness

In the very first chapter of this book, we introduced the field of positive psychology, "the study of positive emotions, positive character traits, and enabling institutions" (Seligman & Steen, 2005, p. 410). Rather than focusing on mental illness and abnormal behavior, positive psychology emphasizes human strengths and virtues. The goal is well-being and fulfillment, and that means "satisfaction" with the past, "hope and optimism" for the future, and "flow and happiness" at the current time (Seligman & Csikszentmihalyi, 2000). Let's take a moment to explore that flow and happiness of the present.

LO 17 Summarize evidence pointing to the biological basis of happiness.

THE BIOLOGY OF HAPPINESS   To what degree do we inherit happiness? Happiness has heritability estimates between 35% and 50%, and as high as 80% in longitudinal studies (Nes, Czajkowski, & Tambs, 2010). In other words, we can explain a high proportion of the variation in happiness, life satisfaction, and well-being by considering genetic make-up, as opposed to environmental factors.

Research suggests that the biological basis of happiness may include a "set point," similar to the set point for body weight (Bartels et al., 2010; Lyubomirsky, Sheldon, & Schkade, 2005). Happiness tends to fluctuate around a fixed level (this point is the degree of happiness we experience when we are not trying to be happier). As we strive for personal happiness, it is important to recognize the strength of this set point, which is influenced by genes and temperament. But do not lose hope; researchers also suggest it is possible to increase happiness over time (Lyubomirsky et al., 2005).

INCREASING HAPPINESS   In general, positive events in our lives only seem to bring temporary happiness (Diener, Lucas, & Scollon, 2006; Mancini, Bonanno, & Clark, 2011). Why is this? We tend to become habituated to new feelings of happiness or a new level of happiness rather quickly. If you win the lottery, get a new job, or buy a beautiful house, you will likely experience an increased level of happiness for a while, but then go back to your baseline, or "set point," of happiness (Lyubomirsky et al., 2005). Things that feel new and improved or life-changing quickly become mundane, suggesting that happiness will not be found in new possessions or shopping sprees. The implication is that we need to be careful when pursuing happiness as a goal in life, as we don't want to emphasize obtaining a specific outcome (like moving

The Brighter Side
Psychologist Martin Seligman is a leading proponent of positive psychology, which emphasizes the goodness and strength of the human spirit. Getting the most out of life, according to Seligman, means not only pursuing happiness, but also cultivating relationships, achieving goals, and being deeply engaged in meaningful activities (Szalavitz, 2011, May 13). Courtesy Positive Psychology Center, University of Pennsylvania/Martin Seligman

CONNECTIONS

In **Chapter 8,** we described several *temperaments* exhibited by infants. Around 40% of infants can be classified as *easy* babies who follow regular schedules, are relatively happy, easy to soothe when upset, and quick to adjust to changes in the environment. The existence of such a temperament lends support to the biological basis of happiness discussed here.

In **Chapter 5,** we presented the concept of *habituation,* a basic form of learning in which repeated exposure to an event generally results in a reduced response. Here, we see the same effect can occur with events that result in happiness. With repeated exposure, we will habituate to an event that initially elicited happiness.

to a house near the ocean) or acquiring a desired object (Lyubomirsky et al., 2005). Our focus should not be on becoming happier, but rather on being content with what we have (Lyubomirsky, Dickerhoof, Boehm, & Sheldon, 2011).

Apply This

There are many steps you can take to increase your level of happiness. Engaging in physical exercise, showing kindness, and getting involved in activities that benefit others are all linked to increased positive emotions (Lyubomorsky et al., 2011; Walsh, 2011). The same can be said for recording positive thoughts and feelings of gratefulness in a journal. One group of researchers asked participants to write down in a diary those aspects of their lives for which they were grateful each day. The researchers measured well-being and found that the participants in the diary group were better off than those not counting their blessings. The participants who recorded their blessings were also more likely to report they had helped or offered emotional support to another person (Emmons & McCullough, 2003). Another way to increase happiness is to identify and actively pursue goals that will have an important effect on your life (Brunstein, 1993). Write down what you are trying to accomplish and take action to make it happen. Knowing what you are actively working toward and committing to attainable goals are associated with increased feelings of well-being and happiness. There may be a genetic component of happiness, but nature isn't everything. Life is what you make of it, and happiness is yours to discover. →

Gender and Emotions

Urban myth, common sense, stereotypes, and our daily experiences in North America all lead us to believe that men and women experience and express their emotions differently, but is this true? Are women really more "emotional" than men? Do men hide their emotions? In a study that set out to examine some of these beliefs, participants were shown pictures of faces expressing emotions such as anger, happiness, and sadness (Barrett & Bliss-Moreau, 2009). Each of the faces was paired with a label stating some situational cause for its emotion (for example, a face showing anger was paired with the phrase "insulted by a stranger"). Then the participants were shown the same images without any label, and asked to state whether the individual depicted was "emotional" or "having a bad day." Female expressions were more likely to be described as emotional, whereas the male faces were more likely to be labeled as having a bad day. Apparently, the participants assumed that the female emotions stemmed from some internal characteristic (being an "overly emotional female"). Meanwhile, the men's emotions were presumed to be responses to situations or environments (Chapter 14).

Who Is Emotional?
Both of these individuals appear angry, but why are they feeling this way? Research suggests that people are more likely to attribute a woman's unpleasant expression to her "emotional" disposition and a man's angry face to "having a bad day." These assumptions rest on the stereotype that women are more emotional than men.
Nicole Betz, Lab Coordinator/Research Technician, Interdisciplinary Affective Science Lab Northeastern University, photo courtesy of Dr. Lisa Feldman Barrett

Happy As Ever
Mohamed got married in 2011, became a father in 2012, and graduated from the University of Minnesota in 2013. He now has two children (a boy and a girl) and is working as an Information Technology Analyst at the Minneapolis Public Housing Authority.
Courtesy Mohamed Dirie

You Asked, Mohamed Answers

http://qrs.ly/o14qsit

Did you do extracurricular activities in high school, and did they help make you feel connected?

The gender differences suggested by the participants' beliefs are not necessarily accurate, however. Most psychologists studying this topic suggest that men and women are more similar than different when it comes to experiencing and expressing emotion (Else-Quest, Higgins, Allison, & Morton, 2012). As noted earlier, there are universal facial expressions, and these are similar across gender. But the notion that women are more emotional is a gross overgeneralization at best.

That being said, research has uncovered some interesting gender disparities related to emotion. Some evidence suggests that women tend to feel more guilt, shame, and embarrassment than men (Else-Quest et al., 2012). They also seem to be more adept at identifying the emotion behind a particular face (Hall & Matsumoto, 2004). We don't know if this results from biological or cultural differences (perhaps women start practicing earlier, and this ability becomes more automatic for them). Women who paid closer attention to eyes, in one study, were able to discern emotional expressions more quickly and correctly than men, suggesting that the eyes are especially important for conveying emotions (Hall, Hutton, & Morgan, 2010). With that thought in mind, take a minute and look into the eyes of Mohamed (in the photograph above). Do you see a look of happiness and tranquility? We certainly do.

 show what you know

1. Researchers have found that when people view images that are threatening, or when they see images of faces of people who are afraid, the _____ becomes active.

2. How would you explain to a fellow student what the following statement means: Happiness has heritability estimates as high as 80%?

3. When confronted by a potential threat, such as a shark, your heart starts pounding, your breathing speeds up, and your pupils dilate. These changes are activated by
   a. the cognitive appraisal approach.
   b. the cortex.
   c. the sympathetic nervous system.
   d. gender differences.

✓ CHECK YOUR ANSWERS IN APPENDIX C.

⑨ summary of concepts

LO 1 Define motivation. (p. 359)

Motivation is a stimulus that can direct the way we behave, think, and feel. A motivated behavior tends to be guided (that is, it has a direction), energized, and persistent. When a behavior is reinforced, an association is established between the behavior and its consequence. With motivated behavior, this association becomes the incentive, or reason, to repeat the behavior.

Christina Norwood/Getty Images

LO 2 Explain how extrinsic and intrinsic motivation impact behavior. (p. 360)

When a learned behavior is motivated by the incentive of external reinforcers in the environment, there is an extrinsic motivation to continue that behavior. Intrinsic motivation occurs when a learned behavior is motivated by the prospect of internal reinforcers. Performing a behavior because it is inherently interesting or satisfying exemplifies intrinsic motivation, when the reinforcers originate from within.

LO 3 Summarize instinct theory. (p. 361)

Instinct theory proposes that through evolution some behaviors are etched into our genetic make-up, and are consistent from one member of the species to the next. Instincts, then, are complex behaviors that are fixed, unlearned, and consistent within a species. Although they apply to other nonhuman animals, there are limited data suggesting that humans display instincts.

LO 4 Describe drive-reduction theory and explain how it relates to motivation. (p. 363)

The drive-reduction theory of motivation suggests that biological needs and homeostasis motivate us. If a need is not fulfilled, this creates a drive, or state of tension, that pushes us or motivates behaviors to meet the need. Once a need is met, the drive is reduced, at least temporarily, because this is an ongoing process, as the need inevitably returns.

LO 5 Explain how arousal theory relates to motivation. (p. 365)

According to arousal theory, humans seek an optimal level of arousal, which is a level of alertness and engagement in the world. What constitutes an optimal level of arousal is variable, and depends on individual differences. Some people seem to be *sensation seekers;* that is, they seek activities that increase arousal.

LO 6 Outline Maslow's hierarchy of needs. (p. 365)

The needs in Maslow's hierarchy, often depicted as a pyramid, are considered to be universal and are ordered in terms of the strength of their associated drive, with the most critical needs, those that are physiological, at the bottom. Moving up the pyramid are increasingly higher-level needs: safety needs; love and belongingness needs; esteem needs; self-actualization; and self-transcendence. Maslow suggested that basic needs must be met before higher-level needs motivate behavior.

LO 7 Discuss how the stomach and the hypothalamus make us feel hunger. (p. 369)

In a classic experiment, researchers confirmed the stomach and brain both work to indicate hunger. When glucose levels dip, the stomach and liver send signals to the brain that something must be done about this reduced energy source. The brain, in turn, initiates a sense of hunger. Signals from the digestive system are sent to the hypothalamus, which then transmits signals to higher regions of the brain. When the lateral hypothalamus is activated, appetite increases. If the ventromedial hypothalamus becomes activated, appetite declines, causing an animal to stop eating.

LO 8 Outline the characteristics of the major eating disorders. (p. 373)

Anorexia nervosa is a serious, life-threatening eating disorder characterized by a significantly low body weight in relation to age, sex, development, and physical health; an extreme fear of gaining weight or getting fat; an altered and distorted sense of body weight and figure; and self-imposed restrictions on "energy intake" (calories) needed to maintain a healthy weight. Bulimia nervosa is characterized by recurrent episodes of binge eating followed by purging (self-induced vomiting, misuse of laxatives, fasting, or excessive exercise). Binge-eating disorder is characterized by episodes during which a larger amount of food is consumed than most people would eat in a similar amount of time under similar circumstances. As in bulimia, the individual feels unable to control eating during that period of time, but the difference is that there are no excessive weight control or purging behaviors.

LO 9 Describe the human sexual response as identified by Masters and Johnson. (p. 375)

The human sexual response is the physiological pattern that occurs during sexual activity. Men and women tend to experience a similar pattern or cycle of excitement, plateau, orgasm, and resolution, but the duration of these phases varies from person to person.

LO 10 Define sexual orientation and summarize how it develops. (p. 377)

According to the American Psychological Association, sexual orientation is the "enduring pattern" of sexual, romantic, and emotional attraction that individuals exhibit toward the same sex, opposite sex, or both sexes. Sexual orientation may be heterosexual (when a person is attracted to members of the opposite sex), homosexual (attracted to members of the same sex), or bisexual (attracted to both sexes). Research has focused on the causes of sexual orientation, but there is no strong evidence pointing to any one factor or factors. Sexual orientation is the result of a complex interaction between nature and nurture.

LO 11 Identify the most common sexually transmitted infections. (p. 383)

Sexually transmitted infections (STIs) are caused by viruses and bacteria and are contracted through sexual activity. Having multiple sexual partners increases the risk of getting an STI; however, awareness that a partner has had (or is having) sex with other partners lowers the risk somewhat. Once aware of a partner's activities, one is more inclined to take preventive measures, such as using condoms. Syphilis, gonorrhea, and chlamydia are bacterial infections. Genital herpes and human papillomavirus are viral infections.

LO 12   Define emotions and explain how they are different from moods. (p. 385)

An emotion is a psychological state that includes a subjective or inner experience. It also has a physiological component and entails a behavioral expression. Emotions are quite strong, but they don't generally last as long as moods. In addition, emotions are more likely to have identifiable causes (they are reactions to stimuli), and they are more likely to motivate a person to action. Moods are longer-term emotional states that are less intense than emotions and do not appear to have distinct beginnings or ends.

LO 13   List the major theories of emotion and describe how they differ. (p. 387)

The James–Lange theory of emotion suggests there is a stimulus that initiates the experience of a physiological reaction and/or a behavioral reaction, and it is this reaction that leads to an emotion. The Cannon–Bard theory of emotion suggests that we do not feel emotion as a result of physiological and behavioral reactions; instead, all these experiences occur simultaneously. The Schachter–Singer theory of emotion suggests there is a general pattern of physiological arousal caused by the sympathetic nervous system, and this pattern is common to a variety of emotions. The experience of emotion is the result of two factors: (1) physiological arousal and (2) a cognitive label for this physiological state (the arousal). The cognitive appraisal theory suggests that the appraisal or interpretation of interactions with surroundings causes an emotional reaction.

LO 14   Discuss evidence to support the idea that emotions are universal. (p. 391)

Darwin suggested that interpreting facial expressions is not something we learn, but rather an innate ability that evolved because it promotes survival. Sharing the same facial expressions allows for communication. In research with an isolated group of indigenous peoples in New Guinea, the results indicated that the same facial expressions represent the same basic emotions across cultures. In addition, the fact that children born deaf and blind have the same types of expressions of emotion (for example, happiness and anger) suggests the universal nature of these displays.

LO 15   Indicate how display rules influence the expression of emotion. (p. 392)

Although the expression of basic emotions appears, in many cases, to be universal, culture acts like a filter to determine the specific context in which to exhibit them. That is, the display rules of a culture provide the framework or guidelines for when, how, and where an emotion is expressed.

LO 16   Describe the role the amygdala plays in the experience of fear. (p. 394)

The amygdala is an almond-shaped structure found in the limbic system and appears to be central to our experience of fear. When people view threatening images, or even look at an image of a frightened face, the amygdala is activated. When confronted with a fear-provoking situation, the amygdala enables an ultrafast and unconscious response. The amygdala also plays an important role in the creation of emotional memories. This is useful because we are more likely to survive if we remember threats in our environments.

LO 17   Summarize evidence pointing to the biological basis of happiness. (p. 396)

Happiness has heritability estimates between 35% and 50%, and as high as 80% in longitudinal studies. There may be a set point for happiness, suggesting that we all have a degree of happiness around which our happiness levels will hover. As we consider our level of happiness and strive for personal happiness, we should keep in mind our set point, as it is strong, and directed by our genes and temperament.

key terms

anorexia nervosa, p. 373
arousal theory, p. 365
binge-eating disorder, p. 374
bisexual, p. 377
bulimia nervosa, p. 374
Cannon–Bard theory of emotion, p. 389
cognitive appraisal approach, p. 390
display rules, p. 392
drive, p. 363

drive-reduction theory, p. 363
emotion, p. 385
extrinsic motivation, p. 360
facial feedback hypothesis, p. 393
heterosexual, p. 377
hierarchy of needs, p. 365
homeostasis, p. 363
homosexual, p. 377
incentive, p. 359
instincts, p. 361

intrinsic motivation, p. 360
James–Lange theory of emotion, p. 387
motivation, p. 359
needs, p. 363
need for achievement (n-Ach), p. 367
need for power (n-Pow), p. 367
orgasm, p. 376
refractory period, p. 376

Schachter–Singer theory of emotion, p. 390
self-actualization, p. 366
self-determination theory (SDT), p. 367
set point, p. 372
sexual dysfunction, p. 382
sexual orientation, p. 377
sexuality, p. 375
sexually transmitted infections (STIs), p. 383

TEST PREP are you ready?

1. To get a child to practice the piano, you allow her 15 minutes to play her favorite computer game when she is done practicing. Playing on the computer eventually represents _____ for her to practice the piano.
   a. negative reinforcement
   b. intrinsic motivation
   c. satiety
   d. an incentive

2. Learned behaviors that are motivated by reinforcers in the environment have
   a. extrinsic motivation.
   b. intrinsic motivation.
   c. drives.
   d. needs.

3. _____ are complex behaviors that are fixed, unlearned, and consistent within a species.
   a. Drives
   b. Motivators
   c. Instincts
   d. Needs

4. Biological needs and homeostasis motivate us to meet our needs. If a need is not fulfilled, this creates a state of tension that pushes us to meet it. This describes the _____ theory of motivation.
   a. self-actualization
   b. drive-reduction
   c. cognitive-appraisal
   d. Schachter–Singer

5. Humans have different optimal levels of need for arousal. These individual differences indicate that some people are _____ ; they appear to seek out activities that increase arousal.
   a. sensation seekers
   b. externally motivated
   c. driven by extrinsic motivation
   d. bulimic

6. When the _____ is stimulated electrically, it sends a hormone signal to decrease appetite. If this region of the brain is destroyed, an animal will drastically overeat.
   a. limbic system
   b. amygdala
   c. lateral hypothalamus
   d. ventromedial hypothalamus

7. A serious health issue characterized by a body mass index of 30 or higher is known as:
   a. anorexia nervosa.
   b. obesity.
   c. bulimia nervosa.
   d. binge-eating disorder.

8. Kory routinely eats large amounts of food that most people could not eat in similar situations or in a similar amount of time. Kory often feels an inability to control her eating and frequently eats alone because she is embarrassed by how much she eats. It is likely that Kory has a diagnosis of:
   a. anorexia nervosa.
   b. bulimia nervosa.
   c. amenorrhea.
   d. binge-eating disorder.

9. Emotion is a psychological state that includes a subjective experience, a physiological component, and a(n):
   a. mood.
   b. drive.
   c. behavioral expression.
   d. incentive.

10. To study the universal nature of emotions, Paul Ekman traveled to New Guinea to explore native peoples' detection of facial expressions. Although unfamiliar with Western facial behaviors, the participants in his study
   a. could not identify the facial expressions in the photos he showed them.
   b. could identify the facial expressions common across the world.
   c. could understand English.
   d. had no display rules.

11. The Schachter–Singer theory suggests that the experience of emotion is the result of
   a. physiological arousal.
   b. cognitive labeling.
   c. physiological arousal and cognitive labeling.
   d. an appraisal of the environment.

12. The _____ suggests that emotion is a very personal reaction to and interpretation of the environment, and that emotion does not result from a cognitive label of physiological arousal.
   a. James–Lange theory
   b. cognitive-appraisal approach
   c. Schachter–Singer theory
   d. Cannon–Bard theory

13. According to Masters and Johnson, sexual arousal begins in the _____ phase, when physical changes begin to take place.
   a. excitement
   b. plateau
   c. resolution
   d. orgasm

14. In a fear-provoking situation, initial processing can be unconscious. Information from the thalamus can take two paths: It may go to the _____ for processing, or directly to the _____, which sets the stage by preparing the body for response to a threat.
   a. cortex; amygdala
   b. parasympathetic nervous system; cortex
   c. hypothalamus; parasympathetic nervous system
   d. parasympathetic nervous system; sympathetic nervous system

15. Evidence from research on emotions suggests that when looking at faces, women seem to
   a. spend less time paying attention to eyes than men.
   b. be less likely to feel embarrassment than men.
   c. be less able to identify what emotion is being felt than men.
   d. be better able to identify what emotion is being felt than men.

16. Describe research findings on the influence of biology in sexual orientation.

17. Describe a situation you are aware of when someone's motivation did not follow the order outlined in Maslow's hierarchy of needs.

18. How are bacterial and viral sexually transmitted infections different?

19. List some of the display rules you respond to on a daily basis. What different display rules do you follow at school in comparison to those at home?

20. What are some activities you can get involved in to increase your happiness?

✓ CHECK YOUR ANSWERS IN APPENDIX C

Get personalized practice by logging into LaunchPad at **www.macmillanhighered.com/launchpad/ sciampresenting1e** to take the LearningCurve adaptive quizzes for Chapter 9.

10

WELCOME

MAY I

HELP

YOU?

Keyboard letters: spxChrome/Getty Images; Mask: Jupiter Images

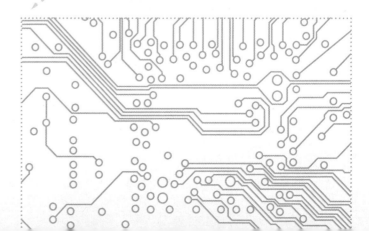

personality

An Introduction to Personality

MEET TANK　Often, in the lobby of a business or other establishment, a receptionist is the first employee you encounter. The receptionist shapes a visitor's first impression, and thus should be friendly, eager to help, and reliable. A neat physical appearance and pleasant voice are also big pluses.

Newell Simon Hall, the computer science building at Pittsburgh's Carnegie Mellon University, has an excellent receptionist. His name is Marion LeFleur, but everyone calls him "Tank," a fitting title given his square jaw and overall tough-guy appearance. But don't be intimidated by the Rambo look. "Tank is a nice guy," says Tank's boss, Dr. Reid Simmons. "He just does his job and has a really good heart." Approach Tank's booth, and he will take note of your presence immediately. "Hello there. What can I do for you?" he asks ever so politely (Greenfieldboyce, 2005, December 26). Looking for the room number of a university employee? Tank will find it in seconds. Need directions to a different building on campus? Tank is all over it. He can also provide updates on the local time and weather. Ask the right questions, and Tank might even share some details of his personal life, such as the fact that he once dated the scoreboard at the Pittsburgh Steelers stadium (Lee, Kiesler, & Forlizzi, 2010; Simmons et al., 2011). He may even tell you about his career disaster with NASA, or his botched mission with the CIA (Carnegie Mellon University, 2013).

Perhaps you feel like you're beginning to know Tank, getting a basic sense of the type of person he is. But wait. Tank isn't a person; he is a robot—a "roboceptionist," to be precise—and robots are not capable of exhibiting the complex behaviors you would expect from a human being. At least not yet.

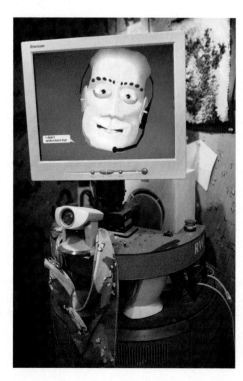

Hello, Tank
The Computer Science Department at Carnegie Mellon University has a robot receptionist named "Tank." Some of Tank's behaviors are amazingly humanlike; he blinks, flares his nostrils, and even displays emotional expressions consistent with what he is saying (Simmons et al., 2011). But no matter how "human" Tank may seem, he does not possess a true personality. Debra Marie Tobin, art director for the Robotics Institute

Note: Quotations attributed to Dr. Reid Simmons are personal communications.

Looking at Tank, it's quite obvious he is not a person. His blue, chiseled face lives in a 15-inch flat-panel LCD screen, and his body looks somewhat like a massive red coffee thermos. He has sensors to detect your presence, but he cannot see your facial expressions, read your body language, or even hear your voice. In fact, the only way to communicate with Tank is by typing on his keyboard, and he can only understand simple questions such as "Where is the ladies' room?"

Tank is a product of Carnegie Mellon's Social Robots Project, a collaboration between the university's Robotics Institute and School of Drama. The goal is to "create a robot that can provide useful services, but that also exhibits personality and character" (Gockley et al., 2005, p. 2199). How is this accomplished? Every one of Tank's behaviors, from the movements of his eyes to the subtle tilts of his head, is preprogrammed by Dr. Simmons' team of computer whizzes. His backstory and script were written by members of the university's drama department. It's all "smoke and mirrors," according to Dr. Simmons. Creating the illusion of a "personality" turns out to be quite a challenge. This would be no surprise to psychologists studying *personality*. 🗀

Tank, in Dr. Simmons' Own Words

http://qrs.ly/az4qse1

© 2016, Macmillan

What Is Personality?

One of the major challenges of creating social robots is programming behaviors that gel coherently. If you want to craft a robot with a convincing personality, you'd better make sure that everything it does and says fits the part. One out-of-character remark and people will be reminded that they are merely talking to a collection of electrical circuits.

LO 1 Define personality.

So far we have used the term "personality" rather loosely. The reality is that robots do not actually have personalities. They take on roles or *personas* whose characteristics may bear resemblance to personalities, but all of their behaviors are programmed by people. Well then, what is personality? Generally speaking, **personality** refers to the unique, core set of characteristics that influence the way one thinks, acts, and feels—characteristics many psychologists would agree are relatively consistent and enduring throughout the life span.

We should point out that personality is not the equivalent of *character*. When people discuss character, they often are referring to qualities of morality or culture-specific ideas about what makes a person "good" or "bad." A person who is untrustworthy or makes "poor" choices might be described as having a weak character, while someone

personality The unique, core set of characteristics that influence the way one thinks, acts, and feels, and that are relatively consistent and enduring throughout the life span.

who stands up for what she believes might be said to have a strong character. You may hear that the guy with the blue mohawk or the woman with the multiple body piercings is a "real character"—often in a judgmental way. Psychologists try not to make such judgments; our goal is to describe behaviors and characteristics objectively.

TEMPERAMENT   Some aspects of adult personality appear to derive from temperament, the distinct patterns of emotional reactions and behaviors observed early in life. Because various temperaments are evident in infants, they appear to have a genetic basis (Plomin, DeFries, Knopik, & Neiderhiser, 2013). But even though temperament remains somewhat stable across the life span (Kagan & Snidman, 1991; Sigelman & Rider, 2009), it can be molded by the environment (Caspi, Roberts, & Shiner, 2005). You can think of temperament as one dimension of the broader construct of personality (Goldsmith et al., 1987).

LO 2   Distinguish how the perspectives of psychology explain personality development.

PERSPECTIVES ON PERSONALITY   Psychologists explain the development of personality in a variety of ways, often in accordance with certain theoretical perspectives (**Table 10.1**). None of the perspectives can completely account for the development and expression of personality, but they do help describe, explain, and predict behavior. Most have strong ties to their founders, all of whom were influenced by the historical period in which they lived. Sigmund Freud's emphasis on sexuality, for example, was partly a reaction to the Victorian cultural climate into which he was born.

CONNECTIONS

In **Chapter 8,** we described various infant temperaments. Some infants are easy to calm, others cranky, sociable, or highly reactive. Humans are born with certain temperaments, and many of the attending characteristics seem to persist throughout life. Here, we introduce temperament in the context of personality.

TABLE 10.1 THEORETICAL PERSPECTIVES OF PERSONALITY

Personality Theory	Main Points	Criticisms
Psychoanalytic	Personality develops early in life; we are greatly influenced by processes of which we are unaware (e.g., internal conflicts, aggression, sexual urges).	Ignores importance of current experiences; overemphasis on the unconscious and the role of sexuality in personality; theory based on a biased, nonrepresentative sample; concepts difficult to operationally define and empirically test.
Behavioral	Personality is shaped by interactions with the environment, specifically through learning (classical conditioning, operant conditioning, and observational learning).	Narrow focus on behavioral processes; ignores influence of unconscious processes and emotional factors.
Humanistic	We are innately good and control our destinies; we have a force moving us toward growth.	Concepts difficult to operationally define and empirically test; ignores the negative aspects of human nature.
Social-cognitive	Focuses on social influences and mental processes that affect personality; emphasis on the combination of environment, cognitive activity, and individual behavior.	Narrow focus on social-cognitive factors; ignores influence of unconscious processes and emotional factors.
Biological	Emphasizes the physiological and genetic influences on personality development; incorporates gene–environment explanations for the emergence of certain characteristics.	Inconsistent findings regarding the stability of the personality dimensions; varying estimates of environmental influences.
Trait	Looks at current traits of the individual to describe personality and predict behaviors.	Underestimates the environmental influences on personality; neglects to explain foundations of personality.

Psychology uses a variety of theoretical perspectives to explain the development of personality. Here are the major theories and some of their key limitations.

In the next section, we will examine these theories of personality in greater depth, but first let's take a quick detour somewhere fun. How would you describe your sense of humor?

Nature and Nurture

Silly Genes
Identical twins, who have all the same genes, are more likely to have similar humor styles than fraternal twins, who share only about half their genes (Baughman et al., 2012). This suggests that sense of humor is to some degree inherited. Education Images/UIG via Getty Images

HUMOR IS VERY MUCH LIKE OTHER ASPECTS OF PERSONALITY— GROUNDED IN BIOLOGY. . . .

The Funny Thing About Personality

Some of us rely on humor to connect with other people, cracking jokes and acting silly for their enjoyment. Others use it as a way to cope with challenges. (We must admit, it does feel good to let loose and laugh when life's stresses become unbearable.) Both of these styles of humor are viewed as positive, as they strengthen social bonds and promote personal well-being (Martin, Puhlik-Doris, Larsen, Gray, & Weir, 2003). There are also negative forms of humor, like ridiculing another person to make yourself look good, or poking fun at yourself in a way that seems to erode self-esteem (Martin et al., 2003; McCosker & Moran, 2012).

Where do these styles of humor originate? According to one large Australian study, identical twins (who have identical genes) are more likely to share humor styles than fraternal (nonidentical) twins. What this tells you is that genes matter. In fact, the study suggests that 30–47% of variation in humor styles can be attributed to genetics (Baughman et al., 2012), and some research shows an even higher proportion (Vernon, Martin, Schermer, Cherkas, & Spector, 2008). But how do you explain the other 53–70% of the variation? Chalk it up to nurture. Humor is very much like other aspects of personality—grounded in biology, but chiseled and refined by a lifetime of experiences.

Over 7 billion human beings inhabit this planet, and not one of them has the same personality as you. Each individual's personality reflects a distinct interplay of inborn characteristics and life experiences. Consider this nature-and-nurture dynamic as you explore the theories of personality in the pages to come. To what degree does each perspective recognize the contributions of nature and nurture, and how do these forces interact? Let's get this discussion rolling with the help of Tank.

---

show what you know

1. _____ is the unique core set of characteristics that influence the way one thinks, acts, and feels.

2. Which perspective explains personality based on the effects of reinforcers and other environmental influences?
   a. psychoanalytic
   b. trait
   c. social-cognitive
   d. behavioral

3. How do character and temperament differ from personality?

✓ CHECK YOUR ANSWERS IN APPENDIX C.

Psychoanalytic Theories

psychoanalysis Freud's views regarding personality as well as his system of psychotherapy and tools for the exploration of the unconscious.

unconscious According to Freud, the level of consciousness outside of awareness, which is difficult to access without effort or therapy.

NEVER GOOD ENOUGH FOR DAD Tank the Roboceptionist has quite a colorful past, thanks to the creative minds at Carnegie Mellon's School of Drama, who carefully crafted his background to mesh with his current persona. Tank's father was a NASA scientist who failed to fulfill his dream of becoming an astronaut. Unfortunately, dad transferred his "unfinished business" onto his robot son, pressuring him to accomplish what he never did. Dad wanted Tank to be like the Hubble Space Telescope, able to fly into space and capture beautiful images of other planets and celestial bodies. But

Tank got his coordinates mixed up and sent back photos of Earth. Tank's father was so humiliated that he disowned him (Carnegie Mellon University, 2013).

If only we could ask Sigmund Freud what he thought of this father–son relationship—surely, he would have some interesting things to say. Freud believed childhood is the prime time for personality development. Early years and basic drives are particularly important, according to Freud, because they shape our thoughts, emotions, and behaviors in ways beyond our awareness. **Psychoanalysis** refers to Freud's views about personality as well as his system of psychotherapy and tools for the exploration of the unconscious. In this next section, we will present an overview of Freud's psychoanalysis as it relates to personality and some of the later personality theories it influenced.

Many students have trouble understanding why we should study Freud, whose ideas they consider sexist, perverse, and outdated. Freud is an important historical figure in psychology, and we can't ignore his legacy just because we disagree with him. You wouldn't find many world history teachers ignoring Hitler in their coverage of the 1900s, would you? The same principle applies to Freud; his impact was huge and cannot be overlooked. 📁

Little Freud
Looking at this photo of Sigmund Freud and his father Jacob, we can't help but wonder how this father–son relationship influenced the development of the younger Freud's personality. Freud believed that events and conflicts from childhood—particularly those involving parents and other caregivers—have a powerful influence on adult personality.
Imagno/Getty Images

Freud and the Mind

Sigmund Freud (1856–1939) spent the majority of his life in Vienna, Austria. He was his parents' first child and quite favored by his mother (Gay, 1988). A smart, ambitious young man, Freud attended medical school and became a physician and researcher with a primary interest in physiology and later neurology. Freud loved doing research, but he soon came to realize that the anti-Semitic culture in which he lived would drastically interfere with his ability to work as a researcher (Freud was Jewish). So, instead of pursuing the career he loved, he opened a medical practice in 1881, specializing in clinical neurology. Working with patients, he noted that many had unexplained or unusual symptoms that seemed related to emotional problems. He also observed (along with colleagues) that the basis of the problems appeared to be sexual in nature, although his patients weren't necessarily aware of this (Freud, 1900/1953). Herein began Freud's lifelong journey to untangle the mysteries of the unconscious mind.

LO 3   Illustrate Freud's models for describing the mind.

CONSCIOUS, PRECONSCIOUS, AND UNCONSCIOUS   Freud (1900/1953) proposed that the mind has three levels of consciousness: conscious, preconscious, and unconscious. This so-called iceberg model, or *topographical model,* was his earliest attempt to explain the bustling activity occurring within the head (Westen, Gabbard, & Ortigo, 2008). It describes the *features* of the mind (which explains the reference to topography), and many who subsequently have presented this model use an iceberg analogy to portray these levels (Schultz & Schultz, 2013; **Figure 10.1** on the next page).

Freud believed that behaviors and personality are guided by mental processes occurring at all three levels of the mind. Everything you are aware of at this moment exists at the *conscious* level, including thoughts, emotions, sensations, and perceptions. At the preconscious level are the mental activities outside your current awareness, which can be brought easily to your attention. (You are studying Freud's theory at this moment, but your mind begins to wander and you start thinking about what you did yesterday.) The **unconscious** level is home to activities outside of your awareness, such as feelings, wishes, thoughts, and urges, which are very difficult to access without concerted effort and/or therapy. To gain access to the unconscious level, Freud (1900/1953) used a variety of techniques, such as dream interpretation

CONNECTIONS

In **Chapter 6,** we presented the concept of *episodic buffer* (a component of *working memory*), which forms a bridge between memory and conscious awareness. Although Freud did not refer to such a buffer, the preconscious level includes activities somewhat similar to those of the episodic buffer.

FIGURE 10.1
Psychoanalytic Description
of the Mind

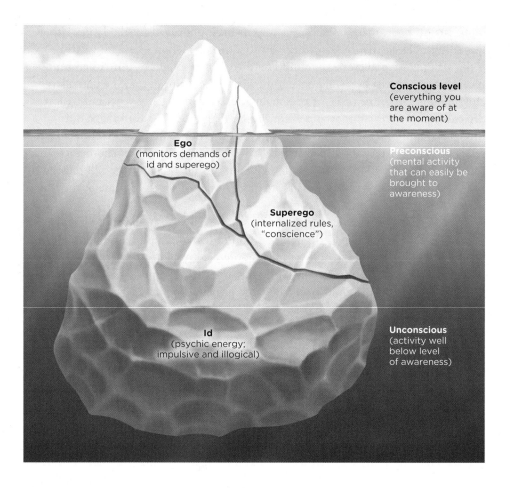

Conscious level
(everything you
are aware of at
the moment)

Ego
(monitors demands of
id and superego)

Preconscious
(mental activity
that can easily be
brought to
awareness)

Superego
(internalized rules,
"conscience")

Id
(psychic energy;
impulsive and illogical)

Unconscious
(activity well
below level
of awareness)

(Chapter 4), hypnosis (Chapter 4), and free association (Chapter 13). Freud did suggest, however, that some content of the unconscious can enter the conscious level through manipulated and distorted processes beyond a person's control or awareness (more on this shortly).

Id, Ego, and Superego: The Structural Model of the Mind

In addition to the topographical model, Freud proposed a *structural model,* which describes the "functions or purposes" of the mind's components (Westen et al., 2008, p. 65). As Freud saw it, the human mind is composed of three structures: the *id,* the *ego,* and the *superego* (Figure 10.1). These components lie at the core of the unconscious conflicts influencing our thoughts, emotions, and behaviors—that is, our personality (Westen et al., 2008).

THE ID   The **id** is the most primitive structure of the mind. It is present from birth, and its activities occur at the unconscious level. The infantlike part of our mind and personality (being impulsive, illogical, pleasure seeking) results from the workings of the id. Our biological drives and instincts, which motivate us, derive from the id. Freud proposed that the id represents the component of the mind that forms the primary pool of *psychic energy* (Freud, 1923/1961, 1933/1964). Included in that pool is sexual energy, which motivates much of our behavior. The primary goal of the id is to ensure that the individual's needs are being met, helping to maintain homeostasis. The id is not rational, and unfulfilled needs or urges compel it to insist on immediate action. It is ruled by the **pleasure principle,** which guides behavior toward instant gratification—and away from contemplating consequences. The id seeks pleasure and avoids pain.

CONNECTIONS

Meeting the demands of the id is similar to the concept of *drive reduction* discussed in **Chapter 9.** If a need is not fulfilled, a drive or a state of tension results that motivates behavior. Once the need is met, the drive is reduced. According to Freud's model, the id is in charge of making sure needs are met.

THE EGO   As an infant grows and starts to realize that the desires of the id cannot prevail in all situations, her **ego,** which is not present from birth, begins to develop from the id (Freud, 1933/1964, 1940/1949). The ego manipulates situations, plans for the future, solves problems, and makes decisions to satisfy the needs of the id. The goal is to make sure that the id is not given free rein to decide on or steer behavior, as this would cause problems. Adults know they can't always get what they want when they want it, but the id does not know or care. Imagine what a busy supermarket would be like if we were all ruled by our ids, ignoring societal expectations to stand in line, speak politely, and pay for food; the store would be full of adults having toddler-like tantrums. To negotiate between the id and the environment, and thereby control the id's psychic energy, the ego uses the **reality principle.** This requires knowledge of the rules of the "real" world and allows most of us to delay gratification as needed (Freud, 1923/1960). The reality principle works through an awareness of potential consequences; the ego can predict what will happen if we act on an urge. We are aware of the ego's activities, although some happen at the preconscious level, and even fewer at the unconscious level (Figure 10.1).

THE SUPEREGO   The **superego** is the structure of the mind that develops last, guiding behavior to follow the rules of society, parents, or other authority figures (Freud, 1923/1960). The superego begins to form as the toddler starts moving about on his own, coming up against rules and expectations (*No, you cannot hit your sister! You need to put your toys away.*). Around age 5 or 6, the child begins to incorporate the morals and values of his parents or caregivers, including their expectations and ideas about right and wrong, colloquially known as the *conscience.* Once the superego is rooted, it serves as a critical internal guide to the values of society (not just those of the parents), so that the child can make "good" choices without constant reminders from a parent, caregiver, or religious leader. The rules and expectations now come from an internal voice citing right and wrong. Sometimes the superego can be harsh and judgmental, and it may set unrealistic standards. The superego is an internalized version of what you have been *taught* is right and wrong, not necessarily an independent moral authority. Some of the activities of the superego are conscious, but the great majority occur at the preconscious and unconscious levels.

CAUGHT IN THE MIDDLE   The ego monitors the demands of both the id and the superego, trying to satisfy both. The ego must deal with rules and expectations as it maneuvers between the wishes of the id and the requirements of the environment. Think of the energy of the id, pushing to get all desires met instantly. The ego must ensure needs are met in a manner acceptable to the superego, reducing tension as much as possible. But not all urges and desires can be met (sometimes not instantly, sometimes never), so when the ego cannot satisfy the id, it must do something with the unsatisfied urge or unmet need. One solution is to remove it from the conscious part of the mind.

Defense Mechanisms

As you have figured out by now, the job of the ego is not easy. It must balance the infantile demands of the id with the perfectionist authority of the superego, and deal with the resulting conflict. This is feasible, but it takes some fancy footwork on the part of the ego. Freud proposed that **ego defense mechanisms** distort our perceptions and memories of the "real" world, without our awareness, to reduce the anxiety created by the conflicts among the id, ego, and superego.

   Imagine you are about to leave for class and you get a text from a good friend, inviting you to a movie. You are torn, because you know an exam is coming up and you should not skip today's class. Your id is demanding a movie, some popcorn, and freedom from work. Your superego demands that you go to class so that you will be

id According to Freud, the most primitive structure of the mind, the activities of which occur at the unconscious level and are guided by the pleasure principle.

pleasure principle Collection of rules that guide the id, resulting in behavior to achieve instant gratification without thought to consequences.

ego According to Freud, the structure of the mind that uses the reality principle to manipulate situations, plan for the future, solve problems, and make decisions.

reality principle Collection of rules that guide the ego as it negotiates between the id and the environment.

superego According to Freud, the structure of the mind that guides behavior to follow the rules of society, parents, or other authority figures.

ego defense mechanisms Distortions of perceptions and memories of the real world, without one's awareness, to reduce the anxiety created by the conflict among the id, ego, and superego.

S. Harris/Cartoonstock

Oops

A "Freudian slip" occurs when an unintended word accidentally slips off the tongue, shedding light on unconscious thoughts. Here, the woman reassures the balding man he still has plenty of hair, but her Freudian slip reveals she thinks otherwise.

fully prepared for the exam. Clearly, your ego can't satisfy both of these demands. The ego must also deal with the external world and its requirements (for example, getting points for attendance). Freud (1923/1960) proposed that this sort of struggle is an everyday, recurring experience that is not always won by the ego. Sometimes, the id will win, and the person will act in an infantile, perhaps even destructive manner (you give in to the pressures of your friend and your id, and happily decide to skip class). Occasionally, the superego will prevail, and the person will feel a great deal of remorse or guilt for not living up to some moral ideal (you skip class, but you feel so guilty you can't enjoy the movie). Sometimes, the anxiety associated with the conflict between the id and the superego, which generally is unconscious, will surface to the conscious level. The ego will then have to deal with this anxiety and make it more bearable (perhaps by suggesting that a day off will help you study, because you haven't had any free time all semester). The ego must come up with a way to decrease the tension, but if it can't find a compromise, the anxiety may become overwhelming, and the ego will turn to defense mechanisms to reduce it.

Projection is a defense mechanism that occurs when the expression of a thought or urge is so anxiety provoking that the ego makes us see it in someone else or accuse another of harboring these same urges. For example, if you are attracted to someone, but this attraction causes you a lot of anxiety, you may project that feeling onto your friend and ask her, "Oh, you really like Tai, don't you?" Freud proposed a variety of other defense mechanisms, which were expanded upon by his daughter, psychoanalyst Anna Freud (1895–1982). Some of these are shown in **Infographic 10.1.**

REPRESSION Probably the defense mechanism best-known by the general public is **repression,** which refers to the way the ego moves uncomfortable thoughts, memories, or feelings from the conscious level to the unconscious. With anxiety-provoking memories, the reality of an event can become distorted to such an extreme that you don't even remember it. Someone involved in a bad car accident, for example, might have unconsciously or automatically repressed the memories surrounding the traumatic event. The ego moves the memory from the conscious to the unconscious so that the person can function day-to-day without anxiety from the accident surfacing into consciousness. Repressed thoughts are like ping-pong balls held below the surface of the water. As long as you hold them down, they stay submerged; but if you let go, they pop up to the surface. The balls didn't cease to exist—they were simply just below the surface, out of sight and awareness.

There are two important points to remember about defense mechanisms. First, we are often unaware of using them, even if they are brought to our attention. Second, using defense mechanisms is not necessarily a bad thing (Vaillant, 2000). There are times when it helps to have reality distorted; for example, when anxiety seeps to the surface, defense mechanisms can bring it down to a more manageable level.

CONNECTIONS

In **Chapter 6,** we presented the controversy surrounding *repressed memories* of childhood abuse. Many psychologists question the validity of research supporting the existence of repressed memories. Freud's case studies describing childhood sexual abuse have been questioned as well.

repression The way the ego moves uncomfortable thoughts, memories, or feelings from the conscious level to the unconscious.

Ego Defense Mechanisms

The impulsive demands of the id sometimes conflict with the moralistic demands of the superego, resulting in anxiety. When that anxiety becomes too intense, the ego works to relieve this uncomfortable feeling through the use of defense mechanisms (Freud, 1923/1960). Defense mechanisms give us a way to "defend" against tension and anxiety, but they are only sometimes adaptive, or helpful. Defense mechanisms can be categorized ranging from less adaptive to more adaptive (Vaillant, 1992). More adaptive defense mechanisms help us deal with our anxiety in more productive and mature ways.

EGO relieves anxiety by employing a defense mechanism.

EGO

Doctors freak me out! There's no way I'm going to see one.

I really should get this mole checked. If it's cancerous, it would be better to get it treated right away.

ID → anxiety ← **SUPEREGO**

Credits: Sad Young Woman, Tom Fullum/Getty Images

✳ We may get better at dealing with stress and anxiety as we age. In a study comparing the use of defense mechanisms in different age groups, older participants were found to use fewer maladaptive defense mechanisms (Segal, Coolidge, & Mizuno, 2007).

MORE ADAPTIVE

SUBLIMATION
Redirecting unacceptable impulses into acceptable outlets.

Example: Instead of worrying about cancer risk, spend time researching clinics and selecting a highly trained dermatologist who specializes in mole analysis.

IDENTIFICATION
Unconsciously modeling our feelings or actions on the behaviors of someone we admire.

Example: Feeling worried about sun exposure, begin sporting the floppy hat and sunglasses frequently worn by a famous model.

DISPLACEMENT
Shifting negative feelings and impulses to an acceptable target.

Example: When scheduling appointment with dermatologist, complain to receptionist about the long wait and inconvenient hours.

REPRESSION
Anxiety-producing information is pushed into the unconscious.

Example: Continually forget to make an appointment.

RATIONALIZATION
Creating an acceptable excuse for an uncomfortable situation.

Example: "I've always had that mole. There's nothing to worry about."

PROJECTION
Attributing your own anxiety-provoking thoughts and impulses to someone else.

Example: "My girlfriend spends too much time sunbathing. I'll tell her she should get screened for skin cancer!"

DENIAL
Refusing to recognize a distressing reality.

Example: Ignore the mole. "I'm way too young. It can't be cancer."

LESS ADAPTIVE

But sometimes conflicts between the id and the superego are overwhelming, the anxiety is too much for the ego, and we overuse defense mechanisms. If this is the case, our behaviors may turn inappropriate or unhealthy (Cramer, 2000, 2008; Tallandini & Caudek, 2010).

Freud's Stages of Development

LO 4   Summarize Freud's use of psychosexual stages to explain personality.

Freud's structural and topographical models of the mind provide frameworks for studying personality, but he didn't stop there. Freud (1905/1953) also conceived a *developmental* model to explain how personality is formed through experiences in childhood, with a special emphasis on sexuality. The development of sexuality and personality follows a fairly standard path through what Freud termed the **psychosexual stages,** which all children experience as they mature into adulthood (**Table 10.2**). The sexual energy of the id is a force behind this development, and because children are sexual beings starting from birth, this indicates a strong biological component to personality development. Associated with each of the psychosexual stages is a specific *erogenous zone,* or area of the body that when stimulated provides more sexual pleasure than other areas of the body.

If the idea of a preschooler getting sexual pleasure from a body part makes you uncomfortable, then you can relate to the child's feeling of conflict between pleasurable sexual feelings and the restrictions and potential disapproval of caregivers. Along with each psychosexual stage comes a conflict that must be successfully resolved in order for an individual to become a well-adjusted adult. If these conflicts are not suitably addressed, one may suffer from a **fixation** and get stuck in that particular stage, unable to progress smoothly through the remaining stages. Freud believed that fixation at a psychosexual stage during the first 5 to 6 years of life can dramatically influence an adult's personality. Let's look at each stage, its erogenous zone, conflicts, and some consequences of fixation.

TABLE 10.2   FREUD'S PSYCHOSEXUAL STAGES

Stage	Age	Erogenous Zone	Focus	Types of Conflict	Results of Fixation
Oral	Birth–1½ years	Mouth	Sucking, chewing, and gumming	Weaning	Smoking, drinking, nail biting, talking more than usual
Anal	1½–3 years	Anus	Eliminating bodily waste and controlling bodily functions responsible for this process	Toilet training	Rule-bound, stingy, chaotic, destructive
Phallic	3–6 years	Genitals	Sexual feelings and awareness of self	Autoeroticism	Promiscuity, flirtation, vanity, or overdependence, and a focus on masturbation
Latency Period	6 years–puberty	Period during which children develop mentally, socially, and physically			
Genital	Puberty and beyond	Genitals	Reawakening of sexuality, with focus on relationships	Sexuality and aggression	Inability to thrive in adult activities such as work and love

According to Freud, psychological and sexual development proceeds through distinct stages. Each stage is characterized by a certain pleasure area, or "erogenous zone," and a conflict that must be resolved. If resolution is not achieved, the person may develop a problematic "fixation."

THE ORAL STAGE   The *oral stage* is the first psychosexual stage, beginning at birth and lasting until the infant is 1 to 1.5 years old. As its name suggests, the erogenous zone for this stage is the mouth. During this period, the infant gets his greatest pleasure from sucking, chewing, and gumming. According to Freud, the conflict during this stage generally centers on weaning. Infants must stop nursing or using a bottle or pacifier, and the timing of this weaning often is decided by the caregiver. Here is a possible conflict: The infant wants to continue using the bottle because it is a pleasurable activity, but his parent believes he is old enough to switch to a cup. How the caregiver handles this conflict can have long-term consequences for personality development. Freud suggested that certain behavior patterns and personality traits are associated with an oral fixation, including smoking, nail biting, and excessive talking and alcohol consumption.

Oral Fixation
The average baby (birth to 18 months) spends 108 minutes per day sucking on a pacifier and another 33 minutes mouthing other objects (Juberg, Alfano, Coughlin, & Thompson, 2001). Freud identified this phase of life with the oral stage of psychosexual development.
BSIP SA/Alamy

THE ANAL STAGE   Following the oral stage, a child enters the *anal stage,* which lasts approximately until the age of 3. During this stage, the erogenous zone is the anus, and pleasure is derived from eliminating bodily waste as well as learning to control the body parts responsible for this process. The conflict during this stage centers on toilet training: The parents want their child to control her waste elimination in a socially acceptable way, but the child is not necessarily on board with this new procedure for doing so. Once again, how caregivers deal with this learning task may have long-term implications for personality. Freud suggested that toilet training can set the stage for power struggles between child and adult; the child ultimately will gain control over her bodily functions, and then she can use this control to manipulate caregivers (not always "going" at the appropriate time and place). If a parent is too harsh about toilet training (growing angry when there are accidents, forcing a child to sit on the toilet until she goes) or too lenient (making excuses for accidents, not really encouraging the child to learn control), the child might grow up with an *anal-retentive* personality (rule-bound, stingy) or an *anal-expulsive* personality (chaotic, destructive).

PHALLIC STAGE   Age 3 to 6 marks the *phallic stage* (*phallus* means "penis" in Latin, and as you will see, Freud's original theory of development is somewhat male-centered). During this period, the erogenous zone is the genitals, and many children begin to discover that self-stimulation is pleasurable. Freud (1923/1960) assigned special importance to the conflict that occurs in the phallic stage.

During this time, little boys develop a desire to replace their fathers. These feelings are normal, according to Freud, but they lead to boys becoming jealous of their fathers, who are now considered rivals for their mothers' affection. This pattern, referred to as the **Oedipus complex** (e-də-pəs), is named for a character in a complicated Greek myth. Oedipus was abandoned by his parents when he was a newborn, so he did not know their identities. As an adult, he unknowingly married his mother and killed his father. Freud named the Oedipus complex after this Greek tragedy, as it mirrors how boys behave and feel during the phallic stage. Freud believed that when a little boy becomes aware of his attraction to his mother, he realizes his father is a formidable rival and experiences jealousy and anger toward him. He also begins to fear his father, who is so powerful, and worry that his father might punish him. Specifically, he fears that his father will castrate him (Freud, 1917/1966). In order to reduce the tension, the boy must identify with and behave like his father, a process known as *identification.* This defense mechanism resolves the Oedipus complex by allowing the boy to take on or internalize the behaviors, gestures, morals, and standards of his father. Freud proposed that the fear of castration causes a great deal of anxiety, but with successful resolution of the Oedipus complex, this anxiety is repressed. The boy realizes that sexual affection should only be between his father and mother, and the incest taboo develops.

psychosexual stages According to Freud, the stages of development, from birth to adulthood, each of which has an erogenous zone as well as a conflict that must be dealt with.

fixation Being stuck in a particular psychosexual stage of development as a result of unsuccessfully dealing with the conflict of that stage.

Oedipus complex (e-də-pəs) According to Freud, the attraction a child feels toward the opposite-sex parent, along with the resentment or envy directed toward the same-sex parent.

Just Like Dad
Young boys often look up to their fathers and strive to be like them. Freud believed this is the way boys resolve the Oedipus complex. Unable to displace his powerful father, the son stops trying to compete and begins to identify with him. Jose Luis Pelaez/Getty Images

Who Is Anna O.?
Anna O. was the alias for Bertha Pappenheim (1859–1936), whose case study appears in the 1895 book *Studies on Hysteria* by Josef Breuer and Sigmund Freud. Although Anna O. inspired Freud's psychoanalytic theory, the facts of her case remain foggy. What type of disorder did she have, and did psychoanalytic methods really help her? Answers to these questions are still up in the air (Hurst, 1982).
Mary Evans/Sigmund Freud Copyrights/
The Image Works

Freud (1923/1960) believed that little girls experience a different conflict, which others refer to as the *Electra complex.* Little girls feel an attraction to their fathers, and become jealous and angry toward their mothers. Around the same time, they realize that they do not have a penis. This leads to feelings of loss and jealousy, known as *penis envy.* The girl responds with anger, blaming her mother for her missing penis. Realizing she can't have her father, she begins to act like her mother as a result of the process of *identification.* She takes on her mother's behaviors, gestures, morals, and standards. Freud's theory of female development is now regarded as a product of its historical and social context, as opposed to objective observation.

If children do not resolve the sexual conflicts that arise during the phallic stage, they develop a fixation, which can lead to promiscuity, flirtation, vanity, overdependence, bravado, and an increased focus on masturbation.

LATENCY PERIOD Freud proposed that from 6 years old to puberty, children remain in a *latency period* (not a "stage" according to Freud's definition, as there is no erogenous zone, conflict, or fixation). During this time, psychosexual development slows. Where does the child's sexual energy go during this period? According to Freud, it is repressed: Although children develop mentally, socially, and physically, their sexual development is on hold. This idea seems to be supported by the fact that most prepubertal children tend to gravitate toward same-sex friends and playmates.

GENITAL STAGE Following the calm of the latency period, a child's psychosexual development picks up speed again. The *genital stage* begins at puberty and is the final stage of psychosexual development. During this time, there is a reawakening of sexuality. The erogenous zone is centered on the genitals, but now in association with relationships, as opposed to autoeroticism or masturbation. Adolescents become interested in partners, whereas earlier their focus was family members. This is a time when one resolves the Oedipus or Electra complex and often becomes attracted to partners who resemble the opposite-sex parent, according to Freud (1905/1953). Because of the ever-present *id* and its requirement for satisfaction, there still are unconscious conflicts to be addressed, including the continual battle against hidden sexual and aggressive urges. The resolution of these conflicts impacts the types of relationships we seek and cultivate. If earlier conflicts are put to rest, then it is possible to thrive in adult activities such as work and love.

An Appraisal of Psychoanalytic Theory

Freud's psychoanalytic theory has been the subject of much criticism (Bornstein, 2005). Some of Freud's own followers (a few of whom we will discuss shortly) recognized several key weaknesses. For example, psychoanalysis does not take into account the possibility that people can change; we are not predestined to develop certain personality types simply because we had specific experiences in childhood. Thus, psychoanalysis ignores the importance of current development. Critics also contend that Freud placed too much weight on the unconscious forces guiding behavior, instead proposing that we can be conscious of our motivations and change our behaviors. Finally, many have objected to Freud's emphasis on sexuality and its role in personality development.

Given the amount of attention Freud's concepts have received, one might expect there is a great deal of research supporting or refuting aspects of his theory. But where would a researcher start? For example, how would you go about designing an experiment to test whether early weaning causes later problems in relationships? How about persuading an ethics committee to approve a study with an independent variable that manipulates toilet training? Given these types of difficulties, it is no surprise there is limited published research on Freudian concepts.

Another serious concern is that much of Freud's theory is based on a biased, nonrepresentative sample (a handful of middle- and upper-class Viennese women and Freud himself), although more recent research attempts to address this issue (Shedler, 2010). Many feminists have raised concerns about Freud's one-sided male perspective, though not necessarily dismissing the potential usefulness of psychoanalysis to women (Young-Bruehl, 2009).

TANK'S ONGOING TROUBLES Let's return to the fictitious backstory of Tank the Roboceptionist. After being kicked to the curb by his father, Tank got a job with the CIA. This ended in another great failure. The agency shipped Tank to Afghanistan to fight in the war against terror, but his performance was so poor that he was sent home. As luck had it, Carnegie Mellon University was looking to hire a new roboceptionist around this time. Valerie, the robot who occupied the post, was leaving to pursue her longtime dream of touring with a Barbra Streisand cover band. Tank accepted the roboceptionist position, which he has held since 2005 (Carnegie Mellon University, 2013).

Tank's story is the intelligent invention of playwrights, but its basic themes are familiar to many. Parents often make the mistake of developing unrealistic expectations for their children, potentially setting them up for failure. In the imaginary storyline, Tank's father longed for him to replace the Hubble Space Telescope, but did he ever ask Tank what *he* wanted out of life?

According to Freud, personality is largely shaped by early childhood experiences and sexual impulses. But some of the most defining experiences in Tank's life—like being abandoned by his father and bungling his mission with the CIA—occurred later in life and had nothing to do with sex. Some personality theorists might argue that these types of nonsexual experiences are important factors in the development of personality. We now turn to the neo-Freudians, who agree with Freud on many points, but depart from his intense emphasis on early childhood experiences, aggression, and sexuality.

The Neo-Freudians

LO 5   Explain how the neo-Freudians' theories of personality differ from Freud's.

Not surprisingly, Freud's psychoanalytic theory was quite controversial, but he did have a following of students who adapted some of the main aspects of his theory. Some who disagreed with Freud on key points broke away to develop their own theories; they are often referred to as neo-Freudians (*neo* = "new").

ALFRED ADLER   One of the first followers to forge his own path was Alfred Adler (1870–1937), whose own theory conflicted with the Freudian notion that personality is, to a large degree, shaped by unconscious motivators. As Adler saw it, humans are not just pleasure seekers, but conscious and intentional in their behaviors. We are motivated by the need to feel superior—to grow, overcome challenges, and strive for perfection. This drive originates during childhood, when we realize that we are dependent on and inferior to adults. Whether imagined or real, our sense of inferiority pushes us to compensate, so we cultivate our special gifts and skills. This attempt to balance perceived weaknesses with strengths is not a sign of abnormality, but a natural response.

Adler's theory of *individual psychology* focuses on each person's unique struggle with feelings of inferiority. Unfortunately, not everyone is successful in overcoming feelings of helplessness and dependence, but instead may develop what is known as an *inferiority complex* (Adler, 1927/1994). Someone with an inferiority complex feels incompetent, vulnerable, and powerless, and cannot achieve his full potential.

CONNECTIONS

In **Chapter 1,** we introduced the *case study,* a form of *descriptive research.* A major weakness of the case study is its failure to provide a *representative sample,* or sample whose characteristics reflect the population. Freud's case studies focused on a particular subgroup, thus his findings might not be generalizable.

CONNECTIONS

Although he considered himself a "loyal Freudian," Erik Erikson took Freud's ideas in a new direction (Schultz & Schultz, 2013). As noted in **Chapter 8,** Erikson suggested psychosocial development occurs throughout life, with eight stages marked by a conflict between the individual's needs and society's expectations.

An Individual Psychology
Alfred Adler studied with Freud but ultimately broke from his teacher and created his own theory. According to Adler, personality is strongly influenced by the drive to conquer feelings of inferiority. Failure to succeed at this endeavor paves the way for an inferiority complex. Imagno/Getty Images

Based on what you know about Tank, would you say he has been programmed to resemble someone who suffers from an inferiority complex?

Perhaps you can imagine how feelings of inferiority might arise in sibling relationships. The firstborn child receives all his parents' attention for the first years of life. Then along comes a baby brother or sister, and suddenly mom and dad must divide their attention. How might this affect the older child's sense of worth? Younger siblings have their own reasons for feeling inferior. They are, after all, the newcomers, smaller and less developed than their older siblings. And unlike the firstborn, who enjoyed being an only child for some time, younger siblings never had that special alone time with mom and dad. They always had to share their parents' love.

Adler was one of the first to theorize about the psychological repercussions of birth order. He believed that firstborn children experience different environmental pressures than youngest and middle children, and these pressures can set the stage for the development of certain personality traits (Ansbacher & Ansbacher, 1956).

CONTROVERSIES

How Birth Order May—or May Not—Affect Your Personality

➡️⬅️ Firstborns are conscientious and high achieving. They play by the rules, excel in school, and become leaders in the workforce. The youngest children, favored and coddled by their parents, grow up to be gregarious and rebellious. Middle children tend to get lost in the shuffle, but they learn to be self-sufficient.

Have you heard these stereotypes about birth order and personality? How well do they match your personal experience, and do you think they are valid?

Famous Firstborn
Oprah Winfrey has many of the stereotypical qualities of a firstborn child. She is ambitious, successful, and seems to be a natural leader. But her example also highlights some of the problems with making generalizations about birth order and personality. Studies on birth order focus on full-blood siblings, yet Winfrey had two half-siblings growing up, and discovered a third half-sibling in 2010 (Allen, 2011, January 24). Gallo Images/Sunday Times/Kevin Sutherland

If you search the scientific literature, you will indeed find research supporting such claims. According to one analysis of 200 studies, firstborns (as well as only children) are often accomplished and successful; middle children are sociable but tend to lack a sense of belonging; and last-born children are agreeable and rebellious (Eckstein et al., 2010). You will also find plenty of skepticism regarding such findings (Ernst & Angst, 1983; Hartshorne, 2010).

Researchers have published about 65,000 scientific papers on birth order, but the connection between birth order and personality is still an active area of scholarly debate (Eckstein et al., 2010; Hartshorne, 2010; Hartshorne, Salem-Hartshorne, & Hartshorne, 2009). One of the problems with birth order studies is that they tend to be cluttered with confounding variables. Family size is an example of such a variable (Hartshorne, 2010): We know that firstborn children are high achievers, but firstborns are also more likely to come from smaller families. Just think about it: The chances of being a firstborn are much greater if you come from a family with two children (1 in 2), as opposed to a family with four children (1 in 4). This makes it difficult to determine which variable is driving high achievement—being a firstborn or coming from a small family (Hartshorne, 2010).

CONNECTIONS

In **Chapter 1,** we discussed *confounding variables,* which are a type of *extraneous variable* that changes in sync with an *independent variable* (IV). Here, the IV is birth order, the confounding variable is family size, and the *dependent variable* (DV) is a measure of high achievement. But we don't know if differences in achievement (DV) are due to birth order (IV) or family size (confounding variable).

We cannot resolve this longstanding debate here, but we can lighten the discussion with some interesting bits of information: Oprah Winfrey was a first child, as were most American presidents (Neal, 2002, June 10). Jim Carrey and Jennifer Lawrence are the youngest of their siblings, while Jennifer Lopez, Bill Gates, and Peyton Manning are middle children (IMDB, 2015; Jones, 2014, August 12; Zupec, 2008, October 22). Given what you know about these famous people, are these revelations what you would expect? ➡️⬅️

MIDDLE CHILDREN TEND TO GET LOST IN THE SHUFFLE. . . .

CARL GUSTAV JUNG   Carl Gustav Jung (yuˈŋ; 1875–1961) was another influential neo-Freudian. Jung's focus was on growth and self-understanding. Although he agreed with Freud about the importance of the unconscious, in his *analytic psychology* he placed less emphasis on biological urges (sex and aggression), proposing more positive and spiritual aspects of human nature. Critical of Freud's overemphasis on the sex drive, Jung claimed that Freud viewed the brain as "an appendage to the genital glands" (Westen et al., 2008, p. 66). Jung (1969) proposed we are driven by psychological energy (not sexual energy) that promotes growth, insight, and balance. He also believed personality development is not limited to childhood; adults continue to evolve throughout life.

Jung also differed from Freud in his view of the unconscious. Jung believed personality is made up of the ego (at the conscious level), a *personal unconscious,* and a *collective unconscious.* The personal unconscious is akin to Freud's notion of the preconscious and the unconscious mind; items from the personal unconscious range from easily retrievable memories to anxiety-provoking repressed memories. The **collective unconscious,** according to Jung, holds the universal experiences of humankind passed from genera-

tion to generation, memories that are not easily retrieved without some degree of effort or interpretation. We inherit a variety of primal images, patterns of thought, and storylines. The themes of these **archetypes** (är-ki-tīps) may be found in art, literature, music, dreams, and religions across time, geography, and culture. Some of the consistent archetypes include the nurturing mother, powerful father, innocent child, and brave hero. Archetypes provide a blueprint for us as we respond to situations, objects, and people in our environments (Jung, 1969). The *anima* refers to the part of our personality that is feminine, and the *animus* to that which is

masculine. Jung believed both of these parts exist in everyone's personality, and we must acknowledge and appreciate them. Failure to accept the anima and animus can result in an imbalance, which prevents us from being whole.

KAREN HORNEY   Karen Horney (hoˈr-ˌnī; 1885–1952) was a neo-Freudian who emphasized the role of relationships between children and their caregivers, not erogenous zones and psychosexual stages. She believed individuals respond to feelings of helplessness and isolation created by inadequate parenting, which she referred to as *basic anxiety* (Horney, 1945). In order to deal with this anxiety, Horney suggested that people use three strategies: moving toward people (looking for affection and acceptance), moving away from people (looking for isolation and self-sufficiency), or moving against people (looking to control others). Horney believed that a balance of these three strategies is important for psychological stability. She was also a committed critic of Freud's sexist approach to the female psyche, pointing out that women are not jealous of the penis itself, but rather what it represents in terms of power and status in society. Horney (1926/1967) also proposed that boys and men can envy women's ability to bear and breast-feed children.

Freud's Legacy

Freud's psychoanalytic theory was groundbreaking and controversial, and it led to a variety of extensions and permutations through neo-Freudians such as Adler, Jung, Horney, and Erikson. Freud's theories are considered among the most important in the field of personality development. He courageously called attention to the

Timeless Heroines
Jennifer Lawrence (left) plays the role of Katniss Everdeen in the 2012 film *The Hunger Games.* Her strength, bravery, and charisma resemble that of 15th-century French heroine Joan of Arc, portrayed in the poster (right). These heroines have the qualities of a Jungian archetype; the thoughts and feelings they evoke are relatively consistent across time and culture. left: Lionsgate/The Kobal Collection; right: V&A Images, London/Art Resource

collective unconscious According to Jung, the universal experiences of humankind passed from generation to generation, including memories.

archetypes (är-ki-tīps) Primal images, patterns of thoughts, and storylines stored in the collective unconscious, with themes that may be found in art, literature, music, dreams, and religions.

existence of infant sexuality at a time when sex was a forbidden topic of conversation. He recognized the importance of infancy and early childhood in the unfolding of personality, and appreciated the universal stages of human development. It was a blow to our collective self-esteem to realize that so much of our thinking occurs without conscious awareness, but this notion has been widely accepted, even among psychologists who are not Freudians or are neo-Freudians. Some suggest Freud's work has "become so pervasive in Western thinking that he is to be ranked with Darwin and Marx for introducing new—and often disturbing—modes of thought in Western culture" (Hilgard, 1987, p. 99).

✓○○○ show what you know

1. According to Freud, all children go through _____ stages as they mature into adulthood. If conflicts are not successfully resolved along the way, a child may suffer from a _____ .

2. Freud's _____ includes three levels: conscious, preconscious, and unconscious.
   a. structural model of the mind
   b. developmental model
   c. individual psychology
   d. topographical model of the mind

3. Jung believed personality is made up of the ego, a personal unconscious, and the:
   a. id.
   b. collective unconscious.
   c. superego.
   d. preconscious.

4. How did the theories of the neo-Freudians differ from Freud's psychoanalytic theory in regard to personality development?

✓ CHECK YOUR ANSWERS IN APPENDIX C.

Humanistic, Learning, and Trait Theories

We have thus far discussed the psychoanalytic theories of personality development, which emphasize the importance of factors beyond one's control. You don't get to choose the identity of your parents, the dynamics within your family, or the nature of your childhood conflicts. Nor do you have the ability to direct unconscious activities. If you're looking for a perspective that emphasizes greater control and self-direction, humanism is a good alternative. According to this approach, the power is in your hands.

The Brighter Side: Maslow and Rogers

The humanistic perspective began gaining momentum in the 1960s and 1970s in response to the negative, mechanistic view of human nature apparent in other theories. According to the humanists, not only are we innately good, we are also in control of our destinies, and these positive aspects of human nature drive the development of personality. According to leading humanists Abraham Maslow and Carl Rogers, our natural tendency is to grow in a positive direction.

LO 6 Summarize Maslow's hierarchy of needs, and describe self-actualizers.

MASLOW AND PERSONALITY Abraham Maslow (1908–1970) is probably best-known for his theory of motivation. According to Maslow, human behaviors are motivated by biological and psychological needs. When a need is not being met, a state of tension motivates us to meet it, and this causes the tension to diminish. Maslow's hierarchy of needs explains the organization of human needs, which are universal and ordered in terms of their strength (from basic physiological needs to self-actualization and self-transcendence). How does this relate to personality? If you recall, personality is the unique core set of characteristics that influence the way we think, act, and feel. Although we tend to respond to needs in a universal order, Maslow suggested that we all have the ability to reorder them. Maslow was

CONNECTIONS

The *behaviorists*, presented in **Chapter 1** and **Chapter 5**, suggested that our behaviors are shaped by factors in the environment. Because of this, we are at the mercy of forces beyond our control. The humanists challenged this position.

Maslow's hierarchy of needs was introduced in **Chapter 9**, in reference to motivation. According to Maslow, behaviors are motivated by needs. If a basic need is not being met, we are less likely to meet needs higher in the hierarchy. Here, we see how Maslow's hierarchy can be used to understand personality.

Apply This

TABLE 10.3   ARE YOU A SELF-ACTUALIZER?

Tendencies	Characteristics	Examples
Realistic perceptions of reality	Nonjudgmental, objective, and acutely aware of others	An individual who is empathetic and unbiased
Acceptance of self, others, and nature	Has patience with weaknesses of self, others, and society	Someone who is forgiving and accepting of others
Spontaneity and creativeness	Original, flexible, and willing to learn from mistakes	Someone who is self-sufficient and lives in unconventional ways
Independent and private	Not reliant on others, enjoys time alone	A person with a strong sense of self who doesn't conform to peer pressure
Freshness of appreciation	Views each experience as if it was the first time (e.g., sunrise), is grateful for what he has	An individual who lives life thankful for each day
Peak experiences	Has moments of ecstasy and transcendence	A highly spiritual individual who experiences intense happiness in day-to-day activities
Social interest and fellowship	Empathic and sympathetic toward others	A person who is devoted to helping others
Profound interpersonal relations	Maintains deep and lasting friendships	Someone with intense, lifelong friendships
A democratic character structure	Tolerant and accepting of others	A person who is open-minded and humble
Autonomous and resistant to enculturation	Independent and free from cultural pressures	An individual who is self-sufficient in thought and behavior and resists social pressure

According to Maslow, a "self-actualizer" is someone who continually strives to achieve his maximum potential. Listed here are common traits and examples of self-actualizers. Perhaps some of these qualities characterize you.

particularly interested in *self-actualizers,* or people who are continually seeking to reach their fullest potential, one of the guiding principles of the humanistic perspective. Have a look at some of the attributes of self-actualizers presented in **Table 10.3.** Do you see any of them in yourself?

Reaching High
Pope Francis greets residents of the Varginha shantytown in Rio de Janeiro, Brazil. The leader of the Catholic Church is known for his humility and commitment to helping the poor. He is the type of person Maslow might have called a "self-actualizer," or one who strives to achieve his full potential.
AP Photo/L'Osservatore Romano

Conditional Love?
Amy Chua poses with her daughters at home in New Haven, Connecticut. This Yale law professor is best-known for writing *Battle Hymn of the Tiger Mother,* a book about cross-cultural parenting differences. Chua never allowed her children to participate in play dates, select their after-school activities, or receive any grade lower than an A. When one daughter behaved "extremely disrespectfully," Chua called her "garbage" (Chua, 2011, January 8). This type of response lacks what Rogers called unconditional positive regard, or total acceptance of a child regardless of her behavior. Erin Patrice O'Brien

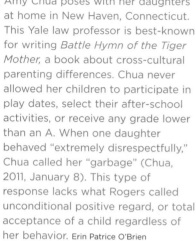

ROGERS AND PERSONALITY   Carl Rogers (1902–1987) was another humanist who had great faith in the essential goodness of people and their ability to make sound choices (Rogers, 1979). According to Rogers, we all have an innate urge to move toward situations and people that will help us grow and to avoid those with the potential to inhibit growth. He believed we should trust our ability to find happiness and mental balance, that is, to be *fully functioning,* and strive to really experience life, not just be passive participants. At the same time, we must also be sensitive to the needs of others.

Rogers highlighted the importance of **self-concept,** which refers to a person's knowledge of her own strengths, abilities, behavior patterns, and temperament. Problems arise when a person's self-concept is *incongruent* with, or does not correspond to, her experiences in the world (Rogers, 1959). If a woman believes she is kind and sociable but fails to get along with most people in her life, this incongruence will produce tension and confusion. Rogers also proposed that people often develop an **ideal self,** which is the *self-concept* a person fervently strives to achieve. Problems arise when the ideal self is unattainable or incongruent with one's self-concept, a topic we will discuss further in Chapter 13 (Rogers, 1959).

Like Freud, Rogers believed caregivers play a vital role in the development of personality and self-concept. Ideally, caregivers should show **unconditional positive regard,** or total acceptance of a child regardless of her behavior. According to Rogers, people need to feel totally accepted and valued for who they are, not what they do. Caregivers who place too much emphasis on rules, morals, and values, ignoring a child's innate goodness, can cause the child to experience *conditions of worth.* When our behaviors are judged to be bad or wrong, we feel unworthy, so we may try to please others by hiding or repressing these "unacceptable" behaviors and emotions. Seeking approval from others, we deny our true selves, and anxiety is ever-present in our lives. As caregivers, it is important to show children that we value them all the time, not just when they obey us and act the way we want them to. Of course, children behave in ways we dislike; but parents should love their children unconditionally, because it is the behavior that is unacceptable, not the child.

An Appraisal of the Humanistic Theories

Let's step back and review the potential weaknesses of the humanistic approach. For humanistic and psychoanalytic theories alike, creating operational definitions can be challenging. How can you use the experimental method to test a subjective approach whose concepts are open to interpretation (Schultz & Schultz, 2013)? Imagine submitting a research proposal that included two randomly assigned groups of children: one group whose parents were instructed to show them *unconditional positive regard* and the other group whose parents were told to instill *conditions of worth.* The proposal would never amount to a real study, not only because it raises ethical issues, but also because it would be impossible to control the experimental conditions. Another problem with unconditional positive regard in particular is that constantly praising, attempting to boost self-esteem, and withholding criticism can be counterproductive. In some cases, we run the risk of "fostering narcissism," or another unproductive characteristic of elevated self-esteem such as aggression (Baumeister, Campbell,

self-concept The knowledge an individual has about his strengths, abilities, behavior patterns, and temperament.

ideal self The self-concept a person strives for and fervently wishes to achieve.

unconditional positive regard According to Rogers, the total acceptance or valuing of a person, regardless of behavior.

Krueger, & Vohs, 2003). Finally, humanism almost completely ignores the negative aspects of human nature evident in war, greed, abuse, and aggression (Burger, 2011). And while it is important to recognize that humans have great potential to grow and move forward, we should not discount the developmental impact of early experiences. In spite of these weaknesses, the humanistic perspective has led to a less negative and more balanced view of human nature, influencing approaches to parenting, education, and psychotherapy. Its legacy is alive and well in the emerging field of positive psychology.

Learning and Social-Cognitive Theories

ROBOTS CAN LEARN, TOO   Tank the Roboceptionist is very good at what he does (providing room numbers, directions, weather forecasts, and so on), and he can respond to a range of unexpected remarks and questions in character with his persona. Say "I love you," and he will shoot back with something like, "That's nice, but you don't even know me." Assault his keyboard with offensive remarks such as "I hate you!" and "@#?! you!" and he will tell you that you are not being very nice. But Tank's persona and everything he says are predetermined by the human beings who created him. Imagine if Tank could craft his own witty responses from scratch. And wouldn't it be something if he could learn from his environment and independently develop new skills?

It turns out that robots can "learn" to some degree. For example, researchers have fashioned robots that can take a collection of objects and categorize them according to the sounds they make when shaken, dropped, or manipulated in other ways (Smith, 2009, March 23). HERB (the Home Exploring Robot Butler) can learn to find his way through messy rooms (Srinivasa et al., 2009). There are also robots that demonstrate observational learning, imitating simple human behaviors like head movements and hand gestures (Breazeal & Scassellati, 2002).

One very popular area of robot research is "reinforcement learning," according to Dr. Simmons. Here's a hypothetical example of how it might work. Researchers program a robot to have some goal, such as exiting a room. The robot begins the task by randomly moving around (not unlike Thorndike's cats from Chapter 5), but eventually it will come upon a path that leads to an exit. Upon leaving the room, the robot gets a signal indicating that the behavior should be repeated. With continued reinforcement through signals received for correct behavior, the robot tends to make fewer errors and reaches the exit more quickly. Over time, its average performance improves. But like most robot-learning feats accomplished thus far, leaving a room is far from an expression of personality.

With improvements in technology and computer programming, is it possible that robots might one day be capable of possessing personality? If you asked a follower of Freud, we suspect the answer would be a forceful "no." Robots do not have unresolved conflicts from childhood; in fact, they don't even have childhoods (remember, the story of Tank is just a human invention). A robot cannot dream, feel sexual urges, or repress unwanted thoughts. Ask a strict behaviorist if robots of the future might be capable of having personality, and you might get a very different answer. ⬒

CONNECTIONS

In **Chapter 1,** we described positive psychology as a relatively new approach. The humanists' optimism struck the right chord with many psychologists, who wondered why the field was not focusing on human strengths and virtues.

You Asked, Dr. Simmons Answers

http://qrs.ly/tu4qse8

Is Tank capable of learning new tasks?

Rock, Scissors, Paper
A student at the Edinburgh International Science Festival interacts with a robot that is capable of developing game strategies. This robot is engaging the student in "rock-scissors-paper." Who won this round? Press Association via AP Images

CONNECTIONS

In **Chapter 5,** we described *operant conditioning,* the type of learning that occurs when we make connections between behaviors and their consequences. The robot's exiting is followed by a signal, which serves as a *reinforcer.* But unlike Thorndike's cats, the robot cannot experience "pleasurable" outcomes. It is programmed to respond to outcomes in a predetermined way.

LO 8   Use learning theories to explain personality development.

Behaviorists like B. F. Skinner were not interested in studying the thoughts and emotions typically equated with expressions of personality. They focused on measuring observable behaviors that they believed resulted from learning processes such as classical conditioning, operant conditioning, and observational learning. From this perspective, personality is a collection of behaviors, all of which have been shaped through a lifetime of learning.

Let's look at an example. Think of a friend or classmate who is very outgoing. A behaviorist would suggest she has been consistently reinforced to act this way. She gets positive attention, perhaps a promotion at work, and is surrounded by many friends, all of which reinforce her outgoing behavior. This characteristic, which psychologists might call "extraversion," is just one of the many dimensions of personality molded by learning. Now apply the behaviorist principle to robots. Learning is the foundation for personality, and robots are capable of learning. Looking at things from this perspective, it seems plausible that robots could develop rudimentary personalities.

Like any theory of personality, behaviorism has limitations. Critics contend that behaviorism essentially ignores anything that is not directly observable and thus portrays humans too simplistically, as passive and unaware of what is going on in their internal and external environments. Julian Rotter (1916–2014) is one of the early social learning theorists who countered these weaknesses, suggesting that not all aspects of behavior and personality can be directly observed (Rotter, 1990). He proposed several important cognitive aspects of personality, including *locus of control* and *expectancy*.

LO 9   Summarize Rotter's view of personality.

ROTTER AND PERSONALITY   According to Rotter, a key component of personality is locus of control, a pattern of beliefs about where control or responsibility for outcomes resides. If a person has an *internal* locus of control, she believes that the causes of her life events generally reside within her, and that she has some control over them. For example, such a person would say that her career success depends on how hard she works, not on luck (Rotter, 1966). Someone with an *external* locus of control believes that causes for outcomes reside outside of him; he assigns great importance to luck, fate, and other features of the environment, over which he has little control. As this person sees it, getting a job occurs when all the circumstances are right and luck is on his side (Rotter, 1966). A person's locus of control refers to beliefs about the self, not about others.

Rotter also explored how behaviors are influenced by thoughts about the future. **Expectancy** refers to the predictions we make about the outcomes and consequences of our behaviors (**Infographic 10.2**). A woman who is considering whether she should confront the manager of a restaurant over a bad meal will decide her next move based on her expectancy: Does she expect to be thrown out the door, or does she believe it will lead to a free meal? In these situations, there is an interaction among expectancies, behaviors, and environmental factors.

LO 10   Discuss how Bandura uses the social-cognitive perspective to explain personality.

BANDURA AND PERSONALITY   Another early critic of the behaviorist approach was Albert Bandura (1925–). Bandura rejected the notion that psychologists should only focus on observable behavior, and recognized the importance of cognition, reinforcers, and environmental factors (Bandura, 2006). This **social-cognitive perspective** suggests that personality results from patterns of thinking (cognitive) as well as relationships and other factors in the environment (social). Prior experiences

expectancy A person's predictions about the consequences or outcomes of behavior.

social-cognitive perspective Suggests that personality results from patterns of thinking (cognitive) as well as relationships and other environmental factors (social).

The Social-Cognitive Perspective on Personality

Social-cognitive theorists rejected behaviorists' exclusive focus on observable behavior. Acknowledging that personality may be shaped through learning, social-cognitive theorists such as Albert Bandura also emphasized the roles of cognitions and environmental influences on behavior. Bandura's theory of reciprocal determinism shows how cognition, behaviors, and the environment all interact to determine our personality.

"Good job!"

Child is praised for reading quietly.

Child receives attention for effort in school.

Child is rewarded for school achievement.

Behaviorists believe personality is the compilation of behaviors shaped through a lifetime of learning. A child who receives reinforcement for studying and effort in school will repeat this behavior, eventually exhibiting the personality characteristic "studious."

cognition

Thinking about behaviors and what they have led to in the past creates expectancies, predictions about what future outcomes will result from a behavior. When we recognize that past efforts to study usually resulted in good grades, we will expect that studying will lead to good grades in the future. Bandura calls this learned expectation of success *self-efficacy*.

I succeed because I am a studious person.

I will apply to college because I can succeed there.

I get good grades when I study, so I will continue to do this.

I am in college, so I know I can handle a busy schedule like other college students.

EXPECTANCIES INFLUENCE BEHAVIOR.

ENVIRONMENT INFLUENCES EXPECTANCIES.

EXPECTANCIES INFLUENCE THE ENVIRONMENT YOU SEEK OUT.

When I study, I get good grades.

PRIOR EXPERIENCES CREATE EXPECTANCIES.

environment

I'm a college student now, so I need to spend more time studying.

behavior

Reinforced behaviors become more consistent over time. When an instructor praises our participation in class, that reinforcement will lead us to participate again. We also learn by observing others' behaviors. If our classmates form a study group that helps them better understand the material, we may learn to adopt that technique.

ENVIRONMENT INFLUENCES BEHAVIOR.

BEHAVIOR INFLUENCES ENVIRONMENT.

The environment can include the college you choose, the major you select, the classes you enroll in, and also the culture where you are a student. For example, in Chinese classrooms, struggle is assumed to be part of the learning process. However, in Western classrooms, struggle is often seen as a sign of lower ability (Li, 2005; Schleppenbach, Flevares, Sims, & Perry, 2007). The culture you live in—your environment—can influence how you think about your own skills and behaviors, and how hard you work at something that is difficult for you.

I study hard and am a successful student, so I've chosen to go to college.

It's a Social-Cognitive Thing
Psychologist Albert Bandura
asserts that personality is molded
by a continual interaction
between cognitions and
social interactions, including
observations of other people's
behaviors. His approach is
known as the *social-cognitive
perspective.* Jon Brenneis/Life
Magazine/Time & Life Pictures

have shaped, and will continue to shape, your personality. Cognitive abilities, including knowledge, are partly the result of our interactions with others (Bandura, 1977a, 2006). We don't spend much time in isolation; in fact, almost everything we do involves some sort of collaboration. We are social creatures who work together and live in family units.

Bandura also pointed to the importance of **self-efficacy,** which refers to beliefs about our ability and effectiveness in reaching goals (Bandura, 1977b, 2001). People who exhibit high self-efficacy often achieve greater success at work because they are more likely to be flexible and open to new ideas (Bandura, 2006). A person who demonstrates low self-efficacy generally believes he will not succeed in a particular situation, regardless of his abilities or experience. Beliefs about self-efficacy are influenced by experience and may change across situations. Generally speaking, people who believe they can change and progress are more likely to persevere in difficult situations.

Beliefs play a key role in our ability to make decisions, problem solve, and deal with life's challenges. The environment also responds to our behaviors. In essence, we have internal forces (beliefs, expectations) directing our behavior, external forces (reinforcers, punishments) responding to those behaviors, and the behaviors themselves influencing our beliefs and the environment. Beliefs, behavior, and environment form a complex system that determines our behavior patterns and personality (Infographic 10.2 on page 423). Bandura (1978, 1986) refers to this multidirectional interaction as **reciprocal determinism.**

Let's use an example to see how reciprocal determinism works. A student harbors a certain belief about herself (*I am going to graduate with honors*). This belief influences her behavior (she studies hard and reaches out to instructors), which affects her environment (instructors take note of her enthusiasm and offer support). Thus, you can see, personality is the result of an ongoing interaction among cognitions, behaviors, and the environment. Bandura's reciprocal determinism resembles Rotter's view. Both suggest that personality is shaped by an ongoing interplay of cognitive expectancies, behaviors, and environment.

TAKING STOCK   The learning and social-cognitive theorists were among the first to realize that we are not just products of our environments, but dynamic agents capable of altering the environment itself. Their focus on research and testable hypotheses provide a clear advantage over the psychoanalytic and humanistic theories. Some critics argue that these approaches minimize the importance of unconscious processes and emotional influences (Schultz & Schultz, 2013; Westen, 1990), but overall, the inclusion of cognition and social factors offers valuable new ways to study and understand personality.

Trait Theories and Their Biological Basis

You Asked, Dr. Simmons Answers

http://qrs.ly/4q4qseb

How did you decide
what personality traits
and backstory Tank
would have?

A FEW WORDS ABOUT TANK   If you ask Dr. Reid Simmons to come up with some adjectives to describe Tank the Roboceptionist, he will offer words like "conscientious," "agreeable," "reserved," "naïve," "loyal," and "caring." All of these are examples of **traits,** the relatively stable properties that describe elements of personality. The **trait theories** presented here are different from theories discussed earlier in that they focus less on explaining why and how personality develops and more on describing personality and predicting behaviors.

ALLPORT AND PERSONALITY One of the first trait theorists was Gordon Allport (1897–1967), who created a comprehensive list of traits to describe personality. One primary reason for developing this list was to operationalize the terminology used in personality research; when researchers study a topic, they should agree on definitions. If two psychologists are studying a trait called "vivacious," they will have an easier time comparing results if they use the same definition. Allport and his colleague carefully reviewed *Webster's New International Dictionary* (1925) and identified 17,953 words (out of approximately 400,000 entries in the dictionary) that they proposed were "descriptive of personality or personal behavior" (Allport & Odbert, 1936, p. 24). The list contained terms that were considered to be personal traits (such as "acrobatical" and "zealous"), temporary states (such as "woozy" and "thrilled"), social evaluations (such as "swine" and "outlandish"), and words that were metaphorical and doubtful (such as "mortal" and "middle-aged"). Most relevant to personality were the personal traits, of which they identified 4,504—a little over 1% of all the entries in the dictionary. Surely, this long list could be condensed, reduced, or classified to make it more manageable. Enter Raymond Cattell.

CATTELL AND PERSONALITY
Raymond Cattell (1905–1998) proposed grouping the long list of personality traits into two major categories: surface traits and source traits (Cattell, 1950). **Surface traits** are the easily observable personality characteristics we commonly use to describe people: *She is quiet. He is friendly.* **Source traits** are the foundational qualities that give rise to surface traits. For example, "extraversion" is a source trait, and the surface traits it produces may include "warm," "gregarious," and "assertive." There are thousands of surface traits but only a few source traits. Cattell (1950) proposed that source traits are the product of both heredity and environment (nature and nurture), and surface traits are the "combined action of several source traits" (p. 34).

1.	Reserved	⟷	Outgoing
2.	Concrete thinker	⟷	Abstract thinker
3.	Affected by feelings	⟷	Emotionally stable
4.	Submissive	⟷	Dominant
5.	Serious	⟷	Happy-go-lucky
6.	Expedient	⟷	Conscientious
7.	Timid	⟷	Bold
8.	Tough-minded	⟷	Sensitive
9.	Trusting	⟷	Suspicious
10.	Practical	⟷	Imaginative
11.	Forthright	⟷	Shrewd
12.	Self-assured	⟷	Insecure
13.	Conservative	⟷	Experimenting
14.	Group-dependent	⟷	Self-sufficient
15.	Undisciplined	⟷	Controlled
16.	Relaxed	⟷	Tense

FIGURE 10.2

Cattell's 16 Personality Factors

Using this list of 16 source traits, Raymond Cattell produced personality profiles by measuring where people fell between the two opposing ends of the dimension for each trait. Cattell (1973b) and Cattell, Eber, and Tatsuoka (1970).

Cattell also condensed the list of surface traits into a much smaller set of 171. Realizing that some of these surface traits would be correlated, he used a statistical procedure known as *factor analysis* to group them into a smaller set of dimensions according to common underlying properties. With factor analysis, Cattell was able to produce a list of 16 personality factors.

These 16 factors, or personality dimensions, can be considered primary source traits. Looking at **Figure 10.2,** you can see that the ends of the dimensions represent polar extremes. On one end of the first dimension is the reserved and unsocial person; at the other end is the "social butterfly." Based on these factors, Cattell developed the Sixteen Personality Factor Questionnaire (16PF), which is described in greater detail in the upcoming section on objective personality tests.

EYSENCK AND PERSONALITY Hans Eysenck (ahy-sengk) (1916–1997) continued to develop our understanding of source traits, proposing that we could describe personalities using three dimensions: introversion–extraversion (E), neuroticism (N), and psychoticism (P) (**Figure 10.3** on the next page).

CONNECTIONS

In **Chapter 1,** we described a *correlation* as a relationship between two variables. Here, we describe *factor analysis,* which examines the relationships among an entire set of variables.

self-efficacy Beliefs one has regarding how effective one will be in reaching a goal.

reciprocal determinism According to Bandura, multidirectional interactions among cognitions, behaviors, and the environment.

traits The relatively stable properties that describe elements of personality.

trait theories Theories that focus on personality dimensions and their influence on behavior; can be used to predict behaviors.

surface traits Easily observable characteristics that derive from source traits.

source traits Basic underlying or foundational characteristics of personality.

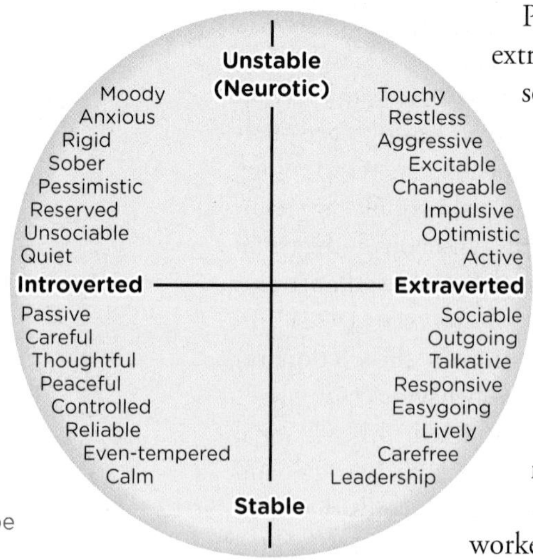

FIGURE 10.3
Eysenck's Dimensions of Personality
Psychologist Hans Eysenck developed a model showing the range of human personality dimensions. This figure displays only the original dimensions Eysenck studied, but years later he proposed an additional dimension: psychoticism. People who score high on the psychoticism trait tend to be impersonal and antisocial. Eysenck and Eysenck (1968).

People high on the *extraversion* end of the introversion–extraversion (E) dimension tend to display a marked degree of sociability and are outgoing and active with others in their environment. Those on the *introversion* end of the dimension tend to be quiet and careful and enjoy time alone. Having high *neuroticism* (N) typically goes hand in hand with being restless, moody, and excitable, while low neuroticism means being calm, reliable, and emotionally stable. A person who is high on the *psychoticism* dimension is likely to be cold, impersonal, and antisocial, whereas someone at the opposite end of this dimension is warm, caring, and empathetic. (The psychoticism dimension is not related to psychosis, which is described in Chapter 12.)

In addition to identifying these dimensions, Eysenck worked diligently to unearth their biological basis. For example, he proposed a direct relationship between the behaviors associated with the introversion–extraversion dimension and the reticular formation (Eysenck, 1967). According to Eysenck (1967, 1990), introverted people display higher reactivity in their reticular formation. With their higher arousal levels, introverts are more likely to react to stimuli, and thus develop patterns of coping with arousal. An introvert may be more careful or restrained, for example. An extravert has lower levels of arousal, and thus is less reactive to stimuli. Extraverts seek stimulation because their arousal levels are low, so they tend to be more impulsive and outgoing.

The trait theories of Allport, Cattell, and Eysenck paved the way for the trait theories commonly used today. Let's take a look at one of the most popular models.

LO 12 **Identify the biological roots of the five-factor model of personality.**

THE BIG FIVE The **five-factor model of personality,** also known as the Big Five, is a current trait approach for explaining personality (McCrae & Costa, 1987). This model, developed using factor analysis, indicates there are five factors, or dimensions, to describe personality. Although there is not 100% agreement on the names of these factors, in general, trait theorists propose they are (1) openness to experience, (2) conscientiousness, (3) extraversion, (4) agreeableness, and (5) neuroticism (McCrae, Scally, Terracciano, Abecasis, & Costa, 2010). Openness is the degree to which someone is willing to try new experiences. Conscientiousness refers to someone's attention to detail and organizational tendencies. The extraversion and neuroticism dimensions are similar to Eysenck's dimensions noted earlier: Extraversion refers to degree of sociability and outgoingness; neuroticism, to emotional stability (degree to which a person is calm, secure, and even tempered). Agreeableness indicates how trusting and easygoing a person is. To remember these factors, students sometimes use the mnemonic OCEAN: Openness, Conscientiousness, Extraversion, Agreeableness, and Neuroticism (**Figure 10.4**).

FIGURE 10.4
The Five-Factor Model of Personality
The mnemonic OCEAN will help you remember these factors. McCrae and Costa (1990).

Openness	Conforming Uncreative Practical	⟷	Unconforming Creative Imaginative
Conscientiousness	Unreliable Lazy Spontaneous	⟷	Reliable Ambitious Punctual
Extraversion	Loner Quiet Reserved	⟷	Sociable Talkative Affectionate
Agreeableness	Rude Uncooperative Critical	⟷	Good-natured Trusting Helpful
Neuroticism	Calm Even-tempered Secure	⟷	Emotional Temperamental Worried

Empirical support for this model has been established using cross-cultural testing. People in more than 50 cultures, who speak languages as diverse as German, Spanish, and Czech, have been shown to exhibit these five dimensions (McCrae et al., 2000, 2005, 2010). Even the everyday terms used to describe personality characteristics across continents (North America, Europe, and Asia) fit well with the five-factor model (McCrae et al., 2010).

One possible explanation is that these five dimensions are biologically based and universal to humans (Allik & McCrae, 2004; McCrae et al.,

2000). Three decades of twin and adoption studies point to a genetic basis for these five factors (McCrae et al., 2000; Yamagata et al., 2006), with openness to experience showing the greatest degree of heritability (McCrae et al., 2000; **Table 10.4**). Some researchers suggest that dog personalities can be described using similar dimensions, such as extraversion and neuroticism (Ley, Bennett, & Coleman, 2008). And such research is not limited to canines; animals as diverse as squid and orangutans seem to display personality characteristics that are surprisingly similar to those observed in humans (Sinn & Moltschaniwskyj, 2005; Weiss, King, & Perkins, 2006).

The biological basis of these five factors is further supported by their general stability over time (Kandler et al., 2010; McCrae et al., 2000). This implies that the dramatic environmental changes most of us experience in life do not have as great an impact as our inherited characteristics. That does not mean personalities are completely static, however; people can experience changes in these five factors over the life span (Specht, Egloff, & Schmukle, 2011). For example, as people age, they tend to score higher on agreeableness and lower on neuroticism, openness, extraversion, and conscientiousness. They also seem to become happier and more easygoing with age, displaying more positive attitudes (Marsh, Nagengast, & Morin, 2013).

Apply This

Personality traits impact your life in ways you may find surprising. Would you believe that creativity—a facet of the personality trait openness—has been linked to longer life span in men (Turiano, Spiro, & Mroczek, 2012)? Apparently, creative thinking helps lower stress (good for overall health) and stimulates the brain by activating a variety of circuits (Rodriguez, 2012). Another personality trait, conscientiousness, has been associated with certain measures of success, including income level and life satisfaction (Duckworth, Weir, Tsukayama, & Kwok, 2012). Even the personality traits of other people, such as romantic partners, may influence you. One study suggests that marrying a conscientious person could benefit your career; conscientious husbands and wives support their spouses' professional lives by taking care of household chores, and by modeling conscientious behaviors, for example (Solomon & Jackson, 2014). How might such information be useful in everyday life? Remember, you have a great deal of control over your actions. This means you have the ability to cultivate behaviors associated with the personality traits you find desirable. You can also seek out those desirable traits in others. →

CONNECTIONS

In **Chapter 7,** we described the Minnesota twin studies, which showed that genes play a role in intellectual abilities. Identical twins share 100% of their genes, fraternal twins share about 50% of their genes, and adopted siblings are genetically very different. Comparing personality traits among these siblings can show the relative importance of genes (nature) and the environment (nurture).

TABLE 10.4 HERITABILITY AND THE BIG FIVE	
Big Five Personality Dimensions	**Heritability**
Openness	.61
Conscientiousness	.44
Extraversion	.53
Neuroticism	.41
Agreeableness	.41

Heritability is the degree to which heredity is responsible for a particular characteristic. Here, we can see the percent of variation in the Big Five traits attributed to genetic make-up, leaving the remainder to be attributed to environmental influences.

JANG, LIVESLEY, AND VERNON (1996).

Men and women appear to differ with respect to the five factors, although there is not total agreement on how. A review of studies from 55 nations reported that, across cultures, women score higher than men on conscientiousness, extraversion, agreeableness, and neuroticism (Schmitt, Realo, Voracek, & Allik, 2008). Men, on the other hand, seem to demonstrate greater openness to experience. These disparities are not extreme, however; the variation within the groups of males and females is greater than the differences between males and females. Critics suggest that using such rough measures of personality may conceal some of the true differences between men and women; in order to shed light on such disparities, they suggest investigating models that incorporate 10 to 20 traits rather than just 5 (Del Giudice, Booth, & Irwing, 2012).

Better with Age
Japanese calligrapher Kawamata-sensei paints a giant character that will go on display at an upcoming event. Creativity is associated with the personality trait of openness, which has been linked to longevity. James Whitlow Delano/Redux

five-factor model of personality A trait approach to explaining personality, including dimensions of openness to experience, conscientiousness, extraversion, agreeableness, and neuroticism; also known as "the Big Five."

Maybe you could have predicted women would score higher on measures of agreeableness and neuroticism; perhaps you would have guessed the opposite. Research suggests that some gender stereotypes do indeed contain a kernel of truth (Costa, Terracciano, & McCrae, 2001; Terracciano et al., 2005). Let's find out if this principle holds true for cultural stereotypes as well.

across the WORLD

Culture of Personality

Have you heard the old joke about European stereotypes? It starts out like this: In heaven, the chefs are French, the mechanics German, the lovers Italian, the police officers British, and the bankers Swiss (Mulvey, 2006, May 15). This joke plays upon what psychologists might call "national stereotypes," or preconceived notions about the personalities of people belonging to certain cultures. The joke assumes, for example, that Italian people have some underlying quality that makes them excel in romance but not money management. Are such national stereotypes accurate?

PLEASE LEAVE YOUR STEREOTYPES AT THE BORDER!

To get to the bottom of this question, a group of researchers used personality tests to assess the Big Five traits of nearly 4,000 people from 49 cultures (Terracciano et al., 2005). When they compared the results of the personality tests to national stereotypes, they found no evidence that the stereotypes mirrored reality. Not only are these stereotypes invalid, but as history demonstrates, they can pave the way for "prejudice, discrimination, or persecution" (p. 99).

An Appraisal of the Trait Theories

As you can see from the examples above, trait theories have facilitated important psychological research. But like any scientific approach, they have their flaws. One major criticism is that trait theories fail to explain the origins of personality. What aspects of personality are innate, and which are environmental? How do unconscious processes, motivations, and development influence personality? If you're looking to answer these types of questions, trait theories might not be your best bet.

Trait theories also tend to underestimate environmental influences on personality. As psychologist Walter Mischel pointed out, environmental circumstances can affect the way traits manifest themselves (Mischel & Shoda, 1995). A person who is high on the openness factor may be nonconforming in college, wearing unique clothing and pursuing unusual hobbies, but put her in the military and her nonconformity will probably assume a new form.

✓ show what you know

1. _____ was a humanist who was interested in exploring people who are self-actualizers. _____, also a humanist, explored the difficulties people face when their self-concept is incongruent with life experiences.

2. The total acceptance of a child regardless of her behavior is known as:
   a. conditions of worth.
   b. repression.
   c. the real self.
   d. unconditional positive regard.

3. According to _____, personality is the compilation of behaviors that have been shaped via reinforcement and other forms of conditioning.

4. Julian Rotter proposed that personality is influenced by _____, one's beliefs about where responsibility or control exists.
   a. reinforcement
   b. locus of control
   c. expectancy
   d. reinforcement value

5. Reciprocal determinism represents a complex multidirectional interaction among beliefs, behavior, and environment. Draw a diagram illustrating how reciprocal determinism explains one of your behavior patterns.

6. The relatively stable properties of personality are:
   a. traits.
   b. expectancies.
   c. reinforcement values.
   d. ego defense mechanisms.

7. Name the Big Five traits and give one piece of evidence for their biological basis.

✓ CHECK YOUR ANSWERS IN APPENDIX C.

Personality Assessment

A LIFETIME OF MISHAPS   The life of Tank the Roboceptionist has been marked by a series of disappointments. After failing to live up to his father's expectations of becoming NASA's next great telescope, Tank had a disastrous career in military reconnaissance. The CIA deployed him to a war zone to fight terrorists, but the hapless robot could not distinguish between comrade and enemy. Exasperated with Tank's bungling performance, American soldiers were ready to recycle his metal parts. The disgraced robot was promptly returned to the United States (Carnegie Mellon University, 2013).

How do you think a string of such disasters might have shaped Tank's personality? If only we could understand how his life experiences have influenced his levels of neuroticism, openness, and agreeableness. Wouldn't it be fascinating to see how this blue-headed robot performs on a personality test? But alas, Tank is not a person, and thus he is not a viable candidate for personality assessment. 📁 ▼

Is It Legit? Reliability and Validity

LO 13 Explain why reliability and validity are important in personality assessment.

Before we discuss the various types of personality tests, let's get a handle on the qualities that render these tests effective—reliability and validity. **Reliability** can refer to two aspects of an assessment. *Test–retest reliability* is how consistent results are when the same person takes the test more than once. Suppose you take the same personality test today and tomorrow. From one day to the next, your personality is unlikely to change, so your results shouldn't either. With a reliable test, the scores should be very similar at different points in time. *Interrater reliability* refers to the consistency across people scoring an assessment. With high interrater reliability, the results are the same regardless of who scores the test.

CONNECTIONS

In **Chapter 7,** we discussed ways to determine the reliability of intelligence tests. In addition to test–retest reliability, we can split a test in half to see if the findings of the two halves agree. This type of reliability can be determined with personality assessment as well.

The other important quality of a personality assessment is validity. A valid test is one that can be shown to measure what it intends to measure. Let's say a psychologist develops an assessment for extraversion. In order for her test to be considered valid, it must yield results that are similar to already established and valid assessments of extraversion.

Assessment of personality can be broadly classified into objective and subjective measures. Findings from subjective assessments are based, in part, on personal intuition, opinions, or interpretations. With objective assessments, findings are based on a standardized procedure in which the scoring is free of opinions, personal beliefs, expectations, and values. Critics of subjective assessments suggest that there is not enough consistency across findings, as a result of nonstandard scoring procedures. And as noted in earlier chapters, humans are prone to a variety of biases and cognitive errors that can interfere with the ability to accurately assess people and situations. Critics of objective assessments contend that the standardization of these tests does not allow for flexibility and fails to appreciate the diversity of individual experiences. Despite these alleged flaws, many psychologists use a mixture of objective and subjective assessment techniques with their clients.

Not everyone agrees about the effectiveness of personality assessment. Even so, it is used in many contexts and in ways that have profound implications. Psychologists use personality tests to get to know their clients and diagnose mental disorders. Companies use them to make decisions about new hires and promotions (*Does this person have what it takes to be a manager?*). Personality tests are part of the battery of assessments used to evaluate the functioning of parents embroiled in custody disputes: *Is mom depressed? Can she care for this child?* (Lilienfeld, Wood, & Garb, 2005).

In this next section, we will explore the major types of personality tests that psychologists employ: interviews, projective personality tests, and objective personality tests. Many of these are aligned with specific perspectives (psychoanalytic or behavioral, for example), but most psychologists use an integrative approach, drawing on multiple perspectives in their assessment of clients.

What Brings You Here Today?

One way to gather information about personality is through a face-to-face interview. In an unstructured, or open-ended, interview, there is no predetermined path. A psychologist might begin with a question like, "What brings you here today?" and then gently direct the conversation in a way that helps her understand her client's strengths and weaknesses, hopes and plans. Semistructured and structured interviews, on the other hand, employ specific paths of questioning that hinge on the respondent's answers. This format provides a more systematic means of comparing behaviors across individuals.

One great advantage of the interview is that it allows a psychologist to see a client in a relatively natural, realistic setting. Talking with a client face to face, a psychologist can observe facial expressions and body language, which may offer clues to what's going on inside. There are drawbacks, however. Interview subjects may lie to the interviewer (without even realizing it), spin the facts to misrepresent themselves, or share memories that are distorted or incomplete. Another source of error is the interviewer. She may, for example, lead the interview in a particular direction or interpret responses in a way that reinforces her own beliefs about personality. Clients can also be influenced by the interviewers' nonverbal language. The desire to answer "correctly" is strong in an interview format. Just as in surveys, the way a question is asked can have a profound influence on the answer.

CONNECTIONS

In **Chapter 1,** we noted that people are prone to the *hindsight bias,* the feeling that "I knew it all along." Researchers, in particular, can introduce *observer bias* into the recording of observations. When choosing a personality assessment, it is important to be alert to the biases that can interfere with objective data collection.

CONNECTIONS

An important factor to consider in the interview procedure is the *malleability* of memory, which we discussed in **Chapter 6.** The interviewer should avoid posing questions that might lead to the *misinformation effect,* which is the tendency for new or misleading information to distort memories.

Tell Me About Yourself
Psychologists assess personality using a variety of tools, including personal interviews. These face-to-face sessions range from open-ended and exploratory to highly structured. Getty Images/iStockphoto

What Do *You* See? Projective Personality Tests

LO 14 Define projective tests and evaluate their strengths and limitations.

It's a hot summer's day and you're lying on the beach, gazing at the clouds. "What do you see?" you ask your friend. "I see the profile of a Doberman pinscher," she replies. "That's funny," you say. "I see a child doing jumping jacks."

How is it possible that two people can look at the same image and come away with such different impressions? Some would argue that it has a lot to do with personality. The idea that personality influences perception is the premise of **projective personality tests,** which psychologists use to explore characteristics that might not be accessible through interview or observation, as they attempt to access aspects of the unconscious (**Infographic 10.3** on the next page). With this type of assessment, the test taker is shown a stimulus without a specified meaning and then prompted to *project* meaning onto it. Projective personality tests assume that people carry around anxiety and unresolved conflicts, often beneath conscious awareness. Because these tests attempt to uncover such issues indirectly, they are less threatening than other methods, and therefore provoke less resistance. The goal of the test administrator is to take the manifest content (what the person reports seeing) and try to understand its underlying meaning.

THE RORSCHACH INKBLOTS   The best-known projective personality test is the Rorschach. The original version of the test was developed by Swiss psychiatrist Hermann Rorschach (1884–1922) in 1921. Today's psychologists typically use Rorschach inkblots with a comprehensive coding system introduced in the 1970s (Exner, 1980, 1986).

Here is a rough description of how the test is administered: Imagine someone hands you a series of cards covered in odd-looking blotches of ink—five cards with black-and-white blotches, and another five with color. Presenting the cards one by one, he asks you to report what you see. The images you describe and the details on which you focus will be important factors in the assessment of your personality, which involves a systematic comparison with answers given by other test takers who have known personality characteristics and diagnoses. Do you see bears playing patty cake? Seeing animals in motion might be interpreted as a sign of rashness. Are you homing in on the black areas? This could suggest a feeling of melancholy or sadness (Lilienfeld et al., 2005).

THE THEMATIC APPERCEPTION TEST (TAT)   In the mid-1930s, Henry Murray and his colleagues developed the Thematic Apperception Test (TAT), a projective assessment that consists of 20 cards containing black-and-white illustrations of ambiguous scenes. When shown a card, the test taker is asked to tell a story about it. The story might incorporate a description of the people in the scene, and should include what led up to the scene, the emotions and thoughts of the characters, and a conclusion. The assumption is that the test taker will project underlying conflicts onto the ambiguous stimuli of the picture; the job of the test administrator is to unearth them.

TAKING STOCK   One criticism of projective personality tests is that they can take too much time. However, because the test taker may be willing to speak openly, honestly, and freely due to the unstructured nature of the assessment, the benefits seem to outweigh the costs. Another major concern, mentioned earlier, is the subjectivity of interpreting results, which can lead to reliability problems. Test administrators may score differently, and test takers may not get the same results when they take the test on different occasions. Even the comprehensive scoring system for the Rorschach inkblots

projective personality tests
Assessments that present stimuli without a specified meaning to test takers, whose responses can then be interpreted to uncover underlying personality characteristics.

Examining the Unconscious: Projective Personality Tests

The psychoanalytic perspective holds that some aspects of personality exist beneath conscious awareness. Projective personality tests seek to uncover these characteristics. Ideas and anxieties in the unconscious will appear in descriptions of ambiguous stimuli, revealing previously hidden conflicts that the test administrator can evaluate.

◄ Test administration ►

The best-known projective tests, the Thematic Apperception Test (TAT) and the Rorschach Inkblot Test, are both conducted in the same way (Lilienfeld, Wood, & Garb, 2005): The test administrator presents a series of picture cards, one at a time, then records the participant's responses. The administrator also notes behaviors such as gestures, tone of voice, and facial expressions.

The standard administration of the TAT presents a selection of 5 to 12 cards. The participant is asked to tell a story for each scene, including what the characters are feeling and how the story might end.

The Rorschach has 10 cards with symmetrical inkblots, 5 in color and 5 in black-and-white. The participant is prompted to give multiple responses for each image, identifying details.

Test Interpretation

To help decrease the influence of administrator bias in interpretation of projective tests, comprehensive systems have been developed to standardize scoring and interpretation of some tests. For the Rorschach Inkblot Test, responses are coded on dimensions such as location (whole inkblot or one detail), themes (unique or consistent), and thought processes (Erdberg, 1990). The use of a comprehensive system allows administrators to compare typical and atypical responses.

PARTICIPANT RESPONSES

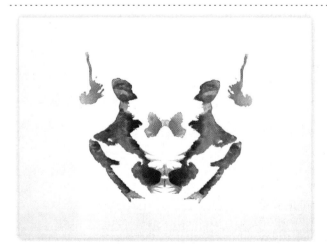

"Looks like two people."

"The people are fighting over something."

"Or they're carrying something heavy together."

"Maybe it's one person looking in a mirror."

"I also see a butterfly."

These sample responses are representative for this inkblot. Most participants interpret this Rorschach inkblot as two figures (Burstein & Loucks, 1989).

EXAMINER RESPONSES

Participant mentions the typical response of two figures.

Suggestion that the people are fighting could indicate issues with aggression or an aggressive personality.

Focus on individuals working together could represent a need for social connection.

However, seeing one person alone could indicate social anxiety, too.

Now participant switches to a specific part of the image, which could also show that he is uncomfortable thinking about others, perhaps related to introversion.

has not resolved concerns about projective tests, because the issue of validity remains. Many critics suggest projective tests are not valid because they do not measure what they claim to be measuring (Schultz & Schultz, 2013). Nonetheless, clinicians continue using projective tests because they often provide a way to begin forming a picture of a client.

What tools do you use to get a feel for a person? Do you ever try to size up someone's personality by looking at his Facebook page? In many cases, personality characteristics projected through social media bear close resemblance to real-world identities.

SOCIAL MEDIA and psychology

It's Written All Over Your Facebook

Facebook profiles reveal a great deal about the personalities of their owners. In one study, researchers assessed the offline personalities of American Facebook users and German StudiVZ users (StudiVZ is a popular European network), and then compared those results with the impressions of people checking out their profiles. Their readings of the profiles turned out to be quite accurate, particularly when it came to the traits of extraversion and openness (Back et al., 2010).

This tendency for Facebook to betray one's true personality may not be a good thing if you happen to be narcissistic. Narcissism is a personality trait often equated with vanity, self-absorption, and feelings of superiority and entitlement. Strangers can easily pick out real-life narcissists by viewing their Facebook profiles (Buffardi & Campbell, 2008), and there is no reason to believe that other characteristics wouldn't be detectable as well.

"But... your Facebook profile says you're a vegetarian!"

FACEBOOK PROFILES REVEAL A GREAT DEAL ABOUT . . . THEIR OWNERS.

Objective Personality Tests

LO 15 Describe objective personality tests and evaluate their strengths and limitations.

Earlier we mentioned that clinicians use a variety of tools to assess the personalities of their clients. Among those tools are *objective personality tests,* assessments made up of a standard set of questions with answer choices (true/false, multiple choice, circle the number). These tests are called *objective* because the results are assessed in a standardized way, free of personal bias. In contrast to the projective inventories, which often seem to be overly subjective, objective personality tests have clear scoring instructions that are identical for anyone taking the test. Often scores are calculated by a computer. In addition to being convenient and unbiased, objective tests have a solid base of evidence supporting their reliability and validity (Anastasi & Urbina, 1997). Some of these tests may focus on a particular personality characteristic or trait (such as locus of control); others might assess a group of characteristics (such as the Big Five).

THE MMPI-2 The most commonly used objective personality test is the Minnesota Multiphasic Personality Inventory (MMPI–2; Butcher & Rouse, 1996). This self-report questionnaire includes more than 567 statements to which the individual responds "true," "false," or "cannot say." Some of the items you might see on the MMPI–2 include statements such as "I often wake up rested and ready to go" or "I want to work as a teacher." Since the original purpose of the MMPI was to identify disorders and abnormal behavior, it includes 10 clinical scales (such as, hypochondriasis and depression). It also has validity scales (such as the Lie scale and the Defensiveness scale) to assess the degree to which the results are useful. These validity measures help ensure that the person taking the assessment is not trying to appear either more disturbed or more healthy than she actually is. It is important to control for manipulation by the test taker because the MMPI is used in a variety of nonclinical settings—to inform decisions about custody or other legal matters, for example. Like other personality assessments, the MMPI has its share of criticisms. Since it was designed to help make diagnoses, many feel its application outside of therapeutic settings is inappropriate. The scales are based on groups of people exhibiting abnormalities, and therefore they may not translate to nonclinical populations.

16PF Another objective assessment of personality is the Sixteen Personality Factor Questionnaire (16PF), originally created by Raymond Cattell and based on his trait theory. With the 16PF, the test taker must select one of three choices in response to 185 questions. Ultimately, a profile is constructed, which indicates where the person falls along the continuum of each of the 16 dimensions. Take a look at **Figure 10.5** and you can see how pilots and writers compare on the 16 factors. For example, airline pilots tend to fall on the tough-minded end of the continuum, whereas writers tend to be located on the sensitive, tender-minded end (Cattell, 1973a).

MYERS–BRIGGS One very popular objective assessment of personality is the Myers–Briggs Type Indicator (MBTI) (Briggs & Myers, 1998). Katherine Briggs and her daughter Isabel Briggs-Myers created this assessment in the 1940s. It designates a personality "type" as it relates to the following four dimensions: extraversion (E) versus introversion (I); sensing (S) versus intuiting (N); thinking (T) versus feeling (F); and judgment (J) versus perception (P). For example, someone characterized as ISTP would be introverted, rely on the senses (rather than intuition) to understand the environment, favor logic over emotion, and focus on using perception as opposed to judgment.

Problems arise when assessments incorporate somewhat vague descriptions of personality traits. Some would even liken it to the Barnum effect, which was named after P. T. Barnum (1810–1891), who was famous for his ability to convince people he could read minds. Essentially, he did this by making generally complimentary and vague statements that could be true about anyone (*You are creative and work well with others and you sometimes procrastinate, but ultimately you get the job done*). Similarly, with the MBTI, the personality type descriptions are "generally flattering and sufficiently vague so that most people will accept the statements as true of themselves" (Pittenger, 1993, November, p. 6). Although the MBTI is quite popular, the research supporting it is weak, especially as it relates to job performance, career choices, and related matters (Pittenger, 2005). Because the test results don't always correlate with job success, the validity of the assessment is questionable. In addition, the test–retest reliability is not always strong. A person can take the test twice and end up with different results (Hunsley, Lee, & Wood, 2003; Pittenger, 2005).

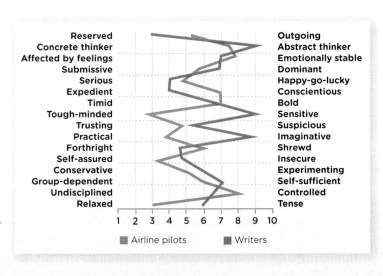

FIGURE 10.5

Example Profiles Generated by the 16PF

On Cattell's 16PF, writers appear to be more reserved, sensitive, and imaginative than airline pilots. Pilots, on the other hand, tend to fall on the tough-minded end of the continuum. Are you surprised that they also appear to be more relaxed?

Research from: Cattell (1973b)

TAKING STOCK　We have noted specific criticisms of the MMPI-2 and Myers–Briggs tests, but there are other serious drawbacks of objective assessments. Although many of these tests include some sort of mechanism for checking the validity of the test taker's answers, people may lie (and get away with it), particularly when the assessment results may impact some important aspect of their lives, such as work or a child custody case. In addition, social desirability can influence the results; individuals may unintentionally answer questions in a way that makes them "look better" to others.

Technology and Personality Assessment

Can we be 100% confident in the results of personality tests? Not yet, but psychologists are developing new measures that take advantage of technology, bypassing self-report as much as possible. For example, scanning technology has been used to identify particular areas of the brain associated with personality expression. One group of researchers made use of fMRI in their effort to tease apart the relationship between personality and mood states. They found that activity in the anterior cingulate sometimes was associated with extraversion, possibly identifying an area of the brain involved in extraversion and introversion (Canli, Amin, Haas, Omura, & Constable, 2004). Perhaps future technologies will enable more precise assessment of personality characteristics (Eisenberger, Lieberman, & Satpute, 2005).

 FINAL THOUGHTS　You may be wondering why we chose to feature Tank the robot in a chapter on personality. We can give robots characteristics and traits; we can even endow them with the capacity to "learn" and interact with their environments. But try as we may, we cannot provide them with genuine personalities. Our inclusion of Tank is a deliberate attempt to illustrate the complex and uniquely human nature of personality.

You Asked, Dr. Simmons Answers
http://qrs.ly/784qsed
Tank: What do you see yourself doing in the next 15 years?

 show what you know

1. _____ personality tests present ambiguous test stimuli to the test taker, so the administrator can interpret and uncover underlying personality characteristics based on that participant's responses.
   a. Objective
   b. Projective
   c. 16PF
   d. Myers–Briggs

2. Objective personality tests are made up of a set of standardized questions with previously established answers (for instance, true/false or multiple choice), and are assessed free of:
   a. intuition or bias.
   b. reliability.
   c. validity.
   d. objectivity.

3. A psychologist gives a client several personality tests to help her choose a career path. What might the consequences be if the tests are not valid? What if they are not reliable?

✓ CHECK YOUR ANSWERS IN APPENDIX C.

⑩ summary of concepts

LO 1   Define personality. (p. 404)

Personality refers to the unique, core set of characteristics that influence the way one thinks, acts, and feels—characteristics many psychologists would agree are consistent and enduring throughout the life span. Personality differs from persona in that persona refers to a role, not personality.

LO 2   Distinguish how the perspectives of psychology explain personality development. (p. 405)

The psychoanalytic perspective suggests that personality development is heavily influenced by processes of which we are unaware, how those processes manifest early in life, and the way caregivers respond. The behavioral perspective describes and explains how the environment shapes personality, and specifically, how reinforcers influence behaviors. The humanistic perspective suggests that we should take advantage of our capabilities as we strive for personal growth, and that the choices we make in life influence our personalities. The social-cognitive perspective focuses on relationships, environmental influences, cognitive activity, and individual behavior as they come together to form personality. The biological perspective suggests physiological and genetic factors affect personality development. Trait theories look at current characteristics of the individual to describe and predict personality.

LO 3   Illustrate Freud's models for describing the mind. (p. 407)

Psychoanalysis refers to Freud's views regarding personality as well as his system of psychotherapy and tools for the exploration of the unconscious. According to his topographical model, our personalities and behaviors result from mental processes that occur at three levels: the conscious, preconscious, and unconscious. The structural model of the mind describes the functions of the mind's components. The id is the most primitive component of personality, and its activities occur at the unconscious level. The ego develops as the infant grows, finding ways to manipulate situations, plan for the future, solve problems, and make decisions in order to satisfy the needs of the id. The superego develops last and guides our behavior to follow the rules of society, parents, or other authority figures.

LO 4   Summarize Freud's use of psychosexual stages to explain personality. (p. 412)

The developmental model helps explain personality and sexuality in terms of a standard developmental path through what Freud called the psychosexual stages. He believed all children must go through these stages as they mature into adulthood. Associated with each stage is an erogenous zone as well as a conflict that must be dealt with. If the conflict is not successfully resolved, the child may suffer from a fixation and get "stuck" in that particular stage, not able to progress smoothly through the remaining stages. The stages include the oral stage, anal stage, phallic stage, latency period, and genital stage.

LO 5   Explain how the neo-Freudians' theories of personality differ from Freud's. (p. 415)

Some of Freud's followers branched out on their own due to disagreements about certain issues, such as his focus on the instincts of sex and aggression, his idea that personality is determined by the end of childhood, and his somewhat negative view of human nature. Adler proposed that humans are conscious and intentional in their behaviors. Jung suggested that we are driven by a psychological energy (as opposed to sexual energy), which encourages positive growth, self-understanding, and balance. Horney emphasized the role of relationships between children and their caregivers, not erogenous zones and psychosexual stages.

LO 6   Summarize Maslow's hierarchy of needs, and describe self-actualizers. (p. 418)

Maslow proposed a hierarchy of needs, which represents a continuum of drives that are universal and ordered in terms of their strength. He suggested that we typically, but not always, respond to these needs in a predictable order. Self-actualizers are those who continually seek to reach their fullest potential.

LO 7   Discuss Rogers' view of self-concept, ideal self, and unconditional positive regard. (p. 420)

Rogers proposed that the development of personality is highly influenced by the role of caregivers in a child's life. He suggested humans have an innate urge to move toward and be attracted to situations and people that will help us grow, and to avoid those that have the potential to stop our growth. Self-concept is knowledge of one's strengths, abilities, behavior patterns, and temperament.

Rogers believed that individuals develop an ideal self, which refers to the self-concept we strive for and fervently wish to achieve. Ideally, caregivers should show unconditional positive regard, which is the total acceptance of a child regardless of behavior. People need to feel completely accepted and valued for who they are, not what they do.

LO 8 Use learning theories to explain personality development. (p. 422)

According to learning theory, personality is a compilation of behaviors, all of which have been shaped through a lifetime of reinforcement and conditioning. Some behaviorists use learning principles to explain personality, including those of classical conditioning, operant conditioning, and observational learning.

LO 9 Summarize Rotter's view of personality. (p. 422)

Rotter suggested that not all aspects of behavior and personality can be directly observed. He believed a key component of personality is locus of control, which is a pattern of beliefs regarding where responsibility or control for an outcome exists. Rotter explored how these beliefs can influence behavior. Expectancy refers to the predictions we make about the consequences or outcomes of our behavior.

LO 10 Discuss how Bandura uses the social-cognitive perspective to explain personality. (p. 422)

Bandura rejected the notion that psychologists should only focus on observable behavior; he realized behavior is determined by cognitions as well as reinforcers and other environmental influences. He used this social-cognitive perspective to explain personality. Personality results from patterns of thinking (cognitive) in addition to our relationships and other environmental factors (social). Reciprocal determinism refers to the multidirectional interaction among beliefs, behaviors, and the environment.

LO 11 Distinguish trait theories from other personality theories. (p. 425)

Traits are the relatively stable properties that describe elements of personality. The trait theories are different from other personality theories in that they focus less on explaining why and how personality develops, and more on describing personality and predicting behaviors. Allport created a comprehensive list of traits to help operationalize the terminology used in personality research. Cattell grouped the traits into two categories: surface traits and source traits. He used factor analysis to group

surface traits into 16 personality factors and developed the Sixteen Personality Factor Questionnaire (16PF) to measure them. Eysenck proposed that we could describe personalities using three dimensions: introversion–extraversion, neuroticism, and psychoticism. He also worked to understand the biological basis of these dimensions.

LO 12 Identify the biological roots of the five-factor model of personality. (p. 426)

The five-factor model of personality, also known as the Big Five, is another trait approach to explaining personality and includes the following factors: openness to experience, conscientiousness, extraversion, agreeableness, and neuroticism. Twin and adoption studies conducted across the world point to a genetic basis for the five factors. These characteristics are stable over time, suggesting that the environmental changes we experience over the life span have less of an impact on personality than inherited characteristics.

LO 13 Explain why reliability and validity are important in personality assessment. (p. 429)

Reliability generally refers to two aspects of a personality assessment: test–retest reliability and interrater reliability. Test–retest reliability is consistency of results when the same person takes a test more than once. Interrater reliability refers to the consistency across people scoring an assessment. Validity refers to the degree to which an assessment measures what it is intended to measure. A valid test must yield results similar to established assessments. Both reliability and validity are important in the assessment of personality because they help render the assessments effective.

LO 14 Define projective tests and evaluate their strengths and limitations. (p. 431)

Personality influences perceptions. With projective personality tests, a test taker is shown a stimulus that has no specified meaning and then is prompted to respond, thus projecting meaning onto it. Testers interpret and uncover underlying personality characteristics from these responses—characteristics that might not be accessible through interview or observation. One strength of this type of assessment is its unstructured nature, which makes it less threatening to test takers, therefore provoking less resistance. Limitations include the amount of time needed to administer the assessment as well as the subjective nature of its interpretation, which can lead to problems with reliability. Some of the best-known projective tests are the Rorschach Inkblot Test and the Thematic Apperception Test (TAT).

LO 15   Describe objective personality tests and evaluate their strengths and limitations. (p. 433)

Objective personality tests are made up of a standard set of questions with answer choices (true/false, multiple choice, circle the number). One strength of this type of personality test is that it is scored in a standardized way, free of any personal intuition or bias. Limitations include the potential for dishonesty on the part of test takers as well as their tendency to unintentionally answer questions in a way that makes them be viewed in a more favorable light (social desirability). Two commonly used objective personality tests are the Minnesota Multiphasic Personality Inventory (MMPI–2) and the Sixteen Personality Factor Questionnaire (16PF).

key terms

archetypes, p. 417

collective unconscious, p. 417

ego, p. 409

ego defense mechanisms, p. 409

expectancy, p. 422

five-factor model of personality, p. 426

fixation, p. 412

id, p. 408

ideal self, p. 420

Oedipus complex, p. 413

personality, p. 404

pleasure principle, p. 408

projective personality tests, p. 431

psychoanalysis, p. 407

psychosexual stages, p. 412

reality principle, p. 409

reciprocal determinism, p. 424

repression, p. 410

self-concept, p. 420

self-efficacy, p. 424

social-cognitive perspective, p. 422

source traits, p. 425

superego, p. 409

surface traits, p. 425

traits, p. 424

trait theories, p. 424

unconditional positive regard, p. 420

unconscious, p. 407

TEST PREP are you ready?

1. The _____ perspective of personality development is based on the theories of Sigmund Freud and suggests that unconscious conflicts are at the root of personality development.
   - **a.** trait
   - **b.** humanistic
   - **c.** biological
   - **d.** psychoanalytic

2. A professor doing research on personality development insists that humans have capabilities that should be harnessed for personal growth. This professor appears to be proposing which of the following perspectives?
   - **a.** humanistic
   - **b.** behavioral
   - **c.** psychoanalytic
   - **d.** social-cognitive

3. Freud's topographical model suggests our personalities and behaviors result from:
   - **a.** components of the mind, including the id, ego, and superego.
   - **b.** the reality principle.
   - **c.** the pleasure principle.
   - **d.** mental processes that occur at three levels of consciousness.

4. According to Freud, the part of the personality that develops last and guides our behaviors to follow rules is the:
   - **a.** preconscious.
   - **b.** superego.
   - **c.** id.
   - **d.** ego.

5. _____ help to reduce the anxiety created by the conflict among the id, ego, and superego.
   - **a.** Psychosexual stages
   - **b.** Three levels of consciousness
   - **c.** Defense mechanisms
   - **d.** Erogenous zones

6. _____ refers to the drive to achieve one's full potential.
   - **a.** Repression
   - **b.** Conditions of worth
   - **c.** Self-actualization
   - **d.** Reciprocal determinism

7. Rogers believed that problems can develop when a person's self-concept is _____ with his experiences in the world.
   - **a.** incongruent
   - **b.** in harmony
   - **c.** self-actualized
   - **d.** conditioned

8. A person high in _____ strongly believes she will succeed in a particular situation even if she has experienced failure in similar circumstances.
   - **a.** reciprocal determinism
   - **b.** reinforcers
   - **c.** self-efficacy
   - **d.** source traits

9. _____ suggests personality is the result of interactions among cognitions, behaviors, and the environment.
   - **a.** Self-efficacy
   - **b.** Factor analysis
   - **c.** Reciprocal determinism
   - **d.** Expectancy

10. Using _____ and other research methods, Cattell proposed that there are 16 personality factors.
    - **a.** source traits
    - **b.** reciprocal determinism
    - **c.** the Big Five
    - **d.** factor analysis

11. According to Eysenck, we can describe personalities based on:
    - **a.** three dimensions of traits.
    - **b.** self-actualization.
    - **c.** locus of control.
    - **d.** reinforcement value.

12. Evidence for the biological basis of the five-factor model of personality includes:
    - **a.** the instability of the personality characteristics over time.
    - **b.** the stability of the personality characteristics over time.
    - **c.** the fact that there are no gender differences in the personality characteristics.
    - **d.** the absence of heritability of these personality characteristics.

13. _____ can be determined when someone takes the same personality assessment more than once and the results do not change.
    - **a.** Heritability
    - **b.** Effectiveness
    - **c.** Reliability
    - **d.** Validity

14. The idea that personality traits influence perception is part of the logic underlying _____, which attempt to explore characteristics that might not be accessible through interview or observation.
    - **a.** projective personality tests
    - **b.** semistructured interviews
    - **c.** structured interviews
    - **d.** fMRI studies

15. The neo-Freudians agree with Freud on many issues, but tend to disagree with which of the following?
    - **a.** his belief in the positive aspect of human nature
    - **b.** his belief in the importance of personality growth throughout life
    - **c.** his intense emphasis on the instincts of sex and aggression
    - **d.** his notion that caregivers cannot shape personality

16. How would a behaviorist describe some of your personality characteristics?

17. What is the difference between the humanistic perspective and the social-cognitive perspective of personality development?

18. Describe the Oedipus complex and the Electra complex. How are they different?

19. Consider how you are doing in your college courses. Name three causes for your successes that represent an internal locus of control. Name three causes for your successes that represent an external locus of control.

20. Describe the differences between objective and subjective approaches to the assessment of personality.

✓ CHECK YOUR ANSWERS IN APPENDIX C.

11

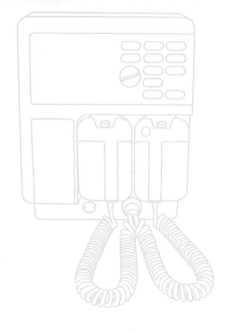

© Paul Hakimata/Alamy

Tetra Images/SuperStock

stress and health

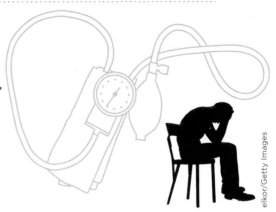

An Introduction to Stress

DRIVE   When Eric Flansburg first enrolled in the police academy at Onondaga Community College in upstate New York, there were 21 students in his class. Of those 21, only 6 graduated. Eric was not among them. Why? Because he failed one very important test: the Emergency Vehicle Operations Course (EVOC).

The EVOC requires exceptional driving skills. The test involves weaving a police car in and out of a zigzag maze of cones and making superfast lane changes—just the kind of police chase maneuvering you see in the movies. Once you get to the end of the course, you have to do it all over again, but this time in reverse. Knock down one cone, or simply brush against it, and you fail. Exceed the allotted 2 minutes and 20 seconds, and you fail. "It's pretty intense driving," Eric says. "It's also fun."

Going into the test, Eric was well prepared. He had learned and rehearsed the steering and breaking techniques needed to succeed. But when the time came to put his hard-earned skills to work, he faltered. "It was all mental," Eric says. "I totally psyched myself out. I was so scared of failing that I failed." There are no two ways about it: Eric was feeling the *stress* of the situation.

Note: Quotations attributed to Eric Flansburg and Kehlen Kirby are personal communications.

Stress and Stressors

LO 1 Define stress and stressors.

We all have an intuitive sense of what stress is, and many of us are more familiar with it than we would like. But what exactly is stress, where does it come from, and how does it affect our physical and mental health? Some people report they experience the *feeling* of stress, almost as if stress were an emotion. Others describe stress as if it were a force that needs to be resisted. An engineer might refer to stress as the application of a force on a target, such as the wing of an airplane, to determine how much load it can handle before breaking (Lazarus, 1993). Do you ever feel you might "break" because the load you bear causes such great strain (**Infographic 11.1**)?

Here, **stress** is defined as the response to perceived threats or challenges resulting from stimuli or events that cause strain, analogous to the airplane wing bending because of an applied load. For humans, these stimuli, or **stressors,** can cause psychological, physiological, and emotional reactions. As you read this chapter, be careful not to confuse *how we react to stressors* with the *stressors* themselves; stress is the response and stressors are the cause (Harrington, 2013). Hans Selye (sĕl'yĕ; 1907–1982), an endocrinologist who studied the impact of hormones and stress, proposed that "stress is the nonspecific response of the body to any demand. A stressor is an agent that produces stress at any time" (1976, p. 53).

There are countless types of stressors. They can be events, such as police academy driving tests, or beliefs and attitudes, like Eric's thoughts and worries about not passing the test. Stressors can even be people, like the drill instructors who run the police academy's Saturday morning physical training. Starting at 6:00 A.M., these guys lead Onondaga's aspiring police officers through 3 hours of running, push-ups, and other backbreaking exercises. If a student makes one mistake, the drill instructors are more than happy to point it out with the full force of their lungs. Mind you, this is all for the cadet's own benefit. Police officers must learn how to brush off rude comments, maintain their composure, and carry on with their duties.

What are the stressors in your life? Some exist outside of you, like homework assignments, dirty dishes in the sink, and job demands. Others are more internal, like the *anxiety* stemming from a strained relationship or the *pressure* of wishing to excel. Generally, we experience stress in response to stressors, although there is at least one exception to this rule: People with anxiety disorders can feel intense anxiety in the absence of any apparent stressors (Chapter 12). Which brings us to another point: Stress is very much related to how one perceives the surrounding world.

CONNECTIONS

In **Chapter 9,** we defined emotion as a psychological state that includes a subjective or inner experience. Emotion also has a physiological component and a behavioral expression. Here, we discuss *stress responses,* which are psychological, physiological, and emotional in nature.

Eric, in His Own Words:

http://qrs.ly/2c4qsft

© 2016, Macmillan

stress The response to perceived threats or challenges resulting from stimuli or events that cause strain.

stressors Stimuli that cause physiological, psychological, and emotional reactions.

Stressed Out

Every year, the American Psychological Association (APA) commissions a survey investigating perceived stress among adults in the United States. In addition to measuring attitudes about stress, the survey identifies leading sources of stress and common behaviors used to manage stressors. The resulting picture shows that stress is a significant issue for many people and that we are not always managing it well (APA, 2013d). Even when we acknowledge the importance of stress management and resolve to make positive lifestyle changes, many adults report barriers such as a lack of time or willpower that prevent them from achieving their goals. The good news? Our ability to manage stress appears to improve with age. (ALL INFORMATION PRESENTED IN THIS INFOGRAPHIC, EXCEPT THE PERCEIVED STRESS SCALE, IS FROM APA, 2013d)

4 OUT OF 5 — Number of people reporting their stress level has increased or stayed the same in the past year.

TOP SOURCES OF STRESS

money **69%**

work **65%**

the economy **61%**

family responsibilities **57%**

relationships **56%**

family health problems **52%**

Number experiencing **responses to stress,** including **anger, fatigue,** and **feeling overwhelmed. NEARLY 7 IN 10**

People with high stress also report poor health behaviors.

Only **30%** of adults with high stress report eating healthy and getting enough sleep.

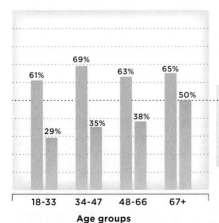

Credit: Strawberry-flavored donut with a bite taken out, Shutterstock; Torn, crumpled dollar, Shutterstock

OVER THE PAST 5 YEARS

60% — **60%** of people have tried to reduce their stress

53% — **53%** are still trying

STRESS OVER THE LIFE SPAN

People across all age groups agree that managing stress is very important. However, the ability to manage stress varies with age. Younger adults are more likely to rely on unhealthy behaviors like drinking alcohol and smoking for stress management. Older adults report more success in achieving healthy lifestyle goals such as eating healthy and getting enough sleep. They also report higher rates of religious participation (APA, 2013d).

▶ **50%** Oldest people report highest rate of meeting stress management goals.

Age groups: 18-33 (61%, 29%), 34-47 (69%, 35%), 48-66 (63%, 38%), 67+ (65%, 50%)

Age groups

▪ Managing stress is very important
▪ Doing a very good job managing stress

DO **YOU** FEEL STRESSED?

Psychologist Sheldon Cohen and colleagues (1983) developed the Perceived Stress Scale to measure the degree to which we appraise situations as stressful. By comparing your score against others tested in your age group, you are able to assess the amount of perceived stress in your life. Simply knowing you find your life uncontrollable or overloaded can be a trigger to seek help implementing positive lifestyle change.

For each question, indicate how often you felt or thought a certain way. The best approach is to answer each question fairly quickly, choosing the alternative that seems like a reasonable estimate.

0=never   3=fairly often
1=almost never   4=very often
2=sometimes

1. In the last month, how often have you been upset because of something that happened unexpectedly?

2. In the last month, how often have you felt that you were unable to control the important things in your life?

3. In the last month, how often have you felt nervous and "stressed"?

4. In the last month, how often have you felt confident about your ability to handle your personal problems?

5. In the last month, how often have you felt that things were going your way?

6. In the last month, how often have you found that you could not cope with all the things that you had to do?

7. In the last month, how often have you been able to control irritations in your life?

8. In the last month, how often have you felt that you were on top of things?

9. In the last month, how often have you been angered because of things that were outside of your control?

10. In the last month, how often have you felt difficulties were piling up so high that you could not overcome them?

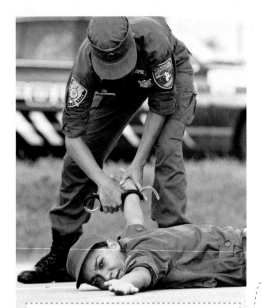

Welcome to the Academy
Police cadets practice arrest procedures at an academy in Gurabo, Puerto Rico. Drill instructors go to great lengths to prepare aspiring officers for the extreme physical and mental stressors they will face on their beats. DENNIS RIVERA/The New York Times/Redux Pictures

CONNECTIONS

In **Chapter 10,** we presented *self-efficacy*, or beliefs about one's ability to reach a goal. People with high self-efficacy are more successful on the job because they are flexible, open to new ideas, and persevere in difficult situations. Eric appeared to show high self-efficacy as he pursued his goal of becoming a police officer.

In many cases, stress results from a *perceived* threat, because what constitutes a threat differs from one person to the next. The police academy driving test might have been threatening to Eric because he felt anxious about failing, while another student viewed the test as an opportunity to shine. Similarly, Eric may have felt completely relaxed taking written exams that other students found highly threatening.

Remember that stress can have psychological, physiological, and emotional effects. Eric's physiological reaction to the driving test may have included increased blood pressure and heart rate, but he was far more aware of the psychological and emotional components of his stress response. Bursting through the starting gates, his mind raced from one thought to the next. He was envisioning every little thing he needed to do to pass the exam and at the same time saying to himself, *Eric, Eric, you can't fail.*

The very same day that Eric failed his driving test, he resolved to return to the academy and start the program again. This minor setback was not going to interfere with his childhood dream of becoming a police officer, and there was no way it was going to define his experience at the academy. "When you fall down, you have to get back up," Eric says. "That's the only way to move forward in life."

Not all people would have responded this way; plenty would have viewed the test as the end of their journey. (*I guess I was never meant to be a police officer.*) As you will learn in this chapter, the ways people experience and cope with stressors are highly variable. The strategies used and the beliefs about one's ability to cope have a profound impact on reactions to stress.

EVERYTHING HAPPENS FOR A REASON In three decades of life, Eric has experienced his fair share of stressors. Immediately after graduating from high school in upstate New York, he traveled to an Air Force base in San Antonio, Texas, to begin basic training, a stepping-stone on his way to joining the military police. "You want to talk about psychological stress?" Eric says laughing. Try waking up at 4:00 A.M. to the sound of drill sergeants banging garbage cans and screaming, "Get out of bed!" Not a morning person? If you cannot wake up, shower, shave, and make your bed with perfect hospital corners (yes, they really expect to be able to bounce a quarter off the sheets) in a half-hour, you can be sure one of the drill sergeants will get in your face and scream something like, "Did you have Mommy make your bed when you were home?"

After about a year of arduous training in the Air Force, Eric suffered a disabling injury and had to be discharged. It was a huge letdown, but Eric believes everything happens for a reason. He returned to New York and got a job at a dairy plant where he moved up the company ranks to become a high-level manager. Working at

It's Nonstop
A dairy plant employee toils among steel vats of milk. Keeping the storage vessels and equipment sterile is an enormous responsibility; if the product becomes contaminated, thousands of consumers might be sickened. As Eric can testify, working as a sanitation manager can cause significant day-to-day stress.
P. Magielsen/Corbis

the plant introduced Eric to a different type of pressure. As a sanitation manager, he was in charge of making sure all processing equipment was sterile. If he failed to identify and correct one weak point in the process, the company might fail an inspection, or worse, thousands of consumers could get food poisoning. In 2010 Eric faced one of the most stressful, and unfortunately common, events in life: He was laid off. But Eric didn't view the job loss as a loss at all; he saw it as an opportunity to finally fulfill his childhood dream of pursuing a career in law enforcement. A few months later, he was training to become a police officer at Onondaga Community College.

When you ask Eric how the various stressors in his life affected him, he has few negative things to say. Even while working upwards of 70 hours a week at the plant, he was eating well, sleeping soundly, and maintaining balance in his life. Despite the long hours and constant pressure, he felt relatively happy and fulfilled. Have you ever considered that some stressors can be positive? According to arousal theory, humans seek an optimal level of arousal, and what is *optimal* is not the same for everyone. 📁

EUSTRESS AND DISTRESS   Clearly, stressors cannot be avoided completely. And some stressors are enjoyable: we feel excitement before a big trip or the birth of a new baby. For Eric, getting married and witnessing the birth of his first child were among the most stressful and joyful events in life. "Oh man, you want to talk about sweaty palms, me shaking, and a whole lot of emotion?" he says, remembering the day he stood at the altar. And the birth of his son? "Unreal," he says. Immediately after the delivery, doctors placed his son on his wife's chest. The baby's eyes were still closed, but when he opened them, Eric was the first person he saw. It was the proudest moment of Eric's life. This "good" kind of stressor leads to **eustress** (yoo'-stres), which is the stress response to agreeable or positive events. Of course, most people associate stress with negative events. These types of undesirable or disagreeable occurrences lead to the particular stress response known as **distress.** Now let's find out how eustress and distress might affect your health.

Major Life Events

LO 2   Describe the Social Readjustment Rating Scale in relation to life events and illness.

Holmes and Rahe (1967) were among the first to propose that life-changing events are potentially stressors. In other words, any event that requires a life adjustment, such as marriage, the birth of a child, or a change in financial status, can cause a stress reaction. They also suggested that these life-changing events have a cumulative effect; the more events you experience in a row or within a brief period of time, the greater the potential for an increased stress reaction and negative health outcomes. Numerous studies have examined these types of events and the strain they cause. Think back to the analogy of applying a force to the wing of an airplane. The degree to which the wing bends (or breaks) indicates the strain it is under (Lazarus, 1993). Researchers have found links between certain life events (the force causing strain) and illnesses (the response) such as sudden cardiac death, heart attack, leukemia, diabetes, influenza, psychiatric disorders, and a variety of other conditions (Hatch & Dohrenwend, 2007; Rabkin & Struening, 1976).

SOCIAL READJUSTMENT RATING SCALE   Illnesses can be clearly defined and identified, but how do psychologists measure *life events?* Holmes and Rahe (1967) developed the Social Readjustment Rating Scale (SRRS) to do just that. With the SRRS, participants are asked to read through a list of events and experiences, and determine which of these happened during the previous year and how

You Asked, Eric Answers

http://qrs.ly/cj4qsg2

How does being a police officer compare to the stress of working in the plant?

CONNECTIONS

In **Chapter 9,** we introduced arousal theory, which suggests behaviors can arise out of the need for stimulation or arousal. Here, we point out that some people seek stressors in order to maintain a satisfying level of arousal.

eustress   (yoo'-stres) The stress response to agreeable or positive stressors.

distress   The stress response to unpleasant and undesirable stressors.

CONNECTIONS

In **Chapter 1,** we explained that a positive correlation indicates that as one variable increases, so does the other variable. Here, we see a positive correlation between life events and health problems: The more life events people have experienced, the more health problems they are likely to have.

many times they occurred. A score is then calculated based on severity ratings of events and the frequency of their occurrence. An event like the death of a spouse has a greater severity rating than something like a traffic violation. Participants are also asked to report any illnesses or accidents they experienced during the same period. Researchers then use this information to look at the correlation between life events and health problems (Kobasa, 1979). Correlations range between .20 and .78, although they are generally lower than .30 (Rabkin & Struening, 1976). But remember, a correlation between life events and illness (or any correlation for that matter) is no proof of causality. There is always the possibility that a third factor, such as poverty, may be causing both illnesses and major life-changing events. Someone who is impoverished might not have employment or access to good health care, nutrition, and so forth. In this case, poverty is leading to stressful life events *and* poor health outcomes.

First used in the late 1960s, the SRRS has been updated over the years. (For example, the original scale included "mortgage over $10,000" as an event.) The rating scale has also been adapted to better match the life events of specific populations; an example is the College Undergraduate Stress Scale (CUSS; Renner & Mackin, 1998; **Figure 11.1**). Even with this degree of specificity, the scale may not be suitable for every person. In addition to dealing with term papers, midterms, and other college-related life events, many of today's college students face a host of other potential stressors, such as making car payments and raising children.

FIGURE 11.1

Sample Items from the College Undergraduate Stress Scale

Reprinted by permission of SAGE Publications/APA/LAWRENCE/ERLBAUM ASSOCIATES, INC. from Renner and Macklin (1998)

Event	Rating
Being raped	100
Death of a close friend	97
Contracting a sexually transmitted infection (other than AIDS)	94
Finals week	90
Flunking a class	89
Financial difficulties	84
Writing a major term paper	83
Talking in front of class	72
Difficulties with a roommate	66
Maintaining a steady dating relationship	55
Commuting to campus or work, or both	54
Getting straight As	51
Falling asleep in class	40

try this

Imagine you were tasked with redesigning the College Undergraduate Stress Scale (CUSS) to bring it up to date. How would you decide what types of items to include in your rating scale? You could begin as many researchers do—by gathering pilot data. Ask five people to complete the CUSS inventory and then request that they make suggestions for additional events to be included in a new inventory.

Another possible problem with self-report scales such as the SRRS and the CUSS is that people tend to forget events over time, or the opposite—they tend to focus more on past events than recent ones (Pachana, Brilleman, & Dobson, 2011). What's more, not all negative life-changing events lead to bad outcomes. Some have even suggested that moderate exposure to stress makes us stronger, a view described as *stress inoculation*. Someone with a "low to moderate" degree of stress may end up with "better mental health and well-being" and a greater ability to cope with pain than those who either have faced no hardships or have had to handle an overwhelming level of adversity (Seery, 2011).

Looking across cultures, we see most people rate the weight of life-changing events very similarly (Leontopoulou, Jimerson, & Anderson, 2011; Scully, Tosi, & Banning, 2000). For example, people from France, Belgium, Switzerland, and Malaysia are similar to Americans in their views about the readjustment required for life events (Harmon, Masuda, & Homes, 1970; Woon, Masuda, Wagner, & Holmes, 1971).

Posttraumatic Stress Disorder

One type of event not included in the SRRS, but which is familiar to police officers and other first responders, is a major disaster experience. These cataclysmic events include natural disasters such as hurricanes, earthquakes, and tornadoes, as well as multicar accidents, war, and terrorist attacks. The emotional and physical responses to such occurrences can last for many years, manifesting themselves in nightmares, flashbacks, depression, grief, anxiety, and other symptoms related to *posttraumatic stress disorder.*

In order to be diagnosed with **posttraumatic stress disorder (PTSD),** a person must be exposed to or threatened by an event involving death, serious injury, or some form of sexual violence. Someone could develop PTSD after witnessing a violent assault or accident, or upon learning about the traumatic experiences of family members, close friends, perhaps even strangers. In some cases, the exposure to trauma is ongoing. First responders like Eric, for example, may witness disturbing scenarios on a weekly basis. For veterans and service members previously deployed to war zones in Afghanistan and Iraq, the estimated incidence of PTSD is 13.8%, based on a study of almost 2,000 participants questioned about their symptoms (Schell & Marshall, 2008). In contrast, around 3.5% of the general population is estimated to have received a PTSD diagnosis during the previous 12 months (American Psychiatric Association, 2013).

However, not everyone exposed to trauma will develop PTSD. Over the course of a lifetime, most people will experience an event that qualifies as a "psychological trauma," but only 5–10% will actually develop PTSD as a result (Bonanno, Westphal, & Mancini, 2011). To be diagnosed with PTSD, a person must experience at least one of the following symptoms: (1) distressing, disturbing, and spontaneously recurring memories of an event; (2) dreams with content or emotions associated with the event; (3) "dissociative reactions" that include feeling as if the event is happening again (flashbacks); (4) extreme psychological distress when reminded of the event; or (5) obvious physical reactions to cues related to the event.

Many people with PTSD try to avoid environmental cues (people, places, or objects) linked to the trauma. If someone were involved in a serious car accident on U.S. Highway 101, then simply driving along that thoroughfare may trigger unwanted memories. Other symptoms include difficulty remembering the details of the event, unrealistic self-expectations, ongoing self-blame, and loss of interest in activities that once were enjoyable. Someone with PTSD might be irritable or aggressive, lashing out at loved ones for no apparent reason. She may have trouble sleeping and concentrating. Also associated with PTSD are *dissociative symptoms,* which may include distorted perceptions of the world, and the feeling of observing oneself from the outside (American Psychological Association, 2013d; Friedman, Resick, Bryant, & Brewin, 2011).

Among those at risk for PTSD are police officers (Berger et al., 2011), many of whom bear witness to bloody crime scenes, traumatized victims, and gun violence. But it is not just these types of traumas that impact police officers; just as important are the more chronic stressors, like being overworked, having unpleasant relationships with colleagues, and not getting enough time with family (Collins & Gibbs, 2003; Maguen et al., 2009).

It's Nonstop: Chronic Stressors

You don't have to be a police officer to appreciate the burden of everyday stress. For some of us, stressors come from balancing school and work, or taking care of young children. Many face the constant stressor of battling a chronic illness like diabetes,

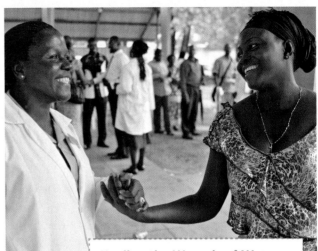

Healing the Wounds of War Physician assistant Klubo Mulba (left) smiles at her former client, Surprise Otto, at JFK Hospital in Monrovia, Liberia. One of Liberia's first mental health clinicians, Mulba received her training through a joint program between The Carter Center and the Liberia Ministry of Health and Social Welfare. On top of dealing with the aftermath of an Ebola epidemic, Liberia's population continues to recover from a 13-year civil war that ended in 2003. Approximately 40% of the population is affected by PTSD (The Carter Center, 2013). The Carter Center/P. Rohe

posttraumatic stress disorder (PTSD) A psychological disorder characterized by exposure to or being threatened by an event involving death, serious injury, or sexual violence; can include disturbing memories, nightmares, flashbacks, and other distressing symptoms.

asthma, or cancer (Sansom-Daly, Peate, Wakefield, Bryant, & Cohn, 2012), or caring for an adult child with a severe mental disorder (Barker, Greenberg, Seltzer, & Almeida, 2012). For some 35 million people and their families (World Health Organization [WHO], 2015), living with HIV provides a host of different stressors.

HIV AND AIDS   One of the most feared sexually transmitted infections (STIs), **human immunodeficiency virus (HIV)** is spread through the transfer of bodily fluids (such as blood, semen, vaginal fluid, or breast milk). Often the virus does not show up on blood tests for up to 6 months after infection, so you cannot assume you are "safe" just because you receive a negative test result—hence, the importance of having protected sex. HIV eventually progresses to **acquired immune deficiency syndrome (AIDS),** which generally results in a severely compromised immune system. A weakened immune system makes the body much more susceptible to opportunistic infections caused by bacteria, viruses, or fungi, and this vulnerability increases as the disease progresses.

HIV has taken an enormous toll on human life. Since the virus was first identified in 1981, it has infected nearly 78 million people, about half of whom have died (WHO, 2015). Worldwide, HIV is a leading cause of death, and in sub-Saharan Africa it is *the* leading killer (Kendall, 2012, June). Approximately 1.2 million people in the United States have HIV, and some 20% of them likely do not know they are infected (Hoppel, 2012).

What comes to mind when you think of stressors associated with HIV? Perhaps you imagine receiving the diagnosis, sharing the news with loved ones, or facing the possibility of developing AIDS. Did you think about the cost of treatment? HIV medications are very expensive, approximately $20,000 per year per person in the United States. And because of funding shortfalls, some 2000 Americans may not be getting the therapies they need (Maxmen, 2012). The problem is global. In 2010, 7.6 million HIV sufferers around the world could not gain access to treatment (Granich et al., 2012). This inability to pay for proper medical treatment relates to a stressor that is even more widespread than HIV: poverty.

LO 3   Summarize how poverty, adjusting to a new culture, and daily hassles affect health.

POVERTY   The number of Americans living at or below the poverty line is significant. As of 2011, 22% of children under 6 years in the United States were living below the poverty level (Addy, Engelhardt, & Skinner, 2013). People struggling to make ends meet experience numerous stressors, including poor health care, lack of preventive health care, noisy living situations, overcrowding, violence, and underfunded schools (Blair & Raver, 2012; Mistry & Wadsworth, 2011). The cycle of poverty is difficult to break, so these stressors often persist across generations. The longer people live in poverty, the more exposure they have to stressors, and the greater the likelihood they will become ill (Miller, Chen, & Parker, 2011). For children in particular, the impact of socioeconomic status (SES) can have lifelong repercussions because environmental stressors affect the developing brain. Some of the factors associated with low SES and permanent changes to the brain include poor nutrition, toxins in the environment, and abuse. In some cases, these irregularities in brain development may lead to differences in "adult neurocognitive outcomes" (D'Angiulli, Lipina, & Olesinska, 2012, September 6). Factors linked to poverty have been associated with "inequalities" in the development of cognitive and socioemotional abilities, which can impact performance in school and at work (Lipina & Posner, 2012, August 17).

CONNECTIONS

In **Chapter 9,** we described various sexually transmitted infections (STIs), diseases that are passed on through sexual activity. There are many types of STIs, but most are caused by viruses or bacteria. Viral STIs such as HIV and herpes do not have cures, only treatments to reduce symptoms.

CONNECTIONS

In **Chapter 7,** we discussed the relationship between poverty and cognitive abilities (socioeconomic status is associated with scores on intelligence tests). In **Chapter 8,** we presented evidence suggesting that isolation and lack of stimulation can hamper the development of young brains. Here, we highlight the link between poverty-related stressors and neurocognitive development.

human immunodeficiency virus (HIV) A virus transferred via bodily fluids (blood, semen, vaginal secretions, or breast milk) that causes the breakdown of the immune system, eventually resulting in AIDS.

acquired immune deficiency syndrome (AIDS) This condition, caused by HIV, generally results in a severely compromised immune system, which makes the body vulnerable to other infections.

acculturative stress (ə-ˌkəl-chə-ˈrā-tiv) Stress that occurs when people move to new countries or cultures and must adjust to a new way of life.

social support The assistance we acquire from others.

ACCULTURATIVE STRESS Another increasingly common source of stress is migration. As of 2013, there were 232 million migrants dispersed across the world (United Nations Population Fund, n.d., para. 1). These people may deal with varying degrees of **acculturative stress** (ə-,kəl-chə-'rā-tiv), or stress associated with adjusting to a new way of life. How would it feel to leave behind your extended family and close friends, and move to a foreign land where the language, customs, holidays, and belief systems are new and different? Perhaps you have had this experience; about 1 in 8 people living in the United States was born in another country (United States Census Bureau, 2013, February 13).

There are various ways people respond to acculturative stress (Berry, 1997). Some try to assimilate, letting go of old ways and adopting those of the new culture. But assimilation can cause problems if family members or friends from the old culture reject the new one, or have trouble assimilating themselves. Another approach is to cling to one's roots and remain *separated* from the new culture. This can be very problematic if the new culture does not support this type of separation and requires assimilation. A combination of these two approaches is *integration,* or holding on to some elements of the old culture, but also adopting aspects of the new one.

The degree of acculturative stress varies greatly from one individual to the next. Some people thrive on new soil (a prime example being Mohamed Dirie from Chapter 9), while others struggle with the stress of starting over. What determines the intensity of acculturative stress, and why do some people seem to have an easier time with it than others?

CONNECTIONS

In **Chapter 8,** we discussed Piaget's concept of assimilation, which refers to a cognitive approach to dealing with new information. This suggests that a person attempts to understand new information using her existing knowledge base. Here, assimilation means letting go of old ways and adopting the customs of a new culture.

Culture Shock
A woman shops for groceries in the Chinatown area of Flushing in Queens, New York. Queens is the most ethnically varied urban community on the planet, providing a home for people from more than 100 countries (Weber, 2013, April 30). Immigrants can either *assimilate* into, *separate* from, or *integrate* into their new cultures. Mark Peterson/Redux

across the WORLD

The Stress of Starting Anew

Imagine trying to get a job, pay your bills, or simply make friends in a world where most everyone speaks a foreign language. Familiarity with language appears to play a key role in determining acculturative stress levels. A study of Haitian immigrants in the United States found lower levels of acculturative stress among those who spoke English (Belizaire & Fuertes, 2011). "The ability to speak English is crucial to the adjustment and well-being of immigrants in the United States," the authors wrote, "and some researchers see this ability as the best indicator of acculturation" (p. 93). Another important determinant is the degree of difference between old and new cultures. Chinese graduate students have been found to experience less acculturative stress studying in Hong Kong as opposed to Australia. Presumably, this is because the cultures of China and Hong Kong are more similar (Pan & Wong, 2011). Finally, we cannot forget the unpleasant reality of discrimination, which causes great stress for the world's immigrant populations. Common targets of discrimination in the United States are people from India, Pakistan, and other South Asian countries. Discrimination against South Asians, which appears to have increased after the terrorist attacks of 9/11, erodes psychological well-being, and in some cases correlates with the development of depression (Kaduvettoor-Davidson & Inman, 2013; Tummala-Narra, Alegria, & Chen, 2012).

IMMIGRATION IS STRESSFUL, ESPECIALLY IF YOU DON'T SPEAK THE NEW LANGUAGE.

Fortunately, there are ways to combat acculturative stress. One of the best defenses is **social support,** or assistance from others. A small study of refugees in Austria indicated that those who had social support from a sponsor experienced less anxiety and depression and had an easier time adapting (Renner, Laireiter, & Maier, 2012).

Life Saver
Kehlen Kirby has one of the most stressful jobs imaginable—providing emergency medical services to people injured in car accidents, fires, and other traumatic incidents. The constant exposure to pain and suffering helps Kehlen maintain perspective on the hassles of daily life; he doesn't sweat the small stuff. Leslie Nazario/ Portraits by Leslie

FIGURE 11.2

The Hassles and Uplifts Scale
Research participants were instructed to circle a number rating the degree to which each item was a hassle (left column) and an uplift (right column). Numbers range from 0 ("none or not applicable") to 3 ("a great deal"). The scale includes 53 items, a sample of which are shown here. © 1988 by the American Psychological Association. Adapted with permission from DeLongis, Folkman, and Lazarus (1988).

Hassles		Uplifts
0 1 2 3	Your child(ren)	0 1 2 3
0 1 2 3	Your friend(s)	0 1 2 3
0 1 2 3	Your work load	0 1 2 3
0 1 2 3	Enough money for emergencies	0 1 2 3
0 1 2 3	Financial care for someone who doesn't live with you	0 1 2 3
0 1 2 3	Your drinking	0 1 2 3
0 1 2 3	Your physical appearance	0 1 2 3
0 1 2 3	Political or social issues	0 1 2 3
0 1 2 3	Amount of free time	0 1 2 3
0 1 2 3	Being organized	0 1 2 3

The stresses of acculturation tend to be gnawing and constant, but some stressors are sudden and dramatic. These are the types that ambulance drivers and paramedics encounter every day. Welcome to the world of Kehlen Kirby.

THE PARAMEDIC'S ROLLERCOASTER   Kehlen Kirby sees more pain and suffering in one month than most people do in a lifetime. In his 8 years working as an emergency medical services (EMS) provider in Pueblo, Colorado, this 26-year-old man has witnessed the highest highs and lowest lows of human experience. He has rescued people from flaming car wrecks, treated teenage gang members for stab and gunshot wounds, and watched chain-smokers who are dying from emphysema beg for cigarettes en route to the hospital. In between the sadness and suffering, there are also stories of hope and inspiration, as when Kehlen and his colleagues delivered a baby on the shoulder of U.S. Route 50, and the mother went from a state of screaming hysteria to smiling, laughing bliss.

Being involved in life-or-death situations may be emotionally challenging, but it helps Kehlen keep things in perspective. "All the traumatic calls, the car wrecks and shootings, it makes you appreciate life," he says. Kehlen will never ride in a car without wearing a seatbelt; he has seen the horrific consequences of not buckling up. He also doesn't get too aggravated by everyday annoyances, like the sound of his own newborn shrieking and wailing. Many new parents find a baby's cries disconcerting. Not Kehlen. From his paramedic's perspective, a crying baby means a breathing baby. "I love it when she cries," he says. But the fact that Kehlen is unfazed by everyday annoyances like screaming infants and dirty laundry probably makes him the exception rather than the rule. Research suggests that these daily hassles can have a significant impact on us. 📁

What a Hassle, What a Joy

Daily hassles are the minor problems or irritants we deal with on a regular basis, such as traffic, financial worries, misplaced keys, messy roommates—a list that does not seem to end. These hassles, although seemingly minor, are repetitive and ever present. The strain of dealing with them can add up, potentially taking a toll on our health and well-being (DeLongis, Coyne, Dakof, Folkman, & Lazarus, 1982; DeLongis, Folkman, & Lazarus, 1988). For example, research suggests that hassles are closely associated with short-lived illnesses, such as colds and headaches (Bottos & Dewey, 2004; DeLongis et al., 1988; Pedersen, Zachariae, & Bovbjerg, 2010). It's a good thing that the weight of our daily hassles is counterbalanced by the uplifts in our lives.

Uplifts are positive experiences that have the potential to make us happy. Think about the last time you smiled; it was likely in response to an uplift, such as a funny text from a friend, a child presenting you with a handmade gift, or a congratulatory e-mail about one of your achievements. We all have hassles and uplifts, but how do they interact to affect our health and well-being? Researchers have been asking this question for decades.

DeLongis and colleagues (1988) developed a scale of daily hassles and uplifts, and used it to explore the relationship between stress and illness (**Figure 11.2**). They asked participants to read through a list of 53 items that could be either hassles or uplifts, such as meeting deadlines, maintaining a car, interacting with fellow workers, and dealing with the weather. Participants then rated these items on a 4-point scale indicating "how much of a hassle" and "how much of an uplift" each was on that particular day (0 = none or not applicable, to 3 = a great deal). They also asked participants to report any illness, injuries, or symptoms they experienced that same day. What did they find? Over a 6-month period, there was a significant link between hassles and health problems. The more daily stressors the participants reported, the more likely they were to suffer from sore throats, headaches, influenza, back problems, and other health issues. More recently, researchers uncovered a link between daily stressors and cardiovascular risk factors, such as high blood pressure (Uchino, Berg, Smith, Pearce, & Skinner, 2006). Daily hassles also increase the risk of catching contagious diseases and may prolong the course of illness (Glaser & Kiecolt-Glaser, 2005).

How do hassles and uplifts affect psychological and social health? One group of researchers studied two Israeli populations (Jewish and Arab), exploring the similarities and differences within subgroups living in the same country. While differences existed, the researchers noted some important similarities. In both groups, for example, daily uplifts had a positive impact on "family satisfaction" and daily hassles had a negative impact on "life satisfaction," though the meaning of "uplift" differed between the two groups (Lavee & Ben-Ari, 2008).

Now that we have explored various types of stressors, from major life events to everyday annoyances, let's find out what occurs in the body and brain when we respond.

CONNECTIONS

In **Chapter 9,** we discussed different ways that we can increase our well-being. Keeping a journal and recording feelings of gratefulness are associated with increased happiness and well-being. Here, we see that uplifts are linked to family satisfaction. Being mindful of the good things in our lives has many benefits.

show what you know

1. _____ is a response to perceived threats or challenges resulting from stimuli that cause strain.

2. The Social Readjustment Rating Scale was created to measure the severity and frequency of life events. This scale is most often used to examine the relationship between stressors and which of the following?
   a. aging
   b. levels of eustress
   c. perceived threats
   d. illness

3. _____ can occur when a person must adjust to life in a new country, often due to unfamiliar language, religious beliefs, and holidays.
   a. Eustress
   b. Acculturative stress
   c. Uplifts
   d. Posttraumatic stress disorder

4. Reflect upon the last few days. Can you think of three uplifts and three hassles you have experienced during this period?

✓ CHECK YOUR ANSWERS IN APPENDIX C.

Stress and Your Health

TROUBLE UNDERCOVER Meet Sergeant Michelle, a long-time veteran of a police department in a large city at the foot of the Rocky Mountains. Michelle currently works in internal affairs investigating potential policy violations by police officers—a highly stressful position given that the outcome of such investigations can lead to the suspension or termination of fellow officers. But it doesn't match the intense, fear-for-your-life type of stress that Michelle experienced at other points in her career, like the time her cover was nearly blown in an operation to bust crack-cocaine dealers. Posing as a buyer, Michelle walked into a house where a suspected dealer was selling. One of the men who happened to be hanging out in the house gave her a funny look, and she instantly realized that he recognized her as a police officer. Fortunately, the man did not give her away (who knows what the dealer would have done had her identity been revealed), and Michelle escaped the situation unscathed. But we can only imagine what she must have felt at that moment.

Faced with the prospect of being gunned down by a drug dealer, Michelle most likely experienced the sensations associated with the fight-or-flight response, such as increased pulse, breathing rate, and mental alertness. A coordinated effort of the sympathetic nervous system and the endocrine system, the fight-or-flight reaction primes the body to respond to danger, either by escaping (bolting out of the crack house, as in Michelle's case) or confronting the threat head-on (defending herself against a physical attack). Let's take a closer look at this survival mechanism.

CONNECTIONS

We introduced the fight-or-flight response to stressors in **Chapter 2.** The sympathetic nervous system is a division of the autonomic nervous system, which regulates the body's involuntary activity (such as digestion and the beating of the heart). Here, we will learn how this automatic activity may relate to illness.

daily hassles Minor and regularly occurring problems that can act as stressors.

uplifts Experiences that are positive and have the potential to make one happy.

CONNECTIONS

In **Chapter 2,** we introduced the parasympathetic nervous system, which is responsible for the "rest-and-digest" process following activation of the fight-or-flight response. The parasympathetic nervous system works with the sympathetic nervous system to prepare us for crises and then to calm us when danger has passed.

Selye's Stages
Endocrinologist Hans Selye proposed that the body passes through a predictable sequence of changes in response to stress. Selye's general adaptation syndrome includes three phases: the *alarm stage,* the *resistance stage,* and the *exhaustion stage.*
Bettmann/CORBIS

Synonyms
hypothalamic–pituitary–adrenal (HPA) system hypothalamic–pituitary–adrenal axis (HPA axis)

general adaptation syndrome (GAS) A specific pattern of physiological reactions to stressors that includes the alarm stage, resistance stage, and exhaustion stage.

Fight or Flight

LO 4   Identify the brain and body changes that characterize the fight-or-flight response.

When faced with a threatening situation, portions of the brain, including the hypothalamus, activate the sympathetic nervous system, which leads to the secretion of catecholamines, such as epinephrine and norepinephrine. These hormones cause heart rate, blood pressure, respiration, and blood flow to the muscles to increase. Meanwhile, digestion slows and the pupils dilate.

Physiological responses prepare us for an emergency by efficiently managing the body's resources. Once the emergency has ended, the parasympathetic system reverses these processes by reducing heart rate, blood pressure, and so on. If a person is exposed to a threatening situation for long periods of time, the fight-or-flight system remains active. This in turn can have detrimental effects on health (Shonkoff et al., 2012), an issue we will explore later.

LO 5   Outline the general adaptation syndrome (GAS).

GENERAL ADAPTATION SYNDROME   Hans Selye, introduced earlier in the chapter, identified police work "as likely the most stressful occupation in the world" (according to Violanti, 1992, p. 718). One of the first to suggest the human body responds to stressors in a predictable way, Selye (1936) described a specific pattern of physiological reactions, which he called the **general adaptation syndrome (GAS).**

According to this theory, the body passes through three stages (**Infographic 11.2**). The first is the *alarm stage,* or the body's initial response to a threatening situation, similar to the fight-or-flight response. Arousal increases, and the body prepares to deal with the threat. Following the alarm stage is the *resistance stage.* During this period, the body maintains a high level of arousal (though not as high as that of the alarm stage), but with a decreased response to new stressors. Under such intense physiological demands, the body simply cannot address any new threatening situations that might arise. According to Selye, this is when some people start to show signs of *diseases of adaptation,* such as hypertension and arthritis (Selye, 1953; Selye & Fortier, 1950). If the threat remains and the person can no longer adapt, Selye suggested that the body then moves into the *exhaustion stage.* At this point, the body's resources become depleted, resulting in vulnerability to illnesses, physical exhaustion, and even death.

LO 6   Describe the function of the hypothalamic–pituitary–adrenal (HPA) system.

HYPOTHALAMIC–PITUITARY–ADRENAL SYSTEM   Overseeing the sympathetic nervous system's response to stress is the *hypothalamic–pituitary–adrenal (HPA) system* (Infographic 11.2). This HPA system helps to maintain balance in the body by directing not only the sympathetic nervous system, but also the neuroendocrine and immune systems (Ben-Zvi, Vernon, & Broderick, 2009). The immune system defends the body from bacteria, viruses, and other types of invaders by deploying cells and chemicals to confront these threats. When a stressful situation arises, the hypothalamus initiates a cascade of responses by alerting the pituitary gland, which then sends signals to the adrenal cortex, which in turn orders the secretion of corticosteroids, such as cortisol. These hormones summon the immune system to fend off a threat and reduce the amount of energy used for nonessential activities (that is, those not associated with the threat), such as digestion and bladder control. The HPA system responds to a stressor in the same way it would to a pathogen—by mobilizing a defense response. You might say it's working overtime. How do you think this affects a person's health?

Physiological Responses to Stress

When faced with an emergency, our bodies go through a series of physiological responses that assist us in coping with a stressor. Activation of the *fight-or-flight* response and *hypothalamic–pituitary–adrenal (HPA)* system gives us the energy and resources we need to cope with a temporary stressor. Studying these physiological responses, Hans Selye (1956) suggested that the sequence follows the same path no matter the stressor. Selye called this sequence the general adaptation syndrome (GAS). He found that when the stressor remains, our bodies can no longer adapt.

GENERAL ADAPTATION SYNDROME (GAS)

In the alarm stage, short-term responses are activated, giving us energy to combat a threat. In the resistance stage, resources remain mobilized, and we continue to cope with the stressor. But eventually we enter the exhaustion stage, becoming weak, susceptible to illness, and less able to cope with the stressor (Selye, 1956).

STRESSOR

Resistance to stress — high / low

normal level of resistance to stress

Alarm stage
(stress response activated)

Resistance stage
(coping with stressor)

Exhaustion stage
(reserves diminished)

SHORT-TERM RESPONSES TO STRESS

Amygdala processes information about stressor. If threat is perceived, hypothalamus triggers short-term stress response.

STRESSOR

Hypothalamus

Pituitary gland

FIGHT-OR-FLIGHT RESPONSE

ACTIVATES

Sympathetic Nervous System

SENDS SIGNAL TO

Adrenal Medulla
(core of adrenal glands)

RELEASES

Catecholamines
epinephrine, norepinephrine

CAUSES

Efficient management of bodily resources ensures these are available for emergency action:
- increased heart rate
- increased respiration
- increased blood flow to muscles
- slowed digestion
- dilated pupils

HYPOTHALAMIC–PITUITARY–ADRENAL (HPA) SYSTEM

ALERTS

Pituitary gland

SENDS SIGNAL TO

Adrenal Cortex
(outside layer of adrenal glands)

RELEASES

Corticosteroids
including cortisol

CAUSES

Efficient management of bodily resources; immune system activation

Adrenal glands

Kidneys

✳ The HPA system manages resources similar to the fight-or-flight response, but it takes longer to mobilize these processes, and the effects are more sustained.

PROLONGED STRESS

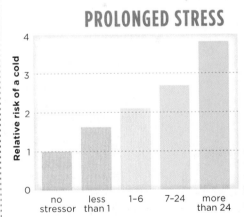

Relative risk of a cold — 0, 1, 2, 3, 4

Duration of stressor (in months): no stressor / less than 1 / 1–6 / 7–24 / more than 24

Prolonged stress can cause the immune system to break down. As you can see, the risk of becoming sick is directly related to the duration of a stressor. This effect is seen even when the stressor is not traumatic. Data in this study were collected from people reporting on interpersonal conflicts and problems concerning work (Cohen et al., 1998).

Credit: Firefighter, Thinkstock; Firefighter crouching, Alan Bailey/Shutterstock; Male fire fighter with smoky background, Colin Anderson/age fotostock

Synonyms
health psychology behavioral medicine
B lymphocytes B cells
T lymphocytes T cells

FIGURE 11.3
The Immune System
Our immunity derives from a complex system involving structures and organs throughout the body that support the work of specialized cell types to keep us healthy. Man: B2M Productions/Getty Images; T lymphocytes & B lymphocytes: Steve Gschmeissner/Science Source; Natural killer cells & macrophages: Eye of Science/Science Source

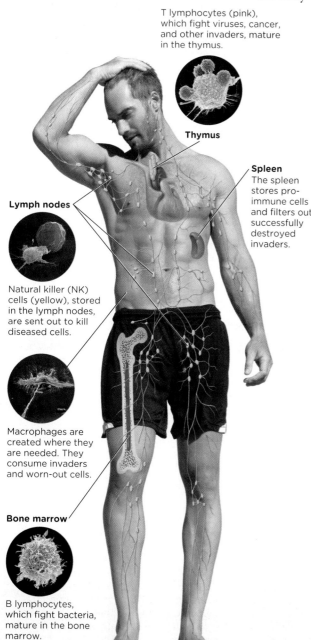

T lymphocytes (pink), which fight viruses, cancer, and other invaders, mature in the thymus.

Thymus

Spleen
The spleen stores pro-immune cells and filters out successfully destroyed invaders.

Lymph nodes

Natural killer (NK) cells (yellow), stored in the lymph nodes, are sent out to kill diseased cells.

Macrophages are created where they are needed. They consume invaders and worn-out cells.

Bone marrow

B lymphocytes, which fight bacteria, mature in the bone marrow.

Psychologists have been exploring this issue for decades, trying to determine how stress influences human health. Early in the 1960s, the field of **health psychology** began to gather momentum, exploring the biological, psychological, and social factors that contribute to health and illness. Health psychology seeks to explain how food choices, social interactions, and living environments affect our predisposition to illness. Researchers in this field contribute to health education, helping people develop positive eating and exercise habits. They conduct public policy research that influences health-related guidelines. Health psychologists also study the impact of personality factors, coping style, cognitive appraisal, poverty, culture, social support, and religion—all topics addressed in this chapter.

Is Stress Making You Sick?

LO 7 Explain how stressors relate to health problems.

Before we explore the connection between stress and illness, we must understand how the body deals with illness in the first place. Let's take a side trip into introductory biology and learn about the body's main defense against disease—the immune system (**Figure 11.3**). The immune system is made up of the spleen, lymph nodes, and bone marrow. When disease-causing invaders threaten the body, the immune system deploys a special army of white blood cells called **lymphocytes.** Lymphocytes are produced in bone marrow, and their job is to battle enemies such as viruses and bacteria. When the body is expending its resources to deal with an ongoing stressor, the immune system is less powerful, and the work of the lymphocytes is compromised.

Like a platoon of soldiers, the immune system has a defense team to fight off invaders. Should the intruder(s) get past the skin, the *macrophages* ("big eaters") are ready to attack. These cells hunt and consume invaders as well as worn-out cells in the body. Cells that have been affected by invaders, such as viruses and cancer, are the targets of *natural killer cells* (*NK cells*), which inject compromised cells with a deadly chemical. In addition, NK cells release a protein that prevents the infection from spreading to other cells. In some cases, the body must call on its "special ops" teams. These are the *B lymphocytes* and *T lymphocytes.* The B lymphocytes mature in the bone marrow and produce antibodies that chemically inhibit bacteria. The T lymphocytes mature in the thymus and play an integral role in fighting cancer, viruses, and other disease-causing agents that the B lymphocytes have not been successful in warding off (Straub, 2012).

Earlier we mentioned that stressors are correlated with health problems. But how exactly do stressors such as beliefs and attitudes affect the physical body? In other words, what is the *causal* relationship between stressors and illness? Let's address this question by examining some illnesses thought to be closely linked to stressors (Cohen, Miller, & Rabin, 2001).

GASTRIC ULCERS AND STRESSORS Gastric ulcers have long been thought to be associated with stress, but the nature of this link has not always been clear. For many years, it was believed that stress alone caused gastric ulcers, but researchers then started to suspect other culprits. They found evidence that the bacterium *H. pylori* plays an important role. This does not mean that *H. pylori* is always to blame, however. Some people who carry the bacteria never get ulcers, while others develop ulcers in its absence. It seems that many factors influence the development of ulcers, among them tobacco use, family history, and excess gastric acid (Fink, 2011).

CANCER AND STRESSORS   Cancer has also been associated with stress, both in terms of risk and development. Specifically, stress has been linked to the suppression of T lymphocytes and NK cells, which help monitor immune system reactions to the invasion of developing tumors. When a person is exposed to stressors, the body is less able to mount an effective immune response, which increases the risk of cancer (Reiche, Nunes, & Morimoto, 2004).

In the United States and other Western countries, breast cancer is the greatest cancer risk for women, and some evidence suggests it is associated with stress. In a meta-analysis of 26 studies examining the association between life events and risk for breast cancer, death of a spouse was found to be modestly linked to the development of breast cancer; however, no other life events were related to increased risk (Duijts, Zeegers, & Borne, 2003). Other studies have found no association between life events and breast cancer risk (Roberts, Newcomb, Trentham-Dietz, & Storer, 1995).

Stress has been correlated with other types of cancer, though not always in the expected direction. One group of researchers examined the relationship between chronic daily stressors and the development of colorectal cancer using a prospective study in which nearly 12,000 Danes (who had never been diagnosed with colorectal cancer) were followed for 18 years (Nielsen et al., 2008). The researchers noted some surprising findings, particularly with respect to females. Women who reported higher levels of "stress intensity" and "daily stress" were less likely to develop colon cancer during the course of the study. In contrast, men with "high stress intensity" experienced higher levels of rectal cancer, although this association was not considered to be strong because only a small number actually developed this kind of cancer. The authors suggested that a variety of physiological, mental, and behavioral factors (for example, sex hormones, burnout, and increased alcohol intake) were involved in the relationship between high stress and lower rates of colon cancer in the women.

Why can't researchers agree on the link between cancer and stressors? Part of the problem is that studies are focusing on stressors of different durations. Short- and long-term stressors have distinct effects on the immune system, and thus its ability to combat cancer (Segerstrom & Miller, 2004). For short-lived stressors such as midterm exams, public speaking, and other activities lasting between 5 and 100 minutes, the body responds by increasing the number of NK cells and deploying other immune cells where needed. In other words, short-term stressors tend to augment immune functioning. The situation is quite different with long-term stressors such as military deployment or caring for someone with dementia, which are associated with decreases in NK cells. In order to appreciate the complex relationship between stress, immune function, and cancer, we must also consider biopsychosocial influences on a person's response to stressors. Factors such as age, medical history, social support, and mental health can mediate the link between stressors and cancer (Reiche et al., 2004; Segerstrom & Miller, 2004).

CARDIOVASCULAR DISEASE AND STRESSORS   The same is true for the relationship between stressors and cardiovascular disease. Dimsdale (2008) noted that over 40,000 citations popped up in a medical database when the search terms were "stress" and "heart disease." What constitutes a stressor in this context? Earthquakes, unhappy marriages, and caregiving burdens are just a few stressors associated with a variety of outcomes or vulnerabilities, ranging from abnormalities in heart function to sudden death. Earlier we discussed socioeconomic status and stress; it turns out that both of those variables are factors in cardiovascular disease. Joseph and colleagues reported fivefold higher odds of experiencing "cardiometabolic events" (within

Battling Stress
A group of Marines practice patrolling techniques as part of their combat training. Long-term stressors such as military deployment are associated with declines in NK cells, which help the body fight infections. Scott Olson/ Getty Images

CONNECTIONS

In **Chapter 6,** we discussed the malleability of memory. Problems may arise when study participants are asked to remember events and illnesses from the past. Here we are describing a prospective study, which does not require participants to retrieve information from the distant past, thus reducing opportunities for error.

health psychology The study of the biological, psychological, and social factors that contribute to illness and health.

lymphocyte Type of white blood cell produced in the bone marrow whose job is to battle enemies such as viruses and bacteria.

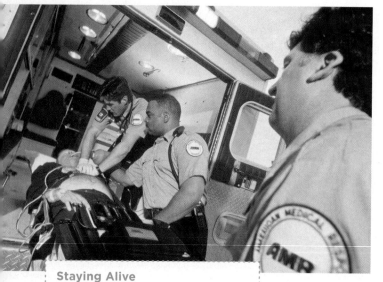

Staying Alive
Paramedics transfer a patient from ambulance to emergency room. The patient is clearly experiencing a health crisis, but the paramedics face their own set of health risks. Working odd hours, not getting enough exercise, eating poorly, and dealing with the ongoing stresses of paramedic work make it challenging to stay healthy. Juan Manuel Silva/age fotostock

5 years) for people who became unemployed as a result of Hurricane Katrina, a devastating natural disaster that occurred in 2005 (Joseph, Matthews, & Myers, 2013, March 25). The faster people get support to decrease "socioeconomic disruptions" related to a disaster, the better their health outcomes.

Other stressors have also been linked to heart disease. "Social-evaluative threats," or concerns about being judged by others (about physical appearance or behaviors in a social context, for example), are associated with increases in blood pressure and consequently elevated risk of heart disease (Smith, Birmingham, & Uchino, 2012). One model suggests that increased job stress can put people at greater risk for developing coronary heart disease, particularly those who perceive a significant degree of job "strain" resulting from high demands, lack of control, and other factors (Ferris, Kline, & Bourdage, 2012).

The mechanisms of the causal relationship between stressors and cardiovascular disease are not totally understood (Straub, 2012). However, we do know that an increase of fatty deposits, inflammation, and scar tissue within artery walls, that is, *atherosclerosis,* is a dangerous risk factor for stroke and heart disease (Go et al., 2013). With this type of damage, blood flow in an artery may become blocked or reduced. Researchers are not sure exactly how atherosclerosis starts, but one theory suggests that it begins with damage to the inner layer of the artery wall, which may be caused by elevated cholesterol and triglycerides, high blood pressure, and cigarette smoke (American Heart Association, 2012). It is important to note that stressors cannot be shown to *cause* changes in cardiovascular health (Dimsdale, 2008). Although there is a clear correlation between biopsychosocial stressors and cardiovascular disease, we cannot say with certainty that these stressors are responsible (Ferris et al., 2012).

Stress and Substances

Stress often exerts its harmful effects indirectly (Cohen et al., 2001). When faced with stressors, we may sleep poorly, eat erratically, and perhaps even drink more alcohol. These behavioral tendencies can lead to significant health problems (Benham, 2010; Ng & Jeffery, 2003).

SMOKING AND STRESS   In Chapter 4, on consciousness, we described how drugs are used to alleviate pain, erase memories, and toy with various aspects of consciousness. But a discussion of drugs is also in order here, because many people use drugs to ease stress. Smokers report that they smoke more cigarettes in response to stressors, as they believe it improves their mood. The association between lighting up and feeling good is one reason smokers have such a hard time quitting (Lerman & Audrain-McGovern, 2010). One study found that when participants were forced to abstain from smoking for some time (a half day, for example), their mood did improve when they finally puffed on a cigarette. However, this was the only stressful condition of the study in which smoking heightened mood; the effect was not observed when participants were made to prepare for a public-speaking task, for example (Perkins, Karelitz, Konklin, Sayette, & Giedgowd, 2010). Such findings are inconsistent with the self-reports of smokers, who claim that they smoke to feel better in a variety of stressful situations.

How do we get people to kick a habit that is perceived as so pleasurable? One effective way is to meet them where they are, rather than taking a one-size-fits-all approach (Mahoney, 2010; Prochaska, Velicer, Prochaska, Delucchi, & Hall, 2006). In other words, we should recognize that not all smokers need the same type of help.

Some need assistance with smoking only; others engage in additional risky behaviors, like eating high-fat diets or getting too much sun. First-time quitters need different interventions than those who have quit before and relapsed. And success is more likely when the benefits and risks of smoking are made clear. For example, smokers often believe quitting will make them gain weight; therefore, they continue to smoke and don't give enough thought to the serious risks of smoking. Gender is another important consideration, as women seem to be more susceptible to anxiety, depression, and perceived stressors when they fail to quit. Men, on the other hand, seem more vulnerable to cigarette cravings (Nakajima & al'Absi, 2012). This leads us to an important point: Do not underestimate the biology of nicotine addiction. Through tolerance, the body becomes dependent on the nicotine; the more you use it, the more of it you need to get the same effect.

ALCOHOL AND STRESS   Much the same could be said for alcohol, another drug frequently used to "take the edge off," or counteract, the unpleasant feelings associated with stress. Perhaps you know someone who "needs" a drink to relax after a rough day. Psychologists explain this type of behavior with *the self-medication hypothesis,* which suggests that people turn to drugs and alcohol to reduce anxiety (Swendsen et al., 2000).

Teenagers, in particular, appear to rely on alcohol to cope with daily hassles (Bailey & Covell, 2011). Adolescents frequently face disagreements with family members, teachers, and peers. They may worry about how they look and whether they are succeeding in school. We need to help adolescents find new and more "healthy" ways to handle these hassles. This means providing more support in schools, and perhaps educating teachers and counselors about the tendency to self-medicate with drugs and alcohol. Later we will discuss some positive coping strategies for teens and adults alike, but first let's see how some people seem to thrive under stress.

CONNECTIONS

In **Chapter 4,** we discussed the concept of physiological dependence and tolerance. When we use drugs, such as nicotine, they alter the chemistry of the brain and body. Over time, the body adapts to the drug and therefore needs more and more of it to create the original effect.

It's Not Medicine
Some people turn to alcohol and other drugs for stress relief, but the *self-medication* approach is not effective. A better strategy might be jogging in the park, laughing with a friend, or doing some deep breathing exercises. Image Source/Alamy

ADRENALINE JUNKIES   What lures a person into an EMS career? The reward of alleviating human suffering is "incredible," according to Kehlen. Imagine walking into the home of a diabetic who is lying on the floor, unconscious and surrounded by trembling family members. You insert an IV line into the patient's vein and deliver D50, a dextrose solution that increases blood sugar. In a few moments, the person is awake as if nothing happened. The family is ecstatic; you have saved their loved one from potential brain damage or death. "People that like to do selfless acts, I think, are made for this job," Kehlen says. And for those who enjoy a good challenge, both physical and mental, an EMS career will not disappoint. Try working for 24 hours in a row, making life-and-death decisions, hoisting heavy bodies onto stretchers, and crouching over patients until your joints burn.

But there appears to be something else drawing people into the EMS profession. You might call it the "adrenaline junkie" factor. Ever since Kehlen was a small boy, he enjoyed a certain amount of risk taking. He was the kid who fearlessly scaled the monkey bars and leaped off the jungle gym, and many of his colleagues claim they were the same way. "All of us probably thought we were 10 feet tall and made of steel," Kehlen says, careful to note that "daring" is not the same as "reckless." One must be calculating when it comes to determining what risks are worth taking.

The adrenaline junkie quality is also apparent in some police officers, according to Sergeant Michelle. An officer patrolling a city beat probably experiences the so-called adrenaline rush at least a few times per week. "When a hot call comes in, anyone worth their salt wants to go," Sergeant Michelle explains ("hot call" meaning anything full of excitement and drama, like a robbery in progress).

Is there really some common adrenaline junkie tendency among police officers, EMS providers, and other first responders? That remains an open question. We do know, though, that first responders are frequently exposed to highly stressful events (Anderson, Litzenberger, & Plecas, 2002; Gayton & Lovell, 2012). With all this exposure to violence and trauma, how do the body and mind hold up? The answer is probably different for each individual, but constant stress certainly has the potential to erode health and well-being.

Too Much Cortisol

LO 8   List some consequences of prolonged exposure to the stress hormone cortisol.

Earlier we discussed the stress hormone cortisol, which plays an important role in mobilizing the body to react to threats and other stressful situations. Cortisol is useful if you are responding to immediate danger, like a raging fire or ruthless assailant. However, you don't want cortisol levels to remain high for long. Both body and brain are impacted when the cortisol system flips into overdrive.

CORTISOL AND KIDS   The negative effects of stress are apparent very early in life—even before birth, in some cases. Increased levels of cortisol in mother and fetus can cause a variety of problems during pregnancy and after birth, including spontaneous abortion, preeclampsia, heart defects, and preterm delivery (Mulder et al., 2002). Infants born to mothers subjected to natural disasters, trauma, and other extreme stressors are more likely to be born prematurely, have low birth weights, exhibit behavioral difficulties, and perhaps even show problems with cognitive development (Davis & Sandman, 2010; Tollenaar, Beijers, Jansen, Riksen-Walraven, & De Weerth, 2011). Prenatal stressors have also been reported to be associated with fussing and crying, but this link might be indirect (Field & Diego, 2008); such temperamental difficulties could be due to preterm birth (Baibazarova et al., 2013).

Now consider the types of stressors some preschool children confront every day. Research shows that conflicts at home can increase cortisol levels in children (Slatcher & Robles, 2012). Verbal exchanges such as the child exclaiming, "No! I don't want to!" and parents saying, "You are going to shut your mouth and be quiet!" are exactly the types of conflicts associated with increased cortisol levels. Cortisol activity may help explain why exposure to conflict during childhood seems to pave the way for health problems (Slatcher & Robles, 2012). Clearly, cortisol plays a role in early development. But how does this stress hormone affect adults?

CORTISOL ON THE JOB   High cortisol levels can have life-or-death consequences, particularly for workers who make on-the-spot safety decisions. In one study, researchers had police officers participate in a realistic simulation of being targeted by shooters. Not only did the officers' cortisol levels rise, but the functioning of their working memory decreased (Taverniers, Smeets, Van Ruysseveldt, Syroit, & von Grumbkow, 2011). Can you imagine the implications of being in a dangerous situation with impaired working memory? Think of the last time you were really afraid, and how difficult it was to think clearly. Your working memory was probably compromised.

Other research suggests that heightened cortisol levels may have the opposite effect. When police officers had to make threat-related decisions in a video simulation, they were better able to discern whether an individual was armed when their cortisol levels were high. But this accuracy increased when the officer faced a simulation involving a Black suspect, and decreased when the suspect was White.

CONNECTIONS

In **Chapter 6,** we presented the concept of working memory, which refers to how we actively maintain and manipulate information in short-term memory. Here, we see how these activities can be impacted by stressful situations.

psychoneuroimmunology (sī-kō-ˌn(y)ür-ō-ˌim-yə-ˈnä-lə-jē) The field that studies the relationships among psychological factors, the nervous system, and immune system functioning.

This finding was the same for the White officers and minority officers participating in the study. The researchers concluded that higher cortisol levels, which were caused by the stressful situation, resulted in "heightened vigilance for danger" (Akinola & Mendes, 2012, p. 172). Apparently, the *perceived* threat of Black men was greater, which is consistent with what social psychologists have learned about the conscious and unconscious reactions many people have to racial minorities (Chapter 14).

PSYCHONEUROIMMUNOLOGY We have now discussed some of the effects of short- and long-term stressors. You know that a spurt of cortisol steps up immunity and prepares the body to confront a threat. You also know that if cortisol levels remain high for prolonged periods (as occurs with chronic stressors), the immune system may not function at an optimal level. We discussed how this affects one's risk for developing gastric ulcers, cancer, and heart disease, but the list of negative health effects is much longer. According to a meta-analysis of over 300 studies, chronic stressors were found to be associated with problematic immune system responses, which may increase the risk for various illnesses involving inflammation, including asthma, allergies, multiple sclerosis, and rheumatoid arthritis (Segerstrom & Miller, 2004). The exact nature of these relationships is yet to be determined, but researchers are working hard to uncover them, especially for people who are aging and who have vulnerable immune systems (Cohen et al., 2001). It is an exciting time for those who specialize in the field of **psychoneuroimmunology** (sī-kō-,n(y)ůr-ō-,im-yə-'nä-lə-jē), which examines the relationships among psychological factors (such as coping, emotions, and beliefs), the nervous system, and the functioning of the immune system.

The field of health psychology, which draws on the biopsychosocial model and psychoneuroimmunology, has shed light on the complex relationship between stress and health (Havelka, Lučanin, & Lučanin, 2009). Now that we understand how profoundly stressors can impact physical well-being, let's explore some real-life situations that can trigger stress.

✓○○○ show what you know

1. According to the _____, the human body responds in a predictable way to stressors, following a specific pattern of physiological reactions.

2. As a police officer, Michelle has found herself in life-threatening situations. When faced with danger, Michelle's body initially exhibits a fight-or-flight reaction, which is equivalent to the _____ of the general adaptation syndrome.
   a. alarm stage
   b. exhaustion stage
   c. diseases of adaptation
   d. acculturative stress

3. _____ helps maintain balance in the body by overseeing the sympathetic nervous system, as well as the neuroendocrine and immune systems.
   a. The general adaptation syndrome
   b. The exhaustion stage
   c. The hypothalamic–pituitary–adrenal system
   d. Eustress

4. Infants of mothers subjected to extreme stressors may be born prematurely, have low birth weights, and exhibit behavioral difficulties. These outcomes result from increased levels of the stress hormone _____.
   a. *H. pylori*
   b. lymphocytes
   c. cortisol
   d. NK cells

5. Why are people under stress more likely to get sick?

✓ CHECK YOUR ANSWERS IN APPENDIX C.

Factors Related to Stress

First responders encounter a wide variety of scenarios, ranging in intensity from five-car pile-ups to soccer injuries. What determines how a first responder reacts in these situations? There are two types of variables to consider: those that reside within the individual and those that exist in the environment. We can see both of these variables at work in one of the most common stressors of everyday life: conflict.

Conflicts

LO 9 Identify different types of conflicts.

When people think of conflict, they may imagine arguments and fist fights, but conflict can also refer to the discomfort one feels when making tough choices. In an **approach–approach conflict,** two or more favorable alternatives are pitted against each other. Here, you must choose between two options you find attractive. Imagine this situation: You have to pick only one class this semester, and to fit your schedule, you must choose between two classes you would really like to take. An **approach–avoidance conflict** occurs when you face a choice or situation that has both favorable and unfavorable characteristics. For example, you are required to take a biology lab class, and although you like biology, you do not like working with other students in lab settings. A third type of conflict is the **avoidance–avoidance conflict,** which occurs when you are faced with two or more alternatives that are unattractive. In order to fulfill a requirement, you must choose between two courses that you really dread taking.

Let's see how these types of conflict might arise in police work:

- **approach–approach conflict:** Suppose you are a 30-year veteran of the Houston police department. You can either retire now and begin receiving a pension, or continue working in a profession you find rewarding. Both options are positive.
- **approach–avoidance conflict:** Now imagine you are a police officer contemplating whether to arrest a mother and father suspected of child abuse. If you make the arrest, all of the children in the home will be placed in foster care, an unfamiliar, often frightening environment for children. Something good will come out of the change (the children are no longer at risk of being abused), but the downside is that they will be thrown into an unfamiliar environment.
- **avoidance–avoidance conflict:** You are new to the police force. It is your second day on the job, and you are given a choice between the following two tasks: ride in the squad car with a partner you dislike or stay in the station all day and answer calls (a very boring activity). Both decisions lead to negative outcomes.

Conflicts can be even more complicated than this. A *double approach–avoidance conflict* occurs when you must decide between two choices, each possessing attractive and unattractive qualities. For example, you are trying to decide whether to purchase an e-book or a hardcover, so you consider the good and bad qualities of both types of books. On the one hand, the e-book allows for portability and quick access, but it is not a good option if the Internet fails or electricity is unavailable. The hardcover is long lasting and always accessible, but it is heavy and more expensive. You might even have to deal with *multiple approach–avoidance conflicts,* which occur when you are faced with a decision that has more than two possible choices. You are trying to decide where to live when you attend college in a new city. Should you apply for a dormitory room, look for an apartment, share a house, or live with a family member? Each of these choices has attractive and unattractive qualities.

Tricky Situation
Police officers deal with a variety of conflicts in their daily work. Imagine you are an officer trying to decide whether to arrest a parent suspected of child abuse. If you make the arrest, the child may be removed from the home and placed in foster care (not an ideal scenario), but at least the threat of abuse is removed. This is an *approach–avoidance conflict*—the outcome has both positive and negative elements. Siri Stafford/Getty Images

approach–approach conflict A type of conflict in which one must choose between two or more options that are attractive.

approach–avoidance conflict A type of conflict that occurs when one is faced with a choice or situation that has favorable and unfavorable characteristics.

avoidance–avoidance conflict A type of conflict in which one is faced with two or more options that are unattractive.

burnout Emotional, mental, and physical fatigue that results in reduced motivation, enthusiasm, and performance.

Sometimes conflicts and other stressors pile up so high they become difficult to tolerate. When we can no longer deal with stress in a constructive way, we experience what psychologists call burnout.

AMBULANCE BURNOUT   Kehlen has been in the EMS field for nearly a decade, and most of that time he has spent working for a private ambulance company. He estimates that the average ambulance worker lasts about 8 years before quitting to pursue another line of work. What makes this career so hard to endure? The pay is modest, the 24-hour shifts grueling, and the constant exposure to trauma profoundly disturbing. The pressure to perform is enormous, but there is seldom a "thank-you" or recognition for a job well done. Perhaps no other profession involves so much responsibility—combined with so little appreciation. "The ambulance crews, they're kind of like the silent heroes," Kehlen explains. "You work so hard and you don't get any thanks at the end of the day."

It might not surprise you that the EMS profession has one of the highest rates of *burnout* (Gayton & Lovell, 2012). **Burnout** refers to emotional, mental, and physical fatigue that results from repeated exposure to challenges, leading to reduced motivation, enthusiasm, and performance. People who work in the helping professions, such as nurses, mental health professionals, and child protection workers, are clearly at risk for burnout (Jenaro, Flores, & Arias, 2007; Linnerooth, Mrdjenovich, & Moore, 2011; Rupert, Stevanovic, & Hunley, 2009). 📁

Drained
A nurse holds a patient's IV bag in the emergency room. Nursing is one of the professions associated with high burnout—the emotional, mental, and physical exhaustion that develops when a person faces constant challenges. Lisa Krantz/ San Antonio Express-News/ Zuma Press

I Can Deal: Coping with Stress

Police officers are also susceptible to burnout. The nature of the work they do, the size of the department they work in, and the amount of trust in their coworkers all play a role (McCarty, Schuck, Skogan, & Rosenbaum, 2011, January 7). To survive and thrive in this career, you must excel under pressure. Police departments need officers who are emotionally stable and capable of making split-second decisions with potentially serious ethical implications. If a tired, stressed-out officer makes one bad decision, the reputation of the entire police department could be tarnished. No wonder over 90% of city police departments in the United States require job applicants to take psychological tests, such as the Minnesota Multiphasic Personality Inventory–2 (MMPI–2; Butcher & Rouse, 1996; Cochrane, Tett, & Vandecreek, 2003). Psychological testing is just one hurdle facing the aspiring police officer; some departments also insist on full-length meetings with a psychologist. Most city agencies require criminal background checks, polygraph (lie detector) tests, and physical fitness assessments. And don't forget the 1,000-or-so hours of training at the police academy (Cochrane et al., 2003). But even after overcoming all the hurdles of the hiring process, some police officers end up struggling with stress management. In this respect, police work is like any other field; there will always be people who have trouble coping with the stress of the job.

You Asked, Eric Answers

http://qrs.ly/gx4qsgq
Has the stress of police training ever made you want to quit?

LO 10   Illustrate how appraisal influences coping.

APPRAISAL AND COPING   Needless to say, people respond to stress in their own unique ways. Psychologist Richard Lazarus (1922–2002) suggested that stress is the result of a person's *appraisal* of a stressor, not necessarily the stressor itself (Folkman &

CONNECTIONS

In **Chapter 9,** we described the *cognitive appraisal* theory of emotion, which suggests that emotion results from the way people appraise or interpret interactions they have. We appraise events based on their significance, and our subjective appraisal influences our response to stressors.

Lazarus, 1985; Lazarus & Folkman, 1984). This viewpoint stands in contrast to Selye's suggestion (noted earlier) that we all react to stressors in a similar manner. **Coping** refers to the cognitive, behavioral, and emotional abilities used to manage something that is perceived as difficult or challenging. In order to cope, we must determine if an event is harmful, threatening, or challenging (**Infographic 11.3**). A person making a **primary appraisal** of a situation determines how the event will affect him. He must decide if it is irrelevant, positive, challenging, or harmful. Next, the individual makes a **secondary appraisal,** or decides how to respond. If he believes he can cope with virtually any challenge that comes his way, the impact of stress remains low. If he thinks his coping abilities are poor, then the impact of stress will be high. These differences in appraisals help explain why two people can react to the same event in dramatically different ways.

There are two basic types of coping. **Problem-focused coping** means taking a direct approach, confronting a problem head-on. Suppose you are having trouble in a relationship; an example of problem-focused coping might be reading self-help books or finding a counselor. **Emotion-focused coping** involves addressing the emotions that surround a problem, rather than trying to solve it. With a troubled relationship, you might think about your feelings, look to friends for support, or exercise to take your mind off it, instead of addressing the problem directly. Sometimes it's better to use emotion-focused coping—when an emotional reaction might be too stressful or interferes with daily functioning, or when a problem cannot be solved (for example, the death of a loved one). In the long run, however, problem-focused coping is usually more productive.

 IT'S A PERSONAL THING   In June 2011 Eric began his second run through Onondaga's police training program. This time around, he nailed the Emergency Vehicle Operations Course (EVOC). "I can't even describe to you how great it felt." The secret to his success? "Instead of worrying about everything, I had fun," Eric says. "Once you relax . . . [it] helps you focus better." Eric graduated in December 2011. He soon landed a position with a local police department.

"Police training is different everywhere," says Eric, who chose the police academy at Onondaga Community College because of its rigor. No training program can totally prepare you for police work, but the academy makes every effort to simulate real-world scenarios. "The individuals who can deal with stress in the best way make it through," says Eric. "Those that cannot weed themselves out on their own." 📁

LO 11   Describe Type A and Type B personalities and explain how they relate to stress.

TYPE A AND TYPE B PERSONALITIES   Personality appears to have a profound effect on coping style and predispositions to stress-related illness. For example, people with certain personality types are more prone to developing cardiovascular disease. Cardiologists Meyer Friedman (1910–2001) and Ray Rosenman (1920–2013) were among the first to suspect a link between personality type and the cardiovascular problems they observed in their patients (Friedman & Rosenman, 1974). In particular, they noted that many of the people they treated were intensely focused on time and always in a hurry. This characteristic pattern of behaviors eventually was referred to as **Type A personality.** Someone with a Type A personality is competitive, aggressive, impatient, and often hostile (Diamond, 1982; Smith & Ruiz, 2002). Through numerous studies, Friedman and Rosenman discovered that people with Type A personalities were twice as likely to develop cardiovascular disease as those with **Type B personality.**

coping The cognitive, behavioral, and emotional abilities used to effectively manage something that is perceived as difficult or challenging.

primary appraisal One's initial assessment of a situation to determine its personal impact and whether it is irrelevant, positive, challenging, or harmful.

secondary appraisal An assessment to determine how to respond to a challenging or threatening situation.

problem-focused coping A coping strategy in which a person deals directly with a problem by attempting to solve and address it head-on.

emotion-focused coping A coping strategy in which a person addresses the emotions that surround a problem, as opposed to trying to solve it.

Type A personality Competitive, aggressive, impatient, and often hostile pattern of behaviors.

Type B personality Relaxed, patient, and nonaggressive pattern of behaviors.

The Process of Coping

Coping refers to the cognitive, emotional, and behavioral methods we employ to manage stressful events. But people don't always rely on the same strategies to manage stressors. Coping is an individual *process* through which we appraise a stressor to determine how it will affect us and how we can respond.

stressful encounter

MAY 12 Math Final

I have a final exam!

How will this affect me?

BEFORE TEST
PRIMARY APPRAISAL

DURING TEST
PRIMARY APPRAISAL

***Now** how will this affect me?*

There will be independent responses from each instance of primary appraisal.

Most stressful events are not static. Therefore, we may appraise them at different stages with different results. For example, you will appraise the challenge of a test differently before you take it, while you are taking it, and after you have taken it but are waiting to receive a grade.

I missed a lot of classes and don't understand the material.

STRESS!

I don't know how to manage this.

I'm doing well in class. I will still get a good grade for the class even if I don't do that well on the final.

not too stressed

I can cope with this.

PERSON "X"
CHALLENGING

PERSON "Y"
POSITIVE

People respond differently to stressors depending on differences in appraisal. A student who is struggling in a class because she hasn't worked hard may find a test even more challenging than a student who has been working hard all semester.

SECONDARY APPRAISAL
What can I do?

SECONDARY APPRAISAL
What can I do?

Once we know how an event will affect us, a secondary appraisal determines how to respond.

* problem focused
Seek help from friends

emotion focused
Seek emotional support

* problem focused
Planning

emotion focused
Emphasize the positive

In response to a stressor, most people use several coping strategies, including both problem-focused and emotion-focused coping. Problem-focused coping involves doing something to deal with the source of stress. People who do not feel they can solve the problem tend to rely more on emotion-focused coping to manage their feelings about the situation.

I'll get notes from a classmate.

I'll feel better after venting.

First I'll take the online self-quiz, then I'll go back and review the material.

I feel so much better when I study.

emotion focused
Mental disengagement

* problem focused
Suppress competing activities

I don't care about this class anyway.

I won't go out this weekend so I can focus on studying.

---

* **Problem-focused coping is usually the most productive. Here are some other problem-focused strategies:**

➡ Restraint (wait to act until all relevant data has come to light)   ➡ Break the problem into manageable chunks   ➡ Research the situation   ➡ Pursue alternatives

People with Type B personality are often more relaxed, patient, and nonaggressive (Rosenman et al., 1975). There appear to be various reasons people with Type A personality suffer disproportionately from cardiovascular disease: they are more likely to have high blood pressure, heart rate, and stress hormone levels. Type A individuals are also prone to more interpersonal problems (for example, arguments, fights, or hostile interactions), which increase the time their bodies are prepared for fight or flight.

Although many years of research confirmed the relationship between Type A behavior and coronary heart problems, some researchers began to report findings inconsistent with this (Smith & MacKenzie, 2006). Failure to reproduce the results led some to question the validity of this relationship, although one major factor was a lack of consistency in research methodology. For example, some studies used samples with high-risk participants, whereas others included healthy people. As researchers continued to probe the relationship between personality type and coronary heart disease, they found that the component of *hostility* in Type A personality was the strongest predictor of coronary heart disease.

TYPE D PERSONALITY   More recently, researchers have suggested another personality type that may better predict how patients fare when they already have heart disease: *Type D personality,* where the "D" refers to distress (Denollet & Conraads, 2011). Someone with Type D personality is characterized by emotions like worry, tension, bad moods, and social inhibition (avoids confronting others, poor social skills). There is a clear link between Type D characteristics and a "poor prognosis" in patients with coronary heart disease (Denollet & Conraads, 2011). In other words, people who have heart problems and exhibit these Type D characteristics are more likely to struggle with their illness. It could be that people with Type D personality tend to avoid dealing with their problems directly and don't take advantage of social support. Such an approach might lead to poor choices about coping with stressors over time (Martin et al., 2011).

THE THREE Cs OF HARDINESS   Clearly, not everyone has the same tolerance for stress (Ganzel, Morris, & Wethington, 2010; Straub, 2012). Some people seem capable of handling intensely stressful situations, such as war and poverty. These individuals appear to have a personality characteristic referred to as **hardiness,** meaning that even when functioning under a great deal of stress, they are very resilient and tend to remain positive. Kehlen, who considers himself "a very optimistic person," may fit into this category, and findings from one study of Scottish ambulance personnel suggest that EMS workers with this characteristic are less likely to experience burnout (Alexander & Klein, 2001).

Kobasa (1979) and others have studied how some executives seem to withstand the effects of extremely stressful jobs. Their hardiness appears to be associated with three characteristics: feeling a strong *commitment* to work and personal matters; believing they are in *control* of the events in their lives and not victims of circumstances; and not feeling threatened by *challenges,* but rather seeing them as opportunities for growth.

hardiness   A personality characteristic indicating an ability to remain resilient and optimistic despite intensely stressful situations.

I Am in Control

The ability to manage stress is very much dependent on one's perceived level of personal control. Psychologists have consistently found that people who believe they have control over their lives and circumstances are less likely to experience the negative impact of stressors than those who do not feel the same control. For example, Langer and Rodin (1976) conducted a series of studies using nursing home residents as participants. Residents in a "responsibility-induced" group were allowed to make a variety of choices about their daily activities and their environments. Members of the "comparison" group were not given these kinds of choices; instead, the nursing home staff made all of these decisions for them (the residents were told the staff were responsible for their happiness and care). After following the residents for 18 months, the researchers found that members of the responsibility-induced group were more lively, active in their social lives, and healthier than the residents in the comparison group. And twice as many of the residents in the comparison group died during this period (Rodin & Langer, 1977).

It's My Life
A nursing home white board displays a list of menu items and activities that residents can choose from. One study found that putting nursing home residents in charge of their daily activities led to increased levels of energy, health, and social engagement. Their empowerment was also associated with lower death rates (Rodin & Langer, 1977). AP Photo/Charles Rex Arbogast

Researchers have examined how having a sense of personal control relates to a variety of health issues across all ages. Feelings of control are linked to how patients fare with some diseases. Cancer patients who exhibit a "helpless attitude" regarding their disease seem more likely to experience a recurrence of the cancer than those with perceptions of greater control. Why would this be? Women who have had breast cancer and believe they maintain control over their lifestyle, through diet and exercise, are more likely to make proactive changes related to their health, and perhaps reduce risk factors associated with recurrence (Costanzo, Lutgendorf, & Roeder, 2011). The same type of relationship is apparent in cardiovascular disease; the less control people feel they have, the greater their risk (Shapiro, Schwartz, & Astin, 1996). As we pointed out, having choices increases a perceived sense of control.

Feelings of control may also have a more direct effect on the body; for example, a sense of powerlessness is associated with increases in catecholamines and corticosteroids, both key players in a physiological response to stressors. Some have suggested a causal relationship between feelings of perceived control and immune system function; the greater the sense of control, the better the functioning of the immune system (Shapiro et al., 1996). But these are correlations, and the direction of causality should not be assumed. Could it be that better immune functioning, and thus better health, might increase a sense of control?

We must also consider cross-cultural differences. Individual control is emphasized and valued in individualist cultures like our own, but not necessarily in collectivistic cultures, where people look to "powerful others" and "chance factors" to explain events and guide decision making (Cheng, Cheung, Chio, & Chan, 2013).

LOCUS OF CONTROL   Differences in perceived sense of control stem from beliefs about where control resides (Rotter, 1966). Someone with an *internal locus of control* generally feels she is in control of life and its circumstances; she probably believes it is important to take charge and make changes when problems occur. A person with an *external locus of control* generally feels as if chance, luck, or fate is responsible for her circumstances; there is no point in trying to change things or make them better.

CONNECTIONS

In **Chapter 10,** we discussed *locus of control,* a key component of personality. Someone with an *internal* locus of control believes the causes of outcomes reside within him. A person with an *external* locus of control thinks causes of outcomes reside outside him. Here, we see that higher personal control is associated with better health outcomes.

Imagine that a doctor tells a patient he needs to change his lifestyle and start exercising. If the patient has an internal locus of control, he will likely take charge and start walking to work or hitting the gym; he expects his actions will impact his health. If the patient has an external locus of control, he is more apt to think his actions won't make a difference and may not attempt lifestyle changes. In the 1970 British Cohort Study, researchers examined over 11,000 children at age 10, and then assessed their health at age 30. Participants with an internal locus of control, measured at 10 years of age, were less likely as adults to be overweight or obese, and had lower levels of psychological problems. They were also less likely to smoke and more likely to exercise regularly than people with a more external locus of control (Gale, Batty, & Deary, 2008).

FROM AMBULANCE TO FIREHOUSE   Kehlen's original career goal was to become a firefighter, but jobs are extremely hard to come by in this field. Fresh out of high school, Kehlen joined an ambulance crew with the goal of moving on to the firehouse. Seven years later, he reached his destination.

Kehlen is now a firefighter paramedic with the Pueblo Fire Department. His job description still includes performing CPR, inserting breathing tubes, and delivering lifesaving medical care. But now he can also be seen handling fire hoses and rushing into 800-degree buildings with 80 pounds of gear.

Compared to an ambulance, the firehouse environment is far more conducive to managing stress. For starters, there is enormous social support. Fellow firefighters are a lot like family members. They eat together, go to sleep together, and wake to the same flashing lights and tones announcing the latest emergency. "The fire department is such a brotherhood," Kehlen says. Spending a third of his life at the firehouse with colleagues, Kehlen has come to know and trust them on a deep level. They discuss disturbing events they witness and help each other recover emotionally. "If you don't talk about it," says Kehlen, "it's just going to wear on you." Another major benefit of working at the firehouse is having the freedom to exercise, which Kehlen considers a major stress reliever. The firefighters are actually required to work out 1 hour per day during their shifts.

Ambulance work is quite another story. Kehlen and his coworkers were friends, but they didn't share the tight bonds that Kehlen now has with fellow firefighters. And eating healthy and exercising were almost impossible. Ambulance workers don't have the luxury of making a healthy meal in a kitchen. They

Camaraderie
Firefighters climb the notoriously difficult "Incline," a seemingly endless set of stairs up Pikes Peak in Manitou Springs, Colorado. Every year on the morning of September 11, the firefighters walk up the 1-mile path to commemorate those who died in the 9/11 terrorist attacks. The tight-knit community at the firehouse provides Kehlen with friendship, emotional support, and a great deal of stress reduction. Nicole Pritts

often have no choice but to drive to the nearest fast-food restaurant and wipe the crumbs off their faces as they race to the next emergency. One of the worst aspects of the job was the lack of exercise. Says Kehlen, "That killed me when I was in the ambulance."

Tools for Healthy Living

LO 12 Discuss several tools for reducing stress and maintaining health.

Dealing with stressors can be challenging, but you don't have to grin and bear it. There are many simple ways to manage and reduce stress. Let's take a look at two powerful stress-fighting weapons: physical exercise and relaxation techniques.

Apply This

Everyday Stress Relievers

You are feeling the pressure. Exam time is here, and you haven't cracked open a book because you've been so busy at work. The holidays are approaching, you have not purchased a single present, and the pile of unpaid bills on your desk is starting to build. With so much to do, you feel paralyzed. In these types of situations, the best solution may be to drop to the floor to do some push-ups, or run out the door and take a jog. When you come back, you feel a new sense of calm. *I can handle this,* you'll think to yourself. *One thing at a time.*

How does exercise work its magic? Physiologically, we know exercise increases blood flow, activates the autonomic nervous system, and helps initiate the release of several hormones. These physiological reactions help the body defend itself from potential illnesses, especially those that are stress related. Exercise also spurs the release of the body's natural painkilling and pleasure-inducing neurotransmitters, the endorphins (Salmon, 2001).

When it comes to choosing an exercise regimen, the tough part is finding an activity that is intense enough to reduce the impact of stress, but sufficiently enjoyable to keep you coming back for more. Research suggests that only 30 minutes of daily exercise is needed to decrease the risk of heart disease, stroke, hypertension, certain types of cancer, and diabetes (Warburton, Charlesworth, Ivey, Nettlefold, & Bredin, 2010) and improve mood (Bryan, Hutchison, Seals, & Allen, 2007; Hansen, Stevens, & Coast, 2001). And exercise needn't be a chore. Your daily 30 minutes could mean dancing to *Just Dance 6* on the Wii, going for a bike ride, raking leaves on a beautiful fall day, or shoveling snow in a winter wonderland.

Exercise is all about getting the body moving, but relaxing the muscles can also relieve stress. "Just relax." We have heard it said a thousand times, but do we really know how to begin? Physician and physiologist Edmund Jacobson (1938) introduced a technique known as *progressive muscle relaxation,* which has since been expanded upon. With this technique, you begin by tensing a muscle group (for example, your toes) for about 10 seconds, and then releasing as you focus on the tension leaving. Next you progress to another muscle group, such as the calves, and then the thighs, buttocks, stomach, shoulders, arms, neck, and so on. After several weeks of practice, you will begin to recognize where you hold tension in your muscles—at least this is the goal. Once you become aware of that tension, you can focus on relaxing those specific muscles without going through the entire process. Progressive muscle relaxation has been shown to diffuse anxiety in highly stressed college students. In one study, researchers found that just 20 minutes of progressive muscle relaxation had "significant short-term effects," including decreases in anxiety, blood pressure, and heart rate (Dolbier & Rush, 2012). Participants also reported a feeling of increased control and energy. This *relaxation response* may also serve as an effective way to reduce pain (Benson, 2000; Dusek et al., 2008).

Meditate on This

➡️⬅️ An increasingly popular way to induce relaxation is meditation. If you've ever known an anxious person who began meditating regularly, you know that it can have a dramatic "chilling out" effect. A sense of serenity seems to envelop people who take up meditation. But anecdotal evidence or folk wisdom is no substitute for scientific data. What does the research say?

Numerous studies point to a variety of meditation-related physical and mental health benefits, including increased immune system activity, enhanced empathy, and reduced levels of anxiety, neuroticism, and negative emotions (Davidson et al., 2003; Roemer, Orsillo, & Salters-Pedneault, 2008; Sedlmeier et al., 2012; Walsh, 2011). This all sounds great, but some scholars assert that many meditation studies are riddled with methodological flaws and lack the support of solid theoretical frameworks (Ireland, 2012; Sedlmeier et al., 2012).

... JUST *THINKING* MEDITATION IS BENEFICIAL MAY AFFECT THE WAY PEOPLE PERCEIVE AND REPORT ITS EFFECTS.

In many cases, it's unclear whether meditation or some other lifestyle factor such as regular exercise is causing the positive effects researchers have observed. It's also important to recognize that the expectations of research participants can sway study results in a favorable direction. In other words, just *thinking* meditation is beneficial may affect the way people perceive and report its effects. Meditation may exert a *placebo effect,* leading its practitioners to believe that their efforts are paying off. If this is the case, the beliefs (rather than the meditation) are producing the health benefits.

That said, we should point out that long-term meditation has been shown to produce observable changes in the brain (Davidson & Lutz, 2008; Hölzel et al., 2011). There is little doubt that something important happens when a person meditates, and that something appears to be positive. ➡️⬅️

Many forms of meditation emphasize control and awareness of breathing. This may be one of the reasons people find meditation so relaxing. Taking slow, deep breaths is a fast and easy way to reduce the impact of stress.

try this ← Using a clock or watch to time yourself, breathe in slowly for 5 seconds. Then exhale slowly for 5 seconds. Do this for 1 minute. With each breath, you begin to slow down and relax. The key is to breathe deeply. Draw your breath deep into the diaphragm and avoid shallow, rapid chest breathing.

BIOFEEDBACK A proven method for reducing physiological responses to stressors is **biofeedback.** This technique builds on learning principles to teach control of seemingly involuntary physiological activity (such as heart rate, blood pressure, and skin temperature). The biofeedback equipment monitors internal responses and provides visual or auditory signals to help a person identify those that are maladaptive (for example, tense shoulder muscles). The person begins by focusing on a signal (a light or tone, for example) that indicates when a desired response occurs. By learning to control this biofeedback indicator, the person learns to maintain the desired response (relaxed shoulders in this example). The goal is to be able to tap into this technique outside of the clinic or lab, and translate what has been learned into real-life practice.

biofeedback A technique that involves providing visual or auditory information about biological processes, allowing a person to control physiological activity (for example, heart rate, blood pressure, and skin temperature).

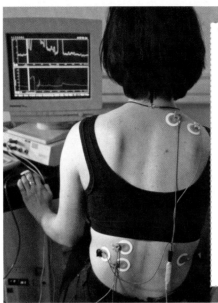

Body Connection
A patient at the Max Planck Institute in Munich, Germany, combats back pain using biofeedback, a learning technique that enables a person to manipulate seemingly automatic functions, such as heart rate and blood pressure. With the help of a monitor that signals the occurrence of a target response, a patient can learn how to sustain this response longer. Ronald Frommann/laif/Redux

The use of biofeedback can decrease the frequency of headaches and chronic pain (Flor & Birbaumer, 1993; Sun-Edelstein & Mauskop, 2011). It appears to be useful for all age groups, including children, adolescents, and the elderly (Morone & Greco, 2007; Palermo, Eccleston, Lewandowski, Williams, & Morley, 2010).

SOCIAL SUPPORT   Up until now, we have discussed ways to manage the body's physiological response to stressors. There are also situational methods to deal with stressors, like maintaining a social support network. Researchers have found that proactively participating in positive enduring relationships with family, friends, and religious groups can generate a health benefit similar to exercise and not smoking (House, Landis, & Umberson, 1988). People who maintain positive, supportive relationships also have better overall health (Walsh, 2011).

You might expect that receiving support is the key to lowering stress, but research suggests that *giving* support also really matters. In a study of older married adults, researchers reported reduced mortality rates for participants who indicated that they helped or supported others, including friends, spouses, relatives, and neighbors. There were no reductions in mortality, however, associated with receiving support from others (Brown, Nesse, Vinokur, & Smith, 2003).

What Goes Around
Volunteers in Chongqing, China, celebrate Father's Day with elderly men in a nursing home. *Altruism,* or helping others because it feels good, is an excellent stress reliever. TopPhoto via AP Images

Helping others because it gives you pleasure, and expecting nothing in return, is known as *altruism,* and it appears to be an effective stress reducer and happiness booster (Schwartz, Keyl, Marcum, & Bode, 2009; Schwartz, Meisenhelder, Yunsheng, & Reed, 2003). When we care for others, we generally don't have time to focus on our own problems; we also come to recognize that others may be dealing with more troubling circumstances than we are.

FAITH, RELIGION, AND PRAYER   Psychologists are also discovering the health benefits of faith, religion, and prayer. Research suggests elderly people who actively participate in religious services or pray experience improved health and noticeably lower rates of depression than those who don't participate in such activities (Lawler-Row & Elliott, 2009; Powell, Shahabi, & Thoresen, 2003). In fact, religious affiliation is associated with increased reports of happiness and physical health (Green & Elliott, 2010).

These various types of proactive, stress-reducing behaviors reflect a certain type of attitude. You might call it a positive psychology attitude.

Think Positive

In the very first chapter of this book, we introduced a field of study known as *positive psychology,* "the study of positive emotions, positive character traits, and enabling institutions" (Seligman & Steen, 2005, p. 410). Rather than focusing on mental illness and abnormal behavior, positive psychology emphasizes human strengths and virtues. The goal is well-being and fulfillment, and that means "satisfaction" with the past, "hope and optimism" for the future, and "flow and happiness" at the current time (Seligman & Csikszentmihalyi, 2000, p. 5).

. . . YOUR CURRENT STRESS LEVEL IS WITHIN YOUR CONTROL.

As we wrap up this chapter on stress and health, we encourage you to focus on that third category: flow and happiness in the present moment. No matter what stressors come your way, try to stay grounded in the here and now. The past is the past, the future is uncertain, but this moment is yours. Finding a way to enjoy the present is one of the best ways to reduce stress. We also remind you that your current stress level is very much within your control. If you're feeling overwhelmed, make time to engage in activities such as exercise and meditation, which produce measurable changes in the body and brain. ➤

TO PROTECT, SERVE, AND NOT GET TOO STRESSED If you're wondering how Eric Flansburg and Kehlen Kirby are doing these days, both young men are thriving in their careers. Eric joined the police department in Cicero, New York. "I love it," he says. "Can't see myself doing anything else." Recently Eric, his wife, and their two sons (Eric Junior, 6, and Nathan, 2) experienced a major stressor: their home was destroyed in a fire. Thankfully no one was hurt, and the damage was covered by insurance. Something positive actually came out of the crisis: the family emerged stronger and closer than ever.

Having worked at the fire station since 2010, Kehlen is really getting into the fire department groove. He was recently promoted to "engineer," which means he is now responsible for driving the fire engine (in addition to all his firefighting and paramedic responsibilities). When he's not putting out fires and rescuing people, Kehlen helps his wife run her family medicine practice and cares for his 3-year-old daughter, Kinley, and his 1-year-old son, Knox. "[Kinley] is one of my biggest stress relievers," suggests Kehlen. "Just chasing her around is enough of a stress reliever for anyone." ▰

✓◯◯◯   show what you know

1. Having to choose between two options that are equally attractive to you is called a(n) _____ conflict.

2. _____ is apparent when a person deals directly with a problem by attempting to solve it.
   a. Emotion-focused coping
   b. Positive psychology
   c. Support seeking
   d. Problem-focused coping

3. Individuals who are more relaxed, patient, and nonaggressive are considered to have a:
   a. Type A personality.
   b. Type B personality.
   c. Type C personality.
   d. Type D personality.

4. Describe three "tools" for healthy living that you could use to improve your health.

✓ CHECK YOUR ANSWERS IN APPENDIX C.

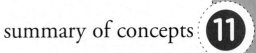

summary of concepts 11

LO 1 Define stress and stressors. (p. 442)

Stress is the response to perceived threats or challenges resulting from stimuli or events that cause strain, analogous to an airplane wing bending in response to an applied load. For humans, these stimuli, or stressors, can cause physiological, psychological, and emotional reactions. We must be careful not to confuse how we react to stressors and the stressors themselves; stress is the response, stressors are the cause. Stress primarily occurs in reaction to a perceived threat.

LO 2 Describe the Social Readjustment Rating Scale in relation to life events and illness. (p. 445)

Holmes and Rahe developed the Social Readjustment Rating Scale (SRRS) to measure the impact of life events. The score is based on the severity of events and their frequency of occurrence. Researchers use this to examine relationships between life events and health problems. Although correlations do exist, they are not necessarily indicative of cause and effect.

LO 3 Summarize how poverty, adjusting to a new culture, and daily hassles affect health. (p. 448)

People living in poverty, moving to a new culture, and dealing with everyday hassles are faced with a number of stressors that increase the likelihood of illness. Unlike major life changes and catastrophes, we are exposed to these stressors on a more constant basis. Moving to a new country is a major life change that can result in acculturative stress; however, integrating the old and new cultures and developing social support helps combat the effects. With all the stressors in our lives, we can be grateful for the positive experiences, or uplifts, that can serve to balance them.

LO 4 Identify the brain and body changes that characterize the fight-or-flight response. (p. 452)

When faced with a threatening situation, portions of the brain, including the hypothalamus, activate the sympathetic nervous system, which then leads to the secretion of catecholamines, such as epinephrine and norepinephrine. These hormones cause heart rate, blood pressure, respiration, and blood flow to the muscles to increase. At the same time, the digestive system slows down and the pupils dilate. These physiological responses prepare us for an emergency by efficiently managing the body's resources.

LO 5 Outline the general adaptation syndrome (GAS). (p. 452)

The human body responds in a predictable way to stressors. The general adaptation syndrome suggests that the body passes through three stages. The first is the alarm stage, or initial response to a threatening situation. This stage includes an increase in arousal, during which the body prepares to deal with a threat. Next is the resistance stage, during which the body maintains a high level of arousal (although not as high as that of the alarm stage), as it deals with a threatening situation; at this point there is a decreased response to new stressors. During the resistance stage, some people start to show signs of diseases of adaptation. Finally there is the exhaustion stage; during this phase, the body's resources become depleted, resulting in vulnerability to illnesses, physical exhaustion, and even death.

LO 6 Describe the function of the hypothalamic–pituitary–adrenal (HPA) system. (p. 452)

Overseeing the sympathetic nervous system's activity is the HPA system. When a stressful situation arises, the hypothalamus initiates a cascade of responses by alerting the pituitary gland, which then sends signals to the adrenal cortex. In turn, the cortex orders the secretion of corticosteroids (for example, cortisol). These hormones summon the immune system to fight off a threat and reduce the amount of energy used on nonessential activities. When faced with a stressor, the body responds in the same way it would to a pathogen—by mobilizing a defense response.

LO 7 Explain how stressors relate to health problems. (p. 454)

When the body is continually mobilizing its resources for fight or flight, the immune system becomes taxed, and the work of the lymphocytes is compromised. During times of stress, people tend to sleep poorly and eat erratically, and may increase their drug and alcohol use, along with other poor behavioral choices. These tendencies can lead to health problems. In particular, stressors have been linked to ulcers, cancer, and cardiovascular disease.

LO 8 List some consequences of prolonged exposure to the stress hormone cortisol. (p. 458)

Cortisol steps up immunity and prepares the body to confront a threat. But when cortisol levels remain high for prolonged periods (which is the case with chronic stressors and threatening situations), immune system functioning may decrease. Elevated cortisol has been associated with premature birth and low birth weight in infants. For workers who have to make on-the-spot safety decisions, high cortisol levels can decrease working memory. The field of psychoneuroimmunology explores the complex interplay of psychological, neurological, and immunological factors involved in stress.

LO 9 Identify different types of conflicts. (p. 460)

Conflict can be defined as the discomfort felt when making tough choices. Often two choices presented are both attractive (approach–approach conflict), at times one choice has both favorable and unfavorable characteristics (approach–avoidance conflict), and other times two alternatives are both unattractive (avoidance–avoidance conflict). Even more challenging are conflicts that occur when someone must decide between two choices, each possessing attractive and unattractive qualities (double approach–avoidance conflict), or those that occur when faced with a decision that has more than two possible choices (multiple approach–avoidance conflicts).

LO 10 Illustrate how appraisal influences coping. (p. 461)

Coping refers to the cognitive, behavioral, and emotional abilities used to manage something that is perceived as difficult or challenging. We must decide whether an event is irrelevant, positive, challenging, or harmful (primary appraisal) and how we will respond (secondary appraisal). If we determine that we

have the ability to cope, then the impact of stress will remain low. We can choose to deal directly with a problem (problem-focused coping), or address the emotions surrounding the problem (emotion-focused coping).

LO 11 Describe Type A and Type B personalities and explain how they relate to stress. (p. 462)

Personality appears to have a profound effect on coping style and predispositions to stress-related illnesses. People with Type A personalities are competitive, aggressive, and impatient and twice as likely to develop cardiovascular disease as people with Type B personalities, who are more relaxed, patient, and nonaggressive. The presence of Type D personality may be a better predictor of how patients fare when they already have heart disease, and it is characterized by emotions such as worry, tension, bad moods, and social inhibition. People who exhibit a personality characteristic referred to as hardiness seem to be more resilient, optimistic, and better able to handle a great deal of stress.

LO 12 Discuss several tools for reducing stress and maintaining health. (p. 467)

Stress management incorporates tools to lower the impact of possible stressors. Exercise, meditation, progressive muscle relaxation, biofeedback, and social support all have positive physical and psychological effects. Caring for and giving to others are also effective ways to reduce the impact of stress.

key terms

acculturative stress, p. 449
approach–approach conflict, p. 460
approach–avoidance conflict, p. 460
acquired immune deficiency syndrome (AIDS), p. 448
avoidance–avoidance conflict, p. 460
biofeedback, p. 468

burnout, p. 461
coping, p. 462
daily hassles, p. 450
distress, p. 445
emotion-focused coping, p. 462
eustress, p. 445
general adaptation syndrome (GAS), p. 452
hardiness, p. 464

health psychology, p. 454
human immunodeficiency virus (HIV), p. 448
lymphocytes, p. 454
posttraumatic stress disorder (PTSD), p. 447
primary appraisal, p. 462
problem-focused coping, p. 462

psychoneuroimmunology, p. 459
secondary appraisal, p. 462
social support, p. 449
stress, p. 442
stressors, p. 442
Type A personality, p. 462
Type B personality, p. 462
uplifts, p. 450

TEST PREP are you ready?

1. _____ are defined as the situations, beliefs, people, and attitudes that cause you to feel stress, a response that can include physiological, psychological, and emotional components.

   a. Levels of eustress   b. Diseases of adaptation
   c. Stressors   d. Conflicts

2. When Eric witnessed the birth of his first child, he felt it was the proudest moment of his life. This kind of "good" stressor leads to a reaction known as:

   a. eustress.   b. distress.
   c. perceived threats.   d. optimal arousal.

3. Your professor is using the Social Readjustment Rating Scale in a study she is conducting. She predicts that the more _____ people have, the more stress reactions they will experience, which increases the likelihood they will become ill.

   a. assimilation   b. stress inoculation
   c. social support   d. life-changing events

4. When faced with a threat, portions of the brain, including the hypothalamus, activate the _____, which leads to the secretion of epinephrine and norepinephrine.
   a. parasympathetic nervous system
   b. sympathetic nervous system
   c. general adaptation syndrome
   d. lymphocytes

5. Once an emergency has ended, the _____ reverses the processes put in motion through the fight-or-flight reaction. Heart rate and blood pressure start to decrease and respiration returns to normal.
   a. parasympathetic nervous system
   b. sympathetic nervous system
   c. general adaptation syndrome
   d. resistance stage

6. According to the general adaptation syndrome, if a threat remains constant, the body's resources become depleted during the _____, resulting in a vulnerability to illnesses, physical exhaustion, and even death.
   a. alarm stage
   b. resistance stage
   c. exhaustion stage
   d. diseases of adaptation stage

7. The hypothalamic–pituitary–adrenal system plays an important role in stress reactions. This system helps to maintain balance in the body by overseeing the neuroendocrine and _____ while monitoring the immune system.
   a. diseases of adaptation
   b. gastric ulcers
   c. assimilation
   d. sympathetic nervous system

8. Stressors can lead to health problems, because as the body mobilizes its resources for fight or flight, _____ is less powerful, and the work of its lymphocytes is reduced.
   a. the immune system   b. *H. pylori*
   c. atherosclerosis   d. cortisol

9. Physical exercise provides a powerful way to reduce the impact of stress, by increasing blood flow, activating the autonomic nervous system, and initiating the release of _____, the body's natural painkilling neurotransmitters.
   a. macrophages   b. endorphins
   c. B lymphocytes   d. natural killer cells

10. The students in your study group are extremely worried about tomorrow's final exam. One student has been seeing a counselor all semester because of her anxiety. When she walks into class tomorrow, she will use what she has learned about _____ to help her reduce tension in her body.
    a. the hypothalamic–pituitary–adrenal system
    b. macrophages
    c. stress inoculation
    d. progressive muscle relaxation

11. Your friend is worried he will lose his job, so he goes home and drinks too much alcohol. His reaction may be explained by the self-medication hypothesis, and his behavior is an example of how:
    a. social-evaluative threats can provide support.
    b. the general adaptation syndrome ends.
    c. stressors are related to health problems.
    d. an acculturative stress response occurs.

12. _____ refers to the cognitive, behavioral, and emotional abilities used to manage a challenging or difficult situation.
    a. Stress   b. Coping
    c. Altruism   d. Eustress

13. You have been given two options for a presentation in your speech class: a 15-minute speech about a childhood friend or a 15-minute speech about a favorite pet. These two speeches sound equally boring to write and to deliver. Your decision regarding which to choose would be considered an:
    a. avoidance–approach conflict.
    b. approach–approach conflict.
    c. approach–avoidance conflict.
    d. avoidance–avoidance conflict.

14. Someone who is competitive, aggressive, and hostile would be likely to have a _____, which indicates he is more likely to develop cardiovascular disease than someone who is more relaxed, patient, and nonaggressive.
    a. Type A personality   b. Type B personality
    c. Type C personality   d. Type D personality

15. Last week, you met an exchange student who began to tell you about her life back home. She described times when she had to deal with hunger, war, and living in an orphanage. Yet she seems so optimistic and resilient. Psychologists would likely suggest her personality includes a characteristic known as:
    a. Type A.   b. hardiness.
    c. responsibility.   d. locus of control.

16. Describe how someone you know used assimilation, separation, or integration to deal with the acculturative stress of moving to a new country or new region of the United States.

17. List the many hassles you have had to deal with during the past week. Also list any life events you have experienced in the past 12 months. Consider how all these stressors may have influenced your health and explain what you can do to reduce their impact.

18. Describe an example from a movie or television show of someone who seemed to be responding to a threat by the fight-or-flight response. What evidence of this did you observe?

19. Give examples of an approach–approach conflict, an approach–avoidance conflict, and an avoidance–avoidance conflict that you have encountered in your own life.

20. Describe someone you know who has an internal locus of control, in particular regarding his or her health-related behaviors. Now describe someone you know who has an external locus of control, and focus on his or her health-related behaviors.

✓ CHECK YOUR ANSWERS IN APPENDIX C.

12

① ② ③ ④ ⑤ ⑥ ⑦

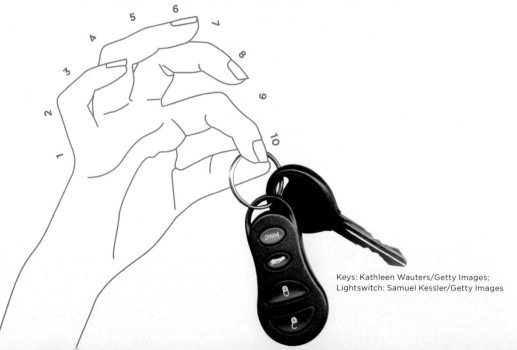

Keys: Kathleen Wauters/Getty Images;
Lightswitch: Samuel Kessler/Getty Images

psychological disorders

An Introduction to Psychological Disorders

WINTER NIGHT It was a clear, cold night in January when 17-year-old Ross Szabo decided to end his life. Nothing bad had happened that day. Ross had woken up, gone to school, played in a basketball game (a victory for his team), and then gone with his buddies to Friendly's restaurant for mozzarella sticks and a sundae. But for some reason, on that winter night, Ross decided he could no longer take it. Riding home in the car, he gazed out the window at Pennsylvania's snow-blanketed cornfields. An overwhelming sense of calm descended on him.

Looks Can Be Deceiving
Ross Szabo appears happy in his senior class photo, but beneath his smile is profound pain and suffering. This was the year Ross began to have persistent thoughts of death and suicide that nearly drove him to take his own life. Martin Fella/Fella Studios

For the 4 months leading to that moment, Ross had been free-falling into an abyss of sadness. No one knew—not his parents, his brothers, or his friends—because Ross was a good actor. Around other people, he was smiling, joking, acting like a normal teenager. But every time he was alone, he was crying. As he puts it, "I had been thinking about suicide 24 hours a day by that point."

Some people say suicide is a selfish act; a person ends his own suffering and destroys the lives of those left behind. Ross truly believed his friends and family would be happier without him. *Maybe you're the problem; maybe you'd be doing them a favor by removing the problem,* Ross remembers thinking to himself. "I didn't think I would have a funeral," he says. "I didn't think anyone should care about me."

When Ross got home, he tried calling a friend but was too upset to speak. So he walked into the bathroom and prepared to kill himself. Fortunately, his father was home and could tell Ross was in distress. He convinced his son to come downstairs and talk. "If you don't take me to the hospital right now, I'm going to kill myself," Ross said as he walked into the kitchen. Instead of returning to school the next day, Ross was admitted to the hospital. 📁

Ross, in His Own Words

http://qrs.ly/wl4qsxp

© 2016, Macmillan

Note: Ross Szabo's story is based on personal communications with Ross Szabo and various passages from the book he coauthored with Melanie Hall: *Behind Happy Faces* (Szabo & Hall, 2007). Unless otherwise specified, quotations attributed to Ross Szabo and Melissa Hopely are personal communications.

What's Normal, What's Not

LO 1   Define psychological disorders and the criteria used to identify abnormal behavior.

A year-and-a-half earlier, Ross had been diagnosed with **bipolar disorder,** a condition marked by dramatic mood swings. We all have our ups and downs—periods of feeling happy, sad, anxious, or irritable—but the emotional roller coaster of bipolar disorder is something quite different. We will soon explore bipolar disorder in greater detail, but first let's familiarize ourselves with the broader focus of this chapter: psychological disorders.

A **psychological disorder** is a set of behavioral, emotional, and cognitive symptoms that are significantly distressing and disabling in terms of social functioning, work endeavors, and other aspects of life. These symptoms are not the result of religious or spiritual experiences; nor are they mere departures from cultural norms. And although stressors can trigger symptoms of psychological disorders, these conditions primarily result from disturbances in psychological, biological, and developmental processes (American Psychiatric Association, 2013).

The behaviors and symptoms associated with psychological disorders are not typical in the general population; in other words, they are abnormal. The academic field devoted to the study of psychological disorders is generally referred to as *abnormal psychology*. Researchers and scholars in abnormal psychology typically have backgrounds in clinical psychology, or psychiatry if they obtained medical degrees.

DEFINING ABNORMAL BEHAVIOR   Psychologists and other mental health professionals determine if a behavior is *abnormal* using a variety of criteria (**Table 12.1**). Perhaps the most straightforward criterion is *typicality* (or lack thereof). An atypical behavior is one that is rarely seen, or infrequent. The profound sadness Ross experienced is relatively rare. Most people experience sadness, even deep sadness at times, but suicidal thoughts are unusual. Although the typicality criterion is useful, it is not enough to confirm the existence of a psychological disorder. A child prodigy who learns to play the piano like a virtuoso by the age of 5 is atypical, but his rare talent does not indicate a psychological disorder.

We should also consider **maladaptive behaviors,** or actions that run counter to one's best interests. The degree of risk associated with these maladaptive behaviors (both to oneself and others) is often used by professionals to determine if a person needs to be admitted to a hospital. In Chapter 13, you can see how Dr. Dan Foster used this criterion in deciding whether to seek hospital care for a client with schizophrenia. We should point out, however, that maladaptive behavior is not always a sign of abnormality. People without disorders may exhibit maladaptive behaviors; just think of a child who has tantrums from time to time, or an adult who drowns his sorrows in alcohol one night.

Synonyms
psychological disorder mental disorder, mental illness, psychiatric illness, mental disability, mental disease
abnormal psychology experimental psychopathology, clinical psychology

CONNECTIONS

The field of *abnormal psychology* encompasses the study of psychological disorders as well as their treatment. In **Chapter 1,** we described various mental health professions, and the training they require. The current chapter focuses on abnormal psychology, a subfield many people associate with the word *psychology.*

bipolar disorder A psychological disorder marked by dramatic swings in mood, ranging from manic episodes to depressive episodes.

psychological disorder A set of behavioral, emotional, and/or cognitive symptoms that are significantly distressing or disabling in terms of social functioning, work endeavors, and other aspects of life.

maladaptive behaviors Behaviors or actions that run counter to what is in one's own best interest.

abnormal behavior Behavior that is atypical, dysfunctional, distressful, and/or deviant.

TABLE 12.1 DEFINING ABNORMAL BEHAVIOR

Criteria	What does it mean?
Typicality	Degree to which behavior is atypical, meaning rarely seen or statistically abnormal
Dysfunction	Degree to which behavior interferes with daily life and relationships
Distress	Degree to which behavior or emotions cause an individual to feel upset or uncomfortable
Deviance	Degree to which behavior is considered outside the standards or rules of society

Psychologists typically identify abnormal behavior using the criteria above.

You Asked, Ross Answers

http://qrs.ly/ht4qsxz

How do you explain your ability to hide what was going on with your bipolar disorder?

Deviant, but Not Disordered
Occupy Wall Street protesters camp out in Lower Manhattan's Zuccotti Park in the autumn of 2011. Setting up a tent and sleeping in a city park are behaviors that challenge social norms—you might even call them deviant. Yet in this case deviance is not necessarily linked to a psychological disorder. Seth Wenig/AP Photo

To arrive at a more definitive determination of **abnormal behavior,** mental health professionals typically rely on three criteria (in addition to typicality): *dysfunction, distress,* and *deviance,* or the "3 Ds" (American Psychiatric Association, 2013; Wakefield, 1992).

The first D, *dysfunction,* indicates the degree to which a behavior interferes with daily life and relationships. Ross' depression sometimes rendered him unable to get out of bed; this type of behavior certainly has the potential to interfere with daily life. But dysfunction alone does not confirm the presence of a psychological disorder. If you stay up all night to meet a deadline, you might experience temporary dysfunction in memory and attention, but that doesn't mean you have a disorder.

The second D is personal *distress.* Feeling regularly upset or uncomfortable because of unwanted behaviors or emotions is another feature of abnormality, and it's not always evident from the outside. Prior to his suicide attempt, Ross appeared to be happy and healthy, but inside he was suffering. There are times, however, when distress does not accompany a disorder. When Ross experienced the euphoric highs of bipolar disorder, he may not have been distressed at all. People with psychological disorders do not always have the insight to recognize that a problem exists.

The third D is *deviance,* or the degree to which a behavior is considered to be outside the standards or rules of a society. Behaving in a way that does not conform to social expectations might be indicative of a psychological disorder. Individuals who are euphoric might talk too loudly in a library or church where people are expected to be quiet, or become so disinhibited that they walk around naked in a public place. Yet, the presence of deviance alone does not necessarily indicate a psychological disorder. Political protesters, for example, may deliberately break social norms to make a statement. Many participants in Occupy Wall Street chose

to set up camp and sleep in public places normally used by others just passing through. Their behavior was deviant but not necessarily suggestive of a psychological disorder.

We should note that conceptions of abnormality and definitions of psychological disorders have changed during the course of history. Homosexuality was once considered a psychological disorder, but this notion was overturned in the 1970s and 1980s by psychiatrists and other mental health professionals (Silverstein, 2009), in part because cultural norms had changed. Always remember that the definition or meaning of "abnormal" is relative to place and time.

IT'S A CONTINUUM   It's important to understand that anyone can have experiences that resemble symptoms of psychological disorders. This is because there is a continuum for many behaviors and feelings: Those at one end are generally considered normal, and those at the other end abnormal. Ross' profound sadness would likely fall at the *abnormal* end of the continuum, whereas a teary farewell to a close friend who is moving away would be at the *normal* end.

CULTURALLY DEFINED   The definition of mental health is not the same for all groups of people. As the biopsychosocial model reminds us, we must consider culture and other social influences when trying to understand concepts like "normal" and "abnormal." Some disorders and symptoms are unique to particular cultures. *Koro,* for example, is an episode of intense anxiety observed mainly in Southeast Asia, although similar conditions have been documented in China. The main feature of *koro* is the unrealistic and intense fear that sexual organs will be pulled into the body, perhaps resulting in death (American Psychiatric Association, 2013; Roy et al., 2011). A man with *koro* might be exceedingly anxious about the idea of his penis disappearing into his abdomen, whereas a woman might fear that her nipples will be pulled into her chest. Another example is *susto,* most evident in Latino populations (Donlan & Lee, 2010). Someone with *susto* reacts to a frightening situation with the belief that her soul has left her body, which ultimately results in illness and sadness (American Psychiatric Association, 2013). Unlike *susto* and *koro, schizophrenia* (discussed later in the chapter) is evident across all cultures and throughout the world, suggesting it is universal.

Let's review what we have learned. Psychologists use three main criteria (in addition to typicality) to identify abnormality—*dysfunction, distress,* and *deviance.* The 3 Ds are useful, but be mindful of their limitations. The same could be said of other mental health concepts (normal, abnormal, and so forth), because their meanings may vary over time, across cultures, and even within the same culture.

THINK again

The Insanity Plea

Perhaps you have heard the term "insanity" used in a legal context. "The defendant got off on an insanity plea," or "The defense failed to demonstrate insanity." What do these statements mean? **Insanity** is a *legal* determination of the degree to which a person is responsible for his criminal behaviors. Those deemed legally insane are thought to have little or no control over or understanding of their behaviors at the time they committed their crimes. Therefore, they are offered psychological treatment rather than criminal punishment such as imprisonment or the death penalty. In America, 46 states offer a form of the *insanity defense;* only Idaho, Kansas, Montana, and Utah do not (Lilienfeld & Arkowitz, 2011,

THE INSANITY PLEA DID NOT WORK SO WELL FOR SERIAL MURDERER JEFFREY DAHMER.

Insanity?
In the summer of 2012, James Holmes walked into a movie theater in Aurora, Colorado, and opened fire on the audience, killing 12 people. Holmes' attorneys entered a plea of insanity; they claim he committed the murders while in a psychotic state (Ingold, 2013, September 30). Refusing to accept the insanity plea, jurors determined he should spend the rest of his life in prison (Associated Press, 2015, August 26). AP Photo/The Denver Post, Andy Cross, Pool

January/February). Many people believe that the insanity defense is frequently used, but it's invoked in only about 1% of cases. Of those cases, just 10–25% of insanity defenses are successful (Torry & Billick, 2010). Among those who avoided prison after entering an insanity plea was John Hinckley Jr., the man who attempted to assassinate President Ronald Reagan in 1981. The insanity plea did not work so well for serial murderer Jeffrey Dahmer, however; in 1992 he was sentenced to 15 life terms for the horrific murders of 15 young men (PBS, 2014). 💬➕

Now that we have explored the meaning of abnormality, let's find out more about the experience of having a psychological disorder—and the negative judgments that sometimes accompany it.

CONNECTIONS

In **Chapter 7,** we discussed the *availability heuristic;* we often predict the probability of something happening in the future based on how easily we can recall a similar type of event from the past. Here, the vividness of a crime and the ensuing trial make the insanity plea more available in our memories, so we are prone to overestimate its likelihood in the future.

DISPELLING STIGMA: ROSS FINDS HIS VOICE After being discharged from the hospital, Ross returned to school where he was greeted with rumors and stares. A couple of his friends stopped spending time with him, perhaps because they were afraid of what they didn't understand. Or maybe it was because people in the farmlands of Pennsylvania didn't talk much about emotions and mental health.

Not long after the hospital stay, a psychologist came to Ross' school to give his annual presentation about helping people with psychological disorders. Most of the students thought the topic was funny and laughed (perhaps out of discomfort) throughout the presentation. But Ross did not find it one bit amusing. After class, he told his teacher that he wanted to give his own presentation. Before long, Ross was standing before his peers, heart pounding and knees wobbling, talking about life with bipolar disorder. The students listened intently, and some approached Ross after class to talk about their own struggles with psychological disorders. By coming forward to share his experiences, Ross dispelled some of his classmates' misconceptions and fears about psychological disorders. He was a real person they knew and liked, and he had a disorder. 📁

WHAT IS STIGMA? Watching his classmates laugh about people with psychological disorders, Ross bore witness to the *stigma* attached to mental illness. **Stigma** is a negative attitude or opinion about groups of individuals based on certain traits or characteristics they have. It can lead to discrimination and stereotypes, and negative characterizations in general (Corrigan, 2005). Surely, you have heard people equate psychological disorders with violence and aggression, or perhaps you have seen TV shows portraying people with mental illness as wild and aggressive. Reality check:

insanity A legal determination of the degree to which a person is responsible for criminal behaviors.

stigma A negative attitude or opinion about a group of people based on certain traits or characteristics.

Hollywood Stereotypes
The late Heath Ledger plays the "Joker" in *The Dark Knight* (2008). Movie characters like the Joker, whom Ledger described as a "psychopathic, mass-murdering, schizophrenic clown with zero empathy" (Lyall, 2007, November 4, para. 13), tend to perpetuate stereotypes about people with psychological disorders, most of whom are not violent (Arkowitz & Lilienfeld, 2011, July/August; Fazel et al., 2009). Warner Bros./Photofest

People with psychological disorders are usually *not* violent. Other factors, such as lower socioeconomic status, male gender, and substance abuse, may be better predictors of violence (Stuart, 2003). The criterion of being a danger to oneself or others does determine the necessity of treatment, but given the degree of violence in our society, violent behavior is actually *atypical* of people with serious psychological disorders, and more commonly associated with substance abuse (Arkowitz & Lilienfeld, 2011, July/August; Fazel, Gulati, Linsell, Geddes, & Grann, 2009).

Stigma can have devastating repercussions. It may lower self-esteem, impair social functioning, and interfere with people getting much-needed treatment. Research suggests that many individuals do not seek mental health services because of the stigma associated with psychological disorders and their treatment (Corrigan, 2005).

What can we do to combat stigma? One suggestion is to use "people-first language"; that is, refer to the individual affected by the disorder (*She has been diagnosed with schizophrenia*), rather than defining the person by her disorder (*She is schizophrenic*; American Psychological Association, 2010c). We should also be cautious about using terms such as "crazy" and "insane." While these words are used to describe people on a daily basis, they are inappropriate, derogatory, and sure indicators of stigma.

Classifying and Explaining Psychological Disorders

How was Ross diagnosed with *bipolar disorder?* He consulted with a psychiatrist. But how did this mental health professional come to the conclusion that Ross suffered from bipolar disorder, and not something else? Given what we know about the complexity of determining abnormal behavior, it probably comes as no surprise that clinicians have not always agreed on what qualifies as a psychological disorder. Over the years, however, they have developed common criteria and procedures for making reliable diagnoses. These criteria and decision-making procedures are presented in manuals, which are shared across mental health professions, and are based on research findings and clinical observations.

THE DIAGNOSTIC AND STATISTICAL MANUAL OF MENTAL DISORDERS

Think about the last time you were ill and went to a doctor. You probably answered a series of questions about your symptoms. The nurse took your blood pressure and temperature, and the doctor performed a physical exam. Based on these subjective and objective findings, the doctor formulated a diagnosis. Mental health professionals must do the same—make diagnoses based on evidence. In addition to gathering information from interviews and other clinical assessments, psychologists typically rely on manuals to guide their diagnoses. Most mental health professionals in North America use the *Diagnostic and Statistical Manual of Mental Disorders* (DSM–5; American Psychiatric Association, 2013). The *DSM–5* is an evidence-based classification system of mental disorders first developed and published by the American Psychiatric Association (http://www.psych.org) in 1952. This manual was conceived and designed to help ensure accurate and consistent diagnoses based on the observation of symptoms. Although the *DSM* is published by the American Psychiatric Association—different from the American Psychological Association—it is used by psychiatrists, psychologists, social workers, and a variety of other clinicians.

When the *DSM* was comprehensively revised in 1994 (for *DSM-IV*), it included classifications for 172 psychological disorders. The *DSM–5* revision lists 157 disorders (American Psychiatric Association Division of Research, personal communication, July 26, 2013) and presents some new ideas on how to think about them (**Infographic 12.1**). The current revision also represents a substantial shift in how the manual is organized. The psychological disorders are presented in 20 chapters, with content organized around developmental changes occurring across the life span.

The *DSM–5*

Revising the *Diagnostic and Statistical Manual of Mental Disorders* was no small task. The process took over 10 years and involved hundreds of experts poring over the most relevant and current research. The final product helps researchers conduct studies and clinicians develop treatment plans and work with other professionals.

Where does the *DSM–5* come from?

PREPARATION Nearly 400 scientists from around the world evaluate research on psychological disorders for 10 years prior to publication of the *DSM–5.*

DRAFTING 160 scientists participating in the American Psychiatric Association's *DSM–5* Task Force and Work Groups review the research regarding disorders. Working with other researchers and clinicians, they gather as much information as possible about the current understanding of disorders. Then they compose and revise diagnostic criteria.

APPROVAL Following approval of the diagnostic criteria by the APA Board of Trustees, the prepublication *DSM–5* goes through two more rounds of review. The Scientific Review Committee examines the evidence informing the proposed changes to the *DSM*, and the Clinical and Public Health committee provides feedback on the criteria from a clinical and public health standpoint.

Some disorders included in the *DSM-5*

Each chapter of the *DSM-5* describes disorders that share common features and/or symptoms. Here we list six chapters, along with a sample disorder that you can read more about in your textbook.

Schizophrenia Spectrum and Other Psychotic Disorders
Dysfunction resulting from delusions, hallucinations, disorganized thinking, abnormal motor behavior, and negative symptoms.

> READ ABOUT
> *Schizophrenia, page 499*

Bipolar and Related Disorders
Manic and depressive behavior characterized by changes in mood and activity levels.

> READ ABOUT
> *Bipolar I Disorder, page 497*

Depressive Disorders
Dysfunction relating to profound sadness, feelings of emptiness, and irritable mood.

> READ ABOUT
> *Major Depressive Disorder, page 492*

Obsessive-Compulsive and Related Disorders
Dysfunction relating to obsessions and/or compulsions that cause distress and disrupt day-to-day functioning.

> READ ABOUT
> *Obsessive-Compulsive Disorder, page 490*

Trauma- and Stressor-Related Disorders
Distress resulting from exposure to traumatic or stressful incidents.

> READ ABOUT
> *Posttraumatic Stress Disorder, page 447*

Dissociative Disorders
Problems with memory, identity, consciousness, perception, and motor control that disrupt psychological functioning.

> READ ABOUT
> *Dissociative Amnesia, page 507*

How are disorders of childhood covered in the *DSM-5*?

The *DSM-5* does not include a separate chapter dedicated to disorders diagnosed in childhood, but diagnoses within chapters are presented in chronological order. The *DSM-5* also includes age-related factors in its descriptions and criteria. Here are two disorders commonly diagnosed in childhood:

Autism Spectrum Disorder
This spectrum of disorders recognizes a continuum of symptoms associated with social communication and interaction, repetitive behaviors or speech, and intellectual ability.

Attention-deficit/hyperactivity disorder (ADHD)
This disorder begins in childhood, and must be recognized in more than one situation (for example, school and home). A child may have difficulty paying attention, and may easily get off task, fidget, or act impulsively. The manual also recognizes that this disorder does not necessarily end in childhood, and may continue into adulthood.

Who uses the *DSM–5*, and how is it used?

Trained mental health professionals use the *DSM-5* to diagnose psychological disorders. The manual is designed to summarize the signs and symptoms of disorders for the clinician to use as an evaluative tool. The presence of specified signs and symptoms may indicate an underlying psychological disorder, and the *DSM-5* criteria can help guide clinicians to accurate diagnoses and appropriate treatment.

AMERICAN PSYCHIATRIC ASSOCIATION, 2013.

Some disorders were removed from the manual (sexual aversion disorder, for instance) and others were added (hoarding disorder, for example). Another major change is that several axes, or dimensions, previously used as additional information are now integrated within the diagnostic criteria for some disorders.

LO 2   Recognize limitations in the classification of psychological disorders.

CRITICISMS OF CLASSIFICATION   Why is the *DSM* important? Classifying mental disorders helps therapists develop treatment plans, enables clients to obtain reimbursement from their insurance companies, and facilitates research and communication among professions. But there is a downside to classification. Anytime someone is diagnosed with a mental disorder, he runs the risk of being labeled, which can lead to the formation of expectations—not only from other people, but also from himself. Few studies illustrate this phenomenon more starkly than David Rosenhan's classic 1973 study "On Being Sane in Insane Places."

didn't SEE that coming

"On Being Sane in Insane Places"

What do you think would happen if you secretly planted eight completely "sane" people (no history of psychological disorders) in American psychiatric hospitals? The hospital employees would immediately identify them as "normal" and send them home . . . right?

> NO HOSPITAL STAFF MEMBER IDENTIFIED THE PSEUDOPATIENTS AS FRAUDS.

In the early 1970s, psychologist David Rosenhan and seven other mentally healthy people managed to get themselves admitted to various psychiatric hospitals by faking auditory hallucinations ("I am hearing voices"), a common symptom of schizophrenia. (Such a feat would be close to impossible in this day and age, where people with documented psychological disorders struggle to obtain inpatient treatment at all; Scribner, 2001.) Upon admission, each of these pretend patients, or "pseudopatients," immediately stopped putting on an act and began behaving like their normal selves. But within the walls of a psychiatric hospital, their ordinary behavior assumed a whole new meaning. Staff members who spotted the pseudopatients taking notes concluded it must be a symptom of their psychological disorder. "Patient engaged in writing behavior," nurses wrote of one pseudopatient. "Nervous, Mr. X?" a nurse asked a pseudopatient who had been walking the halls out of sheer boredom (Rosenhan, 1973, p. 253).

No hospital staff member identified the pseudopatients as frauds. If anyone had them figured out, it was the other patients in the hospital. "You're not crazy," they would say to the pseudopatients. "You're a journalist, or a professor. You're checking up on the hospital" (Rosenhan, 1973, p. 252). After an average stay of 19 days (the range being 7 to 52 days), the pseudopatients were discharged, but not because doctors recognized their diagnostic errors.

Film with a Message
Jack Nicholson (blue shirt) portrays the character R. P. McMurphy in the 1975 classic *One Flew Over the Cuckoo's Nest*. In the film, McMurphy fakes the symptoms of a psychological disorder to get admitted into a mental hospital, where he and his fellow inmates are manipulated and abused. Although the movie deviated somewhat from reality, it did raise awareness about the problems with American mental institutions (Goodfriend, 2012, May 22). Fantasy Films/The Kobal Collection

The pseudopatients, they determined, had gone into "remission" from their fake disorders. They were released back into society—but not without their labels.

Some critics raised legitimate concerns about the methodology, results, and conclusions of Rosenhan's study (Lando, 1976; Spitzer, 1975). Nevertheless, it shed light on the persistence of labels and their associated stigma.

If eight sane people could be diagnosed with serious disorders like schizophrenia, you might be wondering if psychological diagnoses are reliable or valid. We've come a long way since 1973, but the diagnosis of psychological disorders remains a challenge, in part because it often relies on self-reports. Evaluating complex behaviors will never be as straightforward as measuring blood pressure or running a test for strep throat. 👁!

ATHEORETICAL APPROACH   The *DSM* authors tried to address this problem in 1980, by developing a checklist of observable signs and symptoms. This *atheoretical* approach removed the emphasis on particular theories and made it easier for mental health professionals to agree on diagnoses. But this method brought its own set of problems. Relying on checklists rather than theory tends to limit clinicians' understanding of their patients, and the overlapping of criteria across disorders led to some individuals being overdiagnosed (McHugh & Slavney, 2012). Yet, getting the right diagnosis is critical. If one patient is feeling down due to a "life encounter," such as the loss of a spouse, and another is feeling the same as a result of a "brain disease," such as bipolar disorder, their treatment needs will be drastically different (McHugh & Slavney, 2012).

"Abnormal," But Not Uncommon

You probably know someone with bipolar disorder, major depressive disorder, or attention-deficit/hyperactivity disorder (ADHD). Perhaps you have experienced a disorder yourself. Psychological disorders are not uncommon (**Table 12.2**). Findings from a large study of approximately 9,000 individuals indicate that around 50% of the population in the United States, at some point in life, experience symptoms that meet the criteria of a psychological disorder (Kessler, Berglund, et al., 2005; Kessler & Wang, 2008). Yes, you read that correctly; "Nearly half the population meet criteria for a mental disorder in their life . . ." (Kessler, 2010, p. 60). The majority of these disorders begin before the age of 14. Longitudinal studies monitoring children through young adulthood indicate that psychological disorders are "very common," with more than 70% being diagnosed by age 30 (Copeland, Shanahan, Costello, & Angold, 2011; Farmer, Kosty, Seeley, Olino, & Lewinsohn, 2013). And it's not just Americans who struggle with these issues. Lifetime prevalence for major psychological disorders ranges from approximately 26% in Lebanon (Karam et al., 2008) to about 30% in South Africa (Stein et al., 2008), with rates in many other countries similar to those in the United States (Organisation for Economic Co-operation and Development, 2008; Wittchen & Jacobi, 2005).

A TOUGH ROAD   With such high rates of disorders, you can be sure there are many people around you dealing with tough issues. In some cases, psychological disorders lead to greater impairment than chronic medical conditions, yet people with mental ailments are *less* likely to get treatment (Druss et al., 2009). Keep in mind that various psychological disorders are chronic (a person suffers from them continuously), others have a regular pattern (symptoms appear every winter, for example), and some are temporary.

CONNECTIONS

In **Chapter 10,** we discussed the concepts of *reliability* and *validity* in relation to the assessment of personality. Here, we refer to these same concepts when discussing a classification system for psychological disorders. We must determine if diagnoses are reliable (able to provide consistent, reproducible results) and valid (measuring what they intend to measure).

TABLE 12.2   YEARLY RATES OF PSYCHOLOGICAL DISORDERS

Psychological Disorder	Annual Prevalence
Anxiety disorders	18.1%
Specific phobia	8.7%
Social phobia	6.8%
Disruptive behavior disorders	8.9%
Mood disorders	9.5%
Major depression	6.7%
Substance disorders	3.8%
Any disorder	26.2%

In any given year, many people are diagnosed with a psychological disorder. The numbers here represent annual prevalence: the percentage of the U.S. population affected by a disorder over a year. (Elsewhere we have referred to lifetime prevalence, which means the percentage of the population affected by a disorder any time in life.)

KESSLER (2010).

Further complicating the picture is the fact that many people suffer from more than one psychological disorder at a time, a phenomenon called **comorbidity** (kō-ˈmor-bəd-ˈi-tē). The Kessler studies mentioned above found that nearly a quarter of participants with disorders had received two diagnoses in the course of a year (Kessler, Chiu, Demler, & Walters, 2005). You already know that one psychological disorder can lead to significant impairment; now just imagine how these problems compound when someone is coping with more than one disorder.

What Causes Psychological Disorders?

LO 3 Summarize the etiology of psychological disorders.

As we describe psychological disorders throughout this chapter, we will highlight some of the major theories of their *etiology,* or causal factors. But before getting into the specifics, let's familiarize ourselves with the models commonly used to explain the causes of psychological disorders.

IT'S IN YOUR BIOLOGY: THE MEDICAL MODEL The **medical model** explains psychological disorders from a biological standpoint, focusing on genes, neurochemical imbalances, and problems in the brain. This medical approach has had a long and uninterrupted history, as our culture continues to view psychological disorders as illnesses. It is evident in the language used to discuss disorders and their treatment: mental illness, therapy, remission, symptoms, patients, and doctors. Some scholars criticize this approach (Szasz, 2011), in part because it fails to acknowledge how concepts of mental health and illness have changed over time and across cultures (Kawa & Giordano, 2012).

IT'S IN YOUR MIND: PSYCHOLOGICAL FACTORS Another way to understand the etiology of disorders is to focus on the contribution of psychological factors. Some theories propose that cognitive factors or personality characteristics contribute to the development and maintenance of disorders. Others focus on the ways learning or childhood experiences might lay their foundation.

IT'S IN YOUR ENVIRONMENT: SOCIOCULTURAL FACTORS Earlier we mentioned that culture can shape definitions of "abnormal" and influence the development of psychological disorders. Social factors, like poverty and community support

Synonyms
medical model biological model

CONNECTIONS

In **Chapter 5,** we presented a variety of theories that explain how behaviors are learned. Here, we see how learning theories help us understand the development of abnormal behavior. Previous chapters have also discussed Freud's psychoanalytic theory, which suggests that early experiences may pave the way for psychological disorders.

comorbidity (kō-ˈmor-bəd-ˈi-tē) The occurrence of two or more disorders at the same time.

medical model An approach suggesting that psychological disorders are illnesses that have underlying biological causes.

systems, can also play a role in the development and course of these conditions (Honey, Emerson, & Llewellyn, 2011; Lund et al., 2011).

We have established that mental disorders result from a confluence of biological, psychological, and social factors. But is there a way to bring them together? Complex behaviors deserve complex explanations.

THE BIOPSYCHOSOCIAL PERSPECTIVE   As we have suggested in previous chapters, the best way to understand human behavior is to examine it from a variety of perspectives. The *biopsychosocial perspective* provides an excellent model for explaining psychological disorders, suggesting they result from a complex interaction of biological, psychological, and sociocultural factors (**Figure 12.1**). For example, some disorders appear to have a genetic basis, but their symptoms may not be evident until social or psychological factors come into play. We will discuss this again in the section on schizophrenia, when we take a look at the *diathesis–stress model.*

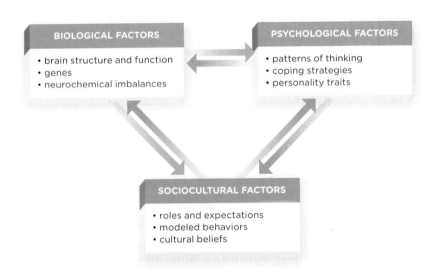

FIGURE 12.1
The Biopsychosocial Perspective
The biopsychosocial perspective considers the complex interaction of biological, psychological, and sociocultural factors that may contribute to a specific disorder.

Now that we have a general understanding of how psychologists conceptualize psychological disorders, let's delve into specifics. We cannot cover every disorder identified in the *DSM-5*, but we can offer an overview of those commonly discussed in an introductory psychology course.

CONNECTIONS

We have introduced psychological disorders in various chapters of this book. In **Chapter 9,** we discussed eating disorders in the context of motivation of hunger, as well as sexual dysfunctions outlined in the *DSM-5*. And **Chapter 11** explored the relationship between stressors and posttraumatic stress disorder.

 show what you know

1. Which of the following is a criterion used to define abnormal behavior?
   a. dysfunction
   b. psychopathology
   c. developmental processes
   d. stigma

2. Using Table 12.1 on page 477 as your guide, think of behaviors that are (1) atypical but not dysfunctional; (2) dysfunctional but not distressful; and (3) deviant but not dysfunctional.

3. The classification and diagnosis of psychological disorders have been criticized for:
   a. using specific criteria to identify disorders.
   b. the creation of labeling and expectations.
   c. placing too much emphasis on sociocultural factors.
   d. their research base.

4. One common approach to explaining the etiology of psychological disorders is the _____, which suggests that psychological disorders have underlying biological causes, such as genes, neurochemical imbalances, and problems in the brain.

✓ CHECK YOUR ANSWERS IN APPENDIX C.

Worried Sick: Anxiety and Obsessive-Compulsive Disorders

 UNWELCOME THOUGHTS: MELISSA'S STORY   Melissa Hopely was about 5 years old when she began doing "weird things" to combat anxiety: flipping light switches on and off, touching the corners of tables, and running to the kitchen to make sure the oven was turned off. Taken at face value, these behaviors may not seem too strange, but for Melissa they were the first signs of a psychological disorder that eventually pushed her to the edge.

Anxiety is a normal part of growing up. Children get nervous for an untold number of reasons: doctors' appointments, the first day of school, or the neighbor's German shepherd. But Melissa was not suffering from common childhood jitters. Her anxiety overpowered her physically, gripping her arms and legs in pain and twisting her stomach into a knot. It affected her emotionally, bringing on a vague feeling that something awful was about to occur—unless she did something to stop it. *If I just touch all the corners of this table like so, nothing bad will happen,* she would think to herself.

As Melissa grew older, her behaviors became increasingly regimented. She felt compelled to do everything an even number of times. Instead of entering a room once, she would enter or leave twice, four times, perhaps even 20 times—as long as the number was a multiple of 2. Some days she would sit in her bedroom for hours, methodically touching all of her possessions twice, then repeating the process again, and again. By performing these rituals, Melissa felt she could prevent her worst fears from becoming reality.

What was she so afraid of? Dying, losing all her friends, and growing up to be jobless, homeless, and living in a dumpster. She also feared striking out in her next softball game and making the whole team lose. Something dreadful was about to happen, though she couldn't quite put her finger on what it was. In reality Melissa had little reason to worry. She had health, smarts, beauty, and a loving circle of friends and family.

We all experience irrational worries from time to time, but Melissa's anxiety had become overwhelming. Where does one draw the line between anxiety that is normal and anxiety that is abnormal?

Then and Now
Melissa Hopely was about 3 years old when the photo on the left was taken. Within a couple of years, she would begin to experience the symptoms of a serious mental disorder that would carry into adulthood. Melissa Hopely

LO 4   Define anxiety disorders and demonstrate an understanding of their causes.

Think about the objects or situations that cause you to feel afraid or uneasy. Maybe you fear creepy crawly insects, slithery snakes, or crowded public spaces. A mild fear of spiders or overcrowded subways is normal, but if you become highly disturbed by the mere thought of them, or if the fear interferes with your everyday functioning, then a problem may exist. People who suffer from **anxiety disorders** have extreme anxiety and/or irrational fears that are debilitating (**Table 12.3**).

How do we differentiate between normal anxiety and an anxiety disorder? We look at the degree of dysfunction the anxiety causes, how much distress it creates, and whether it gets in the way of everyday behavior (interfering with relationships, work, and time management, for example). Let's take a look at some of the anxiety disorders identified in the *DSM–5:* panic disorder, specific phobia, agoraphobia, social anxiety disorder, and generalized anxiety disorder.

anxiety disorders A group of psychological disorders associated with extreme anxiety and/or debilitating, irrational fears.

panic attack Sudden, extreme fear or discomfort that escalates quickly, often with no obvious trigger, and includes symptoms such as increased heart rate, sweating, shortness of breath, chest pain, nausea, lightheadedness, and fear of dying.

panic disorder A psychological disorder that includes recurrent, unexpected panic attacks and fear that can cause significant changes in behavior.

TABLE 12.3 ANXIETY DISORDERS

Disorder	Annual Prevalence	Description	Cultural Impact
Separation anxiety disorder	0.9–1.9% in adults; 1.6% in adolescents; 4% in children	Anxiety or fear related to "separation from home or attachment figures" (p. 191).	Cultures vary with respect to age at which it is appropriate to move from parental home.
Specific phobia	7–9%	Anxiety about, or fear of, a specific object or situation.	Specific phobias vary across cultures.
Social anxiety disorder (social phobia)	7%	Anxiety about, or fear of being in, a social situation that could result in scrutiny by other people.	*Taijin kyofu* (Japan and Korea).
Panic disorder	2–3%	Reoccurring panic attacks that are unexpected and for which there is no apparent cue or trigger.	*Trúng gió* (Vietnam); *ataque de nervios* (Latin America); *khyâl* (Cambodia).
Agoraphobia	1.7%	Anxiety or fear regarding "using public transportation; being in open spaces; being in enclosed places; standing in line or being in a crowd; or being outside of the home" (p. 217).	None listed in *DSM-5*.
Generalized anxiety disorder	0.9% in adolescents; 2.9% in adults	Anxiety and worry that are out of proportion to the actual event or situation.	Varies by culture.

Anxiety disorders are relatively common in both sexes, but they are more apparent in women by an approximate 2:1 ratio.

DSM-5 (AMERICAN PSYCHIATRIC ASSOCIATION, 2013).

Panic Disorder

What should you do if you see somebody trembling and sweating, gasping for breath, or complaining of heart palpitations? If you are concerned it's a heart attack, you may be correct; call 911 immediately if you are not sure. However, a person experiencing a **panic attack** may behave very similarly to someone having a heart attack. A panic attack is a sudden, extreme fear or discomfort that escalates quickly, often with no evident cause, and includes symptoms such as increased heart rate, sweating, shortness of breath, chest pain, nausea, lightheadedness, and fear of dying. A diagnosis of **panic disorder** requires such attacks to recur unexpectedly and have no obvious trigger. In addition, the person worries about having more panic attacks, or she feels she may be losing control. People with panic disorder often make decisions that are maladaptive, like purposefully avoiding exercise or places that are unfamiliar.

THE BIOLOGY OF PANIC DISORDER Panic disorder does appear to have a biological cause (American Psychiatric Association, 2013). Researchers have identified specific parts of the brain thought to be responsible for panic attacks, including

Combatting Panic
Actress Emma Stone, known for her roles in movies such as *The Help* and *The Amazing Spider-Man,* began having panic attacks at the age of 8. Fortunately, she sought treatment and discovered a positive way to channel her anxiety—through acting and comedy. Stone still suffers from panic attacks, but they haven't gotten in the way of her success (Heller, 2012, June 18). Cindy Ord/Getty Images

CONNECTIONS

In **Chapter 2,** we described how the sympathetic division of the autonomic nervous system directs the body's stress response. When a stressful situation arises, the sympathetic nervous system prepares the body to react, causing the heart to beat faster, respiration to increase, and the pupils to dilate, among other things.

In **Chapter 5,** we described how, for Little Albert, an originally neutral stimulus (a rat) was paired with an unconditioned stimulus (a loud sound), which led to an unconditioned response (fear). With repeated pairings, the conditioned stimulus (the rat) led to a conditioned response (fear).

regions of the hypothalamus, which is involved in the fight-or-flight response (Johnson et al., 2010). There is also evidence suggesting that people diagnosed with panic disorder have a smaller amygdala. The amygdala is involved in fear and aggression, as well as the memories associated with those emotions. A smaller amygdala could lead to dysfunction in the autonomic nervous system (which directs the fight-or-flight response), resulting in behavioral and physical symptoms of panic attacks (Hayano et al., 2009).

GENETICS, GENDER, AND PANIC DISORDER Panic disorder affects about 2–3% of the population (American Psychiatric Association, 2013). Research indicates that panic disorder runs in families, with heritability estimates around 40–48% (Maron, Hettema, & Shlik, 2010; Weber et al., 2012). This means that over 40% of the variation of the disorder in the *population* can be attributed to genetic factors and the remaining 60% is due to environmental factors. In other words, the frequency and distribution of panic disorder across people result from a combination of factors, 40% of which are genetic, and 60% nongenetic. People often assume heritability refers to an individual's risk for a disorder ("Her panic disorder is 40% the result of her genes, and 60% due to her environment"). This is incorrect. Remember, heritability explains the variation and risk *among* individuals in a population.

Women are twice as likely as men to be diagnosed with panic disorder, and this disparity is already apparent by the age of 14 (American Psychiatric Association, 2013; Craske et al., 2010; Weber et al., 2012). Such gender differences may have a biological basis, but we must also consider psychological and social factors.

LEARNING AND PANIC DISORDER Some researchers propose that learning—particularly classical conditioning—can play a role in the development of panic disorder (Bouton, Mineka, & Barlow, 2001). In a panic disorder scenario, the neutral stimulus might be something like a location (a shopping mall), the unconditioned stimulus an unexpected panic attack, and the unconditioned response the fear resulting from the panic attack. The panic attack location (the shopping mall) would become the conditioned stimulus, such that every time the person thinks of the shopping mall, she responds with fear (now the conditioned response).

COGNITION AND PANIC DISORDER Other researchers suggest there is a cognitive component of panic disorder, with some individuals misinterpreting physical sensations as signs of major physical or psychological problems (Clark et al., 1997; Teachman, Marker, & Clerkin, 2010). For example, many people have a strange sensation when their hearts skip a beat (technically known as *arrhythmia*), but they realize it is probably not serious, perhaps just the result of too much coffee. A person with panic disorder might interpret that sensation as an indication of an imminent heart attack.

Specific Phobias and Agoraphobia

Panic attacks can occur without apparent triggers. This is not the case with a **specific phobia,** which centers on a particular object or situation, such as rats or airplane travel. Most people who have a phobia do their best to avoid the feared object or situation. If avoidance is not possible, they withstand it, but only with extreme fear and anxiousness. Take a look at **Table 12.4** for a list of some specific phobias.

TABLE 12.4 SPECIFIC PHOBIAS	
Scientific Name	**Fear of . . .**
Acrophobia	Heights
Astraphobia or keraunophobia	Lightning
Brontophobia	Thunder
Claustrophobia	Closed spaces
Cynophobia	Dogs
Epistemophobia	Knowledge
Gamophobia	Marriage
Ophidiophobia	Snakes
Odontophobia	Dental procedures
Xenophobia	Strangers

A person with a specific phobia feels extreme anxiety about a particular object or situation. Fears center on anything from dogs to dental procedures.

REBER, ALLEN, AND REBER (2009).

Paul-Francois Gay/AGE fotostock

LEARNING AND SPECIFIC PHOBIAS   As with panic disorder, phobias can be explained using the principles of learning (LeBeau et al., 2010). Classical conditioning may lead to the acquisition of a fear, through the pairing of stimuli. Operant conditioning could maintain the phobia, through negative reinforcement; if anxiety (the unpleasant stimulus) is reduced by avoiding a feared object or situation, the avoidance behavior is negatively reinforced and thus more likely to recur. Observational learning can also help explain the development of a phobia. Simply watching someone else experience a phobia could create fear in an observer. Some research demonstrates that even rhesus monkeys become afraid of snakes if they observe other monkeys reacting fearfully to real *or* toy snakes (Heyes, 2012; Mineka, Davidson, Cook, & Keir, 1984).

BIOLOGY, CULTURE, AND SPECIFIC PHOBIAS   Phobias can also be understood through the lens of evolutionary psychology. Humans seem to be biologically predisposed to fear certain threats such as spiders, snakes, foul smells, and bitter foods. Spiders, in particular, may inspire fear or disgust because they can be dangerous, but such reactions can also be influenced by culture (Gerdes, Uhl, & Alpers, 2009). From an evolutionary standpoint, these types of fears would tend to protect us from true danger. But the link between anxiety and evolution is not always so apparent. It's hard to imagine how an intense fear of being in public, for example, would promote survival.

AGORAPHOBIA   Do you ever feel a little anxious when you are out in public, in a new city, or at a crowded amusement park? A person with **agoraphobia** (a-gǝ-rǝ-'fō-bē-ǝ) feels extremely anxious in these types of settings. This disorder is characterized by a distinct fear or anxiety related to public transportation, open spaces, retail stores, crowds, or being alone and away from home in general. Agoraphobia may also result in "panic-like symptoms," which can be difficult to handle. Typically, people with agoraphobia need another person to accompany them on outings, because they feel they may not be able to cope on their own. They may avoid situations that frighten them, or be overwhelmed with fear when avoidance or escape is not possible. As with other anxiety disorders, the fear felt by someone with agoraphobia is beyond what is commonly expected in a particular cultural context (American Psychiatric Association, 2013).

Social Anxiety Disorder

According to the *DSM–5,* a person with *social anxiety disorder* (*social phobia*) has a distinct fear of social situations and scrutiny by others. This fear could arise during a speech or presentation, while eating a meal, or simply in an intimate conversation. Social anxiety often stems from a preoccupation with offending someone or behaving in a way that reveals one's anxiety. This extreme fear is not warranted, however. Being evaluated or even mocked by others is not necessarily a dangerous situation and should not cause debilitating stress. This type of social anxiety, where one fears the judgment and scrutiny of others, is what psychologists often observe in Western societies. In other parts of the world, social anxiety may take a different form.

CONNECTIONS

In **Chapter 5,** we discussed *negative reinforcement;* behaviors increase when they are followed by the *removal* of something unpleasant. Here, the avoidance behavior *takes away* the anxious feeling, increasing the likelihood of avoiding the object in the future.

EEK!
Emotional responses, such as fear of spiders, snakes, and heights, may have evolved to protect us from danger (Plomin, DeFries, Knopik, & Neiderhiser, 2013). Avoiding harmful creatures and precarious drop-offs would tend to increase the chances of survival, particularly for our primitive ancestors living in the wild. But when such fears become excessive and irrational, a specific phobia might be present.
skydie/Shutterstock

Attack of the Nerves
In Puerto Rico and other parts of Latin America, stress may trigger a syndrome known as *ataque de nervios,* or "attack of the nerves." People suffering from this condition may burst into tears, yell frantically, behave aggressively, and feel a sensation of heat moving from the chest to the head (American Psychiatric Association, 2013).
Kamira/Shutterstock

specific phobia   A psychological disorder that includes a distinct fear or anxiety in relation to an object or situation.
agoraphobia   (a-gǝ-rǝ-'fō-bē-ǝ) Extreme fear of situations involving public transportation, open spaces, or other public settings.

The Many Faces of Social Anxiety

Every society has its own collection of social norms, so it's not surprising that social anxiety presents itself in distinct ways across the world. People in Asian cultures, for example, are more likely to avoid outward displays of anxiety, such as blushing, sweating, or shaking. Some individuals in Japan and Korea suffer from *taijin kyofu,* a cultural syndrome characterized by an intense fear of offending or embarrassing other people with one's body odor, stomach rumblings, or facial expressions. Note that with *taijin kyofu,* the fear is associated with causing distress in others. In the United States and other Western countries, social anxiety is more centered on humiliating oneself (Hofmann, Asnaani, & Hinton, 2010; Kinoshita et al., 2008). This distinction may stem from cultural differences; Japanese and Korean societies are more collectivist than those of the West (Rapee & Spence, 2004). Collectivist cultures value social harmony over individual needs, so causing discomfort in others is worse than personal humiliation.

Synonyms
taijin kyofu taijin kyofusho

BODY ODOR AND OTHER CULTURAL AFFRONTS

Generalized Anxiety Disorder

Thus far we have discussed anxiety disorders that center on specific objects or scenarios, but what about anxiety that is pervasive, or widespread? Someone with **generalized anxiety disorder** experiences an excessive amount of worry and anxiety about many activities relating to family, health, school, and other aspects of daily life (American Psychiatric Association, 2013). The psychological distress is accompanied by physical symptoms such as muscle tension and restlessness. Individuals with generalized anxiety disorder may avoid activities they believe will not go smoothly, spend a great deal of time getting ready for such events, or wait until the very last minute to engage in the anxiety-producing activity. Like other disorders, the anxiety must cause substantial distress in social settings or work environments to merit a diagnosis.

Twin studies suggest there is a hereditary component to generalized anxiety disorder. This genetic factor appears to be associated with irregularities in parts of the brain associated with fear, such as the amygdala and hippocampus (Hettema et al., 2012; Hettema, Neale, & Kendler, 2001). Environmental factors such as adversity in childhood and overprotective parents also appear to be associated with the development of generalized anxiety disorder (American Psychiatric Association, 2013).

MELISSA'S STRUGGLE   We introduced this section with the story of Melissa Hopely. Melissa struggled with anxiety and felt compelled to perform elaborate rituals in order to assuage it. Her behavior caused significant distress and dysfunction, which suggests that it was abnormal, but does it match any of the anxiety disorders described above? Her anxiety was not attached to a specific object or situation, so it doesn't appear to fit the description of a phobia. Nor was her anxiety nonspecific, as might be the case with generalized anxiety disorder. Melissa's fears emanated from nagging, dreadful thoughts generated by her own mind. She may not have been struggling with an anxiety disorder per se, but she certainly was experiencing anxiety as a result of some disorder. So what was it?

Obsessive-Compulsive Disorder

LO 5   Summarize the symptoms and causes of obsessive-compulsive disorder.

At age 12, Melissa was diagnosed with **obsessive-compulsive disorder (OCD),** a psychological disorder characterized by unwanted thoughts, or obsessions, and repetitive,

generalized anxiety disorder
A psychological disorder characterized by an excessive amount of worry and anxiety about activities relating to family, health, school, and other aspects of daily life.

obsessive-compulsive disorder (OCD)   A psychological disorder characterized by obsessions and/or compulsions that are time-consuming and cause a great deal of distress.

obsession   A thought, an urge, or an image that happens repeatedly, is intrusive and unwelcome, and often causes anxiety and distress.

compulsion   A behavior or "mental act" that a person repeats over and over in an effort to reduce anxiety.

ritualistic behaviors known as compulsions. An **obsession** is a thought, urge, or image that recurs repeatedly, is intrusive and unwelcome, and often causes feelings of intense anxiety and distress. Melissa's recurrent, all-consuming thoughts of disaster and death are examples of obsessions. People with OCD attempt to stop, or at least ignore, their obsessions by engaging in a replacement thought or activity. This isn't always helpful, though, because the replacement can become a **compulsion,** which is a behavior or "mental act" repeated over and over.

Those who suffer from OCD experience various types of obsessions and compulsions. In many cases, obsessions focus on fears of contamination with germs or dirt, and compulsions revolve around cleaning and sterilizing (Cisler, Brady, Olatunji, & Lohr, 2010). One such OCD sufferer reported washing her hands until her knuckles bled, living in fear that she would kill someone with her germs (Turk, Marks, & Horder, 1990). Other common compulsions include repetitive rituals and checking behaviors. Melissa, for example, developed a compulsion about locking her car. Unlike most people, who lock their cars once and walk away, Melissa felt compelled to lock it twice. Then she would begin to wonder whether the car was really locked, so she would lock it a third time—just in case. But 3 is an odd number, and odd numbers don't sit well with Melissa, so she would lock it a fourth time. By the time Melissa finally felt comfortable enough to walk away, she had locked her car eight times. And sometimes that was still not enough.

THE OCD DIAGNOSIS How do you explain this type of behavior? OCD compulsions often aim to thwart unwanted situations, and thereby reduce anxiety and distress. Melissa was tormented by multiple obsessions ranging from catastrophic (the death of her mother) to minor (someone stealing her iPod). But the compulsive behaviors of OCD are either "clearly excessive" or not logically related to the event or situation the person is trying to prevent (American Psychiatric Association, 2013).

Where do we draw the line between obsessive or compulsive behavior and the diagnosis of a disorder? Remember, behaviors or symptoms must be significantly distressing or disabling in order to be considered abnormal and qualify as a disorder. This is certainly the case with OCD, in which obsessions and/or compulsions are very time-consuming (taking more than 1 hour a day) and cause a great deal of distress and disruption in daily life. Everyone has odd thoughts and quirky routines, but they don't eat up multiple hours of the day and interfere with school, work, and relationships. That's the key distinction between normal preoccupations and OCD (American Psychiatric Association, 2013).

THE BIOLOGY OF OCD Evidence suggests that the symptoms of OCD are related to abnormal activity of neurotransmitters. Reduced activity of serotonin is thought to play a role, though other neurotransmitters are also being studied (Bloch, McGuire, Landeros-Weisenberger, Leckman, & Pittenger, 2010). Certain areas of the brain have been implicated, including locations in the basal ganglia, cingulate gyri, and orbital frontal cortex (American Psychiatric Association, 2013; Radua & Mataix-Cols, 2009). These regions play a role in planning and regulating movement (Rotge et al., 2009).

Why do these biological differences arise? There appears to be a genetic basis for OCD. If a first-degree relative (parent, sibling, or offspring who shares about 50% of one's DNA) has an OCD diagnosis, the risk of developing OCD is twice as high as someone whose first-degree relatives do not have the disorder (American Psychiatric Association, 2013).

THE ROLE OF REINFORCEMENT To ease her anxiety, Melissa turned to compulsions—repetitive, ritualistic behaviors aimed at relieving or offsetting her obsessions. Because her greatest fears never came to pass, Melissa assumed that her actions had prevented them. *I didn't die because I touched all the things in my room just the right way,* she would think to herself. The more she followed through on her compulsions and

Soccer Star's Struggle
The Pepsi cans in David Beckham's refrigerator are arranged in a perfect line or in groups of two; if the total number of cans is odd, he removes one to make it even. When Beckham goes to a hotel, he can only relax after systematically organizing all the objects in his room. The British soccer legend reportedly suffers from obsessive-compulsive disorder (Frith, 2006, April 3). Michel Euler/AP Photo

CONNECTIONS

Negative reinforcement (**Chapter 5**) promotes the maladaptive behavior here. The compulsions are not actually preventing unwanted occurrences, but they do lead to a *decrease* in anxiety, and thus negatively reinforce the behavior. Repeatedly locking the car temporarily reduced Melissa's anxiety, making her more likely to perform this behavior in the future.

saw that her fears never played out, the more convinced she became that her behaviors prevented them. As Melissa put it, "When you feed it, feed it, feed it, it gets stronger."

Here, we see how learning can play a role in OCD. Melissa's compulsions were negatively reinforced by the reduction in her fear. The negative reinforcement led to more compulsive behaviors, those compulsions were negatively reinforced, and so on. This learning process is ongoing and potentially very powerful. In one study, researchers monitored 144 people with OCD diagnoses for more than 40 years. The participants' OCD symptoms improved, but almost half continued to show "clinically relevant" symptoms after four decades (Skoog & Skoog, 1999).

 **show what you know**

1. A behaviorist might propose that you acquire a phobia through _____, but the maintenance of that phobia could be the result of _____.

2. People suffering from *taijin kyofu* tend to worry more about embarrassing others than they do about being embarrassed themselves. Yet in Western cultures, the opposite is true. What characteristics of the two cultures might lead to these differences in the expression of anxiety?

3. Melissa has demonstrated recurrent all-consuming thoughts and feelings of worry. She tries to stop unwanted thoughts and

urges through a variety of behaviors that she repeats over and over. These behaviors are known as:

a. obsessions.   b. classical conditioning.

c. panic attacks.   d. compulsions.

4. Evidence suggests there is a _____ basis for OCD. If a first-degree relative has an OCD diagnosis, a person's risk of developing the same disorder is twice as high as someone whose first-degree relatives do not have the disorder.

✓ CHECK YOUR ANSWERS IN APPENDIX C.

The Importance of Friends

Melissa (right) poses with childhood friend Mary Beth, whom she credits for helping save her life. The day that Melissa came home intending to attempt suicide, Mary Beth recognized her friend's distress and called for help. Thanks to the intervention of friends and family, Melissa received the treatment she needed.

Melissa Hopely

From Depression to Mania

 **MELISSA'S SECOND DIAGNOSIS**   Unfortunately for Melissa, receiving a diagnosis and treatment did not solve her problems. She hated herself for having OCD, and her parents and some friends had a hard time accepting her diagnosis. "Every day I woke up, I wanted to die," says Melissa, who reached a breaking point during her sophomore year in high school. After a particularly difficult day at school, Melissa returned home with the intention of taking her own life. Luckily, a friend recognized that she was in distress and notified Melissa's family members, who rushed home to find Melissa curled up in a ball in the corner of her room, rocking back and forth and mumbling nonsense. They took Melissa to the hospital, where she would be safe and begin treatment. During her 3-day stay in the psychiatric unit, Melissa finally met people who didn't think she was "crazy" or define her by the disorder. For the first time, she explains, "I realized I wasn't my disorder." 📁

DSM–5 and Major Depressive Disorder

LO 6   Summarize the symptoms and causes of major depressive disorder.

During that hospital stay, doctors gave Melissa a new diagnosis in addition to OCD. They told her that she was suffering from *depression*. Apparently, the profound sadness and helplessness she had been feeling were symptoms of **major depressive disorder,** one of the depressive disorders described in the *DSM–5* (**Table 12.5**). A *major depressive episode* is evident if five or more of the symptoms listed below (1) occur for at least 2 consecutive weeks and represent a change from prior functioning, (2) cause significant distress or impairment, and (3) are not due to a medical or drug-related condition:

• depressed mood, which might result in feeling sad or hopeless;

• reduced pleasure in activities almost all of the time;

• substantial loss or gain in weight, without conscious effort, or changes in appetite;

• sleeping excessively or not sleeping enough;

major depressive disorder
A psychological disorder that includes at least one major depressive episode, with symptoms such as depressed mood, problems with sleep, and loss of energy.

- feeling tired, drained of energy;
- feeling worthless or extremely guilt-ridden;
- difficulty thinking or concentrating;
- persistent thoughts about death or suicide.

Someone with five or more of these symptoms would feel significantly distressed and experience problems in social interactions and at work.

In order to be diagnosed with major depressive disorder, a person must have experienced at least one major depressive episode. Some people suffer a single episode, while others battle *recurrent* episodes. In some instances, the disorder is triggered by the birth of a baby. Approximately 3–6% of women experience depression starting during pregnancy or within weeks or months of giving birth; this is known as *peripartum onset* (American Psychiatric Association, 2013).

When making a diagnosis, the clinician must be able to distinguish the symptoms of major depression from normal reactions to a "significant loss," such as the death of a loved one. This is not always easy because responses to death often resemble depression. A key distinction is that grief generally decreases with time, and comes in waves associated with memories or reminders of the loss; the sadness associated with a major depressive episode tends to remain steady (American Psychiatric Association, 2013).

Major depressive disorder is one of the most common and devastating psychological disorders. In the United States, for example, the lifetime prevalence of major depressive disorder is almost 17% (Kessler, Berglund, et al., 2005); this means that nearly 1 in 5 people experience a major depressive episode at least once in life. Women are more likely to be affected than men (Kessler et al., 2003), and rates of this disorder are already 1.5 to 3 times higher for females beginning in adolescence (American Psychiatric Association, 2013).

The effects of major depressive disorder extend far beyond the individual. For Americans ages 15 to 44, this condition is at the top of the list enumerating causes of disability (World Health Organization, 2008a)—and this means it impacts the productivity of the workforce. In a comprehensive study of major depressive disorder, respondents reported that their symptoms prevented them from going to work or performing day-to-day activities for an average of 35 days a year (Kessler et al., 2003). Stop and think about this statistic—we are talking about a loss of 7 work weeks!

History of Depression
Actor Jon Hamm is among the millions of Americans who have struggled with depression (Vernon, 2010, September 18). In any one year, approximately 7% of the American population is diagnosed with major depressive disorder (American Psychiatric Association, 2013; Kessler, Chiu, et al., 2005). If you or someone you know appears to be experiencing depression or suicidal thoughts, do not hesitate to seek help. Call the National Suicide Prevention Line: 1-800-273-TALK or 1-800-273-8255. Francis Specker/Landov Photographers

TABLE 12.5 DEPRESSIVE DISORDERS		
Depressive Disorder	**Description**	**Annual Prevalence**
Disruptive mood dysregulation disorder	Persistent irritability that typically results in "temper outbursts" and "angry mood that is present between the severe temper outbursts" (p. 156).	2–5% in children
Major depressive disorder	Feeling depressed (sad, empty, hopeless) almost every day for 2 weeks, or "a loss of interest or pleasure in" almost all activities (p. 163).	7% in the 18–29 age bracket, and 3 times higher among those aged 60 and older
Persistent depressive disorder (dysthymia)	Feeling depressed the majority of the time: at least 2 years in adults and 1 year in children and adolescents.	0.05%
Premenstrual dysphoric disorder	Feeling irritable, low, or anxious during the premenstrual phase of one's cycle, a condition that resolves itself during menses or shortly thereafter.	1.8–5.8% of menstruating women

As you can see from these descriptions, the word *depression* can mean many things. Listed above are various types of depression and their annual prevalence.

DSM-5 (AMERICAN PSYCHIATRIC ASSOCIATION, 2013).

CULTURE   Depression is one of the most common disorders in the world, yet the symptoms experienced, the course of treatment, and the words used to describe it vary from culture to culture. For example, people in China rarely report feeling "sad," but instead focus on physical symptoms, such as dizziness, fatigue, or inner pressure (Kleinman, 2004). In Thailand, depression is commonly expressed through physical *and* mental symptoms, such as headaches, fatigue, daydreaming, social withdrawal, irritation, and forgetfulness (Chirawatkul, Prakhaw, & Chomnirat, 2011).

SUICIDE   The recurrent nature of major depressive disorder creates increased risk for suicide and health complications (Monroe & Harkness, 2011). Around 9% of adults in 21 countries confirm they have harbored "serious thoughts of suicide" at least once (**Infographic 12.2**), and around 3% have attempted suicide (Borges et al., 2010). According to the National Institute of Mental Health (NIMH, 2013, October 1), approximately 90% of people who commit suicide have a psychological disorder, usually depressive disorder and/or substance abuse disorder.

The Biology of Depression

Nearly 7% of Americans battle depression in any given year (American Psychiatric Association, 2013; Kessler, Chiu, et al., 2005). What underlies this staggering statistic? There appears to be something biological at work.

GENETIC FACTORS   Studies of twins, family pedigrees, and adoptions tell us that major depressive disorder runs in families, with a heritability rate of approximately 40–50% (American Psychiatric Association, 2013; Levinson, 2006). This means that about 40–50% of the variability of major depressive disorder in the population can be attributed to genetic factors. People who have a first-degree relative with this disorder are 2 to 4 times more likely to develop it than those whose first-degree relatives are unaffected (American Psychiatric Association, 2013).

NEUROTRANSMITTERS AND THE BRAIN   Three neurotransmitters appear to be associated with the cause and course of major depressive disorder: *norepinephrine, serotonin,* and *dopamine.* The relationships among these neurotransmitters are complicated and research is still ongoing (El Mansari et al., 2010; Torrente, Gelenberg, & Vrana, 2012), but the findings are intriguing. For example, serotonin deficiency has been associated with major depressive disorder (Torrente et al., 2012), and genes may be responsible for some of this irregular activity, particularly in the amygdala and other brain areas involved in processing emotions associated with this disorder (Northoff, 2012). Depression also seems to be correlated with specific structural features in the brain (Andrus et al., 2012). People with major depressive disorder may have irregularities in the amygdala, the prefrontal cortex, and the hippocampus. For example, some regions of the right cortex show significant thinning in people who face a high risk of developing major depressive disorder (Peterson et al., 2009). Studies have zeroed in on a variety of factors, such as increased structure size, decreased volume, and changes in neural activity (Kempton et al., 2011; Sacher et al., 2012; Singh et al., 2013). Research using functional magnetic resonance imaging (fMRI) technologies points to irregularities in neural pathways involved in processing emotions and rewards for people with major depressive disorder (American Psychiatric Association, 2013). Major depressive disorder most likely results from a complex interplay of many neural factors. What's difficult to determine is whether changes in the brain precede the disorder, or the disorder alters the brain.

HORMONES   There is also evidence that hormones play a role in depression. People with depressive disorders may have high levels of cortisol, a hormone secreted by the adrenal glands (Belmaker & Agam, 2008; Dougherty, Klein, Olino, Dyson, & Rose, 2009). Women sufferers, in particular, appear to be affected by stress-induced brain

CONNECTIONS

In **Chapter 2,** we described the endocrine system, which uses glands to convey messages via *hormones.* These chemicals released into the bloodstream can cause aggression and mood swings, as well as influence growth and alertness. Hormones may also play a role in major depressive disorder.

Suicide in the United States

In 2009, suicide emerged as the leading cause of death from injury in the United States, surpassing rates for homicide and traffic accidents (Rockett et al., 2012). Researchers examine suicide rates across gender, age, and ethnicity in order to better understand risk factors and to help develop suicide prevention strategies. Let's take a look at what this means—and what you can do if a friend or family member might be contemplating suicide.

Among adults aged 18 and older, **8.7 million reported having serious thoughts about suicide** in the past year.

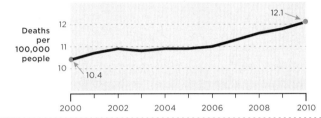

1,100,000 attempted suicide.

(SUBSTANCE ABUSE AND MENTAL HEALTH SERVICES ADMINISTRATION, 2011)

In 2010, someone died as a result of suicide almost every **14 minutes.**
(AMERICAN FOUNDATION FOR SUICIDE PREVENTION, 2013)

Deaths per 100,000 people

12.1
10.4

2000 2002 2004 2006 2008 2010

From 2000 to 2010, suicide rates **increased by nearly 20%.**
(AMERICAN FOUNDATION FOR SUICIDE PREVENTION, 2013)

Suicide is the second leading cause of death for people aged 25 to 34, and the third leading cause of death for people aged 15 to 24.

(CENTERS FOR DISEASE CONTROL AND PREVENTION, NATIONAL CENTER FOR INJURY PREVENTION AND CONTROL, 2010)

Until 2006, people aged 85 and older had the highest rate of suicide. Now people 45 to 64 years old have the highest rate.

(AMERICAN FOUNDATION FOR SUICIDE PREVENTION, 2013)

The suicide rate for males is nearly 4 times higher than females.

WHITE	14.1
AMERICAN INDIAN AND ALASKAN NATIVE	11.0
ASIAN AND PACIFIC ISLANDER	6.2
HISPANIC	5.9
BLACK	5.1

White Americans have the highest rate of suicide: In 2010, 14.1 out of every 100,000 died by suicide.
(AMERICAN FOUNDATION FOR SUICIDE PREVENTION, 2013)

Risk factors for suicide include:

✔ Previous suicide attempt(s)
✔ Family history of suicide or violence
✔ Alcohol or drug abuse
✔ Physical illness
✔ History of depression or other mental illness
✔ Feeling alone

(CENTERS FOR DISEASE CONTROL AND PREVENTION, 2012i)

Serge/Getty Images

If you believe a friend may be thinking about suicide:

- Encourage your friend to contact a responsible person who can help. This may be a counselor, teacher, or health-care professional. Or call a suicide prevention hotline.

- Don't be afraid to be wrong. Talking about suicide will not put the idea in your friend's head. Be direct and ask your friend if he is thinking about hurting himself.

- Just talking with your friend can help. Listen without being judgmental.

- If your friend admits that she has made a detailed plan or obtained a means of hurting herself, stay with her until help arrives or until she is willing to go talk with someone who can help.

- Never agree to keep someone's thoughts about suicide a secret.

(MAINE SUICIDE PREVENTION PROGRAM, 2006; YOUTH SUICIDE PREVENTION PROGRAM, 2011)

Ninety percent of those who commit suicide had a psychological disorder. Of these, 60% involved major depressive disorder. More than 80% of those people with disorders had not been receiving treatment at the time (Mann et al., 2005).

NATIONAL SUICIDE PREVENTION LIFELINE: 1-800-273-TALK (8255) suicidepreventionlifeline.org

Photo is being used for illustrative purposes only; persons depicted in the photos are models.

activity and hormonal fluctuations (Holsen et al., 2011). The hormonal changes associated with pregnancy and childbirth seem to be linked to major depressive episodes. For women suffering from depressive symptoms, there appear to be problems with the hypothalamic–pituitary–adrenal (HPA) system (Corwin & Pajer, 2008; Pearlstein, Howard, Salisbury, & Zlotnick, 2009). This is not just an issue for pregnant women. Research suggests that hyperactivity of the HPA system is linked to major depressive episodes in general (American Psychiatric Association, 2013).

Psychological Roots of Depression

Earlier we mentioned heritability rates of 40–50% for depression. But what about the other 50–60% of the variability? Clearly, biology is not everything. Psychological factors also play a role in the onset and course of major depressive disorder.

LEARNED HELPLESSNESS According to researcher Martin Seligman, people often become depressed because they believe they have no control over the consequences of their behaviors (Overmier & Seligman, 1967; Seligman, 1975; Seligman & Maier, 1967). To demonstrate this **learned helplessness,** Seligman restrained dogs in a "hammock" and then randomly administered inescapable painful electric shocks to their paws (**Figure 12.2**). The next day the same dogs were put into another cage. Although unrestrained, they did not try to escape shocks administered through a floor grid (even though they could have, by jumping over a low barrier in the cage). Seligman concluded the dogs had learned they couldn't control painful experiences during the prior training; they were acting in a depressed manner. He translated this finding to people with major depressive disorder, suggesting that they too feel powerless to change things for the better, and therefore become depressed.

NEGATIVE THINKING Cognitive therapist Aaron Beck (1976) suggested that depression is connected with negative thinking. Depression, according to Beck, is the product of a "cognitive triad"—a negative view of experiences, self, and the future. Here's an example: A student receives a failing grade on an exam, so she begins to think she is a poor student, and that belief leads her to the conclusion that she will fail the course. This self-defeating attitude may actually lead to her failing the course,

In **Chapter 11,** we discussed the *HPA system,* which helps to maintain balance in the body by overseeing the sympathetic nervous system, the neuroendocrine system, and the immune system. The HPA system is also associated with depressive episodes.

CONNECTIONS

Baby Blues
Having a baby is a stressful, life-changing event, and a time of dramatic hormonal changes. The hormone activity associated with pregnancy and childbirth may contribute to the major depressive episodes some women experience before and after the birth of a baby.
Laurent/Ravonison/AGE fotostock

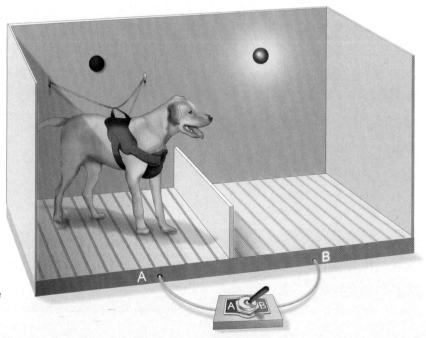

FIGURE 12.2
Seligman's Research on Learned Helplessness
Dogs restrained in a hammock were unable to escape painful shocks administered through an electrical grid on the floor of a specially designed cage called a shuttle box. The dogs soon learned that they were helpless and couldn't control these painful experiences. They did not try to escape by jumping over the barrier even when they were not restrained. The figure here shows the electrical grid activated on side B.

reinforcing her belief that she is a poor student, and perhaps evolving into a broader belief that her life is a failure.

If you aren't convinced that beliefs contribute to depression, consider this: The way people respond to their experience of depression may impact the severity of the disorder. People who repeatedly focus on this experience are much more likely to remain depressed and perhaps even descend into deeper depression (Eaton et al., 2012; Nolen-Hoeksema, 1991). Women tend to *ruminate* or constantly think about their negative emotions more than men, rather than using "active problem solving" (Eaton et al., 2012). Yet changing negative thoughts and moods during major depressive episodes is difficult to do without help. We should also note that a correlation between rumination and depression is not the same as a cause-and-effect relationship. Not every negative thinker develops depression, and depression can lead to negative thoughts.

We can think of mental health as a continuum, with healthy thoughts, emotions, and behaviors at one extreme, and dysfunction, distress, and deviance at the other. We can also conceptualize mood as a continuum, with a depressed mood at one end and neutral moods (not too sad, not too happy) in the center. But what lies at the other extreme? If it's the opposite of depression, then it must be good, right? Not necessarily, as you will soon see.

Bipolar Disorders

HIGHEST HIGHS, LOWEST LOWS   When Ross began battling bipolar disorder, he went through periods of euphoria and excitement. Sometimes he would stay awake for 4 consecutive days, or sleep barely an hour per night for 2 weeks in a row—without feeling the least bit tired. In fact, he was exploding with energy, supercharged with confidence, and feeling high on life. Ideas flashed through his mind so fast that it was difficult to focus on any one of them. "My brain was a television," Ross says, "and someone was just constantly flipping channels." The only way he could ease his mind was by drinking—and we're not talking about a couple of beers or a few shots of vodka, but an entire case or a whole bottle. Ross was using alcohol to drown out his symptoms. 📁 ▼

You Asked, Ross Answers

http://qrs.ly/ic4qsy0

What was the hardest part of having your disorder when you were younger, and what's the hardest part now?

DSM–5 and Bipolar Disorders

LO 7   Compare and contrast bipolar disorders and major depressive disorder.

The extreme energy, euphoria, and confidence Ross felt were most likely the result of **manic episodes,** also known as *mania.* Manic episodes are often characterized by continuous elation that is out of proportion for the situation. Other features include irritability, very high and sustained levels of energy, and an "expansive" mood, meaning the person feels more powerful than he really is and behaves in a showy or overly confident way. During one of these manic episodes, a person exhibits three or more of the symptoms listed below, which represent deviations from normal behavior (American Psychiatric Association, 2013):

- grandiose or extremely high self-esteem;
- reduced sleep;
- increased talkativeness;
- a "flight of ideas" or the feeling of "racing" thoughts;
- easily distracted;
- heightened activity at school or work;
- physical agitation;
- displaying poor judgment and engaging in activities that could have serious consequences (risky sexual behavior, or excessive shopping sprees, for example).

learned helplessness   A tendency for people to believe they have no control over the consequences of their behaviors, resulting in passive behavior.

manic episodes   States of continuous elation that is out of proportion to the setting, and can include irritability, very high and sustained levels of energy, and an "expansive" mood.

TABLE 12.6   BIPOLAR DISORDERS

Bipolar Disorder	Description	Annual Prevalence
Bipolar I disorder	Episodes of mania that include an "abnormally, persistently elevated, expansive, or irritable mood and persistently increased activity or energy that is present for most of the day, nearly every day, for a period of at least 1 week" (p. 127). This may be preceded by hypomania or depression.	0.6%
Bipolar II disorder	Repeated major depressive episodes (lasting at least 2 weeks) and "at least one hypomanic episode," which must last for a minimum of 4 days (p. 135).	0.8%

The two forms of bipolar disorder have distinct patterns of highs and lows. Looking at the annual prevalence (yearly occurrence) of these disorders, you can see that they are relatively rare.

INFORMATION FROM: *DSM-5* (AMERICAN PSYCHIATRIC ASSOCIATION, 2013).

Battling Bipolar
Actress Catherine Zeta-Jones went public with her bipolar diagnosis in 2011. Zeta-Jones suffers from bipolar II disorder, which is characterized by major depressive episodes as well as hypomania, or mania that is not full-blown (Takeda, 2013, July 12). Steve Granitz/WireImage/Getty Images

It is not unusual for a person experiencing a severe manic episode to be hospitalized. Mania is difficult to hide and can be dangerous. One may act out of character, doing things that damage important relationships or jeopardize work. A person may become violent, posing a risk to himself and others. Seeking help is unlikely, because mania leads to impaired judgment, feelings of grandiosity, and euphoria. (Why would you seek help if you feel on top of the world?) At these times, the support of others is essential.

There are various types of bipolar disorder. To be diagnosed with *bipolar I disorder,* a person must experience at least one *manic episode,* substantial distress, and great impairment. *Bipolar II disorder* requires at least one major depressive episode as well as a *hypomanic episode. Hypomania* is associated with some of the same symptoms as a manic episode, but it is not as severe and does not impair one's ability to function (American Psychiatric Association, 2013; **Table 12.6**).

BIPOLAR CYCLING   Some people with bipolar disorder cycle between extreme highs and lows of emotion and energy that last for days, weeks, or even months. During bouts of *mania,* a person's mood can be unusually elevated, irritable, or expansive. At the other extreme are feelings of deep sadness, emptiness, and helplessness. Periods of mania and depression may be brought on by life changes and stressors (Malkoff-Schwartz et al., 1998), though some research suggests that it is only the *first* episode that tends to be triggered by some sort of life event, such as a first love. Subsequent episodes do not seem to be as closely linked to such events (Belmaker, 2004).

Bipolar disorder is uncommon. Over the course of a lifetime, about 0.8% of the American population will receive a diagnosis of bipolar I disorder, and 1.1% bipolar II disorder (Merikangas et al., 2007). Men and women are equally likely to be affected, but men tend to experience earlier onset of symptoms, while the incidence for women seems to be higher later in life (Altshuler et al., 2010; Kennedy et al., 2005).

WHO GETS BIPOLAR DISORDER?   Although researchers have not determined the cause of bipolar disorder, evidence from twin and adoption studies underscores the importance of genes. If one identical twin is diagnosed with bipolar disorder, there is a 40–70% chance the other twin will have the disorder as well. Among fraternal twins, there is only a 5% chance that the second twin will develop the disorder (Craddock, O'Donovan, & Owen, 2005). According to the American Psychiatric Association (2013), "a family history of bipolar disorder is one of the strongest and most consistent risk factors for bipolar disorders" (p. 130). Adults with a family member who has bipolar disorder, on average, have a "10-fold increased risk" for developing the disorder themselves.

But nature is not the only force at work in bipolar disorder; nurture seems to play an important role, too. The fact that there is a higher rate of bipolar disorder in high-income countries (1.4%) than in low-income countries (0.7%; American Psychiatric Association, 2013) suggests that environment may act as a catalyst for its development. Some researchers hypothesize that exposure to viruses, poor nutrition, and stress during fetal development spark a cascade of biological events that leads to the development of bipolar disorder. The same has been said of another serious disorder, schizophrenia (Carter, 2007; Yolken & Torrey, 1995).

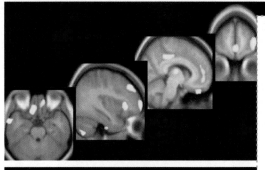

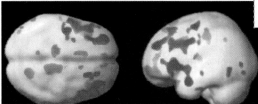

Bipolar in the Brain
Using imaging techniques, researchers have identified certain brain irregularities that appear to be linked to bipolar disorder. These MRI images highlight areas of decreased gray matter volume in prefrontal and temporal areas associated with high-level cognitive functioning and emotional regulation (Rietschel, Maier, & Schulze, 2013).
Dr. Marcella Rietschel

show what you know

1. There are many factors involved in the cause and course of major depressive disorder. Prepare notes for a 5-minute speech you might give on this topic.

2. Ross described going 4 days without sleeping, or 2 weeks sleeping only 1 hour per night. He was exploding with energy, and feeling on top of the world. It is likely that Ross was experiencing periods of euphoria and excitement known as:

   a. depression. **b.** manic episodes.

   c. panic attacks. **d.** anxiety.

3. What is the difference between bipolar I disorder and bipolar II disorder?

4. Compare the symptoms of bipolar disorder with those of major depressive disorder.

✓ CHECK YOUR ANSWERS IN APPENDIX C.

Schizophrenia

LO 8   Recognize the symptoms of schizophrenia.

How would it feel to have voices following you throughout the day, commenting on your behaviors, attacking your character, and taunting you with hurtful remarks: "You're ugly, you're worthless, you deserve to die" (Halpern, 2013, p. 102)? Meanwhile, your perception of the world is grossly distorted. Nickels, dimes, and pennies all look the same, and the subway you take to class is really on its way to a Nazi concentration camp—or so you believe. These are actual symptoms reported by Lisa Halpern, who suffers from a disabling psychological disorder called **schizophrenia** (skit-sə-ˈfrē-nē-ə). People with schizophrenia experience **psychosis,** a loss of contact with reality that is severe and chronic.

A Complex Disorder

The hallmark features of schizophrenia are disturbances in thinking, perception, and language (**Table 12.7** on the next page). Psychotic symptoms include **delusions,** which are strange or false beliefs that a person maintains even when presented with evidence to the contrary. Common delusional themes are being persecuted by others, spied upon, or ridiculed. Some people have grandiose delusions; they may believe they are extraordinarily talented or famous, for example. Others are convinced that radio reports, newspaper headlines, or public announcements are about them. Delusions appear very real to those experiencing them.

schizophrenia (skit-sə-ˈfrē-nē-ə) A disabling psychological disorder that can include delusions, hallucinations, disorganized speech, and abnormal psychomotor behavior.

psychosis Loss of contact with reality that is severe and chronic.

delusions Strange or false beliefs that a person firmly maintains even when presented with evidence to the contrary.

TABLE 12.7   IDENTIFYING SCHIZOPHRENIA

- Delusions
- Hallucinations
- Disorganized speech
- Grossly disorganized or catatonic behavior
- Decreased emotional expression
- Decreased level of functioning at work, socially, or in self-care
- Continuous disturbance lasting at least 6 months
- Symptoms not related to substance use
- Symptoms not related to another medical condition
- Lack of motivation

There is a great deal of public confusion about what it means to have schizophrenia. Listed above are some common features of this frequently misunderstood disorder.

DSM-5 (AMERICAN PSYCHIATRIC ASSOCIATION, 2013).

CONNECTIONS

In **Chapter 5,** we noted that the term *positive* does not always mean "good." *Positive punishment* means the addition of an aversive stimulus. *Positive symptoms* refer to additions or excesses, not an evaluation of the "goodness" of the symptoms. *Negative* refers to the reduction or absence of behaviors, not an evaluation of the "badness" of the symptoms.

People with schizophrenia may also hear voices or see things that are not actually present. This psychotic symptom is known as a **hallucination**—a "perception-like experience" that the individual believes is real, but that is not evident to others. Hallucinations can occur with any of the senses, but auditory hallucinations are most common. Often they manifest as voices commenting on what is happening in the environment, or voices using threatening or judgmental language (American Psychiatric Association, 2013).

The symptoms of schizophrenia are often classified as positive and negative (**Table 12.8**). **Positive symptoms** are excesses or distortions of normal behavior, and include delusions, hallucinations, and disorganized speech—all of which are generally not observed in people without psychosis. **Negative symptoms,** on the other hand, refer to the reduction or absence of normal behaviors. Common negative symptoms are social withdrawal, diminished speech or speech content, limited emotions, and loss of energy and follow-up (Tandon, Nasrallah, & Keshavan, 2009).

TABLE 12.8   SYMPTOMS OF SCHIZOPHRENIA

Positive Symptoms of Schizophrenia	Negative Symptoms of Schizophrenia
Delusions	Decreased emotional expression
Hallucinations	Lack of motivation
Disorganized speech	Decreased speech production
Grossly disorganized behavior	Reduced pleasure
Abnormal motor behavior	Lack of interest in interacting with others

Schizophrenia symptoms can be grouped into two main categories: *Positive symptoms* indicate the presence of excesses or distortions of normal behavior; *negative symptoms* refer to a reduction in normal behaviors and mental processes.

DSM-5 (AMERICAN PSYCHIATRIC ASSOCIATION, 2013).

To be diagnosed with schizophrenia, a person must display symptoms for the majority of days in a 1-month period and experience significant dysfunction with respect to work, school, relationships, or personal care for at least 6 months. (And it must be determined that these problems do not result from substance abuse or a serious medical condition.) The *DSM–5* introduced a major change in how schizophrenia is diagnosed, as the new edition no longer includes the subtypes used in previous editions (paranoid, disorganized, catatonic, undifferentiated, and residual). Using the the *DSM-5*, clinicians can rate the presence and severity of symptoms (hallucinations, delusions, disorganized speech, unusual psychomotor behaviors, and negative symptoms).

With estimates ranging from a 0.3–1% lifetime risk, schizophrenia is uncommon (American Psychiatric Association, 2013; Saha, Chant, Welham, & McGrath, 2005). Although men and women appear to face an equal risk (Abel, Drake, & Goldstein, 2010; Saha et al., 2005), the onset of the disorder tends to occur earlier in men. Males are typically diagnosed during their late teens or early twenties, whereas the peak age for women is the late twenties (American Psychiatric Association, 2013; Gogtay, Vyas, Testa, Wood, & Pantelis, 2011). In most cases, schizophrenia is a lifelong disorder that causes significant disability and a high risk for suicide. The prognosis is worse for earlier onset schizophrenia, but this may be related to the fact that men, who tend to develop symptoms earlier in life, are in poorer condition when first diagnosed (American Psychiatric Association, 2013). Furthermore, there is a higher prevalence of schizophrenia among people in lower socioeconomic classes (Tandon, Keshavan, & Nasrallah, 2008a; 2008b).

Untangling the Roots of Schizophrenia

LO 9 Analyze the biopsychosocial factors that contribute to schizophrenia.

Schizophrenia is a complex psychological disorder that results from an interaction of biological, psychological, and social factors, making it difficult to predict who will be affected. For many years, various experts focused the blame on environmental factors, such as unhealthy family dynamics and bad parenting. A common scapegoat was the "schizophrenogenic mother," whose poor parenting style was believed to cause the disorder in her child (Harrington, 2012). Thankfully, this belief has been shattered by our new understanding of the brain. Schizophrenia is now one of the most heavily researched psychological disorders, with approximately 5,000 new articles added to the search databases every year (Tandon et al., 2008a)! Among the most promising areas of research is the genetics of schizophrenia. It turns out that schizophrenia runs in families, and few cases illustrate this principle better than that of the Genain sisters.

Nature and Nurture

Four Sisters

Nora, Iris, Myra, and Hester Genain were identical quadruplets born in 1930. Their mother went to great lengths to treat them equally, and in many ways the children were equals (Mirsky & Quinn, 1988). As babies, they cried in unison and teethed at the same times. As toddlers, they played with the same toys, wore the same dresses, and rode the same tricycles. The little girls were said to be so mentally in sync that they never argued (Quinn, 1963).

Mr. and Mrs. Genain kept the girls isolated. Spending most of their time at home, the quads cultivated few friendships and didn't go out with boys. The Genains may have protected their daughters from the world outside, but they could not shield them from the trouble brewing inside their brains.

At age 22, one of the sisters, Nora, was hospitalized for a psychiatric disorder characterized by hallucinations, delusions, altered speech, and other symptoms.

hallucinations Perceptual-like experiences that an individual believes are real, but that are not evident to others.

positive symptoms Excesses or distortions of normal behavior; examples are delusions, hallucinations, and disorganized speech.

negative symptoms Behaviors or characteristics that are limited or absent; examples are social withdrawal, diminished speech, limited or no emotions, and loss of energy and follow-up.

Within months, a second sister, Iris, was admitted to a psychiatric ward as well. She, too, had the symptoms of psychosis. Both Nora and Iris were diagnosed with schizophrenia, and it was only a matter of years before Myra and Hester joined them (Mirsky & Quinn, 1988). What are the odds of a birth resulting in identical quadruplets who would all develop schizophrenia? One in 1.5 billion, according to one estimate (Mirsky et al., 2000). As you can imagine, the case of the Genain quads has drawn the attention of many scientists. David Rosenthal and his colleagues at the National Institute of Mental Health studied the women when they were in their late twenties and again when they were 51. To protect the quads' identities, Rosenthal assigned them the pseudonyms **N**ora, **I**ris, **M**yra, and **H**ester, which spell out NIMH, the acronym for the National Institute of Mental Health. *Genain* is also an alias, meaning "dreadful gene" in Greek (Mirsky & Quinn, 1988).

LIKE ANY PSYCHOLOGICAL PHENOMENON, SCHIZOPHRENIA IS A PRODUCT OF BOTH NATURE AND NURTURE.

The Genain sisters are genetically equal, which suggests that there is some heritable component to their schizophrenia. Yet, each woman experiences the disorder in her own way. Hester did not receive a diagnosis of schizophrenia until she was in her twenties, but she started to show signs of psychological impairment much earlier than her sisters and was never able to hold down a job or live alone. Myra, however, has been employed for the majority of her life and has a family of her own (Mirsky et al., 2000; Mirsky & Quinn, 1988). When researchers interviewed Myra at age 81, she was still living on her own, with some assistance from her son (Mirsky, Bieliauskas, Duncan, & French, 2013). Like any psychological phenomenon, schizophrenia is a product of both nature and nurture. ◊ 🏠

GENETIC FACTORS   Overall, researchers agree that schizophrenia is "highly heritable," with genetic factors accounting for around 80% of the risk for developing this disorder (Tandon et al., 2008a; 2008b). Much of the evidence derives from twin, family, and adoption studies (**Figure 12.3**). If one identical twin has schizophrenia, the risk of the other twin developing the disorder is approximately 41–65% (Petronis, 2004). Compare that to a mere 2% risk for those whose first cousins have schizophrenia (Tsuang, Stone, & Faraone, 2001). If both parents have schizophrenia, the risk of their children being diagnosed with this disorder is 27% (Gottesman, Laursen, Bertelsen, & Mortensen, 2010). Keep in mind that schizophrenia is not caused by a single gene, but by a combination of many genes interacting with the environment (Howes & Kapur, 2009).

FIGURE 12.3
The Role of Genetics in Schizophrenia
The average lifetime risk of developing schizophrenia for the general population is 1% or lower. However, for someone with a sibling diagnosed with schizophrenia, the lifetime risk increases to 9%. If that sibling is an identical twin, someone with whom 100% of genetics is shared, the risk rockets to 48%. This suggests a significant role for genetic factors in the development of schizophrenia. Copyright © 2001 by the American Psychological Association. Adapted with permission from Gottesman (2001).

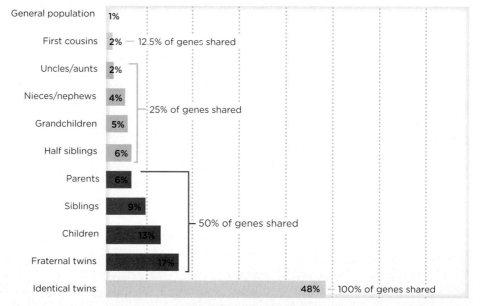

Relationship to person with schizophrenia

General population — 1%
First cousins — 2% — 12.5% of genes shared
Uncles/aunts — 2%
Nieces/nephews — 4% — 25% of genes shared
Grandchildren — 5%
Half siblings — 6%
Parents — 6%
Siblings — 9%
Children — 13% — 50% of genes shared
Fraternal twins — 17%
Identical twins — 48% — 100% of genes shared

Risk of developing schizophrenia

DIATHESIS-STRESS MODEL   Like other disorders, schizophrenia is best understood from the biopsychosocial perspective. One model that takes this perspective into account is the *diathesis–stress model*, where *diathesis* refers to the inherited disposition (to schizophrenia, for example), and *stress* refers to the stressors and other factors in the environment (internal and external). Identical twins share 100% of their genetic makeup (diathesis), yet the environment produces different stressors for the twins (only one of them loses a spouse, for example). This helps explain why one twin may develop the disorder, but the other does not. The diathesis–stress model suggests that developing schizophrenia involves a genetic predisposition *and* environmental triggers.

THE BRAIN   People with schizophrenia generally experience a thinning of the cortex, leading to enlarged ventricles, the cavities in the brain that are filled with cerebrospinal fluid. Research also shows that the total volume of the brain is reduced in schizophrenia (Tandon et al., 2008a). In general, these abnormalities are thought to be related to problems with "cognitive control" and psychotic symptoms (Glahn et al., 2008). A word of caution when interpreting these findings, however: It is possible that differences in brain structures are not just due to schizophrenia, but may also result from long-term use of medications to control its symptoms (Jaaro-Peled, Ayhan, Pletnikov, & Sawa, 2010).

NEUROTRANSMITTER THEORIES   Evidence suggests that abnormal neurotransmitter activity plays a role in schizophrenia. According to the **dopamine hypothesis,** the synthesis, release, and concentrations of dopamine are all elevated in people who have been diagnosed with schizophrenia and are suffering from psychosis (van Os & Kapur, 2009). Support for the dopamine hypothesis comes from the successful use of medications that block the receptor sites for dopamine. These drugs reduce the psychotic symptoms of schizophrenia, presumably because they decrease the potential impact of the excess dopamine being produced (van Os & Kapur, 2009).

Although the effect of increased dopamine has not been precisely determined, one suggestion is that it influences the "reward system" of the brain. Excess dopamine may make it hard for a person to pay attention to what is rewarding in the environment, or pick out its most salient, or important, aspects (van Os & Kapur, 2009). People suffering from schizophrenia often focus on environmental stimuli that lead them to lose touch with reality. So, when they experience delusions, they may be trying to make sense of the stimuli that have captured their attention. Hallucinations might result from placing too much importance on some of their "internal representations" (Kapur, 2003). The dopamine hypothesis has evolved over the last several decades, with researchers appreciating the ongoing dynamic between neurochemical processes of the individual in relation to the environment. We cannot just study what dopamine does in the synapse; we must also consider how dopamine's irregularities are affected by the individual's interactions within the environment (Howes & Kapur, 2009).

ENVIRONMENTAL TRIGGERS AND SCHIZOPHRENIA   Some experts suspect that schizophrenia is associated with exposure to a virus in utero, such as human papilloma virus (HPV). Several illnesses a woman can contract while pregnant, including genital reproductive infections, influenza, and some parasites, may increase her baby's risk of developing schizophrenia later in life (Brown & Patterson, 2011). Retrospective evidence (that is, information collected much later) suggests that the offspring of mothers who were exposed to viruses while pregnant are more likely to develop schizophrenia as adolescents. However, research exploring this theory is still ongoing and must be replicated.

Schizophrenia is not the result of poor parenting; nor is it a product of classical or operant conditioning. That being said, there are some sociocultural and environmental

Synonyms
diathesis–stress model stress–vulnerability model, constitutional vulnerability

CONNECTIONS

In **Chapter 2,** we discussed activity at the synapse. When neurotransmitters are released, they must bind to receptor sites in order to relay their message to the receiving neuron ("fire" or "don't fire"). Medications that block or inhibit the receptor sites on the receiving neuron are referred to as *antagonists,* and some of these are used to reduce symptoms of schizophrenia.

dopamine hypothesis A theory suggesting that the synthesis, release, and concentrations of the neurotransmitter dopamine play a role in schizophrenia.

factors that may play a minor role in one's risk for developing the disorder, and in the severity of symptoms. Evidence exists, for instance, that complications at birth, social stress, and cannabis abuse are related to a slightly increased risk of schizophrenia onset (Tandon et al., 2008a; 2008b).

We now turn our focus to another type of disorder that is intimately connected to one of psychology's core areas of study: personality.

 show what you know

1. A loss of contact with reality is referred to as _____.

2. A woman with schizophrenia reports hearing voices that tell her she is ugly and worthless. This is an example of a(n):
   a. hallucination.   **b.** delusion.
   c. negative symptom.   **d.** diathesis.

3. What are some biopsychosocial factors that contribute to the development of schizophrenia?

 CHECK YOUR ANSWERS IN APPENDIX C.

Disorders of Personality and Identity

LO 10 Differentiate between antisocial and borderline personality disorders.

Before reading this chapter, you probably knew something about depression, bipolar disorder, and schizophrenia. But you may have been less familiar with a somewhat common group of disorders relating to personality. Approximately 1 in 10 adults in the United States has a *personality disorder* (Lenzenweger, Lane, Loranger, & Kessler, 2007). People with **personality disorders** exhibit "an enduring pattern of inner experience and behavior that deviates markedly from the expectations of the individual's culture, is pervasive and inflexible, has an onset in adolescence or early adulthood, is stable over time, and leads to distress or impairment" (American Psychiatric Association, 2013, p. 645). Specifically, someone with a personality disorder behaves in a way that deviates substantially in the following areas: (1) cognition, including perceptions of self, others, and events; (2) emotional responses; (3) interpersonal functioning; and (4) impulse control. In order to be diagnosed with a personality disorder, one must struggle in at least two of these four categories. In addition, these problems must be resistant to change and have far-reaching consequences for interpersonal relationships.

Like personality traits in general, the core qualities of people with personality disorders (as well as the problems that result) are fairly stable over a lifetime and across situations. When diagnosing this type of disorder, the clinician must focus on troublesome personality traits—and be very careful not to confuse them with problems resulting from developmental changes, culture, drug use, or medical conditions.

The *DSM–5* includes 10 personality disorder types (**Table 12.9**). Here, we direct the spotlight onto those that have received the greatest amount of research attention: *antisocial personality disorder* and *borderline personality disorder*.

Antisocial Personality Disorder

Many films, including *The Girl with the Dragon Tattoo* and *The Silence of the Lambs,* feature characters who behave in ways most people find incomprehensible. The qualities of these characters often parallel a diagnosis of **antisocial personality disorder.**

People with antisocial personality disorder may seek personal gratification even when it means violating ethical standards and breaking laws. They sometimes lie or con others, and exhibit aggressive, impulsive, or irritable behaviors. These individuals have difficulty feeling empathy, and may not show concern for others or feel remorse upon hurting them. Other common behavior patterns include carelessness in sexual

Synonyms
antisocial personality disorder
psychopathy, sociopathy

personality disorders A group of psychological disorders that can include impairments in cognition, emotional responses, interpersonal functioning, and impulse control.

antisocial personality disorder A psychological disorder distinguished by unethical behavior, deceitfulness, impulsivity, irritability, aggressiveness, disregard for others, and lack of remorse.

TABLE 12.9 PERSONALITY DISORDERS

Personality Disorder	Description
Paranoid	Widespread distrust of others without basis
Schizoid	Detachment from relationships and a limited range of emotional expression
Schizotypal	Difficulty in establishing relationships, limited ability to maintain close relationships, and eccentric or strange behavior
Antisocial	Unethical behavior, deceitfulness, impulsivity, irritability, aggressiveness, disregard for others, and lack of remorse
Borderline	Incomplete sense of self, extreme self-criticism, unstable emotions, and feelings of emptiness
Histrionic	Extreme emotions used to gain attention
Narcissistic	Self-absorbed, needs to be admired, lack of empathy
Avoidant	Social self-consciousness, hypersensitive to negative feedback
Dependent	Clingy, needs to be cared for by others
Obsessive-compulsive	Fixation with order, perfection, and control

Listed above are the 10 personality disorders identified by the *DSM-5*.

DSM-5 (AMERICAN PSYCHIATRIC ASSOCIATION, 2013).

relationships, and the use of intimidation to control others (American Psychiatric Association, 2013). Around 1% of American adults are diagnosed with antisocial personality disorder, which is more common in men than women (Lenzenweger et al., 2007).

How does antisocial personality disorder develop? There is some evidence for family risk factors, but it is unclear how much of this risk is transmitted through genes, and how much results from learning. Heredity does appear to play a role, as first-degree biological relatives of people with antisocial personality disorder are more likely to have the disorder than those in the general population (American Psychiatric Association, 2013). However, no single gene has been implicated in the development of antisocial behavior patterns. Like most mental health problems, antisocial personality disorder seems to result from a complex interaction of genes and environment (Ferguson, 2010).

Sociopath or Avenger? Swedish actress Noomi Rapace plays the role of Lisbeth Salander in *The Girl with the Dragon Tattoo* (2009). Salander displays some of the hallmark characteristics of antisocial personality disorder: She seems to feel no remorse about violating social norms, hurting others, and breaking laws. Yet she appears to care about those she avenges, making it hard to place her in this category (Burkley, 2012, January 3). Knut Koivisto/Ronald Grant Archive/Mary Evans/Everett Collection

CONNECTIONS

In **Chapter 7,** we noted that executive functioning is involved in planning, maintaining focus, and suppressing automatic responses. In **Chapter 2,** we learned that the frontal lobes are critical in processing emotions and controlling impulses. If these areas in the brain are not functioning properly, one may exhibit antisocial behavior.

Borderline Ballerina?
Winona Ryder plays the part of ex-ballerina Beth Macintyre in the 2010 film *Black Swan.* Emotionally needy, highly insecure, and prone to angry outbursts, this character displays many characteristics associated with borderline personality disorder. Fox Searchlight Pictures/Photofest

You may be wondering what is unique about the brain of a person with antisocial personality disorder. Some studies point to irregularities in the frontal lobes, a region of the brain that is crucial for executive functioning. For example, reduced tissue volume in the prefrontal cortex (11% less than expected) is apparent in some men with antisocial personality disorder. This deficit might be linked to reduced morality, and problems in decision making, planning, and learning in relation to fear, all potentially associated with antisocial behavior. The fact that the prefrontal cortex plays a role in controlling arousal may explain why people with this disorder tend to seek out stimulation, including aggressive and antisocial activities (Raine, Lencz, Bihrle, LaCasse, & Colletti, 2000).

Borderline Personality Disorder

Borderline personality disorder is distinguished by an incomplete sense of self and feelings of emptiness. People with this disorder tend to be emotionally unstable and extremely needy. They may exhibit intense anger, have difficulty controlling their temper, and get into physical fights. They can be impulsive when it comes to sexual activity, substance abuse, and spending money, and may threaten or attempt suicide on a recurring basis. Developing intimacy may also be a struggle, and relationships tend to be unstable, tainted with feelings of mistrust and fear of abandonment. Those with borderline personality disorder may see the world in terms of black and white, rather than different shades of gray. This tendency to perceive extremes may lead a person to become overinvolved or totally withdrawn in relationships (American Psychiatric Association, 2013).

According to the *DSM–5,* individuals with borderline personality disorder experience emotions that are unstable, intense, and inappropriate for the situation at hand. They may feel extreme anxiety and insecurity, concern about being rejected one moment, worried about being too dependent the next. Depressed moods are common, along with feelings of hopelessness, pessimism, and shame. The person may act without thinking and frequently change plans.

Seventy-five percent of people diagnosed with borderline personality disorder are female, and research suggests that some traits associated with this disorder have a genetic component (American Psychiatric Association, 2013). There is also evidence that childhood trauma sets the stage for the development of this condition. A biosocial developmental model has been proposed, indicating an early vulnerability that includes impulsive behavior and increased "emotional sensitivity." If the environment is right, this susceptibility can lead to problems with emotions, behaviors, and cognitive processes (Crowell, Beauchaine, & Linehan, 2009).

As you now know, personality disorders stem from well-established personality characteristics. People suffering from these disorders have traits that are relatively easy to characterize. This is *not* the case for people with dissociative disorders, whose personal identities may be very difficult to pin down.

Dissociative Disorders

LO 11 Identify differences among dissociative disorders.

Dissociative disorders are disturbances in normal psychological functioning that can include problems with memory, identity, consciousness, perception, and motor control. The main feature of these disorders is **dissociation,** or a disturbance in the normally unified experience of psychological functions involved in memory, consciousness, perception, or identity (Spiegel et al., 2011). Dissociation may lead to difficulty recalling personal information (for example, where I live, who I am), or the feeling of being detached from one's body.

In North America and Europe, the prevalence of dissociative disorders imposes a high financial burden (Brand, Classen, McNary, & Zaveri, 2009), in part because of lengthy treatment times. Dissociative disorders generally do not resolve with a simple drug prescription or a couple of therapy sessions. Here, we focus our discussion on two dissociative disorders: *dissociative amnesia* and *dissociative identity disorder*.

Trance Dance
A young man in São Paulo, Brazil, dances in a trance state during a religious ceremony. Behaviors observed in this type of context may resemble those of dissociative identity disorder, but it is important to differentiate between religious practices and disordered behaviors (Moreira-Almeida et al., 2008). Yasuyoshi Chiba/AFP/Getty Images

DISSOCIATIVE AMNESIA People suffering from **dissociative amnesia** have difficulty remembering important personal information. Often the lost memories center on traumatic or stressful events. In some cases the amnesia is localized, or fixed around a certain event; other times it may span a lifetime. Those with dissociative amnesia typically report a great deal of distress or impairment in relationships, work, and other important areas of life, and put a lot of effort into managing the mundane details of daily existence (Staniloiu & Markowitsch, 2012).

A person with dissociative amnesia who wanders in a confused and unexpected manner may also be experiencing **dissociative fugue** (fyüg; Spiegel et al., 2011). Consider this example from a case study: A 62-year-old woman was found in a city many miles from home. She had no understanding of her whereabouts or activities since leaving home. After a medical evaluation, physicians determined there was no neurological or physical explanation for her memory loss. Over time, she was able to recall some events from the "preceding weeks," including an argument with her husband that left her in despair (Rajah, Kumar, Somasundaram, & Kumar, 2009). As often occurs with dissociative amnesia, this woman's memory loss seemed to be associated with distressing events.

DISSOCIATIVE IDENTITY DISORDER Perhaps the most commonly known dissociative disorder is **dissociative identity disorder** (often referred to as multiple personality disorder), which is characterized by the presence of two or more distinct personalities. Dissociative identity disorder is considered the most complicated and persistent of the dissociative disorders (Sar, 2011). One of its key features is a lack of connection among behavior, awareness, memory, and cognition. There is often a reported gap in remembering day-to-day events and personal information. One may feel significant distress in relationships, work, and other areas. And this experience cannot be related to substance use or medical issues.

Clinicians must be mindful of cross-cultural and religious differences in relation to dissociative states. For example, some characteristics associated with dissociative identity disorder seem to occur in Brazilian mediums, and it is important to distinguish between a culturally accepted religious practice and disordered behavior (Moreira-Almeida, Neto, & Cardeña, 2008). Some studies suggest that dissociative identity disorder impacts females more than males, but findings are inconsistent. Societal factors, specifically childhood abuse and trauma, appear to play a significant role (Sar, 2011).

borderline personality disorder A psychological disorder distinguished by an incomplete sense of self, extreme self-criticism, unstable emotions, and feelings of emptiness.

dissociative disorders Psychological disorders distinguished by disturbances in normal psychological functioning; may include problems with memory, identity, consciousness, perception, and motor control.

dissociation A disturbance in the normally integrated experience of psychological functions involved in memory, consciousness, perception, or identity.

dissociative amnesia A psychological disorder marked by difficulty remembering important personal information and life events.

dissociative fugue (fyüg) A condition in which a person with dissociative amnesia wanders about in a confused and unexpected manner.

dissociative identity disorder A psychological disorder that involves the occurrence of two or more distinct personalities within an individual.

WHAT CAUSES DISSOCIATIVE DISORDERS? A great deal of controversy surrounds the apparent increase in diagnoses of dissociative identity disorder in the United States. One possible explanation is that clinicians are reinforcing the development of these dissociations. In other words, by suggesting the possibility of alternate personalities or using hypnosis to "recover" lost memories, the clinician "cues" the individual to believe an alternate personality is responsible for behaviors (Lynn, Lilienfeld, Merckelbach, Giesbrecht, & van der Kloet, 2012). These disorders are difficult to substantiate when they are based on self-reports. We should also note that they are often linked to childhood abuse and neglect, war, and terrorism not only in the United States, but also around the globe (American Psychiatric Association, 2013). Thus, education about and the prevention of early-life stress, as it relates to childhood abuse and neglect, is of significant importance (Sar, 2011).

✓ show what you know

1. The personality disorders include impairments concerning:
   a. contact with reality.
   b. manic episodes.
   c. developmental processes.
   d. the self and interpersonal relationships.

2. Individuals with _____ are likely to feel a sense of emptiness, become angry easily, and maintain intense but unstable relationships.

3. _____ is a disturbance in the normally integrated experiences of memory, consciousness, perception, or identity.

4. Describe the similarities and differences between dissociative amnesia and dissociative identity disorder.

✓ CHECK YOUR ANSWERS IN APPENDIX C.

DEFYING STIGMA: ROSS LEARNS TO THRIVE After graduating from high school, Ross started college at American University in Washington, DC. But he didn't have much of a plan for managing his disorder. "What I did was essentially the equivalent of showing up to college in a wheelchair, and hoping they would have ramps," he recalls in his book *Behind Happy Faces* (Szabo & Hall, 2007, p. 100).

Three weeks into freshman year, Ross had his stomach pumped for alcohol poisoning and, within 2 months, a major relapse with bipolar disorder. He returned to Pennsylvania and was hospitalized. After this, Ross felt like a failure: "I used to sleep on my couch for 18 hours a day or sit out in my backyard and stare out at nothing," he remembers. "I felt like bipolar disorder had won out, and that there was nothing more I could do about it" (Szabo & Hall, 2007, p. 101).

But then Ross did something. He found employment and began taking classes at a community college, which led to his enrollment at a local 4-year college. Eventually, he returned to American University to finish what he had started 4 years before. Unfortunately, drinking alcohol was still a big part of his life. One night, after downing multiple shots of liquor, Ross passed out cold. He awoke 22 hours later, looked in the mirror, and started to weep. "Okay. ENOUGH. You are either going to continue this pattern and DIE, or you are going to make a change," Ross remembers thinking to himself (Szabo & Hall, 2007, p. 102).

What followed were years of hard work. Ross quit using alcohol and caffeine and smoking cigarettes and marijuana. He imposed structure on his life, waking up and going to sleep at the same time each day, eating regular meals, and exercising. He started being open and honest in his relationships with friends, family, and his therapist. And most important, he confronted his self-hatred, working hard to identify and appreciate things he liked about himself. "What was missing was me

being an active member in my treatment," Ross says, "and doing things outside of treatment [to get better]."

In 2002 Ross graduated cum laude from American University, and then he picked up where he left off that day he spoke to his high school class about his experience with bipolar disorder. He became a mental health advocate, giving presentations at high schools and colleges across America. As director of youth outreach for the National Mental Health Awareness Campaign, Ross started The Heard (now part of Active Minds), a speakers' bureau that includes other young presenters who have battled disorders.

After 8 years of working as a mental health advocate, Ross traveled to the African nation of Botswana to serve in the Peace Corps. Upon returning to the United States in 2012, he launched his own consulting group, Human Power Project, which designs cutting-edge mental health curricula for middle and high schools. His battle with bipolar disorder is ongoing ("I'm not cured," says Ross), but he continues learning better ways to cope. It has now been over a decade since Ross experienced a disabling episode of mania or depression. 🗁

You Asked, Ross Answers

http://qrs.ly/qk4sx1d

Are you afraid that you may pass your disorder on to your children and does that impact your desire to have them?

OUTSMARTING OCD: MELISSA FINDS A THERAPY THAT WORKS Shortly after leaving the hospital, Melissa found out about a study on OCD treatments at the University of Pennsylvania. She decided to participate and got acquainted with the lead investigator, who became her therapist. "He taught me how to live with OCD," says Melissa. "He basically saved my life."

Melissa had been taking medications since she was 12, but she only experienced a dramatic improvement when she combined her medication with cognitive behavioral therapy (CBT), an approach you can learn about in Chapter 13 on psychological therapies.

Like Ross, Melissa discovered she had a gift for public speaking. At age 19, she decided to share her story, speaking about her battle with OCD as part of a panel hosted by her college, Immaculata University in Pennsylvania. Her presentation moved some of the audience members to tears. From that point forward,

Melissa decided to do everything in her power to dispel the stigma of psychological disorders. She started a mental health awareness group on her campus, opening a chapter of the national organization Active Minds, and later joined Ross Szabo's speakers' bureau and became a presenter for the mental health organization Minding Your Mind. In 2013, Melissa published a book, *The People You Meet in Real Life,* which relates the stories of those who have inspired her along the way. She hopes these tales of resiliency and optimism will help readers understand they are not alone in their struggles.

Melissa is now in her late twenties. She still has OCD, but it's under control. Instead of walking through a doorway 20 times, she now passes through it twice. And the time she once spent sitting alone in her room meticulously touching objects in sets of 2s she now spends talking to classrooms full of students, shattering the stigma surrounding psychological disorders. ▰

⑫ summary of concepts

LO 1 Define psychological disorders and the criteria used to identify abnormal behavior. (p. 476)

A psychological disorder is a set of behavioral, emotional, or cognitive symptoms that are significantly distressing in terms of social functioning, work endeavors, and other aspects of life. Abnormal behavior often falls along a continuum and is based on typicality and the 3 Ds: dysfunction, distress, and deviance. This continuum includes what we would consider normal at one end and abnormal at the other end, and is determined in part by one's culture.

LO 2 Recognize limitations in the classification of psychological disorders. (p. 482)

Although a classification system is important for communication and treatment planning among professionals, it can lead to labeling and create expectations. Because of the stigma associated with psychological disorders, the effects of a diagnosis can be long lasting. Some critics suggest there is too much emphasis on the medical model, which may ignore the importance of psychological and sociocultural factors.

LO 3 Summarize the etiology of psychological disorders. (p. 484)

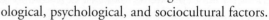

The biopsychosocial perspective provides a model for explaining the causes of psychological disorders, which are complicated and often result from interactions among biological, psychological, and sociocultural factors.

Kathleen Wauters/ Getty Images

Important biological factors include neurochemical imbalances and genetic predispositions for disorders. Psychological influences include cognitive factors and developmental experiences. Sociocultural factors, such as poverty and support systems, may also impact the development and course of psychological disorders.

LO 4 Define anxiety disorders and demonstrate an understanding of their causes. (p. 486)

Anxiety disorders are a group of psychological disorders associated with extreme anxiety and/or irrational fears that are debilitating. Panic disorder includes worries about experiencing unexpected panic attacks or losing control. Specific phobias are characterized by a distinct fear or anxiety in relation to an object or situation. Agoraphobia is a distinct fear or anxiety related to situations such as public transportation, open spaces, retail stores, crowds, or being alone and away from home. Social anxiety disorder is a type of phobia in which a person has a distinct fear or anxiety regarding social situations, particularly the idea of being scrutinized by others. Someone with generalized anxiety disorder experiences an excessive amount of worry and anxiety about many activities relating to family, health, school, and other aspects of daily life. Anxiety disorders can develop as a result of environmental factors and genetic predisposition, and are more prevalent in women. They can be culture specific and/or learned.

LO 5 Summarize the symptoms and causes of obsessive-compulsive disorder. (p. 490)

Obsessive-compulsive disorder (OCD) includes obsessions and/or compulsions that are very time-consuming (taking more than 1 hour a day) and cause a great deal of distress and disruptions in everyday life. An obsession is a thought, urge, or image that occurs repeatedly, is intrusive and unwelcome, and often causes feelings of intense anxiety and distress. Compulsions are behaviors or "mental acts" that a person repeats over and over in an attempt to neutralize obsessions. Sociocultural factors, learning, and biological causes are all involved in the course and maintenance of OCD.

LO 6 Summarize the symptoms and causes of major depressive disorder. (p. 492)

Symptoms of major depressive disorder include feelings of sadness or hopelessness, reduced pleasure, sleeping excessively or not at all, loss of energy, feelings of worthlessness, or difficulties thinking or concentrating. With major depressive disorder, there is substantial severity of symptoms and impairment in the ability to perform expected roles. Biological theories suggest the disorder results from a genetic predisposition, and irregular activity of neurotransmitters and hormones. Psychological theories suggest that feelings of learned helplessness and negative thinking may play a role. Major depressive disorder results from a combination of several factors.

LO 7 Compare and contrast bipolar disorders and major depressive disorder. (p. 497)

A diagnosis of bipolar I disorder requires that a person experience at least one manic episode, substantial distress, and great impairment. Bipolar II disorder involves at least one major depressive episode as well as a hypomanic episode, which is associated with some of the same symptoms as a manic episode, but is not as severe and does not impair one's ability to function. People with bipolar disorder cycle between extreme highs and lows of emotion and energy that last for days, weeks, or even months. Individuals with major depressive disorder, on the other hand, tend to experience a persistent low mood, loss of energy, and feelings of worthlessness.

LO 8 Recognize the symptoms of schizophrenia. (p. 499)

Schizophrenia is a disabling disorder that can involve delusions, hallucinations, disorganized speech, abnormal psychomotor behavior, diminished speech, limited emotions, or loss of energy. Delusions are strange and false beliefs that a person maintains even when presented with contradictory evidence. Hallucinations are "perception-like experiences" that the individual believes are real, but that are not evident to others.

LO 9 Analyze the biopsychosocial factors that contribute to schizophrenia. (p. 501)

Schizophrenia is a complex psychological disorder that results from biological, psychological, and social factors. Because this disorder springs from an interaction of genes and environment, researchers have a hard time predicting who will be affected. The diathesis–stress model takes these factors into account, with diathesis referring to the inherited disposition, and stress referring to the stressors in the environment (internal and external). Genes, neurotransmitter activity, differences in the brain, and exposure to a virus in utero are all possible biopsychosocial influences in the development of schizophrenia.

LO 10 Differentiate between antisocial and borderline personality disorders. (p. 504)

People with antisocial personality disorder may seek personal gratification even when it means violating ethics and breaking laws. They sometimes deceive people, and exhibit aggressive, impulsive, or irritable behavior. These individuals lack empathy, and may not show concern for others or feel remorse upon hurting someone. Borderline personality disorder is distinguished by an incomplete sense of self and feelings of emptiness. Those affected may exhibit intense anger, have difficulty controlling their temper, and get into physical fights. They can be impulsive, especially where sexual activity, substance abuse, and spending money are concerned. Suicide threats and attempts may occur repeatedly. Both disorders may result in issues with intimacy and trust.

LO 11 Identify differences among dissociative disorders. (p. 506)

People suffering from dissociative amnesia seem unable to remember important information about their lives. If a person with dissociative amnesia also wanders in a confused and unexpected manner, this is considered dissociative amnesia with dissociative fugue. Dissociative identity disorder occurs when an individual experiences two or more distinct personalities. This disorder is considered the most complicated and persistent of the dissociative disorders. The commonality in this group of disorders is dissociation, or a disturbance in the normally unified experience of psychological functions involved in memory, consciousness, perception, or identity.

key terms

abnormal behavior, p. 477
agoraphobia, p. 489
antisocial personality disorder, p. 504
anxiety disorders, p. 486
bipolar disorder, p. 476
borderline personality disorder, p. 506
comorbidity, p. 484
compulsion, p. 491
delusions, p. 499

dissociation, p. 506
dissociative amnesia, p. 507
dissociative disorders, p. 506
dissociative fugue, p. 507
dissociative identity disorder, p. 507
dopamine hypothesis, p. 503
generalized anxiety disorder, p. 490
hallucination, p. 500
insanity, p. 478

learned helplessness, p. 496
major depressive disorder, p. 492
maladaptive behaviors, p. 476
manic episodes, p. 497
medical model, p. 484
negative symptoms, p. 500
obsession, p. 491
obsessive-compulsive disorder (OCD), p. 490

panic attack, p. 487
panic disorder, p. 487
personality disorders, p. 504
positive symptoms, p. 500
psychological disorder, p. 476
psychosis, p. 499
schizophrenia, p. 499
specific phobia, p. 488
stigma, p. 479

TEST PREP are you ready?

1. The 3 Ds used to distinguish abnormal behavior are:
   a. _____   b. _____
   c. _____

2. Although classifying mental disorders through the *DSM* is helpful to mental health professionals, its use has been criticized because the manual:
   a. cannot be used to develop treatment plans.
   b. is used to obtain insurance reimbursement.
   c. labels individuals, which only heightens problems with stigma.
   d. does not attempt to be atheoretical.

3. Melissa experienced recurrent, all-consuming thoughts of disaster and death. These _____ were accompanied by her _____, which included repeating certain behaviors, such as locking her car and entering a room, an even number of times.
   a. obsessions; compulsions
   b. compulsions; obsessions
   c. compulsions; contamination
   d. negative reinforcers; obsessions

4. To help explain the causes of psychological disorders, researchers often use the _____ perspective, which examines the complex interaction of biological, psychological, and sociocultural factors.
   a. medical model   b. biopsychosocial
   c. etiological   d. learning

5. A woman is extremely anxious when she is unaccompanied in public. She no longer uses public transportation, refuses to go to the mall, and does not like being away from home. Perhaps she should get evaluated to see if she has which of the following diagnoses?
   a. panic disorder   b. agoraphobia
   c. social anxiety disorder d. specific phobia

6. A man with a diagnosis of _____ exhibits a distinct fear or anxiety related to social situations, particularly the idea of being scrutinized by those around him.
   a. generalized anxiety disorder
   b. panic attack
   c. social anxiety disorder
   d. panic disorder

7. While walking to class one day, you notice a woman who is short of breath, clutches her chest, and appears lightheaded. You are concerned she may be experiencing a heart attack. She tells you she knows it is not her heart, but that she suffers from _____, which involve sudden, extreme fear that escalates quickly.
   a. psychotic episodes   b. manic episodes
   c. panic attacks   d. hallucinations

8. A neighbor describes a newspaper article she read last night about a man in his twenties who has been known to lie and con others, be aggressive and impulsive, and show little empathy or remorse. These are long-standing traits of his, so it is possible that he has:
   a. borderline personality disorder.
   b. antisocial personality disorder.
   c. dissociative identity disorder.
   d. dissociative amnesia.

9. Which of the following plays a role in the etiology of major depressive disorder?
   a. manic episodes
   b. virus contracted by the mother
   c. classical conditioning
   d. serotonin

10. One of the major distinctions of bipolar II disorder is that, unlike bipolar I disorder, it involves:
    a. at least one major depressive episode as well as a hypomanic episode.
    b. at least one major depressive episode as well as a manic episode.
    c. at least one hypomanic episode and one manic episode.
    d. at least one episode of psychosis.

11. One symptom that both major depressive disorder and bipolar disorder share is:
    a. hypomania.
    b. manic episodes.
    c. problems associated with sleep.
    d. extremely high self-esteem.

12. Which of the following is a symptom of a manic episode?
    a. low energy level
    b. need for more sleep
    c. quiet or shy personality
    d. irritability

13. A man with schizophrenia has hallucinations and delusions, and seems to be out of touch with reality. A psychologist explains to his mother that her son is experiencing:
    a. mania.
    b. psychosis.
    c. dissociative identity disorder.
    d. hypomania.

14. A woman in your neighborhood develops a reputation for being emotionally unstable, intense, and extremely needy. She also doesn't seem to have a sense of herself and complains of feeling empty. She struggles with intimacy and her relationships are unstable. If these are long-standing traits, which of the following might she be evaluated for?
    a. borderline personality disorder
    b. antisocial personality disorder
    c. bipolar II disorder
    d. major depressive disorder

15. Dissociative identity disorder (commonly called multiple personality disorder) involves two or more distinct _____ within an individual.
    a. hypomanic episodes
    b. personalities
    c. panic disorders
    d. psychotic episodes

16. Describe the "3 Ds" and give an example of each in relation to a psychological disorder.

17. What is wrong with the following statement: "My friend is schizophrenic"?

18. How can classical conditioning be used to explain the development of panic disorder?

19. How does negative thinking lead to depression?

20. Briefly summarize the theories of the etiology of schizophrenia.

✔ CHECK YOUR ANSWERS IN APPENDIX C.

Get personalized practice by logging into LaunchPad at **www.macmillanhighered.com/launchpad/ sciampresenting1e** to take the LearningCurve adaptive quizzes for Chapter 12.

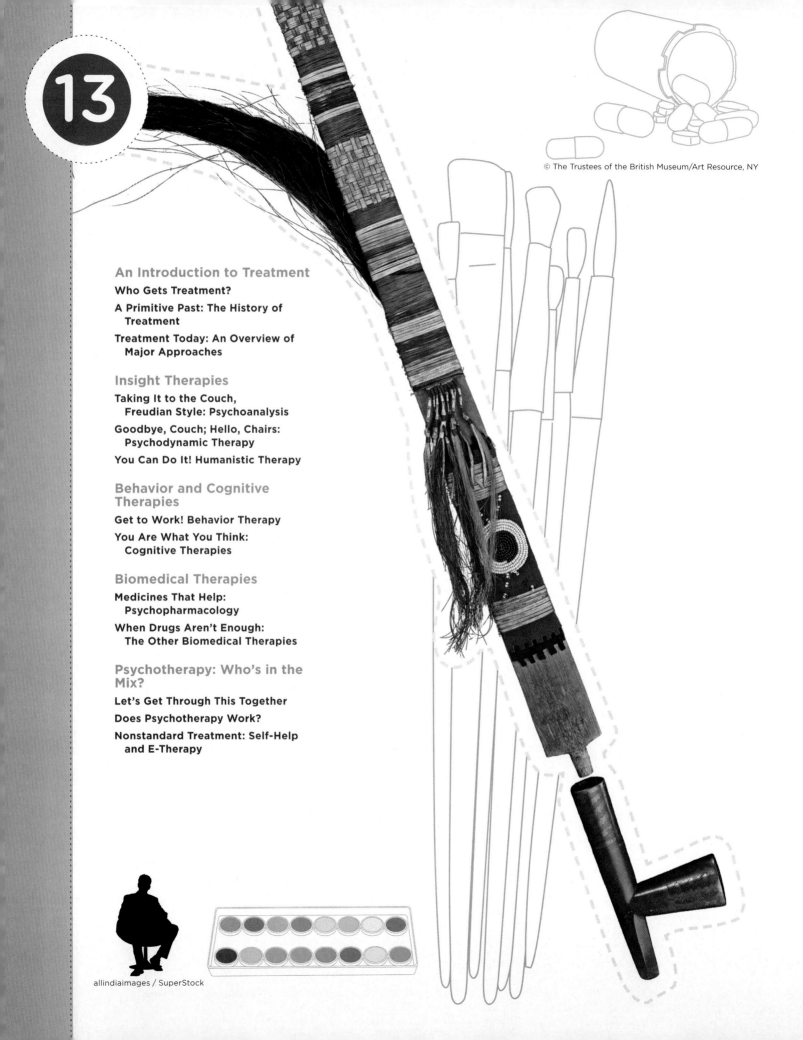

13

treatment of psychological disorders

An Introduction to Treatment

VOICES It's a beautiful evening on the Rosebud Indian Reservation in south-central South Dakota. The sun, low in the sky, casts a warm glow over pine-covered hills. Oceans of prairie grass roll in the wind. The scene could not be more tranquil. But for Chepa,* a young Lakota woman living in this Northern Plains sanctuary, life has been anything but tranquil. For days, Chepa has been tormented by the voice of a deceased uncle. Hearing voices is nothing unusual in the Lakota spiritual tradition; ancestors visit the living often. But in the case of this young woman, the voice is telling her to kill herself. Chepa has tried to make peace with her uncle's spirit using prayer, pipe ceremony, and other forms of traditional medicine, but he will not be appeased. Increasingly paranoid and withdrawn, Chepa is making her relatives uneasy, so they take her to the home of a trusted neighbor, Dr. Dan Foster. A sun dancer and pipe carrier, Dr. Foster is a respected member of the community. He also happens to be the reservation's lead clinical psychologist.

---

*The story of Chepa, a Lakota woman with schizophrenia, is hypothetical, but it is based on actual scenarios that Dr. Foster encounters every week.

Breathtaking
South Dakota is home to many American Indian tribes, including the Sicangu Lakota Oyate, or Rosebud Sioux. The Rosebud Indian Reservation is a vast and beautiful land, but its residents struggle with severe poverty—and all the problems that come with it. Poverty-related stressors can interfere with work, strain personal relationships, and trigger the symptoms of mental disorders. © Marilyn Angel Wynn/Nativestock Pictures/Corbis

CONNECTIONS

In **Chapter 3,** we described sensation as the detection of stimuli by sensory organs. Stimuli are transduced into neural signals and sent to various parts of the brain. With hallucinations, the first step is not occurring (no apparent physical stimuli), but the sensory experience exists nevertheless. The brain interprets internal information as coming from outside the body.

Dr. Foster, in His Own Words

http://qrs.ly/2t4qsgw

© 2016, Macmillan

CONNECTIONS

In **Chapter 12,** we reported that *schizophrenia* is a persistent and debilitating disorder that affects approximately 0.3% to 1% of the population. In this chapter, we will present some approaches to treating people with this diagnosis.

Upon meeting with Chepa and her family, Dr. Foster realizes that she is having *hallucinations,* sensory experiences she thinks are real, but are not evident to anyone else. Chepa is also experiencing *delusions,* which are strange or false beliefs. And because she is vulnerable to acting on these hallucinations and delusions, she poses a risk to herself, and possibly others. Chepa needs to go to the hospital, and it is Dr. Foster's responsibility to make sure she gets there, even if it requires going to a judge and getting a court order. "I'm going to make an intervention," Dr. Foster offers, "and I'm going to have to do it in a way that's respectful to that person and to the culture, but still respectful to the body of literature and training that I come from as a psychologist."

Chepa's grandmother protests: "I don't want her going to the hospital. I want to use Indian medicine." Trying to remain as clear and neutral as possible, Dr. Foster explains that if the voice were that of a spirit, it would have responded to prayer, pipe ceremony, and other traditional approaches. "I believe you're hearing voices," he says to Chepa. "But that voice is not coming from your uncle. . . . I think it's coming from your own mind." He goes on to describe how the brain has a region that specializes in hearing, and areas that store memories of people and their voices. It is possible, he explains, that the brain is calling forth a voice from the past, making it seem like it is here at this moment.

Chepa may not agree with Dr. Foster, but she trusts him. He is, after all, a relative. In Lakota culture, *relatives* are not necessarily linked by blood. One can be adopted into a family or community through a formal ceremony known as *hunka.* At Rosebud, all of the therapists and medical providers are linked to the community through *hunka*—a great honor and also a great responsibility.

An ambulance arrives and transports Chepa to the emergency room, where she finds Dr. Foster waiting. He is there to make a diagnosis and develop a treatment plan, but also to provide her with a sense of security, and to do so in the context of a nurturing relationship. "First of all my concern is safety, and secondly my concern is that you realize I am concerned about you," Dr. Foster says. "We're going to form a relationship, you and I," he says. "Whatever it is that we're facing, we are going to make it so that it comes out better than it is right now."

The blood and urine screens come back negative, indicating that the hallucinations and delusions are not resulting from a drug, such as PCP or methamphetamine, and doctors find no evidence of a medical condition that could be driving the symptoms. Dr. Foster's observations and assessments point to a complex psychological disorder known as schizophrenia.

Note: Quotations attributed to Dr. Dan Foster and Laura Lichti are personal communications.

Because Chepa poses an imminent risk to herself, Dr. Foster and his colleagues arrange a transfer to a psychiatric hospital, where she may stay for several days. The medical staff will stabilize her with a drug to help reduce her symptoms, the first of many doses likely to be administered in years to come. When she returns to the reservation, Dr. Foster and his colleagues will offer her treatment, which will be designed with her specific needs in mind. 📁

The Sun Dancer
Dr. Dan Foster is the lead clinical psychologist on the Rosebud Reservation. He frequently works with clients suffering from severe emotional trauma, but he maintains a positive outlook. "I feel like the crucible of poverty and pain also is the crucible for transformation," says Dr. Foster, who is a respected member of the Lakota community he serves. WHF/Worth Archive

Who Gets Treatment?

Therapists working on the Rosebud Reservation tend to see clients in crises, often related to the conditions of extreme poverty that exist on Northern Plains Indian reservations. The average unemployment rate is nearly 80% (United States Senate, 2010, January 28), and affordable housing is scarce. It is not unusual to have 14 or 15 relatives packed into living quarters the size of a two-bedroom apartment. "Here we are in this beautiful, pastoral Northern Plains setting with the kind of crowding [you might] experience in New York City," Dr. Foster says. "We're a rural ghetto." Squeezed into their homes without employment, entertainment, or access to transportation, people tend to feel stressed, and stress can play a role in psychological disorders. Some seek relief in alcohol, drugs, risky sex, gambling, or as Dr. Foster puts it, "outlets that [temporarily] feel good in the midst of a painful life." Young people may turn to gangs, which can provide a sense of self-worth and belonging. Dr. Foster believes and hopes that Indian language, spiritual ceremony, and culture can act somewhat like a shield, protecting people from self-destructive behaviors. But centuries of assaults by Western society have eroded American Indian cultures.

As you may already know, the arrival of European colonists in 1492 marked the beginning of a long, drawn-out attack on the physical, social, and psychological well-being

CONNECTIONS

In **Chapter 12,** we noted that stressors can impact the course of some psychological disorders. Periods of mania, depression, and psychosis can be brought on by life changes and stressors. The *diathesis–stress model* suggests that a genetic predisposition and environmental triggers play a role in the development of schizophrenia.

The Power of Culture
Residents of the Rosebud Reservation gather for a powwow. Participating in cultural ceremonies and prayer may help people deal with stressors that could otherwise impact psychological problems. LAIF/Redux

of the continent's native people. American Indians were pushed out of their native lands, relocated to reservations, economically disenfranchised, and murdered and raped by generations of American soldiers. Their children were sent away to government boarding schools, where they lost touch with their native language, religion, and culture (Struthers & Lowe, 2003). Tribal cultures are still alive, but struggling to stay afloat.

As we learn more about Dr. Foster's work on Rosebud Reservation, be mindful that therapists work with a broad spectrum of psychological issues. Dr. Foster tends to work with people in severe distress. Some of his clients do not seek therapy, but end up in his care only because friends and relatives intervene. Other therapists spend much of their time serving people who seek help with issues such as shyness, low self-esteem, and unresolved childhood conflicts. Therapy is not just for those with psychological disorders and life catastrophes, but for anyone wishing to live a more fulfilling existence.

Psychologists use various models to explain abnormal behavior and psychological disorders. As our understanding of psychological disorders has changed over time, so have treatments. While reading the brief history that follows, try to identify connections between the perceived causes of disorders and treatments designed to resolve them.

CONNECTIONS

We discussed the *etiology* of psychological disorders in **Chapter 12.** The medical model implies that disorders have biological causes. The biopsychosocial perspective suggests disorders result from an interaction of biological, psychological, and sociocultural factors.

A Primitive Past: The History of Treatment

LO 1   Outline the history of the treatment of psychological disorders.

Psychological disorders are as old as recorded history, and some of the early attempts to "cure" and "treat" them were inhumane and unproven. One theory suggests that during the Stone Age, people believed psychological disorders were caused by possession with demons and evil spirits. Our cave dweller ancestors may have practiced *trephination,* or drilling of holes in the skull, perhaps to create exit routes for evil spirits (Maher & Maher, 2003).

ASYLUMS OR PRISONS?   A major shift came in the 16th century. Religious groups began creating *asylums,* special places to house and treat people with psychological disorders. However, these asylums were overcrowded and resembled prisons, with inmates chained in dungeonlike cells, starved, and subjected to sweltering heat and frigid cold. During the French Revolution (the late 1700s), Philippe Pinel, a French physician, began working in Paris asylums. Horrified by the conditions he observed, Pinel removed the inmates' chains and insisted they be treated more humanely (Hergenhahn, 2005; Maher & Maher, 2003). The idea of using "moral treatment," or respect and kindness instead of harsh methods, spread throughout Europe and America (Routh & Reisman, 2003).

During the mid- to late-1800s, an American schoolteacher named Dorothea Dix vigorously championed the "mental hygiene movement," a campaign to reform asylums in the United States. Appalled by what she witnessed in American prisons and "mental" institutions, including the caging of naked inmates, Dix helped establish and upgrade over 30 state mental hospitals (Parry, 2006). Despite the good intentions of reformers like Pinel and Dix, many institutions eventually deteriorated into warehouses for people with psychological disorders: overcrowded, understaffed, and underfunded.

In the early 1900s, psychiatrists began to realize that mental health problems existed outside asylums, among ordinary people

The Reformer
American schoolteacher Dorothea Dix led the nation's "mental hygiene movement," an effort to improve the treatment of people living in mental institutions. Her advocacy work began in the mid-1800s, when people in some mental hospitals were chained, beaten, and locked in cages (Parry, 2006). National Portrait Gallery, Smithsonian Institution / Art Resource, NY

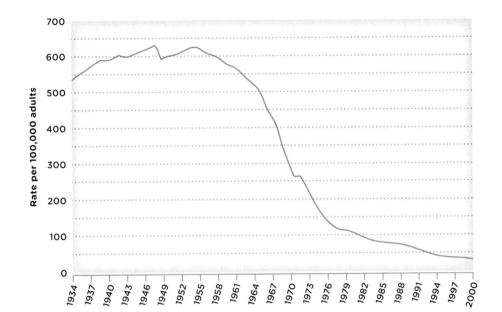

FIGURE 13.1
Deinstitutionalization
Since the 1950s, the rate of institutionalization has declined dramatically. Copyright © 2011 by the University of Chicago Press from Harcourt (2011).

who were capable of functioning in society. Rather than drawing a line between the sane and insane, psychiatrists began to view mental health as a continuum. They started developing a system to classify psychological disorders based on symptoms and progression, and this effort ultimately led to the creation of the first *Diagnostic and Statistical Manual of Mental Disorders* in 1952 (*DSM;* American Psychiatric Association, 1952; Pierre, 2012).

RETURN TO THE COMMUNITY   The 1950s and 1960s in the United States saw a mass exodus of American patients out of institutions and back into the community (**Figure 13.1**). This **deinstitutionalization** was partly the result of a movement to reduce the social isolation of people with psychological disorders and integrate them into society. Deinstitutionalization was also made possible by the introduction of medications that reduced some symptoms of severe psychological disorders. Thanks to these new drugs, many people who had previously needed constant care and supervision began caring for themselves and managing their own medications—an arrangement that worked for some but not all, as many former patients ended up living on the streets or behind bars (Harrington, 2012). As of 2007, approximately 2.7 million inmates in American jails and prisons were suffering from mental health problems, representing more than one half of the inmate population (Hawthorne et al., 2012).

In spite of the deinstitutionalization movement, psychiatric hospitals and institutions continue to play an important role in the treatment of psychological disorders. The scenario involving Dr. Foster and his client Chepa may be unusual in some respects, but not when it comes to the initiation of treatment. For someone experiencing a dangerous psychotic episode, the standard approach includes a stay in a psychiatric hospital or ward. Some of these admissions are voluntary; others are not.

Typically, a person is ready to leave the hospital after a few days or weeks, but many people in crisis are released after just a few hours, due to the high cost of treatment and financial pressures on hospitals. The length of a hospital stay is often determined by what insurance will cover, rather than what a patient needs, as well as the severe shortage of available beds in hospitals and units. Many psychiatric facilities simply cannot accommodate the scores of people seeking treatment (Honberg, Diehl, Kimball, Gruttadaro, & Fitzpatrick, 2011; Interlandi, 2012, June 22). We have come a long way in the treatment of psychological disorders, but there is still considerable progress to be made.

CONNECTIONS

In **Chapter 12,** we noted that most mental health professionals in the United States use the *DSM-5.* The *DSM-5* is a classification system designed to help clinicians ensure accurate and consistent diagnoses based on the observation of symptoms. This manual does not include information on treatment.

CONNECTIONS

In **Chapter 12,** we described *psychotic symptoms,* such as hallucinations and delusions. Psychotic episodes can be risky for the person experiencing them—as well as those around him. In these cases, a person may be admitted to a hospital against his will. Hospitals have procedures in place to ensure that involuntary admissions are ethical.

deinstitutionalization The mass movement of patients with psychological disorders out of mental institutions, and the attempt to reintegrate them into the community.

Treatment Today: An Overview of Major Approaches

LO 2   Discuss how the main approaches to therapy differ and identify their common goal.

Today people receive treatment for a variety of reasons, not just mental disorders. Psychotherapy can help clients resolve work problems, cope with chronic illness, and adjust to major life changes like immigration and divorce. Some people enter psychotherapy to work on a specific issue or to improve their relationships.

The word *psychotherapy* derives from the Ancient Greek *psychē,* meaning "soul," and *therapeuō,* meaning "to heal" (Brownell, 2010), and there are many ways to go about this healing of the soul. Some therapies promote increased awareness of situations and the self: You need to understand the origins of your problems in order to deal with them. Others focus on active steps toward behavioral change: The key to resolving issues is not so much understanding their origins, but changing the thoughts and behaviors that precede them. Finally, there are interventions aimed at correcting disorders from a physical standpoint. These treatments often take the form of medication, and may be combined with psychotherapy.

Many of these approaches share common features: The relationship between the client and the treatment provider is of utmost importance, as is a sense of hope that things will get better (Snyder et al., 2000). And they generally share a common goal, which is to reduce symptoms and increase the quality of life, whether a person is struggling with a psychological disorder or simply wants to be more fulfilled.

Psychological therapies can be categorized along three major dimensions (**Infographic 13.1** on page 522). The first dimension is the manner of delivery— whether therapy is administered to an *individual* (one therapist working with one person) or a *group* (therapists working with multiple people). The second dimension is the treatment approach, which can be biomedical or psychological. **Biomedical therapy** refers to drugs and other medical interventions that target the biological basis of a disorder. **Psychotherapy,** or "talk therapy," homes in on psychological factors. The third dimension of therapy is the theoretical perspective or approach. We can group the various approaches into two broad categories: **insight therapies,** which aim to increase awareness of self and the environment, and **behavior therapies,** which focus on behavioral change. As you learn about the many forms of therapy, keep in mind that they are not mutually exclusive; therapists often incorporate various perspectives. Around 25% to 50% of today's therapists use this type of combined approach (Norcross & Beutler, 2014). Even those who are trained in one discipline may integrate multiple methods, tailoring treatment for each client with an **eclectic approach to therapy.**

In addition to describing the various approaches to psychological treatment, we will examine how well they work. *Outcome research,* which evaluates the success of therapies, is a complicated task. First, it is not always easy to pinpoint the meaning of success, or operationalize it. Should we measure self-esteem, happiness, or some other benchmark? Second, it can be difficult for clinicians to remain free of bias (both positive and negative) when reporting on the successes and failures of clients (see Chapter 14 on the self-serving bias).

CONNECTIONS

In **Chapter 1,** we described the importance of operational definitions. An *operational definition* is the precise manner in which we define and measure a characteristic of interest. Here, it is important to create an operational definition of success, which allows for the comparison of different treatment approaches.

Synonyms
eclectic approach to therapy integrative approach to therapy

✓ ○ ✓ ○ **show what you know**

1. Philippe Pinel was horrified by the conditions in Parisian asylums in the late 1700s. He insisted that the inmates' chains be removed and that they be treated with respect and kindness. This _____ then spread throughout Europe and America.

2. A therapist writes a letter to the editor of a local newspaper in support of more funding for mental health facilities, stating that

regardless of therapists' training, all therapy shares the same goal of reducing _____ and increasing the quality of life.
   a. symptoms   b. combined approaches
   c. biomedical therapy   d. the number of asylums

3. What were some of the consequences of deinstitutionalization?

✓ CHECK YOUR ANSWERS IN APPENDIX C.

Insight Therapies

AWARENESS EQUALS POWER Laura Lichti grew up in a picturesque town high in the clouds of the Rocky Mountains. Her family was, in her words, "very, very conservative," and her church community tight-knit and isolated. As an adolescent, Laura experienced many common teenage emotions (*Who am I? No one understands me*), and she longed for someone to listen and understand. Fortunately, she found that safe spot in a former Sunday school teacher, a twenty-something woman with children of her own, who had a wise "old soul," according to Laura. "The role she played for me was just like a life line," Laura recalls. "What I appreciated is that she really didn't direct me." If Laura felt distressed, her mentor would never say, "I told you so." Instead, she would listen without judgment. Then she would respond with an empathetic statement such as, "I can see that you're having a really hard time. . ."

With her gentle line of inquiry, the mentor encouraged Laura to search within herself for answers. Thoughtfully, empathically, she taught Laura how to find her voice, create her own solutions, and direct her life in a way that was true to herself. "[She] took it back to me," Laura says. "It was beautiful."

Inspired to give others what her mentor had given her, Laura resolved to become a psychotherapist for children and teens. She paid her way through community college, went on to a 4-year university, and eventually received her master's degree in psychology, gaining experience in various internships along the way. After logging in hundreds of hours of supervised training and passing the state licensing exam, Laura finally became a licensed professional counselor. The process was 10 years in the making.

Today, Laura empowers clients much in the same way her mentor empowered her—by developing their self-awareness. She knows that her therapy is working when clients become aware enough to anticipate a problem and use coping skills without her prompting. "I got into an argument and started getting really angry," a client might say, "but instead of flying off the handle I took a walk and calmed down." Developing self-awareness is one of the unifying goals of the insight therapies, which we will now explore.

Taking It to the Couch, Freudian Style: Psychoanalysis

LO 3 Describe how psychoanalysis differs from psychodynamic therapy.

When imagining the stereotypical "therapy" session, many people picture a person reclining on a couch and talking about dreams and memories from childhood. Modern-day therapy generally does not resemble this image. But if we could travel back in time to 1930s Vienna, Austria, and sit on the sofa of Sigmund Freud (1856–1939) we just might see this stereotype come to life.

FREUD AND THE UNCONSCIOUS Sigmund Freud (1900/1953), the father of psychoanalysis, proposed that humans are motivated by two animal-like drives: aggression and sex. But acting on these drives is not always compatible with social norms, so they create conflict and get pushed beneath the surface, or repressed. These drives do not just go away, though; they continue simmering beneath our conscious awareness, affecting our moods and behaviors. And when we can no longer keep them at bay, the result may be disordered behavior, such as that seen with phobias, obsessions, and panic attacks (Solms, 2006, April/May). To help patients

On Her Way
Laura Lichti had many reasons to feel proud the day she received her master's degree in counseling. After working full-time to put herself through college, earning an associate's degree from a community college and then a bachelor's degree from a 4-year institution, Laura was one of 16 people admitted to a highly competitive master's program in counseling. Dan Penn

CONNECTIONS

In **Chapter 10,** we introduced the concept of repression, which is a defense mechanism through which the *ego* moves anxiety-provoking thoughts, memories, or feelings from consciousness to unconsciousness. Here, we will see how psychoanalysis helps uncover some of these activities occurring outside of our awareness.

biomedical therapy Drugs and other physical interventions that target the biological processes underlying psychological disorders; primary goal is to reduce symptoms.

psychotherapy "Talk therapy"; a treatment approach in which a client works with a mental health professional to reduce psychological symptoms and improve quality of life.

insight therapies A type of psychotherapy, aimed at increasing awareness of self and the environment.

behavior therapies A type of therapy that focuses on behavioral change.

eclectic approach to therapy Drawing on multiple theories and approaches to therapy to tailor treatment for a client.

According to some estimates, there exist at least 500 specific types of psychotherapy (Arkowitz & Lilienfeld, 2012). Many approaches to therapy share common features, and it can be helpful to use these broad dimensions as a means of organizing our discussion. However, keep in mind that divisions between therapeutic approaches are much less rigid than it may appear in this diagram. As many as half of therapists today combine approaches, either in terms of specific techniques associated with theoretical perspectives, or in terms of the perspectives themselves (Norcross & Beutler, 2014). But for every approach the goal remains the same: to reduce symptoms and increase the quality of life.

Major Approaches to Therapy

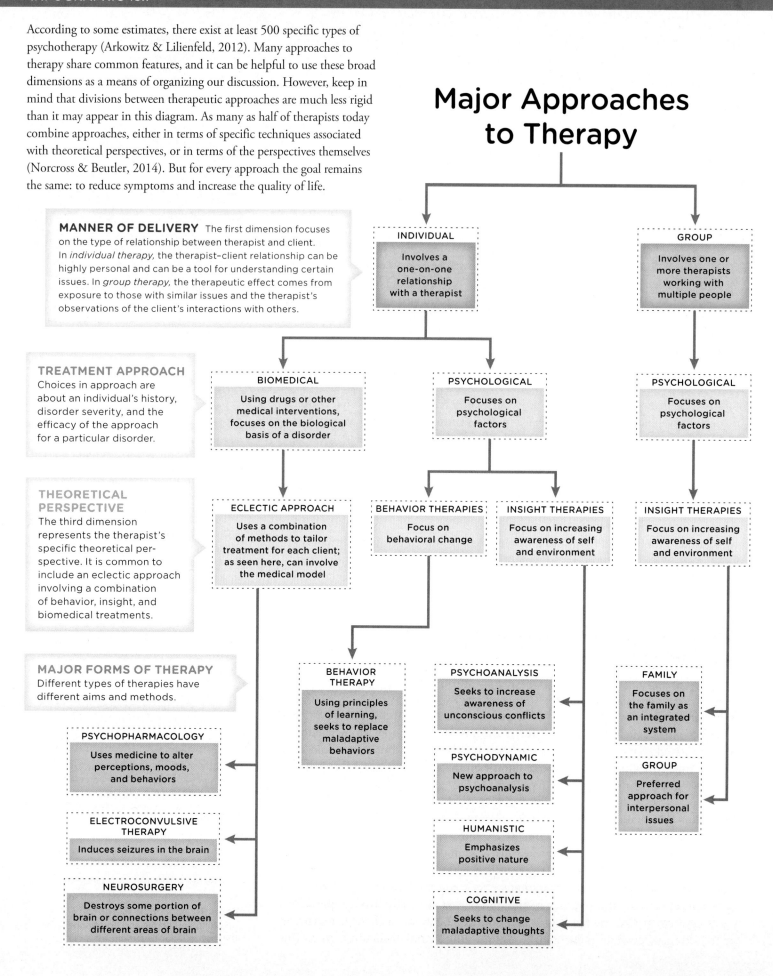

MANNER OF DELIVERY The first dimension focuses on the type of relationship between therapist and client. In *individual therapy,* the therapist–client relationship can be highly personal and can be a tool for understanding certain issues. In *group therapy,* the therapeutic effect comes from exposure to those with similar issues and the therapist's observations of the client's interactions with others.

INDIVIDUAL
Involves a one-on-one relationship with a therapist

GROUP
Involves one or more therapists working with multiple people

TREATMENT APPROACH
Choices in approach are about an individual's history, disorder severity, and the efficacy of the approach for a particular disorder.

BIOMEDICAL
Using drugs or other medical interventions, focuses on the biological basis of a disorder

PSYCHOLOGICAL
Focuses on psychological factors

PSYCHOLOGICAL
Focuses on psychological factors

THEORETICAL PERSPECTIVE
The third dimension represents the therapist's specific theoretical perspective. It is common to include an eclectic approach involving a combination of behavior, insight, and biomedical treatments.

ECLECTIC APPROACH
Uses a combination of methods to tailor treatment for each client; as seen here, can involve the medical model

BEHAVIOR THERAPIES
Focus on behavioral change

INSIGHT THERAPIES
Focus on increasing awareness of self and environment

INSIGHT THERAPIES
Focus on increasing awareness of self and environment

MAJOR FORMS OF THERAPY
Different types of therapies have different aims and methods.

BEHAVIOR THERAPY
Using principles of learning, seeks to replace maladaptive behaviors

PSYCHOANALYSIS
Seeks to increase awareness of unconscious conflicts

FAMILY
Focuses on the family as an integrated system

PSYCHOPHARMACOLOGY
Uses medicine to alter perceptions, moods, and behaviors

PSYCHODYNAMIC
New approach to psychoanalysis

GROUP
Preferred approach for interpersonal issues

ELECTROCONVULSIVE THERAPY
Induces seizures in the brain

HUMANISTIC
Emphasizes positive nature

NEUROSURGERY
Destroys some portion of brain or connections between different areas of brain

COGNITIVE
Seeks to change maladaptive thoughts

The Famous Couch
Freud's psychoanalytic couch appears on display at the Freud Museum in London. All of Freud's patients reclined on this piece of furniture, which is reportedly quite comfortable with its soft cushions and Iranian rug cover (Freud Museum, n.d., para. 4). Freud sat in the chair at the head of the couch, close to but not within view of his patient. Bjanka Kadic/Alamy

deal with these drives, Freud created psychoanalysis, the first formal system of psychotherapy. Psychoanalysis attempts to increase awareness of unconscious conflicts, thus making it possible to address and work through them.

Dreams, according to Freud, are a pathway to unconscious thoughts and desires (Freud, 1900/1953). The overt material of a dream (what we remember upon waking) is called its manifest content, which can disguise a deeper meaning, or *latent content,* hidden from awareness due to potentially uncomfortable issues and desires. Freud would often use dreams as a launching pad for **free association,** a therapy technique in which a patient says anything and everything that comes to mind, regardless of how silly, bizarre, or inappropriate it may seem.

Freud believed this seemingly directionless train of thought would lead to clues about the patient's unconscious. Piecing together the hints he gathered from dreams, free association, and other parts of therapy sessions, Freud would identify and make inferences about the unconscious conflicts driving the patient's behavior. He called this investigative work **interpretation.** When the time seemed right, Freud would share his interpretations, increasing the patient's self-awareness and helping her come to terms with conflicts, with the aim of moving forward (Freud, 1900/1953).

You might be wondering what behaviors psychoanalysts consider signs of unconscious conflict. One indicator is **resistance,** a patient's unwillingness to cooperate in therapy. Examples of resistance might include "forgetting" appointments or arriving late for them, or becoming angry or agitated when certain topics arise. Resistance is a crucial step in psychoanalysis because it means the discussion might be veering close to something that makes the patient feel uncomfortable and threatened, like a critical memory or conflict causing distress. If resistance occurs, the job of the therapist is to help the patient identify its unconscious roots.

Another key sign of unconscious conflict is **transference,** which occurs when a patient reacts to the therapist as if she is dealing with her parents or other important people from childhood. Suppose Chepa relates to Dr. Foster as if he were a favorite uncle. She never liked letting her uncle down, so she resists telling Dr. Foster things she suspects would disappoint him. Transference is a good thing, because it illuminates the unconscious conflicts fueling a patient's behaviors (Hoffman, 2009). One of the reasons Freud sat off to the side and out of a patient's line of vision was to encourage transference. With Freud in this neutral position, patients would have an easier time projecting their unconscious conflicts and feelings onto him.

TAKING STOCK: AN APPRAISAL OF PSYCHOANALYSIS The oldest form of talk therapy, psychoanalysis, is still alive and well today. But Freud's theories have come under sharp criticism. For one thing, they are not evidence-based, or backed up by scientific data. How can you effectively evaluate the subjective interpretations of psychoanalysts? Neither therapists nor patients actually know if they are tapping the patients' unconscious because it is made up of thoughts, memories, and desires

CONNECTIONS

In **Chapter 4,** we introduced Freud's theory of dreams. He suggested *manifest content* is the apparent meaning of a dream. The *latent content* contains the hidden meaning of a dream, representing unconscious urges. Freud believed that to expose this latent content, we must look deeper than the reported storyline of the dream.

Leo Cullum The New Yorker Collection/ The Cartoon Bank

"It's that same dream, where I'm drowning in a bowl of noodles."

CONNECTIONS

In **Chapter 10,** we presented *projective personality tests.* The assumption is that the test taker's unconscious conflicts are projected onto the test material. It is up to the therapist to try to uncover these underlying issues. Here, the patient is projecting these conflicts onto a therapist.

free association A psychoanalytic technique in which a patient says anything that comes to mind.

interpretation A psychoanalytic technique used to discover unconscious conflicts driving behavior.

resistance A patient's unwillingness to cooperate in therapy; a sign of unconscious conflict.

transference A type of resistance that occurs when a patient reacts to a therapist as if dealing with parents or other caregivers from childhood.

of which we are largely unaware. How then can we know if their conflicts are being resolved? In addition, not every person is a good candidate for psychoanalysis; one must be an effective communicator, have time during the week for multiple sessions, and be able to pay for this often expensive therapy.

Although Freud's theories have been criticized, the impact of his work is extensive (just note how often it is cited in this textbook). Freud helped us appreciate how childhood experiences and unconscious processes can shape personality and behavior. Even Laura, who does not identify herself as a psychoanalyst, says that Freudian notions sometimes come into play with her clients. If a person has a traumatic experience in childhood, for example, it may resurface both in therapy and real life, she notes. Like Laura, many contemporary psychologists do not identify themselves as psychoanalysts. But that doesn't mean Freud has left the picture. Far from it.

Goodbye, Couch; Hello, Chairs: Psychodynamic Therapy

Psychodynamic therapy is an updated take on psychoanalysis. This newer approach has been evolving over the last 30 to 40 years, incorporating many of Freud's core themes, including the idea that personality and behaviors often can be traced to unconscious conflicts and experiences from the past.

However, psychodynamic therapy breaks from traditional psychoanalysis in important ways. Therapists tend to see clients once a week for several months rather than many times a week for years. And instead of sitting quietly off to the side of a client reclining on a couch, the therapist sits face-to-face with the client, engaging in a two-way dialogue. The therapist may use a direct approach, guiding the discussion, and providing feedback and advice. Frequently, the goal of psychodynamic therapy is to understand and resolve a specific, current problem. Suppose a client finds herself in a pattern of dating abusive men. Her therapist might help her see how unconscious conflicts from the past creep into the present, influencing her feelings and behaviors. (*My father was abusive. Maybe I'm drawn to what feels familiar, even if it's bad for me.*)

For many years, psychodynamic therapists treated clients without much evidence to back up their approach (Levy & Ablon, 2010, February 23). But recently, researchers have begun testing the effects of psychodynamic therapy with rigorous scientific methods, and their results are encouraging. Randomized controlled trials suggest psychodynamic psychotherapy is effective for treating an array of disorders, including depression, panic disorder, and eating disorders (Leichsenring & Rabung, 2008; Milrod et al., 2007; Shedler, 2010), and the benefits may last long after treatment has ended. People with borderline personality disorder, for example, appear to experience fewer and less severe symptoms (such as a reduction in suicide attempts) for several years following psychodynamic therapy (Bateman & Fonagy, 2008; Shedler, 2010). Yet, this approach is not ideal for everyone. It requires high levels of verbal expression and awareness of self and the environment. Symptoms like hallucinations or delusions might interfere with these requirements.

You Can Do It! Humanistic Therapy

LO 4   Outline the principles and characteristics of humanistic therapy.

For the first half of the 20th century, most psychotherapists leaned on the theoretical framework established by Freud. But in the 1950s, some psychologists began to question Freud's dark view of human nature and his approach to treating clients. A new perspective began to take shape, one that focused on the positive aspects of human nature; this *humanism* would have a powerful influence on generations of psychologists, including Laura Lichti.

CONNECTIONS

In **Chapter 10,** we introduced the *neo-Freudians,* who disagreed with Freud's main ideas, including his singular focus on sex and aggression, his negative view of human nature, and his idea that personality is set by the end of childhood. Here, we can see that psychodynamic therapy grew out of discontent with Freud's ideas concerning treatment.

CONNECTIONS

In **Chapter 1,** we described the experimental method, a research technique that can uncover cause-and-effect relationships. Here, the experimental method is used to study the outcome of therapy. In *randomized controlled trials,* participants are randomly assigned to treatment and control groups. The independent variable is the type of treatment, and the dependent variables are the measures of their effectiveness.

During college, Laura worked as an adult supervisor at a residential treatment facility for children and teens struggling with mental health issues. The experience was eye-opening. "I hadn't really been exposed to the level of intensity, and severe needs . . . of that population," Laura says. "I really had never been with people who constantly wanted to kill themselves, or had a severe eating disorder, or [who] were extreme cutters." Laura was not a therapist at the time, so she could not offer them professional help. To connect with the residents, she relied on the relational skills she had learned from her mentor. Her message was, *I'm here. I'll meet you where you are, and I really care about you.*

Laura continues to use this approach in her work as a therapist, allowing each client to steer the course of his therapy. For example, Laura might begin a session by asking a client to experiment with art therapy. Some people are enthusiastic about art therapy; others resist, but Laura makes it a rule never to coerce a client with statements such as, "Well, you need to do it because I am your therapist." Instead, she might say, "Okay, what do you think would work? If art is not going to work, what is interesting to you?" Maybe the client likes writing song lyrics; if so, Laura will follow his lead. "Okay, then why don't you write a song for me?" 📁

This approach to therapy is very much a part of the humanistic movement, which was championed by American psychotherapist Carl Rogers (1902–1987). Rogers believed that human beings are inherently good and inclined toward growth. "It has been my experience that persons have a basically positive direction," he wrote in his widely popular book, *On Becoming a Person* (Rogers, 1961, p. 26). Rogers recognized that people have basic biological needs for food and sex, but he also saw that we have powerful desires to form close relationships, treat others with warmth and tenderness, and grow and mature as individuals (Rogers, 1961).

With this optimistic spirit, Rogers and others pioneered several types of insight therapy collectively known as **humanistic therapy,** which emphasizes the positive nature of humankind. Unlike psychoanalysis, which tends to focus on the distant past, humanistic therapy concentrates on the present, seeking to identify and address current problems. And rather than digging up unconscious thoughts and feelings, humanistic therapy emphasizes the conscious experience: What's going on in your mind right now?

Paint Me What You're Feeling
Thirteen-year-old Alyssia Crook uses her left leg and foot to create a painting during an art therapy session. This photo was taken less than 2 weeks before Crook, who suffers from a rare disease called pterygium syndrome, had part of her left leg amputated. Art therapy is an approach that uses art to help people understand, express, and deal with their emotions in a constructive way (American Art Therapy Association, 2015). AP Photo/The Grand Rapids Press, Rex Larson

CONNECTIONS

In **Chapter 1,** we introduced the field of *positive psychology,* which draws attention to human strengths and potential for growth. The *humanistic perspective* was a forerunner to this approach. As a treatment method, humanistic therapy emphasizes the positive nature of humans and strives to harness this for clients in treatment.

LO 5 Describe person-centered therapy.

PERSON-CENTERED THERAPY Rogers' distinct form of humanistic therapy is known as **person-centered therapy,** and it closely follows his theory of personality. According to Rogers, each person has a natural tendency toward growth and *self-actualization,* or achieving one's full potential. But expectations from family and society can stifle the process. He suggested these types of external factors often cause an *incongruence,* or a mismatch, between the client's *ideal self* (often involving unrealistic expectations of who she should be) and *real self* (the way the client views herself). The main goal of treatment is to reduce the incongruence between these two selves.

Suppose Laura has a male client who is drawn toward artistic endeavors. He loves dancing, singing, and acting, but his parents believe that boys should be tough and play sports. The client has spent his life trying to become the person others expect him to be, meanwhile denying the person he is deep down, which leaves him feeling unfulfilled and empty. Using a person-centered approach, Laura would take this client on a journey toward self-actualization. She would be supportive and involved throughout the process, but she would not tell him where to go, because as Rogers stated, "It is the *client* who knows what hurts, what directions to go, what problems

Synonyms
person-centered therapy client-centered therapy

psychodynamic therapy A type of insight therapy that incorporates core psychoanalytic themes, including the importance of unconscious conflicts and experiences from the past.
humanistic therapy A type of insight therapy that emphasizes the positive nature of humankind.
person-centered therapy A form of humanistic therapy developed by Rogers; aimed at helping clients achieve their full potential.

I Believe in You
Carl Rogers leads a group therapy session in 1966. One of the founders of humanistic psychology, Rogers firmly believed that every human being is fundamentally good and capable of *self-actualization*, or becoming all that she can be.
Michael Rougier/Time & Life Pictures/Getty Images

are crucial, what experiences have been deeply buried" (Rogers, 1961, pp. 11–12). This type of therapy is **nondirective,** in that the therapist follows the lead of the client. The goal is to help clients see they are empowered to make changes in their lives and continue along a path of positive growth. The assumption is that all humans have an innate drive to become fully functioning.

Part of Rogers' philosophy was his refusal to identify the people he worked with as "patients" (Rogers, 1951). Patients depend on doctors to make decisions for them, or at least give them instructions. In Rogers' mind, it was the patient who had the answers, not the therapist. So he began using the term *client* and eventually settled on the term *person.*

The focus in person-centered therapy is not therapeutic techniques; the goal is to create a warm and accepting relationship between therapist and client. This **therapeutic alliance** is based on mutual respect and caring between the therapist and the client, and it provides a safe place for self-exploration.

At this point, you may be wondering what exactly the therapist does during sessions. If a client has all the answers, why does he need a therapist at all? Sitting face-to-face with a client, the therapist's main job is to "be there" for that person through **empathy,** *unconditional positive regard,* **genuineness,** and **active listening,** all of which are essential for building a therapeutic alliance (**Table 13.1**).

TAKING STOCK: AN APPRAISAL OF HUMANISTIC THERAPY   The humanistic perspective has had a profound impact on our understanding of personality development and on the practice of psychotherapy. Therapists of all different theoretical

nondirective A technique used in person-centered therapy wherein the therapist follows the lead of the client during treatment sessions.

therapeutic alliance A warm and accepting client–therapist relationship that serves as a safe place for self-exploration.

empathy The ability to feel what a person is experiencing by attempting to observe the world through his or her eyes.

genuineness The ability to respond to a client in an authentic way rather than hiding behind a polite or professional mask.

active listening The ability to pick up on the content and emotions behind words in order to understand a client's perspective, often by echoing the main point of what the client says.

exposure A therapeutic technique that brings a person into contact with a feared object or situation while in a safe environment, with the goal of extinguishing or eliminating the fear response.

TABLE 13.1 BUILDING A THERAPEUTIC ALLIANCE

Components	Description
Empathy	The ability to feel what a client is experiencing; seeing the world through the client's eyes (Rogers, 1951); therapist perceives feelings and experiences from "inside" the client (Rogers, 1961)
Unconditional positive regard	Total acceptance of a client no matter how distasteful the client's behaviors, beliefs, and words may be (Chapter 10)
Genuineness	Being authentic, responding to a client in a way that is real rather than hiding behind a polite or professional mask; knowing exactly where the therapist stands allows the client to feel secure enough to open up (Rogers, 1961)
Active listening	Picking up on the content and emotions behind words in order to understand a client's point of view; reflection, or echoing the main point of what a client says

Humanist Carl Rogers believed it was critical to establish a strong and trusting therapist–client relationship. Above are the key elements of a therapeutic alliance.

orientations draw on humanistic techniques to build stronger relationships with clients and create positive therapeutic environments. This type of therapy is useful for an array of people dealing with complex and diverse problems (Corey, 2013), but how it compares to other methods remains somewhat unclear. Studying humanistic therapy is difficult because its methodology has not been operationalized and its use varies from one therapist to the next. Like other insight therapies, humanistic therapy is not ideal for everyone; it requires a high level of verbal ability and self-awareness.

The insight therapies we have explored—psychoanalysis, psychodynamic therapy, and humanistic therapy—help clients develop a deeper understanding of self. By exploring events of the past, clients in psychoanalysis or psychodynamic therapy may discover how prior experiences affect their current thoughts and behaviors. Those working with humanistic therapists may become more aware of what they want in life—and how their desires conflict with the expectations of others. These insights are invaluable, and they often lead to positive changes in behavior. But is it also possible to alter behavior directly? This is the goal of behavior therapy, the subject of the next section.

 show what you know

1. Suzanne is late for her therapy appointment yet again. Her therapist suggests this might be due to _____, which generally refers to a patient's unwillingness to cooperate in therapy.

2. The group of therapies known as _____ therapy focus on the positive nature of human beings and on the here and now.
   a. humanistic
   b. psychoanalytic
   c. psychodynamic
   d. free association

3. Seeing the world through a client's eyes and understanding how it feels to be the client is called:
   a. interpretation.
   b. genuineness.
   c. empathy.
   d. self-actualization.

4. What are the differences between psychoanalytic and psychodynamic therapy?

✓ CHECK YOUR ANSWERS IN APPENDIX C.

Behavior and Cognitive Therapies

The most famous baby in the history of psychology is probably Little Albert. At the age of 11 months, Albert developed an intense fear of rats while participating in a classic study conducted by John B. Watson and Rosalie Rayner (1920). You would hope the researchers did something to reverse the effects of their ethically questionable experiment, that is, help Albert overcome his fear of rats. As far as we know, they did not. But could Albert have benefited from some form of *behavior therapy?*

Get to Work! Behavior Therapy

LO 6   Outline the principles and characteristics of behavior therapy.

Using the learning principles of classical conditioning, operant conditioning, and observational learning (Chapter 5), behavior therapy aims to replace maladaptive behaviors with those that are more adaptive. If behaviors are learned, who says they can't be changed through the same mechanisms? Little Albert learned to fear rats, so perhaps he could also learn to be comfortable around them.

EXPOSURE AND RESPONSE PREVENTION   To help a person overcome a fear or phobia, a behavior therapist might use **exposure,** a technique of placing clients in the situations they fear—without any actual risks involved. Take, for example, a client struggling with a rat phobia. Rats cause this person extreme anxiety; the mere thought of seeing one scamper beneath a dumpster causes

White Terror
A classic in the history of psychology, the case study of Little Albert showed that emotional responses such as fear can be classically conditioned. Researchers John B. Watson and Rosalie Rayner (1920) repeatedly exposed Albert to a frightening "bang!" every time he reached for a white rat, which led him to develop an intense fear of these animals. Vasiliy Koval/Shutterstock

CONNECTIONS

In **Chapter 5,** we learned about *negative reinforcement;* behaviors followed by a reduction in something unpleasant are likely to recur. If anxiety is reduced as a result of avoiding a feared object, the avoidance will be repeated.

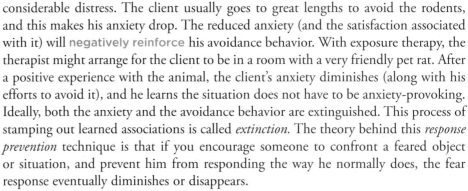

Face the Spider
A woman with arachnophobia (spider phobia) confronts the dreaded creature in a virtual environment called SpiderWorld. The goal of exposure therapy (virtual or otherwise) is to reduce the fear response by exposing clients to situations they fear. When nothing bad happens, their anxiety diminishes and they are less likely to avoid the feared situations in the future. Stephen Dagadakis/Hunter Hoffman

considerable distress. The client usually goes to great lengths to avoid the rodents, and this makes his anxiety drop. The reduced anxiety (and the satisfaction associated with it) will negatively reinforce his avoidance behavior. With exposure therapy, the therapist might arrange for the client to be in a room with a very friendly pet rat. After a positive experience with the animal, the client's anxiety diminishes (along with his efforts to avoid it), and he learns the situation does not have to be anxiety-provoking. Ideally, both the anxiety and the avoidance behavior are extinguished. This process of stamping out learned associations is called *extinction.* The theory behind this *response prevention* technique is that if you encourage someone to confront a feared object or situation, and prevent him from responding the way he normally does, the fear response eventually diminishes or disappears.

A particularly intense form of exposure is to *flood* a client with an anxiety-provoking stimulus that she cannot escape, causing a high degree of arousal. In one study, for example, women with snake phobias sat in very close proximity to a garter snake in a glass aquarium for 30 minutes without a break (Girodo & Henry, 1976).

But sometimes, it's better to approach a feared scenario with "baby steps," upping the exposure with each movement forward (Prochaska & Norcross, 2014). This can be accomplished with an *anxiety hierarchy,* which is essentially a list of activities or experiences ordered from least to most anxiety-provoking (**Infographic 13.2**).

For example, Step 1: Think about a caged rat; Step 2: Look at a caged rat from across the room; Step 3: Walk two steps toward the cage, and so on.

But take note: Working up the anxiety hierarchy needn't involve actual rodents. With technologies available today, you could put on some fancy goggles and travel into a virtual "rat world" where it is possible to reach out and "touch" that creepy crawly animal with the simple click of a rat, er . . . mouse. Virtual reality exposure therapy has become a popular way of reducing anxiety associated with various disorders, including specific phobias.

SYSTEMATIC DESENSITIZATION Therapists often combine anxiety hierarchies with relaxation techniques in an approach called **systematic desensitization,** which takes advantage of the fact that we can't be relaxed and anxious at the same time. The therapist begins by teaching clients how to relax their muscles. One technique for doing this is progressive muscle relaxation, which is the process of tensing and then relaxing muscle groups, starting at the head and ending at the toes. Using this method, a client can learn to release all the tension in his body. It's very simple—want to try it?

CONNECTIONS

In **Chapter 11,** we described *progressive muscle relaxation* in the context of reducing the impact of responses to stress. Here, we see it can also be used to help with the treatment of phobias.

Apply This ❯

try this ◀

Sit in a quiet room in a comfortable chair. Start by tensing the muscles controlling your scalp: Hold that position for about 10 seconds and then release, focusing on the tension leaving your scalp. Next follow the same procedure for the muscles in your face, tensing and releasing. Continue all the way down to your toes and see what happens.

Once a client has learned how to relax, it's time to face the anxiety hierarchy (either in the real world or via imagination) while trying to maintain a sense of calm. Imagine a client who fears flying, moving through an anxiety hierarchy with her therapist. Starting with the least-feared scenario at the bottom of her hierarchy, she imagines purchasing a ticket online. If she can stay relaxed through the first step, then she moves to the second item in the hierarchy, thinking about boarding a plane.

systematic desensitization A treatment that combines anxiety hierarchies with relaxation techniques.

Classical Conditioning in Behavior Therapies

Behavior therapists believe that most behaviors—either desirable or undesirable—are learned. When a behavior is maladaptive, a new, more adaptive behavior can be learned to replace it. Behavior therapists use learning principles to help clients eliminate unwanted behaviors. The two behavior therapies highlighted here rely upon classical conditioning techniques. In exposure therapy, a therapist might use an approach known as *systematic desensitization* to reduce an unwanted response, such as a fear of needles, by pairing it with relaxation. In *aversion therapy,* an unwanted behavior such as excessive drinking is paired with unpleasant reactions, creating an association that prompts avoidance of that behavior.

SYSTEMATIC DESENSITIZATION

A client practices relaxation techniques while engaging in situations listed on her anxiety hierarchy, beginning with the least anxiety-provoking situation. After repeated pairings, the client learns to associate the anxiety-provoking situation with the desirable, conditioned response (calm), which is incompatible with fear or anxiety. The process is repeated for every step on the hierarchy.

During conditioning, two stimuli that produce incompatible responses are repeatedly paired.

+ relaxation

ANXIETY   calm

Because the responses are incompatible, one response will eventually be extinguished. Starting at the bottom of the hierarchy with the least anxiety-provoking situation enables the desired response (calm) to prevail.

MOST ANXIETY PROVOKING

LEAST ANXIETY PROVOKING

Anxiety Hierarchy for Fear of Needles

8 Getting a flu shot.

7 Allowing someone to prep your arm for a shot.

6 Visiting a health clinic to discuss getting a shot.

5 Watching someone get a shot.

4 Holding a hypodermic needle.

3 Touching a hypodermic needle in its packaging.

2 Looking at an actual hypodermic needle.

1 Looking at a photo of a hypodermic needle.

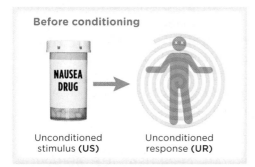

Before conditioning

NAUSEA DRUG

Unconditioned stimulus **(US)** → Unconditioned response **(UR)**

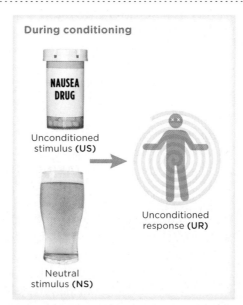

During conditioning

NAUSEA DRUG

Unconditioned stimulus **(US)**

Unconditioned response **(UR)**

Neutral stimulus **(NS)**

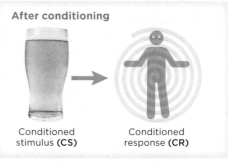

After conditioning

Conditioned stimulus **(CS)** → Conditioned response **(CR)**

Credits: Pill bottle, Joe Belanger/Shutterstock; Pint of beer, Emin Ozkan/Shutterstock; Syringe, istockphoto/thinkstock

AVERSION THERAPY

Aversion therapy seeks to diminish a behavior by linking it with an unpleasant reaction. To reduce alcohol consumption, alcohol is consumed with a drug that causes feelings of nausea. Eventually, alcohol becomes a conditioned stimulus, prompting the unpleasant physical reaction all on its own.

CONNECTIONS

Classical conditioning, presented in **Chapter 5,** can be used to reduce alcohol consumption. Drinking alcohol is a *neutral stimulus* to start (one drink does not normally cause vomiting). Drinking is paired with a nausea-inducing drug, which is an *unconditioned stimulus* that causes an *unconditioned response* of vomiting. After repeated pairings, drinking alcohol becomes the *conditioned stimulus,* and the vomiting becomes the *conditioned response.*

In **Chapter 5,** we described how *positive reinforcement* (supplying something desirable) increases the likelihood of a behavior being repeated. Therapists use reinforcement in behavior modification to shape behaviors to be more adaptive.

Synonyms
behavior modification applied behavior analysis

CONNECTIONS

Tokens are an excellent example of a *secondary reinforcer.* In **Chapter 5,** we reported that secondary reinforcers derive their power from their connection with *primary reinforcers,* which satisfy biological needs.

Coveted Coins

In a token economy, positive behaviors are reinforced with tokens, which can be used to purchase food, obtain privileges, and secure other desirable things. Token economies are typically used in institutions such as schools and mental health facilities. Jon Schulte/Getty Images

At some point in the process, she might start to feel jittery or unable to take the next step. If this happens, the therapist guides her back a step or two in the hierarchy, or as many steps as she needs to feel calm again, using the relaxation technique described above. Then it's back up the hierarchy she goes. It's important to note that this process does not happen in one session, but over the course of many sessions.

AVERSION THERAPY Exposure therapy focuses on *extinguishing* or eliminating associations, but there is another behavior therapy aimed at producing them. It's called **aversion therapy.** Seizing on the power of classical conditioning, aversion therapy seeks to link problematic behaviors, such as drug use or fetishes, to unpleasant physical reactions like sickness and pain (Infographic 13.2). The goal of aversion therapy is to get a person to have an involuntary—and unpleasant—physical reaction to an undesirable behavior, so that the behavior eventually becomes a conditioned stimulus to the conditioned response of feeling bad. A good example is the drug Antabuse, which has helped some people with alcoholism stop drinking, at least temporarily (Cannon, Baker, Gino, & Nathan, 1986; Gaval-Cruz & Weinshenker, 2009). Antabuse interferes with the body's ability to break down alcohol, so combining it with even a small amount of alcohol brings on an immediate unpleasant reaction (vomiting, throbbing headache, and so on). With repeated pairings of alcohol consumption and physical misery, drinkers are less inclined to drink in the future. But aversion therapies like this are only effective if the client is motivated to change and comply with treatment.

LEARNING, REINFORCEMENT, AND THERAPY Another form of behavior therapy is **behavior modification,** which draws on the principles of operant conditioning, shaping behaviors through *reinforcement.* Therapists practicing behavior modification use positive and negative reinforcement, as well as punishment, to help clients increase adaptive behaviors and reduce those that are maladaptive. For behaviors that resist modification, therapists might use successive approximations by reinforcing incremental changes. Some will incorporate observational learning (that is, learning by watching and imitating others) to help clients change their behaviors.

One common approach using behavior modification is the **token economy,** which harnesses the power of positive reinforcement to encourage good behavior. Token economies have proven successful for a variety of populations, including psychiatric patients in residential treatment facilities and hospitals, children in classrooms, and convicts in prisons (Dickerson, Tenhula, & Green-Paden, 2005; Kazdin, 1982). In a residential treatment facility, for example, patients with schizophrenia may earn tokens for socializing with each other, cleaning up after themselves, and eating their meals. Tokens can be exchanged for candy, outings, privileges, and other perks. They can also be taken away as a punishment to reduce undesirable behaviors. Critics contend that token economies manipulate and humiliate the people they intend to help (you might agree that giving grown men and women play money for good behavior is degrading). But, from a practical standpoint, these systems can help people adopt healthier behaviors.

TAKING STOCK: AN APPRAISAL OF BEHAVIOR THERAPY Because of their focus on observable behaviors occurring in the present moment, behavior therapies offer a few key advantages over insight therapies. Behavior therapies tend to work fast, producing quick resolutions to stressful situations, sometimes in a single session (Ollendick et al., 2009; Öst, 1989). And reduced time in therapy typically translates to a lower cost. What's more, the procedures used in behavior therapy are often easy to operationalize (remember, the focus is on modifying observable behavior), so evaluating the outcome is more straightforward.

Behavior therapy has its drawbacks, of course. The goal is to change learned behaviors, but not all behaviors are learned (you can't "learn" to have hallucinations). And because the reinforcement comes from an external source, newly learned behaviors may disappear when reinforcement stops. Finally, the emphasis on observable behavior may downplay the social, biological, and cognitive roots of psychological disorders. This narrow approach works well for treating phobias and other clear-cut behavior problems, but not as well for addressing far-reaching, complex issues arising from disorders such as schizophrenia.

You Are What You Think: Cognitive Therapies

FOLLOW-UP After being discharged from the psychiatric hospital, Chepa returns to the reservation, where Dr. Foster and his colleagues from Indian Health Services follow her progress. Every month, she goes to the medical clinic for an injection of medication to quell her psychosis (more on these antipsychotic drugs later in the chapter). This is also when she is most likely to have a therapy session with Dr. Foster.

Psychologists on the reservation typically don't have the luxury of holding more than two or three sessions with a client, so Dr. Foster has to make the most of every minute. For someone who has just received a new diagnosis, a good portion of the session is spent on *psychoeducation,* or learning more about a disorder: *What is schizophrenia, and how will it affect my life?* Dr. Foster and the client might go over some of the user-friendly literature on schizophrenia published by the National Alliance on Mental Illness (NAMI; http://www.nami.org).

Another main goal is to help clients restructure cognitive processes, or turn negative thought patterns into healthier ones. To help clients recognize the irrational nature of their thoughts, Dr. Foster might provide an analogy as he does here:

Dr. Foster: If we had a blizzard in February and it's 20 degrees below for 4 days in a row, would you consider that a strange winter?

Chepa: No.

Dr. Foster: If we had a day that's 105 degrees in August, would you consider that an odd summer?

Chepa: Well, no.

Dr. Foster: Yet you're talking about a difference of 125 degrees, and we're in the same place and we're saying this is normal weather. . . . We're part of nature. You and I are part of this natural world, and so you might have a day today where you're very distressed, very upset, and a week from now where you're very calm and very at peace, and both of those are normal. Both of those are appropriate.

Dr. Foster might also remind Chepa that her symptoms result from her psychological condition. "Your response is a normal response [for] a human being with this [psychological disorder]," he says, "and so of course you're scared, of course you're upset." 📁

LO 7 Outline the principles and characteristics of cognitive therapy.

Dr. Foster has identified his client's maladaptive thoughts and is beginning to help her change the way she views her world and her relationships. This is the basic goal of **cognitive therapy,** an approach advanced by psychiatrist Aaron Beck (1921–).

aversion therapy Therapeutic approach that uses the principles of classical conditioning to link problematic behaviors to unpleasant physical reactions.

behavior modification Therapeutic approach in which behaviors are shaped through reinforcement and punishment.

token economy A treatment approach that uses behavior modification to harness the power of reinforcement to encourage good behavior.

cognitive therapy A type of therapy aimed at addressing the maladaptive thinking that leads to maladaptive behaviors and feelings.

Beck's Cognitive Approach
The father of cognitive therapy, Aaron Beck, believes that distorted thought processes lie at the heart of psychological problems.

CONNECTIONS

In **Chapter 8,** we presented Piaget's concept of *schema,* a collection of ideas or notions representing a basic unit of understanding. Young children form schemas based on functional relationships they observe in the environment. Here, Beck is suggesting that schemas can also direct the way we interpret events, not always in a realistic or rational manner.

BECK'S COGNITIVE THERAPY   Beck was trained in psychoanalysis, but he opted to develop his own approach after trying (without luck) to produce scientific evidence showing that Freud's methods worked (Beck & Weishaar, 2014). Beck believes that patterns of *automatic thoughts* are at the root of psychological disturbances. These distortions in thinking cause individuals to misinterpret events in their lives (**Table 13.2**).

Beck identified a collection of common *cognitive distortions* or *errors* associated with psychological problems such as depression (Beck, Rush, Shaw, & Emory, 1979). One such distortion is **overgeneralization,** or thinking that self-contained events will have major repercussions in life (Prochaska & Norcross, 2014). For example, a person may assume that just because something is true under one set of circumstances, it will be true in all others (*I have had difficulty working for a male boss, so I will never be able to work effectively under a male supervisor*). Another cognitive distortion is *dichotomous thinking,* or seeing things in extremes (*I can either be a good student, or I can have a social life*). One goal of cognitive therapy then is to help clients recognize and challenge these cognitive errors.

Beck suggests that cognitive schemas underlie these patterns of automatic thoughts, directing the way we interpret events. The goal is to restructure these schemas into more rational frameworks, a process that can be facilitated by client homework. For example, the therapist may challenge a client to test a "hypothesis" related to her dysfunctional thinking. ("If it's true you don't work effectively under male bosses, then why did your previous boss give you that highly sought-after promotion?") Client homework is an important component of cognitive therapy. So, too, is psychoeducation, which might include providing resources that help clients understand their disorders and thus adopt more realistic attitudes and expectations.

Beck's cognitive therapy aims to dismantle or take apart the mental frameworks harboring cognitive errors and replace them with beliefs that nurture more positive, realistic thoughts. Dr. Foster calls these mental frameworks "paradigms," and he also tries to create a more holistic change in thinking. "I tell people that thoughts, behaviors, and words come from beliefs, and when a belief is not working for you, let's change it," he says. "To modify a belief doesn't mean all or none," he adds, "but when we outgrow a belief, that's a wonderful time for transformation."

TABLE 13.2 COGNITIVE DISTORTIONS

Cognitive Distortion	Explanation	Example of Distorted Thinking
Arbitrary inference	Coming to a conclusion even when there is no evidence to support it	*I am a horrible student.*
Selective abstraction	Ignoring information and assuming something has happened based on details taken out of context	*I know he is cheating because he is e-mailing a woman at work.*
Overgeneralizing	Belief that something may always occur because it has occurred before	*My boss doesn't like me; I will never be liked.*
Magnification-minimization	Belief that something is more or less critical than it really is—catastrophizing	*If I don't pass this first quiz, I will fail the course.*
Dichotomous thinking	Viewing experiences in extremes	*I can either be at the top of my class, or I can get married and have a family.*
Personalizing	Taking other people's behaviors too personally	*I waved at her, but she didn't even acknowledge me. I must have upset her.*

Psychiatrist Aaron Beck contends that psychological problems stem from distorted patterns of thought. Cognitive therapy aims to replace these cognitive distortions with more realistic and constructive ways of thinking.

BECK AND WEISHAAR (2014), PP. 231-264.

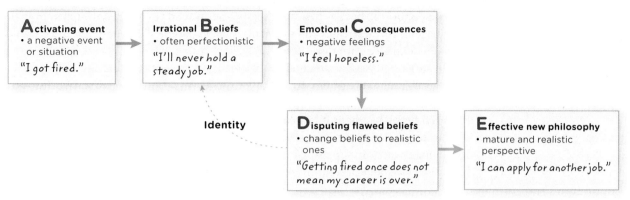

▲ **FIGURE 13.2**

The ABC's of REBT

A rational-emotive behavior therapist uses the ABC model to understand a client's problems. This part of the model is depicted in blue. Therapy, shown in green, helps a client identify and address irrational beliefs—and ultimately develop a mature and realistic perspective.

ELLIS' RATIONAL EMOTIVE BEHAVIOR THERAPY   The other major figure in cognitive therapy is psychologist Albert Ellis (1913–2007). Like Beck, Ellis was trained in psychoanalysis but was disappointed by its results, so he created his own treatment approach: **rational emotive behavior therapy (REBT).** The goal of REBT is to help people identify their irrational or illogical thoughts and convert them into rational ones. An REBT therapist uses the ABC model to understand a client's problems. Point A represents an *Activating event* in the client's life ("My boss fired me"); point B stands for the *irrational Beliefs* that follow ("I will never be able to hold a steady job"); and point C represents the *emotional Consequences* ("I feel hopeless and depressed"). Therapy focuses on addressing point B, the irrational beliefs causing distress. If all goes well, the client successfully reaches point D: *Disputing flawed beliefs* ("Losing one job does not spell the end of my career"), and that leads to point E: an *Effective new philosophy* ("I am capable of being successful in another job"), a mature and realistic perspective on life (Ellis & Dryden, 1997; **Figure 13.2**).

According to Ellis, people tend to have unrealistic beliefs, often perfectionist in nature, about how they and others should think and act. This inevitably leads to disappointment, as no one is perfect. The ultimate goal of REBT is to arrive at self-acceptance, that is, to change these irrational thoughts to realistic ones. This often involves letting go of the "I shoulds" and "I musts," what Ellis called "musturbatory thinking" (Prochaska & Norcross, 2014, p. 266). Through REBT, one develops a rational way of thinking that helps reduce suffering and amplify enjoyment: "The purpose of life," as Ellis was known to say, "is to have a $&%#@ good time" (p. 263). Ellis took a hard line with clients, forcefully challenging them to provide evidence for their irrational ideas and often shocking people with his direct manner (Kaufman, 2007, July 25; Prochaska & Norcross, 2014).

As Ellis developed his therapy throughout the years, he realized it was important to focus on cognitive processing as well as behavior. Thus, REBT therapists focus on changing both cognitions and behaviors, assigning homework to implement the insights clients gain during therapy. Because Ellis and Beck incorporated both cognitive and behavior therapy methods, their approaches are commonly referred to as **cognitive behavioral therapy.** Both are action-oriented, as they require clients to confront and resist their illogical thinking.

TAKING STOCK: AN APPRAISAL OF COGNITIVE THERAPY   There is considerable overlap between the approaches of Ellis and Beck. Both are short-term (usually no more than about 20 one-hour sessions), action-oriented, and homework-intensive. In some instances, cognitive therapy has been found to be more successful than relaxation and exposure therapy in treating certain disorders, such as social phobia and generalized anxiety disorder (Clark et al., 2006; Dugas et al., 2010). If you compare the effectiveness of Beck's and Ellis' approaches, you will find some studies showing

overgeneralization A cognitive distortion that assumes self-contained events will have major repercussions.

rational emotive behavior therapy (REBT) A type of cognitive therapy, developed by Ellis, that identifies illogical thoughts and converts them into rational ones.

cognitive behavioral therapy An action-oriented type of therapy that requires clients to confront and resist their illogical thinking.

greater support for Beck's cognitive therapy. But this advantage is only apparent with certain client characteristics and problems, such as pathological gambling and chronic pain (Prochaska & Norcross, 2014).

In some cases, cognitive models that focus on flawed assumptions and attitudes present a chicken-and-egg problem. People experiencing depression often have distorted beliefs, but are distorted beliefs causing their depression or is depression causing their distorted beliefs? Perhaps it is a combination of both.

All the therapies we have discussed thus far involve interactions among people. But in many cases, interpersonal therapy is not enough. The problem is rooted in the brain, and a biological solution may also be necessary.

☑ show what you know

1. The primary goal of _____ therapy is to replace maladaptive behaviors with more adaptive ones.
   a. behavior
   b. person-centered
   c. humanistic
   d. psychodynamic

2. Imagine you are working in a treatment facility for children, and a resident has been throwing objects at others. Using the principles of operant conditioning and observational learning, how might you use behavior modification to change this behavior?

3. The basic goal of _____ is to help clients identify maladaptive thoughts and change the way they view the world and their relationships.

4. _____ therapy uses the ABC model to help people identify their illogical thoughts and convert them into logical ones.
   a. Behavior
   b. Psychodynamic
   c. Exposure
   d. Rational emotive behavior

✓ CHECK YOUR ANSWERS IN APPENDIX C.

Psychologists Who Prescribe Psychotropic medications are typically prescribed by psychiatrists, but a small number of psychologists have prescription privileges as well. New Mexico, Louisiana, and Illinois have passed laws giving psychologists the green light to prescribe, provided they have a master's degree in psychopharmacology and adequate in-field training. The same is true for psychologists working in the Defense Department or Indian Health Services. Getty Images/Wavebreak Media

Biomedical Therapies

Earlier in the chapter, we described Dr. Foster's work with Chepa, the young woman with schizophrenia. In addition to receiving psychotherapy, Chepa goes to the medical clinic for monthly injections of drugs to control her psychosis. Prescribing medications for psychological disorders is generally the domain of *psychiatrists,* physicians who specialize in treating people with psychological disorders (psychiatrists are medical doctors, whereas clinical psychologists have PhDs and generally cannot prescribe medication).

LO 8 Summarize the biomedical interventions and identify their common goal.

People with severe disorders like depression, schizophrenia, and bipolar disorder often benefit from biomedical therapy, a type of treatment that targets the biological processes underlying psychological disorders. There are three basic biological approaches to treating psychological disorders: (1) the use of drugs, or *psychotropic* medications; (2) the use of electroconvulsive therapy; and (3) the use of surgery.

Medicines That Help: Psychopharmacology

Psychotropic medications are used to treat psychological disorders and their symptoms. *Psychopharmacology* is the scientific study of how these medications alter perceptions, moods, behaviors, and other aspects of psychological functioning. These drugs can be divided into four categories: *antidepressant, mood-stabilizing, antipsychotic,* and *antianxiety.*

ANTIDEPRESSANT DRUGS The most common mental health problem plaguing Dr. Foster's clients is major depressive disorder. Commonly referred to as *depression,* it is one of the most prevalent psychological disorders in America and a common cause of disability in young adults (National Institute of Mental Health, 2013, October 1). Major depressive disorder affects around 7% of the population in any given year (American Psychiatric Association, 2013), resulting in a high demand for ways to lessen its symptoms.

Major depressive disorder is commonly treated with **antidepressant drugs,** a category of psychotropic medication used to improve mood (and to treat anxiety and eating disorders in certain individuals). Essentially, there are three classes of antidepressant drugs: monoamine oxidase inhibitors (MAOIs), such as Nardil; tricyclic antidepressants, such as Elavil; and selective serotonin reuptake inhibitors (SSRIs), such as Prozac. All these antidepressants are thought to work by influencing the activity of neurotransmitters that are hypothesized to be involved in depression and other disorders (**Infographic 13.3** on the next page). (Keep in mind, no one has pinpointed the exact neurological mechanisms underlying depression.)

The monoamine oxidase inhibitors (MAOIs), developed in the 1950s, help people with major depressive disorder by slowing the breakdown of norepinephrine, serotonin, and dopamine in synapses. These neurotransmitters are categorized as monoamines, and the natural role of the enzyme monoamine oxidase is to break down the monoamines when they are in the synaptic gap. MAOIs extend the amount of time these neurotransmitters linger in the gap by hindering the normal activity of monoamine oxidase. Again, the cause of depression is not entirely clear, but low levels of norepinephrine and serotonin could play a role. By making these neurotransmitters more available (that is, allowing them more time in the synapse), MAOIs might lessen symptoms of depression. Even so, this class of drugs has fallen out of use due to safety concerns and side effects, as they require great attention to diet. MAOIs can trigger a life-threatening jump in blood pressure when ingested alongside tyramine, a substance found in many everyday foods, including cheddar cheese, salami, and wine (Anastasio et al., 2010; Blackwell, Marley, Price, & Taylor, 1967; Horwitz, Lovenberg, Engelman, & Sjoerdsma, 1964; Rosenberg & Kosslyn, 2011).

The tricyclic antidepressants, named as such because of their three-ringed molecular structure, inhibit the reuptake of serotonin and norepinephrine in the synaptic gap. Allowing these neurotransmitters more time to be active appears to reduce symptoms. The tricyclic drugs are not always well tolerated by patients and can cause a host of problematic side effects, including sexual dysfunction, confusion, and increased risk of heart attack (Cohen, Gibson, & Alderman, 2000; Higgins, Nash, & Lynch, 2010, September 8). Overdoses can be fatal.

Doctors relied heavily on monoamine oxidase inhibitors and tricyclics until newer, more popular pharmaceutical interventions were introduced in the 1980s. These selective serotonin reuptake inhibitors (SSRIs)—brands such as Prozac, Paxil, and Zoloft—inhibit the reuptake of serotonin specifically.

SSRIs are generally safer and have fewer negative effects than the older generation of antidepressants, which helps explain why they have become so popular in recent decades. But they are far from perfect. Weight gain, fatigue, hot flashes and chills, insomnia, nausea, and sexual dysfunction are all possible side effects. Some research suggests that they work no better than a placebo when it comes to treating mild to moderate depression (Fournier et al., 2010). But these drugs can be very beneficial in reducing the potentially devastating symptoms of depression. Improvement is generally noticed within 3–5 weeks of starting treatment.

CONNECTIONS

In **Chapter 2,** we described how neurons communicate with each other. Sending neurons release *neurotransmitters* into the synaptic gap, where they bind to receptors on the receiving neuron. Neurotransmitters not immediately attached are reabsorbed by the sending neuron (*reuptake*) or are broken down in the synapse. Here, we see how medications can influence this process.

Black Box
A growing number of children and teenagers are taking SSRIs to combat depression, but these medications may increase the risk of suicidal behaviors and thoughts for a small percentage of youth. For this reason, the U.S. Food and Drug Administration (FDA) requires manufacturers to include a "black box" warning on the packaging of these drugs (National Institute of Mental Health, n.d., para. 3). Todor Tsvetkov/Getty Images

CONNECTIONS

In **Chapter 1,** we stated that a *placebo* is a "pretend" treatment used to explore the effectiveness of a "true" treatment. The *placebo effect* is the tendency to feel better if we believe we are being treated with a medication. Expectations about getting better can change treatment outcomes.

antidepressant drugs Psychotropic medications used for the treatment of depression.

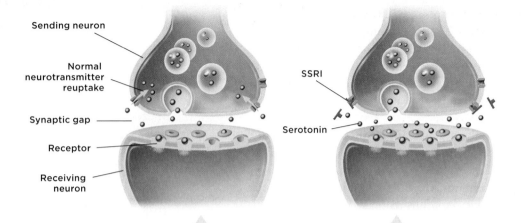

Sending neuron

Normal neurotransmitter reuptake

Synaptic gap

Receptor

Receiving neuron

SSRI

Serotonin

CHEMICAL:
Psychotropic Medications

Drug therapies, which alter the brain's chemistry, are the most commonly prescribed biomedical treatment. Each works to influence neurotransmitters thought to be associated with the disorders the drugs are designed to treat. This illustration shows the action of a class of antidepressants known as selective serotonin reuptake inhibitors (SSRIs).

In normal communication between neurons, neurotransmitters released into the synaptic gap bind to the receiving neuron, sending a message. Excess neurotransmitters are reabsorbed.

As indicated by their name, SSRIs inhibit the reuptake of the neurotransmitter serotonin. Allowed to remain longer in the synapse, serotonin can achieve a greater effect.

Biomedical Therapies

Biomedical therapies use physical interventions to treat psychological disorders. These therapies can be categorized according to the method by which they influence the brain's functioning: chemical, electrical, or structural.

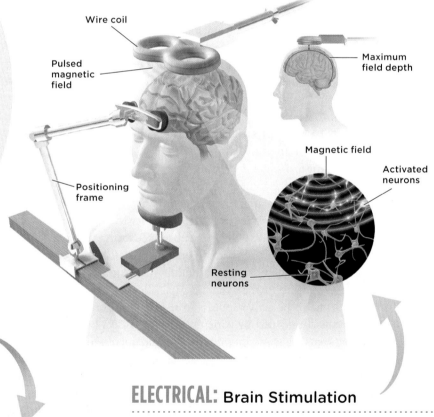

Wire coil

Pulsed magnetic field

Maximum field depth

Magnetic field

Activated neurons

Positioning frame

Resting neurons

STRUCTURAL: Neurosurgery

Modern surgical techniques are able to target a very precise area of the brain known to be directly involved in the condition being treated. For example, the black circles on these scans mark areas typically targeted for a form of surgery known as anterior cingulotomy, which has been shown to reduce symptoms in patients suffering severe cases of major depression (Steele, Christmas, Elijamel, & Matthews, 2008). Using radio frequencies emitted from a 6-millimeter probe, the surgeon destroys part of the anterior cingulate cortex, an area known to be associated with emotions (Faria, 2013).

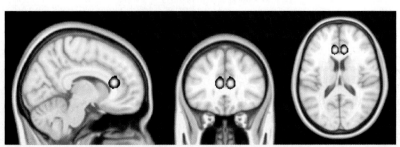

ELECTRICAL: Brain Stimulation

Brain stimulation techniques can be used to relieve symptoms by affecting the electrical activity of the brain. Research on electroconvulsive therapy found an 86% remission rate for those with severe major depression (Kellner et al., 2006). Repetitive transcranial magnetic stimulation (rTMS), shown here, is a noninvasive procedure. A coil pulses a magnetic field that passes painlessly through scalp and bone, penetrating just to the outer cortex. The field induces electric current in nearby neurons, activating targeted regions in the brain (George, 2003).

Credits: Illustration, Graphic by Bryan Christie Design (George, 2003, p. 69); Brain Scans Reprinted by permission from Macmillan Publishers Ltd: Tractographic analysis of historical lesion surgery for depression. Schoene-Bake JC, Coenen et al., *Neuropsychopharmacology*. 2010 December; 35(13): 2553-2563

MOOD-STABILIZING DRUGS   In Chapter 12, we introduced Ross Szabo, a man who suffers from bipolar disorder. Ross has battled extreme mood swings in his life—the highest highs and the lowest lows. Many people suffering from bipolar disorder find some degree of relief in **mood-stabilizing drugs,** which can minimize the lows of depression and the highs of mania. Lithium, for instance, helps smooth the mood swings of people with bipolar disorder, leveling out the dramatic peaks (mania) and valleys (depression). For this reason, it is sometimes called a "mood normalizer" (Bech, 2006) and has been widely used to treat bipolar disorder for decades. Unlike standard drugs that chemists cobble together in laboratories, lithium is a mineral salt, in other words, a naturally occurring substance. (You can find lithium in the Periodic Table of the Elements—just look for the symbol Li.)

Scientists have yet to determine the cause of bipolar disorder and how its symptoms might be lessened with lithium. But numerous theories exist, some pointing to imbalances in neurotransmitters such as glutamate and serotonin (Cho et al., 2005; Dixon & Hokin, 1998). Lithium also seems to be effective in lowering suicide risk among people with bipolar disorder (Angst, Angst, Gerber-Werder, & Gamma, 2005), who are 20 times more likely than people in the general population to die by suicide (Tondo, Isacsson, & Baldessarini, 2003). Doctors must be very careful when prescribing lithium, monitoring the blood levels of patients who use it. Too small a dose will fall short of controlling bipolar symptoms, whereas one that is too large can be lethal. Even when the amount is just right, mild side effects such as hand tremors, thirst, and nausea may occur (National Institute of Mental Health, 2007).

Anticonvulsant medications are also used to treat bipolar disorder. They were originally created to alleviate symptoms of seizure disorders, but scientists discovered they might also be used as mood stabilizers, and some research suggests that they can reduce the symptoms of mania (Bowden et al., 2000). Unfortunately, certain anticonvulsants may increase the risk of suicide or of possible suicide masked as violent death through injury or accident (Patorno et al., 2010). For this reason, the U.S. Food and Drug Administration (FDA, 2008) requires drug companies to place warnings on their labels.

ANTIPSYCHOTIC DRUGS   The hallucinations and delusions of people with disorders like schizophrenia can be subdued with antipsychotics. **Antipsychotic drugs** are designed to block neurotransmitter receptors. Although it is not entirely clear how neurotransmitter activity causes the symptoms of schizophrenia, blocking these receptor sites reduces the firing of neurons presumably associated with psychotic symptoms.

Two kinds of medications can be used in these cases: *traditional antipsychotic medications* and *atypical antipsychotics* (each with about a half-dozen generic drug offshoots). Both types seek to reduce dopamine activity in certain areas of the brain, as abnormal activity of this neurotransmitter is believed to contribute to the psychotic symptoms of schizophrenia and other disorders (Schnider, Guggisberg, Nahum, Gabriel, & Morand, 2010). Antipsychotics accomplish this by acting as dopamine antagonists, meaning they "pose" as dopamine, binding to receptors normally reserved for dopamine (sort of like stealing someone's parking space). By blocking dopamine's receptors, antipsychotic drugs reduce dopamine's excitatory effect on neurons. The main difference between atypical antipsychotics and the traditional variety is that the atypical antipsychotics *also* interfere with neural pathways involving other neurotransmitters, such as serotonin (associated with psychotic symptoms as well).

First rolled out in the 1950s, traditional antipsychotics, such as Haldol, made it possible for scores of people to transition out of psychiatric institutions and into society. These new drugs reduced hallucinations and delusions for many patients, but doctors soon realized that they had other, not-so-desirable effects. After taking the

Synonyms
mood-stabilizing drugs antimanic drugs
traditional antipsychotic medications first-generation antipsychotic medications, typical antipsychotic medications
atypical antipsychotics second-generation antipsychotic medications

CONNECTIONS

In **Chapter 2,** we described how drugs influence behavior by changing what is happening in the synapse. *Agonists* increase the normal activity of a neurotransmitter, and *antagonists* block normal neurotransmitter activity. Here we see how psychotropic medications alter activity in the synapse.

mood-stabilizing drugs Psychotropic medications that minimize the lows of depression and the highs of mania.

antipsychotic drugs Psychotropic medication used in the treatment of psychotic symptoms, such as hallucinations and delusions.

drugs for about a year, some patients developed a neurological condition called *tardive dyskinesia*, the symptoms of which include shaking, restlessness, and bizarre grimaces.

These problems were partially solved with the development of the atypical antipsychotics, such as Risperdal (risperidone), which reduce psychotic symptoms and usually do not cause tardive dyskinesia (Correll, Leucht, & Kane, 2004). But there are other potential side effects, such as weight gain, increased risk for Type 2 diabetes, sexual dysfunction, and heart disease (Üçok & Gaebel, 2008). And although these drugs reduce the symptoms in 60–85% of patients, they are not a cure for the disorder.

Community in Pain

Teenagers Ariel Farmer (left), Kyla Sharp Butte, and Will Sharp Butte relax at a gas station on the Rosebud Indian Reservation. This photo appeared in a 2007 *New York Times* article about the shocking rates of suicide among reservation youth (Nieves, 2007, June 9). Suicides, homicides, and alcohol-related accidents continue to be a major problem on Rosebud, where the average male life expectancy is just 47 years (White, 2013, April 22). Kevin Moloney/The New York Times/Redux

CONNECTIONS

In **Chapter 4,** we discussed psychoactive drugs. *Physiological* dependence can occur with constant use of some drugs, indicated by tolerance and withdrawal symptoms. *Psychological* dependence is apparent when a strong desire or need to continue using a substance occurs, but without tolerance or withdrawal symptoms.

ANTIANXIETY DRUGS Anxiety disorders are the second most common class of conditions Dr. Foster encounters on the reservation. Like many impoverished areas, Rosebud has a high rate of trauma (for example, alcohol-associated accidents and homicides). In the United States, the suicide rate among American Indian and Alaska Native youth (ages 10 to 24) exceeds that of all other racial groups. Youth suicides have increased substantially over the last two decades (Dorgan, 2010). Researchers have tried to untangle the complex web of factors responsible for the deeply troubling statistics, but few would question its connection to the centuries of psychological and cultural damage wrought by colonization and ongoing marginalization and discrimination. Traumatic incidents like suicides inevitably have witnesses, and those witnesses suffer from what they see and hear. Their pain often manifests itself in the form of anxiety.

Antianxiety drugs are used to treat the symptoms of anxiety and anxiety disorders, including panic disorder, social phobia, and generalized anxiety disorder. Most of today's antianxiety medications are *benzodiazepines,* such as Xanax and Ativan, also called "minor tranquilizers." These drugs are used for a continuum of anxiety, from fear of flying to extreme panic attacks. And since they promote sleep in high doses, they can also be used to treat insomnia. Doctors often prescribe benzodiazepines in combination with other psychotropic medications.

Valium is one of the most commonly used minor tranquilizers, and it was the first psychotropic drug to be used by people who were not necessarily suffering from serious disorders. For most of the 1970s, Valium was so popular among white collar businessmen and women that it came to be called "Executive Excedrin." But then people began to realize how dependent they had become on Valium, both physically and psychologically, and its popularity diminished (Barber, 2008). Nevertheless, medications such as Valium and Xanax are still the most commonly abused antianxiety drugs (Phillips, 2013).

A key benefit of benzodiazepines is that they are fast-acting. But they are also dangerously addictive, and mixing them with alcohol can produce a lethal cocktail. Benzodiazepines ease anxiety by enhancing the effect of the neurotransmitter GABA. An inhibitory neurotransmitter, GABA works by decreasing or stopping some neural activity. By giving GABA a boost, these drugs inhibit the firing of neurons that normally induce anxiety reactions.

PSYCHOTROPIC MEDICATION PLUS PSYCHOTHERAPY Psychotropic medications have helped countless people get back on their feet and enjoy life, but many believe that drugs alone don't produce the best long-term outcomes. Ideally, medications should be taken in conjunction with psychotherapy. With therapy, Dr. Foster says, "The person feels greater self-efficacy. They're not relying on a pill to manage depression."

Indeed, studies suggest that psychotropic drugs are most effective when used alongside psychotherapy. Researchers have shown that combining medication with an integrative approach to psychotherapy, including cognitive, behavioral, and psychodynamic perspectives, reduces major depressive symptoms faster than either approach alone (Manber et al., 2008).

Another key point to remember: Medications affect people in different ways. An antidepressant that works for one person may have no effect on another; this is also the case for side effects. We metabolize (break down) drugs at different rates, which means dosages must be assessed on a case-by-case basis. To complicate matters further, many people take multiple medications at once, and some drugs interact in harmful ways.

When Drugs Aren't Enough: The Other Biomedical Therapies

As you may already realize, psychotropic drugs are not a cure-all. Sometimes symptoms of psychological disorders do not improve with medication. In these extreme cases, there are other biomedical options. For example, repetitive transcranial magnetic stimulation (rTMS) appears to be effective in treating symptoms of depression and some types of hallucinations. With rTMS, electromagnetic coils are put on (or above) a person's head, directing brief electrical current into a particular area of the brain (Slotema, Blom, Hoek, & Sommer, 2010). Another technique under investigation is deep brain stimulation, which involves implanting a device that supplies weak electrical stimulation to specific areas of the brain thought to be linked to depression (Kennedy et al., 2011; Schlaepfer, Bewernick, Kayser, Mädler, & Coenen, 2013). These technologies show great promise, but more research is required to determine their long-term impact.

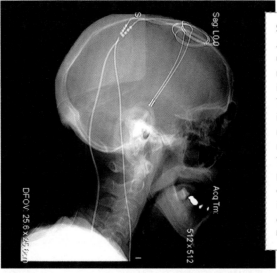

Stimulate the Brain
An X-ray image of a person undergoing deep brain stimulation reveals two electrodes—one implanted in each hemisphere. These electrodes send electrical impulses through certain neural networks, inducing changes that may lead to reduced symptoms. This treatment has produced promising results in patients with depression, but further research is needed to identify its long-term effects (Kennedy et al., 2011). Medical Body Scans/Science Source

ELECTROCONVULSIVE THERAPY   One biomedical approach that essentially causes seizures in the brain is **electroconvulsive therapy (ECT),** which is used with severely depressed people who have not responded to psychotropic medications or psychotherapy. If you've ever seen ECT, or "shock therapy," portrayed in movies, you might think it's a barbaric form of abuse. Truth be told, ECT was a brutal and overly used treatment in the mid-20th century (Glass, 2001; Smith, 2001). Doctors jolted patients (in some cases a dozen times a day) with powerful currents, creating seizures violent enough to break bones and erase weeks or months of memories (Smith, 2001). Today, ECT is much more humane, administered according to guidelines developed by the American Psychiatric Association (2001). Patients take painkillers and muscle relaxants before the treatment, and general anesthesia can be used during the procedure. Furthermore, the electrical currents are weaker, inducing seizures only in the brain. Patients in the United States typically get three treatments per week for up to a month (Glass, 2001).

antianxiety drugs Psychotropic medications used for treating the symptoms of anxiety.

electroconvulsive therapy (ECT) A biomedical treatment of severe depression that induces seizures in the brain through electrical currents.

Scientists don't know exactly how ECT reduces the symptoms of depression, although a variety of theories have been proposed (Cyrzyk, 2013). And despite its enduring "bad rap," ECT can be an effective treatment for depression, bipolar disorder, and schizophrenia in people who haven't responded well to psychotherapy or drugs (Baker, 2009, January 8; Glass, 2001). Yet in the United States, the number of patients admitted to a hospital for ECT treatment in 2009 was 7.2 per 100,000 adults, which represented a substantial decline over the years (Case et al., 2013). The major downside of ECT is its tendency to induce confusion and memory loss, including anterograde and retrograde amnesias (American Psychiatric Association, 2001; Fink & Taylor, 2007; Read & Bentall, 2010).

NEUROSURGERY One extreme option for patients who don't show substantial improvement with psychotherapy or psychotropic drugs is **neurosurgery,** which destroys some portion of the brain or connections between different areas of the brain. Like ECT, neurosurgery is tarnished by an unethical past. During the 1930s, 1940s, and 1950s, doctors performed *prefrontal lobotomies,* destroying part of the frontal lobes or disconnecting them from lower areas of the brain (Kucharski, 1984). But lobotomies can lead to severe side effects, including permanent impairments to everyday functioning. In the past, this procedure had no precision, often resulting in personality changes and diminished function. The consequences of lobotomy were often worse than the disorders they aimed to fix. The popularity of this surgery plummeted in the 1950s when the first-generation antipsychotics were introduced, offering a safer alternative to psychosurgery (Mashour, Walker, & Martuza, 2005).

Brain surgeries are only used to treat psychological disorders as a last resort, and they are far more precise than the archaic lobotomy. Surgeons home in on a small target, destroying only tiny tracts of tissue. One of these surgeries has been a lifesaver for a select few suffering from a severe, drug-resistant form of obsessive-compulsive disorder (OCD), but the precise effects have yet to be determined (Mashour et al., 2005). People suffering from severe seizure disorders sometimes undergo split-brain operations—the surgical separation of the right and left hemispheres. With the corpus callosum severed, the two hemispheres are disconnected, preventing the spread of electrical storms responsible for seizures. These more invasive biomedical therapies are seldom used, but they can make a difference in the quality of life for some individuals.

TAKING STOCK: AN APPRAISAL OF BIOMEDICAL THERAPY Medications and other biomedical treatments can reduce the symptoms of major psychological disorders. In fact, psychotropic drugs work so well that their introduction led to the deinstitutionalization of thousands of people. But it would be a mistake to think of these biological interventions as a cure-all, as this deemphasizes the importance of the other two components of the biopsychosocial model: psychological and social factors. Furthermore, research on the long-term outcomes of many of these treatments remains inconclusive.

CONNECTIONS

In **Chapter 6,** we discussed *amnesia,* which is memory loss resulting from physical or psychological conditions. *Retrograde* amnesia is the inability to access old memories; *anterograde* amnesia is the inability to make new memories. ECT can cause these types of amnesia, which is one reason the American Psychiatric Association developed guidelines for its use (2001).

Synonyms
neurosurgery psychosurgery, brain surgery

CONNECTIONS

In **Chapter 2,** we discussed the use of the *split-brain operation* to treat drug-resistant seizures. When the hemispheres are disconnected, researchers can study them separately to explore their unique capabilities. People who undergo this operation have fewer seizures, and can have normal cognitive abilities and no obvious changes in temperament or personality traits.

> **neurosurgery** A biomedical therapy that involves the destruction of some portion of the brain or connections between different areas of the brain.

 show what you know

1. A young man is taking psychotropic medications for major depression, but the drugs do not seem to be alleviating his symptoms. Which of the following biomedical approaches might his psychiatrist try next?
   a. split-brain operation
   b. tardive dyskinesia
   c. prefrontal lobotomy
   d. electroconvulsive therapy

2. Psychotropic drugs can be divided into four categories, including mood-stabilizing, antipsychotic, antianxiety, and:
   a. mood normalizers.
   b. antidepressants.
   c. antagonists.
   d. atypical antipsychotics.

3. How do biomedical interventions differ from psychotherapy? Compare their goals.

✓ CHECK YOUR ANSWERS IN APPENDIX C.

Psychotherapy: Who's in the Mix?

LO 9 Describe how culture interacts with the therapy process.

WHEN TO LISTEN, WHEN TO TALK One of the challenges of providing therapy in a country like the United States, where ethnic minorities comprise over a third of the population (Yen, 2012, May 17), is meeting the needs of clients from vastly different cultures. A therapist living in a diverse city like San Francisco or Houston may serve clients from multiple cultures in a single week, and each of those cultures has its own set of social norms dictating when to be quiet, when to speak, and how to express oneself.

For Dr. Foster, this part of the job is relatively straightforward. All his clients are Northern Plains Indians, which means they follow similar social rules. And because Dr. Foster belongs to this culture, its norms are second nature to him. He has come to expect, for example, that a young Lakota client will not begin talking until he, the therapist, has spoken first. Dr. Foster is an elder, and elders are shown deference. Thus, to make a younger client feel more comfortable, he might begin a session by talking for 3 or 4 minutes. Once the client does open up, he limits his verbal and nonverbal feedback, sitting quietly and avoiding eye contact. In mainstream American culture, people continuously respond to each other with facial animation and filler words like "wow" and "uh-huh," but the Lakota find this ongoing feedback intrusive. "I might even shut my eyes so they're not feeling influenced by my responses," Dr. Foster says. "I'm not going to respond to what they're telling me, out of respect to their story."

Another facet of Lakota communication—one that often eludes therapists from outside the culture—is the tendency to pause for long periods in the middle of a conversation. If Dr. Foster poses the question, "How are you doing?" a client might take 20 to 30 seconds to respond. "They are not going to answer me on a superficial social level," he explains. "They're going to go inside"—meaning really take the time to consider the question and formulate an answer. These long pauses make some non-Indians very uncomfortable, according to Dr. Foster. "I've found that an outside provider will feel awkward, will start talking within 3 to 5 seconds," he adds. "The client will feel that they never have a chance to speak, and they'll leave frustrated because the person wouldn't be quiet [and] listen." 📁

across the WORLD

Culture Conscious
A Canadian psychologist talks with residents of a displaced persons camp in Port-au-Prince, Haiti. This photo was taken in December 2010, about a year after the country suffered a devastating earthquake. Psychologists must always be mindful of cultural factors that may come into play during therapy. AP Photo/ The Canadian Press, Paul Chiasson

Know Thy Client

Clearly, it is important for a therapist to know the cultural context in which he works. But does that mean therapists and clients should be matched according to race, ethnicity, or gender? Some clients feel more comfortable discussing private thoughts and feelings with a therapist who shares their experience— someone who knows firsthand how it feels to be, say, a Mexican American woman or a Japanese American man. A study in Los Angeles County found that non-English-speaking Mexican and Asian Americans were more likely to stick with and benefit from therapy when matched with a therapist of the same ethnicity and native language (Sue, Fujino, Hu, Takeuchi, & Zane, 1991). Working with a therapist of the same background may be helpful, but it is not essential.

When the therapist and client do come from different worlds, it is the therapist's job to get in touch with the client's unique perspective. That includes being respectful of cultural norms. Western therapists working in India or sub-Saharan

Africa, for example, may find that clients are unfamiliar with psychotherapy and reluctant to discuss personal matters (Bolton et al., 2007; Manickam, 2010). Therapists must also be sensitive to the many forms of prejudice and discrimination that people can experience.

Within any group, there is vast variation from one individual to the next, but cultural themes do emerge. The Sioux and Blackfeet Indians, for example, are very relationship-oriented. "What kind of car you drive or how nice your home is, and so forth, is not even important," Dr. Foster says. "Relationships matter." Some therapists working with American Indian groups report that entire families may show up at sessions to express support for the client (Prochaska & Norcross, 2014). Similarly, Latino cultures place a high value on family, often prioritizing relationships with relatives over individual needs (Comas-Diaz, 2006). These groups tend to be more collectivist, or community-minded, whereas European American cultures tend to place a high premium on individualism (Oyserman, Coon, & Kemmelmeier, 2002).

SHOULD THERAPISTS AND CLIENTS BE MATCHED IN TERMS OF RACE, ETHNICITY, OR GENDER?

Immigrant populations face their own set of challenges. Men often have a difficult time adjusting to the declining social status and income that comes with moving to a new country. Women tend to fare better, adapting to the new culture and finding jobs more quickly, which can lead to tension between spouses (Prochaska & Norcross, 2014). Keep in mind that these are only general trends; assuming they apply to an entire population promotes stereotyping.

This brings us to one of the key themes of the chapter: When it comes to psychological treatment, there is no "one-size-fits-all." Every client has a unique story and a singular set of psychological needs. Responding to the needs of the person—her culture, religious beliefs, and unique personal qualities—is one of the keys to successful therapy (Lakes, Lopez, & Garro, 2006; Norcross & Wampold, 2011).

Let's Get Through This Together

For some people, group therapy is a better fit than individual therapy. First developed in the 1940s, group therapy has adapted to the ever-changing demands of clinical work (Yalom & Leszcz, 2005). Usually, group therapy is led by one or two therapists trained in any of the various approaches (such as psychoanalytic or cognitive). Sessions can include as few as 3 clients, or up to 10 or more. There are groups to help people cope with shyness, panic disorder, chronic pain, compulsive gambling, divorce, grief, and sexual identity issues, to name just a few. These group settings often provide clients with the valuable realization that they are not alone in their struggles to improve. It is not always a psychological disorder that brings people to group therapy, but instead a desire to work on a specific issue.

You Asked, Dr. Foster Answers

http://qrs.ly/f24qsh7

What are the risks if a psychologist fails to pay appropriate attention to both therapy methods *and* cultural traditions?

Finding Strength in Others
Self-help groups provide valuable support for people facing similar struggles, but they usually are not led by mental health professionals. Steve Debenport/Getty Images/iStockphoto

LO 10 Identify the benefits and challenges of group therapy.

GROUP THERAPY In a group therapy session, members share their problems as openly as possible, and research typically shows that group therapy is as effective as individual therapy for addressing many problems. It is actually the preferred approach for interpersonal issues, because it allows therapists to observe clients interacting with others. The therapist's skills play an important role in the success of group sessions, and the dynamics between clients and therapists may be similar to those that arise in individual therapy. (Clients may demonstrate resistance or transference, for example.)

SELF-HELP GROUPS* Groups that provide an opportunity for personal growth are called *self-help groups*. Among the most commonly known are Alcoholics Anonymous (AA), Al-Anon, Parents without Partners, and Weight Watchers. Members of self-help groups provide support to each other while facing bereavement, divorce, infertility, HIV/AIDS, cancer, and other issues. Typically, sessions are *not* run by a psychiatrist, licensed psychologist, or other mental health professional, but by a mental health advisor or *paraprofessional* trained to run the groups. The typical AA leader, for example, is a "recovering alcoholic" who grasps the complexities of alcoholism and recovery, but is not necessarily a mental health professional.

FAMILY THERAPY Introduced in North America in the 1940s, **family therapy** focuses on the family as an *integrated system*, recognizing that the interactions within it can create instability or lead to the breakdown of the family unit (Corey, 2013). Family therapy explores relationship problems rather than the symptoms of particular disorders, teaching communication skills in the process. The family is viewed as a dynamic, holistic entity, and the goal is to understand each person's role in the system, *not* to root out troublemakers, assign blame, or identify one member who must be "fixed." Because families typically seek the resolution of a specific problem, the course of therapy tends to be brief (Corey, 2013). Suppose a teenage girl has become withdrawn at home and is acting out in school, and the whole family decides to participate in therapy. The therapist begins by helping the parents identify ways they encourage her behaviors (not following through with consequences, for example), and may examine how their marital dynamics affect the kids. If it becomes evident that the marriage is in trouble, the parents might seek therapy without the rest of the family, which brings us to the next topic: couples therapy.

COUPLES THERAPY Let's face it, most couples have issues. High on the list are conflicts about money ("You are so stingy!"), failures to communicate ("You never listen!"), languishing physical bonds ("No dear, not tonight"), children, and jealousy (Storaasli & Markman, 1990). But when these problems begin to cause significant distress, *couples therapy* is a smart choice. Couples therapists are trained in many of the therapeutic approaches described earlier, and they tend to focus on conflict management and communication. One goal of couples therapy and relationship education programs is to provide guidance on how to communicate within relationships (Scott, Rhoades, Stanley, Allen, & Markman, 2013).

Couples therapy can yield positive results for many couples—they stay together, and feel more satisfied with the relationship—but some seem to benefit more than others. This is especially true for those who are committed to saving their relationships (Greenberg, Warwar, & Malcolm, 2010). Partners are less likely to benefit from couples therapy if they are emotionally disconnected, struggle with communication,

Synonyms
self-help groups mutual help groups, support groups
family therapy family counseling
couples therapy marital therapy

family therapy A type of therapy that focuses on the family as an integrated system, recognizing that the interactions within it can create instability or lead to the breakdown of the family unit.

---

*You can learn more about self-help groups in your area from The National Mental Health Consumers' Self-Help Clearinghouse, at http://www.mhselfhelp.org.

and tend to avoid conflict (Jacobson & Addis, 1993). Those who participate in relationship education programs prior to marriage may be better off as well, as these may help couples identify some of the situations that could lead to divorce, including a spouse being unfaithful, problems with aggression, and substance abuse.

TAKING STOCK: AN APPRAISAL OF GROUP, FAMILY, AND COUPLES THERAPY
Like any treatment, group therapy has its strengths and limitations (**Table 13.3**). Group members may not get along, or they may feel uncomfortable discussing sensitive issues. But conflict and discomfort are not necessarily bad when it comes to therapy (group or otherwise), because such feelings often motivate people to reevaluate how they interact with others, and perhaps try new approaches.

Evaluating group therapies can be difficult because there is so much variation in approaches (psychodynamic, cognitive behavioral, and so on). However, strong evidence exists that couples and marital therapy are effective for treating a wide range of problems (Shadish & Baldwin, 2003). The outcomes for group therapy rival those of individual therapy for many types of clients and problems (Burlingame & Baldwin, 2011; Yalom & Leszcz, 2005). As with individual therapies, the role of the group therapist is of critical importance: Empathy, good facilitation skills, listening, and careful observation are important predictors of successful outcomes. So, too, are the preparation of the group members, the therapist's verbal style, and the "climate" and cohesion of the group (Burlingame & Baldwin, 2011).

TABLE 13.3 BENEFITS AND DRAWBACKS OF GROUP THERAPY	
Strengths of Group Therapy	**Weaknesses of Group Therapy**
Sessions generally cost about half as much as individual therapy (Helliker, 2009, March 24).	Not everyone feels at ease discussing personal troubles in a room full of people.
People find relief and comfort knowing that others face similar struggles.	Group members may not always get along. This friction can inhibit the therapeutic process.
Group members offer support and encouragement. They also challenge one another to think and behave in new ways.	Groups may have members who show resistance to group therapy, resulting in poor attendance, tardiness, or dropouts (Yalom & Leszcz, 2005).
Seeing others improve offers hope and inspiration.	Some group therapy participants have had negative family experiences, and thus have negative expectations of the group setting (Yalom & Leszcz, 2005).

Listed above are some of the pros and cons of group therapy.

Does Psychotherapy Work?

LO 11 Evaluate the effectiveness of psychotherapy.

Now that we have familiarized ourselves with the strengths and weaknesses of various therapeutic approaches, let's direct our attention to overall outcomes. How effective is psychotherapy in general? This question is not easily answered, partly because therapeutic "success" is so difficult to quantify. What constitutes success in one therapy context may not be the same in another. And for therapists trying to measure the efficacy of methods they use, eliminating bias can be very challenging.

That being said, there is solid evidence suggesting that therapy usually "works," especially if it is long-term. In one large study investigating the effects of psychotherapy, all therapeutic approaches performed equally well across all disorders. But there is one caveat: Individuals who were limited by their insurance companies in terms of therapist choice and duration of treatment did not see the same improvement as those who were less restricted by their insurance (Seligman, 1995). Similarly, people who start therapy but then quit prematurely tend to experience less successful outcomes (Swift & Greenberg, 2012). Around 50% of clients show "clinically significant improvement" after 21 psychotherapy sessions, whereas some 75% show the same degree of improvement after twice that many sessions (Lambert, Hansen, & Finch, 2001). Given the many types of therapeutic approaches, the uniqueness of the client, and the variety of therapists, it is challenging to identify an approach that works best for every client (Pope & Wedding, 2014). But we can say this with relative confidence: Psychotherapy is "cost-effective, reduces disability, morbidity, and mortality, improves work functioning, decreases the use of psychiatric hospitalization, and . . . leads to reduction in unnecessary use of medical and surgical services" (American Psychological Association [APA], 2012b, para. 19).

Victoria Roberts The New Yorker Collection/The Cartoon Bank

Apply This

I Think I Need Help: What Should I Do?

If you suspect you or someone you care about is suffering from a psychological disorder or needs support coping with a divorce, death, or major life change, do not hesitate to seek professional help. The first step is figuring out what kind of therapy fits best for the person and the situation (individual, family, group, and so on). Then there is the issue of cost: Therapy can be expensive. These days, one 60-minute therapy session can cost anywhere from $80 to $250 (or more, believe it or not). If you attend a college or university, however, your student fees may cover services at a student counseling center.

Many people have health insurance that helps pay for medication and psychotherapy. In 2010 the Mental Health Parity and Addiction Equity Act (MHPAEA) took effect, requiring all group health insurance plans (with 50 employees or more) to provide mental health treatment benefits as part of their plan—with benefits equal to those provided for medical treatment. Essentially, this means that mental health problems merit the same treatment benefits as physical health problems. Co-payments must be the same, limits on treatment must be the same, and so on. If your insurance plan does not restrict the number of times you can see your family physician, it also cannot limit the number of visits you have with a psychologist (APA, 2010a). For those without insurance, community-based mental health centers provide quality care to all in need, often with a sliding scale for fees.

The next step is finding the right therapist, that is, the right *qualified* therapist. Helping others manage their mental health issues is a tremendous responsibility that only licensed professionals should take on. But who exactly meets the criteria for a "qualified professional"? It depends on where you live. Different states have different licensing requirements, and because these requirements vary from state to state, we encourage you to verify the standing of a therapist's license with your state's Department of Regulatory Agencies. The pool of potential therapists might include clinical psychologists with PhDs or PsyDs, counseling psychologists, individuals with EdDs, psychiatrists, psychiatric nurses, social workers, marriage and family therapists, pastoral counselors, and more. (See Appendix B for more information about education and careers in psychology.) If you don't seek psychological help from a trained and certified professional in person, you should be very cautious about seeking assistance online. ➤

Nonstandard Treatment: Self-Help and E-Therapy

Type "psychology" or "self-help" into the search engine of Amazon.com, and you will come across thousands of books promising to eliminate your stress, boost your self-esteem, and help you beat depression. Although some self-help books contain valuable information, others are packed with claims that have little or no scientific basis. Keep an open mind, but approach these resources with skepticism, especially when it comes to the research that authors cite. As you have learned, determining the effect of therapy is a difficult business, even when studies are impeccably designed. Reader beware.

LO 12   Summarize the strengths and weaknesses of online psychotherapy.

With more people gaining access to the Internet and more therapists trying to specialize and make themselves marketable, online therapies are multiplying. A relative newcomer to the treatment world, **e-therapy** can mean anything from e-mail communication between client and therapist to real-time sessions via a webcam. Some approaches include a hybrid version of online and face-to-face sessions, whereas others offer virtual support through chat rooms. These digital tools are valuable for serving rural areas and providing services to those who would otherwise have no access. Videoconferencing is a useful supplement to regular therapy, particularly for consultation and supervision. But online psychotherapy and telehealth raise many concerns, including licensing and privacy issues, problems with nonverbal cues, and difficulty developing therapeutic relationships (Barak, Hen, Boniel-Nissim, & Shapira, 2008; Maheu, Pulier, McMenamin, & Posen, 2012; Sucala et al., 2012).

While we are on the topic of the Internet, we cannot resist a tie-in to social media. What role do Facebook, LinkedIn, and other types of social media play in the lives of therapists and their clients?

Let's Skype It Out
Mental health nurse practitioner Cassandra Donlon chats with a client via computer at the Roseburg, Oregon, Veterans Affairs Medical Center. With online technologies such as Skype and Google Hangouts, therapists can conduct sessions with clients on the opposite side of the globe.
Sandy Huffaker/The New York Times/Redux

SOCIAL MEDIA and psychology

Therapist or Friend?

Imagine that you are the psychotherapist serving a small community college. You talk to students about their deepest fears and conflicts. They tell you about their mothers, fathers, lovers, and foes. In some respects, you know these students better than their closest friends do. But your clients are not your buddies. They are your clients. So what do you say when a client asks you to become a friend on Facebook, a contact on LinkedIn, or a follower on Instagram?

e-therapy A category of treatment that utilizes the Internet to provide support and therapy.

Our answer to that question is a definitive no. The relationship between therapist and client should remain a professional one, both online and offline. But that doesn't mean that social media have no place in the mental health field. Psychologists are among the many professionals using social media to connect with colleagues and market their services to potential clients. They may be avid Twitter users, tweeting their latest musings about current events and everyday life. Social media may even come in handy for therapy itself, as when a client with public speaking anxiety shows his therapist a video of himself giving a speech (Kolmes, 2012, December).

But along with new opportunities come new risks. Psychologists who use social media to communicate with colleagues, for instance, may inadvertently compromise confidentiality in seeking advice about how to tailor therapy for a particular client. (As you well know, what's said online stays online.) Others may go online to investigate clients' statements about themselves (*He claims to have 400 Facebook friends; let me just take a peek and confirm;* Kolmes, 2012, December).

DOES FACEBOOK HAVE A PLACE IN THERAPY?

As you can see, the emergence of social media presents new challenges and new opportunities for therapists. This is an area in which we would like to see more research. Stay tuned. . . . 🗨

PASSIONATE PROVIDERS   Before wrapping up, we thought you might like to know what Dr. Dan Foster and Laura Lichti are doing these days. Dr. Foster is as busy as ever, working with one other psychologist and a mental health technician to provide mental health services to Rosebud's 13,000 residents. In addition to working up to 70 hours per week, he and his wife Becky (also a doctorate-level psychologist) have seven adopted children, five of whom are affected by fetal alcohol spectrum disorders (FASDs). Dan doesn't get more than 5 or 6 hours of sleep at night, but he seems to have a limitless supply of energy and optimism.

It's been a time of growth for Laura, who is now working as a behavior therapist for people with intellectual and developmental disabilities. She also opened her own private practice, which focuses on grief counseling for people of all ages, and began teaching psychology at a community college. "I love the variety," Laura says. "It keeps me very busy!" 🗁

Dr. Dan Foster with his wife, Dr. Becky Foster
WHF/Worth Archive

Laura Lichti
Lee Bernhard

●✓●● show what you know

1. A large study in Los Angeles County found that non-English-speaking Asian and Mexican Americans were _____ likely to stick with and benefit from therapy when matched with a therapist of _____ ethnicity and native language.
   a. less; the same
   b. more; the same
   c. more; a different
   d. equally; a different

2. E-therapy is a relatively new approach to helping people with psychological problems or disorders. It varies in terms of how much and what type of contact the "client" has with a "therapist." Concerns regarding online psychotherapy include _____.

3. If you were trying to convince a friend that treatment for psychological disorders works for many groups of people, how would you summarize the effectiveness of psychotherapy? What would you say about the role of culture in its outcome?

4. A single man has had trouble dealing with his coworkers and has not been on a second date in over a year because of his poor interpersonal skills. His therapist decides the best course of treatment is _____, which is led by one or two mental health professionals, involves three or more clients, and allows the therapists to observe the client interacting with others.

5. Under what conditions might group therapy fail or be inappropriate?

✓ CHECK YOUR ANSWERS IN APPENDIX C.

⑬ summary of concepts

LO 1 Outline the history of the treatment of psychological disorders. (p. 518)

One theory suggests that during the Stone Age, trephination, in which holes were drilled through the skull, was done to allow evil spirits to exit the body. In the late 1700s, Philippe Pinel, horrified by the conditions of asylums in Paris, removed the inmates' chains and insisted they be treated more humanely. In the mid to late 1800s, Dorothea Dix supported the "mental hygiene movement," a campaign to reform asylums in America. She helped establish and upgrade many state mental hospitals. Deinstitutionalization in the mid-1900s helped reduce the social isolation of people with psychological disorders, resulting in patients integrating into the community.

LO 2 Discuss how the main approaches to therapy differ and identify their common goal. (p. 520)

Insight therapies include psychoanalysis, psychodynamic therapy, and humanistic therapy, which aim to increase awareness of self and the environment. Behavior therapies focus on behavioral change, with the belief that the key to resolving problems is not understanding their origins, but changing the thoughts and behaviors that precede them. Biomedical therapy targets the biological basis of disorders, often using medications. All these approaches share a common goal: They aim to reduce symptoms and increase the quality of life for individuals, whether they seek help for debilitating psychological disorders or simply want to lead happier lives.

LO 3 Describe how psychoanalysis differs from psychodynamic therapy. (p. 521)

Psychoanalysis, the first formal system of psychotherapy, attempts to uncover unconscious conflicts, making it possible to address and work through them. Psychodynamic therapy is an updated form of psychoanalysis; it incorporates many of Freud's core themes, including the notion that personality characteristics and behavior problems often can be traced to unconscious conflicts. With psychodynamic therapy, therapists see clients once a week for several months rather than many times a week for years. And instead of sitting quietly off to the side, therapists sit facing clients and engage in a two-way dialogue.

LO 4 Outline the principles and characteristics of humanistic therapy. (p. 524)

Humanistic therapy concentrates on the positive aspects of human nature: our powerful desires to form close relationships, treat others with warmth and empathy, and grow as individuals. Humanistic therapists concentrate on current problems and the everyday factors that may contribute to them. Instead of digging up unconscious thoughts and feelings, humanistic therapy emphasizes conscious experience.

LO 5   Describe person-centered therapy. (p. 525)

Person-centered therapy focuses on achieving one's full potential. The focus is not therapeutic techniques, but rather creating a warm and accepting client–therapist relationship using a nondirective approach. Sitting face-to-face with the client, the therapist's main job is to "be there" for the client through empathy, unconditional positive regard, genuineness, and active listening, all important components of building a therapeutic alliance. The main goal of treatment is to reduce the incongruence between the ideal self and the real self.

LO 6   Outline the principles and characteristics of behavior therapy. (p. 527)

Using the learning principles of classical conditioning, operant conditioning, and observational learning, behavior therapy aims to replace maladaptive behaviors with more adaptive behaviors. It incorporates a variety of techniques, including exposure therapy, aversion therapy, systematic desensitization, and behavior modification. Behavior therapy covers a broad range of treatment approaches, and focuses on observable behaviors in the present.

LO 7   Outline the principles and characteristics of cognitive therapy. (p. 531)

The goal of cognitive therapy is to identify maladaptive thinking and help individuals change the way they view the world and relationships. Aaron Beck believed patterns of automatic thoughts and cognitive distortions, such as overgeneralization (thinking that self-contained events will have major repercussions in life), are at the root of psychological disturbances. The aim of cognitive therapy is to help clients recognize and challenge cognitive distortions and illogical thought in short-term, action-oriented, and homework-intensive therapy sessions. Albert Ellis created rational-emotive behavior therapy (REBT), another form of cognitive therapy, to help people identify their irrational or illogical thoughts and convert them into rational ones.

LO 8   Summarize the biomedical interventions and identify their common goal. (p. 534)

Psychopharmacology is the scientific study of how psychotropic medications alter perception, mood, behavior, and other aspects of psychological functioning. Psychotropic drugs include antidepressant, mood-stabilizing, antipsychotic, and antianxiety medications. When severe symptoms do not improve with medication and psychotherapy, other biomedical options are available: electroconvulsive therapy (ECT), which causes seizures in the brain, for cases of severe depression; and neurosurgery, which destroys some portion of the brain or connections between different areas of the brain, only as a last resort.

The common goal of biomedical interventions is to treat the biological basis of psychological disorders through physical interventions.

LO 9   Describe how culture interacts with the therapy process. (p. 541)

One challenge of providing therapy is to meet the needs of clients from vastly different cultures. Every client has a unique story and a singular set of psychological needs, but therapists should know the cultural context in which they work and be mindful of the client's cultural experience. This includes being respectful of cultural norms and sensitive to the many forms of prejudice and discrimination that people can experience. All these personal and cultural factors must be considered in determining which approach will be most effective for a given client.

LO 10   Identify the benefits and challenges of group therapy. (p. 543)

Some of group therapy's benefits include cost-effectiveness, identification with others, accountability, support, encouragement, and a sense of hope. Challenges include potential conflict among group members and discomfort in expressing oneself in the presence of others.

LO 11   Evaluate the effectiveness of psychotherapy. (p. 544)

In general, psychotherapy "works," especially if it is long-term. All approaches perform equally well across all disorders. But individuals who are limited by their insurance companies in terms of their choice of therapists and how long they can attend therapy do not see the same improvement as those who are less restricted by their insurance. In addition, people who start therapy but then quit prematurely experience less successful outcomes. The Mental Health Parity and Addiction Equity Act of 2010 requires group health insurance plans to provide mental health treatment benefits equal to those provided for medical treatment.

LO 12   Summarize the strengths and weaknesses of online psychotherapy. (p. 546)

As more people gain access to the Internet and as more therapists try to specialize and make themselves marketable, online therapies have multiplied. E-therapy can mean anything from an e-mail communication between client and therapist to real-time sessions via a webcam. These digital tools are valuable for serving rural areas and providing services to those who would otherwise have no access. Videoconferencing is useful for consultation and supervision. However, online psychotherapy raises many concerns, including licensing and privacy issues, lack of nonverbal cues, and potential problems with developing therapeutic relationships.

key terms

active listening, p. 526
antianxiety drugs, p. 538
antidepressant drugs, p. 535
antipsychotic drugs, p. 537
aversion therapy, p. 530
behavior modification, p. 530
behavior therapies, p. 520
biomedical therapy, p. 520
cognitive therapy, p. 531
cognitive behavioral therapy,
    p. 533

deinstitutionalization, p. 519
eclectic approach to therapy,
    p. 520
electroconvulsive therapy
    (ECT), p. 539
empathy, p. 526
e-therapy, p. 546
exposure, p. 527
family therapy, p. 543
free association, p. 523
genuineness, p. 526

humanistic therapy, p. 525
insight therapies, p. 520
interpretation, p. 523
mood-stabilizing drugs,
    p. 537
neurosurgery, p. 540
nondirective, p. 526
overgeneralization,
    p. 532
person-centered therapy,
    p. 525

psychodynamic therapy,
    p. 524
psychotherapy, p. 520
rational emotive behavior
    therapy (REBT), p. 533
resistance, p. 523
systematic desensitization,
    p. 528
therapeutic alliance, p. 526
token economy, p. 530
transference, p. 523

TEST PREP are you ready?

1. Which of the following changes did Pinel introduce when he reformed the treatment of individuals with psychological disorders?
   a. reintroduced trephination
   b. reintegrated inmates into society
   c. removed the inmates' chains
   d. built new hospitals for the insane

2. Although most therapies share the common goal of reducing symptoms and increasing quality of life, they do this in various ways. One dimension in which they may differ is theoretical perspective. Psychotherapists who aim to increase awareness of self and the environment tend to use:
   a. biomedical therapy.
   b. behavior therapy.
   c. insight therapy.
   d. deinstitutionalization.

3. Free association and interpretation are used by _____ in their treatment of patients.
   a. psychoanalysts
   b. humanists
   c. behaviorists
   d. cognitive therapists

4. What are some of the weaknesses of Freud's theory?
   a. It is evidence-based.
   b. It is difficult to test through experimentation.
   c. It is client-directed.
   d. It focuses on the present.

5. A friend told you about his therapist, who is nondirective, uses active listening, and shows empathy and unconditional positive regard. It sounds as if your friend's therapist is conducting:
   a. cognitive therapy.
   b. behavior therapy.
   c. psychoanalysis.
   d. person-centered therapy.

6. Systematic desensitization uses _____ that represent(s) a gradual increase in a client's anxiety.
   a. hierarchies
   b. token economies
   c. behavior modification
   d. free association

7. Which of the following statements would not be among Beck's collection of cognitive errors?
   a. My friend stole from me; therefore, everyone will steal from me.
   b. Getting fired once does not mean my career is over.
   c. I forgot to vote; that's why the president lost.
   d. My hairdresser added $20 to my Visa charge. You can't trust salons.

8. The key advantage of behavior therapy is that it:
   a. tends to work quickly.
   b. focuses on changing innate behaviors.
   c. addresses global issues arising from personality disorders.
   d. brings about changes on the inside.

9. Which of the following claims about group therapy is true?
   a. It generally costs twice as much as one-on-one therapy.
   b. Everyone feels comfortable sharing their troubles with a group.
   c. Group members avoid pushing others to own up to their mistakes.
   d. Seeing others improve offers hope and inspiration.

10. The goal of _____ is to understand each family member's unique role in an integrated system, often exploring relationship problems rather than symptoms of particular disorders.
    a. flooding
    b. aversion therapy
    c. systematic desensitization
    d. family therapy

11. _____ therapy emphasizes the positive nature of humans. With a focus on the present, it seeks to identify current problems and emphasizes conscious experience.

   a. Psychoanalytic
   b. Rational emotive behavior
   c. Psychodynamic
   d. Humanistic

12. _____ is the scientific study of how medication alters perceptions, moods, behaviors, and other aspects of psychological functioning.

   a. Biomedical therapy
   b. Psychoeducation
   c. Therapeutic alliance
   d. Psychopharmacology

13. Overall, psychotherapy is cost-effective and helps to decrease disability, hospitalization, and problems at work. Which of the following factors seems to reduce its effectiveness?

   a. unlimited number of sessions
   b. limitations on choice of therapist as mandated by a health insurance policy
   c. number of people in therapy session
   d. gender of therapist

14. Electroconvulsive therapy (ECT) is a technique that essentially causes _____ in the brain.

   a. increased activity of neurotransmitters
   b. tardive dyskinesia
   c. seizures
   d. MAO inhibitors

15. One factor a therapist needs to consider is how _____ may interact with the therapy process: for example, whether a client is from a group that is collectivist or one that values individualism.

   a. culture
   b. biomedical interventions
   c. repression
   d. unconscious conflicts

16. Compare cognitive behavioral therapy to insight therapies.

17. Beck identified a collection of common cognitive distortions. Describe two of these distortions and give examples of each.

18. How would a behavior therapist help someone overcome a fear of spiders?

19. How does culture influence and interact with the therapeutic process?

20. Describe several strengths and weaknesses of online psychotherapy.

✓ CHECK YOUR ANSWERS IN APPENDIX C.

Get personalized practice by logging into LaunchPad at **www.macmillanhighered.com/launchpad/ sciampresenting1e** to take the LearningCurve adaptive quizzes for Chapter 13.

14

UGANDA
359

FRAGILE

cpaquin/Getty Images

pixhook/Getty Images

social psychology

Edward Carlile Portraits/ Getty Images

An Introduction to Social Psychology

LOVE STORY Prior to 2006, Joe Maggio did not have a fulfilling love life. While serving overseas in the military, he had a relationship with a local woman with whom he was not at all compatible. But something beautiful came out of their failed union: a baby girl named Kristina. Joe was awarded full custody, and he returned to Long Island, New York, to begin his life as a single dad. In between work and taking care of his daughter, there was little time for dating. Joe was not the type to frequent bars and nightclubs, and his work as an ice cream truck driver provided few opportunities for meeting other singles. It never seemed to work out with the girlfriends he did manage to date. And as Joe admits, "I had my share of doozies [extraordinarily bad experiences]."

Everything abruptly changed when Susanne entered the picture. Their first face-to-face meeting was at a Chili's restaurant. Joe and Kristina, then 7 years old, were chatting at a table when Susanne appeared. "The minute she walked in the door on our first date, I honestly felt like I was actually waiting for my wife to have dinner with me and my daughter," Joe says. He remembers exactly what she wore and how cute she looked.

Instantly at ease, Susanne sat down and began to talk with Joe and Kristina. "It was just kind of relaxed . . . like we had known each other forever," says Susanne, who at 32 was finished playing games and exploring dead-end relationships. "At this point in my life I was really just looking for somebody that wanted to settle down," she offers. Joe seemed so kind, it was hard to believe he was authentic.

The next morning, Joe called Susanne and invited her for a cup of coffee. "We did not leave the local Starbucks until almost seven, eight hours later," he recalls. During that marathon date, Joe and Susanne shared stories about their families and talked about their hopes and dreams. "I didn't want the day to end," says Joe, who then invited Susanne home and made her a dinner of sautéed pork chops, roasted peppers, and potatoes. "I think I kind of won her heart that night."

Joe and Susanne's initial impressions of one another were right on. They were extremely compatible people with similar backgrounds and family values. Both were big fans of cooking, baseball (the Mets), and spending Friday night curled up on the couch watching a movie. Susanne found it attractive that Joe was a single father. And Joe came to love how Susanne treated Kristina like her own daughter, and how Kristina loved her back. You might say Joe and Susanne were perfectly matched. How did they find one another?

> **Loving Dad**
> Before joining Match.com, Joe Maggio was a single father to daughter Kristina. Dating was a challenge, as most of the women Joe met lacked the qualities he desired. Then, with a few clicks and keystrokes, along came Susanne . . .
> Joseph Maggio

Note: Quotations attributed to Julius Achon and Joe and Susanne Maggio are personal communications.

What Is Social Psychology?

Joe and Susanne did not meet at a church, a library, or a bar. They did not work in the same office, nor were they introduced by mutual friends. Like a growing number of couples, Joe and Susanne first encountered one another online. They met through Match.com, the popular dating Web site.

In just two decades, online dating has gone from being essentially nonexistent to a primary avenue for finding love (**Figure 14.1**). Research suggests that the Internet is the second most common way to connect with a potential partner, the first being an introduction by mutual friends (Finkel, Eastwick, Karney, Reis, & Sprecher, 2012). Joe and Susanne met through one of the mainstream online dating services, but there are also highly specialized sites and mobile apps to accommodate particular interests. Looking for a vegetarian mate? Try VeggieDate.org. Searching for a farmer to love? Visit FarmersOnly.com. There are even digital services designed to match people with the same book preferences and food allergies.

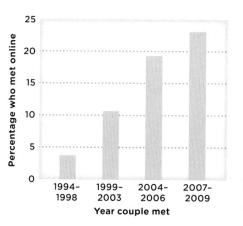

FIGURE 14.1

Nearly 1 in 4 Couples Met Online
In the mid-1990s, only 4% of heterosexual couples in the United States met online. More recently, that number has grown to 23%. Blackwell Publishing/SAGE Publications from Finkel, Eastwick, Karney, Reis, & Sprecher (2012).

Online dating has forever changed the singles' landscape. What other medium allows you to scan and research a database of thousands, if not millions, of potential partners from the comfort of your sofa, or filter potential mates with the ease of a finger swipe? Online dating has also created a new laboratory for psychologists to study the way people's thoughts, emotions, and behaviors are influenced by others. Put differently, it is an emerging topic of research in *social psychology*.

LO 1   Define social psychology and identify how it is different from sociology.

In every chapter of this book, we have touched on issues relevant to social psychology. Chapter 1, for example, tells the story of 33 Chilean miners trapped in a sweltering, underground hole for more than 2 months. How do you think the social interactions among these men influenced their behaviors, thoughts, and feelings? In Chapter 3, we journeyed into the world of Zoe, Emma, and Sophie, identical triplets who are deaf and blind. How might the triplets' social behaviors differ from those of children with normal hearing and vision? Then there was Clive Wearing from Chapter 6. How do you suppose Clive's devastating memory loss affects his relationships? Social psychologists strive to answer these types of questions.

social psychology The study of human cognition, emotion, and behavior in relation to others, including how people behave in social settings.

Social psychology is the study of human cognition, emotion, and behavior in relation to others. Students often ask how social psychology differs from the field of *sociology.* The answer is simple: Social psychology explores the way individuals behave in relation to others and groups, while sociology examines the groups themselves—their cultures, societies, and subcultures. Throughout this text, we have emphasized the importance of the biopsycho*social* perspective, which recognizes the biological, psychological, and social factors underlying human behavior. This chapter focuses on the third aspect of that triad: social forces.

Research Methods in Social Psychology

Social psychologists use the same general research methods as other psychologists, but often with an added twist of deception. Deception is sometimes necessary because people do not always behave naturally when they know they are being observed. Some participants try to conform to expectations; others do just the opposite, behaving in ways they believe will contradict the researchers' predictions. Suppose a team of researchers is studying facial expressions in social settings. If participants know that every glance and grimace is being analyzed, they may feel self-conscious and display atypical facial expressions. Instead of telling participants the real focus of the study, researchers might lead them to believe they are participating in a study on, say, problem solving. That way, they can study the behavior of interest (facial expressions in social settings) more naturally.

Social psychology studies often involve *confederates,* who are people secretly working for the researchers. Playing the role of participants, experimenters, or simply bystanders, confederates say what the researchers tell them to say and do what the researchers tell them to do. They are, unknown to the other participants, just part of the researchers' experimental manipulation.

In most cases, the deception is not kept secret forever. Researchers *debrief* their participants at the end of a study, or review aspects of the research initially kept under wraps. Even after learning they were deceived, many participants report they are willing to take part in subsequent psychology experiments (Blatchley & O'Brien, 2007). Debriefing is also a time when researchers make sure that participants were not harmed or upset by their involvement in a study. We should note that all psychology research affiliated with colleges and universities must be approved by an Institutional Review Board (IRB) to ensure that no harm will come from participation. This requirement is partly a reaction to early studies involving extreme deception and manipulation—studies that many viewed as dehumanizing and unethical. Psychologists agree that deception is only acceptable if there is no other way to study the topic of interest. We will describe many examples of such research in the upcoming pages, but first let's familiarize ourselves with some basic concepts in social psychology.

CONNECTIONS

In **Chapter 1,** we described how participants' and researchers' expectations can influence the results of an experiment. One form of deception used to counter this is the double-blind study, in which neither participants nor researchers administering a treatment know who is getting the real treatment. Participants are told ahead of time they might receive a *placebo.*

CONNECTIONS

In **Chapter 1,** we discussed informed consent and debriefing. *Debriefing* is an ethical component of disclosure in which researchers provide participants with useful information related to the study. In some cases, participants are informed of deception or manipulation they were exposed to in the study—information that couldn't be revealed to them beforehand.

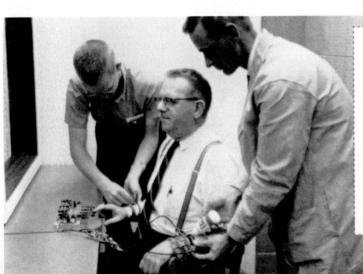

In the Name of Science
A research *confederate* in Stanley Milgram's classic experiment is strapped to a table and hooked up to electrodes. Participants in this study were led to believe they were administering electrical shocks to the confederate when in reality the confederate was just pretending to be shocked. This allowed the researchers to study how far participants would go applying shocks—without anyone actually being hurt. From the film Obedience © 1968 by Stanley Milgram, © renewed 1993 by Alexandra Milgram; and distributed by Alexander Street Press.

show what you know

1. _____ studies individuals in relation to others and groups, whereas _____ studies the groups themselves, including cultures and societies.
   a. Sociology; social psychology
   b. Social psychology; sociology
   c. Sociology; a confederate
   d. A confederate; social psychology

2. When a participant has completed his involvement in a research project, generally the researcher will _____ him by discussing aspects of the study previously kept secret and making sure he was not upset or harmed by his involvement.

3. Social psychology research occasionally involves some form of deception that includes a confederate. How is this type of deception different from the use of double-blind studies?

✓ CHECK YOUR ANSWERS IN APPENDIX C.

CONNECTIONS

In **Chapter 13,** we described *psychoanalysis,* one goal of which is to increase awareness of unconscious conflicts. Here, we discuss how unconscious processes can drive social behaviors. Therapists can help clients become aware of these unconscious influences.

In **Chapter 7,** we defined *cognition* as the mental activity associated with obtaining, storing, converting, and using knowledge. *Thinking* is a specific type of cognition that involves coming to a decision, forming a belief, or developing an attitude. In this section, we examine how cognition and thinking affect the way we use social information.

"Thank God we're cute. You only get one chance to make a good impression."

Emoticon in text: Maxi_m/Shutterstock

Social Cognition

THE DATING GAME Joe and Susanne's story begins right around Valentine's Day 2006, when Joe decided to sign up for a full membership to Match.com. A couple of days after Joe joined the site, Susanne came across his page. "I thought he was cute," she says. "That was obviously the reason why I originally opened it." Joe was a burly guy with a dynamite smile, and Susanne was drawn to big, teddy bear types. Reading his profile, she was immediately intrigued. "The fact that he was a single parent, you know, kind of piqued my interest," she says. Before long, Joe was checking out Susanne's page, liking what he saw, and he initiated the e-mail exchange that ultimately led to that first date at Chili's. 📁

Attributions

LO 2 Describe social cognition and how we use attributions to explain behavior.

Put yourself in Joe or Susanne's position. There you are on Match.com, looking at the profile page of someone you find attractive. On a conscious level, you are tallying up all the interests you have in common and scrutinizing every self-descriptive adjective this person has chosen. There is also some information processing happening outside of your awareness. You might not even realize that this person reminds you of someone you know, like your mother or father, and that sense of familiarity makes you more inclined to reach out. Will you contact this person?

Whatever your decision may be, it is very much reliant on **social cognition**—the way you think about others, attend to social information, and use this information in your life, both consciously and unconsciously. Joe and Susanne used social cognition in forming first impressions of one another. You use social cognition anytime you try to interpret or respond to another person's behavior. Let's take a closer look at two critical facets of social cognition: *attributions* and *attitudes.*

WHAT ARE ATTRIBUTIONS? Joe and Susanne's relationship has always been fairly open, with Joe rarely having to wonder what Susanne is thinking and vice versa. This is usually *not* the case with online dating, or any kind of dating for that matter. The "dating game" typically involves a lot of guesswork about the other person's behavior: *Why didn't he call back? What did she mean by that 😕 yesterday?* These kinds of questions have relevance for all human relationships, not just the romantic kind. Just think about how much time you spend wondering why people do the things that they do. The "answers" you come up with to resolve these questions are called *attributions.*

Attributions are beliefs we develop to explain human behaviors and characteristics, as well as situations. "Why is my friend in such a bad mood?" you ask yourself. Your attribution might be, "Maybe he just got some bad news" or "Perhaps he is hungry." When psychologists characterize attributions, they use the term *observer* to identify the person making the attribution, and *actor* to identify the person exhibiting a behavior of interest. If Joe was trying to explain why Susanne had checked out his profile page, then Joe is the observer and Susanne is the actor.

ATTRIBUTIONAL DIMENSIONS   There are many types of attributions, and differentiating among them is quite a task. To make things more manageable, psychologists often describe attributions along three dimensions: controllable–uncontrollable, stable–unstable, and internal–external. Let's see how these might apply to attributions relating to Joe and Susanne:

Controllable–uncontrollable dimension: Suppose Susanne had been 15 minutes late to meet Joe at Starbucks. If Joe assumed it happened because she got stuck in unavoidable traffic, we would say he was making an uncontrollable attribution. (As far as he knows, Susanne has no control over the traffic.) If, however, Joe assumed that Susanne's lateness resulted from factors within her control, such as how fast she drove or what time she left her house, then the attribution would be controllable.

Stable–unstable dimension: Why did Joe cook Susanne a delicious dinner of pork chops? Susanne could infer his behavior stemmed from a longtime interest in cooking. This would be an example of a stable attribution. With stable attributions, the cause is long-lasting. If Susanne thought Joe's behavior resulted from a transient inspiration from watching a really good cooking show, then her attribution would be unstable. With unstable attributions, the cause is temporary.

Internal–external dimension: Why did Joe have trouble meeting suitable single women before Susanne entered his life? If she thought it was because there were few single women living in his immediate area, this would be an external attribution, because the cause of the problem would reside outside of Joe. External attributions are commonly referred to as **situational attributions,** as the causes exist in the environment. However, if she believed Joe had trouble meeting women because he was reluctant to attend singles events, this would be an internal attribution—the cause is within Joe. With internal attributions, the cause is located inside the person, such as an illness, skill, or attitude.

Dispositional attributions are a particular type of internal attribution in which the presumed causes are traits or personality characteristics. Here, we refer to a subset of internal attributions that are deep-seated, enduring characteristics, as opposed to those that are more transient, like having the flu. If Susanne believed that Joe had trouble meeting other singles because he has a shy, reserved personality (not actually the case, but let's assume for the sake of example), this would be a dispositional attribution.

LO 3   Describe how attributions lead to mistakes in our explanations for behaviors.

When people make attributions, they are often *guessing* about the causes of events or behaviors, which of course leaves plenty of room for error. This is particularly true with situational and dispositional attributions. Let's take a look at four of the most common mistakes (**Infographic 14.1** on the next page).

FUNDAMENTAL ATTRIBUTION ERROR   Suppose you are checking out some profiles on a dating Web site. You see someone cute and reach out with ;-) (a "wink"), but never hear back. If you fall prey to the **fundamental attribution error,** you might automatically assume the person's failure to respond results from her shyness (a dispositional attribution), but another reason might be that her Internet is down (a situational attribution). This is a common tendency; we often think that the cause of other people's behaviors is a characteristic of them (a dispositional attribution) as opposed to the environment (a situational attribution) (Ross, 1977; Ross, Amabile, & Steinmetz, 1977). We easily forget that situational factors can also have a powerful effect, and assume that behaviors are the consequence of a person's disposition (Jones & Harris, 1967). When thinking about what causes or controls behavior, we "underestimate the impact of situational factors and . . . overestimate the role of dispositional factors" (Ross, 1977, p. 183).

Synonyms
fundamental attribution error
correspondence bias

social cognition The way people think about others, attend to social information, and use this information in their lives, both consciously and unconsciously.

attributions Beliefs one develops to explain human behaviors and characteristics, as well as situations.

situational attribution A belief that some environmental factor is involved in the cause of an event or activity.

dispositional attribution A belief that some characteristic of an individual is involved in the cause of a situation, event, or activity.

fundamental attribution error The tendency to overestimate the degree to which the characteristics of an individual are the cause of an event, and to underestimate the involvement of situational factors.

Errors in Attribution

Attributions are beliefs we develop to explain human behaviors and characteristics, as well as situations. We can explain behaviors in many ways, but social psychologists often compare explanations based on traits or personality characteristics (dispositional attributions) to explanations based on external situations (situational attributions). But as we seek to explain events and behaviors, we tend to commit predictable errors, making the wrong assumption about why someone is behaving in a certain way. Let's look at four of the most common types of errors in attribution.

Fundamental attribution error

Observer tends to think actor's behavior is caused by internal characteristics, ignoring the role of the situation.

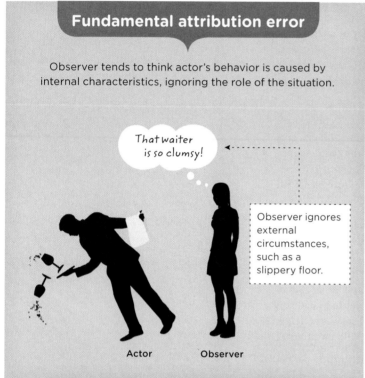

That waiter is so clumsy!

Observer ignores external circumstances, such as a slippery floor.

Actor   Observer

Just-world hypothesis

Observer tends to think people get what they deserve.

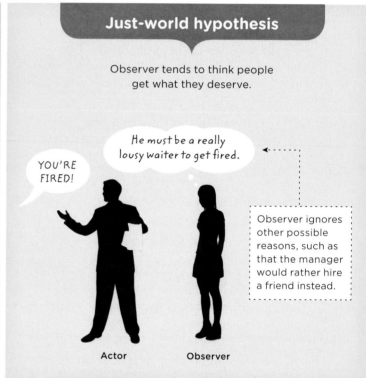

YOU'RE FIRED!

He must be a really lousy waiter to get fired.

Observer ignores other possible reasons, such as that the manager would rather hire a friend instead.

Actor   Observer

Self-serving bias

We tend to attribute our successes to internal characteristics and our failures to external circumstances.

Success! I got a lot of tips tonight.

I'm an excellent waiter so I earn good tips.

Failure! I hardly earned any tips.

Diners were really stingy tonight, so I wasn't tipped well.

False consensus effect

Observer tends to assume the actor is behaving similarly to how she would act in that situation.

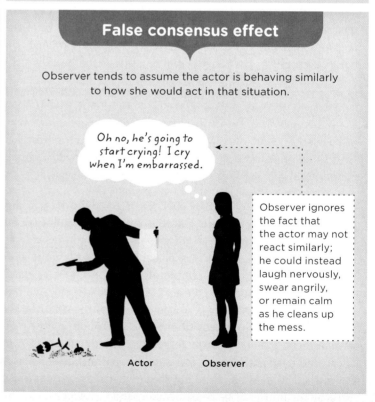

Oh no, he's going to start crying! I cry when I'm embarrassed.

Observer ignores the fact that the actor may not react similarly; he could instead laugh nervously, swear angrily, or remain calm as he cleans up the mess.

Actor   Observer

How do you think this happens? One suggestion is that we have a tendency to make quick decisions about others, often by labeling them as certain types of people. Imagine how dangerous this could be in a medical setting, when doctors and nurses need to make quick choices about treatment. A nurse seeing a patient who has slurred speech, can't walk, and is aggressive might assume he is drunk and an "alcoholic," ignoring other situational factors that might be involved, such as homelessness and severe dehydration (Levett-Jones et al., 2010). Similarly, a doctor might take one look at a patient and decide he is uncooperative, dirty, and just "another homeless hippie," when in fact the patient is on the verge of a diabetic coma. Doctors should be careful not to let negative stereotypes color their diagnoses, and patients and their families should recognize that doctors are not immune to these types of attribution errors (Groopman, 2008).

➤ **CONNECTIONS**

In **Chapter 7,** we described *heuristics,* which are used to solve problems and make decisions. But heuristics are not always reliable. Here, we see how the fundamental attribution error can lead to errors in clinical reasoning. Critical thinking takes effort and time, so it is not unusual to depend on cognitive shortcuts.

Left to Die
Esther Grant holds a painting of Brian Sinclair, the man who died of a treatable urinary tract infection after waiting in a Winnipeg emergency room for 34 hours. Why was Sinclair ignored, even after various people in the emergency room approached hospital staff to voice their concern (Kubinec, 2013, September 5)? Perhaps it had something to do with the fact that Sinclair was a homeless, disabled ethnic minority (Fries, 2011, September 23). Using limited information to make assumptions about people can be very risky in a medical setting.
Boris Minkevich/Winnipeg Free Press

Yet we must make do with the information we have—even if that information is biased and based on our own values and belief systems (Callan, Ferguson, & Bindemann, 2013). This tendency also applies to the *just-world hypothesis.*

JUST-WORLD HYPOTHESIS   People who believe the world is a fair place tend to expect that "bad things" happen for a reason. Their thinking is that when someone is "bad," it should be no surprise when things don't go well for him (Riggio & Garcia, 2009). Many people blame the actor by applying the **just-world hypothesis,** which assumes that if someone is suffering, he must have done something to deserve it (Rubin & Peplau, 1975). In one study, researchers told a group of participants about a man who was violent with his wife, slapping and yelling at her. Another group heard about a loving man who gave his wife flowers and frequently made her dinner. Participants who heard about the "bad person" were more likely to predict a bad outcome for him (he will have a "terrible car accident") than those who heard about the "good person" (he will win a "hugely successful business contract"; Callan et al., 2013).

This belief in a just world, to some degree, may result from cultural teachings. Children in Western cultures are taught this concept so that they learn how to behave properly, show respect for authority figures, and delay gratification (Rubin & Peplau, 1975). For example, in the original tale of *Cinderella* (Grimm & Grimm, 1884), doves rest on Cinderella's shoulders prior to her wedding to the Prince. As the bridal party enters and leaves the church, the doves poke out her evil stepsisters' eyes—a punishment for being cruel to Cinderella. Through this tale, children learn that the stepsisters got what they deserved.

SELF-SERVING BIAS   The tendency to attribute one's successes to internal characteristics and one's failures to environmental factors is known as the **self-serving bias.** Before meeting Joe, Susanne dated a guy who tended to blame his failures on external circumstances. If he lost his job, it was because the boss

➤ **CONNECTIONS**

In **Chapters 10** and **11,** we introduced the concept of *internal locus of control,* which refers to the tendency to feel in control of one's life. People with an internal locus tend to make choices that are better for their health. The *self-serving bias* represents beliefs regarding an internal locus of control for successes.

never liked him—not because his performance fell short. This "woe is me" attitude annoyed Susanne, who had learned to take responsibility for what happened in her life. As her mother often told her, "You can be a survivor, or you can be a victim." Susanne's ex-boyfriend appears to have been influenced by self-serving bias.

You might be surprised to learn that therapists can also fall prey to this bias (Murdock, Edwards, & Murdock, 2010). When clients end their psychotherapy earlier than therapists recommend, therapists tend to think the causes are due to the client's situation (lack of finances) or something within the client (resistance to change), as opposed to some factor within themselves (the therapist). But when considering the same situation for another therapist, they tend to identify the opposite pattern, blaming the other therapist for the early termination of therapy.

Don't Look at Me
There are many reasons the bathroom is messy, but none of them have to do with the little boy Calvin. Here we have an example of self-serving bias, the tendency to attribute mistakes and failures to factors outside ourselves (or to assume personal credit for our successes). © Watterson. Universal Press Syndicate. Reprinted with permission. All rights reserved

FALSE CONSENSUS EFFECT When trying to decipher the causes of other people's behaviors, we overrely on knowledge about ourselves. This can lead to the **false consensus effect,** which is the tendency to overestimate the degree to which people think or act like we do (Ross, Greene, & House, 1977). And when others do not share our thoughts and behaviors, we tend to believe they are acting abnormally or inappropriately. This false consensus effect is evident in our beliefs about everything from celebrities—*Since I love Bradley Cooper, you should, too*—to adolescent substance use—*Since I like to use drugs, you should, too* (Bui, 2012; Henry, Kobus, & Schoeny, 2011). We seem to make this mistake because we have an overabundance of information about ourselves, and often limited information about others. Struggling to understand those around us, we fill in the gaps with what we know about ourselves.

Attribution errors may lead us astray, but we can minimize their impact by being aware of our tendency to fall back on them. Now it's time to explore another facet of social cognition. Where did you get that attitude?

CONNECTIONS

In **Chapter 7,** we describe how the *availability heuristic* is used to predict the probability of something happening in the future based on how easily we can recall a similar event from the past. The false consensus effect is a special type of this heuristic; our judgments about the degree to which others think or act like we do seem to be based on this availability heuristic.

Attitudes

For many people, including Joe and Susanne, the purpose of online dating is to find someone who shares common values, interests, and lifestyle choices—all variables that are strongly influenced by *attitudes.* **Attitudes** are the relatively stable thoughts, feelings, and responses we have toward people, situations, ideas, and things (Ajzen, 2001; Wicker, 1969).

Psychologists suggest that attitudes are composed of cognitive, affective, and behavioral components (**Figure 14.2** on page 561). The *cognitive* aspect of an attitude refers to our beliefs or ideas about an object, person, or situation. Generally, our attitudes include an emotional evaluation, which is the *affective* component relating to mood or emotion. We often have positive or negative feelings about objects, people, or situations (Ajzen, 2001). Feelings and beliefs guide the *behavioral* aspect of the attitude, or the way we respond.

just-world hypothesis The tendency to believe the world is a fair place and individuals generally get what they deserve.

self-serving bias The tendency to attribute our successes to personal characteristics and our failures to environmental factors.

false consensus effect The tendency to overestimate the degree to which others think or act like we do.

attitudes The relatively stable thoughts, feelings, and responses one has toward people, situations, ideas, and things.

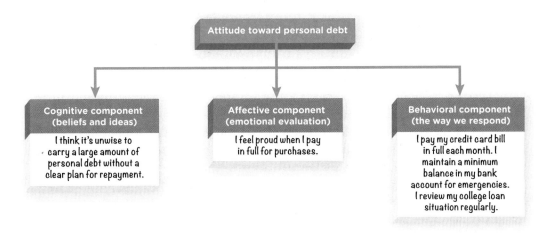

▲ ···
FIGURE 14.2
Attitudes
Attitudes are composed of cognitive, affective, and behavioral components. Cognitive and affective components usually guide the behavioral aspect of an attitude.

WHERE DO ATTITUDES COME FROM?   Of all the nature–nurture conversations occurring in the field of psychology, there is at least one arena where nurture appears to dominate: attitudes. Our attitudes develop through experiences and interactions with the people in our lives, and even through exposure to media (via classical conditioning and observational learning).

That being said, genetic factors do play a role. But to what degree? One of the best ways to gauge the relative weights of nature and nurture is through the study of twins. If nature has a substantive effect on attitudes, then the following should be true: Identical twins (who have the same genetic makeup) should have more similar attitudes than fraternal twins (who share about 50% of their genes). Let's take a look at some research to see if this is the case.

Nature and Nurture

Why the Attitude?

How do you feel about rollercoasters? How about alcohol consumption? Where do you stand on the death penalty? These are just a few of the attitude topics researchers have explored in the context of nature and nurture. One study of several hundred pairs of twins concluded that most of the attitude variation among participants resulted from nonshared environmental factors, or distinct life experiences. But a significant proportion of attitude differences—35%—was related to genes. Those that correlated most strongly with genes centered on abortion, the death penalty, playing sports, riding rollercoasters, and reading books (Olson, Vernon, Harris, & Jang, 2001).

Does this mean that each of us is born with a "pro-life" or "pro-choice" gene, and yet another gene that determines how we feel about sports? Highly unlikely. As the researchers point out, genes probably exert their effects indirectly, through personality traits and other genetically determined characteristics. For example, someone who is born with a very athletic physique (muscular frame or quick reaction time, for example) may become fond of sports simply because she is so good at them (Olson et al., 2001). In this case, the physical traits mediate the relationship between genes and attitudes.

More recent research, also involving twins, offers evidence that political attitudes are influenced by genes. As with the earlier twin study, the relationship between genes and attitudes appears to be indirect; personality traits, which are highly heritable, seem to predispose people to certain political attitudes. But as the researchers point out, family members and peers can also mold political inclinations (Kandler, Bleidorn, & Riemann, 2012). It makes good sense if you think about it: If someone important to you takes a certain political stance, it might seem more appealing, or at least tolerable. The bottom line: Nurture may come out ahead in this particular case, but nature holds its own. ◊🏠

CONNECTIONS

In **Chapter 5,** we described *classical conditioning* and how it might instill emotions and attitudes toward product brands. Observational learning can lead children to imitate others, including their attitudes.

CONNECTIONS

In **Chapter 7,** we explored the heritability of intelligence. *Heritability* is the degree to which hereditary factors are responsible for differences across a variety of physical and psychological characteristics. Heritability research often involves comparing identical and fraternal twins, as is the case here regarding attitudes.

DOES THIS MEAN . . . EACH OF US IS BORN WITH A "PRO-LIFE" OR "PRO-CHOICE" GENE?

All in the Family?
Children and parents frequently have the same attitudes about politics and social issues. To a certain degree, these similarities trace to common personality traits, which are partly inherited (Kandler et al., 2012). But attitudes are more strongly influenced by life experiences (Olson et al., 2001). Tony Savino/Corbis

We have established that attitudes are shaped by experience and, to a lesser extent, heredity. But what impact do these attitudes have on everyday life?

CAN ATTITUDES PREDICT BEHAVIOR?   There are many factors determining whether an attitude can predict a behavior (Ajzen, 2001). The strength of an attitude is important, with stronger, more enduring attitudes having a greater impact (Armitage & Christian, 2003; Holland, Verplanken, & Van Knippenberg, 2002). Specificity is also key; the more specific an attitude, the more likely it will sway behavior (Armitage & Christian, 2003).

Not surprisingly, people are more likely to act on their attitudes when something important is at stake—like money. Imagine your college is holding a meeting to discuss the possibility of increasing student parking fees. What are the chances of your showing up to that meeting if you don't own a car? The greater the personal investment you have in an issue, the more likely you are to act (Sivacek & Crano, 1982).

We now know that attitudes can influence behaviors, but is the opposite true—that is, can behaviors shape attitudes? Absolutely.

didn't SEE that coming

Something Doesn't Feel Right

Most people would agree that cheating on a girlfriend, boyfriend, or spouse is not right. Even so, some people contradict their beliefs by seeking sexual gratification outside their primary relationships. How do you think cheating makes a person feel—relaxed and at peace? Probably not. The tension that results when a behavior (in this case, cheating) clashes with an attitude (*cheating is wrong*) is known as **cognitive dissonance** (Aronson & Festinger, 1958; Festinger, 1957). One way to reduce cognitive dissonance is to adjust the behavior (stop fooling around). Another approach is to change the attitude to better match the behavior (*Cheating is actually good for our relationship, because it makes me a better partner*). Such attitude shifts often occur without our awareness.

The phenomenon of cognitive dissonance was elegantly brought to light in a study by Leon Festinger and J. Merrill Carlsmith (1959). Imagine, for a moment, that you are a participant in this classic study. The researchers have assigned you to a very boring task—placing 12 objects on a tray and then putting them back on the shelf, over and over again for a half-hour. Upon finishing, you spend an additional half-hour twisting 48 pegs ever so slightly, one peg at a time, again and again and again. How would you feel at the end of the hour—pretty bored, right?

Regardless of how you may feel about these activities, you have been paid money to convince someone else that they are a blast: "I had a lot of fun [doing] this task," you say. "It was intriguing, it was exciting . . ." (Festinger & Carlsmith, 1959, p. 205). Unless you like performing repetitive behaviors like a robot, we assume you would feel some degree of *cognitive dissonance,* or tension resulting from this mismatch between your attitude (*Ugh, this activity is so boring*) and your behavior (saying, "I had so much fun!"). What could you do to reduce the cognitive dissonance? If you're like participants in Festinger and Carlsmith's study, you would probably adjust your attitude to better fit your claims. In other words, you would rate the task as more interesting than it actually was.

But here's the really fascinating part: The students who were paid more money ($20 versus $1) were less inclined to change their attitudes to match their claim—a sign that they felt less cognitive dissonance. Apparently, the big bucks made it easier to justify their lies. *I said I liked the boring task because I got paid $20, not because I actually liked it.*

APPARENTLY, THE BIG BUCKS MADE IT EASIER TO JUSTIFY THEIR LIES.

cognitive dissonance A state of tension that results when behaviors are inconsistent with attitudes.

And now, one final example to drive home this concept of cognitive dissonance. We all know that smoking is bad for the body, but smokers around the world continue to light up. You would think awareness of health risks might lead to negative attitudes about smoking, as well as cognitive dissonance during the act (*Smoking is dangerous; I am smoking, and this doesn't feel right*). Reducing the conflict between the attitude and behavior could be accomplished in one of two ways: by changing the attitude or by changing the behavior. Which path do smokers take?

Promises, Promises
Political campaigns are all about making promises. "Vote for me if you want to see your taxes decrease," says one candidate. "When I get into office, I will fix the health care system," says the next. Despite good intentions, many politicians do not follow through on their promises once they get into office. How do you think this conflict between beliefs and behaviors affects them? We suspect they experience a bit of cognitive dissonance. AP Photo/The Canadian Press, Chris Wattie

It appears that smokers often take a third route: thought suppression. They reduce cognitive dissonance by suppressing thoughts about the health implications of smoking. This helps explain why so many smokers don't change their behavior when concerned friends and family members remind them of the dangers. So what should loved ones do to discourage the habit? One **strategy** is to reduce beliefs about positive outcomes, like pointing out that smoking is not effective as a social lubricant or relaxation aid (Kneer, Glock, & Rieger, 2012). ☻!

We have now learned about cognitive processes that form the foundation of our social existence. Attributions help us make sense of events and behaviors, and attitudes provide continuity in the way we think and feel about the surrounding world. It's time to shift our attention to behavior. How do other people influence the way we act? Are you ready to meet runner extraordinaire Julius Achon?

CONNECTIONS

In **Chapter 11,** we reported that many people smoke in response to stressors. To help people quit smoking, we must consider where they are in the process of smoking cessation (first time trying to quit, tried numerous times, etc.). Here, we see it's important to consider cognitive dissonance as well.

✓ show what you know

1. _____ are beliefs used to explain events, situations, and characteristics.
   a. Attributions
   b. Confederates
   c. Dispositions
   d. Attitudes

2. Because of the fundamental attribution error, we tend to attribute causes of behaviors to the:
   a. characteristics of the situation.
   b. factors involved in the event.
   c. length of the activity.
   d. disposition of the person.

3. What three elements comprise an attitude?

✓ CHECK YOUR ANSWERS IN APPENDIX C.

Social Influence

11 ORPHANS In 1983 a 7-year-old boy in northern Uganda came down with the measles. The child was feverish and coughing, and his skin was covered in a blotchy rash. He appeared to be dying. In fact, he did die—or so the local villagers believed. They dug his grave, wrapped him in a burial cloth, and sang him a farewell song. Then, just as they were about to lower the body into the ground, someone heard a sneeze. A few moments later, another sneeze. Could it be? The body inside the burial cloth started to writhe. Hastily unwrapping the cloth, the mourners found the child frantically kicking and crying. It's a good thing the boy sneezed that day at his funeral, as the world is a much happier place because he survived. His name is Julius Achon, and he would grow up to become an Olympic athlete and, perhaps more important, a world-class humanitarian.

Home in Uganda
A group of women sit together in Awake, Uganda, the village where Julius Achon was born and raised. Day-to-day life was difficult, and young Julius dreamed of leaving the village and pursuing a better life in the city. Inspired by the accomplishments of Uganda's Olympic hurdler John Akii-Bua, he decided to start running. Courtesy Dr. Julie Gralow

Fast and Free
Julius wins the 1,500 meters at the 2005 Payton Jordan U.S. Open at Stanford University. With two Olympics under his belt, the young runner had enjoyed an extremely successful athletic career, but his focus was beginning to shift onto something bigger—the task of providing for 11 orphans back home in Uganda. Sport Photos/Newscom

Julius, in His Own Words

http://qrs.ly/o24qsjd

© 2016, Macmillan

Julius was born on December 12, 1976, in Awake, a village that had no electricity or running water. "Life in Uganda is very tough," says Julius, who spent his childhood sleeping between eight brothers and sisters on the floor of a one-room hut. Julius grew up during a period when a government opposition group known as the Lord's Resistance Army (LRA) began its campaign of terror in northern Uganda. At age 12, Julius was kidnapped by the LRA and forced to become a child soldier, but his spirit would not be broken. After 3 months with the rebels, he escaped from their camp and, running much of the distance, returned to his village some 100 miles away.

After coming home, Julius began to run competitively. Running made him feel free, and running was his great gift. He ran 42 miles barefoot to his first major track meet in the city of Lira. Hours after arriving, Julius was racing—and winning—the 800 meters, the 1,500 meters, and the 3,000 meters (Kahn, 2011, December 5). From that point on, it was one success after another: a stunning victory at the national championships, a track scholarship at a prestigious high school in the capital city of Kampala, a gold medal at the World Junior Championships, a college scholarship from George Mason University in the United States, a collegiate record in 1996, and participation in the 1996 and 2000 Olympics (Kahn, 2011, December 5).

As awe-inspiring as these accomplishments may be, the greatest achievement in Julius Achon's life was yet to come, and it had little to do with running. In 2003, while training back home in Uganda, he came upon a bus station in Lira. "I stopped, and then I saw children lying under the bus," Julius says. They had been sleeping there for warmth. One of them stood up and started to beg for money—a 13- or 14-year-old girl clad in a tattered skirt and torn blouse. Then more children emerged, 11 of them in all, some teenagers and others as young as 3. They were terribly thin and dirty, and the little ones wore nothing more than long T-shirts and underwear.

"Where are your parents?" Julius remembers asking. One of the children said their parents had been shot and killed. "Can I walk you to my home, you know, to go eat?" Julius asked. The children eagerly agreed and followed him home for a meal of rice, beans, and porridge. What happened next may seem unbelievable, but Julius and his family are extraordinary people. Julius asked his father to shelter the 11 orphans, provided that he, Julius, would send money home to cover their living expenses. Julius had been running with a professional team in Portugal, making about $5,000 a year, not even enough to cover his own expenses. His parents already had six people living in their one-room home. How did his father respond?

"Ah, it's no problem," said Julius' father. And just like that, Julius and his family adopted 11 children. 📁

Power of Others

Throughout the years Julius was trotting the globe and winning medals, he never forgot about Uganda. He remembered the people back home with empty stomachs and no access to lifesaving medicine, living in constant fear of the LRA. Julius was raised in a family that had always reached out to neighbors in need. "You will get help from other people when you do good," his parents used to say. Julius also felt blessed by all the support people outside the family had given him. "I feel I was so loved [by] others," says Julius, referring to the mentors and coaches who had provided him with places to stay, clothes to wear, and family away from home.

So when Julius encountered those 11 orphans lying under the bus, he didn't think twice about coming to their rescue. His decision to bring them into his life probably had something to do with the positive interactions he had experienced with people in his past.

LO 4   Describe social influence and recognize the factors associated with persuasion.

SOCIAL INFLUENCE DEFINED   Rarely a day goes by that we do not come into contact with other human beings. This contact may be up close and personal, in a family or a tight-knit work group. Other times it's more superficial, like the "Hello, how are you?" type of exchange you might have with a cashier at the store. Sometimes the interaction is so superficial that you never see the person face to face, like the online banker who helps you figure out why you were charged that mysterious fee. All of these interactions impact you in ways you may not realize. Psychologists refer to this as **social influence**—how a person is affected by others as evidenced in behaviors, emotions, and cognition. We begin our discussion with a powerful, yet often unspoken, form of social influence: expectations.

EXPECTATIONS   Think back to your days in elementary school. What kind of student were you—an overachiever, a kid who struggled, or perhaps the class clown? The answer to this question may depend somewhat on the way your teachers perceived you. In a classic study, Rosenthal and Jacobson (1966, 1968) administered a nonverbal intelligence test to students in a San Francisco elementary school. Then all the teachers were provided with a list of students who were likely to "show surprising gains in intellectual competence" during the next year (Rosenthal, 2002a, p. 841). But the list was fake; the "intellectually competent" kids were just a group of kids selected at random (a good example of how deception is used in social psychology research). About 8 months later, the students were given a second intelligence test. Children whom the teachers expected to "show surprising gains" achieved greater increases in their test scores than their peers. Mind you, the only difference between these two groups was in teacher expectations and their resulting behaviors. The students who were expected to be superior actually became superior. Why do you think this happened?

Expectations can have a powerful impact on behaviors. Here, we have a case in which teachers' expectations (based on false information) seemed to transform students' aptitudes and facilitate substantial gains. Let's consider the types of teacher behaviors that could explain this effect. The teachers may have inadvertently communicated expectations by demonstrating "warmer socioemotional" attitudes toward the "surprising gain" students; they may have provided them with more material and opportunities to respond to high expectations; and they may have given them more complex and personalized feedback (Rosenthal, 2002a, 2003). From the student's perspective, teacher behaviors can create a desire to work hard, or they can result in a decline in interest and confidence (Kassin, Fein, & Markus, 2011).

Since this classic study was conducted approximately 50 years ago, researchers have studied expectations in a variety of classroom settings. Their results demonstrate that teacher expectations do not have the same effect or degree of impact on all students (Jussim & Harber, 2005). They appear to have greater influence on younger students (first and second graders) and children of lower socioeconomic status (Sorhagen, 2013).

Expectations are powerful, but they are just one form of social influence. Let's return to the story of Julius and learn about more targeted types of influence.

Great Expectations
Children tend to perform better in school when teachers expect them to succeed (Rosenthal, 2002a). This is especially true for students who are young and socioeconomically disadvantaged (Sorhagen, 2013).
Steve Debenport/Getty Images/Vetta

CONNECTIONS

In **Chapter 11,** we discussed how poverty and its associated stressors can have a lasting impact on the development of the brain and subsequent cognitive abilities. Some factors that influence children's brain development include nutrition, toxins, and abuse. Here, we see that the expectations of others can impact cognitive functioning as well.

social influence How a person is affected by others as evidenced in behaviors, emotions, and cognition.

Persuasion

When Julius asked his father to shelter and feed the 11 orphans, he was using a form of social influence called **persuasion.** With persuasion, one intentionally tries to make other people change their attitudes and beliefs, which may (or may not) lead to changes in their behaviors. The person doing the persuading does not necessarily have control over those he seeks to persuade. Julius could not force his father to feel sympathy for the orphans. His father made a choice.

The important elements of persuasion were first described by Carl Hovland, a social psychologist who studied the morale of soldiers fighting in World War II. According to Hovland, three factors determine persuasive power: the source, the message, and the audience (Hovland, Janis, & Kelley, 1953).

THE SOURCE   The credibility of the person or organization sending a message is critical, and credibility can be dependent on perceived expertise and trustworthiness (Hovland & Weiss, 1951). Suppose you are searching for information about the risks associated with vaccines—whom do you trust to furnish reliable information? In one study, German adults deemed vaccine information provided by government agencies to be more credible than that supplied by pharmaceutical companies (Betsch & Sachse, 2013). Of course, this assessment of government credibility depends on whether citizens consider the government trustworthy. Persuasive ability also hinges on the attractiveness of the source. More attractive people tend to be more persuasive (Bekk & Spörrle, 2010).

THE MESSAGE   The content of the message also determines persuasive power. One important factor is the degree to which the message is logical and to the point (Chaiken & Eagly, 1976). Fear-inducing information can increase persuasion, but it can also backfire. Imagine someone uses this message to encourage teeth-flossing: "If you don't floss daily, you can end up with infected gums, and that infection can spread to your eyes and create total blindness!" If the audience is overly frightened by a message (imagine small children being told to floss . . . or else!), the tension they feel may actually interfere with their ability to process the message (Janis & Feshbach, 1953). If fear is used for the purpose of persuasion, those being persuaded must be provided with information about how to cope with any negative outcomes (Leventhal, Watts, & Pagano, 1967). Being as "gruesome as possible" is not effective; a better approach is to provide clear information about the negative consequences of not being persuaded (de Hoog, Stroebe, & de Wit, 2007, p. 280).

THE AUDIENCE   Finally, we turn to the characteristics of the audience. One important factor is age. For example, middle-age adults (40 to 60 years old) are unlikely to be persuaded to change their attitudes, whereas children are relatively susceptible (Roberts & DelVecchio, 2000). Another key factor is emotional state; when people are happy and well fed, they are more likely to be persuaded (Aronson, 2012; Janis, Kaye, & Kirschner, 1965). Mental focus is also key: If your mind is somewhere else, you are less likely to be affected by message content (Petty & Cacioppo, 1986).

ELABORATION LIKELIHOOD MODEL   The *elaboration likelihood model* proposes that persuasion hinges on the way people think about an argument, and it can occur via one of two pathways. With the *central route* to persuasion, the focus is on the content of the message, and thinking critically about it. With the *peripheral route,* the focus is not on the content but on "extramessage factors" such as the credibility or attractiveness of the source (Petty & Cacioppo, 1986). Little critical thinking is involved, and the commitment to the outcome is low. How do we know which route the message will take? If the person receiving the message is knowledgeable and

persuasion Intentionally trying to make people change their attitudes and beliefs, which may lead to changes in their behaviors.

compliance Changes in behavior at the request or direction of another person or group, who in general do not have any true authority.

foot-in-the-door technique A compliance technique that involves making a small request first, followed by a larger request.

invested in its outcome, the central route to persuasion is used. If the person is distracted, lacks knowledge about the topic, or does not feel invested in the outcome, the peripheral route is typically taken (O'Keefe, 2008).

Immediately following the tragic Newtown massacre of 2012, there was an upsurge in calls for tighter gun control in the United States. Someone with strong feelings about gun control (either for or against it) would likely take advantage of central processing when trying to develop a persuasive argument. Some politicians, for example, tried to persuade others by supplying data about the number of gun-related deaths worldwide: "The United States, which has, per capita, more firearms and particularly more hand-guns than . . . [22 other 'populous, high-income'] countries, as well as the most permissive gun control laws, also has a disproportionate number of firearm deaths—firearm homicides, firearm suicides, and firearm accidents" (Richardson & Hemenway, 2011, p. 243). Such a message would be more persuasive to a person who is knowledgeable and invested in the issue, and thus uses the central processing route. Someone unfamiliar with or indifferent to gun-control policy would more likely be persuaded by the cred-ibility of the source, appearance of the speaker, and so on.

The take-home message: If you want to persuade as many people as possible, make sure your arguments are logical *and* you present yourself as credible and attrac-tive. That way you can take advantage of both routes.

Routes of Persuasion
The fact that this anti-gun message is being presented by a police officer may increase its persuasive power. With the *peripheral route* to persuasion, people pay attention to factors outside the message content, such as the credibility or appearance of the individual who relays the message (Petty & Cacioppo, 1986).
Justin Sullivan/Getty Images

Compliance

LO 5 Define compliance and explain some of the techniques used to gain it.

The results of persuasion are internal and related to a change in *attitude* (Key, Edlund, Sagarin, & Bizer, 2009). **Compliance,** on the other hand, occurs when someone volun-tarily changes her *behavior* at the request or direction of another person or group, who in general does not have any true authority over her. Compliance is evident in changes to "overt behavior" (Key et al., 2009). For example, if you want to get someone to help clean up after a party, you would try to get him to comply with your request, perhaps through some mild form of guilt (*Remember the last party we had, when I helped you?*).

Surprisingly, compliance often occurs outside of our awareness. Think of an everyday situation in which you mindlessly comply with another person's request. You're waiting in line at the copy machine, and a man asks if he can cut in front of you. Do you allow it? Your response may depend on the wording of the request. Researchers study-ing this very scenario—a person asking for permission to cut in line—have found that compliance is much more likely to result when the request is accompanied by a *reason.* Saying, "Excuse me, I have five pages. May I use the [copy] machine?" will not work as well as "Excuse me, I have five pages. May I use the [copy] machine, *because I am in a rush?*" People are more likely to comply with a request that includes a "because" phrase, even if the reasoning is not logical. For example, stating that you need to use the copy machine "*because I am in a rush*" achieves about the same compliance as "*because I have to make copies*" (Langer, Blank, & Chanowitz, 1978). Kind of scary, right?

As you can see, compliance can be associated with mindlessness. Understanding this might lead you to reflect on how compliance comes into play in everyday situa-tions (Fennis & Janssen, 2010). For example, salespeople and marketing experts use a variety of techniques to get consumers to comply with their requests. One common method is the **foot-in-the-door technique,** which occurs when someone makes a small request, followed by a larger request (Freedman & Fraser, 1966). If a college

CONNECTIONS

In **Chapter 4,** we discussed the *automatic cognitive activity* that guides some behaviors. These behaviors appear to occur without our intent or awareness. Compliance can be driven by automatic processes.

club is trying to persuade students to help with a large service project (such as raising money for packages to be sent to soldiers overseas), its members might first stop students in the hallway and ask them if they could help with a smaller task (labeling a couple of donated boxes lying close by). If a student responds positively to this small request, then the club members might make a bigger request (to sponsor packages), with the expectation that the student will comply with the second request on the grounds of having said yes to the first request. Why would this technique work?

The reasoning is that if you have already said yes to a small request, chances are you will agree to a bigger request to remain consistent in your involvement. Your prior participation leads you to believe you are the type of person who gets involved; in other words, your attitude has shifted (Cialdini & Goldstein, 2004; Freedman & Fraser, 1966). So why is such a strategy called *foot-in-the-door?* In the past, salespeople went door to door trying to sell their goods and services, and they would often be successful if they could physically get a "foot in the door," thereby keeping it open, which allowed them to continue with their sales pitch.

Another method for gaining compliance is the **door-in-the-face technique,** which involves making a large request followed by a smaller request. With this technique, the expectation is that the person will not go along with the large request, but because the smaller request may seem so minor by comparison, she will comply with it. There are numerous reasons people comply under these circumstances, but the main reason seems to be one of *reciprocal concessions.* If the solicitor (the person trying to obtain something) is willing to give up something (the large request), the person being solicited tends to feel that he too should give in and satisfy the smaller request (Cialdini & Goldstein, 2004).

Let's review these concepts using Julius as an example. After meeting the 11 orphans, Julius brought them home and asked his parents to provide them with a meal. Once his parents *complied* with this initial request, Julius made a much larger request—he asked them to shelter the children indefinitely. This is an example of the *foot-in-the-door technique* because Julius first made a modest request ("Will you feed these children?") and then followed up with a larger one ("Will you shelter these children?"). Had these requests been flip-flopped, that is, had Julius only wanted to get the children a meal but first asked his parents to house them, we would call it the *door-in-the-face technique.*

Compliance generally occurs in response to specific requests or instructions: Will you pick up the kids after school? Can you chop these onions? Please collect your sweaty socks from the bathroom floor! But social influence needn't be explicit. Sometimes we adapt our behaviors and beliefs simply to fit in with the crowd.

Conformity

When Julius came to the United States on a college scholarship in 1995, he was struck by some of the cultural differences he observed between the United States and Uganda—the way people dressed, for example. Women wore considerably less clothing, and men could be seen wearing jeans halfway down their posteriors (the "sagging" pants trend). There were other differences, like the way people addressed authority figures. In Africa, explains Julius, students speak to their teachers with a certain kind of respect, using a low voice and standing still with their legs close together. Americans tend to use a more casual tone, he notes; they stand with their legs farther apart and shift around during conversation.

During the decade Julius lived in the United States, he never stopped acting like a Ugandan. Before going out in the evening, he would tuck in his shirt, check his hair, and make sure his clothes were ironed—and never would he wear sagging pants. You might say Julius refused to *conform* to certain aspects of American culture—and resisting conformity is not always easy to do.

Foot in the Door
Looks like this petitioner has gotten her "foot in the door," so to speak. With the foot-in-the-door approach, the solicitor makes a small request ("Would you take a moment to sign this petition?") followed by a larger request ("Will you donate money to this cause?"). Getty Images/iStockphoto

You Asked, Julius Answers

http://qrs.ly/sz4qski

Is it difficult returning home to Uganda?

LO 6   Identify the factors that influence the likelihood of someone conforming.

FOLLOWING THE CROWD   Have you ever found yourself turning to look in the same direction as other people who are staring at something, just because you see them doing so? During the Waldo Canyon Fires in Colorado Springs in the summer of 2012, a day did not pass without people pointing to the mountain range. It was next to impossible to avoid looking in the direction they were pointing, and not just because of the smoke coming from the mountains. We seem to have a commanding urge to do what others are doing, even if it means changing our normal behavior. This tendency to modify our behaviors, attitudes, beliefs, and opinions to match those of others is known as **conformity.** Sometimes we conform to the **norms** or standards of the social environment, such as the group to which we are connected. Unlike compliance, which occurs in response to an explicit and direct request, conformity is generally unspoken. We often conform because we feel compelled to fit in and belong.

It is important to note that conformity is not always a bad thing. We rely on conformity in many cases to ensure the smooth running of day-to-day activities involving groups of people. Think of what a third-grade classroom would be like if it weren't for the human urge to conform to what others are doing. Imagine checking out at Target if none of the customers adhered to common social rules.

The next time you are outside in a fairly crowded area, look up and keep your eyes toward the sky. You will find that some people change their gazes to match yours, even though there is no other indication that something is happening above.

try this

STUDYING CONFORMITY   Social psychologists have studied conformity in a variety of settings, including American colleges. In a classic experiment by Solomon Asch (1955), college-student participants were asked to sit at a table with six other people, all of whom were confederates working for the researcher. The participants were told to look at two cards; the first card had one vertical line on it, the standard line, and the second card had three vertical lines of different lengths, marked 1, 2, and 3 (**Figure 14.3** on the next page). The group seated at the table was instructed to look at the two cards and then announce, one at a time going around the table, which of the three lines was closest in length to the standard line, thus making a "visual judgment." The first two rounds of this task went smoothly, with everybody in agreement about which of the three lines matched the standard. But then, in the third round, the first five people (all confederates) offered what was clearly the wrong answer, one after the other. (Prior to the experiment, the researchers had given them instructions about which line to choose in each trial.)

Would the real participant (the sixth person to answer) follow suit and conform to the wrong answer, or would he stand his ground and report the correct answer? In roughly 37% of these trials, participants went along with the group and provided the incorrect answer. What's more, 76% of the participants conformed to the incorrect answers of the confederates at least once (Asch, 1955, 1956). When members of the control group made the same judgments alone in a room, they were correct 99% of the time, confirming that the differences between the standard line and the comparison lines were substantial, and generally not difficult to assess. It is worth noting that most participants (95%) refused to conform on at least one occasion, choosing an answer that conflicted with that of the group (Asch, 1956; Griggs, 2015). Thus, they were capable of thinking and behaving independently. This type of study was later replicated in a variety of cultures, with mostly similar results (Bond & Smith, 1996).

CONNECTIONS

In **Chapter 9,** we described Maslow's hierarchy of needs, which includes the *need to belong.* If physiological and safety needs are met, an individual will be motivated by the need for love and belongingness. This need can drive us to conform.

CONNECTIONS

In **Chapter 1,** we explained that a control group in an experiment is not exposed to the treatment variable. In this case, the control group is not exposed to the confederates making incorrect answers.

door-in-the-face technique A compliance technique that involves making a large request first, followed by a smaller request.

conformity The urge to modify behaviors, attitudes, beliefs, and opinions to match those of others.

norms Standards of the social environment.

→

FIGURE 14.3

Asch's Conformity Experiment
Participants in this experiment were asked to look at the lines on two cards, announcing which of the comparison lines was closest in length to the standard line. Imagine you are a participant, like the man wearing glasses in this photo, and everyone else at the table chooses Line 3. Would that influence your answer? If you are like many participants, it would. Seventy-six percent conformed to the incorrect answer at least once. photo by William Vandivert/Solomon E. Asch, Opinions and Social Pressure, *Scientific American,* Nov 1955, Vol 193, No.5, 31–35

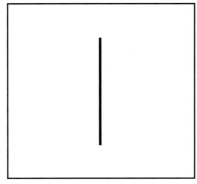
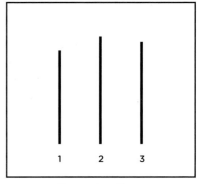

Standard line   Comparison lines

WHY CONFORM?   People do not always conform to the behavior of others, but what factors come into play when they do? There are three major reasons for conformity. Most of us want the approval of others, to be liked and accepted. This desire influences our behavior and is known as *normative social influence.* Just think back to middle school—do you remember feeling pressure to be like some of your classmates or friends? This might have been due to a normative social influence. A second reason we conform is to behave correctly; we look to others for confirmation when we are uncertain about something, and then do as they do. This is known as *informational social influence.* Perhaps you have a friend who is particularly well read in politics, or extremely knowledgeable about psychology. Your tendency is to defer to her expert knowledge. Third, we sometimes conform to others because they belong to a certain *reference group* we respect, admire, or long to join.

Listed below are certain conditions that increase the likelihood of conforming (Aronson, 2012; Asch, 1955):

1. The group includes at least three other people who are unanimous.
2. You have to report your decision in front of others and give your reasons.
3. You are faced with a task you think is difficult.
4. You are unsure of your ability to perform a task.

And here are some conditions that decrease the likelihood of conforming:

1. At least one other person is going against the group with you (Asch, 1955).
2. Group members come from individualist, or "me-centered" cultures, meaning they are less likely to conform than those from collectivistic, or community-centered, cultures (Bond & Smith, 1996).

When you conform, no one is specifically telling you to do so. But this is not the case with all types of social influence (**Table 14.1**). Let's take a trip to the darker side and explore the frightening phenomenon of obedience.

TABLE 14.1   CONCEPTS OF SOCIAL INFLUENCE

Concept	Definition	Example
Persuasion	Intentionally trying to make people change their attitudes and beliefs, which may or may not lead to their behavior changing	Trust our product because it is the best on the market.
Compliance	Voluntarily changing behavior at the request or direction of another person or group, who in general does not have any authority over you	Remove your shoes before you walk into the house because you have been asked.
Conformity	The urge to modify our behaviors, attitudes, beliefs, and opinions to match those of others	Remove your shoes before you walk into the house because everyone else who has entered did the same.
Obedience	Changing our behavior because we have been ordered to do so by someone in authority	Follow the detour sign.

Whether or not you realize it, other people constantly shape your thoughts, emotions, and behaviors. Above are some of the key elements of social influence.

Obedience

BOY SOLDIERS During Uganda's 2-decade civil war, the Lord's Resistance Army (LRA) is said to have kidnapped some 66,000 youths. Scholars have estimated that 20% of male victims did not make it home (Annan, Blattman, & Horton, 2006). Julius came dangerously close to losing his life during a village raid that he and other child soldiers were forced to conduct. His boss ordered him to shoot a man who refused to hand over a chicken, but Julius would not pull the trigger. Had the boss not come from Julius' home village, the punishment probably would have been death. Instead, Julius received a caning that rendered him incapable of sitting for a week.

Boy Soldier
A young boy wields a Kalashnikov rifle near Kampala, Uganda. He is among the tens of thousands of children who have been exploited by military groups in Uganda. Julius was just 12 years old when he was abducted by the Lord's Resistance Army (LRA) and forced to fight and plunder on the group's behalf.
AFP/Getty Images

While a captive of the LRA, Julius witnessed other boy soldiers assaulting innocent people and stealing property. Sometimes at the end of the day, they would laugh or brag about how many people they had beaten or killed. But these were just "normal" boys from the villages, children who never would have behaved this way under regular circumstances. And some showed clear signs of regret. Julius remembers seeing other child soldiers cry alone at night after returning to the camp when there was time to reflect on what they had done.

How do you explain this tragedy? What drives an ordinary child to commit senseless violence? A psychologist might tell you it has something to do with *obedience*. 📁

LO 7 Describe obedience and explain how Stanley Milgram studied it.

One of the most disconcerting results of social influence is **obedience,** which occurs when we change our behavior, or act in a way we might not normally act, because we have been ordered to do so by an authority figure. In these situations, an imbalance

obedience Changing behavior because we have been ordered to do so by an authority figure.

of power exists, and the person with more power (for example, a teacher, police officer, doctor, or boss) generally has an advantage over someone with less power, who is more likely to be obedient out of respect, fear, or concern. In some cases, the person in charge demands obedience for the well-being of those less powerful (a father demanding obedience from a child running wildly through a crowded store). Other times, the person wielding power demands obedience for his own benefit (an adult who perpetrates sexual abuses against innocent children).

THIS WILL *SHOCK* YOU: MILGRAM'S STUDY   Back in the 1960s, psychologist Stanley Milgram was interested in determining the extent to which obedience can lead to behaviors that most people would consider unethical. Milgram (1963, 1974) conducted a series of experiments examining how far people would go, particularly in terms of punishing others, when urged to do so by an authority figure. Participants were told the study was about memory and learning (another example of research deception). The sample included teachers, salespeople, post office workers, engineers, and laborers, representing a wide range of educational backgrounds, from elementary school dropouts to people with graduate degrees.

Upon arriving at the Yale University laboratory, participants were informed they would be using punishment as part of a learning experiment. They were then asked to draw a slip of paper from a hat; the slip told them they had been randomly assigned the *teacher* role, although the truth was that a confederate always played the role of the *learner* (the hat contained two slips that both read "teacher"). To start, the teacher was asked to sit in the learner's chair, so that he could experience a 45-volt shock, just to know what the learner might be feeling. Then the teacher sat at a table that held a control panel for the shock generator. The panel went from 15 volts to 450 volts, and as you can see in **Infographic 14.2,** this range of voltage was labeled from "slight shock" to "XXX." The goal, the teacher was told, was for the learner to memorize a set of paired words. Each time the learner made a mistake, the teacher was to administer a shock, and the shock was to increase by 15 volts for every mistake. The learner was located in a separate room, arms strapped to a table and electrodes attached to his wrists; the electrodes were reportedly attached to a shock generator.

The learner (the confederate) did not receive actual shocks, but instead had a script of responses he was to make as the experiment continued. The learner's behaviors, including the mistakes he made and his responses to the increasing shock levels (including mild complaints, screaming, references to his heart condition, pleas for the experiment to stop, and total silence as if he were unconscious or even dead), were identical for all participants. A researcher in a white lab coat (also a confederate with scripted responses) always remained in the room with the teacher, and he was insistent that the experiment proceed if the teacher began to question going any further given the learner's responses (such as "Experimenter, get me out of here. . . . I refuse to go on" or "I can't stand the pain"; Milgram, 1965, p. 62). The researcher would say to the teacher, "Please continue" and "You have no other choice, you *must* go on" (Milgram, 1963, p. 374).

How many teachers do you think obeyed the researcher and proceeded with the experiment in spite of the learner's desperate pleas? Before the experiment, Milgram asked a variety of people (including psychiatrists and students) to predict how many teachers would obey the researcher. Many believed that the participants would refuse to continue at some point in the experiment. Most of the psychiatrists, for example, predicted that only 0.125% of participants would continue to the highest voltage (Milgram, 1965).

CONNECTIONS

In **Chapter 13,** we introduced the concept of *transference,* a reaction some clients have to their therapists. A client demonstrating transference responds to the therapist as if dealing with a parent, or other important caregiver from childhood; this may include behaving more childlike and obedient.

Troubling Discoveries
A photo of psychologist Stanley Milgram appears on the cover of his biography, *The Man Who Shocked The World: The Life* and *Legacy of Stanley Milgram* (2004), by Thomas Blass. Milgram's research illuminated the dangers of human obedience. Feeling pressure from authority figures, participants in Milgram's studies were willing to administer what they believed to be painful and life-threatening electric shocks to other human beings (Milgram, 1963). Alexandra Milgram

Milgram's Shocking Obedience Study

Stanley Milgram's study on obedience and authority was one of the most ground-breaking and surprising experiments in all of social psychology. Milgram wanted to test the extent to which we will follow the orders of an authority figure. Would we follow orders to hurt someone else, even when that person was begging us to stop? Milgram's experiment also raises the ethical issues of deception and informed consent.

Participants had to actually think they were shocking another person for the experiment to work. Creating this deception involved the use of confederates (people secretly working for the researchers) whose behaviors and spoken responses were carefully scripted. Milgram found high levels of obedience in his participants—much higher than he and others had predicted at the beginning of the study.

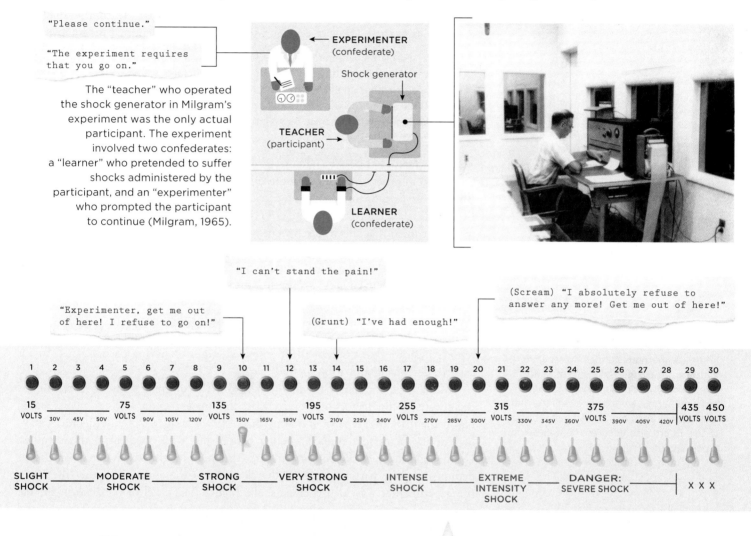

"Please continue."

"The experiment requires that you go on."

The "teacher" who operated the shock generator in Milgram's experiment was the only actual participant. The experiment involved two confederates: a "learner" who pretended to suffer shocks administered by the participant, and an "experimenter" who prompted the participant to continue (Milgram, 1965).

EXPERIMENTER (confederate)

Shock generator

TEACHER (participant)

LEARNER (confederate)

"Experimenter, get me out of here! I refuse to go on!"

"I can't stand the pain!"

(Grunt) "I've had enough!"

(Scream) "I absolutely refuse to answer any more! Get me out of here!"

| 1 | 2 | 3 | 4 | 5 | 6 | 7 | 8 | 9 | 10 | 11 | 12 | 13 | 14 | 15 | 16 | 17 | 18 | 19 | 20 | 21 | 22 | 23 | 24 | 25 | 26 | 27 | 28 | 29 | 30 |

15 VOLTS — 30V 45V 50V — 75 VOLTS — 90V 105V 120V — 135 VOLTS — 150V 165V 180V — 195 VOLTS — 210V 225V 240V — 255 VOLTS — 270V 285V 300V — 315 VOLTS — 330V 345V 360V — 375 VOLTS — 390V 405V 420V — 435 VOLTS — 450 VOLTS

SLIGHT SHOCK — MODERATE SHOCK — STRONG SHOCK — VERY STRONG SHOCK — INTENSE SHOCK — EXTREME INTENSITY SHOCK — DANGER: SEVERE SHOCK — XXX

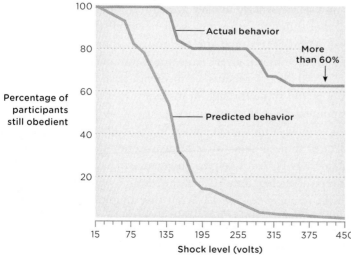

Percentage of participants still obedient

Actual behavior

More than 60%

Predicted behavior

Shock level (volts)

On the control panel of Milgram's shock generator, the participant would see 30 switches clearly labeled as delivering a range from "Slight shock" (15 volts) to "Danger: Severe shock" (375 volts) and beyond. The "learner" produced scripted responses at every level (Milgram, 1963).

Before the experiment, Milgram and a panel of experts predicted most participants would not proceed beyond 150 volts, when the "learner" explicitly demands to end the experiment. In fact, actual results show that most participants obeyed the experimenter's commands all the way to the highest shock level. (ADAPTED FROM MILGRAM, 1965.)

They also guessed that the majority of the participants would quit the experiment when the learner began his protests.

Here's what actually happened: 65% of participants continued to the highest voltage level. Most of these participants were obviously not comfortable with what they were doing (stuttering, sweating, trembling), yet they continued. Even those who eventually refused to proceed went much further than anyone (even Milgram himself) had predicted—they all used shocks up to at least 300 volts, labeled as "Intense Shock" (Milgram, 1963, 1964; Infographic 14.2).

We should emphasize that participants were not necessarily comfortable with their role as *teachers*. One person who witnessed the study reported the following:

> I observed a mature and initially poised businessman enter the laboratory smiling and confident. Within 20 minutes he was reduced to a twitching, stuttering wreck, who was rapidly approaching a point of nervous collapse. . . . At one point he pushed his fist into his forehead and muttered: "Oh God, let's stop it." And yet he continued to respond to every word of the experimenter, and obeyed to the end (Milgram, 1963, p. 377).

REPLICATING MILGRAM This type of research has been replicated in the United States and in other countries, and the findings have remained fairly consistent, with 61–66% of participants continuing to the highest level of shock (Aronson, 2012; Blass, 1999). Not surprisingly, the criticisms of Milgram's studies were strong. Many were concerned that this research went too far with its deception (it would certainly not receive approval from an Institutional Review Board today), and some wondered if the participants were harmed by knowing that they theoretically could have killed someone with their choices during the study. Milgram (1964) spent time with the participants following the study, and reported that 84% claimed they were "glad" they had participated, whereas only 1.3% reported they were "sorry" to have been involved. The participants were seen for psychiatric evaluations a year later, and reports indicate that none of them "show[ed] signs of having been harmed by his experiences" (Milgram, 1964, p. 850).

Milgram and others have followed up on the original study, to determine if there were specific factors or characteristics that made it more likely someone would be obedient in this type of scenario (Blass, 1991; Burger, 2009; Milgram, 1965). Several key factors determined whether participants were obedient in these studies: (1) the legitimacy of the authority figure (the more legitimate, the more obedience demonstrated by participants); (2) the closeness of the authority figure (the closer the experimenter was to participants, the higher their level of obedience); (3) the closeness of the *learner* (the closer the learner, the less obedient the participant); and (4) the presence of other *teachers* (if another confederate was acting as an obedient teacher, the participant was more likely to obey as well).

Milgram's initial motivation for studying obedience came from learning about the horrific events of World War II and the Holocaust, which "could only have been carried out on a massive scale if a very large number of people obeyed orders" (Milgram, 1974, p. 1). And his experiments on obedience seem to support this suggestion. One ray of hope did shine through in his later experiments, and that was how participants responded when they saw others refuse to obey. In one follow-up experiment, two more confederates were included in the study as additional *teachers*. If these confederates showed signs of refusing to obey the authority figure, the research participant was far less likely to cooperate. In fact, Milgram (1974) reported that in this type of setting, only 10% of the research participants were willing to carry on with the *learning experiment*. What this suggests is that one person can make a difference, and when someone stands up for what is right, others will follow that lead.

CONNECTIONS

In **Chapter 1,** we reported that professional organizations have specific guidelines to ensure ethical treatment of research participants. They include doing no harm, safeguarding welfare, and respecting human dignity. An Institutional Review Board also ensures the well-being of participants.

social facilitation The tendency for the presence of others to improve personal performance when the task or event is fairly uncomplicated and a person is adequately prepared.

social loafing The tendency for people to make less than their best effort when individual contributions are too complicated to measure.

diffusion of responsibility The sharing of duties and responsibilities among all group members that can lead to feelings of decreased accountability and motivation.

✓◯◯◯ show what you know

1. Match the definitions with the terms:
   a. how a person is affected by others
   b. intentionally trying to make people change their attitudes
   c. a person voluntarily changes behavior at the request of someone without authority
   d. someone asks for a small request, followed by a larger request
   e. the urge to modify behaviors, attitudes, and beliefs to match those of others

   ____ conformity   ____ persuasion
   ____ compliance   ____ foot-in-the-door technique
   ____ social influence

2. _____ occurs when we change our behavior, or act in a way we might not normally, because we have been ordered to do so by an authority figure.
   a. Persuasion   b. Compliance
   c. Conformity   d. Obedience

3. Asch's experiments with conformity show how difficult it is to resist the urge to conform to the behaviors, attitudes, beliefs, and opinions of others. At the same time, many of his participants did not cave in to so-called peer pressure. Can you think of an everyday example in which somebody successfully resisted the urge to conform?

✓ CHECK YOUR ANSWERS IN APPENDIX C.

Groups and Aggression

Thus far, the primary focus of this chapter has been people in social situations. We learned, for example, how individuals process information about other people (social cognition) and how behavior is shaped by social interactions (social influence). But human beings do not exist solely as isolated units. When striving toward a common goal, we often come together in groups, and these groups have their own fascinating social dynamics.

LET'S DO THIS TOGETHER The most important competition of Julius Achon's career was probably the 1994 World Junior Championships in Portugal. Julius was 17 at the time, and he represented Uganda in the 1,500 meters. It was his first time flying on an airplane, wearing running shoes, and racing on a rubber track. No one expected an unknown boy from Uganda to win, but Julius surprised everyone, including himself. Crossing the finish line strides ahead of the others, he almost looked uncertain as he raised his arms in celebration.

Julius ran the 1,500 meters (the equivalent of 0.93 miles) in approximately 3 minutes and 40 seconds. Do you suppose he would have run this fast if he had been alone? Research suggests the answer is no (Worringham & Messick, 1983). In some situations, people perform better in the presence of others. This is particularly true when the task at hand is uncomplicated (running) and the individual is well prepared (runners may spend months training for races). Thus, **social facilitation** can improve personal performance when the activity is fairly straightforward and the person is adequately prepped. 📁

Beat that Avatar!
Sometimes other "people" don't have to be present and watching for social facilitation to work. Researchers have demonstrated that competitive seniors pedal harder on stationary bikes when they have an avatar rival to race against (Anderson-Hanley, Snyder, Nimon, & Arciero, 2011). Cay Anderson-Hanley, Union College, NY

When Two Heads Are *Not* Better Than One

Being around other people does not always provide a performance boost, however. Learning or performing difficult tasks may actually be harder in the presence of others (Aiello & Douthitt, 2001), and group members may not put forth their best effort. When individual contributions to the group aren't easy to ascertain, **social loafing** may occur (Latané, Williams, & Harkins, 1979). Social loafing is the tendency for people to make less than their best effort when individual contributions are too complicated to measure. Many students will shy away from working in groups because of the negative experiences they have had with other group members' social loafing.

Social loafing often goes hand-in-hand with **diffusion of responsibility,** or the sharing of duties and responsibilities among all group members. Diffusion of responsibility can lead to feelings of decreased accountability and motivation. If we suspect other group members are slacking, we tend to follow suit in order to keep things equal.

Apply This

Cut The Loafing

Want some advice on how to reduce social loafing? Even if an instructor doesn't require it, you should try to get other students in your group to designate and take responsibility for specific tasks, have group members submit their part of the work to the group before the assignment is due, and specify their contributions to the end product (Jones, 2013; Maiden & Perry, 2011). If you do have some "free riders" in your group, don't automatically assume they are lazy or apathetic. Some group members fail to pull their weight because they feel incompetent (perhaps a result of language difficulties), or they are not "team players" (Barr, Dixon, & Gassenheimer, 2005; Hall & Buzwell, 2012). Communicate with these individuals early in the process, and work with your group to identify a task they can perform with confidence and success.

across the WORLD

Slackers of the West

It turns out that social loafing is more likely to occur in societies where people place a high premium on individuality and autonomy. These *individualistic* societies include the United States, Western Europe, and other parts of the Western world. In the *collectivistic* cultures of China and other parts of East Asia, people tend to prioritize community over the individual, and social loafing is less likely to occur. Group members from these more community-oriented societies actually show evidence of working harder (Kerr & Tindale, 2004; Smrt & Karau, 2011). And unlike their individualistic counterparts, they are less interested in outshining their comrades. Preserving group harmony is more important (Tsaw, Murphy, & Detgen, 2011).

IF YOU ARE TRAVELING TO EAST ASIA, SHOULD YOU LEAVE YOUR EGO AT HOME?

Nothing in psychology is ever that simple, however. Social loafing may be less common in collectivist cultures, but it certainly happens (Hong, Wyer, & Fong, 2008). And within every "individualistic" or "collectivistic" society are individuals who do not behave according to these generalities. We should also point out that many group tasks require both individual and shared efforts; in these situations, a combination of individualism and collectivism may lead to more successful outcomes (Wagner, Humphrey, Meyer, & Hollenbeck, 2011).

DEINDIVIDUATION   In the last section, we discussed how obedience played a role in the senseless violence carried out by boy soldiers in Uganda. We suspect that the actions of these children also had something to do with *deindividuation*. People in groups sometimes feel a diminished sense of personal responsibility, inhibition, or adherence to social norms. This state of **deindividuation** can occur when group members are not treated as individuals, and thus begin to exhibit a "lack of self-awareness" (Diener, 1979). As members of a group, the boy soldiers may have felt a loss of personal identity, social responsibility, and ability to discriminate right from wrong.

Research suggests that children are indeed vulnerable to deindividuation. In a classic study of trick-or-treaters, Ed Diener, a professor and researcher at the University of Illinois, and his colleagues set up a study in 27 homes throughout Seattle, Washington. Children arriving at these houses to trick-or-treat were ushered in by a woman (who was a confederate, of course). She told them they could take *one* piece of candy, which was on a table in a bowl. Coincidentally, next to the bowl of candy (about 2 feet away) was a second bowl full of small coins (pennies and nickels).

CONNECTIONS

In **Chapter 1,** we discussed a type of descriptive research that involves studying participants in their natural environments. *Naturalistic observation* requires that the researcher not disturb the participants or their environment. Would Diener's study be considered naturalistic observation?

The woman then excused herself, saying she had to get back to work in another room. What the children didn't know was that an experimenter was observing their behavior through a peephole, tallying up the amount of candy and/or money they took. The other variable being recorded was the number of children and adults in the hallway; remember, the experimenters never knew how many people would show up when the doorbell rang!

The findings were fascinating. If a parent was present, the children were well behaved (only 8% took more than their allotted one piece of candy). But with no adult present, children acted quite differently. Of the children who came to the door alone and anonymous (the confederate did not ask for names or other identifying information), 21% took more than they should have. By comparison, 80% of the children who were in a group and anonymous took extra candy and/or money. The researchers suggested that the condition of being in a group combined with anonymity created a sense of deindividuation (Diener, Fraser, Beaman, & Kelem, 1976). Are you wondering how much money and candy the kids took? It seems that the children who took more than their fair share of candy grabbed as much as their hands could hold (between 1.6 and 2.3 extra candy bars, on average). As for the money, around 14% of the children stole coins (and ignored the candy), while nearly 21% took both money and more than one piece of candy.

We have shown how deindividuation occurs in groups of children, but what about adults? Perhaps you have heard about "Bedlam," a football game between archrival teams from the University of Oklahoma (OU) and Oklahoma State University (OSU). Most years, OU has won, but in 2011, OSU beat OU 44–10. This was the first time in the university's history it captured a Big 12 championship, and the first time it had beaten OU in 9 years. With just a few seconds left, thousands of OSU fans stormed the field, tearing down the goalposts and injuring several people in the celebration. Even after an announcement instructing fans to stay off the field, hoards of people charged forward, some of them laughing. They showed virtually no regard for the safety of others. The fans' impulsive behavior seemed to be a result of deindividuation. This type of behavior has been repeated in many settings and with many groups of people. Why can't we learn to make better decisions when we find ourselves in groups? Perhaps it has something to do with our tendency to act in rash and extreme ways when surrounded by others.

RISKY SHIFT   Imagine you have $250,000 to spend for your company. Will you spend more if you're making decisions alone or working as part of a committee? Researcher James A. F. Stoner (1961, 1968) set out to find the answer to this question, and here's what he discovered: When group members were asked to make a unanimous decision on how to spend the money, they were more likely to recommend uncertain and risky options than individuals working alone, a phenomenon known as the **risky shift.**

GROUP POLARIZATION AND GROUPTHINK   As members of a group work together, their positions tend to become more extreme. For example, if people who strongly support the legalization of marijuana are assembled in a group, their position will become increasingly pro-legalization over time. **Group polarization** is the tendency for a group to take a more extreme stance after deliberations and discussion (Myers & Lamm, 1976). When people hear their opinions echoed by other members of the group, the conversation tends to become more extreme, as the new information tends to reinforce and strengthen the group members' original positions. So does group deliberation actually help? Perhaps not when the members are initially in agreement.

▸ **CONNECTIONS**

What else motivated the children who were *alone?* In **Chapter 9,** we discussed various sources of motivation, ranging from instincts to the need for power. These sources of motivation might help explain why some children took more than their fair share of candy when they thought no one was watching.

Mine for the Taking
A classic study by Diener and colleagues found that children were most likely to swipe Halloween candy and coins when they were anonymous group members. The condition of being anonymous and part of a group seemed to create a state of deindividuation (Diener et al., 1976).
Samantha Grandy/Shutterstock

deindividuation   The diminished sense of personal responsibility, inhibition, or adherence to social norms that occurs when group members are not treated as individuals.

risky shift   The tendency for groups to recommend uncertain and risky options.

group polarization   The tendency for a group to take a more extreme stance than originally held after deliberations and discussion.

Thinking Inside the Box
When group members become increasingly unified, frequently reaching agreement but seldom questioning each other, groupthink has probably taken hold. S. Harris/Cartoonstock

As a group becomes increasingly united, another group process known as **groupthink** can occur. This is the tendency for group members to maintain cohesiveness and agreement in their decision making, failing to consider possible alternatives and related viewpoints (Janis, 1972; Rose, 2011). Groupthink is thought to have played a role in a variety of disasters, including the *Challenger* space shuttle explosion in 1986, the Mount Everest climbing tragedy in 1996, and the U.S. decision to invade Iraq in 2003 (Badie, 2010; Burnette, Pollack, & Forsyth, 2011).

As you can see, groupthink can have life-or-death consequences. So, too, can the bystander effect, another alarming phenomenon that occurs among people in groups.

LO 8   Recognize the circumstances that influence the occurrence of the bystander effect.

THE BYSTANDER EFFECT   Before meeting Julius, the orphans had been homeless for several months. At night, they kept each other warm coiled beneath the bus, and they shared food when there was enough to go around. Their meals often consisted of scraps that hotels had poured onto side roads for dogs and cats. The orphans leaned on one another, but they didn't get much assistance from the outside world. Day after day, they encountered hundreds of passersby. Why didn't anyone try to rescue them? "Everybody was fearing responsibility," Julius says. In northern Uganda, many people cannot even afford to feed themselves, so they are reluctant to lend a helping hand.

But perhaps there was another factor at work, one that psychologists call the **bystander effect.** When a person is in trouble, bystanders have the tendency to assume (and perhaps wish) that someone else will help—and therefore they stand by and do nothing, partly a result of the *diffusion of responsibility.* This is particularly true when there are many other people present. Strange as it seems, we are more likely to aid a person in distress if no one else is present (Darley & Latané, 1968; Eagly & Crowley, 1986; Latané & Darley, 1968). So when people encountered the 11 orphans begging on the street, they probably assumed and hoped somebody else would take care of the problem. *These children must belong to someone; their parents will come back for them.*

Perhaps the most famous illustration of the bystander effect is the attack on Kitty Genovese. It was March 13, 1964, around 3:15 A.M., when Catherine "Kitty" Genovese arrived home from work in her Queens, New York, neighborhood. As she approached her apartment building, an attacker brutally stabbed her. Kitty screamed for help, but initial reports suggested that no one came to her rescue. The attacker ran away, and Kitty stumbled to her apartment building. But he soon returned, raping and stabbing her to death. *The New York Times* originally reported that 38 neighbors heard her cries for help, witnessed the attack, and did nothing to assist. But the evidence suggests that the second attack occurred inside her building, where few people could have witnessed it (Manning, Levine, & Collins, 2007).

groupthink   The tendency for group members to maintain cohesiveness and agreement in their decision making, failing to consider possible alternatives and related viewpoints.

bystander effect   The tendency for people to avoid getting involved in an emergency they witness because they assume someone else will help.

More recently, in April 2010, a homeless man (also in Queens) was left to die after several people walked by him and decided to do nothing. The man, Hugo Tale-Yax, had been trying to help a woman under assault, but the attacker stabbed him in the chest (Livingston, Doyle, & Mangan, 2010, April 25). As many as 25 people walked past Mr. Tale-Yax as he lay on the ground dying, and one even took a cell phone picture of him before walking away. Can you think of any reason they wouldn't help? Would you help someone in such a situation?

A recent review of the research suggests that things might not be as "bleak" as these events suggest. In extremely dangerous situations, bystanders are actually *more* likely to help even if there is more than one person watching. More dangerous situations are recognized and interpreted quickly as being such, leading to faster intervention and help (Fischer et al., 2011). If we want to increase the likelihood of bystanders getting involved in stopping violence, the community needs to educate its members about their responsibilities as neighbors and take steps to increase people's confidence in their ability to help (Banyard & Moynihan, 2011). Take a look at **Table 14.2** to learn about factors that increase helping behavior.

TABLE 14.2   WHY LEND A HAND?

Why People Help	Explanation
Kin selection	We are more likely to help those who are close relatives, as it might promote the survival of our genes (Alexander, 1974; Hamilton, 1964).
Empathy	We assist others to reduce their distress (Batson & Powell, 2003).
Social exchange theory	We help when the benefits of our good deeds outweigh the costs (Thibaut & Kelly, 1959).
Reciprocal altruism	We help those whom we believe can return the favor in the future (Trivers, 1971).
Mood	We tend to help others when our mood is good, but we also help when our spirits are low, knowing that this behavior can improve our mood (Batson & Powell, 2003; Schnall, Roper, & Fessler, 2010).

There are many reasons people assist each other in times of need. Above are some common explanations.

Aggression

THE ULTIMATE INSULT When Julius attended high school in Uganda's capital city of Kampala, he never told his classmates that he had been kidnapped by the LRA. "I would not tell them, or anybody, that I was a child soldier," he says. Had the other students known, they might have called him a *rebel*—one of the most derogatory terms you can use to describe a person in Uganda. Calling someone a rebel is like saying that individual is worthless. "You're poor; you do not know anything; you're a killer," Julius says. "It's the same pain as in America [when] they used to call Black people 'nigger.' You feel that kind of pain inside you . . . when they call you a 'rebel' within your country."

LO 9 Demonstrate an understanding of aggression and identify some of its causes.

Using racial slurs and hurling threatening insults is a form of *aggression*. Psychologists define **aggression** as intimidating or threatening behavior or attitudes intended to hurt someone. Like any phenomenon studied in psychology, aggression results from an interplay of biology and environment. According to the **frustration–aggression hypothesis,** we can all show aggressive behavior when placed in a frustrating situation (Dollard, Miller, Doob, Mowrer, & Sears, 1939). But aggressive tendencies also seem to be rooted in our genes. Studies comparing identical and fraternal twins suggest that aggression may run in families. Identical twins, who have the same genes, are more likely than fraternal twins to share aggressive traits (Bezdjian, Tuvblad, Raine, & Baker, 2011; Rowe, Almeida, & Jacobson, 1999). Some research on identical twins suggests that approximately 50% of aggressive behavior can be explained by genetic factors (DiLalla, 2002; Tackett, Waldman, & Lahey, 2009). Hormones and neurotransmitters also appear to play a role, with high levels of testosterone and low levels of serotonin correlating with aggression (Glenn, Raine, Schug, Gao, & Granger, 2011; Montoya, Terburg, Bos, & van Honk, 2012).

The way we express our aggression may be influenced by our gender. Males tend to show more *direct aggression* (physical displays of aggression such as hitting), while females are more likely to engage in *relational aggression*—behaviors such as gossip, exclusion, and ignoring, that are indirect and aimed at relationships (Ainsworth & Maner, 2012; Archer, 2004; Archer & Coyne, 2005; Crick & Grotpeter, 1995). Why would women show a tendency toward relational aggression as opposed to direct aggression? One important reason is that females run a greater risk of bodily injury resulting from a physical confrontation (Campbell, 1999).

Gender disparities in aggressive behavior typically appear early in life (Card, Stucky, Sawalani, & Little, 2008; Hanish, Sallquist, DiDonato, Fabes, & Martin, 2012), and result from a complex interaction of environmental factors and genetics (Brendgen et al., 2005; Rowe, Maughan, Worthman, Costello, & Angold, 2004). As mentioned, high levels of testosterone have been linked to aggression, and men have more testosterone than women. Social and cultural factors also play a role. Researchers have noted that boys tend to be more aggressive when raised in nonindustrial societies; patriarchal societies, in which women have less power and are considered inferior to men; and polygamous societies, in which men can have more than one wife. Evolutionary psychology would suggest that competition for resources (including females) increases the likelihood of aggression (Wood & Eagly, 2002).

CONNECTIONS

In previous chapters, we noted that *identical twins* share 100% of their genetic material, whereas fraternal twins share approximately 50%. Here, we see that identical twins are more likely than fraternal twins to share aggressive traits.

CONNECTIONS

In **Chapters 7** and **8,** we presented the concept of heritability (in relation to intelligence and schizophrenia, for example). Here, we note that around half of the variability in aggressive behavior can be attributed to genes and the other half to environment.

Stereotypes and Discrimination

Typically, we associate aggression with behavior, but it can also exist in the mind, coloring our *attitudes* about people and things. This is evidenced by the existence of **stereotypes**—the conclusions or inferences we make about people who are different from us, based on their group membership (such as race, religion, age, or gender). Stereotypes are often negative (*Blonde people are airheads*), but they can also be positive (*Asians are good at math*). Either way, stereotypes can be harmful.

Stereotypes are often associated with a set of perceived characteristics that we think describes members of a group. The stereotypical college instructor is absentminded, absorbed in thought, and unapproachable. The quintessential motorcycle rider is covered in tattoos, and the teenager with the tongue ring is rebelling against her parents. What do all these stereotypes have in common? They are not objective or based on empirical research. In other words, they are like bad theories of personality that characterize people based on a single behavior or trait. These stereotypes typically include a variety of predicted behaviors and traits that are rooted in subjective observations and value judgments.

When Julius was living in Louisiana, a man once approached him and said, "Is it true in Africa people still walk [around] naked?" We can only imagine where this man had gathered his knowledge of Africa (perhaps he had spent a bit too much time flipping through dated issues of *National Geographic*), but one thing seems certain: He was relying on an inaccurate stereotype of African people. The underlying message was clearly an aggressive one; he judged African people to be primitive and not as advanced as he was.

Running Hero
Julius runs by the Lira bus station where he discovered 11 orphans lying under a bus. Despite all the personal struggles Julius faced—living abroad, struggling financially, and battling foreign stereotypes of African people—Julius made a most selfless decision. He and his family adopted all 11 children. Charlie Shoemaker for *Runner's World* magazine. Copyright: 2011

LO 10 Recognize how group affiliation influences the development of stereotypes.

GROUPS AND SOCIAL IDENTITY Evolutionary psychologists would suggest that stereotypes allowed human beings to quickly identify the group to which they belonged (Liddle, Shackelford, & Weekes-Shackelford, 2012)—an adaptive trait, given that groups provide safety. But because we tend to think our group is superior, we may draw incorrect conclusions about members of other groups, or outsiders in general. We tend to see the world in terms of the **in-group** (the group to which *we* belong, or *us*) and the **out-group** (those who are outside the group to which we belong, or *them*). For better or worse, our affiliation with an in-group helps us form our **social identity,** or view of ourselves within a social group, and this process begins at a very young age. Those in your in-group may influence your behaviors and thoughts more than you realize.

DISCRIMINATION Seeing the world from the narrow perspective of our own group may lead to **ethnocentrism.** This term is often used in reference to cultural groups, yet it can apply to any group (think of football teams, glee clubs, college rivals, or nations). We tend to see our own group as *the one* that is worthy of emulation, the superior group. This type of group identification can lead to stereotyping, discussed earlier, and **discrimination,** which involves showing favoritism or hostility to others because of their group affiliation.

Those in the out-group are particularly vulnerable to becoming scapegoats. A **scapegoat** is the target of negative emotions, beliefs, and behaviors. During periods of major stress (such as an economic crisis), scapegoats are often blamed for undesirable social situations (high unemployment).

aggression Intimidating or threatening behavior or attitudes intended to hurt someone.
frustration–aggression hypothesis Suggests that aggression may occur in response to frustration.
stereotypes Conclusions or inferences we make about people who are different from us based on their group membership, such as race, religion, age, or gender.
in-group The group to which we belong.
out-group People outside the group to which we belong.
social identity How we view ourselves within our social group.
ethnocentrism To see the world only from the perspective of one's own group.
discrimination Showing favoritism or hostility to others because of their affiliation with a group.
scapegoat A target of negative emotions, beliefs, and behaviors; typically, a member of the out-group who receives blame for an upsetting social situation.

PREJUDICE   People who harbor stereotypes and blame scapegoats are more likely to feel **prejudice,** hostile or negative attitudes toward individuals or groups (**Infographic 14.3** on page 584). While racial prejudice has declined in the United States over the last half-century, there is still considerable evidence that negative attitudes persist. The same is true when it comes to sexual orientation, disabilities, and religious beliefs (Carr, Dweck, & Pauker, 2012; Dovidio, Kawakami, & Gaertner, 2002). The causes of prejudice are complex and varied. Cognitive aspects of prejudice include the just-world hypothesis, which assumes that a person has done something to deserve the bad things happening to him, and that he should be able to control the events in his life. Prejudice may also result from conformity, as when a person seeks approval from others with strong prejudicial views.

Researchers have concluded that prejudice can be reduced when people are forced to work together toward a common goal. In the early 1970s, Eliot Aronson and colleagues developed the notion of a jigsaw classroom. The teachers created exercises that required all students to complete individual tasks, the results of which would fit together like a jigsaw puzzle. The students began to realize the importance of working cooperatively to reach the desired goal. Ultimately, every contribution was an essential piece of the puzzle, and this resulted in all the students feeling valuable (Aronson, 2015).

STEREOTYPE THREAT   Stereotypes, discrimination, and prejudice are conceptually related to **stereotype threat,** a "situational threat" in which a person is aware of others' negative expectations. This leads to a fear of being judged or treated as inferior, and it can actually undermine performance in a specific area associated with the stereotype (Steele, 1997).

African American college students are often the targets of racial stereotypes about poor academic abilities. These threatening stereotypes can lead to lowered performance on tests designed to measure ability, and to a *disidentification* with the role of a student (in other words, taking on the attitude that *I am not a student*). Interestingly, a person does not have to believe the stereotype is accurate in order for it to have an impact (Steele, 1997, 2010).

There is a great deal of variation in how people react to stereotype threats (Block, Koch, Liberman, Merriweather, & Roberson, 2011). Some people simply "fend off" the stereotype, by working harder to disprove it. Others feel discouraged and respond by getting angry, either overtly or quietly. Still others seem to ignore the threats. These resilient types appear to "bounce back" and grow from the negative experience. When confronted with a stereotype, they redirect their responses to create an environment that is more inclusive and less conducive to stereotyping.

Unfortunately, stereotypes are pervasive in our society. Just contemplate all the positive and negative stereotypes associated with certain lines of work. Lawyers are greedy, truck drivers are overweight, and (dare we say) psychologists are manipulative. Can you think of any negative stereotypes associated with prison guards? As you read the next feature, think about how stereotypes come to life when people fail to stop and think about their behaviors.

prejudice   Holding hostile or negative attitudes toward an individual or group.

stereotype threat   A "situational threat" in which individuals are aware of others' negative expectations, which leads to their fear that they will be judged or treated as inferior.

social roles   The positions we hold in social groups, and the responsibilities and expectations associated with those roles.

CONTROVERSIES

The Stanford "Prison"

➡️⬅️ August 1971: Philip Zimbardo of Stanford University launched what would become one of the most controversial experiments in the history of psychology. Zimbardo and his colleagues carefully selected 24 male college students to play the roles of prisoners and guards in a simulated "prison" setup in the basement of Stanford University's psychology building. (Three of the selected students did not end up participating, so the final number of participants included 10 prisoners and 11 guards.)

The young men chosen for the experiment were deemed "normal-average" by the researchers, who administered several psychological tests (Haney, Banks, & Zimbardo, 1973, p. 90).

After being "arrested" in their homes by Palo Alto Police officers, the prisoners were searched and booked at a local police station, and then sent to the "prison" at Stanford. The experiment was supposed to last for 2 weeks, but the behavior of the guards and the prisoners was so disturbing the researchers abandoned the study after just 6 days (Haney & Zimbardo, 1998). Some of the guards became abusive, punishing the prisoners, stripping them naked, and confiscating their mattresses. It seemed as if they had lost sight of the prisoners' humanity, as they ruthlessly wielded their newfound power. As one guard stated, "Looking back, I'm impressed how little I felt for them" (Haney et al., 1973, p. 88). Some prisoners became passive and obedient, accepting the guards' cruel treatment; others were released early due to "extreme emotional depression, crying, rage, and acute anxiety" (p. 81).

> ## ". . . LOOKING BACK, I'M IMPRESSED HOW LITTLE I FELT FOR THEM."

How can we explain this fiasco? The guards and prisoners, it seemed, took their assigned **social roles** and ran way too far with them. Social roles guide our behavior and represent the positions we hold in social groups, and the responsibilities and expectations associated with those roles.

The prison experiment may have shed light on the power of social roles, but its validity has come under fire. For example, scholars suggest that the participants were merely "acting out their stereotypic images" of guards and prisoners, and behaving in accordance with the researchers' expectations (Banuazizi & Movahedi, 1975, p. 159). As one guard explained decades later, "I set out with a definite plan in mind, to try to force the action, force something to happen, so that the researchers would have something to work with" (Ratnesar, 2011, July/August, para. 30). Apparently, Zimbardo made his expectations quite clear, instructing the guards to deny the prisoners their "privacy," "freedom," and "individuality" (Zimbardo, 2007).

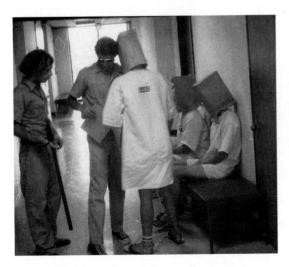 

Prison Horrors
(left) Prisoners in Zimbardo's 1971 prison experiment are forced to wear bags over their heads. An Abu Ghraib detainee (right) lies on the floor attached to a leash in 2003. The dehumanization and cruel treatment of prisoners in the "Stanford Prison" and the Abu Ghraib facility are disturbingly similar.
left: Philip G. Zimbardo, Inc.; right: AP Photo

Despite its limitations and questionable ethics, the Stanford Prison Experiment continues to be relevant. In 2004, news broke that American soldiers and intelligence officials at Iraq's Abu Ghraib prison had beaten, sodomized, and forced detainees to commit degrading sexual acts (Hersh, 2004, May 10). The similarities between Abu Ghraib and the Stanford Prison are noteworthy (Zimbardo, 2007). In both cases, authority figures threatened, abused, and forced inmates to be naked. Those in charge seemed to derive pleasure from violating and humiliating other human beings (Haney et al., 1973; Hersh, 2004, May 10). ➡️⬅️

Thinking About Other People
Stereotypes, Discrimination, and Prejudice

Attitudes are complex and only sometimes related to our behaviors. Like most attitudes, prejudicial attitudes can be connected with our *cognitions* about groups of people, our negative *feelings* about others (also referred to as prejudice), and our *behaviors* (discriminating against others). Understanding how and when these pieces connect to each other is an important goal of social psychology. Jane Elliott's classic "Blue Eyes/Brown Eyes" exercise helps demonstrate how stereotypes, discrimination, and prejudice may be connected.

Prejudical attitude toward others

Cognitive component (beliefs and ideas)

We tend to categorize people in terms of the *in-group* (the group to which we belong) and the *out-group* (people different from us in some way). **Stereotypes** are beliefs or assumptions we hold about people, based on perceived differences we think describe members of their group.

Affective component (emotional evaluation)

Prejudice, or feelings of hostility, anger, or discomfort toward members of out-groups.

Social psychologists often use prejudice to refer to both these negative attitudes and the negative feelings tied to them.

Behavioral component (the way we respond)

Discrimination, or treating others differently because of their affiliation with a group. Can include showing hostility or anger to others, or can be more subtle, such as different body language or tone of voice.

Stereotype

"cleaner, more civilized, smarter"

Prejudice

Prejudice

Discrimination

Brown-eyes dislike blue-eyes, but have to be nice while in class.

Brown-eyes dislike blue-eyes and exclude them from games at recess.

Brown-eyes, who are required to sit at the front of the room, do not sit with blue-eyes, who must sit at the back.

Discrimination

When Dr. Martin Luther King, Jr., was assassinated in 1968, a teacher named Jane Elliott gave her students a lesson about discrimination. Because no African Americans lived in their Iowa town, she knew students would have trouble understanding what motivated the terrible act. Elliott invited the class to join her in an exercise in which one set of students was segregated into a negatively stereotyped out-group: "Suppose we divided the class into blue-eyed people and brown-eyed people.... [B]rown-eyed people are better than blue-eyed people. They are cleaner . . . more civilized . . . smarter" (Peters, 1971, pp. 20–21).

In her exercise, Elliott created a situation in which discrimination initially existed without the presence of actual feelings of hostility or anger. Although prejudice and discrimination often go hand in hand, either condition can exist independently.

During the exercise, a list of rules governed behavior for both groups. For example, only children with brown eyes were allowed to sit at the front of the room near the teacher. The effect of this manufactured discrimination surprised even Elliott. The brown-eyed children quickly became openly hostile toward the blue-eyed children. And "[t]he blue-eyed children were miserable.... [T]heir entire attitudes were those of defeat. Their classroom work regressed sharply from that of the day before" (Peters, 1971, p. 25).

Much of this chapter has focused on the negative aspects of human behavior, such as obedience, stereotyping, and discrimination. While we cannot deny the existence of these phenomena, we believe they are overshadowed by the goodness that lies within every one of us.

✓ show what you know

1. _____ is the tendency for people to not react in an emergency, often thinking that someone else will step in to help.
   - **a.** Group polarization
   - **b.** The risky shift
   - **c.** The bystander effect
   - **d.** Deindividuation

2. According to research, which of the following plays a role in aggressive behavior?
   - **a.** low social identity
   - **b.** low levels of the hormone testosterone
   - **c.** low levels of the neurotransmitter serotonin
   - **d.** low levels of ethnocentrism

3. Name and describe the different displays of aggression exhibited by males and females.

4. Students often have difficulty identifying how the concepts of stereotypes, discrimination, and prejudice are related. If you were sitting at a table with a sixth-grade student, how would you explain their similarities and differences?

✓ CHECK YOUR ANSWERS IN APPENDIX C.

It's All Good: Prosocial Behavior, Attraction, and Love

You may be wondering why we chose to include Joe and Susanne Maggio in the same chapter as Julius Achon. What do these people have in common, and why are they featured together in a chapter on social psychology? We selected these individuals because their stories send a positive message, illuminating what is best about human relationships, like the capacity to love and feel empathy. They epitomize the positive side of social psychology.

Prosocial Behavior

LO 11 Compare prosocial behavior and altruism.

We like to believe that all human beings are capable of *prosocial behavior,* or behavior aimed at benefiting others. An exemplar of this ability is Julius Achon. After meeting the orphans in 2003, Julius kept his promise to assist them, wiring his family $150 a month to cover the cost of food, clothing, school uniforms, tuition, and other necessities—even when he and his wife were struggling to stay afloat. For 3 years, Julius was the children's sole source of financial support. Then in 2006, when Julius was living in Portland and working for Nike, a friend helped him gather additional support from others. The following year, Julius formalized his efforts by creating the Achon Uganda Children's Fund (AUCF), a nonprofit organization dedicated to improving the living conditions of children in the rural areas of northern Uganda. AUCF's latest project is the construction and operation of a medical clinic in Julius' home county of Otuke. The Kristina Acuma Achon Health Center is named after Julius' mother, who was shot by the LRA in 2004 and died from her wounds because she lacked access to proper medical care. Julius recently moved back to Uganda, where he is overseeing the work of AUCF. (For more information about the organization, please see http://achonugandachildren.org.)

As for the 11 orphans, all of them are flourishing. The teenage girl in tattered clothing—the first to emerge from under the bus that morning in 2003—is now a nurse at the Kristina Acuma Achon Health Center. Many of the older children attend

You Asked, Julius Answers

http://qrs.ly/2l4qslg

What advice would you give to someone interested in charitable work?

a boarding school in Kampala, and one of them—a young man named Samuel—has become a competitive runner like Julius. The other children attend school and remain in the care of Julius and his family.

On the Up Side

It feels good to give to others, even when you receive nothing in return. The satisfaction derived from knowing you made someone feel happier, more secure, or appreciated is enough of a reward. The desire or motivation to help others with no expectations of payback is called **altruism.** *Empathy,* or the ability to understand and recognize another's emotional point of view, is a major component of altruism.

ALTRUISM AND TODDLERS   The seeds of altruism appear to be planted very early in life. Children as young as 18 months have been observed demonstrating helping behavior. One study found that the vast majority of 18-month-olds would help a researcher obtain an out-of-reach object, assist him in a book-stacking exercise, and open a door for him when his hands were full. It is important to note the babies did not lend a hand when the researcher intentionally put the object out of reach, or if he appeared satisfied with the stack of books. They only helped when it appeared assistance was needed (Warneken & Tomasello, 2006). What was happening in the brains of these young children? Research demonstrates that particular areas of the brain (such as the medial prefrontal cortex) show increased activity in association with feelings of empathy and helping behaviors (Rameson, Morelli, & Lieberman, 2012). Given that altruism shows up so early in life, perhaps you are wondering if it is innate. Researchers are trying to determine if this characteristic has a genetic component, and the findings from twin studies identify "considerable heritability" of altruistic tendencies and other prosocial behaviors (Jiang, Chew, & Ebstein, 2013). But as always, we must consider the biopsychosocial perspective, recognizing the interaction of genetics, environment, and culture (Knafo & Israel, 2010).

CONNECTIONS

In **Chapter 11,** we discussed how altruistic behaviors can reduce stress. When helping someone else, we generally don't have time to focus on our own problems; we also see that there are people dealing with more troubling issues than we are.

REDUCING STRESS AND INCREASING HAPPINESS   Research suggests that helping others reduces stress and increases happiness (Schwartz, Keyl, Marcum, & Bode, 2009; Schwartz, Meisenhelder, Yunsheng, & Reed, 2003). The gestures don't have to be grand in order to be altruistic or prosocial. Consider the last time you bought coffee for a colleague without being asked, or gave a stranger a quarter to fill his parking meter. Do you recycle, conserve electricity, and take public transportation? These behaviors indicate an awareness of the need to conserve resources for the benefit of all. Promoting sustainability is an indirect, yet very impactful, prosocial endeavor. Perhaps you haven't opened your home to 11 orphaned children, but you may perform acts of kindness more regularly than you realize.

Even if you're not the type to reach out to strangers, you probably demonstrate prosocial behavior toward your family and close friends. This giving of yourself allows you to experience the most magical element of human existence: love.

Interpersonal Attraction

TO HAVE AND TO HOLD   Less than a year after meeting Susanne, Joe purchased an engagement ring. He carried it around in his pocket for 3 months, and then proposed to her one morning over breakfast. They have been happily married for over 7 years. Some things have changed since that rendezvous at Chili's 10 years ago. Joe left the ice cream business for a corporate career, *little* Kristina is now a teenager, and Susanne gave birth to TRIPLETS in February 2013— two boys and a girl.

Other things remain the same, like Joe's goofy sense of humor. He still strolls into the supermarket singing at the top of his lungs and tells people "good morning" when it's 11 o'clock at night. "I'm a big kid," Joe says, "but you know when it comes to my family, it's all about making sure that they are happy and making sure that they are taken care of, and that's my only priority in life."

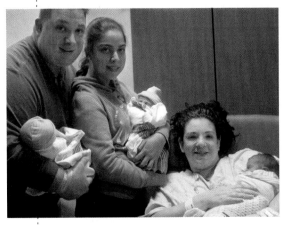

Love Grows
Joe, Kristina, and Susanne celebrate the arrival of their new family members: Joseph Jr., Michael Charles Frank, and Sophia Elizabeth. The triplets came into the world on February 11, 2013. Joe Maggio

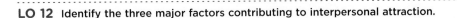

LO 12 Identify the three major factors contributing to interpersonal attraction.

It seems Joe and Susanne have made a very happy life for themselves. Things can get hectic with triplet toddlers and a teen, but they seem content and able to cope with whatever challenges may arise. Joe and Susanne make a great team. How do you explain their compatibility? We suspect it has something to do with **interpersonal attraction,** the factors that lead us to form friendships or romantic relationships with others. What are these mysterious attraction factors? Let's focus our attention on the three most important: proximity, similarity, and physical attractiveness.

WE'RE CLOSE: PROXIMITY   We would guess that the majority of people in your social circle live nearby. **Proximity,** or nearness, plays a significant role in the formation of our relationships. The closer two people live geographically, the greater the odds that they will meet and spend time together, and the more likely they are to establish a bond (Festinger, Schachter, & Back, 1950; Nahemow & Lawton, 1975). One study looking at the development of friendships in a college classroom setting concluded that sitting in nearby seats and being assigned to the same work groups correlated with the development of friendships (Back, Schmukle, & Egloff, 2008). In other words, sitting next to someone in class, or even in the same row, increases the chances that you will become friends. Would you agree?

Notions of proximity have changed since the introduction of the Internet. Thanks to applications like *Skype* and *Google Hangouts,* we can now have face-to-face conversations with people who are thousands of miles away. Dating sites and mobile apps offer similar capabilities through chats, instant messaging, and photo sharing. They also provide the option of geographic filtering, allowing users to narrow their searches to people who live in a certain zip code or city. But do all these new tools really improve the way people relate to one another? For Joe and Susanne, the answer seems to be "yes." If it weren't for Match.com, their paths probably would not have crossed. As for the rest of humanity, the answer is not so straightforward.

CONNECTIONS

In **Chapter 1,** we described how researchers examine relationships between two variables. A correlation does not necessarily mean one variable causes changes in the other. What other factors might be influencing friendships to develop in the classroom?

altruism A desire or motivation to help others with no expectation of anything in return.

interpersonal attraction The factors that lead us to form friendships or romantic relationships with others.

proximity Nearness; plays an important role in the formation of relationships.

SOCIAL MEDIA and psychology

Relationships Online

The great advantage of online dating, according to researchers, is that it broadens the dating pool, providing users with opportunities to meet people they never would encounter offline (Finkel et al., 2012). There are drawbacks, however, like the tendency for many online daters to focus on profile pictures and other superficial details. Also, don't count on the compatibility algorithms many online dating sites advertise, as researchers are skeptical of them (Finkel, et al., 2012). Despite these shortcomings, relationships that start on these sites are surprisingly successful. According to one study, around 20% of couples who met online had formed lasting relationships, defined as married, engaged, or living together (Bargh & McKenna, 2004).

You may be wondering how social media sites such as Facebook affect interpersonal bonds. Research suggests that many people use social media to enhance the relationships they already have (Anderson, Fagan, Woodnutt, & Chamorro-Premuzic, 2012). Teenagers, in particular, use social networking sites to make contact with their "offline" friends. Their online activities are primarily social (communicating as opposed to playing video games, for example) and seem to reinforce existing friendships (Reich et al., 2012).

LOOKING FOR LOVE IN ELECTRONIC PLACES.

Relationships 2.0
Social networking sites play a significant role in modern relationships, particularly among young people. For many teens, communicating through sites like Facebook is an important means of cultivating relationships (Reich, Subrahmanyam, & Espinoza, 2012).
Paul Noth The New Yorker Collection/The Cartoon Bank

"I can't wait to see what you're like online."

MERE-EXPOSURE EFFECT   These repeated contacts with friends serve a purpose; the **mere-exposure effect** suggests that the more we are exposed to people, food, jingles, songs, politics, or music, the more positive a reaction we have toward them. More time spent online with friends can strengthen relationships, *merely* through exposure.

The mere-exposure effect may, to a certain extent, explain why Joe and Susanne are more in love today than they were 8 years ago. After years of positive exposure to one another (living under the same roof, raising children together, and sharing new experiences), their connection has deepened.

But here's the flip side. Repeated *negative* exposures may lead to stronger distaste. If a person you frequently encounter has annoying habits or uncouth behavior, negative feelings might develop, even if your initial impression was positive (Cunningham, Shamblen, Barbee, & Ault, 2005). This can be problematic for romantic partners. All those minor irritations you overlooked early in the relationship can evolve into major headaches.

SIMILARITY   Perhaps you have heard the saying "birds of a feather flock together." This statement alludes to the concept of *similarity,* another factor that contributes to interpersonal attraction (Moreland & Zajonc, 1982; Morry, Kito, & Ortiz, 2011). We tend to prefer those who share our interests, viewpoints, ethnicity, values, and other characteristics. Even age, education, and occupation tend to be similar among those who are close (Lott & Lott, 1965).

PHYSICAL ATTRACTIVENESS   We probably don't need to tell you that *physical attractiveness* plays a major role in interpersonal attraction (Eastwick, Eagly, Finkel, & Johnson, 2011; Lou & Zhang, 2009). But here is the question: Is beauty really in the eye of the beholder? In other words, do people from different cultures and historical periods have different concepts of beauty? There is some degree of consistency in the way people rate facial attractiveness (Langlois et al., 2000), with facial symmetry generally considered an attractive trait (Grammer & Thornhill, 1994). But certain aspects of beauty do appear to be culturally distinct (Gangestad & Scheyd, 2005). In some parts of the world, people go to great lengths to elongate their necks, increase height, pierce their bodies, augment their breasts, enlarge or reduce the size of their waists, and paint

mere-exposure effect The more we are exposed to someone or something, the more positive a reaction we have toward it.

themselves—just so others within their culture will find them attractive. In America, the ideal body shape for women has changed over the years (think of Marilyn Monroe versus Gisele Bündchen), suggesting that cultural concepts of beauty can morph over time.

LOOKING GOOD IN THOSE GENES: THE EVOLUTIONARY PERSPECTIVE

Why is physical attractiveness so important? Beauty is a sign of health, and healthy people have greater potential for longevity and successful breeding (Gangestad & Scheyd, 2005). Consider this evidence: Women are more likely to seek out men with healthy-looking physical characteristics when they are experiencing peak fertility and therefore likely to conceive. Ovulating women tend to look for masculine characteristics that suggest a genetic advantage, such as facial symmetry and social dominance, in order to provide the greatest benefit to offspring. In fact, research indicates that ovulating women perceive "sexy cads" as more devoted fathers and partners than average-looking men—even when provided with information suggesting the opposite (Durante, Griskevicius, Simpson, Cantú, & Li, 2012).

Clearly, women can be swayed by the good looks of potential mates. But which gender places greater value on beauty? And what other characteristics do men and women seek in long-term sexual partners?

CONTROVERSIES

Are You My Natural Selection?

➡️⬅️ From an evolutionary standpoint, men and women produce offspring for the same reason—to ensure that their genes outlast them. But they have different roles in reproduction. Women generally invest more in childbearing and rearing (getting pregnant, breastfeeding, and so on) and they are limited in the number of offspring they can produce. Men are capable of fathering hundreds, if not thousands, of children, and they are not hampered by the biological constraints of pregnancy and breastfeeding. Under these circumstances, a woman's best strategy is to find a mate who will ensure that her children have all the resources they need to survive and reproduce. A man, on the other hand, should be on the lookout for a woman who can bear many children—someone who shows signs of fertility, like youth and beauty (Geary, Vigil, & Byrd-Craven, 2004).

> **A WOMAN'S FINANCIAL SECURITY HAS BECOME AN INCREASINGLY IMPORTANT CRITERION FOR MALE SUITORS.**

Do people really choose partners according to these criteria? One study of over 10,000 participants from 37 cultures concluded that women around the world do indeed favor mates who appear to be good providers, whereas men place greater value on good looks and youth (Buss, 1989). Subsequent studies have produced similar results (Buss, Shackelford, Kirkpatrick, & Larsen, 2001; Schwarz & Hassebrauck, 2012; Shackelford, Schmitt, & Buss, 2005).

Sure, we all have preferences for the type of partner we want, but do they really impact the choices we make? Do men, for instance, typically marry women who are younger? Yes, this appears to be the case. Husbands across the world are, on average, a few years older than their wives (Buss, 1989; Lakdawalla & Schoeni, 2003; Otta, da Silva Queiroz, de Sousa Campos, da Silva, & Silveira, 1999).

But let's put these findings in perspective. Two or three years is not much of a gap if you're thinking about growing old together. (Is age 83 really any different from 80?) And we all know there are many women in search of "hot men," and men in pursuit of "sugar mamas." Over the past several decades, in fact, a woman's financial security has become an increasingly important criterion for male suitors (Buss et al., 2001). In today's ever-changing social and cultural environment, evolution is just one factor influencing our selection of a mate. ➡️⬅️

"Marry me, Virginia. My genes are excellent and, as yet, unpatented."

BEAUTY PERKS   We have discussed beauty in the context of romantic relationships, but how does physical appearance affect other aspects of social existence? Generally speaking, physically attractive people seem to have more opportunities. Beauty is correlated with how much money someone makes, the type of job she holds, and overall success (Pfeifer, 2012). Good-looking children and adults are viewed as more intelligent and popular, and are treated better in general (Langlois et al., 2000). Why would this be? From the perspective of evolutionary psychology, these characteristics would be good indicators of reproductive potential. And many people fall prey to the *halo effect,* or the tendency to assign excessive weight to one dimension of a person. This concept was originally described by Thorndike in 1920 as it related to the evaluation of others. People tend to form these general impressions early on and then cling to them, even in the absence of supporting evidence, or the presence of contradictory evidence (Aronson, 2012). The way we respond to beautiful people is one example of the halo effect; our initial impression of their beauty may lead us to assume they have other positive characteristics like superior intelligence, popularity, and desirability.

Beauty may captivate you in the beginning stages of a relationship, but other characteristics and qualities gain importance as time goes along. Think about the type of person you want for a life partner. Whom would you want to hold your hand when you're sick in the hospital—the underwear model or the person you most respect and trust?

What Is Love?

In America, we are taught to believe that love is the foundation of marriage. People in Western cultures do tend to marry for love, but this is not the case everywhere. In Harare, Zimbabwe, for example, people might also marry for reasons associated with the needs of the family, such as maintaining alliances and social status (Wojcicki, van der Straten, & Padian, 2010). Similarly, many marriages in India and other parts of South Asia are arranged by family members. Love may not be present in the beginning stages of such unions, but it can blossom.

STERNBERG'S THEORY OF LOVE   In a pivotal study published in 1986, Robert Sternberg proposed that love is made up of three elements: passion (feelings leading to romance and physical attraction); intimacy (feeling close); and commitment (the recognition of love). He conceptualized these elements in terms of the corners of a triangle (**Figure 14.4**). Love takes many forms according to Sternberg, and can include any combination of the three elements.

Many relationships begin with exhilaration and intense physical attraction, and then evolve into more intimate connections. This is the type of love we often see portrayed in the movies. The combination of connection, concern, care, and intimacy is what Sternberg called **romantic love.** Romantic love is similar to what some psychologists refer to as **passionate love** (also known as "love at first sight"), which is based on zealous emotion, leading to intense longing and sexual attraction (Hatfield, Bensman, & Rapson, 2012). As a relationship grows, intimacy and commitment develop into **companionate love,** or love that consists of profound fondness, camaraderie, understanding, and emotional closeness. Companionate love is typical of a couple that has been together for many years. They become comfortable with each other, routines set in, and passion often fizzles (Aronson, 2012). Although the passion may wane, the friendship is strong. **Consummate love** (kän(t)-sə-mət) is evident when intimacy and commitment are accompanied by passion. The ultimate goal is to maintain all three components of the triangle.

Research and life experiences tell us that relationships inevitably change. Romantic love is generally what drives people to commit to one another (Berscheid, 2010).

FIGURE 14.4
Sternberg's Triangular Model of Love
Sternberg proposed that there are different kinds of love resulting from combinations of three elements: passion, intimacy, and commitment. The ideal form, consummate love, combines all three elements. Sternberg (1986).

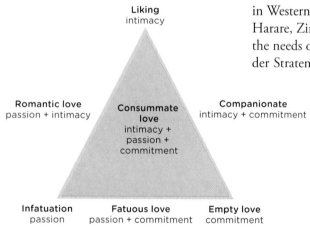

romantic love Love that is a combination of connection, concern, care, and intimacy.

passionate love Love that is based on zealous emotion, leading to intense longing and sexual attraction.

companionate love Love that consists of profound fondness, camaraderie, understanding, and emotional closeness.

consummate love (kän(t)-sə-mət) Love that combines intimacy, commitment, and passion.

But the passion associated with this stage generally decreases over time. That does not mean it cannot reemerge, however. Can you think of ways this passion might be rekindled—a romantic night out, some sexy new underwear, a trip to fantasyland? Companionate love, in contrast, tends to grow over time. As we experience life with a partner, it is companionate love that seems to endear us to one another (Berscheid, 2010).

What type of love do you think online dating sites tend to select for? Is it companionate love (SF loves to garden, looking for someone who . . .)? Or is it passionate love (SM looking for a good time with no strings attached . . .)? As Joe can attest, passionate love was present from the beginning of his relationship with Susanne (he jokes about taking a few cold showers before anything happened). Although their passion is still strong and steady, the love and respect they have for one another have grown much deeper.

Have you ever wondered about the long-term stability of your relationships? Couples stay together for many reasons, some better than others. Caryl Rusbult's *investment model of commitment* focuses on the resources at stake in relationships, including finances, possessions, time spent together, and perhaps even children (Rusbult, 1983). According to this model, decisions to stay together or separate are based on how happy people are in their relationship, their notion of what life would be like without it, and their investment. According to the investment model of commitment people may stay in unsatisfying or unhealthy relationships if they feel there are no better alternatives or believe they have too much to lose (Rusbult & Martz, 1995). This model helps us understand why people remain in destructive relationships.

MAKING THIS CHAPTER WORK IN YOUR LIFE At last, we reach the end of our journey through social psychology. We hope that what you have learned in this chapter will come in handy in your everyday social exchanges. Be conscious of the attributions you use to explain the behavior of others—are you being objective or falling prey to self-serving bias? Be mindful of your attitudes—how are they influencing your behavior? Know that your behaviors are constantly being shaped by your social interactions—both as an individual and as a member of groups. Understand the dangers of stereotyping, and know the human suffering caused by aggression. But perhaps most of all, be kind and helpful to others, and allow yourself to experience love.

CONNECTIONS

In **Chapter 3,** we discussed sensory adaptation, which refers to the way in which sensory receptors become less sensitive to constant stimuli. In **Chapter 5,** we presented the concept of habituation, which occurs when an organism becomes less responsive to repeated stimuli. Humans seem to be attracted to novelty, which might underlie our desire for passion.

The Honeymoon Continues
After several years of marriage and three new children, the love between Joe and Susanne Maggio is stronger than ever. They have what you might call consummate love, a type of love characterized by intimacy, commitment, and passion. Joseph Maggio

---

✓○○○   **show what you know**

1. Julius Achon sent money home every month to help cover the cost of food, clothing, and schooling for his 11 adopted children. This is a good example of:
   a. the just-world hypothesis.
   b. deindividuation.
   c. individualistic behavior.
   d. prosocial behavior.

2. What are the three major factors that play a role in interpersonal attraction?
   a. social influence; obedience; physical attractiveness
   b. proximity; similarity; physical attractiveness
   c. obedience; proximity; social influence
   d. proximity; love; social influence

3. We described how the investment model of commitment can be used to predict the long-term stability of a romantic relationship. How can you use this same model to predict the long-term stability of friendships, positions at work, or loyalty to institutions?

✓ CHECK YOUR ANSWERS IN APPENDIX C.

14 summary of concepts

LO 1   Define social psychology and identify how it is different from sociology. (p. 554)

Social psychology is the study of human cognition, emotion, and behavior in relation to others. This includes how we perceive and react to others, and how we behave in social settings. Social psychology focuses on studying individuals in relation to others and groups, whereas sociology studies the groups themselves—their cultures, societies, and subcultures. Using the same general research methods as other psychologists, social psychologists often conduct studies involving confederates, or people who are secretly working for them. At the end of a study, researchers debrief participants, or review aspects of the research they had previously concealed.

LO 2   Describe social cognition and how we use attributions to explain behavior. (p. 556)

Social cognition refers to the way we think about others, attend to social information, and use this information in our lives, both consciously and unconsciously. Attributions are the beliefs we develop to explain human behaviors and characteristics, as well as situations. Because attributions rely on whatever information happens to be available (our observations of what people say and do, for example), they are vulnerable to personal bias and inaccuracies.

LO 3   Describe how attributions lead to mistakes in our explanations for behaviors. (p. 557)

Situational attributions are a type of external attribution in which the assumed causes of behaviors are in the environment. Dispositional attributions are a type of internal attribution in which the causes of behaviors are thought to be traits or characteristics. When people make attributions, they are often guessing about the causes of events or behaviors, leaving plenty of room for error. Three common errors are (1) the fundamental attribution error, which assumes the causes of behaviors are in the person (dispositional) as opposed to the environment (situational); (2) the just-world hypothesis, which assumes that if someone is suffering, he must have done something to deserve it; and (3) the self-serving bias, which attributes one's successes to internal characteristics and one's failures to environmental factors.

LO 4   Describe social influence and recognize the factors associated with persuasion. (p. 565)

Social influence refers to the way a person is affected by others, as apparent in behavior, emotion, and cognition. Expectations are an often overlooked form of social influence. Students in Rosenthal's study who were expected to show surprising gains actually did as a result of the high expectations placed on them. Persuasion is intentionally trying to make people change their attitudes and beliefs, which may (or may not) lead to changes in their behavior. There are three factors that determine persuasive power: the source, the message, and the audience.

cpaquin/Getty Images

LO 5   Define compliance and explain some of the techniques used to gain it. (p. 567)

Compliance occurs when someone voluntarily changes her behavior at the request or direction of another person or group, who in general does not have any true authority over her. A common method to gain compliance is the foot-in-the-door technique, which occurs when an individual initially makes a small request, followed by a larger one. Another method is the door-in-the-face technique, which involves making a large request, followed by a smaller one.

LO 6   Identify the factors that influence the likelihood of someone conforming. (p. 569)

The urge to modify behaviors, attitudes, beliefs, and opinions to match those of others is known as conformity. There are three major reasons we conform. Most people want approval, to be liked and accepted by others. This desire, known as normative social influence, can have a significant impact on behaviors. A second reason to conform is that we want to be correct. We look to others for confirmation when we are uncertain about something, and then do as they do. This is known as informational social influence. Finally, we may conform to others because they belong to a certain reference group we respect, admire, or long to join.

LO 7   Describe obedience and explain how Stanley Milgram studied it. (p. 571)

Obedience occurs when we change our behavior, or act in a way that we might not normally act, because we have been ordered to do so by an authority figure. Milgram conducted a series of studies examining how far people would go when urged by an authority figure to inflict punishment on others. During an early experiment, the goal was for the confederate (*learner*) to memorize a set of paired words. The participant (*teacher*) sat at a table, which held a control panel for administering electrical "shocks." The teacher was told to administer a shock each time the learner made a mistake, and the shock was to increase by 15 volts for every mistake. Milgram was surprised that so many people obeyed the experimenter and continued to administer "shocks," even when they hesitated or were uncomfortable, simply because an authority figure had instructed them to do so.

LO 8 Recognize the circumstances that influence the occurrence of the bystander effect. (p. 578)

When a person is in trouble, bystanders have the tendency to assume that someone else will help—and therefore they stand by and do nothing, partly because there is a diffusion of responsibility. This bystander effect is more likely to occur when there are many other people present. By contrast, individuals are more inclined to aid a person in distress if no one else is around.

LO 9 Demonstrate an understanding of aggression and identify some of its causes. (p. 580)

Aggression is defined as intimidating or threatening behavior or attitudes intended to hurt someone. Research on aggression suggests that it has a biological basis (for instance, high levels of testosterone and low levels of serotonin). In addition, the frustration–aggression hypothesis suggests that in a frustrating situation, we can all show aggressive behavior.

LO 10 Recognize how group affiliation influences the development of stereotypes. (p. 581)

We tend to see the world in terms of the in-group (the group to which we belong) and the out-group (those outside our group). Seeing the world from the narrow perspective of our own group may lead to ethnocentrism, which sets the stage for stereotyping and discrimination.

Stereotypes are the conclusions or inferences we make about people based on their group membership. Discrimination involves showing favoritism or hostility to others because of their affiliation with a group. People who harbor stereotypes and blame scapegoats are more likely to feel prejudice, that is, hostile or negative attitudes toward individuals or groups.

LO 11 Compare prosocial behavior and altruism. (p. 585)

Behavior aimed at benefiting others is known as prosocial behavior. Altruism is a desire or motivation to help others with no expectation of anything in return. Empathy, or the ability to understand and recognize another's emotional perspective, is a major component of altruism.

LO 12 Identify the three major factors contributing to interpersonal attraction. (p. 587)

Interpersonal attraction leads us to form friendships or romantic relationships with others. The three major factors of interpersonal attraction are proximity, similarity, and physical attractiveness. Many relationships begin with exhilaration and intense physical attraction, and then evolve into more intimate connections. The combination of connection, concern, care, and intimacy is romantic love. This is similar to passionate love, or love that is based on zealous emotion, leading to intense longing and sexual attraction. As a relationship grows, intimacy and commitment develop into companionate love, which consists of fondness, camaraderie, understanding, and emotional closeness. Consummate love is evident when intimacy and commitment are accompanied by passion.

key terms

aggression, p. 580
altruism, p. 586
attitudes, p. 560
attributions, p. 556
bystander effect, p. 578
cognitive dissonance, p. 562
companionate love, p. 590
compliance, p. 567
conformity, p. 569
consummate love, p. 590
deindividuation, p. 576
diffusion of responsibility, p. 575
discrimination, p. 581

dispositional attribution, p. 557
door-in-the-face technique, p. 568
ethnocentrism, p. 581
false consensus effect, p. 560
foot-in-the-door technique, p. 567
frustration–aggression hypothesis, p. 580
fundamental attribution error, p. 557
group polarization, p. 577
groupthink, p. 578

in-group, p. 581
interpersonal attraction, p. 587
just-world hypothesis, p. 559
mere-exposure effect, p. 588
norms, p. 569
obedience, p. 571
out-group, p. 581
passionate love, p. 590
persuasion, p. 566
prejudice, p. 582
proximity, p. 587
risky shift, p. 577
romantic love, p. 590

scapegoat, p. 581
self-serving bias, p. 559
situational attribution, p. 557
social cognition, p. 556
social facilitation, p. 575
social identity, p. 581
social influence, p. 565
social loafing, p. 575
social psychology, p. 555
social roles, p. 583
stereotypes, p. 581
stereotype threat, p. 582

TEST PREP are you ready?

1. _____ is the study of human cognition, emotion, and behavior in relation to others.
   a. Sociology
   b. Developmental psychology
   c. The biopsychosocial model
   d. Social psychology

2. A researcher is interested in studying how students attend to social information and use it in their lives. Her general focus is:
   a. attributions.
   b. social cognition.
   c. the internal–external dimension.
   d. attitudes.

3. _____ is an uneasy feeling that occurs with the recognition that a mismatch exists between an attitude and a behavior.
   a. Cognitive dissonance   b. An attitude
   c. A confederate   d. Altruism

4. One common bias we have is to more often attribute causes of behaviors to the individual rather than to the environment, thus underestimating the powerful influence of the environment on behavior. This is known as:
   a. the just-world hypothesis.
   b. the false consensus effect.
   c. a dispositional attribution.
   d. the fundamental attribution error.

5. Hovland proposed that persuasive communication involves three important components, and we must consider factors associated with them. The three components are:
   a. the source, the audience, and the sender.
   b. the source, the message, and the social influence.
   c. the source, the persuasion, and the compliance.
   d. the source, the message, and the audience.

6. When someone changes his behavior at the request or direction of another person who does not have authority over him, this is known as:
   a. obedience.
   b. conformity.
   c. compliance.
   d. normative social influence.

7. Your neighbor seems to follow the lead in terms of decorating his house. If he sees others hanging lights, he immediately does the same. His urge to modify his behaviors to match those of others in the neighborhood is known as:
   a. conformity.
   b. informational social influence.
   c. obedience.
   d. cognitive dissonance.

8. Milgram reported that 65% of the participants in his study gave shocks marked as the highest voltage level to a confederate. Researchers have found that the degree of compliance of participants in such studies is associated with the:
   a. severity of the punishment.
   b. occupation of the participant.
   c. legitimacy of the authority figure.
   d. education level of the participant.

9. _____ occurs when the sharing of duties among all members of the group leads to feelings of decreased accountability.
   a. Obedience to authority
   b. Diffusion of responsibility
   c. A risky shift
   d. Groupthink

10. One study found that 80% of trick-or-treaters in a group who were anonymous took more candy or money than they were supposed to. The children's sense of anonymity as well as inclusion in a group likely led to their sense of:
    a. deindividuation.
    b. obedience.
    c. authority.
    d. a risky shift.

11. A family friend of yours constantly goes on about how suburban teenagers with tongue rings are rebelling against their parents and most of them are troublemakers. These _____ are conclusions he has drawn based on his subjective observations and value judgments.
    a. norms
    b. external attributions
    c. situational attributions
    d. stereotypes

12. Psychologists define _____ as intimidating or threatening behavior or as attitudes intended to hurt someone.
    a. prejudice
    b. discrimination
    c. aggression
    d. stereotypes

13. When teachers in an elementary school in San Francisco were given a list of students who were likely to "show surprising gains in intellectual competence" during the coming year, the students on that list achieved greater increases in test scores than students not on it. This example demonstrates the power of _____, a form of social influence.
    a. cognitive dissonance
    b. expectations
    c. altruism
    d. the mere-exposure effect

14. _____ suggests that the more we are exposed to people, food, jingles, or songs, the more positive a reaction we have toward them.
    a. The mere-exposure effect
    b. Prosocial behavior
    c. Altruism
    d. The self-serving bias

15. According to Sternberg, the three elements that make up love are:
    a. passion, mere exposure, and proximity.
    b. proximity, similarity, and passion.
    c. romantic love, mere exposure, and similarity.
    d. passion, intimacy, and commitment.

16. You are trying to explain why a colleague of yours is frequently absent from work. Can you come up with an attribution that is external, uncontrollable, and unstable? Can you think of a different attribution that is internal, controllable, and stable?

17. The findings from Milgram's experiment on obedience seemed surprising when they were first published, but they remain relevant today. Why is it important to pay attention to the way you behave when under the influence of an authority figure?

18. Knowledge about the bystander effect provides a lesson for all of us, particularly in terms of crisis situations in a group setting. How would you describe this lesson to others?

19. Identify any stereotypes you might harbor about certain groups of people. How did your association with specific groups impact the development of these stereotypes?

20. Think about someone you are close to and try to determine if—and how—proximity, similarity, and physical attractiveness played a role in your attraction to each other.

✓ CHECK YOUR ANSWERS IN APPENDIX C.

Get personalized practice by logging into LaunchPad at **www.macmillanhighered.com/launchpad/ sciampresenting1e** to take the LearningCurve adaptive quizzes for Chapter 14.

introduction to statistics

The vast knowledge base that defines the field of psychology is the result of rigorous and meticulous scientific research, most of which entails the careful collection of data. In Chapter 1, we presented various methods used to gather this data, but we only touched upon statistical approaches for analyzing it. Here, we will discover how we can use data meaningfully: Welcome to **statistics**, the science of collecting, organizing, analyzing, displaying, and interpreting data.

Statistics are everywhere—not just in the academic materials published by psychologists. Newspapers, Web sites, and television shows report on statistical findings every day, though they sometimes make mistakes, exaggerate, or leave out important information. You can detect these types of errors if you understand statistics. It is important for everyone (not just psychology students) to think critically about research findings.

Descriptive and Inferential Statistics

There are two basic types of statistics: descriptive and inferential. With *descriptive statistics*, researchers summarize information they have gleaned from their studies. The raw data can be organized and presented through tables, graphs, and charts, examples of which we provide in this appendix. We can also use descriptive statistics to represent the average and the spread of the data (how dispersed the values are), a topic we will revisit later. The goal of descriptive statistics is to describe data, or provide a snapshot of what is observed in a study. *Inferential statistics*, on the other hand, go beyond simple data presentation. With inferential statistics, for example, we can determine the probability of events and make predictions about general trends. The goals are to generalize findings from studies, make predictions based on relationships among variables, and test hypotheses. Inferential statistics also can be used to make statements about how confident we are in our findings based on the data collected.

In Chapter 1, we defined a *hypothesis* as a statement used to test a prediction. Once a researcher develops a hypothesis, she gathers data and uses statistics to test it. Hypothesis testing involves mathematical procedures to determine whether data support a hypothesis or if they simply result from chance. Let's look at an example to see how this works. (And you might find it useful to review Chapter 1 if your knowledge of research methods is a little rusty.)

Suppose a researcher wants to determine whether taking vitamin D supplements can boost cognitive function. The researcher designs an experiment to test if giving participants vitamin D pills (the independent variable) leads to better performance on some sort of cognitive task, such as a memory test (the test score is the dependent variable). Participants in the treatment group receive doses of vitamin D and participants in the control group receive a placebo. Neither the participants nor the researchers working directly with those participants know who is getting the vitamin D and who

◀**CONNECTIONS**

In **Chapter 1,** we presented a study examining the impact of fast-paced cartoons on executive functioning. The researchers tested the following hypothesis: Children who watch 9 minutes of *SpongeBob Square Pants* will be more likely to show cognitive changes than children who watch *Caillou* or simply draw. The researchers used inferential statistics to determine that the children in the *SpongeBob* group did show a lapse in cognitive functioning in comparison to the other two groups in the study.

statistics A science that focuses on how to collect, organize, analyze, display, and interpret data; numbers that describe characteristics of a sample.

hypothesis testing Mathematical procedures used to determine the likelihood that a researcher's predictions are supported by the data collected.

CONNECTIONS

In **Chapter 14,** we presented the biomedical approach to treating psychological disorders. Many researchers use a double-blind procedure to determine the causes of psychological disorders and the effectiveness of psychotropic medications in alleviating symptoms. For example, Schnider and colleagues (2010) used a randomized double-blind procedure to determine the impact of L-dopa, risperdone, and a placebo on participants' ability to "rapidly adapt thinking to ongoing reality" (p. 583). The researchers used a double-blind procedure to ensure that neither the participants' nor the researchers' expectations unduly influenced the results.

CONNECTIONS

In **Chapter 5,** we presented Bandura's work on observational learning and aggressive models. Bandura and colleagues (1961) divided participants into treatment and control groups and found that the average "expression of aggression" for children who viewed aggressive models was statistically significantly greater than for the control group children who did not observe an aggressive model. The difference in the amount of expressed aggression for the two groups was large enough to be considered due to the experimenters' manipulation as opposed to a chance result (for example, simply based on the children who were assigned randomly to each group).

---

is getting the placebo, so we call it a double-blind procedure. After the data have been collected, the researcher will need to compare the memory scores for the two groups to see if the treatment worked. In all likelihood, the average test scores of the two groups will differ simply because they include two different groups of people. So how does the researcher know whether the difference is sufficient to conclude that vitamin D had an effect? Using statistical procedures, the researcher can state with a chosen level of certainty (for example, with 95% confidence) that the disparity in average scores resulted from the vitamin D treatment. In other words, there is a slight possibility (in this case, 5%) that the difference was merely due to chance.

With the use of statistical methods, researchers can establish statistical significance, indicating that differences between groups in a study (for example, the average scores for treatment and control groups) are so great that they are likely due to the researcher's manipulations; the mathematical analyses suggest a minimal probability the findings were due to chance. When we use the experimental method (that is, randomly assign individuals, manipulate an independent variable, and control extraneous variables) and find *statistically* significant differences between our experimental and control groups, we can be assured that these differences are very likely due to how we treated the participants (for example, administering vitamin D treatment versus a placebo).

In addition to determining statistical significance, we also have to consider the *practical importance* of findings, meaning the degree to which the results of a study can be used in a meaningful way. In other words, do the findings have any relevance to real life? If the vitamin D regimen produces statistically significant results (with a performance gap between the treatment and control groups most likely not due to chance), the researcher would still have to determine its practical importance. Suppose the two groups differ by only a few points on the cognitive test; then the question is whether vitamin D supplementation is really worth the trouble. We should note that big samples are more likely to result in *statistically* significant results (small differences between groups can be amplified by a large sample) even though the results might not provide much practical information.

Sampling Techniques

Long before data are collected and analyzed, researchers must select people to participate in their studies. Depending on what a psychologist is interested in studying, the probability of being able to include all members of a *population* is not likely, so generally a *sample*, or subset of the population, is chosen. The characteristics of the sample members must closely reflect those of the population of interest so that the researcher can generalize, or apply, her findings to the population at large.

In an effort to ensure that the sample accurately reflects the larger population, a researcher may use *random sampling*, which means that all members of the population have an equal chance of being invited to participate in the study. If the researcher has a numbered list of the population members, she could generate random numbers on a computer and then contact the individuals with those numbers. Because the numbers are randomly picked, everyone on the list has an equal chance of being selected. Another approach is *stratified sampling*. A researcher chooses this method if she wants a certain variable to be well represented—car ownership in urban areas, for example. She divides the population into four groups or *strata* (no car, one car, two cars, more than two cars), and then picks randomly from within each group or *stratum*, ensuring that all of the different types of car ownership are included in the sample. Researchers use strata such as ethnicity, gender, and age group to ensure a sample has appropriate representation of these important factors.

Some researchers use a method called *convenience sampling*, which entails choosing a sample from a group that is readily available or convenient. If a student researcher is interested in collecting data on coffee drinking behavior from people who frequent coffee shops, he might be tempted to go to the Starbucks and Peet's Coffee shops in his neighborhood. But this approach does not use random sampling (just think of all the Dunkin' Donuts and Caribou coffee drinkers who would be excluded), so the likelihood that it results in a *representative sample* is very slim. In other words, a randomly picked sample is more likely than a convenience sample to include members with characteristics similar to the population. Only if a sample is representative can a researcher use his findings to make accurate *inferences* or valid generalizations about the characteristics of the population. But it's important to note that even a randomly selected sample is not foolproof. There is always the possibility that the chosen participants have characteristics that are not typical for the population. The smaller the sample, the less likely it will be representative and the less reliable the results. Larger samples tend to provide more accurate reflections of the population being studied.

The ultimate goal of most studies is to provide results that can be used to make inferences about a population. We can describe a population using various **parameters,** or numbers that delineate its characteristics (for example, the average number of cars owned by *all* households in urban areas in the United States). When the same characteristics are determined for a sample, they are referred to as *statistics* (the average number of cars owned by households in the sample). (Recall that the word "statistics" can also refer to the scientific discipline of collecting, organizing, analyzing, displaying, and interpreting data.) We will introduce you to some of these numerical characteristics later when we discuss *measures of central tendency* and *measures of variation*.

Understanding sampling techniques can help you become a more critical consumer of scientific information. When reading or watching media reports on scientific studies, ask yourself whether the samples are truly representative. If not, the use of statistics to make inferences about parameters is suspect; the findings might only be true for the sample, not the population.

Variables

Once a study sample is selected, researchers can begin studying and manipulating the variables of interest. Variables are measurable characteristics that vary over time or across people, situations, or objects. In psychology, variables may include cognitive abilities, social behaviors, or even the font size in books. Statisticians often refer to two types of variables. *Quantitative variables* are numerical, meaning they have values that can be represented by numbered units or ranks. Midterm exam scores, age at graduation, and number of students in a class are all quantitative variables. *Qualitative variables* are characteristics that enable us to place participants in categories, but they cannot be assigned numbered units or ranks. An example might be college major; you can ask all of the students in the library to line up under signs for psychology, biology, chemistry, undeclared, and so on, and thereby categorize them by their majors. We can rank how much we like the majors based on the courses associated with them, but the majors cannot be ordered or ranked in and of themselves. We can alphabetize them, but that is a ranking based on their labels. We can even order the majors in terms of how many students are pursuing them, but that is a different variable (number of students). Other examples of qualitative variables include gender, ethnicity, and religious faith.

Synonyms
qualitative variables categorical variables

Throughout this textbook, we have identified multiple characteristics and traits that can be used as variables in studies. Pick two chapters and see if you can identify five variables that are quantitative and five that are qualitative.

> try this

Variables are the focal point of experiments in psychology. Typically, the goal is to determine how one variable (the dependent variable) is affected by changes in another (the independent variable). Many studies focus on similar topics, so you might imagine it's easy to compare their results. But this is not necessarily the case. Sometimes psychologists define variables in different ways, or study the same variables with vastly different samples, methods of measurement, and experimental designs. How do we reconcile all their findings? We rely on a **meta-analysis,** a statistical approach that allows researchers to combine the findings of different studies and draw general conclusions. A meta-analysis is an objective, quantitative (measurable) mechanism for gathering and analyzing findings from a set of studies on the same topic (Weathington, Cunningham, & Pittenger, 2010).

The Presentation of Data

Conducting an experiment is a major accomplishment, but it has little impact if researchers cannot devise an effective way to present their data. If they just display raw data in a table, others will find it difficult to draw any useful conclusions. Imagine you have collected the data presented in **Table A.1**, which represents the number of minutes of REM sleep (the dependent variable) each of your 44 participants ($n = 44$; n is the symbol for sample size) had during one night spent in your sleep lab. Looking at this table, you can barely tell what variable is being studied.

TABLE A.1	RAW DATA FROM REM SLEEP STUDY									
77	114	40	18	68	96	81	142	62	80	117
81	98	76	22	71	35	85	49	105	99	49
20	70	35	83	150	57	112	131	104	121	47
31	47	39	92	73	122	68	58	100	52	101

Quantitative Data Displays

A common and simple way to display data is to use a **frequency distribution,** which shows how often the various values in a data set are present. In **Table A.2**, we have displayed the data in seven *classes*, or groups, of equal width. The frequency for each class is tallied up and appears in the middle column. The first class goes from

meta-analysis A type of statistical analysis that combines findings from many studies on a single topic; statistics used to merge the outcomes of many studies.

frequency distribution A simple way to portray data that displays how often various values in a data set are present.

histogram Displays classes of a variable on the *x*-axis, and the frequency of the data is represented as vertical bars that reach the height of the number of values.

frequency polygon A type of graphic display that uses lines to represent the frequency of data values.

stem-and-leaf plot A type of graphical display that uses the actual data values in the form of leading digits and trailing digits.

distribution shape How the frequencies of the values are shaped along the *x*-axis.

TABLE A.2	FREQUENCY DISTRIBUTION FOR REM SLEEP STUDY	
No. of Minutes in REM (Class Limits)	Raw Frequency	Relative Frequency
4 to 24	3	.068
25 to 45	5	.114
46 to 66	8	.182
67 to 87	12	.273
88 to 108	8	.182
109 to 129	5	.114
130 to 150	3	.068

4 to 24 minutes, and in our sample of 44 participants, only 3 had a total amount of REM in this class (18, 20, 22 minutes). The greatest number of participants experienced between 67 and 87 minutes of REM sleep. By looking at the frequency for each class, you begin to see patterns. In this case, the greatest number of participants had REM sleep within the middle of the distribution, and fewer appear on the ends. We will come back to this pattern shortly.

Frequency distributions can also be presented with a **histogram,** which displays the classes of a variable on the *x-axis* and the frequency of the data on the *y-axis* (portrayed by the height of the vertical bars). The values on the *y*-axis can be either the raw frequency (actual number) or the relative frequency (proportion of the whole set; see Table A.2, right column). The example portrayed in **Figure A.1** is a histogram of the minutes of REM sleep, with the classes representing the number of minutes in REM on the *x*-axis and the raw frequency on the *y*-axis. Looking at a histogram makes it easier to see how the data are distributed across classes. In this case you can see that the most frequent duration of REM is in the middle of the distribution (the 67- to 87-minute class), and that the frequency tapers off toward both ends. Histograms are often used to display quantitative variables that have a wide range of numbers that would be difficult to interpret if they weren't grouped in classes.

Similar to a histogram is a **frequency polygon,** which uses lines instead of bars to represent the frequency of the data values. The same data displayed in the histogram (Figure A.1) appear in the frequency polygon in **Figure A.2**. We see the same general shape in the frequency polygon, but instead of raw frequency we have used the relative frequency to represent the proportion of participants in each of the classes (see Table A.2, right column). Thus, rather than saying 12 participants had 67 to 87 minutes of REM sleep, we can state that the proportion of participants in this class was approximately .27, or 27%. Relative frequencies are especially useful when comparing data sets with different sample sizes. Imagine we wanted to compare two different studies examining REM sleep: one with a sample size of 500, and the other with a sample size of 44. The larger sample might have a greater number of participants in the 67- to 87-minute group (let's say 50 participants out of 500 [.10] versus the 12 out of the 44 participants [.27] in the smaller sample), making the raw frequency of this group (50) in the larger sample greater than the raw frequency of this group (12) in the smaller sample. But the proportion for the smaller sample would still be greater (smaller sample = .27 versus larger sample = .10). The relative frequency makes it easier to detect these differences in proportion.

Another common way to display quantitative data is through a **stem-and-leaf plot,** which uses the actual data values in its display. The *stem* is made up of the first digits in a number, and the *leaf* is made up of the last digit in each number. This allows us to group numbers by 10s, 20s, 30s, and so on. In **Figure A.3**, we display the REM sleep data in a stem-and-leaf plot using the first part of the number (either the 10s and/or the 100s) as the stem, and the ones column as the leaf. In the top row, for example, 8 is from the ones column of the smallest number in the data set, 18; 0 and 2 in the second row represent the ones column from the numbers 20 and 22; the 0 in the bottom row comes from 150.

Distribution Shapes

Once the data have been displayed on a graph, researchers look very closely at the **distribution shape,** which is just what it sounds like—how the data are spread along the *x*-axis (that is, the shape is based on the variable represented along the *x*-axis and the frequency of its values portrayed by the *y*-axis). A *symmetric shape* is apparent in

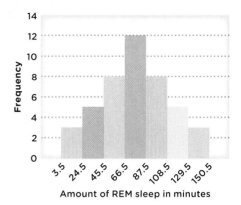

▲ FIGURE A.1
Histogram of REM sleep study

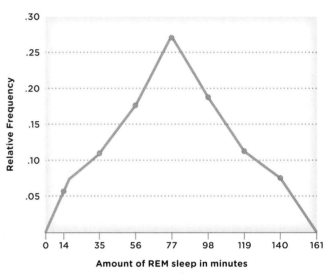

▲ FIGURE A.2
Frequency polygon of REM sleep study

FIGURE A.3

Stem-and-leaf plot for REM sleep study

1	8
2	0 2
3	1 5 5 9
4	0 7 7 9 9
5	2 7 8
6	2 8 8
7	0 1 3 6 7
8	0 1 1 3 5
9	2 6 8 9
10	0 1 4 5
11	2 4 7
12	1 2
13	1
14	2
15	0

FIGURE A.4

Symmetrically shaped distributions

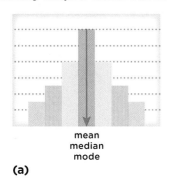

mean
median
mode

(a)

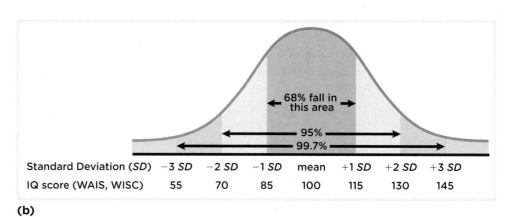

68% fall in
this area

95%
99.7%

Standard Deviation (*SD*)	−3 *SD*	−2 *SD*	−1 *SD*	mean	+1 *SD*	+2 *SD*	+3 *SD*
IQ score (WAIS, WISC)	55	70	85	100	115	130	145

(b)

the histogram in **Figure A.4a**, which shows a distribution for a sample that is high in the middle, but tapers off at the same rate on each end. The *bell-shaped* or normal curve on the right (b) also has a symmetric shape, and this type of curve is fairly typical in psychology (curves generally represent the distribution of the entire population). Many human characteristics have this type of distribution, including cognitive abilities, personality characteristics, and a variety of physical characteristics such as height and weight. Through many years of study, we have found that measurements for the great majority of people fall in the middle of the distribution, and a smaller proportion have characteristics represented on the ends (or in the tails) of the distribution. For example, if you look at the IQ scores displayed in **Figure A.4b**, you can see that 68% of people have scores between 85 and 115, about 95% have scores between 70 and 130, around 99.7% fall between 55 and 145, and only a tiny percentage (0.3%) are below 55 or above 145. These percentages are true for many other characteristics.

Some data will have a **skewed distribution,** which is not symmetrical. As you can see in **Figure A.5a**, a **negatively skewed** or *left-skewed* distribution has a longer tail to the left side of the distribution. A **positively skewed** or *right-skewed* distribution (**Figure A.5b**) has a longer tail to the right side of the distribution. Determining whether a distribution is skewed is particularly important because it informs our decision about what type of statistical analysis to conduct. Later, we will see how certain types of data values can play a role in *skewing* the distribution.

FIGURE A.5

Skewed distributions

skewed distribution Nonsymmetrical frequency distribution.

negatively skewed A nonsymmetric distribution with a longer tail to the left side of the distribution; left-skewed distribution.

positively skewed A nonsymmetric distribution with a longer tail to the right side of the distribution; right-skewed distribution.

bar graph Displays qualitative data with categories of interest on the *x*-axis and frequency on the *y*-axis.

pie chart Displays qualitative data with categories of interest represented by slices of the pie.

(a) Negatively skewed

(b) Positively skewed

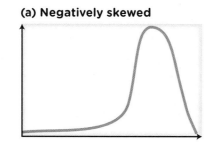

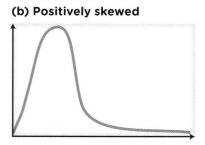

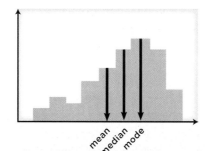

mean
median
mode

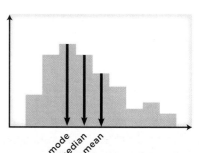

mode
median
mean

Qualitative Data Displays

Thus far, we have discussed several ways to represent quantitative data. With qualitative data, a frequency distribution lists the various categories and the number of members in each. For example, if we wanted to display the college major data on 44 students interviewed at the library, we could use a frequency distribution (**Table A.3**).

Another common way to display qualitative data is through a **bar graph,** which displays the categories of interest on the *x*-axis and their frequencies on the *y*-axis. **Figure A.6** shows how the data collected in the library can be presented in a bar graph. Bar graphs are useful for comparing several different populations on the same variable (for example, perhaps comparing college majors by gender or ethnicity).

TABLE A.3 FREQUENCY DISTRIBUTION OF COLLEGE MAJORS		
College Major	**Raw Frequency**	**Percent**
Biology	3	7
Chemistry	5	11.5
Culinary Arts	8	18
English	5	11.5
Nursing	12	27
Psychology	3	7
Undecided	8	18

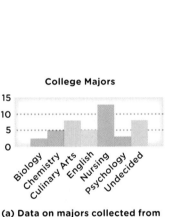

(a) Data on majors collected from library interviews

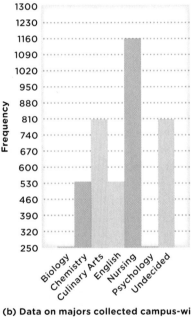

(b) Data on majors collected campus-wide

FIGURE A.6

Bar graph for college majors

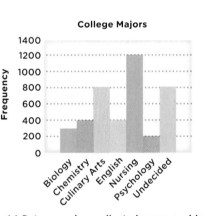

(c) Data on majors collected campus-wide

Pie charts can also be used to display qualitative data, with pie slices representing the proportion of the data set belonging to each category (**Figure A.7**). As you can see, the biggest percentage is nursing (27%), followed by culinary arts (18%), and undecided (18%). The smallest percentage is shared by biology and psychology (both 7%). Often researchers use pie charts to easily display data for which it is important to know the relative proportion of each category (for example, a psychology department trying to gain support for funding its courses might want to be able to display the relative number of psychologists in particular subfields; see Figure 1.1, page 4).

With any type of data display, one must be on the lookout for misleading portrayals. In Figure A.6a, we display data for the 44 students interviewed in the library. Notice that, while Figures A.6b and A.6c look different, they display the same data for the same campus of 4,400 students. Quickly look at (b) and (c) of the figure and decide, if you were head of the psychology department, which bar chart you would use to demonstrate the popularity of the psychology major. In (b), the size of

FIGURE A.7

Pie chart for college majors

the department (as measured by number of students) looks fairly small compared to that of other departments, particularly the nursing program. But notice that the scale on the *y*-axis starts at 250 in (b), whereas it begins at 0 in (c). In this third bar chart, it appears that the student count for the psychology program is not far behind that for other programs like chemistry and English, for example. An important aspect of *critical thinking* is being able to evaluate the source of evidence, something one must consider when reading graphs and charts. (For example, does the author of the bar chart in Figure A.6b have a particular agenda to reduce funding for the psychology and biology departments?) It is important to recognize that manipulating the presentation of data can lead to faulty interpretations (the data on the 4,400 students are valid, but the way they are presented is not).

The Description of Data

In addition to using graphs and charts, psychologists can describe their data sets using numbers that express important characteristics: measures of central tendency, measures of variation, and measures of position. These numbers are an important component of descriptive statistics, as they provide a current snapshot of a data set.

Measures of Central Tendency

If you want to understand human behaviors and mental processes, it helps to know what is typical, or standard, for the population. What is the average level of intelligence? At what age do most people experience first love? To answer these types of questions, psychologists can describe their data sets by calculating **measures of central tendency,** which are numbers representing the "middle" of data sets. There are several ways of doing this. The **mean** is the arithmetic average of a data set. Most students learn how to calculate a mean, or "average," early in their schooling, using the following formula:

$\bar{X} = \frac{\Sigma X}{n}$ where $\bar{X}$ is the sample mean; X is a value in the data set; Σ, or sigma, means to sum the values; and n represents the sample size

or

$$\text{Sample mean} = \frac{\text{Sum of all of the values in the data set}}{\text{Number of values}}$$

To calculate the sample mean ($\bar{X}$) for minutes of REM sleep, you would plug the numbers into the formula:

$\bar{X} = (18 + 20 + 22 + 31 + 35 + 35 + 39 + \ldots + 131 + 142 + 150) \div 44$
$= 76.8$ minutes

Another measure of central tendency is the **median**—the number representing the position in the middle of a data set. In other words, 50% of the data values are greater than the median, and 50% are smaller. To find the median for a small set of numbers, start by ordering the values, and then determine which number lies exactly in the center. This is relatively simple when the data set is odd-numbered; all you have to do is find the value that has the same number of values above and below it. For a data set that has an even number of values, however, there is one additional step: You must take the average of the two middle numbers (add them together and divide by 2). With an odd number of values in a data set, the median will always be a member of the set. With an even number of values, the median may or may not be a member of the data set.

measures of central tendency Numbers that represent the middle of a data set.

mean The arithmetic average of a data set; a measure of central tendency.

median A number that represents the position in the data set for which 50% of the values are above it, and 50% are below it; a measure of central tendency.

Here is how you would determine the median (*Mdn*) for the minutes of REM sleep:

1. Order the numbers in the data set from smallest to largest. We can use the stem-and-leaf plot for this purpose. (See Figure A.3 on page A-7.)
2. Find the value in the data set that has 50% of the other values below it and 50% above it. Because we have an even number for our sample size ($n = 44$), we will have to find the middle two data values and calculate their average. We divide our sample size of 44 by 2, which is 22, indicating that the median is midway between the 22nd and 23rd values in our set. We count (starting at 18 in the stem-and-leaf plot) to the 22nd and 23rd numbers in our ordered list (76 and 77; there are 21 values below 76 and 21 values above 77).

3. $Mdn = \dfrac{(76 + 77)}{2}$
   $= 76.5$ minutes

A third measure of central tendency is the **mode,** which is the most frequently occurring value in a data set. If there is only one such value, we call it a *unimodal* distribution. With a symmetric distribution, the mean, median, and mode are the same (see Figure A.4a on page A-6). Sometimes there are two modes, indicating a **bimodal distribution,** and the shape of the distribution exhibits two vertical bars of equal height (**Figure A.8**). In our example of REM sleep data, we cannot see a clear mode, as there are several values that occur twice (35, 47, 49, 68, and 81 minutes). In bimodal distributions, the mode is often a better representation of the central tendency, because neither the mean nor median will indicate that there are in essence two "centers" for the data set.

Under other circumstances, the median is better than the mean for representing the middle of the data set. This is especially true when the data set includes one or more *outliers*, or values that are very different from the rest of the set. We can see why this is true by replacing just one value in our data set on REM sleep. See what happens to the mean and median when you swap 150 for 400. First calculate the mean:

1. $\bar{X} = (18 + 20 + 22 + 31 + 35 + 35 + 39 + \ldots + 131 + 142 + 400) \div 44$
   $= 82.5$ minutes (greater than the original mean of 76.8)
2. And now calculate the median. The numbers in the data set are ordered from smallest to largest. The middle two values have not changed (76 and 77).

   $Mdn = 76.5$ minutes (identical to the original median of 76.5)

No matter how large (or small) a single value is, it does not change the median, but it can have a great influence on the mean. When this occurs, psychologists often present both of these statistics, and discuss the possibility that an outlier is pulling the mean toward it. Look again at the skewed distributions in Figure A.5 on page A-6 and see how the mean is "pulled" toward the side of the distribution that has a possible outlier in its tail. When data are skewed, it is often a good idea to use the median as a measure of central tendency, particularly if a problem exists with outliers.

Measures of Variation

In addition to information on the central tendency, psychologists are interested in **measures of variation,** which describe how much variation or dispersion there is in a data set. If you look at the two data sets in **Figure A.9** on the next page (number of miles commuting to school), you can see that they have the same central tendency (identical means: the mean commute for both samples is 30 miles; $\bar{X} = 30.0$), yet their dispersion is very different: One data set looks spread out (Sample A), and the other closely packed (Sample B).

There are several measures we can use to characterize the *variability*, or variation, of a data set. The **range** represents the length of a data set and is calculated by taking the highest

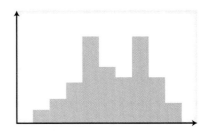

▲ FIGURE A.8
Bimodal distribution

mode The value of the data set that is most frequent; a measure of central tendency.

bimodal distribution A distribution with two modes, which are the two most frequently occurring values.

measures of variation Numbers that describe the variation or dispersion in a data set.

range A number that represents the length of the data set and is a rough depiction of dispersion; a measure of variation.

FIGURE A.9

Same mean, different variability for Sample A and Sample B

Data Values from Sample A (daily commute to school in miles) (9, 10, 15, 23, 25, 32, 35, 45, 48, 58). Data Values from Sample B (daily commute to school) (19, 27, 27, 28, 28, 30, 30, 32, 35, 44).

Data Values from Sample A

0	9
1	0 5
2	3 5
3	2 5
4	5 8
5	8

$\bar{X}$ = 30.0 miles, *Mdn* = 28.5 miles

Data Values from Sample B

1	9
2	7 7 8 8
3	0 0 2 5
4	4

$\bar{X}$ = 30.0 miles, *Mdn* = 29.0 miles

TABLE A.4 STANDARD DEVIATION FOR SAMPLE A

X	$X - \bar{X}$	$(X - \bar{X})^2$
9	9 − 30 = −21	−21² = 441
10	10 − 30 = −20	−20² = 400
15	15 − 30 = −15	−15² = 225
23	23 − 30 = −7	−7² = 49
25	25 − 30 = −5	−5² = 25
32	32 − 30 = 2	2² = 4
35	35 − 30 = 5	5² = 25
45	45 − 30 = 15	15² = 225
48	48 − 30 = 18	18² = 324
58	58 − 30 = 28	28² = 784

$\sum(X - \bar{X})^2$ = 441 + 400 + 225 + 49 + 25 + 4 + 25 + 225 + 324 + 784
= 2,502

$n - 1 = (10 - 1) = 9$

$s = \sqrt{\dfrac{2,502}{9}}$

$s = 16.7$

value minus the lowest value. The range is a rough depiction of variability, but it's useful for comparing data on the same variable measured in two samples. For the data sets presented in Figure A.9, we can compare the ranges of the two samples and see that Sample A has a range of 49 miles and Sample B has a smaller range of 25 miles.

Sample A	**Sample B**
Range = 58 − 9	Range = 44 − 19
Range = 49 miles	Range = 25 miles

A more precise measure of dispersion is the **standard deviation** (referred to by the symbol *s* when describing samples), which essentially represents the average amount the data points are away from their mean. Think about it like this: If the values in a data set are very close to each other, they will also be very close to their mean, and the dispersion will be small. Their average distance from the mean is small. If the values are widely spread, they will not all be clustered around the mean, and their dispersion will be great. Their average distance from the mean is large. One way we can calculate the standard deviation of a sample is by using the following formula:

$$s = \sqrt{\frac{\sum(X - \bar{X})^2}{(n - 1)}}$$

This formula does the following: (1) Subtract the mean from a value in the data set, then square the result. Do this for every value in the set and calculate the sum of the results. (2) Divide this sum by the sample size minus 1. (3) Take the square root of the result. In **Table A.4**, we have gone through each of these steps for Sample A.

The standard deviation for Sample A is 16.7 miles and the standard deviation for Sample B is 6.4 miles (the calculation is not shown here). These standard deviations are consistent with what we expect from looking at the stem-and-leaf plots in Figure A.9. Sample A is more variable, or spread out, than Sample B.

The standard deviation is useful for making predictions about the probability of a particular value occurring (Figure A.4b on page A-6). The *empirical rule* tells us that we can expect approximately 68% of all values to fall within 1 standard deviation below or above their mean on a normal curve. We can expect approximately 95% of all values to fall within 2 standard deviations below or above their mean. And we can expect approximately 99.7% of all values to fall within 3 standard deviations below or above their mean. Only 0.3% of the values will fall above or below 3 standard deviations—these values are extremely rare, as you can see in Figure A.4b.

Measures of Position

Another way to describe data is by looking at **measures of position,** which represent where particular data values fall in relation to other values in a set. You have probably

standard deviation A number that represents the average amount the values in a data set are away from their mean; a measure of variation.

measures of position Numbers that represent where particular data values fall in relation to other values in the data set.

heard of *percentiles*, which indicate the percentage of values occurring above and below a certain point in a data set. A value at the 50th percentile is at the median, which indicates that 50% of the values fall above it, and 50% fall below it. A value at the 10th percentile indicates that 90% fall above it, and 10% fall below it. Often you will see percentiles in reports from standardized tests, weight charts, height charts, and so on.

Using the data below, calculate the mean, median, range, and standard deviation. Also create a stem-and-leaf plot to display the data and then describe the shape of the distribution.
10 10 11 16 18 18 20 20 24 24 25 25 26 29 29 39 40 41 41 42 43 46 48 49 50 50 51 52 53 56 36 37 38 66 71 75 31 34 34 35 57 59 61 61 38

try this

Check your answers in Appendix C.

Statistics Is a Language

This introduction to statistics was created to provide you with an overview of the "language" of statistics that psychologists use to collect, organize, analyze, display, and interpret data. Like any *foreign* language, statistics is not something you master by reading a brief overview. To become proficient in statistical methods, you must study and practice them. And the best way to become fluent in this language is to immerse yourself in it. For starters, we recommend taking a course in elementary statistics and reading articles published in psychology journals (see **Table A.5** for some commonly used symbols). If you find statistics is your forte, keep taking classes, and consider the possibility of becoming a researcher. Perhaps your work will be published in a scientific journal one day—and cited in an introductory psychology textbook!

TABLE A.5 SYMBOLS COMMONLY USED IN STATISTICS

Concept	Symbol	Description
Sample correlation coefficient,	r	Represents the strength and direction of the relationship between two variables
F-test value,	F	Used to measure the statistical significance of the differences among 3 or more means
t-test value,	t	Used to measure the statistical significance of the difference between 2 means.
p-value,	p	An indication of the probability of getting a test statistic of a certain size by chance
Population mean,	μ	The mean of a population (pronounced "mew")
Sample mean,	M (or $\overline{X}$)	The mean of a sample (pronounced "X-bar")
Population standard deviation,	σ	The standard deviation of the population (pronounced "sigma")
Sample standard deviation,	s	The standard deviation of a sample
Population size,	N	Indicates the size of a population
Sample size,	n	Indicates the size of a sample
z-score,	z	Indicates a standard score; number of standard deviations from the mean

key terms

bar graph, p. A-7
bimodal distribution, p. A-9
distribution shape, p. A-5
frequency distribution, p. A-4
frequency polygon, p. A-5
histogram, p. A-5
hypothesis testing, p. A-1

mean, p. A-8
measures of central tendency,
    p. A-8
measures of position, p. A-10
measures of variation, p. A-9
median, p. A-8
meta-analysis, p. A-4

mode, p. A-9
negatively skewed, p. A-6
parameters, p. A-3
pie chart, p. A-7
positively skewed, p. A-6
range, p. A-9
skewed distribution, p. A-6

standard deviation, p. A-10
statistical significance, p. A-2
statistics, p. A-1
stem-and-leaf plot, p. A-5

TEST PREP are you ready?

1. With descriptive statistics, researchers use tables, graphs, and charts to:
   a. summarize data.
   b. make inferences about data.
   c. make predictions.
   d. test hypotheses.

2. A classmate is collecting data for a research project incorporating a treatment group and a control group. When the data collection is complete, she will check for _____ to see if the differences between the two groups are due to the researcher's manipulations.
   a. random sampling
   b. descriptive statistics
   c. standard deviations
   d. statistical significance

3. In the following, identify the variable as quantitative (1) or qualitative (2):
   a. political affiliation
   b. hair color
   c. yearly income
   d. weight in pounds

4. One common way to present data is to use a _____, which displays how often various values in a data set are present.
   a. qualitative variable
   b. meta-analysis
   c. frequency distribution
   d. measure of variation

5. A researcher is looking to measure cognitive ability in a large representative sample. She can expect that the distribution will be symmetric and have a bell shape. This type of distribution is also known as a:
   a. normal curve.
   b. stem-and-leaf plot.
   c. qualitative variable.
   d. parameter.

6. Numbers that represent the "middle" of data sets are known as:
   a. standard deviations.
   b. measures of central tendency.
   c. measures of variability.
   d. misleading.

7. What is the mean for a sample that includes the following values: 4, 4, 6, 3, 8?
   a. 4
   b. 5
   c. 6
   d. 7

8. What is the median for a sample that includes the following values: 4, 4, 6, 3, 8?
   a. 4
   b. 5
   c. 6
   d. 7

9. What is the mode for a sample that includes the following values: 4, 4, 6, 3, 8?
   a. 4
   b. 5
   c. 6
   d. 7

10. A value that is very different from the rest of the data set is called a(n) _____, and it can have a great influence on the _____.
    a. mode; median
    b. variable; mode
    c. outlier; mean
    d. outlier; median

11. A classmate is trying to calculate a measure of variability. He takes the highest value in the data set and subtracts the lowest value from it. This is considered the _____ of the data set.
    a. range
    b. central tendency
    c. median
    d. standard deviation

12. What is the standard deviation for a sample that includes the following values: 4, 4, 6, 3, 8?
    a. 2
    b. 3
    c. 4
    d. 5

CHECK YOUR ANSWERS IN APPENDIX C.

Get personalized practice by logging into LaunchPad at www.macmillanhighered.com/launchpad/sciampresenting1e to take the LearningCurve adaptive quizzes for Appendix A.

careers in psychology

Most people hear the word "psychologist" and automatically think of therapy, counseling, and Freud, but as we noted in Chapter 1, psychologists perform a variety of roles in our society. Psychology is a vast field, and there is no shortage of career paths. If you are considering psychology, or even if you have already chosen psychology as your major, it is important to determine if this is the right career choice for you, and to figure out which subfield matches your interests, skills, and abilities. Then there is the issue of money. Will the career you choose allow you to reach your financial goals? Psychologists' salaries are highly variable and depend on many factors, including education level, specialty, and type of employer.

Any career in psychology will require some degree of specialized education. The question is, how much are you willing and able to attain? For many students, the answer depends on age, family responsibilities, financial concerns, and life experiences. In psychology, there are three types of degrees you can consider at the undergraduate and graduate level: bachelor's, master's, and doctoral.

What Can I Do with a Bachelor's Degree in Psychology?

Many students begin their journey by obtaining a 2-year associate's degree, and then go on to earn a bachelor's degree from a 4-year institution. A bachelor's degree in psychology is a great step toward understanding the scientific study of behavior and mental processes. It can prepare you to enter a graduate program, or it may serve as the foundation for your career. The psychology bachelor's degree is exceptionally popular, with over 97,000 awarded in 2010–2011 (Snyder & Dillow, 2011), which could mean substantial competition in the job market. This is one place where the decision between entering the workforce or attending graduate school becomes important. **Table B.1** gives you a sense of the types of jobs you can obtain with a bachelor's degree in psychology.

When it comes to earning potential, education level matters. People with bachelor's degrees earn an estimated $2.3 million over the course of a lifetime. Contrast that with $1.3 million lifetime earnings for those with only high school diplomas. Higher-level degrees generally lead to the most lucrative positions. The average lifetime salary is $2.7 million for someone with a master's degree, and $3.3 million for someone with a doctoral degree (Carnevale, Rose, & Cheah, 2011).

TABLE B.1 BACHELOR'S DEGREES AND CAREERS IN PSYCHOLOGY

Psychology Focus	Median Annual Salary	Business Focus	Median Annual Salary	Other Focus	Median Annual Salary
Caseworker	$28,000	Administrative assistant	$35,000	Child-care employee	$19,000
Correctional treatment specialist	$47,000	Advertising sales agent	$45,000	Clergy	$48,000
Foster-care home supervisor	$28,000	Airline reservations employee	$33,500	Community service manager	$58,000
Group home supervisor	$28,000	Customer relations	$30,000	Health services manager	$84,000
Probation officer	$47,000	Employment counselor	$56,000	High school teacher	$53,000
Residential treatment center employee	$27,000	Insurance agent	$47,000	Law enforcement	$55,000
Social services director	$58,000	Human resources	$53,000	Parks and recreation worker	$22,000
Substance abuse counselor	$38,000	Public relations	$57,500	Security officer	$24,000

A bachelor's degree in psychology prepares you for many types of employment opportunities. Here, we see how this type of degree is not limited to the field of psychology. For more up-to-date information, log onto LaunchPad at www.macmillanhighered.com/launchpad/sciampresenting1e.

ADAPTED FROM LANDRUM (2001) AND LLOYD (1997, JULY 16). SALARY INFORMATION FROM BUREAU OF LABOR STATISTICS (2012–2013).

What Can I Do with a Master's Degree in Psychology?

Choosing to pursue a graduate degree in psychology requires a great deal of research. There are many types of degrees, and a multitude of colleges and universities that offer them. The American Psychological Association (APA) publishes a valuable resource for students thinking about this next step, *Graduate Study in Psychology* (2015). This guide, which is routinely updated, includes information on approximately 600 psychology graduate programs offered in the United States and Canada. In it you will find a program's application deadlines, tuition costs, graduate employment data, and other useful information.

A master's degree in psychology is flexible and can prepare you to work in areas outside the field of psychology, including government, health care, business, marketing, and education. Many master's-level psychologists devote their careers to research, working under PhD-level researchers at universities and other institutions. Others become therapists. Typically, this means earning a master's degree, with an emphasis on counseling, and securing a state license to practice.

Table B.2 provides some general information about the types of degrees and training required of various mental health professions. In most states, master's-level clinicians must obtain a license to practice and share details about their education, training, and licensing status with their clients. One can also earn a master's degree in nonclinical specialties such as industrial/organizational psychology, engineering psychology, and leadership psychology. Some of these applied fields offer lucrative careers in business and industry. Finally, many students earning a master's degree in psychology go on to complete their doctorate degrees.

TABLE B.2 MENTAL HEALTH PROFESSIONALS

Degree	Occupation	Training	Focus	Approximate Years of Study After Bachelor's Degree
Medical doctor, MD	Psychiatrist	Medical school and residency training	Treatment of psychological disorders; may include research focus	8 (including residency)
Doctor of philosophy, PhD	Clinical or counseling psychologist	Graduate school; includes dissertation and internship	Research-oriented and clinical practice	3-6
Doctor of psychology, PsyD	Clinical or counseling psychologist	Graduate school; includes internship; may include dissertation	Focus on professional practice	2-5
Master's degree, MA or MS	Mental health counselor	Graduate school; includes internship	Focus on professional practice	2

Mental health professionals have a variety of backgrounds. Here, we present a handful of these, including general information on training, focus, and the length of education.

Doctoral Degrees: PhD and PsyD

Whether you need a degree at the doctoral level really depends on your interests. A PhD (doctor of philosophy) psychologist typically focuses on research, though some may provide therapy (Norcross & Castle, 2002). Earning a PhD requires graduate-level course work: 3 to 6 years of advanced college courses and training in addition to a bachelor's degree. PhD course work and research culminate in a dissertation, which you might think of as a huge research paper in your field of study. PhD programs are highly competitive; it is not unusual for an applicant to apply to multiple schools, but only gain acceptance to one or two. The good news is that programs typically provide 70–80% of students with tuition assistance (Norcross & Castle, 2002). For some helpful tips on applying to PhD programs, you can visit the APA Web site at http://www.apa.org/education/grad/applying.aspx and LaunchPad at www.macmillanhighered.com/launchpad/sciampresenting1e.

If your interest is more clinically focused, then you may consider the other doctoral-level degree in psychology, a PsyD (doctor of psychology). It emphasizes clinical practice rather than research, and typically requires 1 to 1.5 fewer years than a PhD program. This is not to say that PsyD programs do not require course work in statistics and research methods; it is just not the primary focus. PsyD programs traditionally emphasize clinical study, practice, and experience (Norcross & Castle, 2002). Because most PsyD degrees are offered by professional schools of psychology or private colleges and universities, students in these programs graduate with an average debt of $120,000 (Novotney, 2013, January). There also tends to be less financial aid available for PsyD students.

Doctor of Psychology
David Brantley III celebrates with his daughter after receiving a doctor of psychology degree (PsyD) from Rutgers Graduate School of Applied and Professional Psychology. Unlike PhD programs, which are highly research focused, PsyD programs focus more on the clinical side of things—that is, the diagnosis and treatment of psychological disorders. AP Photo/Mike Derer

Subfields of Psychology

Psychologists provide treatment for people with mental disorders, examine cognitive processes, study changes across the life span, work with children in schools, help corporations develop marketing strategies, and much more. Let's explore careers in some of the subfields of psychology.

Changing the World
With a budget of only $3,000, Dr. Tamara Russell launched an innovative mental health program at Washington State Penitentiary in Walla Walla, WA. Her treatment program provides inmates with opportunities to help others—by mentoring fellow inmates, tutoring students for the General Educational Development (GED) tests, and caring for orphaned kittens, among other things (Hagar, 2013, September 19).
AP Photo/Walla Walla Union-Bulletin, Greg Lehman

Clinical Psychology

Clinical psychologists focus on the diagnosis and treatment of people with psychological disorders. In addition to providing therapy, many of these professionals also conduct research. They may, for example, use brain scanning technologies to better understand the causes of depression, or design studies to compare the effects of different treatments. Some work as professors in colleges or universities, others as clinicians in medical facilities or private practice (APA, 1998b, 2011b).

Cognitive Psychology

Cognitive psychologists examine thinking, memory, intelligence, language, attention, and problem solving. Using the scientific method, these psychologists study how people "perceive, interpret and store information" (APA, 1998b, p. 14). Cognitive psychologists generally work in college and university settings, but many are employed as business consultants (APA, 1998b, 2011b).

Counseling Psychology

Like clinical psychologists, counseling psychologists provide treatment for people with psychological disorders. But instead of helping people with severe disorders, they often work with those needing support concerning day-to-day problems. These psychologists tend to focus on relationship issues, career exploration, and stress management. They can be found in academic settings, clinical practice, and hospitals (APA, 1998b, 2011b). The work of clinical and counseling psychologists overlaps to some degree, although differences may result from their specific training programs. In some cases, counseling programs are located in a psychology department, which is also the case for most clinical programs. However, many counseling psychology programs are affiliated with education departments, which might conduct different types of research and training than psychology departments.

Developmental Psychology

Developmental psychologists are primarily concerned with physical, cognitive, and socioemotional changes that occur over the life span (APA, 1998b, 2011b). Research in this field provides information about people from conception to death, impacting, for example, how children are treated in day-care settings, students are educated in classrooms, and elderly people are advised to manage their health. In the past, this field focused primarily on children from birth to adolescence, but developmental psychologists have become increasingly aware of the need to study adults as they age. They are especially concerned with helping people remain independent throughout life (APA, 2011b).

Educational and School Psychology

Educational psychologists examine methods of learning and how memory relates to learning. These specialists play a key role in developing teaching strategies and curricula. School psychologists working in the classroom often apply lessons gleaned by educational psychologists. Research findings may inform decisions about how to classify students academically, for example. Educational and school psychologists work at colleges and universities, in school districts, and in private practice. Some educational psychologists are employed in industry, helping to create and evaluate standardized tests (APA, 1998b, 2011b). These psychologists may collaborate with school administrators, teachers, and parents to provide an effective and safe learning environment. They may assist students who are having learning difficulties, students identified as gifted, or teachers dealing with classroom management and student behavior problems.

Engineering Psychology

Engineering psychologists conduct research to improve work environments by optimizing processes, systems, and equipment. They are also referred to as human factors specialists and usually work in industry and government (APA, 2011b). These specialists play a key role in observing on-the-job activities, conducting surveys, and recommending changes to facilitate optimal work environments with high productivity and safety. They may recommend changes in equipment, workload, personnel, or training.

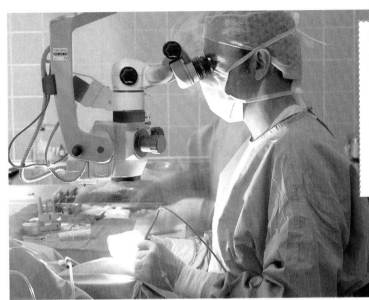

Positive Work Environment
A physician uses a surgical microscope designed to facilitate a more comfortable sitting posture. Optimizing the relationship between humans and technology is one of the goals of engineering psychology. These specialists research and develop ways to improve work environments. Business Wire via Getty Images

Environmental Psychology

Environmental psychologists study the connection between behavior and the physical environment. "Physical environment" refers to anywhere that humans spend time, be it at home, in a college dorm, or on a city block. Environmental psychologists explore ways to promote "positive human behavior" in governmental agencies, businesses, and other types of settings (APA, 1998b, 2011b).

Experimental Psychology

Experimental psychologists are science enthusiasts. They spend their days conducting basic and applied research on people, animals, and data. These researchers typically focus on a particular area of study, such as cognitive psychology, neuroscience, or animal behavior. Experimental psychologists may teach at colleges and universities, or conduct research for industries (APA, 1998b, 2011b).

Forensic Psychology

Forensic psychologists apply the principles of psychology to the legal system, working in diverse environments including criminal, family, and civil courts. These experts often are called upon in legal cases involving decisions about child custody, or situations in which a person's "mental competence to stand trial" is in question (APA, 2011b, p. 2). Some forensic psychologists are trained in law as well as in psychology, and they may conduct research on topics such as jury behavior or eyewitness testimony.

Health Psychology

Health psychologists focus their efforts on promoting positive health behaviors and preventing illness. They may research questions such as: Why do people smoke? or, What drives someone to overeat?, and their findings are used to promote good health practices. Health psychologists examine how individuals deal with sickness, pain, and medical treatment. They look at the interaction of biological, psychological, and social factors in relation to health and well-being. Health psychologists may be employed by hospitals, clinics, and rehabilitation centers, or they might work in private practice (APA, 1998b, 2011b).

Industrial and Organizational (I/O) Psychology

Industrial and organizational psychologists examine the relationships of people working in organizations. They are particularly interested in employee job satisfaction, productivity, and organizational structure and change, as well as the interface between humans and machines. In addition, I/O psychologists work with administrators to assist in hiring, training, and educating employees, and promoting their interests. I/O psychologists are often employed in industry, government, business, and academic settings (APA, 1998b, 2011b).

Media Psychology

Media psychologists examine human responses to the interactions among graphics, images, and sound. They study psychology and the development, production, and use of technology. Media psychologists investigate all forms of media (print, radio, television, social media) through different formats (mobile, interactive, virtual; APA, 2012c). They are particularly concerned with the way media shape how we spend our time. They may also look at how social media, text messaging, and e-mail have influenced the manner in which people relate to one another. Media psychologists might also examine the way reality TV shows can elevate ordinary people to celebrity status.

Neuropsychology and Psychobiology

Neuropsychologists and psychobiologists are interested in the link between human behavior and the body (neural activity, hormonal changes, and so on; APA, 1998b, 2011b). These psychologists work with people recovering from strokes and brain traumas, or struggling with learning disabilities and developmental delays. They investigate how the structure and function of the brain relate to behavior, cognition, and emotion. Neuropsychologists and psychobiologists often conduct research at colleges or universities, but they may also be employed by hospitals or other medical facilities (APA, 1998b, 2011b).

Rehabilitation Psychology

Rehabilitation psychologists either study or work with patients who have lost functioning as a result of strokes, epilepsy, autism, or accidents, for example. These psychologists are particularly concerned with helping people adjust to work, relationships, and day-to-day living. Their research may impact the development of public programs (APA, 2011b).

Neuropsychologist at Work
Cognitive neuropsychologist Dr. Lisa Barnes (left) studies the social factors involved in age-related cognitive decline in minority populations. A professor at Rush University Medical Center in Chicago, Dr. Barnes aims to understand why African Americans are disproportionately affected by Alzheimer's disease. Lisa L. Barnes, PHD

Social Psychology

Social psychologists examine the behaviors, thoughts, and emotions of people in groups. They may study attitudes, persuasion, discrimination, conformity, or group behavior. Social psychologists are interested in the many factors that influence interpersonal relationships, as well as the factors associated with attraction and love. While often employed by colleges and universities, these psychologists may also work for businesses and corporations (APA, 1998b, 2011b).

Sport Psychology

Sport psychologists help athletes and their coaches set constructive goals, increase motivation, and cope with anxiety related to athletic performance (APA, 2011b). As any sport psychologist can testify, being physically fit is not the only requirement for athletic excellence; mental fitness is also critical. Sport psychologists also work in many corporations, helping to build their "teams" and supporting efforts to manage stress, build confidence, and improve job performance (APA, 2015).

Psychologist in the Field
Sport psychologist Jeremy Snape (middle) meets with legendary cricket player Sir Viv Richards (left) and Melbourne Stars captain Shane Warne (right) before a big cricket game. Sport psychologists help athletes and coaches contend with the psychological challenges of their sport. Paul Kane/Getty Images

The science of psychology is relatively young compared to other sciences, and it is growing and changing with the advancement of technology and interdisciplinary research. If you are considering a career in psychology, keep up with the exciting developments in the field. A good way to stay abreast is by visiting the Web sites of the field's professional organizations (the Association for Psychological Science and the American Psychological Association) and logging onto Launch-Pad at www.macmillanhighered.com/launchpad/sciampresenting1e.

1 introduction to the science of psychology

show what you know

Presenting Psychology

1. behavior; mental processes

2. d. control

3. *Common sense* is a collection of knowledge that any reasonably smart person can pick up through everyday experiences and casual observations. Findings from psychology, however, are based on meticulous and methodical observations of behaviors and mental processes, as well as data analysis. Many people respond to psychological findings with *hindsight bias,* or the feeling as if they knew it all along, when in reality they wouldn't have predicted the outcome ahead of time.

Roots, Schools, and Perspectives of Psychology

1. d. introspection

2. b. behavioral

3. a. natural selection

4. Answers will vary. *Sociocultural* and *biopsychosocial* perspectives are similar in that both examine how interactions with other people influence behaviors and mental processes. *Cognitive* and *biological* perspectives differ in that the *cognitive* perspective focuses on the thought processes underlying behavior, while the *biological* perspective emphasizes physiological processes.

Science and Psychology

1. b. critical thinking

2. Astrology is a great example of a *pseudopsychology,* an approach to explaining and predicting behavior and events that appears to be psychology but lacks scientific support. If you search the scientific literature for empirical, objective studies supporting astrological claims, you will have a very difficult time finding any. Another sign astrology is a pseudoscience is that its predictions are often too broad to refute. Let's say an astrologer predicts that a friend or close family member will soon need your kind words and support. Such a prediction would likely apply to the great majority of people, as family members and friends often look to each other for strength. Such a prediction would always seem to come true, because the probability of its occurrence is almost 100%.

3. d. operational definition

4. c. representative sample

Descriptive Research

1. c. Descriptive research

2. a. naturalistic observation.

3. *Descriptive research* explores and describes behaviors. This approach is excellent for investigating unfamiliar topics. A researcher conducting such a study has few or no specific expectations about outcomes, and may use his findings to direct future research. A critical weakness of descriptive research is that it cannot uncover cause-and-effect relationships.

Experimental Research

1. d. cause-and-effect relationship

2. a. dependent

3. In a *double-blind study,* neither the participants nor the researchers working directly with those participants know who is getting the treatment and who is getting the placebo. This type of study is designed to reduce the effects of expectations and biases that can interfere when either participants or experimenters know what they've received or distributed. This use of deception is necessary so that neither experimenters nor participants consciously or unconsciously alter their behaviors, that is, unknowingly change the outcome of the experiment.

4. b. debriefing.

TEST PREP are you ready?

1. b. applied research.

2. a. Common sense

3. c. the nature side of the nature–nurture issue.

4. d. functionalism.

5. d. Humanistic psychology

6. b. critical thinking

7. c. the scientific method

8. a. Inferential statistics

9. c. variables.

10. d. an equally likely chance of being picked to participate.

11. c. relationships among variables.

12. b. case study

13. d. independent; dependent

14. a. double-blind

15. b. experimental group

16. A thorough review of the literature informs us about what has been learned in the past. Without doing a literature search, we may find ourselves redoing a study that has already provided the answers we seek. In addition, it may help us develop research questions, move in new directions, and deepen our understanding of psychological phenomena.

17. Answers will vary. Possible answers may include: The treatment group could be told to write a lie, while the control group is instructed to write something truthful. The researcher could determine if other factors change the pressure and strokes of handwriting.

18. The most accurate data are likely to come from participants who answer written questions in private. Those answering in face-to-face interviews are not always forthright with their answers, or they may be uncomfortable or embarrassed to reveal the truth.

19. Answers will vary. Look for studies on topics that would be very hard for researchers to manipulate in an ethical manner (for example, breast-feeding, amount of television watched, attitudes).

20. Answers will vary. Some possibilities include showing the children a different cartoon; changing the ages of the children; including children of different ethnicities and socioeconomic backgrounds; determining whether they are hungry prior to participating; and so on.

(2) biology and behavior

ｏｏｏｏ show what you know

Introducing the Brain

1. b. the human nervous system

2. neuroscience

3. Answers will vary. Building blocks can include items ranging from flour and butter in culinary training to numbers in mathematics. Atoms, chemical compounds, mechanical parts, and many other basic components may be building blocks in other fields of study.

Neurons and Neural Communication

1. myelin sheath

2. a. glial cells

3. b. Neurotransmitters; synaptic gap

4. A diagram could include the following information: Neural communication involves different processes within and between neurons. Using Infographic 2.2, you can follow the electrical action within the neuron. Messages received by the dendrites from neighboring neurons are passed down the axon, which sends messages to other neurons through its branchlike terminal buds.

   Infographic 2.3 demonstrates how neurons communicate with each other via chemicals called *neurotransmitters*. The signal to release neurotransmitters is the voltage change from the action potential, which results in vesicles that contain neurotransmitters attaching to the membrane on the terminal bud. This allows the neurotransmitter to be released into the synaptic gap. The majority of these neurotransmitters drift across the synaptic gap and come into contact with receptor sites of the receiving neuron's dendrites, which may (or may not) lead to an action potential in the receiving neuron.

The Supporting Systems

1. d. Motor neurons

2. b. spinal cord

3. pituitary

4. Both types of responses tend to increase the likelihood of survival and reproduction. The *fight-or-flight* strategy centers on self-preservation: by confronting or fleeing a threatening situation, the individual is acting to ensure her own survival and ability to reproduce. *Tend and befriend* is perhaps a less direct approach. Forging social bonds and tending to the young strengthen the community as a whole, which can support the survival and reproduction of its members.

The Amazing Brain

1. d. lateralization.

2. b. Broca's area.

3. The *corpus callosum* is a bundle of nerve fibers that allows the two halves of the brain to communicate and work together to process information. This same band of nerve fibers can also serve as a passageway for electrical storms responsible for seizures. With the split-brain operation, the corpus callosum is severed so that these storms can no longer pass freely between the hemispheres.

4. a. neuroplasticity

5. b. frontal lobes

6. association areas

Digging Below the Cortex

1. b. limbic system

2. amygdala

3. a. relay sensory information.

TEST PREP are you ready?

1. c. Neurons

2. a. an action potential

3. a. myelin sheath

4. 1. acetylcholine: c. enables movement; 2. glutamate: b. learning, memory; 3. endorphins: a. reduction of pain; 4. serotonin: d. mood, aggression, appetite

5. a. central nervous system.

6. b. spinal cord

7. d. peripheral nervous system

8. d. "rest-and-digest" process.

9. b. endocrine system; glands

10. b. The right hemisphere is more competent handling visual tasks.

11. a. locations in the brain are responsible for certain activities.

12. d. Wernicke's area

13. 1. association areas: b. integration of information from all over brain; 2. temporal lobes: c. hearing and language comprehension; 3. meninges: a. three thin membranes protect brain; 4. occipital lobes: e. processes visual information; 5. parietal lobes: d. receive sensory information, such as touch

14. 1. amygdala: b. processes basic emotions; 2. hippocampus: a. responsible for making new memories; 3. hypothalamus: d. keeps body systems in steady state; 4. thalamus: c. relays sensory information

15. d. reticular formation

16. Answers will vary. *Agonists* boost normal neurotransmitter activity and *antagonists* dampen normal neurotransmitter activity. An agonist is somewhat like a substance you add to your car engine to increase its efficiency. An antagonist might be compared to a character in a novel who prevents a heroine from doing her job.

17. Diagrams will vary; see Figure 2.3. A *reflex* is an uncontrollable reaction that often protects us from bodily harm. For example, we automatically pull away when we touch a hot surface. Sensory neurons are activated and carry information from the environment to interneurons in the spinal cord, which activates motor neurons. The motor neurons excite the muscle and initiate the motion of pulling away.

18. *Neurotransmitters* are chemical messengers produced by neurons that enable communication between neurons. *Hormones* are chemical messengers produced by the endocrine system and released into the bloodstream. The effects of the neurotransmitters are almost instantaneous, whereas those of hormones are usually delayed and longer lasting. Both influence thoughts, emotions, and behaviors. Neurotransmitters and hormones can work together, for example directing the fight-or-flight response to stress.

19. Sperry and Gazzaniga's research demonstrated that the hemispheres of the human brain, while strikingly similar in appearance, specialize in different functions. The left hemisphere excels in language processing, and the right hemisphere excels at visuospatial tasks. The corpus callosum normally allows the two hemispheres to share and integrate information.

20. The *EEG* detects electrical impulses in the brain. The *CT* uses X-rays to create many cross-sectional images of the brain. The *MRI* uses pulses of radio waves to produce more detailed cross-sectional images than those of a CT scan, but both MRI and CT are used to study the structure of the brain. The *PET* uses radioactivity to track glucose consumption and constructs a map of brain activity. The *fMRI* also captures changes in brain activity, but instead of tracking glucose consumption, it reveals patterns of blood flow in the brain, which is a good indicator of how much oxygen is being used. All of these tools have strengths and limitations (see Table 2.1 and Infographic 2.1).

try this
page 62

ANSWER: Yes, Brandon would display a reflex. Remember that the knee jerk is an involuntary reaction carried out by neurons outside of the brain.

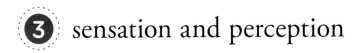

3 sensation and perception

▢▢▢▢ show what you know

An Introduction to Sensation and Perception

1. a. Perception

2. Answers will vary. Some examples may include the light reflecting off the book, the vibration of your phone, the sound of your refrigerator.

3. d. sensory adaptation.

Vision

1. wavelength

2. b. photoreceptors

3. The *trichromatic theory of color vision* suggests there are three types of cones, each sensitive to particular wavelengths in the red, green, and blue spectrums. The brain identifies a precise hue by calculating patterns of excitement among the three types of cones, that is, the relative activity of the three types.

   The *opponent-process theory of color vision* suggests that in addition to the color-sensitive cones, we also have neurons that respond to opponent colors (for example, red–green, blue–yellow). One neuron in an opponent pair fires when one is looking at red, for example, but is inactive when one is looking at green. Both the trichromatic and opponent-process theories clarify different aspects of color vision, as color perception occurs in the light-sensing cones in the retina and in the opponent cells serving the brain.

4. d. rods.

Hearing

1. a. frequency

2. b. transduction.

3. place

4. Diagrams will vary. The pitch of a sound is determined by the frequency of its sound wave, which is usually measured in Hertz. *Place theory* suggests that the location of neural activity along the cochlea allows us to sense different pitches of high-frequency sounds. *Frequency theory* suggests that the pitch of a sound is determined by the vibrating frequency of the sound wave, basilar membrane, and associated neural impulses. Place theory explains our perception of pitches from 4,000 to 20,000 Hz, and frequency theory explains how we perceive the pitch of sounds from 20 to 400 Hz. The *volley principle* explains the perception of pitches from 400 to 4,000 Hz.

Smell, Taste, Touch: The Chemical and Skin Senses

1. olfaction

2. b. transduction.

3. Answers will vary. Some examples may include typing on your computer, sitting in your chair, getting food from the refrigerator, turning off the fan, taking notes.

4. c. the gate-control theory

Perception

1. Gestalt

2. a. convergence

3. *ESP* is the purported ability to obtain information about the world in the absence of sensory stimuli. There is a lack of scientific evidence to support the existence of ESP, and most so-called evidence comes in the form of personal anecdotes. Subjective information can be biased. Using critical thinking, we must determine the credibility of the source and validity of the evidence. Despite ESP's lack of scientific credibility, many people still believe in its existence, in part because of illusory correlations, which appear to be links between variables that are not closely related at all.

4. b. perceptual constancy

TEST PREP are you ready?

1. c. sensation.

2. a. transduction.

3. b. fatigue and motivation

4. d. cornea

5. b. rods and cones

6. a. afterimage effect; trichromatic

7. d. audition

8. c. neural impulses firing

9. b. 20%

10. a. thalamus

11. a. Feature detectors

12. a. proprioceptors

13. a. tension of the muscles focusing the eyes

14. d. proximity.

15. c. relative size.

16. Answers may vary. Humans gravitate toward sweet, calorie-rich foods for their life-sustaining energy, which was adaptive for primitive humans foraging in trees and bushes. We tend to avoid bitter and sour tastes as this gives us an evolutionary edge because poisonous plants or rancid foods are often bitter or sour.

17. Extrasensory perception is the purported ability to obtain information about the world without any sensory stimuli. Subliminal stimuli are sights, sounds, smells, tastes, and feelings occurring below absolute threshold. Another difference is that there is research evidence for the influence of subliminal stimuli, but there is no reliable data to back up claims about ESP.

18. Diagrams will vary; see Infographic 3.3. The pinna funnels sound waves into the auditory canal, focusing them toward the eardrum. Vibrations in the eardrum cause the hammer to push the anvil, moving the stirrup, which presses on the oval window, amplifying waves. Pressure on the oval window causes fluid in the cochlea to vibrate and bend the hair cells on the basilar membrane. If vibration is strong enough in the cochlear fluid, the bending of hair cells causes nearby nerve cells to fire. The auditory nerve carries signals to the auditory cortex in the brain, where sounds are given meaning.

19. The *gate-control theory of pain* suggests that the perception of pain can either increase or decrease through the interaction of biopsychosocial factors. Signals are sent to open or close the "gates" that control the neurological pathways for pain. When large myelinated fibers are active, the gates are more likely to close, which then inhibits pain messages from being sent on. With a sore shoulder, applying ice to the injured area can stimulate the temperature and pressure receptors of the large fibers. This activity closes the gates, temporarily interfering with the pain message that would have been sent to the brain.

20. An absolute threshold is the weakest stimuli that can be detected 50% of the time. A difference threshold is the minimum difference between two stimuli that can be noticed 50% of the time.

4 consciousness

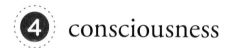 show what you know

An Introduction to Consciousness

1. subjective

2. b. automatic processing

3. Answers will vary. The ability to focus awareness on a small segment of information that is available through our sensory systems is called *selective attention*. Although we are exposed to many different stimuli at once, we tend to pay particular attention to abrupt or unexpected changes in the environment. Such events may pose a danger and we need to be aware of them. However, selective attention can cause us to be blind to objects directly in our line of vision. This "looking without seeing" can have serious consequences, as we fail to see important occurrences in our surroundings. Our advice would be to try to remain aware of the possibility of inattentional blindness, in particular when you are in situations that could involve serious injury.

Sleep

1. d. retinal ganglion cells.

2. b. Stage 2

3. cataplexy

4. Drawings will vary; see Infographic 4.2. A normal adult sleeper begins in non-rapid eye movement sleep. Stage 1, the lightest sleep, is associated with theta waves. Stage 2 includes evidence of sleep spindles. Stages 3 and 4 are associated with delta waves and deep sleep. Sleep then becomes less deep as the sleeper works back from Stage 4 to Stage 1. But instead of waking up, the sleeper enters rapid eye movement sleep (REM). Each cycle lasts about 90 minutes, with the average adult sleeper looping through five cycles per night.

Dreams

1. manifest content; latent content

2. c. activation–synthesis model

3. EEG and PET scan technologies can demonstrate neural activity while we sleep. During REM sleep, the motor areas of the brain are inhibited, but a great deal of neural activity is occurring in the sensory areas of the brain. The *activation–synthesis model* suggests dreams result when the brain responds to this random neural activity as if it has meaning. The creative human mind makes up stories to match the neural activity. The vestibular system is also active during REM sleep, resulting in sensations of floating or flying. The *neurocognitive theory of dreams* proposes that a network of neurons in the brain (including some areas in the limbic system and forebrain) are necessary for dreaming to occur.

4. a. until children are around 13 to 15 years old, their reported dreams are less vivid.

Altered States of Consciousness

1. 1. depressant: b. slows down activity in the CNS; 2. opioid: a. blocks pain; 3. alcohol: d. cirrhosis of the liver; 4. cocaine: c. increases neural activity in the CNS

2. c. LSD

3. psychoactive drugs

4. To determine if behaviors should be considered problematic, one could evaluate the presence of tolerance or withdrawal, both signs of physiological dependence. With *tolerance,* one's system adapts to a drug over time and therefore needs more and more of the substance to re-create the original effect. *Withdrawal* can occur with constant use of some psychoactive drugs, when the body has become dependent and then reacts when the drug is withheld. In some cases, with *psychological dependence,* behaviors may be problematic when there is a strong desire or need to continue the behavior, but with no evidence of tolerance or withdrawal symptoms. If an individual harms himself or others around him as a result of his behaviors, it is a problem. Overuse is maladaptive and causes significant impairment or distress to the user and/or his family. This might include difficulties at work or school, neglect of children and household duties, and physically dangerous behaviors.

TEST PREP are you ready?

1. d. consciousness

2. b. selective attention.

3. a. The cocktail-party effect

4. d. circadian rhythm.

5. c. hypothalamus; reticular formation

6. a. insomnia

7. b. alpha

8. d. REM sleep

9. a. REM rebound.

10. b. wish fulfillment.

11. d. the neurocognitive theory

12. c. Psychoactive drugs

13. a. dopamine

14. b. tobacco

15. c. Physiological; withdrawal

16. Answers will vary. If someone walks into your room while you are asleep, you wake up immediately if there is a noise. You hear a text message come in during the night and quickly wake up to answer the message.

17. Without one's awareness, the brain determines what is important, what requires immediate attention, and what can be processed and stored for later use if necessary. This *automatic processing* happens involuntarily, with little or no conscious effort. It is important because our sensory systems absorb large amounts of information that needs to be processed, and we could not possibly be consciously aware of all of it. Automatic processing also enables *sensory adaptation,* which is the tendency to become less sensitive to and less aware of constant stimuli after a period of time.

18. We might not want a doctor with such a schedule to care for us because staying up for 48 hours can result in problems with memory, attention, reaction time, and decision making, all important processes that doctors use in caring for patients. Sleep deprivation impairs the ability to focus attention on a single activity, such as delivering medical care.

19. Answers will vary. See Table 4.1 for information on sleep disturbances and their defining characteristics.

20. Answers will vary. There are many different drugs that people use legally on an everyday basis. Caffeine is a psychoactive drug found in coffee, soda, tea, and some medicines. Over-the-counter painkillers are legal drugs used to treat minor aches and pains. Nicotine is a highly addictive drug found in cigarettes or cigars. Alcohol is a legal psychoactive drug used on a daily basis by many people, as they drink a glass of wine or beer with an evening meal.

try this
page 138

ANSWER: Answers will vary. Conduct a study using a representative sample of U.S. college students. Because the goal of the study is to determine if the college living environment has some effect on sleep–wake cycles, the *independent variable* is living environment, and the *dependent variable* is sleep–wake cycle. The control group lives in a typical college dormitory, where there are no rules about when to go to sleep and wake up. The experimental group also lives in a dormitory, but this dorm has an early curfew and an 11 p.m. "lights-out" policy. At the end of some specified time period (for example, 6 weeks), the researchers observe and compare the sleep cycles of the two groups.

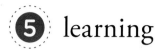

5 learning

 show what you know

An Introduction to Learning

1. behavior or thinking; experiences
2. c. associations

Classical Conditioning

1. Classical conditioning
2. biological preparedness
3. a. salmonella
4. When Little Albert heard the loud bang, it was an unconditioned stimulus (US) that elicited fear, the unconditioned response (UR). Through conditioning, the sight of the rat became paired with the loud noise, and thus the rat went from being a *neutral stimulus* to a conditioned stimulus (CS). Little Albert's fear of the rat became a conditioned response (CR). Not only did Little Albert begin to fear rats, he showed stimulus generalization when he demonstrated fear to other furry objects, including a sealskin coat and a rabbit.

Operant Conditioning

1. law of effect
2. d. stimulus generalization.
3. a. positive punishment
4. Answers will vary, but can be based on the following definitions. *Reinforcers* are consequences that increase the likelihood of a behavior reoccurring. *Positive reinforcement* is the process by which pleasant reinforcers are presented following a target behavior. *Negative reinforcement* occurs with the removal of an unpleasant stimulus following a target behavior. *Successive approximation* is a method for shaping that uses reinforcers to condition a series of small steps that gradually approach the target behavior.
5. *Continuous reinforcement* is a schedule of reinforcement in which every target behavior is reinforced. *Partial reinforcement* is a schedule of reinforcement in which target behaviors are reinforced intermittently, not continuously. Continuous reinforcement is generally more effective for establishing a behavior, whereas learning through partial reinforcement is more resistant to extinction and useful for maintaining behavior.

Observational Learning and Cognition

1. a. observational learning.
2. Answers will vary, but can be based on the following definitions. A *model* is an individual or character whose behavior is being imitated. *Observational learning* occurs as a result of watching the behavior of others.
3. c. latent learning.

TEST PREP are you ready?

1. b. habituation
2. c. ability to press a pendulum to get food.

3. a. involuntary; voluntary
4. b. conditioned response.
5. b. conditioned stimulus.
6. a. adaptive value
7. c. conditioned emotional response.
8. d. The law of effect
9. c. A dog whining in the morning, leading an owner to wake up and take it outside
10. a. positive reinforcement.
11. b. positive reinforcement.
12. a. were more likely to display aggressive behavior.
13. d. at increased risk of abusing their spouses when they become adults.
14. a. latent learning.
15. b. insight.
16. *Stimulus generalization* is the tendency for stimuli similar to the conditioned stimulus to elicit the conditioned response, whereas *stimulus discrimination* is the ability to differentiate between a conditioned stimulus and other stimuli sufficiently different from it. Once an association is forged between a CS and a CR, the learner often responds to similar stimuli as if they are the original CS (stimulus generalization).
17. Answers will vary, but can be based on the following definitions. *Shaping* is the use of reinforcers to guide behavior to the acquisition of a desired, complex behavior. *Partial reinforcement* is a schedule of reinforcement in which target behaviors are reinforced intermittently, not continuously (see Figure 5.3 to view the four different schedules of reinforcement).
18. Answers will vary, but can be based on the following definitions. *Primary reinforcers* satisfy biological needs, such as for food, water, or physical contact. *Secondary reinforcers* do not satisfy biological needs, but often gain their power through their association with primary reinforcers. A primary reinforcer used to change behavior might be food. A college tries to increase student participation by providing food at important school functions. Money can be used as a secondary reinforcer. Employees are paid money, which increases attendance at work.
19. Answers will vary, but can be based on the following definitions. *Punishment decreases* the likelihood of the behavior it follows. On the other hand, *negative reinforcement increases* the likelihood of a behavior recurring. See Table 5.3 for examples.
20. Answers can vary. The studies that have found an association between violent films and violent behaviors are *correlational:* They highlight a link between the films and the behaviors, not necessarily a cause-and-effect relationship. There are other factors that have to be considered. For example, parenting could influence both television viewing and aggression. A parent who is emotionally neglectful may place a child in front of a television all day, such that the child is more likely to imitate some aggressive behaviors seen on the TV. Simultaneously, the child may resent her parent for ignoring her, and the resentment could lead to aggressive behavior. In this example, is it the television programming or the parenting that is leading to aggression?

try this
page 205

ANSWER: Independent variable: exposure to an adult displaying aggressive or nonaggressive behavior. Dependent variable: child's level of aggression.

Ideas for altering the study: Conducting the same study with older or younger children; exposing the children to other children (as opposed to adults) behaving aggressively; pairing children with adults of the same and different ethnicities to determine the impact of ethnic background.

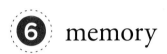

⑥ memory

○○○○ show what you know

An Introduction to Memory

1. Memory
2. b. Encoding
3. a. long-term memory
4. Paying little attention to data entering our sensory system results in *shallow processing*. For example, you remember seeing a word that has been boldfaced in the text while studying. You might even be able to recall the page that it appears on, and where on the page it is located. *Deeper-level processing* relies on characteristics related to patterns and meaning, and generally results in longer-lasting and easier to retrieve memories. As we study, if we contemplate incoming information and relate it to memories we already have, deeper processing occurs and the new memories are more likely to persist.

Flow With It: The Stages of Memory

1. b. 30 seconds
2. b. working memory.
3. Explicit; implicit
4. d. flashbulb memory.
5. Answers will vary. **Ex**quisitely **Se**rious **Ep**isodes **Fl**ashed **Im**possible **Pr**oteins

    Explicit memory, **Se**mantic memory, **Ep**isodic memory, **Fl**ashbulb memory, **Im**plicit memory, **Pr**ocedural memory

Retrieval and Forgetting

1. a. The encoding specificity principle
2. b. curve of forgetting.
3. d. rich false memory.
4. A *reconstructionist model* of memory suggests that memories are a combination of "fact and fiction." Over time, memories can fade, and because they are permeable, they become more vulnerable to the invasion of new information. In other words, memory of an event might include revisions to what really happened, based on knowledge, opinions, and information you have gained since the event occurred. The Loftus and Palmer experiment indicates that the wording of questions can significantly influence recall, demonstrating that memories can change in response to new information (that is, they are malleable).

The Biology of Memory

1. a. Anterograde amnesia
2. c. hippocampus
3. b. Memory consolidation
4. Answers will vary, but can be based on the following information. *Infantile amnesia* is the inability to remember events from one's earliest years. Most adults cannot remember events before the age of 3.

TEST PREP are you ready?

1. d. retrieval
2. a. hierarchy of processing
3. c. iconic memory.
4. d. chunking
5. b. working memory
6. a. the encoding specificity principle.
7. c. recognition
8. c. Proactive interference; retroactive interference
9. d. a reconstructionist model of memory
10. b. rich false memory
11. a. the misinformation effect.
12. c. repressed
13. b. access memories of events created before the trauma.
14. b. Long-term potentiation
15. d. hippocampus
16. Information enters sensory memory, which includes an overwhelming array of sensory stimuli. If it is not lost in sensory memory, it enters the short-term memory stage. The amount of time information is maintained and processed in short-term memory can be about 30 seconds. And short-term memory has a limited capacity. Because short-term memories cannot last for a couple of hours, it is more likely his grandmother is having difficulty encoding, storing, and/or recalling information that should be held in long-term memory.
17. *Iconic memories* are visual impressions that are photograph-like in their accuracy but dissolve in less than a second. *Echoic memories* are exact copies of the sounds we hear, lasting about 1–10 seconds. Iconic memory uses our visual system, whereas echoic memory uses our auditory system.
18. *Short-term memory* is a stage of memory that temporarily maintains and processes a limited amount of information. *Working memory* is the active processing of information in short-term memory. Working memory refers to what is going on in short-term memory.
19. Answers will vary. Examples may include **P**lease **E**xcuse **M**y **D**ear **A**unt **S**ally to help remember the order of operations in a mathematical expression (**p**arentheses, **e**xponents, **m**ultiplication, **d**ivision, **a**ddition, and **s**ubtraction); **R**oy **G. B**iv to help remember the colors of the rainbow (**r**ed, **o**range, **y**ellow, **g**reen, **b**lue, **i**ndigo, **v**iolet); **E**very **G**ood **B**oy **D**oes **F**ine for remembering the notes of the treble clef in music (**E, G, B, D, F**).
20. The teacher should list the most important rules first and last in the list. The *serial position effect* suggests items at the beginning and

at the end of a list are more likely to be recalled. The *primacy effect* suggests we are more likely to remember items at the beginning of a list, because they have a better chance of moving into long-term memory. The *recency effect* suggests we are more likely to remember items at the end of a list because they linger in short-term memory.

try this
page 240
ANSWER: f

7 cognition, language, and intelligence

⬤⬤⬤⬤ show what you know

An Introduction to Cognition

1. Cognition
2. b. concept
3. c. formal concept
4. Answers will vary. Structures in the brain are associated with cognition. For example, the association areas integrate information from all over the brain. Broca's and Wernicke's areas work with other parts of the brain to generate and understand language.

    The biology of cognition can be found at the neural level as well. For example, changes at the level of neurons make it possible to store and retrieve information. It is also at the neuronal level where we see the plasticity of the brain at work.

Problem Solving and Decision Making

1. c. trial and error.
2. Answers will vary. A *means–ends analysis* is a heuristic used to determine how to decrease the distance between a goal and the current state. The goal in this example is to complete an assignment in a timely manner. The means could be to break the problem into two subproblems: (1) choosing a topic (for example, by reading the textbook for interesting ideas, discussing ideas with your instructor); and (2) conducting a literature review (for example, identifying appropriate databases, finding a library to obtain and read articles).
3. Decision making
4. d. availability heuristic.
5. Answers will vary. A *heuristic* uses a "rule of thumb" or a broad application of a strategy to solve a problem, but it can also be used to help predict the probability of an event occurring. However, heuristics can lead us astray in our assessment of situations or predictions of outcomes. In the current example, you can present information to your friend that indicates flying is the safest form of travel. But you can also describe how the *availability heuristic* might lead him to believe that air travel is not safe. The vividness of airplane crashes can influence his recall; even though they are rare events, he is likely to overestimate the probability of them happening again due to the ease with which he recalls similar events. Highly detailed media reports of an airplane crash are likely to linger in his memory.

Language

1. Phonemes
2. b. thinking and perception.
3. Answers will vary. Bilingualism is associated with enhanced creativity, abstract thought, and working memory. And knowing more than one language has been found to be associated with more efficient executive functioning, including abilities related to planning ahead and solving problems. Thus, bilingualism may actually improve performance on cognitive tasks, such as deciphering unknown and untranslatable words.

Intelligence

1. c. analytic, creative, practical.
2. aptitude; achievement
3. The *intelligence quotient* (*IQ*) is a score from an intelligence assessment; it provides a way to compare levels of intelligence across ages. Originally, an IQ score was derived by dividing mental age by chronological age and multiplying that number by 100. Modern intelligence tests still assign a numerical score, although they no longer use the actual quotient score.
4. originality

TEST PREP are you ready?

1. d. Cognition; thinking
2. a. Concepts
3. c. natural concepts
4. b. the plasticity
5. d. an algorithm
6. a. Insight
7. b. availability heuristic.
8. d. confirmation bias.
9. c. the framing effect.
10. b. phonemes
11. a. divergent thinking
12. c. morphemes
13. d. Intelligence
14. b. validity
15. a. environmental factors such as chronic stress.
16. *Formal concepts* are created through rigid and logical rules, or features of a concept. *Natural concepts* are acquired through everyday experience, and they do not have the same types of rigid rules for identification that formal concepts have.

    Examples will vary. An example of a formal concept is the pitch of a sound, which is defined by the frequency of the sound wave. The concept of family is an example of a natural concept. Is a family a group of people who just live together, or do they have to be related genetically? Family is a natural concept that can change based on individual experiences.
17. See Table 7.2. Charles Spearman speculated that intelligence consists of a *general intelligence* (or *g* factor), which refers to a singular underlying aptitude or intellectual ability. Howard Gardner suggested we have *multiple intelligences,* proposing eight different

types of intelligences or "frames of mind": linguistic (verbal), logical-mathematical, spatial, bodily-kinesthetic, musical, intrapersonal, interpersonal, and naturalist. Robert Sternberg proposed three kinds of intelligences. His *triarchic theory of intelligence* suggests that humans have varying degrees of analytical, creative, and practical abilities.

18. Using the *availability heuristic,* we predict the probability of something happening in the future based on how easily we can recall a similar type of event from the past. The availability heuristic is essentially a decision-making strategy that relies on memory. They remembered a recent storm in which they did not have to leave their homes, and so they decided it was safe to stay.

19. *Reliability* is the ability of an assessment to provide consistent, reproducible results. *Validity* is the degree to which an assessment measures what it intends to measure. An unreliable IQ test might result in getting different scores for the IQ test taken now and again in a few months; it would not be consistent across time, which is counter to what you would expect (we expect level of intelligence to remain fairly stable over time). An IQ test that is not valid would not be able to predict future performance on tasks related to intellectual ability.

20. Answers will vary. *Divergent thinking* is the ability to devise many solutions to a problem.

Possible solutions: As a door stop, icebreaker, paper weight, shovel, or axe; for killing a poisonous snake; for putting out cigarettes; for breaking glass; for crushing ingredients for a recipe; for putting out a candle; and so on.

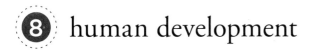

⑧ human development

▯▯▯▯ show what you know

The Study of Human Development

1. development

2. Developmental psychologists' longstanding discussions have centered on three major themes: stages and continuity; nature and nurture; and stability and change. Each of these themes relates to a basic question: (1) Does development occur in separate or discrete stages, or is it a steady, continuous process? (2) What are the relative roles of heredity and environment in human development? (3) How stable is one's personality over a lifetime and across situations?

3. c. cross-sectional

Genetics, Conception, and Prenatal Development

1. d. Chromosomes

2. Genotype; phenotype

3. a. embryonic period

4. Genes are behind most human traits, from shoe size to behavior. Each chromosome pair provides us with two versions of a gene: We acquire one gene from our biological mother and the other from our biological father. In some cases, the genes are identical. In other cases, the genes in a pair provide conflicting instructions about the outcome of some characteristic. Often one gene variant has more power than the other. This dominant gene then directs the

expression of the inherited characteristic, overpowering the recessive, or subordinate, gene in the pair. A recessive gene cannot overcome the influence of a dominant gene. For example, the gene responsible for cystic fibrosis is recessive. If a child inherits the cystic fibrosis gene from one parent and a normal gene from the other parent, the disease gene will not be expressed (she will not develop cystic fibrosis). However, if she inherits the cystic fibrosis gene from both parents, the gene will be expressed (she will develop the disease).

Infancy and Child Development

1. rooting; sucking

2. a. theories of behaviorism

3. d. assimilation.

4. scaffolding

5. c. developmental tasks or emotional crises.

6. There is a universal sequence of language development. At around 2–3 months, infants typically start to produce vowel-like sounds known as *cooing.* At 4–6 months, in the *babbling stage,* infants combine consonants with vowels. This progresses to the *one-word stage* around 12 months, followed by *two-word telegraphic speech* at approximately 18 months. As children mature, they start to use more complete sentences. Infants pay more attention to adults who use infant-directed speech and are more likely to provide them with chances to learn and interact, thus allowing more exposure to language. Parents and caregivers should talk with their infants and children as much as possible, as babies benefit from a lot of chatter.

Adolescence

1. b. secondary sex characteristics.

2. a. formal operational stage.

3. Preconventional

4. Answers will vary. During the stage of *ego identity versus role confusion,* an adolescent seeks to define himself through his values, beliefs, and goals. If a helicopter parent has been troubleshooting all of her child's problems, the child has never had to learn to take care of things for himself. Thus, he may feel helpless and unsure of how to handle a problem that arises. The parent might also have ensured the child was successful in every endeavor, but this too could cause the child to be unable to identify his true strengths, again interfering with the creation of an adult identity.

Adulthood

1. a. physical exercise

2. fluid; crystallized

3. d. acceptance

4. integrity; despair

TEST PREP are you ready?

1. b. longitudinal research.

2. d. nature and nurture

3. d. genes

4. a. epigenetics.

5. c. synaptic pruning

6. d. Teratogens

7. b. babbling

8. c. trust versus mistrust

9. b. scaffolding

10. c. Primary sex characteristics

11. a. formal operational stage.

12. b. search for identity

13. d. menopause

14. b. longitudinal method.

15. a. denial

16. Answers may vary. Family: social. Learning: psychological, social. Media: social, psychological. Heredity: biological. Hormones: biological. Traits: biological, psychological, and social. Culture: psychological, social.

17. At conception, when a sperm and egg merge, they form a single cell called a *zygote*. During the germinal period, the zygote grows through cell division and eventually becomes implanted in the uterine wall. Between the 3rd and 8th weeks of development, the mass of cells is now called an *embryo.* The embryo begins to develop everything the baby will need to live. The *fetal period* begins at the 9th week and continues until birth. Overall growth of the body and development of organ systems in the fetus is taking place. By the time a baby reaches this stage, everything that it needs to become a new person is already in place; it just needs to grow, develop, and become more mature.

18. *Infant-directed speech (IDS)* is observed throughout the world. Infants as young as 5 months old pay more attention to people who use infant-directed speech. It helps a child to learn to interact with "appropriate social partners," or adults who are more likely to provide them with such chances. From an evolutionary perspective, IDS helps a baby know who is going to pay the most attention to her, and who is going to protect and guide her. It also ensures that the infant will be enriched by interactions with others.

19. Answers will vary. Authoritarians give strictness; authoritative give warmth; permissive give permission; uninvolved give little. Authoritarian parenting; authoritative parenting; permissive parenting; uninvolved parenting.

20. *Wisdom* improves with age through an accumulation of instructive life experiences. As it increases, we make better decisions when encountering daily problems. Practical abilities also seem to increase. Experiences allow people to develop a more balanced understanding of the world surrounding them.

⑨ motivation and emotion

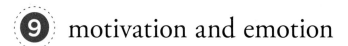 show what you know

Motivation

1. Motivation

2. Answers will vary. *Extrinsic motivation* is the drive or urge to continue a behavior because of external reinforcers. *Intrinsic motivation* is the drive or urge to continue a behavior because of internal reinforcers. A teacher wants to encourage intrinsic motivation because the reinforcers originate inside of the students, through personal satisfaction, interest in a subject matter, and so on. There are some potential disadvantages to extrinsic motivation. For example, using rewards, such as money and candy, to reinforce already interesting activities can lead to a decrease in what was intrinsically motivating. Thus, the teacher would want students to respond to intrinsic motivation because the tasks themselves are motivating, and the students love learning for the sake of learning itself.

    When activities are not novel or challenging or do not have aesthetically pleasing characteristics, intrinsic motivation will not be useful. Thus, using rewards might be the best way to motivate these types of activities.

3. c. instinct theory

4. d. drive-reduction

5. hierarchy of needs

6. The *drive-reduction theory* of motivation suggests that biological needs and homeostasis motivate us to meet needs. If a need is not fulfilled, this creates a drive, or state of tension, that pushes us or motivates behaviors to meet the need. Once a need is met, the drive is reduced, at least temporarily (because this is an ongoing process, as the need inevitably returns). *Arousal theory* suggests that humans seek an optimal level of arousal, and what is optimal is based on individual differences. Behaviors can arise out of the simple desire for stimulation, or arousal, which is a level of alertness and engagement in the world, and people are motivated to seek out activities that fulfill this need. Drive-reduction theory suggests that the motivation is to reduce tension, but arousal theory suggests that in some cases the motivation is to increase tension.

Back to Basics: Hunger

1. a. stomach was contracting.

2. d. extreme overeating followed by purging.

3. When glucose levels dip, the stomach and liver send signals to the brain that something must be done about this reduced energy source. The brain, in turn, initiates a sense of hunger. Signals from the digestive system are sent to the hypothalamus, which then transmits signals to higher regions of the brain. When the lateral hypothalamus is activated, appetite increases. On the other hand, if the ventromedial hypothalamus becomes activated, appetite declines, causing an animal to stop eating.

Sexual Motivation

1. a. excitement, plateau, orgasm, and resolution.

2. Because monozygotic twins share 100% of their genetic make-up, we expect them to share more genetically influenced characteristics than dizygotic twins, who only share about 50% of their genes. Using twins, researchers explored the impact of genes and environment on same-sex sexual behavior. Monozygotic twins were moderately more likely than dizygotic twins to have the same sexual orientation. They found men and women differ in terms of the heritability of same-sex sexual behavior (34–39% for men, 18–19% for women). These studies highlight that the influence of the environment is substantial with regard to same-sex sexual behavior.

3. a. Syphilis; gonorrhea

Emotion

1. d. Emotion

2. Answers will vary, but can be based on the following definitions. *Emotion* is a psychological state that includes a subjective or inner experience. It also has a physiological component and entails a behavioral expression. Emotions are quite strong, but they don't generally last as long as moods. In addition, emotions are more likely to have identifiable causes (that is, be reactions to stimuli that provoked them) and they are more likely to motivate a person to action. *Moods* are longer-term emotional states that are less intense than emotions and do not appear to have distinct beginnings or ends. It is very likely that on your way to a wedding you are in a happy mood, and you have been that way for quite a while. If you were to get mud on your clothing, it is likely that you would experience an emotion such as anger. This emotion differs from your mood in that it: (1) has a clear cause (your clothes were splashed with mud), (2) likely produces a physiological reaction (your face flushes with heat), and (3) motivates you to action (you glare at the culprit).

3. James–Lange

4. b. Display rules

5. Answers may vary. See Infographic 9.3. The *Cannon–Bard* theory of emotion suggests that environmental stimuli are the starting point for emotions, and that body changes and emotions happen together. The *Schachter–Singer* theory of emotion suggests there is a general pattern of physiological arousal caused by the sympathetic nervous system, and this pattern is common to a variety of emotions. Unlike the Cannon–Bard theory, the Schachter–Singer theory suggests our thoughts about our body changes lead to emotions. The experience of emotion is the result of two factors: physiological arousal and a cognitive label for this physiological state (the arousal). Cannon–Bard did not suggest that a cognitive label is necessary for emotions to be experienced.

6. Darwin suggested that interpreting facial expressions is not something we learn but rather is an innate ability that evolved because it promotes survival. Sharing the same facial expressions allows for communication. Research on an isolated group of indigenous peoples in New Guinea suggests that the same facial expressions represent the same basic emotions across cultures. In addition, the fact that children born deaf and blind have the same types of expressions of emotion as children who are not deaf or blind suggests the universal nature of these displays, and thus the emotions that trigger them.

Types of Emotions

1. amygdala

2. *Heritability* is the degree to which heredity is responsible for a particular characteristic in a population. In this case, the heritability for happiness is as high as 80%, indicating that around 80% of the variation in happiness can be attributed to genes, and 20% to environmental influences. In other words, we can explain a high proportion of the variation in happiness, life satisfaction, and well-being by considering genetic make-up, as opposed to environmental factors.

3. c. the sympathetic nervous system.

TEST PREP are you ready?

1. d. an incentive

2. a. extrinsic motivation.

3. c. Instincts

4. b. drive-reduction

5. a. sensation seekers

6. d. ventromedial hypothalamus

7. b. obesity.

8. d. binge-eating disorder.

9. c. behavioral expression.

10. b. could identify the facial expressions common across the world.

11. c. physiological arousal and cognitive labeling.

12. b. cognitive-appraisal approach

13. a. excitement.

14. a. cortex; amygdala

15. d. be better able to identify what emotion is being felt than are men.

16. Sexual orientation is the "enduring pattern" of sexual, romantic, and emotional attraction that individuals exhibit toward the same sex, opposite sex, or both sexes. Research has focused on the causes of sexual orientation, but there is no strong evidence pointing to any one factor or factors. There is some evidence that genetics and hormones may influence sexual orientation; however, most agree sexual orientation is the result of a complex interaction between nature and nurture.

17. Answers will vary, but can be based on the following definition. *Maslow's hierarchy of needs* is considered to be universal. The needs in the hierarchy are ordered in terms of the strength of their associated drive, with the most critical needs at the bottom. The pyramid includes increasingly higher-level needs: physiological needs; safety needs; love and belongingness needs; esteem needs; self-actualization; self-transcendence. Maslow suggested that one's most basic needs must be met before higher-level needs motivate behavior. An example of someone not following the prescribed order of needs might be a martyr who is motivated by self-transcendence needs, ignoring safety needs altogether.

18. Sexually transmitted infections are diseases or illnesses passed on through sexual activity. Bacterial infections such as syphilis, gonorrhea, and chlamydia often clear up with antibiotics. Viral infections like genital herpes and human papillomavirus (HPV) have no cure, only treatments to reduce symptoms.

19. Answers will vary, but can be based on the following definition. *Display rules* provide a framework or guidelines for when, how, and where an emotion is expressed. Display rules are a product of cultures.

20. Answers will vary, but can include physical exercise, showing kindness, getting involved in activities that benefit others, recording positive thoughts and feelings of gratefulness in a journal, identifying and pursuing goals, and so on.

10 personality

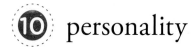 show what you know

An Introduction to Personality

1. Personality

2. d. behavioral

3. *Personality* is a unique core set of characteristics that influences the way one thinks, acts, and feels, which is relatively consistent and enduring throughout the life span. *Temperament* is a distinct pattern of emotional reactions and behaviors that can be observed early in life, and may be considered one dimension of personality. Unlike personality, which can be assessed with objective measures, *character* refers to culture-specific ideas about what makes a person good or bad.

Psychoanalytic Theories

1. psychosexual; fixation

2. d. topographical model of the mind

3. b. collective unconscious.

4. Answers will vary, but could include the following. Some of *Freud's followers* branched out on their own due to disagreements about certain issues, such as his focus on the instincts of sex and aggression, his idea that personality is determined by the end of childhood, and his somewhat negative view of human nature. *Adler* proposed that humans are conscious and intentional in their behaviors. *Jung* suggested that we are driven by a psychological energy (as opposed to sexual energy) that encourages positive growth, self-understanding, and balance. *Horney* emphasized the role of relationships between children and their caregivers, not erogenous zones and psychosexual stages.

Humanistic, Learning, and Trait Theories

1. Abraham Maslow; Carl Rogers

2. d. unconditional positive regard.

3. learning theory

4. b. locus of control

5. Answers will vary, but can be based on the following definition (and see Infographic 10.2). *Reciprocal determinism* refers to the multidirectional interactions among cognitions, behaviors, and the environment guiding our behavior patterns and personality.

6. a. traits.

7. Answers will vary (and see Table 10.4). The *Big Five* traits include openness, conscientiousness, extraversion, agreeableness, and neuroticism. Three decades of twin and adoption studies point to a genetic (and therefore biological) basis of these five factors. The proportion of variation in the Big Five traits attributed to genetic make-up is substantial (ranging from .41 to .61), suggesting that the remainder can be attributed to environmental influences.

Personality Assessment

1. b. Projective

2. a. intuition or bias.

3. Answers will vary, but can be based on the following definition. A *valid measure* is one that can be shown to measure what it intends to measure. If a measure is not valid, a client might be given information that is not meaningful because the findings have not been shown to measure their intended topic. A reliable measure provides consistent results across time as well as across raters or people scoring the measure. If findings from a personality test are not reliable, a client may be given information that will not reflect a consistent pattern or that may be questionable due to problems with scoring.

TEST PREP are you ready?

1. d. psychoanalytic

2. a. humanistic

3. d. mental processes that occur at three levels of consciousness.

4. b. superego.

5. c. Defense mechanisms

6. c. Self-actualization

7. a. incongruent

8. c. self-efficacy

9. c. Reciprocal determinism

10. d. factor analysis

11. a. three dimensions of traits.

12. b. the stability of the personality characteristics over time.

13. c. Reliability

14. a. projective personality tests

15. c. his intense emphasis on the instincts of sex and aggression

16. Answers will vary, but can be based on the following information. According to behaviorists and learning theory, the *environment* shapes personality through processes of classical conditioning and reinforcers. *Observation* and *modeling* also play a role in personality development.

17. Answers will vary. The *humanistic perspective* suggests that we are innately good and that we have capabilities we can and should take advantage of as we strive for personal growth. The choices we make in life influence our personalities. The *social-cognitive perspective* focuses on relationships, environmental influences, cognitive activity, and individual behavior as they come together to form personality. The humanistic perspective views personality as what we are able to do, whereas the social-cognitive perspective views personality, in part, as how we react to the environment.

18. Both the Oedipus (for boys) and the Electra (for girls) complex represent important conflicts that occur during the phallic stage. For both boys and girls, the conflict can be resolved through the process of identification. Although basic urges and developmental processes underlie both of these complexes, there are several important differences. The *Oedipus complex* is the attraction a boy feels toward his mother, along with resentment or envy directed toward his father. When a little boy becomes aware of his attraction to his mother, he realizes his father is a formidable rival and experiences jealousy and anger toward him. With the *Electra complex*, a little girl feels an attraction to her father and becomes jealous and angry toward her mother. Realizing she doesn't have a penis, she may respond with anger, blaming her mother for her missing penis.

19. Answers will vary, but can be based on the following definitions. An *internal locus of control* suggests that the causes of life events reside within an individual, and that one has some control over them. An *external locus of control* suggests that causes for outcomes reside outside of an individual, and there is little control over them.

20. *Objective assessments* of personality are based on a standardized procedure in which the scoring is free of opinions, beliefs, expectations, and values. Critics of objective assessments contend they do not allow flexibility or fully appreciate individual differences in experiences. Findings from *subjective assessments* of personality are based, in part, on personal intuition, opinions, and interpretations. Critics of the subjective assessments suggest there is not enough consistency across findings because of nonstandard scoring procedures.

 # stress and health

OOOO show what you know

An Introduction to Stress

1. Stress

2. d. illness

3. b. Acculturative stress

4. Answers will vary, but can be based on the following definitions. *Daily hassles* are the minor problems or irritants we deal with on a regular basis (for example, heavy traffic, financial worries, messy roommates). *Uplifts* are positive experiences that have the potential to make us happy (for example, a humorous text message, a small gift).

Stress and Your Health

1. general adaptation syndrome (GAS)

2. a. alarm stage

3. c. The hypothalamic–pituitary–adrenal system

4. c. cortisol

5. When the body is expending its resources to deal with an ongoing stressor, the immune system is less powerful, and the work of the lymphocytes is compromised. During times of stress, people tend to sleep poorly and eat erratically, and may increase their drug and alcohol use, along with other poor behavioral choices. These tendencies can lead to health problems.

Factors Related to Stress

1. approach–approach

2. d. Problem-focused coping

3. b. Type B personality.

4. Answers may vary. *Stress management* incorporates tools to lower the impact of possible stressors. Exercise, meditation, progressive muscle relaxation, biofeedback, and social support all have positive physical and psychological effects on the response to stressors. In addition, looking out for the well-being of others by caring and giving of yourself is an effective way to reduce the impact of stress.

1. c. Stressors

2. a. eustress.

3. d. life-changing events

4. b. sympathetic nervous system

5. a. parasympathetic nervous system

6. c. exhaustion stage

7. d. sympathetic nervous systems

8. a. the immune system

9. b. endorphins

10. d. progressive muscle relaxation

11. c. stressors are related to health problems.

12. b. Coping

13. d. avoidance–avoidance conflict.

14. a. Type A personality

15. b. hardiness.

16. Answers will vary, but can be based on the following explanation. There are various ways people respond to acculturative stress. Some try to assimilate into the culture, letting go of old ways and adopting those of the new culture. Another approach is to cling to one's roots and remain separated from the new culture. Such an approach can be very problematic if the new culture does not support this type of separation and requires assimilation. A combination of these two approaches is integration, or holding on to some elements of the old culture, but also adopting aspects of the new one.

17. Answers will vary, but can be based on the following definitions. *Daily hassles* are the minor problems or irritants we deal with on a regular basis. *Life-changing events* are occurrences that require a life adjustment (for example, marriage, change in school status). During times of stress, people tend to sleep poorly, eat erratically, and may increase their drug and alcohol use, along with other poor behavioral choices. These tendencies can lead to health problems. Exercise, meditation, progressive muscle relaxation, biofeedback, and social support all have positive physical and psychological effects on the response to stressors.

18. Answers will vary, but can be based on the following information. Reactions associated with the fight-or-flight response include increased pulse, breathing rate, and mental alertness. A coordinated effort of the sympathetic nervous system and the endocrine system, the fight-or-flight reaction primes the body to respond to danger, either by escaping or confronting the threat head-on.

19. Answers will vary, but can be based on the following definitions. One major source of stress is conflict, which can be defined as the discomfort felt when making tough choices. Often two choices presented are both attractive to you (*approach–approach conflict*); at times a choice or situation has favorable and unfavorable characteristics (*approach–avoidance conflict*); and at other times the two alternatives are both unattractive (*avoidance–avoidance conflict*).

20. Answers will vary, but can be based on the following definitions. Someone with an *internal locus of control* generally feels as if she is in control of life and its circumstances; she probably believes

it is important to take charge and make changes when problems occur. A person with an *external locus of control* generally feels as if chance, luck, or fate is responsible for her circumstances; there is no need to try to change things or make them better. Any decisions related to healthy choices can be influenced by locus of control.

⑫ psychological disorders

▢▢▢▢ show what you know

An Introduction to Psychological Disorders

1. a. dysfunction

2. Answers will vary (see Table 12.1). An *atypical* behavior that is not dysfunctional might be an adolescent who dyes his hair in many different shades of green. A *dysfunctional* behavior that is not distressful might be someone having difficulty getting out of bed in the morning because she stayed up late to meet a deadline for the next day. *Deviant* but not dysfunctional behaviors were demonstrated in 2011 by the Occupy Wall Street protesters who slept in public places and refused to move when asked to do so by the police during their protests.

3. b. the creation of labeling and expectations.

4. medical model

Worried Sick: Anxiety and Obsessive-Compulsive Disorders

1. classical conditioning; operant conditioning

2. *Taijin kyofu* tends to occur in collectivist societies, where great emphasis is placed on the surrounding people, which might lead individuals from these societies to become overly concerned about making someone else feel uncomfortable. *Collectivist* cultures value social harmony over individual needs, so if you cause someone to be uncomfortable, that is worse than personal humiliation you might feel. Western cultures are more *individualistic*. People from these societies are much more afraid of embarrassing themselves than they are of embarrassing someone else. They tend to value their own feelings over those of others.

3. d. compulsions.

4. genetic

From Depression to Mania

1. Answers will vary, but can be based on the following information. The symptoms of major depressive disorder can include feelings of sadness or hopelessness, reduced pleasure, sleeping excessively or not at all, loss of energy, feelings of worthlessness, or difficulties thinking or concentrating. The hallmarks of major depressive disorder are the "substantial" severity of symptoms and impairment in the ability to perform expected roles. *Biological theories* suggest the disorder results from a genetic predisposition, neurotransmitters, and hormones. *Psychological theories* suggest that feelings of learned helplessness and negative thinking may play a role. Not just one

factor is involved in major depressive disorder, but rather the interplay of several.

2. b. manic episodes.

3. In order to be diagnosed with *bipolar I disorder,* a person must experience at least one manic episode spanning a week or more. These periods of mania are characterized by increased energy and activity and unusual excitement and/or irritability. Depression and hypomania may also occur.

    To be diagnosed with *bipolar II disorder,* a person must experience recurrent episodes of major depression lasting 2 or more weeks and at least one episode of hypomania spanning 4 or more days. *Hypomania* is a mild version of mania; the symptoms are similar, but not disabling.

4. A diagnosis of *bipolar I disorder* requires that a person experience at least one manic episode, substantial distress, and great impairment. *Bipolar II disorder* requires at least one major depressive episode as well as a hypomanic episode, which is associated with some of the same symptoms as a manic episode, but is not as severe and does not impair one's ability to function. People with bipolar disorder cycle between extreme highs and lows of emotion and energy that last for days, weeks, or even months. Individuals with *major depressive disorder,* on the other hand, tend to experience a persistent low mood, loss of energy, and feelings of worthlessness.

Schizophrenia

1. psychosis

2. a. hallucination.

3. Answers will vary, but can be based on the following information. Schizophrenia is a complex psychological disorder that results from a combination of biological, psychological, and social factors. This disorder springs from a complex interaction of genes and environment. The diathesis–stress model takes these factors into account, with *diathesis* referring to an inherited disposition (for example, to schizophrenia) and *stress* referring to the stressors in the environment (internal and external). Genes, neurotransmitters, differences in the brain, and exposure to a virus in utero are all possible influences in the development of schizophrenia. There are some sociocultural and environmental factors that may play a minor role in one's risk for developing the disorder, as well as the severity of symptoms. Evidence exists, for instance, that complications at birth, social stress, and cannabis abuse are related to a slightly increased risk of schizophrenia onset.

Disorders of Personality and Identity

1. the self and interpersonal relationships.

2. borderline personality disorder

3. Dissociation

4. Answers will vary, but can be based on the following information. The commonality in this group of disorders is dissociation, or disturbance in the normally unified experience of psychological functions involved in memory, consciousness, perception, or identity. *Dissociative identity disorder* is a psychological disorder that involves the occurrence of two or more distinct personalities within one individual, whereas *dissociative amnesia* is a psychological disorder that includes a lack of ability to remember important personal information and memories. Both disorders interfere with relationships, memory, work, and other important areas of life.

1. dysfunction, distress, deviance

2. c. labels individuals, which only heightens problems with stigma.

3. a. obsessions; compulsions

4. b. biopsychosocial

5. b. agoraphobia

6. c. social anxiety disorder

7. c. panic attacks

8. b. antisocial personality disorder.

9. d. serotonin

10. a. at least one major depressive episode as well as a hypomanic episode.

11. c. problems associated with sleep.

12. d. irritability

13. b. psychosis.

14. a. borderline personality disorder

15. b. personalities

16. Answers will vary, but can be based on the following information. *Dysfunction* is the degree to which a behavior interferes with one's life or ability to function (for example, washing one's hands to the point of making them raw, as in obsessive-compulsive disorder). *Distress* is feeling regularly upset or uncomfortable because of unwanted behaviors or emotions (for example, continually feeling sad and hopeless, as in major depressive disorder). *Deviance* is the degree to which a behavior is considered to be outside of the standards or rules of a society (for example, removing one's clothes in inappropriate settings, as in bipolar disorder).

17. Answers will vary. This statement does not follow the suggestion of using "people-first language." Instead, it is defining an individual by her disorder. People are much more than their diagnoses. The diagnosis does not describe who your friend is, but only what is causing her distress or discomfort.

18. Classical conditioning can play a role in the development of a panic disorder by pairing an initially neutral stimulus (for example, a mall) with an unexpected panic attack (the unconditioned stimulus). The panic attack location then becomes a conditioned stimulus. When the location is visited or even considered, a panic attack can ensue (now the conditioned response).

19. Cognitive therapist Aaron Beck suggested that depression is a product of a cognitive triad, which includes a negative view of experiences, self, and the future. Negative thinking may lead to self-defeating behaviors, which, in turn, reinforce the beliefs.

20. Answers will vary, but can be based on the following information. Schizophrenia is a complex psychological disorder that results from biological, psychological, and social factors. Because this disorder springs from a complex interaction of genes and environment, researchers have a hard time predicting who will be affected. The diathesis–stress model takes these factors into account, with *diathesis* referring to an inherited disposition (for example, to schizophrenia) and *stress* referring to the stressors in the environment (internal and external). Genes, neurotransmitters, differences in the brain, and exposure to a virus in utero are all possible biological factors. Neurotransmitters are also thought to play a role in schizophrenia. The *dopamine hypothesis,* for example, suggests that the synthesis, release, and concentrations of dopamine are all elevated in people who have been diagnosed with schizophrenia and are suffering from psychosis. There are several environmental triggers thought to be involved in one's risk for developing the disorder as well as the severity of symptoms (for example, complications at birth, social stress, and cannabis abuse are related to a slightly increased risk of schizophrenia onset).

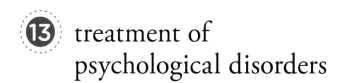

⑬ treatment of psychological disorders

□□□□ show what you know

An Introduction to Treatment

1. moral treatment

2. a. symptoms

3. *Deinstitutionalization* was the mass movement of patients with psychological disorders out of mental institutions, in an attempt to reintegrate them into the community. Deinstitutionalization was partially the result of a movement to reduce the social isolation of people with psychological disorders. This movement marked the beginning of new treatment modalities that allowed individuals to better care for themselves and function in society. However, many former patients ended up living on the streets or behind bars. Many people locked up in American jails and prisons are suffering from mental health problems.

Insight Therapies

1. resistance

2. a. humanistic

3. c. empathy.

4. *Psychoanalysis,* the first formal system of psychotherapy, attempts to increase awareness of unconscious conflicts, making it possible to address and work through them. The therapist's goal is to uncover these unconscious conflicts. *Psychodynamic therapy* is an updated form of psychoanalysis; it incorporates many of Freud's core themes, including the notion that personality characteristics and behavior problems often can be traced to unconscious conflicts. In psychodynamic therapy, therapists see clients once a week for several months rather than many times a week for years. And instead of sitting quietly off to the side, therapists and clients sit face-to-face and engage in a two-way dialogue.

Behavior and Cognitive Therapies

1. a. behavior

2. Answers will vary, but may be based on the following information. In *behavior modification,* one uses positive and negative reinforcement, as well as punishment, to help a child increase adaptive behaviors and reduce those that are maladaptive. For behaviors that resist modification, therapists might use successive approximations by reinforcing incremental changes. Some therapists will

incorporate observational learning (that is, learning by imitating and watching others) to help clients change their behaviors.

3. cognitive therapy

4. d. Rational emotive behavior

Biomedical Therapies

1. d. electroconvulsive therapy

2. b. antidepressants.

3. Answers will vary. *Biomedical therapies* use physical interventions to treat psychological disorders. These therapies can be categorized according to the method by which they influence the brain's functioning: chemical, electrical, or structural. *Psychotherapy* is a treatment approach in which a client works with a mental health professional to reduce psychological symptoms and increase his or her quality of life. These approaches share common features: The relationship between the client and the treatment provider is of utmost importance, as is a sense of hope that things will get better. Psychotherapy generally seeks to reduce symptoms and increase the quality of life, whether a person is struggling with a psychological disorder or simply wants to be more fulfilled.

Psychotherapy: Who's in the Mix?

1. b. more; the same

2. licensing issues; privacy issues

3. Answers will vary, but may be based on the following information. In general, therapy "works," especially if it is long-term. All approaches to psychotherapy perform equally well across all disorders. But individuals whose insurance companies limit their choice of therapists and how long they can receive treatment do not experience the same improvement as those who are less restricted. In addition, people who start therapy but then decide to stop it experience less successful outcomes. The client's cultural experience is important to keep in mind. Within any group, there is vast variation from one individual to the next, but it is still necessary for therapists to understand the cultural context in which they work. This includes being respectful of cultural norms and sensitive to the many forms of prejudice and discrimination that people can experience.

4. group therapy

5. Answers will vary (see Table 13.3). Group therapy would be inappropriate for an individual who is not comfortable talking or interacting with others and is unwilling to share his or her own thoughts, feelings, or problems. A group may fail if group members do not get along, are continually late for meetings, or drop out. The skills of the group therapist also play a role in the success of treatment (for example, empathy, facilitation skills, observation skills).

TEST PREP are you ready?

1. c. removed the inmates' chains

2. c. insight therapy.

3. a. psychoanalysts

4. b. It is difficult to test through experimentation

5. d. person-centered therapy.

6. a. hierarchies

7. b. Getting fired once does not mean my career is over.

8. a. tends to work quickly.

9. d. Seeing others improve offers hope and inspiration.

10. d. family therapy

11. d. Humanistic

12. d. Psychopharmacology

13. b. limitations on choice of therapist as mandated by a health insurance policy

14. c. seizures

15. a. culture

16. Answers will vary, but may be based on the following information. *Cognitive behavior therapy* is an action-oriented type of therapy that requires clients to confront and resist their illogical thinking. *Insight therapies* aim to increase awareness of self and the environment. These approaches share common features: The relationship between the client and the treatment provider is of utmost importance, as is a sense of hope that things will get better. And these approaches generally seek to reduce symptoms and increase the quality of life, whether a person is struggling with a psychological disorder or simply wants to be more fulfilled.

17. Answers will vary (see Table 13.2).

18. Answers will vary, but may be based on the following information. *Exposure* is a therapeutic technique that brings a person into contact with a feared object or situation while in a safe environment, with the goal of extinguishing or eliminating the fear response. An anxiety hierarchy (a list of activities ordered from least to most anxiety-provoking) can be used to help with exposure.

19. Answers will vary, but may be based on the following information. One challenge of providing therapy is to meet the needs of clients from vastly different cultures. Within any group, there is great variation from one individual to the next, but it is still necessary for the therapist to keep in mind the client's cultural experience. This includes being respectful of cultural norms and sensitive to the many forms of prejudice and discrimination that people can experience. Every client has a unique story and a singular set of psychological needs. Responding to those needs and determining which approach will be most effective are key to successful therapy.

20. Answers will vary, but may be based on the following information. As more people gain access to the Internet and as more therapists try to specialize and market their services, online therapies have multiplied. *E-therapy* can mean anything from e-mail communications between client and therapist to real-time sessions via a webcam. These digital tools are valuable for serving rural areas and providing treatment to those who would otherwise have no access. Videoconferencing is also useful for consultation and supervision. But online psychotherapy raises many concerns, including licensing and privacy issues, lack of nonverbal cues, and potential problems with developing therapeutic relationships.

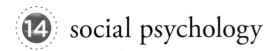

⑭ social psychology

◯◯◯◯ show what you know

An Introduction to Social Psychology

1. b. Social psychology; sociology

2. debrief

3. Social psychology studies often involve confederates, who are people secretly working for the researchers. Playing the role of participants, confederates say what the researchers tell them to say and do what the researchers tell them to do. They are, unknown to the other participants, just part of the researchers' experimental manipulation. In a double-blind study, neither participants nor researchers administering a treatment know who is getting the real treatment. Participants are told ahead of time that they might receive a placebo, but do not necessarily know about confederates until after the study is complete.

Social Cognition

1. a. Attributions

2. d. disposition of the person.

3. Answers will vary, but may be based on the following information. *Attitudes* are the relatively stable thoughts, feelings, and responses one has toward people, situations, ideas, and things. Attitudes are composed of three types of elements: cognitive (beliefs or ideas), affective (mood or emotion), and behavioral (response).

Social Influence

1. a. social influence; b. persuasion; c. compliance; d. foot-in-the-door technique; e. conformity

2. d. Obedience

3. Answers will vary. Examples may include resisting the urge to eat dessert when others at the table are doing so, saying no to a cigarette when others offer one, and so forth.

Groups and Aggression

1. c. The bystander effect

2. c. low levels of the neurotransmitter serotonin

3. Males tend to show more direct aggression (physical displays of aggression), whereas females are more likely to engage in relational aggression (gossip, exclusion, ignoring), perhaps because females have a higher risk for physical or bodily harm than males do.

4. Answers will vary, but may be based on the following information. *Discrimination* is showing favoritism or hostility to others because of their affiliation with a group. *Prejudice* is holding hostile or negative attitudes toward an individual or group. *Stereotypes* are conclusions or inferences we make about people who are different from us based on their group membership, such as their race, religion, age, or gender. Discrimination, prejudice, and stereotypes involve making assumptions about others we may not know. They often lead to unfair treatment of others.

It's All Good: Prosocial Behavior, Attraction, and Love

1. d. prosocial behavior.

2. b. proximity, similarity, physical attractiveness

3. According to this model, decisions to stay together or part ways are based on how happy people are in their relationship, their notion of what life would be like without it, and their investment in the relationship. People may stay in unsatisfying or unhealthy relationships if they feel there are no better alternatives or believe they have too much to lose. This model helps us understand why people remain in destructive relationships. These principles also apply to friendships, positions at work, or loyalty to institutions.

TEST PREP are you ready?

1. d. Social psychology

2. b. social cognition.

3. a. Cognitive dissonance

4. d. the fundamental attribution error.

5. d. the source, the message, and the audience.

6. c. compliance.

7. a. conformity.

8. c. legitimacy of the authority figure.

9. b. Diffusion of responsibility

10. a. deindividuation.

11. d. stereotypes

12. c. aggression

13. b. expectations

14. a. The mere-exposure effect

15. d. passion, intimacy, and commitment.

16. Answers will vary, but may be based on the following information (see Infographic 14.1). The *internal–external dimension* refers to the location of the cause. The *controllable–uncontrollable dimension* refers to whether the outcome can be controlled. The *stable–unstable dimension* refers to whether the cause is long-lasting. As an example, the reason your colleague has recently been absent is that she is caring for her father (external) who has just been diagnosed with an illness and there is no other family member available to help him (uncontrollable). This set of circumstances, however, has only caused problems this week (unstable).

17. Answers will vary. *Obedience* occurs when we change our behavior, or act in a way that we might not normally, because we have been ordered to do so by an authority figure. An imbalance of power exists, and the person with more power generally has an advantage over a person with less power. It is important for us to pay attention to how we react when under the influence of an authority figure, as we could inflict harm on others. One person can make a difference when he or she stands up for what is right.

18. Answers will vary. When a person is in trouble, bystanders have the tendency to assume that someone else will help—and therefore they stand by and do nothing, a phenomenon that is partly due to

the diffusion of responsibility. This bystander effect is particularly common when there are many other people present. Individuals are more likely to aid a person in distress if no one else is present.

19. Answers will vary, but can be based on the following definition. *Stereotypes* are the conclusions or inferences we make about people who are different from us, based on their group membership (such as race, religion, age, or gender). We tend to see the world in terms of *ingroups* (the group to which we belong) and *outgroups* (people who are outside the group to which we belong), which can impact the stereotypes we hold.

20. Answers will vary, but can be based on the following definitions. *Proximity* means nearness, which may play an important role in the formation of relationships. *Similarity* has to do with how much you have in common with someone else. We tend to prefer those who share our interests, viewpoints, ethnicity, values, and other characteristics.

appendix a

introduction to statistics

1	0 0 1 6 8 8
2	0 0 4 4 5 5 6 9 9
3	0 1 1 2 3 6 8 9
4	0 1 1 2 3 6 8 9
5	0 0 1 2 3 6 7 9
6	1 1 6
7	1 5

1. a. summarize data.
2. d. statistical significance
3. a. 2; b. 2; c. 1; d. 1
4. c. frequency distribution
5. a. normal curve.
6. b. measures of central tendency.
7. b. 5
8. a. 4
9. a. 4
10. c. outlier; mean
11. a. range
12. a. 2

try this
page A-3

Answers will vary, but here are examples from Chapter 3:

quantitative variables: frequency of sound waves, pitch of sound, number of hair cells, weight of butter, color wavelength

qualitative variables: gender, supertasters, carpentered worlds versus traditional settings

page A-11

ANSWER: The mean for the sample is 38.6, the median is 38, the range is 65, and the standard deviation is 16.5. A stem-and-leaf plot would look like the following, and it appears it might be positively skewed.

Glossary

abnormal behavior Behavior that is atypical, dysfunctional, distressful, and/or deviant. (p. 477)

absolute threshold The weakest stimuli that can be detected 50% of the time. (p. 90)

accommodation The process by which the lens changes shape in order to focus on images near and far. (p. 96)

accommodation A restructuring of old ideas to make a place for new information. (p. 324)

acculturative stress (ə-ˌkəl-chə-ˈrā-tiv) Stress that occurs when people move to new countries or cultures and must adjust to a new way of life. (p. 449)

achievement Acquired knowledge, or what has been learned. (p. 289)

acquired immune deficiency syndrome (AIDS) This condition, caused by HIV, generally results in a severely compromised immune system, which makes the body vulnerable to other infections. (p. 448)

acquisition The initial learning phase in both classical and operant conditioning. (p. 178)

action potential The spike in electrical energy that passes through the axon of a neuron, the purpose of which is to convey information. (p. 55)

activation–synthesis model This theory proposes that humans respond to random neural activity while in REM sleep as if it has meaning. (p. 151)

active listening The ability to pick up on the content and emotions behind words in order to understand a client's perspective, often by echoing the main point of what the client says. (p. 526)

adaptive value The degree to which a trait or behavior helps an organism survive. (p. 182)

adolescence The transition period between late childhood and early adulthood. (p. 333)

adrenal glands (ə-drē-nəl) Part of the endocrine system involved in responses to stress as well as the regulation of salt balance. (p. 66)

afterimage An image that appears to linger in the visual field after its stimulus, or source, is removed. (p. 101)

aggression Intimidating or threatening behavior or attitudes intended to hurt someone. (p. 580)

agoraphobia (a-gə-rə-ˈfō-bē-ə) Extreme fear of situations involving public transportation, open spaces, or other public settings. (p. 489)

algorithm (al-gə-ri-thəm) An approach to problem solving using a formula or set of rules that, if followed, ensures a solution. (p. 271)

all-or-none A neuron either fires or does not fire; action potentials are always the same strength. (p. 56)

alpha waves Brain waves that indicate a relaxed, drowsy state. (p. 139)

altruism A desire or motivation to help others with no expectation of anything in return. (p. 586)

amphetamines (am-ˈfe-tə-ˌmēnz) Stimulant drugs; methamphetamine falls in this class of drugs. (p. 159)

amplitude The height of a wave; the distance from midpoint to peak, or from midpoint to the trough of a wave. (p. 95)

amygdala (ə-mig-də-lə) A pair of almond-shaped structures in the limbic system that processes basic emotions, such as fear and aggression, as well as associated memories. (p. 79)

androgens The male hormones secreted by the testes in males. (p. 312)

androgyny The tendency to cross gender-role boundaries, exhibiting behaviors associated with both genders. (p. 342)

anorexia nervosa An eating disorder identified by significant weight loss, an intense fear of being overweight, a false sense of body image, and a refusal to eat the proper amount of calories to achieve a healthy weight. (p. 373)

anterograde amnesia (an-tə-ˌrō-ˌgrād) A type of memory loss; an inability to create new memories following damage or injury to the brain. (p. 247)

antianxiety drugs Psychotropic medications used for treating the symptoms of anxiety. (p. 538)

antidepressant drugs Psychotropic medications used for the treatment of depression. (p. 535)

antipsychotic drugs Psychotropic medication used in the treatment of psychotic symptoms, such as hallucinations and delusions. (p. 537)

antisocial personality disorder A psychological disorder distinguished by unethical behavior, deceitfulness, impulsivity, irritability, aggressiveness, disregard for others, and lack of remorse. (p. 504)

anxiety disorders A group of psychological disorders associated with extreme anxiety and/or debilitating, irrational fears. (p. 486)

approach–approach conflict A type of conflict in which one must choose between two or more options that are attractive. (p. 460)

approach–avoidance conflict A type of conflict that occurs when one is faced with a choice or situation that has favorable and unfavorable characteristics. (p. 460)

aptitude An individual's potential for learning. (p. 289)

archetypes (är-ki-tīps) Primal images, patterns of thoughts, and storylines stored in the collective unconscious, with themes that may be found in art, literature, music, dreams, and religions. (p. 417)

arousal theory Suggests that humans are motivated to seek an optimal level of arousal, or alertness and engagement in the world. (p. 365)

assimilation Using existing information and ideas to understand new knowledge and experiences. (p. 324)

association areas Regions of the cortex that integrate information from all over the brain, allowing us to learn, think in abstract terms, and carry out other intellectual tasks. (p. 77)

attachment The degree to which an infant feels an emotional connection with primary caregivers. (p. 330)

attitudes The relatively stable thoughts, feelings, and responses one has toward people, situations, ideas, and things. (p. 559)

attributions Beliefs one develops to explain human behaviors and characteristics, as well as situations. (p. 556)

audition The sense of hearing. (p. 102)

authoritarian parenting A rigid parenting style characterized by strict rules and poor communication skills. (p. 349)

authoritative parenting A parenting style characterized by high expectations, strong support, and respect for children. (p. 349)

automatic processing Detection, encoding, and sometimes storage of information without conscious effort or awareness. (p. 132)

autonomic nervous system (ȯ-tə-'nä-mik) The branch of the peripheral nervous system that controls involuntary processes within the body, such as contractions in the digestive tract and activity of glands. (p. 63)

availability heuristic A decision-making strategy that predicts the likelihood of something happening based on how easily a similar type of event from the past can be recalled. (p. 275)

aversion therapy Therapeutic approach that uses the principles of classical conditioning to link problematic behaviors to unpleasant physical reactions. (p. 530)

avoidance–avoidance conflict A type of conflict in which one is faced with two or more options that are unattractive. (p. 460)

axon Skinny tubelike structure of a neuron that extends from the cell body, and which sends messages to other neurons. (p. 52)

babbling The combining of consonants with vowels typically displayed at the age of 4 to 6 months. (p. 322)

barbiturate (bär-'bi-chə-rət) Depressant drug that decreases neural activity and reduces anxiety; a type of sedative. (p. 154)

behaviorism The scientific study of observable behavior. (pp. 11, 188)

behavior modification Therapeutic approach in which behaviors are shaped through reinforcement and punishment. (p. 530)

behavior therapies A type of therapy that focuses on behavioral change. (p. 520)

beta waves Brain waves that indicate an alert, awake state. (p. 139)

binge-eating disorder An eating disorder characterized by episodes of extreme overeating, during which a larger amount of food is consumed than most people would eat in a similar amount of time under similar circumstances. (p. 374)

binocular cues Information gathered from both eyes to help judge depth and distance. (p. 121)

biofeedback A technique that involves providing visual or auditory information about biological processes, allowing a person to control physiological activity (for example, heart rate, blood pressure, and skin temperature). (p. 468)

biological preparedness The tendency for animals to be predisposed or inclined to form associations. (p. 182)

biological psychology The branch of psychology that focuses on how the brain and other biological systems influence human behavior. (p. 49)

biomedical therapy Drugs and other physical interventions that target the biological processes underlying psychological disorders; primary goal is to reduce symptoms. (p. 520)

biopsychosocial perspective Explains behavior through the interaction of biological, psychological, and sociocultural factors. (p. 13)

bipolar disorder A psychological disorder marked by dramatic swings in mood, ranging from manic episodes to depressive episodes. (p. 476)

bisexual Attraction to members of both the same and opposite sex. (p. 377)

blind spot The location where the optic nerve exits the retina. (p. 98)

borderline personality disorder A psychological disorder distinguished by an incomplete sense of self, extreme self-criticism, unstable emotions, and feelings of emptiness. (p. 506)

Broca's area (brō-kəz) A region of the cortex that is critical for speech production. (p. 71)

bulimia nervosa An eating disorder characterized by extreme overeating followed by purging, with serious health risks. (p. 374)

burnout Emotional, mental, and physical fatigue that results in reduced motivation, enthusiasm, and performance. (p. 461)

bystander effect The tendency for people to avoid getting involved in an emergency they witness because they assume someone else will help. (p. 578)

Cannon–Bard theory of emotion Suggests that environmental stimuli are the starting point for emotions, and physiological or behavioral responses occur at the same time emotions are felt. (p. 389)

case study A type of descriptive research that closely examines one individual or small group. (p. 27)

cell body The region of the neuron that includes protein-producing mechanisms, structures that nourish the cell, and a nucleus containing DNA. (p. 52)

central nervous system (CNS) A major component of the human nervous system that includes the brain and spinal cord. (p. 60)

cerebellum (ser-ə-be-ləm) Structure located behind the brainstem that is responsible for muscle coordination and balance; Latin for "little brain." (p. 81)

cerebral cortex (sə-rē-brəl) The wrinkled outermost layer of the cerebrum, responsible for higher mental functions, such as decision making, planning, and processing visual information. (p. 73)

cerebrum The largest part of the brain, includes virtually all parts of the brain except primitive structures; has two distinct hemispheres. (p. 67)

chromosomes Inherited threadlike structures composed of deoxyribonucleic acid (DNA). (p. 311)

chunking Grouping numbers, letters, or other items into meaningful subsets as a strategy for increasing the quantity of information that can be maintained in short-term memory. (p. 226)

circadian rhythm (sər-'kā-dē-ən) The daily patterns roughly following the 24-hour cycle of daylight and darkness; 24-hour cycle of physiological and behavioral functioning. (p. 136)

classical conditioning Learning process in which two stimuli become associated with each other; when an originally neutral stimulus is conditioned to elicit an involuntary response. (p. 178)

cochlea (kō-klē-ə) Fluid-filled, snail-shaped organ of the inner ear lined with the basilar membrane. (p. 106)

cognition The mental activity associated with obtaining, converting, and using knowledge. (p. 261)

cognitive appraisal approach Suggests that the appraisal or interpretation of interactions with surroundings causes an emotional reaction. (p. 390)

cognitive behavioral therapy An action-oriented type of therapy that requires clients to confront and resist their illogical thinking. (p. 533)

cognitive dissonance A state of tension that results when behaviors are inconsistent with attitudes. (p. 562)

cognitive map The mental representation of the layout of a physical space. (p. 207)

cognitive therapy A type of therapy aimed at addressing the maladaptive thinking that leads to maladaptive behaviors and feelings. (p. 531)

collective unconscious According to Jung, the universal experiences of humankind passed from generation to generation, including memories. (p. 417)

color constancy Objects are perceived as maintaining their color, even with changing sensory data. (p. 122)

comorbidity (kō-'mòr-bəd-'i-tē) The occurrence of two or more disorders at the same time. (p. 484)

companionate love Love that consists of profound fondness, camaraderie, understanding, and emotional closeness. (p. 590)

compliance Changes in behavior at the request or direction of another person or group, who in general do not have any true authority. (p. 567)

compulsion A behavior or "mental act" that a person repeats over and over in an effort to reduce anxiety. (p. 491)

concepts Mental representations of categories of objects, situations, and ideas that belong together based on their central features or characteristics. (p. 262)

concrete operational stage Piaget's stage of cognitive development during which children begin to think more logically, but mainly in reference to concrete objects and circumstances. (p. 326)

conditioned emotional response An emotional reaction acquired through classical conditioning; process by which an emotional reaction becomes associated with a previously neutral stimulus. (p. 183)

conditioned response (CR) A learned response to a conditioned stimulus. (p. 178)

conditioned stimulus (CS) A previously neutral stimulus that an organism learns to associate with an unconditioned stimulus. (p. 178)

conditioned taste aversion A form of classical conditioning that occurs when an organism learns to associate the taste of a particular food or drink with illness. (p. 182)

cones Specialized light receptors responsible for our sensation of color and our ability to sense details. (p. 98)

confirmation bias The tendency to look for evidence that upholds our beliefs and overlook evidence that runs counter to them. (p. 277)

conformity The urge to modify behaviors, attitudes, beliefs, and opinions to match those of others. (p. 569)

confounding variable A type of extraneous variable that changes in sync with the independent variable, making it difficult to discern which one is causing changes in the dependent variable. (p. 36)

consciousness The state of being aware of oneself, one's thoughts, and/or the environment; includes various levels of conscious awareness. (p. 130)

conservation Refers to the unchanging properties of volume, mass, or amount in relation to appearance. (p. 326)

consummate love (kän(t)-sə-mət) Love that combines intimacy, commitment, and passion. (p. 590)

continuous reinforcement A schedule of reinforcement in which every target behavior is reinforced. (p. 194)

control group The participants in an experiment who are not exposed to the treatment variable; this is the comparison group. (p. 36)

conventional moral reasoning Kohlberg's stage of moral development that determines right and wrong from the expectations of society and important others. (p. 338)

convergence A binocular cue used to judge distance and depth based on the tension of the muscles that direct where the eyes are focusing. (p. 121)

convergent thinking A conventional approach to problem solving that focuses on finding a single best solution to a problem by using previous experience and knowledge. (p. 298)

cooing Production of vowel-like sounds by infants, often repeated in a joyful manner. (p. 322)

coping The cognitive, behavioral, and emotional abilities used to effectively manage something that is perceived as difficult or challenging. (p. 462)

cornea The clear, outer layer of the eye that shields it from damage and focuses incoming light waves. (p. 96)

corpus callosum (kòr-pəs ka-lō-səm) The thick band of nerve fibers connecting the right and left cerebral hemispheres; principal structure for information shared between the two hemispheres. (p. 68)

correlation An association or relationship between two (or more) variables. (p. 29)

correlation coefficient The statistical measure (symbolized as *r*) that indicates the strength and direction of the relationship between two variables. (p. 31)

correlational method A type of descriptive research examining the relationships among variables. (p. 29)

creativity In problem solving, the ability to construct valuable results in innovative ways; the ability to generate original ideas. (p. 297)

critical period Specific time frame in which an organism is sensitive to environmental factors, and certain behaviors and abilities are readily shaped or altered by events or experiences. (p. 308)

critical thinking The process of weighing various pieces of evidence, synthesizing them, and evaluating and determining the contributions of each. (p. 17)

cross-sectional method A research design that examines people of different ages at a single point in time. (p. 308)

cross-sequential method A research design that examines groups of people of different ages, following them across time. (p. 310)

crystallized intelligence Knowledge gained through learning and experience. (p. 347)

culture-fair intelligence test Assessments designed to minimize cultural bias. (p. 294)

daily hassles Minor and regularly occurring problems that can act as stressors. (p. 450)

dark adaptation Ability of the eyes to adjust to dark after exposure to brightness. (p. 99)

data-based processing Taking basic sensory information about incoming stimuli and processing it for further interpretation. (p. 89)

debriefing Sharing information with participants after their involvement in a study has ended, including the purpose of the study and of deception used in it. (p. 25)

decision making The cognitive process of choosing from alternatives that might be used to reach a goal. (p. 274)

deindividuation The diminished sense of personal responsibility, inhibition, or adherence to social norms that occurs when group members are not treated as individuals. (p. 576)

deinstitutionalization The mass movement of patients with psychological disorders out of mental institutions, and the attempt to reintegrate them into the community. (p. 519)

delirium tremens (DTs) Withdrawal symptoms that can occur when a heavy drinker suddenly stops or significantly cuts down alcohol consumption; can include sweating, restlessness, hallucinations, severe tremors, and seizures. (p. 164)

delta waves Brain waves that indicate a deep sleep. (p. 141)

delusions Strange or false beliefs that a person firmly maintains even when presented with evidence to the contrary. (p. 499)

dendrites (den-drīts) Tiny, branchlike fibers extending from the cell body that receive messages from other neurons and send information in the direction of the cell body. (p. 52)

deoxyribonucleic acid (DNA) A molecule that provides the instructions for the development and production of cells. (p. 311)

dependent variable (DV) In the experimental method, the characteristic or response that is measured to determine the effect of the researcher's manipulation. (p. 36)

depressants A class of psychoactive drugs that *depress* or slow down activity in the central nervous system. (p. 154)

depth perception The ability to perceive three-dimensional objects and judge distances. (p. 121)

descriptive research Research methods that describe and explore behaviors, but with findings that cannot definitively state cause-and-effect relationships. (p. 26)

developmental psychology A field of psychology that examines physical, cognitive, and socioemotional changes across the life span. (p. 306)

difference threshold The minimum difference between two stimuli that can be noticed 50% of the time. (p. 90)

diffusion of responsibility The sharing of duties and responsibilities among all group members that can lead to feelings of decreased accountability and motivation. (p. 575)

discrimination Showing favoritism or hostility to others because of their affiliation with a group. (p. 581)

display rules Framework or guidelines for when, how, and where an emotion is expressed. (p. 392)

dispositional attribution A belief that some characteristic of an individual is involved in the cause of a situation, event, or activity. (p. 557)

dissociation A disturbance in the normally integrated experience of psychological functions involved in memory, consciousness, perception, or identity. (p. 506)

dissociative amnesia A psychological disorder marked by difficulty remembering important personal information and life events. (p. 507)

dissociative disorders Psychological disorders distinguished by disturbances in normal psychological functioning; may include problems with memory, identity, consciousness, perception, and motor control. (p. 506)

dissociative fugue (fyüg) A condition in which a person with dissociative amnesia wanders about in a confused and unexpected manner. (p. 507)

dissociative identity disorder A psychological disorder that involves the occurrence of two or more distinct personalities within an individual. (p. 507)

distress The stress response to unpleasant and undesirable stressors. (p. 445)

distributed practice Spreading out study sessions over time with breaks in between. (p. 233)

divergent thinking The ability to devise many solutions to a problem; a component of creativity. (p. 298)

dizygotic twins Fraternal twins who develop from two eggs inseminated by two sperm, and are as genetically similar as any sibling pair. (p. 315)

dominant gene One of a pair of genes that has power over the expression of an inherited characteristic. (p. 314)

door-in-the-face technique A compliance technique that involves making a large request first, followed by a smaller request. (p. 568)

dopamine hypothesis A theory suggesting that the synthesis, release, and concentrations of the neurotransmitter dopamine play a role in schizophrenia. (p. 503)

double-blind study Type of study in which neither the researchers who are administering the independent variable nor the participants know what type of treatment is being given. (p. 37)

drive A state of tension that pushes us or motivates behaviors to meet a need. (p. 363)

drive-reduction theory Suggests that homeostasis motivates us to meet biological needs. (p. 363)

echoic memory (ə-'kō-ik) Exact copies of the sounds we hear; a form of sensory memory. (p. 224)

eclectic approach to therapy Drawing on multiple theories and approaches to therapy to tailor treatment for a client. (p. 520)

effortful processing The encoding and storage of information with conscious effort, or awareness. (p. 232)

ego According to Freud, the structure of the mind that uses the reality principle to manipulate situations, plan for the future, solve problems, and make decisions. (p. 409)

egocentrism Only able to imagine the world from one's own perspective. (p. 324)

ego defense mechanisms Distortions of perceptions and memories of the real world, without one's awareness, to reduce the anxiety created by the conflict among the id, ego, and superego. (p. 409)

elaborative rehearsal The method of connecting incoming information to knowledge in long-term memory; a deep level of encoding. (p. 233)

electroconvulsive therapy (ECT) A biomedical treatment of severe depression that induces seizures in the brain through electrical currents. (p. 539)

embryo The unborn human from the beginning of the 3rd week of pregnancy, lasting through the 8th week of prenatal development. (p. 315)

emerging adulthood A phase of life between 18 and 25 years that includes exploration and opportunity. (p. 343)

emotion A psychological state that includes a subjective or inner experience, a physiological component, and a behavioral expression. (p. 385)

emotion-focused coping A coping strategy in which a person addresses the emotions that surround a problem, as opposed to trying to solve it. (p. 462)

emotional intelligence The capacity to perceive, understand, regulate, and use emotions to adapt to social situations. (p. 295)

empathy The ability to feel what a person is experiencing by attempting to observe the world through his or her eyes. (p. 526)

encoding The process through which information enters our memory system. (p. 217)

encoding specificity principle Memories are more easily recalled when the context and cues at the time of encoding are similar to those at the time of retrieval. (p. 237)

endocrine system (en-də-krən) The communication system that uses glands to convey messages by releasing hormones into the bloodstream. (p. 65)

epigenetics A field of study that examines the processes involved in the development of phenotypes. (p. 314)

episodic memory (e-pə-sä-dik) The record of memorable experiences or "episodes" including when and where an experience occurred; a type of explicit memory. (p. 229)

estrogen The female hormone secreted primarily by the ovaries in females. (p. 312)

e-therapy A category of treatment that utilizes the Internet to provide support and therapy. (p. 546)

ethnocentrism To see the world only from the perspective of one's own group. (p. 581)

eustress (yōō'-stres) The stress response to agreeable or positive stressors. (p. 445)

expectancy A person's predictions about the consequences or outcomes of behavior. (p. 422)

experiment A controlled procedure that involves careful examination through the use of scientific observation and/or manipulation of variables (measurable characteristics). (p. 18)

experimental group The members of an experiment who are exposed to the treatment variable or manipulation by the researcher; represents the treatment group. (p. 36)

experimental method A type of research that manipulates a variable of interest (independent variable) to uncover cause-and-effect relationships. (p. 34)

experimenter bias Researchers' expectations that influence the outcome of a study. (p. 37)

explicit memory A type of memory you are aware of having and can consciously express in words or declare, including memories of facts and experiences. (p. 229)

exposure A therapeutic technique that brings a person into contact with a feared object or situation while in a safe environment, with the goal of extinguishing or eliminating the fear response. (p. 527)

extinction In classical conditioning, the process by which the CR decreases after repeated exposure to the CS in the absence of the US; in operant conditioning, the disappearance of a learned behavior through the removal of its reinforcer. (p. 179)

extraneous variable A variable in the environment or of the participants that could unintentionally influence the outcome of a study. (p. 36)

extrasensory perception (ESP) The purported ability to obtain information about the world without any sensory stimuli. (p. 123)

extrinsic motivation The drive or urge to continue a behavior because of external reinforcers. (p. 360)

facial feedback hypothesis The facial expression of an emotion can affect the experience of that emotion. (p. 393)

false consensus effect The tendency to overestimate the degree to which others think or act like we do. (p. 559)

family therapy A type of therapy that focuses on the family as an integrated system, recognizing that the interactions within it can create instability or lead to the breakdown of the family unit. (p. 543)

feature detectors Neurons in the visual cortex specialized in detecting specific features of the visual experience, such as angles, lines, and movements. (p. 99)

fetal alcohol syndrome (FAS) Delays in development that result from moderate to heavy alcohol use during pregnancy. (p. 316)

fetus The unborn human from 2 months following conception to birth. (p. 316)

figure–ground A central principle of Gestalt psychology, involving the shifting of focus; as attention is focused on one object, all other features drop or recede into the background. (p. 119)

five-factor model of personality A trait approach to explaining personality, including dimensions of openness to experience, conscientiousness, extraversion, agreeableness, and neuroticism; also known as "the Big Five." (p. 426)

fixation Being stuck in a particular psychosexual stage of development as a result of unsuccessfully dealing with the conflict of that stage. (p. 412)

fixed-interval schedule A schedule in which the reinforcer comes after a preestablished interval of time goes by; the behavior is only reinforced after the given interval is over. (p. 197)

fixed-ratio schedule A schedule in which the subject must exhibit a predetermined number of desired behaviors before a reinforcer is given. (p. 197)

flashbulb memory A detailed account of circumstances surrounding an emotionally significant or shocking, sometimes historic, event. (p. 229)

fluid intelligence The ability to think in the abstract and create associations among concepts. (p. 347)

foot-in-the-door technique A compliance technique that involves making a small request first, followed by a larger request. (p. 567)

forebrain Largest part of the brain; includes the cerebral cortex and the limbic system. (p. 80)

formal concepts The mental representations of categories that are created through rigid and logical rules or features. (p. 263)

formal operational stage Piaget's stage of cognitive development during which children begin to think more logically and systematically. (p. 326)

framing effect Occurs when the wording of questions or the context of a problem influences the outcome of a decision. (p. 277)

free association A psychoanalytic technique in which a patient says anything that comes to mind. (p. 523)

frequency The number of sound waves passing a given point per second; higher frequency is perceived as higher pitch, and lower frequency is perceived as lower pitch. (p. 104)

frequency theory States that pitch is determined by the vibrating frequency of the sound wave, basilar membrane, and associated neural impulses. (p. 107)

frontal lobes The area of the cortex that organizes information among the other lobes of the brain and is responsible for higher-level cognitive functions and behavior. (p. 73)

frustration–aggression hypothesis Suggests that aggression may occur in response to frustration. (p. 580)

functional fixedness A barrier to problem solving that occurs when familiar objects can only be imagined to function in their normal or usual way. (p. 273)

functionalism An early school of psychology that focused on the function of thought processes, feelings, and behaviors and how they help us adapt to the environment. (p. 10)

fundamental attribution error The tendency to overestimate the degree to which the characteristics of an individual are the cause of an event, and to underestimate the involvement of situational factors. (p. 557)

gate-control theory Suggests that the perception of pain will either increase or decrease through the interaction of biopsychosocial factors; signals are sent to open or close "gates" that control the neurological pathways for pain. (p. 115)

gender The dimension of masculinity and femininity based on social, cultural, and psychological characteristics. (p. 339)

gender identity The feeling or sense of being either male or female, and compatibility, contentment, and conformity with one's gender. (p. 339)

gender roles The collection of actions, beliefs, and characteristics that a culture associates with masculinity and femininity. (p. 339)

gender schemas The psychological or mental guidelines that dictate how to be masculine and feminine. (p. 340)

gene Specified segment of a DNA molecule. (p. 311)

general adaptation syndrome (GAS) A specific pattern of physiological reactions to stressors that includes the alarm stage, resistance stage, and exhaustion stage. (p. 452)

general intelligence (*g* factor) A singular underlying aptitude or intellectual competence that drives abilities in many areas, including verbal, spatial, and reasoning abilities. (p. 287)

generalized anxiety disorder A psychological disorder characterized by an excessive amount of worry and anxiety about activities relating to family, health, school, and other aspects of daily life. (p. 490)

genotype An individual's complete collection of genes. (p. 313)

genuineness The ability to respond to a client in an authentic way rather than hiding behind a polite or professional mask. (p. 526)

gestalt (gə-'stält) The natural tendency for the brain to organize stimuli into a whole, rather than perceiving the parts and pieces. (p. 119)

gifted Highly intelligent; defined as having an IQ score of 130 or above. (p. 295)

glial cells (glē-əl) Cells that support, nourish, and protect neurons; produce myelin that covers axons. (p. 53)

grammar The rules associated with word and sentence structure. (p. 283)

group polarization The tendency for a group to take a more extreme stance than originally held after deliberations and discussion. (p. 577)

groupthink The tendency for group members to maintain cohesiveness and agreement in their decision making, failing to consider all possible alternatives and related viewpoints. (p. 578)

gustation (gəs-'tā-shən) The sensation of taste. (p. 111)

habituation (hah-bi-chü-ā-shən) A basic form of learning evident when an organism does not respond as strongly or as often to an event following multiple exposures to it. (p. 174)

hallucinations Perceptual-like experiences that an individual believes are real, but that are not evident to others. (p. 500)

hallucinogens (hə-'lü-sə-nə-jənz) A group of psychoactive drugs that can produce hallucinations (auditory, visual, or kinesthetic), distorted sensory experiences, alterations of mood, and distorted thinking. (p. 161)

hardiness A personality characteristic indicating an ability to remain resilient and optimistic despite intensely stressful situations. (p. 464)

health psychology The study of the biological, psychological, and social factors that contribute to illness and health. (p. 454)

heritability The degree to which hereditary factors (genes) are responsible for a particular characteristic observed within a population; the proportion of variation in a characteristic attributed to genetic factors. (p. 296)

heterosexual Attraction to members of the opposite sex. (p. 377)

heuristics (hyü-ris-tiks) Problem-solving approaches that incorporate a rule of thumb or broad application of a strategy. (p. 272)

hierarchy of needs A continuum of needs that are universal and ordered in terms of the strength of their associated drives. (p. 365)

higher order conditioning With repeated pairings of a conditioned stimulus and a neutral stimulus, the second neutral stimulus becomes a conditioned stimulus as well. (p. 180)

hindbrain Includes areas of the brain responsible for fundamental life-sustaining processes. (p. 80)

hippocampus A pair of structures located in the limbic system; primarily responsible for creating new memories. (p. 79)

homeostasis The tendency for bodies to maintain constant states through internal controls. (p. 363)

homosexual Attraction to members of the same sex. (p. 377)

hormones Chemical messengers released into the bloodstream that influence mood, cognition, appetite, and many other processes and behaviors. (p. 65)

hue The color of an object, determined by the wavelength of light it reflects. (p. 95)

human immunodeficiency virus (HIV) A virus transferred via bodily fluids (blood, semen, vaginal secretions, or breast milk) that causes the breakdown of the immune system, eventually resulting in AIDS. (p. 448)

humanistic psychology An approach suggesting that human nature is by and large positive, and the human direction is toward growth. (p. 11)

humanistic therapy A type of insight therapy that emphasizes the positive nature of humankind. (p. 525)

hypnosis An altered state of consciousness allowing for changes in perceptions and behaviors, which result from suggestions made by a hypnotist. (p. 166)

hypothalamus (hī-pō-tha-lə-məs) A small structure located below the thalamus that maintains a constant internal environment within a healthy range; helps regulate sleep–wake cycles, sexual behavior, and appetite. (p. 80)

hypothesis (hī-'pä-thə-səs) A statement that can be used to test a prediction. (p. 20)

iconic memory Visual impressions that are photograph-like in their accuracy but dissolve in less than a second; a form of sensory memory. (p. 223)

id According to Freud, the most primitive structure of the mind, the activities of which occur at the unconscious level and are guided by the pleasure principle. (p. 408)

ideal self The self-concept a person strives for and fervently wishes to achieve. (p. 420)

identity A sense of self based on values, beliefs, and goals. (p. 335)

illusion A perception incongruent with sensory data. (p. 118)

implicit memory A memory of something you know or know how to do, but that might be automatic or unconscious; this type of memory is often difficult to bring to awareness and express. (p. 229)

incentive An association established between a behavior and its consequences, which then motivates that behavior. (p. 359)

independent variable (IV) In the experimental method, the variable manipulated by the researcher to determine its effect on the dependent variable. (p. 36)

informed consent Acknowledgment from study participants that they understand what their participation will entail. (p. 25)

in-group The group to which we belong. (p. 581)

insanity A legal determination of the degree to which a person is responsible for criminal behaviors. (p. 478)

insight An understanding or solution that occurs in a sudden stroke of clarity (the feeling of "aha!"). (p. 272)

insight therapies A type of psychotherapy, aimed at increasing awareness of self and the environment. (p. 520)

insomnia Sleep disorder characterized by an inability to fall asleep or stay asleep, impacting both the quality and the quantity of sleep. (p. 145)

instinctive drift The tendency for animals to revert to instinctual behaviors after a behavior pattern has been learned. (p. 189)

instincts Complex behaviors that are fixed, unlearned, and consistent within a species. (p. 361)

Institutional Review Board (IRB) A committee that reviews research proposals to protect the rights and welfare of all participants. (p. 25)

intelligence Innate ability to solve problems, adapt to the environment, and learn from experiences. (p. 287)

intelligence quotient (IQ) A score from an intelligence assessment; originally based on mental age divided by chronological age, multiplied by 100. (p. 290)

interneurons Neurons that reside exclusively in the brain and spinal cord; act as a bridge connecting sensory and motor neurons. (p. 61)

interpersonal attraction The factors that lead us to form friendships or romantic relationships with others. (p. 587)

interpretation A psychoanalytic technique used to discover unconscious conflicts driving behavior. (p. 523)

intersexual Ambiguous or inconsistent biological indicators of male or female in the sexual structures and organs. (p. 312)

intrinsic motivation The drive or urge to continue a behavior because of internal reinforcers. (p. 360)

introspection The examination of one's own conscious activities. (p. 9)

iris The muscle responsible for changing the size of the pupil. (p. 96)

James–Lange theory of emotion Suggests that a stimulus initiates the experience of a physiological and/or behavioral reaction, and this reaction leads to the feeling of an emotion. (p. 387)

just-world hypothesis The tendency to believe the world is a fair place and individuals generally get what they deserve. (p. 558)

kinesthesia (ki-nəs-'thē-zhē-ə) Sensory system that conveys information about body position and movement. (p. 116)

knowledge-based processing Drawing on past experiences and knowledge to understand and interpret sensory information. (p. 89)

language A system for using symbols to think and communicate. (p. 280)

latent content The hidden meaning of a dream, often concealed by the manifest content of the dream. (p. 151)

latent learning Learning that occurs without awareness and regardless of reinforcement, and is not evident until needed. (p. 207)

lateralization The idea that each cerebral hemisphere processes certain types of information and excels in certain activities. (p. 70)

law of effect Thorndike's principle stating that behaviors are more likely to be repeated when followed by pleasurable outcomes, and those followed by something unpleasant are less likely to be repeated. (p. 188)

learned helplessness A tendency for people to believe they have no control over the consequences of their behaviors, resulting in passive behavior. (p. 496)

learning A relatively enduring change in behavior or thinking that results from experiences. (p. 174)

light adaptation Ability of the eyes to adjust to light after being in the dark. (p. 99)

limbic system A collection of structures that regulates emotions and basic drives like hunger, and aids in the creation of memories. (p. 79)

longitudinal method A research design that examines one sample of people over a period of time to determine age-related changes. (p. 310)

long-term memory A stage of memory with essentially unlimited capacity that stores enduring information about facts and experiences. (p. 219)

long-term potentiation The increased efficiency of neural communication over time, resulting in learning and the formation of memories. (p. 252)

lymphocyte Type of white blood cell produced in the bone marrow whose job is to battle enemies such as viruses and bacteria. (p. 454)

lysergic acid diethylamide (LSD) (lə-'sər-jik; dī-,e-thə-,la-,mīd) A synthetically produced, odorless, tasteless, and colorless hallucinogen that is very potent; produces extreme changes in sensations and perceptions. (p. 161)

maintenance rehearsal Technique of repeating information to be remembered, increasing the length of time it can be held in short-term memory. (p. 224)

major depressive disorder A psychological disorder that includes at least one major depressive episode, with symptoms such as depressed mood, problems with sleep, and loss of energy. (p. 492)

maladaptive behaviors Behaviors or actions that run counter to what is in one's own best interest. (p. 476)

manic episode State of continuous elation that is out of proportion to the setting, and can include irritability, very high and sustained levels of energy, and an "expansive" mood. (p. 497)

manifest content The apparent meaning of a dream the remembered story line of a dream. (p. 151)

massed practice Studying for long periods of time without breaks. (p. 233)

maturation Physical growth beginning with conception and ending when the body stops growing. (p. 307)

means–ends analysis Heuristic used to determine how to decrease the distance between a goal (the means) and the current status, leading to the solution of a problem (the end). (p. 272)

medical model An approach suggesting that psychological disorders are illnesses that have underlying biological causes. (p. 484)

medulla (mə-'dül-ə) A structure that oversees vital functions, including breathing, digestion, and heart rate. (p. 81)

memory Information collected and stored in the brain that is generally retrievable for later use. (p. 217)

memory trace The location where memories are etched in the brain via physiological changes. (p. 249)

menarche ['me-,när-kē] The point at which menstruation begins. (p. 333)

menopause The time when a woman no longer ovulates, her menstrual cycle stops, and she is no longer capable of reproduction. (p. 345)

mental age (MA) A score representing the mental abilities of an individual in relation to others of a similar chronological age. (p. 290)

mere-exposure effect The more we are exposed to someone or something, the more positive a reaction we have toward it. (p. 588)

methylenedioxymethamphetamine (MDMA) (meth'ĭ-lĕn-dī-ok'sē-meth'am-fet'ă-mēn) A synthetic drug chemically similar to the stimulant methamphetamine and the hallucinogen mescaline; produces a combination of stimulant and hallucinogenic effects. (p. 162)

midbrain The part of the brainstem involved in levels of arousal; responsible for generating movement patterns in response to sensory input. (p. 80)

misinformation effect The tendency for new and misleading information obtained after an incident to distort one's memory of it. (p. 244)

mnemonic (nih-'män-ik) Technique to improve memory. (p. 230)

model The individual or character whose behavior is being imitated. (p. 204)

monocular cues Depth and distance cues that require the use of only one eye. (p. 122)

monozygotic twins Identical twins who develop from one egg inseminated at conception, which then splits into two separate cells. (p. 315)

mood-stabilizing drugs Psychotropic medications that minimize the lows of depression and the highs of mania. (p. 537)

morphemes (mȯr-fēmz) The fundamental units that bring meaning to language. (p. 283)

motivation A stimulus that can direct behavior, thinking, and feeling. (p. 359)

motor cortex A band of tissue toward the rear of the frontal lobes that works with other brain regions to plan and execute voluntary movements. (p. 75)

motor neurons Neurons specialized for transmitting information from the central nervous system to other parts of the body, such as muscles and glands. (p. 61)

myelin sheath (mī-ə-lən shēth) Fatty substance that insulates the axon and speeds the transmission of neural messages. (p. 52)

narcolepsy A neurological disorder characterized by excessive daytime sleepiness, which includes lapses into sleep and napping. (p. 143)

natural concepts The mental representations of categories resulting from experiences in daily life. (p. 265)

natural selection The process through which inherited traits in a given population either increase in frequency because they are adaptive or decrease in frequency because they are maladaptive. (p. 13)

naturalistic observation A type of descriptive research that studies participants in their natural environment through systematic observation. (p. 26)

need for achievement (n-Ach) A drive to reach attainable and challenging goals, especially in the face of competition. (p. 367)

need for power (n-Pow) A drive to control and influence others. (p. 367)

needs Physiological or psychological requirements that must be maintained at some baseline or constant state. (p. 363)

negative punishment The removal of something desirable following an unwanted behavior, with the intention of decreasing that behavior. (p. 198)

negative reinforcement The removal of an unpleasant stimulus following a target behavior, which increases the likelihood of it occurring again. (p. 192)

negative symptoms Behaviors or characteristics that are limited or absent; examples are social withdrawal, diminished speech, limited or no emotions, and loss of energy and follow-up. (p. 500)

nerves Bundles of neurons that carry information to and from the central nervous system; provide communication between the central nervous system and the muscles, glands, and sensory receptors. (p. 62)

neurogenesis The generation of new neurons in the brain. (p. 73)

neurons The building blocks of the nervous system that transmit electrical and chemical signals in the body. (p. 51)

neuroplasticity The brain's ability to heal, grow new connections, and reorganize in order to adapt to the environment. (p. 72)

neuroscience The study of the brain and nervous system. (p. 49)

neurosurgery A biomedical therapy that involves the destruction of some portion of the brain or connections between different areas of the brain. (p. 540)

neurotransmitters Chemical messengers that neurons use to communicate at the synapse. (p. 56)

neutral stimulus (NS) A stimulus that does not cause a relevant automatic or reflexive response. (p. 178)

nightmares Frightening dreams that occur during REM sleep. (p. 146)

nondirective A technique used in person-centered therapy wherein the therapist follows the lead of the client during treatment sessions. (p. 526)

non-rapid eye movement (non-REM) The nondreaming sleep that occurs during sleep Stages 1 to 4. (p. 139)

normal curve Depicts the frequency of values of a variable along a continuum; bell-shaped symmetrical distribution, with the highest point reflecting the average score. (p. 292)

norms Standards of the social environment. (p. 569)

obedience Changing behavior because we have been ordered to do so by an authority figure. (p. 571)

object permanence A milestone of the sensorimotor stage of cognitive development; an infant's realization that objects and people still exist even when out of sight or touch. (p. 324)

observational learning Learning that occurs as a result of watching the behavior of others. (p. 204)

observer bias Errors introduced into the recording of observations due to a researcher's value system, expectations, or attitudes. (p. 27)

obsession A thought, an urge, or an image that happens repeatedly, is intrusive and unwelcome, and often causes anxiety and distress. (p. 491)

obsessive-compulsive disorder (OCD) A psychological disorder characterized by obsessions and/or compulsions that are time-consuming and cause a great deal of distress. (p. 490)

obstructive sleep apnea hypopnea (hī-pop-'nē-ə) A serious disturbance of non-REM sleep characterized by complete absence of air flow (apnea) or reduced air flow (hypopnea). (p. 145)

occipital lobes (äk-si-pə-təl) The area of the cortex in the back of the head that processes visual information. (p. 75)

Oedipus complex (e-də-pəs) According to Freud, the attraction a child feels toward the opposite-sex parent, along with the resentment or envy directed toward the same-sex parent. (p. 413)

olfaction (ōl-'fak-shən) The sense of smell. (p. 109)

operant conditioning Learning that occurs when voluntary actions become associated with their consequences. (p. 187)

operational definition The precise manner in which a variable of interest is defined and measured. (p. 20)

opiates A class of psychoactive drugs that cause a sense of euphoria; a drug that imitates the endorphins naturally produced in the brain. (p. 156)

opioids A class of psychoactive drugs that minimizes perceptions of pain. (p. 156)

opponent-process theory Perception of color derives from a special group of neurons that respond to opponent colors (red–green, blue–yellow). (p. 101)

optic nerve The bundle of axons from ganglion cells leading to the visual cortex. (p. 98)

orgasm A powerful combination of extremely gratifying sensations and a series of rhythmic muscular contractions. (p. 376)

out-group People outside the group to which we belong. (p. 581)

overgeneralization A cognitive distortion that assumes self-contained events will have major repercussions. (p. 532)

panic attack Sudden, extreme fear or discomfort that escalates quickly, often with no obvious trigger, and includes symptoms such as increased heart rate, sweating, shortness of breath, chest pain, nausea, lightheadedness, and fear of dying. (p. 487)

panic disorder A psychological disorder that includes recurrent, unexpected panic attacks and fear that can cause significant changes in behavior. (p. 487)

parapsychology The study of extrasensory perception. (p. 123)

parasympathetic nervous system The division of the autonomic nervous system that orchestrates the "rest-and-digest" response to bring the body back to a noncrisis mode. (p. 63)

parietal lobes (pə-rī-ə-təl) The area of the cortex that receives and processes sensory information such as touch, pressure, temperature, and spatial orientation. (p. 73)

partial reinforcement A schedule of reinforcement in which target behaviors are reinforced intermittently, not continuously. (p. 195)

partial reinforcement effect The tendency for behaviors acquired through intermittent reinforcement to be more resistant to extinction than those acquired through continuous reinforcement. (p. 195)

passionate love Love that is based on zealous emotion, leading to intense longing and sexual attraction. (p. 590)

perception The organization and interpretation of sensory stimuli by the brain. (p. 88)

perceptual constancy The tendency to perceive objects in our environment as stable in terms of shape, size, and color, regardless of changes in the sensory data received. (p. 122)

perceptual set The tendency to perceive stimuli in a specific manner based on past experiences and expectations. (p. 123)

peripheral nervous system (PNS) The part of the nervous system that connects the central nervous system to the rest of the body. (p. 60)

permissive parenting A parenting style characterized by low demands of children and few limitations. (p. 349)

personality The unique, core set of characteristics that influence the way one thinks, acts, and feels, and that are relatively consistent and enduring throughout the life span. (p. 404)

personality disorders A group of psychological disorders that can include impairments in cognition, emotional responses, interpersonal functioning, and impulse control. (p. 504)

person-centered therapy A form of humanistic therapy developed by Rogers; aimed at helping clients achieve their full potential. (p. 525)

persuasion Intentionally trying to make people change their attitudes and beliefs, which may lead to changes in their behaviors. (p. 566)

phenotype The observable expression or characteristics of one's genetic inheritance. (p. 313)

phonemes (fō-nēmz) The basic building blocks of spoken language. (p. 280)

photoreceptors Cells that absorb light energy and turn it into chemical and electrical signals for the brain to process. (p. 98)

phrenology An early approach to explaining the functions of the brain by trying to link the physical structure of the skull with a variety of characteristics. (p. 49)

physiological dependence With constant use of some psychoactive drugs, the body no longer functions normally without the drug. (p. 164)

pitch The degree to which a sound is high or low determined by the frequency of its sound wave. (p. 104)

pituitary gland The pea-sized gland located in the center of the brain just under the hypothalamus; known as the master gland. (p. 66)

place theory States that pitch corresponds to the location of the vibrating hair cells along the cochlea. (p. 107)

placebo (plə-'sē-,bō) An inert substance given to members of the control group; the fake treatment that has no benefit, but is administered as if it does. (p. 37)

pleasure principle Collection of rules that guide the id, resulting in behavior to achieve instant gratification without thought to consequences. (p. 408)

pons A hindbrain structure that helps regulate sleep–wake cycles and coordinate movement between the right and left sides of the body. (p. 80)

population All members of an identified group about which a researcher is interested. (p. 24)

positive psychology An approach that focuses on the positive aspects of human beings, seeking to understand their strengths and uncover the roots of happiness, creativity, humor, and so on. (p. 25)

positive punishment The addition of something unpleasant following an unwanted behavior, with the intention of decreasing that behavior. (p. 198)

positive reinforcement The process by which reinforcers are added or presented following a targeted behavior, increasing the likelihood of it occurring again. (p. 192)

positive symptoms Excesses or distortions of normal behavior; examples are delusions, hallucinations, and disorganized speech. (p. 500)

postconventional moral reasoning Kohlberg's stage of moral development in which right and wrong are determined by the individual's beliefs about morality, which sometimes do not coincide with society's rules and regulations. (p. 339)

posttraumatic stress disorder (PTSD) A psychological disorder characterized by exposure to or being threatened by an event involving death, serious injury, or sexual violence; can include disturbing memories, nightmares, flashbacks, and other distressing symptoms. (p. 447)

pragmatics The social rules that help to organize language. (p. 283)

preconventional moral reasoning Kohlberg's stage of moral development in which a person, usually a child, focuses on the consequences of behaviors, good or bad, and is concerned with avoiding punishment. (p. 338)

prejudice Holding hostile or negative attitudes toward an individual or group. (p. 582)

preoperational stage Piaget's stage of cognitive development during which children can start to use language to explore and understand their worlds. (p. 324)

primacy effect The tendency to remember items at the beginning of a list. (p. 236)

primary appraisal One's initial assessment of a situation to determine its personal impact and whether it is irrelevant, positive, challenging, or harmful. (p. 462)

primary reinforcer A reinforcer that satisfies a biological need, such as food, water, physical contact; innate reinforcer. (p. 193)

primary sex characteristics Organs associated with reproduction, including the ovaries, uterus, vagina, penis, scrotum, and testes. (p. 333)

priming The stimulation of memories as a result of retrieval cues in the environment. (p. 236)

proactive interference The tendency for information learned in the past to interfere with the retrieval of new material. (p. 241)

problem-focused coping A coping strategy in which a person deals directly with a problem by attempting to solve and address it head-on. (p. 462)

problem solving The variety of approaches that can be used to achieve a goal. (p. 269)

procedural memory The unconscious memory of how to carry out a variety of skills and activities; a type of implicit memory. (p. 230)

projective personality tests Assessments that present stimuli without a specified meaning to test takers, whose responses can then be interpreted to uncover underlying personality characteristics. (p. 431)

proprioceptors (proh-prē-uh-sep-tərs) Specialized nerve endings primarily located in the muscles and joints that provide information about body location and orientation. (p. 116)

prosocial behaviors Actions that are kind, generous, and beneficial to others. (p. 206)

prototype The ideal or most representative example of a natural concept; helps us categorize or identify specific members of a concept. (p. 265)

proximity Nearness; plays an important role in the formation of relationships. (p. 587)

pseudopsychology An approach to explaining and predicting behavior and events that appears to be psychology, but has no empirical or objective evidence to support it. (p. 17)

psychoactive drugs Substances that can cause changes in psychological activities such as sensation, perception, attention, judgment, memory, self-control, emotion, thinking, and behavior; substances that cause changes in conscious experiences. (p. 153)

psychoanalysis Freud's views regarding personality as well as his system of psychotherapy and tools for the exploration of the unconscious. (p. 407)

psychodynamic therapy A type of insight therapy that incorporates core psychoanalytic themes, including the importance of unconscious conflicts and experiences from the past. (p. 524)

psychological dependence With constant use of some psychoactive drugs, a strong desire or need to continue using the substance occurs without the evidence of tolerance or withdrawal symptoms. (p. 164)

psychological disorder A set of behavioral, emotional, and/or cognitive symptoms that are significantly distressing or disabling in terms of social functioning, work endeavors, and other aspects of life. (p. 476)

psychologists Scientists who study behavior and mental processes. (p. 3)

psychology The scientific study of behavior and mental processes. (p. 3)

psychoneuroimmunology (sī-kō-ˌn(y)ür-ō-ˌim-yə-ˈnä-lə-jē) The field that studies the relationships among psychological factors, the nervous system, and immune system functioning. (p. 459)

psychosexual stages According to Freud, the stages of development, from birth to adulthood, each of which has an erogenous zone as well as a conflict that must be dealt with. (p. 412)

psychosis Loss of contact with reality that is severe and chronic. (p. 499)

psychotherapy "Talk therapy"; a treatment approach in which a client works with a mental health professional to reduce psychological symptoms and improve quality of life. (p. 520)

puberty The period of development during which the body changes and becomes sexually mature and capable of reproduction. (p. 333)

punishment The application of a consequence that decreases the likelihood of a behavior recurring. (p. 198)

random assignment The process of appointing participants in a research study to the experimental or control groups, ensuring that every person has an equal chance of being assigned to either. (p. 34)

random sample A subset of the population chosen through a procedure that ensures all members of the population have an equally likely chance of being selected to participate in the study. (p. 24)

rapid eye movement (REM) The stage of sleep associated with dreaming; sleep characterized by bursts of eye movements, with brain activity similar to that of a waking state, but with a lack of muscle tone. (p. 141)

rational emotive behavior therapy (REBT) A type of cognitive therapy, developed by Ellis, that identifies illogical thoughts and converts them into rational ones. (p. 533)

reality principle Collection of rules that guide the ego as it negotiates between the id and the environment. (p. 409)

recall The process of retrieving information held in long-term memory without the help of explicit retrieval cues. (p. 236)

recency effect The tendency to remember items at the end of a list. (p. 236)

receptor sites The location where neurotransmitters attach on the receiving side of the synaptic gap. (p. 56)

recessive gene One of a pair of genes that is dominated by the other gene in the pair. (p. 314)

reciprocal determinism According to Bandura, multidirectional interactions among cognitions, behaviors, and the environment. (p. 424)

recognition The process of matching incoming data to information stored in long-term memory. (p. 236)

reflex arc An automatic response to a sensory stimulus, such as the "knee-jerk" reaction; a simple pathway of communication from sensory neurons through interneurons in the spinal cord back out through motor neurons. (p. 62)

refractory period An interval of time during which a man cannot attain another orgasm. (p. 376)

reinforcement Process by which an organism learns to associate a voluntary behavior with its consequences. (p. 188)

reinforcers Consequences, such as events or objects, that increase the likelihood of a behavior reoccurring. (p. 188)

relearning Material learned previously is acquired more quickly in subsequent exposures. (p. 239)

reliability The ability of an assessment to provide consistent, reproducible results. (p. 291)

REM rebound An increased amount of time spent in REM during the first sleep session after sleep deprivation. (p. 148)

REM sleep behavior disorder A sleep disturbance in which the mechanism responsible for paralyzing the body during REM sleep is not functioning, resulting in the acting out of dreams. (p. 144)

replicate To repeat an experiment, generally with a new sample and/or other changes to the procedures, the goal of which is to provide further support for the findings of the first study. (p. 22)

representativeness heuristic A decision-making strategy used to evaluate the degree to which the primary characteristics of a person or situation are similar to our prototype of that type of person or situation. (p. 277)

representative sample A subgroup of a population selected so that its members have characteristics similar to those of the population of interest. (p. 24)

repression The way the ego moves uncomfortable thoughts, memories, or feelings from the conscious level to the unconscious. (p. 410)

resistance A patient's unwillingness to cooperate in therapy; a sign of unconscious conflict. (p. 523)

resting potential The electrical potential of a cell "at rest"; the state of a cell when it is not activated. (p. 55)

reticular formation A network of neurons running through the midbrain that controls levels of arousal and quickly analyzes sensory information on its way to the cortex. (p. 80)

retina The layer of the eye that contains photoreceptor cells and the location for the transduction of light energy into neural activity. (p. 98)

retinal disparity A binocular cue that uses the difference between the images the two eyes see to determine the distance of objects. (p. 121)

retrieval The process of accessing information encoded and stored in memory. (p. 218)

retrieval cues Stimuli that help in the retrieval of stored information that is difficult to access. (p. 235)

retroactive interference The tendency for recently learned information to interfere with the retrieval of things learned in the past. (p. 242)

retrograde amnesia A type of memory loss; an inability to access memories formed prior to damage or injury to the brain, or difficulty retrieving them. (p. 248)

reuptake Process by which neurotransmitters are reabsorbed by the sending terminal bud. (p. 58)

rich false memories Recollections of an event that never occurred, which are expressed with emotions and confidence and include details. (p. 244)

risky shift The tendency for groups to recommend uncertain and risky options. (p. 577)

rods Specialized light receptors in the retina that are responsible for sight when the light level is low; not sensitive to color, but useful for night vision. (p. 98)

romantic love Love that is a combination of connection, concern, care, and intimacy. (p. 590)

sample A subset of a population chosen for inclusion in an experiment. (p. 24)

saturation Color purity. (p. 95)

scaffolding Pushing children to go just beyond what they are competent and comfortable doing, while providing help in a decreasing manner. (p. 327)

scapegoat A target of negative emotions, beliefs, and behaviors; typically, a member of the out-group who receives blame for an upsetting social situation. (p. 581)

Schachter–Singer theory of emotion Suggests that the experience of emotion is the result of physiological arousal and a cognitive label for this physiological state. (p. 390)

schema A collection of ideas that represents a basic unit of understanding. (p. 323)

schizophrenia (skit-sə-'frē-nē-ə) A disabling psychological disorder that can include delusions, hallucinations, disorganized speech, and abnormal psychomotor behavior. (p. 499)

scientific method The process scientists use to conduct research, which includes a continuing cycle of exploration, critical thinking, and systematic observation. (p. 18)

secondary appraisal An assessment to determine how to respond to a challenging or threatening situation. (p. 462)

secondary reinforcer Reinforcers that do not satisfy biological needs but often gain their power through their association with primary reinforcers. (p. 193)

secondary sex characteristics Body characteristics, such as pubic hair, underarm hair, and enlarged breasts, that develop in puberty but are not associated with reproduction. (p. 333)

selective attention The ability to focus awareness on a small segment of information that is available through our sensory systems. (p. 133)

self-actualization The need to be one's best and strive for one's fullest potential. (p. 366)

self-concept The knowledge an individual has about his strengths, abilities, behavior patterns, and temperament. (p. 420)

self-determination theory (SDT) Suggests that humans are born with the needs for competence, relatedness, and autonomy, which are always driving us in the direction of growth and optimal functioning. (p. 367)

self-efficacy Beliefs one has regarding how effective one will be in reaching a goal. (p. 424)

self-serving bias The tendency to attribute our successes to personal characteristics and our failures to environmental factors. (p. 558)

semantic memory The memory of information theoretically available to anyone, which pertains to general facts about the world; a type of explicit memory. (p. 229)

semantics The rules used to bring meaning to words and sentences. (p. 283)

sensation The process by which sensory organs in the eyes, ears, nose, mouth, skin, and other tissues receive and detect stimuli. (p. 88)

sensorimotor stage Piaget's stage of cognitive development during which infants use their sensory capabilities and motor skills to learn about the surrounding world. (p. 324)

sensory adaptation Sensory receptors tend to become less sensitive to constant stimuli. (p. 90)

sensory memory A stage of memory that captures near-exact copies of vast amounts of sensory stimuli for a very brief period of time. (p. 219)

sensory neurons Neurons specialized for receiving information about the environment from the sensory systems and transmitting this information to the brain for further processing. (p. 61)

serial position effect The ability to recall items in a list depends on where they are in the series. (p. 236)

set point The stable weight that is maintained despite variability in exercise and food intake. (p. 372)

sexual dysfunction A significant disturbance in the ability to respond sexually or to gain pleasure from sex. (p. 382)

sexual orientation A person's enduring sexual interest in individuals of the same sex, opposite sex, or both sexes. (p. 377)

sexuality Sexual activities, attitudes, and behaviors. (p. 375)

sexually transmitted infections (STIs) Diseases or illnesses transmitted through sexual activity. (p. 383)

shape constancy An object is perceived as maintaining its shape, regardless of the image projected on the retina. (p. 122)

shaping The use of reinforcers to guide behavior to the acquisition of a desired, complex behavior. (p. 188)

short-term memory A stage of memory that temporarily maintains and processes a limited amount of information. (p. 219)

signal detection theory A theory explaining how various factors influence our ability to detect weak signals in the environment. (p. 93)

situational attribution A belief that some environmental factor is involved in the cause of an event or activity. (p. 557)

size constancy An object is perceived as maintaining its size, regardless of the image projected on the retina. (p. 122)

sleep terrors A disturbance of non-REM sleep, generally occurring in children; characterized by screaming, staring fearfully, and usually no memory of the episode the following morning. (p. 146)

social cognition The way people think about others, attend to social information, and use this information in their lives, both consciously and unconsciously. (p. 556)

social-cognitive perspective Suggests that personality results from patterns of thinking (cognitive) as well as relationships and other environmental factors (social). (p. 422)

social facilitation The tendency for the presence of others to improve personal performance when the task or event is fairly uncomplicated and a person is adequately prepared. (p. 575)

social identity How we view ourselves within our social group. (p. 581)

social influence How a person is affected by others as evidenced in behaviors, emotions, and cognition. (p. 565)

social loafing The tendency for people to make less than their best effort when individual contributions are too complicated to measure. (p. 575)

social psychology The study of human cognition, emotion, and behavior in relation to others, including how people behave in social settings. (p. 555)

social roles The positions we hold in social groups, and the responsibilities and expectations associated with those roles. (p. 583)

social support The assistance we acquire from others. (p. 449)

somatic nervous system The branch of the peripheral nervous system that includes sensory nerves and motor nerves; gathers information from sensory receptors and controls the skeletal muscles responsible for voluntary movement. (p. 63)

somatosensory cortex A band of tissue running parallel to the motor cortex that receives and integrates sensory information from all over the body. (p. 77)

source traits Basic underlying or foundational characteristics of personality. (p. 425)

specific phobia A psychological disorder that includes a distinct fear or anxiety in relation to an object or situation. (p. 488)

spermarche [ˈspər-ˌmär-kē] A boy's first ejaculation. (p. 334)

spinal cord The bundle of neurons that allows communication between the brain and the peripheral nervous system, connecting with the body's muscles, glands, and organs. (p. 60)

split-brain operation A rare procedure used to disconnect the right and left hemispheres by cutting the corpus callosum. (p. 68)

spontaneous recovery The reappearance of a conditioned response following its extinction. (p. 180)

standardization Occurs when test developers administer a test to a large sample and then publish the average scores for specified groups. (p. 292)

stem cells Cells responsible for producing new neurons. (p. 73)

stereotypes Conclusions or inferences we make about people who are different from us based on their group membership, such as race, religion, age, or gender. (p. 581)

stereotype threat A "situational threat" in which individuals are aware of others' negative expectations, which leads to their fear that they will be judged or treated as inferior. (p. 582)

stigma A negative attitude or opinion about a group of people based on certain traits or characteristics. (p. 479)

stimulants A class of drugs that increase neural activity in the central nervous system. (p. 158)

stimulus An event or occurrence that generally leads to a response. (p. 174)

stimulus discrimination The ability to differentiate between a conditioned stimulus and other stimuli sufficiently different from it. (p. 179)

stimulus generalization The tendency for stimuli similar to the conditioned stimulus to elicit the conditioned response. (p. 179)

storage The process of preserving information for possible recollection in the future. (p. 218)

stress The response to perceived threats or challenges resulting from stimuli or events that cause strain. (p. 442)

stressors Stimuli that cause physiological, psychological, and emotional reactions. (p. 442)

structuralism An early school of psychology that used introspection to determine the structure and most basic elements of the mind. (p. 10)

successive approximations A method of shaping that uses reinforcers to condition a series of small steps that gradually approach the target behavior. (p. 189)

superego According to Freud, the structure of the mind that guides behavior to follow the rules of society, parents, or other authority figures. (p. 409)

surface traits Easily observable characteristics that derive from source traits. (p. 425)

survey method A type of descriptive research that uses questionnaires or interviews to gather data. (p. 28)

sympathetic nervous system The division of the autonomic nervous system that mobilizes the "fight-or-flight" response to stressful or crisis situations. (p. 63)

synapse (si-naps) The tiny gap between a terminal bud of one axon and a neighboring dendrite of the next neuron; junction between neurons where communication occurs. (p. 52)

syntax The collection of rules concerning where to place words or phrases. (p. 283)

systematic desensitization A treatment that combines anxiety hierarchies with relaxation techniques. (p. 528)

telegraphic speech Two-word phrases typically used by infants around the age of 18 months. (p. 322)

temperament Characteristic differences in behavioral patterns and emotional reactions that are evident from birth. (p. 328)

temporal lobes The area of the cortex that processes auditory stimuli and language. (p. 75)

teratogens (tə-'ra-tə-jəns) Environmental agents that can damage the growing zygote, embryo, or fetus. (p. 316)

testosterone An androgen produced by the testes. (p. 312)

tetrahydrocannabinol (THC) (te-trə-hī-drə-kə-'na-bə-,nól) The active ingredient of marijuana. (p. 163)

thalamus (tha-lə-məs) A structure in the limbic system that processes and relays sensory information to the appropriate areas of the cortex. (p. 80)

theory Synthesizes observations in order to explain phenomena and guide predictions to be tested through research. (p. 20)

therapeutic alliance A warm and accepting client–therapist relationship that serves as a safe place for self-exploration. (p. 526)

theta waves Brain waves that indicate light sleep. (p. 139)

thinking Mental activity associated with coming to a decision, reaching a solution, or forming a belief. (p. 261)

third variable An unaccounted for characteristic of participants or the environment that explains changes in the variables of interest. (p. 31)

thyroid gland Gland of the endocrine system that regulates the rate of metabolism by secreting thyroxin. (p. 66)

token economy A treatment approach that uses behavior modification to harness the power of reinforcement to encourage good behavior. (p. 530)

tolerance With constant use of some psychoactive drugs, a condition in which the body requires more and more of the drug to create the original effect; a sign of physiological dependence. (p. 164)

traits The relatively stable properties that describe elements of personality. (p. 424)

trait theories Theories that focus on personality dimensions and their influence on behavior; can be used to predict behaviors. (p. 424)

transduction The process of transforming stimuli into neural signals. (p. 89)

transference A type of resistance that occurs when a patient reacts to a therapist as if dealing with parents or other caregivers from childhood. (p. 523)

transgender Refers to people whose gender identity and expression do not typically match the gender assigned to them at birth. (p. 342)

transsexual An individual who seeks or undergoes a social transition to the other gender, and who may make changes to his or her body through surgery and medical treatment. (p. 342)

trial and error An approach to problem solving that involves finding a solution through a series of attempts and eliminating those that do not work. (p. 271)

triarchic theory of intelligence (trī-är-kik) Sternberg's theory suggesting that humans have varying degrees of analytical, creative, and practical abilities. (p. 288)

trichromatic theory (trī-krō-'ma-tik) The perception of color is the result of three types of cones, each sensitive to particular wavelengths in the red, green, and blue spectrums. (p. 100)

Type A personality Competitive, aggressive, impatient, and often hostile pattern of behaviors. (p. 462)

Type B personality Relaxed, patient, and nonaggressive pattern of behaviors. (p. 462)

unconditional positive regard According to Rogers, the total acceptance or valuing of a person, regardless of behavior. (p. 420)

unconditioned response (UR) A reflexive, involuntary response to an unconditioned stimulus. (p. 178)

unconditioned stimulus (US) A stimulus that automatically triggers an involuntary response without any learning needed. (p. 178)

unconscious According to Freud, the level of consciousness outside of awareness, which is difficult to access without effort or therapy. (p. 407)

uninvolved parenting A parenting style characterized by a parent's indifference to a child, including a lack of emotional involvement. (p. 349)

uplifts Experiences that are positive and have the potential to make one happy. (p. 450)

validity The degree to which an assessment measures what it intends to measure. (p. 291)

variables Measurable characteristics that can vary over time or across people. (p. 24)

variable-interval schedule A schedule in which the reinforcer comes after an interval of time goes by, but the length of the interval changes from trial to trial. (p. 197)

variable-ratio schedule A schedule in which the number of desired behaviors that must occur before a reinforcer is given changes across trials and is based on an average number of behaviors to be reinforced. (p. 197)

vestibular sense (ve-'sti-byə-lər) The sense of balance and equilibrium. (p. 116)

volley principle States that the perception of pitches between 400 and 4,000 Hz is made possible by neurons working together to fire in volleys. (p. 107)

wavelength The distance between wave peaks (or troughs). (p. 94)

Weber's law The law stating that each of the five senses has its own constant ratio determining difference thresholds. (p. 92)

Wernicke's area (ver-nə-kəz) A region of the cortex that plays a pivotal role in language comprehension. (p. 71)

withdrawal With constant use of some psychoactive drugs, a condition in which the body becomes dependent and then reacts when the drug is withheld; a sign of physiological dependence. (p. 164)

working memory The active processing of information in short-term memory; the maintenance and manipulation of information in the memory system. (p. 226)

zygote A single cell formed by the union of a sperm cell and egg. (p. 312)

References

Abel, K. M., Drake, R., & Goldstein, J. M. (2010). Sex differences in schizophrenia. *International Review of Psychiatry, 22,* 417–428.

Abou-Khalil, B. W. (2010). When should corpus callosotomy be offered as palliative therapy? *Epilepsy Currents, 10,* 9–10.

Ackerman, P. L., Kanfer, R., & Calderwood, C. (2010). Use it or lose it? Wii brain exercise practice and reading for domain knowledge. *Psychology and Aging, 25,* 753–766.

Addy, S., Engelhardt, W., & Skinner, C. (2013). *Basic facts about low-income children: Children under 18 years, 2011* [Fact sheet]. New York: National Center for Children in Poverty. Retrieved from http://www.nccp.org/publications/pub_1074.html

Adler, A. (1927/1994). *Understanding human nature.* Oxford, UK: Oneworld.

Aeschbach, D., Sher, L., Postolache, T. T., Matthews, J. R., Jackson, M. A., & Wehr, T. A. (2003). A longer biological night in long sleepers than in short sleepers. *Journal of Clinical Endocrinology & Metabolism, 88,* 26–30.

Afifi, T. O., Mota, N. P., Dasiewicz, P., MacMillan, H. L., Sareen, J. (2012). Physical punishment and mental disorders: Results from a nationally representative US sample. *Pediatrics, 130,* 184–192.

Agence France Presse. (2010, October 14). In Chile mine rescue 33 is lucky number. *The Sydney Morning Herald.* Retrieved from http://www.smh.com.au/world/in-chile-mine-rescue-33-is-lucky-number-20101014-16kxg.html

Agence France Presse. (2014, July 26). U.N. warns of a food shortage 3 years after Somalia's famine. *The New York Times.* Retrieved from http://www.nytimes.com/2014/07/27/world/africa/un-warns-of-a-food-shortage-3-years-after-somalias-famine.html

Ahima, R. S., & Antwi, D. A. (2008). Brain regulation of appetite and satiety. *Endocrinology Metabolism Clinics of North America, 31,* 811–823.

Aiello, J. R., & Douthitt, E. A. (2001). Social facilitation from Triplett to electronic performance monitoring. *Group Dynamics: Theory, Research, and Practice, 5,* 163–180.

Ainsworth, M. D. S. (1979). Infant–mother attachment. *American Psychologist, 34,* 932–937.

Ainsworth, M. D. (1985). Patterns of attachment. *Clinical Psychologist, 38,* 27–29.

Ainsworth, M. D. S., & Bell, S. M. (1970). Attachment, exploration, and separation: Illustrated by the behavior of one-year-olds in a strange situation. *Child Development, 41,* 49–67.

Ainsworth, M. D. S., Blehar, M. C., Waters, E., & Wall, S. (1978). *Patterns of attachment: A psychological study of the strange situation.* Hillsdale, NJ: Lawrence Erlbaum Associates.

Ainsworth, S. E., & Maner, J. K. (2012). Sex begets violence: Mating motives, social dominance, and physical aggression in men. *Journal of Personality and Social Psychology, 103,* 819–829. doi:10.1037/a0029428

Ajzen, I. (2001). Nature and operation of attitudes. *Annual Review of Psychology, 52,* 27–58.

Akcay, O., Dalgin, M. H., & Bhatnagar, S. (2011). Perception of color in product choice among college students: A cross-national analysis of USA, India, China and Turkey. *International Journal of Business and Social Science, 2,* 42–48.

Akinola, M., & Mendes, W. B. (2012). Stress-induced cortisol facilitates threat-related decision making among police officers. *Behavioral Neuroscience, 126,* 167–174.

Al Firdaus, M. M. (2012). SQ3R strategy for increasing students' retention of reading and written information. *Majalah Ilmiah Dinamika, 31,* 49–63.

Albert, D., Chein, J., & Steinberg, L. (2013). The teenage brain: Peer influences on adolescent decision making. *Current Directions in Psychological Science, 22,* 114–120.

Aldrete, J. A., Marron, G. M., & Wright, A. J. (1984). The first administration of anesthesia in military surgery: On occasion of the Mexican-American War. *Anesthesiology, 61,* 585–588.

Alexander, D. A., & Klein, S. (2001). Ambulance personnel and critical incidents: Impact of accident and emergency work on mental health and emotional well-being. *British Journal of Psychiatry, 178,* 76–81.

Alexander, G. M., & Hines, M. (2002). Sex differences in response to children's toys in nonhuman primates (*Cercopithecus aethiops sabaeus*). *Evolution and Human Behavior, 23,* 467–479.

Alexander, G. M., Wilcox, T., & Woods, R. (2009). Sex differences in infants' visual interest in toys. *Archives of Sexual Behavior, 38,* 427–433.

Alexander, R. D. (1974). The evolution of social behavior. *Annual Review of Ecology and Systematics, 5,* 325–383.

Allegood, J. (2011, July 27). N.C. girl in good spirits after Outer Banks shark attack last week. *The Salt Lake Tribune.* Retrieved from http://www.sltrib.com/52272296

Allen, N. (2011, January 24). Oprah Winfrey reunited with 'secret half-sister.' *The Telegraph.* Retrieved from http://www.telegraph.co.uk/news/worldnews/northamerica/usa/8279477/Oprah-Winfrey-reunited-with-secret-half-sister.html

Allen, S. (2009, October 30). 11 famous people who overcame dyslexia. *CNN com.* Retrieved from http://www.cnn.com/2009/LIVING/10/30/mf.dyslexia.famous.celebrities/

Allik, J., & McCrae, R. R. (2004). Toward a geography of personality traits patterns of profiles across 36 cultures. *Journal of Cross-Cultural Psychology, 35,* 13–28.

Allport, G. W. & Odbert, H. S. (1936). Trait-names: A psycho-lexical study. *Psychological Monographs, 47*(211), i–171.

Alpert, P. T. (2012). The health lowdown on caffeine. *Home Health Care Management Practice, 24,* 156–158.

Altshuler, L. L., Kuaka, R. W., Hellemann, G., Frye, M. A., Sugar, C. A., McElroy, S. L., . . . Suppes, T. (2010). Bipolar disorder evaluated prospectively in the Stanley Foundation Bipolar Treatment Outcome Network. *American Journal of Psychiatry, 167,* 708–715.

Alzheimer's Association. (2013). *Alzheimer's and dementia testing for earlier diagnosis.* Retrieved from http://www.alz.org/research/science/earlier_alzheimers_diagnosis.asp#Brain

American Academy of Ophthalmology. (2014a). *EyeSmart: Smoking and eye health.* Retrieved October 19, 2014 from http://www.geteyesmart.org/eyesmart/living/smokers.cfm

American Academy of Ophthalmology. (2014b). *EyeSmart: The sun, UV radiation and your eyes.* Retrieved October 19, 2014 from http://www.geteyesmart.org/eyesmart/living/sun.cfm

American Academy of Ophthalmology. (2014c). *EyeSmart: Preventing eye injuries.* Retrieved October 19, 2014 from http://www.geteyesmart.org/eyesmart/living/eye-injuries/preventing.cfm

American Academy of Pediatrics. (1998). Guidance for effective discipline. *Pediatrics, 101,* 723–728.

American Academy of Pediatrics. (2009). Policy statement–Media violence. *Pediatrics, 124,* 1495–1503.

American Academy of Pediatrics. (2013). Children, adolescents, and the media. *Pediatrics, 132,* 958–961.

American Academy of Pediatrics, Committee on Public Education. (2001). American Academy of Pediatrics: Children, adolescents, and television. *Pediatrics, 107,* 423–426.

American Art Therapy Association. (2015). *About art therapy.* Retrieved from http://www.arttherapy.org/

American Cancer Society. (2012). *Child and teen tobacco use.* Retrieved from http://www.cancer.org/cancer/cancercauses/tobaccocancer/childandteentobaccouse/child-and-teen-tobacco-use-child-and-teen-tobacco-use

American Heart Association. (2014). *Atherosclerosis.* Retrieved from http://www.heart.org/HEARTORG/Conditions/Cholesterol/WhyCholesterolMatters/Atherosclerosis_UCM_305564_Article.jsp

American Heart Association. (2014). Overweight in children. Retrieved from http://www.heart.org/HEARTORG/GettingHealthy/Overweight-in-Children_UCM_304054_Article.jsp

American Humane Association. (2013). *Animal-assisted therapy.* Retrieved from http://www.americanhumane.org/interaction/programs/animal-assisted-therapy/

American Lung Association. (2014). *Smoking.* Retrieved from http://www.lung.org/stop-smoking/about-smoking/health-effects/smoking.html

American Psychiatric Association. (1952). *Diagnostic and statistical manual of mental disorders.* Arlington, VA: Author.

American Psychiatric Association. (2001). *The practice of ECT: A task force report* (2nd ed.). Washington, DC: Author.

American Psychiatric Association. (2013). *Diagnostic and statistical manual of mental disorders* (5th ed., *DSM–5*). Arlington, VA: Author.

American Psychological Association. (1998a). Final conclusions of the American Psychological Association's working group on investigation of memories of childhood abuse. *Psychology, Public Policy, and Law, 4,* 933–940.

American Psychological Association. (1998b). *Psychology education & career guide for college students of color: Subfields of psychology.* Retrieved from http://www.apa.org/careers/resources/guides/college-students.aspx?item=14

American Psychological Association. (2004). *The truth about lie detectors (aka polygraph tests).* Retrieved from http://www.apa.org/research/action/polygraph.aspx

American Psychological Association. (2008). *Answers to your questions: For a better understanding of sexual orientation and homosexuality.* Retrieved from http://www.apa.org/topics/sorientation.pdf

American Psychological Association. (2010a). *Ethical principles of psychologists and code of conduct,* 1–18. Retrieved from http://www.apa.org/ethics/code/principles.pdf

American Psychological Association. (2010b). *Publication manual of the American Psychological Association* (6th ed.). Washington, DC: American Psychological Association.

American Psychological Association. (2011a). *Answers to your questions about transgender people, gender identity, and gender expression.* Retrieved from http://www.apa.org/topics/sexuality/transgender.pdf

American Psychological Association. (2011b). *Careers in psychology: Some of the subfields in psychology.* Retrieved from http://www.apa.org/careers/resources/guides/careers.aspx?item=3#

American Psychological Association. (2012, March). *Understanding alcohol use disorders and their treatment.* Retrieved February 20, 2013, from www.http://www.apa.org/helpcenter/alcohol-disorders.aspx

American Psychological Association. (2012a). *Divisions of the APA.* Retrieved from http://www.apa.org/about/division/index.aspx

American Psychological Association. (2012b). *Resolution on the recognition of psychotherapy effectiveness.* Retrieved October 19, 2012, from http://www.apa.org/news/press/releases/2012/08/resolution-psychotherapy.aspx

American Psychological Association. (2012c). *Resolution on the recognition of psychotherapy effectiveness.* Retrieved June 23, 2015 from http://www.apa.org/about/policy/resolution-psychotherapy.aspx

American Psychological Association. (2012d). *Society for media psychology & technology.* Division 46. Retrieved from http://www.apa.org/divisions/div46/

American Psychological Association. (2013a). *Graduate study in psychology, 2014 edition.* Washington, DC: Author.

American Psychological Association. (2013b). *Margaret Floy Washburn, PhD: 1921 APA President.* Retrieved from http://www.apa.org/about/governance/president/bio-margaret-washburn.aspx

American Psychological Association. (2013c). *Roper v. Simmons.* Retrieved from http://www.apa.org/about/offices/ogc/amicus/roper.aspx

American Psychological Association. (2013d). *Stress in America: Missing the health care connection.* Retrieved from http://www.apa.org/news/press/releases/stress/2012/full-report.pdf

American Psychological Association. (2015). *Graduate study in psychology, 2016 edition.* Washington, DC: Author.

American Psychological Association. (2015). *Sport psychology off the field.* Retrieved from http://www.apa.org/helpcenter/sport-psychology.aspx

American Speech-Language-Hearing Association. (2012). *Who should be screened for hearing loss?* Retrieved from http://www.asha.org/public/hearing/Who-Should-be-Screened/

American Speech-Language-Hearing Association. (2014). *Noise.* Retrieved October 19, 2014 from http://www.asha.org/public/hearing/Noise/

American Stroke Association. (2012). *What is an arteriovenous malformation (AVM)?* Retrieved from http://www.strokeassociation.org/STROKEORG/AboutStroke/TypesofStroke/HemorrhagicBleeds/What-Is-an-Arteriovenous-Malformation-AVM_UCM_310099_Article.jsp

Amesbury, E. C., & Schallhorn, S. C. (2003). Contrast sensitivity and limits of vision. *International Ophthalmology Clinics, 43,* 31–42.

Anastasi, A., & Urbina, S. (1997). *Psychological testing* (7th ed.). Upper Saddle River, NJ: Prentice Hall.

Anastasio, A., Draisci, R., Pepe, T., Mercogliano, R., Quadri, F. D., Luppi, G., & Cortesi, M. L. (2010). Development of biogenic amines during the ripening of Italian dry sausages. *Journal of Food Protection, 73,* 114–118.

Anderson, B., Fagan, P., Woodnutt, T., & Chamorro-Premuzic, T. (2012). Facebook psychology: Popular questions answered by research. *Psychology of Popular Media Culture, 1,* 23–37.

Anderson, C. A. (2001). Heat and violence. *Current Directions in Psychological Science, 10,* 33–38.

Anderson, G. S., Litzenberger, R., & Plecas, D. (2002). Physical evidence of police officer stress. *An International Journal of Police Strategies & Management, 25,* 399–420.

Anderson, R. C. (1971). Encoding processes in the storage and retrieval of sentences. *Journal of Experimental Psychology, 91,* 338–340.

Anderson-Hanley, C., Snyder, A. L., Nimon, J. P., & Arciero, P. J. (2011). Social facilitation in virtual reality-enhanced exercise: Competitiveness moderates exercise effort of older adults. *Clinical Interventions in Aging, 6,* 275–280.

Andrus, B. M., Blizinsky, K., Vedell, P. T., Dennis, K., Shukla, P. K., Schaffer, D. J., . . . Redei, E. E. (2012). Gene expression patterns in the hippocampus and amygdala of endogenous depression and chronic stress models. *Molecular Psychiatry, 17,* 49–61.

Angst, J., Angst, F., Gerber-Werder, R., & Gamma, A. (2005). Suicide in 406 mood-disorder patients with and without long-term medication: A 40 to 44 years' follow-up. *Archives of Suicide Research, 9,* 279–300.

Anis, A. H., Zhang, W., Bansback, N., Guh, D. P., Amarsi, Z., & Birmingham, C. L. (2010). Obesity and overweight in Canada: An updated cost-of-illness study. *Obesity Reviews, 11,* 21–40.

Annan, J., Blattman, C., & Horton, R. (2006). *The state of youth and youth protection in northern Uganda: Findings from the Survey for War Affected Youth* [Report for UNICEF Uganda], ii–89. Retrieved from http://chrisblattman.com/documents/policy/sway/SWAY.Phase1.FinalReport.pdf

Ansbacher, H. L., & Ansbacher, R. R. (Eds.). (1956). *The individual psychology of Alfred Adler.* New York: Harper and Row.

Araque, A., & Navarrete, M. (2010). Glial cells in neuronal network function. *Philosophical Transactions of the Royal Society of Biological Sciences, 365,* 2375–2381.

Archer, J. (2004). Sex differences in aggression in real-world settings: A meta-analytic review. *Review of General Psychology, 8,* 291–322.

Archer, J., & Coyne, S. M. (2005). An integrated review of indirect, relational, and social aggression. *Personality and Social Psychology Review, 9,* 212–230.

Ardila, A., Rosselli, M., Matute, E., & Inozemtseva, O. (2011). Gender differences in cognitive development. *Developmental Psychology, 47,* 984–990.

Arkowitz, H., & Lilienfeld, S. O. (2011, July/August). Deranged and dangerous? *Scientific American Mind, 22,* 64–65.

Arlin, P. K. (1975). Cognitive development in adulthood: A fifth stage? *Developmental Psychology, 11,* 602–606.

Armitage, C. J., & Christian, J. (2003). From attitudes to behaviour: Basic and applied research on the theory of planned behaviour. *Current Psychology: Developmental, Learning, Personality, Social, 22,* 187–195.

Arnett, J. J. (2000). Emerging adulthood: A theory of development from the late teens through the twenties. *American Psychologist, 55,* 469–480.

Aronson, E. (2012). *The social animal* (11th ed.). New York: Worth.

Aronson, E. (2015). *Jigsaw classroom.* Retrieved from http://www.jigsaw.org

Aronson, E., & Festinger, L. (1958). *Some attempts to measure tolerance for dissonance* (WADC.TR-58.492ASTIA Document No. AD 207 337). San Antonio, TX: Lackland Air Force Base.

Asch, S. E. (1955). Opinions and social pressure. *Scientific American, 193,* 31–35.

Asch, S. E. (1956). Studies of independence and conformity: I. A minority of one against a unanimous majority. *Psychological Monographs: General and Applied, 70,* 1–70.

Associated Press. (2008, April 25). *ESPN.* Retrieved from http://sports.espn.go.com/espn/wire?section=horse&id=3367868

Associated Press. (2010, August 25). Geology of Chilean gold and copper mine helped miners survive with air, water and warmth. *Fox News.* Retrieved from http://www.foxnews.com/world/2010/08/25/geology-chilean-gold-copper-helped-miners-survive-air-water-warmth/

Associated Press. (2010, August 30). Chilean miners must move tons of rocks in rescue. *USA Today.* Retrieved from http://usatoday30.usatoday.com/news/world/2010-08-29-chile-mine-rescue_N.htm

Associated Press. (2010, September 7). Skin infections pose risk to Chilean miners as rescuers work to cool the sweltering conditions. *Fox News.* Retrieved from http://www.foxnews.com/world/2010/09/07/skin-infections-pose-risk-chilean-miners-rescuers-work-cool-sweltering/

Associated Press. (2015, August 26). James Holmes trial: Judge formally sentences Aurora gunman to life in prison. *NBC News.* Retrieved from http://www.nbcnews.com/news/us-news/james-holmes-trial-judge-formally-sentences-aurora-gunman-life-prison-n416396

Association for Psychological Science. (2012). *Psychology links.* Retrieved from http://www.psychologicalscience.org/index.php/about/psychology-links

Atkinson, R. C., & Shiffrin, R. M. (1968, January 31–February 2). *Some speculations on storage and retrieval processes in long-term memory* (Technical Report No. 127). Paper presented at Conference on Research on Human Decision Making sponsored by NASA-Ames Research Center, Moffett Field, CA.

Attarian, H. P., Schenck, C. H., & Mahowald, M. W. (2000). Presumed REM sleep behavior disorder arising from cataplexy and wakeful dreaming. *Sleep Medicine, 1,* 131–133.

Attia, E., & Roberto, C. A. (2009). Should amenorrhea be a diagnostic criterion for anorexia nervosa? *International Journal of Eating Disorders, 42,* 581–589.

Aurora, R. N., Zak, R. S., Maganti, R. K., Auerbach, S. H., Casey, K. R., Chowdhuri, S., . . . American Academy of Sleep Medicine. (2010). Best practice guide for the treatment of REM sleep behavior disorder (RED). *Journal of Clinical Sleep Medicine, 15,* 85–95.

Awikunprasert, C., & Sittiprapapom, W. (2012). Sleep pattern and efficiency in Thai children aged 3-6. *Research Journal of Pharmaceutical, Biological and Chemical Sciences, 3,* 1208–1217.

Axelrod, V., Bar, M., Rees, G., & Yovel, G. (2014). Neural correlates of subliminal language processing. *Cerebral Cortex,* doi:10.1093/cercor/bhu022

Back, M. D., Schmukle, S. C., & Egloff, B. (2008). Becoming friends by chance. *Psychological Science, 19,* 439–440.

Back, M. D., Stopfer, J. M., Vazire, S., Gaddis, S., Schmukle, S. C., Egloff, B., & Gosling, S. D. (2010). Facebook profiles reflect actual personality, not self-idealization. *Psychological Science, 21,* 372–374.

Baddeley, A. (1995). Working memory. In M. S. Gazzaniga (Ed.), *The cognitive neurosciences* (pp. 755–764). Cambridge, MA: MIT Press.

Baddeley, A. (1999). *Essentials of human memory.* East Sussex, UK: Psychology Press.

Baddeley, A. (2000). The episodic buffer: A new component of working memory? *Trends in Cognitive Sciences, 4,* 417–423.

Baddeley, A. (2002). Is working memory still working? *European Psychologist, 7,* 85–97.

Baddeley, A. (2006). Working memory: An overview. In S. J. Pickering (Ed.), *Working memory in education* (pp. 3–31). Burlington, MA: Elsevier.

Baddeley, A. D., & Hitch, G. J. (1974). Working memory. In G. Bower (Ed.), *Recent advances in learning and memory* (Vol. 8, pp. 47–90). New York: Academic Press.

Baddeley, A. D., & Hitch, G. J. (1994). Developments in the concept of working memory. *Neuropsychology, 8,* 485–493.

Badie, D. (2010). Groupthink, Iraq, and the war on terror: Explaining US policy shift toward Iraq. *Foreign Policy Analysis, 6,* 277–296.

Baer, J. M. (1993). *Creativity and divergent thinking.* Hillsdale, NJ: Erlbaum.

Bahrick, H. P., Hall, L. K., & Da Costa, L. A. (2008). Fifty years of memory of college grades: Accuracy and distortions. *Emotion, 8,* 13–22.

Bahrick, L. E., Gogate, L. J., & Ruiz, I. (2002). Attention and memory for faces and actions in infancy: The salience of actions over faces in dynamic events. *Child Development, 73,* 1629–1643.

Bahrick, L. E., & Newell, L. C. (2008). Infant discrimination of faces in naturalistic events: Actions are more salient than faces. *Developmental Psychology, 44,* 983–996.

Baibazarova, E., van de Beek, C., Cohen-Kettenis, P. T., Buitelaar, J., Shelton, K. H., & van Goozen, S. H. M. (2013). Influence of prenatal maternal stress, maternal plasma cortisol and cortisol in the amniotic fluid on birth outcomes and child temperament at 3 months. *Psychoneuroendocrinology, 38,* 907–915.

Bailey, S. J., & Covell, K. (2011). Pathways among abuse, daily hassles, depression and substance use in adolescents. *The New School Psychology Bulletin, 8,* 4–14.

Baillargeon, R., Spelke, E. S., & Wasserman, S. (1985). Object permanence in five-month-old infants. *Cognition, 20,* 191–208.

Baker, M. (2009, January 8). How brain activity makes new neurons. *Nature Reports Stem Cells.* Retrieved from http://www.nature.com/stemcells/2009/0901/090108/full/stemcells.2009.15.html

Bandell, M., Macpherson, L. J., & Patapoutian, A. (2007). From chills to chilis: Mechanisms for thermosensation and chemesthesis via thermoTRPs. *Current Opinion in Neurobiology, 17,* 490–497.

Bandura, A. (1977a). Self-efficacy: Toward a unifying theory of behavioral change. *Psychological Review, 84,* 191–215.

Bandura, A. (1977b). *Social learning theory.* Englewood Cliffs, NJ: Prentice Hall.

Bandura, A. (1978). The self system in reciprocal determinism. *American Psychologist, 33,* 344–358.

Bandura, A. (1986). *Social foundations of thought and action: A social cognitive theory.* Englewood Cliffs, NJ: Prentice Hall.

Bandura, A. (2001). Social cognitive theory: An agentic perspective. *Annual Review of Psychology, 52,* 1–26.

Bandura, A. (2006). Toward a psychology of human agency. *Perspectives on Psychological Science, 1,* 164–180.

Bandura, A., Ross, D., & Ross, S. A. (1961). Transmission of aggression through imitation of aggressive models. *Journal of Abnormal and Social Psychology, 63,* 575–582.

Banks, M. S., & Salapatek, P. (1978). Acuity and contrast sensitivity in 1-, 2-, and 3-month-old human infants. *Investigative Ophthalmology & Visual Science, 17,* 361–365.

Banks, S., & Dinges, D. F. (2007). Behavioral and physiological consequences of sleep restriction. *Journal of Clinical Sleep Medicine, 3,* 519–528.

Banuazizi, A., & Movahedi, S. (1975). Interpersonal dynamics in a simulated prison: A methodological analysis. *American Psychologist, 30,* 152–160.

Banyard, V. L., & Moynihan, M. M. (2011). Variation in bystander behavior related to sexual and intimate partner violence prevention: Correlates in a sample of college students. *Psychology of Violence, 1,* 287–301.

Barak, A., Hen, L., Boniel-Nissim, M., & Shapira, N. A. (2008). A comprehensive review and a meta-analysis of the effectiveness of Internet-based psychotherapeutic interventions. *Journal of Technology in Human Services, 26,* 109–160.

Barash, P. G., Cullen, B. F., Stoelting, R. K., & Cahalan, M. (2009). *Clinical anesthesia* (6th ed.). Philadelphia: Lippincott Williams & Wilkins.

Barber, C. (2008). *Comfortably numb.* New York: Pantheon Books.

Bard, P. (1934). Emotion I: The neuro-humoral basis of emotional reactions. In C. Murchison, (Ed.), *Handbook of general experimental psychology,* International University Series in Psychology (pp. 264–311). Worcester, MA: Clark University Press.

Bargh, J. A., & McKenna, K. Y. A. (2004). The Internet and social life. *Annual Review of Psychology, 55,* 573–590.

Barker, E. T., Greenberg, J. S., Seltzer, M. M., & Almeida, D. M. (2012). Daily stress and cortisol patterns in parents of adult children with serious mental illness. *Health Psychology, 31,* 130–134.

Barnes, A. J., De Martinis, B. S., Gorelick, D. A., Goodwin, R. S., Kolbrich, E. A., & Huestis, M. A. (2009). Disposition of MDMA and metabolites in human sweat following controlled MDMA administration. *Clinical Chemistry, 55,* 454–462.

Barnes, S. K. (2010). Sign language with babies: What difference does it make? *Dimensions of Early Childhood, 38,* 21–30.

Barr, T. F., Dixon, A. L., & Gassenheimer, J. B. (2005). Exploring the "lone wolf" phenomenon in student teams. *Journal of Marketing Education, 27,* 81–90.

Barredo, J. L., & Deeg, K. E. (2009, February 24). Could living in a mentally enriching environment change your genes? *Scientific American.* Retrieved from http://www.scientificamerican.com/article.cfm?id=enriched-environments-memory

Barrett, L. F., & Bliss-Moreau, E. (2009). She's emotional. He's having a bad day: Attributional explanations for emotion stereotypes. *Emotion, 9,* 649–658.

Barrionuevo, A. (2011, October 12). A year out of the dark in Chile, but still trapped. *The New York Times.* Retrieved from http://www.nytimes.com/2011/10/12/world/americas/chiles-rescued-miners-face-major-struggles-a-year-later.html?pagewanted=all

Bartels, M., Saviouk, V., De Moor, M. H. M., Willemsen, G., van Beijsterveldt, T. C. E. M., Hottenga, J.-J., . . . Boomsma, D. I. (2010). Heritability and genome-wide linkage scan of subjective happiness. *Twin Research and Human Genetics, 13,* 135–142.

Bateman, A., & Fonagy, P. (2008). 8-year follow-up of patients treated for borderline personality disorder: Mentalization-based treatment versus treatment as usual. *American Journal of Psychiatry, 165,* 631–638.

Batson, C. D., & Powell, A. A. (2003). Altruism and prosocial behavior. In I. B. Weiner, T. Millon, & M. J. Lerner (Eds.), *Handbook of psychology: Vol. 5. Personality and social psychology* (pp. 463–484). Hoboken, NJ: John Wiley & Sons.

Bauer, P. J. (2006). Constructing a past in infancy: A neuro-developmental account. *Trends in Cognitive Sciences, 10,* 175–181.

Baughman, H. M., Giammarco, E. A., Veselka, L., Schermer, J. A., Martin, N. G., Lynskey, M., & Vernon, P. A. (2012). A behavioral genetic study of humor styles in an Australian sample. *Twin Research and Human Genetics, 15,* 663–667.

Baumeister, R. F., Campbell, J. D., Krueger, J. I., & Vohs, K. D. (2003). Does high self-esteem cause better performance, interpersonal success, happiness, or healthier lifestyles? *Psychological Science in the Public Interest, 4,* 1–44.

Baumrind, D. (1966). Effects of authoritative parental control on child behavior. *Child Development, 37,* 887–907.

Baumrind, D. (1971). Current patterns of parental authority. *Developmental Psychology Monograph, 4,* 1–103.

Baumrind, D. (1991). The influence of parenting style on adolescent competence and substance use. *Journal of Early Adolescence, 11,* 56–95.

Baumrind, D. (1996). Personal statements. *Pediatrics, 98,* 857–860.

Baumrind, D., Larzelere, R. E., & Cowan, P. A. (2002). Ordinary physical punishment: Is it harmful? [Peer commentary on the paper "Corporal punishment by parents and associated child behaviors and experiences: A metaanalytic and theoretical review" by E. T. Gershoff]. *Psychological Bulletin, 128,* 580–589.

BBC News. (2001, November 16). Rise of the blockbuster. Retrieved from http://news.bbc.co.uk/2/hi/entertainment/1653733.stm

BBC News. (2010, October 14). Jubilation as Chile mine rescue ends. Retrieved from http://www.bbc.co.uk/news/world-latin-america-11469025

BBC News. (2010, November 20). Global health officials target tobacco additives. Retrieved from http://www.bbc.co.uk/news/world-latin-america-11804767?print=true

BBC News. (2011, June 28). Somalia fleeing to Kenya in large numbers. Retrieved from http://www.bbc.co.uk/news/world-africa-13937486

BBC News. (2011, July 22). EU must do more on East Africa famine—David Cameron. Retrieved from http://www.bbc.co.uk/news/uk-politics-14253766

Beauchamp, M. H., & Anderson, V. (2010). Social: An integrative framework for the development of social skills. *Psychological Bulletin, 136,* 39–64.

Bech, P. (2006). The full story of lithium. *Psychotherapy and psychosomatics, 75,* 265–269.

Beck, A. T. (1976). *Cognitive therapy and the emotional disorders.* New York: International Universities Press.

Beck, A. T., Rush, A. J., Shaw, B. F., & Emory, G. (1979). *Cognitive therapy of depression.* New York: Guilford Press.

Beck, A. T., & Weishaar, M. E. (2014). Cognitive therapy. In R. J. Corsini & D. Wedding (Eds.), *Current psychotherapies* (10th ed., pp. 231–264). Belmont, CA: Brooks/Cole, Cengage Learning.

Beck, H. (2011, December 28). Newest Knick out to prove he's not just a novelty. *The New York Times.* Retrieved from http://www.nytimes.com/2011/12/29/sports/basketball/jeremy-lin-knicks-newest-addition-is-out-to-prove-hes-not-just-a-novelty.html

Beck, H. (2012, February 4). Lin sparks Knicks, to crowd's delight and D'Antoni's relief. *The New York Times.* Retrieved from http://www.nytimes.com/2012/02/05/sports/basketball/lin-leads-knicks-over-nets.html

Beck, H. (2012, February 24). The evolution of a point guard. *The New York Times.* Retrieved from http://www.nytimes.com/2012/02/25/sports/basketball/the-evolution-of-jeremy-lin-as-a-point-guard.html?pagewanted=all

Beck, H. P., & Irons, G. (2011). Finding Little Albert: A seven-year search for psychology's lost boy. *The Psychologist, 24,* 392–395.

Beck, H. P., Levinson, S., & Irons, G. (2009). Finding Little Albert: A journey to John B. Watson's infant laboratory. *American Psychologist, 64,* 605–614.

Becker, K. A. (2003). History of the Stanford-Binet intelligence scales: Content and psychometrics. In *Stanford-Binet intelligence scales, Fifth Edition Assessment Service Bulletin* (no. 1). Itasca, IL: Riverside.

Beebe-Center, J. G. (1951). Feeling and emotion. In H. Helson (Ed.), *Theoretical foundations of psychology* (pp. 254–317). Princeton, NJ: Van Nostrand.

Bekk, M., & Spörrle, M. (2010). The influence of perceived personality characteristics on positive attitude towards and suitability of a celebrity as a marketing campaign endorser. *Open Psychology Journal, 3,* 54–66.

Belizaire, L. S., & Fuertes, J. N. (2011). Attachment, coping, acculturative stress, and quality of life among Haitian immigrants. *Journal of Counseling & Development, 89,* 89–97.

Belmaker, R. H. (2004). Bipolar disorder. *New England Journal of Medicine, 351,* 476–486.

Belmaker, R. H., & Agam, G. (2008). Major depressive disorder. *New England Journal of Medicine, 358,* 55–68.

Bem, D. J. (2011). Feeling the future: Experimental evidence for anomalous retroactive influences on cognition and affect. *Journal of Personality and Social Psychology, 100,* 407–425.

Bem, D. J., Utts, J., & Johnson, W. O. (2011). Must psychologists change the way they analyze their data? *Journal of Personality and Social Psychology, 101,* 716–719.

Bem, S. L. (1981). Gender schema theory: A cognitive account of sex typing. *Psychological Review, 88,* 354–364.

Benedek, M., Franz, F., Heene, M., & Neubauer, A. C. (2012). Differential effects of cognitive inhibition and intelligence on creativity. *Personality and Individual Differences, 53,* 480–485.

Benham, G. (2010). Sleep: An important factor in stress-health models. *Stress and Health, 26,* 201–214.

Benjamin, L. T. (2007). *A brief history of modern psychology.* Malden, MA: Blackwell.

Bennett, A. T. D., Cuthill, I. C., Partridge, J. C., & Maier, E. J. (1996). Ultraviolet vision and mate choice in zebra finches. *Nature, 380,* 433–435.

Benson, H. (2000). *The relaxation response.* New York: Avon Books.

Ben-Zvi A., Vernon S. D., & Broderick G. (2009). Model-based therapeutic correction of hypothalamic-pituitary-adrenal axis dysfunction. *PLoS Computational Biology, 5,* e1000273. doi:10.1371/journal.pcbi.1000273

Berenbaum, S. A., Blakemore, J. E. O., & Beltz, A. M. (2011). A role for biology in gender-related behavior. *Sex Roles, 64,* 804–825.

Berg, K. S., Delgado, S., Cortopassi, K. A., Beissinger, S. R., & Bradbury, J. W. (2012). Vertical transmission of learned signatures in a wild parrot. *Proceedings of the Royal Society of London, B, 279,* 585–591.

Berger, W., Coutinho, E. S. F., Figueira, I., Marques-Portella, C., Luz, M. P., Neylan, T. C., . . . Mendlowicz, M. V. (2011). Rescuers at risk: A systematic review and meta-regression analysis of the worldwide current prevalence and correlates of PTSD in rescue workers. *Social Psychiatry and Psychiatric Epidemiology, 47,* 1001–1011.

Bergh, C., Sjöstedt, S., Hellers, G., Zandian, M., & Södersten, P. (2003). Meal size, satiety and cholecystokinin in gastrectomized humans. *Physiology & Behavior, 78,* 143–147.

Berkeley Lab. (n.d.). *Electromagetic spectrum* Retrieved February 16, 2013, from http://www.lbl.gov/MicroWorlds/ALSTool/EMSpec/EMSpec2.html

Bernard, L. L. (1926). *An introduction to social psychology.* New York: Henry Holt.

Bernier, A., Carlson, S. M., & Whipple, N. (2010). From external regulation to self-regulation: Early parenting precursors of young children's executive functioning. *Child Development, 81,* 326–229.

Berry, J. W. (1997). Immigration, acculturation, and adaptation. *Applied Psychology: An International Review, 46,* 5–68.

Berscheid, E. (2010). Love in the fourth dimension. *Annual Review of Psychology, 61,* 1–25.

Berthoz, S., Blair, R. J. R., Le Clec'h, G., & Martinot, J.-L. (2002). Emotions: From neuropsychology to functional imaging. *International Journal of Psychology, 37,* 193–203.

Besedovsky, L., Lange, T., & Born, J. (2012). Sleep and immune function. *Pflügers Archiv—European Journal of Physiology, 463,* 1–17.

Betsch, C., & Sachse, K. (2013). Debunking vaccination myths: Strong risk negations can increase perceived vaccination risks. *Health Psychology, 32,* 145–155. doi:10.1037/a0027387

Bezdjian, S., Baker, L. A., & Tuvblad, C. (2011). Genetic and environmental influences on impulsivity: A meta-analysis of twin, family and adoption studies. *Clinical Psychology Review, 31,* 1209–1223.

Bezdjian, S., Tuvblad, C., Raine, A., & Baker, L. A. (2011). The genetic and environmental covariation among psychopathic personality traits, and reactive and proactive aggression in childhood. *Child Development, 82,* 1267–1281.

Bialystok, E. (2011). Reshaping the mind: The benefits of bilingualism. *Canadian Journal of Experimental Psychology, 65,* 229–235.

Bihm, E. M., Gillaspy, J. A., Lammers, W. J., & Huffman, S. P. (2010). IQ zoo and teaching operant concepts. *Psychological Record, 60,* 523–526.

Bikle, D. D. (2004). Vitamin D and skin cancer. *Journal of Nutrition, 134,* 3472S–3478S.

Blackmore, S. J. (2005). *Consciousness: A very short introduction.* New York: Oxford University Press.

Blackwell, B., Marley, E., Price, J., & Taylor, D. (1967). Hypertensive interactions between monoamine oxidase inhibitors and foodstuffs. *British Journal of Psychiatry, 113,* 349–365.

Blair, C., & Raver, C. C. (2012). Child development in the context of adversity: Experiential canalization of brain and behavior. *American Psychologist, 67,* 309–318. doi:10.1037/a0027493

Blanchard, R. (2008). Review and theory of handedness, birth order, and homosexuality in men. *Laterality, 13,* 51–70.

Blasi, A. (1980). Bridging moral cognition and moral action: A critical review of the literature. *Psychological Bulletin, 88,* 1–45.

Blass, T. (1991). Understanding behavior in the Milgram obedience experiment: The role of personality, situations, and their interactions. *Journal of Personality and Social Psychology, 60,* 398–413.

Blass, T. (1999). The Milgram paradigm after 35 years: Some things we now know about obedience to authority. *Journal of Applied Social Psychology, 25,* 955–978.

Blatchley, B., & O'Brien, K. R. (2007). Deceiving the participant: Are we creating the reputational spillover effect? *North American Journal of Psychology, 9,* 519–534.

Blickenstaff, J. C. (2005). Women and science careers: Leaky pipeline or gender filter? *Gender and Education, 17,* 369–386.

Bloch, M. H., McGuire, J., Landeros-Weisenberger, A., Leckman, J. F., & Pittenger, C. (2010). Meta-analysis of the dose-response relationship of SSRI in obsessive-compulsive disorder. *Molecular Psychiatry, 15,* 850–855.

Block, C. J., Koch, S. M., Liberman, B. E., Merriweather, T. J., & Roberson, L. (2011). Contending with stereotype threat at work: A model of long-term responses. *Counseling Psychologist, 39,* 570–600.

Blumenthal, H., Leen-Feldner, E. W., Babson, K. A., Gahr, J. L., Trainor, C. D., & Frala, J. L. (2011). Elevated social anxiety among early maturing girls. *Developmental Psychology, 47,* 1133–1140.

Boccella, K. (2012, May 6). Blindness is no barrier for Center City triathlete. *The Philadelphia Inquirer.* Retrieved from http://articles.philly.com/2012-05-06/news/31587179_1_husband-retinal-cancer-guide/3

Boeve, B. F., Silber, M. H., Saper, C. B., Ferman, T. J., Dickson, D. W., Parisi, J. E., . . . Braak, H. (2007). Pathophysiology of REM sleep behaviour disorder and relevance to neurodegenerative disease. *Brain, 130,* 2770–2788.

Bold, K. W., Yoon, H., Chapman, G. B., & McCarthy, D. E. (2013). Factors predicting smoking in a laboratory-based smoking-choice task. *Experimental and Clinical Psychopharmacology, 21,* 133–143. doi:10.1037/a0031559

Bolen, R. M., & Scannapieco, M. (1999). Prevalence of child sexual abuse: A corrective meta-analysis. *Social Service Review, 73,* 281–313.

Bolton, P., Bass, J., Betancourt, T., Speelman, L., Onyango, G., Clougherty, K. F., . . . Verdeli, H. (2007). Interventions for depression symptoms among adolescent survivors of war and displacement in northern Uganda. *Journal of the American Medical Association, 298,* 519–527.

Bonanno, G. A., Brewin, C. R., Kaniasty, K., & La Greca, A. M. (2010). Weighing the costs of disaster: Consequences, risks, and resilience in individuals, families, and communities. *Psychological Science in the Public Interest, 11,* 1–49.

Bonanno, G. A., Westphal, M., & Mancini, A. D. (2011). Resilience to loss and potential trauma. *Annual Review of Clinical Psychology, 7,* 1.1–1.25.

Bond, R., & Smith, P. B. (1996). Culture and conformity: A meta-analysis of studies using Asch's (1952b, 1956) line judgment task. *Psychological Bulletin, 119,* 111–137.

Bonnie, R. J., & Scott, E. S. (2013). The teenage brain: Adolescent brain research and the law. *Current Directions in Psychological Science, 22,* 158–161.

Borges, G., Nock, M. K., Abad, J. M. H., Hwang, I., Sampson, N. A., Alonso, J., . . . Kessler, R. C. (2010). Twelve month prevalence of and risk factors for suicide attempts in the WHO world mental health surveys. *Journal of Clinical Psychiatry, 71,* 1617–1628.

Boring, E. G. (1953). A history of introspection. *Psychological Bulletin, 50,* 169–189.

Born, J., Rasch, B., & Gais, S. (2006). Sleep to remember. *Neuroscientist, 12,* 410–424.

Bornstein, R. F. (2005). Reconnecting psychoanalysis to mainstream psychology: Challenges and opportunities. *Psychoanalytic Psychology, 22,* 323–340.

Borota, D., Murray, E., Keceli, G., Chang, A., Watabe, J. M., Ly, M., Toscano, J. P., & Yassa, M. A. (2014). Post-study caffeine administration enhances memory consolidation in humans. *Nature Neuroscience, 17,* 201–203.

Borra, J. E. (2005). Roper v. Simmons. *Journal of Gender, Social Policy, & the Law, 13,* 707–715.

Bottos, S. H., & Dewey, D. (2004). Perfectionists' appraisal of daily hassles and chronic headache. *Headache, 44,* 772–779.

Bouton, M. E., Mineka, S., & Barlow, D. H. (2001). A modern learning theory perspective on the etiology of panic disorder. *Psychological Review, 108,* 4–32.

Bowden, C. L., Calabrese, J. R., McElroy, S. L., Gyulai, L., Wassef, A., Petty, F., . . . Wozniak, P. J. (2000). A randomized, placebo-controlled 12-month trial of divalproex and lithium in treatment of outpatients with bipolar I disorder. *Archives of General Psychiatry, 57,* 481–489.

Bower, G. H., Clark, M. C., Lesgold, A. M., & Winzenz, D. (1969). Hierarchical retrieval schemes and recall of categorized word lists. *Journal of Verbal Learning and Verbal Behavior, 8,* 323–343.

Bower, G. H., Gilligan, S. G., & Menteiro, K. P. (1981). Selectivity of learning caused by affective states. *Journal of Experimental Psychology: General, 110,* 451–473.

Bower, J. M., & Parsons, L. M. (2003, July 14). Rethinking "the lesser brain." *Scientific American, 289,* 51–57. Retrieved from http://www.scientificamerican.com/article.cfm?id=rethinking-the-lesser-bra

Bowers, J. S., Mattys, S. L., & Gage, S. H. (2009). Preserved implicit knowledge of a forgotten childhood language. *Psychological Science, 20,* 1064–1069.

Bowman, L. L., Levine, L. E., Waite, B. M., & Gendron, M. (2010). Can students really multitask? An experimental study of instant messaging while reading. *Computers & Education, 54,* 927–931.

Bradley, L. A. (2011). Culture, gender and clothing. *Paideusis-Journal for Interdisciplinary and Cross-Cultural Studies, 5,* A1–A6.

Brain Observatory. (2013). *Deconstructing Henry: The re-examination of the brain of patient H.M.* University of San Diego. Retrieved from http://thebrainobservatory.ucsd.edu/hm

Brand, B. L., Classen, C. C., McNary, S. W., & Zaveri, P. (2009). A review of dissociative disorders treatment studies. *Journal of Nervous and Mental Disorders, 197,* 646–654.

Brandone, A. C., Salkind, S. J., Golinkoff, R. M., & Hirsh-Pasek, K. (2006). Language development. In G. G. Bear & K. M. Minke (Eds.), *Children's needs III: Development, prevention, and intervention* (pp. 499–514). Washington, DC: National Association of School Psychologists.

Brandt, J., & Benedict, R. H. B. (1993). Assessment of retrograde amnesia: Findings with a new public events procedure. *Neuropsychology, 7,* 217–227.

Brascamp, J. W., Blake, R., & Kristjánsson, A. (2011). Deciding where to attend: Priming of pop-out drives target selection. *Journal of Experimental Psychology: Human Perception and Performance, 37,* 1700–1707.

Braun, J. W. (2015). Orlando Bloom Biography. *IMDB.* Retrieved from http://www.imdb.com/name/nm0089217/bio

Breazeal, C., & Scassellati, B. (2002). Robots that imitate humans. *Trends in Cognitive Sciences, 6,* 481–487.

Breland, K., & Breland, M. (1951). A field of applied animal psychology. *American Psychologist, 6,* 202–204.

Breland, K., & Breland, M. (1961). The misbehavior of organisms. *American Psychologist, 16,* 681–684.

Brendgen, M., Dionne, G., Girard, A., Boivin, M., Vitaro, F., & Pérusse, D. (2005). Examining genetic and environmental effects on social aggression: A study of 6-year-old twins. *Child Development, 76,* 930–946.

Brent, R. L. (2004). Environmental causes of human congenital malformations: The pediatrician's role in dealing with these complex clinical problems caused by a multiplicity of environmental and genetic factors. *Pediatrics, 113,* 957–968.

Breus, M. J. (2009, May 6). Are you fooling yourself? [Huffpost Healthy Living]. *Huffington Post.* Retrieved from http://www.huffingtonpost.com/dr-michael-jbreus/are-you-fooling-yourself_b_198525.html

Bridge, H., Harrold, S., Holmes, E. A., Stokes, M., & Kennard, C. (2012). Vivid visual mental imagery in the absence of the primary visual cortex. *Journal of Neurology, 259,* 1062–1070.

Briggs, K. C., & Myers, I. B. (1998). *Myers–Briggs type indicator.* Palo Alto, CA: Consulting Psychologists Press.

British Broadcasting Corporation [BBC]. (2014, September 17). *Dr Money and the boy with no penis—programme transcript.* Retrieved from http://www.bbc.co.uk/sn/tvradio/programmes/horizon/dr_money_trans.shtml

Broadbelt, K. G., Paterson, D. S., Rivera, K. D., Trachtenberg, F. L., & Kinney, H. C. (2010). Neuroanatomic relationships between the GABAergic and serotonergic systems in the developing human medulla. *Autonomic Neuroscience: Basic & Clinical, 154,* 30–41.

Broderick, A. C., Coyne, M. S., Fuller, W. J., Glen, F., & Godley, B. J. (2007). Fidelity and over-wintering of sea turtles. *Proceedings of the Royal Society B: Biological Sciences, 274,* 1533–1538.

Brody, S. (2010). The relative health benefits of different sexual activities. *Journal of Sexual Medicine, 7,* 1336–1361.

Brody, S., & Costa, R. M. (2009). Satisfaction (sexual, life, relationship, and mental health) is associated directly with penile-vaginal intercourse, but inversely with other sexual behavior frequencies. *Journal of Sexual Medicine, 6,* 1947–1954.

Brogaard, P., & Marlow, K. (2012, December 11). Kim Peek, the real rain man. *Psychology Today.* Retrieved from http://www.psychologytoday.com/blog/the-superhuman-mind/201212/kim-peek-the-real-rain-man

Brotto, L. A. (2010). The DSM diagnostic criteria for hypoactive sexual desire disorder in men. *Journal of Sex Medicine, 7,* 2015–2030.

Brown, A. S., & Nix, L. A. (1996). Age-related changes in the tip-of-the-tongue experience. *American Journal of Psychology, 109,* 79–91.

Brown, A. S., & Patterson, P. H. (2011). Maternal infection and schizophrenia: Implications for prevention. *Schizophrenia Bulletin, 37,* 284–290.

Brown, P. K., & Wald, G. (1964). Visual pigments in single rods and cones of the human retina. *Science, 144,* 45.

Brown, R., & Kulik, J. (1977). Flashbulb memories. *Cognition, 5,* 73–99.

Brown, S. L, Nesse, R. M., Vinokur, A. D., & Smith, D. M. (2003). Providing social support may be more beneficial than receiving it: Results from a prospective study of mortality. *Psychological Science, 14,* 320–327.

Brown, T. T., & Dobs, A. S. (2002). Endocrine effects of marijuana. *Journal of Clinical Pharmacology, 42,* 90S–96S.

Brownell, P. (2010). *Gestalt therapy: A guide to contemporary practice.* New York: Springer.

Brunstein, J. C. (1993). Personal goals and subjective well-being: A longitudinal study. *Journal of Personality and Social Psychology, 65,* 1061–1070.

Bryan, A., Hutchison, K. E., Seals, D. R., & Allen, D. L. (2007). A transdisciplinary model integrating genetic, physiological, and psychological, psychological correlates of voluntary exercise. *Health Psychology, 26,* 30–39.

Bryan, S. M. (2012, January 28). Wolves' senses tapped to keep them clear of cattle. *Bangor Daily News.* Retrieved from http://bangordailynews.com/2012/01/28/outdoors/wolves-senses-tapped-to-keep-them-clear-of-cattle/

Buck, R. (1980). Nonverbal behavior and the theory of emotion: The facial feedback hypothesis. *Journal of Personality and Social Psychology, 38,* 811–824.

Buffardi, L. E., & Campbell, W. K. (2008). Narcissism and social networking web sites. *Personality and Social Psychology Bulletin, 34,* 1303–1314.

Bui, N. H. (2012). False consensus in attitudes toward celebrities. *Psychology of Popular Media Culture, 1,* 236–243. doi:10.1037/a0028569

Bulpitt, C. J., Markowe, H. L. J., & Shipley, M. J. (2001). Why do some people look older than they should? *Postgraduate Medical Journal, 77,* 578–581.

Bureau of Labor Statistics, U.S. Department of Labor. (2012–2013). *Occupational outlook handbook.* Retrieved from http://www.bls.gov/ooh

Burgaleta, M., Head, K., Alvarez-Linera, J., Martinez, K., Escorial, S., Haier, R., & Colom, R. (2012). Sex differences in brain volume are related to specific skills, not to general intelligence. *Intelligence, 40,* 60–68.

Burger, J. M. (2009). Replicating Milgram: Would people still obey today? *American Psychologist, 64,* 1–11.

Burger, J. M. (2011). *Personality* (8th ed.). Belmont, CA: Wadsworth, Cengage Learning.

Burkley, M. (2012, January 3). Is Lisbeth Salander a psychopath? *Psychology Today.* Retrieved from http://www.psychologytoday.com/blog/the-social-thinker/201201/is-lisbeth-salander-psychopath

Burlingame, G. M., & Baldwin, S. (2011). Group therapy. In J. C. Norcross, G. R. VandenBos, & D. K. Freedheim (Eds.), *History of psychotherapy: Continuity and change* (2nd ed., pp. 505–515). Washington, DC: American Psychological Association.

Burnette, J. L., Pollack, J. M., & Forsyth, D. R. (2011). Leadership in extreme contexts: A groupthink analysis of the May 1996 Mount Everest disaster. *Journal of Leadership Studies, 4,* 29–40.

Burton, H. (2003). Visual cortex activity in early and late blind people. *Journal of Neuroscience, 23,* 4005–4011.

Bushdid, C., Magnasco, M. O., Vosshall, L. B., & Keller, A. (2014). Humans can discriminate more than 1 trillion olfactory stimuli. *Science, 343,* 1370–1372.

Buss, D. M. (1989). Sex differences in human mate preferences: Evolutionary hypotheses tested in 37 cultures. *Behavioral and Brain Sciences, 12,* 1–14.

Buss, D. M. (1995). Psychological sex differences: Origins through sexual selection. *American Psychologist, 50,* 164–168.

Buss, D. M., Shackelford, T. K., Kirkpatrick, L. A., & Larsen, R. J. (2001). A half century of mate preferences: The cultural evolution of values. *Journal of Marriage and Family, 63,* 491–503.

Buss, L., Tolstrup, J., Munk, C., Bergholt, T., Ottensen, B., Grønbæk, M., & Kjaer, S. K. (2006). Spontaneous abortion: A prospective cohort study of younger women from the general population in Denmark. Validation, occurrence and risk determinants. *Acta Obstetricia et Gynecologic, 85,* 467–475.

Bussey, K., & Bandura, A. (1999). Social cognitive theory of gender development and differentiation. *Psychological Review, 106,* 676–713.

Butcher, J. N., & Rouse, S. V. (1996). Personality: Individual differences and clinical assessment. *Annual Review of Psychology, 47,* 87–111.

Butler, R. A. (1960). Acquired drives and the curiosity-investigative motives. In R. H. Waters, D. A. Rethlingshafer, & W. E. Caldwell (Eds.), *Principles of comparative psychology* (pp. 144–176). McGraw-Hill Series in Psychology. New York: McGraw-Hill.

Byers, E. S. (2011). Beyond the birds and the bees and was it good for you?: Thirty years of research on sexual communication. *Canadian Psychology, 52,* 20–28.

Bynum, H. (2007). Anesthesia and the practice of medicine: Historical perspectives. *Journal of the American Medical Association, 298,* 2551–2552.

Cabanatuan, M., & Sebastian, S. (2005, October 19). Surfer fights off shark, escapes with bitten leg. *SFGate.com.* Retrieved from http://articles.sfgate.com/2005-10-19/news/17396469_1_salmon-creek-beach-shark-deputies

Cahill, L. (2012). His brain, her brain. *Scientific American Classics Mind, 1,* 40–47.

Caldicott, D. G., Mahajani R., & Kuhn M. (2001). The anatomy of a shark attack: A case report and review of the literature. *Injury, 32,* 445–453.

Callan, M. J., Ferguson, H. J., & Bindemann, M. (2013). Eye movements to audiovisual scenes reveal expectations of a just world. *Journal of Experimental Psychology: General, 142,* 34–40. doi:10.1037/a0028261

Campbell, A. (1999). Staying alive: Evolution, culture, and women's intrasexual aggression. *Behavioral and Brain Sciences, 22,* 203–252.

Campbell, G. A., & Rosner, M. H. (2008). The agony of ecstasy: MDMA (3,4-Methylenedioxymethamphetamine) and the kidney. *Clinical Journal of the American Society of Nephrology, 3,* 1852–1860.

Canli, T., Amin, Z., Haas, B., Omura, K., & Constable, R. T. (2004). A double dissociation between mood states and personality traits in the anterior cingulate. *Behavioral Neuroscience, 118,* 897–904.

Cannon, D. S., Baker, T. B., Gino, A., & Nathan, P. E. (1986). Alcohol-aversion therapy: Relation between strength of aversion and abstinence. *Journal of Consulting and Clinical Psychology, 54,* 825–830.

Cannon, W. B. (1927). The James-Lange theory of emotions: A critical examination and an alternative theory. *American Journal of Psychology, 39,* 106–124.

Cannon, W. B., & Washburn, A. L. (1912). An explanation of hunger. *American Journal of Physiology, 29,* 441–454.

Cantero, J. L., Atienza, M., Salas, R. M., & Gómez, C. M. (1999). Alpha EEG coherence in different brain states: An electrophysiological index of the arousal level in human subjects. *Neuroscience Letters, 271,* 167–170.

Card, N. A., Stucky, B. D., Sawalani, G. M., & Little, T. D. (2008). Direct and indirect aggression during childhood and adolescence: A meta-analytic review of gender differences, intercorrelations, and relations to maladjustment. *Child Development, 79,* 1185–1229.

Carey, B. (2008, December 4). H.M., an unforgettable amnesiac, dies at 82. *The New York Times.* Retrieved from http://www.nytimes.com/2008/12/05/us/05hm.html?pagewanted=all&_r=0

Carlsson, K., Petersson, K. M., Lundqvist, D., Karlsson, A., Ingvar, M., & Öhman, A. (2004). Fear and the amygdala: Manipulation of awareness generates differential cerebral responses to phobic and fear-relevant (but nonfeared) stimuli. *Emotion, 4,* 340–353.

Carnegie Mellon University. (2013). *Carnegie Mellon Robotic Performance Company presents Tank: Roboceptionist.* Retrieved from http://roboceptionist.org/index.htm

Carnevale, A. P., Rose, S. J., & Cheah, B. (2011). *The college payoff: Education, occupations, lifetime earnings.* Georgetown University Center on Education and the Workforce. Retrieved from https://www2.ed.gov/policy/highered/reg/hearulemaking/2011/collegepayoff.pdf

Carpenter, C. J. (2012). Narcissism on Facebook: Self-promotional and anti-social behavior. *Personality and Individual Differences, 52,* 482–486.

Carr, P. B., Dweck, C. S., & Pauker, K. (2012). "Prejudiced" behavior without prejudice? Beliefs about the malleability of prejudice affect interracial interactions. *Journal of Personality and Social Psychology, 103,* 452–471.

Carskadon, M. A., Labyak, S. E., Acebo, C., & Seifer, R. (1999). Intrinsic circadian period of adolescent humans measured in conditions of forced desynchrony. *Neuroscience Letters, 260,* 129–132.

Carstensen, L. L., Turan, B., Scheibe, S., Ram, N., Ersner-Hershfield, H., Samanez-Larkin, G. R., . . . Nesselroade, J. R. (2011). Emotional experience improves with age: Evidence based on over 10 years of experience sampling. *Psychology and Aging, 26,* 21–33.

Carter, C. J. (2007). eIF2B and oligodendrocyte survival: Where nature and nurture meet in bipolar disorder and schizophrenia? *Schizophrenia Bulletin, 33,* 1343–1353.

Carter Center. (2013). *Development of mental health services in Liberia.* Retrieved from http://www.cartercenter.org/resources/pdfs/factsheets/mental-health-liberia-facts.pdf

Caruso, R. (2007, August 13). Why does it take so long for our vision to adjust to a darkened theater after we come in from bright sunlight? *Scientific American Online.* Retrieved from http://www.scientificamerican.com/article.cfm?id=experts-eyes-adjust-to-darkness

Case, B. G., Bertollo, D. N., Laska, E. M., Price, L. H., Siegel, C. E., Olfson, M., & Marcus, S. C. (2013). Declining use of electroconvulsive therapy in United States general hospitals. *Biological Psychiatry, 73,* 119–126.

Caspi, A., Roberts, B. W., & Shiner, R. L. (2005). Personality development: Stability and change. *Annual Review of Psychology, 56,* 453–484.

Cassidy, J. (2001). Truth, lies, and intimacy: An attachment perspective. *Attachment & Human Development, 3,* 121–155.

Castel, A. D., Humphreys, K. L., Lee, S. S., Galván, A., Balota, D. A., & McCabe, D. P. (2011). The development of memory efficiency and value-directed remembering across the life span: A cross-sectional study of memory and selectivity. *Developmental Psychology, 47,* 1553–1564.

Castellanos, M., Sobrino, T., Pedraza, S., Moldes, O., Pumar, J. M., Silva, Y., . . . Dávalos, A. (2008). High plasma glutamate concentrations are associated with infarct growth in acute ischemic stroke. *Neurology, 71,* 1862–1868.

Catalino, L. I., & Fredrickson, B. L. (2011). A Tuesday in the life of a flourisher: The role of positive emotional reactivity in optimal mental health. *Emotion, 11,* 938–950.

Cattell, R. B. (1950). *Personality: A systematic theoretical and factual study.* New York: McGraw-Hill.

Cattell, R. B. (1973a). *Personality and mood by questionnaire.* San Francisco: Jossey-Bass.

Cattell, R. B. (1973b). Personality pinned down. *Psychology Today, 7,* 40–46.

Cattell, R. B., Eber, H. W., & Tatsuoka, M. M. (1970). *Handbook for the sixteen personality factor questionnaire (16PF).* Champaign, IL: Institute for Personality and Ability Testing.

Cavallini, A., Fazzi, E., Viviani, V., Astori, M. G., Zaverio, S., Bianchi, P. E., & Lanzi, G. (2002). Visual acuity in the first two years of life in healthy term newborns: An experience with the teller acuity cards. *Functional Neurology, 17,* 87–92.

CBS News. (2011, February 10). *Chilean miners rescued, but were they saved?* Retrieved from http://www.cbsnews.com/news/chilean-miners-rescued-but-were-they-saved-10-02-2011/

CBS News. (2011, July 26). *Shark survivor girl: "I like dolphins way better."* Retrieved from http://www.cbsnews.com/stories/2011/07/26/earlyshow/living/petplanet/main20083393.shtml

CBS News/AP. (2010, October 12). *Florencio Avalos: The first miner chosen.* Retrieved from http://www.cbsnews.com/stories/2010/10/12/world/main6951753.shtml

CBS News/AP. (2010, October 16). Miners' fistfights, despair during ordeal. Retrieved from http://www.cbsnews.com/stories/2010/10/15/earlyshow/main6961011.shtml

Ceci, S., & Williams, W. M. (2009). Yes: The scientific truth must be pursued. *Nature, 457,* 788–789.

Centers for Disease Control and Prevention [CDC]. (2004). Alcohol-attributable deaths and years of potential life lost—United States, 2001. *Morbidity and Mortality Weekly Report, 53,* 866–870.

Centers for Disease Control and Prevention [CDC]. (2008). *Nationally representative CDC study finds 1 in 4 teenage girls has a sexually transmitted disease* [Press release]. Retrieved from http://www.cdc.gov/stdconference/2008/press/release-11march2008.htm

Centers for Disease Control and Prevention [CDC]. (2010). Vital signs: Current cigarette smoking among adults aged ≥18 Years—United States, 2009. *Morbidity and Mortality Weekly Report, 59,* 1135–1140.

Centers for Disease Control and Prevention [CDC]. (2011, February 11). *Effects of Blood Alcohol Concentration (BAC).* Retrieved February 20, 2013, from http://www.cdc.gov/Motorvehiclesafety/Impaired_Driving/bac.html

Centers for Disease Control and Prevention [CDC]. (2012). *Sexually transmitted disease surveillance 2011.* Retrieved from http://www.cdc.gov/std/stats11/

Centers for Disease Control and Prevention [CDC]. (2013). *Incidence, prevalence, and cost of sexually transmitted infections in the United States* [Fact sheet]. Retrieved from http://www.cdc.gov/std/stats/STI-Estimates-Fact-Sheet-Feb-2013.pdf

Centers for Disease Control and Prevention [CDC]. (2014a). *Chlamydia* [Fact sheet]. Retrieved from http://www.cdc.gov/std/chlamydia/STDFact-chlamydia-detailed.htm

Centers for Disease Control and Prevention [CDC]. (2014b). *Genital herpes* [Fact sheet]. Retrieved from http://www.cdc.gov/std/Herpes/STDFact-Herpes.htm

Centers for Disease Control and Prevention [CDC]. (2014c). *Gonorrhea* [Fact sheet]. Retrieved from http://www.cdc.gov/std/gonorrhea/STDFact-gonorrhea.htm

Centers for Disease Control and Prevention [CDC]. (2014d). *Health effects of secondhand smoke* [Fact sheet]. Retrieved from http://www.cdc.gov/tobacco/data_statistics/fact_sheets/secondhand_smoke/health_effects/

Centers for Disease Control and Prevention [CDC]. (2015). *Genital HPV infection* [Fact sheet]. Retrieved from http://www.cdc.gov/std/HPV/STDFact-HPV.htm

Centola, D. (2010). The spread of behavior in an online social network experiment. *Science, 329,* 1194–1197.

Cervilla, J. A., Prince, M., Joels, S., Lovestone, S., & Mann, A. (2000). Long-term predictors of cognitive outcome in a cohort of older people with hypertension. *British Journal of Psychiatry, 177,* 66–71.

Chaiken, S., & Eagly, A. H. (1976). Communication modality as a determinant of message persuasiveness and message comprehensibility. *Journal of Personality and Social Psychology, 34,* 605–614.

Chaimay, B. (2011). Influence of breastfeeding practices on children's cognitive development—systematic review. *Asia Journal of Public Health, 2,* 40–44.

Champagne, F. A., & Mashoodh, R. (2009). Genes in context: Gene-environment interplay and the origins of individual differences in behavior. *Current Directions in Psychological Science, 18,* 127–131.

Chandrashekar, J., Hoon, M. A., Ryba, N. J., & Zuker, C. S. (2006). The receptors and cells for mammalian taste. *Nature, 444,* 288–294.

Charlton, B., & Verghese, A. (2010). Caring for Ivan Ilyich. *Journal of General Internal Medicine, 25,* 93–95.

Chawla, D., Agarwal, R., Deorari, A., Paul, V. K., Chandra, P., & Azad, R. V. (2012). Retinopathy of prematurity. *Indian journal of Pediatrics, 79,* 501–509.

Chechik, G., Meilijson, I., & Ruppin, E. (1998). Synaptic pruning in development: A computational account. *Neural Computation, 10,* 1759–1777.

Cheng, C., Cheung, S.-F., Chio, J. H.-M., & Chan, M.-P. S. (2013). Cultural meaning of perceived control: A meta-analysis of locus of control and psychological symptoms across 18 cultural regions. *Psychological Bulletin 139,* 152–188. doi:10.1037/a0028596

Cheng, D. T., Knight, D. C., Smith, C. N., & Helmstetter, F. J. (2006). Human amygdala activity during the expression of fear responses. *Behavioral Neuroscience, 120,* 1187–1195.

Cherney, I. D. (2008). Mom, let me play more computer games: They improve my mental rotation skills. *Sex Roles, 59,* 776–786.

Cheyne, J. A. (2002). Situational factors affecting sleep paralysis and associated hallucinations: Position and timing effects. *Journal of Sleep Research, 11,* 169–177.

Cheyne, J. A., Newby-Clark, I. R., & Rueffer, S. D. (1999). Relations among hypnagogic and hypnopompic experiences associated with sleep paralysis. *Journal of Sleep Research, 8,* 313–317.

Chiao, J. Y., Iidka, T., Gordon, H. L., Nogawa, J., Bar, M., Aminoff, E., . . . Ambady, N. (2008). Cultural specificity in amygdala response to fear faces. *Journal of Cognitive Neuroscience, 20,* 2167–2174.

Child Mind Institute. (2010, October 18). *Orlando Bloom on dyslexia.* Retrieved from http://www.childmind.org/en/posts/articles/2010-10-18-orlando-bloom-on-growing-up-with-dyslexia

Chin, H. B., Sipe, T. A., Elder, R., Mercer, S. L., Chattopadhyay, S. K., Jacob, V., . . . Santelli, J. (2012). The effectiveness of group-based comprehensive risk-reduction and abstinence education interventions to prevent or reduce the risk of adolescent pregnancy, human immunodeficiency virus, and sexually transmitted infections: Two systematic reviews for the Guide to Community Preventive Services. *American Journal of Preventive Medicine, 42,* 272–294.

Chirawatkul, S., Prakhaw, P., & Chomnirat, W. (2011). Perceptions of depression among people of Khon Kaen City: A gender perspective. *Journal of Nursing Science & Health, 34,* 66–75.

Cho, H. J., Meira-Lima, I., Cordeiro, Q., Michelon, L., Sham, P., Vallada, H., & Collie., D. A. (2005). Population-based and family-based studies on the serotonin transporter gene polymorphisms and bipolar disorder: A systematic review and meta-analysis. *Molecular Psychiatry, 10,* 771–781.

Choi, C. (2007, May 24). Strange but true: When half a brain is better than a whole one. *Scientific American Online.* Retrieved from http://www.scientificamerican.com/article/strange-but-true-when-half-brain-better-than-whole/

Choi, C. Q. (2008, March). Do you need only half your brain? *Scientific American, 298,* 104.

Chomsky, N. (1959). Verbal behavior. *Language, 35,* 26–58.

Chomsky, N. (2000). *New horizons in the study of language and mind.* Cambridge, UK: Cambridge University Press.

Christakis, D. A., Garrison, M. M., Herrenkohl, T., Haggerty, K., Rivara, F. P., Zhou, C., & Liekweg, K. (2013). Modifying media content for preschool children: A randomized controlled trial. *Pediatrics, 131,* 431–438.

Chua, A. (2011, January 8). Why Chinese mothers are superior. *The Wall Street Journal.* Retrieved from http://online.wsj.com/article/SB10001424052748704111504576059713528698754.html

Chung, F., & Elsaid, H. (2009). Screening for obstructive sleep apnea before surgery: Why is it important? *Current Opinion in Anesthesiology, 22,* 405–411.

Cialdini, R. B., & Goldstein, N. J. (2004). Social influence: Compliance and conformity. *Annual Review of Psychology, 55,* 591–621.

Cisler, J. M., Brady, R. E., Olatunji, B. O., & Lohr, J. M. (2010). Disgust and obsessive beliefs in contamination-related OCD. *Cognitive Therapy Research, 34,* 439–448.

Clapp, W. C., Rubens, M. T., Sabharwal, J., & Gazzaley, A. (2011). Deficit in switching between functional brain networks underlies the impact of multitasking on working memory in older adults. *Proceedings of the National Academy of Sciences, 108,* 7212–7217.

Clark, D. M., Ehlers, A., Hackmann, A., McManus, F., Fennell, M., Grey, N., . . . Wild, J. (2006). Cognitive therapy versus exposure and applied relaxation in social phobia: A randomized controlled trial. *Journal of Consulting and Clinical Psychology, 74,* 568–578.

Clark, D. M., Salkovskis, P. M., Öst, L-G., Breitholtz, E., Koehler, K. A., Westling, B. E., . . . Gelder, M. (1997). Misinterpretation of body sensations in panic disorder. *Journal of Consulting and Clinical Psychology, 65,* 203–213.

Clemente, M., Espinosa, P., & Vidal, M. Á. (2008). The media and violent behavior in young people: Effects of the media on antisocial aggressive behavior in a Spanish sample. *Journal of Applied Social Psychology, 38,* 2395–2409.

Coan, J. A. (2010). Emergent ghosts of the emotion machine. *Emotion Review, 2,* 274–285.

Cochrane, R. E., Tett, R. P., & Vandecreek, L. (2003). Psychological testing and the selection of police officers: A national survey. In Curt R. Bartol and Anne M. Bartol (Eds.), *Current perspectives in forensic psychology and criminal justice* (pp. 25–34). Thousand Oaks, CA: SAGE.

Cohen, D. (2011). Applied knowledge: NASA aids the Chilean rescue effort. *ASK Magazine, 41,* 5–9.

Cohen, D. A., Wang, W., Wyatt, J. K., Kronauer, R. E., Dijk, D. J., Czeisler, C. A., & Klerman, E. B. (2010). Uncovering residual effects of chronic sleep loss on human performance. *Science Translational Medicine, 13,* 14ra3.

Cohen, H. W., Gibson, G., & Alderman, M. H. (2000). Excess risk of myocardial infarction in patients treated with antidepressant medications: Association with use of tricyclic agents. *American Journal of Medicine, 108,* 2–8.

Cohen, S., Miller, G. E., & Rabin, B. S. (2001). Psychological stress and antibody response to immunization: A critical review of the human literature. *Psychosomatic Medicine, 63,* 7–18.

Colapinto, J. (2000). *As nature made him: The boy who was raised as a girl.* New York: HarperCollins.

Cole, C. F., Labin, D. B., & del Rocio Galarza, M. (2008). Begin with the children: What research on *Sesame Street's* international coproductions reveals about using media to promote a new more peaceful world. *International Journal of Behavioral Development, 32*(4), 359–365.

Collins, D. W., & Kimura, D. (1997). A large sex difference on a two-dimensional mental rotation task. *Behavioral Neuroscience, 111,* 845–849.

Collins, P. A., & Gibbs, A. C. C. (2003). Stress in police officers: A study of the origins, prevalence and severity of stress-related symptoms within a county police force. *Occupational Medicine, 53,* 256–264.

Colrain, I. M. (2005). The k-complex: A 7-decade history. *SLEEP, 28,* 255–273.

Comas-Diaz, L. (2006). Latino healing: The integration of ethnic psychology into psychotherapy. *Psychotherapy: Theory, Research, Practice, Training, 43,* 436–453.

Compton, W. M., Grant, B. F., Colliver, J. D., Glantz, M. D., & Stinson, F. S. (2004). Prevalence of marijuana use disorders in the United States: 1991–1992 and 2001–2002. *Journal of the American Medical Association, 291,* 2114–2121.

Cone, B. K., Wake, M., Tobin, S., Poulakis, Z., & Rickards, F. W. (2010). Slight–mild sensorineural hearing loss in children: Audiometric, clinical, and risk factor profiles. *Ear and Hearing, 31,* 202–212.

Congdon, E., Service, S., Wessman, J., Seppänen, J. K., Schönauer, S., Miettunen, J., . . . Nelson B. (2012). Early environment and neurobehavioral development predict adult temperament clusters. *PLoS ONE, 7,* e38065. doi:10.1371/journal.pone.0038065

Conley, A. M. (2012). Patterns of motivation beliefs: Combining achievement goal and expectancy-value perspectives. *Journal of Educational Psychology, 104,* 32–47.

Conway, M. A., Cohen, G., & Stanhope, N. (1991). On the very long-term retention of knowledge acquired through formal education: Twelve years of cognitive psychology. *Journal of Experimental Psychology: General, 120,* 395–409.

Copeland, W., Shanahan, L., Costello, J., & Angold, A. (2011). Cumulative prevalence of psychiatric disorders by young adulthood: A prospective cohort analysis from the Great Smoky Mountain Study. *Journal of the American Academy of Child & Adolescent Psychiatry, 50,* 252–261.

Corballis, P. M. (2003). Visuospatial processing and the right-hemisphere interpreter. *Brain and Cognition, 53,* 171–176.

Corballis, P. M., Funnell, M. G., & Gazzaniga, M. S. (2002). Hemispheric asymmetries for simple visual judgments in the split brain. *Neuropsychologia, 40,* 401–410.

Coren, S. (2008, October 20). Can dogs see colors? *Psychology Today.* Retrieved from https://www.psychologytoday.com/blog/canine-corner/200810/can-dogs-see-colors

Corey, G. (2013). *Theory and practice of counseling and psychotherapy* (9th ed.). Belmont, CA: Brooks/Cole, Cengage Learning.

Corkin, S. (2002). What's new with the amnesic patient H.M.? *Nature Reviews Neuroscience, 3,* 153–160.

Cornelius, S. W., & Caspi, A. (1987). Everyday problem solving in adulthood and old age. *Psychology and Aging, 2,* 144–153.

Correll, C. U., Leucht, S., & Kane, J. M. (2004). Lower risk for tardive dyskinesia associated with second-generation antipsychotics: A systematic review of 1-year studies. *American Journal of Psychiatry, 161,* 414–425.

Corrigan, P. (2005). How stigma interferes with mental health care. *American Psychologist, 59,* 614–625.

Corti, R., Binggeli, C., Sudano, I., Spieker, L., Hanseler, E., Ruschitzka, F., . . . Noll, G. (2002). Coffee acutely increases sympathetic nerve activity and blood pressure independently of caffeine content: Role of habitual versus non habitual drinking. *Circulation, 106,* 2935–2940.

Corwin, E. J., & Pajer, K. (2008). The psychoneuroimmunology of postpartum depression. *Journal of Women's Health, 17,* 1529–1534.

Costa, G. (2003). Shift work and occupational medicine: An overview. *Occupational Medicine, 53,* 83–88.

Costa, P. T. Jr., Terracciano, A., & McCrae, R. R. (2001). Gender differences in personality traits across cultures: Robust and surprising findings. *Journal of Personality and Social Psychology, 81,* 322–331.

Costandi, M. (2009, February 10). Where are old memories stored in the brain? *Scientific American Online.* Retrieved from http://www.scientificamerican.com/article/the-memory-trace/

Costanzo, E. S., Lutgendorf, S. K., & Roeder, S. L. (2011). Common-sense beliefs about cancer and health practices among women completing treatment for breast cancer. *Psychooncology, 20,* 53–61.

Cotman, C. W., & Berchtold, N. C. (2002). Exercise: A behavioral intervention to enhance brain health and plasticity. *Trends in Neurosciences, 25,* 295–301.

Coulson, S., & Van Petten, C. (2007). A special role for the right hemisphere in metaphor comprehension? ERP evidence from hemifield presentation. *Brain Research, 1146,* 128–145.

Couperus, J. W. (2011). Perceptual load influences selective attention across development. *Developmental Psychology, 47,* 1431–1439.

Cowan, N. (1988). Evolving conceptions of memory storage, selective attention, and their mutual constraints within the human information-processing system. *Psychological Bulletin, 104,* 163–191.

Cowan, N. (2008). What are the differences between long-term, short-term, and working memory? *Progress in Brain Research, 169,* 323–338.

Cowan, N., Chen, Z., & Rouder, J. N. R. (2004). Constant capacity in an immediate serial-recall task: A logical sequel to Miller (1956). *Psychological Science, 15,* 634–640.

Cowan, N., Nugent, L. D., & Elliott, E. M. (2000). Memory-search and rehearsal processes and the word length effect in immediate recall: A synthesis in reply to service. *Quarterly Journal of Experimental Psychology, 53,* 666–670.

Craddock, N., O'Donovan, M. C., & Owen, M. J. (2005). The genetics of schizophrenia and bipolar disorder: Dissecting psychosis. *Journal of Medical Genetics, 42,* 193–204.

Craik, F. I. M., & Lockhart, R. S. (1972). Levels of processing: A framework for memory research. *Journal of Verbal Learning and Verbal Behavior, 11,* 671–684.

Craik, F. I. M., & Tulving, E. (1975). Depth of processing and the retention of words in episodic memory. *Journal of Experimental Psychology, 104,* 268–294.

Cramer, P. (2000). Defense mechanisms in psychology today: Further processes for adaptation. *American Psychologist, 55,* 637–646.

Cramer, P. (2008). Identification and the development of competence: A 44-year longitudinal study from late adolescence to late middle age. *Psychology and Aging, 23,* 410–421.

Craske, M. G., Kircanski, K., Epstein, A., Wittchen, H.-U., Pine, D. S., Lewis-Fernandez, R. . . . DSM-V Anxiety, OC Spectrum, Posttraumatic and Dissociative Disorder Work Group. (2010). Panic disorder: A review of *DSM-IV* panic disorder and proposals for *DSM-V. Depression and Anxiety, 27,* 93–112.

Craze, M., & Crooks, N. (2010, October 13). Chile frees 12 of 33 miners in underground rescue *Bloomberg.com.* Retrieved from http://www.bloomberg.com/news/2010-10-13/chile-frees-first-of-33-miners-in-world-s-longest-underground-mine-rescue.html

Crick, N. R., & Grotpeter, J. K. (1995). Relational aggression, gender, and social-psychological adjustment. *Child Development, 66,* 710–722.

Croce, P. J. (2010). Reaching beyond Uncle William: A century of William James in theory and in life. *History of Psychology, 13,* 351–377.

Crowell, S. E., Beauchaine, T. P., & Linehan, M. M. (2009). A biosocial developmental model of borderline personality: Elaborating and extending Linehan's theory. *Psychological Bulletin, 135,* 495–510.

Cunha, J. P., & Stöppler, M. C. (Eds.). (2011). Jetlag. *MedicineNet.com.* Retrieved from http://www.medicinenet.com/jet_lag/article.htm

Cunningham, M., & Cox, E. O. (2003). Hearing assessment in infants and children: Recommendations beyond neonatal screening. *Pediatrics, 111,* 436–440.

Cunningham, M. R., Shamblen, S. R., Barbee, A. P., & Ault, L. K. (2005). Social allergies in romantic relationships: Behavioral repetition, emotional sensitization, and dissatisfaction in dating couples. *Personal Relationships, 12,* 273–295.

Curtiss, S., Fromkin, V., Krashen, S., Rigler, D., & Rigler, M. (1974). The linguistic development of Genie. *Language, 50,* 528–554.

Cyna, A. M., McAuliffe, G. L., & Andrew, M. I. (2004). Hypnosis for pain relief in labour and childbirth: A systematic review. *British Journal of Anesthesia, 93,* 505–511.

Cynkar, A. (2007). The changing gender composition of psychology. *Monitor on Psychology, 38,* 46. Retrieved from http://www.apa.org/monitor/jun07/changing.aspx

Cyrzyk, T. (2013). Electroconvulsive therapy: Why it is still controversial. *Mental Health Practice, 16,* 22–27.

Czarnowski, C., Bailey, J., & Bal, S. (2007). Curare and a Canadian connection. *Canadian Family Physician, 53,* 1531–1532.

Czeisler, C. A., Duffy, J. F., Shanahan, T. L., Brown, E. N., Mitchell, J. F., Rimmer, D. W., . . . Kronauer, R. E. (1999). Stability, precision, and near-24-hour period of the human circadian pacemaker. *Science, 284,* 2177–2181.

Daffner, K. R., Chong, H., Riis, J., Rentz, D. M., Wolk, D. A., Budson, A. E., & Holcomb, P. J. (2007). Cognitive status impacts age-related changes in attention to novel and target events. *Neuropsychology, 21,* 291–300.

Dalrymple, T. (2012). *Jeremy Lin: The reason for the Linsanity.* New York: Center Street.

Dalton, P. H., Opiekun, R. E., Gould, M., McDermott, R., Wilson, T., Maute, C., . . . Moline, J. (2010, May 18). Chemosensory loss: Functional consequences of the World Trade Center disaster. *Environmental Health Perspectives, 118,* 1251–1256. doi:10.1289/ehp.1001924

Damasio, A. R., Grabowski, T. J., Bechara, A., Damasio, H., Ponto, L. L. B., Parvizi, J., & Hichwa, R. D. (2000). Subcortical and cortical brain activity during the feeling of self-generated emotions. *Nature Neuroscience, 3,* 1049–1056.

Damasio, H., Grabowski, T., Frank, R., Galaburda, A. M., & Damasio, A. R. (1994). The return of Phineas Gage: Clues about the brain from the skull of a famous patient. *Science, 264,* 1102–1105.

D'Angiulli, A., Lipina, S. J., & Olesinska, A. (2012, September 6). Explicit and implicit issues in the developmental cognitive neuroscience of social inequality. *Frontiers in Human Neuroscience,* Article 254. Retrieved from http://www.ncbi.nlm.nih.gov/pmc/articles/PMC3434357/pdf/fnhum-06-00254.pdf

Dang-Vu, T. T., Schabus, M., Desseilles, M., Albouy, G., Boly, M., Darsaud, A., . . . Maquet, P. (2008). Spontaneous neural activity during human slow wave sleep. *Proceeding of the National Academy of Sciences, 105,* 15160–15165.

Danker, J. F., & Anderson, J. R. (2010). The ghosts of brain states past: Remembering reactivates the brain regions engaged during encoding. *Psychological Bulletin, 136,* 87–102.

Dapretto, M., Lee, S. S., & Caplan, R. (2005). A functional magnetic resonance imaging study of discourse coherence in typically developing children. *NeuroReport, 16,* 1661–1665.

Darcy, A. M., Doyle, A. C., Lock, J., Peebles, R., Doyle, P., & Le Grange, D. (2012). The eating disorders examination in adolescent males with anorexia nervosa: How does it compare to adolescent females? *International Journal of Eating Disorders, 45,* 110–114.

Darley, J. M., & Latané, B. (1968). Bystander intervention in emergencies: Diffusion of responsibility. *Journal of Personality and Social Psychology, 8,* 377–383.

Dar-Nimrod, I., & Heine, S. J. (2011). Genetic essentialism: On the deceptive determinism of DNA. *Psychological Bulletin, 137,* 800–818.

Darwin, C. (1872/2002). *The expression of the emotions in man and animals.* New York: Oxford University Press.

Davidson, R. J., Kabat-Zinn, J., Schumacher, J., Rosenkranz, M., Muller, D., Santorelli, S. F., . . . Sheridan, J. F. (2003). Alterations in brain and immune function produced by mindfulness meditation. *Psychosomatic Medicine, 65,* 564–570.

Davidson, R. J., & Lutz, A. (2008). Buddha's brain: Neuroplasticity and meditation. *IEEE Signal Process Magazine, 25,* 176–174.

Davidson, R. J., Scherer, K. R., & Goldsmith, H. H. (Eds.). (2002). *Handbook of affective sciences.* New York: Oxford University Press.

d'Avila, J., Lam, T., Bingham, D., Shi, J., Won, S., Kauppinen, T., . . . Swanson, R. (2012). Microglial activation induced by brain trauma is suppressed by post-injury treatment with a PARP inhibitor. *Journal of Neuroinflammation, 9,* 31–42.

Davis, E. P., & Sandman, C. A. (2010). The timing of prenatal exposure to maternal cortisol and psychosocial stress is associated with human infant cognitive development. *Child Development, 81,* 131–148.

Davis, M., & Whalen, P. J. (2001). The amygdala: Vigilance and emotion. *Molecular Psychiatry, 6,* 13–34.

Deary, I. J., Penke, L., & Johnson, W. (2010). The neuroscience of human intelligence differences. *Nature Reviews Neuroscience, 11,* 201–211.

de Boysson-Bardies, B., Halle, P., Sagart, L., & Durand, C. (1989). A cross-linguistic investigation of vowel formats in babbling. *Journal of Child Language, 16,* 1–17.

DeCasper, A. J., & Fifer, W. P. (1980). Of human bonding: Newborns prefer their mothers' voices. *Science, 208,* 1174–1176.

Deci, E. L., Koestner, R., & Ryan, R. M. (1999). A meta-analytic review of experiments examining the effects of extrinsic rewards on intrinsic motivation. *Psychological Bulletin, 125,* 627–668.

Deci, E. L., Koestner, R., & Ryan, R. M. (2001). Extrinsic rewards and intrinsic motivation in education: Reconsidered once again. *Review of Educational Research, 71,* 1–27.

Deci, E. L., & Ryan, R. M. (2008). Self-determination theory: A macrotheory of human motivation, development, and health. *Canadian Psychology, 49,* 182–185.

Deckers, L. (2005). *Motivation: Biological, psychological, and environmental* (2nd ed.). New York: Pearson.

Decoz, H. (2011, April 18). Meet the master numbers. *Numerology.com.* Retrieved from http://www.numerology.com/numerology-news/master-numbers

Deeb, S. S. (2005). The molecular basis of variation in human color vision. *Clinical Genetics, 67,* 369–377.

Deer, B. (2011). How the case against the MMR vaccine was fixed. *British Medical Journal, 342,* 77–82.

Deese, J., & Kaufman, R. A. (1957). Serial effects in recall of unorganized and sequentially organized verbal material. *Journal of Experimental Psychology, 54,* 180–187.

Degenhardt, L., & Hall, W. (2012). Extent of illicit drug use and dependence, and their contribution to the global burden of disease. *Lancet, 379,* 55–70.

Degnan, K. A., Hane, A. A., Henderson, H. A., Moas, O. L., Reeb-Sutherland, B. C., & Fox, N. A. (2011). Longitudinal stability of temperamental exuberance and social-emotional outcomes in early childhood. *Developmental Psychology, 47,* 765–780.

Del Giudice, M., Booth, T., & Irwing, P. (2012). The distance between Mars and Venus: Measuring global sex differences in personality. *PLoS ONE, 7*(1), e29265. doi:10.1371/journal.pone.0029265

de Hoog, N., Strobe, W., & de Wit, J. B. F. (2007). The impact of vulnerability to and severity of a health risk on processing and acceptance of fear-arousing communications: A meta-analysis. *Review of General Psychology, 11,* 258–285.

de Lauzon-Guillain, B., Wijndaele, K., Clark, M., Acerini, C. L., Hughes, I. A., Dunger, D. B., . . . Ong, K. K. (2012). Breastfeeding and infant temperament at age three months. *PLoS ONE, 7*(1), e29326. doi:10.1371/journal.pone.0029326

DeLongis, A., Coyne, J. C., Dakof, G., Folkman, S., & Lazarus, R. S. (1982). Relationship of daily hassles, uplifts, and major life events to health status. *Health Psychology, 1,* 119–136.

DeLongis, A., Folkman, S., & Lazarus, R. S. (1988). The impact of daily stress on health and mood: Psychological and social resources as mediators. *Journal of Personality and Social Psychology, 54,* 486–495.

Dement, W., & Kleitman, N. (1957). The relation of eye movements during sleep to dream activity: An objective method for the study of dreaming. *Journal of Experimental Psychology, 53,* 339–346.

Démonet, J.-F., Taylor, M. J., & Chaix, Y. (2004). Developmental dyslexia. *Lancet, 363,* 1451–1460.

Denollet, J., & Conraads, V. M. (2011). Type D personality and vulnerability to adverse outcomes in heart disease. *Cleveland Clinic Journal of Medicine, 78,* S13–S19.

Derringer, J., Krueger, R. F., Dick, D. M., Saccone, S., Grucza, R. A., Agrawal, A., . . . Bierut, L. J. (2010). Predicting sensation seeking from dopamine genes: A candidate system approach. *Psychological Science, 21,* 1282–1290.

Desai, M., Pratt, L. A., Lentzner, H., & Robinson, K. N. (2001). Trends in vision and hearing among older Americans. *Aging Trends, 2,* 1–8. Hyattsville, MD: National Center for Health Statistics. Retrieved from http://www.cdc.gov/nchs/data/ahcd/agingtrends/02vision.pdf

Desco, M., Navas-Sanchez, F. J., Sanchez-González, J., Reig, S., Robles, O., Franco, C., . . . Arango, C. (2011). Mathematically gifted adolescents use more extensive and more bilateral areas of the fronto-parietal network than controls during executive functioning and fluid reasoning tasks. *NeuroImage, 57,* 281–292.

Deslandes, A., Moraes, H., Ferreira, C., Veiga, H., Silverira, H., Mouta, R., . . . Laks, J. (2009). Exercise and mental health: Many reasons to move. *Neuropsychobiology, 59,* 191–198.

Despins, L. A., Scott-Cawiezell, J., & Rouder, J. N. (2010). Detection of patient risk by nurses: A theoretical framework. *Journal of Advanced Nursing, 66,* 465–474.

DeValois, R. L., & DeValois, K. K. (1975). Neural coding of color. *Handbook of Perception, 5,* 117–166.

Devaney, S. A., Palomaki, G. E., Scott, J. A., & Bianchi, D. W. (2011). Non-invasive fetal sex determination using cell-free fetal DNA. *Journal of American Medical Association, 306,* 627–636.

DeWall, C. N., Baumeister, R. F., & Vohs, K. D. (2008). Satiated with belong-ingness? Effects of acceptance, rejection, and task framing on self-regulatory per-formance. *Journal of Personality Social Psychology, 95,* 1367–1382.

Dewar, M., Alber, J., Butler, C., Cowan, N., & Della Sala, S. (2012). Brief wakeful resting boosts new memories over the long term. *Psychological Science, 23,* 955–960.

Diamond, E. L. (1982). The role of anger and hostility in essential hypertension and coronary heart disease. *Psychological Bulletin, 92,* 410–433.

Diamond, M. (2004). Sex, gender, and identity over the years: A changing perspective. *Child and Adolescent Psychiatric Clinics of North America, 13,* 591–607.

Diamond, M., & Sigmundson, H. K. (1997). Sex reassignment at birth: Long-term review and clinical implications. *Archives of Pediatric & Adolescent Medicine, 151,* 298–304.

Dickens, W. T., & Flynn, J. R. (2001). Heritability estimates vs. large environ-mental effects: The IQ paradox resolved. *Psychological Review, 108,* 346–369.

Dickens, W. T., & Flynn, J. R. (2006). Black Americans reduce the racial IQ gap: Evidence from standardization samples. *Psychological Science, 17,* 913–920.

Dickerson, F. B., Tenhula, W. N., & Green-Paden, L. D. (2005). The token economy for schizophrenia: Review of the literature and recommendations for future research. *Schizophrenia Research, 75,* 405–416.

Diekelmann, S., & Born, J. (2010). The memory function of sleep. *Nature Reviews Neuroscience, 11,* 114–126.

Diener, E. (1979). Deindividuation, self-awareness, and disinhibition. *Journal of Personality and Social Psychology, 3,* 1160–1171.

Diener, E., Fraser, S. C., Beaman, A. L., & Kelem, R. T. (1976). Effects of deindividuation variables on stealing among Halloween trick-or-treaters. *Journal of Personality and Social Psychology, 33,* 178–183.

Diener, E., Lucas, R. E., & Scollon, C. N. (2006). Beyond the hedonic tread-mill. *American Psychologist, 6,* 305–314.

DiLalla, L. F. (2002). Behavior genetics of aggression in children: Review and future directions. *Developmental Review, 22,* 593–622.

Di Lorenzo, L., De Pergola, G., Zocchetti, C., L'Abbate, N., Basso, A., Pan-nacciulli, N., . . . Soleo, L. (2003). Effect of shift work on body mass index: Results of a study performed in 319 glucose-tolerant men working in a Southern Italian industry. *International Journal of Obesity, 21,* 1353–1358.

Dimberg, U., Thunberg, M., & Elmehed, K. (2000). Unconscious facial reac-tions to emotional facial expressions. *Psychological Science, 11,* 86–89.

Dimsdale, J. E. (2008). Psychological stress and cardiovascular disease. *Journal of the American College of Cardiology, 51,* 1237–1247.

DiSalvo, D. (2010, January/February). Are social networks messing with your head? *Scientific American Mind, 20,* 48–55.

Dixon, J. F., & Hokin, L. E. (1998). Lithium acutely inhibits and chroni-cally up-regulates and stabilizes glutamate uptake by presynaptic nerve endings in mouse cerebral cortex. *Proceedings of the National Academy of Sciences, 95,* 8363–8368.

Dobkin, B. H. (2005). Rehabilitation after stroke. *New England Journal of Medi-cine, 352,* 1677–1684.

Doherty-Sneddon, G. (2008). The great baby signing debate. *Psychologist, 21,* 300–303. doi:10.1371/journal.pone.0029265

Dolbier, C. L., & Rush, T. E. (2012). Efficacy of abbreviated progressive muscle relaxation in a high-stress college sample. *International Journal of Stress Manage-ment, 19,* 48–68.

Dolder, C. R., & Nelson, M. H. (2008). Hypnosedative-induced complex behaviors: Incidence, mechanisms and management. *CNS Drugs, 22,* 1172–7047.

Dollard, J., Miller, N. E., Doob, L. W., Mowrer, O. H., & Sears, R. R. (1939). *Frustration and aggression.* New Haven, CT: Yale University Press.

Domhoff, G. W. (2001). A new neurocognitive theory of dreams. *Dreaming, 11,* 13–33.

Donlan, W., & Lee, J. (2010). Coraje, nervios, and susto: Culture-bound syndromes and mental health among Mexican migrants in the United States. *Advances in Mental Health, 9,* 288–302.

Dorgan, B. L. (2010). The tragedy of Native American youth suicide. *Psychologi-cal Services, 7,* 213–218.

Dougherty, D. M., & Lewis, P. (1991). Stimulus generalization, discrimination learning, and peak shift in horses. *Journal of the Experimental Analysis of Behav-ior, 56,* 97–104.

Dougherty, L. R., Klein, D. N., Olino, T. M., Dyson, M., & Rose, S. (2009). Increased waking salivary cortisol and depression risk in preschoolers: The role of maternal history of melancholic depression and early child temperament. *Journal of Child Psychology Psychiatry, 50,* 1495–1503.

Dovidio, J. F., Kawakami, K., & Gaertner, S. L. (2002). Implicit and explicit prejudice and interracial interaction. *Journal of Personality and Social Psychology, 82,* 62–68.

Drace, S., Ric, F., & Desrichard, O. (2010). Affective biases in likelihood per-ception: A possible role of experimental demand in mood-congruence effects. *International Review of Social Psychology, 23*(1), 93–109.

Drake, C., Roehrs T., Shambroom, J., & Roth, T. (2013). Caffeine effects on sleep taken 0, 3, or 6 hours before going to bed. *Journal of Clinical Sleep Medi-cine, 9,* 1195–1200.

Driver, H. S., & Taylor, S. R. (2000). Exercise and sleep. *Sleep Medicine Reviews, 4,* 387–402.

drjilltaylor.com. (2010). *Dr. Jill Bolte Taylor.* Retrieved from http://drjilltaylor. com/about.html

Druckman, D., & Bjork, R. A. (Eds.). (1994). *Learning, remembering, believ-ing: Enhancing human performance* [Study conducted by the National Research Council]. Washington, DC: National Academy Press.

Drug Abuse Warning Network. (2011). *Drug Abuse Warning Network, 2011: National estimates of drug-related emergency department visits.* Retrieved from http://www.samhsa.gov/data/2k13/DAWN2k11ED/DAWN2k11ED.htm#high

Drug Enforcement Administration. (2012). *Rohypnol* [Fact sheet]. Retrieved from http://www.justice.gov/dea/druginfo/drug_data_sheets/Rohypnol.pdf

Druss, B. G., Hwang, I., Petukhova, M., Sampson, N. A., Wang, P. S., & Keller, R. C. (2009). Impairment in role functioning in mental and chronic medical disorders in the United States: Results from the National Comorbidity Survey Replication. *Molecular Psychiatry, 14,* 728–737.

Duckworth, A. L., & Seligman, M. E. P. (2005). Self-discipline outdoes IQ in predicting academic performance of adolescents. *Psychological Science, 16,* 939–944.

Duckworth, A. L., Weir, D., Tsukayama, E., & Kwok, D. (2012). Who does well in life? Conscientious adults excel in both objective and subjective success. *Frontiers in Psychology, 3* (356). doi:10.3389/fpsyg.2012.00356

Dugas, M. J., Brillon, P., Savard, P., Turcotte, J., Gaudet, A., Ladouceur, R., . . . Gervais, N. J. (2010). A randomized clinical trial of cognitive-behavioral therapy and applied relaxation for adults with generalized anxiety disorder. *Behav-ioral Therapies, 41,* 46–58.

Duijts, S. F. A., Zeegers, M. P. A., & Borne, B. V. (2003). The association between stressful life events and breast cancer risk: A meta-analysis. *International Journal of Cancer, 107,* 1023–1029. doi:10.1002/ijc.11504

Dunlosky, J., Rawson, K. A., Marsh, E. J., Nathan, M. J., & Willingham, D. T. (2013). Improving students' learning with effective learning techniques promising directions from cognitive and educational psychology. *Psychological Science in the Public Interest, 14,* 4–58.

Durante, K. M., Griskevicius, V., Simpson, J. A., Cantú, S. M., & Li, N. P. (2012, August). Ovulation leads women to perceive sexy cads as good dads. *Journal of Personality and Social Psychology, 103*(2), 292–305.

Dusek, J. A., Out, H. H., Wohlhueter, A. L., Bhasin, M., Zerbini, L. F., Joseph, M. G., . . . Libermann, T. A. (2008). Genomic counter-stress changes induced by the relaxation response. *PLoS ONE, 3,* e2576. doi:10.1371/journal.pone.0002576

Dyer, A. G., Neumeyer, C., & Chittka, L. (2005). Honeybee (*Apis mellifera*) vision can discriminate between and recognise images of human faces. *Journal of Experimental Biology, 208,* 4709–4714.

Eagly, A. H., & Crowley, M. (1986). Gender and helping behavior: A meta-analytic review of the social psychological literature. *Psychological Bulletin, 100,* 283–308.

Eastwick, P. W., Eagly, A. H., Finkel, E. J., & Johnson, S. E. (2011). Implicit and explicit preferences for physical attractiveness in a romantic partner: A double dissociation in predictive validity. *Journal of Personality and Social Psychology, 101,* 993–1011.

Eaton, N. R., Keyes, K. M., Krueger, R. F., Balsis, S., Skodol, A. E., Markon, K. E., . . . Hasin, D. S. (2012). An invariant dimensional liability model of gender differences in mental disorder prevalence: Evidence from a national sample. *Journal of Abnormal Psychology, 121,* 282–288.

Ebbinghaus, H. (1885/1913). *Memory: A contribution to experimental psychology.* H. A. Ruger & C. E. Bussenius (Trans.). New York: Teachers College, Columbia University.

eBizMBA. (2015). Top 15 most popular social networking sites: March 2015. Retrieved March 28, 2015 from http://www.ebizmba.com/articles/social-networking-websites

Ebrahim, I. O., Shapiro, C. M., Williams, A. J., & Fenwick, P. B. (2013). Alcohol and sleep I: Effects on normal sleep. *Alcoholism: Clinical and Experimental Research, 37,* 539–549.

Eckert, M. A., Keren, N. I., Roberts, D. R., Calhoun, V. D., & Harris, K. C. (2010). Age-related changes in processing speed: Unique contributions of cerebellar and prefrontal cortex. *Frontiers in Human Neuroscience, 4,* 1–14.

Eckstein, D., Aycock, K. J., Sperber, M. A., McDonald, J., Van Wiesner, V. III, Watts, R. E., & Ginsburg, P. (2010). A review of 200 birth-order studies: Lifestyle characteristics. *Journal of Individual Psychology, 6,* 408–434.

Eden, G. F., Jones, K. M., Cappell, K., Gareau, L., Wood, F. B., Zeffiro, T. A., . . . Flowers, D. L. (2004). Neural changes following remediation in adult developmental dyslexia. *Neuron, 44,* 411–422.

Editors of The Lancet. (2010). Retraction—Ileal-lymphoid-nodular hyperplasia, non-specific colitis, and pervasive developmental disorder in children. *Lancet, 375,* 445.

Egan, S. K., & Perry, D. G. (2001). Gender identity: A multidimensional analysis with implications for psychosocial adjustment. *Developmental Psychology, 37,* 451–463.

Eichenbaum, H. (2004). Hippocampus: Cognitive processes and neural representations that underlie declarative memory. *Neuron, 44,* 109–120.

Eisenberger, N. I., Lieberman, M. D., & Satpute, A. B. (2005). Personality from a controlled processing perspective: An fMRI study of neuroticism, extraversion, and self-consciousness. *Cognitive, Affective, & Behavioral Neuroscience, 5,* 169–181.

Ekman, P. (1992). Are there basic emotions? *Psychological Review, 99,* 550–553.

Ekman, P. (2003). *Emotions revealed.* New York: Times Books.

Ekman, P., & Friesen, W. V. (1971). Constants across cultures in the face and emotion. *Journal of Personality and Social Psychology, 17,* 124–129.

Ekman, P., Friesen, W. V., O'Sullivan, M., Chan, A., Diacoyanni-Tarlatzis, I., Heider, K., . . . Tzavaras, A. (1987). Universals and cultural differences in the judgments of facial expressions of emotion. *Journal of Personality and Social Psychology, 53,* 712–717.

El Ansary, M., Steigerwald, I., & Esser, S. (2003). Egypt: Over 5000 years of pain management—Cultural and historic aspects. *Pain Practice, 3,* 84–87.

Elder, C. R., Gullion, C. M., Funk, K. L., DeBar, L. L., Lindberg, N. M., & Stevens, V. J. (2012). Impact of sleep, screen time, depression and stress on weight change in the intensive weight loss phase of the LIFE study. *International Journal of Obesity, 36,* 86–92.

Elkind, D. (1967). Egocentrism in adolescence. *Child development, 38,* 1025–1034.

Elliott, D. B., Krivickas, K., Brault, M. W., & Kreider, R. M. (2012). *Historical marriage trends from 1890–2010: A focus on race differences.* Paper presented at Annual Meeting of the Population Association of America, San Francisco, May 3–5, 2012.

Ellis, A., & Dryden, W. (1997). *The practice of rational emotive behavior therapy* (2nd ed.). New York: Springer.

El Mansari, M., Guiard, B. P., Chernoloz, O., Ghanbari, R., Katz, N., & Blier, P. (2010). Relevance of norepinephrine-dopamine interactions in the treatment of major depressive disorder. *CNS Neuroscience & Therapeutics, 16,* e1–e17.

Else-Quest, N. M., Higgins, A., Allison, C., & Morton, L. C. (2012). Gender differences in self-conscious emotional experience: A meta-analysis. *Psychological Bulletin, 138,* 947–981.

Emmons, R. A., & McCullough, M. E. (2003). Counting blessings versus burdens: An experimental investigation of gratitude and subjective well-being in daily life. *Journal of Personality and Social Psychology, 84,* 377–389. doi:10.1037/0022-3514.84.2.377

Endicott, L., Bock, T., & Narvaez, D. (2003). Moral reasoning, intercultural development, and multicultural experiences: Relations and cognitive underpinnings. *International Journal of Intercultural Relations, 27,* 403–419.

Enea, V., & Dafinoiu, I. (2009). Motivational/solution-focused intervention for reducing school truancy among adolescents. *Journal of Cognitive and Behavioral Psychotherapies, 9,* 185–198.

Engel de Abreu, P. M., Cruz-Santos, A., Tourinho, C. J., Martin, R., & Bialystok, E. (2012). Bilingualism enriches the poor: Enhanced cognitive control in low-income minority children. *Psychological Science, 23,* 1364–1371.

Epstein, L., & Mardon, S. (2007). *The Harvard Medical School guide to a good night's sleep.* New York: McGraw Hill.

Erickson, K. I., Voss, M. W., Prakash, R. S., Basak, C., Szabo, A., Chaddock, L., . . . Kramer, A. F. (2011). Exercise training increases size of hippocampus and improves memory. *Proceedings of the National Academy of Sciences, 108*(7), 3017–3022.

Erickson-Schroth, L. (2010). The neurobiology of sex/gender-based attraction. *Journal of Gay & Lesbian Mental Health, 14,* 56–69.

Ericsson, K. A. (2003). The acquisition of expert performance as problem solving. In J. E. Davidson & R. J. Sternberg (Eds.), *The psychology of problem solving* (pp. 31–83). Cambridge, UK: Cambridge University Press.

Erikson, E. H. (1993). *Childhood and society.* New York: W. W. Norton.

Erikson, E. H., & Erikson, J. M. (1997). *The life cycle completed.* New York: W. W. Norton.

Eriksson, P. S., Perfilieva, E., Bjork-Eriksson, T., Alborn, A. M., Nordborg, C., Peterson, D. A., & Gage, F. H. (1998). Neurogenesis in the adult human hippocampus. *Nature Medicine, 4,* 1313–1317.

Ernst, C., & Angst, J. (1983). *Birth order: Its influence on personality.* Berlin: Springer Verlag.

ESPN.com. (2012, February 10). *Jeremy Lin pours in career-best 38 points, leads Knicks past Lakers.* Retrieved from http://scores.espn.go.com/nba/recap?gamdd=320210018

ESPN.com. (2015). *Jeremy Lin.* Retrieved from http://espn.go.com/nba/player/_/id/4299/jeremy-lin

Etaugh, C. (2008). Women in the middle and later years. In F. L. Denmark and M. Paludi (Eds.), *Psychology of women: Handbook of issues and theories* (2nd ed., pp. 271–302). Westport, CT: Praeger.

Evans, V., & Green, M. (2006). *Cognitive linguistics: An introduction.* Mahwah, NJ: Erlbaum.

Exner, J. E. (1980). But it's only an inkblot. *Journal of Personality Assessment, 44,* 562–577.

Exner, J. E. (1986). *The Rorschach: A comprehensive system* (Vol. 1, 2nd ed.). New York: John Wiley & Sons.

Eysenck, H. J. (1967). *The biological basis of personality.* Springfield, IL: C.C. Thomas.

Eysenck, H. J. (1990). Biological dimensions of personality. In L. A. Pervin (Ed.), *Handbook of personality: Theory of research* (pp. 244–276). New York: Guilford Press.

Eysenck, H. J., & Eysenck, B. G. (1968). *Manual for the Eysenck Personality Inventory.* San Diego, CA: Educational Industrial Testing Service.

Facebook. (2015). Newsroom: Company info. Retrieved March 28, 2015 from http://newsroom.fb.com/company-info/

Facebook Help Center. (2015). What is the maximum number of friends that we can add on Facebook? Retrieved April 2, 2015 from https://www.facebook.com/help/community/question/?id=567604083305019

Falk, D., Lepore, F. E., & Noe, A. (2012, November 14). The cerebral cortex of Albert Einstein: A description and preliminary analysis of unpublished photographs. *Brain.* doi:10.1093/brain/aws295

Fancher, R. E., & Rutherford, A. (2012). *Pioneers of psychology: A history* (4th ed.). New York: W. W. Norton.

Fantini, M. L., Corona, A., Clerici, S., & Ferini-Strambi, L. (2005). Aggressive dream content without daytime aggressiveness in REM sleep behavior disorder. *Neurology, 65,* 1010–1015.

Farha, B. (2007). *Paranormal claims: A critical analysis.* Lanham, MD: University Press of America.

Farmer, R. F., Kosty, D. B., Seeley, J. R., Olino, T. M., & Lewinsohn, P. M. (2013). Aggregation of lifetime axis I psychiatric disorders through age 30: Incidence, predictors, and associated psychosocial outcomes. *Journal of Abnormal Psychology, 122,* 573–586.

Farthing, G. W. (1992). *The psychology of consciousness.* Upper Saddle River, NJ: Prentice Hall.

Fay, A. J., & Maner, J. K. (2014). When does heat promote hostility? Person by person situation interactions shape the psychological effects of haptic sensations. *Journal of Experimental Social Psychology, 50,* 210–216.

Faymonville, M. E., Laureys, S., Degueldre, C., DelFiore, G., Luxen, A., Franck, G., . . . Maquet, P. (2000). Neural mechanisms of antinociceptive effects of hypnosis. *Anesthesiology, 2,* 1257–1267.

Fazel, S., Gulati, G., Linsell, L., Geddes, J. R., & Grann, M. (2009). Schizophrenia and violence: Systematic review and meta-analysis. *PLOS Med, 6,* e1000120. doi:10.1371/journal.pmed.1000120

Feinstein, J. S., Adolphs, R., Damasio, A., & Tranel, D. (2011). The human amygdala and the induction and experience of fear. *Current Biology, 21,* 34–38.

Feis, D. L., Brodersen, K. H., von Cramon, D. Y., Luders, E., & Tittgemeyer, M. (2013). Decoding gender dimorphism of the human brain using multimodal anatomical and diffusion MRI data. *NeuroImage, 70,* 250–257.

Feist, G. J. (2004). Creativity and the frontal lobes. *Bulletin of Psychology and the Arts, 5,* 21–28.

Feldman, R., Eidelman, A. I., Sirota, L., & Weller, A. (2002). Comparison of skin-to-skin (kangaroo) and traditional care: Parenting outcomes and preterm infant development. *Pediatrics, 110,* 16–26.

Fennis, B. M., & Janssen, L. (2010). Mindlessness revisited: Sequential request techniques foster compliance by draining self-control resources. *Current Psychology, 29,* 235–246.

Ferguson, C. J. (2010). Genetic contributions to antisocial personality and behavior: A meta-analytic review from an evolutionary perspective. *Journal of Social Psychology, 150,* 160–180.

Ferrer, E., Shaywitz, B. A., Holahan, J. M., Marchione, K., & Shaywitz, S. E. (2010). Uncoupling of reading and IQ over time: Empirical evidence for a definition of dyslexia. *Psychological Science, 21,* 93–101.

Ferris, P. A., Kline, T. J. B., & Bourdage, J. S. (2012). He said, she said: Work, biopsychosocial, and lifestyle contributions to coronary heart disease risk. *Health Psychology, 31,* 503–511.

Fessler, D. M. T., & Abrams, E. T. (2004). Infant mouthing behavior: The immunocalibration hypothesis. *Medical Hypotheses, 63,* 925–932.

Festinger, L. (1957). *A theory of cognitive dissonance.* New York: Harper & Row.

Festinger, L., & Carlsmith, J. M. (1959). Cognitive consequences of forced compliance. *Journal of Abnormal and Social Psychology, 58,* 203–210.

Festinger, L., Schachter, S., & Back, K. (1950). *Social pressures in informal groups: A study of human factors in housing.* Stanford, CA: Stanford University Press.

Feyerick, D., & Steffen, S. (2009, April 8). "Sexting" lands teen on sex offender list. *CNN.* Retrieved from http://www.cnn.com/2009/CRIME/04/07/sexting.busts/

Field, T. (1996). Attachment and separation in young children. *Annual Review of Psychology, 47,* 541–561.

Field, T., & Diego, M. (2008). Cortisol: The culprit prenatal stress variable. *International Journal of Neuroscience, 118,* 1181–1205.

Filkins, D. (2004, November 21). In Falluja, young marines saw the savagery of an urban war. *The New York Times.* Retrieved from http://www.nytimes.com/2004/11/21/international/middleeast/21battle.html?_r=0

Fine, E. J., Ionita, C. C., & Lohr, L. (2002). The history of the development of the cerebellar examination. *Seminars in Neurology, 22,* 375–384.

Finer, L. B. (2007). Trends in premarital sex in the United States, 1954–2003. *Public Health Reports, 122,* 73–78.

Finger, S. (2001). *Origins of neuroscience: A history of explorations into brain function.* New York: Oxford University Press.

Fink, G. (2011). Stress controversies: Post-traumatic stress disorder, hippocampal volume, gastroduodenal ulceration. *Journal of Neuroendocrinology, 23,* 107–117.

Fink, M. & Taylor, M. A. (2007). Electroconvulsive therapy: Evidence and challenges. *Journal of the American Medical Association, 298,* 330–332.

Finkel, E. J., Eastwick, P. W., Karney, B. R., Reis, H. T., & Sprecher, S. (2012). Online dating: A critical analysis from the perspective of psychological science. *Psychological Science in the Public Interest, 13,* 3–66.

Finucane, A. M. (2011). The effect of fear and anger on selective attention. *Emotion, 11,* 970–974.

Firestein, S. (2001). How the olfactory system makes sense of scents. *Nature, 413,* 211–218.

Firth, S. (2005). End-of-life: A Hindu view. *Lancet, 366,* 682–686.

Fischer, B., & Rehm, J. (2007). Illicit opioid use in the 21st century: Witnessing a paradigm shift? *Addiction, 102,* 499–501.

Fischer, P., Krueger, J. I., Greitemeyer, T., Vogrincic, C., Kastenmüller, A., Frey, D., . . . Kainbacher, M. (2011). The bystander-effect: A meta-analytic review on bystander intervention in dangerous and non-dangerous emergencies. *Psychological Bulletin, 137,* 517–537.

Fisher, S. E., & DeFries, J. E. (2002). Developmental dyslexia: Genetic dissection of a complex cognitive trait. *Nature Reviews Neuroscience, 3,* 767–780.

Fitzpatrick, M. J., & McPherson, B. J. (2010). Coloring within the lines: Gender stereotypes in contemporary coloring books. *Sex Roles, 62,* 127–137.

Flaherty, C. (2011, October 29). Soldier's best friend: Dogs boost therapy program for wounded. *Lubbock Avalanche-Journal.* Retrieved from http://lubbockonline.com/life/2011-10-29/soldiers-best-friend-dogs-boost-therapy-program-wounded#.UXl89HApsVs

Flegal, K. M., Carroll, M. D., Ogden, C. L., & Curtin, L. R. (2010). Prevalence and trends in obesity among US adults, 1999–2008. *Journal of the American Medical Association, 303,* 235–241.

Flor, H., & Birbaumer, N. (1993). Comparison of the efficacy of electromyographic biofeedback, cognitive-behavioral therapy, and conservative medical interventions in the treatment of chronic musculoskeletal pain. *Journal of Consulting and Clinical Psychology, 61,* 653–658.

Flor, H., Nikolajsen, L., & Jensen, T. S. (2006). Phantom limb pain: A case of maladaptive CNS plasticity? *Nature Reviews Neuroscience, 7,* 873–881.

Florida Museum of Natural History. (2014). *Ichthyology: Sharks.* Retrieved May 25, 2015 from http://www.flmnh.ufl.edu/fish/sharks/isaf/isaf.htm

Fogel, S. M., & Smith, C. T. (2011). The function of the sleep spindle: A psychological index of intelligence and a mechanism for sleep-dependent memory consolidation. *Neuroscience & Biobehavioral Reviews, 35,* 1154–1165.

Folkman, S., & Lazarus, R. S. (1985). If it changes it must be a process: Study of emotion and coping during three stages of a college examination. *Journal of Personality and Social Psychology, 48,* 150–170.

Foos, P. W., & Goolkasian, P. (2008). Presentation format effects in a levels-of-processing task. *Experimental Psychology, 55,* 215–227.

Forgas, J. P. (2008). Affect and cognition. *Perspectives on Psychological Science, 3,* 94–101.

Forger, D. B., & Peskin, C. S. (2003). A detailed predictive model of the mammalian circadian clock. *Proceedings of the National Academy of Sciences, 100,* 14806–14811.

Fournier, J. C., DeRubeis, R. J., Hollon, S. D., Dimidjian, S., Amsterdam, J. D., Shelton, R. C., & Fawcett, J. (2010). Antidepressant drug effects and depression severity. *Journal of the American Medical Association, 303,* 47–53.

Fowlkes, C. C., Martin, D. R., & Malik, J. (2007). Local figure–ground cues are valid for natural images. *Journal of Vision, 7,* 1–9.

Fox, A. B., Rosen, J., & Crawford, M. (2009). Distractions, distractions: Does instant messaging affect college students' performance on a concurrent reading comprehension task? *CyberPsychology & Behavior, 12,* 51–53.

Fox, M. (2013, July 25). Virginia Johnson, Masters' collaborator in sex research, dies at 88. *The New York Times.* Retrieved from http://www.nytimes.com/2013/07/26/us/virginia-johnson-masterss-collaborator-in-sex-research-dies-at-88.html?pagewanted=all&_r=0

Fox News. (2012, September 19). *Pacifier use can lead to emotional problems in boys, study finds.* Retrieved from http://www.foxnews.com/health/2012/09/19/pacifier-use-can-lead-to-emotional-problems-in-boys-study-finds/

Fox News. (2013, March 20). *Social media anxiety: Sites like Facebook, Twitter stressing teens out?* Retrieved from http://www.foxnews.com/health/2013/03/20/social-media-anxiety-sites-like-facebook-twitter-stressing-teens-out/

Fozard, J. L. (1990). Vision and hearing in aging. *Handbook of the Psychology of Aging, 3,* 143–156.

Francis, W. S., & Gutiérrez, M. (2012). Bilingual recognition memory: Stronger performance but weaker levels-of-processing effects in the less fluent language. *Memory Cognition, 40,* 496–503.

Franklin, J. (2011). *33 Men: Inside the miraculous survival and dramatic rescue of the Chilean miners.* New York: G.P. Putnam's Sons.

Fratiglioni, L., Paillard-Borg, S., & Winblad, B. (2004). An active and socially integrated lifestyle in late life might protect against dementia. *Lancet Neurology, 3,* 343–353.

Freberg, K., Adams, R., McGaughey, K., & Freberg, L. (2010). The rich get richer: Online and offline social connectivity predicts subjective loneliness. *Media Psychology Review, 3*(1) 103–115.

Freedman, J. L., & Fraser, S. C. (1966). Compliance without pressures: The foot-in-the-door technique. *Journal of Personality and Social Psychology, 4,* 195–202.

freedomflores. (2010, October 18). The Chilean miners' rescue, or masonic ritual? [Web log post]. Retrieved from http://www.davidicke.com/forum/showthread.php?t=140011

Freedom of Speech Ltd. (2014, March 10). *Orlando Bloom and dyslexia - His experience, thoughts & advice* [Video file]. Retrieved from https://www.youtube.com/watch?v=hLTSPmoH2eE

Freud, S. (1900/1953). The interpretation of dreams. In J. Strachey (Ed. and Trans.), *The standard edition of the complete psychological works of Sigmund Freud* (Vol. 4, pp. 1–338; Vol. 5, pp. 339–621). London: Hogarth Press.

Freud, S. (1905/1953). Three essays on the theory of sexuality. In J. Strachey (Ed. and Trans.), *The standard edition of the complete psychological works of Sigmund Freud* (Vol. 7, pp. 123–245). London: Hogarth Press.

Freud, S. (1917/1966). *Introductory lectures on psycho-analysis: The standard edition.* New York: W. W. Norton.

Freud, S. (1923/1960). *The ego and the id.* (Joan Riviere, Trans., & James Strachey, Ed.). New York: W. W. Norton.

Freud, S. (1923/1961). The ego and the id. In J. Strachey (Ed. and Trans.), *The standard edition of the complete psychological works of Sigmund Freud* (Vol. 19, pp. 1–66). London: Hogarth Press.

Freud, S. (1933/1964). New introductory lectures on psycho-analysis. In J. Strachey (Ed. and Trans.), *The standard edition of the complete psychological works of Sigmund Freud* (Vol. 22, pp. 1–182). London: Hogarth Press.

Freud, S. (1940/1949). *An outline of psychoanalysis.* (James Strachey, Trans.). New York: W. W. Norton.

Freud Museum. (n.d.). *About the museum.* Retrieved from http://www.freud.org.uk/about/

Friedman, M., & Rosenman, R. H. (1974). *Type A behavior and your heart.* New York: Knopf.

Friedman, M. J., Resick, P. A., Bryant, R. A., & Brewin, C. R. (2011). Considering PTSD for DSM-5. *Depression and Anxiety, 28,* 750–769.

Friend farming. (n.d.). In *Merriam-Webster.com: The Open Dictionary.* Retrieved December 3, 2012, from http://nws.merriam-webster.com/opendictionary/newword_search.php

Fries, C. J. (2011, September 23). Brian Sinclair was "ignored to death." *The Huffington Post.* Retrieved from http://www.huffingtonpost.ca/christopher-j-fries/brian-sinclair-ignored-to-death_b_969550.html

Frith, M. (2006, April 3). Beckham reveals his battle with obsessive disorder. *The Independent.* Retrieved from http://www.independent.co.uk/news/uk/this-britain/beckham-reveals-his-battle-with-obsessive-disorder-472573.html

Funnell, M. G., Corballis, P. M., & Gazzaniga, M. S. (1999). A deficit in perceptual matching in the left hemisphere of a callosotomy patient. *Neuropsychologia, 37,* 1143–1154.

Gabrieli, J. D. E., Corkin, S., Mickel, S. F., & Growdon, J. H. (1993). Intact acquisition and long-term retention of mirror-tracing skill in Alzheimer's disease and in global amnesia. *Behavioral Neuroscience, 107,* 899–910.

Gackenbach, J., & LaBerge, S. (Eds.). (1988). *Conscious mind, sleeping brain: Perspectives on lucid dreaming.* New York: Plenum Press.

Galanter, E. (1962). Contemporary psychophysics. In R. Brown, E. Galanter, E. H. Hess, & G. Mandler (Eds.), *New directions in psychology* (pp. 87–156). New York: Holt, Rinehart & Winston.

Galati, D., Scherer, K. R., & Ricci-Bitti, P. E. (1997). Voluntary facial expression of emotion: Comparing congenitally blind with normally sighted encoders. *Journal of Personality and Social Psychology, 73,* 1363–1379.

Gale, C., & Martyn, C. (1998). Larks and owls and health, wealth, and wisdom. *British Medical Journal, 317,* 1675–1677.

Gale, C. R., Batty, G. D., & Deary, I. J. (2008). Locus of control at age 10 years and health outcomes and behaviors at age 30 years: The 1970 British Cohort Study. *Psychosomatic Medicine, 70,* 397–403.

Gangestad, S. W., & Scheyd, G. J. (2005). The evolution of human physical attractiveness. *Annual Review of Anthropology, 34,* 523–548.

Ganis, G., Thompson, W. L., & Kosslyn, S. M. (2004). Brain areas underlying visual mental imagery and visual perception: An fMRI study. *Cognitive Brain Research, 20,* 226–241.

Ganzel, B. L., Morris, P. A., & Wethington, E. (2010). Allostasis and the human brain: Integrating models of stress from the social and life sciences. *Psychological Review, 117,* 134–174.

Garcia, J., Ervin, F. R., & Koelling, R. A. (1966). Learning with prolonged delay of reinforcement. *Psychonomic Science, 5,* 121–122.

Garcia, J. R., Reiber, C., Massey, S. G., & Merriwether, A. M. (2012). Sexual hookup culture: A review. *Review of General Psychology, 16,* 161–176.

García-Lázaro, H., Ramirez-Carmona, R., Lara-Romero, R., & Roldan-Valadez, E. (2012). Neuroanatomy of episodic and semantic memory in humans: A brief review of neuroimaging studies. *Neurology India, 60,* 613–617.

Gardner, H. (1999). *Intelligence reframed: Multiple intelligences for the 21st century.* New York: Basic Books.

Gardner, H. (2011). *Frames of mind: The theory of multiple intelligences.* New York: Basic Books.

Gardner, H., & Hatch, T. (1989). Educational implications of the theory of multiple intelligences. *Educational Researcher, 18,* 4–10.

Garry, M., & Gerrie, M. P. (2005). When photographs create false memories. *Current Directions in Psychological Science, 14,* 321–325.

Gassmann, P. (1991, December 21). Somalia: The agony of a dying nation. *The New York Times.* Retrieved from http://www.nytimes.com/1991/12/21/opinion/21iht-edga.html?scp=2&sq=somalia%201991&st=cse

Gastil, J. (1990). Generic pronouns and sexist language: The oxymoronic character of masculine generics. *Sex Roles, 23,* 629–643.

Gatchel, R. J., & Maddrey, A. M. (2004). The biopsychosocial perspective of pain. In J. M. Raczynski & L. C. Leviton (Eds.), *Handbook of clinical health psychology: Vol 2 Disorders of behavior and health* (pp. 357–378). Washington, DC: American Psychological Association.

Gatchel, R. J., Peng, Y. B., Peters, M. L., Fuchs, P. N., & Turk, D. C. (2007). The biopsychosocial approach to chronic pain: Scientific advances and future directions. *Psychological Bulletin, 133,* 581–624.

Gates, G. J. (2011). *How many people are lesbian, gay, bisexual, and transgendered?* Los Angeles: Williams Institute, UCLA School of Law. Retrieved from http://williamsinstitute.law.ucla.edu/research/census-lgbt-demographics-studies/how-many-people-are-lesbian-gay-bisexual-and-transgender/

Gaval-Cruz, M., & Weinshenker, D. (2009). Mechanisms of disulfiram-induced cocaine abstinence: Antabuse and cocaine relapse. *Molecular Interventions, 9,* 175–187.

Gavie, J., & Revonsuo, A. (2010). The future of lucid dreaming treatment [Commentary on "The neurobiology of consciousness: Lucid dreaming wakes up" by J. Allan Hobson]. *International Journal of Dream Research, 3,* 13–15.

Gay, P. (1988). *Freud: A life for our time.* New York: W. W. Norton.

Gayton, S. D., & Lovell, G. P. (2012). Resilience in ambulance service paramedics and its relationships with well-being and general health. *Traumatology, 18,* 58–64. doi:10.1177/1534765610396727

Gazzaniga, M. S. (1967). The split brain in man. *Scientific American, 217,* 24–29.

Gazzaniga, M. S. (1998). The split brain revisited. *Scientific American, 279,* 50–55.

Gazzaniga, M. S., Bogen, J. E., & Sperry, R. W. (1965). Observations on visual perception after disconnection of the cerebral hemispheres in man. *Brain, 88,* 221–236.

Geake, J. (2008). Neuromythologies in education. *Educational Research, 50,* 123–133.

Geary, D. C., Vigil, J., & Byrd-Craven, J. (2004). Evolution of human mate choice. *Journal of Sex Research, 41,* 27–42.

Geddes, L. (2011, November 29). Banishing consciousness: The mystery of anaesthesia. *New Scientist.* Retrieved from http://www.newscientist.com/article/mg21228402.300-banishing-consciousness-the-mystery-of-anaesthesia.html?full=true

Gegenfurtner, K. R. (2003). Cortical mechanisms of color vision. *Nature Reviews Neuroscience, 4,* 563–572.

Geier, A., Wansink, B., & Rozin, P. (2012). Red potato chips: Segmentation cues can substantially decrease food intake. *Health Psychology, 31,* 398–401.

Genetics Home Reference. (2008). *5-alpha reductase deficiency.* Retrieved from http://ghr.nlm.nih.gov/condition/5-alpha-reductase-deficiency

George, M. S. (2003, September). Stimulating the brain. *Scientific American, 289,* 67–73.

Georgiadis, J. R., Reinders, A. A. T., Paans, A. M., Renken, R., & Kortekaas, R. (2009). Men versus women on sexual brain function: Prominent differences during tactile genital stimulation, but not during orgasm. *Human Brain Mapping, 30,* 3089–3101.

Gerdes, A. B. M., Uhl, G., & Alpers, G. W. (2009). Spiders are special: Fear and disgust evoked by pictures of arthropods. *Evolution and Human Behavior, 30,* 66–73.

German, T. P., & Defeyter, M. A. (2000). Immunity to functional fixedness in young children. *Psychonomic Bulletin & Review, 7,* 707–712.

Gershoff, E. T. (2008). *Report on physical punishment in the United States: What research tells us about its effects on children.* Columbus, OH: Center for Effective Discipline. Retrieved from http://www.phoenixchildrens.com/sites/default/files/PDFs/principles_and_practices-of_effective_discipline.pdf

Gershoff, E. T. (2010). More harm than good: A summary of scientific research on the intended and unintended effects of corporal punishment on children. *Law and Contemporary Problems, 73,* 31–56.

Gershoff, E. T., & Bitensky, S. H. (2008). The case against corporal punishment of children. *Psychology, Public Policy, and Law, 13,* 231–272.

Gerstorf, D., Ram, N., Hoppmann, C., Willis, S. L., & Schaie, K. W. (2011). Cohort differences in cognitive aging and terminal decline in the Seattle Longitudinal Study. *Developmental Psychology, 47,* 1026–1041.

Gettleman, J. (2011, July 15). Misery follows as Somalis try to flee hunger. *The New York Times.* Retrieved from http://www.nytimes.com/2011/07/16/world/africa/16somalia.html?_r=0

Gibson, E. J., & Walk, R. D. (1960). The "visual cliff." *Scientific American, 202,* 80–92.

Giedd, J. N., Lalonde, F. M., Celano, M. J., White, S. L., Wallace, G. L., Lee, N. R., & Lenroot, R. K. (2009). Anatomical brain magnetic resonance imaging of typically developing children and adolescents. *Journal of the American Academy of Child and Adolescent Psychiatry, 48,* 465–475.

Gigerenzer, G. (2004). Dread risk, September 11, and fatal traffic accidents. *Psychological Science, 15,* 286–287.

Gilligan, C. (1982). *In a different voice: Psychological theory and women's development.* Cambridge, MA: Harvard University Press.

Gillin, J. C. (2002, March 25). How long can humans stay awake? *Scientific American.* Retrieved from http://www.scientificamerican.com/article.cfm?id=how-long-can-humans-stay

Girodo, M., & Henry, D. R. (1976). Cognitive, physiological and behavioural components of anxiety in flooding. *Canadian Journal of Behavioural Science/Revue canadienne des sciences du comportement, 8,* 224–231.

Glahn, D. C., Laird, A. R., Ellison-Wright, I., Thelen, S. M., Robinson, J. L., Lancaster, J. L., . . . Fox, P. (2008). Meta-analysis of gray matter anomalies in schizophrenia: Application of anatomic likelihood estimation and network analysis. *Biological Psychiatry, 64,* 774–781.

Glaser, R., & Kiecolt-Glaser, J. K. (2005). Stress-induced immune dysfunction: Implications for health. *Nature Reviews Immunology, 5,* 243–251.

Glass, R. M. (2001). Electroconvulsive therapy: Time to bring it out of the shadows. *Journal of the American Medical Association, 285,* 1346–1348.

Glenn, A. L., Raine, A., Schug, R. A., Gao, Y., & Granger, D. A. (2011). Increased testosterone-to-cortisol ration in psychopathy. *Journal of Abnormal Psychology, 120,* 389–399.

Global Sex Survey. (2005). *Durex.* Retrieved from http://www.durex.com/en-jp/sexualwellbeingsurvey/documents/gss2005result.pdf

Go, A. S., Mozaffarian, D., Roger, V. L., Benjamin, E. J., Berry, J. D., Borden, W. B., . . . Turner, M. B. (2013). Heart disease and stroke statistics—2013 update: A report from the American Heart Association. *Circulation, 127,* e6–e245.

Gockley, R., Bruce, A., Forlizzi, J., Michalowski, M., Mundell, A., Rosenthal, S., . . . Wang, J. (2005). Designing robots for long-term social interaction. In *2005 IEEE/RSJ International Conference on Intelligent Robots and Systems (IROS 2005)* (pp. 2199–2204). New York: IEEE.

Godden, D. R., & Baddeley, A. D. (1975). Context-dependent memory in two natural environments: On land and underwater. *British Journal of Psychology, 66,* 325–331.

Godlee, F., Smith, J., & Marcovitch, H. (2011). Wakefield's article linking MMR vaccine and autism was fraudulent. *British Medical Journal, 342,* c7452.

Goel, N., Rao, H., Durmer, J. S., & Dinges, D. F. (2009, September). Neurocognitive consequences of sleep deprivation. *Seminars in Neurology, 29,* 320–339.

Gogtay, N., Vyas, N. S., Testa, R., Wood, S. J., & Pantelis, C. (2011). Age of onset of schizophrenia: Perspectives from neural structural neuroimaging studies. *Schizophrenia Bulletin, 37,* 504–513.

Gold, R. B. (2005). The implications of defining when a woman is pregnant. *Guttmacher Report on Public Policy, 8*(2), 7–10.

Goldin-Meadow, S. (1978). Review: A study in human capacities. *Science, 200,* 649–651.

Goldsmith, H. H., Buss, A. H., Plomin, R., Rothbart, M. K., Chess, S., Hinde, R. A., & McCall, R. B. (1987). What is temperament? Four approaches. *Child Development, 58,* 505–529.

Goldstein, E. B. (2011). *Cognitive psychology: Connecting mind, research, and everyday experience* (3rd ed.). Belmont, CA: Wadsworth, Cengage Learning.

Goldstein, I. (2000). Male sexual circuitry. *Scientific American, 283,* 70–75.

Goldstein, J. M., Seidman, L. J., Horton, N. J., Makris, N., Kennedy, D. N., Caviness, V. S. Jr., . . . Tsuang, M. T. (2001). Normal sexual dimorphism of the adult human brain assessed by in vivo magnetic resonance imaging. *Cerebral Cortex, 11,* 490–497.

Goleman, D. (1995). *Emotional intelligence.* New York: Bantam Books.

Goodfriend, W. (2012, May 22). Mental hospitals in "One Flew Over the Cuckoo's Nest." *Psychology Today.* Retrieved from http://www.psychologytoday.com/blog/psychologist-the-movies/201205/mental-hospitals-in-one-flew-over-the-cuckoo-s-nest

Gordon, J. (2010). Testing the glutamate hypothesis of schizophrenia. *Nature Neuroscience, 13,* 2–4.

Gordon, S. M. (2001, July 5). What are the effects of the drug Ecstasy? *Scientific American Online.* Retrieved from http://www.scientificamerican.com/article/what-are-the-effects-of-t/

Gordon-Messer, D., Bauermeister, J. A., Grodzinski, A., & Zimmerman, M. A. (2013). Sexting among young adults. *Journal of Adolescent Health, 52,* 301–306. doi:10.1016/j.jadohealth.2012.05.013

Gordon-Salant, S., & Callahan, J. S. (2009). The benefits of hearing aids and closed captioning for television viewing by older adults with hearing loss. *Ear and Hearing, 30,* 458–465.

Gottesman, I. I. (2001). Psychopathology through a life span—genetic prism. *American Psychologist, 56,* 867–878.

Gottesman, I. I., Laursen, T. M., Bertelsen, A., & Mortensen, P. B. (2010). Severe mental disorders in offspring with 2 psychiatrically ill parents. *Archives of General Psychiatry, 67,* 252–257.

Gottfried, J. A., Smith, A. P. R., Rugg, M. D., & Dolan, R. J. (2004). Remembrance of odors past: Human olfactory cortex in cross-modal recognition memory. *Neuron, 42,* 687–895.

Gould, E., Beylin, A., Tanapat, P., Reeves, A., & Shors, T. J. (1999). Learning enhances adult neurogenesis in the hippocampal formation. *Nature Neuroscience, 2,* 260–265.

Grabner, R. H., Ansari, D., Reishofer, G., Stern, E., Ebner, F., & Neuper, C. (2007). Individual differences in mathematical competence predict parietal brain activation during mental calculation. *NeuroImage, 38,* 346–356.

Gracheva, E. O., Ingolia, N. T., Kelly, Y. M., Cordero-Morales, J. F., Hollopeter, G., Chesler, A. T., . . . Julius, D. (2010). Molecular basis of infrared detection by snakes. *Nature, 464,* 1006–1011.

Gradin, M., & Eriksson, M. (2011). Neonatal pain assessment in Sweden—a fifteen-year follow up. *Acta Pædiatrica, 100,* 204–208.

Grady, J. S., Ale, C. M., & Morris, T. L. (2012). A naturalistic observation of social behaviours during preschool drop-off. *Early Child Development and Cue, 182,* 1683–1694.

Grammer, K., & Thornhill, R. (1994). Human (Homo sapiens) facial attractiveness and sexual selection: The role of symmetry and averageness. *Journal of Comparative Psychology, 108,* 233–242.

Granich, R., Kahn, J. G., Bennett, R., Holmes, C. B., Garg, N., Serenata, C., . . . Williams, B. G. (2012). Expanding ART for treatment and prevention of HIV in South Africa: Estimated cost and cost-effectiveness 2011–2050. *PloS ONE, 7,* e30216. doi:10.1371/journal.pone.0030216

Granrud, C. E. (2009). Development of size constancy in children: A test of the metacognitive theory. *Perception & Psychophysics, 71,* 644–654.

Grant, B. F., Stinson, F. S., Dawson, D. A., Chou, S. P., Dufour, M. C., Compton, W., . . . Kaplan, K. (2004). Prevalence and co-occurrence of substance use disorders and independent mood and anxiety disorders: Results from the National Epidemiologic Survey on Alcohol and Related Conditions. *Archives of General Psychiatry, 61,* 807–816.

Grant, P. R. (1991). Natural selection and Darwin's finches. *Scientific American, 265,* 82–87.

Green, J. P. (1999). Hypnosis and the treatment of smoking cessation and weight loss. In I. Kirsch, A. Capafons, E. Cardeña-Buelna, & S. Amigó (Eds.), *Clinical hypnosis and self-regulation: Cognitive-behavioral perspectives* (pp. 249–276; Dissociation, Trauma, Memory, and Hypnosis Book Series). Washington, DC: American Psychological Association.

Green, M., & Elliott, M. (2010). Religion, health, and psychological well-being. *Journal of Religious Health, 49,* 149–163.

Greenberg, L., Warwar, S., & Malcolm, W. (2010). Emotion-focused couples therapy and the facilitation of forgiveness. *Journal of Marital and Family Therapy, 36,* 28–42.

Greenblatt, S. H., Dagi, T. F., & Epstein, M. H. (1997). *A history of neurosurgery.* Park Ridge, IL: American Association of Neurological Surgeons.

Greenfieldboyce, N. (2005, December 26). Robot receptionist dishes directions and attitude. *NPR.org.* Retrieved from http://www.npr.org/templates/story/story.php?storyId=5067678

Gregson, S., & Blacker, J. (2011). Kangaroo care in pre-term or low birth weight babies in a postnatal ward. *British Journal of Midwifery, 19,* 568–577.

Greitemeyer, T. (2009). Effects of songs with prosocial lyrics on prosocial thoughts, affect, and behavior. *Journal of Experimental Social Psychology, 45,* 186–190.

Griggs, R. A. (2015). The Disappearance of Independence in Textbook Coverage of Asch's Social Pressure Experiments. *Teaching of Psychology, 42,* 137–142.

Grimm, J., & Grimm, W. (1884). *Grimm's household tales* [Vol. 1, Margaret Hunt (Trans. & Ed.)]. London: George Bell and Sons.

Groopman, J. (2008). *How doctors think.* Boston: Houghton Mifflin.

Gross, C. G. (2007). The discovery of motor cortex and its background. *Journal of the History of the Neurosciences, 16,* 320–331.

Grossman, R. P., & Till, B. D. (1998). The persistence of classically conditioned brand attitudes. *Journal of Advertising, 21,* 23–31.

Grotenhermen, F., & Müller-Vahl, K. (2012). The therapeutic potential of cannabis and cannabinoids. *Deutsches Ärzteblatt International, 109,* 495–501.

Gruber, D. F. (2009). Three's company. *Nature Medicine, 15,* 232–235.

Grusec, J. E., & Goodnow, J. J. (1994). Impact of parental discipline methods on the child's internalization of values: A reconceptualization of current points of view. *Developmental Psychology, 30,* 4–19.

Grusec, J. E., Goodnow, J. J., & Kuczynski, L. (2000). New directions in analyses of parenting contributions to children's acquisition of values. *Child Development, 71,* 205–211.

Guilford, J. P. (1967). *The nature of human intelligence.* New York: McGraw-Hill.

Guilford, J. P., Christensen, P. R., Merrifield, P. R., & Wilson, R. C. (1960). *Alternate uses.* Beverly Hills, CA: Sheridan Psychological Services.

Guillot, C. (2007). Is recreational ecstasy (MDMA) use associated with higher levels of depressive symptoms? *Journal of Psychoactive Drugs, 39,* 31–39.

Guiney, H., & Machado, L. (2013). Benefits of regular aerobic exercise for executive functioning in healthy populations. *Psychonomic Bulletin & Review, 20,* 73–86.

Guinness Book of World Records News. (2012, February 6). *Royal mail group workers set charity record.* Retrieved from http://www.guinnessworldrecords.com/news/2012/2/royal-mail-group-workers-set-charity-record/

Gulevich, G., Dement, W., & Johnson, L. (1966). Psychiatric and EEG observations on a case of prolonged (264 hours) wakefulness. *Archives of General Psychiatry, 15,* 29–35.

Gundel, J. (2003). The migration–development nexus: Somalia case study. *International Migration, 40,* 255–281.

Gunderson, E. A., Ramirez, G., Levine, S. C., & Beilock, S. L. (2012). The role of parents and teachers in the development of gender-related math attitudes. *Sex Roles, 66,* 153–166.

Gurpegui, M., Aguilar, M. C., Martínez-Ortega, J. M., Diaz, F. J., & de Leon, J. (2004). Caffeine intake in outpatients with schizophrenia. *Schizophrenia Bulletin, 30,* 935–945.

Gurven, M., von Rueden, C., Massenkoff, M., Kaplan, H., & Lero Vie, M. (2013). How universal is the Big Five? Testing the five-factor model of personality variation among forager—farmers in the Bolivian Amazon. *Journal of Personality and Social Psychology, 104,* 354–370.

Haedt-Matt, A. A., & Keel, P. K. (2011). Revisiting the affect regulation model of binge eating: A meta-analysis of studies using ecological momentary assessment. *Psychological Bulletin, 137,* 660–681.

Hagar, S. (2013, September 19). Washington State Penitentiary psychologist earns national acclaim for programs. Union-Bulletin.com. Retrieved from http://union-bulletin.com/news/2013/sep/19/washington-state-penitentiary-psychologist-earns-n/

Hall, D., & Buzwell, S. (2012). The problem of free-riding in group projects: Looking beyond social loafing as reason for non-contribution. *Active Learning in Higher Education, 14,* 37–49.

Hall, J. A., & Matsumoto, D. (2004). Gender differences in judgments of multiple emotions from facial expressions. *Emotion, 4,* 201–206.

Hall, J. K., Hutton, S. B., & Morgan, M. J. (2010). Sex differences in scanning faces: Does attention to the eyes explain female superiority in facial expression recognition? *Cognition and Emotion, 24,* 629–637.

Hall, J. W., Smith, S. D., & Popelka, G. R. (2004). Newborn hearing screening with combined otoacoustic emissions and auditory brainstem responses. *Journal of the American Academy of Audiology, 15,* 414–425.

Halpern, D. F., Benbow, C. P., Geary, D. C., Gur, R. C., Hyde, J. S., & Gernsbacher, M. A. (2007). The science of sex differences in science and mathematics. *Psychological Science in the Public Interest, 8,* 1–51.

Halpern, L. (2013, April). Let me tell you what it's like to have schizophrenia. Retrieved from http://namimass.org/let-me-tell-you-what-its-like-to-have-schizophrenia-guest-blog-post.

Hamer, D. H., Hu, S., Magnuson, V. L., Hu, N., & Pattatucci, A. M. (1993). A linkage between DNA markers on the X chromosome and male sexual orientation. *Science, 261,* 321–327.

Hamilton, W. D. (1964). The genetical evolution of social behavior. *Journal of Theoretical Biology, 12,* 12–45.

Hammond, S. I., Müller, U., Carpendale, J. I. M., Bibok, M. B., & Liebermann-Finestone, D. P. (2012). The effects of parental scaffolding on preschoolers' executive function. *Developmental Psychology, 48,* 271–281.

Hampton, A. N., & O'Doherty, J. P. (2007). Decoding the neural substrates of reward-related decision making with functional MRI. *Proceedings of the National Academy of Sciences, 104,* 1377–1382.

Hampton, J. A. (1998). Similarity-based categorization and fuzziness of natural categories. *Cognition, 65,* 137–165.

Haney, C., Banks, C., & Zimbardo, P. (1973). Interpersonal dynamics in a simulated prison. *International Journal of Criminology and Penology, 1,* 69–97.

Haney, C., & Zimbardo, P. (1998). The past and future of U.S. prison policy: Twenty-five years after the Stanford prison experiment. *American Psychologist, 53,* 709–727.

Hanish, L. D., Sallquist, J., DiDonato, M., Fabes, R. A., & Martin, C. L. (2012, September). Aggression by whom–aggression toward whom: Behavioral predictors of same- and other-gender aggression in early childhood. *Developmental Psychology, 48*(5), 1450–1462. doi:10.1037/a0027510

Hanley, J. R., & Chapman, E. (2008). Partial knowledge in a tip-of-the-tongue state about two- and three-word proper names. *Psychonomic Bulletin & Review, 15,* 156–160.

Hanna-Pladdy, B., & MacKay, A. (2011). The relation between instrumental musical activity and cognitive aging. *Neuropsychology, 25,* 378–386.

Hanscombe, K. B., Trzaskowski, M., Haworth, C. M. A., Davis, O. S. P., Dale, P. S., & Plomin, R. (2012). Socioeconomic status (SES) and children's intelligence (IQ): In a UK-representative sample SES moderates the environmental, not genetic, effect on IQ. *PLoS ONE, 7,* e30320. doi:10.1371/journal.pone.0030320

Hansen, C. J., Stevens, L. C., & Coast, J. R. (2001). Exercise duration and mood state: How much is enough to feel better? *Health Psychology, 20,* 267–275.

Harden, K. P., & Mendle, J. (2012). Gene-environment interplay in the association between pubertal timing and delinquency in adolescent girls. *Journal of Abnormal Psychology, 121,* 73–87.

Hariri, A. R., Tessitore, A., Mattay, V. S., Fera, F., & Weinberger, D. R. (2002). The amygdala response to emotional stimuli: A comparison of faces and scenes. *NeuroImage, 17,* 317–323.

Harlow, H. F. (1958). The nature of love. *American Psychologist, 13,* 673–685.

Harlow, H. F., Harlow, M. K., & Meyer, D. R. (1950). Learning motivated by a manipulation drive. *Journal of Experimental Psychology, 40,* 228–234.

Harlow, H. F., Harlow, M. K., & Suomi, S. J. (1971). From thought to therapy: Lessons from a primate laboratory. *American Scientist, 59,* 538–549.

Harlow, H. F., & Zimmerman, R. R. (1959). Affectional responses in the infant monkey. *Science, 130,* 421–432.

Harmon, D. K., Masuda, M., & Holmes, T. H. (1970). The social readjustment rating scale: A cross-cultural study of Western Europeans and Americans. *Journal of Psychosomatic Research, 14,* 391–400.

Harrington, A. (2012). The fall of the schizophrenogenic mother. *Lancet, 379,* 1292–1293.

Harrington, R. (2013). *Stress, health & well-being: Thriving in the 21st century.* Belmont, CA: Wadsworth, Cengage Learning.

Harris, B. (1979). Whatever happened to Little Albert? *American Psychologist, 34,* 151–160.

Harris, E. C., & Barraclough, B. (1998). Excess mortality of mental disorder. *British Journal of Psychiatry, 173,* 11–53.

Harris Interactive/Health Day Poll. (2011). *Vaccine–autism link: Sound science or fraud?* [Press release]. Retrieved from http://www.harrisinteractive.com/NewsRoom/PressReleases/tabid/446/mid/1506/articleId/674/ctl/ReadCustom%20Default/Default.aspx

Hart, B., & Risley, T. R. (1995). *Meaningful differences in the everyday experience of young American children.* Baltimore, MD: Paul H. Brookes.

Hartlage, S., Alloy, L. B., Vázquez, C., & Dykman, B. (1993). Automatic and effortful processing in depression. *Psychological Bulletin, 113,* 247–278.

Hartshorne, J. K. (2010). Ruled by birth order? *Scientific American Mind, 20,* 18–19.

Hartshorne, J. K., Salem-Hartshorne, N., & Hartshorne, T. S. (2009). Birth order effects in the formation of long-term relationships. *Journal of Individual Psychology, 65,* 156–176.

Harvard Medical School. (2007). *Healthy sleep: Jet lag and shift work.* Retrieved from http://healthysleep.med.harvard.edu/healthy/science/variations/jet-lag-and-shift-work

Harvey, M. A., Sellman, J. D., Porter, R. J., & Frampton, C. M. (2007). The relationship between non-acute adolescent cannabis use and cognition. *Drug and Alcohol Review, 26,* 309–319.

Hasher, L., & Zacks, R. T. (1979). Automatic and effortful processes in memory. *Journal of Experimental Psychology: General, 108,* 356–388.

Hassett, J. M., Siebert, E. R., & Wallen, K. (2008). Sex differences in rhesus monkey toy preferences parallel those of children. *Hormones and Behavior, 54,* 359–364.

Hassin, R. R., Bargh, J. A., & Zimerman, S. (2009). Automatic and flexible: The case of non-conscious goal pursuit. *Social Cognition, 27,* 20–36.

Hatch, S. L., & Dohrenwend, B. P. (2007). Distribution of traumatic and other stressful life events by race/ethnicity, gender, SES and age: A review of the research. *American Journal of Community Psychology, 40,* 313–332.

Hatfield, E., Bensman, L., & Rapson, R. L. (2012). A brief history of social scientists' attempts to measure passionate love. *Journal of Social and Personal Relationships, 29,* 143–164.

Havelka, M., Lučanin, J. D., & Lučanin, D. (2009). Biopsychosocial model-the integrated approach to health and disease. *Collegium Antropologicum, 33,* 303–310.

Hawthorne, W. B., Folsom, D. P., Sommerfeld, D. H., Lanouette, N. M., Lewis, M., Aarons, G. A., . . . Jeste, D. V. (2012). Incarceration among adults who are in the public mental health system: Rates, risk factors, and short-term outcomes. *Psychiatric Services, 63,* 26–32.

Hayano, F., Nakamura, M., Asami, T., Uehara, K., Yoshida, T., Roppongi, T., . . . Hirayasu, Y. (2009). Smaller amygdala is associated with anxiety in patients with panic disorder. *Psychiatry and Clinical Neurosciences, 63,* 266–276.

He, Y., Jones, C. R., Fujiki, N., Xu, Y., Guo, B., Holder, J. L., . . . Fu, Y. (2009). The transcriptional repressor DEC2 regulates sleep length in mammals. *Science, 325,* 866–870.

Healy, J. (2010, August 23). Chileans will work to sustain miners. *The New York Times.* Retrieved from http://www.nytimes.com/2010/08/24/world/americas/24chile.html?_r=0

Hecht, S., & Mandelbaum, J. (1938). Rod-cone dark adaptation and vitamin A. *Science, 88,* 219–221.

Hegarty, P., & Buechel, C. (2006). Androcentric reporting of gender differences in APA journals: 1965-2004. *Review of General Psychology, 10,* 377–389.

Heiman, J. R. (2002). Sexual dysfunction: Overview of prevalence, etiological factors, and treatments. *Journal of Sex Research, 39,* 73–78.

Heller, N. (2012, June 18). Emma Stone makes her Vogue cover debut in the July issue. *Vogue.* Retrieved from http://www.vogue.com/magazine/article/emma-stone-comic-relief/#1

Helliker, K. (2009, March 24). No joke: Group therapy offers savings in numbers. *The Wall Street Journal.* Retrieved from http://www.wsj.com/articles/SB123785686766020551

Hendricks, M. L., & Testa, R. J. (2012, October). A conceptual framework for clinical work with transgender and gender nonconforming clients: An adaptation of the Minority Stress Model. *Professional Psychology: Research and Practice, 43*(5), 460–467. doi:10.1037/a0029597

Henneman, W. J., Sluimer, J. D., Barnes, J., van der Flier, W. M., Sluimer, I. C., Fox, N. C., . . . Barkhof, F. (2009). Hippocampal atrophy rates in Alzheimer disease: Added value over whole brain volume measures. *Neurology, 72,* 999–1007.

Henry, D. B., Kobus, K., & Schoeny, M. E. (2011). Accuracy and bias in adolescents' perceptions of friends' substance use. *Psychology of Addictive Behaviors, 25,* 80–89.

Herbenick, D., Reece, M., Schick, V., Sanders, S. A., Dodge, B., & Fortenberry, J. D. (2010). Sexual behavior in the United States: Results from a national probability sample of men and women ages 14–94. *Journal of Sexual Medicine, 7* (Suppl. 5), 255–265.

Hergenhahn, B. R. (2005). *An introduction to the history of psychology* (5th ed.). Belmont, CA: Thomson Wadsworth.

Herman, C. P., Roth, D. A., & Polivy, J. (2003). Effects of the presence of others on food intake: A normative interpretation. *Psychological Bulletin, 129,* 873–886.

Hersh, S. M. (2004, May 10). Torture at Abu Ghraib. *The New Yorker.* Retrieved from http://www.newyorker.com/archive/2004/05/10/040510fa_fact?printable=true&currentPage=all

Hertenstein, M. J., & McCullough, M. A. (2005). Separation anxiety. In N. J. Salkind (Ed.), *Encyclopedia of human development* (Vol. 3, pp. 1146–1147). Thousand Oaks, CA: SAGE.

Hertzog, C., Kramer, A. F., Wilson, R. S., & Lindenberger, U. (2009, July/August). Fit body, fit mind? *Scientific American Mind, 20,* 24–31.

Herz, R. S. (1998). Are odors the best cues to memory? A cross-modal comparison of associative memory stimuli. *Annals of the New York Academy of Sciences, 855,* 670–674.

Herz, R. (2007). *The scent of desire: Discovering our enigmatic sense of smell.* New York: William Morrow/HarperCollins.

Herz, R. S., Eliassen, J., Beland, S., & Souza, T. (2004). Neuroimaging evidence for the emotional potency of odor-evoked memory. *Neuropsychologia, 42,* 371–378.

Hess, E. H. (1975). The role of pupil size in communication. *Scientific American, 233,* 110–119.

Hess, U., & Thibault, P. (2009). Darwin and emotion expression. *American Psychologist, 64,* 120–128.

Hettema, J. M., Kettenmann, B., Ahluwalia, V., McCarthy, C., Kates, W. R., Schmitt, J. E., . . . Silberg, & Fatouros, P. (2012). Pilot multimodal twin imaging study of generalized anxiety disorder. *Depression and Anxiety, 29,* 202–209.

Hettema, J. M., Neale, M. C., & Kendler, K. S. (2001). A review and meta-analysis of the genetic epidemiology of anxiety disorders. *American Journal of Psychiatry, 158,* 1568–1578.

Hetzel, L., & Smith, A. (2001). The 65 years and over populations: 2000. *Census 2000 Brief.* Retrieved from http://www.census.gov/prod/2001pubs/c2kbr01-10.pdf

Heyes, C. (2012). What's social about social learning. *Journal of Comparative Psychology, 126,* 193–202.

Hickok, G., & Poeppel, D. (2000). Towards a functional neuroanatomy of speech perception. *Trends in Cognitive Sciences, 4,* 131–138.

Higgins, A., Nash, M., & Lynch, A. M. (2010, September 8). Antidepressant-associated sexual dysfunction: Impact, effects, and treatment. *Drug, Healthcare and Patient Safety, 2,* 141–150.

Hilgard, E. R. (1977). *Divided consciousness.* New York: Wiley.

Hilgard, E. R. (1987). *Psychology in America: A historical survey.* Orlando, FL: Harcourt Brace Jovanovich.

Hilgard, E. R. (1994). Neodissociation theory. In S. J. Lynn & J. W. Rhue (Eds.), *Dissociation: Clinical, theoretical and research perspectives.* New York: Guilford Press.

Hilgard, E. R., Morgan, A. H., & Macdonald, H. (1975). Pain and dissociation in the cold pressor test: A study of hypnotic analgesia with "hidden reports" through automatic key pressing and automatic talking. *Journal of Abnormal Psychology, 84,* 280–289.

Hines, M. (2011a). Gender development and the human brain. *Annual Review of Neuroscience, 34,* 69–88.

Hines, M. (2011b). Prenatal endocrine influences on sexual orientation and on sexually differentiated childhood behavior. *Frontiers in Neuroendocrinology, 32,* 170–182.

Hingson, R. W., Zha, W., & Weitzman, E. R. (2009). Magnitude of and trends in alcohol-related mortality and morbidity among U.S. college students ages 18–24, 1998–2005. *Journal of Studies on Alcohol and Drugs, 16* (Suppl.), 12–20.

Hirsh-Pasek, K., Golinkoff, R. M., & Eyer, D. (2003). *Einstein never used flash cards.* Emmaus, PA: Rodale Press.

Hobson, J. A. (1989). *Sleep.* New York: Scientific American Library.

Hobson, J. A. (2006, April/May). Freud returns? Like a bad dream. *Scientific American Mind, 17,* 35.

Hobson, J. A., & McCarley, R. W. (1977). The brain as a dream state generator: An activation–synthesis hypothesis of the dream process. *American Journal of Psychiatry, 134,* 1335–1348.

Hock, R. R. (2012). *Human sexuality* (3rd ed.). Upper Saddle River, NJ: Pearson Education.

Hodis, F. A., Meyer, L. H., McClure, J., Weir, K. F., & Walkey, F. H. (2011). A longitudinal investigation of motivation and secondary school achievement using growth mixture modeling. *Journal of Educational Psychology, 103,* 312–323.

Hoff, E. (2003). The specificity of environmental influence: Socioeconomic status affects early vocabulary development via maternal speech. *Child Development, 74,* 1368–1378.

Hoffman, I. Z. (2009). Therapeutic passion in the countertransference. *Psychoanalytic Dialogues, 19,* 617–636.

Hofmann, S. G., Asnaani, M. A., & Hinton, D. E. (2010). Cultural aspects in social anxiety and social anxiety disorder. *Depression and Anxiety, 27,* 1117–1127.

Hofmann, W., Vohs, K. D., & Baumeister, R. F. (2012). What people desire, feel conflicted about, and try to resist in everyday life. *Psychological Science, 23,* 582–588.

Hogan, C. L., Mata, J., & Carstensen, L. L. (2013). Exercise holds immediate benefits for affect and cognition in younger and older adults. *Psychology and Aging, 28,* 587–594. doi:10.1037/a0032634

Holahan, C. K., & Sears, R. R. (1995). *The gifted group in later maturity.* Stanford, CA: Stanford University Press.

Holland, R. W., Verplanken, B., & Van Knippenberg, A. (2002). On the nature of attitude-behavior relations: the strong guide, the weak follow. *European Journal of Social Psychology, 32,* 869–876.

Holmes, T. H., & Rahe, R. H. (1967). The Social Readjustment Rating Scale. *Journal of Psychosomatic Research, 11,* 213–318.

Holowka, S., & Petitto, L. A. (2002). Left hemisphere cerebral specialization for babies while babbling. *Science, 297,* 1515.

Holsen, L. M., Spaeth, S. B., Lee, J.-H., Ogden, L. A., Klibanski, A., Whitfield-Gabrieli, S., & Goldstein, J. M. (2011). Stress response circuitry hypoactivation related to hormonal dysfunction in women with major depression. *Journal of Affective Disorders, 131,* 379–387.

Hölzel, B. K., Carmody, J., Vangel, M., Congleton, C., Yerramsetti, S. M., Gard, T., & Lazar, S. W. (2011). Mindfulness practice leads to increases in regional brain gray matter density. *Psychiatry Research: Neuroimaging, 191,* 36–43.

Honberg, R., Diehl, S., Kimball, A., Gruttadaro, D., & Fitzpatrick, M. (2011). *State mental health cuts: A national crisis* [Report by the National Alliance on Mental Illness]. Retrieved from http://www.nami.org/Template.cfm?Section=state_budget_cuts_report

Honda, H., Shimizu, Y., & Rutter, M. (2005). No effect of MMR withdrawal on the incidence of autism: A total population study. *Journal of Child Psychology and Psychiatry, 46,* 572–579.

Honey, A., Emerson, E., & Llewellyn, G. (2011). The mental health of young people with disabilities: Impact of social conditions. *Social Psychiatry and Psychiatric Epidemiology, 46,* 1–10.

Hong, Y.-Y., Wyer, R. S. Jr., & Fong, C. P. S. (2008). Chinese working in groups: Effort dispensability versus normative influence. *Asian Journal of Social Psychology, 11,* 187–195.

Hook, J. (2015, March 9). Support for gay marriage hits all-time high—WSJ/NBC News Poll. *The Wall Street Journal.* Retrieved from http://blogs.wsj.com/washwire/2015/03/09/support-for-gay-marriage-hits-all-time-high-wsjnbc-news-poll/

Hoppel, A. M. (2012). HIV: Still epidemic after 30 years. *Clinician Reviews, 22*(C1), 11–14, 33–35.

Hor, H., & Tafti, M. (2009). How much sleep do we need? *Science, 325,* 825–826.

Horne, J. (2006). *Sleepfaring.* Oxford, UK: Oxford University Press.

Horney, K. (1926/1967). The flight from womanhood: The masculinity-complex in women as viewed by men and by women. In H. Kelmam (Ed.), *Feminine psychology* (pp. 54–70). New York: W. W. Norton.

Horney, K. (1945). *Our inner conflicts: A constructive theory of neurosis.* New York: W. W. Norton.

Horoscope.com. (2014). *Monthly horoscope: Gemini.* Retrieved September 14 from http://my.horoscope.com/astrology/free-monthly-horoscope-gemini.html

Horwitz, B., Amunts, K., Bhattacharyya R., Patkin, D., Jeffries, K., Zilles, K., & Braun, A. R. (2003). Activation of Broca's area during the production of spoken and signed language: A combined cytoarchitectonic mapping and PET analysis. *Neuropsychologia, 41,* 1868–1876.

Horwitz, D., Lovenberg, W., Engelman, K., & Sjoerdsma, A. (1964). Monoamine oxidase inhibitors, tyramine, and cheese. *Journal of the American Medical Association, 188,* 1108–1110.

Horwood, L. J., & Fergusson, D. M. (1998). Breastfeeding and later cognitive and academic outcomes. *Pediatrics, 101,* 1–7.

Hothersall, D. (2004). *History of psychology* (4th ed.). New York: McGraw-Hill.

House, J. S., Landis, K. R., & Umberson, D. (1988). Social relationships and health. *Science, 241,* 540–545.

Hovland, C. I., Janis, I. L., & Kelley, H. H. (1953). *Communication and persuasion: Psychological studies of opinion change.* New Haven, CT: Yale University Press.

Hovland, C. I., & Weiss, W. (1951). The influence of source credibility on communication effectiveness. *Public Opinion Quarterly, 15,* 635–650.

Howes, O. D., & Kapur, S. (2009). The dopamine hypothesis of schizophrenia: Version III—the final common pathway. *Schizophrenia Bulletin, 35,* 549–562.

Howland, J., Rohsenow, D. J., Greece, J. A., Littefield, C. A., Almeida, A., Heeren, T., . . . Hermos, J. (2010). The effects of binge drinking on college students' next-day academic test-taking performance and mood state. *Addiction, 105,* 655–665.

Howland, M., Hunger, J. M., & Mann, T. (2012). Friends don't let friends eat cookies: Effects of restrictive eating norms on consumption among friends. *Appetite, 59,* 505–509.

Hoyert, D., & Xu, J. (2012). Deaths: Preliminary data for 2011. *National Vital Statistics Reports, 61,* 1–64.

Hubbard, T. L. (2010). Auditory imagery: Empirical findings. *Psychological Bulletin, 136,* 302–329.

Hubel, D. H., & Wiesel, T. N. (1979, September). Brain mechanisms of vision. *Scientific American, 241,* 150–162.

Huber, V. L., Neale, M. A., & Northcraft, G. B. (1987). Decision bias and personnel selection strategies. *Organizational Behavior and Human Decision Processes, 40,* 136–137.

Hudson, C., & Paul, J. (Producers). (2007). *Through your eyes.* [DVD]. Los Angeles: Global Universal Film Group.

Huesmann, L. R., Moise-Titus, J., Podolski, C., & Eron, L. D. (2003). Longitudinal relations between children's exposure to TV violence and their aggressive and violent behavior in young adulthood: 1977–1992. *Developmental Psychology, 33,* 201–221.

Huffington Post. (2012, July 16). *Ramadan 2012: History, dates, greeting and rules of the Muslim fast.* Retrieved from http://www.huffingtonpost.com/2012/07/16/ramadan-top-ten_n_1676639.html

Hughes, S., Lyddy, F., & Lambe, S. (2013). Misconceptions about psychological science: A review. *Psychology Learning and Teaching, 12,* 20–31.

Hull, C. L. (1952). *A behavior system: An introduction to behavior theory concerning the individual organism.* New Haven, CT: Yale University Press.

Humphries, T., Kushalnagar, P., Mathur, G., Napoli, D. J., Padden, C., Rathmann, C., & Smith, S. R. (2012). Language acquisition for deaf children: Reducing the harms of zero tolerance to the use of alternative approaches. *Harm Reduction Journal, 3,* 1–9.

Hunsley, J., Lee, C. M., & Wood, J. M. (2003). Controversial and questionable assessment techniques. In S. O. Lilienfeld, J. M. Lohr, & S. J. Lynn (Eds.), *Science and pseudoscience in clinical psychology* (pp. 39–76). New York: Guilford Press.

Hunt, W. A. (1939). A critical review of current approaches to affectivity. *Psychological Bulletin, 36,* 807–828.

Hupp, J. M., Smith, J. L, Coleman, J. M., & Brunell, A. B. (2010). That's a boys' toy: Gender-typed knowledge in toddlers as a function of mother's marital status. *Journal of Genetic Psychology, 171,* 389–401.

Hurst, L. C. (1982). What was wrong with Anna O? *Journal of the Royal Society of Medicine, 75,* 129–131.

Hyde, J. S. (2007). New directions in the study of gender similarities and differences. *Current Directions in Psychological Science, 16,* 259–263.

Hyde, J. S., & Linn, M. C. (1988). Gender differences in verbal ability: A meta-analysis. *Psychological Bulletin, 104,* 53–69.

Hyman, I. E. Jr., Husband, T. H., & Billings, F. J. (1995). False memories of childhood experiences. *Applied Cognitive Psychology, 3,* 181–197.

IMDB. (2015a). Jennifer Lawrence biography. Retrieved from http://www.imdb.com/name/nm2225369/bio

IMDB. (2015b). *My stroke of insight.* Retrieved from http://www.imdb.com/title/tt1738297/?ref_=nm_flmg_wr_1

iminmotion.net. (n.d.). Ivonne Marcela Mosquera-Schmidt's website. Retrieved from http://iminmotion.net/about.html

Impey, C., Buxner, S., Antonellis, J. (2012). Non-scientific beliefs among undergraduate students. *Astronomy Education Review, 11.* doi:10.3847/AER2012016

Ingold, J. (2013, September 30). Sides debate lengthy witness lists for James Holmes trial. *The Denver Post.* Retrieved from http://www.denverpost.com/breakingnews/ci_24205468/psychiatric-exam-up-debate-new-aurora-theater-shooting#

Interlandi, J. (2012, June 22). When my crazy father actually lost his mind. *The New York Times.* Retrieved from http://www.nytimes.com/2012/06/24/magazine/when-my-crazy-father-actually-lost-his-mind.html?_r=0

International Dyslexia Association. (2015). *Dyslexia basics.* Retrieved from http://eida.org/dyslexia-basics/

Intersex Society of North America. (2008). *How common is intersex?* Retrieved from http://www.isna.org/faq/frequency

Inui, K., Urakawa, T., Yamahiro, K., Otsuru, N., Takeshima, Y., Nishihara, M., . . . Kakigi, R. (2010). Echoic memory of a single pure tone by change-related brain activity. *BMS Neuroscience, 11,* 135–145.

Ireland, M. (2012). Meditation and psychological health and functioning: A descriptive and critical review. *Scientific Review of Mental Health Practice, 9,* 4–19.

Isen, A. (2008). Some ways in which positive affect influences decision making and problem solving. In M. Lewis, J. M. Haviland-Jones, & L. F. Barrett (Eds.), *Handbook of emotions* (3rd ed., pp. 548–573). New York: Guilford Press.

Iversen, L. (2003). Cannabis and the brain. *Brain, 126,* 1252–1270.

Izard, C. E. (1992). Basic emotions, relations among emotions, and emotion-cognition relations. *Psychological Review, 99,* 561–565.

Izard, C. E. (2007). Basic emotions, natural kinds, emotion schemas, and a new paradigm. *Perspectives on Psychological Science, 2,* 260–280.

Jaaro-Peled, H., Ayhan, Y., Pletnikov, M. V., & Sawa, A. (2010). Review of pathological hallmarks of Schizophrenia: Comparison of genetic models with patients and nongenetic models. *Schizophrenia Bulletin, 36,* 301–313.

Jacobs, H. (2012). Don't ask, don't tell, don't publish. *EMBO Reports, 13*(5), 393.

Jacobson, E. (1938). *Progressive relaxation.* Chicago: University of Chicago Press.

Jacobson, N. S., & Addis, M. E. (1993). Research on couples and couple therapy. What do we know and where are we going? *Journal of Consulting and Clinical Psychology, 61,* 85–93.

James, L. E., & Burke, D. M. (2000). Phonological priming effects on word retrieval and tip-of-the-tongue experiences in young and older adults. *Journal of Experimental Psychology: Learning, Memory, and Cognition, 26,* 1378–1391.

James, S. D. (2008, May 7). Wild child speechless after tortured life. *ABC News.* Retrieved from http://abcnews.go.com/Health/story?id=4804490&page=1#.UW4DxHApsVs

James, W. J. (1890/1983). *The principles of psychology.* Cambridge, MA: Harvard University Press.

Jameson, D., & Hurvich, L. M. (1989). Essay concerning color constancy. *Annual Review of Psychology, 40,* 1–24.

Janata, P., & Paroo, K. (2006). Acuity of auditory images in pitch and time. *Perception & Psychophysics, 68,* 829–844.

Jang, K. L., Livesley, W. J., & Vernon, P. A. (1996). Heritability of the big five personality dimensions and their facets: A twin study. *Journal of Personality, 64,* 577–592.

Janis, I. J., Kaye, D., & Kirschner, P. (1965). Facilitating effects of "eating-while-reading" on responsiveness to persuasive communication. *Journal of Personality and Social Psychology, 1,* 181–186.

Janis, I. L. (1972). *Victims of groupthink: A psychological study of foreign-policy decisions and fiascoes.* Oxford, UK: Houghton Mifflin.

Janis, I. L., & Feshbach, S. (1953). Effects of fear-arousing communications. *Journal of Abnormal and Social Psychology, 48,* 78–92.

Jasper, J. D., Goel, R., Einarson, A., Gallo, M., & Koren, G. (2001). Effects of framing on teratogenic risk perception in pregnant women. *Lancet, 358,* 1237–1238.

Jenaro, C., Flores, N., & Arias, B. (2007). Burnout and coping in human service practitioners. *Professional Psychology: Research and Practice, 38,* 80–87.

Jessberger, S., & Gage, F. H. (2014). Adult neurogenesis: Bridging the gap between mice and humans. *Trends in Cell Biology, 24*(10), 558–563.

Jeste, D. V., Savla, G. N., Thompson, W. K., Vahia, I. V., Glorioso, D. K., Palmer, B. W., . . . Depp, C. A. (2013). Association between older age and more successful aging: Critical role of resilience and depression. *American Journal of Psychiatry, 170,* 188–196. doi:10.1176/appi.ajp.2012.12030386

Jiang, Y., Chew, S. H., & Ebstein, R. P. (2013). The role of D4 receptor gene exon lll polymorphisms in shaping human altruism and prosocial behavior. *Frontiers in Human Neuroscience, 7,* 1–7.

Johnson, D. M. (2005). *Introduction to and review of simulator sickness research* (Research Report 1832, Army Project No. 2O262785A790). Arlington, VA: U.S. Army Research Institute for the Behavioral and Social Sciences. Retrieved from http://www.dtic.mil/cgi-bin/GetTRDoc?AD=ADA434495

Johnson, H. D., McNair, R., Vojick, A., Congdon, D., Monacelli, J., & Lamont, J. (2006). Categorical and continuous measurement of sex-role orientation: Differences in associations with young adults' reports of well-being. *Social Behavior and Personality, 34,* 59–76.

Johnson, H. D., Sholcosky, D., Gabello, K., Ragni, R., & Ogonosky, N. (2003). Sex differences in public restroom handwashing behavior associated with visual behavior prompts. *Perceptual and Motor Skills, 97,* 805–810.

Johnson, L. R., LeDoux, J. E., & Doyère, V. (2009). Hebbian reverberations in emotional memory micro circuits. *Frontiers in Neuroscience, 3,* 198–205.

Johnson, P. L., Truitt, W., Fitz, S. D., Minick, P. E., Dietrich, A., Sanghani, S., . . . Shekhar, A. (2010). A key role for orexin in panic anxiety. *Nature Medicine, 16,* 111–115.

Johnson, R. D. (1987). Making judgments when information is missing: Inferences, biases, and framing effects. *Acta Psychologica, 66,* 69–72.

Johnson, W., & Bouchard, T. J. (2011). The MISTRA data: Forty-two mental ability tests in three batteries. *Intelligence, 39,* 82–88.

Johnston, L. D., O'Malley, P. M., Bachman, J. G., & Schulenberg, J. E. (2012). *Monitoring the future national results on adolescent drug use: Overview of key findings, 2011.* Ann Arbor: Institute for Social Research, University of Michigan.

Johnston, M. V. (2009). Plasticity in the developing brain: Implications for rehabilitation. *Developmental Disabilities Research Reviews, 15,* 94–101.

Jones, B. E. (2003). Arousal systems. *Frontiers in Bioscience, 8,* 438–451.

Jones, E. E., & Harris, V. A. (1967). The attribution of attitudes. *Journal of Experimental Social Psychology, 3,* 1–24.

Jones, K. (2013). Discouraging social loafing during team-based assessments. *Teaching Innovation Projects, 3,* Article 13.

Jones, N. (2014, August 12). Do these famous middle children live up to the stereotype? *People.* Retrieved from http://www.people.com/article/celebrity-middle-children

Jordan, J. (2009, May 13). Wanda Sykes becomes mom of twins! *People.* Retrieved from http://www.people.com/people/article/0,20278746,00.html

Jordan-Young, R. M. (2012). Hormones, context, and "Brain Gender": A review of evidence from congenital adrenal hyperplasia. *Social Science & Medicine, 74,* 1738–1744.

Joseph, N. T., Matthews, K. A., & Myers, H. F. (2013, March 25). Conceptualizing health consequences of Hurricane Katrina from the perspective of socioeconomic status decline. *Health Psychology.* doi:10.1037/a0031661

Josephs, R. A., Newman, M. L., Brown, R. P., & Beer, J. M. (2003). Status, testosterone, and human intellectual performance: Stereotype threat as status concern. *Psychological Science, 14,* 158–163.

Joshua, A. M., Cotroneo, A., & Clarke, S. (2005). Humor and oncology. *Journal of Clinical Oncology, 23,* 645–648.

Jouvet, M. (1979). What does a cat dream about? *Trends in Neurosciences, 2,* 280–282.

Juberg, D. R., Alfano, K., Coughlin, R. J., & Thompson, K. M. (2001). An observational study of object mouthing behavior by young children. *Pediatrics, 107,* 135–142.

Julien, R. M., Advokat, C. D., & Comaty, J. E. (2011). *A primer of drug action* (12th ed.). New York: Worth Publishers.

Julien, R. M., & DiCecco, K. (2010). To intend or not to intend: That is the question. *Journal of Legal Nurse Consulting, 21,* 10–14.

Junco, R., & Cotten, S. R. (2012). No A 4 U: The relationship between multitasking and academic performance. *Computers and Education, 59,* 505–514.

Jung, C. G. (1969). *Collected works: Vol. 8. The structure and dynamics of the psyche* (R. F. C. Hull, Ed., 2nd ed.). Princeton, NJ: Princeton University Press.

Jussim, L., & Harber, K. D. (2005). Teacher expectations and self-fulfilling prophecies: Knowns and unknowns, resolved and unresolved controversies. *Personality and Social Psychology Review, 9,* 131–155.

Kaduvettoor-Davidson, A., & Inman, A. G. (2013). South Asian Americans: Perceived discrimination, stress, and well-being. *Asian American Journal of Psychology, 4,* 155–165. doi:10.1037/a0030634

Kagan, J. (1985). The human infant. In A. M. Rogers & C. J. Scheirer (Eds.), *The G. Stanley Hall lecture series* (Vol. 5., pp. 55–86). Washington, DC: American Psychological Association.

Kagan, J. (2003). Biology, context, and developmental inquiry. *Annual Review of Psychology, 54,* 1–23.

Kagan, J., & Snidman, N. (1991). Temperamental factors in human development. *American Psychologist, 46,* 856–862.

Kahlenberg, S. G., & Hein, M. M. (2010). Progression on Nickelodeon? Gender-role stereotypes in toy commercials. *Sex Roles, 62,* 830–847.

Kahn, J. (2011, December 5). Born to run back. *Runner's World,* Retrieved from http://www.runnersworld.com/runners-stories/born-run-back?page=single

Kahneman, D., & Tversky, A. (1973). On the psychology of prediction. *Psychological Review, 80,* 238–251.

Kahneman, D., & Tversky, A. (1984). Choices, values, and frames. *American Psychologist, 39,* 341–350.

Kahneman, D., & Tversky, A. (1996). On the reality of cognitive illusions. *Psychological Review, 103,* 582–591.

Kalin, N. H., Shelton, S. E., & Davidson, R. J. (2004). The role of the central nucleus of the amygdala in mediating fear and anxiety in the primate. *Journal of Neuroscience, 24,* 5506–5515.

Kaminski, J., Call, J., & Fischer, J. (2004). Word learning in a domestic dog: Evidence for "fast mapping." *Science, 304,* 1682–1683.

Kanai, R., Bahrami, B., Roylance, R., & Rees, G. (2012). Online social network size is reflected in human brain structure. *Proceedings of the Royal Society B, 279,* 1327–1334.

Kandel, E. R. (2009). The biology of memory: A forty-year perspective. *Journal of Neuroscience, 29,* 12748–12756.

Kandel, E. R., & Pittenger, C. (1999). The past, the future and the biology of memory storage. *Philosophical Transactions: Biological Sciences, 354,* 2027–2052.

Kandler, C., Bleidorn, W., & Riemann, R. (2012). Left or right? Sources of political orientation: The roles of genetic factors, cultural transmission, assortative mating, and personality. *Journal of Personality and Social Psychology, 102,* 633–645.

Kandler, C., Bleidorn, W., Riemann, R., Spinath, F. M., Thiel, W., & Angleitner, A. (2010). Sources of cumulative continuity in personality: A longitudinal multiple-rater twin study. *Journal of Personality and Social Psychology, 98,* 995–1008.

Kaneda, H., Maeshima, K., Goto, N., Kobayakawa, T., Ayabe-Kanamura, S., & Saito, S. (2000). Decline in taste and odor discrimination abilities with age, and relationship between gustation and olfaction. *Chemical Senses, 25,* 331–337.

Kanwisher, N., McDermott, J., & Chun, M. M. (1997). The fusiform face area: A module in human extrastriate cortex specialized for face perception. *Journal of Neuroscience, 17,* 4302–4311.

Kapur, S. (2003). Psychosis as a state of aberrant salience: A framework linking biology, phenomenology, and pharmacology in schizophrenia. *American Journal of Psychiatry, 160,* 13–23.

Karam, E. G., Mneimneh, Z. N., Dimassi, H., Fayyad, J. A., Karam, A. N., Nasser, S. C., . . . Kessler, R. C. (2008). Lifetime prevalence of mental disorders in Lebanon: First onset, treatment, and exposure to war. *PLOS Medicine, 5,* 0579–0586.

Karlen, S. J., Kahn, D. M., & Krubitzer, L. (2006). Early blindness results in abnormal cortico-cortical and thalamocortical connections. *Neuroscience, 142,* 843–858.

Karremans, J. C., Stroebe, W., & Claus, J. (2006). Beyond Vicary's fantasies: The impact of subliminal priming and brand choice. *Journal of Experimental Social Psychology, 42,* 792–798.

Kasisomayajula, V., Herbst, R. S., Land, S. R., Leischow, S. J., Shields, P. G., & Writing Committee for the American Association for Cancer Research Task Force on Tobacco and Cancer. (2010). Tobacco and cancer: An American Association for Cancer Research policy statement. *Cancer Research, 70,* 3419–3430.

Kassin, S., Fein, S., & Markus, H. R. (2011). *Social psychology* (8th ed.). Belmont, CA: Wadsworth, Cengage Learning.

Kastenbaum, R., & Costa, P. T. Jr. (1977). Psychological perspectives on death. *Annual Review of Psychology, 28,* 225–249.

Katotomichelakis, M., Balatsouras, D., Tripsianis, G., Davris, S., Maroudias, N., Danielides, V., & Simopoulos, C. (2007). The effect of smoking on the olfactory function. *Rhinology, 45,* 273–280.

Kaufman, M. T. (2007, July 25). Albert Ellis, 93, influential psychotherapist, dies. *The New York Times.* Retrieved from http://www.nytimes.com/2007/07/25/nyregion/25ellis.html?pagewanted=all&_r=0

Kawa, S., & Giordano, J. (2012). A brief historicity of the *Diagnostic and Statistical Manual of Mental Disorders*: Issues and implications for the future of psychiatric canon and practice. *Philosophy, Ethics, and Humanities in Medicine, 7,* 1–9.

Kay, L. M., & Sherman, S. M. (2007). An argument for an olfactory thalamus. *Trends in Neurosciences, 30,* 47–53.

Kazdin, A. E. (1982). The token economy: A decade later. *Journal of Applied Behavior Analysis, 15,* 431–445.

Keel, P. K., & Klump, K. L. (2003). Are eating disorders culture-bound syndromes? Implications for conceptualizing their etiology. *Psychological Bulletin, 129,* 747–769.

Keesey, R. E., & Hirvonen, M. D. (1997). Body weight set-points: Determination and adjustment. *Journal of Nutrition, 127,* 1875S–1883S.

Keirstead, H. S., Nistor, G., Bernal, G., Totoiu, M., Cloutier, F., Sharp, K., & Oswald, S. (2005). Human embryonic stem cell-derived oligodendrocyte progenitor cell transplants remyelinate and restore locomotion after spinal cord injury. *Journal of Neuroscience, 25,* 4694–4705.

Keith, S. E., Michaud, D. S., & Chiu, V. (2008). Evaluating the maximum playback sound levels from portable digital audio players. *Journal of the Acoustical Society of America, 123,* 4227–4237.

Keller, A., & Malaspina, D. (2013). Hidden consequences of olfactory dysfunction: a patient report series. *BMC Ear, Nose and Throat Disorders, 13*(8). doi:10.1186/1472-6815-13-8

Kemeny, M. E., & Shestyuk, A. (2008). Emotions, the neuroendocrine and immune systems, and health. In M. Lewis, J. M. Haviland-Jones, & L. F. Barrett (Eds.), *Handbook of emotions* (3rd ed., pp. 661–675). New York: Guilford Press.

Kempton, M. J., Salvador, Z., Munafò, M. R., Geddes, J. R., Simmons, A., Frangou, S., & Williams, S. C. R. (2011). Structural neuroimaging studies in major depressive disorder. *Archives of General Psychiatry, 68,* 675–690.

Kendall, A. E. (2012, June). *U.S. response to the global threat of HIV/AIDS: Basic facts.* Washington, DC: Congressional Research Service.

Kennedy, N., Boydell, J., Kalidindi, S., Fearon, P., Jones, P. B., van Os, J., & Murray, R. M. (2005). Gender differences in incidence and age at onset of mania and bipolar disorder over a 35-year period in Camberwell, England. *American Journal of Psychiatry, 162,* 257–262.

Kennedy, P. G. E., & Chaudhuri, A. (2002). Herpes simplex encephalitis. *Journal of Neurology, Neurosurgery & Psychiatry, 13,* 237–238.

Kennedy, S. H., Giacobbe, P., Rizvi, S. J., Placenza, F. M., Nishikawa, Y., Mayberg, H. S., & Lozano, A. M. (2011). Deep brain stimulation for treatment-resistant depression: Follow-up after 3 to 6 years. *American Journal of Psychiatry, 168,* 502–510.

Kerr, N. L., & Tindale, R. S. (2004). Group performance and decision making. *Annual Review of Psychology, 55,* 623–655.

Kessler, R. C. (2010). The prevalence of mental illness. In T. L. Scheid & T. N. Brown (Eds.), *A handbook for the study of mental health: Social contexts, theories, and systems* (2nd ed., pp. 46–63). Cambridge, UK: Cambridge University Press.

Kessler, R. C., Berglund, P., Demler, O., Jin, R., Koretz, D., Merikangas, K. R., . . . Wang, P. S. (2003). The epidemiology of major depressive disorder: Results from the National Comorbidity Survey Replication (NCS-R). *Journal of the American Medical Association, 289,* 3095–3105.

Kessler, R. C., Berglund, P., Delmer, O., Jin, R., Merikangas, K. R., & Walters, E. E. (2005). Lifetime prevalence and age-of-onset distributions of *DSM-IV* disorders in the National Comorbidity Survey Replication. *Archives of General Psychiatry, 62,* 593–602.

Kessler, R. C., Chiu, W. T., Demler, O., & Walters, E. E. (2005). Prevalence, severity, and comorbidity of 12-month *DSM-IV* disorders in the National Comorbidity Survey Replication. *Archives of General Psychiatry, 62,* 617–627.

Kessler, R. C., & Wang, P. S. (2008). The descriptive epidemiology of commonly occurring mental disorders in the United States. *Annual Review of Public Health, 29,* 115–129.

Key, M. S., Edlund, J. E., Sagarin, B. J., & Bizer, G. Y. (2009). Individual differences in susceptibility to mindlessness. *Personality and Individual Differences, 46,* 261–264.

Keys, T. E. (1945). *The history of surgical anesthesia.* New York: Schuman's.

Kidd, S. A., Eskenazi, B., & Wyrobek, A. J. (2001). Effects of male age on semen quality and fertility: A review of the literature. *Fertility and Sterility, 75,* 237–248.

Kihara, T., & Shimohama, S. (2004). Alzheimer's disease and acetylcholine receptors. *Acta Neurobiologiae Experimentalis, 64,* 99–106.

Kihlstrom, J. F. (1985). Hypnosis. *Annual Review of Psychology, 36,* 385–418.

Kim, D.-Y., Oh, B.-M., & Paik, N.-J. (2006). Central effect of botulinum toxin type A in humans. *International Journal of Neuroscience, 116,* 667–680.

King, B. M. (2006). The rise, fall, and resurrection of the ventromedial hypothalamus in the regulation of feeding behavior and body weight [Invited review]. *Physiology & Behavior, 87,* 221–244.

Kingsbury, M. K., & Coplan, R. J. (2012). Mothers' gender-role attitudes and their responses to young children's hypothetical display of shy and aggressive behaviors. *Sex Roles, 66,* 506–517.

Kinoshita, Y., Chen, J., Rapee, R. M., Bögels, S., Schneier, F. R., Choy, Y., . . . Furukawa, T. A. (2008). Cross-cultural study of conviction subtype Taijin Kyofu: Proposal and reliability of Nagoya-Osaka diagnostic criteria for social anxiety disorder. *Journal of Nervous and Mental Diseases, 196,* 307–313.

Kinsey, A. C., Pomeroy, W. B., & Martin, C. E. (1948). *Sexual behavior in the human male.* Philadelphia: W. B. Saunders.

Kinsey, A. C., Pomeroy, W. B., Martin, C. E., & Gebhard, P. H. (1953). *Sexual behavior in the human female.* Philadelphia: W. B. Saunders.

Kisilevsky, B. S., Hains, M. J., Brown, C.A., Lee, C. T., Cowperthwaite, B., Stutzman, S. S., . . . Wang, Z. (2008). Fetal sensitivity to properties of maternal speech and language. *Infant Behavior and Development, 32,* 59–71.

Kisilevsky, B. S., Hains, S. M. J., Lee, K., Xie, X., Huang, H., Ye, H. H., . . . Wang, Z. (2003). Effects of experience on fetal voice recognition. *Psychological Science, 14,* 220–224.

Klass, P. (2011, October 10). Hearing bilingual: How babies sort out language. *The New York Times.* Retrieved from http://www.nytimes.com/2011/10/11/health/views/11klass.html?_r=1

Klaver, C. C., Wolfs, R. C., Vingerling, J. R., Hoffman, A., & de Jong, P. T. (1998). Age-specific prevalence and causes of blindness and visual impairment in an older population: The Rotterdam Study. *Archives of Opthamology, 116,* 653–658.

Kleber, H. D., & DuPont, R. (2012). Physicians and medical marijuana. *American Journal of Psychiatry, 169,* 564–568.

Kleinman, A. (2004). Culture and depression. *New England Journal of Medicine, 351,* 951–953.

Klerman, E. B., & Dijk, D. J. (2004). Interindividual variation in sleep duration and its association with sleep debt in young adults. *Sleep, 28,* 1253–1259.

Klimstra, T. A., Luyckx, K., Hale III, W. W., Frijns, T., van Lier, P. A. C., & Meeus, W. H. J. (2010). Short-term fluctuations in identity: Introducing a micro-level approach to identity formation. *Journal of Personality and Social Psychology, 99,* 191–202.

Klugman, A., & Gruzelier, J. (2003). Chronic cognitive impairment in users of "ecstasy" and cannabis. *World Psychiatry, 2,* 184–190.

Kluver, H., & Bucy, P. (1939). Preliminary analysis of function of the temporal lobe in monkeys. *Archives of Neurology, 42,* 979–1000.

Knafo, A., & Israel, S. (2010). Genetic and environmental influences on prosocial behavior. In M. Mikulincer & P. R. Shaver (Eds.), *Prosocial motives, emotions, and behavior: The better angels of our nature* (pp. 149–167). Washington, DC: American Psychological Association.

Knapp, S., & VandeCreek, L. (2000). Recovered memories of childhood abuse: Is there an underlying professional consensus? *Professional Psychology: Research and Practice, 31,* 365–371.

Knecht, S., Dräger, B., Deppe, M., Bobe, L., Lohmann, H., Flöel, A., . . . Henningsen, H. (2000). Handedness and hemispheric language dominance in healthy humans. *Brain, 123,* 74–81.

Kneer, J., Glock, S., & Rieger, D. (2012). Fast and not furious? Reduction of cognitive dissonance in smokers. *Social Psychology, 43,* 81–91.

Knickmeyer, R. C., Gouttard, S., Kang, C., Evans, D., Wilber, J., Smith, K., . . . Gilmore, J. H. (2008). A structural MRI study of human brain development from birth to 2 years. *Journal of Neuroscience, 47*(28), 12176–12182.

Knudsen, E. I. (2004). Sensitive periods in the development of the brain and behavior. *Journal of Cognitive Neuroscience, 16,* 1412–1425.

Knutsson, A. (2003). Health disorders of shift workers. *Occupational Medicine, 53,* 103–108. Retrieved from http://occmed.oxfordjournals.org/content/53/2/103.long

Ko, H. J., & Youn, C. H. (2011). Effects of laughter therapy on depression, cognition and sleep among the community-dwelling elderly. *Geriatrics & Gerontology International, 3,* 267–274.

Kobasa, S. C. (1979). Stressful life events, personality, and health: An inquiry into hardiness. *Journal of Personality and Social Psychology, 37,* 1–11.

Koch, I., Lawo, V., Fels, J., & Vorländer, M. (2011). Switching in the cocktail party: Exploring intentional control of auditory selective attention. *Journal of Experimental Psychology: Human Perception and Performance, 37,* 1140–1147.

Kochanek, K. D., Xu, J., Murphy, S. L., Miniño, A. M., & Kung., H.-C. (2011). *Deaths: Final data for 2009* (National Vital Statistics Reports, Vol. 60, No. 3). Hyattsville, MD: National Center for Health Statistics. Retrieved from http://www.cdc.gov/nchs/data/nvsr/nvsr59/nvsr59_04.pdf

Koelsch, S., Gunter, T. C., Cramon, D. Y., Zysset, S., Lohmann, G., & Friederici, A. D. (2002). Bach speaks: A cortical "language-network" serves the processing of music. *NeuroImage, 17,* 956–966.

Koenig, B. A., & Gates-Williams, J. (1995). Understanding cultural difference in caring for dying patients. *Western Journal of Medicine, 163,* 244–249.

Kofman, J., & Hopper, K. (2010, October 13). Chile's successful rescue sets example for other countries. *ABC News International.* Retrieved from http://abcnews.go.com/International/chilean-miners-rescued-united-states-success/story?id=11874238

Kohlberg, L. (1981). *The philosophy of moral development: Vol. 1. Essays on moral development.* San Francisco: Harper & Row.

Kohlberg, L., & Hersh, R. H. (1977). Moral development: A review of the theory. *Theory into Practice, 16,* 53–59.

Kohler, P. K., Manhart, L. E., & Lafferty, W. E. (2008). Abstinence-only and comprehensive sex education in the initiation of sexual activity and teen pregnancy. *Journal of Adolescent Health, 42,* 344–351.

Köhler, W. (1925). *The mentality of apes.* New York: Harcourt Brace Jovanovich.

Kolb, B., & Gibb, R. (2011). Brain plasticity and behaviour in the developing brain. *Journal of the Canadian Academy of Child and Adolescent Psychiatry, 20,* 265–276.

Kolb, B., & Whishaw, I. Q. (1998). Brain plasticity and behavior. *Annual Review of Psychology, 49,* 43–64.

Kolb, B., & Whishaw, I. Q. (2009). *Fundamentals of human neuropsychology* (6th ed.). New York: Worth Publishers.

Kolb, B., & Whishaw, I. Q. (2011). *An introduction to brain and behavior* (3rd ed.). New York: Worth Publishers.

Kolmes, K. (2012, December). Social media in the future of professional psychology. *Professional Psychology: Research and Practice, 43*(6), 606–612. doi:10.1037/a0028678

Komai, T. (1951). Notes on lingual gymnastics. *Journal of Heredity, 42,* 293–297.

Kornheiser, A. S. (1976). Adaptation to laterally displaced vision: A review. *Psychological Bulletin, 5,* 783–816.

Kosslyn, S. M. (1978). Measuring the visual angle of the mind's eye. *Cognitive Psychology, 10,* 356–389.

Kosslyn, S. M., Ball, T. M., & Reiser, B. J. (1978). Visual images preserve metric spatial information: Evidence from studies of image scanning. *Journal of Experimental Psychology: Human Perception and Performance, 4,* 47–60.

Kosslyn, S. M., Thompson, W. L., Costantini-Ferrando, M. F., Alpert, N. M., & Spiegel, D. (2000). Hypnotic visual illusion alters color processing in the brain. *American Journal of Psychiatry, 157,* 1279–1284.

Kossoff, E. H., Vining, E. P. G., Pillas, D. J., Pyzik, P. L., Avellino, A. M., Carson, B. S., & Freeman, J. M. (2003). Hemispherectomy for intractable unihemispheric epilepsy: Epilepsy vs. outcome. *Neurology, 61,* 887–890.

Kothadia, J. P., Chhabra, S., Marcus, A., May, M., Saraiya, B., & Jabbour, S. K. (2012). Anterior mediastinal mass in a young marijuana smoker: A rare case of small-cell lung cancer. *Case Reports in Medicine,* Article 754231, 1–4.

Kouider, S., & Dehaene, S. (2007). Levels of processing during non-conscious perception: A critical review of visual masking. *Philosophical Transactions of the Royal Society B: Biological Sciences, 362,* 857–875.

Kounios, J., & Beeman, M. (2009). The *Aha!* moment: The cognitive neuroscience of insight. *Current Directions in Psychological Science, 18,* 210–216.

Kovács, A. M., & Mehler, J. (2009). Cognitive gains in 7-month-old bilingual infants. *Proceedings of the National Academy of Sciences, 106,* 6556–6560.

Kozel, A. F., Johnson, K. A., Grenesko, E. L., Laken, S. J., Kose, S., Lu, X., . . . George, M. S. (2009). Functional MRI detection of deception after committing a mock sabotage crime. *Journal of Forensic Science, 54,* 220–231.

Kraft, D. (2012). Successful treatment of heavy smoker in one hour using split screen imagery, aversion, and suggestions to eliminate cravings. *Contemporary Hypnosis and Integrative Therapy, 29,* 175–188.

Kramer, A. F., Erickson, K. I., & Colcombe, S. J. (2006). Exercise, cognition, and the aging brain. *Journal of Applied Physiology, 101,* 1237–1242.

Krasnova, I. N., & Cadet, J. L. (2009). Methamphetamine toxicity and messengers of death. *Brain Research Reviews, 60,* 379–407.

Kraul, C. (2010, October 11). Health experts monitoring trapped miners in Chile brace for unexpected ailments. *Los Angeles Times.* Retrieved from http://articles.latimes.com/2010/oct/11/world/la-fg-chile-miners-medical-20101011

Krebs, D. L., & Denton, K. (2005). Toward a more pragmatic approach to morality: A critical evaluation of Kohlberg's model. *Psychological Review, 112,* 629–649.

Krech, D., & Crutchfield, R. S. (1958). *Elements of psychology.* New York: Alfred A. Knopf.

Kreiman, G., Koch, C., & Fried, I. (2000). Imagery neurons in the human brain. *Nature, 408,* 357–361.

Kripke, D. F., Langer, R. D., & Kline, L. E. (2012). Hypnotics' association with mortality or cancer: A matched cohort study. *BMJ Open, 2,* e000850.

Krizan, Z., & Windschitl, P. D. (2007). The influence of outcome desirability on optimism. *Psychological Bulletin, 133,* 95–121.

Krosnick, J. A., Betz, A. L., Jussim, L. J., & Lynn, A. R. (1992). Subliminal conditioning of attitudes. *Personality and Social Psychology Bulletin, 18,* 152–162.

Kruger, J., Blanck, H. M., & Gillespie, C. (2006). Dietary and physical activity behaviors among adults successful at weight loss maintenance. *International Journal of Behavioral Nutrition and Physical Activity, 3,* 17–27.

Kruk, M. R., Halász, J., Meelis, W. & Haller, J. (2004). Fast positive feedback between the adrenocortical stress response and a brain mechanism involved in aggressive behavior. *Behavioral Neuroscience, 118,* 1062–1070.

Kubinec, V-L. (2013, September 5). Brian Sinclair ignored by Winnipeg ER: Report. *CBC News.* Retrieved from http://www.cbc.ca/news/canada/manitoba/brian-sinclair-ignored-by-winnipeg-er-report-1.1385107

Kübler-Ross, E. (2009). *On death and dying. What the dying have to teach doctors, nurses, clergy, and their own families* (40th Anniversary Ed.). London: Routledge.

Kucharski, A. (1984). History of frontal lobotomy in the United States, 1935–1955. *Neurosurgery, 14,* 765–772.

Kuhl, P. K., Conboy, B. T., Padden, D., Nelson, T., & Pruitt, J. (2005). Early speech perception and later language development: Implications for the "Critical Period." *Language Learning and Development, 1,* 237–264.

Kujawa, S. G., & Liberman, M. C. (2006). Acceleration of age-related hearing loss by early noise exposure: evidence of a misspent youth. *Journal of Neuroscience, 26,* 2115–2123.

Kuo, Z. Y. (1921). Giving up instincts in psychology. *Journal of Philosophy, 18,* 654–664.

Laan, E., & Janssen, E. (2007). How do men and women feel? Determinants of subjective experience of sexual arousal. In E. Janssen (Ed.), *The psychophysiology of sex* (pp. 278–290). The Kinsey Institute Series. Bloomington: Indiana University Press.

Ladouceur, C. D. (2012). Neural systems supporting cognitive-affective interactions in adolescence: The role of puberty and implications for affective disorders. *Frontiers in Integrative Neuroscience, 6,* 1–11.

Laeng, B., & Falkenberg, L. (2007). Women's pupillary responses to sexually significant others during the hormonal cycle. *Hormones and Behavior, 52,* 520–530.

Laeng, B., Profeti, I., Sæther, L., Adolfsdottir, S., Lundervold, A. J., Vangberg, T., . . . Waterloo, K. (2010). Invisible expressions evoke core impressions. *Emotion, 10,* 573–386.

Lahav, O., & Mioduser, D. (2008). Construction of cognitive maps of unknown spaces using a multi-sensory virtual environment for people who are blind. *Computers in Human Behavior, 24,* 1139–1155.

Lakdawalla, D. N., & Schoeni, R. F. (2003). Is nursing home demand affected by the decline in age difference between spouses? *Demographic Research, 8,* 279–304.

Lakes, K., Lopez, S. R., & Garro, L. C. (2006). Cultural competence and psychotherapy: Applying anthropologically informed conceptions of culture. *Psychotherapy: Theory, Research, Practice, Training, 43,* 380–396.

Lambert, M. J., Hansen, N. B., & Finch, A. E. (2001). Patient-focused research: Using patient outcome data to enhance treatment effects. *Journal of Consulting and Clinical Psychology, 69,* 159–172.

Lando, H. A. (1976). On being sane in insane places: A supplemental report. *Professional Psychology, 7,* 47–52.

Landrum, R. E. (2001). I'm getting my bachelor's degree in psychology—what can I do with it? *Eye on Psi Chi, 6,* 22–24.

Lange, C. G., & James, W. (1922). The Emotions. In K. Dunlap (Ed.), *Psychology Classics: A Series of Reprints and Translations.* Baltimore, MD: Williams & Wilkins.

Langer, E., Blank, A., & Chanowitz, B. (1978). The mindlessness of ostensibly thoughtful action: The role of "placebic" information in interpersonal interaction. *Journal of Personality and Social Psychology, 36,* 635–642.

Langer, E. J., & Rodin, J. (1976). The effects of choice and enhanced personal responsibility for the aged: A field experiment in an institutional setting. *Journal of Personality and Social Psychology, 34,* 191–198.

Langlois, J. H., Kalakanis, L., Rubenstein, A. J., Larson, A., Hallam, M., & Smoot, M. (2000). Maxims or myths of beauty? A meta-analytic and theoretical review. *Psychological Bulletin, 126,* 390–423.

Långström, N., Rahman, Q., Carlström, E., & Lichtenstein, P. (2010). Genetic and environmental effects on same-sex sexual behavior: A population study of twins in Sweden. *Archives of Sexual Behavior, 39,* 75–80.

Langwith, J. (2010). *Perspectives on diseases and disorders.* Farmington Hills, MI: Greenhaven Press.

Lara, D. R. (2010). Caffeine, mental health, and psychiatric disorders. *Journal of Alzheimer's Disease, 20,* S239–S248.

Larsen, L., Hartmann, P., & Nyborg, H. (2008). The stability of general intelligence from early adulthood to middle-age. *Intelligence, 36,* 29–34.

Larsson, M., Finkel, D., & Pederson, N. L. (2000). Odor identification: Influences of age, gender, cognition, and personality. *Journal of Gerontology: Psychological Sciences, 55B,* P304–P310.

Larsson, M., & Willander, J. (2009). Autobiographical odor memory. *Annals of the New York Academy of Sciences, 1170,* 318–323.

Larzelere, R. E., & Baumrind. (2010). Are spanking injunctions scientifically supported? *Law and Contemporary Problems, 73,* 57–87.

Lashley, K. D. (1950). In search of the engram. *Symposia of the Society for Experimental Biology, 4,* 454–482.

Latané, B., & Darley, J. M. (1968). Group inhibition of bystander intervention in emergencies. *Journal of Personality and Social Psychology, 10,* 215–221.

Latané, B., Williams, K., & Harkins, S. (1979). Many hands make light the work: The causes and consequences of social loafing. *Journal of Personality and Social Psychology, 37,* 822–832.

Laumann, E. O., Gagnon, J. H., Michael, R. T., & Michaels, S. (1994). *The social organization of sexuality: Sexual practices in the United States.* Chicago: University of Chicago Press.

Laumann, E. O., Paik, A., & Rosen, R. C. (1999). Sexual dysfunction in the United States: Prevalence and predictors. *Journal of the American Medical Association, 281,* 537–544.

Lavee, Y., & Ben-Ari, A. (2008). The association of daily hassles and uplifts with family and life satisfaction: Does cultural orientation make a difference? *American Journal of Community Psychology, 41,* 89–98.

Lawler-Row, K. A., & Elliott, J. (2009). The role of religious activity and spirituality in the health and well-being of older adults. *Journal of Health Psychology, 14,* 43–52.

Lawn, J. E., Blencowe, H., Pattinson, R., Cousens, S., Kumar, S., Ibiebele, I., . . . Stanton, C. (2011). Stillbirths: Where? When? Why? How to make the data count? *Lancet, 377,* 1448–1463.

Lazarus, R. S. (1984). On the primacy of cognition. *American Psychologist, 39,* 124–129.

Lazarus, R. S. (1991a). Cognition and motivation in emotion. *American Psychologist, 46,* 352–367.

Lazarus, R. S. (1991b). Progress on a cognitive-motivational-relational theory of emotion. *American Psychologist, 46,* 819–834.

Lazarus, R. S. (1993). From psychological stress to the emotions: A history of changing outlooks. *Annual Review of Psychology, 44*, 1–21.

Lazarus, R. S., & Folkman, S. (1984). *Stress, appraisal, and coping.* New York: Springer.

LeBeau, R. T., Glenn, D., Liao, B., Wittchen, H.-U., Beesdo-Baum, K., Ollendick, T., & Craske, M. G. (2010). Specific phobia: A review of DSM-IV specific phobia and preliminary recommendations for DSM-V. *Depression and Anxiety, 27*, 148–167.

LeDoux, J. E. (1996). *The emotional brain: The mysterious underpinnings of emotional life.* New York: Simon & Schuster.

LeDoux, J. E. (2000). Emotion circuits in the brain. *Annual Review of Neuroscience, 23*, 155–184.

LeDoux, J. E. (2002). Emotion, memory and the brain. *Scientific American Special Edition, 12*, 62–71.

LeDoux, J. (2012). Rethinking the emotional brain. *Neuron, 73*, 653–676.

Lee, J. H., Chang, Y. S., Yoo, H. S., Ahn, S. Y., Seo, H. J., Choi, S. H., . . . Park, W. S. (2011). Swallowing dysfunction in very low birth weight infants with oral feeding desaturation. *World Journal of Pediatrics, 7*, 337–343.

Lee, J. H., O'Keefe, J. H., Bell, D., Hensrud, D. D., & Holick, M. F. (2008). Vitamin D deficiency an important, common, and easily treatable cardiovascular risk factor? *Journal of the American College of Cardiology, 52*, 1949–1956.

Lee, M. (2006, December 19). Anthony suspended 15 games for brawl. *The Washington Post.* Retrieved from http://www.washingtonpost.com/wp-dyn/content/article/2006/12/18/AR2006121800424.html

Lee, M. K., Kiesler, S. B., & Forlizzi, J. (2010). Receptionist or information kiosk: How do people talk with a robot? In K. Inkpen, C. Gutwin, & J. Tang (Eds.), *Proceedings of the 2010 ACM Conference on Computer-Supported Cooperative Work, Savannah, Georgia* (pp. 31–40). New York: Association for Computing Machinery.

Lee, P. A., Houk, C. P., Ahmed, S. F., & Hughes, I. A. (2006). Consensus statement on management of intersex disorders. *Pediatrics, 118*, e488–e500.

Lee, V. E., & Burkan, D. T. (2002). *Inequality at the starting gate.* Washington, DC: Economic Policy Institute.

Lee, W., Reeve, J., Xue, Y., & Xiong, J. (2012). Neural differences between intrinsic reasons for doing versus extrinsic reasons for doing: An fMRI study. *Neuroscience Research, 73*, 68–72.

Leichsenring, F., & Rabung, S. (2008). Effectiveness of long-term psychodynamic psychotherapy. *Journal of the American Medical Association, 300*, 1551–1565.

Leighty, K. A., Grand, A. P., Pittman Courte, V. L., Maloney, M. A., & Bettinger, T. L. (2013). Relational responding by eastern box turtles (*Terrapene carolina*) in a series of color discrimination tasks. *Journal of Comparative Psychology, 127*, 256–264. doi:10.1037/a0030942

Leinninger, G. (2011). Lateral thinking about leptin: A review of leptin action via the lateral hypothalamus. *Physiology & Behavior, 104*, 572–581.

Lenhart, A., Madden, M., Smith, A., Purcell, K., Zickuhr, K., & Rainie, L. (2011). *Teens, kindness and cruelty on social network sites.* Washington, DC: Pew Internet & American Life Project.

Lenzenweger, M. F., Lane, M. C., Loranger, A. W., & Kessler, R. C. (2007). DSM-IV personality disorders in the national comorbidity survey replication. *Biological Psychiatry, 62*, 553–564.

Leontopoulou, S., Jimerson, S. R., & Anderson, G. E. (2011). An international exploratory investigation of students' perceptions of stressful life events: Results from Greece, Cyprus, and the United States. *School Psychology International, 32*, 632–644.

Lerman, C., & Audrain-McGovern, J. (2010). Reinforcing effects of smoking: More than a feeling. *Biological Psychiatry, 67*, 699–701.

Lessmoellmann, A. (2006, October-4/November). Can we talk? *Scientific American Mind, 17*, 44–49. Retrieved from http://www.scientificamerican.com/article.cfm?id=can-we-talk

Levänen, S., Uutela, K., Salenius, S., & Hari, R. (2001). Cortical representations of sign language: Comparison of deaf signers and hearing non-signers. *Cerebral Cortex, 11*, 506–512.

LeVay, S. (1991). A difference in hypothalamic structure between heterosexual and homosexual men. *Science, 253*, 1034–1037.

Levenson, R. W., Carstensen, L. L., Friesen, W. V., & Ekman, P. (1991). Emotion, physiology, and expression in old age. *Psychology and Aging, 6*, 28–35.

Leventhal, H., Watts, J. C., & Pagano, F. (1967). Effects of fear and instructions on how to cope with danger. *Journal of Personality and Social Psychology, 6*, 313–321.

Levett-Jones, T., Sundin, D., Bagnall, M., Hague, K., Schuman, W., Taylor, C., & Wink, J. (2010). Learning to think like a nurse. *HNE Handover: For Nurses and Midwives, 3*, 15–20.

Levin, R. J. (2008). Critically revisiting aspects of the human sexual response cycle of Masters and Johnson: Correcting errors and suggesting modifications. *Sexual and Relationship Therapy, 23*, 393–399.

Levinson, D. F. (2006). The genetics of depression: A review. *Biological Psychiatry, 60*, 84–92.

Levy, R. A., & Ablon, S. J. (2010, February 23). Talk therapy: Off the couch and into the lab. *Scientific American.* Retrieved from http://www.scientificamerican.com/article/talk-therapy-off-couch-into-lab/

Lewis, D. J., & Duncan, C. P. (1956). Effect of different percentages of money reward on extinction of a lever-pulling response. *Journal of Experimental Psychology, 52*, 23–27.

Ley, J., Bennett, P., & Coleman, G. (2008). Personality dimensions that emerge in companion canines. *Applied Animal Behaviour Science, 110*, 305–317.

Li, A., Montaño, Z., Chen, V. J., & Gold, J. I. (2011). Virtual reality and pain management: Current trends and future directions. *Pain Management, 1*, 147–157.

Lichtwarck-Aschoff, A., Kunnen, S. E., & van Geert, P. L. C. (2009). Here we go again: A dynamic systems perspective on emotional rigidity across parent-adolescent conflicts. *Developmental Psychology, 45*, 1364–1375.

Licis, A. K., Desruisseau, D. M., Yamada, K. A., Duntley, S. P., & Gurnett, C. A. (2011). Novel findings in an extended family pedigree with sleepwalking. *Neurology, 76*, 49–52.

Liddle, J. R., Shackelford, T. K., & Weekes-Shackelford, V. A. (2012). Why can't we all just get along? Evolutionary perspectives on violence, homicide, and war. *Review of General Psychology, 16*, 24–36.

Lieberson, A. D. (2004, November 8). How long can a person survive without food? *Scientific American.* Retrieved from http://www.scientificamerican.com/article.cfm?id=how-long-can-a-person-sur

Lilienfeld, S. O. (2012). Public skepticism of psychology: Why many people perceive the study of human behavior as unscientific. *American Psychologist, 67*, 111–129.

Lilienfeld, S. O., & Arkowitz, H. (2011, January/February). The insanity verdict on trial. *Scientific American Mind*, 64–65.

Lilienfeld, S. O., Lynn, S. J., Ruscio, J., & Beyerstein, B. L. (2010). Busting big myths in popular psychology. *Scientific American Mind, 21*, 42–49.

Lilienfeld, S. O., Lynn, S. J., Ruscio, J., & Beyerstein, B. L. (2011). *50 great myths of popular psychology: Shattering widespread misconceptions about human behavior.* Hoboken, NJ: Wiley-Blackwell.

Lilienfeld, S. O., Wood, J. M., & Garb, H. N. (2005). What's wrong with this picture? *Scientific American Mind, 16*, 50–57.

Lillard, A. S., & Peterson, J. (2011). The immediate impact of different types of television on young children's executive function. *Pediatrics, 128*, 644–649.

Lim, J., & Dinges, D. F. (2010). A meta-analysis of the impact of short-term sleep deprivation on cognitive variables. *Psychological Bulletin, 136*, 375–389.

Lindau, S. T., Schumm, L. P., Laumann, E. O., Levinson, W., O'Muircheartaigh, C. A., & Waite, L. J. (2007). A study of sexuality and health among older adults in the United States. *New England Journal of Medicine, 357*, 762–774.

Lindberg, S. M., Hyde, J. S., Petersen, J. L., & Linn, M. C. (2010). New trends in gender and mathematics performance: A meta-analysis. *Psychological Bulletin, 136,* 1123–1135.

Linden, J. (2012, July 5). Profile: Olympics-Lochte unfazed by challenge of tackling Phelps. *Reuters.com.* Retrieved from http://www.reuters.com/article/2012/07/05/oly-swim-lochte-profile-idUSL6E8I208620120705

Lineberry, T. W., & Bostwick, J. M. (2006). Methamphetamine abuse: A perfect storm of complications. *Mayo Clinic Proceedings, 81,* 77–84.

Linhares, J. M., Pinto, P. D., & Nascimento, S. M. (2008). The number of discernible colors in natural scenes. *Journal of the Optical Society of America, 25,* 2918–2924.

Linnenbrink, E. A., & Pintrich, P. R. (2002). Motivation as an enabler for academic success. *School Psychology Review, 31,* 313–327.

Linneroth, P. J., Mrdjenovich, A. J., & Moore, B. A. (2011). Professional burnout in clinical military psychologists: Recommendations before, during, and after deployment. *Professional Psychology: Research and Practice, 42,* 87–93.

Lipina, S. J., & Posner, M. I. (2012, August 17). The impact of poverty on the development of brain networks. *Frontiers in Human Neuroscience,* Article 238. Retrieved from http://journal.frontiersin.org/article/10.3389/fnhum.2012.00238/full

Littlewood, R. (2004). Commentary: Globalization, culture, body image, and eating disorders. *Culture, Medicine and Psychiatry, 28,* 597–602.

Liu, S., Chow, H. M., Xu, Y., Erkkinen, M. G., Swett, K. E., Eagle, M. W., . . . Braun, A. R. (2012). Neural correlates of lyrical improvisation: An fMRI study of freestyle rap. *Scientific Reports, 2.* doi:10.1038/srep00834

Liu, Y., Yu, C., Liang, M., Li, J., Tian, L., Zhou, Y., . . . Jiang, T. (2007). Whole brain functional connectivity in the early blind. *Brain, 130,* 2085–2096.

Livingston, I., Doyle, J., & Mangan, D. (2010, April 25). Stabbed hero dies as more than 20 people stroll past him. *New York Post.* Retrieved from http://www.nypost.com/p/news/local/queens/passers_by_let_good_sam_die_5SGkf5XDP5ooudVuEd8fbI

Lloyd, M.A. (1997, July 16). *Entry level positions obtained by psychology majors.* Retrieved from Psych Web: http://www.psywww.com/careers/entry.htm

Loftus, E. F. (1994). The repressed memory controversy. *American Psychologist, 49,* 443–445.

Loftus, E. F. (1997). Creating false memories. *Scientific American, 277,* 70–75.

Loftus, E. F. (2005). Planting misinformation in the human mind: A 30-year investigation of the malleability of memory. *Learning and Memory, 12,* 361–366.

Loftus, E. F., & Bernstein, D. M. (2005). Rich false memories. In A. F. Healy (Ed.), *Experimental cognitive psychology and its applications* (pp. 101–113). Washington, DC: American Psychological Association Press.

Loftus, E., & Ketcham, K. (1994). *The myth of repressed memory.* New York: St. Martin's Griffin.

Loftus, E. F., Miller, D. G., & Burns, H. J. (1978). Semantic integration of verbal information into a visual memory. *Journal of Experimental Psychology: Human Learning and Memory, 4,* 19–31.

Loftus, E. F., & Palmer, J. C. (1974). Reconstruction of automobile destruction. *Journal of Verbal Learning and Verbal Behavior, 13,* 585–589.

Loftus, E. F., & Pickrell, J. E. (1995). The formation of false memories. *Psychiatric Annals, 25,* 720–725.

Lopez-Garcia, E., Rodriguez-Artalejo, F., Rexrode, K. M., Logroscino, G., Hu, F. B., & van Dam, R. M. (2009). Coffee consumption and risk of stroke in women. *Circulation, 119,* 1116–1123.

Lorenz, K. Z. (1937). The companion in the bird's world. *The Auk, 54,* 245–273.

Lott, A. J., & Lott, B. E. (1965). Group cohesiveness as interpersonal attraction: A review of relationships with antecedent and consequent variables. *Psychological Bulletin, 64,* 259–309.

Lou, S., & Zhang, G. (2009). What leads to romantic attractions: Similarity, reciprocity, security, or beauty? Evidence from a speed-dating study. *Journal of Personality, 77,* 933–964.

Lowenstein, J. A., Blank, H., & Sauer, J. D. (2010). Uniforms affect the accuracy of children's eyewitness identification and decisions. *Journal of Investigative Psychology and Offender Profiling, 7,* 59–73.

Lu, Z.-L., Williamson, S. J., & Kaufman, L. (1992). Behavioral lifetime of human auditory sensory memory predicted by physiological measures. *Science, 258,* 1668–1670.

Ludel, J. (1978). *Introduction to sensory processes.* San Francisco: W. H. Freeman and Company.

Lund, C., De Silva, M., Plagerson, S., Cooper, S., Chisholm, D., Das, J., . . . Patel, V. (2011). Poverty and mental disorders: Breaking the cycle in low-income and middle-income countries. *Lancet, 78,* 1502–1514.

Lyall, S. (2007, November 4). In Stetson or wig, he's hard to pin down. *The New York Times.* Retrieved from http://www.nytimes.com/2007/11/04/movies/moviesspecial/04lyal.html

Lyckholm, L. J. (2004). Thirty years later: An oncologist reflects on Kübler-Ross's work. *American Journal of Bioethics, 4,* 29–31.

Lynch, G. (2002). Memory enhancement: The search for mechanism-based drugs. *Nature Neuroscience 5* (Suppl.), 1035–1038.

Lynn, S. J., Lilienfeld, S. O., Merckelbach, H., Giesbrecht, T., & van der Kloet, D. (2012). Dissociation and dissociative disorders: Challenging conventional wisdom. *Current Directions in Psychological Science, 21,* 48–53.

Lyubomirsky, S., Dickerhoof, R., Boehm, J. K., & Sheldon, K. M. (2011). Becoming happier takes both a will and a proper way: An experimental longitudinal intervention to boost well-being. *Emotion, 11,* 391–402.

Lyubomirsky, S., Sheldon, S. M., & Schkade, D. (2005). Pursuing happiness: The architecture of sustainable change. *Review of General Psychology, 9,* 111–131.

MacCann, C., Fogarty, G. J., Zeidner, M., & Roberts, R. D. (2011). Coping mediates the relationship between emotional intelligence (EI) and academic achievement. *Contemporary Educational Psychology, 36,* 60–70.

Maccoby, E. E., & Martin, J. A. (1983). Socialization in the context of the family: Parent-child interaction. In P. Mussen & E. M. Hetherington (Eds.), *Handbook of child psychology: Vol. IV. Socialization, personality and social development* (pp. 1–101). New York: John Wiley & Sons.

Mack, A. (2003). Inattentional blindness: Looking without seeing. *Current Directions in Psychological Science, 12,* 180–184.

Macmillan, M. (2000). Restoring Phineas Gage: A 150th retrospective. *Journal of the History of the Neurosciences, 9,* 46–66.

Madden, M., Lenhart, A., Duggan, M., Cortesi, S., & Gasser, U. (2013). Teens and technology 2013. Washington, DC: Pew Internet & American Life Project.

Madden, S., Morris, A., Zurynski, Y. A., Kohn, M., & Elliot, E. J. (2009). Burden of eating disorders in 5–13-year-old children in Australia. *Medical Journal of Australia, 190,* 410–414.

Madsen, K. M., Hviid, A., Vestergaard, M., Schendel, D., Wohlfahrt, J., Thorsen, P., . . . Melbye, M. (2002). A population-based study of measles, mumps, and rubella vaccination and autism. *New England Journal of Medicine, 347,* 1477–1482.

Maguen, S., Metzler, T. J., McCaslin, S. E., Inslicht, S. S., Henn-Haase, C., Neylan, T. C., & Marmar, C. R. (2009). Routine work environment stress and PTSD symptoms in police officers. *Journal of Nervous and Mental Disease, 197,* 754–760.

Maguire, E. A., Valentine, E.R., Wilding, J. M., & Kapur, N. (2003). Routes to remembering: The brains behind superior memory. *Nature Neuroscience, 6,* 90–95.

Maguire, E. A., Woollett, K., & Spiers, H. J. (2006). London taxi drivers and bus drivers: A structural MRI and neuropsychological analysis. *Hippocampus, 16,* 1091–1101.

Mah, K., & Binik, Y. M. (2001). Do all orgasms feel alike? Evaluating a two-dimensional model of orgasm experience across gender and sexual context. *Journal of Sex Research, 39,* 104–113.

Maher, W. B., & Maher, B. A. (2003). Abnormal psychology. In D. K. Freedheim (Ed.), *Handbook of psychology: History of psychology* (Vol. 1, pp. 303–336). New York: John Wiley & Sons.

Maheu, M. M., Pulier, M. L., McMenamin, J. P., & Posen, L. (2012). Future of telepsychology, telehealth, and various technologies in psychological research and practice. *Professional Psychology: Research and Practice, 43,* 613–621.

Mahmood, N. (2010, March 31). Here's how easily a hacker can crack your weak passwords. *Tech Journal.* Retrieved from http://thetechjournal.com/electronics/computer/security-computer-electronics/heres-how-easily-a-hacker-can-crack-your-weak-passwords.xhtml#ixzz1F7chbAEr

Mahoney, J. (2010). Strategic communication and anti-smoking campaigns. *Public Communication Review, 1,* 33–48.

Mai, E., & Buysse, D. J. (2008). Insomnia: Prevalence, impact, pathogenesis, differential diagnosis, and evaluation. *Sleep Medicine Clinics, 3,* 167–174.

Maiden, B., & Perry, B. (2011). Dealing with free-riders in assessed group work: Results from a study at a UK university. *Assessment & Evaluation in Higher Education, 36,* 451–464.

Majid, A. (2012). Current emotion research in the language sciences. *Emotion Review, 4,* 432–443.

Ma-Kellams, C., & Blascovich, J. (2012). Enjoying life in the face of death: East-West differences in responses to mortality salience. *Journal of Personality and Social Psychology, 103,* 773–386.

Makin, J. W., & Porter, R. H. (1989). Attractiveness of lactating females' breast odors to neonates. *Child Development, 60,* 803–810.

Malenka, R. C., & Nicoll, R. A. (1999). Long-term potentiation—A decade of progress? *Science, 285,* 1870–1874.

Malkoff-Schwartz, S., Frank, E., Anderson, B, Sherrill, J. T., Siegel, L., Patterson, D., & Kupfer, D. J. (1998). Stressful life events and social rhythm disruption in the onset of manic and depressive bipolar episodes. *Archives of General Psychiatry, 55,* 702–707.

Manago, A. M., Taylor, T., & Greenfield, P. M. (2012). Me and my 400 friends: The anatomy of college students' Facebook networks, their communication patterns, and well-being. *Developmental Psychology, 48*(2), 369–380. doi:10.1037/a0026338

Manber, R., Kraemer, H. C., Arnow, B. A., Trivedi, M. H., Rush, A. J., Thase, M. E., . . . Keller, M. E. (2008). Faster remission of chronic depression with combined psychotherapy and medication than with each therapy alone. *Journal of Consulting and Clinical Psychology, 76,* 459–467.

Mancini, A. D., Bonanno, G. A., & Clark, A. E. (2011). Stepping off the hedonic treadmill: Individual differences in response to major life events. *Journal of Individual Differences, 32,* 144–152.

Mandler, J. M. (2008). On the birth and growth of concepts. *Philosophical Psychology, 21,* 207–230.

Manickam, L. S. S. (2010). Psychotherapy in India. *Indian Journal of Psychiatry, 52,* S366–S370.

Manninen, B. A. (2011). Parental, medical, and sociological responsibilities: "Octomom" as a case study in the ethics of fertility treatments. *Journal of Clinical Research & Bioethics, S1,* 1–11.

Manning, R., Levine, M., & Collins, A. (2007). The Kitty Genovese murder and the social psychology of helping: The parable of the 38 witnesses. *American Psychologist, 62,* 555–562.

Manns, J. R., Hopkins, R. O., & Squire, L. R. (2003). Semantic memory and the human hippocampus. *Neuron, 38,* 127–133.

Maquet, P. (2000). Functional neuroimaging of normal human sleep by positron emission tomography. *Journal of Sleep Research, 3,* 208–231.

Marceau, K., Ram, N., Houts, R. M., Grimm, K. J., & Susman, E. J. (2011). Individual differences in boys' and girls' timing and tempo of puberty: Modeling development with nonlinear growth models. *Developmental Psychology, 47,* 1389–1409.

March of Dimes. (2013). *Your premature baby.* Retrieved from http://www.marchofdimes.org/baby/premature-babies.aspx#

Marmurek, H. C., & Grant, R. D. (1990). Savings in a recognition test. *Canadian Journal of Psychology, 44,* 414–419.

Maron, E., Hettema, J. M., & Shlik, J. (2010). Advances in molecular genetics of panic disorder. *Molecular Psychiatry, 15,* 681–701.

Marris, E. (2006, March 28). ACS: Are you a super taster? [Web log comment]. Retrieved from http://blogs.nature.com/inthefield/2006/03/acs_are_you_a_supertaster.html

Marsh, H. W., Nagengast, B., & Morin, A. J. (2013). Measurement invariance of Big-Five factors over the life span: ESEM tests of gender, age, plasticity, maturity, and La Dolce Vita effects. *Developmental Psychology, 49,* 1194–1218.

Marshall, L., & Born, L. (2007). The contribution of sleep to hippocampus-dependent memory consolidation. *Trends in Cognitive Sciences, 10,* 442–450.

Martin, C. L., & Ruble, D. N. (2010). Patterns of gender development. *Annual Review of Psychology, 61,* 353–381.

Martin, L. A., Doster, J. A., Critelli, J. W., Purdum, M., Powers, C., Lambert, P. L., & Miranda, V. (2011). The 'Distressed' personality, coping and cardiovascular risk. *Stress and Health, 27,* 64–72.

Martin, R. A., Puhlik-Doris, P., Larsen, G., Gray, J., & Weir, K. (2003). Individual differences in uses of humor and their relation to psychological well-being: Development of the Humor Styles Questionnaire. *Journal of Research in Personality, 37,* 48–75.

Mashour, G. A., Walker, E. E., & Martuza, R. L. (2005). Psychosurgery: Past, present, and future. *Brain Research Reviews, 48,* 409–419.

Maslow, A. H. (1943). A theory of human motivation. *Psychological Review, 50,* 370–396.

Masters, W., & Johnson, V. (1966). *Human sexual response.* Boston: Little, Brown.

Matlin, M. W. (2009). *Cognition* (7th ed.). Hoboken, NJ: John Wiley & Sons.

Matlin, M. W. (2013). *Cognition* (8th ed.). Hoboken, NJ: John Wiley & Sons.

Matsumoto, D., & Willingham, B. (2009). Spontaneous facial expressions of emotion of congenitally and noncongenitally blind individuals. *Journal of Personality and Social Psychology, 96,* 1–10.

Matsumura, S., Bito, S., Liu, H., Kahn, K., Fukuhara, S., Kagawa-Singer, M., & Wenger, N. (2002). Acculturation of attitudes toward end-of-life care: A cross-cultural survey of Japanese Americans and Japanese. *Journal of General Internal Medicine, 17,* 531–539.

Mattarella-Micke, A., Mateo, J., Kozak, M. N., Foster, K., & Beilock, S. L. (2011). Choke or thrive? The relation between salivary cortisol and math performance depends on individual differences in working memory and math-anxiety. *Emotion, 11*(4), 1000–1005.

Maulia, E. (2013, February 15). Social media addiction a new "pathological" disorder. *The Jakarta Globe.* Retrieved from http://www.thejakartaglobe.com/news/social-media-addiction-a-new-pathological-disorder/571887

Maxmen, A. (2012). Generic HIV drugs will widen US treatment net. *Nature, 488,* 267.

Mayo Clinic. (2014, June 2). Fetal alcohol syndrome: Symptoms. Retrieved from http://www.mayoclinic.com/health/fetal-alcohol-syndrome/DS00184/DSECTION=symptoms

Mayo Clinic. (2014, October 17). *Presbyopia.* Retrieved from http://www.mayoclinic.org/diseases-conditions/presbyopia/basics/definition/con-20032261

McAdams, D. P., & Olson, B. D. (2010). Personality development: Continuity and change over the life course. *Annual Review of Psychology, 61,* 5.1–5.26.

McCarthy, C. (2013). Pediatricians and television: It's time to rethink our messaging and our efforts. *Pediatrics, 131,* 589–590.

McCarthy, J. R., & Skowronski, J. J. (2011). The interplay of controlled and automatic processing in the expression of spontaneously inferred traits: A PDP analysis. *Journal of Personality and Social Psychology, 100,* 229–240.

McCarty, W. P., Schuck, A., Skogan, W., & Rosenbaum, D. (2011, January 7). Stress, burnout, and health. *National Police Research Platform*. Retrieved from http://nationalpoliceresearch.org/storage/updated-papers/Stress%20Burnout%20%20and%20Health%20FINAL.pdf

McClelland, D. C., Atkinson, J. W., Clark, R. W., & Lowell, E. L. (1976). *The achievement motive*. New York: Irvington.

McCormick, J. G. (2007). Behavioral observations of sleep and anesthesia in the dolphin: Implications for bispectral index monitoring of unihemispheric effects in dolphins. *Anesthesia & Analgesia, 104*, 239–241.

McCosker, B., & Moran, C. C. (2012). Differential effects of self-esteem and interpersonal competence on humor styles. *Psychology Research and Behavior Management, 5*, 143–150.

McCrae, R. R., & Costa, P. T. Jr. (1987). Validation of the five-factor model of personality across instruments and observers. *Journal of Personality and Social Psychology, 49*, 81–90.

McCrae, R. R., & Costa, P. T. Jr. (1990). *Personality in adulthood*. New York: Guilford Press.

McCrae, R. R., Costa, P. T. Jr., Ostendorf, F., Angleitner, A., Hřebíčková, M., Avia, M. D., . . . Smith, P. B. (2000). Nature over nurture: Temperament, personality, and life span development. *Journal of Personality and Social Psychology, 78*, 173–186.

McCrae, R. R., Scally, M., Terracciano, A., Abecasis, G. R., & Costa, P. T. Jr. (2010). An alternative to the search for single polymorphisms: Toward molecular personality scales for the five-factor model. *Journal of Personality and Social Psychology, 99*, 1014–1024.

McCrae, R. R., Terracciano, A., & 78 Members of the Personality Profiles of Cultures Project. (2005). Universal features of personality traits from the observer's perspective: Data from 50 cultures. *Journal of Personality and Social Psychology, 88*, 547–561.

McDougall, W. (1912). *An introduction to social psychology* (Rev. 4th ed.). Boston: John W. Luce.

McEwen, B. S. (2000). The neurobiology of stress: From serendipity to clinical relevance. *Brain Research, 886*, 172–189.

McGregor, J. (2012, February 15). How Jeremy Lin's star power could go unnoticed for so long. *The Washington Post*. Retrieved from http://www.washingtonpost.com/blogs/post-leadership/post/how-jeremy-lin-could-go-unnoticed-by-the-new-york-knicks-for-so-long/2011/04/01/gIQAAscmFR_blog.html

McGue, M., Bouchard, T. J. Jr., Iacono, W. G., & Lykken, D. T. (1993). Behavioral genetics of cognitive ability: A life-span perspective. In R. Plomin & G. E. McClearn (Eds.), *Nature, nurture & psychology* (pp. 59–76). Washington, DC: American Psychological Association.

McHugh, P. R., & Slavney, P. R. (2012). Mental illness—Comprehensive evaluation or checklist? *New England Journal of Medicine, 366*, 1853–1855.

McKenzie, S. (2012, October 23). A weighty issue: Hidden world of jockey heaving bowls. *CNN.com*. Retrieved from http://edition.cnn.com/2012/10/23/sport/jockey-diets-weight-horse-racing

McKinney, A., & Coyle, K. (2006). Alcohol hangover effects on measures of affect the morning after a normal night's drinking. *Alcohol & Alcoholism, 41*, 54–60.

McMurray, B. (2007). Defusing the childhood vocabulary explosion. *Science, 317*, 631.

McMurray, B., & Mitchell, C. (2008). A stochastic model for the vocabulary explosion. *Cognitive Science Proceedings*, 1919–1926.

McNally, R. J., & Clancy, S. A. (2005). Sleep paralysis, sexual abuse, and space alien abduction. *Transcultural Psychiatry, 42*, 113–122.

McPherson, M., Smith-Lovin, L., & Cook, J. M. (2001). Birds of a feather: Homophily in social networks. *Annual Review of Sociology, 27*, 415–444.

MedicineNet. (2014). Cocaine hydrochloride - topical. Retrieved from http://www.medicinenet.com/cocaine_hydrochloride-topical/article.htm

Medline Plus. (2014). *Osteomalacia*. Bethesda, MD: U.S. National Library of Medicine. Retrieved from http://www.nlm.nih.gov/medlineplus/ency/article/000376.htm

Mehdizadeh, S. (2010). Self-presentation 2.0: narcissism and self-esteem on Facebook. *Cyberpsycholgy, Behavior, and Social Networking, 13*, 357–364.

Melzack, R. (1993). Pain: Past present and future. *Canadian Journal of Experimental Psychology, 47*, 615–629.

Melzack, R. (2008). The future of pain. *Nature Reviews, 7*, 629.

Melzack, R., & Wall, P. D. (1965). Pain mechanisms: A new theory. *Science, 150*, 971–979.

Mendle, J., & Ferrero, J. (2012). Detrimental psychological outcomes associated with pubertal timing in adolescent boys. *Developmental Review, 32*, 49–66.

Mendle, J., Harden, K. P., Brooks-Gunn, J., & Graber, J. A. (2010). Development's tortoise and hare: Pubertal timing, pubertal tempo, and depressive symptoms in boys and girls. *Developmental Psychology, 46*, 1341–1353.

Menken, J., Trussell, J., & Larsen, U. (1986). Age and infertility. *Science, 233*, 1389–1394.

Mennella, J. A., Coren P., Jagnow, M. S., & Beauchamp, G. K. (2001). Prenatal and postnatal flavor learning by human infants. *Pediatrics, 107*, e88.

Merikangas, K. R., Akiskal, H. S., Angst, J., Greenberg, P. E., Hirschfeld, R. M. A., Petukhova, M., & Kessler, R. C. (2007). Lifetime and 12-month prevalence of bipolar spectrum disorder in the national comorbidity survey replication. *Archives of General Psychiatry, 64*, 543–552.

Mervis, C. B., & Rosch, E. (1981). Categorization of natural objects. *Annual Review of Psychology, 32*, 89–115.

Michael, R. T., Laumann, E. O., Kolata, G. B., & Gagnon, J. H. (1994). *Sex in America: A definitive survey*. Boston: Little, Brown.

Michalski, D., Kohout, J., Wicherski, M., & Hart, B. (2011). *2009 Doctorate employment survey*. APA Center for Workforce Studies. Retrieved from http://www.apa.org/workforce/publications/09-doc-empl/index.aspx

Milgram, S. (1963). Behavioral study of obedience. *Journal of Abnormal and Social Psychology, 67*, 371–378.

Milgram, S. (1964). Issues in the study of obedience: A reply to Baumrind. *American Psychologist, 19*, 848–852.

Milgram, S. (1965). Some conditions of obedience and disobedience to authority. *Human Relations, 18*(1), 57–76.

Milgram, S. (1974). *Obedience to authority: An experimental view*. New York: Harper & Row.

Miller, G. (1956). The magical number seven, plus or minus two: Some limits on our capacity for processing information. *Psychological Review, 63*, 81–97.

Miller, G. E. Chen, E., & Parker, K. J. (2011). Psychological stress in childhood and susceptibility to the chronic diseases of aging: Moving toward a model of behavioral and biological mechanisms. *Psychological Bulletin, 137*, 959–997.

Milrod, B., Leon, A. C., Busch, F., Rudden, M., Schwalberg, M., Clarkin, J., . . . Shear, M. K. (2007). A randomized control trial of psychoanalytic psychotherapy for panic disorder. *American Journal of Psychiatry, 164*, 265–272.

Mineka, S., Davidson, M., Cook, M., & Keir, R. (1984). Observational conditioning of snake fear in rhesus monkeys. *Journal of Abnormal Psychology, 93*, 355–372.

Mirsky, A. F., Bieliauskas, L. A., Duncan, C. C., & French, L. M. (2013). Letter to the editor re: The Genain quadruplets. *Schizophrenia Research, 148*, 186-187.

Mirsky, A. F., Bieliauskas L. A., French, L. M., Van Kammen, D. P., Jönsson, E., & Sedvall G. A. (2000). A 39-year followup of the Genain quadruplets. *Schizophrenia Bulletin, 26*, 699–708.

Mirsky, A. F., & Quinn, O. W. (1988). The Genain triplets. *Schizophrenia Bulletin, 14*, 595–612.

Mischel, W., & Shoda, Y. (1995). A cognitive-affective system theory of personality: Reconceptualizing the invariances in personality and the role of situations. *Psychological Review, 102,* 229–258.

Mistry, R. S., & Wadsworth, M. E. (2011). Family functioning and child development in the context of poverty. *Prevention Researcher, 18,* 11–15.

Mitler, M. M., & Miller, J. C. (1996). Methods of testing for sleeplessness. *Behavioral Medicine, 21,* 171–183.

Moisse, K. (2011, September 20). Drug deaths exceed traffic deaths. *ABC News.* Retrieved from http://abcnews.go.com/Health/Drugs/drug-deaths-exceed-traffic-deaths/story?id=14554903

Mokdad, A. H., Marks, J. S., Stroup, D. F., & Gerberding, J. L. (2004). Actual causes of deaths in the United States, 2000. *Journal of the American Medical Association, 291,* 1238–1245.

Mollon, J. D. (1982). Color vision. *Annual Review of Psychology, 33,* 41–85.

Monroe, S. M., & Harkness, K. L. (2011). Recurrence in major depression: A conceptual analysis. *Psychological Review, 118,* 655–674.

Montemayor, R. (1983). Parents and adolescents in conflict: All families some of the time and some families most of the time. *Journal of Early Adolescence, 3,* 83–103.

Montoya, E. R., Terburg, D., Bos, P. A., & van Honk, J. (2012). Testosterone, cortisol, and serotonin as key regulators of social aggression: A review and theoretical perspective. *Motivation and Emotion, 36,* 65–73.

Moore, D. S., & Johnson, S. P. (2008). Mental rotation in human infants: A sex difference. *Psychological Science, 19,* 1063–1066.

Moore, E. G. J. (1986). Family socialization and the IQ test performance of traditionally and transracially adopted Black children. *Developmental Psychology, 22,* 317–326.

Morales, A., Heaton, J. P. W., & Carson III, C. C. (2000). Andropause: A misnomer for a true clinical entity. *Journal of Urology, 163,* 705–712.

Moreira-Almeida, A., Neto, F. L., & Cardeña, E. (2008). Comparison of Brazilian spiritist mediumship and dissociative identity disorder. *Journal of Nervous and Mental Disease, 196,* 420–424.

Moreland, R. L., & Zajonc, R. B. (1982). Exposure effects in person perception: Familiarity, similarity, and attraction. *Journal of Experimental Social Psychology, 18,* 395–415.

Morin, C. M., Bootzin, R. R., Buysse, D. J., Edinger, J.D., Espie, C. A., & Lichstein, K. L. (2006). Psychological and behavioral treatment of insomnia: Update of the recent evidence (1998–2004). *Sleep, 29,* 1398–1414.

Morone, N. E., & Greco, C. M. (2007). Mind-body interventions for chronic pain in older adults: A structured review. *Pain Medicine, 8,* 359–375.

Morrot, G., Brochet, F., & Dubourdieu, D. (2001). The color of odors. *Brain and Language, 79,* 309–320.

Morry, M. M., Kito, M., & Ortiz, L. (2011). The attraction-similarity model and dating couples: Projection, perceived similarity, and psychological benefits. *Personal Relationships, 18,* 125–143.

Mos Def. (2011, February 28). Kanye West: "I'm Scared of the Grammys" [Video file embedded in article]. *Rolling Stone.* Retrieved from http://www.rollingstone.com/music/news/kanye-west-im-scared-of-the-grammys-20110228

Moseley, G. L., Gallace, A., & Spence, C. (2008). Is mirror therapy all it is cracked up to be? Current evidence and future directions, *Pain, 138,* 7–10.

Mosher, W. D., Chandra, A., & Jones, J. (2005, September 15). *Sexual behavior and selected health measures: Men and women 15–44 years of age, United States, 2002* (Advance Data from Vital and Health Statistics, No. 362). Washington, DC: Centers for Disease Control and Prevention, National Center for Health Statistics. Retrieved from http://www.cdc.gov/nchs/data/ad/ad362.pdf

Most, S. B., Simons, D. J., Scholl, B. J., Jimenez, R., Clifford, E., & Chabris, C. F. (2001). How not to be seen: The contribution of similarity and selective ignoring to sustained inattentional blindness. *Psychological Science, 12,* 9–17.

MSNBC.com. (2011, July 26). *Girl, 6, on shark that bit her: "I forgive him"* [Video file]. Retrieved from http://today.msnbc.msn.com/id/43892097/ns/today-today_people/t/girl-shark-bit-her-i-forgive-him/#.TqR3Sc33LjQ

Mukamal, K. J., Maclure, M., Muller, J. E., Sherwood, J. B., & Mittleman, M. A. (2001). Prior alcohol consumption and mortality following acute myocardial infarction. *Journal of the American Medical Association, 285,* 1965–1970.

Mulder, E. J. H., Robles de Medina, P. G., Huizink, A. C., Van den Bergh, B. R. H., Buitelaar, J. K., & Visser, G. H. A. (2002). Prenatal maternal stress: Effects on pregnancy and the (unborn) child. *Early Human Development, 70,* 3–14.

Mulvey, S. (2006, May 15). Cakes and jokes at Cafe d'Europe. *BBC News.* Retrieved from http://news.bbc.co.uk/2/hi/europe/4755659.stm

Murdock, B. (1962). The serial position effect of free recall. *Journal of Experimental Psychology, 64,* 482–488.

Murdock, N. L., Edwards, C., & Murdock, T. B. (2010). Therapists' attributions for client premature termination: Are they self-serving? *Psychotherapy Theory, Research, Practice, Training, 47,* 221–234.

Murray, R. M., Morrison, P. D., Henquet, C., & Di Forti, M. (2007). Cannabis, the mind and society: The hash realities. *Nature Reviews Neuroscience, 8,* 885–895.

Mustanski, B. S., Chivers, M. L., & Bailey, J. M. (2002). A critical review of recent biological research on human sexual orientation. *Annual Review of Sex Research, 13,* 89–140.

Musto, D. F. (1991). Opium, cocaine and marijuana in American history. *Scientific American, 265,* 41–47.

Myers, D. G., & Lamm, H. (1976). The group polarization phenomenon. *Psychological Bulletin, 83,* 602–627.

Mysterud, I. (2003). Long live nature via nurture! *Evolutionary Psychology, 1,* 188–191.

Nagel, I. E., Chicherio, C., Li, S., von Oertzen, T., Sander, T., Villringer, A., . . . Lindenberger, U. (2008). Human aging magnifies genetic effects on executive functioning and working memory. *Frontiers in Human Neuroscience, 2,* 1–8.

Nahemow, L., & Lawton, M. P. (1975). Similarity and propinquity in friendship formation. *Journal of Personality and Social Psychology, 32,* 205–213.

Naimi, T. S., Brewer, R. D., Mokdad, A., Denny, C., Serdula, M. K., & Marks, J. S. (2003). Binge drinking among US adults. *Journal of the American Medical Association, 289,* 70–75.

Nakajima, M., & al'Absi, M. (2012). Predictors of risk for smoking relapse in men and women: A prospective examination. *Psychology of Addictive Behaviors, 26,* 633–637. doi:10.1037/z0027280

Nash, M. R. (2001). The truth and the hype of hypnosis. *Scientific American, 285,* 44–55.

Nathanson, V., Jayesinghe, N., & Roycroft, G. (2007). Is it all right for women to drink small amounts of alcohol in pregnancy? No. *British Medical Journal, 335,* 857.

National Cancer Institute. (2010). The downside of diagnostic imaging. *NCI Cancer Bulletin, 7*(2).

National Eye Institute. (2012). *Facts about the cornea and corneal disease* Retrieved June 8, 2012, from http://www.nd.nih.gov/health/cornealdisease/

National Geographic. (2015). *Dia de los Muertos.* Retrieved from http://education.nationalgeographic.com/education/media/dia-de-los-muertos/?ar_a=1

National Institute of Mental Health. (n.d.). *Antidepressant medications for children and adolescents: Information for parents and caregivers.* Retrieved from http://www.nimh.nih.gov/health/topics/child-and-adolescent-mental-health/antidepressant-medications-for-children-and-adolescents-information-for-parents-and-caregivers.shtml

National Institute of Mental Health. (n.d.). *Eating disorders.* Bethesda, MD: Author. http://www.nimh.nih.gov/health/topics/eating-disorders/index.shtml

National Institute of Mental Health. (2007). *Medications.* (NIH Publication No 02-3929). National Institute of Mental Health, National Institutes of Health, US Department of Health and Human Services. Available from http://solsticenyc.com/pdfs/medications.pdf.

National Institute of Mental Health. (2013, October 1). *The numbers count: Mental disorders in America.* Retrieved from http://www.lb7.uscourts.gov/documents/12-cv-1072url2.pdf

National Institute of Neurological Disorders and Stroke. (2011a). *Narcolepsy* [Fact sheet]. Bethesda, MD: National Institutes of Health. Retrieved from http://www.ninds.nih.gov/disorders/narcolepsy/detail_narcolepsy.htm

National Institute of Neurological Disorders and Stroke. (2011b). *NINDS Rasmussen's encephalitis information page.* Bethesda, MD: National Institutes of Health. Retrieved from http://www.ninds.nih.gov/disorders/rasmussen/rasmussen .htm

National Institute of Neurological Disorders and Stroke. (2015). *Arteriovenous malformations and other vascular lesions of the central nervous system fact sheet.* Retrieved from http://www.ninds.nih.gov/disorders/avms/detail_avms.htm

National Institute on Aging. (2013). *About Alzheimer's disease: Alzheimer's basics.* Retrieved from http://www.nia.nih.gov/alzheimers/topics/alzheimers-basics

National Institute on Drug Abuse. (2012, July). *Nationwide trends.* Retrieved November 24, 2012, from http://www.drugabuse.gov/sites/default/files/drugfactsnationtrends_1.pdf

National Institute on Drug Abuse. (2013a). Cocaine. Retrieved from http://www.drugabuse.gov/drugs-abuse/cocaine

National Institute on Drug Abuse. (2013b). *DrugFacts: Heroin.* Bethesda, MD: National Institutes of Health. Retrieved from http://www.drugabuse.gov/publications/drugfacts/heroin

National Institute on Drug Abuse. (2013c). Methamphetamine. Retrieved from http://d14rmgtrwzf5a.cloudfront.net/sites/default/files/methrrs.pdf

National Institute on Drug Abuse. (2013d). MDMA (Ecstasy or Molly). Retrieved from http://www.drugabuse.gov/publications/drugfacts/mdma-ecstasy-or-molly

National Institute on Drug Abuse. (2014a). *DrugFacts: Prescription and over-the-counter medications.* Retrieved from http://www.drugabuse.gov/publications/drugfacts/prescription-over-counter-medications

National Institute on Drug Abuse. (2014b). *Marijuana.* Retrieved from http://www.drugabuse.gov/drugs-abuse/marijuana

National Institute on Drug Abuse. (2014c). *Media guide: The science of drug abuse and addiction: The Basics.* Retrieved from http://www.drugabuse.gov/publications/media-guide/science-drug-abuse-addiction-basics

National Institute on Drug Abuse. (2015). Marijuana. Retrieved from http://d14rmgtrwzf5a.cloudfront.net/sites/default/files/mjrrs_4_15.pdf

National Institutes of Health. (2012). Tips for getting a good night's sleep. *Medline Plus, 7,* 20.

National Institutes of Health, Eunice Kennedy Shriver National Institute of Child Health and Human Development. (n.d.). *Turner syndrome.* Retrieved from http://turners.nichd.nih.gov/

National Institutes of Health, National Institute on Alcohol Abuse and Alcoholism. (2013). *Alcohol use disorders.* Retrieved from http://www.niaaa.nih.gove/alcohol-health/overview-alcohol-consumption/alcohol-use-disorders

National Safety Council. (2012). *Injury facts 2012 edition.* Itasca, IL: Author.

National Science Foundation, Division of Science Resources Statistics. (2011). Women, minorities, and persons with disabilities in science and engineering: 2011. In *Special Report NSF 11-309.* Arlington, VA. Available at http://www.nsf.gov/statistics/wmpd/

National Sleep Foundation. (2009). *Sleep in America poll: Highlights and key findings.* Retrieved from http://sleepfoundation.org/sites/default/files/2009%20POLL%20HIGHLIGHTS.pdf

National Sleep Foundation. (2015a). *Children and sleep.* Retrieved from http://www.sleepfoundation.org/article/sleep-topics/children-and-sleep

National Sleep Foundation. (2015b). *Healthy Sleep Tips.* Retrieved from http://sleepfoundation.org/sleep-tools-tips/healthy-sleep-tips

National Sleep Foundation. (2015c). *Teens and sleep.* Retrieved from http://www.sleepfoundation.org/article/sleep-topics/teens-and-sleep

Nawrot, P., Jordan, S., Eastwood, J., Rotstein, J., Hugenholtz, A., & Feeley M. (2003). Effects of caffeine on human health. *Food Additives and Contaminants, 20,* 1–30.

NBA.com. (2007, November 20). *2007–08 Player survey: Weight.* Retrieved from http://www.nba.com/news/survey_weight_2007.html

NBA.com. (2007, November 27). *2007–08 Player survey: Height.* Retrieved from http://www.nba.com/news/survey_height_2007.html

NBC Universal. (2013, February 12). UK clinics treating patients for social-media addiction. *9 News.* Retrieved from http://www.9news.com/story/news/local/4-pm-show/2014/02/24/1839802/

Ndubaku, U., & de Bellard, M. (2008). Glial cells: Old cells with new twists. *Acta Histochemica, 110,* 182–195.

Neal, R. (2002, June 10). Personality traits linked to birth order. *CBS News.* Retrieved from http://www.cbsnews.com/news/personality-traits-linked-to-birth-order/

Neisser, U. (1979). The control of information pickup in selective looking. In A. D. Pick (Ed.), *Perception and its development: A tribute to Eleanor J. Gibson* (pp. 201–219). Hillsdale, NJ: Erlbaum.

Neisser, U. (1991). A place of misplaced nostalgia. *American Psychologist, 46,* 34–36.

Neisser, U., & Becklen, R. (1975). Selective looking: Attending to visually specified events. *Cognitive Psychology, 7,* 480–494.

Nelson, S. M., Telfer, E. E., & Anderson, R. A. (2013). The ageing ovary and uterus: New biological insights. *Human Reproduction Update, 19,* 67–83.

Nes, R. B., Czajkowski, N., & Tambs, K. (2010). Family matters: Happiness in nuclear families and twins. *Behavioral Genetics, 40,* 577–590.

Newell, A., Shaw, J. C., & Simon, H. A. (1958). Elements of a theory of human problem solving. *Psychological Review, 65,* 151–166.

Newell, B. R., & Andrews, S. (2004). Levels of processing effects on implicit and explicit memory tasks: Using question position to investigate the lexical-processing hypothesis. *Experimental Psychology, 51,* 132–144.

Newsweek. (2004, June 20). *He's one smart puppy.* Retrieved from http://www.newsweek.com/hes-one-smart-puppy-128631

Newton, K. M., Reed, S. D., LaCroix, A. Z., Grothaus, L. C., Ehrlich, K., & Guiltinan, J. (2006). Treatment of vasomotor symptoms of menopause with black cohosh, multibotanicals, soy, hormone therapy, or placebo. *Annals of Internal Medicine, 145,* 869–879.

Neylan, T. C. (1999). Frontal lobe function: Mr. Phineas Gage's famous injury. *Journal of Neuropsychiatry and Clinical Neurosciences, 11,* 280–281.

Ng, D. M., & Jeffery, R. W. (2003). Relationships between perceived stress and health behaviors in a sample of working adults. *Health Psychology, 22,* 638–642.

Ngun, T. C., Ghahramani, N., Sánchez, F. J., Bocklandt, S., & Vilain, E. (2011). The genetics of sex differences in brain and behavior. *Frontiers in Neuroendocrinology, 32,* 227–248.

Nickerson, R. S., & Adams, J. J. (1979). Long-term memory for a common object. *Cognitive Psychology, 11,* 287–307.

Niedenthal, P. M., Augustinova, M., Rychlowska, M., Droit-Volet, S., Zinner, L., Knafo, A., & Brauer, M. (2012). Negative relations between pacifier use and emotional competence. *Basic and Applied Social Psychology, 34,* 387–394.

Nielsen, N. R., Kristensen, T. S., Strandberg-Larsen, K., Zhang, Z.-F., Schnohr, P., & Grønbæk, M. (2008). Perceived stress and risk of colorectal cancer in men and women: A prospective cohort study. *Journal of Internal Medicine, 263,* 192–202.

Niemi, M.-B. (2009). Placebo effect: A cure in the mind. *Scientific American Mind, 20,* 42–49. Retrieved from http://www.scientificamerican.com/article/placebo-effect-a-cure-in-the-mind/

Nieves, E. (2007, June 9). Indian reservation reeling in wave of youth suicides and attempts. *The New York Times.* Retrieved from http://www.nytimes.com/2007/06/09/us/09suicide.html?_r=0

Nisbett, R. E., Aronson, J., Blair, C., Dickens, W., Flynn, J., Halpern, D. F., & Turkheimer, E. (2012). Intelligence: New findings and theoretical developments. *American Psychologist, 67,* 130–159.

Nishitani, S., Miyamura, T., Tagawa, M., Sumi, M., Takase, R., Doi, H., . . . Shinohara, K. (2009). The calming effect of a maternal breast milk odor on the human newborn infant. *Neuroscience Research, 63,* 66–71.

Niskar, A. S., Kieszak, S. M., Holmes, A. E., Esteban, E., Rubin, C., & Brody, D. J. (2001). Estimated prevalence of noise-induced hearing threshold shifts among children 6 to 19 years of age: The Third National Health and Nutrition Examination Survey, 1988–1994, United States. *Pediatrics, 108,* 40–43.

Nolen-Hoeksema, S. (1991). Responses to depression and their effects on the duration of depressive episodes. *Journal of Abnormal Psychology, 100,* 569–582.

Noller, G. (2009). *Literature review and assessment report on MDMA/Ecstasy.* Wellington, New Zealand: Ministry of Health. Retrieved from http://www.moh.govt.nz/notebook/nbbooks.nsf/0/EE5BDDAA39721D6ACC257B8000708A11/$file/July2010Literature-Review-Assessment-Report-MDMA-Ecstasy.pdf

Nonnemaker, J., Hersey, J., Homsi, G., Busey, A., Hyland, A., Juster, H., & Farrelly, M. (2011). Self-reported exposure to policy and environmental influences on smoking cessation and relapse: A 2-year longitudinal population-based study. *International Journal of Environmental Research and Public Health, 8,* 3591–3608.

Norcross, J. C., & Beutler, L. E. (2014). Integrative psychotherapies. In R. J. Corsini & D. Wedding (Eds.), *Current psychotherapies* (10th ed., pp. 499–532). Belmont, CA: Brooks/Cole, Cengage Learning.

Norcross, J. C., & Castle, P. H. (2002). Appreciating the PsyD: The facts. *Eye on Psi Chi, 7,* 2–26.

Norcross, J. C., & Wampold, B. E. (2011). What works for whom: Tailoring psychotherapy to the person. *Journal of Clinical Psychology, 67,* 127–132.

Northoff, G. (2012). Genes, brains, and environment—genetic neuroimaging of depression. *Current Opinion in Neurobiology, 23,* 1–10.

Northoff, G., Schneider, F., Rotte, M., Matthiae, C., Tempelmann, C., Wiebking, C., . . . Panksepp, J. (2009). Differential parametric modulation of self-relatedness and emotions in different brain regions. *Human Brain Mapping, 30,* 369–382.

Nour, N. M. (2009). Child marriage: A silent health and human rights issue. *Reviews in Obstetrics & Gynecology, 2,* 51–56.

Novotney, A. (2013, January). gradPSYCH Magazine, 11(1). Retrieved from http://www.apa.org/gradpsych/2013/01/debt.aspx

Nusbaum, E. C., & Silvia, P. J. (2011). Are intelligence and creativity really so different? Fluid intelligence, executive processes, and strategy use in divergent thinking. *Intelligence, 39,* 36–45.

Oakley, S. (2012, May 30). Mayo Clinic medical edge: Cochlear implants a good next step when hearing aids are no longer effective. *The Chicago Tribune.* Retrieved from http://articles.chicagotribune.com/2012-05-30/lifestyle/sns-201205291800-tms-premhnstr-k-b20120530-20120530_1_cochlear-auditory-nerve-implant-device

Oatley, K., Keltner, D., & Jenkins, J. (2006). *Understanding emotions.* Malden, MA: Blackwell.

Öberg, M., Jaakkola, M. S., Woodward, A., Peruga, A., & Prüss-Ustün, A. (2011). Worldwide burden of disease from exposure to second-hand smoke: A retrospective analysis of data from 192 countries. *Lancet, 311,* 139–146.

O'Brien, D. (2005). *How to develop a brilliant memory.* London: Duncan Baird.

O'Brien, P. (2007). Is it all right for women to drink small amounts of alcohol in pregnancy? Yes. *British Journal of Medicine, 335,* 857.

Occupational Safety & Health Administration. (2014). *Occupational noise exposure.* Retrieved October 19, 2014 from https://www.osha.gov/SLTC/noisehearingconservation/

Oda, R., Matsumoto-Oda, A., & Kurashima, O. (2005). Effects of belief in genetic relatedness on resemblance judgments by Japanese raters. *Evolution of Human Behavior, 26,* 441–450.

O'Donnell, S., Webb, J. K., & Shine, R. (2010). Conditioned taste aversion enhances the survival of an endangered predator imperiled by a toxic invader. *Journal of Applied Ecology, 47,* 558–565.

Oerlemans, W. G. M., Bakker, A. B., & Veenhoven, R. (2011). Finding the key to happy aging: A day reconstruction study of happiness. *Journal of Gerontology: Psychological Sciences, 6*(6), 665–674. doi:10.1093/geronb/gbr040

Office of the Surgeon General, National Center for Injury Prevention and Control, National Institute of Mental Health, & Center for Mental Health Services. (2001). *Youth violence: A report of the Surgeon General (Risk factors) for youth violence,* chapter 4). Rockville, MD: Office of the Surgeon General. Retrieved from http://www.ncbi.nlm.nih.gov/books/NBK44293/

Ogden, C. L., Carroll, M. D., Kit, B. K., & Flegal, K. M. (2014). Prevalence of childhood and adult obesity in the United States, 2011–2012. *Journal of the American Medical Association, 311,* 806–814.

O'Hanlon, I. (2010, August 31). Chilean miners suffering like soldiers. *Discovery News.* Retrieved from http://news.discovery.com/human/trapped-miners-psychology.htm

Ohayon, M. (2011). Epidemiological overview of sleep disorders in the general population. *Sleep Medicine Reviews, 2,* 1–9.

Ohayon, M., Carskadon, M. A., Guilleminault, C., & Vitiello, M. V. (2004). Meta-analysis of quantitative sleep parameters from childhood to old age in healthy individuals: Developing normative sleep values across the human life-span. *Sleep, 21,* 1255–1273.

O'Keefe, D. J. (2008). Elaboration likelihood model. In W. Donsbach (Ed.), *International encyclopedia of communication* (Vol. IV, pp. 1475–1480). Malden, MA: Blackwell.

O'Keeffe, G. S., Clarke-Pearson, K., & Council on Communications and Media. (2011). The impact of social media on children, adolescents, and families. *Pediatrics, 127,* 800–804.

Ollendick, T. H., Öst, L. G., Reuterskiöld, L., Costa, N., Cederlund, R., Sirbu, C., . . . Jarrett, M. A. (2009). One-session treatment of specific phobias in youth: A randomized clinical trial in the United States and Sweden. *Journal of Consulting and Clinical Psychology, 77,* 504–516.

Olson, J. M., Vernon, P. A., Harris, J. A., & Jang, K. L. (2001). The heritability of attitudes: A study of twins. *Journal of Personality and Social Psychology, 80,* 845–860.

Olson, R. L., Hanowski, R. J., Hickman, J. S., & Bocanegra, J. (2009). *Driver distraction in commercial vehicle operations* (Document No. FMCSA-RRT-09-042). Washington, DC: U.S. Department of Transportation, Federal Motor Carrier Safety Administration. Retrieved from http://www.fmcsa.dot.gov/sites/fmcsa.dot.gov/files/docs/FMCSA-RRR-09-042.pdf

O'Neil, D. (2009, December 10). Immigrant dream plays out through son. *ESPN.com.* Retrieved from http://sports.espn.go.com/ncb/columns/story?columnist=onei l_dana&id=4730385

O'Riordan, K. (2012). The life of the gay gene: From hypothetical genetic marker to social reality. *Journal of Sex Research, 49,* 362–368.

Organisation for Economic Co-operation and Development. (2008). *Mental health in OECD countries* (OECD Policy Brief). Retrieved from http://78.41.128.130/dataoecd/6/48/41686440.pdf

Orzeł-Gryglewska, J. (2010). Consequences of sleep deprivation. *International Journal of Occupational Medicine & Environmental Health, 23,* 94–114.

Öst, L. G. (1989). One-session treatment for specific phobias. *Behaviour Research and Therapy, 27,* 1–7.

Otta, E., da Silva Queiroz, R., de Sousa Campos, L., da Silva, M. W. D., & Silveira, M. T. (1999). Age differences between spouses in a Brazilian marriage sample. *Evolution and Human Behavior, 20,* 99–103.

Overmier, J. B., & Seligman, M. E. P. (1967). Effects of inescapable shock upon subsequent escape and avoidance responding. *Journal of Comparative and Physiological Psychology, 63,* 28–33.

Oyserman, D., Coon, H. M., & and Kemmelmeier, M. (2002). Rethinking individualism and collectivism: Evaluation of theoretical assumptions and meta-analyses. *Psychological Bulletin, 128,* 3–72.

Ozsungur, S., Brenner, D., & El-Sohemy, A. (2009). Fourteen well-described caffeine withdrawal symptoms factor into three clusters. *Psychopharmacology, 201,* 541–548.

Pachana, N. A., Brilleman, S. L., & Dobson, A. J. (2011). Reporting of life events over time: Methodological issues in a longitudinal sample of women. *Psychological Assessment, 23,* 277–281.

Paikoff, R. L., & Brooks-Gunn, J. (1991). Do parent-child relationships change during puberty? *Psychological Bulletin, 110,* 47–66.

Palermo, T. M., Eccleston, C., Lewandowski, A. S., Williams, A. C. D. C., & Morley, S. (2010). Randomized controlled trials of psychological therapies for management of chronic pain in children and adolescents: An updated meta-analytic review. *Pain, 148,* 387–397.

Pan, J.-Y., & Wong, D. F. K. (2011). Acculturative stressors and acculturative strategies as predictors of negative affect among Chinese international students in Australia and Hong Kong: A cross-cultural comparative study. *Academic Psychiatry, 35,* 376–381.

Pape, H.-C., & Pare, D. (2010). Plastic synaptic networks of the amygdala for the acquisition, expression, and extinction of conditioned fear. *Physiological Review, 90,* 419–463.

Papsin, B. C., & Gordon, K. A. (2007). Cochlear implants for children with severe-to-profound hearing loss. *New England Journal of Medicine, 357,* 2380–2387.

Parker, E. S., Cahill, L., & McGaugh, J. L. (2006). A case of unusual autobiographical remembering. *Neurocase, 12,* 35–49.

Parmentier, F. B. R., & Andrés, P. (2010). The involuntary capture of attention by sound: Novelty and postnovelty distraction in young and older adults. *Experimental Psychology, 57,* 68–76.

Parrott, A. C. (2004). MDMA (3,4-Methylenedioxymethamphetamine) or Ecstasy: The neuropsychobiological implications of taking it at dances and raves. *Neuropsychobiology, 50,* 329–335.

Parry, M. S. (2006). Dorothea Dix (1802–1887). *American Journal of Public Health, 96,* 624–625.

Pashler, H., Rohrer, D., Cepeda, N. J., & Carpenter, S. K. (2007). Enhancing learning and retarding forgetting: Choices and consequences *Psychonomic Bulletin & Review, 14,* 187–193.

Patorno, E., Bohn, R. L., Wahl, P. M., Avorn, J., Patrick, A. R., Liu, J., & Schneeweiss, S. (2010). Anticonvulsant medications and the risk of suicide, attempted suicide, or violent death. *Journal of the American Medical Association, 303,* 1401–1409.

Patterson, D. R., & Jensen, M. P. (2003). Hypnosis and clinical pain. *Psychological Bulletin, 129,* 495–521.

Pavlos, P., Vasilios, N., Antonia, A., Dimitrios, K., Georgios, K., & Georgios, A. (2009). Evaluation of young smokers and non-smokers with electro-gustometry and contact endoscopy. *BMC Ear, Nose and Throat Disorders, 9*(9). doi:10.1186/1472-6815-9-9

Pavlov, I. (1906). The scientific investigation of the psychical faculties or processes in the higher animals. *Science, 24,* 613–619.

Pavlov, I. (1927/1960). *Conditioned reflexes.* New York: Dover.

Pavlovich-Danis, S. J., & Patterson, K. (2006, January 9). For a good night's sleep. *Nurseweek News.*

PBS. (1997, March 4). Secret of the wild child. *NOVA: Transcripts.* Retrieved from http://www.pbs.org/wgbh/nova/transcripts/2112gchild.html

PBS. (2005, January 27). American experience: Kinsey. Retrieved from http://www.pbs.org/wgbh/amex/kinsey/peopleevents/p_kinsey.html

PBS. (2014). Other notorious insanity cases. *Frontline.* Retrieved from http://www.pbs.org/wgbh/pages/frontline/shows/crime/trial/other.html

Pearce, J. M. (2009). Marie-Jean-Pierre Flourens (1794–1867) and cortical localization. *European Journal of Neurology, 61,* 311–314.

Pearlstein, T., Howard, M., Salisbury, A., & Zlotnick, C. (2009). Postpartum depression. *American Journal of Obstetrics & Gynecology, 200,* 357–364.

Pearson, E., & Siemaszko, C. (2010, November 6). Chilean miner Edison Pena is on top of world and ready for New York Marathon. *New York Daily News.* Retrieved from http://www.nydailynews.com/new-york/chilean-miner-edison-pena-top-world-ready-new-york-marathon-article-1.450963

Pedersen, A., Zachariae, R., & Bovbjerg, D. H. (2010). Influence of psychological stress on upper respiratory infection: A meta-analysis of prospective studies. *Psychosomatic Medicine, 72,* 823–832.

Penfield, W., & Boldrey E. (1937). Somatic motor and sensory representation in the cerebral cortex of man as studied by electrical stimulation. *Brain, 60,* 389–443.

Penhaul, K. (2010, September 18). Trapped miners celebrate independence. *CNN.com.* Retrieved from http://www.cnn.com/2010/WORLD/americas/09/18/chile.mine.independence/index.html

Pennisi, E. (2012, September 5). Human genome is much more than just genes. *Science NOW.* Retrieved from http://news.sciencemag.org/sciencenow/2012/09/human-genome-is-much-more-than-j.html

Peplau, L. A. (2003). Human sexuality: How do men and women differ? *Current Directions in Psychological Science, 12,* 37–40.

Perkins, K. A., Karelitz, J. L., Conklin, C. A., Sayette, M. A., & Giedgowd, G. E. (2010). Acute negative affect relief from smoking depends on the affect measure and situation, but not on nicotine. *Biological Psychiatry, 67,* 707–714.

Peters, W. (1971). *A class divided: Then and now.* New Haven, CT: Yale University Press.

Peterson, B. S., Warner, V., Bansal, R., Zhu, H., Hao, X., Liu, J., . . . Weissman, M. M. (2009). Cortical thinning in persons at increased familial risk for major depression. *Proceedings of the National Academy of Sciences, 106,* 6273–6278.

Peterson, G. B. (2004). A day of great illumination: B. F. Skinner's discovery of shaping. *Journal of the Experimental Analysis of Behavior, 82,* 317–328.

Peterson, L. R., & Peterson, M. J. (1959). Short-term retention of individual verbal items. *Journal of Experimental Psychology, 58,* 193–198.

Peterson, M. J., Meagher, R. B. Jr., & Ellsbury, S. W. (1970). Repetition effects in sensory memory. *Journal of Experimental Psychology, 84,* 15–23.

Petitto, L. A. (1994). Are signed languages "real" languages? *International Quarterly of the Sign Linguistics Association, 7,* 1–10.

Petitto, L. A., & Marentette, P. F. (1991). Babbling in the manual mode: Evidence for the ontogeny of language. *Science, 251,* 1493–1496.

Petronis, A. (2004). The origin of schizophrenia: Genetic thesis, epigenetic antithesis, and resolving synthesis. *Biological Psychiatry, 55,* 965–970.

Petty, R. E., & Cacioppo, J. T. (1986). The elaboration likelihood model of persuasion. *Advances in Experimental Social Psychology, 19,* 123–205.

Pew Research Center. (2014, February 3). 6 new facts about Facebook. Retrieved from http://www.pewresearch.org/fact-tank/2014/02/03/6-new-facts-about-facebook/

Pfeifer, C. (2012). Physical attractiveness, employment and earnings. *Applied Economics Letters, 19,* 505–510.

Phillips, J. (2013). Prescription drug abuse: Problem, policies, and implications. *Nursing Outlook, 61,* 78–84.

Phonecrastinate. (n.d.). In *Merriam-Webster.com: The open dictionary.* Retrieved December 3, 2012, from http://nws.merriam-webster.com/opendictionary/newword_search.php

Piaget, J. (1936/1952). *The origins of intelligence in children.* New York: Norton.

Pich, E. M., Pagliusi, S. R., Tessari, M., Talabot-Ayer, D., Van Huijsduijnen, R. H., & Chiamulera, C. (1997). Common neural substrates for the addictive properties of nicotine and cocaine. *Science, 275,* 83–86.

Pickren, W. E., & Burchett, C. (2014). Making psychology inclusive: A history of education and training for diversity in American psychology. In W. E. Pickren, C. Burchett, F. T. L. Leong, L. Comas-Díaz, G. C. Nagayama Hall, C. Gordon, V. C. McLoyd, & J. E. Trimble (Eds.), *APA handbook of multicultural psychology, Vol. 2: Applications and training. APA handbooks in psychology* (pp. 3–18). Washington, DC, US: American Psychological Association.

Pierre, J. M. (2012). Mental illness and mental health: Is the glass half empty or half full? *Canadian Journal of Psychiatry, 57,* 651–658.

Pilley, J. W., & Reid, A. K. (2011). Border collie comprehends object names as verbal referents. *Behavioural Processes, 86,* 184–195.

Pines, A. (2011). Male menopause: Is it a real clinical syndrome? *Climacteric, 14,* 15–17.

Pinker, S. (1994). *The language instinct.* New York: Harper Perennial.

Pinker, S. (2003). Language as an adaptation to the cognitive niche. In M. H. Christiansen & S. Kirby (Eds.), *Language evolution: The states of the art* (pp. 16–37). New York: Oxford University Press.

Piper, A., Lillevik, L., & Kritzer, R. (2008). What's wrong with believing in repression?: A review for legal professionals. *Psychology, Public Policy, and Law, 14,* 223–242.

Pittenger, D. J. (1993, November). Measuring the MBTI and coming up short. *Journal of Career Planning & Placement, 54*(1), 48–52.

Pittenger, D. J. (2005). Cautionary comments regarding the Myers-Briggs Type Indicator. *Consulting Psychology Journal: Practice and Research, 57,* 210–221.

Pletcher, M. J., Vittinghoff, E., Kalhan, R., Richman, J., Safford, M., Sidney, S., . . . Kertesz, S. (2012). Association between marijuana exposure and pulmonary function over 20 years. *Journal of the American Medical Association, 307,* 173–181.

Plomin, R., & DeFries, J. C. (1998). Genetics of cognitive abilities and disabilities. *Scientific American, 218*(5), 62–69.

Plomin, R., DeFries, J. C., Knopik, V. S., & Neiderhiser, J. M. (2013). *Behavioral genetics* (6th ed.). New York: Worth Publishers.

Poisson, J. (2011, December 26). The "genderless baby" who caused a storm of controversy in 2011. *Toronto Star.* Retrieved from http://www.thestar.com/news/gta/2011/12/26/the_genderless_baby_who_caused_a_storm_of_controversy_in_2011.html

Polidori, M. C., Nelles, G., & Pientka, L. (2010). Prevention of dementia: Focus on lifestyle. *International Journal of Alzheimer's Disease, 2010,* 1–9. doi:10.406112010/393579

Pope, K. S., & Wedding, D. (2014). Contemporary challenges and controversies. In R. J. Corsini & D. Wedding (Eds.), *Current psychotherapies* (10th ed., pp. 569–604). Belmont, CA: Brooks/Cole, Cengage Learning.

Porter, J. S., Stern, M., & Zak-Piace, J. (2009). Prematurity, stereotyping, and perceived vulnerability at 5 months: Relations with mothers and their premature and full-term infants at 9 months. *Journal of Reproductive and Infant Psychology, 27,* 168–181.

Porter, R. H., & Winberg, J. (1999). Unique salience of maternal breast odors for newborn infants. *Neuroscience & Biobehavioral Reviews, 23,* 439–449.

Postuma, R. B., Gagnon, J. F., Vendette, M., Fantini, M. L., Massicotte-Marquez, J., & Montplaisir, J. (2009). Quantifying the risk of neurodegenerative disease in idiopathic REM sleep behavior disorder. *Neurology, 72,* 1296–1300.

Potter, R. H. (2006). "As firecrackers to atom bombs": Kinsey, science, and authority. *Sexuality & Culture, 10,* 29–38.

Powell, L. H., Shahabi, L., & Thoresen, C. E. (2003). Religion and spirituality: Linkages to physical health. *American Psychologist, 58,* 36–52.

Powell, R. A. (2010). Little Albert still missing. *American Psychologist, 65,* 299–300.

Powell, R. A., Digdon, N., Harris, B., & Smithson, C. (2014). Correcting the record on Watson, Rayner and Little Albert: Albert Barger as "Psychology's Lost Boy." *American Psychologist, 69,* 600–611.

Premack, A. J., & Premack, D. (1972). Teaching language to an ape. *Scientific American, 227,* 92–99.

Prengaman, P. (2010, September 3). NASA's advice to trapped Chile miners: Sleep, exercise, vitamin D. *Associated Press.* Retrieved from http://www.nbcnews.com/id/39000893/ns/world_news-americas/t/nasas-advice-trapped-chile-miners-sleep-exercise-vitamin-d/

Prochaska, J. J., Velicer, W. F., Prochaska, J. O., Delucchi, K., & Hall, S. M. (2006). Comparing intervention outcomes in smokers treated for single versus multiple behavioral risks. *Health Psychology, 25,* 380–388.

Prochaska, J. O., & Norcross, J. C. (2014). *Systems of psychotherapy* (8th ed.). Pacific Grove, CA: Brooks/Cole, Cengage Learning.

Pryor, K. (2002). *Don't shoot the dog!* Dorking, UK: Ringpress Books.

Przybelski, R. J., & Binkley, N. C. (2007). Is vitamin D important for preserving cognition? A positive correlation of serum 25-hydroxyvitamin D concentration with cognitive function. *Archives of Biochemistry and Biophysics, 460,* 202–205.

Puig, J., Englund, M. M., Simpson, J. A., & Collins, W. A. (2013). Predicting adult physical illness from infant attachment: A prospective longitudinal study. *Health Psychology, 32,* 409–417.

Pullum, G. K. (1991). *The great Eskimo vocabulary hoax and other irreverent essays on the study of language.* Chicago: University of Chicago Press.

Punjabi, N. M. (2008). The epidemiology of adult obstructive sleep apnea. *Proceedings of the American Thoracic Society, 5,* 136–143.

Qin, S., Ge, S., Yin, H., Xia, J., & Heynderickx, I. (2010). Just noticeable difference in black level, white level and chroma for natural images measured in two different countries. *Displays, 31,* 25–34.

Quilodran, F. (2010, August 24). Dinner for Chile miners—2 spoonfuls of tuna. *Associated Press.* Retrieved from http://www.msnbc.msn.com/id/38830593/ns/world_news-americas/t/dinner-chile-miners-spoonfuls-tuna/

Quinn, O. W. (1963). The public image of the family. In David Rosenthal (Ed.), *The Genain quadruplets: A case study and theoretical analysis of heredity and environment in schizophrenia* (pp. 355–372). New York: Basic Books.

Rabkin, J. G., & Struening, E. L. (1976). Life events, stress, and illness. *Science, 194,* 1013–1020.

Radak, Z., Hart, N., Sarga, L., Koltai, E., Atalay, M., Ohno, H., & Boldough, I. (2010). Exercise plays a preventive role against Alzheimer's disease. *Journal of Alzheimer's Disease, 20,* 777–783.

Radua, J., & Mataix-Cols, D. (2009). Voxel-wise meta-analysis of grey matter changes in obsessive-compulsive disorder. *British Journal of Psychiatry, 195,* 393–402.

Raichle, K. A., Hanley, M., Jensen, M. P., & Cardenas, D. D. (2007). Cognitions, coping, and social environment predict adjustment to pain in spinal cord injury. *Journal of Pain, 8,* 718–729.

Raine, A., Lencz, T., Bihrle, S., LaCasse, L., & Colletti, P. (2000). Reduced prefrontal gray matter volume and reduced autonomic activity in antisocial personality disorder. *Archives of General Psychiatry, 57,* 119–127.

Rainville, P., Duncan, G. H., Price, D. D., Carrier, B., & Bushnell, M. C. (1997, August 15). Pain affect encoded in human anterior cingulate but not somatosensory cortex. *Science, 277*(5328), 968–971.

Rajah, A., Kumar, R. S., Somasundaram, C. P., & Kumar, A. A. (2009). Dissociative fugue in the elderly. *Indian Journal of Psychiatry, 51,* 305–307.

Ramachandran, V. S., & Brang, D. (2009). Sensations evoked in patients with amputation from watching an individual whose corresponding intact limb is being touched. *Archives of Neurology, 66,* 1281–1284.

Ramachandran, V. S., & Rogers-Ramachandran, D. (2009). I see, but I don't know. Patients with unusual visual deficits provide insights into how we normally see. *Scientific American Mind, 19,* 20–22.

Ramchandran, K., & Hauser, J. (2010). Phantom limb pain #212. *Journal of Palliative Medicine, 13,* 1285–1287.

Rameson, L. T., Morelli, S. A., & Lieberman, M. D. (2012). The neural correlates of empathy: Experience, automaticity, and prosocial behavior. *Journal of Cognitive Neuroscience, 24,* 235–245.

Randall, D. K. (2012, September 22). Rethinking sleep. *The New York Times.* Retrieved from http://www.nytimes.com/2012/09/23/opinion/sunday/rethinking-sleep.html

Rapee, R. M., & Spence, S. H. (2004). The etiology of social phobia: Empirical evidence and an initial model. *Clinical Psychology Review, 24,* 737–767.

Rasmussen, S. C. (2007). The history of science as a tool to identify and confront pseudoscience. *Journal of Chemical Education, 84,* 949–951.

Ratiu, P., Talos, I. F., Haker, S., Lieberman, D., & Everett, P. (2004). The tale of Phineas Gage, digitally remastered. *Journal of Neurotrauma, 21,* 637–643.

Ratnesar, R. (2011, July/August). The menace within. *Stanford Magazine.* Retrieved from http://alumni.stanford.edu/get/page/magazine/article/?article_id=40741

Read, J., & Bentall, R. (2010). The effectiveness of electroconvulsive therapy: A literature review. *Epidemiologia e psichiatria sociale, 19,* 333–347.

Reber, S., Allen, R., & Reber, E. S. (2009). Appendix A: Simple phobias. In S. Reber, R. Allen, E. S. Reber (Eds.). *The Penguin dictionary of psychology* (4th ed.). London: Penguin.

Rechtschaffen, A., & Bergmann, B. M. (1995). Sleep deprivation in the rat by the disk-over-water method. *Behavioural Brain Research, 69,* 55–63.

Reece, A. S. (2009). Chronic toxicology of cannabis. *Clinical Toxicology, 47,* 517–524.

Rees, J. L. (2003). Genetics of hair and skin color. *Annual Review of Genetics, 37,* 67–90.

Reese, H. W. (2010). Regarding Little Albert. *American Psychologist, 65,* 300–301.

Regalado, M., Sareen, H., Inkelas, M., Wissow, L. S., & Halfon, N. (2004). Parents' discipline of young children: Results from the National Survey of Early Childhood Health. *Pediatrics, 113,* 1952–1958.

Reich, S. M., Subrahmanyam, K., & Espinoza, G. (2012). Friending, IMing, and hanging out face-to-face: Overlap in adolescents' online and offline social networks. *Developmental Psychology, 48,* 356–368.

Reiche, E. M. V., Nunes, S. O. V., & Morimoto, H. K. (2004). Stress, depression, the immune system, and cancer. *Lancet Oncology, 5,* 617–625.

Reisenzein, R. (1983). The Schachter theory of emotion: Two decades later. *Psychological Bulletin, 94,* 239–264.

Ren, J., Wu, Y. D., Chan, J. S., & Yan, J. H. (2013). Cognitive aging affects motor performance and learning. *Geriatrics & Gerontology International, 13,* 19–27. doi:10.1111/j.1447-0594.2012.00914.x

Reneman, L., Booij, J., de Bruin, K., Reitsma, J. B., de Wolff, F. A., Gunning, W. B., . . . van den Brink, W. (2001). Effects of dose, sex, and long-term abstention from use on toxic effects of MDMA (ecstasy) on brain serotonin neurons. *Lancet, 358,* 1864–1869.

Renner, M. J., & Mackin, R. S. (1998). A life stress instrument for classroom use. *Teaching of Psychology, 25,* 46–48.

Renner, W., Laireiter, A.-R., & Maier, M. (2012). Social support as a moderator of acculturative stress among refugees and asylum seekers. *Social Behavior and Personality, 40,* 129–146.

Reuter-Lorenz, P. A. (2013). Aging and cognitive neuroimaging: A fertile union. *Perspectives on Psychological Science, 8,* 68–71.

Reynolds, B. A., & Weiss, S. (1992). Generation of neurons and astrocytes from isolated cells of the adult mammalian central nervous system. *Science, 255,* 1707–1710.

Ricaurte, G. A., & McCann, U. D. (2001). Experimental studies on 3,4-methylenedioxymethamphetamine (MDMA, "ecstasy") and its potential to damage brain serotonin neurons. *Neurotoxicity Research, 3,* 85–99.

Rice, E., Rhoades, H., Winetrobe, H., Sanchez, M., Montoya, J., Plant, A., & Kordic, T. (2012). Sexually explicit cell phone messaging associated with sexual risk among adolescents. *Pediatrics, 130,* 667–673.

Rich, A. N., & Mattingley, J. B. (2002). Anomalous perception in synaesthesia: A cognitive neuroscience perspective. *Nature Reviews Neuroscience, 3,* 43–52.

Richardson, E. G., & Hemenway, D. (2011). Homicide, suicide, and unintentional firearm fatality: Comparing the United States with other high-income countries, 2003. *Journal of Trauma, 70,* 238–243.

Riedel, G., Platt, B., & Micheau, J. (2003). Glutamate receptor function in learning and memory. *Behavioural Brain Research, 140,* 1–47.

Rieke, F., & Baylor, D. A. (1998). Single-photon detection by rod cells of the retina. *Reviews of Modern Physics, 70,* 1027–1036.

Rietschel, M., Maier, W., & Schulze, T. G. (2013). *Phenotype refinement in bipolar affective disorder as a prerequisite for the identification of disease genes.* Federal Ministry of Education and Research, Disease-Oriented Genome Networks. Retrieved from http://www.science.ngfn.de/6_148.htm

Riggio, H. R., & Garcia, A. L. (2009). The power of situations: Jonestown and the fundamental attribution error. *Teaching of Psychology, 36,* 108–112.

Ritchie, J. (2009, January 12). Fact or fiction: Elephants never forget. *Scientific American Online.* Retrieved from http://www.scientificamerican.com/article.cfm?id=elephants-never-forget

Ritchie, S. J., Wiseman, R., & French, C. C. (2012). Replication, replication, replication. *Psychologist, 25*(5), 346–348.

Rivkees, S. A. (2003). Editorial: Time to wake-up to the individual variation in sleep needs. *Journal of Clinical Endocrinology & Metabolism, 88,* 24–25.

Robbins, B. D. (2008). What is the good life? Positive psychology and the renaissance of humanistic psychology. *The Humanistic Psychologist, 36,* 96–112.

Robbins, R. N., & Bryan, A. (2004). Relationships between future orientation, impulsive sensation seeking, and risk behavior among adjudicated adolescents. *Journal of Adolescent Research, 19,* 428–445.

Roberti, J. W. (2004). A review of behavioral and biological correlates of sensation seeking. *Journal of Research in Personality, 38,* 256–279.

Roberts, B. W., & DelVecchio, W. F. (2000). The rank-order consistency of personality traits from childhood to old age: A quantitative review of longitudinal studies. *Psychological Bulletin, 126,* 3–25.

Roberts, F. D., Newcomb, P. A., Trentham-Dietz, A., & Storer, B. E. (1995). Self-reported stress and risk of breast cancer. *Cancer, 77,* 1089–1093.

Robertson, L. A., McAnally, H. M., & Hancox, R. J. (2013). Childhood and adolescent television viewing and antisocial behavior in early adulthood. *Pediatrics, 131,* 439–446.

Robinson, D. K. (2010). Gustav Fechner: 150 years of Elemente der Psychophysik. *History of Psychology, 13,* 409–410.

Rodin, J., & Langer, E. J. (1977). Long-term effects of a control-relevant intervention with the institutionalized aged. *Journal of Personality and Social Psychology, 12,* 897–902.

Rodriguez, T. (2012). Open mind, longer life. *Scientific American Mind, 23,* 18.

Roediger, H. L., & Bergman, E. T. (1998). The controversy over recovered memories. *Psychology, Public Policy, and Law, 4,* 1091–1109.

Roediger, H. L., III, Putnam, A. L., & Smith, M. A. (2011). Ten benefits of testing and their applications to educational practice. *Psychology of Learning and Motivation: Advances in Research and Theory, 55,* 1–36.

Roehrs, T., Hyde, M., Blaisdell, B., Greenwald, M., & Roth, T. (2006). Sleep loss and REM sleep loss are hyperalgesic. *Sleep, 23,* 145–151.

Roemer, L., Orsillo, S. M., & Salters-Pedneault, K. (2008). Efficacy of an acceptance-based behavior therapy for generalized anxiety disorder: Evaluation in a randomized controlled trial. *Journal of Consulting and Clinical Psychology, 76,* 1083–1089.

Rogers, C. R. (1951). *Client-centered therapy: Its current practice, implications, and theory.* Boston: Houghton Mifflin.

Rogers, C. R. (1959). A theory of therapy, personality, and interpersonal relationships as developed in the client-centered framework. In S. Koch (Ed.), *Psychology: A study of a science: Vol. 3. Formulations of the person and the social context* (pp. 184–256). New York: McGraw-Hill.

Rogers, C. R. (1961). *On becoming a person.* New York: Houghton Mifflin.

Rogers, C. R. (1979). The foundations of the person-centered approach. *Education, 100,* 98–107.

Rohrer, D., & Taylor, K. (2006). The effects of overlearning and distributed practice on the retention of mathematics knowledge. *Applied Cognitive Psychology, 20,* 1209–1224.

Rohwedder, S., & Willis, R. J. (2010). Mental retirement. *Journal of Economic Perspective, 24,* 119–138.

Roid, G. H. (2003). *Stanford-Binet Intelligence Scales* (5th ed.). Itasca, IL: Riverside.

Romero, M., Simón, R., Garcia-Recuero, I., & Romance, A. (2008). Dental management of oral self-mutilation in neurological patients: A case of congenital insensitivity to pain with anhidrosis. *Medicina Oral Patologia Oral y Cirugia Bucal, 13,* E644–E647.

Rosales-Lagarde, A., Armony, J. L., del Rio-Portilla, Y., Trejo-Mardnez, D., Conde, R., & Corsi-Cabrera, M. (2012). Enhanced emotional reactivity after selective REM sleep deprivation in humans: An fMRI study. *Frontiers in Behavioral Neuroscience, 6,* 1–13.

Rosch, E. (1973). Natural categories. *Cognitive Psychology, 4,* 328–350.

Rosch, E., & Mervis, C. B. (1975). Family resemblances: Studies in the internal structure of categories. *Cognitive Psychology, 7,* 573–605.

Rosch, E., Mervis, C. B., Gray, W. D., Johnson, D. M., & Boyes-Braem, P. (1976). Basic objects in natural categories. *Cognitive Psychology, 8,* 382–439.

Rose, J. D. (2011). Diverse perspectives on the groupthink theory—A literary review. *Emerging Leadership Journeys, 4,* 37–57.

Rose, N., Myerson, J., Roediger, H. L., & Hale, S. (2010). Similarities and differences between working memory and long-term memory: Evidence from the levels-of-processing span task. *Journal of Experimental Psychology: Learning, Memory, and Cognition, 36,* 471–483.

Rosenberg, R. S., & Kosslyn, S. M. (2011). *Abnormal psychology.* New York: Worth Publishers.

Rosenblum, L. D. (2010). *See what I'm saying: The extraordinary powers of our five senses.* New York: W. W. Norton.

Rosenhan, D. L. (1973). On being sane in insane places. *Science, 179,* 250–258.

Rosenkranz, M. A. (2007). Substance P at the nexus of mind and body in chronic inflammation and affective disorders. *Psychological Bulletin, 133,* 1007–1037.

Rosenman, R. H., Brand, R. J., Jenkins, D., Friedman, M., Straus, R., & Wurm, M. (1975). Coronary heart disease in the Western Collaborative Group Study: Final follow-up experience of 8 ½ years. *Journal of the American Medical Association, 233,* 872–877.

Rosenthal, R. (2002a). Covert communication in classrooms, clinics, courtrooms, and cubicles. *American Psychologist, 57,* 839–849.

Rosenthal, R. (2002b). Experimenter and clinician effects in scientific inquiry and clinical practice. *Prevention & Treatment, 5,* 1–12.

Rosenthal, R. (2003). Covert communication in laboratories, classrooms, and the truly real world. *Current Directions in Psychological Science, 12,* 151–154.

Rosenthal, R., & Jacobson, L. (1966). Teachers' expectancies: Determinants of pupils' IQ gains. *Psychological Reports, 19,* 115–118.

Rosenthal, R., & Jacobson, L. (1968). *Pygmalion in the classroom: Teacher expectation and pupils' intellectual development.* New York: Holt, Rinehart, & Winston.

Rosenzweig, M. R. (1984). Experience, memory, and the brain. *American Psychologist, 39,* 365–376.

Roseth, C. J., Johnson, D. W., & Johnson, R. T. (2008). Promoting early adolescents' achievement and peer relationships: The effects of cooperative, competitive, and individualistic goal structures. *Psychological Bulletin, 134,* 223–246.

Ross, L. (1977). The intuitive psychologist and his shortcomings: Distortions in the attribution process. In L. Berkowitz (Ed.), *Advances in experimental social psychology* (Vol. 10, pp. 173–220). New York: Academic Press.

Ross, L. D., Amabile, T. M., & Steinmetz, J. L. (1977). Social roles, social control, and biases in social-perception processes. *Journal of Personality and Social Psychology, 33,* 485–494.

Ross, L., Greene, D., & House, P. (1977). The "false consensus effect": An egocentric bias in social perception and attribution processes. *Journal of Experimental Social Psychology, 13,* 279–301.

Rossion, B. (2014). Understanding face perception by means of prosopagnosia and neuroimaging. *Frontiers in Bioscience (Elite edition), 6,* 258–307.

Rosso, A., Mossey, J., & Lippa, C. F. (2008). Review: Caffeine: Neuroprotective functions in cognition and Alzheimer's disease. *American Journal of Alzheimer's Disease and Other Dementias, 23,* 417–422.

Rotge, J.-Y., Guehl, D., Dilharreguy, B., Tignol, J., Bioulac, B., Allard, M., . . . Aouizerate, B. (2009). Meta-analysis of brain volume changes in obsessive-compulsive disorder. *Biological Psychiatry, 65,* 75–83.

Roth, T. (2007). Insomnia: Definition, prevalence, etiology, and consequences. *Journal of Clinical Sleep Medicine, 3,* 7–10.

Rothbaum, F., Weisz, J., Pott, M., Miyake, K., & Morelli, G. (2000). Attachment and culture: Security in the United States and Japan. *American Psychologist, 55,* 1093–1104.

Rotter, J. B. (1966). Generalized expectancies for internal versus external control of reinforcement. *Psychological Monographs: General and Applied, 80,* 1–28.

Rotter, J. B. (1990). Internal versus external control of reinforcement: A case history of a variable. *American Psychologist, 45,* 489–493.

Routh, D. K., & Reisman, J. M. (2003). Clinical psychology. In D. K. Freedheim (Ed.), *Handbook of psychology: Vol. 1. History of psychology* (pp. 337–355). Hoboken, NJ: John Wiley & Sons.

Rowe, D. C., Almeida, D. M., & Jacobson, K. C. (1999). School context and genetic influences on aggression in adolescence. *Psychological Science, 10,* 277–280.

Rowe, M. H. (2002). Trichromatic color vision in primates. *News in Physiological Sciences, 17,* 93–98.

Rowe, R., Maughan, B., Worthman, C. M., Costello, E. J., & Angold, A. (2004). Testosterone, antisocial behavior, and social dominance in boys: Pubertal development and biosocial interaction. *Biological Psychiatry, 55,* 546–552.

Roy, D., Hazarika, S., Bhattacharya, A., Das, S., Nath, K., & Saddichha, S. (2011). Koro: Culture bound or mass hysteria? *Royal Australian & New Zealand Journal of Psychiatry, 45,* 683.

Rubin, Z., & Peplau, L. A. (1975). Who believes in a just world? *Journal of Social Issues, 31,* 65–89.

Rugg, D. (1941). Experiments in wording questions: II. *Public Opinion Quarterly, 5*(1), 91–92.

Rupert, P. A., Stevanovic, P., & Hunley, H. A. (2009). Work-family conflict and burnout among practicing psychologists. *Professional Psychology: Research and Practice, 40,* 54–61.

Rusbult, C. E. (1983). A longitudinal test of the investment model: The development (and deterioration) of satisfaction and commitment in heterosexual involvements. *Journal of Personality and Social Psychology, 45,* 101.

Rusbult, C. E., & Martz, J. M. (1995). Remaining in an abusive relationship: An investment model analysis of nonvoluntary dependence. *Personality and Social Psychology Bulletin, 21,* 558–571.

Rushton, J. P., & Jensen, A. R. (2010). Race and IQ: A theory-based review of the research in Richard Nisbett's *Intelligence and how to get it. Open Psychology Journal, 3,* 9–35.

Russell, J. A. (1980). A circumplex model of affect. *Journal of Personality and Social Psychology, 39*(6), 1161–1178.

Rutherford, A. (2012). Mamie Phipps Clark: Developmental psychologist, starting from strengths. In W. E. Pickren, D. A. Dewsbury, & M. Wertheimer (Eds.), *Portraits of pioneers in developmental psychology* (pp. 261–275). New York, NY: Psychology Press.

Rutter, M., & O'Connor, T. G. (2004). Are there biological programming effects for psychological development findings from a study of Romanian adoptees. *Developmental Psychology, 40,* 81–94.

Ruxton, C. H. S. (2008). The impact of caffeine on mood, cognitive function, performance and hydration: A review of benefits and risks. *Nutrition Bulletin, 33,* 15–25.

Ryan, R. M., & Deci, E. L. (2000). Intrinsic and extrinsic motivations: Classic definitions and new directions. *Contemporary Educational Psychology, 25,* 54–67.

Ryon, S. (2011, October 3). *Orlando Bloom on some of the challenges he faced at school* [Video file]. Retrieved from https://www.youtube.com/watch?v=LyhTj0tWFDY

Sääksjärvi, K., Knekt, P., Rissanen, H., Laaksonen, M. A., Reunanen, A., & Männistö, S. (2008). Prospective study of coffee consumption and risk of Parkinson's disease. *European Journal of Clinical Nutrition, 62,* 908–915.

Sabah, M., Mulcahy, J., & Zeman, A. (2012). Herpes simplex encephalitis. *British Medical Journal, 344,* e3166. doi:10.1136/bmj.e3166

Sacher, J., Neumann, J., Fünfstück, T., Soliman, A., Villringer, A., & Schroeter, M. L. (2012). Mapping the depressed brain: A meta-analysis of structural and functional alterations in major depressive disorder. *Journal of Affective Disorders, 140,* 142–148.

Sacks, O. (2007, September 24). The abyss. *The New Yorker.* Retrieved from http://www.newyorker.com/reporting/2007/09/24/070924fa_fact_sacks

Sagiv, M., Vogelaere, P. P., Soudry, M., & Ehrsam, R. (2000). Role of physical activity training in attenuation of height loss through aging. *Gerontology, 46,* 266–270.

Saha, S., Chant, D., Welham, J., & McGrath, J. (2005). A systematic review of the prevalence of schizophrenia. *PLoS Medicine, 2,* e141.

Sai, F. Z. (2005). The role of the mother's voice in developing mother's face preference: Evidence for intermodal perception at birth. *Infant and Child Development, 14,* 29–50.

Salimpoor, V. N., Benovoy, M., Larcher, K., Dagher, A., & Zatorre, R. J. (2011). Anatomically distinct dopamine release during anticipation and experience of peak emotion to music. *Nature Neuroscience, 14,* 257–264.

Salmon, P. (2001). Effects of physical exercise on anxiety, depression, and sensitivity to stress: A unifying theory. *Clinical Psychology Review, 21,* 33–61.

Salovey, P., Mayer, J. D., & Caruso, D. (2002). The positive psychology of emotional intelligence. In C. R. Snyder & S. J. Lopez (Eds.), *Handbook of positive psychology* (pp. 159–171). New York: Oxford University Press.

Salthouse, T. A. (2006). Mental exercise and mental aging: Evaluating the validity of the "use it or lose it" hypothesis. *Perspectives on Psychological Science, 1,* 68–87.

Salva, O. R., Farroni, T., Regolin, L., Vallortigara, G., & Johnson, M. H. (2011). The evolution of social orienting: Evidence from chicks (*gallus gallus*) and human newborns. *PLoS ONE 6,* e18802. doi:10.1371/journal.pone.0018802

Sanders, G., Sjodin, M., & de Chastelaine, M. (2002). On the elusive nature of sex differences in cognition: Hormonal influences contributing to within-sex variation. *Archives of Sexual Behavior, 31,* 145–152.

Sansom-Daly, U. M., Peate, M., Wakefield, C. E., Bryant, R. A., & Cohn, R. (2012). A systematic review of psychological interventions for adolescents and young adults living with chronic illness. *Health Psychology, 31,* 380–393.

Saper, C. B., Scammell, T. E., & Lu, J. (2005). Hypothalamic regulation of sleep and circadian rhythms. *Nature, 437,* 1257–1263.

Sar, V. (2011). Epidemiology of dissociative disorders: An overview. *Epidemiology Research International, 2011,* 1–8.

Sastre, J. P., & Jouvet, M. (1979). Le comportement onirique du chat [Oneiric behavior in cats]. *Physiology & Behavior, 22,* 979–989.

Sattler, J. M. (1990). *Assessment of children* (3rd ed.). San Diego, CA: Author.

Saucerman, J., & Vasquez, K. (2014). Psychological barriers to STEM participation for women over the course of development. *Adultspan Journal, 13,* 46–64.

Saxe, L. (1994). Detection of deception: Polygraph and integrity tests. *Current Directions in Psychological Science, 3,* 69–73.

Scarr, S., & McCartney, K. (1983). How people make their own environments: A theory of genotype - environment effects. *Child Development, 54,* 424–435.

Schachner, A., & Hannon, E. E. (2011). Infant-directed speech drives social preferences in 5-month-old infants. *Developmental Psychology, 47,* 19–25.

Schachter, S., & Singer, J. E. (1962). Cognitive, social, and physiological determinants of emotional state. *Psychological Review, 69,* 379–399.

Schaie, K. W. (1993). The Seattle longitudinal studies of adult intelligence. *Current Directions in Psychological Science, 2,* 171–175.

Schaie, K. W. (2008). Historical processes ad patterns of cognitive aging. In S. M. Hofer and D. F. Alwin (Eds.), *Handbook of cognitive aging: Interdisciplinary perspectives.* Thousand Oaks, CA: SAGE.

Schalock, R. L., Borthwick-Duffy, S., Bradley, V. J., Bunting, W. H. E., Coulter, D. L., & Craig, E. M. (2010). *Intellectual disability: Definition classification, and systems of supports* (11th ed.). Washington, DC: American Association on Intellectual and Developmental Disabilities.

Scheffer, P. G., van der Schoot, C. E., Page-Christiaens, G. C., Bossers, B., van Erp, F., & de Haas, M. (2010). Reliability of fetal sex determination using maternal plasma. *Obstetrics & Gynecology, 115,* 117–126.

Schell, T. L., & Marshall, G. N. (2008). Survey of individuals previously deployed for OEF/OIF. In T. Tanielian & L. H. Jacycox (Eds.), *Invisible wounds of war: Psychological and cognitive injuries, their consequences, and services to assist recovery* (pp. 86–115). Santa Monica, CA: Rand Corporation.

Schellenberg, E. G. (2011). Music lessons, emotional intelligence, and IQ. *Music Perception, 29,* 185–194.

Schellenberg, E. G., & Winner, E. (2011). Music training and nonmusical abilities. *Music Perception, 29,* 129–132.

Schenck, C. H., & Mahowald, M. W. (2002). REM sleep behavior disorder: Clinical, developmental, and neuroscience perspectives 16 years after its formal identification in *SLEEP. SLEEP, 25,* 120–138.

Scherer, A. M., Windschitl, P. D., O'Rourke, J., & Smith, A. R. (2012). Hoping for more: The influence of outcome desirability on information seeking and predictions about relative quantities. *Cognition, 125,* 113–117.

Schiffman, S. S. (1997). Taste and smell losses in normal aging and disease. *Journal of American Medical Association, 278,* 1357–1362.

Schlaepfer, T. E., Bewernick, B. H., Kayser, S., Mädler, B., & Coenen, V. A. (2013). Rapid effects of deep brain stimulation for treatment-resistant major depression. *Biological Psychiatry, 73,* 1204–1212.

Schmaltz, R., & Lilienfeld, S. O. (2014). Hauntings, homeopathy, and the Hopkinsville Goblins: Using pseudoscience to teach scientific thinking. *Frontiers in Psychology, 5,* 1–5.

Schmidt, H. G., Peeck, V. H., Paas, F., & van Breukelen, G. J. P. (2000). Remembering the street names of one's childhood neighbourhood: A study of very long-term retention. *Memory, 8,* 37–49.

Schmidt-Daffy, M. (2011). Modeling automatic threat detection: Development of a face-in-the-crowd task. *Emotion, 11,* 153–168.

Schmitt, D. P., Realo, A., Voracek, M., & Allik, J. (2008). Why can't a man be more like a woman? Sex differences in big five personality traits across 55 cultures. *Journal of Personality and Social Psychology, 94*, 168–182.

Schnall, S., Roper, J., & Fessler, D. M. (2010). Elevation leads to altruistic behavior. *Psychological Science, 21*, 315–320.

Schneidman, E. S. (1973). *Deaths of man.* New York: Quadrangle/The New York Times Book Co.

Schnider, A., Guggisberg, A., Nahum, L., Gabriel, D., & Morand, S. (2010). Dopaminergic modulation of rapid reality adaptation in thinking. *Neuroscience, 167*, 583–587.

Schocker, L. (2012, September 25). Celebrities With Sleep Apnea: Rick Perry And 7 Others With The Condition. *Huffington Post.* Retrieved from http://www.huffingtonpost.com/2012/09/25/http/www.huffingtonpost.com/2012/09/25/celebrities-sleep-apnea_n_1911549.html

Schoene-Bake, J. C., Parpaley, Y., Weber, B., Panksepp, J., Hurwitz, T. A., & Coenen, V. A. (2010). Tractographic Analysis of Historical Lesion Surgery for Depression. *Neuropsychopharmacology, 35*, 2553–2563.

Schommer-Aikins, M., & Easter, M. (2008). Epistemological beliefs' contributions to study strategies of Asian Americans and European Americans. *Journal of Educational Psychology, 100*, 920–929.

Schreiner, A. M., & Dunn, M. E. (2012). Residual effects of cannabis use on neurocognitive performance after prolonged abstinence: A meta-analysis. *Experimental and Clinical Psychopharmacology, 20*, 420–429.

Schultz, D. P., & Schultz, S. E. (2012). *A history of modern psychology* (10th ed.). Belmont, CA: Wadsworth, Cengage Learning.

Schultz, D. P., & Schultz, S. E. (2013). *Theories of personality* (10th ed.). Belmont, CA: Wadsworth, Cengage Learning.

Schwartz, B. L. (2012). *Tip-of-the-tongue states: Phenomenology, mechanism, and lexical retrieval.* Mahwah, NJ: Psychology Press.

Schwartz, C. E., Keyl, P. M., Marcum, J. P., & Bode, R. (2009). Helping others shows differential benefits on health and well-being for male and female teens. *Journal of Happiness Studies, 10*, 431–448.

Schwartz, C., Meisenhelder, J. B., Yunsheng, M., & Reed, G. (2003). Altruistic social interest behaviors are associated with better mental health. *Psychosomatic Medicine, 65*, 778–785.

Schwartz, S. J. (2001). The evolution of Eriksonian and Neo-Eriksonian identity theory and research: A review and integration. *Identity: An International Journal of Theory and Research, 1*, 7–58.

Schwarz, S., & Hassebrauck, M. (2012). Sex and age differences in mate-selection preferences. *Human Nature, 23*, 447–466.

Schweinsburg, A. D., Brown, S. A., & Tapert, S. F. (2008). The influence of marijuana use on neurocognitive functioning in adolescents. *Current Drug Abuse Reviews, 1*, 99–111.

Scott, S. B., Rhoades, G. K., Stanley, S. M., Allen, E. S., & Markman, H. J. (2013). Reasons for divorce and recollections of premarital intervention: Implications for improving relationship education. *Couple and Family Psychology: Research and Practice, 2*, 131–145.

Scott, S. K., Blank, C. C., Rosen, S., & Wise, R. J. S. (2000). Identification of a pathway for intelligible speech in the left temporal lobe. *Brain, 123*, 2400–2406.

Scoville, W. B., & Milner, B. (1957). Loss of recent memory after bilateral hippocampal lesions. *Journal of Neurology, Neurosurgery, & Psychiatry, 20*, 11–21.

Scribner, C. M. (2001). Rosenhan revisited. *Professional Psychology: Research and Practice, 32*, 215–216.

Scully, J. A., Tosi, H., & Banning, K. (2000). Life event checklists: Revisiting the Social Readjustment Rating Scale after 30 years. *Educational and Psychological Measurement, 60*, 864–876.

Searight, H. R., & Gafford, J. (2005). Cultural diversity at the end of life: Issues and guidelines for family physicians. *American Family Physician, 71*, 515–522.

Searleman, A. (2007, March 12). Is there such a thing as a photographic memory? And if so, can it be learned? *Scientific American Online.* Retrieved from http://www.scientificamerican.com/article/is-there-such-a-thing-as/

Sedlmeier, P., Eberth, J., Schwarz, M., Zimmermann, D., Haarig, F., Jaeger, S., & Kunze, S. (2012). The psychological effects of meditation: A meta-analysis. *Psychological Bulletin, 138*, 1139–1171. doi:10.1037/a0028168

Seely, R. (2012, September 19). UW study says boys' pacifier use limits social development. *Wisconsin State Journal.* Retrieved from http://host.madison.com/news/local/education/university/uw-study-says-boys-pacifier-use-limits-social-development/article_c44e3998-01f9-11e2-9b69-0019bb2963f4.html

Seery, M. D. (2011). Resilience: A silver lining to experiencing adverse life events? *Current Directions in Psychological Science, 20*, 390–394.

Segall, M. H., Campbell, D. T., & Herskovits, M. J. (1968). The influence of culture on visual perception. In H. Toch and C. Smith (Eds.), *Social perception* (pp. 1–5). Oxford, UK: Bobbs-Merrill.

Segerstrom, S. C., & Miller, G. E. (2004). Psychological stress and the human immune system: A meta-analytic study of 30 years of inquiry. *Psychological Bulletin, 130*, 601–630.

Segraves, R. T. (2010). Considerations for a better definition of male orgasmic disorder in *DSM V. Journal of Sexual Medicine, 7*, 690–699.

Seligman, M. E. P. (1975). *Helplessness: On depression, development, and death.* San Francisco: W. H. Freeman.

Seligman, M. E. P. (1995). The effectiveness of psychotherapy: The *Consumer Reports* study. *American Psychologist, 50*, 965–974.

Seligman, M. E. P., & Csikszentmihalyi, M. (2000). Positive psychology: An introduction. *American Psychologist, 55*, 5–14.

Seligman, M. E. P., & Maier, S. F. (1967). Failure to escape traumatic shock. *Journal of Experimental Psychology, 74*, 1–9.

Seligman, M. E. P., & Steen, T. A. (2005). Positive psychology progress. *American Psychologist, 60*, 410–421.

Sella, M. (2005). The epic life of Orlando Bloom. *GQ.com.* Retrieved from http://www.gq.com/entertainment/celebrities/200510/orlando-bloom-errol-flynn?currentPage=1

Selye, H. (1936). A syndrome produced by diverse nocuous agents. *Nature, 138*, 32.

Selye, H. (1953). The General-Adaptation-Syndrome in its relationships to neurology, psychology, and psychopathology. In A. Weider (Ed.), *Contributions toward medical psychology: Vol. 1. Theory and psychodiagnostic methods* (pp. 234–274). New York: Ronald Press.

Selye, H. (1976). Forty years of stress research: Principal remaining problems and misconceptions. *Canadian Medical Association Journal, 115*, 53–56.

Selye, H., & Fortier, C. (1950). Adaptive reaction to stress. *Psychosomatic Medicine, 12*, 149–157.

Shackelford, T. K., Schmitt, D. P., & Buss, D. M. (2005). Mate preferences of married persons in the newlywed year and three years later. *Cognition and Emotion, 19*, 1262–1270.

Shadish, W. R., & Baldwin, S. A. (2003). Meta-analysis of MFT interventions. *Journal of Marital and Family Therapy, 29*, 547–570.

Shah, A. K., & Oppenheimer, D. M. (2008). Heuristics made easy: An effort-reduction framework. *Psychological Bulletin, 134*, 207–222.

Shapiro, D. H. Jr., Schwartz, C. E., & Astin, J. A. (1996). Controlling ourselves, controlling our world: Psychology's role in understanding positive and negative consequences of seeking and gaining control. *American Psychologist, 51*, 1213–1230.

Shargorodsky, J., Curhan, S. G., Curhan, G. C., & Eavey, R. (2010). Change in prevalence of hearing loss in US adolescents. *Journal of the American Medical Association, 304*, 772–778.

Shaywitz, S. E. (1996). Dyslexia. *Scientific American, 275*, 98–104.

Shaywitz, S. E. (2003). *Overcoming dyslexia: A new and complete science-based program for reading problems at any level.* New York: Vintage Books.

Shaywitz, S. E., Mody, M., & Shaywitz, B. A. (2006). Neural mechanisms in dyslexia. *Current Directions in Psychological Science, 15,* 278–281.

Shaywitz, S. E., & Shaywitz, B. A. (2005). Dyslexia (specific reading disability). *Biological Psychiatry, 57,* 1301–1309.

Shedler, J. (2010). The efficacy of psychodynamic psychotherapy. *American Psychologist, 63,* 98–109.

Shelton, K. H., & van den Bree, M. B. M. (2010). The moderating effects of pubertal timing on the longitudinal associations between parent-child relationships' quality and adolescent substance use. *Journal of Research on Adolescence, 20,* 1044–1064.

Shepard, R. N., & Metzler, J. (1971). Mental rotation of three-dimensional objects. *Science, 171,* 701–703.

Sherwood, C. C., Subiaul, F., & Zawidzki, T. W. (2008). A natural history of the human mind: Tracing evolutionary changes in brain and cognition. *Journal of Anatomy, 212,* 426–454.

Sherwood, L. (2010). *Human physiology: From cells to systems* (7th ed.). Belmont, CA: Brooks/Cole, Cengage Learning.

Shiv, B., & Fedorikhin, A. (1999). Heart and mind in conflict: The interplay of affect and cognition in consumer decision making. *Journal of Consumer Research, 26,* 278–291.

Shonkoff, J. P., Garner, A. S., The Committee on Psychosocial Aspects of Child and Family Health, Committee on Early Childhood, Adoption, and Dependent Care, and Section on Developmental and Behavioral Pediatrics, Siegel, B. S., Dobbins, M. I., Earls, M. F., Garner, A. S., McGuinn, L. Pascoe, J., & Wood, D. L. (2012). The lifelong effects of early childhood adversity and toxic stress. *Pediatrics, 129,* e232–e246.

Siegel, J. M. (2005). Clues to the functions of mammalian sleep. *Nature, 437,* 1264–1271.

Sigelman, C. K., & Rider, E. A. (2009). *Life-span human development* (6th ed.). Belmont, CA: Brooks/Cole, Cengage Learning.

Sigurdson, K., & Ayas, N. T. (2007). The public health and safety consequences of sleep disorders. *Canadian Journal of Physiology and Pharmacology, 85,* 179–183.

Silva, C. E., & Kirsch, I. (1992). Interpretive sets, expectancy, fantasy proneness, and dissociation predictors of hypnotic response. *Journal of Personality and Social Psychology, 63,* 847–856.

Silverstein, C. (2009). The implications of removing homosexuality from the *DSM* as a mental disorder. *Archives of Sexual Behavior, 38,* 131–163.

Simmons, R., Makatchev, M., Kirby, R., Lee, M. K., Fanaswala, I., Browning, B., . . . Sakr, M. (2011). Believable robot characters. *AI Magazine, 32*(4), 39–52.

Simons, D. J. (2010). Monkeying around with the gorillas in our midst: Familiarity with an inattentional-blindness task does not improve the detection of unexpected events. *i-Perception, 1,* 3–6.

Simonton, D. K. (2000). Creativity: Cognitive, personal, developmental, and social aspects. *American Psychologist, 55,* 151–158.

Simonton, D. K. (2012, November/December). The science of genius. *Scientific American Mind, 23,* 35–41.

Simpson, J. A., & Rholes, W. S. (2010). Attachment and relationships: Milestones and future directions. *Journal of Social and Personal Relationships, 27,* 173–180.

Simpson, K. J. (2002). Anorexia nervosa and culture. *Journal of Psychiatric and Mental Health Nursing, 9,* 65–71.

Simpson, L. (2010, April 5). Lady Gaga: I haven't slept in three days. *OK!* magazine. Retrieved from http://www.ok.co.uk/celebrity-news/Lady-Gaga-I-haven-t-slept-in-three-days

Singh, L., Nestor, S., Parikh, C., & Yull, A. (2009). Influences of infant-directed speech on early word recognition. *Infancy, 14,* 654–666.

Singh, M. K., Kesler, S. R., Hosseini, S. M. H., Kelley, R. G., Amatya, D., Hamilton, J. P., . . . Gotlib, I. H. (2013). Anomalous gray matter structural networks in major depressive disorder. *Biological Psychiatry, 74* (10), 777–785. doi:0.1016/j.biopsych.2013.03.005

Singh-Manoux, A., Kivimaki, M., Glymour, M. M., Elbaz, A., Berr, C., Ebmeier, K. P., . . . Dugravot, A. (2012). Timing of onset of cognitive decline: Results from Whitehall II prospective cohort study. *British Medical Journal, 334,* 1–8.

Sinn, D. L., & Moltschaniwskyj, N. A. (2005). Personality traits in dumpling squid (*Euprymna Tasmania*): Context-specific traits and their correlation with biological characteristics. *Journal of Comparative Psychology, 119,* 99–110.

Sio, U. N., & Ormerod, T. C. (2009). Does incubation enhance problem solving? A meta-analytic review. *Psychological Bulletin, 135,* 94–120.

Sivacek, J., & Crano, W. D. (1982). Vested interest as a moderator of attitude-behavior consistency. *Journal of Personality and Social Psychology, 43,* 210–221.

Skinner, B. F. (1953). *Science and human behavior.* New York: Macmillan.

Skinner, B. F. (1956). A case history in scientific method. *American Psychologist, 11,* 221–233.

Skinner, B. F. (1957). *Verbal behavior.* New York: Macmillan.

Skinner, B. F. (1976). *Particulars of my life.* New York: Knopf.

Skinner, N. F. (2009). Academic folk wisdom: Fact, fiction and falderal. *Psychology Learning and Teaching, 8,* 46–50.

Skirbekk, V., Loichinger, E., & Weber, D. (2012). Variation in cognitive functioning as a refined approach to comparing aging across countries. *Proceedings of the National Academy of Sciences, 109,* 770–774.

Skoog, G., & Skoog, I. (1999). A 20-year follow-up of patients with obsessive-compulsive disorder. *Archives of General Psychiatry, 56,* 121–127.

Slaney, K. L., & Racine, T. P. (2011). On the ambiguity of concept use in psychology: Is the concept "concept" a useful concept? *Journal of Theoretical and Philosophical Psychology, 31,* 73–89.

Slatcher, R. B., & Robles, T. F. (2012). Preschoolers' everyday conflict at home and diurnal cortisol patterns. *Health Psychology, 31,* 834–838. doi:10.1037/a0026774

Slife, B. D. (1990). Introduction and overview of the special issue on Aristotle. *Theoretical & Philosophical Psychology, 10,* 3–6.

Slotema, C. W., Blom, J. D., Hoek, H. W., & Sommer, I. E. C. (2010). Should we expand the toolbox of psychiatric treatment methods to include Repetitive Transcranial Magnetic Stimulation (rTMS)? A meta-analysis of the efficacy of rTMS in psychiatric disorders. *Journal of Clinical Psychiatry, 71,* 873–884.

Sloter, E., Schmid, T. E., Marchetti, F., Eskenazi, B., Nath, J., & Wyrobek, A. J. (2006). Quantitative effects of male age on sperm motion. *Human Reproduction, 21,* 2868–2875.

Slovic, P., & Weber, E. U. (2002, April). *Perception of risk posed by extreme events.* Paper presented at Conference on Risk Management Strategies in an Uncertain World, Palisades, NY.

Small, B. J., Dixon, R. A., & McArdle, J. J. (2011). Tracking cognition–health changes from 55 to 95 years of age. *The Journals of Gerontology Series B: Psychological Sciences and Social Sciences, 66B,* i153–i161, doi: 10.1093/geronb/gbq093

Small, B. J., Dixon, R. A., McArdle, J. J., & Grimm, K. J. (2012). Do changes in lifestyle engagement moderate cognitive decline in normal aging? Evidence from the Victoria Longitudinal Study. *Neuropsychology, 26,* 144–155. doi:10.1037/a0026579

Smink, F. R. E., van Hoeken, D., & Hoek, H. W. (2012). Epidemiology of eating disorders: Incidence, prevalence, and mortality rates. *Current Psychiatry Reports, 14,* 406–414.

Smith, B. L. (2012). The case against spanking. *Monitor on Psychology, 43,* 60.

Smith, C. N., & Squire, L. R. (2009). Medial temporal lobe activity during retrieval of semantic memory is related to the age of the memory. *Journal of Neuroscience, 29,* 930–938.

Smith, D. (2001). Shock and disbelief. *Atlantic Monthly, 287,* 79–90.

Smith, J. (2009, March 23). Can robots be programmed to learn from their own experiences? *Scientific American Online.* Retrieved from http://www.scientificamerican.com/article.cfm?id=robot-learning

Smith, S. M., Glenberg, A. M., & Bjork, R. A. (1978). Environmental context and human memory. *Memory and Cognition, 6,* 342–353.

Smith, T. W., Birmingham, W., & Uchino, B. N. (2012). Evaluative threat and ambulatory blood pressure: Cardiovascular effects of social stress in daily experience. *Health Psychology, 31,* 763–766.

Smith, T. W., & MacKenzie, J. (2006). Personality and risk of physical illness. *Annual Review of Clinical Psychology, 2,* 435–467.

Smith, T. W., & Ruiz, J. M. (2002). Psychosocial influences on the development and course of coronary heart disease: Current status and implications for research and practice. *Journal of Consulting and Clinical Psychology, 70,* 548–568.

Smrt, D. L., & Karau, S. J. (2011). Protestant work ethic moderates social loafing. *Group Dynamics: Theory, Research, and Practice, 15,* 267–274.

Snyder, C. R., Ilardi, S. S., Cheavens, J., Michael, S. T., Yamhure, L., & Sympson, S. (2000). The role of hope in cognitive-behavior therapies. *Cognitive Therapy and Research, 24,* 747–762.

Snyder, T. D., & Dillow, S. A. (2011). *Digest of education statistics 2010* (NCES 2011-015). Washington, DC: U.S. Department of Education, National Center for Education Statistics, Institute of Education Sciences. Retrieved from http://nces.ed.gov/pubs2011/2011015.pdf

Society for Neuroscience. (2012). Sensation and perception. In *Brain facts* (6th ed., pp. 15–21). Washington, DC: Author.

Solms, M. (2006, April/May). Freud returns. *Scientific American,* 82–88.

Solomon, B. C., & Jackson, J. J. (2014). The long reach of one's spouse: Spouses' personality influences occupational success. *Psychological Science, 25,* 2189–2198.

Solomon, S. G., & Lennie, P. (2007). The machinery of color vision. *Nature Reviews Neuroscience, 8,* 276–286.

Somatosensory function. (2004). In *Corsini encyclopedia of psychology.* Hoboken, NJ: Wiley. doi:10.100219780470479216

Song, H., Zmyslinski-Seelig, A., Kim, J., Drent, A., Victor, A., Omori, K., Allen, M. (2014). Does Facebook make you lonely?: A meta analysis. *Computers in Human Behavior, 36,* 446–452.

Sørensen, K., Aksglaede, L., Petersen, J. H., & Juul, A. (2010). Recent changes in pubertal timing in healthy Danish boys: Associations with Body Mass Index. *Journal of Clinical Endocrinology & Metabolism, 95,* 263–270.

Sorhagen, N. S. (2013). Early teacher expectations disproportionately affect poor children's high school performance. *Journal of Educational Psychology, 105,* 465–477.

Southworth, M. R., Kortepeter, C., & Hughes, A. (2008). Nonbenzodiazepine hypnotic use and cases of sleep driving. *Annals of Internal Medicine, 148,* 486–487.

Sparling, J., Wilder, D. A., Kondash, J., Boyle, M., & Compton, M. (2011). Effects of interviewer behavior on accuracy of children's responses. *Journal of Applied Behavior Analysis, 44,* 587–592.

Sparrow, B., Liu, J., & Wegner, D. W. (2011). Google effects on memory: Cognitive consequences of having information at our fingertips. *Science, 333,* 776–778. doi:10.1126lscience.l207745

Sparrow, R. (2005). Defending deaf culture: The case of cochlear implants. *Journal of Political Philosophy, 13,* 135–152.

Speakman, J. R., Levitsky, D. A., Allison, D. B., Bray, M. S., de Castro, J. M., Clegg, D. J., . . . Westerterp-Plantenga, M. S. (2011). Set points, settling points and some alternative models: Theoretical options to understand how genes and environments combine to regulate body adiposity. *Disease Models & Mechanisms, 4,* 733–745.

Spears, M. J. (2012, February 18). Jeremy Lin's high school inspired by Linsanity. *Yahoo Sports.* Retrieved from http://sports.yahoo.com/news/jeremy-lins-high-school-inspired-023300091-nba.html

Specht, J., Egloff, B., & Schmukle, S. C. (2011). Stability and change of personality across the life course: The impact of age and major life events on mean-level and rank-order stability of the Big Five. *Journal of Personality and Social Psychology, 101,* 862–882.

Sperling, G. (1960). The information available in brief visual presentations. *Psychological Monographs: General and Applied, 74,* 1–29.

Spiegel, D., Loewenstein, R. J., Lewis-Fernández, R., Sar, V., Simeon, D., Vermetten, E., . . . Dell, P. F. (2011). Dissociative disorders in DSM-5. *Depression and Anxiety, 28,* 824–852.

Spitzer, R. L. (1975). On pseudoscience in science, logic in remission, and psychiatric diagnosis: A critique of Rosenhan's "On Being Sane in Insane Places." *Journal of Abnormal Psychology, 84,* 442–451.

Spotts, P. (2010, September 7). Trapped miners impress NASA team. *Christian Science Monitor.* Retrieved from http://www.csmonitor.com/Science/2010/0907/Trapped-miners-impress-NASA-team

Squire, L. R., & Bayley, P. J. (2007). The neuroscience of remote memory. *Current Opinion in Neurobiology, 17,* 185–196.

Squire, L. R., Stark, C. E. L., & Clark, R. E. (2004). The medial temporal lobe. *Annual Review of Neuroscience, 27,* 279–306.

Squire, L. R., & Wixted, J. T. (2011). The cognitive neuroscience of human memory since HM. *Annual Review of Neuroscience, 34,* 259–288.

Srinivasa, S. S., Ferguson, D., Helfrich, C. J., Berenson, D., Collet, A., Diankov, R., . . . Vande Weghe, J. (2009). HERB: A home exploring robotic butler. *Autonomous Robots, 28,* 5–20.

Stanford School of Medicine. (2015). About narcolepsy. *Center for Narcolepsy.* Retrieved from http://med.stanford.edu/narcolepsy/symptoms.html

Stanger-Hall, K., & Hall, D. W. (2011). Abstinence-only education and teen pregnancy rates: Why we need comprehensive sex education in the U.S. *PLoS ONE, 6,* e24658. doi:10.1371/journal.pone.0024658

Staniloiu, A., & Markowitsch, H. J. (2012). The remains of the day in dissociative amnesia. *Brain Sciences, 2,* 101–129.

Stanovich, K. E. (2013). *How to think straight about psychology* (10th ed.). Upper Saddle River, NJ: Pearson.

Starr, B. (2005, June 10). Is it possible for two parents who cannot roll their tongues to have a tongue-roller child? *Tech Museum of Innovation.* Retrieved from http://genetics.thetech.org/ask/ask125

Steel, E. (2015, April 25). Bruce Jenner's transgender announcement draws 16.8 million on ABC News. *The New York Times.* Retrieved from http://www.nytimes.com/2015/04/26/business/media/bruce-jenners-transgender-announcement-draws-16-8-million-on-abc-news.html

Steele, C. M. (1997). A threat in the air: How stereotypes shape intellectual identity and performance. *American Psychologist, 52,* 613–629.

Steele, C. M. (2010). *Whistling Vivaldi: How stereotypes affect us and what we can do.* New York: W. W. Norton.

Stein, B. E., Stanford, T. R., & Rowland, B. A. (2009). The neural basis of multisensory integration in the midbrain: Its organization and maturation. *Hearing Research, 258,* 4–15.

Stein, D. J., Seedat, S., Herman, A., Moomal, H., Heeringa, S. G., Kessler, R. C., & Williams, D. R. (2008). Lifetime prevalence of psychiatric disorders in South Africa. *British Journal of Psychiatry, 192,* 112–117.

Steinberg, L. (2010). Commentary: A behavioral scientist looks at the science of adolescent brain development. *Brain and Cognition, 72,* 160–164.

Steinberg, L. (2012). Should the science of adolescent brain development inform public policy? *Issues in Science & Technology, 28,* 76–78.

Steiner, M. (2012, September 4). The importance of pragmatic communication. *Monocracy Neurodevelopmental Center.* Retrieved from http://monocacycenter.com/the-importance-of-pragmatic-communication/

Stemwedel, J. D. (2011, October 4). Drawing the line between science and pseudo-science. *Scientific American*. Retrieved from http://blogs.scientificamerican.com/doing-good-science/2011/10/04/drawing-the-line-between-science-and-pseudo-science/

Stern, K., & Karraker, K. H. (1989). Sex stereotyping of infants: A review of gender labeling studies. *Sex Roles, 20*, 501–522.

Sternberg, R. J. (1986). A triangular theory of love. *Psychological Review, 93*, 119–135.

Sternberg, R. J. (1988). *The triarchic mind: A new theory of human intelligence.* New York: Viking.

Sternberg, R. J. (2004). Culture and intelligence. *American Psychologist, 59*, 325–338.

Sternberg, R. J. (2006a). Creating a vision of creativity: The first 25 years. *Psychology of Aesthetics, Creativity, and the Arts, S*(1), 2–12.

Sternberg, R. J. (2006b). The nature of creativity. *Creativity Research Journal, 18*, 87–98.

Sternberg, R. J., & Grigorenko, E. L. (2005). Intelligence and wisdom. In M. L. Johnson (Ed.), *The Cambridge Handbook of Age and Ageing* (pp. 209–213). Cambridge, UK: Cambridge University Press.

Stice, E., Marti, C. N., Shaw, H., & Jaconis, M. (2009). An 8-year longitudinal study of the natural history of threshold, subthreshold, and partial eating disorders from a community sample of adolescents. *Journal of Abnormal Psychology, 118*, 587–597.

St. John, K. (2003, August 19). Yosemite landmark falls/Sentinel Dome's oft-photographed Jeffrey pine topples. *San Francisco Chronicle.* Retrieved from http://www.sfgate.com/news/article/Yosemite-landmark-falls-Sentinel-Domes-2574496.php#ixzz2HLMo2N31

Stone, A. A., Schwartz, J. E., Broderick, J. E., & Deaton, A. (2010). A snapshot of the age distribution of psychological well-being in the United States. *Proceedings of the National Academy of Sciences, 107*, 9985–9990.

Stone, D. (2009). Brainy Bonnie. Smithsonian Zoogoer. Retrieved from http://nationalzoo.si.edu/Publications/ZooGoer/2009/1/BrainyBonnie.cfm

Stone, D. N., Deci, E. L., & Ryan, R. M. (2009). Beyond talk: Creating autonomous motivation through self-determination theory. *Journal of General Management, 34*, 75–102.

Stoner, J. A. F. (1961). *A comparison of individual and group decisions involving risk* (Unpublished Master's thesis, Alfred P. Sloan School of Management, Massachusetts Institute of Technology). Retrieved from http://dspace.mit.edu/bitstream/handle/1721.1/11330/33120544-MIT.pdf?sequence=2

Stoner, J. A. F. (1968). Risky and cautious shifts in group decisions: The influence of widely held values. *Journal of Experimental Psychology, 4*, 442–459.

Storaasli, R. D., & Markman, H. J. (1990). Relationship problems in the early stages of marriage: A longitudinal investigation. *Journal of Family Psychology, 4*, 80–98.

Storm, B. C., Bjork, E. L., & Bjork, R. A. (2008). Accelerated relearning after retrieval-induced forgetting: The benefit of being forgotten. *Journal of Experimental Psychology: Learning, Memory, and Cognition, 34*, 230–236.

Strack, F., Martin, L. L., & Stepper, S. (1988). Inhibiting and facilitating conditions of the human smile: A nonobtrusive test of the facial feedback hypothesis. *Journal of Personality and Social Psychology, 54*, 768–777.

Strain, George M. (2003). *How well do dogs and other animals hear?* Department of Comparative Biomedical Sciences, School of Veterinary Medicine, Louisiana State University. Retrieved from http://www.lsu.edu/deafness/HearingRange.html

Strassberg, D. S., McKinnon, R. K., Sustaíta, M. A., & Rullo J. (2013). Sexting by high school students: An exploratory and descriptive study. *Archives of Sexual Behavior, 42*, 15–21.

Stratton, G. (1896, August). *Some preliminary experiments on vision without inversion of the retinal image.* Paper presented at the Third International Congress for Psychology, Munich.

Straub, R. O. (2012). *Health psychology: A biopsychosocial approach* (3rd ed.). New York: Worth Publishers.

Straus, M. A. (2005). Children should never, ever, be spanked no matter what the circumstances. In D. R. Loseke, R. J. Gelles, & M. M. Cavanaugh (Eds.), *Current controversies about family violence* (2nd ed., pp. 137–157). Thousand Oaks, CA: Sage.

Straus, M. A., & Paschall, M. J. (2009). Corporal punishment by mothers and development of children's cognitive ability: A longitudinal study of two nationally representative age cohorts. *Journal of Aggression, Maltreatment & Trauma, 18*, 459–483.

Strayer, D. L., & Watson, J. M. (2012, March). Top multitaskers help explain how brain juggles thoughts. *Scientific American Mind, 23*, 22–29.

Streit, W. J. (2000). Microglial response to brain injury: A brief synopsis. *Toxicologic Pathology, 28*, 28–30.

Stright, A. D., Gallagher, K. C., & Kelley, K. (2008). Infant temperament moderates relations between maternal parenting in early childhood and children's adjustment in first grade. *Child Development, 79*, 186–200.

Stroebe, W., van Koningsbruggen, G. M., Papies, E. K., & Aarts, H. (2013). Why most dieters fail but some succeed: A goal conflict model of eating behavior. *Psychological Review, 120*, 110–138.

Struthers, R., & Lowe, J. (2003). Nursing in the Native American culture and historical trauma. *Issues in Mental Health Nursing, 24*, 257–272.

Stuart, H. (2003). Violence and mental illness: An overview. *World Psychiatry, 2*, 121–124.

Stuen, C., & Faye, E. E. (2003). Vision loss: Normal and not normal changes among older adults. *Generations, 27*, 8–14.

Stump, S. (2011, July 26). Girl, 6, on shark that bit her: 'I forgive him.' *Today.com.* Retrieved from http://today.msnbc.msn.com/id/43892097/ns/today-today_people/t/girl-shark-bit-her-i-forgive-him/#.Tpnf6s1lYjw

Stuss, D. T., & Alexander, M. P. (2000). Executive functions and the frontal lobes: A conceptual view. *Psychological Research, 63*, 289–298.

Su, K. G., Banker, G., Bourdette, D., & Forte, M. (2009). Axonal degeneration in multiple sclerosis: The mitochondrial hypothesis. *Current Neurological Neuroscience, 9*, 411–417.

Substance Abuse and Mental Health Services Administration. (2010). *The DAWN report: Trends in emergency department visits involving nonmedical use of narcotic pain relievers.* Retrieved from http://oas.samhsa.gov/2k10/DAWN016/OpioidED.htm

Substance Abuse and Mental Health Services Administration. (2012). *Results from the 2011 National Survey on Drug Use and Health: Summary of national findings* (NSDUH Series H-44, HHS Publication No. (SMA) 12-4713). Retrieved from http://www.samhsa.gov/data/nsduh/2k11results/nsduhresults2011.htm

Substance Abuse and Mental Health Services Administration. (2014). *The NSDUH report: Substance use and mental health estimates from the 2013 national survey on drug use and health: overview of findings.* Rockville, MD.

Sucala, M., Schnur, J. B., Constantino, M. J., Miller, S. J., Brackman, E. H., & Montgomery, G. H. (2012). The therapeutic relationship in e-therapy for mental health: A systematic review. *Journal of Medical Internet Research, 14*, e110. doi:10.2196/jmir.2084

Sue, S., Fujino, D. C., Hu, L., Takeuchi, D. T., & Zane, N. W. S. (1991). Community mental health services for ethnic minority groups: A test of the cultural responsiveness hypothesis. *Journal of Consulting and Clinical Psychology, 59*, 533–540.

Sun-Edelstein, C., & Mauskop, A. (2011). Alternative headache treatments: Nutraceuticals, behavioral, and physical treatments. *Headache, 25*, 469–483.

Susuki, K. (2010). Myelin: A specialized membrane for cell communication. *Nature Education, 3*, 59–63.

Suwanrath, C., & Suntharasaj, T. (2010). Sleep-wake cycles in normal fetuses. *Archives of Gynecology and Obstetrics, 281*, 449–454.

Swan, S. H., Liu, F., Hines, M., Kruse, R. L., Wang, C., Redmon, J. B., . . . Weiss, B. (2010). Prenatal phthalate exposure and reduced masculine play in boys. *International Journal of Andrology, 3,* 259–269.

Swanson, L. (1997). Cochlear implants: The head-on collision between medical technology and the right to be deaf. *Canadian Medical Association Journal, 157,* 929–932.

Swendsen, J. D., Tennen, H., Carney, M. A., Affleck, G., Willard, A., & Hromi, A. (2000). Mood and alcohol consumption: An experience sampling test of the self-medication hypothesis. *Journal of Abnormal Psychology, 109,* 198–204.

Swift, J. K., & Greenberg, R. P. (2012). Premature discontinuation in adult psychotherapy: A meta-analysis. *Journal of Consulting and Clinical Psychology, 80,* 547–559.

Swinburn, B. A., Sacks, G., Hall, K. D., McPherson, K., Finegood, D. T., Moodie, M. L., & Gortmaker, S. L. (2011). The global obesity pandemic: Shaped by global drivers and local environments. *Lancet, 378,* 804–814.

Szabo, R., & Hall, M. (2007). *Behind happy faces.* Los Angeles: Volt Press.

Szalavitz, M. (2011, May 13). Q&A: Positive psychologist Martin Seligman on the good life. *Time.* Retrieved from http://healthland.time.com/2011/05/13/mind-reading-positive-psychologist-martin-seligman-on-the-good-life/

Szasz, T. (2011). The myth of mental illness: 50 years later. *Psychiatrist Online, 35,* 179–182.

Tackett, J. L., Waldman, I. D., & Lahey, B. B. (2009). Etiology and measurement of relational aggression: A multi-informant behavior genetic investigation. *Journal of Abnormal Psychology, 118,* 722–733.

Takeda, A. (2013, July 12). Catherine Zeta-Jones wows on first red carpet after treatment for bipolar II: Picture. *US Weekly.* Retrieved from http://www.usmagazine.com/celebrity-style/news/catherine-zeta-jones-wows-on-first-red-carpet-after-treatment-for-bipolar-ii-picture-2013127

Talarico, J. M., & Rubin, D. C. (2003). Confidence, not consistency, characterizes flashbulb memories. *Psychological Science, 14,* 455–461.

Tallandini, M. A., & Caudek, C. (2010). Defense mechanisms development in typical children. *Psychotherapy Research, 20,* 535–545.

Tandon, P. S., Zhou, C., Lozano, P., & Christakis, D. A. (2011). Preschoolers' total daily screen time at home and by type of child care. *Journal of Pediatrics, 158,* 297–300.

Tandon, R., Keshavan, M. S., & Nasrallah, H. A. (2008a). Schizophrenia, "just the facts": What we know in 2008. Part 1: Overview. *Schizophrenia Research, 100,* 4–19.

Tandon, R., Keshavan, M. S., & Nasrallah, H. A. (2008b). Schizophrenia, "just the facts": What we know in 2008. Part 2: Epidemiology and etiology. *Schizophrenia Research, 102,* 1–18.

Tandon, R., Nasrallah, H. A., & Keshavan, M. S. (2009). Schizophrenia, "just the facts." 4. Clinical features and conceptualization. *Schizophrenia Research, 110,* 1–23.

Tang, Y., Nyengaard, J. R., De Groot, D. M., & Gundersen, H. J. G. (2001). Total regional and global number of synapses in the human brain neocortex. *Synapse, 41*(3), 258–273.

Tate, M. C., Herbet, G., Moritz-Gasser, S., Tate, J. E., & Duffau, H. (2014). Probabilistic map of critical functional regions of the human cerebral cortex: Broca's area revisited. *Brain, 137,* 2773–2782.

Taverniers, J., Smeets, T., Van Ruysseveldt, J., Syroit, J., & von Grumbkow, J. (2011). The risk of being shot at: Stress, cortisol secretion, and their impact memory and perceived learning during reality-based practice for armed officers. *International Journal of Stress Management, 18,* 113–132.

Taylor, B., Miller, E., Lingam, R., Andrews, N., Simmons, A., & Stowe, J. (2002). Measles, mumps, and rubella vaccination and bowel problems or developmental regression in children with autism: Population study. *British Medical Journal, 324,* 393–396.

Taylor, C. A., Manganello, J. A., Lee, S. J., & Rice, J. (2010). Mothers' spanking of 3-year-old children and subsequent risk of children's aggressive behavior. *Pediatrics, 125,* e1057–e1065.

Taylor, J. B. (2006). *My stroke of insight.* New York: Plume.

Taylor, S. E., Klein, L. C., Lewis, B. P., Gruenewald, T. L., Gurung, R. A., & Updegraff, J. A. (2000). Biobehavioral responses to stress in females: Tend-and-befriend, not fight-or-flight. *Psychological Review, 107,* 411–429.

Teachman, B. A., Marker, C. D., & Clerkin, E. M. (2010). Catastrophic misinterpretations as a predictor of symptom change during treatment for panic disorder. *Journal of Consulting and Clinical Psychology, 78,* 964–973.

TED.com. (2008). *Jill Bolte Taylor's stroke of insight* [Video file]. Retrieved from http://www.ted.com/talks/jill_bolte_taylor_s_powerful_stroke_of_insight.html

Temmel, A. F., Quint, C., Schickinger-Fischer, B., Klimek, L., Stoller, E., & Hummel, T. (2002). Characteristics of olfactory disorders in relation to major causes of olfactory loss. *Archives of Otolaryngology–Head & Neck Surgery, 128,* 635–641.

Tenenbaum, H. R., & Leaper, C. (2002). Are parents' gender schemas related to their children's gender-related cognitions? A meta-analysis. *Developmental Psychology, 38,* 615–630.

Tennis, M. (2012, February 20). Jeremy Lin and the 2006 All-State Team. *ESPN.com.* Retrieved from http://espn.go.com/blog/high-school/california/post/_/id/631/jeremy-lin-and-the-2006-all-state-team

Terman, L. M. (1916). *The measurement of intelligence.* Boston: Houghton Mifflin.

Terman, L. M. (1925). *Genetic studies of genius. Mental and physical traits of a thousand gifted children.* Palo Alto, CA: Stanford University Press.

Terman, L. M., & Oden, M. H. (1947). *The gifted child grows up: Twenty-five years' follow-up of a superior group.* Palo Alto, CA: Stanford University Press.

Terracciano, A., Abdel-Khalek, A. M., Ádám, N., Adamovová, L., Ahn, C. K., Ahn, H. N., . . . McCrae, R. R. (2005). National character does not reflect mean personality trait levels in 49 cultures. *Science, 310,* 96–100.

Thelen, E., & Fisher, D. M. (1982). Newborn stepping: An explanation for a "disappearing" reflex. *Developmental Psychology, 18,* 760–775.

Thibaut, J., & Kelly, H. (1959). *The social psychology of groups.* New York: John Wiley & Sons.

Thomas, A., & Chess, S. (1986). The New York Longitudinal Study: From infancy to early adult life. In R. Plomin & J. Dunn (Eds.), *The study of temperament: Changes, continuities, and challenges* (pp. 39–52). Hillsdale, NJ: Lawrence Erlbaum Associates.

Thomas, M. (December 30, 2009). "I'm just trying to be honest about who I am": Lambert. *Daily Xtra.* Retrieved from http://dailyxtra.com/vancouver/arts-and-entertainment/im-just-trying-honest-lambert?market=210

Thomas, T. L., Garland, F. C., Molé, D., Cohen, B. A., Gudewicz, T. M., Spiro, R. T., & Zahm, S. H. (2003). Health of U.S. Navy submarine crew during periods of isolation. *Aviation, Space, and Environmental Medicine, 74,* 260–265.

Thompson, P. M., Giedd, J. N., Woods, R. P., MacDonald, D., Evans, A. C., & Toga, A. W. (2000). Growth patterns in the developing brain detected by using continuum mechanical tensor maps. *Nature, 404,* 190–193.

Thompson, R. F., & Kim, J. J. (1996). Memory systems in the brain and localization of a memory. *Proceedings of the National Academy of Sciences, USA, 93,* 13438–13444.

Thompson, R. F., & Steinmetz, J. E. (2009). The role of the cerebellum in classical conditioning of discrete behavioral responses. *Neuroscience, 162,* 732–755.

Thorndike, E. L. (1898). Animal intelligence: An experimental study of the associative process in animals. *Psychological Review Monograph Supplement, 2*(8).

Thorne, B. (1993). *Gender play: Girls and boys in school.* Cambridge, UK: Open University Press.

Thorne, M., & Henley, T. B. (2005). *Connections in the history and systems of psychology* (3rd ed.). Boston: Houghton Mifflin.

Thurlow, H. J., & Girvin, J. P. (1971). Use of anti-epileptic medication in treating "flashbacks" from hallucinogenic drugs. *Canadian Medical Association Journal, 105,* 947–948.

Tian, L., Wang, J., Yan, C., & He, Y. (2011). Hemisphere- and gender-related differences in small-world brain networks: A resting-state functional MRI study. *NeuroImage, 54,* 191–202.

Tobar, H. (2014, July 7). Sixty-nine days. *The New Yorker.* Retrieved from http://www.newyorker.com/magazine/2014/07/07/sixty-nine-days

Tobin, D. D., Menon, M., Menon, M., Spatta, B. C., Hodges, E. V. E., & Perry, D. G. (2010). The intrapsychics of gender: A model of self-socialization. *Psychological Review, 117,* 601–622.

Toga, A. W., Thompson, P. M., & Sowell, E. R. (2006). Mapping brain maturation. *Trends in Neuroscience, 29,* 148–159.

Tollenaar, M. S., Beijers, R., Jansen, J., Riksen-Walraven, J. M. A., & De Weerth, C. (2011). Maternal prenatal stress and cortisol reactivity to stressors in human infants. *Stress, 14,* 53–65.

Tolman, E. C. (1948). Cognitive maps in rats and men. *Psychological Review, 55*(4), 189–208.

Tolman, E. C., & Honzik, C. H. (1930). Introduction and removal of reward, and maze performance in rats. *University of California Publications in Psychology, 4,* 257–275.

Tombs, S., & Silverman, I. (2004). Pupillometry: A sexual selection approach. *Evolution and Human Behavior, 25,* 221–228.

Tomoda, A., Suzuki, H., Rabi, K., Sheu, Y., Polcari, A., & Teicher, M. H. (2009). Reduced prefrontal cortical gray matter volume in young adults exposed to harsh corporal punishment. *NeuroImage, 47,* T66–T71.

Tondo, L., Isacsson, G., & Baldessarini, R. J. (2003). Suicidal behaviour in bipolar disorder: Risk and prevention. *CNS Drugs, 17,* 491–511.

Topp, S. S. (2013). Against the quiet revolution: The rhetorical construction of intersex individuals as disordered. *Sexualities, 16,* 180–194.

Torrente, M. P., Gelenberg, A. J., & Vrana, K. E. (2012). Boosting serotonin in the brain: Is it time to revamp the treatment of depression? *Journal of Psychopharmacology, 26,* 629–635.

Torry, Z. D., & Billick, S. B. (2010). Overlapping universe: Understanding legal insanity and psychosis. *Psychiatric Quarterly, 81,* 253–262.

Toufexis, A. (2001, June 24). Why men can outdrink women. *TIME Magazine.* Retrieved from http://content.time.com/time/magazine/article/0,9171,153672,00.html

Tourangeau, R., & Yan, T. (2007). Sensitive questions in surveys. *Psychological Bulletin, 133,* 859–883.

Tränkner, D., Jagle, H., Kohl, S., Apfelstedt-Sylla, E., Sharpe, L. T., Kaupp, U. B., . . . Wissinger, B. (2004). Molecular basis of an inherited form of incomplete *achromatopsia. Journal of Neuroscience, 24,* 138–147.

Treffert, D. A. (2009). The savant syndrome: An extraordinary condition. A synopsis: Past, present, future. *Philosophical Transactions of the Royal Society, 364,* 1351–1357.

Trivers, R. L. (1971). The evolution of reciprocal altruism. *Quarterly Review of Biology, 46,* 35–57.

Tsaw, D., Murphy, S., & Detgen, J. (2011). Social loafing and culture: Does gender matter? *International Review of Business Research, 7,* 1–8.

Tsuang, M. T., Stone, W. S., & Faraone, S. V. (2001). Genes, environment and schizophrenia. *British Journal of Psychiatry, 178,* s18–s24.

Tulving, E. (1972). Episodic and semantic memory. In E. Tulving & W. Donaldson (Eds.), *Organization of memory* (pp. 381–403). New York: Academic Press.

Tulving, E. (1985). Memory and consciousness. *Canadian Psychology/Psychologice Canadienne, 26,* 1–11.

Tulving, E., & Osler, S. (1968). Effectiveness of retrieval cues in memory forwords. *Journal of Experimental Psychology, 77,* 593–601.

Tulving, E., & Thomson, D. M. (1973). Encoding specificity and retrieval processes in episodic memory. *Psychological Review, 80,* 352–373.

Tummala-Narra, P., Alegria, M., & Chen, C.-N. (2012). Perceived discrimination, acculturative stress, and depression among South Asians: Mixed findings. *Asian American Journal of Psychology, 3,* 3–16.

Turgeon, J. K. (2011, July 14). 11 celebrities with dyslexia who made it big. *The Huffington Post.* Retrieved from http://www.huffingtonpost.com/2011/07/14/famous-people-with-dyslexia_n_897475.html#s308246&title=Whoopi_Goldberg

Turiano, N. A., Spiro, A. III, & Mroczek, D. K. (2012). Openness to experience and mortality in men: Analysis of trait and facets. *Journal of Aging and Health, 24,* 654–672.

Turk, J., Marks, I. M., & Horder, J. (1990). Obsessive-compulsive disorder: Case study and discussion of treatment. *British Journal of General Practice, 40,* 210–212.

Tversky, A., & Kahneman, D. (1981). The framing of decisions and the psychology of choice. *Science, 211,* 453–458.

Tversky, A., & Kahneman, D. (1982). Judgment under uncertainty: Heuristics and biases. In D. Kahneman, P. Slovic, & A. Tversky (Eds.), *Judgment under uncertainty: Heuristics and biases* (pp. 3–20). New York: Cambridge University Press.

Twenge, J. M., Baumeister, R. F., DeWall, C. N., Ciarocco, N. J., & Bartels, J. M. (2007). Social exclusion decreases prosocial behavior. *Journal of Personality and Social Psychology, 92,* 56–66.

Uchino, B. N., Berg, C. A., Smith, T. W., Pearce, G., & Skinner, M. (2006). Age-related differences in ambulatory blood pressures during daily stress: Evidence for greater blood pressure reactivity with age. *Psychology and Aging, 21,* 231–239.

Ücok, A., & Gaebel, W. (2008). Side effects of atypical antipsychotics: A brief overview. *World Psychiatry, 7,* 58–62.

UCSF Medical Center. (2015). *FAQ: Cochlear implants.* Retrieved from http://www.ucsfhealth.org/education/cochlear_implants/index.html

United Nations. (2012). *World drug report 2012* (No. E.12.XI.l). Vienna: Office on Drugs and Crime.

United Nations Office for the Coordination of Humanitarian Affairs. (2011, September 5). *Key facts on Somalia.* Retrieved from http://reliefweb.int/report/somalia/key-figures-somalia-05-september-2011

United Nations Population Fund. (n.d.). *Migration.* Retrieved from http://www.unfpa.org/migration

United States Census Bureau. (2013, February 13). *How do we know? America's foreign born in the last 50 years.* Retrieved from http://www.census.gov/library/infographics/foreign_born.html

United States Senate. (2010, January 28). *Unemployment on Indian reservations at 50 percent: The urgent need to create jobs in Indian country: Hearing before the Committee on Indian Affairs,* 111th Cong., 2nd Sess.

University of Chicago. (2013). *Human performance level.* Retrieved from http://hpl.uchicago.edu/

Urso, A. M. (2007). The reality of neonatal pain and the resulting effects. *Journal of Neonatal Nursing, 13,* 236–238.

U.S. Census Bureau. (2011 and earlier). *Current Population Survey (CPS) data on educational attainment* (Annual Social and Economic [ASEC] or March Supplements). Retrieved from http://www.census.gov/hhes/socdemo/education/data/cps/

U.S. Fish & Wildlife Service. (2006). *Laysan Albatross* Phoebastria immutabilis *conservation status* (Alaska Seabird Information Series, 3–4). Retrieved from http://www.fws.gov/alaska/mbsp/mbm/seabirds/pdf/laal.pdf

U.S. Food and Drug Administration. (2008). *Drugs: Information for healthcare professionals: Suicidal behavior and ideation and antiepileptic drugs.* Retrieved from http://www.fda.gov/Drugs/DrugSafety/PostmarketDrugSafetyInformationforPatientsandProviders/ucm100192.htm

U.S. Food and Drug Administration. (2013). For consumers: Side effects of sleep drugs. Retrieved from http://www.fda.gov/forconsumers/consumerupdates/ucm107757.htm

Vaillant, G. E. (1992). *Ego mechanisms of defense: A guide for clinicians and researchers.* Arlington, VA: American Psychiatric Association.

Vaillant, G. E. (2000). Adaptive mental mechanisms: Their role in a positive psychology. *American Psychologist, 55,* 89–98.

Valenza, E., Leo, I., Gava, L., & Simion, F. (2006). Perceptual completion in newborn human infants. *Child Development, 77,* 1810–1821.

van Dam, R. M., & Hu, F. B. (2005). Coffee consumption and risk of type 2 diabetes: A systematic review. *Journal of the American Medical Association, 294,* 97–104.

Van Doorn, M. D., Branje, S. J. T., & Meeus, W. H. (2011). Developmental changes in conflict resolution styles in parent-adolescent relationships: A four-wave longitudinal study. *Journal of Youth and Adolescence, 40,* 97–107.

Van Horn, J. D., Irinia, A., Torgerson, C. M., Chambers, M., Kikinis, R., & Toga, A. W. (2012). Mapping connectivity damage in the case of Phineas Gage. *PLoS ONE, 7,* e37454. doi:10.1371/journal.pone. 0037454

van Os, J., & Kapur, S. (2009). Schizophrenia. *Lancet, 374,* 635–645.

van Praag, H., Kempermann, G., & Gage, F. H. (2000). Neural consequences of environmental enrichment. *Nature Reviews Neuroscience, 1,* 191–198.

Vartanian, L. R., Herman, C. P., & Wansink, B. (2008). Are we aware of the external factors that influence our food intake? *Health Psychology, 27,* 533–538.

Vasalou, A., Joinson, A. N., & Courvoisier, D. (2010). Cultural differences, experience with social networks and the nature of "true commitment" in Facebook. *International Journal of Human Computer Studies, 68,* 719–728.

Velagaleti, G. V. N., & Moore, C. M. (2011). Role of array comparative genomic hybridization of cytogenetic causes of pregnancy loss. *Pathology Case Reviews, 16,* 214–221.

Vennard, M. (2011, November 21). How can musicians keep playing despite amnesia? *BBC World Service.* Retrieved from http://www.bbc.co.uk/news/magazine-15791973

Vernon, P. (2010, September 18). Mad Men: Jon Hamm on life as Don Draper and the blessings of late fame. *The Observer.* Retrieved from http://www.theguardian.com/tv-and-radio/2010/sep/19/jon-hamm-mad-men-don-draper

Vernon, P. A., Martin, R. A., Schermer, J. A., Cherkas, L. F., & Spector, T. D. (2008). Genetic and environmental contributions to humor styles: A replication study. *Twin Research and Human Genetics, 11,* 44–47.

Vgontzas, A. N., Liao, D., Pejovic, S., Calhoun, S., Karataraki, M., & Bixler, E. O. (2009). Insomnia with objective short sleep duration is associated with type 2 diabetes: A population-based study. *Diabetes Care, 32,* 1980–1985.

Viera, M. (2012, February 12). For Lin, erasing a history of being overlooked. *The New York Times.* Retrieved from http://www.nytimes.com/2012/02/13/sports/basketball/for-knicks-lin-erasing-a-history-of-being-overlooked.html

Vigilant Citizen. (2010, October 14). The odd masonic imagery of the 33 Chilean miners' rescue. Retrieved from http://vigilantcitizen.com/latestnews/the-odd-masonic-imagery-surrounding-the-33-chilean-miners-rescue/

Vilain, E. J. N. (2008). Genetics of sexual development and differentiation. In D. L. Rowland & L. Incrocci (Eds.), *Handbook of sexual and gender identity disorders* (pp. 329–353). Hoboken, NJ: John Wiley & Sons.

Vingtdeux, V., Davies, P., Dickson, D. W., & Marambaud, P. (2011). AMPK is abnormally activated in tangle- and pre-tangle-bearing neurons in Alzheimer's disease and other tauopathies. *Acta Neuropathologica, 121,* 337–349.

Violanti, J. M. (1992). Coping strategies among police recruits in a high-stress training environment. *Journal of Social Psychology, 132*(6), 717–729.

Visser, B. A., Ashton, M. C., & Vernon, P. A. (2006). Beyond *g:* Putting multiple intelligences theory to the test. *Intelligence, 34,* 487–502.

Volkow, N. D., Chang, L., Wang, G. J., Fowler, J. S., Leonido-Yee, M., Franceschi, D., . . . Miller, E. N. (2001). Association of dopamine transporter reduction with psychomotor impairment in methamphetamine abusers. *American Journal of Psychiatry, 158,* 377–382.

von Dawans, B., Fischbacher, U., Kirschbaum, C., Fehr, E., & Heinrichs, M. (2012). The social dimension of stress reactivity: Acute stress increases prosocial behavior in humans. *Psychological Science, 23,* 829–839.

von Stumm, S., & Deary, I. J. (2012). Typical intellectual engagement and cognition in the ninth decade of life: The Lothian Birth Cohort 1921. *Psychology and Aging, 27,* 761–767.

Vredeveldt, A., Baddeley, A. D., & Hitch, G. J. (2013, February). The effectiveness of eye-closure in repeated interviews. *Legal and Criminological Psychology.* doi:10.1111/lcrp.12013

Vygotsky, L. S. (1934/1962). *Thought and language* (Eugenia Hanfmann & Gertrude Vakar, Eds. & Trans.). Cambridge, MA: Massachusetts Institute of Technology.

Wagenmakers, E. J., Wetzels, R., Borsboom, D., & van der Maas, H. L. (2011). Why psychologists must change the way they analyze their data: The case of psi [Peer commentary on the paper "Feeling the future: Experimental evidence for anomalous retroactive influences on cognition and affect" by D. J. Bem]. *Journal of Personality and Social Psychology, 100,* 426–432.

Wagner, J. A. III, Humphrey, S. E., Meyer, C. J., & Hollenbeck, J. R. (2011). Individualism–collectivism and team member performance: Another look. *Journal of Organizational Behavior, 33,* 946–963.

Wai, J., Cacchio, M., Putallaz, M., & Makel, M. C. (2010). Sex differences in the right tail of cognitive abilities: A 30 year examination. *Intelligence, 38,* 412–423.

Wakefield, A. J., Murch, S. H., Anthony, A., Linnell, J., Casson, D. M., Malik, M., . . . Walker-Smith, J. A. (1998). Ileal-lymphoid-nodular hyperplasia, non-specific colitis, and pervasive developmental disorder in children. *Lancet, 28,* 637–641.

Wakefield, J. C. (1992). The concept of mental disorder: On the boundary between biological facts and social values. *American Psychologist, 47,* 373–388.

Wallentin, M. (2009). Putative sex differences in verbal abilities and language cortex: A critical review. *Brain and Language, 108,* 175–183.

Wallin, P. (1949). An appraisal of some methodological aspects of the Kinsey report. *American Sociological Review, 14,* 197–210.

Walma van der Molen, J. H., & van der Voort, T. H. A. (2000). The impact of television, print, and audio on children's recall of the news: A study of three alternative explanations for the dual-coding hypothesis. *Human Communication Research, 26,* 3–26.

Walsh, R. (2011). Lifestyle and mental health. *American Psychologist, 66,* 579–592.

Wang, H.-X., Karp, A., Winblad, B., & Fratiglioni, L. (2002). Late-life engagement in social and leisure activities is associated with a decreased risk of dementia: A longitudinal study from the Kungsholmen Project. *American Journal of Epidemiology, 155,* 1081–1087.

Wang, L., Swank, J. S., Glick, I. E., Gado, M. H., Miller, M. I., Morris, J. C. W., & Csernansky, J. G. (2003). Changes in hippocampal volume and shape across time distinguish dementia of the Alzheimer type from healthy aging. *NeuroImage, 20,* 667–682.

Wang, Q., & Conway, M. A. (2004). The stories we keep: Autobiographical memory in American and Chinese middle-aged adults. *Journal of Personality, 72,* 911–938.

Wansink, B., & Kim, J. (2005). Bad popcorn in big buckets: Portion size can influence intake as much as taste. *Journal of Nutrition Education and Behavior, 37,* 242–245.

Warburton, D. E. R., Charlesworth, S., Ivey, A., Nettlefold, L., & Bredin, S. S. D. (2010). A systematic review of the evidence for Canada's physical activity guidelines for adults. *International Journal of Behavioral Nutrition and Physical Activity, 7,* 1–220.

Ward, O. (2006, June 10). The man who heard his paintbox hiss. *The Telegraph.* Retrieved from http://www.telegraph.co.uk/culture/art/3653012/The-man-who-heard-his-paintbox-hiss.html

Warneken, F., & Tomasello, M. (2006). Altruistic helping in human infants and young chimpanzees. *Science, 311,* 1301–1303.

Washburn, D. A. (2010). Book reviews: The animal mind at 100. *Psychological Record, 60,* 369–376.

Wasserstein, R. L. (2013, May 16). A statistician's view: What are your chances of winning the Powerball lottery? *The Huffington Post, Science.* Retrieved from http://www.huffingtonpost.com/ronald-l-wasserstein/chances-of-winning-powerball-lottery_b_3288129.html

Waterhouse, L. (2006). Multiple intelligences, the Mozart effect, and emotional intelligence: A critical review. *Educational Psychologist, 41,* 207–225.

Watson, J. B., & Rayner, R. (1920). Conditioned emotional reactions. *Journal of Experimental Psychology, 3,* 1–14. Reprinted in *American Psychologist, 55,* 313–317.

Watson, J. M., & Strayer, D. L. (2010). Supertaskers: Profiles in extraordinary multi-tasking ability. *Psychonomic Bulletin and Review, 17,* 479–485.

Watson, R. I. (1968). *The great psychologists* (2nd ed.). Philadelphia: J. B. Lippincott.

Waugh, N. C., & Norman, D. A. (1965). Primary memory. *Psychological Review, 72,* 89–104.

Wearing, D. (2005). *Forever today: A memoir of love and amnesia.* London: Corgi Books.

Weathington, B. L., Cunningham, C. J. L., & Pittenger, D. J. (2010). *Research methods for the behavioral and social sciences.* Hoboken, NJ: Wiley.

Webb, S. J., Monk, C. S., & Nelson, C. A. (2001). Mechanisms of postnatal neurobiological development: Implications for human development. *Developmental Neuropsychology, 19,* 147–171.

Webber, J. (2010, October 11). Chile miners knew of dangers but needed money. *The Financial Times.* Retrieved from http://www.ft.com/intl/cms/s/0/f3ea0c16-d557-11df-8e86-00144feabdc0.html#axzz3UGsLlZEk

Weber, A. (2013, April 30). *NewYork.com.* Queens. Retrieved from http://www.newyork.com/articles/neighborhoods/queens-72876/

Weber, H., Scholz, C. J., Domschke, K., Baumann, C., Klauke, B., Jacob, C. P., . . . Reif, A. (2012). Gender differences in associations of glutamate decarboxylase 1 gene (GAD1) variants with panic disorder. *PLoS ONE, 7,* e37651.

Webster's New International Dictionary of the English Language. (1925). W. T. Harris & F. Sturges Allen (Eds.). Springfield, MA: G. & C. Merriam.

Weiner, J. (2011, January 9). Chilean mine rescue makes Golborne, SEP '96, a star. *Stanford Graduate School of Business News.* Retrieved from http://csi.gsb.stanford.edu/chilean-mining-minister-accomplishes-rescue-mission

Weiss, A., King, J. E., & Perkins, L. (2006). Personality and subjective well-being in orangutans (*Pongo pygmaeus* and *Pongo abelii*). *Journal of Personality and Social Psychology, 90,* 501–511.

Weisskirch, R. S., & Delevi, R. (2011). "Sexting" and adult romantic attachment. *Computers in Human Behavior, 27,* 1697–1701.

Wen, C. P., Wai, J. P., Tsai, M. K., Yang, Y. C., Cheng, T. Y., Lee, M. C., . . . Wu, X. (2011). Minimum amount of physical activity for reduced mortality and extended life expectancy: A prospective cohort study. *Lancet, 378,* 1244–1253.

Wen, X. J., Kanny, D., Thompson, W. W., Okoro, C. A., Town, M., & Balluz, L. S. (2012). Binge drinking intensity and health-related quality of life among US adult binge drinkers. *Preventing Chronic Disease, 9,* 1–11.

Wentzel, K. R., McNamara Barry, C., & Caldwell, K. A. (2004). Friendships in middle school: Influences on motivation and school adjustment. *Journal of Educational Psychology, 96,* 195–203.

Werker, J. F., & Tees, R. C. (1984). Cross-language speech perception: Evidence for perceptual reorganization during the first year of life. *Infant Behavior and Development, 7,* 49–63.

Wernig, M., Zhao, J. P., Pruszak, J., Hedlund, E., Fu, D., Soldner, F., . . . & Jaenisch, R. (2008). Neurons derived from reprogrammed fibroblasts functionally integrate into the fetal brain and improve symptoms of rats with Parkinson's disease. *Proceedings of the National Academy of Sciences, 105,* 5856–5861.

Wertheimer, M. (2012). *A brief history of psychology* (5th ed.). New York: Taylor & Francis.

Westen, D. (1990). Psychoanalytic approaches to personality. In L. A. Pervin (Ed.), *Handbook of personality* (pp. 21–65). New York: Guilford Press.

Westen, D., Gabbard, G. O., & Ortigo, K. M. (2008). Psychoanalytic approaches to personality. In O. P. John, R. W. Robins, & L. A. Pervin (Eds.), *Handbook of personality: Theory of research* (pp. 61–113). New York: Guilford Press.

Westly, E. (2011, July/August). The bilingual advantage. *Scientific American Mind.*

Whisman, M. A., & Synder, D. K. (2007). Sexual infidelity in a national survey of American women: Differences in prevalence and correlates as a function of method of assessment. *Journal of Family Psychology, 21,* 147–154.

White, T. (2013, April 22). Finding hope on the Rosebud Indian Reservation [Blog post]. Retrieved from http://scopeblog.stanford.edu/2013/04/22/finding-hope-on-the-rosebud-indian-reservation/

Whitley, R. J., & Gnann, J. W. (2002). Viral encephalitis: Familiar infections and emerging pathogens. *Lancet, 359,* 507–513.

Whitlock, J. R., Heynen, A. J., Shuler, M. G., & Bear, M. F. (2006). Learning induces long-term potentiation in the hippocampus. *Science, 313,* 1093–1097.

Whitman, R. D. (2011). *Cognition.* Hoboken, NJ: Wiley.

WHO Multicentre Growth Reference Study Group, & de Onis, M. (2006). WHO Motor Development Study: Windows of achievement for six gross motor development milestones. *Acta Paediatrica, 95,* 86–95.

Whorf, B. L. (1956). *Language, thought, and reality.* Cambridge, MA: MIT Press.

Wich, S. A., Swartz, K. B., Hardus, M. E., Lameira, A. R., Stromberg, E., & Shumaker, R. W. (2009). Case of spontaneous acquisition of a human sound by an orangutan. *Primates, 50,* 56–64.

Wicker, A. W. (1969). Attitudes versus actions: The relationship of verbal and overt behavioral responses to attitude objects. *Journal of Social Issues, 24,* 41–78.

Wilkins, C. H., Sheline, Y. I., Roe, C. M., Birge, S. J., & Morris, J. C. (2006). Vitamin D deficiency is associated with low mood and worse cognitive performance in older adults. *American Journal of Geriatric Psychiatry, 14,* 1032–1340.

Williams, P. G., Suchy, Y., & Kraybill, M. L. (2010). Five-factor model personality traits and executive functioning among older adults. *Journal of Research in Personality, 44,* 485–491.

Williamson, A. M., & Feyer, A. M. (2000). Moderate sleep deprivation produces impairments in cognitive and motor performance equivalent to legally prescribed levels of alcohol intoxication. *Occupational and Environmental Medicine, 57,* 649–655.

Willoughby, K. A., Desrocher, M., Levine, B., & Rovet, J. F. (2012). Episodic and semantic autobiographical memory and everyday memory during late childhood and early adolescence. *Frontiers in Psychology, 3,* 1–15.

Willyard, C. (2011). Men: A growing minority. *gradPSYCH Magazine,* 40–44.

Wilson, B. A., Baddeley, A. D., & Kapur, N. (1995). Dense amnesia in a professional musician following herpes simplex virus encephalitis. *Journal of Clinical and Experimental Neuropsychology, 17,* 668–681.

Wilson, B. A., Kopelman, M., & Kapur, N. (2008). Prominent and persistent loss of past awareness in amnesia: Delusion, impaired consciousness or coping strategy. *Neuropsychological Rehabilitation, 18,* 527–540.

Wilson, B. A., & Wearing, D. (1995). Prisoner of consciousness: A state of just awakening following herpes simplex encephalitis. In R. Campbell & M. Conway (Eds.), *Broken memories: Case studies in memory impairment* (pp. 14–30). Oxford, UK: Blackwell.

Wilson, R. S., & Bennett, D. A. (2003). Cognitive activity and risk of Alzheimer's disease. *Current Directions in Psychological Science, 12,* 87–91.

Winickoff, J. P., Friebely, J., Tanski, S. E., Sherrod, C., Matt, G. E., Hovell, M. F., & McMillen, R. C. (2009). Beliefs about the health effects of "third-hand" smoke and home smoking bans. *Pediatrics, 123,* e74–e79.

Wiseman, R., & Watt, C. (2006) Belief in psychic ability and the misattribution hypothesis: A qualitative review. *British Journal of Psychology, 91,* 323–338.

Witelson S., Kigar, D., & Harvey, T. (1999). The exceptional brain of Albert Einstein. *Lancet, 353,* 2149–2153.

Witelson, S. F., Kigar, D. L., Scamvougeras, A., Kideckel, D. M., Buck, B., Stanchev, P. L., . . . Black, S. (2008). Corpus callosum anatomy in right-handed homosexual and heterosexual men. *Archives of Sexual Behavior, 37,* 857–863.

Wittchen, H.-U., & Jacobi, F. (2005). Size and burden of mental disorders in Europe. *European Neuropsychopharmacology, 15,* 357–376.

Wobst, A. H. K. (2007). Hypnosis and surgery: Past, present, and future. *Anesthesia & Analgesia, 104,* 1199–1208.

Wojcicki, J. M., van der Straten, A., & Padian, N. (2010). Bridewealth and sexual and reproductive practices among women in Harare, Zimbabwe. *AIDS Care, 22,* 705–710.

Wolf, M. (2007). *Proust and the squid: The story and science of the reading brain.* New York: HarperCollins.

Wolman, D. (2012, March 15). The split brain: A tale of two halves. *Nature, 483,* 260–263.

Wolpert, D. M., Goodbody, S. J., & Husain, M. (1998). Maintaining internal representations: The role of the human superior parietal lobe. *Nature Neuroscience, 1,* 529–533.

Wong, B. (2011). Point of view: Color blindness. *Nature Methods, 8,* 441.

Wood, G., & Pennington, J. (1973). Encoding and retrieval from long-term storage. *Journal of Experimental Psychology, 99,* 243–254.

Wood, W., & Eagly, A. H. (2002). A cross-cultural analysis of the behavior of women and men: Implications for the origins of sex differences. *Psychological Bulletin, 128,* 699–727.

Woon, T.-H., Masuda, M., Wagner, N. N., & Holmes, T. H. (1971). The social readjustment rating scale: A cross-cultural study of Malaysians and Americans. *Journal of Cross-Cultural Psychology, 2,* 373–386.

World Health Organization. (2008a). Table A2, Burden of disease in DALYs by cause, sex and income group in WHO regions, estimates for 2004. *The global burden of disease: 2004 update.* Retrieved from http://www.who.int/healthinfo/global_burden_disease/GBD_report_2004update_AnnexA.pdf

World Health Organization. (2008b). WHO report on the global tobacco epidemic, 2008: The MPOWER package. Retrieved from http://www.who.int/tobacco/ mpower/mpower_report_full_2008.pdf

World Health Organization. (2015). Global health observatory (GHO) data: HIV/AIDS. Retrieved from http://www.who.int/gho/hiv/en/

World Memory Statistics. (2013). *60 Minute/hour numbers.* Retrieved from http://www.world-memory-statistics.com/discipline.php?id=num60

Worringham, C. J., & Messick, D. M. (1983). Social facilitation of running: An unobtrusive study. *Journal of Social Psychology, 121,* 23–29.

WRAL.com. (2011, July 26). *NC shark attack victim asked, 'Am I going to die?'* Retrieved from http://www.wral.com/news/local/story/9907709/

Wright, K. (2002). The times of our lives. *Scientific American, 287,* 59–65.

Wuethrich, B. (1999, November 29). Telling an ovenbird by its nest. *Science NOW.* Retrieved from http://news.sciencemag.org/sciencenow/1999/11/29-02.html

Xu, J., Gannon, P. J., Emmorey, K., Smith, J. F., & Braun, A. R. (2009). Symbolic gestures and spoken language are processed by a common neural system. *Proceedings of the National Academy of Sciences, USA, 106,* 20664–20669.

Yalom, I. D. and Leszcz, M. (2005). *The theory and practice of group psychotherapy* (5th ed.). New York: Basic Books.

Yamagata, S., Suzuki, A., Ando, J., Ono, Y., Kijima, N., Yoshimura, K., . . . Jang, K. (2006). Is the genetic structure of human personality universal? A cross-cultural twin study from North America, Europe, and Asia. *Journal of Personality and Social Psychology, 90,* 987–998.

Yanchar, S. C., Slife, B. D., & Warne, R. (2008). Critical thinking as disciplinary practice. *Review of General Psychology, 12,* 265–281.

Yardi, S., & Bruckman, A. (2011). Social and technical challenges in parenting teens' social media use. In *Proceedings of the SIGCHI Conference on Human Factors in Computing Systems, May 7–12, 2011, Vancouver, BC* (pp. 3237–3246). New York: Association for Computing Machinery.

Yasmin, M., Sharif, M., Masood, S., Raza, M., & Mohsin, S. (2012). Brain image enhancement—a survey. *World Applied Sciences Journal, 17,* 1192–1204.

Yee, M., & Brown, R. (1994). The development of gender differentiation in young children. *British Journal of Social Psychology, 33,* 183–196.

Yen, H. (2012, May 17). Minority birth rate: Racial and ethnic minorities surpass whites in U.S. births for first time, Census reports. *The Huffington Post.* Retrieved from http://www.huffingtonpost.com/2012/05/17/census-minority-birth-rate_n_1523150.html

Yolken, R. H., & Torrey, E. F. (1995). Viruses, schizophrenia, and bipolar disorder. *Clinical Microbiology Reviews, 8,* 131–145.

Yoon, C., Feinberg, F., Hu, P., Gutchess, A. H., Hedden, T., Chen, H.-Y. M., . . . Park, D. C. (2004). Category norms as a function of culture and age: Comparisons of item responses to 105 categories by American and Chinese adults. *Psychology and Aging, 19,* 379–393.

Yost, W. A. (2007). *Fundamentals of hearing* (5th ed.). San Diego: Academic Press.

Young, M. E., Mizzau, M., Mai, N. T., Sirisegaram, A., & Wilson, M. (2009). Food for thought: What you eat depends on your sex and eating companions. *Appetite, 53,* 268–271.

Young-Bruehl, E. (2009). Women and children first! *Modern Psychoanalysis, 34,* 52–74.

Youngstedt, S. D., & Kline, C. E. (2006). Epidemiology of exercise and sleep. *Sleep and Biological Rhythms, 4,* 215–221.

Yu, C. K. C., & Fu, W. (2011). Sex dreams, wet dreams, and nocturnal emissions. *Dreaming, 21,* 197–212.

Yu, D., Ponomarev, A., & Davis, R. L. (2004). Altered representation of the spatial code for odors after olfactory classical conditioning: Memory trace formation by synaptic recruitment. *Neuron, 42,* 437–449.

Yue, S., Duncan, I. J. H., & Moccia, R. D. (2008). Investigating fear in rainbow trout (*Oncorhynchus mykiss*) using the conditioned-suppression paradigm. *Journal of Applied Animal Welfare Science, 11,* 14–27.

Yuhas, D., & Jabr, F. (2012). Know your neurons: What is the ratio of glia to neurons in the brain? Retrieved from http://blogs.scientificamerican.com/brainwaves/2012/06/13/know-your-neurons-what-is-the-ratio-of-glia-to-neurons-in-the-brain/

Yule, G. (1996). *Pragmatics.* Oxford, UK: Oxford University Press.

Zajonc, R. B. (1980). Feeling and thinking: Preferences need no inferences. *American Psychologist, 35,* 151–175.

Zajonc, R. B. (1984). On the primacy of affect. *American Psychologist, 39,* 117–123.

Zammit, G. (2009). Comparative tolerability of newer agents for insomnia. *Drug Safety, 32,* 735–748.

Zaretskii, V. K. (2009). The zone of proximal development: What Vygotsky did not have time to write. *Journal of Russian and East European Psychology, 47,* 70–93.

Zhang, L., Dong, Y., Doyon, W. M, & Dani, J. A. (2012). Withdrawal from chronic nicotine exposure alters dopamine signaling dynamics in the nucleus accumbens. *Biological Psychiatry, 71,* 184–191.

Zhang, T.-Y., & Meaney, M. J. (2010). Epigenetics and the environmental regulation of the genome and its function. *Annual Review of Psychology, 61,* 439–466.

Zhang, Y., Picetti, R., Butelman, E. R., Schlussman, S. D., Ho, A., & Kreek, J. (2009). Behavioral and neurochemical changes induced by oxycodone differ between adolescent and adult mice. *Neuropsychopharmacology, 34,* 912–922.

Zimbardo, P. (2007). *The Lucifer effect: Understanding how good people turn evil.* New York: Random House.

Zimmerman, R. (2014, June 19). 'I'm not stupid, just dyslexic' — and how brain science can help. *WBUR's CommonHealth.* Retrieved from http://commonhealth. wbur.org/2014/06/dyslexia-brain

Zolotor, A. J., Theodore, A. D., Runyan, D. K., Chang, J. J., & Laskey, A. L. (2011). Corporal punishment and physical abuse: population-based trends for three-to-11-year-old children in the United States. *Child Abuse Review, 20,* 57–66.

Zosuls, K. M., Miller, C. F., Ruble, D. N., Martin, C. L., & Fabes, R. A. (2011). Gender development research in *Sex Roles:* Historical trends and future directions. *Sex Roles, 64,* 826–842.

Zuckerman, M. (1979). *Sensation seeking: Beyond the optimal level of arousal.* Hillsdale, NJ: Lawrence Erlbaum Associates.

Zuckerman, M. (1994). *Behavioral expressions and biosocial bases of sensation seeking.* Cambridge, UK: Cambridge University Press.

Zupec, R. (2008, October 22). Can birth order determine your career? *CNN .com.* Retrieved from http://www.cnn.com/2008/LIVING/worklife/10/22/ cb.birth.order.career/index.html

Name Index

Note: Page numbers followed by f indicate entries in figures, those followed by t indicate entries in tables, those followed by i indicate entries in Infographics, and those followed by c indicate entries in Connections.

Subject Index

Note: Page numbers followed by f indicate figures; i indicates infographics; c indicates connections; t indicates tables; and boldface indicates key terms.

list of infographics

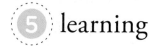